THE COMPLETE
EUROPEAN FOOTBALL
CHAMPIONSHIPS
2002-2024

Dirk Karsdorp

British Library Cataloguing in Publication Data
A catalogue record for this book is available from the British Library

ISBN: 978-1-86223-526-7

Copyright © 2024, SOCCER BOOKS LIMITED (01472 696226)
72 St. Peter's Avenue, Cleethorpes, N.E. Lincolnshire, DN35 8HU, England

Website   www.soccer-books.co.uk
e-mail   info@soccer-books.co.uk

Printed in the UK by 4edge Ltd.

AN INTRODUCTION TO THE EUROPEAN FOOTBALL CHAMPIONSHIPS

ALTHOUGH the European Championship itself did not get underway until 5th April 1958, organised regional international tournaments were already well established throughout Europe.

Way back in 1883 England, Northern Ireland (then just Ireland), Scotland and Wales kicked-off the British Championship (known as the Home International Championship) followed, in 1924, by Denmark, Finland, Norway and Sweden with the Scandinavian Championship (the Nordic Cup). In 1927 Hugo Meisl, that great Austrian champion of the game, originated the Central European Championship between Austria, Czechoslovakia, Hungary, Italy and Switzerland. Indeed, although known as the Dr. Gero Cup from 1955, this tournament was variously called *The Nations Cup*, *The International Cup* and *The Europe Cup*!

Just as we have to thank a Frenchman, Jules Rimet, for the conception of the FIFA World Cup in 1930, we are indebted to another Frenchman, Henri Delaunay, for the European Championship. Monsieur Delaunay, the secretary of the French Football Federation, proposed the tournament in the mid-1950s but, sadly, died before the competition got under way, although the trophy still bears his name.

Originally known as *The European Nations' Cup*, the first tournament struggled to get off the ground and was poorly supported by the major footballing countries of Europe with just 17 entrants taking part.

However, following the success of the first series which ran between the years of 1958 and 1960, most eligible countries entered the second series running from 1962 to 1964 and now it would be unthinkable for any of the members of UEFA to boycott such an important event.

The official name of the competition was changed to *The European Football Championship* in 1966 and it is now considered to rank second only to the FIFA World Cup in order of importance in the world game.

The number of teams entering the competition has risen ever higher following the break up of the Soviet Union, the subsequent independence of nations from a number of other Eastern European countries and the recognition of smaller nations by UEFA. In total, 53 of the 55 UEFA members entered the qualification process for the Euro 2024 competition. The Russian team was ineligible to compete as it was suspended from UEFA and FIFA competitions following their country's invasion of Ukraine in 2022.

This book covers the European Football Championship for every tournament from Euro 2004 held in Portugal through to Euro 2024 which was played in Germany. Complete and comprehensive statistics are included for every game played from the first qualifiers in 2002 through to the Euro 2024 Final match played in Berlin.

A sister-publication containing collated statistics for the competition from the very first game played in 1958 through to the Euro 2000 Final match is also available from Soccer Books. Please see the back of this book for a list of many other statistical publications about European and World football which we also publish.

UEFA Euro 2004

QUALIFYING ROUND

GROUP 1

07-09-2002	Nicosia	Cyprus – France	1-2 (1-1)
07-09-2002	Ljubljana	Slovenia – Malta	3-0 (1-0)
12-10-2002	Ta'Qali	Malta – Israel	0-2 (0-0)
12-10-2002	Saint-Denis	France – Slovenia	5-0 (2-0)
16-10-2002	Ta'Qali	Malta – France	0-4 (0-2)
20-11-2002	Nicosia	Cyprus – Malta	2-1 (0-0)
29-03-2003	Limassol	Cyprus – Israel	1-1 (0-1)
29-03-2003	Lens	France – Malta	6-0 (2-0)
02-04-2003	Ljubljana	Slovenia – Cyprus	4-1 (4-1)
02-04-2003	Palermo	Israel – France	1-2 (1-2)
30-04-2003	Palermo	Israel – Cyprus	2-0 (0-0)
30-04-2003	Ta'Qali	Malta – Slovenia	1-3 (0-2)
07-06-2003	Ta'Qali	Malta – Cyprus	1-2 (0-1)
07-06-2003	Antalya	Israel – Slovenia	0-0
06-09-2003	Ljubljana	Slovenia – Israel	3-1 (2-0)
06-09-2003	Saint-Denis	France – Cyprus	5-0 (3-0)
10-09-2003	Antalya	Israel – Malta	2-2 (1-0)
10-09-2003	Ljubljana	Slovenia – France	0-2 (0-1)
11-10-2003	Limassol	Cyprus – Slovenia	2-2 (0-2)
11-10-2003	Saint-Denis	France – Israel	3-0 (3-0)

FINAL STANDING

Pos	Team	Pld	W	D	L	GF	GA	GD	Pts
1	France	8	8	0	0	29	2	+27	24
2	Slovenia	8	4	2	2	15	12	+3	14
3	Israel	8	2	3	3	9	11	-2	9
4	Cyprus	8	2	2	4	9	18	-9	8
5	Malta	8	0	1	7	5	24	-19	1

France qualified for the Final Tournament in Portugal.

Slovenia qualified for the play-offs.

07-09-2002   GSP Stadium, Nicosia: Cyprus – France   1-2 (1-1)
Cyprus: Nicos Panagiotou (C), Georgois Theodotou, Panagiotis Spyrou (YC58), Nikos
Nicolaou (74' Marios Agathocleous), Petros Konnafis, Demetris Daskalakis (68'
Chrysostomos Michail), Marinos Satsias, Costas Kaiafas, Akis Ioakim, Rainer Rauffmann (62'
Yiasoumi Yiasemakis), Ioannis Okkas. (Coach: Momcilo Vukotic (CYP)).
France: Grégory Coupet, Lilian Thuram, Mikaël Silvestre, Marcel Desailly (C) (YC61),
Philippe Christanval, Zinédine Zidane, Patrick Vieira, Claude Makélélé, Sylvain Wiltord (79'
Olivier Kapo), Steve Marlet (70' Sidney Govou), Djibril Cissé. (Coach: Jacques Santini
(FRA)).
Goals: Cyprus: 1-0 Ioannis Okkas (14').
France: 1-1 Djibril Cissé (39'), 1-2 Sylvain Wiltord (51').
Referee: Herbert Fandel (GER)   Attendance: 11.898

07-09-2002   Bezigrad Stadium, Ljubljana: Slovenia – Malta   3-0 (1-0)
Slovenia: Marko Simeunovic, Muamer Vugdalic (YC80), Aleksander Knavs, Spasoje Bulajic,
Goran Sukalo (73' Sasa Gajser), Miran Pavlin (C), Amir Karic, Milenko Acimovic (86'
Aleksander Radosavljevic), Ermin Siljak (90' Ermin Rakovic), Sebastjan Cimirotic, Zlatko
Zahovic. (Coach: Bojan Prasnikar (SLO)).
Malta: Mario Muscat, Brian Said (YC28), Luke Dimech, Darren Debono (YC85), Jeffrey
Chetcuti, Stefan Giglio (YC42,YC90), David Carabott (C), Chucks Nwoko, George Mallia
(71' Daniel Bogdanovic), Michael Mifsud (88' Adrian Mifsud), Gilbert Agius (YC51).
(Coach: Sigfried Held (GER)).
Goals: Slovenia: 1-0 Darren Debono (37' *own goal*), 2-0 Ermin Siljak (59'), 3-0 Sebastjan
Cimirotic (90').
Referee: Georgios Borovilos (GRE)   Attendance: 7.800

12-10-2002   Ta'Qali National Stadium, Ta'Qali: Malta – Israel   0-2 (0-0)
Malta: Mario Muscat, Brian Said, Luke Dimech, Darren Debono, Jeffrey Chetcuti, Noel
Turner, David Carabott (C) (YC60), Joe Brincat (YC38) (76' Adrian Mifsud), Chucks Nwoko
(64' Daniel Bogdanovic), Michael Mifsud, Gilbert Agius (82' George Mallia). (Coach:
Sigfried Held (GER)).
Israel: Dudu Aouate, Avishay Zano, Adoram Keisi, Asaf Domb, Arik Benado, Idan Tal (84'
Yagal Antebi (YC86)), Haim Revivo, Eyal Berkovic (89' Avi Nimni), Tal Banin, Walid
Badier, Pini Balili (72' Yossi Benayoun). (Coach: Avram Grant (ISR)).
Goals: Israel: 0-1 Pini Balili (56'), 0-2 Haim Revivo (76').
Referee: Sergiy Shebek (UKR)   Attendance: 5.200

12-10-2002   Stade de France, Saint-Denis: France – Slovenia   5-0 (2-0)
France: Fabien Barthez, Lilian Thuram (84' Willy Sagnol), Mikaël Silvestre, William Gallas,
Marcel Desailly (C), Zinédine Zidane, Patrick Vieira, Claude Makélélé, Sylvain Wiltord (87'
Bruno Cheyrou), Steve Marlet (80' Sidney Govou), Thierry Henry. (Coach: Jacques Santini
(FRA)).
Slovenia: Marko Simeunovic, Muamer Vugdalic, Fabijan Cipot, Goran Sukalo, Miran Pavlin
(C), Amir Karic (89' Suad Filekovic), Sasa Gajser (RC90+2), Aleksander Radosavljevic (68'
Anton Zlogar), Zlatko Zahovic, Ermin Siljak, Sebastjan Cimirotic (46' Nastja Ceh). (Coach:
Bojan Prasnikar (SLO)).
Goals: France: 1-0 Patrick Vieira (10'), 2-0 Steve Marlet (35'), 3-0 Steve Marlet (64'), 4-0
Sylvain Wiltord (79'), 5-0 Sidney Govou (86').
Referee: Kim Milton Nielsen (DEN)   Attendance: 77.619

6

16-10-2002   Ta'Qali National Stadium, Ta'Qali: Malta – France   0-4 (0-2)
Malta: Mario Muscat, Brian Said, Luke Dimech, Darren Debono (88' Miguel Mifsud), Jeffrey Chetcuti, Stefan Giglio (YC34), David Carabott (C), Joe Brincat (YC51) (70' George Mallia), Chucks Nwoko (46' Daniel Bogdanovic), Michael Mifsud, Gilbert Agius. (Coach: Sigfried Held (GER)).
France: Fabien Barthez, Lilian Thuram (85' Philippe Mexès), Mikaël Silvestre, William Gallas, Marcel Desailly (C), Zinédine Zidane, Patrick Vieira (70' Olivier Dacourt), Claude Makélélé, Sylvain Wiltord, Steve Marlet, Thierry Henry (78' Éric Carrière). (Coach: Jacques Santini (FRA)).
Goals: France: 0-1 Thierry Henry (26'), 0-2 Thierry Henry (36'), 0-3 Sylvain Wiltord (59'), 0-4 Éric Carrière (84').
Referee: Alexandru Dan Tudor (ROM)   Attendance: 9.175

20-11-2002   GSP Stadium, Nicosia: Cyprus – Malta   2-1 (0-0)
Cyprus: Nicos Panagiotou (C), Georgois Theodotou, Panagiotis Spyrou, Stelios Okkarides, Petros Konnafis, Marinos Satsias (61' Chrysostomos Michail), Costas Kaiafas, Akis Ioakim (YC75), Rainer Rauffmann (71' Yiasoumi Yiasemakis (YC84)), Ioannis Okkas, Michalis Konstantinou (66' Nikos Nicolaou). (Coach: Momcilo Vukotic (CYP)).
Malta: Mario Muscat, Brian Said, Carlo Mamo (YC68) (74' Miguel Mifsud), Luke Dimech, Jeffrey Chetcuti (YC14), Stefan Giglio (YC55) (80' Daniel Theuma), David Carabott (C), Michael Mifsud, Adrian Mifsud (61' George Mallia), Daniel Bogdanovic, Gilbert Agius. (Coach: Sigfried Held (GER)).
Goals: Cyprus: 1-0 Rainer Rauffmann (50'), 2-0 Ioannis Okkas (74').
Malta 2-1 Michael Mifsud (90').
Referee: Anton Guenov (BUL)   Attendance: 5.000

29-03-2003   Tsirion Stadium, Limassol: Cyprus – Israel   1-1 (0-1)
Cyprus: Nicos Panagiotou (C), Georgois Theodotou, Panagiotis Spyrou, Stelios Okkarides, Petros Konnafis, Panagiotis Engomitis (60' Rainer Rauffmann), Vladan Tomic (YC63), Costas Kaiafas, Akis Ioakim (46' Nikos Nicolaou, 76' Demetris Daskalakis), Ioannis Okkas, Michalis Konstantinou. (Coach: Momcilo Vukotic (CYP)).
Israel: Dudu Aouate, Alon Harazi, Adoram Keisi (YC12), Arik Benado, Tal Ben Haim, Idan Tal, Haim Revivo, Tal Banin (YC56), Walid Badier (83' Yossi Abukasis), Omri Afek (72' Yossi Benayoun), Michael Zandberg (66' Avi Nimni). (Coach: Avram Grant (ISR)).
Goals: Cyprus: 1-1 Rainer Rauffmann (61').
Israel: 0-1 Omri Afek (2').
Referee: Thomas Michael (Mike) McCurry (SCO)   Attendance: 5.500

29-03-2003   Stade Félix-Bollaert, Lens: France – Malta   6-0 (2-0)
France: Fabien Barthez (YC1), Bixente Lizarazu, Lilian Thuram (65' Willy Sagnol), Mikaël Silvestre, William Gallas, Zinédine Zidane, Claude Makélélé, Benoît Pedretti, Sylvain Wiltord (75' Sidney Govou), Thierry Henry (80' Jérôme Rothen), David Trézéguet. (Coach: Jacques Santini (FRA)).
Malta: Mario Muscat, Brian Said, Carlo Mamo (71' Jeffrey Chetcuti (YC86)), Luke Dimech, Ian Ciantar, Simon Vella, Michael Mifsud, David Carabott (C), Chucks Nwoko, George Mallia, Daniel Bogdanovic (62' Noel Turner). (Coach: Sigfried Held (GER)).
Goals: France: 1-0 Sylvain Wiltord (36'), 2-0 Thierry Henry (38'), 3-0 Thierry Henry (54'), 4-0 Zinédine Zidane (57' penalty), 5-0 David Trézéguet (70'), 6-0 Zinédine Zidane (80').
Referee: Emil Bozonovski (MCD)   Attendance: 40.775

02-04-2003   Bezigrad Stadium, Ljubljana: Slovenia – Cyprus   4-1 (4-1)
Slovenia: Marko Simeunovic, Muamer Vugdalic, Fabijan Cipot, Spasoje Bulajic, Goran
Sukalo, Miran Pavlin (C) (YC59), Robert Koren (85' Mladen Rudonja), Amir Karic, Nastja
Ceh (90' Anton Zlogar), Zlatko Zahovic, Ermin Siljak (90'+1' Ermin Rakovic). (Coach: Bojan
Prasnikar (SLO)).
Cyprus: Nicos Panagiotou (C), Georgois Theodotou, Panagiotis Spyrou (75' Georgios
Konstanti), Stelios Okkarides, Petros Konnafis (46' Akis Ioakim (YC61)), Demetris
Daskalakis, Vladan Tomic, Costas Kaiafas, Rainer Rauffmann (63' Constantinos
Charalambides), Ioannis Okkas, Michalis Konstantinou. (Coach: Momcilo Vukotic (CYP)).
Goals: Slovenia: 1-0 Ermin Siljak (4'), 2-1 Ermin Siljak (14'), 3-1 Zlatko Zahovic (38'
penalty), 4-1 Nastja Ceh (43').
Cyprus: 1-1 Michalis Konstantinou (10').
Referee: Paulo Manuel Gomes da Costa (POR)   Attendance: 4.000

02-04-2003   Renzo Barbera Stadium, Palermo (ITA): Israel – France   1-2 (1-2)
Israel: Dudu Aouate, Adoram Keisi, Alon Harazi, Arik Benado (YC12), Tal Ben Haim, Idan
Tal (56' Walid Badier), Haim Revivo, Tal Banin (C) (75' Yossi Benayoun), Omri Afek, Yossi
Abukasis, Amir Torjman (46' Michael Zandberg). (Coach: Avram Grant (ISR)).
France: Fabien Barthez, Lilian Thuram, Mikaël Silvestre, Bixente Lizarazu, William Gallas,
Zinédine Zidane (C), Patrick Vieira (YC62), Claude Makélélé, Sylvain Wiltord (66' Sidney
Govou), David Trézéguet (75' Djibril Cissé), Thierry Henry. (Coach: Jacques Santini (FRA)).
Goals: Israel: 1-0 Omri Afek (2').
France: 1-1 David Trézéguet (23'), 1-2 Zinédine Zidane (45'+1').
Referee: Graham Barber (ENG)   Attendance: 2.455

30-04-2003   Renzo Barbera Stadium, Palermo (ITA): Israel – Cyprus   2-0 (0-0)
Israel: Shavit Elimelech, Avishay Zano, Adoram Keisi, Arik Benado, Tal Ben Haim, Haim
Revivo, Tal Banin (C) (84' Walid Badier), Omri Afek, Yossi Abukasis, Michael Zandberg (67'
Shay Holtzman), Amir Torjman (52' Yossi Benayoun). (Coach: Avram Grant (ISR)).
Cyprus: Nicos Panagiotou (C), Stelios Okkarides, Nikos Nikolaou, Petros Konnafis, Christos
Germanos (YC87), Georgios Theodotou, Panagiotis Engomitis (80' Chrysostomos Michail),
Vladan Tomic (YC46) (62' Costas Kaiafas), Charis Nicolaou (89' Yiasoumi Yiasemakis),
Ioannis Okkas, Michalis Konstantinou. (Coach: Momcilo Vukotic (CYP)).
Goals: Israel: 1-0 Walid Badier (88'), 2-0 Shay Holtzman (90'+5').
Referee: Michal Benes (CZE)   Attendance: 300

30-04-2003   Ta'Qali National Stadium, Ta'Qali: Malta – Slovenia   1-3 (0-2)
Malta: Mario Muscat, Simon Vella, Brian Said, Luke Dimech, Ian Ciantar (YC48), Noel
Turner, Stefan Giglio (YC68) (69' William Camenzuli), David Carabott (C), Chucks Nwoko
(63' Daniel Bogdanovic), George Mallia (YC22), Michael Mifsud. (Coach: Sigfried Held
(GER)).
Slovenia: Marko Simeunovic, Damjan Oslaj (61' Matej Snofl), Muamer Vugdalic, Fabijan
Cipot, Goran Sukalo, Miran Pavlin (C), Amir Karic, Sasa Gajser (YC32) (78' Robert Koren),
Nastja Ceh, Zlatko Zahovic, Ermin Siljak (90' Ermin Rakovic). (Coach: Bojan Prasnikar
(SLO)).
Goals: Malta: 1-3 Michael Mifsud (90'+1').
Slovenia: 0-1 Zlatko Zahovic (15'), 0-2 Ermin Siljak (36'), 0-3 Ermin Siljak (57').
Referee: Attila Hanacsek (HUN)   Attendance: 802

8

07-06-2003   Ta'Qali National Stadium, Ta'Qali: Malta – Cyprus 1-2 (0-1)
Malta: Saviour Darmanin (RC21), Simon Vella (YC43), Brian Said (85' Daniel Bogdanovic),
Luke Dimech, William Camenzuli, Noel Turner, Stefan Giglio, David Carabott (C), Chucks
Nwoko (23' Mario Muscat (YC73) goalkeeper), George Mallia (65' Gilbert Agius (YC78)),
Michael Mifsud. (Coach: Sigfried Held (GER)).
Cyprus: Nicos Panagiotou (C), Marios Elia, Stelios Okkarides, Petros Konnafis (YC90+2),
Demetris Daskalakis (65' Stavros Foukaris), Marinos Satsias, Chrysostomos Michail,
Constantinos Charalambides (90'+2' Alexandros Garpozis), Marios Christodoulou (YC64),
Ioannis Okkas (78' Yiasoumi Yiasemakis), Michalis Konstantinou (YC73). (Coach: Momcilo
Vukotic (CYP)).
Goals: Malta: 1-2 Luke Dimech (73').
Cyprus: 0-1 Michalis Konstantinou (23' penalty), 0-2 Michalis Konstantinou (52').
Referee: Bernhard Brugger (AUT)   Attendance: 851

07-06-2003   Atatürk Stadium, Antalya (TUR): Israel – Slovenia 0-0
Israel: Shavit Elimelech, Arik Benado, Avishay Zano (YC23), Adoram Keisi, Tal Ben Haim,
Idan Tal (YC52) (76' Walid Badier), Haim Revivo (C), Avi Nimni, Omri Afek (71' Michael
Zandberg), Yossi Abukasis (85' Shay Holtzman), Yossi Benayoun. (Coach: Avram Grant
(ISR)).
Slovenia: Marko Simeunovic, Fabijan Cipot (YC31), Muamer Vugdalic (YC29), Aleksander
Knavs, Sasa Gajser (YC66) (71' Robert Koren), Milenko Acimovic (YC77) (87' Matej Snofl),
Goran Sukalo, Miran Pavlin (C) (YC50), Amir Karic, Zlatko Zahovic (YC82), Ermin Siljak.
(Coach: Bojan Prasnikar (SLO)).
Referee: Massimo Busacca (SUI)   Attendance: 1.800

06-09-2003   Bezigrad Stadium, Ljubljana: Slovenia – Israel 3-1 (2-0)
Slovenia: Marko Simeunovic, Matej Snofl, Aleksander Knavs, Fabijan Cipot, Goran Sukalo,
Amir Karic (YC40), Nastja Ceh (90' Mladen Rudonja), Milenko Acimovic, Adem Kapic (83'
Simon Seslar), Ermin Siljak (YC14) (63' Sebastjan Cimirotic), Zlatko Zahovic (C). (Coach:
Bojan Prasnikar (SLO)).
Israel: Shavit Elimelech, Adoram Keisi (YC34) (46' Pini Balili), Alon Harazi, Arik Benado,
Tal Ben Haim (YC22,RC90), Haim Revivo (C), Avi Nimni (RC87), Eyal Berkovic (YC70),
Idan Tal, Yossi Benayoun (82' Michael Zandberg), Yossi Abukasis (YC64) (75' Walid
Badier). (Coach: Avram Grant (ISR)).
Goals: Slovenia: 1-0 Ermin Siljak (35'), 2-0 Aleksander Knavs (37'), 3-1 Nastja Ceh (78').
Israel: 2-1 Haim Revivo (69').
Referee: Herbert Fandel (GER)   Attendance: 8.500

06-09-2003   Stade de France, Saint-Denis: France – Cyprus 5-0 (3-0)
France: Fabien Barthez, Bixente Lizarazu, Marcel Desailly (C), Lilian Thuram (65' Willy
Sagnol), Mikaël Silvestre, Claude Makélélé, Robert Pirès, Patrick Vieira (71' Olivier Dacourt),
Thierry Henry (78' Steve Marlet), Sylvain Wiltord, David Trézéguet. (Coach: Jacques Santini
(FRA)).
Cyprus: Nicos Panagiotou (C), Petros Konnafis (46' Akis Ioakim), Nicolaos Georgiou,
Georgios Theodotou, Stelios Okkarides, Nikos Nicolaou, Costas Kaiafas, Panagiotis Engomitis
(58' Chrysostomos Michail), Marinos Satsias, Michalis Konstantinou (68' Yiasoumi
Yiasemakis), Ioannis Okkas. (Coach: Momcilo Vukotic (CYP)).
Goals: France: 1-0 David Trézéguet (8'), 2-0 Sylvain Wiltord (20'), 3-0 Sylvain Wiltord (41'),
4-0 Thierry Henry (60'), 5-0 David Trézéguet (82').
Referee: Leslie John Irvine (NIR)   Attendance: 50.132

9

10-09-2003   Atatürk Stadium, Antalya (TUR): Israel – Malta   2-2 (1-0)
Israel: Shavit Elimelech, Arik Benado, Alon Harazi, Shimon Gershon (YC80), Eyal Berkovic (43' Omri Afek), Walid Badier (75' Shay Holtzman), Idan Tal, Haim Revivo (C), Yossi Abukasis, Pini Balili, Michael Zandberg (60' Yossi Benayoun). (Coach: Avram Grant (ISR)).
Malta: Mario Muscat, Jeffrey Chetcuti, William Camenzuli (YC34), Brian Said, Stefan Giglio (79' Daniel Theuma), David Carabott (C) (YC90+2), Noel Turner, Etienne Barbara (YC23), Chucks Nwoko (88' Adrian Mifsud), Michael Mifsud, Daniel Bogdanovic (69' Michael Galea). (Coach: Sigfried Held (GER)).
Goals: Israel: 1-0 Haim Revivo (16'), 2-2 Pini Balili (79').
Malta: 1-1 Michael Mifsud (51' penalty), 1-2 David Carabott (52').
Referee: Eric Blareau (BEL)   Attendance: 250

10-09-2003   Bezigrad Stadium, Ljubljana: Slovenia – France   0-2 (0-1)
Slovenia: Marko Simeunovic, Aleksander Knavs, Fabijan Cipot, Muamer Vugdalic (82' Matej Snofl), Amir Karic (YC32), Nastja Ceh, Milenko Acimovic, Goran Sukalo (54' Adem Kapic (YC87)), Miran Pavlin (C), Zlatko Zahovic (64' Sebastjan Cimirotic), Ermin Siljak. (Coach: Bojan Prasnikar (SLO)).
France: Fabien Barthez, Bixente Lizarazu, Marcel Desailly (C), Lilian Thuram, Mikaël Silvestre, Claude Makélélé (YC43,YC66), Zinédine Zidane (YC39) (78' Robert Pirès), Patrick Vieira (YC74), Thierry Henry, Sylvain Wiltord (75' Willy Sagnol), David Trézéguet (67' Olivier Dacourt). (Coach: Jacques Santini (FRA)).
Goals: France: 0-1 David Trézéguet (9'), 0-2 Olivier Dacourt (71').
Referee: Domenico Messina (ITA)   Attendance: 8.500

11-10-2003   Tsirion Stadium, Limassol: Cyprus – Slovenia   2-2 (0-2)
Cyprus: Nicos Panagiotou (C), Stelios Okkarides, Nikos Nicolaou (YC31), Marios Elia (YC90), Nicolaos Georgiou (78' Lambros Lambrou (YC87)), Lazaros Iacovou, Marios Antoniou, Stavros Georgiou, Panagiotis Engomitis (43' Eleftherakis Eleftheriou), Georgios Konstanti (YC41) (46' Elias Charalambous), Yiasoumi Yiasemakis. (Coach: Momcilo Vukotic (CYP)).
Slovenia: Marko Simeunovic, Aleksander Knavs (46' Matej Snofl (YC66)), Fabijan Cipot (24' Spasoje Bulajic), Muamer Vugdalic, Miran Pavlin (C), Adem Kapic, Nastja Ceh, Milenko Acimovic, Goran Sukalo, Mladen Rudonja (86' Robert Koren), Ermin Siljak. (Coach: Bojan Prasnikar (SLO)).
Goals: Cyprus: 1-2 Stavros Georgiou (70'), 2-2 Yiasoumi Yiasemakis (82').
Slovenia: 0-1 Ermin Siljak (12'), 0-2 Ermin Siljak (42').
Referee: Tom Henning Øvrebø (NOR)   Attendance: 242

11-10-2003   Stade de France, Saint-Denis: France – Israel   3-0 (3-0)
France: Fabien Barthez, Lilian Thuram, Anthony Réveillère, Bixente Lizarazu, Jean-Alain Boumsong, Zinédine Zidane (C), Robert Pirès (85' Ludovic Giuly), Benoît Pedretti, Olivier Dacourt, David Trézéguet (85' Steve Marlet), Thierry Henry (76' Djibril Cissé). (Coach: Jacques Santini (FRA)).
Israel: Nir Davidovitch, Adoram Keisi, Alon Harazi, Shimon Gershon, Arik Benado, Oren Zitoni (88' Pini Balili), Idan Tal, Haim Revivo (C), Walid Badier (75' Kfir Udi), Yossi Benayoun, Michael Zandberg (46' Yossi Abukasis). (Coach: Avram Grant (ISR)).
Goals: France: 1-0 Thierry Henry (8'), 2-0 David Trézéguet (24'), 3-0 Jean-Alain Boumsong (42').
Referee: Cosimo-Giancarlo Bolognino (ITA)   Attendance: 57.009

GROUP 2

07-09-2002	Oslo	Norway - Denmark	2-2 (0-1)
07-09-2002	Sarajevo	Bosnia-Herzegovina – Romania	0-3 (0-3)
12-10-2002	Bucharest	Romania –Norway	0-1 (0-0)
12-10-2002	Copenhagen	Denmark – Luxembourg	2-0 (0-0)
16-10-2002	Oslo	Norway – Bosnia-Herzegovina	2-0 (2-0)
16-10-2002	Luxembourg	Luxembourg – Romania	0-7 (0-4)
29-03-2003	Bucharest	Romania – Denmark	2-5 (1-1)
29-03-2003	Zenica	Bosnia-Herzegovina – Luxembourg	2-0 (0-0)
02-04-2003	Copenhagen	Denmark – Bosnia-Herzegovina	0-2 (0-2)
02-04-2003	Luxembourg	Luxembourg – Norway	0-2 (0-0)
07-06-2003	Craiova	Romania – Bosnia-Herzegovina	2-0 (0-0)
07-06-2003	Copenhagen	Denmark – Norway	1-0 (1-0)
11-06-2003	Oslo	Norway – Romania	1-1 (0-0)
11-06-2003	Luxembourg	Luxembourg – Denmark	0-2 (0-1)
06-09-2003	Ploiesti	Romania – Luxembourg	4-0 (3-0)
06-09-2003	Zenica	Bosnia-Herzegovina – Norway	1-0 (0-0)
10-09-2003	Copenhagen	Denmark – Romania	2-2 (1-0)
10-09-2003	Luxembourg	Luxembourg – Bosnia-Herzegovina	0-1 (0-1)
11-10-2003	Oslo	Norway – Luxembourg	1-0 (1-0)
11-10-2003	Sarajevo	Bosnia-Herzegovina – Denmark	1-1 (1-1)

FINAL STANDING

Pos	Team	Pld	W	D	L	GF	GA	GD	Pts
1	*Denmark*	8	4	3	1	15	9	+6	15
2	Norway	8	4	2	2	9	5	+4	14
3	Romania	8	4	2	2	21	9	+12	14
4	Bosnia-Herzegovina	8	4	1	3	7	8	-1	13
5	Luxembourg	8	0	0	8	0	21	-21	0

Denmark qualified for the Final Tournament in Portugal.

Norway qualified for the play-offs due to a better head to head record against Romania.

07-09-2002   Ullevaal Stadion, Oslo: Norway – Denmark   2-2 (0-1)
Norway: Frode Grodås, Ronny Johnsen, André Bergdølmo, Henning Berg (C), Christer Basma, Trond Andersen (77' Roar Strand), John Arne Riise, Øyvind Leonhardsen (77' John Carew), Eirik Bakke (YC13) (88' Tommy Svindal Larsen), Ole Gunnar Solskjær, Steffen Iversen. (Coach: Nils Johan Semb (NOR)).
Denmark: Thomas Sørensen, Steven Lustü, Martin Laursen (YC41), Niclas Jensen, Thomas Helveg, Christian Poulsen, Jesper Grønkjær (69' Claus Jensen), Thomas Gravesen, Dennis Rommedahl (59' Jan Michaelsen), Jon Dahl Tomassen (90'+2' Per Nielsen), Ebbe Sand (C). (Coach: Morten Per Olsen (DEN)).
Goals: Norway: 1-1 John Arne Riise (54'), 2-2 John Carew (90'+2').
Denmark: 0-1 Jon Dahl Tomasson (22'), 1-2 Jon Dahl Tomasson (72').
Referee: Hugh Dallas (SCO)   Attendance: 25.114

11

07-09-2002   Kosevo Stadium, Sarajevo: Bosnia-Herzegovina – Romania   0-3 (0-3)
Bosnia-Herzegovina: Tomislav Piplica, Munever Rizvic (YC49), Asmir Ikanovic (37' Jasmin
Huric), Mirsad Hibic (C) (YC52), Hasan Salihamidzic (YC86), Vedin Music, Sinisa Mulina,
Almedin Hota, Mirsad Beslija (41' Senad Brkic (YC63)), Zlatan Bajramovic (45' Bruno
Akrapovic (YC65)), Samir Muratovic. (Coach: Blaz Sliskovic (BOS)).
Romania: Bogdan Stelea (33' Bogdan Vintila), Gheorghe Popescu (C) (YC39), Cristian Chivu,
Iulian Filipescu, Cosmin Contra, Adrian Mutu, Dorinel Munteanu, Paul Codrea (84' Tiberiu
Ghioane), Mirel Radoi, Marius Niculae (66' Florin Cernat), Ioan Ganea. (Coach: Anghel
Iordanescu (ROM)).
Goals: Romania: 0-1 Cristian Chivu (7'), 0-2 Dorinel Munteanu (8'), 0-3 Ioan Ganea (27').
Referee: Lucílio Cardoso Cortez Batista (POR)   Attendance: 1.830

12-10-2002   Stadionul Steaua, Bucharest: Romania – Norway   0-1 (0-0)
Romania: Bogdan Vintila, Razvan Rat, Gheorghe Popescu (C), Cristian Chivu (YC16),
Cosmin Contra, Adrian Mutu, Dorinel Munteanu (85' Daniel Pancu), Paul Codrea, Mirel
Radoi, Ioan Ganea (63' Adrian Ilie), Viorel Moldovan (63' Marius Niculae). (Coach: Anghel
Iordanescu (ROM)).
Norway: Thomas Myhre, Claus Lundekvam, André Bergdølmo, Henning Berg (C), Christer
Basma, Trond Andersen, John Arne Riise (YC41), Eirik Bakke, Ole Gunnar Solskjær (90'
Sigurd Rushfeldt), John Carew (YC36) (78' Øyvind Leonhardsen), Steffen Iversen. (Coach:
Nils Johan Semb (NOR)).
Goal: Norway: 0-1 Steffen Iversen (83').
Referee: Valentin Valentinovich Ivanov (RUS)   Attendance: 20.000

12-10-2002   Parken Stadium, Copenhagen: Denmark – Luxembourg   2-0 (0-0)
Denmark: Peter Skov-Jensen, Niclas Jensen, René Henriksen, Kasper Bøgelund, Christian
Poulsen, Claus Jensen (84' Peter Løvenkrands), Martin Jørgensen (75' Thomas Røll Larsen),
Thomas Gravesen (YC29), Ebbe Sand, Dennis Rommedahl (66' Jesper Grønkjær), Jon Dahl
Tomassen. (Coach: Morten Per Olsen (DEN)).
Luxembourg: Alija Besic, Jeff Strasser, Claude Reiter, Eric Hoffmann, Ralph Ferron (YC43),
Frank Deville (YC28), Sébastien Remy, Fons Leweck, Manuel Cardoni, Luc Holtz (84' Sven
Di Domenico), Gordon Braun (79' Daniel Huss). (Coach: Allan Rodenkam Simonsen (DEN)).
Goals: Denmark: 1-0 Jon Dahl Tomasson (52' penalty), 2-0 Ebbe Sand (72').
Referee: Ferenc Bede (HUN)   Attendance: 40.259

16-10-2002   Ullevaal Stadion, Oslo: Norway – Bosnia-Herzegovina   2-0 (2-0)
Norway: Frode Olsen, Claus Lundekvam, André Bergdølmo, Henning Berg (C), Christer
Basma, Trond Andersen (90' Tommy Svindal Larsen), John Arne Riise, Øyvind Leonhardsen
(65' John Carew (YC69)), Eirik Bakke, Ole Gunnar Solskjær (90' Sigurd Rushfeldt), Steffen
Iversen. (Coach: Nils Johan Semb (NOR)).
Bosnia-Herzegovina: Almir Tolja, Sasa Papac (YC45), Muhamed Konjic, Mirsad Hibic
(YC26), Spomenko Bosnjak (65' Edin Mujcin), Hasan Salihamidzic (YC67) (84' Nenad
Miskovic), Nermin Sabic (57' Jasmin Huric), Vedin Music, Vladan Grujic, Zlatan Bajramovic,
Elvir Baljic. (Coach: Blaz Sliskovic (BOS)).
Goals: Norway: 1-0 Claus Lundekvam (7'), 2-0 John Arne Riise (27').
Referee: Michael Benes (CZE)   Attendance: 24.169

16-10-2002   Stade Josy Barthel, Luxembourg: Luxembourg – Romania   0-7 (0-4)
Luxembourg: Alija Besic, Jeff Strasser, Claude Reiter, Eric Hoffmann, Ralph Ferron, Frank Deville, Sébastien Remy, Fons Leweck, Manuel Cardoni (C) (60' Sacha Schneider), Luc Holtz (77' Sach Rohmann), Gordon Braun (72' Daniel Huss). (Coach: Allan Rodenkam Simonsen (DEN)).
Romania: Bogdan Vintila, Razvan Rat, Gheorghe Popescu (C), Ilie Miu, Cosmin Contra, Dorinel Munteanu, Paul Codrea (36' Tiberiu Ghioane), Mirel Radoi, Adrian Ilie, Ioan Ganea (46' Daniel Pancu), Viorel Moldovan (70' Florin Cernat). (Coach: Anghel Iordanescu (ROM)).
Goals: Romania: 0-1 Viorel Moldovan (2'), 0-2 Viorel Moldovan (5'), 0-3 Mirel Radoi (25'), 0-4 Cosmin Contra (45'+1'), 0-5 Cosmin Contra (47'), 0-6 Tiberiu Ghioane (81'), 0-7 Cosmin Contra (86').
Referee: Romans Lajuks (LAT)   Attendance: 2.056

29-03-2003   Stadionul National, Bucharest: Romania – Denmark   2-5 (1-1)
Romania: Bogdan Lobont, Gheorghe Popescu (C), Cristian Chivu, Iulian Filipescu, Cosmin Contra (YC70), Adrian Mutu (YC50), Dorinel Munteanu, Paul Codrea (YC54) (62' Laurentiu Reghecampf), Mirel Radoi, Daniel Pancu (67' Florin Bratu), Ioan Ganea. (Coach: Anghel Iordanescu (ROM)).
Denmark: Thomas Sørensen, Thomas Rytter (34' Jan Michaelsen), Martin Laursen (YC15), Niclas Jensen, René Henriksen, Christian Poulsen (67' Morten Wieghorst), Thomas Gravesen, Jon Dahl Tomassen, Ebbe Sand, Dennis Rommedahl, Peter Løvenkrands (46' Martin Jørgensen). (Coach: Morten Per Olsen (DEN)).
Goals: Romania: 1-0 Adrian Mutu (5'), 2-1 Dorinel Munteanu (47').
Denmark: 1-1 Dennis Rommedahl (8'), 2-2 Thomas Gravesen (53'), 2-3 Jon Dahl Tomassen (71'), 2-4 Cosmin Contra (73' own goal), 2-5 Dennis Rommedahl (90'+2').
Referee: Manuel Enrique Mejuto González (ESP)   Attendance: 52.000

29-03-2003   Bilino Polje, Zenica: Bosnia-Herzegovina – Luxembourg   2-0 (0-0)
Bosnia-Herzegovina: Kenan Hasagic, Muhamed Konjic, Haris Alihodzic, Vladan Grujic, Mirsad Beslija (79' Mirko Hrgovic), Zlatan Bajramovic, Vedin Music, Bulent Biscevic (YC45+2) (68' Dzemal Berberovic), Sergej Barbarez, Elvir Bolic (81' Almir Turkovic), Elvir Baljic (YC32). (Coach: Blaz Sliskovic (BOS)).
Luxembourg: Alija Besic (YC75), Jeff Strasser (C), Eric Hoffmann (YC71), Manou Schauls, Sébastien Remy, Fons Leweck (77' Sven Di Domenico), Gregory Molitor, Ben Federspiel, René Peters, Gordon Braun (88' Sacha Schneider), Marcel Christophe (85' Daniel Huss). (Coach: Allan Rodenkam Simonsen (DEN)).
Goals: Bosnia-Herzegovina: 1-0 Elvir Bolic (58'), 2-0 Sergej Barbarez (75').
Referee: Jouni Hyytiä (FIN)   Attendance: 7.380

02-04-2003   Parken Stadium, Copenhagen: Denmark – Bosnia-Herzegovina   0-2 (0-2)
Denmark: Thomas Sørensen, Niclas Jensen (81' Per Frandsen), René Henriksen, Martin Albrechtsen, Jan Michaelsen, Claus Jensen (60' Morten Wieghorst (YC70)), Martin Jørgensen, Thomas Gravesen, Jon Dahl Tomassen (85' Søren Berg), Ebbe Sand, Dennis Rommedahl. (Coach: Morten Per Olsen (DEN)).
Bosnia-Herzegovina: Kenan Hasagic, Muhamed Konjic, Mirsad Hibic (C), Dzemal Berberovic, Vedin Music, Mirko Hrgovic (67' Vladan Grujic), Mirsad Beslija (82' Sinisa Mulina), Zlatan Bajramovic (YC70), Bulent Biscevic (YC73), Sergej Barbarez, Elvir Baljic (76' Dragan Blatnjak). (Coach: Blaz Sliskovic (BOS)).
Goals: Bosnia-Herzegovina: 0-1 Sergej Barbarez (23'), 0-2 Elvir Baljic (29').
Referee: Anton Stredák (SVK)   Attendance: 30.845

02-04-2003   Stade Josy Barthel, Luxembourg: Luxembourg – Norway   0-2 (0-0)
Luxembourg: Alija Besic, Jeff Strasser (C), Manou Schauls, Eric Hoffmann (YC7), Sébastien
Remy, René Peters, Gregory Molitor, Fons Leweck (90'+2' Patrick Lassine), Ben Federspiel,
Marcel Christophe (83' Daniel Huss), Gordon Braun (75' Sacha Schneider). (Coach: Allan
Rodenkam Simonsen (DEN)).
Norway: Frode Olsen, Ronny Johnsen, André Bergdølmo, Henning Berg (C) (YC30), Christer
Basma, Trond Andersen (YC10), John Arne Riise, Petter Rudi (46' Jo Tessem), Eirik Bakke
(85' Tommy Svindal Larsen), Tore André Flo (46' Sigurd Rushfeldt), Ole Gunnar Solskjær.
(Coach: Nils Johan Semb (NOR)).
Goals: Norway: 0-1 Sigurd Rushfeldt (57'), 0-2 Ole Gunnar Solskjær (73').
Referee: Ivan Dobrinov (BUL)   Attendance: 2.900

07-06-2003   Stadionul Ion Oblemenco, Craiova: Romania – Bosnia-Herzegovina   2-0 (0-0)
Romania: Bogdan Lobont, Adrian Iencsi, Cristian Chivu (C), Razvan Rat, Cosmin Contra,
Adrian Mutu (87' Ilie Miu), Ioan Ganea, Paul Codrea (65' Zeno Marius Bundea), Mirel Radoi,
Adrian Ilie (79' Florin Soava), Daniel Pancu (YC52). (Coach: Anghel Iordanescu (ROM)).
Bosnia-Herzegovina: Kenan Hasagic, Mirsad Hibic (C), Muhamed Konjic, Dzemal Berberovic
(79' Dragan Blatnjak), Vladan Grujic, Mirsad Beslija (YC22) (50' Mladen Bartolovic), Zlatan
Bajramovic, Vedin Music, Mirko Hrgovic (72' Emir Spahic), Elvir Bolic (YC53), Sergej
Barbarez. (Coach: Blaz Sliskovic (BOS)).
Goals: Romania: 1-0 Adrian Mutu (46'), 2-0 Ioan Ganea (87').
Referee: Ruud Bossen (HOL)   Attendance: 19.900

07-06-2003   Parken Stadium, Copenhagen: Denmark – Norway   1-0 (1-0)
Denmark: Thomas Sørensen, Martin Laursen, Niclas Jensen, René Henriksen (C), Thomas
Helveg, Claus Jensen (62' Thomas Røll Larsen), Morten Wieghorst, Martin Jørgensen (83' Per
Nielsen), Jesper Grønkjær (71' Dennis Rommedahl), Thomas Gravesen, Ebbe Sand (YC89).
(Coach: Morten Per Olsen (DEN)).
Norway: Frode Olsen, Claus Lundekvam, Ronny Johnsen, Christer Basma, Trond Andersen
(46' André Bergdølmo (YC60)), John Arne Riise, Øyvind Leonhardsen (62' Tore André Flo),
Eirik Bakke, Ole Gunnar Solskjær (C) (89' Haavard Flo), John Carew, Steffen Iversen.
(Coach: Nils Johan Semb (NOR)).
Goal: Denmark: 1-0 Jesper Grønkjær (5').
Referee: Graham Poll (ENG)   Attendance: 41.824

11-06-2003   Ullevaal Stadion, Oslo: Norway – Romania   1-1 (0-0)
Norway: Frode Olsen, André Bergdølmo, Henning Berg (C) (85' Claus Lundekvam), Christer
Basma, Trond Andersen, Ronny Johnsen, John Arne Riise, Eirik Bakke, Ole Gunnar Solskjær,
Frode Johnsen (70' Tore André Flo), John Carew (81' Steffen Iversen). (Coach: Nils Johan
Semb (NOR)).
Romania: Bogdan Lobont, Adrian Iencsi, Cristian Chivu (C), Razvan Rat, Cosmin Contra
(YC24), Florin Soava, Adrian Mutu, Mirel Radoi (YC76), Adrian Ilie (46' Alin Stoica), Ioan
Ganea (YC66), Daniel Pancu (85' Florin Bratu). (Coach: Anghel Iordanescu (ROM)).
Goals: Norway: 1-1 Ole Gunnar Solskjær (78' penalty).
Romania: 0-1 Ioan Ganea (64').
Referee: Lubos Michel (SVK)   Attendance: 24.890

14

11-06-2003   Stade Josy Barthel, Luxembourg: Luxembourg – Denmark   0-2 (0-1)
Luxembourg: Alija Besic, Jeff Strasser, Manou Schauls, Claude Reiter, Sébastien Remy, Gregory Molitor, Fons Leweck (YC43), Ben Federspiel, Manuel Cardoni (C), Patrick Posing, Gordon Braun (71' Marcel Christophe). (Coach: Allan Rodenkam Simonsen (DEN)).
Denmark: Thomas Sørensen, Martin Laursen, Niclas Jensen, René Henriksen (C), Kasper Bøgelund, Claus Jensen, Martin Jørgensen, Jesper Grønkjær (64' Dennis Rommedahl), Thomas Gravesen, Morten Wieghorst (53' Thomas Røll Larsen), Ebbe Sand (74' Morten Skoubo). (Coach: Morten Per Olsen (DEN)).
Goals: Denmark: 0-1 Claus Jensen (22'), 0-2 Thomas Gravesen (50').
Referee: Yuri Valeryevich Baskakov (RUS)   Attendance: 6.869

06-09-2003   Stadionul Astra, Ploiesti: Romania – Luxembourg   4-0 (3-0)
Romania: Bogdan Lobont, Razvan Rat, Cristian Chivu (C) (46' Florin Soava), Adrian Iencsi, Adrian Mutu (46' Florin Bratu), Dorinel Munteanu, Flavius Stoican, Florentin Dumitru, Mirel Radoi, Daniel Pancu (76' Alin Stoica), Ioan Ganea. (Coach: Anghel Iordanescu (ROM)).
Luxembourg: Alija Besic, Jeff Strasser, Manou Schauls, Claude Reiter, Eric Hoffmann, Sébastien Remy, René Peters, Fons Leweck, Ben Federspiel, Manuel Cardoni (C) (85' Daniel Huss), Gordon Braun (85' Paul Mannon). (Coach: Allan Rodenkam Simonsen (DEN)).
Goals: Romania: 1-0 Adrian Mutu (38'), 2-0 Daniel Pancu (40'), 3-0 Ioan Ganea (43'), 4-0 Florin Bratu (77').
Referee: Alon Yefet (ISR)   Attendance: 2.457

06-09-2003   Bilino Polje, Zenica: Bosnia-Herzegovina – Norway   1-0 (0-0)
Bosnia-Herzegovina: Kenan Hasagic, Sasa Papac, Muhamed Konjic, Mirsad Hibic (C), Emir Spahic, Hasan Salihamidzic (65' Mirsad Beslija), Vedin Music (69' Mirko Hrgovic), Vladan Grujic, Zlatan Bajramovic, Elvir Bolic, Sergej Barbarez (YC38) (89' Bulent Biscevic). (Coach: Blaz Sliskovic (BOS)).
Norway: Espen Johnsen, Ronny Johnsen (YC15), André Bergdølmo (YC90+3), Henning Berg (C), Christer Basma, John Arne Riise, Brede Hangeland (YC72), Martin Andresen (YC58), Roar Strand (88' Jan Gunnar Solli), Ole Gunnar Solskjær (86' Steffen Iversen), John Carew (YC70) (73' Tore André Flo). (Coach: Nils Johan Semb (NOR)).
Goal: Bosnia-Herzegovina: 1-0 Zlatan Bajramovic (87').
Referee: Stéphane Bré (FRA)   Attendance: 22.000

10-09-2003   Parken Stadium, Copenhagen: Denmark – Romania   2-2 (1-0)
Denmark: Thomas Sørensen, Martin Laursen, Niclas Jensen, René Henriksen (C), Thomas Helveg, Morten Wieghorst (64' Christian Poulsen), Martin Jørgensen, Jesper Grønkjær (YC74) (80' Dennis Rommedahl), Thomas Gravesen, Jon Dahl Tomassen (55' Peter Madsen), Ebbe Sand. (Coach: Morten Per Olsen (DEN)).
Romania: Bogdan Lobont, Cristian Chivu (C), Razvan Rat (YC69), Adrian Iencsi, Flavius Stoican, Adrian Mutu (YC81) (90'+2 Florin Soava), Dorinel Munteanu (YC49), Florentin Dumitru (70' Florin Cernat), Mirel Radoi, Daniel Pancu, Ioan Ganea (67' Florin Bratu). (Coach: Anghel Iordanescu (ROM)).
Goals: Denmark: 1-0 Jon Dahl Tomassen (35' penalty), 2-2 Martin Laursen (90'+5').
Romania: 1-1 Adrian Mutu (61'), 1-2 Daniel Pancu (72').
Referee: Urs Meier (SUI)   Attendance: 42.049

15

10-09-2003   Stade Josy Barthel, Luxembourg:
               Luxembourg – Bosnia-Herzegovina   0-1 (0-1)
Luxembourg: Alija Besic, Jeff Strasser (C), Manou Schauls, Claude Reiter, Eric Hoffmann, Sébastien Remy, René Peters, Fons Leweck, Ben Federspiel (YC16) (55' Gilles Engeldinger (YC87)), Daniel Huss, Gordon Braun (22' Paul Mannon (YC57)). (Coach: Allan Rodenkam Simonsen (DEN)).
Bosnia-Herzegovina: Kenan Hasagic, Muhamed Konjic, Vladan Grujic (62' Mirsad Beslija), Mirsad Hibic (C) (YC51), Emir Spahic, Hasan Salihamidzic, Mirko Hrgovic (78' Sasa Papac), Zlatan Bajramovic, Vedin Music, Elvir Bolic (62' Bulent Biscevic), Sergej Barbarez. (Coach: Blaz Sliskovic (BOS)).
Goal: Bosnia-Herzegovina: 0-1 Sergej Barbarez (35').
Referee: Costas Kapitanis (CYP)   Attendance: 3.425

11-10-2003   Ullevaal Stadion, Oslo: Norway – Luxembourg   1-0 (1-0)
Norway: Espen Johnsen, Claus Lundekvam, Henning Berg (C), Christer Basma, John Arne Riise, Fredrik Winsnes (81' Trond Andersen), Roar Strand, Martin Andresen, Harald Brattbakk, Håvard Flo (69' Frode Johnsen), Tore André Flo (85' Sigurd Rushfeldt). (Coach: Nils Johan Semb (NOR)).
Luxembourg: Alija Besic, Jeff Strasser (C), Manou Schauls, Eric Hoffmann, Sébastien Remy, René Peters (YC72), Fons Leweck (YC28), Ben Federspiel, Paul Mannon (71' Sven Di Domenico), Daniel Huss, Gordon Braun. (Coach: Allan Rodenkam Simonsen (DEN)).
Goal: Norway: 1-0 Tore André Flo (19').
Referee: Zsolt Szabó (HUN)   Attendance: 22.255

11-10-2003   Kosevo Stadium, Sarajevo: Bosnia-Herzegovina – Denmark   1-1 (1-1)
Bosnia-Herzegovina: Kenan Hasagic, Muhamed Konjic (80' Mirko Hrgovic (YC82)), Mirsad Hibic (C), Emir Spahic (YC27) (46' Elvir Baljic (YC67)), Hasan Salihamidzic, Vedin Music, Vladan Grujic, Mirsad Beslija (YC50), Zlatan Bajramovic (85' Bulent Biscevic), Elvir Bolic, Sergej Barbarez. (Coach: Blaz Sliskovic (BOS)).
Denmark: Thomas Sørensen, Martin Laursen, Niclas Jensen (YC69) (90' Per Nielsen), René Henriksen (C), Thomas Helveg, Christian Poulsen, Morten Wieghorst, Martin Jørgensen (55' Dennis Rommedahl), Jesper Grønkjær (85' Thomas Røll Larsen), Thomas Gravesen (YC31,YC90+1), Jon Dahl Tomassen. (Coach: Morten Per Olsen (DEN)).
Goals: Bosnia-Herzegovina: 1-1 Elvir Bolic (39').
Denmark: 0-1 Martin Jørgensen (12').
Referee: Graham Peter Barber (ENG)   Attendance: 32.000

16

GROUP 3

07-09-2002	Vienna	Austria –Moldova	2-0 (2-0)
07-09-2002	Eindhoven	Netherlands – Belarus	3-0 (2-0)
12-10-2002	Chisinau	Moldova – Czech Republic	0-2 (0-0)
12-10-2002	Minsk	Belarus – Austria	0-2 (0-0)
16-10-2002	Teplice	Czech Republic – Belarus	2-0 (2-0)
16-10-2002	Vienna	Austria – Netherlands	0-3 (0-3)
29-03-2003	Minsk	Belarus – Moldova	2-1 (1-1)
29-03-2003	Rotterdam	Netherlands – Czech Republic	1-1 (1-0)
02-04-2003	Tiraspol	Moldova – Netherlands	1-2 (1-1)
02-04-2003	Prague	Czech Republic – Austria	4-0 (2-0)
07-06-2003	Tiraspol	Moldova – Austria	1-0 (0-0)
07-06-2003	Minsk	Belarus – Netherlands	0-2 (0-0)
11-06-2003	Olomouc	Czech Republic – Moldova	5-0 (1-0)
11-06-2003	Innsbruck	Austria – Belarus	5-0 (1-0)
06-09-2003	Minsk	Belarus – Czech Republic	1-3 (1-1)
06-09-2003	Rotterdam	Netherlands – Austria	3-1 (1-1)
10-09-2003	Tiraspol	Moldova – Belarus	2-1 (1-0)
10-09-2003	Prague	Czech Republic – Netherlands	3-1 (2-0)
11-10-2003	Vienna	Austria – Czech Republic	2-3 (0-1)
11-10-2003	Eindhoven	Netherlands – Moldova	5-0 (1-0)

FINAL STANDING

Pos	Team	Pld	W	D	L	GF	GA	GD	Pts
1	Czech Republic	8	7	1	0	23	5	+18	22
2	Netherlands	8	6	1	1	20	6	+14	19
3	Austria	8	3	0	5	12	14	-2	9
4	Moldova	8	2	0	6	5	19	-14	6
5	Belarus	8	1	0	7	4	20	-16	3

Czech Republic qualified for the Final Tournament in Portugal.

Netherlands qualified for the play-offs.

07-09-2002   Ernst-Happel-Stadion, Vienna: Austria – Moldova 2-0 (2-0)
Austria: Alexander Manninger, Martin Hiden, Ernst Dospel, Michael Baur, René Aufhauser, Jürgen Panis, Thomas Flögel, Markus Schopp (58' Gerd Wimmer), Andreas Herzog (C), Roman Wallner (67' Roland Linz), Ivica Vastic (81' Michael Wagner). (Coach: Johann Hans Krankl (AUT)).
Moldova: Evgeni Hmaruc, Aleksandr Covalenco (YC62), Andrian Sosnovschi, Radu Rebeja, Ghenadie Olexic (YC3), Iurie Priganiuc (67' Vadim Boret), Stanislav Ivanov, Eugeniu Boicenco (46' Boris Cebotari), Serghei Rogaciov, Serghei Clescenco (C), Victor Berco (46' Valeriu Catinsus). (Coach: Viktor Vasilevich Pasulko (UKR)).
Goals: Austria: 1-0 Andreas Herzog (4' penalty), 2-0 Andreas Herzog (29' penalty).
Referee: Stuart Dougal (SCO)   Attendance: 18.300

07-09-2002   Philips Stadion, Eindhoven: Netherlands – Belarus   3-0 (2-0)
Netherlands: Edwin van der Sar, Fernando Ricksen, Jaap Stam, Frank de Boer (C), Edgar
Davids (70' Rafael van der Vaart, 83' Michael Reiziger), Andy van der Meyde, Mark van
Bommel, Phillip Cocu, Boudewijn Zenden, Ruud van Nistelrooy (70' Jimmy Floyd
Hasselbaink), Patrick Kluivert. (Coach: Dick Nicolaas Advocaat (HOL)).
Belarus: Valeri Shantalosov (89' Vasili Khomutovski), Aleksandr Lukhvich, Andrei Ostrovski
(YC85), Sergei Omelyanchuk (YC34) (76' Vladimir Shuneiko), Sergei Gurenko, Maksim
Romashchenko (YC29,YC84), Sergei Shtaniuk, Aleksandr Kulchiy, Aleksandr Khatskevich
(82' Denis Kovba), Aleksandr Hleb, Vitali Kutuzov. (Coach: Eduard Vasilevich Malofeev
(BLS)).
Goals: Netherlands: 1-0 Edgar Davids (35'), 2-0 Patrick Kluivert (37'), 3-0 Jimmy Floyd
Hasselbaink (73').
Referee: Graham Peter Barber (ENG)   Attendance: 32.000

12-10-2002   Stadionul Republican, Chisinau: Moldova – Czech Republic   0-2 (0-0)
Moldova: Evgeni Hmaruc, Aleksandr Covalenco, Andrian Sosnovschi (YC,YC69), Radu
Rebeja, Ghenadie Olexic, Valeriu Catinsus, Vadim Boret (65' Stanislav Ivanov), Boris
Cebotari, Ghenadie Pusca, Serghei Rogaciov (71' Alexandru Budanov), Serghei Clescenco (C)
(46' Evgeni Patula). (Coach: Viktor Vasilevich Pasulko (UKR)).
Czech Republic: Petr Cech, René Bolf, Tomás Ujfalusi, Zdenek Grygera (YC36), Marek
Jankulovski, Stepán Vachousek (87' Richard Dostálek), Tomás Rosicky (YC73) (81' Vratislav
Lokvenc), Karel Poborsky (C), Tomás Galásek (56' Jirí Jarosík (YC56)), Jirí Stajner, Jan
Koller. (Coach: Karel Brückner (CZE)).
Goals: Czech Republic: 0-1 Marek Jankulovski (69' penalty), 0-2 Tomás Rosicky (79').
Referee: Leslie John R.Irvine (NIR)   Attendance: 3.000

12-10-2002   Dinamo Stadium, Minsk: Belarus – Austria   0-2 (0-0)
Belarus: Gennadi Tumilovich, Andrei Ostrovski (YC66), Sergei Yaskovich (52' Sergei
Omelyanchuk), Vladimir Shuneiko (64' Roman Vasilyuk), Aleksandr Lukhvich (RC85),
Sergei Gurenko (C), Sergei Shtaniuk (YC79), Aleksandr Kulchiy, Aleksandr Khatskevich,
Aleksandr Hleb, Vitali Kutuzov (83' Nikolai Ryndyuk). (Coach: Eduard Vasilevich Malofeev
(BLS)).
Austria: Alexander Manninger, Martin Hiden (YC50), Ernst Dospel, Michael Baur (YC69),
Michael Wagner, Bozo Kovacevic (YC53) (89' René Aufhauser), Volkan Kahraman (83'
Andreas Herzog), Thomas Flögel, Harald Cerny (YC42), Markus Schopp, Roman Wallner (75'
Muhammet Akagündüz). (Coach: Johann Hans Krankl (AUT)).
Goals: Austria: 0-1 Markus Schopp (58'), 0-2 Muhammet Akagündüz (88').
Referee: Éric Poulat (FRA)   Attendance: 15.082

16-10-2002   Na Stínadlech, Teplice: Czech Republic – Belarus   2-0 (2-0)
Czech Republic: Petr Cech, Tomás Ujfalusi, Martin Jiránek (86' Zdenek Grygera), René Bolf,
Marek Jankulovski, Tomás Rosicky (90' Jirí Jarosík (YC90+2)), Karel Poborsky, Pavel
Nedved (C), Tomás Galásek (YC78), Jan Koller (57' Stepán Vachousek), Milan Baros.
(Coach: Karel Brückner (CZE)).
Belarus: Gennadi Tumilovich, Sergei Yaskovich (26' Andrei Lavrik), Vladimir Shuneiko (46'
Sergei Omelyanchuk), Aleksandr Khrapkovskiy (YC12), Sergei Gurenko (C), Maksim
Romashchenko, Sergei Shtaniuk (YC39), Aleksandr Kulchiy, Aleksandr Khatskevich,
Aleksandr Hleb (69' Nikolai Ryndyuk), Vitali Kutuzov. (Coach: Eduard Vasilevich Malofeev
(BLS)).
Goals: Czech Republic: 1-0 Karel Poborsky (6'), 2-0 Milan Baros (23').
Referee: Dr.Helmut Fleischer (GER)   Attendance: 12.851

18

16-10-2002   Ernst-Happel-Stadion, Vienna: Austria – Netherlands   0-3 (0-3)
Austria: Alexander Manninger, Martin Hiden (YC18,YC78), Ernst Dospel, Michael Baur,
Michael Wagner, Thomas Flögel, Harald Cerny, Markus Schopp (YC5), Andreas Herzog (46'
René Aufhauser), Markus Weissenberger (77' Muhammet Akagündüz), Roman Wallner (80'
Paul Scharner). (Coach: Johann Hans Krankl (AUT)).
Netherlands: Edwin van der Sar, Fernando Ricksen, Jaap Stam, Frank de Boer (C), Clarence
Seedorf (YC39), Edgar Davids, Mark van Bommel (77' Ronald de Boer), Phillip Cocu,
Boudewijn Zenden (YC8) (70' Wilfred Bouma), Roy Makaay (80' Jimmy Floyd Hasselbaink),
Patrick Kluivert. (Coach: Dick Nicolaas Advocaat (HOL)).
Goals: Netherlands: 0-1 Clarence Seedorf (15'), 0-2 Phillip Cocu (20'), 0-3 Roy Makaay (30').
Referee: Pierluigi Collina (ITA)   Attendance: 46.100

29-03-2002   Dinamo Stadium, Minsk: Belarus – Moldova   2-1 (1-1)
Belarus: Gennadi Tumilovich, Andrei Ostrovski, Vladimir Shuneiko (YC26), Sergei
Omelyanchuk, Sergei Gurenko (C), Andrei Lavrik, Aleksandr Kulchiy, Aleksandr
Khatskevich, Aleksandr Hleb (80' Maksim Romashchenko), Valentin Belkevich, Vitali
Kutuzov (88' Denis Kovba). (Coach: Eduard Vasilevich Malofeev (BLS)).
Moldova: Evgeni Hmaruc, Radu Rebeja, Ghenadie Olexic, Valeriu Catinsus, Aleksandr
Covalenco, Ion Testemitanu, Iurie Priganiuc, Serghei Covalciuc, Boris Cebotari (YC51) (80'
Alexandru Golban), Serghei Clescenco (C), Serghei Rogaciov (26' Alexandru Popovici, 62'
Victor Berco). (Coach: Viktor Vasilevich Pasulko (UKR)).
Goals: Belarus: 1-1 Vitali Kutuzov (43'), 2-1 Sergei Gurenko (58').
Moldova: 0-1 Boris Cebotari (14').
Referee: Johan Verbist (BEL)   Attendance: 7.700

29-03-2003   De Kuip, Rotterdam: Netherlands – Czech Republic   1-1 (1-0)
Netherlands: Ronald Waterreus, Fernando Ricksen, Jaap Stam, Frank de Boer (C), Clarence
Seedorf, Edgar Davids, Giovanni van Bronckhorst (39' Rafael van der Vaart), Mark van
Bommel (YC79), Boudewijn Zenden, Ruud van Nistelrooy (YC75) (81' Roy Makaay), Patrick
Kluivert. (Coach: Dick Nicolaas Advocaat (HOL)).
Czech Republic: Petr Cech, Tomás Ujfalusi, Zdenek Grygera, René Bolf, Marek Jankulovski,
Vladimír Smicer (YC26) (79' Martin Jiránek), Tomás Rosicky (68' Milan Baros), Karel
Poborsky, Pavel Nedved (C), Tomás Galásek, Jan Koller (87' Vratislav Lokvenc). (Coach:
Karel Brückner (CZE)).
Goals: Netherlands: 1-0 Ruud van Nistelrooy (45'+1').
Czech Republic: 1-1 Jan Koller (68').
Referee: Kim Milton Nielsen (DEN)   Attendance: 48.378

02-04-2003   Sheriff Stadium, Tiraspol: Moldova – Netherlands   1-2 (1-1)
Moldova: Evgeni Hmaruc, Aleksandr Covalenco (YC42), Ion Testemitanu, Ghenadie Olexic,
Valeriu Catinsus, Iurie Priganiuc, Stanislav Ivanov, Serghei Covalciuc (80' Victor Berco),
Boris Cebotari (88' Serghei Pogreban), Vadim Boret, Serghei Clescenco (C) (62' Alexandru
Golban). (Coach: Viktor Vasilevich Pasulko (UKR)).
Netherlands: Ronald Waterreus, Michael Reiziger, Jaap Stam (62' Fernando Ricksen), Frank
de Boer (C) (YC45+1), Edgar Davids, Rafael van der Vaart (75' Pierre van Hooijdonk),
Clarence Seedorf (66' Ronald de Boer), Mark van Bommel, Boudewijn Zenden, Ruud van
Nistelrooy, Patrick Kluivert. (Coach: Dick Nicolaas Advocaat (HOL)).
Goals: Moldova: 1-0 Vadim Boret (16').
Netherlands: 1-1 Ruud van Nistelrooy (37'), 1-2 Mark van Bommel (85').
Referee: Alain Sars (FRA)   Attendance: 9.500

02-04-2003   Toyota Arena, Prague: Czech Republic – Austria   4-0 (2-0)
Czech Republic: Petr Cech, Tomás Ujfalusi, Zdenek Grygera, René Bolf, Marek Jankulovski
(YC7), Vladimír Smicer (62' Tomás Rosicky), Karel Poborsky, Pavel Nedved (C) (73' Stepán
Vachousek), Tomás Galásek, Jan Koller (78' Vratislav Lokvenc), Milan Baros. (Coach: Karel
Brückner (CZE)).
Austria: Thomas Mandl, Mario Hieblinger (YC89), Emanuel Pogatetz, Martin Stranzl, Paul
Scharner, René Aufhauser, Thomas Flögel (C) (45'+1' Michael Wagner), Markus
Weissenberger, Markus Schopp, Andreas Herzog (YC21) (53' Bozo Kovacevic (RC55)),
Mario Haas (62' Ernst Dospel). (Coach: Johann Hans Krankl (AUT)).
Goals: Czech Republic: 1-0 Pavel Nedved (18'), 2-0 Jan Koller (32'), 3-0 Marek Jankulovsky
(56' penalty), 4-0 Jan Koller (62').
Referee: Antonio Jesús López Nieto (ESP)   Attendance: 17.150

07-06-2003   Sheriff Stadium, Tiraspol: Moldova – Austria   1-0 (0-0)
Moldova: Evgeni Hmaruc, Ghenadie Olexic, Valeriu Catinsus (C), Ion Testemitanu, Iurie
Priganiuc (YC87), Stanislav Ivanov, Serghei Covalciuc, Boris Cebotari, Vadim Boret (68'
Liviu Andriuta), Viorel Frunza (85' Eduard Valuta), Serghei Rogaciov (78' Evgeni Patula).
(Coach: Viktor Vasilevich Pasulko (UKR)).
Austria: Thomas Mandl, Ernst Dospel (56' Harald Cerny), Anton Ehmann (YC41), Paul
Scharner (YC76) (80' Thomas Eder), René Aufhauser, Martin Stranzl, Thomas Flögel (C),
Roland Kirchler, Michael Wagner (70' Roman Wallner), Markus Schopp (YC87), Mario Haas.
(Coach: Johann Hans Krankl (AUT)).
Goal: Moldova: 1-0 Viorel Frunza (60').
Referee: Joaquim Paulo Gomes Ferreira Paraty da Silva (POR)   Attendance: 3.864

07-06-2003   Dinamo Stadium, Minsk: Belarus – Netherlands   0-2 (0-0)
Belarus: Gennadi Tumilovich, Andrei Ostrovski, Vladimir Shuneiko (YC5) (75' Denis Kovba),
Aleksandr Lukhvich, Sergei Gurenko (C), Maksim Romashchenko (51' Aleksandr Hleb),
Sergei Shtanyuk (90' Sergei Omelyanchuk), Andrei Lavrik, Aleksandr Kulchiy (YC18),
Valentin Belkevich, Vitali Kutuzov. (Coach: Eduard Vasilevich Malofeev (BLS)).
Netherlands: Edwin van der Sar, Michael Reiziger (45' Paul Bosvelt), Jaap Stam, Frank de
Boer (C), Clarence Seedorf, Giovanni van Bronckhorst (60' Marc Overmars), Mark van
Bommel, Phillip Cocu, Boudewijn Zenden, Ruud van Nistelrooy (YC43) (76' Rafael van der
Vaart), Patrick Kluivert. (Coach: Dick Nicolaas Advocaat (HOL)).
Goals: Netherlands: 0-1 Marc Overmars (61'), 0-2 Patrick Kluivert (68').
Referee: Tom Henning Øvrebø (NOR)   Attendance: 19.309

11-06-2003   Andruv Stadion, Olomouc: Czech Republic – Moldova   5-0 (1-0)
Czech Republic: Petr Cech, Zdenek Grygera, René Bolf, Tomás Ujfalusi (YC53), Marek
Jankulovski, Vladimír Smicer (59' Milan Baros), Tomás Rosicky, Karel Poborsky (65' Jirí
Stajner), Pavel Nedved (C), Tomás Galásek, Jan Koller (80' Vratislav Lokvenc). (Coach: Karel
Brückner (CZE)).
Moldova: Evgeni Hmaruc, Valeriu Catinsus (C), Alexandr Covalenco (YC19), Ion
Testemitanu, Ghenadie Olexic, Iurie Priganiuc (YC36,YC78), Serghei Covalciuc (83' Serghei
Pogreban), Boris Cebotari (76' Evgeni Patula), Vadim Boret, Stanislav Ivanov, Serghei
Rogaciov (76' Viorel Frunza). (Coach: Viktor Vasilevich Pasulko (UKR)).
Goals: Czech Republic: 1-0 Vladimír Smicer (41'), 2-0 Jan Koller (73' penalty), 3-0 Jirí
Stajner (82'), 4-0 Vratislav Lokvenc (88'), 5-0 Vratislav Lokvenc (90'+2').
Referee: Kristinn Jakobsson (ISL)   Attendance: 12.097
(Marek Jankulovski missed a penalty in the 35th minute)

20

11-06-2003   Tivoli Neu, Innsbruck: Austria – Belarus   5-0 (1-0)
Austria: Thomas Mandl (86' Helge Payer), Anton Ehmann, Ernst Dospel, Martin Stranzl (46' Mario Hieblinger), Paul Scharner, René Aufhauser, Michael Wagner (YC78), Roland Kirchler, Thomas Flögel (C), Harald Cerny, Mario Haas (60' Roman Wallner). (Coach: Johann Hans Krankl (AUT)).
Belarus: Gennadi Tumilovich, Andrei Ostrovski, Aleksandr Lukhvich, Sergei Omelyanchuk (YC87), Sergei Gurenko (C), Maksim Romashchenko, Sergei Shtanyuk (66' Aleksandr Khrapkovskiy), Andrei Lavrik, Aleksandr Kulchiy, Valentin Belkevich (55' Denis Kovba), Vitali Kutuzov (46' Roman Vasilyuk). (Coach: Eduard Vasilevich Malofeev (BLS)).
Goals: Austria: 1-0 René Aufhauser (33'), 2-0 Mario Haas (47'), 3-0 Roland Kirchler (52'), 4-0 Roman Wallner (62'), 5-0 Harald Cerny (70').
Referee: Peter Fröjdfeldt (SWE)   Attendance: 8.100

06-09-2003   Dinamo Stadium, Minsk: Belarus – Czech Republic   1-3 (1-1)
Belarus: Gennadi Tumilovich (YC42), Andrei Ostrovski, Dmitri Rovneiko (90'+2' Aleksandr Khrapkovskiy), Aleksandr Lukhvich (YC36), Sergei Gurenko (C) (82' Vitali Volodenkov), Vyacheslav Geraschenko, Maksim Romashchenko (YC31), Sergei Shtanyuk, Aleksandr Kulchiy, Vitali Bulyga, Vitali Kutuzov (56' Aleksandr Hleb (YC79)). (Coach: Anatoliy Baydachnyi (RUS)).
Czech Republic: Petr Cech, René Bolf, Tomáš Ujfalusi, Zdenek Grygera, Marek Jankulovski (YC51), Roman Tyce (35' Vladimír Smicer) Tomáš Rosicky (83' Stepán Vachousek), Karel Poborsky (YC42), Pavel Nedved (C), Milan Baros (65' Tomáš Hübschman), Jan Koller. (Coach: Karel Brückner (CZE)).
Goals: Belarus: 1-0 Vitali Bulyga (14').
Czech Republic: 1-1 Pavel Nedved (36'), 1-2 Milan Baros (53'), 1-3 Vladimír Smicer (85').
Referee: Thomas Michael McCurry (SCO)   Attendance: 7.500

06-09-2003   De Kuip, Rotterdam: Netherlands – Austria   3-1 (1-1)
Netherlands: Edwin van der Sar, Michael Reiziger, Jaap Stam, Frank de Boer (C), Rafael van der Vaart, Edgar Davids (46' Marc Overmars), Andy van der Meyde (71' Arjen Robben), Mark van Bommel, Phillip Cocu, Boudewijn Zenden (46' Pierre van Hooijdonk), Patrick Kluivert. (Coach: Dick Nicolaas Advocaat (HOL)).
Austria: Thomas Mandl, Anton Ehmann (YC73), Ernst Dospel, Emanuel Pogatetz, Martin Hiden, René Aufhauser, Thomas Flögel (C), Andreas Ivanschitz (83' Matthias Dollinger), Markus Schopp, Roland Kollmann (65' Roland Kirchler), Edi Glieder (65' Mario Haas). (Coach: Johann Hans Krankl (AUT)).
Goals: Netherlands: 1-0 Rafael van der Vaart (29'), 2-1 Patrick Kluivert (60'), 3-1 Phillip Cocu (62').
Austria: 1-1 Emanuel Pogatetz (32').
Referee: Éric Poulat (FRA)   Attendance: 48.000

10-09-2003   Sheriff Stadium, Tiraspol: Moldova – Belarus   2-1 (1-0)
Moldova: Evgeni Hmaruc, Valeriu Catinsus (C), Alexandr Covalenco (74' Alexei Savinov), Eduard Valuta (69' Vadim Boret), Ghenadie Olexic (YC81), Serghei Covalciuc, Boris Cebotari, Victor Barisev, Stanislav Ivanov (YC53), Serghei Rogaciov, Serghei Dadu (67' Serghei Clescenco). (Coach: Viktor Vasilevich Pasulko (UKR)).
Belarus: Gennadi Tumilovich, Aleksandr Lukhvich, Andrei Ostrovski, Dmitri Rovneiko (YC7), Sergei Gurenko (C), Vyacheslav Geraschenko, Maksim Romashchenko (YC28) (64' Roman Vasilyuk), Aleksandr Kulchiy (YC81), Sergei Shtanyuk (41' Sergei Omelyanchuk), Vitali Kutuzov (51' Vitali Volodenkov), Vitali Bulyga. (Coach: Anatoliy Baydachnyi (RUS)).
Goals: Moldova: 1-0 Serghei Dadu (26'), 2-0 Serghei Covalciuc (87').
Belarus: 2-1 Roman Vasilyuk (90' penalty).
Referee: Dejan Delevic (SBM)   Attendance: 5.500

10-09-2003   Toyota Arena, Prague: Czech Republic – Netherlands   3-1 (2-0)
Czech Republic: Petr Cech, Tomás Ujfalusi (YC36), Martin Jiránek, Zdenek Grygera (25' Tomás Hübschman), René Bolf (YC38), Vladimír Smicer (81' Stepán Vachousek), Tomás Rosicky (59' Milan Baros (YC90+3)), Karel Poborsky (YC15), Pavel Nedved (C), Tomás Galásek, Jan Koller. (Coach: Karel Brückner (CZE)).
Netherlands: Edwin van der Sar, Michael Reiziger, Jaap Stam, Frank de Boer (C) (46' André Ooijer), Rafael van der Vaart, Edgar Davids (YC10,YC13), Mark van Bommel (YC90), Phillip Cocu, Marc Overmars (20' Paul Bosvelt), Ruud van Nistelrooy (YC45) (70' Pierre van Hooijdonk), Patrick Kluivert. (Coach: Dick Nicolaas Advocaat (HOL)).
Goals: Czech Republic: 1-0 Jan Koller (14' penalty), 2-0 Karel Poborsky (37'), 3-1 Milan Baros (90'+3').
Netherlands: 2-1 Rafael van der Vaart (60').
Referee: Lucílio Cardoso Cortez Batista (POR)   Attendance: 18.356

11-10-2003   Ernst-Happel-Stadion, Vienna: Austria – Czech Republic   2-3 (0-1)
Austria: Thomas Mandl, Emanuel Pogatetz, Martin Hiden (YC61), Martin Stranzl (YC54), René Aufhauser, Thomas Flögel (C) (69' Ernst Dospel), Markus Schopp (YC22,YC65), Andreas Ivanschitz, Joachim Standfest (YC52), Mario Haas (77' Roland Linz), Edi Glieder (69' Michael Wagner). (Coach: Johann Hans Krankl (AUT)).
Czech Republic: Petr Cech, Adam Petrous, Martin Jiránek (42' Roman Tyce), René Bolf, Marek Jankulovsky (84' Petr Vorísek), Stepán Vachousek, Pavel Nedved (C) (YC89), Tomás Galásek, Jirí Stajner, Vratislav Lokvenc, Marek Heinz (69' Jan Koller). (Coach: Karel Brückner (CZE)).
Goals: Austria: 1-1 Mario Haas (50'), 2-1 Andreas Ivanschitz (78').
Czech Republic: 0-1 Marek Jankulovsky (26'), 2-2 Stepán Vachousek (79'), 2-3 Jan Koller (90'+2').
Referee: Georgios Kasnaferis (GRE)   Attendance: 32.350

11-10-2003   Philips Stadion, Eindhoven: Netherlands – Moldova 5-0 (1-0)
Netherlands: Edwin van der Sar, Michael Reiziger (33' Roy Makaay), Jaap Stam (YC29),
André Ooijer, Rafael van der Vaart, Wesley Sneijder, Andy van der Meyde, Giovanni van
Bronckhorst, Phillip Cocu, Marc Overmars (65' Arjen Robben), Patrick Kluivert (71' Pierre
van Hooijdonk). (Coach: Dick Nicolaas Advocaat (HOL)).
Moldova: Evgeni Hmaruc, Alexandr Covalenco (63' Ion Testemitanu), Eduard Valuta, Valeriu
Catinsus (C), Iurie Priganiuc (YC74), Stanislav Ivanov (82' Iuri Miterev), Serghei Covalciuc,
Boris Cebotari, Victor Barisev, Alexei Savinov (YC79), Serghei Dadu (75' Alexandru
Golban). (Coach: Viktor Vasilevich Pasulko (UKR)).
Goals: Netherlands: 1-0 Patrick Kluivert (44'), 2-0 Wesley Sneijder (51'), 3-0 Pierre van
Hooijdonk (74' penalty), 4-0 Rafael van der Vaart (80'), 5-0 Arjen Robben (89').
Referee: Zeljko Siric (CRO)   Attendance: 30.995

GROUP 4

07-09-2002	Riga	Latvia – Sweden	0-0
07-09-2002	Serravalle	San Marino – Poland	0-2 (0-0)
12-10-2002	Solna	Sweden – Hungary	1-1 (0-1)
12-10-2002	Warsaw	Poland – Latvia	0-1 (0-1)
16-10-2002	Budapest	Hungary – San Marino	3-0 (0-0)
20-11-2002	Serravalle	San Marino – Latvia	0-1 (0-0)
29-03-2003	Chorzów	Poland – Hungary	0-0
02-04-2003	Ostrowiec Swietokrzyski	Poland – San Marino	5-0 (2-0)
02-04-2003	Budapest	Hungary – Sweden	1-2 (0-1)
30-04-2003	Riga	Latvia – San Marino	3-0 (2-0)
07-06-2003	Budapest	Hungary – Latvia	3-1 (0-1)
07-06-2003	Serravalle	San Marino – Sweden	0-6 (0-1)
11-06-2003	Solna	Sweden – Poland	3-0 (2-0)
11-06-2003	Serravalle	San Marino – Hungary	0-5 (0-2)
06-09-2003	Gothenburg	Sweden – San Marino	5-0 (1-0)
06-09-2003	Riga	Latvia – Poland	0-2 (0-2)
10-09-2003	Riga	Latvia – Hungary	3-1 (2-0)
10-09-2003	Chorzów	Poland – Sweden	0-2 (0-2)
11-10-2003	Solna	Sweden – Latvia	0-1 (0-1)
11-10-2003	Budapest	Hungary – Poland	1-2 (0-1)

FINAL STANDING

Pos	Team	Pld	W	D	L	GF	GA	GD	Pts
1	Sweden	8	5	2	1	19	3	+16	17
2	Latvia	8	5	1	2	10	6	+4	16
3	Poland	8	4	1	3	11	7	+4	13
4	Hungary	8	3	2	3	15	9	+6	11
5	San Marino	8	0	0	8	0	30	-30	0

Sweden qualified for the Final Tournament in Portugal.

Latvia qualified for the play-offs.

07-09-2002   Skonto stadions, Riga: Latvia – Sweden   0-0
Latvia: Aleksandrs Kolinko, Igors Stepanovs, Aleksandrs Isakovs, Olegs Blagonadezdins, Mihails Zemlinskis (YC12), Andrejs Rubins, Juris Laizāns (YC84), Imants Bleidelis, Vitālijs Astafjevs, Māris Verpakovskis, Marians Pahars (79' Andrejs Stolcers). (Coach: Aleksandrs Starkovs (LAT)).
Sweden: Magnus Hedman, Andreas Jakobsson, Tomas Gustafsson-Antonelius, Michael Svensson, Olof Mellberg, Pontus Farnerud (55' Mattias Jonson), Niclas Alexandersson, Magnus Svensson (79' Andreas Johansson), Tobias Linderoth, Zlatan Ibrahimovic (YC61) (64' Kim Källström), Marcus Allbäck (YC74). (Coaches: Lars Lagerbäck (SWE) & Tommy Söderberg (SWE)).
Referee: Frank de Bleeckere (BEL)   Attendance: 8.500

07-09-2002   Stadio Olimpico, Serravalle: San Marino – Poland   0-2 (0-0)
San Marino: Federico Gasperoni, Mirco Gennari, Damiano Vannucci (82' Roberto Selva), Simone Bacciocchi, Nicola Albani, Lorenzo Moretti (70' Ermanno Zonzini), Ivan Matteoni (C), Michele Marani (YC26), Mauro Marani, Andrea Ugolini (78' Marco De Luigi), Andy Selva. (Coach: Giampaolo Mazza (SMR)).
Poland: Wojciech Kowalewski, Mariusz Kukielka, Tomasz Klos, Arkadiusz Glowacki (YC40), Jacek Bak (C), Kamil Kosowski, Radoslaw Kaluzny (60' Marcin Zewlakow), Pawel Kaczorowski, Artur Wichniarek (46' Tomasz Dawidowski), Maciej Zurawski, Emmanuel Olisadebe (80' Mariusz Lewandowski). (Coach: Zbigniew Boniek (POL)).
Goals: Poland: 0-1 Pawel Kaczorowski (75'), 0-2 Mariusz Kukielka (88').
Referee: Paul McKeon (IRL)   Attendance: 2.421

12-10-2002   Råsunda Stadium, Solna: Sweden – Hungary   1-1 (0-1)
Sweden: Andreas Isaksson, Michael Svensson (YC85), Olof Mellberg, Andreas Jakobsson, Tomas Gustafsson-Antonelius (67' Mattias Jonson), Fredrik Ljungberg, Tobias Linderoth (YC53), Niclas Alexandersson (59' Kim Källström), Anders Svensson, Anders Andersson, Zlatan Ibrahimovic (YC41) (78' Marcus Allbäck). (Coaches: Lars Lagerbäck (SWE) & Tommy Söderberg (SWE)).
Hungary: Gábor Király, Flórián Urbán, Zsolt Löw, Gábor Gyepes, Csaba Fehér (YC37), Attila Dragóner, Krisztián Lisztes (YC38), Péter Lipcsei (YC25), Pál Dárdai, Attila Tököli (59' Miklós Fehér), Krisztián Kenesei (70' Zoltán Gera). (Coach: Imre Gellei (HUN)).
Goals: Sweden: 1-1 Zlatan Ibrahimovic (76').
Hungary: 0-1 Krisztián Kenesei (5').
Referee: Wolfgang Stark (GER)   Attendance: 35.084

12-10-2002   Polish Army Stadium, Warsaw: Poland – Latvia   0-1 (0-1)
Poland: Jerzy Dudek, Krzysztof Ratajczyk, Mariusz Kukielka, Tomasz Hajto, Jacek Zielinski, Michal Zewlakow (46' Lukasz Surma), Kamil Kosowski (63' Marcin Mieciel), Mariusz Lewandowski, Artur Wichniarek (46' Marcin Zewlakow), Maciej Zurawski, Tomasz Dawidowski. (Coach: Zbigniew Boniek (POL)).
Latvia: Aleksandrs Kolinko, Igors Stepanovs, Aleksandrs Isakovs, Olegs Blagonadezdins, Mihails Zemlinskis, Andrejs Rubins, Juris Laizāns, Imants Bleidelis, Vitālijs Astafjevs (YC78), Māris Verpakovskis (89' Andrejs Stolcers), Marians Pahars (58' Andrejs Prohorenkovs). (Coach: Aleksandrs Starkovs (LAT)).
Goal: Latvia: 0-1 Juris Laizāns (30').
Referee: Massimo Busacca (SUI)   Attendance: 11.814

24

16-10-2002   Szusza Ferenc Stadium, Budapest: Hungary – San Marino   3-0 (0-0)
Hungary: Gábor Király, Csaba Fehér, Attila Dragóner, Flórián Urbán (YC58), Zsolt Löw,
Gábor Gyepes, Krisztián Lisztes (84' Vasile László Miriuta), Péter Lipcsei, Pál Dárdai (78'
Miklós Fehér), Attila Tököli, Krisztián Kenesei (46' Zoltán Gera). (Coach: Imre Gellei
(HUN)).
San Marino: Federico Gasperoni, Mirco Gennari, Simone Bacciocchi, Nicola Albani, Luca
Gobbi, Damiano Vannucci (YC68), Carlo Valentini (YC67) (81' Ermanno Zonzini), Riccardo
Muccioli (73' Paolo Montagna), Lorenzo Moretti (55' Roberto Selva (YC64)), Michele
Marani, Andy Selva. (Coach: Giampaolo Mazza (SMR)).
Goals: Hungary: 1-0 Zoltán Gera (49'), 2-0 Zoltán Gera (60'), 3-0 Zoltán Gera (85').
Referee: Gylfi Thór Orrason (ISL)   Attendance: 4.136

20-11-2002   Stadio Olimpico, Serravalle: San Marino – Latvia   0-1 (0-0)
San Marino: Federico Gasperoni, Luca Gobbi, Mirco Gennari (86' Nicola Albani), Simone
Bacciocchi, Damiano Vannucci, Carlo Valentini (YC20), Ivan Matteoni (C), Riccardo
Muccioli (YC88), Michele Marani (53' Ermanno Zonzini), Paolo Montagna (59' Marco De
Luigi), Andy Selva. (Coach: Giampaolo Mazza (SMR)).
Latvia: Aleksandrs Kolinko, Aleksandrs Isakovs, Olegs Blagonadezdins, Igors Stepanovs,
Mihails Zemlinskis, Vladimirs Kolesnicenko (57' Andrejs Prohorenkovs), Imants Bleidelis
(46' Andrejs Stolcers), Vitālijs Astafjevs (C), Andrejs Rubins, Māris Verpakovskis (63'
Mihails Miholaps), Marians Pahars. (Coach: Aleksandrs Starkovs (LAT)).
Goal: Latvia: 0-1 Carlo Valentini (89' *own goal*).
Referee: Asim Khudiev (AZE)   Attendance: 637

29-03-2003   Silesian Stadium, Chorzów: Poland – Hungary   0-0
Poland: Jerzy Dudek, Maciej Stolarczyk (YC25), Tomasz Hajto, Jacek Bak (YC79), Piotr
Swierczewski, Kamil Kosowski, Radoslaw Kaluzny, Miroslaw Szymkowiak, Emmanuel
Olisadebe, Marcin Zajac (71' Tomasz Dawidowski), Marcin Kuzba. (Coach: Pawel Janas
(POL)).
Hungary: Gábor Király, Tamás Juhár, Csaba Fehér, Attila Dragóner (YC33), Pál Dárdai, Zsolt
Löw, Krisztián Lisztes, Péter Lipcsei, Flórián Urbán, Krisztián Kenesei (69' József Sebök),
Attila Tököli (85' Zoltan Böör). (Coach: Imre Gellei (HUN)).
Referee: Massimo de Santis (ITA)   Attendance: 42.200

02-04-2003   Miejski Stadion Sportowy "KSZO" w Ostrowcu., Ostrowiec Swietokryski:
                Poland – San Marino   5-0 (2-0)
Poland: Jerzy Dudek, Jacek Bak (63' Marcin Wasilewski), Miroslaw Sznaucner, Jacek
Zielinski, Miroslaw Szymkowiak, Kamil Kosowski, Marcin Burkhardt, Maciej Zurawski,
Marcin Zajac (46' Bartosz Karwan), Emmanuel Olisadebe (39' Jacek Krzynówek), Marcin
Kuzba. (Coach: Pawel Janas (POL)).
San Marino: Federico Gasperoni, Ermanno Zonzini (67' Bryan Gasperoni), Simone
Bacciocchi, Nicola Albani, Damiano Vannucci, Riccardo Muccioli, Lorenzo Moretti, Ivan
Matteoni (C), Michele Marani, Paolo Montagna (75' Marco De Luigi), Andy Selva (90'+1'
Andrea Ugolini). (Coach: Giampaolo Mazza (SMR)).
Goals: Poland: 1-0 Miroslaw Szymkowiak (3'), 2-0 Kamil Kosowski (26'), 3-0 Marcin Kuzba
(54'), 4-0 Bartosz Karwan (81'), 5-0 Marcin Kuzba (90'+3').
Referee: Loizos Loizou (CYP)   Attendance: 8.500

25

02-04-2003   Stadium Puskás Ferenc, Budapest: Hungary – Sweden   1-2 (0-1)
Hungary: Gábor Király, Zsolt Löw, Tamás Juhár, Csaba Fehér, Attila Dragóner, Flórián Urbán (60' László Bodnár), Krisztián Lisztes, Péter Lipcsei (79' Zoltan Böör), Pál Dárdai, Krisztián Kenesei, Attila Tököli (67' József Sebök (YC74)). (Coach: Imre Gellei (HUN)).
Sweden: Andreas Isaksson, Johan Mjällby (YC41), Olof Mellberg, Teddy Lucic, Erik Edman, Michael Svensson (YC68), Fredrik Ljungberg (YC90+2), Anders Svensson (YC51) (59' Kim Källström (YC90+1)), Anders Andersson, Marcus Allbäck (90'+2' Mattias Jonson), Henrik Larsson. (Coaches: Lars Lagerbäck (SWE) & Tommy Söderberg (SWE)).
Goals: Hungary: 1-1 Krisztián Lisztes (64').
Sweden: 0-1 Marcus Allbäck (33'), 1-2 Marcus Allbäck (66').
Referee: Lucílio Cardoso Cortez Batista (POR)   Attendance: 22.162

30-04-2003   Skonto stadions, Riga: Latvia – San Marino   3-0 (2-0)
Latvia: Aleksandrs Kolinko, Igors Stepanovs, Aleksandrs Isakovs (YC86), Dzintars Zirnis, Mihails Zemlinskis (C), Andrejs Rubins, Juris Laizāns, Imants Bleidelis (85' Viktors Dobrecovs), Māris Verpakovskis (60' Vits Rimkus), Andrejs Prohorenkovs, Mihails Miholaps (79' Andrejs Stolcers). (Coach: Aleksandrs Starkovs (LAT)).
San Marino: Federico Gasperoni, Carlo Valentini, Mirco Gennari (77' Lorenzo Moretti), Damiano Vannucci, Simone Bacciocchi, Nicola Albani, Riccardo Muccioli (YC35) (90' Bryan Gasperoni), Ivan Matteoni (C), Michele Marani (YC50), Paolo Montagna (65' Marco De Luigi), Andy Selva. (Coach: Giampaolo Mazza (SMR)).
Goals: Latvia: 1-0 Andrejs Prohorenkovs (10'), 2-0 Imants Bleidelis (21'), 3-0 Imants Bleidelis (74').
Referee: Hubert Byrne (IRL)   Attendance: 7.500

07-06-2003   Stadium Puskás Ferenc, Budapest: Hungary – Latvia   3-1 (0-1)
Hungary: Zoltán Végh, Flórián Urbán (YC4), Zsolt Löw, Tamás Juhár (RC61), Csaba Fehér (YC80), Attila Dragóner (38' Zoltán Gera), Krisztián Lisztes (77' Zoltan Böör), Péter Lipcsei, Pál Dárdai, Krisztián Kenesei (64' Miklós Lendvai), Imre Szabics. (Coach: Imre Gellei (HUN)).
Latvia: Aleksandrs Kolinko (YC32), Igors Stepanovs, Valentins Lobanovs (70' Mihails Miholaps), Aleksandrs Isakovs, Olegs Blagonadezdins, Mihails Zemlinskis (C), Vitalijs Astafjevs (YC81) (86' Igors Semjonovs), Andrejs Rubins, Juris Laizāns, Imants Bleidelis (71' Andrejs Stolcers), Māris Verpakovskis. (Coach: Aleksandrs Starkovs (LAT)).
Goals: Hungary: 1-1 Imre Szabics (51'), 2-1 Imre Szabics (58'), 3-1 Zoltán Gera (87').
Latvia: 0-1 Māris Verpakovskis (38').
Referee: Dr.Markus Merk (GER)   Attendance: 4.000

07-06-2003   Stadio Olimpico, Serravalle: San Marino – Sweden   0-6 (0-1)
San Marino: Federico Gasperoni, Mirco Gennari, Simone Bacciocchi, Nicola Albani, Damiano Vannucci (77' Marco De Luigi), Carlo Valentini (66' Ermanno Zonzini), Lorenzo Moretti (YC53) (86' Roberto Selva), Ivan Matteoni (C), Bryan Gasperoni, Paolo Montagna, Andy Selva. (Coach: Giampaolo Mazza (SMR)).
Sweden: Andreas Isaksson, Erik Edman, Johan Mjällby (73' Andreas Johansson), Olof Mellberg, Teddy Lucic, Andreas Jakobsson, Fredrik Ljungberg (73' Mikael Nilsson), Kim Källström (57' Anders Svensson), Anders Andersson, Marcus Allbäck, Mattias Jonson. (Coaches: Lars Lagerbäck (SWE) & Tommy Söderberg (SWE)).
Goals: Sweden: 0-1 Mattias Jonson (16'), 0-2 Marcus Allbäck (49'), 0-3 Fredrik Ljungberg (55'), 0-4 Mattias Jonson (60'), 0-5 Mattias Jonson (70'), 0-6 Marcus Allbäck (85').
Referee: Dejan Delevic (SBM)   Attendance: 2.184

26

11-06-2003   Råsunda Stadium, Solna: Sweden – Poland   3-0 (2-0)
Sweden: Andreas Isaksson, Johan Mjällby (C), Olof Mellberg, Teddy Lucic (88' Michael Svensson), Andreas Jakobsson (YC25), Erik Edman, Mikael Nilsson, Fredrik Ljungberg (YC64), Anders Svensson, Mattias Jonson (69' Magnus Svensson), Marcus Allbäck. (Coaches: Lars Lagerbäck (SWE) & Tommy Söderberg (SWE)).
Poland: Jerzy Dudek, Maciej Stolarczyk, Tomasz Hajto, Jacek Bak, Marcin Baszczynski (YC29) (46' Tomasz Klos), Miroslaw Szymkowiak (76' Marcin Burkhardt), Kamil Kosowski (64' Marcin Zajac), Thomas Zdebel (YC74), Jacek Krzynówek, Tomasz Dawidowski (YC24), Artur Wichniarek. (Coach: Pawel Janas (POL)).
Goals: Sweden: 1-0 Anders Svensson (16'), 2-0 Marcus Allbäck (43'), 3-0 Anders Svensson (72').
Referee: Gilles Veissière (FRA)   Attendance: 35.220
11-06-2003   Stadio Olimpico, Serravalle: San Marino – Hungary   0-5 (0-2)
San Marino: Federico Gasperoni, Ermanno Zonzini, Nicola Albani (YC8), Damiano Vannucci (65' Mirco Gennari), Carlo Valentini, Simone Bacciocchi, Ivan Matteoni (C), Bryan Gasperoni, Michele Marani, (YC57) Marco De Luigi (73' Paolo Montagna (YC90+1)), Andy Selva. (Coach: Giampaolo Mazza (SMR)).
Hungary: Zoltán Végh, Tamás Szekeres (55' Ákos Füzi), Tamás Bódog, Zsolt Löw, Attila Dragóner, Zoltan Böör, Krisztián Lisztes, Péter Lipcsei (73' Miklós Lendvai), Pál Dárdai (YC58) (79' Gábor Zavadszky), Krisztián Kenesei, Imre Szabics. (Coach: Imre Gellei (HUN)).
Goals: Hungary: 0-1 Zoltan Böör (4'), 0-2 Krisztián Lisztes (20'), 0-3 Krisztián Kenesei (60'), 0-4 Imre Szabics (76'), 0-5 Krisztián Lisztes (81').
Referee: Kenneth William Clark (SCO)   Attendance: 1.410
(Andy Selva misses a penalty in the 75th minute)

06-09-2003   Ullevi, Gothenburg: Sweden – San Marino   5-0 (1-0)
Sweden: Andreas Isaksson, Michael Svensson, Olof Mellberg, Teddy Lucic, Andreas Jakobsson (64' Tobias Linderoth), Erik Edman, Mikael Nilsson, Kim Källström, Anders Svensson (64' Andreas Johansson), Mattias Jonson (72' Niklas Skoog), Zlatan Ibrahimovic. (Coaches: Lars Lagerbäck (SWE) & Tommy Söderberg (SWE)).
San Marino: Federico Gasperoni, Mirco Gennari (25' Luca Nanni), Damiano Vannucci, Carlo Valentini, Simone Bacciocchi, Nicola Albani, Lorenzo Moretti, Ivan Matteoni (C) (YC68), Alex Gasperoni (8' Ermanno Zonzini, 85' Roberto Selva), Michele Marani, Paolo Montagna. (Coach: Giampaolo Mazza (SMR)).
Goals: Sweden: 1-0 Mattias Jonson (32'), 2-0 Andreas Jakobsson (48'), 3-0 Zlatan Ibrahimovic (53'), 4-0 Kim Källström (66' penalty), 5-0 Zlatan Ibrahimovic (81' penalty).
Referee: Stefan Messner (AUT)   Attendance: 31.098

06-09-2003   Skonto stadions, Riga: Latvia – Poland   0-2 (0-2)
Latvia: Aleksandrs Kolinko, Valentins Lobanovs (YC63), Aleksandrs Isakovs (YC42), Olegs Blagonadezdins (YC84), Igors Stepanovs, Mihails Zemlinskis (C), Andrejs Rubins (YC65) (76' Igors Semjonovs), Juris Laizāns (RC60), Imants Bleidelis, Andrejs Prohorenkovs (79' Vits Rimkus), Māris Verpakovskis (82' Andrejs Stolcers). (Coach: Aleksandrs Starkovs (LAT)).
Poland: Jerzy Dudek, Krzysztof Ratajczyk, Tomasz Klos, Tomasz Hajto (YC66), Jacek Bak, Radoslaw Sobolewski, Miroslaw Szymkowiak (89' Thomas Zdebel), Mariusz Lewandowski (YC36) (68' Kamil Kosowski), Jacek Krzynówek, Pawel Kryszalowicz (46' Marek Saganowski), Maciej Zurawski (YC64). (Coach: Pawel Janas (POL)).
Goals: Poland: 0-1 Miroslaw Szymkowiak (36'), 0-2 Tomasz Klos (39').
Referee: Kyros Vassaras (GRE)   Attendance: 6.500

27

10-09-2003   Skonto stadions, Riga: Latvia – Hungary 3-1 (2-0)
Latvia: Aleksandrs Kolinko, Valentins Lobanovs, Olegs Blagonadezdins, Igors Stepanovs, Dzintars Zirnis, Mihails Zemlinskis, Imants Bleidelis, Vitalijs Astafjevs (C), Andrejs Rubins, Vits Rimkus (76' Igors Semjonovs), Māris Verpakovskis (89' Vladimirs Kolesnicenko). (Coach: Aleksandrs Starkovs (LAT)).
Hungary: Gábor Király (C), Tamás Juhár, Csaba Fehér (YC19), Attila Dragóner, Zsolt Löw (46' Zoltan Böör), Krisztián Lisztes, Péter Lipcsei, Pál Dárdai, Miklós Fehér (46' Krisztián Kenesei), Zoltán Gera (87' Zoltán Kovács), Imre Szabics. (Coach: Imre Gellei (HUN)).
Goals: Latvia: 1-0 Māris Verpakovskis (38'), 2-0 Vits Rimkus (43'), 3-0 Māris Verpakovskis (51').
Hungary: 3-1 Krisztián Lisztes (53').
Referee: Claus Bo Larsen (DEN)   Attendance: 4.500

10-09-2003   Silisian Stadium, Chorzów: Poland – Sweden 0-2 (0-2)
Poland: Jerzy Dudek, Tomasz Klos (YC58), Tomasz Hajto (C) (YC36,RC63), Jacek Bak, Radoslaw Sobolewski, Michal Zewlakow, Miroslaw Szymkowiak, Jacek Krzynówek, Mariusz Lewandowski (67' Kamil Kosowski), Maciej Zurawski (74' Pawel Kryszalowicz), Marek Saganowski (YC60) (63' Grzegorz Rasiak (YC)). (Coach: Pawel Janas (POL)).
Sweden: Andreas Isaksson, Andreas Jakobsson, Erik Edman, Michael Svensson (YC10), Olof Mellberg (C), Teddy Lucic, Mikael Nilsson, Fredrik Ljungberg, Anders Svensson, Mattias Jonson (86' Anders Andersson), Marcus Allbäck (89' Zlatan Ibrahimovic). (Coaches: Lars Lagerbäck (SWE) & Tommy Söderberg (SWE)).
Goals: Sweden: 0-1 Mikael Nilsson (3'), 0-2 Olof Mellberg (38').
Referee: Michael (Mike) Riley (ENG)   Attendance: 18.500

11-10-2003   Råsunda Stadium, Solna: Sweden – Latvia 0-1 (0-1)
Sweden: Andreas Isaksson, Michael Svensson (YC44), Olof Mellberg (C), Teddy Lucic (46' Mikael Dorsin), Andreas Jakobsson, Christoffer Andersson (80' Andreas Johansson), Mikael Nilsson, Kim Källström (63' Zlatan Ibrahimovic), Anders Svensson, Mattias Jonson, Marcus Allbäck. (Coaches: Lars Lagerbäck (SWE) & Tommy Söderberg (SWE)).
Latvia: Aleksandrs Kolinko, Igors Stepanovs, Valentins Lobanovs, Olegs Blagonadezdins, Dzintars Zirnis (RC72), Mihails Zemlinskis (YC36), Andrejs Rubins (80' Jurgis Pucinskis), Imants Bleidelis, Vitalijs Astafjevs (C), Māris Verpakovskis (88' Andrejs Stolcers), Vits Rimkus (74' Aleksandrs Isakovs). (Coach: Aleksandrs Starkovs (LAT)).
Goal: Latvia: 0-1 Māris Verpakovskis (22').
Referee: Massimo de Santis (ITA)   Attendance: 32.095

11-10-2003   Stadium Puskás Ferenc, Budapest: Hungary – Poland 1-2 (0-1)
Hungary: Gábor Király (C), Tamás Bódog (YC90+2), Tamás Juhár (YC69), Ákos Füzi, Attila Dragóner, Zoltan Böör (YC62), Krisztián Lisztes (YC45), Péter Lipcsei (46' Zoltán Gera), Pál Dárdai, Miklós Fehér (64' Krisztián Kenesei), Imre Szabics. (Coach: Imre Gellei (HUN)).
Poland: Jerzy Dudek, Tomasz Klos, Jacek Bak (C), Tomasz Rzasa, Radoslaw Sobolewski (YC38), Michal Zewlakow, Sebastian Mila (52' Kamil Kosowski), Miroslaw Szymkowiak (85' Mariusz Lewandowski), Jacek Krzynówek, Andrzej Niedzielan (87' Marek Saganowski), Grzegorz Rasiak. (Coach: Pawel Janas (POL)).
Goals: Hungary: 1-1 Imre Szabics (48').
Poland: 0-1 Andrzej Niedzielan (10'), 1-2 Andrzej Niedzielan (62').
Referee: Manuel Enrique Mejuto González (ESP)   Attendance: 13.800

28

07-09-2002	Toftir	Faroe Islands – Scotland	2-2 (2-0)
07-09-2002	Kaunas	Lithuania – Germany	0-2 (0-1)
12-10-2002	Reykjavik	Iceland – Scotland	0-2 (0-1)
12-10-2002	Kaunas	Lithuania – Faroe Islands	2-0 (2-0)
16-10-2002	Reykjavik	Iceland – Lithuania	3-0 (0-0)
16-10-2002	Hanover	Germany – Faroe Islands	2-1 (1-1)
29-03-2003	Glasgow	Scotland – Iceland	2-1 (1-0)
29-03-2003	Nuremberg	Germany – Lithuania	1-1 (1-0)
02-04-2003	Kaunas	Lithuania – Scotland	1-0 (0-0)
07-06-2003	Glasgow	Scotland – Germany	1-1 (0-1)
07-06-2003	Reykjavik	Iceland – Faroe Islands	2-1 (0-0)
11-06-2003	Kaunas	Lithuania – Iceland	0-3 (0-0)
11-06-2003	Tórshavn	Faroe Islands – Germany	0-2 (0-0)
20-08-2003	Tórshavn	Faroe Islands – Iceland	1-2 (0-1)
06-09-2003	Glasgow	Scotland – Faroe Islands	3-1 (2-1)
06-09-2003	Reykjavik	Iceland – Germany	0-0
10-09-2003	Toftir	Faroe Islands – Lithuania	1-3 (1-1)
10-09-2003	Dortmund	Germany – Scotland	2-1 (1-0)
11-10-2003	Glasgow	Scotland – Lithuania	1-0 (0-0)
11-10-2003	Hamburg	Germany – Iceland	3-0 (1-0)

FINAL STANDING

Pos	Team	Pld	W	D	L	GF	GA	GD	Pts
1	*Germany*	*8*	*5*	*3*	*0*	*13*	*4*	*+9*	*18*
2	Scotland	8	4	2	2	12	8	+4	14
3	Iceland	8	4	1	3	11	9	+2	13
4	Lithuania	8	3	1	4	7	11	-4	10
5	Faroe Islands	8	0	1	7	7	18	-11	1

Germany qualified for the Final Tournament in Portugal.

Scotland qualified for the play-offs.

07-09-2002   Svangaskard, Toftir: Faroe Islands – Scotland 2-2 (2-0)
Faroe Islands: Jens Martin Knudsen (YC78), Jens Kristian Hansen, Pól Thorsteinsson, Óli Johannesen, Hjalgrím Elttør (89' Hedin á Lakjuni), Fródi Benjaminsen, Julian Schantz Johnsson, John Petersen (80' Andrew av Fløtum), Christian Jacobsen (75' Rógvi Jacobsen), Jákup á Borg (YC18), Jón Jacobsen. (Coach: Henrik Larsen (DEN)).
Scotland: Robert James (Rab) Douglas, Christian Dailly, Stephen Crainey, Maurice Ross (YC45+1) (75' Graham Alexander), David Weir (YC71), Paul Lambert (C), Allan Johnston, Barry Ferguson, Scott Dobie (83' Steven Thompson (YC88)), Paul Dickov (46' Steven Crawford), Kevin Kyle. (Coach: Hans-Hubert (Berti) Vogts (GER)).
Goals: Faroe Islands: 1-0 John Petersen (7'), 2-0 John Petersen (13').
Scotland: 2-1 Paul Lambert (62'), 2-2 Barry Ferguson (83').
Referee: Jacek Granat (POL)   Attendance: 4.000

07-09-2002   S.Darius and S.Girénas Stadium. Kaunas: Lithuania – Germany   0-2 (0-1)
Lithuania: Gintaras Staucé, Dainius Gleveckas, Marius Stankevicius, Aurelijus Skarbalius, Ignas Dedura, Deividas Semberas (YC60), Saulius Mikalajūnas, Tomas Razanauskas (71' Igoris Morinas), Raimondas Zutautas, Robertas Poskus, Edgaras Jankauskas (78' Artūras Fomenka). (Coach: Benjaminas Zelkevicius (LIT)).
Germany: Oliver Kahn, Christoph Metzelder (YC34), Thomas Linke, Dietmar Hamann, Torsten Frings (YC49), Jörg Böhme, Michael Ballack, Bernd Schneider (81' Jens Jeremies), Carsten Ramelow, Carsten Jancker (YC53) (69' Oliver Neuville), Miroslav Klose. (Coach: Rudolf (Rudi) Völler (GER)).
Goals: Germany: 0-1 Michael Ballack (27'), 0-2 Marius Stankevicius (59' *own goal*).
Referee: Graham Poll (ENG)   Attendance: 8.244

12-10-2002   Laugardalsvöllur, Reykjavik: Iceland – Scotland   0-2 (0-1)
Iceland: Árni Arason, Bjarni Thorsteinsson, Lárus Sigurdsson, Hermann Hreidarsson, Brynjar Gunnarsson, Rúnar Kristinsson (C) (YC32), Ívar Ingimarsson, Arnar Vidarsson (66' Marel Baldvinsson), Helgi Sigurdsson (46' Heidar Helguson), Haukur Ingi Gudnason (88' Bjarni Gudjónsson), Eidur Gudjohnsen. (Coach: Atli Edvaldsson (ISL)).
Scotland: Robert James (Rab) Douglas, Lee Wilkie, Maurice Ross (YC23), Steven Pressley, Gary Naysmith (89' Russell Anderson), Christian Dailly, Jackie McNamara (34' Callum Davidson (YC72)), Paul Lambert (C), Barry Ferguson, Steven Thompson (YC41) (85' Scott Severin), Steven Crawford. (Coach: Hans-Hubert (Berti) Vogts (GER)).
Goals: Scotland: 0-1 Christian Dailly (6'), 0-2 Gary Naysmith (63').
Referee: Alain Sars (FRA)   Attendance: 7.056

12-10-2002   S.Darius and S.Girénas Stadium, Kaunas: Lithuania – Faroe Islands   2-0 (2-0)
Lithuania: Gintaras Staucé, Aurelijus Skarbalius, Dainius Gleveckas (YC77), Andrius Skerla, Rolandas Dziaukstas, Tomas Razanauskas, Saulius Mikalajūnas, Deividas Cesnauskis (77' Giedrius Slavickas, 84' Marius Stankevicius), Raimondas Zutautas (75' Nerijus Barasa), Robertas Poskus (YC50), Artūras Fomenka (YC61). (Coach: Benjaminas Zelkevicius (LIT)).
Faroe Islands: Jákup Mikkelsen, Óli Johannesen (YC47), Jens Kristian Hansen, Pól Thorsteinsson (YC49) (73' Jóhannis Sámal Joensen), Øssur Hansen, Fródi Benjaminsen (YC14), Julian Schantz Johnsson (68' Rógvi Jacobsen), John Petersen, Jón Jacobsen, Christian Jacobsen (60' Andrew av Fløtum (YC89)), Jákup á Borg. (Coach: Henrik Larsen (DEN)).
Goals: Lithiania: 1-0 Tomas Razanauskas (23' penalty), 2-0 Robertas Poskus (37').
Referee: Dejan Delevic (SBM)   Attendance: 1.200

16-10-2002   Laugardalsvöllur, Reykjavik: Iceland – Lithiania   3-0 (0-0)
Iceland: Árni Arason, Bjarni Thorsteinsson (38' Bjarni Gudjónsson (YC40)), Hermann Hreidarsson (C), Brynjar Gunnarsson, Ólafur Stígsson (YC24) (66' Gylfi Einarsson), Ívar Ingimarsson, Jóhannes Gudjónsson (80' Helgi Sigurdsson), Arnar Vidarsson (YC25), Heidar Helguson, Haukur Ingi Gudnason, Eidur Gudjohnsen. (Coach: Atli Edvaldsson (ISL)).
Lithuania: Gintaras Staucé, Marius Stankevicius, Andrius Skerla, Dainius Gleveckas, Nerijus Barasa, Rolandas Dziaukstas, Tomas Razanauskas, Saulius Mikalajūnas (C), Deividas Cesnauskis (RC21), Robertas Poskus, Artūras Fomenka. (Coach: Benjaminas Zelkevicius (LIT)).
Goals: Iceland: 1-0 Heidar Helguson (50'), 2-0 Eidur Gudjohnsen (61'), 3-0 Eidur Gudjohnsen (74').
Referee: Grzegorz Gilewski (POL)   Attendance: 3.513

16-10-2002   AWD-Arena, Hanover: Germany – Faroe Islands   2-1 (1-1)
Germany: Oliver Kahn, Arne Friedrich, Christian Wörns (YC67), Jens Jeremies, Dietmar Hamann, Torsten Frings, Michael Ballack, Bernd Schneider (87' Sebastian Kehl), Carsten Ramelow (46' Paul Freier), Miroslav Klose, Carsten Jancker (69' Oliver Neuville). (Coach: Rudolf (Rudi) Völler (GER)).
Faroe Islands: Jákup Mikkelsen, Óli Johannesen (YC1), Jens Kristian Hansen, Pól Thorsteinsson (YC74), Julian Schantz Johnsson, Øssur Hansen, Fródi Benjaminsen, John Petersen (87' Helgi Petersen), Jón Jacobsen, Andrew av Fløtum (78' Christian Jacobsen), Jákup á Borg (71' Hjalgrím Elttør). (Coach: Henrik Larsen (DEN)).
Goals: Germany: 1-0 Michael Ballack (2' penalty), 2-1 Miroslav Klose (59').
Faroe Islands: 1-1 Arne Friedrich (45' *own goal*).
Referee: Dani Koren (ISR)   Attendance: 36.628

29-03-2003   Hampden Park, Glasgow: Scotland – Iceland   2-1 (1-0)
Scotland: Robert James (Rab) Douglas, Christian Dailly, Graham Alexander, Lee Wilkie, Steven Pressley (YC25), Gary Naysmith, Paul Lambert (C) (YC90+3), Barry Ferguson, Don Hutchison (64' Paul Devlin), Steven Crawford (YC77), Kenny Miller (81' Jackie McNamara). (Coach: Hans-Hubert (Berti) Vogts (GER)).
Iceland: Árni Arason, Brynjar Gunnarsson (73' Thordur Gudjónsson), Gudni Bergsson, Bjarni Thorsteinsson, Lárus Sigurdsson, Rúnar Kristinsson (C), Ívar Ingimarsson, Jóhannes Gudjónsson, Arnar Grétarsson, Arnar Vidarsson (82' Indridi Sigurdsson (YC84)), Eidur Gudjohnsen (88' Tryggvi Gudmundsson). (Coach: Atli Edvaldsson (ISL)).
Goals: Scotland: 1-0 Kenny Miller (12'), 2-1 Lee Wilkie (71').
Iceland: 1-1 Eidur Gudjohnsen (49').
Referee: René H.J.Temmink (HOL)   Attendance: 37.938

29-03-2003   Frankenstadion, Nuremberg: Germany – Lithuania   1-1 (1-0)
Germany: Oliver Kahn (C), Christian Wörns, Arne Friedrich, Bernd Schneider, Tobias Rau (YC21) (82' Paul Freier), Carsten Ramelow, Dietmar Hamann, Torsten Frings, Jörg Böhme (YC42) (46' Marko Rehmer), Miroslav Klose, Fredi Bobic (71' Kevin Kurányi). (Coach: Rudolf (Rudi) Völler (GER)).
Lithuania: Gintaras Staucé (C), Tomas Zvirgzdauskas, Nerijus Barasa, Deividas Semberas, Ignas Dedura, Vadimas Petrenko (YC47) (86' Rolandas Dziaukstas), Tomas Razanauskas, Saulius Mikalajūnas, Arunas Pukelevicius (46' Darius Maciulevicius (YC88)), Igoris Morinas (YC83), Edgaras Jankauskas (90'+4' Artūras Fomenka). (Coach: Algimantas Liubinskas (LIT)).
Goals: Germany: 1-0 Carsten Ramelow (7').
Lithuania: 1-1 Tomas Razanauskas (72').
Referee: Victor José Esquinas Torres (ESP)   Attendance: 40.754

02-04-2003   S.Darius and S.Girénas Stadium, Kaunas: Lithuania – Scotland   1-0 (0-0)
Lithuania: Gintaras Staucé (C), Tomas Zvirgzdauskas, Dainius Gleveckas (YC32), Nerijus Barasa, Deividas Semberas, Ignas Dedura, Tomas Razanauskas, Vadimas Petrenko (70' Darius Maciulevicius), Saulius Mikalajūnas (88' Orestas Buitkus), Igoris Morinas, Edgaras Jankauskas (62' Artūras Fomenka (YC66)). (Coach: Algimantas Liubinskas (LIT)).
Scotland: Paul Gallacher, Lee Wilkie, Steven Pressley, Gary Naysmith, Christian Dailly (YC75), Graham Alexander, Jackie McNamara (78' Andy Gray), Paul Lambert (C), Don Hutchison (YC77) (83' Colin Cameron), Kenny Miller, Steven Crawford (56' Paul Devlin). (Coach: Hans-Hubert (Berti) Vogts (GER)).
Goal: Lithuania: 1-0 Tomas Razanauskas (74' penalty).
Referee: Fritz Stuchlik (AUT)   Attendance: 8.244

31

07-06-2003   Hampden Park, Glasgow: Scotland – Germany   1-1 (0-1)
Scotland: Robert James (Rab) Douglas, Andy Webster, Maurice Ross (74' Jackie McNamara),
Steven Pressley (YC81), Gary Naysmith, Christian Dailly (YC64), Paul Lambert (C), Paul
Devlin (YC31) (59' Gavin Rae), Colin Cameron, Kenny Miller (89' Steven Thompson
(YC90+2)), Steven Crawford. (Coach: Hans-Hubert (Berti) Vogts (GER)).
Germany: Oliver Kahn (C), Christian Wörns, Arne Friedrich, Bernd Schneider (86' Sebastian
Kehl), Tobias Rau (57' Paul Freier (YC59)), Carsten Ramelow, Jens Jeremies, Torsten Frings
(YC33), Michael Ballack (YC64), Miroslav Klose (74' Olivier Neuville), Fredi Bobic. (Coach:
Rudolf (Rudi) Völler (GER)).
Goals: Scotland: 1-1 Kenny Miller (68').
Germany: 0-1 Fredi Bobic (22').
Referee: Domenico Messina (ITA)   Attendance: 48.047

07-06-2003   Laugardalsvöllur, Reykjavik: Iceland – Faroe Islands   2-1 (0-0)
Iceland: Árni Arason, Lárus Sigurdsson, Hermann Hreidarsson, Gudni Bergsson, Indridi
Sigurdsson (76' Arnar Grétarsson), Thordur Gudjónsson, Rúnar Kristinsson (C), Jóhannes
Gudjónsson (YC53), Arnar Vidarsson, Helgi Sigurdsson (76' Tryggvi Gudmundsson), Eidur
Gudjohnsen. (Coach: Ásgeir (Sigi) Sigurvinsson (ISL)).
Faroe Islands: Jákup Mikkelsen, Jóhannis Sámal Joensen (YC44), Jann Ingi Petersen (YC5)
(62' Julian Schantz Johnsson), Rógvi Jacobsen, Fródi Benjaminsen, Súni Olsen, John Petersen,
Jón Jacobsen, Christian Jacobsen, Andrew av Fløtum (YC55) (65' Hjalgrím Elttør), Jákup á
Borg. (Coach: Henrik Larsen (DEN)).
Goals: Iceland: 1-0 Helgi Sigurdsson (51'), 2-1 Tryggvi Gudmundsson (90'+2').
Faroe Islands: 1-1 Rógvi Jacobsen (63').
Referee: Miroslav Liba (CZE)   Attendance: 6.038

11-06-2003   S.Darius and S.Girénas Stadium, Kaunas: Lithuania – Iceland   0-3 (0-0)
Lithuania: Gintaras Staucé (C), Aurelijus Skarbalius, Nerijus Barasa (71' Darius
Maciulevicius), Tomas Zvirgzdauskas (YC36), Deividas Semberas (YC55,RC85), Ignas
Dedura, Tomas Razanauskas, Vadimas Petrenko, Raimondas Zutautas (63' Tomas
Danilevicius), Igoris Morinas, Edgaras Jankauskas (76' Dimitrijus Guscinas). (Coach:
Algimantas Liubinskas (LIT)).
Iceland: Árni Arason, Hermann Hreidarsson, Brynjar Gunnarsson (90' Arnar Grétarsson),
Gudni Bergsson, Lárus Sigurdsson, Rúnar Kristinsson, Thordur Gudjónsson, Jóhannes
Gudjónsson (90'+2' Indridi Sigurdsson), Helgi Sigurdsson (81' Tryggvi
Gudmundsson (YC89)), Eidur Gudjohnsen (C). (Coach: Ásgeir (Sigi) Sigurvinsson (ISL)).
Goals: Iceland: 0-1 Thordur Gudjónsson (60'), 0-2 Eidur Gudjohnsen (71'), 0-3 Hermann
Hreidarsson (90'+3').
Referee: Sorin Corpodean (ROM)   Attendance: 6.500

11-06-2003   Tórsvøllur, Tórshavn: Faroe Islands – Germany   0-2 (0-0)
Faroe Islands: Jákup Mikkelsen, Pól Thorsteinsson, Óli Johannesen (C), Jóhannis Sámal
Joensen, Rógvi Jacobsen, Julian Schantz Johnsson, Fródi Benjaminsen (YC33), John Petersen,
Jákup á Borg (YC55) (61' Hjalgrím Elttør), Jón Jacobsen, Christian Jacobsen (YC31) (77'
Jann Ingi Petersen). (Coach: Henrik Larsen (DEN)).
Germany: Oliver Kahn (C) (46' Frank Rost), Christian Wörns, Arne Friedrich, Sebastian Kehl,
Bernd Schneider, Tobias Rau (YC70) (72' Michael Hartmann), Carsten Ramelow (YC31), Jens
Jeremies (65' Miroslav Klose), Paul Freier, Olivier Neuville (YC79), Fredi Bobic. (Coach:
Rudolf (Rudi) Völler (GER)).
Goals: Germany: 0-1 Miroslav Klose (89'), 0-2 Fredi Bobic (90'+2').
Referee: Jan Willem Wegereef (HOL)   Attendance: 6.140

32

20-08-2003   Tórsvøllur, Tórshavn: Faroe Islands – Iceland   1-2 (0-1)
Faroe Islands: Jákup Mikkelsen, Pól Thorsteinsson (80' Jóhannis Sámal Joensen), Óli
Johannesen (C), Jann Ingi Petersen, Julian Schantz Johnsson, Rógvi Jacobsen, Súni Olsen,
John Petersen (80' Helgi Petersen), Jón Jacobsen, Christian Jacobsen (YC75), Andrew av
Fløtum (56' Hjalgrím Elttør). (Coach: Henrik Larsen (DEN)).
Iceland: Árni Arason, Hermann Hreidarsson, Brynjar Gunnarsson (71' Arnar Grétarsson),
Pétur Marteinsson, Rúnar Kristinsson (78' Heidar Helguson), Thordur Gudjónsson, Jóhannes
Gudjónsson, Ólafur Örn Bjarnason, Arnar Vidarsson, Helgi Sigurdsson (86' Indridi
Sigurdsson), Eidur Gudjohnsen (C). (Coach: Ásgeir (Sigi) Sigurvinsson (ISL)).
Goals: Faroe Islands: 1-1 Rógvi Jacobsen (65').
Iceland: 0-1 Eidur Gudjohnsen (6'), 1-2 Pétur Marteinsson (70').
Referee: Eduardo Iturralde González (ESP)   Attendance: 3.402

06-09-2003   Hampden Park, Glasgow: Scotland – Faroe Islands   3-1 (2-1)
Scotland: Robert James (Rab) Douglas, Andy Webster, Gary Naysmith, Lee Wilkie, Jackie
McNamara, Neil McCann, Barry Ferguson (C), Paul Devlin (58' James McFadden), Colin
Cameron, Paul Dickov (67' Gavin Rae), Steven Crawford (YC61) (75' Steven Thompson).
(Coach: Hans-Hubert (Berti) Vogts (GER)).
Faroe Islands: Jákup Mikkelsen, Pól Thorsteinsson, Óli Johannesen (C), Jann Ingi Petersen,
Julian Schantz Johnsson (84' Christian Holst), Rógvi Jacobsen (YC86), Fródi Benjaminsen
(YC29), John Petersen, Helgi Petersen (65' Tór-Ingar Akselsen), Jón Jacobsen, Jákup á Borg
(84' Atli Danielsen). (Coach: Henrik Larsen (DEN)).
Goals: Scotland: 1-0 Neil McCann (8'), 2-1 Paul Dickov (45'+1'), 3-1 James McFadden (73').
Faroe Islands: 1-1 Julian Schantz Johnsson (35').
Referee: Darko Ceferin (SLO)   Attendance: 40.901

06-09-2003   Laugardalsvøllur, Reykjavik: Iceland – Germany   0-0
Iceland: Árni Arason, Lárus Sigurdsson, Hermann Hreidarsson, Indridi Sigurdsson (84' Arnar
Vidarsson), Ólafur Örn Bjarnason, Pétur Marteinsson (75' Arnar Grétarsson), Rúnar
Kristinsson, Thordur Gudjónsson, Jóhannes Gudjónsson (YC87), Heidar Helguson (78' Helgi
Sigurdsson), Eidur Gudjohnsen (C). (Coach: Ásgeir (Sigi) Sigurvinsson (ISL)).
Germany: Oliver Kahn (C), Christian Wörns, Arne Friedrich, Frank Baumann, Christian Rahn
(YC5) (60' Michael Hartmann (YC88)), Bernd Schneider (70' Sebastian Deisler), Carsten
Ramelow, Sebastian Kehl (YC28), Michael Ballack, Olivier Neuville (46' Kevin Kurányi),
Miroslav Klose (YC47). (Coach: Rudolf (Rudi) Völler (GER)).
Referee: Graham Barber (ENG)   Attendance: 7.065

10-09-2003   Svangaskard, Toftir: Faroe Islands – Lithuania   1-3 (1-1)
Faroe Islands: Jens Martin Knudsen (C) (YC79), Pól Thorsteinsson (50' Rógvi Jacobsen),
Hans Fródi Hansen, Jann Ingi Petersen, Julian Schantz Johnsson (80' Atli Danielsen), Fródi
Benjaminsen, Súni Olsen (YC6), John Petersen, Jón Jacobsen (YC85), Christian Jacobsen,
Jákup á Borg (YC54) (77' Tór-Ingar Akselsen). (Coach: Henrik Larsen (DEN)).
Lithuania: Eduardas Kurskis, Tomas Zvirgzdauskas, Nerijus Barasa, Rolandas Dziaukstas
(YC34), Ignas Dedura, Donatas Vencevicius (90' Dimitrijus Guscinas), Edgaras Cesnauskis
(YC40), Deividas Cesnauskis, Eimantas Poderis (46' Tomas Tamosauskas), Igoris Morinas
(77' Aurimas Kucys), Edgaras Jankauskas (YC73). (Coach: Algimantas Liubinskas (LIT)).
Goals: Faroe Islands: 1-1 Súni Olsen (42').
Lithuania: 0-1 Igoris Morinas (22'), 1-2 Igoris Morinas (57'), 1-3 Donatas Vencevicius (88').
Referee: Edo Trivkovic (CRO)   Attendance: 2.175

33

10-09-2003   Westfalenstadion, Dortmund: Germany – Scotland 2-1 (1-0)
Germany: Oliver Kahn (C), Marko Rehmer, Christian Wörns, Arne Friedrich, Frank Baumann, Bernd Schneider (81' Sebastian Kehl), Tobias Rau (YC55), Carsten Ramelow, Michael Ballack, Kevin Kurányi, Fredi Bobic (76' Miroslav Klose). (Coach: Rudolf (Rudi) Völler (GER)).
Scotland: Robert James (Rab) Douglas, Steven Pressley (YC50), Gary Naysmith, Christian Dailly (YC70), Paul Lambert (46' Maurice Ross (YC56,YC66)), Jackie McNamara, Neil McCann, Barry Ferguson (C) (YC55), Colin Cameron, Steven Thompson, James McFadden (53' Gavin Rae). (Coach: Hans-Hubert (Berti) Vogts (GER)).
Goals: Germany: 1-0 Fredi Bobic (25'), 2-0 Michael Ballack (50' penalty).
Scotland: 2-1 Neil McCann (60').
Referee: Anders Frisk (SWE)   Attendance: 66.000

11-10-2003   Hampden Park, Glasgow: Scotland – Lithuania 1-0 (0-0)
Scotland: Robert James (Rab) Douglas, Christian Dailly, Steven Pressley, Gary Naysmith (YC21) (65' Darren Fletcher), Barry Ferguson (C), Colin Cameron (65' Don Hutchison), Gavin Rae, Jackie McNamara (YC25), Steven Crawford, Kenny Miller, James McFadden (89' Graham Alexander). (Coach: Hans-Hubert (Berti) Vogts (GER)).
Lithuania: Gintaras Staucé (C), Nerijus Barasa, Darius Regelskis (86' Ricardas Beniusis), Tomas Zvirgzdauskas, Rolandas Dziaukstas, Ignas Dedura, Donatas Vencevicius (YC25) (79' Darius Maciulevicius), Tomas Razanauskas, Giedrius Barevicius (46' Deividas Cesnauskis), Robertas Poskus (YC63), Edgaras Jankauskas. (Coach: Algimantas Liubinskas (LIT)).
Goal: Scotland: 1-0 Darren Fletcher (70').
Referee: Claude Colombo (FRA)   Attendance: 50.343

11-10-2003   AOL Arena, Hamburg: Germany – Iceland 3-0 (1-0)
Germany: Oliver Kahn (C), Andreas Hinkel, Arne Friedrich (YC34), Frank Baumann, Christian Wörns (YC67), Carsten Ramelow (YC90), Christian Rahn, Michael Ballack, Bernd Schneider, Kevin Kurányi (85' Oliver Neuville), Fredi Bobic (70' Miroslav Klose). (Coach: Rudolf (Rudi) Völler (GER)).
Iceland: Árni Arason, Hermann Hreidarsson, Indridi Sigurdsson (65' Ríkhardur Dadason), Rúnar Kristinsson (YC61), Thordur Gudjónsson, Arnar Grétarsson (80' Veigar Gunnarsson), Ólafur Örn Bjarnason, Ívar Ingimarsson, Arnar Vidarsson (YC60), Eidur Gudjohnsen (C) (YC27), Helgi Sigurdsson (80' Brynjar Gunnarsson (YC85)). (Coach: Ásgeir (Sigi) Sigurvinsson (ISL)).
Goals: Germany: 1-0 Michael Ballack (9'), 2-0 Fredi Bobic (60'), 3-0 Kevin Kurányi (79').
Referee: Valentin Valentinovich Ivanov (RUS)   Attendance: 50.785

34

07-09-2002	Yerevan	Armenia – Ukraine	2-2 (0-2)
07-09-2002	Athens	Greece – Spain	0-2 (0-1)
12-10-2002	Kiev	Ukraine – Greece	2-0 (0-0)
12-10-2002	Albacete	Spain – Northern Ireland	3-0 (1-0)
16-10-2002	Athens	Greece – Armenia	2-0 (1-0)
16-10-2002	Belfast	Northern Ireland – Ukraine	0-0
29-03-2003	Yerevan	Armenia – Northern Ireland	1-0 (0-0)
29-03-2003	Kiev	Ukraine – Spain	2-2 (1-0)
02-04-2003	Belfast	Northern Ireland – Greece	0-2 (0-1)
02-04-2003	León	Spain – Armenia	3-0 (0-0)
07-06-2003	Lviv	Ukraine – Armenia	4-3 (1-1)
07-06-2003	Zaragoza	Spain- Greece	0-1 (0-1)
11-06-2003	Athens	Greece – Ukraine	1-0 (0-0)
11-06-2003	Belfast	Northern Ireland – Spain	0-0
06-09-2003	Yerevan	Armenia – Greece	0-1 (0-1)
06-09-2003	Donetsk	Ukraine – Northern Ireland	0-0
10-09-2003	Belfast	Northern Ireland – Armenia	0-1 (0-1)
10-09-2003	Elche	Spain – Ukraine	2-1 (0-0)
11-10-2003	Yerevan	Armenia – Spain	0-4 (0-1)
11-10-2003	Athens	Greece – Northern Ireland	1-0 (0-0)

FINAL STANDING

Pos	Team	Pld	W	D	L	GF	GA	GD	Pts
1	Greece	8	6	0	2	8	4	+4	18
2	Spain	8	5	2	1	16	4	+12	17
3	Ukraine	8	2	4	2	11	10	+1	10
4	Armenia	8	2	1	5	7	16	-9	7
5	Northern Ireland	8	0	3	5	0	8	-8	3

Greece qualified for the Final Tournament in Portugal.

Spain qualified for the play-offs.

07-09-2002   Hanrapetakan Stadium, Yerevan: Armenia – Ukraine   2-2 (0-2)
Armenia: Roman Berezovski, Harutyun Vardanyan (YC7), Artur Mkrtchyan (60' Albert Sarkisyan), Karen Dokhoyan, José Andrés Bilibio Estigarribia, Sargis Hovsepyan, Artur Petrosyan, Romik Khàchatryan, Artavazd Karamyan, Vardan Minasyan (46' Artur Voskanyan), Arman Karamyan (71' Andrey Movsisyan). (Coach: Oskar López (ARG)).
Ukraine: Vitaliy Reva, Volodymyr Yezerskiy (YC90+3,RC90+3), Andriy Nesmachniy, Oleg Luzhny (YC20), Hennadiy Zubov (69' Olexandr Spivak), Serhiy Kormiltsev, Andriy Gusin (65' Roman Maksymyuk, 90'+3 Serhiy Popov), Anatoliy Tymoshchuk (YC70), Serhiy Serebrennikov (YC81), Gennadiy Moroz, Andriy Vorobey. (Coach: Leonid Buryak (UKR)).
Goals: Armenia: 1-2 Artur Petrosyan (73'), 2-2 Albert Sarkisyan (90'+3' penalty).
Ukraine: 0-1 Serhiy Serebrennikov (2'), 0-2 Hennadiy Zubov (33').
Referee: Mikko Vuorela (FIN)   Attendance: 9.000

07-09-2002   Apostolos Nikolaidis Stadium, Athens: Greece – Spain   0-2 (0-1)
Greece: Antonis Nikopolidis, Nikolaos (Nikos) Dabizas, Panagiotis (Takis) Fyssas (72' Zisis Vryzas), Traianos Dellas, Christos Patsatzoglou, Konstantinos (Kostas) Konstantinidis (40' Giorgios Karagounis (YC44)), Theodoros Zagorakis (C) (46' Angelos Basinas), Vasilios Tsiartas, Stylianos Giannakopoulos, Angelos Charisteas, Themistoklis (Demis) Nikolaidis. (Coach: Otto-Heinz Rehhagel (GER)).
Spain: IKER CASILLAS Fernández, José Antonio GARCÍA CALVO, RAÚL BRAVO Sanfélix, MÍCHEL Ángel SALGADO Fernández (YC48), Carlos MARCHENA López, IVÁN HELGUERA Bujía (YC66), VICENTE Rodríguez Guillén, Juan Carlos VALERÓN Santana (87' CÉSAR MARTÍN Villar), JOAQUÍN Sánchez Rodríguez (59' Rubén BARAJA Vegas), Xavier "XAVI" Hernández i Creus (59' Gaizka MENDIETA Zabala), RAÚL González Blanco (C). (Coach: José Ignacio "Iñaki" Sáez Ruiz (ESP)).
Goals: Spain: 0-1 RAÚL González Blanco (8'), 0-2 Juan Carlos VALERÓN Santana (77').
Referee: Dr.Markus Merk (GER)   Attendance: 14.206

12-10-2002   Olimpiysky National Sports Complex, Kyiv: Ukraine – Greece   2-0 (0-0)
Ukraine: Vitaliy Reva, Mykhaylo Starostyak, Oleg Luzhny (C), Hennadiy Zubov, Serhiy Kormiltsev (71' Serhiy Rebrov), Andriy Gusin, Anatoliy Tymoshchuk, Serhiy Serebrennikov (23' Andriy Voronin), Gennadiy Moroz (YC22) (24' Olexandr Radchenko), Maxym Kalynychenko, Andriy Vorobey. (Coach: Leonid Buryak (UKR)).
Greece: Antonis Nikopolidis, Stelios Venetidis, Giorgios (Giourkas) Seitaridis, Traianos Dellas (YC81), Nikolaos (Nikos) Dabizas, Theodoros Zagorakis (C) (69' Angelos Basinas), Vasilios Tsiartas, Vassilios Lakis (66' Zisis Vryzas), Giorgios Karagounis (YC87), Themistoklis (Demis) Nikolaidis (66' Stylianos Giannakopoulos), Angelos Charisteas. (Coach: Otto-Heinz Rehhagel (GER)).
Goals: Ukraine: 1-0 Andriy Vorobey (51'), 2-0 Andriy Voronin (90'+1').
Referee: René H.J.Temmink (HOL)   Attendance: 40.000

12-10-2002   Estadio Carlos Belomte, Albacete: Spain – Northern Ireland   3-0 (1-0)
Spain: IKER CASILLAS Fernández, MÍCHEL Ángel SALGADO Fernández, RAÚL BRAVO Sanfélix, IVÁN HELGUERA Bujía (YC34), Carles PUYOL Saforcada, JOAQUÍN Sánchez Rodríguez (76' Gaizka MENDIETA Zabala), Rubén BARAJA Vegas, VICENTE Rodríguez Guillén, Xavier "XAVI" Hernández i Creus, José María "GUTI" Gutiérrez Hernández (83' Jesús "CAPI" Capitán Prada), RAÚL González Blanco (C) (63' Fernando MORIENTES Sánchez). (Coach: José Ignacio "Iñaki" Sáez Ruiz (ESP)).
Northern Ireland: Maik Taylor, George McCartney, Gerry Taggart (69' Grant McCann), Colin Murdock, Aaron Hughes, Steve Lomas, Kevin Horlock (65' David Healy), Philip Mulryne, Damien Johnson, Keith Gillespie (YC34), Paul McVeigh (65' Michael Hughes). (Coach: Samuel Baxter (Sammy) McIlroy (NIR)).
Goals: Spain: 1-0 Rubén BARAJA Vegas (19'), 2-0 José María "GUTI" Gutiérrez Hernández (59'), 3-0 Rubén BARAJA Vegas (89').
Referee: Lubos Michel (SVK)   Attendance: 15.150

16-10-2002   Apostolos Nikolaidis Stadium, Athens: Greece – Armenia   2-0 (1-0)
Greece: Antonis Nikopolidis, Stelios Venetidis (60' Zisis Vryzas), Giorgios (Giourkas) Seitaridis, Traianos Dellas (YC75), Nikolaos (Nikos) Dabizas (C), Angelos Basinas (YC73), Vasilios Tsiartas (46' Theodoros Zagorakis), Pantelis Kafes, Giorgos Georgiadis (46' Stylianos Giannakopoulos), Themistoklis (Demis) Nikolaidis, Angelos Charisteas. (Coach: Otto-Heinz Rehhagel (GER)).
Armenia: Roman Berezovski, Harutyun Vardanyan (C), Karen Dokhoyan, José Andrés Bilibio Estigarribia (YC73), Sargis Hovsepyan, Artur Voskanyan, Albert Sarkisyan (82' Egishe Melikyan), Artur Petrosyan, Romik Khachatryan (46' Vardan Minasyan), Artavazd Karamyan, Arman Karamyan (66' Hamlet Vladi Mkhitaryan). (Coach: Oskar López (ARG)).
Goals: Greece: 1-0 Themistoklis (Demis) Nikolaidis (2'), 2-0 Themistoklis (Demis) Nikolaidis (59').
Referee: Darko Ceferin (SLO)   Attendance: 6.000

16-10-2002   Windsor Park, Belfast: Northern Ireland – Ukraine   0-0
Northern Ireland: Maik Taylor, George McCartney, Aaron Hughes, Philip Mulryne (90'+2' Grant McCann), Steve Lomas (C), Michael Hughes (YC27), Kevin Horlock, Damien Johnson (82' Colin Murdock), Keith Gillespie, Paul McVeigh (63' Andrew Kirk), David Healy. (Coach: Samuel Baxter (Sammy) McIlroy (NIR)).
Ukraine: Vitaliy Reva, Mykhaylo Starostyak, Olexandr Radchenko, Oleg Luzhny (C), Andriy Gusin (YC24), Hennadiy Zubov, Serhiy Kormiltsev (83' Vitaliy Lysytskiy), Anatoliy Tymoshchuk, Maxym Kalynychenko (54' Serhiy Rebrov), Andriy Vorobey (75' Olexandr Melashchenko), Andriy Voronin. (Coach: Leonid Buryak (UKR)).
Referee: Cosimo-Giancarlo Bolognino (ITA)   Attendance: 9.288

29-03-2003   Hanrapetakan Stadium, Yerevan: Armenia – Northern Ireland   1-0 (0-0)
Armenia: Roman Berezovski, Karen Dokhoyan, José Andrés Bilibio Estigarribia, Harutyun Vardanyan (C), Sargis Hovsepyan (YC23), Artur Voskanyan, Albert Sarkisyan (90'+2' Artur Mkrtchyan), Artur Petrosyan (90'+3' Hamlet Vladi Mkhitaryan), Egishe Melikyan (YC12), Artavazd Karamyan (89' Aghvan Mkrtchyan), Arman Karamyan. (Coach: Mihai Stoichita (ROM)).
Northern Ireland: Maik Taylor, Mark Williams, Aaron Hughes, Stephen Craigan (YC63), Grant McCann, Steve Lomas (C), Damien Johnson, David Healy, Keith Gillespie, Paul McVeigh, James Quinn (71' Stuart Elliott). (Coach: Samuel Baxter (Sammy) McIlroy (NIR)).
Goal: Armenia: 1-0 Artur Petrosyan (86').
Referee: Roland Beck (LIE)   Attendance: 10.321

29-03-2003   Olimpiyski National Sports Complex, Kyiv: Ukraine – Spain   2-2 (1-0)
Ukraine: Olexandr Shovkovskiy, Serhiy Fedorov, Yuriy Dmytrulin, Andriy Nesmachniy, Olexandr Gorshkov, Serhiy Kormiltsev (62' Maxym Kalynychenko), Andriy Gusin (YC10), Anatoliy Tymoshchuk (YC33), Andriy Vorobey, Andriy Voronin, Andriy Shevchenko (C) (67' Serhiy Serebrennikov). (Coach: Leonid Buryak (UKR)).
Spain: IKER CASILLAS Fernández, MÍCHEL Ángel SALGADO Fernández, CÉSAR MARTÍN Villar (YC73), Carlos MARCHENA López, Agustín Alkorta ARANZÁBAL, Rubén BARAJA Vegas (YC59), David ALBELDA Aliqués (65' Xavier "XAVI" Hernández i Creus), VICENTE Rodríguez Guillén (77' DIEGO TRISTÁN Herrera), José María "GUTI" Gutiérrez Hernández (65' Juan Carlos VALERÓN Santana), Joseba Andoni ETXEBERRIA Lizardi, RAÚL González Blanco (C). (Coach: José Ignacio "Iñaki" Sáez Ruiz (ESP)).
Goals: Ukraine: 1-1 Andriy Voronin (11'), 2-2 Olexandr Gorshkov (90'+2').
Spain: 1-1 RAÚL González Blanco (83'), 1-2 Joseba Andoni ETXEBERRIA Lizardi (87').
Referee: Michael (Mike) Riley (ENG)   Attendance: 83.400

02-04-2003   Windsor Park, Belfast: Northern Ireland – Greece   0-2 (0-1)
Northern Ireland: Maik Taylor, Stephen Craigan, Mark Williams (YC36), George McCartney,
Aaron Hughes, Grant McCann (67' Andrew Kirk), Steve Lomas (C) (YC88), Damien Johnson,
David Healy (67' Paul McVeigh), Keith Gillespie (YC26,YC69), James Quinn (RC39).
(Coach: Samuel Baxter (Sammy) McIlroy (NIR)).
Greece: Antonis Nikopolidis, Stelios Venetidis (YC11) (71' Panagiotis (Takis) Fyssas),
Sotirios Kyrgiakos (YC62), Nikolaos (Nikos) Dabizas (C), Theodoros Zagorakis, Vasilios
Tsiartas (74' Pantelis Kafes), Konstantinos (Kostas) Konstantinidis, Giorgios Karagounis
(YC26), Stylianos Giannakopoulos, Themistoklis (Demis) Nikolaidis (40' Zisis Vryzas),
Angelos Charisteas. (Coach: Otto-Heinz Rehhagel (GER)).
Goals: Greece: 0-1 Angelos Charisteas (4'), 0-2 Angelos Charisteas (55').
Referee: Grzegorz Gilewski (POL)   Attendance: 7.196

02-04-2003   Nuevo Estadio Antonio Amilivia, León: Spain – Armenia   3-0 (0-0)
Spain: IKER CASILLAS Fernández, RAÚL BRAVO Sanfélix, MÍCHEL Ángel SALGADO
Fernández, Carlos MARCHENA López, IVÁN HELGUERA Bujía, David ALBELDA
Aliqués, Juan Carlos VALERÓN Santana (YC58) (64' Rubén BARAJA Vegas (YC66)),
Xavier "XAVI" Hernández i Creus (53' VICENTE Rodríguez Guillén), Joseba Andoni
ETXEBERRIA Lizardi (41' JOAQUÍN Sánchez Rodríguez), DIEGO TRISTÁN Herrera,
RAÚL González Blanco (C). (Coach: José Ignacio "Iñaki" Sáez Ruiz (ESP)).
Armenia: Roman Berezovski, Karen Dokhoyan, Harutyun Vardanyan (C), Sargis Hovsepyan,
Artur Voskanyan, Albert Sarkisyan, Artur Petrosyan (80' Hamlet Vladi Mkhitaryan), Egishe
Melikyan (YC1), Romik Khachatryan (83' Vardan Minasyan), Artavazd Karamyan (90'+3'
José Andrés Bilibio Estigarribia), Arman Karamyan. (Coach: Mihai Stoichita (ROM)).
Goals: Spain: 1-0 DIEGO TRISTÁN Herrera (64'), 2-0 IVÁN HELGUERA Bujía (69'), 3-0
JOAQUÍN Sánchez Rodríguez (90'+3').
Referee: Alon Yefet (ISR)   Attendance: 13.500

07-06-2003   Ukraina Stadium, Lviv: Ukraine – Armenia   4-3 (1-1)
Ukraine: Dmitro Shutkov, Serhiy Popov (65' Maxym Kalynychenko), Andriy Nesmachniy,
Oleg Luzhny (YC14), Serhiy Fedorov, Olexandr Gorshkov, Serhiy Zakarlyuka (59' Olexandr
Radchenko), Andriy Vorobey (YC67), Serhiy Rebrov (YC17) (81' Oleg Venhlinskiy), Andriy
Voronin, Andriy Shevchenko (C). (Coach: Leonid Buryak (UKR)).
Armenia: Roman Berezovski (YC83), Karen Dokhoyan, Harutyun Vardanyan (C), Sargis
Hovsepyan (YC64), Romik Khachatryan, Artavazd Karamyan, Edouard Partsikyan (YC16),
Artur Voskanyan, Albert Sarkisyan, Artur Petrosyan (80' José Andrés Bilibio Estigarribia),
Arman Karamyan (84' Ararat Harutyunyan). (Coach: Mihai Stoichita (ROM)).
Goals: Ukraine: 1-1 Olexandr Gorshkov (28'), 2-2 Andriy Shevchenko (65' penalty), 3-2
Andriy Shevchenko (73'), 4-3 Serhiy Fedorov (90'+2').
Armenia: 0-1 Albert Sarkisyan (15' penalty), 1-2 Albert Sarkisyan (52'), 3-3 Artur Petrosyan
(74').
Referee: Hermann Albrecht (GER)   Attendance: 23.600

07-06-2003   La Romareda, Zaragoza: Spain – Greece   0-1 (0-1)
Spain: IKER CASILLAS Fernández, MÍCHEL Ángel SALGADO Fernández, Carlos
MARCHENA López (YC74) (76' SERGIO González Soriano), RAÚL BRAVO Sanfélix,
IVÁN HELGUERA Bujía (YC85), Carles PUYOL Saforcada, VICENTE Rodríguez Guillén
(57' JOAQUÍN Sánchez Rodríguez), Juan Carlos VALERÓN Santana, Fernando
MORIENTES Sánchez, Joseba Andoni ETXEBERRIA Lizardi (YC47) (57' Francisco Javier
"Javi" DE PEDRO Falque), RAÚL González Blanco (C). (Coach: José Ignacio "Iñaki" Sáez
Ruiz (ESP)).
Greece: Antonis Nikopolidis, Traianos Dellas, Nikolaos (Nikos) Dabizas (YC52), Mihalis
Kapsis (C), Stelios Venetidis (YC15,YC79), Giorgios (Giourkas) Seitaridis, Stylianos
Giannakopoulos, Theodoros Zagorakis, Vasilios Tsiartas (36' Giorgios Karagounis), Angelos
Charisteas (34' Vassilios Lakis), Zisis Vryzas. (Coach: Otto-Heinz Rehhagel (GER)).
Goal: Greece: 0-1 Stylianos Giannakopoulos (42').
Referee: Alain Sars (FRA)   Attendance: 29.500

11-06-2003   Apostolos Nikolaidis Stadium, Athens: Greece – Ukraine   1-0 (0-0)
Greece: Antonis Nikopolidis, Giorgios (Giourkas) Seitaridis, Mihalis Kapsis, Panagiotis
(Takis) Fyssas, Traianos Dellas, Nikolaos (Nikos) Dabizas, Theodoros Zagorakis (C) (71'
Vasilios Tsiartas), Vassilios Lakis (65' Lampros Choutos), Giorgios Karagounis, Stylianos
Giannakopoulos, Zisis Vryzas (46' Angelos Charisteas). (Coach: Otto-Heinz Rehhagel (GER)).
Ukraine: Olexandr Shovkovskiy, Olexandr Golovko (YC23), Andriy Nesmachniy, Serhiy
Fedorov, Vyacheslav Shevchuk, Serhiy Zakarlyuka (89' Maxym Kalynychenko), Andriy
Gusin, Anatoliy Tymoshchuk (YC51), Serhiy Rebrov (61' Andriy Vorobey), Andriy Voronin
(90'+1' Adrian Pukanych), Andriy Shevchenko (C). (Coach: Leonid Buryak (UKR)).
Goal: Greece: 1-0 Angelos Charisteas (86').
Referee: Frank de Bleeckere (BEL)   Attendance: 14.314
(Stylianos Giannakopoulos missed a penalty in the 16th minute)

11-06-2003   Windsor Park, Belfast: Northern Ireland – Spain   0-0
Northern Ireland: Maik Taylor, George McCartney, Danny Griffin, Aaron Hughes (C), Chris
Baird, Stephen Jones (73' Paul McVeigh), Tommy Doherty (80' Ciarán Toner), Peter
Kennedy, Damien Johnson (YC54), Andy Smith (90'+2' Mark Williams), David Healy.
(Coach: Samuel Baxter (Sammy) McIlroy (NIR)).
Spain: IKER CASILLAS Fernández, "JUANFRAN" Juan Francisco García García, Carlos
MARCHENA López, Carles PUYOL Saforcada, IVÁN HELGUERA Bujía, VICENTE
Rodríguez Guillén (66' JOAQUÍN Sánchez Rodríguez), Juan Carlos VALERÓN Santana,
SERGIO González Soriano (66' Fernando MORIENTES Sánchez), Rubén BARAJA Vegas,
RAÚL González Blanco (C), Joseba Andoni ETXEBERRIA Lizardi (79' Francisco Javier
"Javi" DE PEDRO Falque (YC85)). (Coach: José Ignacio "Iñaki" Sáez Ruiz (ESP)).
Referee: Claus Bo Laren (DEN)   Attendance: 11.365

06-09-2003   Hanrapetakan Stadium, Yerevan: Armenia – Greece   0-1 (0-1)
Armenia: Roman Berezovski, José Andrés Bilibio Estigarribia, Harutyun Vardanyan (C) (YC47), Albert Sarkisyan, Artur Petrosyan, Egishe Melikyan, Romik Khachatryan (YC8), Artavazd Karamyan, Tudor Marian Zeciu (YC52), Artur Voskanyan (88' Ara Hakobyan), Arman Karamyan (64' Andrey Movsisyan). (Coach: Mihai Stoichita (ROM)).
Greece: Antonis Nikopolidis, Mihalis Kapsis, Panagiotis (Takis) Fyssas, Traianos Dellas, Paraskevas Antzas (YC18), Giorgios (Giourkas) Seitaridis, Giorgios Karagounis (84' Theodoros Zagorakis), Stylianos Giannakopoulos (YC33) (67' Giorgos Georgiadis), Angelos Basinas, Angelos Charisteas (46' Themistoklis (Demis) Nikolaidis), Zisis Vryzas (YC83). (Coach: Otto-Heinz Rehhagel (GER)).
Goal: Greece: 0-1 Zisis Vryzas (36').
Referee: René H.J.Temmink (HOL)   Attendance: 6.500

06-09-2003   Shakhtar Stadium, Donetsk: Ukraine – Northern Ireland   0-0
Ukraine: Olexandr Shovkovskiy, Oleg Luzhny (C), Serhiy Fedorov, Andriy Nesmachniy (YC87), Andriy Gusin (16' Oleg Gusev), Olexandr Gorshkov, Hennadiy Zubov, Anatoliy Tymoshchuk, Andriy Vorobey, Serhiy Rebrov (72' Olexandr Melashchenko), Andriy Voronin. (Coach: Leonid Buryak (UKR)).
Northern Ireland: Maik Taylor, Danny Griffin (YC90+1), George McCartney, Chris Baird, Aaron Hughes (C), Tommy Doherty (YC47) (67' Philip Mulryne), Peter Kennedy, Michael Hughes (YC38) (81' Stephen Jones), Damien Johnson, David Healy (62' Andy Smith), Keith Gillespie. (Coach: Samuel Baxter (Sammy) McIlroy (NIR)).
Referee: Wolfgang Stark (GER)   Attendance: 25.700

10-09-2003   Windsor Park, Belfast: Northern Ireland – Armenia   0-1 (0-1)
Northern Ireland: Maik Taylor, Danny Griffin, George McCartney, Aaron Hughes (C), Chris Baird, Grant McCann, Tommy Doherty (29' Stephen Jones), Damien Johnson (YC75), David Healy (78' Paul McVeigh), Keith Gillespie (29' Philip Mulryne), Andy Smith. (Coach: Samuel Baxter (Sammy) McIlroy (NIR)).
Armenia: Roman Berezovski, José Andrés Bilibio Estigarribia, Sargis Hovsepyan (C), Egishe Melikyan (YC73), Romik Khachatryan, Artavazd Karamyan (87' Edouard Partsikyan), Albert Sarkisyan, Tudor Marian Zeciu, Artur Voskanyan, Artur Petrosyan (12' Arman Karamyan), Andrey Movsisyan (75' Ara Hakobyan). (Coach: Mihai Stoichita (ROM)).
Goal: Armenia: 0-1 Artavazd Karamyan (27').
Referee: Anton Stredák (SVK)   Attendance: 8.616

10-09-2003   Estadio Manuel Martínez Valero, Elche: Spain – Ukraine   2-1 (0-0)
Spain: IKER CASILLAS Fernández, "JUANITO" Juan Gutierrez Moreno, MÍCHEL Ángel SALGADO Fernández, Carlos MARCHENA López, Carles PUYOL Saforcada, VICENTE Rodríguez Guillén (63' José Antonio REYES Calderón), Rubén BARAJA Vegas (84' Xavier "XAVI" Hernández i Creus), Xabier "XABI" ALONSO Olano, RAÚL González Blanco (C), Joseba Andoni ETXEBERRIA Lizardi, FERNANDO José TORRES Sanz (63' Juan Carlos VALERÓN Santana). (Coach: José Ignacio "Iñaki" Sáez Ruiz (ESP)).
Ukraine: Olexandr Shovkovskiy, Serhiy Popov (18' Serhiy Serebrennikov), Andriy Nesmachniy, Oleg Luzhny (C), Serhiy Fedorov (YC25), Yuriy Dmytrulin (63' Hennadiy Zubov), Olexandr Gorshkov, Anatoliy Tymoshchuk (YC67), Andriy Vorobey, Andriy Voronin (51' Oleg Gusev), Andriy Shevchenko. (Coach: Leonid Buryak (UKR)).
Goals: Spain: 1-0 RAÚL González Blanco (59'), 2-0 RAÚL González Blanco (71').
Ukraine: 2-1 Andriy Shevchenko (84').
Referee: Terje Hauge (NOR)   Attendance: 33.847
(FERNANDO José TORRES Sanz missed a penalty in the 54th minute)

40

11-10-2003   Hanrapetakan Stadium, Yerevan: Armenia – Spain   0-4 (0-1)
Armenia: Roman Berezovski, Harutyan Vardanyan (C), Karen Dokhoyan, Sargis Hovsepyan, Tudor Marian Zeciu (88' José Andrés Bilibio Estigarribia), Artur Voskanyan (78' Andrey Movsisyan), Albert Sarkisyan (YC71), Egishe Melikyan, Romik Khachatryan (YC44), Artavazd Karamyan, Arman Karamyan (YC49) (87' Artur Petrosyan). (Coach: Mihai Stoichita (ROM)).
Spain: IKER CASILLAS Fernández, MÍCHEL Ángel SALGADO Fernández, Carlos MARCHENA López, Carles PUYOL Saforcada, IVÁN HELGUERA Bujía, VICENTE Rodríguez Guillén (61' José Antonio REYES Calderón), Juan Carlos VALERÓN Santana, Rubén BARAJA Vegas (66' Xabier "XABI" ALONSO Olano), David ALBELDA Aliqués, RAÚL González Blanco (C) (78' ALBERT LUQUE Martos), Joseba Andoni ETXEBERRIA Lizardi. (Coach: José Ignacio "Iñaki" Sáez Ruiz (ESP)).
Goals: Spain: 0-1 Juan Carlos VALERÓN Santana (7'), 0-2 RAÚL González Blanco (76'), 0-3 José Antonio REYES Calderón (86'), 0-4 José Antonio REYES Calderón (90'+1').
Referee: Urs Meier (SUI)   Attendance: 15.000

11-10-2003   Apostolos Nikolaidis Stadium, Athens: Greece – Northern Ireland   1-0 (0-0)
Greece: Antonis Nikopolidis, Giorgios (Giourkas) Seitaridis, Panagiotis (Takis) Fyssas, Traianos Dellas (YC57), Nikolaos (Nikos) Dabizas (C) (46' Giorgos Georgiadis), Paraskevas Antzas, Vasilios Tsiartas, Stylianos Giannakopoulos, Angelos Basinas (89' Theodoros Zagorakis), Zisis Vryzas, Angelos Charisteas (YC19) (46' Themistoklis (Demis) Nikolaidis). (Coach: Otto-Heinz Rehhagel (GER)).
Northern Ireland: Maik Taylor (YC12), George McCartney (YC65,RC67), Danny Griffin (88' Stephen Jones), Aaron Hughes, Chris Baird, Jeff Whitley (YC88), Peter Kennedy, Michael Hughes (YC58), Stuart Elliott (70' Colin Murdock), David Healy (YC90+1), Keith Gillespie (C) (64' Andy Smith). (Coach: Samuel Baxter (Sammy) McIlroy (NIR)).
Goal: Greece: 1-0 Vasilios Tsiartas (68' penalty).
Referee: Lucílio Cardoso Cortez Batista (POR)   Attendance: 14.585

GROUP 7

07-09-2002	Istanbul	Turkey – Slovakia	3-0 (2-0)
08-09-2002	Vaduz	Liechtenstein – Macedonia	1-1 (0-1)
12-10-2002	Skopje	Macedonia – Turkey	1-2 (1-1)
12-10-2002	Bratislava	Slovakia – England	1-2 (1-0)
16-10-2002	Istanbul	Turkey – Liechtenstein	5-0 (3-0)
16-10-2002	Southampton	England – Macedonia	2-2 (2-2)
29-03-2003	Vaduz	Liechtenstein – England	0-2 (0-1)
29-03-2003	Skopje	Macedonia – Slovakia	0-2 (0-1)
02-04-2003	Trnava	Slovakia – Liechtenstein	4-0 (1-0)
02-04-2003	Sunderland	England – Turkey	2-0 (0-0)
07-06-2003	Skopje	Macedonia – Liechtenstein	3-1 (1-1)
07-06-2003	Bratislava	Slovakia - Turkey	0-1 (0-1)
11-06-2003	Istanbul	Turkey – Macedonia	3-2 (1-2)
11-06-2003	Middlesbrough	England – Slovakia	2-1 (0-1)
06-09-2003	Skopje	Macedonia – England	1-2 (1-0)
06-09-2003	Vaduz	Liechtenstein – Turkey	0-3 (0-2)
10-09-2003	Zilina	Slovakia – Macedonia	1-1 (1-0)
10-09-2003	Manchester	England – Liechtenstein	2-0 (0-0)
11-10-2003	Istanbul	Turkey – England	0-0
11-10-2003	Vaduz	Liechtenstein – Slovakia	0-2 (0-1)

FINAL STANDING

Pos	Team	Pld	W	D	L	GF	GA	GD	Pts
1	England	8	6	2	0	14	5	+9	20
2	Turkey	8	6	1	1	17	5	+12	19
3	Slovakia	8	3	1	4	11	9	+2	10
4	Macedonia	8	1	3	4	11	14	-3	6
5	Liechtenstein	8	0	1	7	2	22	-20	1

England qualified for the Final Tournament in Portugal.

Turkey qualified for the play-offs.

07-09-2002   Ali Sami Yen Stadium, Istanbul: Turkey – Slovakia   3-0 (2-0)
Turkey: Rüstü Reçber, Fatih Akyel, Alpay Özalan, Hakan Ünsal, Bülent Korkmaz, Emre Belözoglu (78' Cihan Haspolatli), Yildiray Bastürk, Tugay Kerimoglu, Okan Buruk (63' Nihat Kahveci), Arif Erdem, Serhat Akin (87' Ümit Davala). (Coach: Senol Günes (TUR)).
Slovakia: Juraj Bucek, Marek Spilár, Vladimír Labant (61' Rastislav Michalík), Vladimír Janocko, Vratislav Gresko (72' Peter Hlinka), Peter Dzúrik, Marián Cisovsky, Karol Kisel, Miroslav Karhan, Róbert Vittek, Jozef Kozlej (55' Lubomír (Lubos) Reiter). (Coach: Ladislav Jurkemik (SVK)).
Goals: Turkey: 1-0 Serhat Akin (14'), 2-0 Arif Erdem (44'), 3-0 Arif Erdem (65').
Referee: Antonio Jesús López Nieto (ESP)   Attendance: 17.300

08-09-2002   Rheinpark Stadion, Vaduz: Liechtenstein – Macedonia   1-1 (0-1)
Liechtenstein: Peter Jehle, Christof Ritter, Michael Stocklasa, Martin Stocklasa (YC25), Daniel Hasler (C), Andreas Gerster, Frédéric Gigon (83' Franz Burgmeier), Martin Telser (83' Fabio D'Elia), Mario Frick, Matthias Beck (46' Ronny Büchel), Thomas Beck. (Coach: Ralf Loose (GER)).
Macedonia: Petar Milosevski, Igor Nikolovski, Goce Sedloski, Robert Petrov (YC77), Igor Mitreski, Aleksandar Mitreski, Artim Shakiri (YC84), Aguinaldo Braga de Jesus (85' Boban Grncarov (YC90+2)), Goran Pandev (70' Aco Stojkov), Velice Sumulikoski, Georgi Hristov (58' Robert Popov). (Coach: Nikola Ilievski (MCD)).
Goals: Liechtenstein: 1-1 Michael Stocklasa (90'+3').
Macedonia: 0-1 Georgi Hristov (8').
Referee: Vitaliy Godulyan (UKR)   Attendance: 2.650

12-10-2002   Gradski Stadium, Skopje: Macedonia – Turkey   1-2 (1-1)
Macedonia: Petar Milosevski, Milan Stojanoski, Igor Mitreski, Aleksandar Mitreski (YC12), Aleksandar Vasoski (YC21), Goce Sedloski, Artim Shakiri, Vlatko Grozdanoski, Vanco Trajanov (YC4) (65' Dragan Nacevski), Velice Sumulikoski (45'+1' Robert Popov), Georgi Hristov (C) (YC41) (45'+1' Robert Petrov). (Coach: Nikola Ilievski (MCD)).
Turkey: Rüstü Reçber, Fatih Akyel, Alpay Özalan, Bülent Korkmaz (C), Emre Belözoglu, Yildiray Bastürk (YC36), Ergün Penbe, Tugay Kerimoglu (46' Hasan Sas (YC90+1)), Okan Buruk (82' Ümit Davala), Arif Erdem (46' Serhat Akin), Nihat Kahveci. (Coach: Senol Günes (TUR)).
Goals: Macedonia: 1-0 Vlatko Grozdanoski (2').
Turkey: 1-1 Okan Buruk (29'), 1-2 Nihat Kahveci (53').
Referee: Knud Erik Fisker (DEN)   Attendance: 9.000

12-10-2002   Tehelné pole, Bratislava: Slovakia – England 1-2 (1-0)
Slovakia: Miroslav König, Marián Zeman (YC84), Martin Petrás, Vladimír Leitner (YC62),
Vladimír Janocko (88' Marek Mintál), Peter Hlinka, Peter Dzúrik (C), Attila Pinte (88' Jozef
Kozlej), Miroslav Karhan, Róbert Vittek (YC31) (80' Lubomír (Lubos) Reiter), Szilárd
Németh. (Coach: Ladislav Jurkemik (SVK)).
England: David Seaman, Ashley Cole, Jonathan Woodgate, Gareth Southgate, Gary Neville,
Nicky Butt, Paul Scholes (YC68), Steven Gerrard (YC42) (77' Kieron Dyer), David Beckham
(C), Emile Heskey (90'+3' Alan Smith), Michael Owen (86' Owen Hargreaves). (Coach:
Sven-Göran Eriksson (SWE)).
Goals: Slovakia: 1-0 Szilárd Németh (23').
England: 1-1 David Beckham (64'), 1-2 Michael Owen (82').
Referee: Domenico Messina (ITA)   Attendance: 28.500

16-10-2002   Ali Sami Yen Stadium, Istanbul: Turkey – Liechtenstein 5-0 (3-0)
Turkey: Rüstü Reçber, Alpay Özalan, Bülent Korkmaz (C) (46' Fatih Akyel), Ergün Penbe,
Tugay Kerimoglu, Ümit Davala (YC53), Emre Belözoglu, Okan Buruk (60' Hakan Ünsal),
Ilhan Mansiz (79' Serhat Akin), Nihat Kahveci, Arif Erdem. (Coach: Senol Günes (TUR)).
Liechtenstein: Peter Jehle, Michael Stocklasa, Martin Stocklasa (79' Matthias Beck), Daniel
Hasler (C), Fabio D'Elia, Thomas Nigg (72' Franz Burgmeier), Andreas Gerster, Martin
Telser, Mario Frick, Ronny Büchel (85' Jürgen Ospelt), Thomas Beck (YC45). (Coach: Ralf
Loose (GER)).
Goals: Turkey: 1-0 Okan Buruk (7'), 2-0 Ümit Davala (14'), 3-0 Ilhan Mansiz (23'), 4-0 Serhat
Akin (81'), 5-0 Serhat Akin (90').
Referee: Yuri Valeryevich Baskakov (RUS)   Attendance: 10.890
(Mario Frick missed a penalty in the 92nd minute)

16-10-2002   St Mary's Stadium, Southampton: England – Macedonia 2-2 (2-2)
England: David Seaman, Jonathan Woodgate, Ashley Cole, Wayne Bridge (58' Darius
Vassell), Gary Neville, Sol Campbell, Paul Scholes, David Beckham (C) (YC40), Steven
Gerrard (55' Nicky Butt), Alan Smith (YC69,YC90+3), Michael Owen. (Coach: Sven-Göran
Eriksson (SWE)).
Macedonia: Petar Milosevski, Aleksandar Vasoski (YC45+1), Goce Sedloski (C), Robert
Petrov, Aleksandar Mitreski, Artim Shakiri, Robert Popov, Vlatko Grozdanoski, Vanco
Trajanov (90'+3' Milan Stojanoski), Velice Sumulikoski, Goce Toleski (62' Goran Pandev).
(Coach: Nikola Ilievski (MCD)).
Goals: England: 1-1 David Beckham (13'), 2-2 Steven Gerrard (35').
Macedonia: 0-1 Artim Shakiri (10'), 1-2 Vanco Trajanov (24').
Referee: Arturo Daudén Ibáñez (ESP)   Attendance: 32.095

29-03-2003   Rheinpark Stadion, Vaduz: Liechtenstein – England 0-2 (0-1)
Liechtenstein: Peter Jehle, Harry Zech (YC59) (62' Franz Burgmeier), Michael Stocklasa,
Martin Stocklasa, Daniel Hasler (C), Fabio D'Elia, Andreas Gerster, Martin Telser, Mario
Frick (82' Thomas Nigg), Ronny Büchel (86' Matthias Beck), Thomas Beck. (Coach: Ralf
Loose (GER)).
England: David James, Gareth Southgate, Wayne Bridge, Gary Neville, Rio Ferdinand, Paul
Scholes, Kieron Dyer, Steven Gerrard (66' Nicky Butt), David Beckham (C) (70' Danny
Murphy), Emile Heskey (80' Wayne Rooney), Michael Owen. (Coach: Sven-Göran Eriksson
(SWE)).
Goals: England: 0-1 Michael Owen (28'), 0-2 David Beckham (53').
Referee: Georgios Kasnaferis (GRE)   Attendance: 3.548

29-03-2003   Gradski Stadium, Skopje: Macedonia – Slovakia   0-2 (0-1)
Macedonia: Petar Milosevski, Saso Lazarevski (81' Aco Stojkov), Igor Mitreski, Goce
Sedloski (YC61), Mile Krstev (YC49), Aguinaldo Braga de Jesus, Igor Jancevski, Artim
Shakiri (C), Goran Pandev, Velice Sumulikoski (51' Ilco Naumoski (YC87)), Saso Krstev (61'
Vlatko Grozdanoski). (Coach: Nikola Ilievski (MCD)).
Slovakia: Miroslav König, Vladimír Leitner, Maros Klimpl (YC90), Martin Petrás, Vladimír
Janocko, Peter Hlinka, Igor Demo (C) (80' Vladimír Labant), Rastislav Michalík (YC64),
Miroslav Karhan (89' Michal Hanek), Róbert Vittek (YC36), Szilárd Németh (75' Lubomír
(Lubos) Reiter). (Coach: Ladislav Jurkemik (SVK)).
Goals: Slovakia: 0-1 Martin Petrás (28'), 0-2 Lubomír (Lubos) Reiter (90').
Referee: Laurent Duhamel (FRA)   Attendance: 7.000

02-04-2003   Stadion Antona Malatinského, Trnava: Slovakia – Liechtenstein   4-0 (1-0)
Slovakia: Miroslav König, Martin Petrás, Vladimír Leitner (YC22), Maros Klimpl, Igor Demo
(68' Vladimír Labant), Rastislav Michalík (81' Marek Mintál), Vladimír Janocko (YC59),
Peter Hlinka, Miroslav Karhan (C), Lubomír (Lubos) Reiter, Jozef Kozlej (46' Szilárd
Németh). (Coach: Ladislav Jurkemik (SVK)).
Liechtenstein: Peter Jehle, Michael Stocklasa, Martin Stocklasa (YC77), Daniel Hasler (C),
Fabio D'Elia, Andreas Gerster (YC80) (83' Jürgen Ospelt), Martin Telser (YC53), Franz
Burgmeier (YC84), Mario Frick (59' Thomas Nigg), Thomas Beck (YC56), Ronny Büchel
(71' Frédéric Gigon). (Coach: Ralf Loose (GER)).
Goals: Slovakia: 1-0 Lubomír (Lubos) Reiter (19'), 2-0 Szilárd Németh (50'), 3-0 Szilárd
Németh (64'), 4-0 Vladimír Janocko (89').
Referee: Darko Ceferin (SLO)   Attendance: behind closed doors

02-04-2003   Stadium of Light, Sunderland: England – Turkey   2-0 (0-0)
England: David James, Wayne Bridge, Gary Neville, Rio Ferdinand (YC90+1), Sol Campbell,
Paul Scholes, Nicky Butt, Steven Gerrard, David Beckham (C) (YC9), Wayne Rooney (88'
Kieron Dyer), Michael Owen (57' Darius Vassell). (Coach: Sven-Göran Eriksson (SWE)).
Turkey: Rüstü Reçber, Alpay Özalan, Bülent Korkmaz (C) (YC90+1), Fatih Akyel (YC49)
(78' Hakan Sükür), Ergün Penbe, Tugay Kerimoglu, Emre Belözoglu, Yildiray Bastürk (70'
Hasan Sas), Okan Buruk (YC34) (59' Ümit Davala), Ilhan Mansiz, Nihat Kahveci. (Coach:
Senol Günes (TUR)).
Goals: England: 1-0 Darius Vassell (75'), 2-0 David Beckham (90'+2 penalty).
Referee: Urs Meier (SUI)   Attendance: 47.667

07-06-2003   Gradski Stadium, Skopje: Macedonia – Liechtenstein   3-1 (1-1)
Macedonia: Petar Milosevski, Saso Lazarevski, Aleksandar Vasoski (YC86), Goce Sedloski
(C), Aleksandar Mitreski, Artim Shakiri (55' Aleksandar Bajevski), Mile Krstev (YC32),
Vanco Trajanov (60' Igor Jancevski (YC72)), Velice Sumulikoski, Ilco Naumoski (YC44) (46'
Dragan Dimitrovski), Aco Stojkov. (Coach: Nikola Ilievski (MCD)).
Liechtenstein: Peter Jehle (YC38), Sandro Maierhofer (89' Franz-Josef Vogt), Daniel Hasler
(C) (YC39), Fabio D'Elia, Jürgen Ospelt (YC40), Andreas Gerster, Roger Beck (79' Raphael
Rohrer), Martin Telser, Frédéric Gigon, Matthias Beck (89' Mario Wolfinger), Mario Frick.
(Coach: Ralf Loose (GER)).
Goals: Macedonia: 1-1 Goce Sedloski (39' penalty), 2-1 Mile Krstev (52'), 3-1 Aco Stojkov
(82').
Liechtenstein: 0-1 Roger Beck (20').
Referee: Jaroslav Jára (CZE)   Attendance: 2.500

44

07-06-2003   Tehelné pole, Bratislava: Slovakia – Turkey   0-1 (0-1)
Slovakia: Miroslav König, Vladimír Labant, Maros Klimpl (YC18), Marián Zeman, Martin Petrás, Rastislav Michalík (77' Karol Kisel), Vladimír Janocko, Peter Hlinka (46' Róbert Vittek), Igor Demo (YC65), Miroslav Karhan (C) (71' Marek Mintál), Szilárd Németh. (Coach: Ladislav Jurkemik (SVK)).
Turkey: Rüstü Reçber, Bülent Korkmaz (C), Fatih Akyel, Alpay Özalan, Ergün Penbe, Tugay Kerimoglu, Emre Belözoglu (YC84) (90' Ibrahim Üzülmez), Yildiray Bastürk (YC48) (80' Volkan Arslan), Okan Buruk (YC52) (59' Tayfun Korkut), Nihat Kahveci, Hakan Sükür. (Coach: Senol Günes (TUR)).
Goal: Turkey: 0-1 Nihat Kahveci (12').
Referee: Terje Hauge (NOR)   Attendance: 18.000

11-06-2003   BJK Inönü Stadium, Istanbul: Turkey – Macedonia   3-2 (1-2)
Turkey: Rüstü Reçber, Bülent Korkmaz (C), Fatih Akyel, Alpay Özalan, Ibrahim Üzülmez, Ergün Penbe, Tugay Kerimoglu, Emre Belözoglu (YC31) (43' Gökdeniz Karadeniz), Tayfun Korkut (46' Okan Yilmaz), Nihat Kahveci, Hakan Sükür (78' Volkan Arslan). (Coach: Senol Günes (TUR)).
Macedonia: Petar Milosevski, Saso Lazarevski, Vasko Bozinovski (YC53) (75' Goce Toleski), Goce Sedloski (C) (YC31), Aleksandar Mitreski, Aleksandar Vasoski (YC82), Artim Shakiri, Igor Jancevski (YC68) (71' Goran Stankovski), Vlatko Grozdanoski (85' Arben Nuhiji), Velice Sumulikoski (YC15), Aco Stojkov. (Coach: Nikola Ilievski (MCD)).
Goals: Turkey: 1-1 Nihat Kahveci (25'), 2-2 Gökdeniz Karadeniz (47'), 3-2 Hakan Sükür (57').
Macedonia: 0-1 Vlatko Grozdanoski (23'), 1-2 Artim Shakiri (27').
Referee: Roberto Rosetti (ITA)   Attendance: 20.900

11-06-2003   Riverside Stadium, Middlesbrough: England – Slovakia   2-1 (0-1)
England: David James, Matthew Upson, Phil Neville, Gareth Southgate, Danny Mills (43' Owen Hargreaves), Ashley Cole, Paul Scholes, Frank Lampard, Steven Gerrard, Wayne Rooney (58' Darius Vassell), Michael Owen (C). (Coach: Sven-Göran Eriksson (SWE)).
Slovakia: Miroslav König, Marián Zeman, Martin Petrás, Vladimír Labant (39' Ondrej Debnár (YC89)), Michal Hanek (YC60), Rastislav Michalík, Vladimír Janocko, Igor Demo (56' Marek Mintál), Radoslav Zabavník, Róbert Vittek (YC64), Szilárd Németh (76' Lubomír (Lubos) Reiter). (Coach: Ladislav Jurkemik (SVK)).
Goals: England: 1-1 Michael Owen (61' penalty), 2-1 Michael Owen (72').
Slovakia: 0-1 Vladimír Janocko (31').
Referee: Wolfgang Stark (GER)   Attendance: 33.106

06-09-2003   Gradski Stadium, Skopje: Macedonia – England   1-2 (1-0)
Macedonia: Petar Milosevski, Goran Stavrevski, Milan Stojanoski, Igor Mitreski, Artim Shakiri (C), Vanco Trajanov, Velice Sumulikoski (YC90+2), Goran Pandev (47' Igor Gjuzelov), Vlatko Grozdanoski (56' Aguinaldo Braga de Jesus (YC65)), Ilco Naumoski (YC2), Georgi Hristov (YC70) (88' Dragan Dimitrovski). (Coach: Dragan (Dragi) Kanatlarovski (MCD)).
England: David James, Gary Neville, Ashley Cole, John Terry, Sol Campbell (YC24), Owen Hargreaves, Nicky Butt, Frank Lampard (46' Emile Heskey), David Beckham (C) (YC42), Wayne Rooney (74' Phil Neville), Michael Owen (84' Kieron Dyer). (Coach: Sven-Göran Eriksson (SWE)).
Goals: Macedonia: 1-0 Georgi Hristov (28').
England: 1-1 Wayne Rooney (52'), 1-2 David Beckham (63' penalty).
Referee: Frank de Bleeckere (BEL)   Attendance: 4.500

45

06-09-2003   Rheinpark Stadion, Vaduz: Liechtenstein – Turkey   0-3 (0-2)
Liechtenstein: Peter Jehle, Christof Ritter, Michael Stocklasa (YC28) (83' Sandro Maierhofer),
Martin Stocklasa, Daniel Hasler (C), Fabio D'Elia, Andreas Gerster, Martin Telser, Franz
Burgmeier (60' Ronny Büchel), Mario Frick, Thomas Beck (60' Roger Beck). (Coach: Walter
Hörmann (AUT)).
Turkey: Rüstü Reçber, Bülent Korkmaz (C) (63' Deniz Baris), Alpay Özalan, Ibrahim
Üzülmez, Tümer Metin (63' Hasan Sas), Tugay Kerimoglu, Ergün Penbe, Ümit Davala, Okan
Buruk (75' Gökdeniz Karadeniz), Tuncay Sanli, Hakan Sükür. (Coach: Senol Günes (TUR)).
Goals: Turkey: 0-1 Tümer Metin (14'), 0-2 Okan Buruk (41'), 0-3 Hakan Sükür (50').
Referee: Dick J.H.van Egmond (HOL)   Attendance: 3.548

10-09-2003   Stadium Pod Dubnom, Zilina: Slovakia – Macedonia   1-1 (1-0)
Slovakia: Miroslav König, Branislav Labant, Martin Petrás, Vladimír Labant, Maros Klimpl,
Martin Durica (72' Karol Kisel), Vladimír Janocko (89' Dusan Sninsky), Radoslav Zabavník
(YC31), Marek Mintál (72' Rudolf Urban), Tomás Oravec, Szilárd Németh. (Coach: Ladislav
Jurkemik (SVK)).
Macedonia: Petar Milosevski, Milan Stojanoski, Goran Stavrevski, Goce Sedloski, Igor
Mitreski, Artim Shakiri (C), Igor Jancevski, Vanco Trajanov, Goran Pandev (74' Dimitar
Kapinkovski), Vlatko Grozdanoski (90'+1' Slavco Georgievski), Ilco Naumoski (38' Dragan
Dimitrovski). (Coach: Dragan (Dragi) Kanatlarovski (MCD)).
Goals: Slovakia: 1-0 Szilárd Németh (25').
Macedonia: 1-1 Dragan Dimitrovski (62').
Referee: Leif Sundell (SWE)   Attendance: 2.286

10-09-2003   Old Trafford, Manchester: England – Liechtenstein   2-0 (0-0)
England: David James, Wayne Bridge (YC59), Matthew Upson, Gary Neville, John Terry,
Frank Lampard, Steven Gerrard (57' Owen Hargreaves), David Beckham (C) (57' Phil
Neville), James Beattie, Wayne Rooney (67' Joe Cole), Michael Owen. (Coach: Sven-Göran
Eriksson (SWE)).
Liechtenstein: Peter Jehle (YC27), Christof Ritter, Daniel Hasler (C), Fabio D'Elia (71' Ronny
Büchel), Michael Stocklasa, Martin Stocklasa (YC20) (46' Sandro Maierhofer), Andreas
Gerster (YC55), Franz Burgmeier, Roger Beck (56' Thomas Beck), Martin Telser, Mario
Frick. (Coach: Walter Hörmann (AUT)).
Goals: England: 1-0 Michael Owen (46'), 2-0 Wayne Rooney (52').
Referee: Knud Erik Fisker (DEN)   Attendance: 64.931

11-10-2003   Sükrü Saracoglu Stadium, Istanbul: Turkey – England   0-0
Turkey: Rüstü Reçber (YC81), Bülent Korkmaz (C), Alpay Özalan, Fatih Akyel, Ibrahim
Üzülmez, Emre Belözoglu (79' Ergün Penbe), Sergen Yalçin (61' Tuncay Sanli), Tugay
Kerimoglu (YC62), Okan Buruk (67' Ilhan Mansiz), Nihat Kahveci, Hakan Sükür (YC58).
(Coach: Senol Günes (TUR)).
England: David James, Ashley Cole, Sol Campbell, John Terry, Gary Neville, Nicky Butt
(YC80), Paul Scholes (90' Frank Lampard), Steven Gerrard, David Beckham (C), Emile
Heskey (67' Darius Vassell), Wayne Rooney (72' Kieron Dyer). (Coach: Sven-Göran Eriksson
(SWE)).
Referee: Pierluigi Collina (ITA)   Attendance: 42.000
(David Beckham missed a penalty in the 37th minute)

11-10-2003   Rheinpark Stadion, Vaduz: Liechtenstein – Slovakia   0-2 (0-1)
Liechtenstein: Martin Heeb, Christof Ritter, Sandro Maierhofer, Michael Stocklasa, Daniel
Hasler (C), Fabio D'Elia (YC39) (76' Ronny Büchel), Martin Telser, Franz Burgmeier, Mario
Frick (YC80), Matthias Beck (46' Raphael Rohrer), Thomas Beck (46' Roger Beck). (Coach:
Walter Hörmann (AUT)).
Slovakia: Miroslav König (C), Stanislav Varga, Vladimír Leitner, Branislav Labant, Maros
Klimpl (YC51), Rastislav Michalík (84' Peter Babnic), Karol Kisel (46' Rudolf Urban),
Vladimír Janocko (YC90+2), Radoslav Zabavník, Róbert Vittek, Szilárd Németh (76' Tomás
Oravec). (Coach: Ladislav Jurkemik (SVK)).
Goals: Slovakia: 0-1 Róbert Vittek (40'), 0-2 Róbert Vittek (56').
Referee: Jouni Hyytiä (FIN)   Attendance: 955

GROUP 8

07-09-2002	Osijek	Croatia – Estonia	0-0
07-09-2002	Brussels	Belgium – Bulgaria	0-2 (0-1)
12-10-2002	Sofia	Bulgaria – Croatia	2-0 (2-0)
12-10-2002	Andorra la Vella	Andorra – Belgium	0-1 (0-0)
16-10-2002	Sofia	Bulgaria – Andorra	2-1 (1-0)
16-10-2002	Tallinn	Estonia – Belgium	0-1 (0-1)
29-03-2003	Zagreb	Croatia – Belgium	4-0 (1-0)
02-04-2003	Tallinn	Estonia – Bulgaria	0-0
02-04-2003	Varazdin	Croatia – Andorra	2-0 (2-0)
30-04-2003	Andorra la Vella	Andorra – Estonia	0-2 (0-1)
07-06-2003	Tallinn	Estonia – Andorra	2-0 (2-0)
07-06-2003	Sofia	Bulgaria – Belgium	2-2 (0-1)
11-06-2003	Tallinn	Estonia – Croatia	0-1 (0-0)
11-06-2003	Ghent	Belgium – Andorra	3-0 (2-0)
06-09-2003	Andorra la Vella	Andorra – Croatia	0-3 (0-2)
06-09-2003	Sofia	Bulgaria – Estonia	2-0 (1-0)
10-09-2003	Andorra la Vella	Andorra – Bulgaria	0-3 (0-2)
10-09-2003	Brussels	Belgium – Croatia	2-1 (2-1)
11-10-2003	Zagreb	Croatia – Bulgaria	1-0 (0-0)
11-10-2003	Liège	Belgium – Estonia	2-0 (1-0)

FINAL STANDING

Pos	Team	Pld	W	D	L	GF	GA	GD	Pts
1	*Bulgaria*	*8*	*5*	*2*	*1*	*13*	*4*	*+9*	*17*
2	Croatia	8	5	1	2	12	4	+8	16
3	Belgium	8	5	1	2	11	9	+2	16
4	Estonia	8	2	2	4	4	6	-2	8
5	Andorra	8	0	0	8	1	18	-17	0

Bulgaria qualified for the Final Tournament in Portugal.

Croatia qualified for the play-offs.

07-09-2002   Stadion Gradski vrt, Osijek: Croatia – Estonia   0-0
Croatia: Stipe Pletikosa, Boris Zivkovic (YC71), Mario Tokic, Filip Tapalovic, Dario Simic (C), Daniel Saric, Silvio Maric (45' Milan Rapaic), Marko Babic (YC63), Tomislav Maric (60' Mladen Petric), Davor Vugrinec (79' Stjepan Tomas), Ivica Olic. (Coach: Otto Baric (CRO)).
Estonia: Mart Poom, Andrei Stepanov, Erko Saviauk, Teet Allas (YC90), Raio Piiroja, Marko Kristal, Meelis Rooba, Martin Reim (C), Joel Lindpere (59' Urmas Rooba (YC79)), Indrek Zelinski (YC50), Andres Oper. (Coach: Arnoldus Dick (Arno) Pijpers (HOL)).
Referee: Juan Antonio Fernández Marín (ESP)   Attendance: 10.766

07-09-2002   King Baudouin Stadium, Brussels: Belgium – Bulgaria   0-2 (0-1)
Belgium: Geert de Vlieger, Peter van der Heyden (64' Bob Peeters), Stijn Vreven (YC90), Daniel van Buyten, Yves Vanderhaeghe (YC11), Timmy Simons, Bart Goor (C), Gaëtan Englebert (53' Mbo Mpenza), Walter Baseggio, Wesley Sonck, Emile Mpenza (70' Bernd Thijs). (Coach: Aimé Anthuenis (BEL)).
Bulgaria: Zdravko Zdravkov, Predrag Pazin, Radostin Kishishev, Rosen Kirilov, Stilian Petrov, Milen Petkov (YC40) (90' Zlatomir Zagorcic), Georgi Peev (83' Georgi Petrov), Krasimir Balakov (C), Martin Petrov, Ivaylo Petkov (YC59), Zoran Jankovic (YC70) (77' Georgi Chilikov). (Coach: Plamen Markov (BUL)).
Goals: Bulgaria: 0-1 Zoran Jankovic (17'), 0-2 Stilian Petrov (63').
Referee: Terje Hauge (NOR)   Attendance: 30.950

12-10-2002   Vasil Levski National Stadium, Sofia: Bulgaria – Croatia   2-0 (2-0)
Bulgaria: Zdravko Zdravkov, Predrag Pazin, Radostin Kishishev, Rosen Kirilov, Stilian Petrov, Georgi Peev (90' Georgi Ivanov), Krasimir Balakov (C) (YC76), Martin Petrov (66' Georgi Petrov (YC87)), Ivaylo Petkov, Zoran Jankovic, Dimitar Berbatov (YC37) (38' Georgi Chilikov). (Coach: Plamen Markov (BUL)).
Croatia: Stipe Pletikosa, Boris Zivkovic, Igor Tudor (YC75), Stjepan Tomas, Dario Simic (C) (46' Ivica Olic), Robert Kovac, Mario Stanic (YC78), Milan Rapaic (46' Marijo Maric), Jerko Leko (YC13), Alen Boksic (69' Silvio Maric), Davor Vugrinec. (Coach: Otto Baric (CRO)).
Goals: Bulgaria: 1-0 Stilian Petrov (22'), 2-0 Dimitar Berbatov (37').
Referee: Anders Frisk (SWE)   Attendance: 37.500

12-10-2002   Estadi Comunal d'Aixovall, Andorra la Vella: Andorra – Belgium   0-1 (0-0)
Andorra: Jesús Luis Álvarez de Eulate Güergue "Koldo", Antonio "Toni" Lima Sola, Roberto Jonás Alonso Martinez (YC56), José Manuel "Txema" García Luema (66' Jordi Escura Aixas), Julià "Juli" Fernández Ariza, José Manuel Díaz "Josep" Ayala, Óscar Masand Sonejee, Manolo "Manel" Jiménez Soria (76' Jesús Julian Lucendo Heredia), Juli Sánchez Soto (9' Fernando José Silva García), Emiliano González Arquez, Justo Ruíz González (C) (YC40). (Coach: David Rodrigo Lo (ESP)).
Belgium: Geert de Vlieger, Joos Valgaeren, Didier Dheedene (YC90), Olivier de Cock, Yves Vanderhaeghe, Timmy Simons, Bart Goor (C), Thomas Buffel, Walter Baseggio (81' Bernd Thijs), Peter van Houdt, Wesley Sonck (90' Tom Soetaers). (Coach: Aimé Anthuenis (BEL)).
Goal: Belgium: 0-1 Wesley Sonck (61').
Referee: Karen Nalbandyan (ARM)   Attendance: 1.100

16-10-2002   Vasil Levski National Stadium, Sofia: Bulgaria – Andorra 2-1 (1-0)
Bulgaria: Zdravko Zdravkov, Predrag Pazin, Radostin Kishishev, Rosen Kirilov, Georgi Peev, Krasimir Balakov (C) (61' Svetoslav Petrov), Stilian Petrov, Martin Petrov (75' Vladimir Manchev), Ivaylo Petkov, Zoran Jankovic (77' Georgi Ivanov), Georgi Chilikov. (Coach: Plamen Markov (BUL)).
Andorra: Jesús Luis Álvarez de Eulate Güergue "Koldo", Antonio "Toni" Lima Sola (YC58,RC83), Roberto Jonás Alonso Martinez, Jordi Escura Aixas, Ildefons Lima Solà (YC44), Julià "Juli" Fernández Ariza, José Manuel Díaz "Josep" Ayala (YC22), Manolo "Manel" Jiménez Soria (80' Marc Pujol Pons), Óscar Masand Sonejee, Emiliano González Arquez (63' Fernando José Silva García), Justo Ruíz González (C). (Coach: David Rodrigo Lo (ESP)).
Goals: Bulgaria: 1-0 Georgi Chilikov (37'), 2-0 Krasimir Balakov (58').
Andorra: 2-1 Antonio "Toni" Lima Sola (80').
Referee: David Ceri Richards (WAL)   Attendance: 25.500

16-10-2002   A. Le Coq Arena, Tallinn: Estonia – Belgium 0-1 (0-1)
Estonia: Mart Poom, Andrei Stepanov, Urmas Rooba, Teet Allas, Raio Piiroja (YC7), Marko Kristal (83' Aleksander Saharov), Aivar Anniste (46' Kert Haavistu), Martin Reim (C), Indrek Zelinski, Andres Oper (YC26), Sergei Terehhov (60' Kristen Viikmäe). (Coach: Arnoldus Dick (Arno) Pijpers (HOL)).
Belgium: Geert de Vlieger, Joos Valgaeren, Didier Dheedene, Olivier de Cock, Yves Vanderhaeghe, Timmy Simons, Bart Goor (C), Thomas Buffel (88' Joris van Hout), Walter Baseggio, Peter van Houdt, Wesley Sonck. (Coach: Aimé Anthuenis (BEL)).
Goal: Belgium: 0-1 Wesley Sonck (2').
Referee: Michael (Mike) Riley (ENG)   Attendance: 5.200

29-03-2003   Stadion Maksimir, Zagreb: Croatia – Belgium 4-0 (1-0)
Croatia: Stipe Pletikosa, Boris Zivkovic (C), Igor Tudor (77' Niko Kovac), Josip Simunic, Dario Simic, Robert Kovac, Djovani Roso (YC26) (46' Jerko Leko), Milan Rapaic, Darijo Srna (YC34), Dado Prso (71' Mario Stanic), Tomislav Maric. (Coach: Otto Baric (CRO)).
Belgium: Franky Vanderdriessche, Peter van der Heyden, Joos Valgaeren (67' Jelle van Damme), Olivier de Cock (YC20) (56' Eric Deflandre (YC70)), Daniel van Buyten, Timmy Simons, Bart Goor (C), Gaëtan Englebert (55' Walter Baseggio), Thomas Buffel, Wesley Sonck, Emile Mpenza. (Coach: Aimé Anthuenis (BEL)).
Goals: Croatia: 1-0 Darijo Srna (9'), 2-0 Dado Prso (55'), 3-0 Tomislav Maric (70'), 4-0 Jerko Leko (76').
Referee: Herbert Fandel (GER)   Attendance: 18.117
(Djovani Roso also known as Giovanni Rosso)

02-04-2003   A. Le Coq Arena, Tallinn: Estonia – Bulgaria 0-0
Estonia: Mart Poom (C), Marek Lemsalu, Urmas Rooba, Teet Allas, Enar Jääger, Liivo Leetma, Marko Kristal, Kert Haavistu (62' Ott Reinumäe), Indrek Zelinski (56' Kristen Viikmäe (YC73)), Andres Oper, Sergei Terehhov. (Coach: Arnoldus Dick (Arno) Pijpers (HOL)).
Bulgaria: Zdravko Zdravkov, Predrag Pazin, Radostin Kishishev, Rosen Kirilov, Stilian Petrov, Georgi Peev, Krasimir Balakov (C) (YC80), Martin Petrov (71' Milen Petkov), Ivaylo Petkov, Zoran Jankovic (YC24) (46' Svetoslav Todorov (YC82)), Dimitar Berbatov. (Coach: Plamen Markov (BUL)).
Referee: Konrad Plautz (AUT)   Attendance: 3.000

02-04-2003   Stadion Andjelko Herjavec, Varazdin: Croatia – Andorra   2-0 (2-0)
Croatia: Stipe Pletikosa, Boris Zivkovic (C), Igor Tudor (YC63), Josip Simunic (46' Mario
Stanic), Dario Simic, Robert Kovac, Darijo Srna, Milan Rapaic (65' Marko Babic), Jerko
Leko, Dado Prso, Tomislav Maric (46' Niko Kovac (YC73)). (Coach: Otto Baric (CRO)).
Andorra: Jesús Luis Álvarez de Eulate Güergue "Koldo", Roberto Jonás Alonso Martinez
(YC10), José Manuel "Txema" García Luema, Julià "Juli" Fernández Ariza, José Manuel Díaz
"Josep" Ayala, Óscar Masand Sonejee, Manolo "Manel" Jiménez Soria (54' Jordi Escura
Aixas), Juli Sánchez Soto, Agusti Pol Pérez (84' Jesús Julian Lucendo Heredia), Marc Pujol
Pons, Emiliano González Arquez (90'+1' Alain-Kumar Montwani Marina). (Coach: David
Rodrigo Lo (ESP)).
Goals: Croatia: 1-0 Milan Rapaic (10' penalty), 2-0 Milan Rapaic (43').
Referee: Marian Mircea Salomir (ROM)   Attendance: 7.290

30-04-2003   Estadi Comunal d'Aixovall, Andorra la Vella: Andorra – Estonia   0-2 (0-1)
Andorra: Jesús Luis Álvarez de Eulate Güergue "Koldo", José Manuel "Txema" García Luema,
Jordi Escura Aixas, Julià "Juli" Fernández Ariza, José Manuel Díaz "Josep" Ayala (YC35) (89'
Fernando José Silva García), Óscar Masand Sonejee, Manolo "Manel" Jiménez Soria (70'
Jesús Julian Lucendo Heredia), Juli Sánchez Soto, Marc Pujol Pons (80' Josep Felix Álvarez
Blázquez), Emiliano González Arquez, Justo Ruíz González (C). (Coach: David Rodrigo Lo
(ESP)).
Estonia: Mart Poom (C), Andrei Stepanov, Urmas Rooba, Marek Lemsalu, Teet Allas, Marko
Kristal, Martin Reim, Kert Haavistu (69' Ott Reinumäe), Indrek Zelinski (YC15), Kristen
Viikmäe (89' Meelis Rooba), Sergei Terehhov (55' Joel Lindpere). (Coach: Arnoldus Dick
(Arno) Pijpers (HOL)).
Goals: Estonia: 0-1 Indrek Zelinski (26'), 0-2 Indrek Zelinski (74').
Referee: Ali Aydin (TUR)   Attendance: 850

07-06-2003   A. Le Coq Arena, Tallinn: Estonia – Andorra   2-0 (2-0)
Estonia: Mart Poom (C), Andrei Stepanov, Urmas Rooba (49' Erko Saviauk), Teet Allas, Raio
Piiroja, Liivo Leetma, Marko Kristal, Joel Lindpere (89' Ott Reinumäe), Kert Haavistu (70'
Meelis Rooba), Kristen Viikmäe (YC89), Vjatseslav Zahovaiko (YC16). (Coach: Arnoldus
Dick (Arno) Pijpers (HOL)).
Andorra: Jesús Luis Álvarez de Eulate Güergue "Koldo", Antonio "Toni" Lima Sola, José
Manuel "Txema" García Luema, Jordi Escura Aixas, Ildefons Lima Solà, Julià "Juli"
Fernández Ariza, Óscar Masand Sonejee, Manolo "Manel" Jiménez Soria (72' Marc Pujol Pons
(YC87)), Juli Sánchez Soto (YC36), Emiliano González Arquez (83' Fernando José Silva
García), Justo Ruíz González (C) (YC90). (Coach: David Rodrigo Lo (ESP)).
Goals: Estonia: 1-0 Teet Allas (22'), 2-0 Kristen Viikmäe (31').
Referee: Attila Juhos (HUN)   Attendance: 2.700

07-06-2003   Vasil Levski National Stadium, Sofia: Bulgaria – Belgium   2-2 (0-1)
Bulgaria: Zdravko Zdravkov, Martin Stankov, Ilian Stoyanov (YC64), Rosen Kirilov, Mariyan
Hristov (71' Vladimir Manchev), Daniel Borimirov, Stilian Petrov (C), Ivaylo Petkov, Martin
Petrov, Velizar Dimitrov (80' Aleksander Yordanov Aleksandrov), Dimitar Berbatov (53'
Svetoslav Todorov). (Coach: Plamen Markov (BUL)).
Belgium: Geert de Vlieger, Philippe Clement, Didier Dheedene, Eric Deflandre (YC42),
Daniel van Buyten, Timmy Simons, Bart Goor (C), Thomas Buffel, Walter Baseggio, Wesley
Sonck (74' Emile Mpenza), Mbo Mpenza. (Coach: Aimé Anthuenis (BEL)).
Goals: Bulgaria: 1-1 Dimitar Berbatov (52'), 2-2 Svetoslav Todorov (71' penalty).
Belgium: 0-1 Stilian Petrov (30' *own goal*), 1-2 Philippe Clement (55').
Referee: Pierluigi Collina (ITA)   Attendance: 37.200

50

11-06-2003   A. Le Coq Arena, Tallinn: Estonia – Croatia   0-1 (0-0)
Estonia: Mart Poom (C), Andrei Stepanov, Urmas Rooba, Teet Allas (82' Vjatseslav
Zahovaiko), Raio Piiroja (YC38), Liivo Leetma, Marko Kristal (YC20), Meelis Rooba (71' Ott
Reinumäe), Joel Lindpere (83' Marek Lemsalu), Indrek Zelinski, Andres Oper. (Coach:
Arnoldus Dick (Arno) Pijpers (HOL)).
Croatia: Stipe Pletikosa, Boris Zivkovic (C) (YC66), Stjepan Tomas, Josip Simunic, Dario
Simic (YC12) (60' Tomislav Maric), Marko Babic (73' Jerko Leko), Milan Rapaic (79'
Djovani Roso), Niko Kovac, Darijo Srna (YC32), Dado Prso, Ivica Olic (YC90+3). (Coach:
Otto Baric (CRO)).
Goal: Croatia: 0-1 Niko Kovac (76').
Referee: Alain Hamer (LUX)   Attendance: 4.000

11-06-2003   Jules Ottenstadion, Ghent: Belgium – Andorra   3-0 (2-0)
Belgium: Geert de Vlieger, Didier Dheedene (80' Peter van der Heyden), Olivier de Cock
(YC35), Philippe Clement, Daniel van Buyten, Timmy Simons, Bart Goor (C) (84' Tom
Soetaers), Thomas Buffel (73' Sandy Martens), Walter Baseggio, Wesley Sonck, Mbo
Mpenza. (Coach: Aimé Anthuenis (BEL)).
Andorra: Jesús Luis Álvarez de Eulate Güergue "Koldo", Antonio "Toni" Lima Sola (C),
Roberto Jonás Alonso Martinez, José Manuel "Txema" García Luema (YC56), Ildefons Lima
Solà, Julià "Juli" Fernández Ariza, José Manuel Díaz "Josep" Ayala, Óscar Masand Sonejee
(83' Jesús Julian Lucendo Heredia), Juli Sánchez Soto (59' Jordi Escura Aixas), Marc Pujol
Pons (YC28), Emiliano González Arquez (71' Josep Felix Álvarez Blázquez). (Coach: David
Rodrigo Lo (ESP)).
Goals: Belgium: 1-0 Bart Goor (21'), 2-0 Wesley Sonck (45'), 3-0 Bart Goor (69').
Referee: Siarhei Shmolik (BLS)   Attendance: 11.747

06-09-2003   Estadi Comunal d'Aixovall, Andorra la Vella: Andorra – Croatia   0-3 (0-2)
Andorra: Jesús Luis Álvarez de Eulate Güergue "Koldo", Francesc Javier Ramírez Palomo
(YC18), Antonio "Toni" Lima Sola, Roberto Jonás Alonso Martinez (69' Genís García Iscla),
José Manuel "Txema" García Luema, Julià "Juli" Fernández Ariza, José Manuel Díaz "Josep"
Ayala, Óscar Masand Sonejee (YC67), Juli Sánchez Soto (73' Manolo "Manel" Jiménez
Soria), Emiliano González Arquez (50' Fernando José Silva García), Justo Ruíz González (C)
(YC12). (Coach: David Rodrigo Lo (ESP)).
Croatia: Stipe Pletikosa, Stjepan Tomas (YC87), Josip Simunic, Dario Simic (C), Robert
Kovac (YC78), Djovani Roso, Milan Rapaic, Jerko Leko (YC32) (46' Igor Tudor), Niko
Kovac (33' Jurica Vranjes), Ivica Mornar, Ivica Olic (58' Dado Prso). (Coach: Otto Baric
(CRO)).
Goals: Croatia: 0-1 Niko Kovac (4'), 0-2 Josip Simunic (16'), 0-3 Djovani Roso (71').
Referee: Miroslav Liba (CZE)   Attendance: 900

06-09-2003   Vasil Levski National Stadium, Sofia: Bulgaria – Estonia   2-0 (1-0)
Bulgaria: Dimitar Ivankov, Ilian Stoyanov (YC36) (87' Zhivko Zhelev), Rosen Kirilov, Stilian
Petrov (C), Mariyan Hristov, Daniel Borimirov, Martin Petrov, Ivaylo Petkov, Velizar
Dimitrov (71' Georgi Peev), Zoran Jankovic (62' Nikolai Krastev (YC89)), Dimitar Berbatov.
(Coach: Plamen Markov (BUL)).
Estonia: Mart Poom (C), Andrei Stepanov, Urmas Rooba, Teet Allas (YC57), Enar Jääger,
Liivo Leetma (YC52), Marko Kristal (YC13), Meelis Rooba (61' Ott Reinumäe), Joel
Lindpere (75' Ragnar Klavan), Kristen Viikmäe, Andres Oper (RC70). (Coach: Arnoldus Dick
(Arno) Pijpers (HOL)).
Goals: Bulgaria: 1-0 Martin Petrov (16'), 2-0 Dimitar Berbatov (66').
Referee: Dr.Franz-Xaver Wack (GER)   Attendance: 25.128

51

10-09-2003   Estadi Comunal d'Aixovall, Andorra la Vella: Andorra – Bulgaria   0-3 (0-2)
Andorra: Jesús Luis Álvarez de Eulate Güergue "Koldo", Francesc Javier Ramírez Palomo
(RC86), Antonio "Toni" Lima Sola (YC75), Roberto Jonás Alonso Martinez (61' Juli Sánchez
Soto (YC67)), José Manuel "Txema" García Luema, Julià "Juli" Fernández Ariza, José Manuel
Díaz "Josep" Ayala (80' Jordi Escura Aixas), Óscar Masand Sonejee (YC54), Manolo "Manel"
Jiménez Soria (YC53), Marc Pujol Pons (YC68), Justo Ruíz González (C) (90'+3' Jesús Julian
Lucendo Heredia). (Coach: David Rodrigo Lo (ESP)).
Bulgaria: Dimitar Ivankov, Predrag Pazin, Rosen Kirilov, Stilian Petrov (C), Georgi Peev (64'
Vladimir Manchev), Mariyan Hristov (YC74), Daniel Borimirov, Martin Petrov, Ivaylo
Petkov, Zoran Jankovic (59' Velizar Dimitrov), Dimitar Berbatov. (Coach: Plamen Markov
(BUL)).
Goals: Bulgaria: 0-1 Dimitar Berbatov (11'), 0-2 Dimitar Berbatov (24'), 0-3 Mariyan Hristov
(58').
Referee: Tomasz Mikulski (POL)   Attendance: 450

10-09-2003   King Baudouin Stadium, Brussels: Belgium – Croatia   2-1 (2-1)
Belgium: Geert de Vlieger, Jelle van Damme, Philippe Clement, Eric Deflandre, Daniel van
Buyten (YC18), Jonathan Walasiak, Timmy Simons, Bart Goor (C), Thomas Buffel (88' Sandy
Martens (YC90)), Walter Baseggio, Wesley Sonck (90'+2' Tom Soetaers). (Coach: Aimé
Anthuenis (BEL)).
Croatia: Stipe Pletikosa, Boris Zivkovic (C) (YC68), Stjepan Tomas (YC75), Josip Simunic
(YC17,YC72), Dario Simic, Robert Kovac, Djovani Roso (63' Darijo Srna), Milan Rapaic (78'
Marijo Maric), Niko Kovac (YC83), Ivica Mornar (YC4), Ivica Olic (46' Dado Prso). (Coach:
Otto Baric (CRO)).
Goals: Belgium: 1-0 Wesley Sonck (35'), 2-1 Wesley Sonck (43').
Croatia: 1-1 Milan Rapaic (37').
Referee: Graham Poll (ENG)   Attendance: 35.682

11-10-2003   Stadion Maksimir, Zagreb: Croatia – Bulgaria   1-0 (0-0)
Croatia: Stipe Pletikosa, Boris Zivkovic (C), Igor Tudor (YC38), Dario Simic, Robert Kovac
(YC41), Jurica Vranjes, Milan Rapaic (75' Marko Babic), Darijo Srna (46' Ivica Olic), Jerko
Leko (YC89), Dado Prso, Ivica Mornar (54' Djovani Roso). (Coach: Otto Baric (CRO)).
Bulgaria: Zdravko Zdravkov, Predrag Pazin, Nikolai Krastev (YC35), Rosen Kirilov, Stilian
Petrov (C) (YC82), Georgi Peev (72' Zoran Jankovic), Mariyan Hristov, Daniel Borimirov,
Ivaylo Petkov, Velizar Dimitrov (YC14) (63' Vladimir Manchev), Dimitar Berbatov. (Coach:
Plamen Markov (BUL)).
Goal: Croatia: 1-0 Ivica Olic (48').
Referee: Gilles Veissière (FRA)   Attendance: 31.363

11-10-2003   Stade Maurice Dufrasne, Liège: Belgium – Estonia   2-0 (1-0)
Belgium: Geert de Vlieger, Jelle van Damme (56' Olivier Deschacht), Eric Deflandre, Philippe
Clement, Daniel van Buyten, Timmy Simons, Bart Goor (C), Thomas Buffel (87' Cédric
Roussel), Walter Baseggio, Wesley Sonck (80' Emile Mpenza), Mbo Mpenza. (Coach: Aimé
Anthuenis (BEL)).
Estonia: Mart Poom, Urmas Rooba, Marek Lemsalu, Raio Piiroja, Ragnar Klavan (64' Sergei
Terehhov), Enar Jääger, Ott Reinumäe, Meelis Rooba, Martin Reim (C), Kert Haavistu (78'
Vjatseslav Zahovaiko), Kristen Viikmäe. (Coach: Arnoldus Dick (Arno) Pijpers (HOL)).
Goals: Belgium: 1-0 Raio Piiroja (44' *own goal*), 2-0 Thomas Buffel (60').
Referee: Massimo Busacca (ITA)   Attendance: 22.408

GROUP 9

07-09-2002	Helsinki	Finland – Wales	0-2 (0-1)
07-09-2002	Baku	Azerbaijan – Italy	0-2 (0-1)
12-10-2002	Helsinki	Finland – Azerbaijan	3-0 (1-0)
12-10-2002	Naples	Italy –Yugoslavia	1-1 (1-1)
16-10-2002	Belgrade	Yugoslavia – Finland	2-0 (0-0)
16-10-2002	Cardiff	Wales – Italy	2-1 (1-1)
30-11-2002	Baku	Azerbaijan – Wales	0-2 (0-1)
12-02-2003	Podgorica	Serbia and Montenegro – Azerbaijan	2-2 (1-0)
29-03-2003	Cardiff	Wales –Azerbaijan	4-0 (3-0)
29-03-2003	Palermo	Italy – Finland	2-0 (2-0)
07-06-2003	Helsinki	Finland – Serbia and Montenegro	3-0 (2-0)
11-06-2003	Baku	Azerbaijan – Serbia and Montenegro	2-1 (0-1)
11-06-2003	Helsinki	Finland – Italy	0-2 (0-1)
20-08-2003	Belgrade	Serbia and Montenegro – Wales	1-0 (0-0)
06-09-2003	Baku	Azerbaijan – Finland	1-2 (0-0)
06-09-2003	Milan	Italy – Wales	4-0 (0-0)
10-09-2003	Cardiff	Wales – Finland	1-1 (1-0)
10-09-2003	Belgrade	Serbia and Montenegro – Italy	1-1 (0-1)
11-10-2003	Cardiff	Wales – Serbia and Montenegro	2-3 (1-1)
11-10-2003	Reggio Calabria	Italy – Azerbaijan	4-0 (2-0)

FINAL STANDING

Pos	Team	Pld	W	D	L	GF	GA	GD	Pts
1	*Italy*	*8*	*5*	*2*	*1*	*17*	*4*	*+13*	*17*
2	Wales	8	4	1	3	13	10	+3	13
3	Serbia and Montenegro	8	3	3	2	11	11	+0	12
4	Finland	8	3	1	4	9	19	-1	10
5	Azerbaijan	8	1	1	6	5	20	-15	4

Italy qualified for the Final Tournament in Portugal.
Wales qualified for the play-offs.

Serbia and Montenegro began the campaign as Yugoslavia, but officially changed their name in February 2003.

07-09-2002   Helsinki Olympic Stadium, Helsinki: Finland – Wales   0-2 (0-1)
Finland: Antti Niemi, Hannu Tihinen (YC21), Janne Saarinen (78' Peter Kopteff), Ville Nylund (70' Jonatan Johansson), Sami Hyypiä (YC45), Teemu Tainio (YC90+3), Aki Riihilahti (YC86), Mika Nurmela (85' Mika Kottila), Joonas Kolkka, Jari Litmanen (C), Shefki Kuqi. (Coach: Antti Muurinen (FIN)).
Wales: Paul Jones, Andy Melville, Daniel (Danny) Gabbidon, Mark Delaney, Robbie Savage, Mark Pembridge (YC10), Andy Johnson (YC63) (76' Craig Bellamy), Simon Davies, John Hartson, Ryan Giggs, Gary Speed (C). (Coach: Mark Hughes (WAL)).
Goals: Wales: 0-1 John Hartson (30'), 0-2 Simon Davies (72').
Referee: Konrad Plautz (AUT)   Attendance: 35.833

07-09-2002   Tofiq Bahramov Stadium, Baku: Azerbaijan – Italy   0-2 (0-1)
Azerbaijan: Dmitriy Kramarenko, Emin Agayev, Aslan Kerimov, Emin Guliyev (YC15),
Tarlan Akhmedov (C), Emin Imamaliyev, Makhmud Gurbanov (66' Ruslan Musayev (YC71)),
Kamal Guliyev (YC77), Rashad Farhad oglu Sadygov, Samir Aliyev (87' Nadir Nabiyev),
Gurban Gurbanov. (Coach: Vagif Sadykov (AZE)).
Italy: Gianluigi Buffon, Fabio Cannavaro (C) (YC62), Alessandro Nesta, Francesco Coco,
Christian Panucci, Damiano Tommasi, Gennaro Gattuso, Luigi Di Biagio (58' Massimo
Ambrosini), Christian Vieri (58' Vincenzo Montella), Filippo Inzaghi (76' Andrea Pirlo),
Alessandro Del Piero. (Coach: Giovanni Trapattoni (ITA)).
Goals: Italy: 0-1 Tarlan Akhmadov (33' *own goal*), 0-2 Alessandro Del Piero (65').
Referee: Kyros Vassaras (GRE)   Attendance: 28.000

12-10-2002   Helsinki Olympic Stadium, Helsinki: Finland – Azerbaijan   3-0 (1-0)
Finland: Antti Niemi, Hannu Tihinen (YC37), Janne Saarinen, Petri Pasanen, Sami Hyypiä
(79' Toni Kuivasto), Teemu Tainio (74' Jarkko Wiss), Aki Riihilahti, Mika Nurmela, Joonas
Kolkka, Antti Sumiala (86' Shefki Kuqi), Jari Litmanen (C). (Coach: Antti Muurinen (FIN)).
Azerbaijan: Jahangir Hasanzade, Aslan Kerimov (YC37), Emin Agayev, Emin Guliyev
(YC58), Ramiz Mammadov (YC59) (90'+2' Fizuli Mamedov), Emin Imamaliyev (83' Vadim
Vasilyev), Makhmud Gurbanov (65' Rashad Farhad oglu Sadygov), Kamal Guliyev (YC69),
Tarlan Akhmedov (C) (YC41), Gurban Gurbanov, Samir Aliyev (YC73). (Coach: Vagif
Sadykov (AZE)).
Goals: Finland: 1-0 Emin Agayev (14' *own goal*), 2-0 Hannu Tihinen (60'), 3-0 Sami Hyypiä
(72').
Referee: Alain Hamer (LUX)   Attendance: 11.853

12-10-2002   Stadio San Paolo, Naples: Italy – Yugoslavia   1-1 (1-1)
Italy: Gianluigi Buffon, Alessandro Nesta, Fabio Cannavaro (C), Luciano Zauri (80' Massimo
Oddo), Christian Panucci, Damiano Tommasi (YC78), Gennaro Gattuso, Cristiano Doni (46'
Vincenzo Montella), Andrea Pirlo (78' Massimo Ambrosini), Filippo Inzaghi, Alessandro Del
Piero. (Coach: Giovanni Trapattoni (ITA)).
Yugoslavia: Dragoslav Jevric, Zoran Mirkovic (8' Igor Duljaj), Mladen Krstajic, Ivica
Dragutinovic, Nemanja Vidic, Sinisa Mihajlovic, Goran Trobok (YC69), Dejan Stankovic,
Nikola Lazetic (YC36), Predrag Mijatovic (YC89) (65' Mateja Kezman), Darko Kovacevic
(YC72) (72' Savo Milosevic). (Coach: Dejan Savicevic (YUG)).
Goals: Italy: 1-1 Alessandro Del Piero (38').
Yugoslavia: 0-1 Predrag Mijatovic (27').
Referee: Manuel Enrique Mejuto González (ESP)   Attendance: 43.661

16-10-2002   Stadion Crvena Zvezda, Belgrade: Yugoslavia – Finland   2-0 (0-0)
Yugoslavia: Dragoslav Jevric, Nemanja Vidic (YC31), Sinisa Mihajlovic (YC48), Ivica
Dragutinovic, Dejan Stankovic (YC8), Zoran Njegus (46' Mladen Krstajic), Nikola Lazetic,
Igor Duljaj, Predrag Mijatovic (C), Darko Kovacevic (YC40) (71' Savo Milosevic), Mateja
Kezman (62' Nenad Brnovic). (Coach: Dejan Savicevic (YUG)).
Finland: Antti Niemi, Janne Saarinen, Petri Pasanen (63' Juha Reini (RC83)), Toni Kuivasto,
Sami Hyypiä, Teemu Tainio (82' Shefki Kuqi), Aki Riihilahti, Mika Nurmela (YC41), Joonas
Kolkka, Antti Sumiala (57' Jonatan Johansson), Jari Litmanen (C). (Coach: Antti Muurinen
(FIN)).
Goals: Yugoslavia: 1-0 Darko Kovacevic (55'), 2-0 Predrag Mijatovic (84' penalty).
Referee: Dick J.H.van Egmond (HOL)   Attendance: 22.113

16-10-2002   Millennium Stadium, Cardiff: Wales – Italy   2-1 (1-1)
Wales: Paul Jones, Andy Melville, Daniel (Danny) Gabbidon, Mark Delaney, Robbie Savage (YC20), Mark Pembridge, Simon Davies, John Hartson, Ryan Giggs, Craig Bellamy (YC30) (90' Nathan Blake), Gary Speed (C). (Coach: Mark Hughes (WAL)).
Italy: Gianluigi Buffon, Alessandro Nesta, Fabio Cannavaro (C), Luciano Zauri (YC90), Christian Panucci, Massimo Ambrosini, Damiano Tommasi, Luigi Di Biagio (YC6) (65' Gennaro Gattuso, 84' Massimo Marazzina), Andrea Pirlo, Vincenzo Montella (69' Massimo Maccarone), Alessandro Del Piero. (Coach: Giovanni Trapattoni (ITA)).
Goals: Wales: 1-0 Simon Davies (11'), 2-1 Craig Bellamy (70').
Italy: 1-1 Alessandro Del Piero (31').
Referee: Gilles Veissière (FRA)   Attendance: 71.000

20-11-2002   Tofiq Bahramov Stadium, Baku: Azerbaijan – Wales   0-2 (0-1)
Azerbaijan: Jahangir Hasanzade, Ilham Yadullayev, Adaim Niftaliyev, Aslan Kerimov (46' Fizuli Mamedov), Emin Imamaliyev, Makhmud Gurbanov (62' Farrukh Ismayilov (YC65)), Tarlan Akhmedov (C) (75' Arif Asadov), Rashad Farhad oglu Sadygov (YC32), Vadim Vasilyev, Gurban Gurbanov, Samir Aliyev. (Coach: Asgar Abdullayev (AZE)).
Wales: Paul Jones, Robert (Rob) Page (YC34), Andy Melville, Mark Delaney (71' Rhys Weston), Darren Barnard (YC69), Carl Robinson (90'+2' Paul Trollope), Simon Davies, John Hartson, Ryan Giggs, Robert (Rob) Earnshaw (90' Neil Roberts), Gary Speed (C). (Coach: Mark Hughes (WAL)).
Goals: Wales: 0-1 Gary Speed (10'), 0-2 Robert (Rob) Page (68').
Referee: Luc Huyghe (BEL)   Attendance: 9.500

12-02-2003   Podgorica City Stadium, Podgorica:
                    Serbia and Montenegro – Azerbaijan   2-2 (1-0)
Serbia and Montenegro: Dragoslav Jevric, Milan Dudic, Nenad Djordjevic, Goran Bunjevcevic, Branko Boskovic, Zvonimir Vukic, Dejan Stankovic, Nikola Lazetic (74' Marjan Markovic), Savo Milosevic, Predrag Mijatovic (C) (70' Danijel Ljuboja), Mateja Kezman (59' Igor Duljaj). (Coach: Dejan Savicevic (SBM)).
Azerbaijan: Jahangir Hasanzade (YC52), Ramiz Mammadov, Emin Guliyev, Kamal Guliyev, Tarlan Akhmedov (C), Emin Imamaliyev, Makhmud Gurbanov (90'+3' Fizuli Mamedov), Rashad Farhad oglu Sadygov (YC29), Samir Aliyev (87' Khagani Mammadov), Farrukh Ismayilov (YC44) (55' Ruslan Musayev), Gurban Gurbanov. (Coach: Asgar Abdullayev (AZE)).
Goals: Serbia and Montenegro: 1-0 Predrag Mijatovic (33' penalty), 2-0 Nikola Lazetic (52').
Azerbaijan: 2-1 Gurban Gurbanov (58'), 2-2 Gurban Gurbanov (77').
Referee: Jacek Granat (POL)   Attendance: 6.500

29-03-2003   Millennium Stadium, Cardiff: Wales – Azerbaijan   4-0 (3-0)
Wales: Paul Jones, Robert (Rob) Page, Andy Melville, John Oster, Robbie Savage (19' Carl Robinson), Mark Pembridge, Simon Davies, John Hartson, Ryan Giggs, Craig Bellamy (71' Robert (Rob) Edwards), Gary Speed (C) (45' Paul Trollope). (Coach: Mark Hughes (WAL)).
Azerbaijan: Jahangir Hasanzade, Emin Guliyev (46' Fizuli Mamedov (YC46)), Ruslan Musayev, Ramiz Mammadov (YC38), Emin Imamaliyev, Aftandil Hadjiev (46' Ilham Yadullayev), Makhmud Gurbanov (YC68), Kamal Guliyev, Tarlan Akhmedov (C), Gurban Gurbanov, Samir Aliyev (78' Zaur Tagizade). (Coach: Asgar Abdullayev (AZE)).
Goals: Wales: 1-0 Simon Davies (1'), 2-0 Gary Speed (40'), 3-0 John Hartson (43'), 4-0 Ryan Giggs (52').
Referee: Philippe Leuba (SUI)   Attendance: 73.500

29-03-2003   Stadio Renzo Barbera, Palermo: Italy – Finland   2-0 (2-0)
Italy: Gianluigi Buffon, Alessandro Nesta, Fabio Cannavaro (C), Gianluca Zambrotta,
Christian Panucci, Simone Perrotta, Mauro Camoranesi, Cristiano Zanetti, Marco Delvecchio
(68' Alessandro Birindelli), Christian Vieri (82' Bernardo Corradi), Francesco Totti (86'
Fabrizio Miccoli). (Coach: Giovanni Trapattoni (ITA)).
Finland: Antti Niemi, Hannu Tihinen, Janne Saarinen, Petri Pasanen (YC71), Sami Hyypiä (C),
Teemu Tainio, Aki Riihilahti (35' Jonatan Johansson), Mika Nurmela (75' Peter Kopteff),
Joonas Kolkka (88' Shefki Kuqi), Jari Olola, Mikael Forssell. (Coach: Antti Muurinen (FIN)).
Goals: Italy: 1-0 Christian Vieri (6'), 2-0 Christian Vieri (23').
Referee: Valentin Valentinovich Ivanov (RUS)   Attendance: 34.074

07-06-2003   Helsinki Olympic Stadium, Helsinki:
              Finland – Serbia and Montenegro   3-0 (2-0)
Finland: Jussi Jääskeläinen, Hannu Tihinen, Janne Saarinen, Petri Pasanen, Sami Hyypiä, Mika
Väyrynen, Simo Valakari (YC31), Mika Nurmela (87' Aki Riihilahti), Joonas Kolkka (66'
Peter Kopteff), Jari Litmanen (C), Mikael Forssell (79' Shefki Kuqi). (Coach: Antti Muurinen
(FIN)).
Serbia and Montenegro: Dragoslav Jevric, Zoran Mirkovic (80' Nenad Kovacevic), Slobodan
Markovic (YC49), Mladen Krstajic, Nemanja Vidic, Sinisa Mihajlovic (RC26), Igor Duljaj,
Boban Dmitrovic (YC28), Savo Milosevic (46' Nenad Jestrovic), Predrag Mijatovic (C) (46'
Zvonimir Vukic), Darko Kovacevic. (Coach: Dejan Savicevic (SBM)).
Goals: Finland: 1-0 Sami Hyypiä (19'), 2-0 Joonas Kolkka (45'), 3-0 Mikael Forssell (56').
Referee: Claude Colombo (FRA)   Attendance: 17.343

11-06-2003   Shafa Stadium, Baku: Azerbaijan – Serbia and Montenegro   2-1 (0-1)
Azerbaijan: Dmitriy Kramarenko, Emin Agayev (84' Zaur Tagizade), Aslan Kerimov (YC20),
Emin Guliyev, Kamal Guliyev (YC38), Tarlan Akhmedov (C), Ruslan Musayev (59' Farrukh
Ismayilov), Makhmud Gurbanov, Rashad Farhad oglu Sadygov, Samir Aliyev, Gurban
Gurbanov (90'+4' Ilham Yadullayev). (Coach: Asgar Abdullayev (AZE)).
Serbia and Montenegro: Dragoslav Jevric (46' Dragan Zilic), Nenad Djordjevic, Nikola
Malbasa (YC16), Zoran Mirkovic (YC86), Mladen Krstajic (YC69), Igor Duljaj (88' Savo
Milosevic), Branko Boskovic (YC53), Zvonimir Vukic (YC23), Zoran Njegus, Darko
Kovacevic, Predrag Mijatovic (C) (69' Nenad Kovacevic). (Coach: Dejan Savicevic (SBM)).
Goals: Azerbaijan: 1-1 Gurban Gurbanov (88' penalty), 2-1 Farrukh Ismayilov (90'+1').
Serbia and Montenegro:0-1 Branko Boskovic (27').
Referee: Knud Erik Fisker (DEN)   Attendance: 1.500

11-06-2003   Helsinki Olympic Stadium, Helsinki: Finland – Italy   0-2 (0-1)
Finland: Jussi Jääskeläinen, Hannu Tihinen, Janne Saarinen, Petri Pasanen, Sami Hyypiä, Mika
Väyrynen, Simo Valakari (81' Aki Riihilahti), Mika Nurmela (68' Peter Kopteff), Joonas
Kolkka (78' Jonatan Johansson), Jari Litmanen (C), Mikael Forssell. (Coach: Antti Muurinen
(FIN)).
Italy: Gianluigi Buffon, Alessandro Nesta, Fabio Cannavaro (C) (89' Nicola Legrottaglie),
Gianluca Zambrotta, Christian Panucci, Stefano Fiore (80' Massimo Oddo), Cristiano Zanetti,
Simone Perrotta, Alessandro Del Piero, Bernardo Corradi (84' Marco Delvecchio), Francesco
Totti. (Coach: Giovanni Trapattoni (ITA)).
Goals: Italy: 0-1 Francesco Totti (31'), 0-2 Alessandro Del Piero (73').
Referee: Zeljko Siric (CRO)   Attendance: 36.850

20-08-2003   Stadion Crvena Zvezda, Belgrade: Serbia and Montenegro – Wales   1-0 (0-0)
Serbia and Montenegro: Dragoslav Jevric (YC88), Milivoje Cirkovic, Goran Gavrancic, Dejan
Stefanovic, Mladen Krstajic, Ivica Dragutinovic, Dragan Mladenovic, Zvonimir Vukic (YC17)
(67' Sasa Ilic), Dejan Stankovic (YC20) (81' Predrag Djordjevic), Darko Kovacevic (C),
Mateja Kezman (71' Savo Milosevic (YC90+3)). (Coach: Ilja Petkovic (SBM)).
Wales: Paul Jones, Robert (Rob) Page, Daniel (Danny) Gabbidon, Mark Delaney (YC61),
Robbie Savage, Mark Pembridge, Simon Davies, Ryan Giggs, Nathan Blake (78' Robert (Rob)
Earnshaw), Craig Bellamy, Gary Speed (C). (Coach: Mark Hughes (WAL)).
Goal: Serbia and Montenegro: 1-0 Dragan Mladenovic (73').
Referee: Anders Frisk (SWE)   Attendance: 19.752

06-09-2003   Shafa Stadium, Baku: Azerbaijan – Finland   1-2 (0-0)
Azerbaijan: Dmitriy Kramarenko, Ilham Yadullayev (YC33), Emin Agayev (58' Ruslan
Musayev (YC84)), Emin Guliyev, Makhmud Gurbanov, Kamal Guliyev, Tarlan Akhmedov
(C) (YC14,YC41), Rashad Farhad oglu Sadygov, Vadim Vasilyev (59' Zaur Tagizade),
Farrukh Ismayilov, Samir Aliyev (46' Emin Imamaliyev). (Coach: Asgar Abdullayev (AZE)).
Finland: Antti Niemi, Janne Saarinen (YC71), Juha Reini (YC90), Petri Pasanen, Sami Hyypiä
(C), Mika Väyrynen (YC69) (71' Aki Riihilahti), Teemu Tainio (86' Simo Valakari), Mika
Nurmela, Joonas Kolkka, Jonatan Johansson (46' Peter Kopteff), Mikael Forssell. (Coach:
Antti Muurinen (FIN)).
Goals: Azerbaijan: 1-2 Farrukh Ismayilov (89').
Finland: 0-1 Teemu Tainio (52'), 0-2 Mika Nurmela (75').
Referee: Vladimir Hrinák (SVK)   Attendance: 6.500

06-09-2003   Stadio Giuseppe Meazza, Milan: Italy – Wales   4-0 (0-0)
Italy: Gianluigi Buffon (YC27), Alessandro Nesta, Fabio Cannavaro (C), Gianluca Zambrotta,
Christian Panucci (58' Massimo Oddo), Mauro Camoranesi, Cristiano Zanetti, Simone Perrotta
(86' Stefano Fiore), Filippo Inzaghi (74' Gennaro Gattuso), Alessandro Del Piero, Christian
Vieri. (Coach: Giovanni Trapattoni (ITA)).
Wales: Paul Jones, Mark Delaney (YC51), Robert (Rob) Page, Jason Koumas (71' Robert
(Rob) Earnshaw), Simon Davies, Robbie Savage (YC25), Mark Pembridge (78' Andy
Johnson), John Hartson (82' Nathan Blake), Ryan Giggs, Craig Bellamy (YC27), Gary Speed
(C). (Coach: Mark Hughes (WAL)).
Goals: Italy: 1-0 Filippo Inzaghi (59'), 2-0 Filippo Inzaghi (63'), 3-0 Filippo Inzaghi (70'), 4-0
Alessandro Del Piero (76' penalty).
Referee: Dr.Markus Merk (GER)   Attendance: 69.000

10-09-2003   Millennium Stadium, Cardiff: Wales – Finland   1-1 (1-0)
Wales: Paul Jones, Rhys Weston (73' Andy Johnson), Robert (Rob) Page, Andy Melville
(YC70), Mark Pembridge, Jason Koumas (YC47,YC63), Simon Davies, John Hartson (82'
Nathan Blake), Ryan Giggs, Robert (Rob) Earnshaw, Gary Speed (C). (Coach: Mark Hughes
(WAL)).
Finland: Antti Niemi, Hannu Tihinen, Janne Saarinen (46' Juha Reini), Petri Pasanen (YC58)
(82' Peter Kopteff), Sami Hyypiä (C), Mika Väyrynen (57' Shefki Kuqi), Teemu Tainio, Aki
Riihilahti, Mika Nurmela, Joonas Kolkka, Mikael Forssell. (Coach: Antti Muurinen (FIN)).
Goals: Wales: 1-0 Simon Davies (3').
Finland: 1-1 Mikael Forssell (79').
Referee: Arturo Daudén Ibáñez (ESP)   Attendance: 73.411

57

10-09-2003   Stadion Crvena Zvezda, Belgrade: Serbia and Montenegro – Italy 1-1 (0-1)
Serbia and Montenegro: Dragoslav Jevric, Dejan Stefanovic (YC64), Mladen Krstajic (YC72),
Goran Gavrancic, Milivoje Cirkovic, Ivica Dragutinovic (70' Branko Boskovic), Dragan
Mladenovic (YC45), Predrag Djordjevic, Sasa Ilic, Savo Milosevic (C), Mateja Kezman (59'
Danijel Ljuboja). (Coach: Ilja Petkovic (SBM)).
Italy: Gianluigi Buffon, Alessandro Nesta, Fabio Cannavaro (C), Gianluca Zambrotta (YC38),
Christian Panucci (YC78), Alessio Tacchinardi, Simone Perrotta, Mauro Camoranesi (52'
Gennaro Gattuso), Christian Vieri (79' Bernardo Corradi (YC90)), Filippo Inzaghi (64'
Stefano Fiore), Alessandro Del Piero (YC83). (Coach: Giovanni Trapattoni (ITA)).
Goals: Serbia and Montenegro: 1-1 Sasa Ilic (82').
Italy: 0-1 Filippo Inzaghi (22').
Referee: Alain Hamer (LUX)   Attendance: 25.631

11-10-2003   Millennium Stadium, Cardiff: Wales – Serbia and Montenegro 2-3 (1-1)
Wales: Paul Jones, Darren Barnard, Rhys Weston (YC48) (73' Robert (Rob) Edwards), Daniel
(Danny) Gabbidon, Mark Delaney, Carl Robinson (89' John Oster), John Hartson (86' Nathan
Blake), Ryan Giggs, Robert (Rob) Earnshaw, Craig Bellamy (YC60), Gary Speed (C). (Coach:
Mark Hughes (WAL)).
Serbia and Montenegro: Dragoslav Jevric, Goran Bunjevcevic (YC25), Goran Gavrancic,
Nenad Djordjevic (YC37), Milivoje Cirkovic (75' Nenad Brnovic), Branko Boskovic (YC),
Dragan Sarac, Zvonimir Vukic, Dragan Mladenovic, Darko Kovacevic (C) (YC79) (79'
Danijel Ljuboja), Mateja Kezman (YC36) (54' Savo Milosevic). (Coach: Ilja Petkovic (SBM)).
Goals: Wales: 1-1 John Hartson (25' penalty), 2-3 Robert (Rob) Earnshaw (90'+2').
Serbia and Montenegro: 0-1 Zvonimir Vukic (4'), 1-2 Savo Milosevic (82'), 1-3 Danijel
Ljuboja (87').
Referee: Fritz Stuchlik (AUT)   Attendance: 72.514

11-10-2003   Stadio Orest Granillo, Reggio Calabria: Italy – Azerbaijan 4-0 (2-0)
Italy: Gianluigi Buffon, Massimo Oddo, Alessandro Nesta (76' Matteo Ferrari), Fabio
Cannavaro (C), Gianluca Zambrotta, Cristiano Zanetti, Simone Perrotta, Mauro Camoranesi
(86' Gennaro Gattuso), Christian Vieri (55' Marco Di Vaio), Filippo Inzaghi, Francesco Totti.
(Coach: Giovanni Trapattoni (ITA)).
Azerbaijan: Dmitriy Kramarenko (56' Jahangir Hasanzade), Emin Agayev (C), Ilham
Yadullayev, Aslan Kerimov, Emin Guliyev, Emin Imamaliyev, Makhmud Gurbanov (82'
Ramiz Mammadov), Kamal Guliyev (YC44), Rashad Farhad oglu Sadygov, Zaur Tagizade
(73' Vadim Vasilyev), Samir Aliyev. (Coach: Asgar Abdullayev (AZE)).
Goals: Italy: 1-0 Christian Vieri (15'), 2-0 Filippo Inzaghi (23'), 3-0 Marco Di Vaio (64'), 4-0
Filippo Inzaghi (86').
Referee: Stuart Dougal (SCO)   Attendance: 22.100

07-09-2002	Moscow	Russia – Republic of Ireland	4-2 (2-0)
08-09-2002	Basel	Switzerland – Georgia	4-1 (1-0)
12-10-2002	Tirana	Albania – Switserland	1-1 (0-1)
16-10-2002	Volgograd	Russia – Albania	4-1 (2-1)
16-10-2002	Dublin	Republic of Ireland – Switzerland	1-2 (0-1)
29-03-2003	Shkodër	Albania – Russia	3-1 (1-0)
29-03-2003	Tbilisi	Georgia – Republic of Ireland	1-2 (0-1)
02-04-2003	Tbilisi	Georgia – Switzerland	0-0
02-04-2003	Tirana	Albania – Republic of Ireland	0-0
30-04-2003	Tbilisi	Georgia – Russia	1-0 (1-0)
07-06-2003	Dublin	Rupublic of Ireland – Albania	2-1 (1-1)
07-06-2003	Basel	Switzerland – Russia	2-2 (2-1)
11-06-2003	Geneva	Switzerland – Albania	3-2 (2-1)
11-06-2003	Dublin	Republic of Ireland – Georgia	2-0 (1-0)
06-09-2003	Dublin	Republic of Ireland – Russia	1-1 (1-1)
06-09-2003	Tbilisi	Georgia – Albania	3-0 (3-0)
10-09-2003	Moscow	Russia – Switzerland	4-1 (2-1)
10-09-2003	Tirana	Albania – Georgia	3-1 (0-0)
11-10-2003	Moscow	Russia – Georgia	3-1 (2-1)
11-10-2003	Basel	Switzerland – Republic of Ireland	2-0 (1-0)

FINAL STANDING

Pos	Team	Pld	W	D	L	GF	GA	GD	Pts
1	Switzerland	8	4	3	1	15	11	+4	15
2	Russia	8	4	2	2	19	12	+7	14
3	Republic of Ireland	8	3	2	3	10	11	-1	11
4	Albania	8	2	2	4	11	15	-4	8
5	Georgia	8	2	1	5	8	14	-6	7

Switzerland qualified for the Final Tournament in Portugal.
Russia qualified for the play-offs.

07-09-2002   Lokomotiv Stadium, Moscow: Russia – Republic of Ireland 4-2 (2-0)
Russia: Sergei Ovchinnikov (YC89), Viktor Onopko, Gennadi Nizhegorodov, Sergei Ignashevich, Igor Yanovski, Sergei Semak (C) (75' Dmitri Khokhlov), Dmitri Loskov, Andrei Kayaka, Rolan Gusev (29' Andrei Solomatin), Evgeni Aldonin, Vladimir Beschastnykh (46' Aleksandr Kerzhakov). (Coach: Valeri Georgievich Gazzaev (RUS)).
Republic of Ireland: Shay Given, Ian Harte, Steve Finnan, Kenny Cunningham (C), Gary Breen, Jason McAteer (65' Gary Doherty), Mark Kinsella, Kevin Kilbane (86' Phil Babb), Matt Holland, Damien Duff (17' Clinton Morrison), Robbie Keane. (Coach: Michael Joseph (Mick) McCarthy (IRL)).
Goals: Russia: 1-0 Andrei Karyaka (20'), 2-0 Vladimir Beschastnykh (24'), 3-1 Aleksandr Kerzhakov (71'), 4-2 Phil Babb (88' own goal).
Republic of Ireland: 2-1 Gary Doherty (69'), 3-2 Clinton Morrison (76').
Referee: Claude Colombo (FRA)   Attendance: 26.000

08-09-2002   St. Jakob-Park, Basel: Switzerland – Georgia   4-1 (1-0)
Switzerland: Jörg Stiel (C), Murat Yakin, Patrick Müller, Stéphane Henchoz, Bernt Haas
(YC79), Ludovic Magnin (82' Bruno Berner), Johann Vogel (68' Fabio Celestini), Ricardo
Cabanas Rey, Hakan Yakin (73' Raphaël Wicky), Stéphane Chapuisat, Alexander Frei.
(Coach: Jakob (Köbi) Kuhn (SUI)).
Georgia: David Gvaramadze, Gela Shekiladze (YC33), Edik Sadjaia (46' Aleksandr
Rekhviashvili (YC71), 84' Mikheil Kavelashvili), Kakha Kaladze (YC35), Levan Tskitishvili,
Georgi Nemsadze (C), Levan Kobiashvili (YC65), Giorgi Kinkladze (46' Vladimir (Lado)
Burduli), Gocha Jamarauli, Shota Arveladze, Georgi Demetradze. (Coach: Alexandre Chivadze
(GEO)).
Goals: Switzerland: 1-0 Alexander Frei (37'), 2-1 Hakan Yakin (62'), 3-1 Patrick Müller (74'),
4-1 Stéphane Chapuisat (81').
Georgia: 1-1 Shota Arveladze (62').
Referee: Vladimír Hrinák (SVK)   Attendance: 20.500

12-10-2002   Qemal Stafa Stadium, Tirana: Albania – Switzerland   1-1 (0-1)
Albania: Fotaq Strakosha, Altin Haxhi (60' Alban Bushi), Ervin Fakaj (89' Elvis Sina), Geri
Çipi, Arian Xhumba, Edvin Murati, Besnik Hasi, Klodian Duro (YC70), Fatmir Vata, Altin
Lala, Igli Tare (71' Florian Myrtaj). (Coach: Giuseppe Dossena (ITA)).
Switzerland: Jörg Stiel (C) (YC83), Patrick Müller (YC12), Bernt Haas, Murat Yakin, Raphaël
Wicky, Ludovic Magnin, Johann Vogel, Ricardo Cabanas Rey (YC63) (81' Mario Cantaluppi
(YC82)), Hakan Yakin (63' Fabio Celestini), Stéphane Chapuisat, Alexander Frei (YC8) (84'
Léonard Thurre). (Coach: Jakob (Köbi) Kuhn (SUI)).
Goals: Albania: 1-1 Edvin Murati (79').
Switzerland: 0-1 Murat Yakin (37').
Referee: Orhan Erdemir (TUR)   Attendance: 12.000

12-10-2002   Mikheil Meskhi Stadium, Tbilisi: Georgia – Russia   0-0
Georgia: Georgi Lomaia, Aleksandr Rekhviashvili, Giorgi Shashiashvili, Kakha Kaladze (C),
Aleksandre Amisulashvili, Givi Didava, Levan Tskitishvili, Vladimir (Lado) Burduli,
Aleksandre Iashvili, Levan Kobiashvili, Shota Arveladze (23' Georgi Demetradze). (Coach:
Alexandre Chivadze (GEO)).
Russia: Sergei Ovchinnikov, Gennadi Nizhegorodov, Sergei Ignashevich, Aleksei Smertin (C),
Sergei Semak, Igor Yanovski, Viktor Onopko, Rolan Gusev, Andrei Solomatin (45' Ruslan
Pimenov), Dmitri Loskov, Vladimir Beschastnykh. (Coach: Valeri Georgievich Gazzaev
(RUS)).
Referee: Tom Henning Øvrebø (NOR)
(Match was abandoned at half-time due to floodlight failure and replayed on 30-04-2003)

16-10-2002   Central Stadium, Volgograd: Russia – Albania   4-1 (2-1)
Russia: Sergei Ovchinnikov, Viktor Onopko, Gennadi Nizhegorodov, Andrei Solomatin,
Sergei Ignashevich, Sergei Semak (C), Dmitri Loskov (46' Evgeni Aldonin), Rolan Gusev (79'
Vadim Evseev), Igor Yanovski (YC54), Aleksei Smertin, Aleksandr Kerzhakov (64' Denis
Popov). (Coach: Valeri Georgievich Gazzaev (RUS)).
Albania: Fotaq Strakosha, Altin Haxhi (56' Alban Bushi (YC90)), Ervin Fakaj, Geri Çipi,
Arian Xhumba, Edvin Murati, Besnik Hasi (YC87), Klodian Duro, Fatmir Vata (60' Elvis
Sina), Altin Lala, Igli Tare (69' Florian Myrtaj). (Coach: Giuseppe Dossena (ITA)).
Goals: Russia: 1-0 Aleksandr Kerzhakov (3'), 2-1 Sergei Semak (42'), 3-1 Viktor Onopko
(52'), 4-1 Sergei Semak (55').
Albania: 1-1 Klodian Duro (13').
Referee: Leif Sundell (SWE)   Attendance: 17.200

16-10-2002   Lansdowne Road, Dublin: Republic of Ireland – Switzerland   1-2 (0-1)
Republic of Ireland: Shay Given, Gary Kelly, Ian Harte (87' Gary Doherty), Kenny
Cunningham (C) (YC44), Gary Breen, Mark Kinsella, Kevin Kilbane (62' Clinton Morrison),
Matt Holland, Colin Healy, Damien Duff (82' Thomas Butler), Robbie Keane. (Coach:
Michael Joseph (Mick) McCarthy (IRL)).
Switzerland: Jörg Stiel (C) (YC64), Murat Yakin, Raphaël Wicky (85' Mario Cantaluppi),
Patrick Müller, Bernt Haas, Ludovic Magnin, Johann Vogel, Ricardo Cabanas Rey, Hakan
Yakin (85' Fabio Celestini), Stéphane Chapuisat, Alexander Frei (71' Léonard Thurre).
(Coach: Jakob (Köbi) Kuhn (SUI)).
Goals: Republic of Ireland: 1-1 Ludovic Magnin (78' *own goal*).
Switzerland: 0-1 Hakan Yakin (45'), 1-2 Fabio Celestini (87').
Referee: Rune Pedersen (NOR)   Attendance: 36.000

29-03-2003   Loro Boriçi Stadium, Shkodër: Albania – Russia   3-1 (1-0)
Albania: Fotaq Strakosha (C), Geri Çipi, Adrian Aliaj, Ardit Beqiri, Ervin Skela (83' Nevil
Dede), Edvin Murati (67' Arian Bellaj), Besnik Hasi, Klodian Duro, Altin Lala, Igli Tare, Altin
Rraklli (70' Florian Myrtaj). (Coach: Hans-Peter Briegel (GER)).
Russia: Sergei Ovchinnikov, Gennadi Nizhegorodov (YC17), Sergei Ignashevich, Aleksei
Berezutskiy, Aleksandr Tochilin (46' Andrei Karyaka), Aleksei Smertin (C) (72' Igor
Yanovski), Sergei Semak, Dmitri Loskov, Rolan Gusev (54' Vladimir Beschastnykh), Evgeni
Aldonin, Aleksandr Kerzhakov. (Coach: Valeri Georgievich Gazzaev (RUS)).
Goals: Albania: 1-0 Altin Rraklli (20'), 2-1 Altin Lala (79'), 3-1 Igli Tare (82').
Russia: 1-1 Andrei Karyaka (76').
Referee: Paul Allaerts (BEL)   Attendance: 13.000
(Klodian Duro missed a penalty in the 18th minute)

29-03-2003   Mikheil Meskhi Stadium, Tbilisi: Georgia – Republic of Ireland   1-2 (0-1)
Georgia: Georgi Lomaia, Giorgi Shashiashvili, Otar Khizaneishvili (YC76), Aleksandre
Amisulashvili, Levan Tskitishvili, Georgi Nemsadze (C), Levan Kobiashvili, Giorgi Kinkladze
(71' Givi Didava), Gocha Jamarauli, Temur Ketsbaia (46' Georgi Demetradze), Aleksandr
Iashvili. (Coach: Aleksandre Chivadze (GEO)).
Republic of Ireland: Shay Given, Stephen Carr, John O'Shea, Kenny Cunningham (C), Gary
Breen, Mark Kinsella, Kevin Kilbane, Matt Holland, Lee Carsley, Damien Duff, Gary Doherty
(YC32). (Coach: Brian Kerr (IRL)).
Goals: Georgia: 1-1 Levan Kobiashvili (61').
Republic of Ireland: 0-1 Damien Duff (18'), 1-2 Gary Doherty (85').
Referee: Kyris Vassaras (GRE)   Attendance: 10.000

02-04-2003   Mikheil Meskhi Stadium, Tbilisi: Georgia – Switzerland   0-0
Georgia: Georgi Lomaia, Zurab Khizanishvili, Otar Khizaneishvili, Dato Kvirkvelia, Levan
Tskitishvili, Aleksandr Rekhviashvili (YC18), Georgi Nemsadze (C) (46' Givi Didava), Levan
Kobiashvili (YC76), Revaz Kemoklidze, Aleksandr Iashvili (46' Shota Arceladze), Georgi
Demetradze (73' Mikheil Ashvetia (YC83)). (Coach: Aleksandre Chivadze (GEO)).
Switzerland: Pascal Zuberbühler, Murat Yakin, Raphaël Wicky, Patrick Müller, Bernt Haas,
Bruno Berner, Ricardo Cabanas Rey (69' Mario Cantaluppi), Johann Vogel, Hakan Yakin (90'
Léonard Thurre), Stéphane Chapuisat (C) (YC5), Alexander Frei (60' Fabio Celestini). (Coach:
Jakob (Köbi) Kuhn (SUI)).
Referee: Edo Trivkovic (CRO)   Attendance: 3.017

02-04-2003   Qemal Stafa Stadium, Tirana: Albania – Republic of Ireland   0-0
Albania: Fotaq Strakosha (C), Geri Çipi, Adrian Aliaj, Elvin Beqiri, Ervin Skela (85' Alban Bushi (YC86)), Edvin Murati (66' Arian Bellaj), Besnik Hasi, Klodian Duro, Altin Lala, Igli Tare, Altin Rraklli (69' Florian Myrtaj). (Coach: Hans-Peter Briegel (GER)).
Republic of Ireland: Shay Given, Kenny Cunningham (C), Stephen Carr, Gary Breen, John O'Shea, Lee Carsley, Mark Kinsella, Kevin Kilbane, Matt Holland, Damien Duff, Robbie Keane (66' Gary Doherty). (Coach: Brian Kerr (IRL)).
Referee: Stefano Farina (ITA)   Attendance: 16.000

30-04-2003   Mikheil Meskhi Stadium, Tbilisi: Georgia – Russia   1-0 (1-0)
Georgia: Georgi Lomaia, Zurab Khizanishvili, Otar Khizaneishvili, Kakha Kaladze, Dato Kvirkvelia (15' Givi Didava), Malkhaz Asatiani, Levan Tskitishvili, Georgi Nemsadze (C) (YC71), Vladimir (Lado) Burduli (80' Giorgi Shashiashvili), Georgi Demetradze, Mikheil Ashvetia (YC81) (84' Rati Aleksidze). (Coach: Ivo Susak (CRO)).
Russia: Veniamin Mandrykin, Viktor Onopko, Gennadi Nizhegorodov (YC60), Sergei Ignashevich (15' Denis Evsikov), Marat Izmailov (46' Aleksandr Kerzhakov), Yegor Titov, Dmitri Alenichev, Aleksei Smertin (C), Sergei Semak, Andrei Karyaka, Evgeni Aldonin (80' Dmitri Sychev). (Coach: Valeri Georgievich Gazzaev (RUS)).
Goal: Georgia: 1-0 Malkhaz Asatiani (12').
Referee: Dr.Franz-Xaver Wack (GER)   Attendance: 11.000
(Match was originally played on 12-10-2002 but suspended due to floodlight failure and fully replayed)

07-06-2003   Lansdowne Road, Dublin: Republic of Ireland – Albania   2-1 (1-1)
Republic of Ireland: Shay Given, John O'Shea, Kenny Cunningham (C), Stephen Carr (YC36), Gary Breen, Mark Kinsella (YC41) (55' Lee Carsley), Kevin Kilbane (76' Steven Reid), Matt Holland, Damien Duff, David Connolly (65' Gary Doherty), Robbie Keane. (Coach: Brian Kerr (IRL)).
Albania: Fotaq Strakosha (C) (78' Arjan Beqaj), Geri Çipi (YC89), Adrian Aliaj, Elvin Beqiri (YC81), Klodian Duro, Ervin Skela, Edvin Murati (58' Arian Bellaj), Besnik Hasi, Altin Lala (YC26), Igli Tare, Altin Rraklli (85' Florian Myrtaj). (Coach: Hans-Peter Briegel (GER)).
Goals: Republic of Ireland: 1-1 Robbie Keane (6'), 2-1 Adrian Aliaj (90'+2' *own goal*).
Albania: 1-1 Ervin Skela (8').
Referee: Tomasz Mikulski (POL)   Attendance: 35.900

07-06-2003   St. Jakob-Park, Basel: Switzerland – Russia   2-2 (2-1)
Switzerland: Jörg Stiel (C), Murat Yakin (YC66), Raphaël Wicky (YC67) (70' Johann Vogel), Patrick Müller (YC58) (81' Stéphane Henchoz), Bernt Haas, Ludovic Magnin (60' Bruno Berner), Fabio Celestini, Ricardo Cabanas Rey, Hakan Yakin, Stéphane Chapuisat, Alexander Frei. (Coach: Jakob (Köbi) Kuhn (SUI)).
Russia: Sergei Ovchinnikov, Yuri Kovtun, Sergei Ignashevich, Vasili Berezutskiy, Evgeni Aldonin, Igor Yanovski (YC25), Aleksei Smertin (C), Sergei Semak (81' Denis Evsikov), Andrei Karyaka (51' Petr Bystrov (YC82)), Rolan Gusev, Denis Popov (46' Dmitri Sychev). (Coach: Valeri Georgievich Gazzaev (RUS)).
Goals: Switzerland: 1-0 Alexander Frei (13'), 2-0 Alexander Frei (15').
Russia: 2-1 Sergei Ignashevich (23'), 2-2 Sergei Ignashevich (67' penalty).
Referee: Arturo Daudén Ibáñez (ESP)   Attendance: 30.500

11-06-2003   Stade de Genève, Geneva: Switzerland – Albania 3-2 (2-1)
Switzerland: Jörg Stiel (C), Murat Yakin, Raphaël Wicky (64' Christoph Spycher), Stéphane
Henchoz (75' Marco Zwyssig), Bernt Haas, Bruno Berner (YC79), Johann Vogel, Ricardo
Cabanas Rey, Hakan Yakin, Stéphane Chapuisat, Alexander Frei (83' Fabio Celestini). (Coach:
Jakob (Köbi) Kuhn (SUI)).
Albania: Fotaq Strakosha (C), Geri Çipi (46' Lorik Cana), Arian Bellaj, Adrian Aliaj (YC71),
Elvin Beqiri (YC13), Ervin Skela, Besnik Hasi, Klodian Duro (74' Mehmet Dragusha), Altin
Lala (YC44), Igli Tare (YC5), Alban Bushi (62' Altin Rraklli). (Coach: Hans-Peter Briegel
(GER)).
Goals: Switzerland: 1-0 Bernt Haas (10'), 2-1 Alexander Frei (32'), 3-1 Ricardo Cabanas Rey
(71').
Albania: 1-1 Altin Lala (22'), 3-2 Ervin Skela (86' penalty).
Referee: Stephen Graham (Steve) Bennett (ENG)   Attendance: 26.000

11-06-2003   Lansdowne Road, Dublin: Republic of Ireland – Georgia 2-0 (1-0)
Republic of Ireland: Shay Given, Kenny Cunningham (C), Stephen Carr, Gary Breen, John
O'Shea, Matt Holland, Colin Healy (86' Mark Kinsella), Lee Carsley, Kevin Kilbane, Robbie
Keane, Gary Doherty (88' Alan Lee). (Coach: Brian Kerr (IRL)).
Georgia: Georgi Lomaia, Kakha Kaladze (C), Givi Didava (76' Rati Aleksidze), Aleksandre
Amisulashvili, Zurab Khizanishvili, Otar Khizaneishvili (YC38), Vladimir (Lado) Burduli,
Malkhaz Asatiani, Aleksandr Rekhviashvili, Georgi Demetradze (59' Vitali Daraselia Jr.),
Shota Arveladze. (Coach: Ivo Susak (CRO)).
Goals: Republic of Ireland: 1-0 Gary Doherty (43'), 2-0 Robbie Keane (59').
Referee: Eduardo Iturralde González (ESP)   Attendance: 36.000

06-09-2003   Lansdowne Road, Dublin: Republic of Ireland – Russia 1-1 (1-1)
Republic of Ireland: Shay Given, John O'Shea (26' Ian Harte), Kenny Cunningham (C)
(YC67), Stephen Carr, Gary Breen, Kevin Kilbane (YC81), Matt Holland, Colin Healy, Lee
Carsley (46' Steven Reid), Damien Duff, Clinton Morrison (74' Gary Doherty). (Coach: Brian
Kerr (IRL)).
Russia: Sergei Ovchinnikov, Dmitri Sennikov, Viktor Onopko (C), Sergei Ignashevich
(YC64), Aleksandr Mostovoy (YC81), Aleksei Smertin, Rolan Gusev (YC24), Vadim Evseev
(YC70), Dmitri Alenichev (39' Evgeni Aldonin), Dmitri Bulykin, Valeri Esipov (34'
Aleksandr Kerzhakov). (Coach: Georgi Aleksandrovich Yartsev (RUS)).
Goals: Republic of Ireland: 1-0 Damien Duff (35').
Russia: 1-1 Sergei Ignashevich (42').
Referee: Lubos Michel (SVK)   Attendance: 36.000

06-09-2003   Boris Paichadze Stadium, Tbilisi: Georgia – Albania 3-0 (3-0)
Georgia: Georgi Lomaia, Zurab Khizanishvili, Dato Kvirkvelia, Georgi Nemsadze, Levan
Kobiashvili, Revaz Kemoklidze, Gocha Jamarauli (58' Malkhaz Asatiani), Vladimir (Lado)
Burduli (70' Aleksandr Rekhviashvili (YC79)), Aleksandr Iashvili, Mikheil Ashvetia, Shota
Arveladze (60' Georgi Demetradze). (Coach: Merab Jordania (GEO)).
Albania: Fotaq Strakosha (C), Nevil Dede (10' Redi Jupi (YC75)), Geri Çipi, Arian Bellaj (46'
Klodian Duro), Adrian Aliaj, Ervin Skela, Edvin Murati, Besnik Hasi, Mehmet Dragusha,
Lorik Cana (YC72), Alban Bushi (61' Igli Tare). (Coach: Hans-Peter Briegel (GER)).
Goals: Georgia: 1-0 Shota Arveladze (8'), 2-0 Mikheil Ashvetia (17'), 3-0 Shota Arveladze
(43').
Referee: Nicolai Vollquartz (DEN)   Attendance: 3.200

10-09-2003   Lokomotiv Stadium, Moscow: Russia – Switzerland   4-1 (2-1)
Russia: Sergei Ovchinnikov, Andrei Solomatin (YC42) (46' Dmitri Sennikov), Viktor Onopko
(C), Sergei Ignashevich, Vladislav Radimov (YC88), Aleksei Smertin, Aleksandr Mostovoy,
Andrei Karyaka, Rolan Gusev (55' Marat Izmailov), Dmitri Bulykin, Aleksandr Kerzhakov
(76' Dmitri Sychev). (Coach: Georgi Aleksandrovich Yartsev (RUS)).
Switzerland: Pascal Zuberbühler, Murat Yakin, Patrick Müller (63' Benjamin Huggel), Remo
Meyer, Stéphane Henchoz (C) (YC49), Bruno Berner (70' Raphaël Wicky), Johann Vogel
(YC77), Fabio Celestini, Ricardo Cabanas Rey (RC88), Stéphane Chapuisat, Alexander Frei
(78' Milaim Rama). (Coach: Jakob (Köbi) Kuhn (SUI)).
Goals: Russia: 1-1 Dmitri Bulykin (19'), 2-1 Dmitri Bulykin (32'), 3-1 Dmitri Bulykin (58'),
4-1 Aleksandr Mostovoy (72').
Switzerland: 0-1 Andrei Karyaka (12' *own goal*).
Referee: Pierluigi Collina (ITA)   Attendance: 28.800

10-09-2003   Qemal Stafa Stadium, Tirana: Albania – Georgia   3-1 (0-0)
Albania: Fotaq Strakosha (C), Geri Çipi (YC9), Adrian Aliaj, Elvin Beqiri, Blendi Shkëmbi,
Edvin Murati (18' Altin Haxhi), Besnik Hasi, Klodian Duro (YC90+1), Lorik Cana (85' Devis
Mukaj), Igli Tare, Altin Rraklli (58' Alban Bushi (YC80)). (Coach: Hans-Peter Briegel
(GER)).
Georgia: Georgi Lomaia, Zurab Khizanishvili, Givi Didava (54' Giorgi Kinkladze), Dato
Kvirkvelia, Georgi Nemsadze (C), Levan Kobiashvili, Revaz Kemoklidze (40' Aleksandr
Rekhviashvili (YC65)), Gocha Jamarauli, Aleksandr Iashvili (54' Georgi Demetradze (YC61)),
Mikheil Ashvetia, Shota Arveladze. (Coach: Merab Jordania (GEO)). (Not used sub: Georgi
Gakhokidze (YC54,RC54)).
Goals: Albania: 1-0 Besnik Hasi (51'), 2-0 Igli Tare (53'), 3-1 Alban Bushi (80').
Georgia: 2-1 Shota Arveladze (64').
Referee: Marian Mirceo Salomir (ROM)   Attendance: 1.200

11-10-2003   Lokomoitv Stadium, Moscow: Russia – Georgia   3-1 (2-1)
Russia: Sergei Ovchinnikov, Dmitri Sennikov, Viktor Onopko (C), Sergei Ignashevich, Yegor
Titov, Aleksandr Mostovoy, Andrei Karyaka (46' Marat Izmailov), Rolan Gusev (63' Evgeni
Aldonin), Vadim Evseev, Dmitri Bulykin, Aleksandr Kerzhakov (56' Dmitri Sychev (YC70)).
(Coach: Georgi Aleksandrovich Yartsev (RUS)).
Georgia: Georgi Lomaia, Zurab Khizanishvili, Dato Kvirkvelia, Levan Tskitishvili (54'
Malkhaz Asatiani), Georgi Nemsadze (C) (YC80), Levan Kobiashvili, Revaz Kemoklidze
(YC31), Gocha Jamarauli (46' Vladimir (Lado) Burduli), Aleksandr Iashvili, Georgi
Demetradze (YC1), Mikheil Ashvetia (58' Vitali Daraselia Jr.). (Coach: Merab Jordania
(GEO)).
Goals: Russia: 1-1 Dmitri Bulykin (29'), 2-1 Yegor Titov (45'+1'), 3-1 Dmitri Sychev (73').
Georgia: 0-1 Aleksandr Iashvili (3').
Referee: Konrad Plautz (AUT)   Attendance: 30.000

11-10-2003   St. Jakob-Park, Basel: Switzerland – Repulic of Ireland   2-0 (1-0)
Switzerland: Jörg Stiel (C), Murat Yakin, Raphaël Wicky (YC54), Patrick Müller, Bernt Haas (YC24), Christoph Spycher, Johann Vogel, Benjamin Huggel, Hakan Yakin (56' Fabio Celestini), Stéphane Chapuisat (69' Marco Streller), Alexander Frei (90'+1' Stéphane Henchoz). (Coach: Jakob (Köbi) Kuhn (SUI)).
Republic of Ireland: Shay Given, John O'Shea, Ian Harte (YC90+1), Stephen Carr (YC28), Gary Breen, Kevin Kilbane (74' Steve Finnan), Matt Holland (74' Mark Kinsella (YC88)), Colin Healy, Damien Duff, Robbie Keane, David Connolly (58' Clinton Morrison). (Coach: Brian Kerr (IRL)).
Goals: Switzerland: 1-0 Hakan Yakin (6'), 2-0 Alexander Frei (60').
Referee: Anders Frisk (SWE)   Attendance: 31.006

QUALIFICATION PLAY-OFFS

15-11-2003   Hampden Park, Glasgow: Scotland – Netherlands   1-0 (1-0)
Scotland: Robert James (Rab) Douglas, Lee Wilkie, Steven Pressley, Gary Naysmith, Christian Dailly (YC42), Jackie McNamara, Neil McCann (71' Stephen Pearson), Darren Fletcher, Barry Ferguson (C), Paul Dickov (66' Kenny Miller), James McFadden (YC26) (90' Don Hutchison). (Coach: Hans-Hubert (Berti) Vogts (GER)).
Netherlands: Edwin van der Sar, Jaap Stam (YC82), André Ooijer (YC59), Frank de Boer, Edgar Davids (60' Rafael van der Vaart), Andy van der Meyde, Giovanni van Bronckhorst (46' Clarence Seedorf), Phillip Cocu, Marc Overmars, Ruud van Nistelrooy, Patrick Kluivert (77' Roy Makaay). (Coach: Dick Nicolaas Advocaat (HOL)).
Goal: Scotland: 1-0 James McFadden (22').
Referee: Terje Hauge (NOR)   Attendance: 52.063

15-11-2003   Lokomotiv Stadium, Moscow: Russia – Wales   0-0
Russia: Sergei Ovchinnikov (YC46), Dmitri Sennikov, Viktor Onopko (C), Sergei Ignashevich, Dmitri Alenichev, Aleksei Smertin (59' Rolan Gusev), Aleksandr Mostovoy (YC68), Dmitri Loskov, Vadim Evseev, Dmitri Sychev (46' Marat Izmailov), Dmitri Bulykin. (Coach: Georgi Aleksandrovich Yartsev (RUS)).
Wales: Paul Jones, Darren Barnard, Andy Melville, Daniel (Danny) Gabbidon, Mark Delaney (YC41), Robbie Savage (YC68), Jason Koumas (YC63), Andy Johnson, John Hartson (83' Nathan Blake), Ryan Giggs, Gary Speed (C) (YC68). (Coach: Mark Hughes (WAL)).
Referee: Lucílio Cardoso Cortez Batista (POR)   Attendance: 28.500

15-11-2003   Maksimir Stadion, Zagreb: Croatia – Slovenia   1-1 (1-1)
Croatia: Stipe Pletikosa, Mato Neretljak (YC47), Boris Zivkovic (C) (58' Darijo Srna (YC83)), Igor Tudor, Stjepan Tomas (YC72), Dario Simic, Jerko Leko (46' Milan Rapaic), Niko Kovac, Dado Prso (YC86), Ivica Mornar, Ivica Olic (YC32) (46' Djovani Roso). (Coach: Otto Baric (CRO)).
Slovenia: Mladen Dabanovic, Fabijan Cipot, Muamer Vugdalic, Aleksander Knavs, Nastja Ceh (87' Spasoje Bulajic), Milenko Acimovic (75' Adem Kapic), Goran Sukalo (YC80), Miran Pavlin (C), Amir Karic (YC4), Zlatko Zahovic, Ermin Siljak (YC32) (90'+3' Bostjan Cesar). (Coach: Bojan Prasnikar (SLO)).
Goals: Croatia: 1-0 Dado Prso (5').
Slovenia: 1-1 Ermin Siljak (22').
Referee: Dr.Markus Merk (GER)   Attendance: 34.657

15-11-2003   Skonto Stadium, Riga: Latvia – Turkey 1-0 (1-0)
Latvia: Aleksandrs Kolinko, Igors Korablovs, Igors Stepanovs, Valentins Lobanovs (YC30), Aleksandrs Isakovs, Andrejs Rubins (82' Jurgis Pucinskis), Juris Laizāns, Imants Bleidelis, Vitalijs Astafjevs (C), Māris Verpakovskis (YC12) (89' Vladimirs Kolesnicenko), Vits Rimkus (85' Andrejs Stolcers). (Coach: Aleksandrs Starkovs (LAT)).
Turkey: Rüstü Reçber (YC59), Bülent Korkmaz (C), Emre Asik (YC63,RC73), Fatih Akyel (YC69), Ibrahim Üzülmez, Tugay Kerimoglu, Ergün Penbe, Emre Belözoglu (YC13) (86' Tümer Metin), Okan Buruk (YC23) (83' Gökdeniz Karadeniz), Nihat Kahveci (76' Deniz Baris), Ilhan Mansiz. (Coach: Senol Günes (TUR)).
Goal: Latvia: 1-0 Māris Verpakovskis (29').
Referee: Gilles Veissière (FRA)   Attendance: 8.800

15-11-2003   Mestalla, Valencia: Spain – Norway 2-1 (1-1)
Spain: IKER CASILLAS Fernández, MÍCHEL Ángel SALGADO Fernández, Carlos MARCHENA López (YC70), Carles PUYOL Saforcada, IVÁN HELGUERA Bujía, Rubén BARAJA Vegas, David ALBELDA Aliqués, José Antonio REYES Calderón (78' VICENTE Rodríguez Guillén), RAÚL González Blanco (C), Joseba Andoni ETXEBERRIA Lizardi (78' JOAQUÍN Sánchez Rodríguez), FERNANDO José TORRES Sanz (69' Juan Carlos VALERÓN Santana). (Coach: José Ignacio "Iñaki" Sáez Ruiz (ESP)).
Norway: Espen Johnsen, Claus Lundekvam (YC65), Henning Berg (C) (YC34), Christer Basma, Trond Andersen, John Arne Riise, Roar Strand (25' Harald Brattbakk), Jan Gunnar Solli, Martin Andresen (87' Runar Berg), Tore André Flo, Steffen Iversen (YC63) (78' Frode Johnsen). (Coach: Nils Johan Semb (NOR)).
Goals: Spain: 1-1 RAÚL González Blanco (21'), 2-1 Rubén BARAJA Vegas (85').
Norway: 0-1 Steffen Iversen (15').
Referee: Graham Poll (ENG)   Attendance: 45.648

19-11-2003   Bezigrad Stadium, Ljubljana: Slovenia – Croatia 0-1 (0-0)
Slovenia: Mladen Dabanovic, Aleksander Knavs, Fabijan Cipot (89' Spasoje Bulajic), Muamer Vugdalic, Goran Sukalo (68' Ermin Rakovic), Miran Pavlin (C), Amir Karic (YC11), Nastja Ceh, Milenko Acimovic, Mladen Rudonja (46' Adem Kapic), Zlatko Zahovic. (Coach: Bojan Prasnikar (SLO)).
Croatia: Stipe Pletikosa, Boris Zivkovic (C), Igor Tudor (YC36,YC59), Josip Simunic (52' Marko Babic), Robert Kovac, Djovani Roso, Milan Rapaic (68' Stjepan Tomas), Darijo Srna, Niko Kovac, Tomo Sokota, Dado Prso (75' Jerko Leko (YC90)). (Coach: Otto Baric (CRO)).
Goal: Croatia: 0-1 Dado Prso (61').
Referee: Urs Meier (SUI)   Attendance: 8.500

19-11-2003   Ullevaal Stadion, Oslo: Norway – Spain 0-3 (0-1)
Norway: Espen Johnsen (62' Frode Olsen), Ståle Stensaas, Claus Lundekvam (C), Ronny Johnsen, Christer Basma, Trond Andersen (46' Håvard Flo), John Arne Riise, Jan Gunnar Solli, Martin Andresen (74' Frode Johnsen), Tore André Flo, Steffen Iversen (YC39). (Coach: Nils Johan Semb (NOR)).
Spain: IKER CASILLAS Fernández, MÍCHEL Ángel SALGADO Fernández, CÉSAR MARTÍN Villar, Carles PUYOL Saforcada, IVÁN HELGUERA Bujía, VICENTE Rodríguez Guillén, Juan Carlos VALERÓN Santana (74' José María "GUTI" Gutiérrez Hernández), David ALBELDA Aliqués (YC36) (87' Rubén BARAJA Vegas), Xabier "XABI" ALONSO Olano, RAÚL González Blanco (C), Joseba Andoni ETXEBERRIA Lizardi (78' JOAQUÍN Sánchez Rodríguez). (Coach: José Ignacio "Iñaki" Sáez Ruiz (ESP)).
Goals: Spain: 0-1 RAÚL González Blanco (34'), 0-2 VICENTE Rodríguez Guillén (50'), 0-3 Joseba Andoni ETXEBERRIA Lizardi (56').
Referee: Pierluigi Collina (ITA)   Attendance: 25.106

66

19-11-2003   Inönü Stadium, Istanbul: Turkey – Latvia   2-2 (1-0)
Turkey: Ömer Çatkiç, Bülent Korkmaz (C), Ibrahim Üzülmez, Ümit Davala (YC10) (77'
Hasan Sas), Emre Belözoglu, Tugay Kerimoglu (79' Tuncay Sanli), Tümer Metin (60'
Gökdeniz Karadeniz), Deniz Baris, Ilhan Mansiz, Hakan Sükür, Nihat Kahveci. (Coach: Senol
Günes (TUR)).
Latvia: Aleksandrs Kolinko, Aleksandrs Isakovs, Igors Stepanovs, Dzintars Zirnis, Mihails
Zemlinskis, Juris Laizāns, Imants Bleidelis (YC35), Vitalijs Astafjevs (C), Andrejs Rubins,
Vits Rimkus (YC45+2) (79' Andrejs Stolcers), Māris Verpakovskis (90'+1' Marians Pahars).
(Coach: Aleksandrs Starkovs (LAT)).
Goals: Turkey: 1-0 Ilhan Mansiz (20'), 2-0 Hakan Sükür (64').
Latvia: 2-1 Juris Laizāns (65'), 2-2 Māris Verpakovskis (76').
Referee: Anders Frisk (SWE)   Attendance: 17.500

19-11-2003   Amsterdam ArenA, Amsterdam: Netherlands – Scotland   6-0 (3-0)
Netherlands: Edwin van der Sar, Michael Reiziger, André Ooijer (46' Frank de Boer), Wilfred
Bouma (68' Clarence Seedorf), Rafael van der Vaart, Edgar Davids (YC47), Andy van der
Meyde, Wesley Sneijder, Phillip Cocu, Marc Overmars, Ruud van Nistelrooy (YC4) (77'
Patrick Kluivert). (Coach: Dick Nicolaas Advocaat (HOL)).
Scotland: Robert James (Rab) Douglas, Lee Wilkie, Steven Pressley (YC10), Gary Naysmith
(YC44) (46' Steven (Stevie) Crawford), Gavin Rae, Jackie McNamara, Neil McCann (63'
Kenny Miller), Darren Fletcher, Barry Ferguson (C) (YC4), Paul Dickov (YC17) (46' Maurice
Ross), James McFadden. (Coach: Hans-Hubert (Berti) Vogts (GER)).
Goals: Netherlands: 1-0 Wesley Sneijder (14'), 2-0 André Ooijer (32'), 3-0 Ruud van
Nistelrooy (37'), 4-0 Ruud van Nistelrooy (51'), 5-0 Frank de Boer (65'), 6-0 Ruud van
Nistelrooy (67').
Referee: Lubos Michel (SVK)   Attendance: 49.656

19-11-2003   Millennium Stadium, Cardiff: Wales – Russia   0-1 (0-1)
Wales: Paul Jones, Andy Melville, Daniel (Danny) Gabbidon, Mark Delaney, Darren Barnard
(YC65), Robbie Savage (YC58), Jason Koumas (74' Nathan Blake), Andy Johnson (58'
Robert (Rob) Earnshaw), John Hartson, Ryan Giggs, Gary Speed (C). (Coach: Mark Hughes
(WAL)).
Russia: Vyacheslav Malafeev, Dmitri Sennikov, Viktor Onopko (C), Sergei Ignashevich,
Yegor Titov (59' Vladislav Radimov (YC89)), Aleksei Smertin, Marat Izmailov, Rolan Gusev,
Vadim Evseev, Dmitri Alenichev (YC60), Dmitri Bulykin (YC74). (Coach: Georgi
Aleksandrovich Yartsev (RUS)).
Goal: Russia: 0-1 Vadim Evseev (21').
Referee: Manuel Enrique Mejuto González (ESP)   Attendance: 73.062

FINAL TOURNAMENT IN PORTUGAL

Portugal automatically qualified for the Final Tournament as hosts.

GROUP STAGE

GROUP A

12-06-2004   Estádio do Dragão, Porto: Portugal – Greece   1-2 (0-1)
Portugal: RICARDO Alexandre Martins Soares Pereira, PAULO Renato Rebocho FERREIRA, JORGE Manuel Almeida Gomes de ANDRADE, FERNANDO Manuel Silva COUTO (C), RUI JORGE de Sousa Dias Macedo de Oliveira, Nuno Ricardo de Oliveira Ribeiro "MANICHE", Francisco José Rodrigues da Costa "COSTINHA" (YC21) (66' NUNO "GOMES" Miguel Soares Pereira Ribeiro), LUÍS Filipe Madeira Caeiro FIGO, RUI Manuel César COSTA (46' Anderson Luís de Souza "DECO"), SIMÃO Pedro Fonseca Sabrosa (46' CRISTIANO RONALDO dos Santos Aveiro), Pedro Miguel Carreiro Resendes "PAULETA" (YC57). (Coach: Luiz Felipe Scolari (BRA)).
Greece: Antonis Nikopolidis, Giorgios (Giourkas) Seitaridis (YC76), Traianos Dellas, Michalis Kapsis, Panagiotis (Takis) Fyssas, Giorgios Karagounis (YC39) (46' Konstantinos (Kostas) Katsouranis), Theodoros Zagorakis (C), Angelos Basinas, Stylianos Giannakopoulos (68' Themistoklis (Demis) Nikolaidis), Angelos Charisteas (74' Vassilis Lakis), Zisis Vryzas. (Coach: Otto-Heinz Rehhagel (GER)).
Goals: Portugal: 1-2 CRISTIANO RONALDO dos Santos Aveiro (90'+3').
Greece: 0-1 Giorgios Karagounis (7'), 0-2 Angelos Basinas (51' penalty).
Referee: Pierlugi Collina (ITA)   Attendance: 48.761

12-06-2004   Estádio do Algarve, Faro-Loulé: Spain – Russia   1-0 (0-0)
Spain: IKER CASILLAS Fernández, Carles PUYOL Saforcada, IVÁN HELGUERA Bujía, Carlos MARCHENA López (YC66), RAÚL BRAVO Sanfélix, David ALBELDA Aliqués (YC85), Rubén BARAJA Vegas (YC43) (59' Xabier "XABI" ALONSO Olano), Joseba Andoni ETXEBERRIA Lizardi, RAÚL González Blanco (C) (78' FERNANDO José TORRES Sanz), VICENTE Rodríguez Guillén, Fernando MORIENTES Sánchez (59' Juan Carlos VALERÓN Santana). (Coach: José Ignacio "Iñaki" Sáez Ruiz (ESP)).
Russia: Sergei Ovchinnikov, Vadim Evseev, Aleksei Smertin (C) (YC29), Roman Sharonov (YC27,YC88), Dmitri Sennikov, Evgeni Aldonin (YC32) (68' Dmitri Sychev), Rolan Gusev (YC12) (46' Vladislav Radimov (YC90+3)), Dmitri Alenichev, Aleksandr Mostovoy, Marat Izmailov (74' Andrei Karyaka), Dmitri Bulykin. (Coach: Georgi Aleksandrovich Yartsev (RUS)).
Goal: Spain: 1-0 Juan Carlos VALERÓN Santana (60').
Referee: Urs Meier (SUI)   Attendance: 28.182

16-06-2004   Estádio do Bessa, Porto: Greece – Spain   1-1 (0-1)
Greece: Antonis Nikopolidis, Giorgios (Giourkas) Seitaridis, Traianos Dellas, Michalis Kapsis, Panagiotis (Takis) Fyssas (86' Stylianos Venetidis), Giorgios Karagounis (YC27) (53' Vasilios Tsiartas), Theodoros Zagorakis (C) (YC61), Konstantinos (Kostas) Katsouranis (YC7), Stylianos Giannakopoulos (YC24) (49' Themistoklis (Demis) Nikolaidis), Angelos Charisteas, Zisis Vryzas (YC90+1). (Coach: Otto-Heinz Rehhagel (GER)).

Spain: IKER CASILLAS Fernández, Carles PUYOL Saforcada, IVÁN HELGUERA Bujía (YC37), Carlos MARCHENA López (YC16), RAÚL BRAVO Sanfélix, David ALBELDA Aliqués, Rubén BARAJA Vegas, Joseba Andoni ETXEBERRIA Lizardi (46' JOAQUÍN Sánchez Rodríguez), RAÚL González Blanco (C) (80' FERNANDO José TORRES Sanz), VICENTE Rodríguez Guillén, Fernando MORIENTES Sánchez (65' Juan Carlos VALERÓN Santana). (Coach: José Ignacio "Iñaki" Sáez Ruiz (ESP)).
Goals: Greece: 1-1 Angelos Charisteas (66').
Spain: 0-1 Fernando MORIENTES Sánchez (28').
Referee: Lubos Michel (SVK)   Attendance: 25.444

16-06-2004   Estádio da Luz, Lisbon: Russia – Portugal   0-2 (0-1)
Russia: Sergei Ovchinnikov (RC45), Vadim Evseev (YC21), Aleksei Smertin (C) (YC16), Aleksei Bugayev, Dmitri Sennikov, Evgeni Aldonin (45'+2' Vyacheslav Malafeev goalkeeper), Dmitri Alenichev (YC87), Dmitri Loskov, Marat Izmailov (72' Vladimir Bystrov), Andrei Karyaka (79' Dmitri Bulykin), Aleksandr Kerzhakov. (Coach: Georgi Aleksandrovich Yartsev (RUS)).
Portugal: RICARDO Alexandre Martins Soares Pereira, Luís MIGUEL Brito Garcia Monteiro, JORGE Manuel Almeida Gomes de ANDRADE, RICARDO Alberto Silveira de CARVALHO (YC24), NUNO Jorge Pereira da Silva VALENTE, Nuno Ricardo de Oliveira Ribeiro "MANICHE", Francisco José Rodrigues da Costa "COSTINHA", LUÍS Filipe Madeira Caeiro FIGO (C) (78' CRISTIANO RONALDO dos Santos Aveiro), Anderson Luís de Souza "DECO" (YC85), SIMÃO Pedro Fonseca Sabrosa (63' RUI Manuel César COSTA), Pedro Miguel Carreiro Resendes "PAULETA" (57' NUNO "GOMES" Miguel Soares Pereira Ribeiro). (Coach: Luiz Felipe Scolari (BRA)).
Goals: Portugal: 0-1 Nuno Ricardo de Oliveira Ribeiro "MANICHE" (7'), 0-2 RUI Manuel César COSTA (89').
Referee: Terje Hauge (NOR)   Attendance: 59.273

20-06-2004   Estádio José Alvalade, Lisbon: Spain – Portugal   0-1 (0-0)
Spain: IKER CASILLAS Fernández, Carles PUYOL Saforcada (YC74), IVÁN HELGUERA Bujía, Juan Gutiérrez Moreno "JUANITO" (YC68) (79' Fernando MORIENTES Sánchez), RAÚL BRAVO Sanfélix, Xabier "XABI" ALONSO Olano, David ALBELDA Aliqués (YC8) (65' Rubén BARAJA Vegas), JOAQUÍN Sánchez Rodríguez (71' ALBERT LUQUE Martos), RAÚL González Blanco (C), VICENTE Rodríguez Guillén, FERNANDO José TORRES Sanz. (Coach: José Ignacio "Iñaki" Sáez Ruiz (ESP)).
Portugal: RICARDO Alexandre Martins Soares Pereira, Luís MIGUEL Brito Garcia Monteiro, JORGE Manuel Almeida Gomes de ANDRADE, RICARDO Alberto Silveira de CARVALHO, NUNO Jorge Pereira da Silva VALENTE, Francisco José Rodrigues da Costa "COSTINHA", Nuno Ricardo de Oliveira Ribeiro "MANICHE", LUÍS Filipe Madeira Caeiro FIGO (C) (77' Armando Gonçalves Teixeira "PETIT"), Anderson Luís de Souza "DECO", CRISTIANO RONALDO dos Santos Aveiro (84' FERNANDO Manuel Silva COUTO), Pedro Miguel Carreiro Resendes "PAULETA" (YC7) (46' NUNO "GOMES" Miguel Soares Pereira Ribeiro (YC65)). (Coach: Luiz Felipe Scolari (BRA)).
Goal: Portugal: 0-1 NUNO "GOMES" Miguel Soares Pereira Ribeiro (57').
Referee: Anders Frisk (SWE)   Attendance: 47.491

69

20-06-2004   Estádio do Algarve, Faro-Loulé: Russia – Greece   2-1 (2-1)
Russia: Vyacheslav Malafeev (YC88), Aleksandr Anyukov (YC28), Roman Sharonov (YC15)
(56' Dmitri Sennikov), Aleksei Bugayev, Vadim Evseev, Rolan Gusev, Dmitri Alenichev (C)
(YC65), Vladislav Radimov (YC71), Andrei Karyaka (YC39) (46' Igor Semshov), Dmitri
Bulykin (46' Dmitri Sychev), Dmitri Kirichenko. (Coach: Georgi Aleksandrovich Yartsev
(RUS)).
Greece: Antonis Nikopolidis, Giorgios (Giourkas) Seitaridis, Traianos Dellas (YC86), Michalis
Kapsis, Stylianos Venetidis (89' Panagiotis (Takis) Fyssas), Angelos Basinas (42' Vasilios
Tsiartas), Konstantinos (Kostas) Katsouranis, Theodoros Zagorakis (C), Angelos Charisteas,
Dimitrios Papadopoulos (70' Themistoklis (Demis) Nikolaidis), Zisis Vryzas (YC45). (Coach:
Otto-Heinz Rehhagel (GER)).
Goals: Russia: 1-0 Dmitri Kirichenko (2'), 2-0 Dmitri Bulykin (17').
Greece: 2-1 Zisis Vryzas (43').
Referee: Gilles Veissière (FRA)   Attendance: 24.347

STANDINGS

Pos	Team	Pld	W	D	L	GF	GA	GD	Pts
1	Portugal	3	2	0	1	4	2	+2	6
2	Greece	3	1	1	1	4	4	+0	4
3	Spain	3	1	1	1	2	2	+0	4
4	Russia	3	1	0	2	2	4	-2	3

Portugal and Greece qualified for the Quarter-finals.

GROUP   B

13-06-2004   Estádio Dr.Magalhães Pessoa, Leiria: Switzerland – Croatia   0-0
Switzerland: Jörg Stiel (C) (YC73), Bernt Haas, Murat Yakin, Patrick Müller, Christoph
Spycher, Benjamin Huggel (YC41), Johann Vogel (YC4,YC50), Raphaël Wicky (83' Stéphane
Henchoz), Hakan Yakin (87' Daniel Gygax), Stéphane Chapuisat (55' Fabio Celestini),
Alexander Frei. (Coach: Jakob (Köbi) Kuhn (SUI)).
Croatia: Tomislav Butina, Dario Simic (61' Darijo Srna), Robert Kovac, Josip Simunic, Boris
Zivkovic (C) (YC51), Ivica Mornar (YC52), Niko Kovac, Nenad Bjelica (YC30) (74' Djovani
Roso), Ivica Olic (46' Milan Rapaic (YC48)), Dado Prso (YC13), Tomo Sokota. (Coach: Otto
Baric (CRO)).
Referee: Lucílio Cardoso Cortez Batista (POR)   Attendance: 24.090

13-06-2004   Estádio da Luz, Lisbon: France – England   2-1 (0-1)
France: Fabien Barthez, William Gallas, Lilian Thuram, Mikaël Silvestre (YC72) (79' Willy
Sagnol), Bixente Lizarazu, Robert Pirès (YC49) (76' Sylvain Wiltord), Patrick Vieira, Claude
Makélélé (90'+4' Olivier Dacourt), Zinédine Zidane (C), David Trézéguet, Thierry Henry.
(Coach: Jacques Santini (FRA)).
England: David James (YC90+2), Gary Neville, Ledley King, Sol Campbell, Ashley Cole,
David Beckham (C), Frank Lampard (YC71), Steven Gerrard, Paul Scholes (YC54) (76' Owen
Hargreaves), Wayne Rooney (76' Emile Heskey), Michael Owen (69' Darius Vassell). (Coach:
Sven-Göran Eriksson (SWE)).
Goals: France: 1-1 Zinédine Zidane (90'+1'), 2-1 Zinédine Zidane (90'+3' penalty).
England: 0-1 Frank Lampard (38').
Referee: Dr.Markus Merk (GER)   Attendance; 62.487
(David Beckham missed a penalty in the 73rd minnute)

70

17-06-2004   Estádio Cidade de Coimbra, Coimbra: England – Switzerland   3-0 (1-0)
England: David James, Gary Neville, John Terry, Sol Campbell, Ashley Cole, David Beckham (C), Steven Gerrard, Frank Lampard, Paul Scholes (70' Owen Hargreaves), Michael Owen (72' Darius Vassell), Wayne Rooney (YC18) (83' Kieron Dyer). (Coach: Sven-Göran Eriksson (SWE)).
Switzerland: Jörg Stiel (C), Bernt Haas (YC49,YC60), Murat Yakin, Patrick Müller, Christoph Spycher, Benjamin Huggel, Fabio Celestini (YC23) (54' Ricardo Cabanas Rey), Raphaël Wicky, Hakan Yakin (84' Johan Vonlanthen), Stéphane Chapuisat (46' Daniel Gygax), Alexander Frei. (Coach: Jakob (Köbi) Kuhn (SUI)).
Goals: England: 1-0 Wayne Rooney (23'), 2-0 Wayne Rooney (75'), 3-0 Steven Gerrard (82').
Referee: Valentin Valentinovich Ivanov (RUS)   Attendance: 28.214

17-06-2004   Estádio Dr. Magalhães Pessoa, Leiria: Croatia – France   2-2 (0-1)
Croatia: Tomislav Butina, Dario Simic (C), Igor Tudor (YC39), Robert Kovac (YC64), Josip Simunic, Djovani Roso (YC61), Niko Kovac, Nenad Bjelica (68' Jerko Leko (YC78)), Milan Rapaic (87' Ivica Mornar), Dado Prso, Tomo Sokota (73' Ivica Olic). (Coach: Otto Baric (CRO)).
France: Fabien Barthez, William Gallas (81' Willy Sagnol), Lilian Thuram, Marcel Desailly (C), Mikaël Silvestre, Sylvain Wiltord (70' Robert Pirès), Olivier Dacourt (YC60) (79' Benoît Pedretti), Patrick Vieira (YC32), Zinédine Zidane (C), David Trézéguet, Thierry Henry. (Coach: Jacques Santini (FRA)).
Goals: Croatia: 1-1 Milan Rapaic (48' penalty), 2-1 Dado Prso (52').
France: 0-1 Igor Tudor (22' own goal), 2-2 David Trézéguet (64').
Referee: Kim Milton Nielsen (DEN)   Attendance: 29.160

21-06-2004   Estádio da Luz, Lisbon: Croatia – England   2-4 (1-2)
Croatia: Tomislav Butina, Dario Simic (YC63) (67' Darijo Srna), Igor Tudor, Robert Kovac (46' Ivica Mornar), Josip Simunic, Djovani Roso, Niko Kovac, Boris Zivkovic (C), Milan Rapaic (55' Ivica Olic), Dado Prso, Tomo Sokota. (Coach: Otto Baric (CRO)).
England: David James, Gary Neville, John Terry, Sol Campbell, Ashley Cole, David Beckham (C), Frank Lampard (84' Phil Neville), Steven Gerrard, Paul Scholes (70' Ledley King), Michael Owen, Wayne Rooney (72' Darius Vassell). (Coach: Sven-Göran Eriksson (SWE)).
Goals: Croatia: 1-0 Niko Kovac (5'), 2-3 Igor Tudor (73').
England: 1-1 Paul Scholes (40'), 1-2 Wayne Rooney (45'+1'), 1-3 Wayne Rooney (68'), 2-4 Frank Lampard(79').
Referee: Pierluigi Collina (ITA)   Attendance: 57.047

21-06-2004   Estádio Cidade de Coimbra, Coimbra: Switzerland – France   1-3 (1-1)
Switzerland: Jörg Stiel (C), Stéphane Henchoz (85' Ludovic Magnin), Murat Yakin, Patrick Müller, Christoph Spycher, Ricardo Cabanas Rey, Johann Vogel, Raphaël Wicky (YC66), Daniel Gygax (85' Milaim Rama), Hakan Yakin (YC43) (60' Benjamin Huggel (YC75)), Johan Vonlanthen. (Coach: Jakob (Köbi) Kuhn (SUI)).
France: Fabien Barthez, Willy Sagnol (46' William Gallas, 90'+2' Jean-Alain Boumsong), Lilian Thuram, Mikaël Silvestre, Bixente Lizarazu, Zinédine Zidane (C), Patrick Vieira, Claude Makélélé, Robert Pirès, David Trézéguet (75' Louis Saha), Thierry Henry (YC47). (Coach: Jacques Santini (FRA)).
Goals: Switzerland: 1-1 Johan Vonlanthen (26').
France: 0-1 Zinédine Zidane (20'), 1-2 Thierry Henry (76'), 1-3 Thierry Henry (84').
Referee: Lubos Michel (SVK)   Attendance; 28.111

71

STANDINGS

Pos	Team	Pld	W	D	L	GF	GA	GD	Pts
1	*France*	*3*	*2*	*1*	*0*	*7*	*4*	*+3*	*7*
2	*England*	*3*	*2*	*0*	*1*	*8*	*4*	*+4*	*6*
3	Croatia	3	0	2	1	4	6	-2	2
4	Switzerland	3	0	1	2	1	6	-5	1

France and England qualified for the Quarter-finals.

GROUP C

14-06-2004   Estádio D. Afonso Henriques, Guimarães: Denmark – Italy   0-0
Denmark: Thomas Sørensen, Thomas Helveg (YC67), Martin Laursen, René Henriksen (C),
Niclas Jensen, Daniel Jensen, Christian Poulsen (76' Brian Priske), Dennis Rommedahl, Jon
Dahl Tomassen (YC29), Martin Jørgensen (72' Kenneth Perez), Ebbe Sand (69' Claus Jensen).
(Coach: Morten Per Olsen (DEN)).
Italy: Gianluigi Buffon, Christian Panucci, Alessandro Nesta, Fabio Cannavaro (C) (YC62),
Gianluca Zambrotta, Cristiano Zanetti (57' Gennaro Gattuso (YC81)), Simone Perrotta, Mauro
Camoranesi (68' Stefano Fiore), Francesco Totti YC90+3), Alessandro Del Piero (64' Antonio
Cassano (YC70)), Christian Vieri. (Coach: Giovanni Trapattoni (ITA)).
Goals: Manuel Enrique Mejuto González (ESP)   Attendance: 29.595

14-06-2004   Estádio José Alvalade, Lisbon: Sweden – Bulgaria   5-0 (1-0)
Sweden: Andreas Isaksson, Teddy Lucic (41' Christian Wilhelmsson), Olof Mellberg (C),
Andreas Jakobsson, Erik Edman, Tobias Linderoth (YC52), Mikael Nilsson, Anders Svensson
(77' Kim Källström), Fredrik Ljungberg, Zlatan Ibrahimovic (YC65) (81' Marcus Allbäck),
Henrik Larsson. (Coaches: Lars Lagerbäck (SWE) & Tommy Söderberg (SWE)).
Bulgaria: Zdravko Zdravkov, Vladimir Ivanov (YC70), Rosen Kirilov (YC22), Predrag Pazin,
Ivaylo Petkov (YC18), Georgi Peev, Stilian Petrov (C), Mariyan Hristov, Martin Petrov (84'
Zdravko Lazarov), Zoran Jankovic (YC23) (62' Velizar Dimitrov), Dimitar Berbatov (76'
Vladimir Manchev). (Coach: Plamen Markov (BUL)).
Goals: Sweden: 1-0 Fredrik Ljungberg (32'), 2-0 Henrik Larsson (57'), 3-0 Henrik Larsson
(58'), 4-0 Zlatan Ibrahimovic (78' penalty), 5-0 Marcus Allbäck (90'+1').
Referee: Michael (Mike) Riley (ENG)   Attendance: 31.652

18-06-2004   Estádio Municipal de Braga, Braga: Bulgaria – Denmark   0-2 (0-1)
Bulgaria: Zdravko Zdravkov, Vladimir Ivanov (51' Zdravko Lazarov), Rosen Kirilov (YC4),
Ilian Stoyanov (YC50), Ivaylo Petkov (40' Zlatomir Zagorcic (YC80)), Georgi Peev, Mariyan
Hristov (YC82), Stilian Petrov (C) (YC77,YC83), Martin Petrov (YC84), Zoran Jankovic (81'
Milen Petkov), Dimitar Berbatov. (Coach: Plamen Markov (BUL)).
Denmark: Thomas Sørensen, Thomas Helveg, Martin Laursen, René Henriksen (C), Niclas
Jensen (YC10), Daniel Jensen, Thomas Gravesen, Jon Dahl Tomassen, Dennis Rommedahl
(23' Jesper Grønkjær), Martin Jørgensen (72' Claus Jensen), Ebbe Sand (YC58). (Coach:
Morten Per Olsen (DEN)).
Goals: Denmark: 0-1 Jon Dahl Tomassen (44'), 0-2 Jesper Grønkjær (90'+2').
Referee: Lucílio Cardoso Cortez Batista (POR)   Attendance: 24.131

18-06-2004   Estádio do Dragão, Porto: Italy – Sweden   1-1 (1-0)
Italy: Gianluigi Buffon, Christian Panucci, Fabio Cannavaro (C) (YC46), Alessandro Nesta, Gianluca Zambrotta (YC58), Gennaro Gattuso (YC39) (76' Giuseppe Favalli), Andrea Pirlo, Simone Perrotta, Antonio Cassano (70' Stefano Fiore), Christian Vieri, Alessandro Del Piero (82' Mauro Camoranesi). (Coach: Giovanni Trapattoni (ITA)).
Sweden: Andreas Isaksson, Mikael Nilsson, Olof Mellberg (C), Andreas Jakobsson, Erik Edman (YC54) (77' Marcus Allbäck), Tobias Linderoth (YC75), Christian Wilhelmsson (67' Mattias Jonson), Anders Svensson (55' Kim Källström), Fredrik Ljungberg, Zlatan Ibrahimovic, Henrik Larsson. (Coaches: Lars Lagerbäck (SWE) & Tommy Söderberg (SWE)).
Goals: Italy: 1-0 Antonio Cassano (37').
Sweden: 1-1 Zlatan Ibrahimovic (85').
Referee: Urs Meier (SUI)   Attendance: 44.926

22-06-2004   Estádio D. Afonso Henriques, Guimarães: Italy – Bulgaria   2-1 (0-1)
Italy: Gianluigi Buffon, Christian Panucci, Alessandro Nesta, Marco Materazzi (YC44) (83' Marco Di Vaio), Gianluca Zambrotta, Simone Perrotta (68' Massimo Oddo), Andrea Pirlo, Stefano Fiore, Antonio Cassano, Bernardo Corradi (53' Christian Vieri), Alessandro Del Piero (C). (Coach: Giovanni Trapattoni (ITA)).
Bulgaria: Zdravko Zdravkov (C), Daniel Borimirov, Predrag Pazin (64' Kiril Kotev), Zlatomir Zagorcic, Ilian Stoyanov (YC66), Mariyan Hristov (79' Velizar Dimitrov), Milen Petkov, Zdravko Lazarov (YC80), Zoran Jankovic (46' Valeri Bojinov (YC49)), Martin Petrov (YC45+1), Dimitar Berbatov. (Coach: Plamen Markov (BUL)).
Goals: Italy: 1-1 Simone Perrotta (48'), 2-1 Antonio Cassano (90'+4').
Bulgaria: 0-1 Martin Petrov (45' penalty).
Referee: Valentin Valentinovich Ivanov (RUS)   Attendance: 16.002

22-06-2004   Estádio do Bessa, Porto: Denmark – Sweden   2-2 (1-0)
Denmark: Thomas Sørensen, Thomas Helveg, Martin Laursen, René Henriksen (C), Niclas Jensen (46' Kasper Bøgelund), Daniel Jensen (66' Christian Poulsen), Thomas Gravesen, Jon Dahl Tomassen, Jesper Grønkjær, Martin Jørgensen (57' Dennis Rommedahl), Ebbe Sand. (Coach: Morten Per Olsen (DEN)).
Sweden: Andreas Isaksson, Mikael Nilsson, Olof Mellberg (C), Andreas Jakobsson, Erik Edman (YC36), Anders Andersson (81' Marcus Allbäck), Mattias Jonson, Kim Källström (YC63) (72' Christian Wilhelmsson), Fredrik Ljungberg, Zlatan Ibrahimovic, Henrik Larsson. (Coaches: Lars Lagerbäck (SWE) & Tommy Söderberg (SWE)).
Goals: Denmark: 1-0 Jon Dahl Tomassen (28'), 2-1 Jon Dahl Tomassen (66').
Sweden: 1-1 Henrik Larsson (47' penalty), 2-2 Mattias Jonson (89').
Referee: Dr.Markus Merk (GER)   Attendance: 26.115

STANDINGS

Pos	Team	Pld	W	D	L	GF	GA	GD	Pts
1	Sweden	3	1	2	0	8	3	+5	5
2	Denmark	3	1	2	0	4	2	+2	5
3	Italy	3	1	2	0	3	2	+1	5
4	Bulgaria	3	0	0	3	1	9	-8	0

Sweden and Denmark qualified for the Quarter-finals.

The three teams, Italy, Denmark and Sweden, all finished with 5 points, with each team having defeated Bulgaria but drawn their other games. As all results between the three teams in question were draws, both the points won in these games and the goal difference accrued in these games still left the teams undivided. The decisive tiebreaker was therefore the goals scored during the games between one another: Italy having scored the fewest goals of the three teams were therefore eliminated.

GROUP D

15-06-2004   Estádio Municipal de Aveiro, Aveiro: Czech Republic – Latvia 2-1 (0-1)
Czech Republic: Petr Cech, Zdenek Grygera (56' Marek Heinz), René Bolf, Tomás Ujfalusi, Marek Jankulovsky, Tomás Galásek (64' Vladimír Smicer), Karel Poborsky, Tomás Rosicky, Pavel Nedved (C), Milan Baros (87' Martin Jiránek), Jan Koller. (Coach: Karel Brückner (CZE)).
Latvia: Aleksandrs Kolinko, Aleksandrs Isakovs, Mihails Zemlinskis, Igors Stepanovs, Olegs Blagonadezdins, Imants Bleidelis, Vitalijs Astafjevs (C), Valetīns Lobanovs (90' Vits Rimkus), Andrejs Rubins, Andrejs Prohorenkovs (71' Juris Laizāns), Māris Verpakovskis (81' Marians Pahars). (Coach: Aleksandrs Starkovs (LAT)).
Goals: Czech Republic: 1-1 Milan Baros (73'), 2-1 Marek Heinz (85').
Latvia: 0-1 Māris Verpakovskis (45'+1').
Referee: Gilles Veissière (FRA)   Attendance: 21.744

15-06-2004   Estádio do Dragão, Porto: Germany – Netherlands 1-1 (1-0)
Germany: Oliver Kahn (C), Arne Friedrich, Christian Wörns, Jens Nowotny, Philipp Lahm, Dietmar Hamann, Frank Baumann, Bernd Schneider (68' Bastian Schweinsteiger), Michael Ballack (YC90+1), Torsten Frings (79' Fabian Ernst), Kevin Kurányi (YC12) (85' Fredi Bobic). (Coach: Rudolf (Rudi) Völler (GER)).
Netherlands: Edwin van der Sar, John Heitinga (74' Pierre van Hooijdonk), Jaap Stam (YC73), Wilfred Bouma, Giovanni van Bronckhorst, Phillip Cocu (YC29), Edgar Davids (46' Wesley Sneijder), Andy van der Meyde, Rafael van der Vaart, Boudewijn Zenden (46' Marc Overmars), Ruud van Nistelrooy. (Coach: Dick Nicolaas Advocaat (HOL)).
Goals: Germany: 1-0 Torsten Frings (30').
Netherlands: 1-1 Ruud van Nistelrooy (81').
Referee: Anders Frisk (SWE)   Attendance: 48.197

19-06-2004   Estádio do Bessa, Porto: Latvia – Germany 0-0
Latvia: Aleksandrs Kolinko, Aleksandrs Isakovs (YC1), Mihails Zemlinskis, Igors Stepanovs, Olegs Blagonadezdins, Imants Bleidelis, Vitalijs Astafjevs (C) (YC79), Valentīns Lobanovs (70' Juris Laizāns), Andrejs Rubins, Andrejs Prohorenkovs (67' Marians Pahars), Māris Verpakovskis (90'+2' Dzintars Zirnis). (Coach: Aleksandrs Starkovs (LAT)).
Germany: Oliver Kahn (C), Arne Friedrich (YC21), Christian Wörns, Frank Baumann, Philipp Lahm, Bernd Schneider (46' Bastian Schweinsteiger), Dietmar Hamann (YC42), Michael Ballack, Torsten Frings (YC53), Fredi Bobic (67' Miroslav Klose), Kevin Kurányi (78' Thomas Brdaric). (Coach: Rudolf (Rudi) Völler (GER)).
Referee: Michael (Mike) Riley (ENG)   Attendance: 22.344

19-06-2004   Estádio Municipal de Aveiro, Aveiro: Netherlands – Czech Republic   2-3 (2-1)
Netherlands: Edwin van der Sar, John Heitinga (YC26,YC75), Jaap Stam, Wilfred Bouma, Giovanni van Bronckhorst, Phillip Cocu (C), Clarence Seedorf (YC9) (86' Rafael van der Vaart), Edgar Davids, Andy van der Meyde (79' Michael Reiziger), Arjen Robben (58' Paul Bosvelt), Ruud van Nistelrooy. (Coach: Dick Nicolaas Advocaat (HOL)).
Czech Republic: Petr Cech, Zdenek Grygera (25' Vladimír Smicer), Martin Jiránek, Tomás Ujfalusi, Marek Jankulovsky, Karel Poborsky, Tomás Rosicky, Tomás Galásek (YC55) (62' Marek Heinz), Pavel Nedved (C), Jan Koller (75' David Rozehnal), Milan Baros. (Coach: Karel Brückner (CZE)).
Goals: Netherlands: 1-0 Wilfred Bouma (4'), 2-0 Ruud van Nistelrooy (19').
Czech Republic: 2-1 Jan Koller (23'), 2-2 Milan Baros (71'), 2-3 Vladimír Smicer (88').
Referee: Manuel Enrique Mejuto González (ESP)   Attendance: 29.935

23-06-2004   Estádio Municipal de Braga, Braga: Netherlands – Latvia   3-0 (2-0)
Netherlands: Edwin van der Sar, Michael Reiziger, Jaap Stam, Frank de Boer (C), Giovanni van Bronckhorst, Clarence Seedorf, Phillip Cocu, Edgar Davids (77' Wesley Sneijder), Andy van der Meyde (63' Marc Overmars), Arjen Robben, Ruud van Nistelrooy (70' Roy Makaay). (Coach: Dick Nicolaas Advocaat (HOL)).
Latvia: Aleksandrs Kolinko, Aleksandrs Isakovs, Mihails Zemlinskis, Igors Stepanovs, Olegs Blagonadezdins, Imants Bleidelis (83' Andrejs Stolcers), Valentīns Lobanovs (YC53), Vitalijs Astafjevs (C), Andrejs Rubins, Andrejs Prohorenkovs (74' Juris Laizāns), Māris Verpakovskis (62' Marians Pahars). (Coach: Aleksandrs Starkovs (LAT)).
Goals: Netherlands: 1-0 Ruud van Nistelrooy (27' penalty), 2-0 Ruud van Nistelrooy (35'), 3-0 Roy Makaay (84').
Referee: Kim Milton Nielsen (DEN)   Attendance: 27.904

23-06-2004   Estádio José Alvalade, Lisbon: Germany – Czech Republic   1-2 (1-1)
Germany: Oliver Kahn (C), Arne Friedrich, Jens Nowotny (YC38), Christian Wörns (YC83), Torsten Frings (46' Lukas Podolski), Dietmar Hamann (79' Miroslav Klose), Philipp Lahm (YC74), Bernd Schneider, Michael Ballack, Bastian Schweinsteiger (86' Jens Jeremies), Kevin Kurányi. (Coach: Rudolf (Rudi) Völler (GER)).
Czech Republic: Jaromír Blazek, Martin Jiránek, René Bolf, David Rozehnal, Pavel Mares, Roman Tyce (YC48), Tomás Galásek (C) (46' Tomás Hübschman), Jaroslav Plasil (70' Karel Poborsky), Marek Heinz, Stepán Vachousek, Vratislav Lokvenc (59' Milan Baros). (Coach: Karel Brückner (CZE)).
Goals: Germany: 1-0 Michael Ballack (21').
Czech Republic: 1-1 Marek Heinz (30'), 1-2 Milan Baros (77').
Referee: Terje Hauge (NOR)   Attendance: 46.849

STANDINGS

Pos	Team	Pld	W	D	L	GF	GA	GD	Pts
1	Czech Republic	3	3	0	0	7	4	+3	9
2	Netherlands	3	1	1	1	6	4	+2	4
3	Germany	3	0	2	1	2	3	-1	2
4	Latvia	3	0	1	2	1	5	-4	1

Czech Republic and Netherlands qualified for the Quarter-finals.

24-06-2004   Estádio da Luz, Lisbon: Portugal – England   2-2 (0-1, 1-1) (AET)
Portugal: RICARDO Alexandre Martins Soares Pereira, Luís MIGUEL Brito Garcia Monteiro
(79' RUI Manuel César COSTA), RICARDO Alberto Silveira de CARVALHO (YC119),
JORGE Manuel Almeida Gomes de ANDRADE, NUNO Jorge Pereira da Silva VALENTE,
Francisco José Rodrigues da Costa "COSTINHA" (YC56) (63' SIMÃO Pedro Fonseca
Sabrosa), Nuno Ricardo de Oliveira Ribeiro "MANICHE", LUÍS Filipe Madeira Caeiro FIGO
(C) (75' HÉLDER Manuel Marques POSTIGA), Anderson Luís de Souza "DECO" (YC85),
CRISTIANO RONALDO dos Santos Aveiro, NUNO "GOMES" Miguel Soares Pereira
Ribeiro. (Coach: Luiz Felipe Scolari (BRA)).
England: David James, Gary Neville (YC45), John Terry, Sol Campbell, Ashley Cole, David
Beckham (C), Frank Lampard, Steven Gerrard (YC37) (81' Owen Hargreaves), Paul Scholes
(57' Phil Neville (YC92)), Michael Owen, Wayne Rooney (27' Darius Vassell). (Coach: Sven-
Göran Eriksson (SWE)).
Goals: Portugal: 1-1 HÉLDER Manuel Marques POSTIGA (83'), 2-1 RUI Manuel César
COSTA (110').
England: 0-1 Michael Owen (3'), 2-2 Frank Lampard (115').
Referee: Urs Meier (SUI)   Attendance: 65.000
Penalties:
* David Beckham   1 Anderson Luís de Souza "DECO"
1 Michael Owen   2 SIMÃO Pedro Fonseca Sabrosa
2 Frank Lampard   * RUI Manuel César COSTA
3 John Terry   3 CRISTIANO RONALDO dos Santos Aveiro
4 Owen Hargreaves   4 Nuno Ricardo de Oliveira Ribeiro "MANICHE"
5 Ashley Cole   5 HÉLDER Manuel Marques POSTIGA
* Darius Vassell   6 RICARDO Alexandre Martins Soares Pereira

25-06-2004   Estádio José Alvalade, Lisbon: France – Greece   0-1 (0-0)
France: Fabien Barthez, William Gallas, Lilian Thuram, Mikaël Silvestre, Bixente Lizarazu,
Zinédine Zidane (C) (YC44), Olivier Dacourt (72' Sylvain Wiltord), Claude Makélélé, Robert
Pirès (79' Jérôme Rothen), David Trézéguet (72' Louis Saha (YC86)), Thierry Henry. (Coach:
Jacques Santini (FRA)).
Greece: Antonis Nikopolidis, Giorgios (Giourkas) Seitaridis, Traianos Dellas, Michalis Kapsis,
Panagiotis (Takis) Fyssas, Angelos Basinas (85' Vasilios Tsiartas), Konstantinos (Kostas)
Katsouranis, Giorgios Karagounis (YC6), Theodoros Zagorakis (C) (YC50), Themistoklis
(Demis) Nikolaidis (61' Vassilis Lakis), Angelos Charisteas. (Coach: Otto-Heinz Rehhagel
(GER)).
Goal: Greece: 0-1 Angelos Charisteas (64').
Referee: Anders Frisk (SWE)   Attendance: 45.390

26-06-2004   Estádio do Algarve, Faro-Louié: Sweden – Netherlands 0-0 (AET)
Sweden: Andreas Isaksson, Alexander Östlund (YC88), Olof Mellberg (C), Andreas
Jakobsson, Mikael Nilsson, Tobias Linderoth, Mattias Jonson (64' Christian Wilhelmsson),
Fredrik Ljungberg, Anders Svensson (81' Kim Källström), Zlatan Ibrahimovic (YC58), Henrik
Larsson. (Coaches: Lars Lagerbäck (SWE) & Tommy Söderberg (SWE)).
Netherlands: Edwin van der Sar, Michael Reiziger, Jaap Stam, Frank de Boer (C) (YC30) (35'
Wilfred Bouma), Giovanni van Bronckhorst, Edgar Davids (61' John Heitinga), Clarence
Seedorf, Phillip Cocu, Andy van der Meyde (YC48) (87' Roy Makaay (YC116)), Arjen
Robben, Ruud van Nistelrooy. (Coach: Dick Nicolaas Advocaat (HOL)).
Referee: Lubos Michel (SVK)   Attendance: 27.762
Penalties:
1 Kim Källström   1 Ruud van Nistelrooy
2 Henrik Larsson   2 John Heitinga
* Zlatan Ibrahimovic   3 Michael Reiziger
3 Fredrik Ljungberg   * Phillip Cocu
4 Christian Wilhelmsson   4 Roy Makaay
* Olof Mellberg   5 Arjen Robben

27-06-2004   Estádio do Dragão, Porto: Czech Republic – Denmark 3-0 (0-0)
Czech Republic: Petr Cech, Martin Jiránek (39' Zdenek Grygera), Tomás Ujfalusi (YC45),
René Bolf (65' David Rozehnal), Marek Jankulovski (YC10), Tomás Galásek, Karel Poborsky,
Tomás Rosicky, Pavel Nedved (C) (YC61), Jan Koller, Milan Baros (70' Marek Heinz).
(Coach: Karel Brückner (CZE)).
Denmark: Thomas Sørensen, Thomas Helveg, Martin Laursen, René Henriksen (C), Kasper
Bøgelund (YC56), Christian Poulsen (YC51), Claus Jensen (71' Peter Madsen), Thomas
Gravesen (YC77), Jesper Grønkjær (77' Dennis Rommedahl), Martin Jørgensen (85' Peter
Løvenkrands), Jon Dahl Tomassen. (Coach: Morten Per Olsen (DEN)).
Goals: Czech Republic: 1-0 Jan Koller (49'), 2-0 Milan Baros (63'), 3-0 Milan Baros (65').
Referee: Valentin Valentinovich Ivanov (RUS)   Attendance: 41.092

SEMI-FINALS

30-06-2004   Estádio José Alvalade, Lisbon: Portugal – Netherlands 2-1 (1-0)
Portugal: RICARDO Alexandre Martins Soares Pereira, Luís MIGUEL Brito Garcia Monteiro,
JORGE Manuel Almeida Gomes de ANDRADE, RICARDO Alberto Silveira de
CARVALHO, NUNO Jorge Pereira da Silva VALENTE (YC44), Nuno Ricardo de Oliveira
Ribeiro "MANICHE" (87' FERNANDO Manuel Silva COUTO), Francisco José Rodrigues da
Costa "COSTINHA", CRISTIANO RONALDO dos Santos Aveiro (YC27) (68' Armando
Gonçalves Teixeira "PETIT"), Anderson Luís de Souza "DECO", LUÍS Filipe Madeira Caeiro
FIGO (C) (YC90), Pedro Miguel Carreiro Resendes "PAULETA" (75' NUNO "GOMES"
Miguel Soares Pereira Ribeiro). (Coach: Luiz Felipe Scolari (BRA)).
Netherlands: Edwin van der Sar, Michael Reiziger, Jaap Stam, Wilfred Bouma (56' Rafael van
der Vaart), Giovanni van Bronckhorst, Edgar Davids, Clarence Seedorf, Phillip Cocu (C),
Marc Overmars (YC39) (46' Roy Makaay), Arjen Robben (YC71) (81' Pierre van Hooijdonk),
Ruud van Nistelrooy. (Coach: Dick Nicolaas Advocaat (HOL)).
Goals: Portugal: 1-0 CRISTIANO RONALDO dos Santos Aveiro (26'), 2-0 Nuno Ricardo de
Oliveira Ribeiro "MANICHE" (58').
Netherlands: 2-1 JORGE Manuel Almeida Gomes de ANDRADE (63' *own goal*).
Referee: Anders Frisk (SWE)   Attendance: 46.679

01-07-2004   Estádio do Dragão, Porto: Greece – Czech Republic   1-0 (0-0) (AET)
Greece: Antonis Nikopolidis, Giorgios (Giourkas) Seitaridis (YC23), Michalis Kapsis,
Traianos Dellas, Panagiotis (Takis) Fyssas, Theodoros Zagorakis (C), Konstantinos (Kostas)
Katsouranis, Angelos Basinas (72' Stylianos Giannakopoulos), Angelos Charisteas (YC70),
Zisis Vryzas (91' Vasilios Tsiartas), Giorgios Karagounis (YC87). (Coach: Otto-Heinz
Rehhagel (GER)).
Czech Republic: Petr Cech, Zdenek Grygera, René Bolf, Tomás Ujfalusi, Marek Jankulovski,
Tomás Galásek (YC48), Karel Poborsky, Tomás Rosicky, Pavel Nedved (C) (40' Vladimír
Smicer (YC55)), Jan Koller, Milan Baros (YC102). (Coach: Karel Brückner (CZE)).
Goal: Greece: 1-0 Traianos Dellas (105'+1' *silver goal*).
Referee: Pierluigi Collina (ITA)   Attendance: 42.449

FINAL

04-07-2004   Estádio da Luz, Lisbon: Portugal – Greece   0-1 (0-0)
Portugal: RICARDO Alexandre Martins Soares Pereira, Luís MIGUEL Brito Garcia Monteiro
(43' PAULO Renato Rebocho FERREIRA), JORGE Manuel Almeida Gomes de ANDRADE,
RICARDO Alberto Silveira de CARVALHO, NUNO Jorge Pereira da Silva VALENTE
(YC90+3), Nuno Ricardo de Oliveira Ribeiro "MANICHE", Francisco José Rodrigues da
Costa "COSTINHA" (YC12) (60' RUI Manuel César COSTA), CRISTIANO RONALDO dos
Santos Aveiro, Anderson Luís de Souza "DECO", LUÍS Filipe Madeira Caeiro FIGO (C),
Pedro Miguel Carreiro Resendes "PAULETA" (74' NUNO "GOMES" Miguel Soares Pereira
Ribeiro). (Coach: Luiz Felipe Scolari (BRA)).
Greece: Antonis Nikopolidis, Giorgios (Giourkas) Seitaridis (YC63), Michalis Kapsis,
Traianos Dellas, Panagiotis (Takis) Fyssas (YC67), Konstantinos (Kostas) Katsouranis,
Theodoros Zagorakis (C), Angelos Basinas (YC45+2), Angelos Charisteas, Stylianos
Giannakopoulos (76' Stylianos Venetidis), Zisis Vryzas (81' Dimitrios Papadopoulos (YC85)).
(Coach: Otto-Heinz Rehhagel (GER)).
Goal: Greece: 0-1 Angelos Charisteas (57').
Referee: Dr.Markus Merk (GER)   Attendance: 62.865

*** Greece European Champion ***

GOALSCORERS TOURNAMENT 2002-2004:

Goals	Players
9	Ruud van Nistelrooy (HOL), Ermin Siljak (SLO)
8	Milan Baros (CZE), Jan Koller (CZE), Jon Dahl Tomasson (DEN), Thierry Henry (FRA)
7	RAÚL González Blanco (ESP), David Trézéguet (FRA), Māris Verpakovskis (LAT)
6	Michael Owen (ENG), Wayen Rooney (ENG), Sylvain Wiltord (FRA), Zinédine Zidane (FRA), Angelos Charisteas (GRE), Filippo Inzhagi (ITA), Marcus Allbäck (SWE)
5	Wesley Sonck (BEL), Dimitar Berbatov (BUL), David Beckham (ENG), Michael Ballack (GER), Eidur Gudjohnsen (ISL), Alessandro Del Piero (ITA), Dmitri Bulykin (RUS), Alexander Frei (SUI), Zlatan Ibrahimovic (SWE), Mattias Jonson (SWE)
4	Dado Prso (CRO), Milan Rapaic (CRO), Shota Arveladze (GEO), Fredi Bobic (GER), Patrick Kluivert (HOL), Zoltán Gera (HUN), Krisztián Lisztes (HUN), Imre Szabics (HUN), Ionel Ganea (ROM), Adrian Mutu (ROM), Szilárd Neméth (SVK), Simon Davies (WAL)
3	Artur Petrosyan (ARM), Albert Sarkisyan (ARM), Gurban Gurbanov (AZE), Sergej Barbarez (BOS), Niko Kovac (CRO), Mihalis Konstantinou (CYP), Marek Jankulovski (CZE), Vladimír Smicer (CZE), Frank Lampard (ENG), Juan Carlos VALERÓN Santana (ESP), Rafael van der Vaart (HOL), Gary Doherty (IRL), Heim Revivo (ISR), Christian Vieri (ITA), Tomas Razanauskas (LIT), Michael Mifsud (MLT), Cosmin Contra (ROM), Sergei Ignashevich (RUS), Hakan Yakin (SUI), Henrik Larsson (SWE), Serhat Akin (TUR), Okan Buruk (TUR), Nihat Kahveci (TUR), Hakan Sükür (TUR), Andriy Shevchenko (UKR)
2	Altin Lala (ALB), Ervin Skela (ALB), Igli Tare (ALB), Mario Haas (AUT), Andreas Herzog (AUT), Farrukh Ismayilov (AZE), Bart Goor (BEL), Elvir Bolic (BOS), Martin Petrov (BUL), Stilian Petrov (BUL), Ioannis Okkas (CYP), Rainer Rauffmann (CYP), Marek Heinz (CZE), Vratislav Lokvenc (CZE), Pavel Nedved (CZE), Karel Poborsky (CZE), Thomas Gravesen (DEN), Jesper Grønkjær (DEN), Dennis Rommedahl (DEN), Steven Gerrard (ENG), Rubén BARAJA Vegas (ESP), Joseba Andoni EXTEBERRÍA Lizardi (ESP), José Antonio REYES Calderón (ESP), Indrek Zelinski (EST), Rógvi Jacobsen (FAR), John Petersen (FAR), Mikael Forssell (FIN), Sami Hyypiä (FIN), Steve Marlet (FRA), Miroslav Klose (GER), Themistoklis (Demis) Nikolaidis (GRE), Zisis Vryzas (GRE), Philip Cocu (HOL), Roy Makaay (HOL), Wesley Sneijder (HOL), Krisztián Kenesei (HUN), Damien Duff (IRL), Robbie Keane (IRL), Omri Afek (ISR), Pini Balili (ISR), Antonio Cassano (ITA), Imants Bleidelis (LAT), Juris Ļaizāns (LAT), Igoris Morinas (LIT), Vlatko Grozdanoski (MCD), Georgi Hristov (MCD), Artim Sakiri (MCD), Steffen Iversen (NOR), John Arne Riise (NOR), Ole Gunnar Solskjær (NOR), Marcin Kuzba (POL), Andrzej Niedzielan (POL), Miroslaw Szymkowiak (POL), CRISTIANO RONALDO dos Santos Aveiro (POR), Nuno Ricardo de Oliveira Ribeiro "MANICHE" (POR), RUI Manuel César COSTA (POR), Viorel Moldovan (ROM), Dorinel Munteanu (ROM), Daniel Pancu (ROM), Andrei Karyaka (RUS), Aleksandr Kerzhakov (RUS), Sergei Semak (RUS), Predrag Mijatovic (SBM), Neil McCann (SCO), James McFadden (SCO), Kenny

	Miller (SCO), Nastja Ceh (SLO), Zlato Zahovic (SLO), Vladimír Janocko (SVK), Lubomír (Lubos) Reiter (SVK), Róbert Vittek (SVK), Fredrik Ljungberg (SWE), Anders Svensson (SWE), Arif Erdem (TUR), Ilhan Mansiz (TUR), Andriy Voronin (UKR), Olexandr Gorshkov (UKR), John Hartson (WAL), Gary Speed (WAL)
1	Alban Bushi (ALB), Klodian Duro (ALB), Besnik Hasi (ALB), Edvin Murati (ALB), Altin Rraklli (ALB), Antonio "Toni"Lima Sola (AND), Arman Karamyan (ARM), Muhammet Akagündüz (AUT), René Aufhauser (AUT), Harald Cerny (AUT), Andreas Ivanschitz (AUT), Roland Kirchler (AUT), Emanuel Pogatetz (AUT), Markus Schopp (AUT), Roman Wallner (AUT), Thomas Buffel (BEL), Philippe Clement (BEL), Vital Bulyha (BLS), Sergei Gurenko (BLS), Vitali Kutuzov (BLS), Roman Vasilyuk (BLS), Zlatan Bajramovic (BOS), Elvir Baljic (BOS), Krassimir Balakov (BUL), Georgi Chilikov (BUL), Mariyan Hristov (BUL), Zoran Jankovic (BUL), Svetoslav Todorov (BUL), Tomislav Maric (CRO), Jerko Leko (CRO), Ivica Olic (CRO), Djovani Roso (CRO), Josip Simunic (CRO), Darijo Srna (CRO), Igor Tudor (CRO), Stavros Georgiou (CYP), Yiasoumis Yiasoumi (CYP), Tomás Rosicky (CZE), Jirí Stajner (CZE), Stepán Vachousek (CZE), Claus Jensen (DEN), Martin Jørgensen (DEN), Martin Laursen (DEN), Ebbe Sand (DEN), Paul Scholes (ENG), Darius Vassell (ENG), DIEGO TRISTÁN Herrera (ESP), José María "GUTI" Gutiérrez Hernández (ESP), IVÁN HELGUERA Bujía (ESP), JOAQUÍN Sánchez Rodríguez (ESP), Fernando MORIENTES Sánchez (ESP), VICENTE Rodríguez Guillén (ESP), Teet Allas (EST),.Kristen Viikmäe (EST), Julian Schantz Johnsson (FAR), Súni Olsen (FAR), Joonas Kolkka (FIN), Mika Nurmela (FIN), Teemu Tainio (FIN), Hannu Tihinen (FIN), Jean-Alain Boumsong (FRA), Eric Carrière (FRA), Djibril Cissé (FRA), Olivier Dacourt (FRA), Sidney Govou (FRA), Patrick Vieira (FRA), Malkhaz Asatiani (GEO), Mikheil Ashvetia (GEO), Aleksandre Iashvili (GEO), Levan Kobiashvili (GEO), Torsten Frings (GER), Kevin Kurányi (GER), Carsten Ramelow (GER), Angelos Basinas (GRE), Traianos Dellas (GRE), Stylianos Giannakopoulos (GRE), Giorgios Karagounis (GRE), Vasilios Tsiartas (GRE), Frank de Boer (HOL), Mark van Bommel (HOL), Wilfred Bouma (HOL), Edgar Davids (HOL), Jimmy Floyd Hasselbaink (HOL), Pierre van Hooijdonck (HOL), André Ooijer (HOL), Marc Overmars (HOL), Arjen Robben (HOL), Clarence Seedorf (HOL), Zoltán Böör (HUN), Clinton Morrison (IRL), Thórdur Gudjónsson (ISL), Tryggvi Gudmundsson (ISL), Heidar Helgason (ISL), Hermann Hreidarsson (ISL), Petur Marteinsson (ISL), Helgi Sigurdsson (ISL), Walid Badier (ISR), Shay Holtzman (ISR), Marco Di Vaio (ITA), Simone Perrotta (ITA), Francesco Totti (ITA), Andrejs Prohorenkovs (LAT), Roger Beck (LIE), Michael Stocklasa (LIE), Robertas Poskus (LIT), Donatas Vencevicius (LIT), Dragan Dimitrovski (MCD), Mile Krstev (MCD), Goce Sedloski (MCD), Aco Stojkov (MCD), Vanco Trajanov (MCD), David Carabott (MLT), Luke Dimech (MLT), Vadim Boret (MOL), Boris Cebotari (MOL), Serghei Covalciuc (MOL), Serghei Dadu (MOL), Viorel Frunza (MOL), John Carew (NOR), Tore André Flo (NOR), Claus Lundekvam (NOR), Sigurd Rushfeldt (NOR), Pawel Kaczorowski (POL), Bartosz Karwan (POL), Tomasz Klos (POL), Kamil Kosowski (POL), Mariusz Kukielka (POL), HÉLDER Manuel Marques POSTIGA (POR), NUNO "GOMES" Miguel Soares Ribeiro (POR), Florin Bratu (ROM), Cristian Chivu (ROM), Tiberiu Ghioane (ROM), Mirel Radoi (ROM), Vladimir Beschastnykh (RUS),

	Vadim Evseev (RUS), Dmitri Kirichenko (RUS), Aleksandr Mostovoy (RUS), Viktor Onopko (RUS), Dmitri Sychev (RUS), Yegor Titov (RUS), Branko Boskovic (SBM), Goran Gavrancic (SBM), Sasa Ilic (SBM), Darko Kovacevic (SBM), Nikola Lazetic (SBM), Sinisa Mihajlovic (SBM), Savo Milosevic (SBM), Dragan Mladenovic (SBM), Zvonimir Vukic (SBM), Christian Dailly (SCO), Paul Dickov (SCO), Barry Ferguson (SCO), Darren Fletcher (SCO), Paul Lambert (SCO), Gary Naysmith (SCO), Lee Wilkie (SCO), Sebastjan Cimirotic (SLO), Aleksander Knavs (SLO), Ricardo Cabanas Rey (SUI), Fabio Celestini (SUI), Stéphane Chapuisat (SUI), Bernt Haas (SUI), Patrick Müller (SUI), Johan Vonlanthen (SUI), Murat Yakin (SUI), Martin Petráš (SVK), Andreas Jakobsson (SWE), Kim Källström (SWE), Olof Mellberg (SWE), Mikael Nilsson (SWE), Ümit Davala (TUR), Gökdeniz Karadeniz (TUR), Tümer Metin (TUR), Serhiy Fedorov (UKR), Serhiy Serebrennikov (UKR), Andriy Vorobey (UKR), Hennadiy Zubov (UKR), Craig Bellamy (WAL), Robert (Rob) Earnshaw (WAL), Ryan Giggs (WAL)
1 own goal	Ardian Aliaj (ALB) for Republic of Ireland, Emin Agayev (AZE) for Finland, Tarlan Akhmedov (AZE) for Italy, Stilian Petrov (BUL) for Belgium, Igor Tudor (CRO) for France Raio Piiroja (EST) for Belgium, Arne Friedrich (GER) for Faroe Islands, Phil Babb (IRL) for Russia, Marius Stankevicius (LIT) for Germany, Darren Debono (MLT) for Slovenia, Henning Berg (NOR) for Spain, JORGE Manuel Almeida Gomes de ANDRADE (POR) for the Netherlands, Cosmin Contra (ROM) for Denmark, Andrei Karyaka (RUS) for Switzerland, Carlo Valentini (SMR) for Latvia, Ludovic Magnin (SUI) for Republic of Ireland

UEFA Euro 2008

16-08-2006	Brussels	Belgium – Kazakhstan	0-0
02-09-2006	Belgrade	Serbia – Azerbaijan	1-0 (0-0)
02-09-2006	Bydgoszcz	Poland – Finland	1-3 (0-0)
06-09-2006	Baku	Azerbaijan – Kazakhstan	1-1 (1-1)
06-09-2006	Yerevan	Armenia – Belgium	0-1 (0-1)
06-09-2006	Helsinki	Finland – Portugal	1-1 (1-1)
06-09-2006	Warsaw	Poland – Serbia	1-1 (1-0)
07-10-2006	Almaty	Kazakhstan – Poland	0-1 (0-0)
07-10-2006	Yerevan	Armenia – Finland	0-0
07-10-2006	Belgrade	Serbia – Belgium	1-0 (0-0)
07-10-2006	Porto	Portugal – Azerbaijan	3-0 (2-0)
11-10-2006	Almaty	Kazakhstan – Finland	0-2 (0-1)
11-10-2006	Belgrade	Serbia – Armenia	3-0 (0-0)
11-10-2006	Chorzów	Poland – Portugal	2-1 (2-0)
11-10-2006	Brussels	Belgium – Azerbaijan	3-0 (1-0)
15-11-2006	Helsinki	Finland – Armenia	1-0 (1-0)
15-11-2006	Brussels	Belgium – Poland	0-1 (0-1)
15-11-2006	Coimbra	Portugal – Kazakhstan	3-0 (2-0)
24-03-2007	Almaty	Kazakhstan – Serbia	2-1 (0-0)
24-03-2007	Warsaw	Poland – Azerbaijan	5-0 (3-0)
24-03-2007	Lisbon	Portugal – Belgium	4-0 (0-0)
28-03-2007	Baku	Azerbaijan – Finland	1-0 (0-0)
28-03-2007	Kielce	Poland – Armenia	1-0 (1-0)
28-03-2007	Belgrade	Serbia – Portugal	1-1 (1-1)
02-06-2007	Almaty	Kazakhstan – Armenia	1-2 (0-2)
02-06-2007	Baku	Azerbaijan – Poland	1-3 (1-0)
02-06-2007	Helsinki	Finland – Serbia	0-2 (0-1)
02-06-2007	Brussels	Belgium – Portugal	1-2 (0-1)
06-06-2007	Almaty	Kazakhstan – Azerbaijan	1-1 (0-1)
06-06-2007	Helsinki	Finland – Belgium	2-0 (1-0)
06-06-2007	Yerevan	Armenia – Poland	1-0 (0-0)
22-08-2007	Yerevan	Armenia – Portugal	1-1 (1-1)
22-08-2007	Tampere	Finland – Kazakhstan	2-1 (1-1)
22-08-2007	Brussels	Belgium – Serbia	3-2 (2-0)
08-09-2007		Azerbaijan – Armenia	Cancelled
08-09-2007	Belgrade	Serbia – Finland	0-0
08-09-2007	Lisbon	Portugal – Poland	2-2 (0-1)
12-09-2007		Armenia – Azerbaijan	Cancelled
12-09-2007	Almaty	Kazakhstan – Belgium	2-2 (1-2)
12-09-2007	Helsinki	Finland – Poland	0-0
12-09-2007	Lisbon	Portugal – Serbia	1-1 (1-0)
13-10-2007	Yerevan	Armenia – Serbia	0-0

13-10-2007	Baku	Azerbaijan – Portugal	0-2 (0-2)
13-10-2007	Warsaw	Poland – Kazakhstan	3-1 (0-1)
13-10-2007	Brussels	Belgium – Finland	0-0
17-10-2007	Almaty	Kazakhstan – Portugal	1-2 (0-0)
17-10-2007	Baku	Azerbaijan – Serbia	1-6 (1-4)
17-10-2007	Brussels	Belgium – Armenia	3-0 (0-0)
17-11-2007	Helsinki	Finland – Azerbaijan	2-1 (0-0)
17-11-2007	Chorzów	Poland – Belgium	2-0 (1-0)
17-11-2007	Leiria	Portugal – Armenia	1-0 (1-0)
21-11-2007	Yerevan	Armenia – Kazakhstan	0-1 (0-0)
21-11-2007	Baku	Azerbaijan – Belgium	0-1 (0-0)
21-11-2007	Porto	Portugal – Finland	0-0
21-11-2007	Belgrade	Serbia – Poland	2-2 (0-1)
24-11-2007	Belgrade	Serbia – Kazakhstan	1-0 (0-0)

FINAL STANDING

Pos	Team	Pld	W	D	L	GF	GA	GD	Pts
1	*Poland*	*14*	*8*	*4*	*2*	*24*	*12*	*+12*	*28*
2	*Portugal*	*14*	*7*	*6*	*1*	*24*	*10*	*+14*	*27*
3	Serbia	14	6	6	2	22	11	+11	24
4	Finland	14	6	6	2	13	7	+6	24
5	Belgium	14	5	3	6	14	16	-2	18
6	Kazakhstan	14	2	4	8	11	21	-10	10
7	Armenia	12	2	3	7	4	13	-9	9
8	Azerbaijan	12	1	2	9	6	28	-22	5

Poland and Portugal qualified for the Final Tournament in Austria and Switzerland.

Armenia and Azerbaijan played only 12 matches due to UEFA's decision to cancel the two fixtures between these countries, with no points awarded to either team for the cancelled matches.

16-08-2006   Constant Vanden Stock, Brussels: Belgium – Kazakhstan   0-0
Belgium: Stijn Stijnen, Carl Hoefkens (75' Anthony vanden Borre), Jelle van Damme (60' Luigi Pieroni), Daniel van Buyten, Vincent Kompany (39' Stein Huysegems), Thomas Vermaelen, Timmy Simons (C), Bart Goor, Karel Geraerts, Thomas Buffel, Mousa Dembélé. (Coach: René Vandereycken (BEL)).
Kazakhstan: David Loria, Maksim Zhalmagambetov, Aleksandr Kuchma, Yegor Azovskiy, Eduard Sergienko (YC55), Nikita Khokhlov, Dmitriy Byakov, Samat Smakov (YC59), Andrei Karpovich (YC49) (53' Andrei Travin), Ruslan Baltiev (YC66), Nurbol Zhumaskaliyev (C). (Coach: Arnoldus Dick (Arno) Pijpers (HOL)).
Referee: Mark Courtney (NIR)   Attendance: 15.495

02-09-2006   Stadion Crvena Zvezda, Belgrade: Serbia – Azerbaijan   1-0 (0-0)
Serbia: Vladimir Stojkovic, Milan Stepanov, Marjan Markovic, Aleksandar Lukovic, Mladen
Krstajic, Dejan Stankovic (C), Igor Duljaj (YC30), Ognjen Koroman (64' Sasa Ilic), Nikola
Zigic, Marko Pantelic (81' Danijel Ljuboja), Danko Lazovic (74' Ivan Ergic). (Coach: Javier
Clemente Lázaro (ESP)).
Azerbaijan: Farkhad Veliyev, Sergei Sokolov, Aslan Kerimov (C), Zaur Gashimov, André
Luiz Ladaga (YC75) (77' Vagif Javadov), Yuri Muzika (62' Ilgar Gurbanov), Emin
Imamaliyev, Aleksandr Chertoganov, Ruslan Abbasov (YC65), Elmar Baxsiyev (YC20),
Farrukh Ismayilov (71' Samir Musaev). (Coach: Shahin Diniyev (AZE)).
Goal: Serbia: 1-0 Nikola Zigic (72').
Referee: Knut Kircher (GER)   Attendance: behind closed doors

02-09-2006   Zdzislaw Krzyszkowiak, Budgoszcz: Poland – Finland   1-3 (0-0)
Poland: Jerzy Dudek, Jacek Bak, Marcin Wasilewski, Arkadiusz Glowacki (RC74), Michal
Zewlakow, Jakub Blaszczykowski (46' Euzebiusz (Ebi) Smolarek), Miroslaw Szymkowiak
(46' Ireneusz Jelen), Arkadiusz (Arek) Radomski, Jacek Krzynówek, Tomasz Frankowski (73'
Lukasz Gargula), Maciej Zurawski (C). (Coach: Leo Beenhakker (HOL)).
Finland: Jussi Jääskeläinen, Sami Hyypiä, Hannu Tihinen, Petri Pasanen, Toni Kallio, Markus
Heikkinen, Mika Väyrynen (YC80), Teemu Tainio, Joonas Kolkka (79' Mika Nurmela),
Jonatan Johansson (67' Aleksei Eremenko), Jari Litmanen (C) (87' Mikael Forssell). (Coach:
Roy Hodgson (ENG)).
Goals: Poland: 1-3 Lukasz Gargula (90').
Finland: 0-1 Jari Litmanen (54'), 0-2 Jari Litmanen (76' penalty), 0-3 Mika Väyrynen (84').
Referee: Laurent Duhamel (FRA)   Attendance: 13.000

06-09-2006   Tofiq Bakhramov Stadium, Baku: Azerbaijan – Kazakhstan   1-1 (1-1)
Azerbaijan: Farkhad Veliyev, Sergei Sokolov (59' Yuri Muzika), Aslan Kerimov (C), André
Luiz Ladaga, Dzeykhun Sultanov (65' Samir Musaev), Emin Imamaliyev, Aleksandr
Chertoganov, Ruslan Abbasov (46' Rail Melikov), Leandro Melino Gomes (YC20), Ilgar
Gurbanov, Vagif Javadov. (Coach: Shahin Diniyev (AZE)).
Kazakhstan: David Loria, Aleksandr Kuchma, Yegor Azovskiy, Maksim Zhalmagambetov,
Eduard Sergienko, Nikita Khokhlov (YC90), Dmitriy Byakov, Samat Smakov, Andrei
Karpovich (67' Andrei Travin), Ruslan Baltiev (YC78), Nurbol Zhumaskaliyev (C) (75' Kairat
Utabayev). (Coach: Arnoldus Dick (Arno) Pijpers (HOL)).
Goals: Azerbaijan: 1-0 André Luiz Ladaga (16').
Kazakhstan: 1-1 Dmitriy Byakov (35').
Referee: Zsolt Szabó (HUN)   Attendance: 8.500

06-09-2006   Hanrapetakan Stadium, Yerevan: Armenia – Belgium   0-1 (0-1)
Armenia: Gevorg Kasparov, Karen Dokhoyan, Robert Arzumanyan, Sargis Hovsepyan (C),
Agvan Mkrtchyan (76' Arman Karamyan), Hamlet Vladi Mkhitaryan (82' Galust Petrosyan),
Egishe Melikyan, Romik Khachatryan (YC89), Karen Aleksanyan, Armen Shahgeldyan (72'
Aram Hakobyan), Samvel Melkonyan. (Coach: John (Ian) Porterfield (SCO)).
Belgium: Stijn Stijnen, Jelle van Damme (YC67), Carl Hoefkens, Pieter Collen (60' Anthony
vanden Borre (YC78)), Daniel van Buyten, Timmy Simons (C), Karel Geraerts, Gaëtan
Englebert, Koen Daerden (YC28) (66' Wim de Decker), Luigi Pieroni (YC86), Mousa
Dembélé (78' Steven Defour). (Coach: René Vandereycken (BEL)).
Goal: Belgium: 0-1 Daniel van Buyten (41').
Referee: Gerald Lehner (AUT)   Attendance: 4.122

84

06-09-2006 Olympic Stadium, Helsinki: Finland – Portugal 1-1 (1-1)
Finland: Jussi Jääskeläinen, Hannu Tihinen, Petri Pasanen, Toni Kallio, Sami Hyypiä, Mika Väyrynen, Teemu Tainio, Joonas Kolkka (81' Aleksei Eremenko (YC90+3)), Markus Heikkinen (YC66), Jari Litmanen (C) (YC30), Jonatan Johansson (65' Shefki Kuqi). (Coach: Roy Hodgson (ENG)).
Portugal: RICARDO Alexandre Martins Soares Pereira, RICARDO Miguel Moreira da COSTA (YC35,YC54), RICARDO Alberto Silveira de CARVALHO, NUNO Jorge Pereira Silva VALENTE, MARCO António Simões CANEIRA, Luís Carlos Almeida da Cunha "NANI" (57' Sergio Azevedo RICARDO ROCHA), Armando Gonçalves Teixeira PETIT (YC69), Anderson Luís de Souza "DECO" (86' TIAGO Cardoso Mendes), Francisco José Rodrigues Costa "COSTINHA" (C), NUNO "GOMES" Miguel Soares Pereira Ribeiro (76' JOÃO Filipe Iria Santos MOUTINHO), CRISTIANO RONALDO dos Santos Aveiro. (Coach: Luiz Felipe Scolari (BRA)).
Goals: Finland: 1-0 Jonatan Johansson (23').
Portugal: NUNO "GOMES" Miguel Soares Pereira Ribeiro (41').
Referee: Konrad Plautz (AUT)   Attendance: 38.015

06-09-2006 Stadion Wojska Polskiego, Warsaw: Poland – Serbia 1-1 (1-0)
Poland: Wojciech Kowalewski (YC90+2), Mariusz Jop, Jacek Bak, Michal Zewlakow, Pawel Golanski (YC20) (72' Marcin Wasilewski), Arkadiusz (Arek) Radomski, Mariusz Lewandowski, Jacek Krzynówek, Maciej Zurawski (C), Radoslaw Matusiak, Ireneusz Jelen (74' Jakub Blaszczykowski (YC79)). (Coach: Leo Beenhakker (HOL)).
Serbia: Vladimir Stojkovic, Milan Stepanov (YC55), Marjan Markovic (YC42), Mladen Krstajic (YC86), Milan Bisevac, Nenad Kovacevic, Aleksandar Trisovic (60' Danko Lazovic), Dejan Stankovic (C) (YC42), Igor Duljaj (66' Ivan Ergic), Nikola Zigic, Marko Pantelic (82' Ognjen Koroman). (Coach: Javier Clemente Lázaro (ESP)).
Goals: Poland: 1-0 Radoslaw Matusiak (30').
Serbia: 1-1 Danko Lazovic (73').
Referee: Graham Poll (ENG)   Attendance: 4.918

07-10-2006 Almaty Central Stadium, Almaty: Kazakhstan – Poland 0-1 (0-0)
Kazakhstan: David Loria, Aleksandr Kuchma, Yegor Azovskiy, Maksim Zhalmagambetov, Kairat Utabayev (YC32) (68' Kairat Ashirbekov (YC87)), Nikita Khokhlov, Dmitriy Byakov (YC63), Eduard Sergienko (81' Sergey Larin), Andrei Karpovich (59' Andrei Travin), Samat Smakov, Nurbol Zhumaskaliyev (C). (Coach: Arnoldus Dick (Arno) Pijpers (HOL)).
Poland: Wojciech Kowalewski, Grzegorz Bronowicki, Jacek Bak, Pawel Golanski, Jakub Blaszczykowski (87' Rafal Grzelak), Radoslaw Sobolewski, Arkadiusz (Arek) Radomski, Mariusz Lewandowski (30' Przemyslaw Kazmierczak), Maciej Zurawski (C) (71' Radoslaw Matusiak), Grzegorz Rasiak, Euzebiusz (Ebi) Smolarek. (Coach: Leo Beenhakker (HOL)).
Goal: Poland: 0-1 Euzebiusz (Ebi) Smolarek (52').
Referee: Edo Trivkovic (CRO)   Attendance: 18.000

85

07-10-2006   Hanrapetakan Stadium, Yerevan: Armenia – Finland   0-0
Armenia: Gevorg Kasparov, Karen Dokhoyan, Robert Arzumanyan (YC59), Sargis Hovsepyan
(C), Armen Tigranyan, Egishe Melikyan, Karen Aleksanyan (YC33) (56' Aram
Kh.Hakobyan), Edgar Manucharyan (78' Ara Hakobyan (YC87)), Armen Shahgeldyan,
Samvel Melkonyan (YC90), Arman Karamyan (46' Agvan Mkrtchyan). (Coach: John (Ian)
Porterfield (SCO)).
Finland: Jussi Jääskeläinen, Hannu Tihinen, Petri Pasanen, Toni Kallio, Sami Hyypiä (YC28),
Mika Väyrynen (72' Mika Nurmela), Joonas Kolkka, Markus Heikkinen (YC50), Jari
Litmanen (C), Shefki Kuqi (66' Mikael Forssell), Jonatan Johansson (83' Aki Riihilahti).
(Coach: Roy Hodgson (ENG)).
Referee: Damir Skomina (SLO)   Attendance: 2.800

07-10-2006   Stadion Crvena Zvezda, Belgrade: Serbia – Belgium   1-0 (0-0)
Serbia: Vladimir Stojkovic, Marjan Markovic (YC79), Mladen Krstajic, Nemanja Vidic, Ivica
Dragutinovic, Aleksandar Trisovic (59' Danko Lazovic), Dejan Stankovic (C), Nenad
Kovacevic, Ognjen Koroman (YC58) (72' Ivan Ergic), Nikola Zigic, Marko Pantelic (90' Igor
Duljaj). (Coach: Javier Clemente Lázaro (ESP)).
Belgium: Stijn Stijnen, Carl Hoefkens, Thomas Vermaelen, Daniel van Buyten, Vincent
Kompany (YC81), Timmy Simons (C) (YC86), Bart Goor (85' Kevin Vandenbergh), Karel
Geraerts, Gaby Mudingayi (75' Luigi Pieroni), Emile Mpenza, Mousa Dembélé (63' Mbo
Mpenza). (Coach: René Vandereycken (BEL)).
Goal: Serbia: 1-0 Nikola Zigic (54').
Referee: Domenico Messina (ITA)   Attendance: 16.901

07-10-2006   Bessa XXI, Porto: Portugal – Azerbaijan   3-0 (2-0)
Portugal: RICARDO Alexandre Martins Soares Pereira, Sergio Azevedo RICARDO ROCHA
(YC54), RICARDO Alberto Silveira de CARVALHO, NUNO Jorge Pereira Silva VALENTE
(YC23) (46' MARCO António Simões CANEIRA), Luis MIGUEL Brito Garcia Monteiro,
Nuno Ricardo de Oliveira Ribeiro "MANICHE" (63' TIAGO Cardoso Mendes), Anderson
Luís de Souza "DECO", Francisco José Rodrigues Costa "COSTINHA" (C), NUNO
"GOMES" Miguel Soares Pereira Ribeiro, SIMÃO Pedro Fonseca Sabrosa, CRISTIANO
RONALDO dos Santos Aveiro (73' Luís Carlos Almeida da Cunha "NANI"). (Coach: Luiz
Felipe Scolari (BRA)).
Azerbaijan: Farkhad Veliyev, Sergei Sokolov (YC29), Aslan Kerimov (C), Zaur Gashimov,
André Luiz Ladaga, Dzeykhun Sultanov (YC15) (63' Farrukh Ismayilov), Ernani Pereira
(YC44), Yuri Muzika (66' Ilgar Gurbanov), Emin Imamaliyev, Aleksandr Chertoganov,
Leandro Melino Gomes (76' Vagif Javadov). (Coach: Shahin Diniyev (AZE)).
Goals: Portugal: 1-0 CRISTIANO RONALDO dos Santos Aveiro (24'), 2-0 RICARDO
Alberto Silveira de CARVALHO (30'), 3-0 CRISTIANO RONALDO dos Santos Aveiro
(63').
Referee: Mark Richard Halsey (ENG)   Attendance: 14.000

11-10-2006   Almaty Central Stadium, Almaty: Kazakhstan – Finland   0-2 (0-1)
Kazakhstan: David Loria, Maksim Zhalmagambetov, Aleksandr Kuchma, Yegor Azovskiy,
Andrei Travin (82' Maksim Azovskiy), Eduard Sergienko (76' Sergey Larin), Nikita
Khokhlov, Dmitriy Byakov, Samat Smakov, Ruslan Baltiev, Nurbol Zhumaskaliyev (C) (63'
Kairat Ashirbekov). (Coach: Arnoldus Dick (Arno) Pijpers (HOL)).
Finland: Jussi Jääskeläinen, Hannu Tihinen, Petri Pasanen, Toni Kallio (YC25), Sami Hyypiä,
Mika Väyrynen (90' Aki Riihilahti), Mika Nurmela, Joonas Kolkka, Jari Ilola, Jari Litmanen
(C), Mikael Forssell (72' Shefki Kuqi). (Coach: Roy Hodgson (ENG)).
Goals: Finland: 0-1 Jari Litmanen (28'), 0-2 Sami Hyypiä (64').
Referee: Athanassios Briakos (GRE)   Attendance: 17.863

11-10-2006   Stadion Crvena Zvezda, Belgrade: Serbia – Armenia   3-0 (0-0)
Serbia: Vladimir Stojkovic, Milan Stepanov, Mladen Krstajic, Ivica Dragutinovic, Aleksandar Trisovic (46' Danko Lazovic), Dejan Stankovic (C) (YC47), Nenad Kovacevic, Igor Duljaj, Ognjen Koroman (71' Ivan Ergic), Nikola Zigic, Marko Pantelic (46' Sasa Ilic). (Coach: Javier Clemente Lázaro (ESP)).
Armenia: Gevorg Kasparov (YC52), Karen Dokhoyan, Robert Arzumanyan (YC13), Sargis Hovsepyan (C), Rafael Nazaryan (YC13,YC76), Agvan Mkrtchyan, Egishe Melikyan, Edgar Manucharyan (78' Armen Tigranyan), Armen Shahgeldyan (64' Nshan Erzrumyan), Samvel Melkonyan, Aram Kh.Hakobyan (68' Artur Hrantovich Minasyan). (Coach: John (Ian) Porterfield (SCO)).
Goals: Serbia: 1-0 Dejan Stankovic (53' penalty), 2-0 Danko Lazovic (61'), 3-0 Nikola Zigic (90'+2').
Referee: Georgios Kasnaferis (GRE)   Attendance: 10.987

11-10-2006   Stadion Slaski, Chorzów: Poland – Portugal   2-1 (2-0)
Poland: Wojciech Kowalewski (YC90+2), Grzegorz Bronowicki, Jacek Bak, Pawel Golanski, Radoslaw Sobolewski, Arkadiusz (Arek) Radomski, Jakub Blaszczykowski (66' Jacek Krzynówek), Mariusz Lewandowski (YC20), Maciej Zurawski (C), Grzegorz Rasiak (74' Radoslaw Matusiak), Euzebiusz (Ebi) Smolarek. (Coach: Leo Beenhakker (HOL)).
Portugal: RICARDO Alexandre Martins Soares Pereira, Sergio Azevedo RICARDO ROCHA (YC62), RICARDO Alberto Silveira de CARVALHO, NUNO Jorge Pereira Silva VALENTE, Luis MIGUEL Brito Garcia Monteiro, Armando Gonçalves Teixeira PETIT (68' Luís Carlos Almeida da Cunha "NANI"), Anderson Luís de Souza "DECO" (83' Nuno Ricardo de Oliveira Ribeiro "MANICHE"), Francisco José Rodrigues Costa "COSTINHA" (C) (46' TIAGO Cardoso Mendes), NUNO "GOMES" Miguel Soares Pereira Ribeiro, SIMÃO Pedro Fonseca Sabrosa (YC44), CRISTIANO RONALDO dos Santos Aveiro. (Coach: Luiz Felipe Scolari (BRA)).
Goals: Poland: 1-0 Euzebiusz (Ebi) Smolarek (9'), 2-0 Euzebiusz (Ebi) Smolarek (18').
Portugal: 2-1 NUNO "GOMES" Miguel Soares Pereira Ribeiro (90'+2').
Referee: Wolfgang Stark (GER)   Attendance: 38.199

11-10-2006   Constant Vanden Stock, Brussels: Belgium – Azerbaijan   3-0 (1-0)
Belgium: Stijn Stijnen, Philippe Léonard, Carl Hoefkens, Thomas Vermaelen, Anthony vanden Borre (77' Mbo Mpenza), Daniel van Buyten (YC14), Timmy Simons (C), Bart Goor (YC15), Karel Geraerts, Kevin Vandenbergh (86' Luigi Pieroni), Emile Mpenza (70' Mousa Dembélé (RC86)). (Coach: René Vandereycken (BEL)).
Azerbaijan: Farkhad Veliyev (YC23), Sergei Sokolov, Aslan Kerimov (C) (YC86), Zaur Gashimov (77' Vüqar Nadirov), André Luiz Ladaga, Dzeykhun Sultanov (55' Vagif Javadov), Ernani Pereira, Yuri Muzika (YC29,RC45+3) (33' Ilgar Gurbanov), Emin Imamaliyev, Aleksandr Chertoganov, Leandro Melino Gomes. (Coach: Shahin Diniyev (AZE)).
Goals: Belgium: 1-0 Timmy Simons (24' penalty), 2-0 Kevin Vandenbergh (47'), 3-0 Mousa Dembélé (82').
Referee: Romans Lajuks (LAT)   Attendance: 11.917

15-11-2006   Finnair Stadium, Helsinki: Finland – Armenia   1-0 (1-0)
Finland: Jussi Jääskeläinen, Hannu Tihinen, Ari Nyman, Toni Kallio, Sami Hyypiä (C), Mika Väyrynen (46' Jari Ilola), Mika Nurmela, Joonas Kolkka, Markus Heikkinen, Aleksei Eremenko (88' Shefki Kuqi), Jonatan Johansson. (Coach: Roy Hodgson (ENG)).
Armenia: Gevorg Kasparov, Aleksandr Tadevosyan (YC62), Karen Dokhoyan (46' Valeri Aleksanyan), Sargis Hovsepyan (C), Levon Pachajyan (YC26), Agvan Mkrtchyan, Hamlet Vladi Mkhitaryan (74' Ara Hakobyan), Romik Khachatryan, Artavazd Karamyan (YC27), Robert Zebelyan (YC72) (79' Arman Karamyan), Armen Shahgeldyan (YC89). (Coach: John (Ian) Porterfield (SCO)).
Goal: Finland: 1-0 Mika Nurmela (8').
Referee: Craig Alexander Thomson (SCO)   Attendance: 9.445

15-11-2006   King Baudouin Stadium, Brussels: Belgium – Poland   0-1 (0-1)
Belgium: Stijn Stijnen, Philippe Léonard (YC57) (79' Gaby Mudingayi), Carl Hoefkens, Daniel van Buyten, Thomas Vermaelen (YC25), Anthony vanden Borre (46' Stein Huysegems), Timmy Simons (C) (YC88), Bart Goor (YC88), Karel Geraerts (YC12), Emile Mpenza, Kevin Vandenbergh (62' Luigi Pieroni). (Coach: René Vandereycken (BEL)).
Poland: Artur Boruc, Grzegorz Bronowicki, Jacek Bak, Marcin Wasilewski, Michal Zewlakow, Radoslaw Sobolewski (YC26), Jakub Blaszczykowski (YC58), Dariusz Dudka (79' Rafal Murawski), Radoslaw Matusiak (88' Przemyslaw Kazmierczak), Maciej Zurawski (C) (62' Lukasz Gargula), Euzebiusz (Ebi) Smolarek. (Coach: Leo Beenhakker (HOL)).
Goal: Poland: 0-1 Radoslaw Matusiak (19').
Referee: Stuart Dougal (SCO)   Attendance: 37.978

15-11-2006   Estádio Cidade de Coimbra, Coimbra: Portugal – Kazakhstan   3-0 (2-0)
Portugal: RICARDO Alexandre Martins Soares Pereira, António Leonel Vilar Nogueira Sousa "TONEL" (76' JORGE Manuel Almeida Gomez de ANDRADE), RICARDO Alberto Silveira de CARVALHO, PAULO Renato Rebocho FERREIRA, Luis MIGUEL Brito Garcia Monteiro, TIAGO Cardoso Mendes, RAÚL José Trindade MEIRELES, Anderson Luís de Souza "DECO" (63' CARLOS Jorge Neto MARTINS), NUNO "GOMES" Miguel Soares Pereira Ribeiro (C), SIMÃO Pedro Fonseca Sabrosa (YC50), CRISTIANO RONALDO dos Santos Aveiro (56' RICARDO Andrade QUARESMA Bernardo). (Coach: Luiz Felipe Scolari (BRA)).
Kazakhstan: David Loria, Maksim Zhalmagambetov, Aleksandr Kuchma, Yegor Azovskiy, Andrei Travin (YC65), Eduard Sergienko (73' Sergey Larin), Nikita Khokhlov, Dmitriy Byakov, Samat Smakov, Ruslan Baltiev, Nurbol Zhumaskaliyev (C). (Coach: Arnoldus Dick (Arno) Pijpers (HOL)).
Goals: Portugal: 1-0 SIMÃO Pedro Fonseca Sabrosa (8'), 2-0 CRISTIANO RONALDO dos Santos Aveiro (30'), 3-0 SIMÃO Pedro Fonseca Sabrosa (84').
Referee: René Rogalla (SUI)   Attendance: 29.500

24-03-2007   Almaty Central Stadium, Almaty: Kazakhstan – Serbia   2-1 (0-0)
Kazakhstan: David Loria (YC59), Maksim Zhalmagambetov, Aleksandr Kuchma, Farkhadbek Irismetov (YC7), Eduard Sergienko (58' Anton Chichulin), Kairat Ashirbekov (71' Dmitriy Byakov), Sergei Skorykh, Samat Smakov, Ruslan Baltiev (YC42), Nurbol Zhumaskaliyev (C), Murat Suyumagambetov (80' Andrei Finonchenko). (Coach: Arnoldus Dick (Arno) Pijpers (HOL)).
Serbia: Vladimir Stojkovic, Milan Stepanov, Marjan Markovic, Nemanja Vidic (C) (YC63), Dusko Tosic, Milos Krasic (YC56), Nenad Kovacevic, Ivan Ergic (70' Ognjen Koroman), Bosko Jankovic, Nikola Zigic (RC90), Marko Pantelic (69' Danko Lazovic). (Coach: Javier Clemente Lázaro (ESP)).
Goals: Kazakhstan: 1-0 Kairat Ashirbekov (47'), 2-0 Nurbol Zhumaskaliyev (61').
Serbia: 2-1 Nikola Zigic (68').
Referee: Vladimír Hrinák (SVK)   Attendance: 19.600

24-03-2007   Stadion Wojska Polskiego, Warsaw: Poland – Azerbaijan   5-0 (3-0)
Poland: Artur Boruc, Marcin Wasilewski, Jacek Bak, Michal Zewlakow, Wojciech Lobodzinski, Mariusz Lewandowski, Jacek Krzynówek (79' Ireneusz Jelen), Lukasz Gargula, Dariusz Dudka, Maciej Zurawski (C), Radoslaw Matusiak (69' Przemyslaw Kazmierczak). (Coach: Leo Beenhakker (HOL)).
Azerbaijan: Jahangir Hasanzade, Aslan Kerimov (C), Ernani Pereira, Emin Imamaliyev (65' Murad Aghakishiyev), Aleksandr Chertoganov, Samir Abbasov, Elmar Baxsiyev, Branimir Subasic, Ilgar Gurbanov (YC61), Leandro Melino Gomes (62' André Luiz Ladaga), Kanan Kerimov (YC29) (67' Vagif Javadov (YC78)). (Coach: Shahin Diniyev (AZE)).
Goals: Poland: 1-0 Jacek Bak (3'), 2-0 Dariusz Dudka (6'), 3-0 Wojciech Lobodzinski (34'), 4-0 Jacek Krzynówek (58'), 5-0 Przemyslaw Kazmierczak (84').
Referee: Kristinn Jakobsson (ISL)   Attendance: 12.000

24-03-2007   José Alvalade, Lisbon: Portugal – Belgium   4-0 (0-0)
Portugal: RICARDO Alexandre Martins Soares Pereira, PAULO Renato Rebocho FERREIRA, RICARDO Alberto Silveira de CARVALHO, Luis MIGUEL Brito Garcia Monteiro, JORGE Manuel Almeida Gomez de ANDRADE (C), TIAGO Cardoso Mendes, RICARDO Andrade QUARESMA Bernardo (70' Luís Carlos Almeida da Cunha "NANI" (YC80)), Armando Gonçalves Teixeira PETIT (76' FERNANDO José da Silva Freitas MEIRA), JOÃO Filipe Iria Santos MOUTINHO, NUNO "GOMES" Miguel Soares Pereira Ribeiro, CRISTIANO RONALDO dos Santos Aveiro (YC45) (78' HUGO Miguel Ferreira Gomes VIANA). (Coach: Luiz Felipe Scolari (BRA)).
Belgium: Stijn Stijnen, Peter van der Heyden, Carl Hoefkens (YC15) (64' François Sterchele), Philippe Clement, Daniel van Buyten (C), Maarten Martens (56' Thomas Chatelle), Mark de Man (YC38), Gaby Mudingayi, Marouane Fellaini (YC58), Steven Defour, Mbo Mpenza (81' Jelle van Damme (YC89)). (Coach: René Vandereycken (BEL)).
Goals: Portugal: 1-0 NUNO "GOMES" Miguel Soares Pereira Ribeiro (53'), 2-0 CRISTIANO RONALDO dos Santos Aveiro (55'), 3-0 RICARDO Andrade QUARESMA Bernardo (69'), 4-0 CRISTIANO RONALDO dos Santos Aveiro (75').
Referee: Kyros Vassaras (GRE)   Attendance: 47.009

28-03-2007   Tofiw Bakhramov Stadium, Baku: Azerbaijan – Finland 1-0 (0-0)
Azerbaijan: Farkhad Veliyev, Aslan Kerimov (C), André Luiz Ladaga (66' Emin Imamaliyev),
Ramin Guliyev, Dzeykhun Sultanov (YC59) (76' Ilgar Gurbanov), Ernani Pereira, Aleksandr
Chertoganov (YC69), Samir Abbasov, Branimir Subasic, Leandro Melino Gomes (10' Vüqar
Nadirov (YC49)), Murad Aghakishiyev. (Coach: Shahin Diniyev (AZE)).
Finland: Jussi Jääskeläinen, Hannu Tihinen, Petri Pasanen, Toni Kallio, Sami Hyypiä, Aleksei
Eremenko (YC28), Mika Väyrynen, Joonas Kolkka (85' Shefki Kuqi), Markus Heikkinen, Jari
Litmanen (C), Jonatan Johansson (86' Mikael Forssell). (Coach: Roy Hodgson (ENG)).
Goal: Azerbaijan: 1-0 Emin Imamaliyev (82').
Referee: Domenico Messina (ITA)   Attendance: 14.500

28-03-2007   Kielce City Stadium, Kielce: Poland – Armenia 1-0 (1-0)
Poland: Artur Boruc, Marcin Wasilewski, Jacek Bak, Michal Zewlakow, Przemyslaw
Kazmierczak (61' Radoslaw Sobolewski), Jakub Blaszczykowski, Mariusz Lewandowski,
Jacek Krzynówek (83' Ireneusz Jelen), Lukasz Gargula, Dariusz Dudka, Maciej Zurawski (C).
(Coach: Leo Beenhakker (HOL)).
Armenia: Roman Berezovskiy, Karen Dokhoyan (YC80), Robert Arzumanyan, Sargis
Hovsepyan (C), Levon Pachajyan (YC60), Rafael Nazaryan (46' Edgar Manucharyan), Egishe
Melikyan (YC28), Romik Khachatryan (YC82), Artavazd Karamyan (68' Samvel Melkonyan),
Robert Zebelyan, Armen Shahgeldyan (75' Hamlet Vladi Mkhitaryan). (Coach: John (Ian)
Porterfield (SCO)).
Goal: Poland: 1-0 Maciej Zurawski (26').
Referee: Alberto Undiano Mallenco (ESP)   Attendance: 13.450

28-03-2007   Stadion Crvena Zvezda, Belgrade: Serbia – Portugal 1-1 (1-1)
Serbia: Vladimir Stojkovic, Mladen Krstajic, Ivica Dragutinovic (YC62), Nemanja Vidic,
Dusko Tosic (84' Danko Lazovic), Milos Krasic, Nenad Kovacevic, Igor Duljaj, Dejan
Stankovic (C) (YC7) (78' Marjan Markovic), Bosko Jankovic (YC40) (64' Ognjen Koroman),
Marko Pantelic (YC35). (Coach: Javier Clemente Lázaro (ESP)).
Portugal: RICARDO Alexandre Martins Soares Pereira, PAULO Renato Rebocho FERREIRA
(YC50), Luis MIGUEL Brito Garcia Monteiro (72' MARCO António Simões CANEIRA),
JORGE Manuel Almeida Gomez de ANDRADE (C), RICARDO Alberto Silveira de
CARVALHO, JOÃO Filipe Iria Santos MOUTINHO (77' RAÚL José Trindade MEIRELES),
TIAGO Cardoso Mendes (YC59), Armando Gonçalves Teixeira PETIT, NUNO "GOMES"
Miguel Soares Pereira Ribeiro (82' RICARDO Andrade QUARESMA Bernardo),
CRISTIANO RONALDO dos Santos Aveiro (YC36), SIMÃO Pedro Fonseca Sabrosa.
(Coach: Luiz Felipe Scolari (BRA)).
Goals: Serbia: 1-1 Bosko Jankovic (37').
Portugal: 0-1 TIAGO Cardoso Mendes (5').
Referee: Bertrand Layec (FRA)   Attendance: 46.810

02-06-2007   Almaty Central Stadium, Almaty: Kazakhstan – Armenia 1-2 (0-2)
Kazakhstan: David Loria, Aleksandr Kuchma (YC35), Farkhadbek Irismetov, Maksim Zhalmagambetov, Eduard Sergienko (36' Dmitriy Byakov), Samat Smakov, Anton Chichulin, Ruslan Baltiev, Zhambyl Kukeyev (57' Murat Tleshev), Nurbol Zhumaskaliyev (C) (78' Oleg Kornienko), Murat Suyumagambetov. (Coach: Arnoldus Dick (Arno) Pijpers (HOL)).
Armenia: Gevorg Kasparov, Aleksandr Tadevosyan, Robert Arzumanyan, Ararat Arakelyan (80' Aram Hakobyan), Vahagn Minasyan, Sargis Hovsepyan (C), Artur Voskanyan, Agvan Mkrtchyan, Egishe Melikyan, Hamlet Vladi Mkhitaryan (YC67) (75' Armen Shahgeldyan), Samvel Melkonyan (YC66) (90' Arman Karamyan). (Coach: John (Ian) Porterfield (SCO)).
Goals: Kazakhstan: 1-2 Ruslan Baltiev (88' penalty).
Armenia: 0-1 Robert Arzumanyan (31'), 0-2 Sargis Hovsepyan (39' penalty).
Referee: Pavel Královec (CZE)   Attendance: 17.100

02-06-2007   Tofiq Bakhramov Stadium, Baku: Azerbaijan – Poland 1-3 (1-0)
Azerbaijan: Farkhad Veliyev (YC25), Aslan Kerimov (C), Samir Abbasov, Emin Guliyev, Ramin Guliyev, Emin Imamaliyev (70' Zaur Gashimov), Aleksandr Chertoganov, Ramazan Abbasov (YC5), Alim Gurbanov (YC33) (65' Ilgar Gurbanov), Branimir Subasic, Khagani Mammadov (53' Vagif Javadov (YC62)). (Coach: Shahin Diniyev (AZE)).
Poland: Artur Boruc, Marcin Wasilewski (YC80), Jacek Bak, Michal Zewlakow, Jakub Blaszczykowski (57' Wojciech Lobodzinski), Mariusz Lewandowski, Jacek Krzynówek, Dariusz Dudka, Maciej Zurawski (C) (57' Marek Saganowski), Grzegorz Rasiak (81' Radoslaw Sobolewski), Euzebiusz (Ebi) Smolarek. (Coach: Leo Beenhakker (HOL)).
Goals: Azerbaijan: 1-0 Branimir Subasic (6').
Poland: 1-1 Euzebiusz (Ebi) Smolarek (63'), 1-2 Jacek Krzynówek (66'), 1-3 Jacek Krzynówek (90').
Referee: Costas Kapitanis (CYP)   Attendance: 25.800

02-06-2007   Olympic Stadium, Helsinki: Finland – Serbia 0-2 (0-1)
Finland: Jussi Jääskeläinen, Hannu Tihinen, Petri Pasanen, Toni Kallio, Sami Hyypiä (C) (YC77), Mika Väyrynen, Teemu Tainio (28' Joonas Kolkka), Jari Ilola, Markus Heikkinen, Shefki Kuqi (70' Jari Litmanen), Mikael Forssell (62' Jonatan Johansson). (Coach: Roy Hodgson (ENG)).
Serbia: Vladimir Stojkovic, Mladen Krstajic, Nemanja Vidic, Antonio Rukavina, Ivica Dragutinovic, Dejan Stankovic (C) (YC77), Milos Krasic (85' Igor Duljaj), Nenad Kovacevic (YC27), Zdravko Kuzmanovic, Bosko Jankovic (67' Danko Lazovic), Marko Pantelic (60' Milan Jovanovic). (Coach: Javier Clemente Lázaro (ESP)).
Goals: Serbia: 0-1 Bosko Jankovic (3'), 0-2 Milan Jovanovic (86').
Referee: Manuel Enrique Mejuto González (ESP)   Attendance: 33.615

91

02-06-2007   King Baudouin Stadium, Brussels: Belgium – Portugal 1-2 (0-1)
Belgium: Stijn Stijnen, Carl Hoefkens (45'+2' Mark de Man), Philippe Clement, Thomas
Vermaelen, Timmy Simons (C), Jan Vertonghen, Gaby Mudingayi (76' Karel Geraerts),
Marouane Fellaini, Steven Defour (YC63), François Sterchele (61' Tom de Mul), Emile
Mpenza. (Coach: René Vandereycken (BEL)).
Portugal: RICARDO Alexandre Martins Soares Pereira, PAULO Renato Rebocho FERREIRA,
Luís MIGUEL Brito Garcia Monteiro (53' José BOSINGWA da Silva), JORGE Manuel
Almeida Gomez de ANDRADE (C), FERNANDO José da Silva Freitas MEIRA, TIAGO
Cardoso Mendes, RICARDO Andrade QUARESMA Bernardo (YC76), Armando Gonçalves
Teixeira PETIT (YC78), Luís Carlos Almeida da Cunha "NANI" (86' Sergio Paulo Barbosa
Valente "DUDA"), Anderson Luís de Souza "DECO", HÉLDER Manuel Marques POSTIGA
(YC52) (79' HUGO Miguel Pereira de ALMEIDA (RC90+4)). (Coach: Luiz Felipe Scolari
(BRA)).
Goals: Belgium: 1-1 Marouane Fellaini (55').
Portugal: 0-1 Luís Carlos Almeida da Cunha "NANI" (43'), 1-2 HÉLDER Manuel Marques
POSTIGA (64').
Referee: Martin Hansson (SWE)   Attendance: 45.383

06-06-2007   Almaty Central Stadium, Almaty: Kazakhstan – Azerbaijan 1-1 (0-1)
Kazakhstan: David Loria, Maksim Zhalmagambetov (RC45), Aleksandr Kuchma, Farkhadbek
Irismetov, Dmitriy Byakov, Samat Smakov, Andrei Karpovich, Anton Chichulin, Ruslan
Baltiev, Nurbol Zhumaskaliyev (C) (90'+3' Kairat Utabayev), Sergei Ostapenko (69' Murat
Tleshev). (Coach: Arnoldus Dick (Arno) Pijpers (HOL)).
Azerbaijan: Jahangir Hasanzade, Zaur Gashimov, Ramin Guliyev, Emin Guliyev (YC70),
Samir Abbasov, Dzeykhun Sultanov (74' Alim Gurbanov), Aleksandr Chertoganov, Ramazan
Abbasov, Branimir Subasic, Vüqar Nadirov (84' Khagani Mammadov), Kanan Kerimov (C)
(58' Emin Imamaliyev). (Coach: Shahin Diniyev (AZE)).
Goals: Kazakhstan: 1-1 Ruslan Baltiev (53').
Azerbaijan: 0-1 Vüqar Nadirov (30').
Referee: Albert (Abby) Toussaint (LUX)   Attendance: 11.800

06-06-2007   Olympic Stadium, Helsinki: Finland – Belgium 2-0 (1-0)
Finland: Jussi Jääskeläinen, Hannu Tihinen (C), Petri Pasanen, Ari Nyman, Toni Kallio,
Roman Eremenko, Aleksei Eremenko (89' Mikael Forssell), Mika Väyrynen (YC36), Joonas
Kolkka (88' Mika Nurmela), Markus Heikkinen, Jonatan Johansson. (Coach: Roy Hodgson
(ENG)).
Belgium: Stijn Stijnen, Jan Vertonghen, Jelle van Damme (YC85), Philippe Clement, Thomas
Vermaelen (45'+2' Maarten Martens), Timmy Simons (C), Mark de Man, Marouane Fellaini
(YC16,YC51), Steven Defour, Emile Mpenza (86' François Sterchele), Tom de Mul (55' Faris
Haroun). (Coach: René Vandereycken (BEL)).
Goals: Finland: 1-0 Jonatan Johansson (27'), 2-0 Aleksei Eremenko (71').
Referee: Michael (Mike) Riley (ENG)   Attendance: 34.818

92

06-06-2007   Habrapetakan Stadium, Yerevan: Armenia – Poland   1-0 (0-0)
Armenia: Gevorg Kasparov, Aleksandr Tadevosyan, Robert Arzumanyan, Ararat Arakelyan, Sargis Hovsepyan (C), Vahagn Minasyan (78' Levon Pachajyan), Hamlet Vladi Mkhitaryan (74' Arman Karamyan), Artur Voskanyan, Agvan Mkrtchyan (YC41), Egishe Melikyan, Armen Shahgeldyan (46' Aram Hakobyan). (Coach: John (Ian) Porterfield (SCO)).
Poland: Artur Boruc, Marcin Wasilewski, Grzegorz Bronowicki (YC84), Jacek Bak (C) (65' Radoslaw Sobolewski), Michal Zewlakow, Wojciech Lobodzinski (60' Jakub Blaszczykowski), Mariusz Lewandowski, Jacek Krzynówek, Dariusz Dudka, Euzebiusz (Ebi) Smolarek (60' Maciej Zurawski), Marek Saganowski. (Coach: Leo Beenhakker (HOL)).
Goal: Armenia: 1-0 Hamlet Vladi Mkhitaryan (66').
Referee: Pavel Cristian Balaj (ROM)   Attendance: 9.800

22-08-2007   HanrapetakanStadium, Yereven: Armenia – Portugal   1-1 (1-1)
Armenia: Roman Berezovskiy, Aleksandr Tadevosyan, Robert Arzumanyan, Ararat Arakelyan, Sargis Hovsepyan (C), Hamlet Vladi Mkhitaryan (59' Gevorg Ghazaryan), Artavazd Karamyan (70' Egishe Melikyan), Artur Voskanyan, Levon Pachajyan, Agvan Mkrtchyan, Samvel Melkonyan (90' Romik Khachatryan). (Coach: John (Ian) Porterfield (SCO)).
Portugal: RICARDO Alexandre Martins Soares Pereira, PAULO Renato Rebocho FERREIRA, Luis MIGUEL Brito Garcia Monteiro, JORGE Manuel Almeida Gomez de ANDRADE (C) (YC69) (76' BRUNO Eduardo Regufe ALVES), FERNANDO José da Silva Freitas MEIRA, TIAGO Cardoso Mendes, RAÚL José Trindade MEIRELES, Anderson Luís de Souza "DECO", HÉLDER Manuel Marques POSTIGA (61' NUNO "GOMES" Miguel Soares Pereira Ribeiro), SIMÃO Pedro Fonseca Sabrosa (63' RICARDO Andrade QUARESMA Bernardo), CRISTIANO RONALDO dos Santos Aveiro. (Coach: Luiz Felipe Scolari (BRA)).
Goals: Armenia: 1-0 Robert Arzumanyan (11').
Portugal: 1-1 CRISTIANO RONALDO dos Santos Aveiro (37').
Referee: Claus Bo Larsen (DEN)   Attendance: 14.935

22-08-2007   Ratina Stadion, Tampere: Finland – Kazakhstan   2-1 (1-1)
Finland: Jussi Jääskeläinen (YC79), Hannu Tihinen, Petri Pasanen, Toni Kallio (YC82), Sami Hyypiä (C), Aleksei Eremenko, Teemu Tainio (76' Aki Riihilahti), Joonas Kolkka (88' Mika Nurmela), Markus Heikkinen (YC56), Roman Eremenko (46' Daniel Sjölund), Jonatan Johansson. (Coach: Roy Hodgson (ENG)).
Kazakhstan: David Loria, Aleksandr Kuchma, Farkhadbek Irismetov, Yegor Azovskiy, Sergey Larin (78' Kairat Ashirbekov), Dmitriy Byakov, Samat Smakov, Sergei Skorykh (YC41) (69' Anton Chichulin), Ruslan Baltiev (YC32), Nurbol Zhumaskaliyev (C), Sergei Ostapenko (70' Murat Suyumagambetov). (Coach: Arnoldus Dick (Arno) Pijpers (HOL)).
Goals: Finland: 1-0 Aleksei Eremenko (13'), 2-1 Teemu Tainio (61').
Kazakhstan: 1-1 Dmitriy Byakov (23').
Referee: Viktor Kassai (HUN)   Attendance: 13.407

93

22-08-2007   King Baudouin Stadium, Brussels: Belgium – Serbia 3-2 (2-0)
Belgium: Stijn Stijnen, Carl Hoefkens, Thomas Vermaelen,Vincent Kompany, Timmy Simons (C), Bart Goor (YC32), Karel Geraerts, Gaby Mudingayi, Steven Defour (86' Mpo Mpenza), Kevin Mirallas (67' Anthony vanden Borre), Mousa Dembélé (90' Nicolas Lombaerts). (Coach: René Vandereycken (BEL)).
Serbia: Vladimir Stojkovic, Mladen Krstajic (C) (YC78), Nemanja Vidic (YC90+4), Antonio Rukavina, Ivica Dragutinovic, Nenad Kovacevic, Zdravko Kuzmanovic, Ognjen Koroman (56' Milos Krasic), Bosko Jankovic, Marko Pantelic (56' Milan Jovanovic), Danko Lazovic (70' Milan Smiljanic). (Coach: Javier Clemente Lázaro (ESP)).
Goals: Belgium: 1-0 Mousa Dembélé (10'), 2-0 Kevin Mirallas (30'), 3-1 Mousa Dembélé (88').
Serbia: 2-1 Zdravko Kuzmanovic (73'), 3-2 Zdravko Kuzmanovic (90'+1').
Referee: Terje Hauge (NOR)   Attendance: 19.202

08-09-2007   Azerbaijan – Armenia   Cancelled

08-09-2007   Stadion Crvena Zvezda, Belgrade: Serbia – Finland 0-0
Serbia: Vladimir Stojkovic, Dusko Tosic (53' Zoran Tosic (YC77)), Antonio Rukavina, Branislav Ivanovic, Ivica Dragutinovic, Dejan Stankovic (C), Milos Krasic, Nenad Kovacevic, Zdravko Kuzmanovic, Bosko Jankovic YC20) (54' Milan Jovanovic), Danko Lazovic (62' Nikola Zigic). (Coach: Javier Clemente Lázaro (ESP)).
Finland: Jussi Jääskeläinen, Hannu Tihinen, Petri Pasanen, Toni Kuivasto, Sami Hyypiä (C) (YC19), Teemu Tainio (YC71), Mika Nurmela, Markus Heikkinen, Aleksei Eremenko (74' Mikael Forssell), Daniel Sjölund, Jonatan Johansson (78' Jarkko Wiss). (Coach: Roy Hodgson (ENG)).
Referee: Eric Frederikus Johannes Braamhaar (HOL)   Attendance: 10.530

08-09-2007   Estádio da Luz, Lisbon: Portugal – Poland 2-2 (0-1)
Portugal: RICARDO Alexandre Martins Soares Pereira, FERNANDO José da Silva Freitas MEIRA, MARCO António Simões CANEIRA (12' Luis MIGUEL Brito Garcia Monteiro), BRUNO Eduardo Regufe ALVES, José BOSINGWA da Silva, Nuno Ricardo de Oliveira Ribeiro "MANICHE", Anderson Luís de Souza "DECO", Armando Gonçalves Teixeira PETIT, NUNO "GOMES" Miguel Soares Pereira Ribeiro (C) (69' RICARDO Andrade QUARESMA Bernardo), CRISTIANO RONALDO dos Santos Aveiro, SIMÃO Pedro Fonseca Sabrosa (81' JOÃO Filipe Iria Santos MOUTINHO). (Coach: Luiz Felipe Scolari (BRA)).
Poland: Artur Boruc (YC20), Mariusz Jop, Grzegorz Bronowicki (YC37) (55' Pawel Golanski), Marcin Wasilewski (YC29), Michal Zewlakow, Jakub Blaszczykowski, Mariusz Lewandowski, Dariusz Dudka, Jacek Krzynówek, Maciej Zurawski (C) (56' Radoslaw Matusiak), Euzebiusz (Ebi) Smolarek (73' Wojciech Lobodzinski). (Coach: Leo Beenhakker (HOL)).
Goals: Portugal: 1-1 Nuno Ricardo de Oliveira Ribeiro "MANICHE" (50'), 2-1 CRISTIANO RONALDO dos Santos Aveiro (73').
Poland: 0-1 Mariusz Lewandowski (44'), 2-2 Jacek Krzynówek (88').
Referee: Roberto Rosetti (ITA)   Attendance: 48.000

12-09-2007   Armenia – Azerbaijan   Cancelled

12-09-2007   Almaty Central Stadium, Almaty: Kazakhstan – Belgium   2-2 (1-2)
Kazakhstan: David Loria, Aleksandr Kuchma, Farkhadbek Irismetov (YC42), Yegor Azovskiy
(66' Dmitri Lyapkin), Sergey Larin (73' Murat Suyumagambetov), Dmitriy Byakov, Samat
Smakov, Sergei Skorykh, Andrei Karpovich, Nurbol Zhumaskaliyev (C), Sergei Ostapenko.
(Coach: Arnoldus Dick (Arno) Pijpers (HOL)).
Belgium: Stijn Stijnen, Carl Hoefkens, Thomas Vermaelen, Vincent Kompany, Timmy Simons
(C), Bart Goor (84' Mpo Mpenza), Karel Geraerts (77' Faris Haroun), Marouane Fellaini
(YC75), Steven Defour (YC51), Kevin Mirallas (63' Jan Vertonghen), Mousa Dembélé.
(Coach: René Vandereycken (BEL)).
Goals: Kazakhstan: 1-2 Dmitriy Byakov (39'), 2-2 Samat Smakov (77' penalty).
Belgium: 0-1 Karel Geraerts (13'), 0-2 Kevin Mirallas (24').
Referee: Alexandru Dan Tudor (ROM)   Attendance: 18.100

12-09-2007   Olympic Stadium, Helsinki: Finland – Poland   0-0
Finland: Jussi Jääskeläinen, Hannu Tihinen, Petri Pasanen, Toni Kuivasto, Sami Hyypiä (C),
Teemu Tainio, Joonas Kolkka, Markus Heikkinen (90'+1' Jarkko Wiss), Aleksei Eremenko
(YC25), Daniel Sjölund, Jonatan Johansson (72' Mikael Forssell). (Coach: Roy Hodgson
(ENG)).
Poland: Artur Boruc, Mariusz Jop (YC33), Michal Zewlakow, Pawel Golanski, Radoslaw
Sobolewski, Jakub Blaszczykowski (YC89), Mariusz Lewandowski (C), Jacek Krzynówek,
Dariusz Dudka, Grzegorz Rasiak (65' Marek Saganowski), Euzebiusz (Ebi) Smolarek (80'
Maciej Zurawski). (Coach: Leo Beenhakker (HOL)).
Referee: Herbert Fandel (GER)   Attendance: 34.088

12-09-2007   Estádio José Alvalade, Lisbon: Portugal – Serbia   1-1 (1-0)
Portugal: RICARDO Alexandre Martins Soares Pereira, PAULO Renato Rebocho FERREIRA,
FERNANDO José da Silva Freitas MEIRA, BRUNO Eduardo Regufe ALVES, José
BOSINGWA da Silva, Armando Gonçalves Teixeira PETIT (YC86), Nuno Ricardo de
Oliveira Ribeiro "MANICHE" (83' RAÚL José Trindade MEIRELES), Anderson Luís de
Souza "DECO" (77' JOÃO Filipe Iria Santos MOUTINHO), NUNO "GOMES" Miguel Soares
Pereira Ribeiro (C) (65' RICARDO Andrade QUARESMA Bernardo), SIMÃO Pedro Fonseca
Sabrosa, CRISTIANO RONALDO dos Santos Aveiro. (Coach: Luiz Felipe Scolari (BRA)).
Serbia: Vladimir Stojkovic (YC36), Nemanja Vidic (YC59), Antonio Rukavina, Branislav
Ivanovic, Ivica Dragutinovic (YC51,RC90+2), Zoran Tosic (61' Marko Pantelic), Dejan
Stankovic (C), Milos Krasic (61' Nikola Zigic), Nenad Kovacevic, Zdravko Kuzmanovic (71'
Igor Duljaj), Milan Jovanovic. (Coach: Javier Clemente Lázaro (ESP)).
Goals: Portugal: 1-0 SIMÃO Pedro Fonseca Sabrosa (11').
Serbia: 1-1 Branislav Ivanovic (88').
Referee: Dr.Markus Merk (GER)   Attendance: 47.000

13-10-2007   Hanrapetakan Stadium, Yerevan: Armenia – Serbia   0-0
Armenia: Roman Berezovskiy, Aleksandr Tadevosyan, Karen Dokhoyan, Robert Arzumanyan,
Ararat Arakelyan (YC37), Sargis Hovsepyan (C), Artavazd Karamyan, Artur Voskanyan (70'
Romik Khachatryan), Levon Pachajyan, Hamlet Vladi Mkhitaryan (YC23) (82' Aram
Hakobyan), Samvel Melkonyan (62' Robert Zebelyan). (Coach: Vardan Razmik Minasyan
(ARM)).
Serbia: Vladimir Stojkovic, Milan Stepanov (YC90), Dusko Tosic, Antonio Rukavina (YC60),
Branislav Ivanovic, Dejan Stankovic (C) (YC51), Milos Krasic (73' Bosko Jankovic), Nenad
Kovacevic, Zdravko Kuzmanovic (61' Zoran Tosic), Nikola Zigic, Marko Pantelic (62' Danko
Lazovic). (Coach: Javier Clemente Lázaro (ESP)).
Referee: Stefan Johannesson (SWE)   Attendance: 7.150

95

13-10-2007   Tofiq Bakhramov Stadium, Baku: Azerbaijan – Portugal   0-2 (0-2)
Azerbaijan: Farkhad Veliyev, Sasa Yunisoglu (YC66), Aslan Kerimov (RC29), Emin Guliyev,
Samir Abbasov, Elvin Aliyev, Emin Imamaliyev (7' Zaur Gashimov), Aleksandr Chertoganov,
Branimir Subasic, Ilgar Gurbanov (56' Khagani Mammadov), Samir Aliyev (73' Alim
Gurbanov). (Coach: Shahin Diniyev (AZE)).
Portugal: RICARDO Alexandre Martins Soares Pereira (YC28), RICARDO Alberto Silveira
de CARVALHO, PAULO Renato Rebocho FERREIRA, Luis MIGUEL Brito Garcia Monteiro
(75' JORGE Miguel de Oliveira RIBEIRO (YC90+3)), BRUNO Eduardo Regufe ALVES,
MIGUEL Luís Pinto VELOSO, RICARDO Andrade QUARESMA Bernardo (70' Luís Carlos
Almeida da Cunha "NANI"), Nuno Ricardo de Oliveira Ribeiro "MANICHE", Anderson Luís
de Souza "DECO", HUGO Miguel Pereira de ALMEIDA, CRISTIANO RONALDO dos
Santos Aveiro (C). (Coach: Luiz Felipe Scolari (BRA)).
Goals: Portugal: 0-1 BRUNO Eduardo Regufe ALVES (12'), 0-2 HUGO Miguel Pereira de
ALMEIDA (45').
Referee: Ivan Bebek (CRO)   Attendance: 25.000

13-10-2007   Stadion Wojska Polskiego, Warsaw: Poland – Kazakhstan   3-1 (0-1)
Poland: Artur Boruc, Mariusz Jop, Grzegorz Bronowicki, Jacek Bak (C), Michal Zewlakow
(46' Maciej Zurawski), Wojciech Lobodzinski (80' Kamil Kosowski), Mariusz Lewandowski,
Jacek Krzynówek, Dariusz Dudka, Marek Saganowski (46' Marcin Wasilewski), Euzebiusz
(Ebi) Smolarek. (Coach: Leo Beenhakker (HOL)).
Kazakhstan: David Loria, Dmitri Lyapkin (YC40), Aleksandr Kuchma, Kairat Nurdauletov,
Sergey Larin (73' Murat Suyumagambetov), Dmitriy Byakov (85' Kairat Ashirbekov), Samat
Smakov, Sergei Skorykh (81' Andrei Karpovich), Ruslan Baltiev, Nurbol Zhumaskaliyev (C),
Sergei Ostapenko. (Coach: Arnoldus Dick (Arno) Pijpers (HOL)).
Goals: Poland: 1-1 Euzebiusz (Ebi) Smolarek (56'), 2-1 Euzebiusz (Ebi) Smolarek (65'), 3-1
Euzebiusz (Ebi) Smolarek (66').
Kazakhstan: 0-1 Dmitriy Byakov (20').
Referee: Espen Berntsen (NOR)   Attendance: 11.040

13-10-2007   King Baudouin Stadium, Brussels: Belgium – Finland   0-0
Belgium: Stijn Stijnen, Daniel van Buyten, Nicolas Lombaerts, Vincent Kompany, Timmy
Simons (C), Faris Haroun (67' Bart Goor), Christophe Grégoire (67' Wesley Sonck), Gaby
Mudingayi, Guillaume Gillet, Mousa Dembélé, Kevin Mirallas (YC73) (84' François
Sterchele). (Coach: René Vandereycken (BEL)).
Finland: Jussi Jääskeläinen, Hannu Tihinen, Petri Pasanen, Toni Kallio, Sami Hyypiä (C),
Aleksei Eremenko (YC43), Aki Riihilahti, Joonas Kolkka, Roman Eremenko, Daniel Sjölund
(90'+2' Mika Nurmela), Jonatan Johansson (90' Shefki Kuqi). (Coach: Roy Hodgson (ENG)).
Referee: Costas Kapitanis (CYP)   Attendance: 21.393

17-10-2007   Almaty Central Stadium, Almaty: Kazakhstan – Portugal   1-2 (0-0)
Kazakhstan: David Loria, Maksim Zhalmagambetov, Aleksandr Kuchma, Farkhadbek
Irismetov (YC36), Dmitriy Byakov, Sergey Larin (37' Dmitri Lyapkin), Samat Smakov
(YC40), Sergei Skorykh, Andrei Karpovich (YC6) (89' Kairat Nurdauletov), Nurbol
Zhumaskaliyev (C), Sergei Ostapenko. (Coach: Arnoldus Dick (Arno) Pijpers (HOL)).
Portugal: RICARDO Alexandre Martins Soares Pereira, BRUNO Eduardo Regufe ALVES,
RICARDO Alberto Silveira de CARVALHO, PAULO Renato Rebocho FERREIRA, Luis
MIGUEL Brito Garcia Monteiro, MIGUEL Luís Pinto VELOSO, RICARDO Andrade
QUARESMA Bernardo (85' JOÃO Filipe Iria Santos MOUTINHO), Nuno Ricardo de
Oliveira Ribeiro "MANICHE" (YC33) (59' Luís Carlos Almeida da Cunha "NANI"),
Anderson Luís de Souza "DECO", HUGO Miguel Pereira de ALMEIDA (63' Ariza
Makukula), CRISTIANO RONALDO dos Santos Aveiro (C). (Coach: Luiz Felipe Scolari
(BRA)).
Goals: Kazakhstan: 1-2 Dmitriy Byakov (90'+3').
Portugal: 0-1 Ariza Makukula (84'), 0-2 CRISTIANO RONALDO dos Santos Aveiro
(90'+1').
Referee: Jan Willem Wegereef (HOL)   Attendance: 25.057

17-10-2007   Tofiq Bakhramov Stadium, Baku: Azerbaijan – Serbia   1-6 (1-4)
Azerbaijan: Farkhad Veliyev (45' Jahangir Hasanzade), Zaur Gashimov (50' Elmar Baxsiyev
(YC69)), Ramin Guliyev, Emin Guliyev, Samir Abbasov, Dzeykhun Sultanov (C) (YC28) (69'
Farrukh Ismayilov), Aleksandr Chertoganov, Ramazan Abbasov, Alim Gurbanov, Branimir
Subasic, Samir Aliyev. (Coach: Shahin Diniyev (AZE)).
Serbia: Vladimir Stojkovic, Milan Bisevac, Dusko Tosic, Antonio Rukavina, Branislav
Ivanovic, Zoran Tosic, Nenad Kovacevic (65' Milan Jovanovic), Igor Duljaj (C), Zdravko
Kuzmanovic (YC37), Bosko Jankovic (68' Danko Lazovic), Nikola Zigic (73' Marko
Pantelic). (Coach: Javier Clemente Lázaro (ESP)).
Goals: Azerbaijan: 1-2 Samir Aliyev (26').
Serbia: 0-1 Dusko Tosic (4'), 0-2 Nikola Zigic (17'), 1-3 Bosko Jankovic (41'), 1-4 Nikola
Zigic (42'), 1-5 Milan Jovanovic (75'), 1-6 Danko Lazovic (81').
Referee: Thomas Einwaller (AUT)   Attendance: 3.100

17-10-2007   King Baudouin Stadium, Brussels: Belgium – Armenia   3-0 (0-0)
Belgium: Stijn Stijnen, Nicolas Lombaerts (83' Jan Vertonghen), Gill Swerts (YC2), Daniel
van Buyten (60' Vincent Kompany), Bart Goor, Karel Geraerts, Timmy Simons (C), Marouane
Fellaini, Steven Defour, Kevin Mirallas (46' Wesley Sonck), Mousa Dembélé. (Coach: René
Vandereycken (BEL)).
Armenia: Gevorg Kasparov, Karen Dokhoyan, Robert Arzumanyan, Ararat Arakelyan,
Aleksandr Tadevosyan (C) (82' Agvan Mkrtchyan), Sargis Hovsepyan, Romik Khachatryan
(57' Aram Hakobyan), Artavazd Karamyan, Artur Voskanyan, Levon Pachajyan, Samvel
Melkonyan (70' Robert Zebelyan). (Coach: Vardan Razmik Minasyan (ARM)).
Goals: Belgium: 1-0 Wesley Sonck (63'), 2-0 Mousa Dembélé (69'), 3-0 Karel Geraerts (76').
Referee: Jóhannes Valgeirsson (ISL)   Attendance: 14.812

17-11-2007   Olympic Stadium, Helsinki: Finland – Azerbaijan   2-1 (0-0)
Finland: Jussi Jääskeläinen, Hannu Tihinen (C), Petri Pasanen (YC39), Toni Kallio (66' Mika
Väyrynen), Sami Hyypiä, Teemu Tainio, Joonas Kolkka, Roman Eremenko (80' Shefki Kuqi),
Daniel Sjölund, Jonatan Johansson (59' Jari Litmanen), Mikael Forssell. (Coach: Roy Hodgson
(ENG)).
Azerbaijan: Farkhad Veliyev, Usim Charles Nduko (YC23) (46' Elvin Aliyev (YC54)), Sasa
Yunisoglu (YC33), Ramin Guliyev (61' André Luiz Ladaga), Samir Abbasov, Jemshid
Maharramov, Makhmud Gurbanov (YC45), Rashad Farhad oglu Sadygov (C), Zaur
Ramazanov, Zaur Tagizade, Branimir Subasic (YC85). (Coach: Gjokica (Gjoko) Hadzievski
(MCD)).
Goals: Finland: 1-1 Mikael Forssell (79'), 2-1 Shefki Kuqi (86').
Azerbaijan: 0-1 Makhmud Gurbanov (63').
Referee: Alain Hamer (LUX)   Attendance: 10.325

17-11-2007   Stadion Slaski, Chorzów: Poland – Belgium   2-0 (1-0)
Poland: Artur Boruc, Grzegorz Bronowicki, Jacek Bak (YC33), Marcin Wasilewski, Michal
Zewlakow, Radoslaw Sobolewski, Wojciech Lobodzinski (46' Jakub Blaszczykowski
(YC90+1)), Mariusz Lewandowski, Jacek Krzynówek, Maciej Zurawski (C) (82' Rafal
Murawski), Euzebiusz (Ebi) Smolarek (85' Kamil Kosowski). (Coach: Leo Beenhakker
(HOL)).
Belgium: Stijn Stijnen, Daniel van Buyten (C), Vincent Kompany, Faris Haroun (84' Karel
Geraerts), Bart Goor, Marouane Fellaini, Steven Defour (61' Luigi Pieroni), Jan Vertonghen,
Guillaume Gillet, Mousa Dembélé, Kevin Mirallas (76' Stein Huysegems). (Coach: René
Vandereycken (BEL)).
Goals: Poland: 1-0 Euzebiusz (Ebi) Smolarek (45'), 2-0 Euzebiusz (Ebi) Smolarek (49').
Referee: Claus Bo Larsen (DEN)   Attendance: 41.450

17-11-2007   Estádio Dr. Magalhães Pessoa, Leiria: Portugal – Armenia   1-0 (1-0)
Portugal: RICARDO Alexandre Martins Soares Pereira, FERNANDO José da Silva Freitas
MEIRA, MARCO António Simões CANEIRA (YC64), BRUNO Eduardo Regufe ALVES,
MIGUEL Luís Pinto VELOSO, José BOSINGWA da Silva (YC78), RICARDO Andrade
QUARESMA Bernardo (60' MANUEL Henriques Tavares FERNANDES), Nuno Ricardo de
Oliveira Ribeiro "MANICHE", HUGO Miguel Pereira de ALMEIDA (68' Ariza Makukula),
SIMÃO Pedro Fonseca Sabrosa (77' Luís Carlos Almeida da Cunha "NANI"), CRISTIANO
RONALDO dos Santos Aveiro (C). (Coach: Luiz Felipe Scolari (BRA)).
Armenia: Roman Berezovskiy, Aleksandr Tadevosyan, Karen Dokhoyan, Robert Arzumanyan
(YC70), Ararat Arakelyan, Sargis Hovsepyan (C), Artur Voskanyan, Levon Pachajyan (YC45),
Romik Khachatryan (59' Hamlet Vladi Mkhitaryan), Artavazd Karamyan (76' Agvan
Mkrtchyan), Samvel Melkonyan (63' Edgar Manucharyan). (Coach: Vardan Razmik Minasyan
(ARM)).
Goal: Portugal: 1-0 HUGO Miguel Pereira de ALMEIDA (42').
Referee: Michael (Mike) Riley (ENG)   Attendance: 22.048

21-11-2007   Hanrapetakan Stadium, Yerevan: Armenia – Kazakhstan 0-1 (0-0)
Armenia: Roman Berezovskiy, Aleksandr Tadevosyan, Karen Dokhoyan, Robert Arzumanyan, Ararat Arakelyan (56' Romik Khachatryan), Sargis Hovsepyan (C), Artavazd Karamyan, Artur Voskanyan (80' Gevorg Ghazaryan (YC82)), Levon Pachajyan, Hamlet Vladi Mkhitaryan, Samvel Melkonyan (59' Edgar Manucharyan). (Coach: Vardan Razmik Minasyan (ARM)).
Kazakhstan: David Loria, Maksim Zhalmagambetov (YC41), Aleksandr Kuchma (YC63), Farkhadbek Irismetov, Kairat Nurdauletov, Sergey Larin (61' Dmitri Lyapkin), Dmitriy Byakov, Sergei Skorykh, Ruslan Baltiev, Nurbol Zhumaskaliyev (C), Sergei Ostapenko. (Coach: Arnoldus Dick (Arno) Pijpers (HOL)).
Goal: Kazakhstan: 0-1 Sergei Ostapenko (64').
Referee: Fredy Fautrel (FRA)   Attendance: 3.100

21-11-2007   Tofiq Bakhramov Stadium, Baku: Azerbaijan – Belgium 0-1 (0-0)
Azerbaijan: Farkhad Veliyev, Aslan Kerimov (84' Khagani Mammadov), Rail Malikov, Ramin Guliyev, Samir Abbasov, Jemshid Maharramov (77' Anatoliy Ponomaryov), Makhmud Gurbanov, Rashad Farhad oglu Sadygov (C), Zaur Ramazanov, Zaur Tagizade (YC27) (70' Leandro Melino Gomes), Branimir Subasic. (Coach: Gjokica (Gjoko) Hadzievski (MCD)).
Belgium: Brian Vandenbussche, Jelle van Damme, Gill Swerts, Daniel van Buyten (C), Christophe Grégoire (68' Bart Goor), Karel Geraerts (YC35) (46' Steven Defour), Guillaume Gillet, Marouane Fellaini (YC81), Jan Vertonghen, Luigi Pieroni (YC41) (81' Kevin Mirallas), Mousa Dembélé (YC45). (Coach: René Vandereycken (BEL)).
Goal: Belgium: 0-1 Luigi Pieroni (52').
Referee: Asaf Kenan (ISR)   Attendance: 7.000

21-11-2007   Estádio do Dragão, Porto: Portugal – Finland 0-0
Portugal: RICARDO Alexandre Martins Soares Pereira, FERNANDO José da Silva Freitas MEIRA, MARCO António Simões CANEIRA (YC68), BRUNO Eduardo Regufe ALVES, Képler Laveran Lima Ferreira "PEPE", MIGUEL Luís Pinto VELOSO, José BOSINGWA da Silva, RICARDO Andrade QUARESMA Bernardo (84' Luís Carlos Almeida da Cunha "NANI"), Nuno Ricardo de Oliveira Ribeiro "MANICHE" (73' RAÚL José Trindade MEIRELES), NUNO "GOMES" Miguel Soares Pereira Ribeiro (C) (77' Ariza Makukula (YC90)), CRISTIANO RONALDO dos Santos Aveiro. (Coach: Luiz Felipe Scolari (BRA)).
Finland: Jussi Jääskeläinen, Petri Pasanen (YC88), Toni Kallio, Sami Hyypiä (YC47), Hannu Tihinen, Joonas Kolkka (75' Jonatan Johansson), Markus Heikkinen, Teemu Tainio (69' Roman Eremenko), Daniel Sjölund (YC39), Jari Litmanen (C) (67' Mika Väyrynen), Mikael Forssell (YC62). (Coach: Roy Hodgson (ENG)).
Referee: Lubos Michel (SVK)   Attendance: 49.000

21-11-2007   Stadion Crvena Zvezda, Belgrade: Serbia – Poland 2-2 (0-1)
Serbia: Vlada Avramov, Mladen Krstajic (C) (64' Dusko Tosic), Antonio Rukavina (YC30), Branislav Ivanovic, Ivica Dragutinovic, Milos Krasic (76' Bosko Jankovic), Nenad Kovacevic, Igor Duljaj (46' Danko Lazovic (YC88)), Zdravko Kuzmanovic, Nikola Zigic (YC90), Milan Jovanovic. (Coach: Javier Clemente Lázaro (ESP)).
Poland: Lukasz Fabianski, Marcin Wasilewski, Mariusz Jop, Grzegorz Bronowicki, Jacek Bak (C) (YC72) (77' Michal Zewlakow), Jakub Wawrzyniak (YC42), Kamil Kosowski (19' Tomasz Zahorski (YC43)), Rafal Murawski, Wojciech Lobodzinski, Mariusz Lewandowski, Grzegorz Rasiak (46' Radoslaw Matusiak). (Coach: Leo Beenhakker (HOL)).
Goals: Serbia: 1-2 Nikola Zigic (68'), 2-2 Danko Lazovic (70').
Poland: 0-1 Rafal Murawski (28'), 0-2 Radoslaw Matusiak (46').
Referee: Massimo Busacca (SUI)   Attendance: 3.247

99

24-11-2007   Stadion Partizani, Belgrade: Serbia – Kazakhstan   1-0 (0-0)
Serbia: Vlada Avramov (YC90+3), Dusan Andjelkovic, Djordje Tutoric, Ivan Stevanovic, Branislav Ivanovic, Milos Krasic (YC19) (24' Bosko Jankovic), Gojko Kacar (YC43), Igor Duljaj (C), Ranko Despotovic, Nikola Zigic (70' Ljubomir Fejsa), Milan Jovanovic (63' Stefan Babovic). (Coach: Javier Clemente Lázaro (ESP)).
Kazakhstan: David Loria, Maksim Zhalmagambetov (YC90+3), Dmitri Lyapkin (73' Nurbol Zhumaskaliyev), Farkhadbek Irismetov, Kairat Nurdauletov, Dmitriy Byakov (YC68), Samat Smakov (C), Sergei Skorykh, Andrei Karpovich, Ruslan Baltiev (YC86) (86' Kairat Ashirbekov), Murat Suyumagambetov (73' Sergei Ostapenko). (Coach: Arnoldus Dick (Arno) Pijpers (HOL)).
Goal: Serbia: 1-0 Sergei Ostapenko (79' own goal).
Referee: Kyros Vassaras (GRE)   Attendance: 400

GROUP   B

16-08-2006	Toftir	Faroe Islands – Georgia	0-6 (0-3)
02-09-2006	Glasgow	Scotland – Faroe Islands	6-0 (5-0)
02-09-2006	Tbilisi	Georgia – France	0-3 (0-2)
02-09-2006	Naples	Italy – Lithuania	1-1 (1-1)
06-09-2006	Kiev	Ukraine – Georgia	3-2 (1-1)
06-09-2006	Kaunas	Lithuania – Scotland	1-2 (0-0)
06-09-2006	Saint-Denis	France – Italy	3-1 (2-1)
07-10-2006	Tórshavn	Faroe Irlands – Lithiania	0-1 (0-0)
07-10-2006	Glasgow	Scotland – France	1-0 (0-0)
07-10-2006	Rome	Italy –Ukraine	2-0 (0-0)
11-10-2006	Kiev	Ukraine – Scotland	2-0 (0-0)
11-10-2006	Tbilisi	Georgia – Italy	1-3 (1-1)
11-10-2006	Montbéliard	France – Faroe Islands	5-0 (2-0)
24-03-2007	Glasgow	Scotland – Georgia	2-1 (1-1)
24-03-2007	Toftir	Faroe Islands – Ukraine	0-2 (0-1)
24-03-2007	Kaunas	Lithuania – France	0-1 (0-0)
28-03-2007	Odessa	Ukraine – Lithuania	1-0 (0-0)
28-03-2007	Tbilisi	Georgia – Faroe Irlands	3-1 (2-0)
28-03-2007	Bari	Italy – Scotland	2-0 (1-0)
02-06-2007	Kaunas	Lithuania – Georgia	1-0 (0-0)
02-06-2007	Saint-Denis	France – Ukraine	2-0 (0-0)
02-06-2007	Tórshavn	Faroe Islands – Italy	1-2 (0-1)
06-06-2007	Toftir	Faroe Islands – Scotland	0-2 (0-2)
06-06-2007	Auxerre	France – Georgia	1-0 (1-0)
06-06-2007	Kaunas	Lithuania – Italy	0-2 (0-2)
08-09-2007	Glasgow	Scotland – Lithuania	3-1 (1-0)
08-09-2007	Tbilisi	Georgia – Ukraine	1-1 (0-1)
08-09-2007	Milan	Italy – France	0-0
12-09-2007	Kaunas	Lithuania – Faroe Islands	2-1 (1-0)
12-09-2007	Kiev	Ukraine – Italy	1-2 (0-1)
12-09-2007	Paris	France – Scotland	0-1 (0-0)
13-10-2007	Glasgow	Scotland – Ukraine	3-1 (2-1)
13-10-2007	Tórshavn	Faroe Islands – France	0-6 (0-2)
13-10-2007	Genoa	Italy – Georgia	2-0 (1-0)

17-10-2007	Kiev	Ukraine – Faroe Islands	5-0 (3-0)
17-10-2007	Tbilisi	Georgia – Scotland	2-0 (1-0)
17-10-2007	Nantes	France – Lithuania	2-0 (0-0)
17-11-2007	Glasgow	Scotland – Italy	1-2 (0-1)
17-11-2007	Kaunas	Lithuania – Ukraine	2-0 (1-0)
21-11-2007	Tbilisi	Georgia – Lithuania	0-2 (0-0)
21-11-2007	Modena	Italy – Faroe Islands	3-1 (3-0)
21-11-2007	Kiev	Ukraine – France	2-2 (1-2)

FINAL STANDING

Pos	Team	Pld	W	D	L	GF	GA	GD	Pts
1	Italy	12	9	2	1	22	9	+13	29
2	France	12	8	2	2	25	5	+20	26
3	Scotland	12	8	0	4	21	12	+9	24
4	Ukraine	12	5	2	5	18	16	+2	17
5	Lithuania	12	5	1	6	11	13	-2	16
6	Georgia	12	3	1	8	16	19	-3	10
7	Faroe Islands	12	0	0	12	4	43	-39	0

Italy and France qualified for the Final Tournament in Austria and Switzerland.

16-08-2006   Svangaskard, Toftir: Faroe Islands – Georgia   0-6 (0-3)
Faroe Islands: Jákup Mikkelsen, Óli Johannesen (C) (YC43), Janus Joensen, Atli Danielsen, Kári Nielsen, Claus Jørgensen (46' Pauli Hansen), Rógvi Jacobsen (YC27) (72' Jónhard Frederiksberg), Fródi Benjaminsen, Símun Samuelsen (61' Hans Pauli Samuelsen), Christian Jacobsen, Jákup á Borg. (Coach: Jógvan Martin Olsen (FAR)).
Georgia: Grigol Chanturia, Giorgi Shashiashvili, Ilia Kandelaki (66' Dato Kvirkvelia), Levan Kobiashvili (C), Jaba Kankava, Gogita Gogua (58' Georgi Demetradze), Malkhaz Asatiani, Kakhaber Aladashvili (72' Georgi Gakhokidze), David Mujiri, Aleksandr Iashvili, Shota Arveladze. (Coach: Klaus Toppmöller (GER)).
Goals: Georgia: 0-1 David Mujiri (17'), 0-2 Aleksandr Iashvili (19'), 0-3 Shota Arveladze (37'), 0-4 Levan Kobiashvili (50' penalty), 0-5 Shota Arveladze (62'), 0-6 Shota Arveladze (82').
Referee: Michael Thomas Ross (NIR)   Attendance: 2.114

02-09-2006   Celtic Park, Glasgow: Scotland – Faroe Islands   6-0 (5-0)
Scotland: Craig Gordon, Steven Pressley, Gary Naysmith, Christian Dailly, David Weir (C), Nigel Quashie (85' Scott Severin), Paul Hartley, Darren Fletcher (YC40) (46' Gary Stewart Teale), Kenny Miller (YC43) (61' Garry O'Connor), James McFadden, Kris Boyd. (Coach: Walter Ferguson Smith (SCO)).
Faroe Islands: Jákup Mikkelsen, Óli Johannesen (C) (YC58), Janus Joensen, Atli Danielsen, Julian Schantz Johnsson (75' Símun Samuelsen), Rógvi Jacobsen (84' Kári Nielsen), Pauli Hansen, Fródi Benjaminsen (YC40), Christian Jacobsen, Jónhard Frederiksberg (YC51) (60' Hanus Thorleifsson), Jákup á Borg (YC24). (Coach: Jógvan Martin Olsen (FAR)).
Goals: Scotland: 1-0 Darren Fletcher (7'), 2-0 James McFadden (10'), 3-0 Kris Boyd (24' penalty), 4-0 Kenny Miller (30' penalty), 5-0 Kris Boyd (38'), 6-0 Garry O'Connor (86').
Referee: Igor Vyacheslavovich Egorov (RUS)   Attendance: 50.059

02-09-2006   Boris Paichadze Stadium, Tbilisi: Georgia – France   0-3 (0-2)
Georgia: Grigol Chanturia, Zurab Khizanishvili, Levan Kobiashvili (C) (YC11), Jaba Kankava
(YC45), Gogita Gogua (YC53), Malkhaz Asatiani, Kakhaber Aladashvili (37' Ilia Kandelaki),
David Mujiri (82' Zurab Menteshashvili), Aleksandre Iashvili (46' Dato Kvirkvelia), Georgi
Demetradze (YC81), Shota Arveladze. (Coach: Klaus Toppmöller (GER)).
France: Grégory Coupet, Lilian Thuram, Willy Sagnol, William Gallas, Éric Abidal, Patrick
Vieira (C), Franck Ribéry (68' Sidney Govou), Florent Malouda, Claude Makélélé (57' Rio
Mavuba), Louis Saha (86' Sylvain Wiltord), Thierry Henry. (Coach: Raymond Domenech
(FRA)).
Goals: France: 0-1 Florent Malouda (7'), 0-2 Louis Saha (15'), 0-3 Malkhaz Asatiani (47' *own
goal*).
Referee: Jan Willem Wegereef (HOL)   Attendance: 54.000

02-09-2006   Stadio San Paolo, Naples: Italy – Lithuania   1-1 (1-1)
Italy: Gianluigi Buffon, Massimo Oddo, Fabio Cannavaro (C), Fabio Grosso, Andrea Barzagli,
Simone Perrotta (YC28) (72' Alberto Gilardino), Gennaro Gattuso (YC90+5), Andrea Pirlo,
Daniele De Rossi (62' Marco Marchionni), Filippo Inzaghi (88' David Di Michele), Antonio
Cassano. (Coach: Roberto Donadoni (ITA)).
Lithuania: Zydrūnas Karcemarskas (YC87), Tomas Zvirgzdauskas, Marius Stankevicius,
Andrius Skerla, Rolandas Dziaukstas (YC17), Aidas Preiksaitis, Mantas Savénas (66'
Mindaugas Kalonas), Saulius Mikoliūnas (84' Tomas Tamosauskas), Deividas Cesnauskis,
Robertas Poskus (80' Tadas Labukas), Tomas Danilevicius (C). (Coach: Algimantas
Liubinskas (LIT)).
Goals: Italy: 1-1 Filippo Inzaghi (30').
Lithuania: 0-1 Tomas Danilevicius (21').
Referee: Martin Hansson (SWE)   Attendance: 43.440

06-09-2006   NSC Olimpiysky, Kiev: Ukraine – Georgia   3-2 (1-1)
Ukraine: Olexandr Shovkovskiy, Andriy Nesmachniy, Andriy Rusol, Serhiy Tkachenko (86'
Andriy Vorobey), Oleh Shelayev, Ruslan Rotan, Andriy Gusin (46' Volodymyr Yezerskiy
(YC59)), Oleh Gusev, Anatoliy Tymoshchuk, Serhiy Rebrov (56' Andriy Voronin), Andriy
Shevchenko (C). (Coach: Oleh Vladimirovich Blokhin (UKR)).
Georgia: Grigol Chanturia, Dato Kvirkvelia (81' David Mujiri), Zurab Khizanishvili (YC88),
Davit Imedashvili (34' Ilia Kandelaki), Zurab Menteshashvili (82' Mikheil Ashvetia), Levan
Kobiashvili (C) (YC32), Jaba Kankava, Gogita Gogua (YC25), Malkhaz Asatiani, Georgi
Demetradze (YC39), Shota Arveladze YC88). (Coach: Klaus Toppmöller (GER)).
Goals: Ukraine: 1-0 Andriy Shevchenko (31'), 2-2 Ruslan Rotan (61'), 3-2 Andriy Rusol (80').
Georgia: 1-1 Shota Arveladze (38'), 1-2 Georgi Demetradze (60').
Referee: Jaroslav Jára (CZE)   Attendance: 25.000

06-09-2006   S.Darius and S.Girénas, Kaunas: Lithuania – Scotland   1-2 (0-0)
Lithuania: Zydrūnas Karcemarskas, Tomas Zvirgzdauskas (YC9), Marius Stankevicius,
Andrius Skerla, Rolandas Dziaukstas, Aidas Preiksaitis (YC14) (81' Darius Miceika),
Mindaugas Kalonas (YC78), Mantas Savénas (50' Tomas Tamosauskas), Saulius Mikoliūnas
(66' Tadas Labukas), Robertas Poskus (YC62), Tomas Danilevicius (C). (Coach: Algimantas
Liubinskas (LIT)).
Scotland: Craig Gordon, Steven Pressley, Gary Naysmith, Christian Dailly (YC39), David
Weir (C), Gary Caldwell (YC56), Nigel Quashie (43' Kris Boyd), Paul Hartley (88' Scott
Severin), Darren Fletcher, Kenny Miller (YC29), James McFadden (21' Graham Alexander).
(Coach: Walter Ferguson Smith (SCO)).
Goals: Lithuania: 1-2 Darius Miceika (85').
Scotland: 0-1 Christian Dailly (46'), 0-2 Kenny Miller (63').
Referee: Vladimír Hrinák (SVK)   Attendance: 6.500

06-09-2006   Stade de France, Saint-Denis: France – Italy   3-1 (2-1)
France: Grégory Coupet, Lilian Thuram, Willy Sagnol, William Gallas, Éric Abidal, Patrick
Vieira (C), Franck Ribéry (88' Louis Saha), Florent Malouda, Claude Makélélé, Thierry Henry
(YC37), Sidney Govou (75' Sylvain Wiltord). (Coach: Raymond Domenech (FRA)).
Italy: Gianluigi Buffon, Fabio Cannavaro (C) (YC29), Gianluca Zambrotta, Fabio Grosso
(YC90+1), Andrea Barzagli, Franco Semioli (54' David Di Michele), Simone Perrotta (YC44),
Gennaro Gattuso, Andrea Pirlo, Alberto Gilardino (YC65) (87' Daniele De Rossi), Antonio
Cassano (73' Filippo Inzaghi). (Coach: Roberto Donadoni (ITA)).
Goals: France: 1-0 Sidney Govou (2'), 2-0 Thierry Henry (17'), 3-1 Sidney Govou (57').
Italy: 2-1 Alberto Gilardino (20').
Referee: Herbert Fandel (GER)   Attendance: 78.831

07-10-2006   Tórshavn: Faroe Islands – Lithuania   0-1 (0-0)
Faroe Islands: Jákup Mikkelsen (C) (YC87), Marni Djurhuus, Atli Danielsen, Vagnur Mohr
Mortensen, Rógvi Jacobsen (81' Kári Nielsen), Pauli Hansen (YC69) (89' Arnbjørn Hansen),
Fródi Benjaminsen, Mikkjal Thomassen (YC52), Símun Samuelsen (73' Jónhard
Frederiksberg), Christian Jacobsen, Jákup á Borg. (Coach: Jógvan Martin Olsen (FAR)).
Lithuania: Zydrūnas Karcemarskas, Tomas Zvirgzdauskas, Marius Stankevicius, Andrius
Skerla, Gediminas Paulauskas, Darius Miceika, Mantas Savénas (46' Mindaugas Kalonas),
Saulius Mikoliūnas (62' Vitalijus Kavaliauskas), Deividas Cesnauskis, Robertas Poskus (70'
Ricardas Beniusis), Tomas Danilevicius (C). (Coach: Algimantas Liubinskas (LIT)).
Goal: Lithuania: 0-1 Andrius Skerla (88').
Referee: Anthony Buttimer (IRL)   Attendance: 1.982

07-10-2006   Hampden Park, Glasgow: Scotland – France   1-0 (0-0)
Scotland: Craig Gordon, Steven Pressley, Christian Dailly (YC71), Graham Alexander, David
Weir, Gary Caldwell, Paul Hartley, Darren Fletcher, Barry Ferguson (C), James McFadden
(YC29) (73' Garry O'Connor), Lee McCulloch (YC32) (58' Gary Stewart Teale). (Coach:
Walter Ferguson Smith (SCO)).
France: Grégory Coupet, Lilian Thuram, Willy Sagnol, Jean-Alain Boumsong, Éric Abidal,
Patrick Vieira (C), Franck Ribéry (74' Sylvain Wiltord), Florent Malouda, Claude Makélélé,
David Trézéguet (62' Louis Saha), Thierry Henry. (Coach: Raymond Domenech (FRA)).
Goal: Scotland: 1-0 Gary Caldwell (66').
Referee: Massimo Busacca (SUI)   Attendance: 50.456

07-10-2006   Stadio Olimpico, Rome: Italy – Ukraine   2-0 (0-0)
Italy: Gianluigi Buffon, Massimo Oddo, Marco Materazzi, Fabio Cannavaro (C), Gianluca
Zambrotta, Gennaro Gattuso (YC43), Andrea Pirlo, Daniele De Rossi, Luca Toni (85' Filippo
Inzaghi), Vincenzo Iaquinta (76' Mauro Camoranesi), Alessandro Del Piero (61' Antonio Di
Natale). (Coach: Roberto Donadoni (ITA)).
Ukraine: Olexandr Shovkovsky (C), Volodymyr Yezerskiy (YC75), Bohdan Shershun
(YC30), Andriy Nesmachniy, Andriy Rusol (YC68), Oleh Shelayev, Oleh Gusev, Anatoliy
Tymoshchuk, Serhiy Nazarenko (60' Maxym Kalynychenko), Andriy Vorobey (74' Artem
Milevskiy), Andriy Voronin (YC40). (Coach: Oleh Vladimirovich Blokhin (UKR)).
Goals: Italy: 1-0 Massimo Oddo (68' penalty), 2-0 Luca Toni (79').
Referee: Kyros Vassaras (GRE)   Attendance: 49.149

11-10-2006   NSC Olimpiysky, Kiev: Ukraine – Scotland   2-0 (0-0)
Ukraine: Olexandr Shovkovsky, Vyacheslav Sviderskiy, Andriy Nesmachniy, Andriy Rusol,
Olexandr Kucher (YC30), Oleh Shelayev, Oleh Gusev (60' Artem Milevskiy), Anatoliy
Tymoshchuk, Maxym Kalynychenko (78' Andriy Vorobey), Andriy Voronin (90'+3' Bohdan
Shershun), Andriy Shevchenko (C). (Coach: Oleh Vladimirovich Blokhin (UKR)).
Scotland: Craig Gordon, Steven Pressley (RC86), Robbie Neilson (YC74) (90' Stephen
McManus), Graham Alexander, David Weir, Gary Caldwell, Paul Hartley, Darren Fletcher
(YC21), Barry Ferguson (C), Kenny Miller, James McFadden (YC9) (75' Kris Boyd). (Coach:
Walter Ferguson Smith (SCO)).
Goals: Ukraine: 1-0 Olexandr Kucher (60'), 2-0 Andriy Shevchenko (90' penalty).
Referee: Martin Hansson (SWE)   Attendance: 50.000

11-10-2006   Boris Paichadze Stadium, Tbilisi: Georgia – Italy   1-3 (1-1)
Georgia: Georgi Lomaia, Giorgi Shashiashvili (YC29), Dato Kvirkvelia, Zurab Khizanishvili,
Otar Khizaneishvili, Kakha Kaladze (C), Levan Tskitishvili (YC45+2) (75' Ilia Kandelaki),
Zurab Menteshashvili, Jaba Kankava (YC20,YC60), Otar Martsvaladze (85' Vasil Gigiadze),
Mikheil Ashvetia (70' Aleksandre Iashvili). (Coach: Klaus Toppmöller (GER)).
Italy: Gianluigi Buffon, Massimo Oddo, Alessandro Nesta, Fabio Cannavaro (C) (74' Marco
Materazzi), Gianluca Zambrotta (YC86), Simone Perrotta, Mauro Camoranesi (88' Vincenzo
Iaquinta), Andrea Pirlo (62' Stefano Mauri), Daniele De Rossi, Luca Toni, Antonio Di Natale.
(Coach: Roberto Donadoni (ITA)).
Goals: Georgia: 1-1 Giorgi Shashiashvili (25').
Italy: 0-1 Daniele De Rossi (22'), 1-2 Mauro Camoranesi (61'), 1-3 Simone Perrotta (71').
Referee: Michael (Mike) Riley (ENG)   Attendance: 48.000

11-10-2006   Stade Auguste Bonal, Montbéliard: France – Faroe Islands   5-0 (2-0)
France: Mickaël Landreau, Lilian Thuram, Willy Sagnol (78' François Clerc), William Gallas,
Julian Escudé, Patrick Vieira (C), Jérémy Toulalan, Franck Ribéry, Florent Malouda, Louis
Saha (61' David Trézéguet), Thierry Henry (61' Nicolas Anelka). (Coach: Raymond
Domenech (FRA)).
Faroe Islands: Jákup Mikkelsen (C), Marni Djurhuus (YC18), Atli Danielsen, Vagnur Mohr
Mortensen, Rógvi Jacobsen, Pauli Hansen (46' Kári Nielsen), Fródi Benjaminsen, Mikkjal
Thomassen, Símun Samuelsen, Christian Jacobsen, Jákup á Borg (88' Jónhard Frederiksberg).
(Coach: Jógvan Martin Olsen (FAR)).
Goals: France: 1-0 Louis Saha (1'), 2-0 Thierry Henry (22'), 3-0 Nicolas Anelka (76'), 4-0
David Trézéguet (77'), 5-0 David Trézéguet (84').
Referee: Sorin Corpodean (ROM)   Attendance: 19.314

24-03-2007   Hampden Park, Glasgow: Scotland – Georgia 2-1 (1-1)
Scotland: Craig Gordon, Gary Naysmith, Stephen McManus, Graham Alexander, David Weir,
Paul Hartley, Barry Ferguson (C) (YC90+3), Gary Stewart Teale (60' Scott Brown), Kenny
Miller (90'+2' Shaun Maloney), Lee McCulloch, Kris Boyd (76' Craig Beattie). (Coach:
Alexander (Alex) McLeish (SCO)).
Georgia: Georgi Lomaia, Lasha Salukvadze (YC62), Zurab Khizanishvili, Zaal Eliava, Giorgi
Shashiashvili, Zurab Menteshashvili (YC11) (46' Gogita Gogua), Levan Kobiashvili (C),
Vladimer Burduli (57' David Siradze), Levan Tskitishvili (90'+2' David Mujiri), Georgi
Demetradze (YC85), Shota Arveladze. (Coach: Klaus Toppmöller (GER)).
Goals: Scotland: 1-0 Kris Boyd (11'), 2-1 Craig Beattie (89').
Georgia: 1-1 Shota Arveladze (41').
Referee: Nicolai Vollquartz (DEN)   Attendance: 52.063

24-03-2007   Svangaskard, Toftir: Faroe Islands – Ukraine 0-2 (0-1)
Faroe Islands: Jákup Mikkelsen, Óli Johannesen (C), Marni Djurhuus, Atli Danielsen (YC9),
Rógvi Jacobsen, Fródi Benjaminsen, Mikkjal Thomassen (78' Sámal Joensen), Súni Olsen (74'
Tem Hansen), Símun Samuelsen (66' Christian Holst), Christian Jacobsen, Jákup á Borg.
(Coach: Jógvan Martin Olsen (FAR)).
Ukraine: Olexandr Shovkovskiy (C), Volodymyr Yezerskiy, Andriy Nesmachniy, Andriy
Rusol, Taras Mikhalik, Dmytro Chygrynskiy, Oleh Gusev (60' Andriy Vorobey), Anatoliy
Tymoshchuk (82' Oleh Shelayev), Maxym Kalynychenko, Olexiy Bielik, Andriy Voronin (75'
Serhiy Nazarenko). (Coach: Oleh Vladimirovich Blokhin (UKR)).
Goals: Ukraine: 0-1 Volodymyr Yezerskiy (20'), 0-2 Oleh Gusev (57').
Referee: Damir Skomina (SLO)   Attendance: 717

24-03-2007   S.Darius and S.Girénas, Kaunas: Lithuania – France 0-1 (0-0)
Lithuania: Zydrūnas Karcemarskas, Tomas Zvirgzdauskas, Andrius Skerla, Arūnas
Klimavicius (YC30), Marius Stankevicius, Gediminas Paulauskas, Deividas Semberas, Mantas
Savénas (77' Mindaugas Kalonas), Igoris Morinas (82' Ricardas Beniusis), Tomas
Danilevicius (C), Robertas Poskus (86' Tomas Radzinevicius). (Coach: Algimantas Liubinskas
(LIT)).
France: Grégory Coupet, William Gallas, Éric Abidal, Lilian Thuram (C), Willy Sagnol,
Claude Makéléle, Lassana Diarra (YC79), Jérémy Toulalan, Florent Malouda (89' Abou
Diaby), Sidney Govou (62' Djibril Cissé), Nicolas Anelka. (Coach: Raymond Domenech
(FRA)).
Goals: France: 0-1 Nicolas Anelka (73').
Referee: Howard Melton Webb (ENG)   Attendance: 8.740

28-03-2007   Chornomorets Stadium, Odessa: Ukraine – Lithuania 1-0 (0-0)
Ukraine: Olexandr Shovkovskiy, Volodymyr Yezerskiy (YC17), Andriy Nesmachniy, Andriy
Rusol, Taras Mikhalik (70' Oleh Shelayev), Olexandr Kucher, Oleh Gusev (79' Andriy
Vorobey), Anatoliy Tymoshchuk, Maxym Kalynychenko (82' Dmytro Chygrynskiy), Andriy
Voronin, Andriy Shevchenko (C). (Coach: Oleh Vladimirovich Blokhin (UKR)).
Lithuania: Paulius Grybauskas, Tomas Zvirgzdauskas, Marius Stankevicius, Andrius Skerla,
Arūnas Klimavicius, Deividas Semberas, Gediminas Paulauskas, Mantas Savénas (YC39) (51'
Mindaugas Kalonas), Robertas Poskus (64' Tomas Radzinevicius), Igoris Morinas (56'
Andrius Gedgaudas), Tomas Danilevicius (C) (YC24). (Coach: Algimantas Liubinskas (LIT)).
Goal: Ukraine: 1-0 Oleh Gusev (47').
Referee: Florian Meyer (GER)   Attendance: 33.600

28-03-2007   Boris Paichadze Stadium, Tbilisi: Georgia – Faroe Islands 3-1 (2-0)
Georgia: Georgi Lomaia, Giorgi Shashiashvili, Lasha Salukvadze, Dato Kvirkvelia, Levan
Kobiashvili (C) (YC55) (61' Zurab Menteshashvili), Jaba Kankava, Levan Tskitishvili, David
Siradze (YC63), David Mujiri, Aleksandre Iashvili, Georgi Demetradze. (Coach: Klaus
Toppmöller (GER)).
Faroe Islands: Jákup Mikkelsen, Óli Johannesen (C), Marni Djurhuus, Atli Danielsen, Rógvi
Jacobsen, Fródi Benjaminsen (YC58,YC63), Súni Olsen, Mikkjal Thomassen, Christian
Jacobsen, Jákup á Borg (90'+1' Símun Samuelsen), Andrew av Fløtum (43' Christian Holst).
(Coach: Jógvan Martin Olsen (FAR)).
Goals: Georgia: 1-0 David Siradze (26'), 2-0 Aleksandre Iashvili (45'+1'), 3-1 Aleksandre
Iashvili (90'+2' penalty).
Faroe Islands: 2-1 Rógvi Jacobsen (56').
Referee: Pavel Saliy (KAZ)   Attendance: 12.000

28-03-2007   Stadio San Nicola, Bari: Italy – Scotland 2-0 (1-0)
Italy: Gianluigi Buffon, Massimo Oddo, Marco Materazzi, Fabio Cannavaro (C), Gianluca
Zambrotta, Simone Perrotta (77' Andrea Pirlo), Gennaro Gattuso, Mauro Camoranesi, Daniele
De Rossi, Luca Toni (87' Fabio Quagliarella), Antonio Di Natale (66' Alessandro Del Piero).
(Coach: Roberto Donadoni (ITA)).
Scotland: Craig Gordon, Graham Alexander, Gary Naysmith, Stephen McManus, David Weir,
Gary Stewart Teale (66' Shaun Maloney), Paul Hartley, Barry Ferguson (C), Scott Brown (86'
Craig Beattie), Kenny Miller, Lee McCulloch (81' Kris Boyd). (Coach: Alexander (Alex)
McLeish (SCO)).
Goals: Italy: 1-0 Luca Toni (12'), 2-0 Luca Toni (70').
Referee: Frank de Bleeckere (BEL)   Attendance: 37.600

02-06-2007   S.Darius And S.Girénas, Kaunas: Lithuania – Georgia 1-0 (0-0)
Lithuania: Zydrūnas Karcemarskas (YC90+4), Tomas Zvirgzdauskas, Marius Stankevicius,
Andrius Skerla, Arūnas Klimavicius, Deividas Semberas, Gediminas Paulauskas, Mantas
Savénas (55' Mindaugas Kalonas), Igoris Morinas (62' Saulius Mikoliūnas (YC79)), Tomas
Danilevicius (C), Ricardas Beniusis (75' Tadas Labukas). (Coach: Algimantas Liubinskas
(LIT)).
Georgia: Georgi Lomaia, Dato Kvirkvelia, Zurab Khizanishvili, Otar Khizaneishvili, Kakha
Kaladze (C), Zaal Eliava, Levan Tskitishvili (YC73) (80' David Mujiri), Zurab Menteshashvili
(64' Otar Martsvaladze), Levan Kobiashvili (YC53), Aleksandre Iashvili, Georgi Demetradze
(YC45+1). (Coach: Klaus Toppmöller (GER)).
Goal: Lithuania: 1-0 Saulius Mikoliūnas (78').
Referee: Claudio Circhetta (SUI)   Attendance: 6.400

02-06-2007   Stade de France, Saint-Denis: France – Ukraine 2-0 (0-0)
France: Grégory Coupet, Lilian Thuram (C), William Gallas (YC78), François Clerc, Éric
Abidal, Jérémy Toulalan, Franck Ribéry, Samir Nasri (81' Lassana Diarra), Florent Malouda,
Claude Makéléle, Nicolas Anelka (77' Djibril Cissé). (Coach: Raymond Domenech (FRA)).
Ukraine: Olexandr Shovkovskiy (C), Volodymyr Yezerskiy (78' Evgeniy Levchenko), Andriy
Nesmachniy, Andriy Rusol, Taras Mikhalik, Dmytro Chygrynskiy, Oleh Gusev, Olexiy Gai,
Anatoliy Tymoshchuk (YC85), Maxym Kalynychenko (64' Ruslan Rotan), Andriy Voronin
(72' Andriy Vorobey). (Coach: Oleh Vladimirovich Blokhin (UKR)).
Goals: France: 1-0 Franck Ribéry (57'), 2-0 Nicolas Anelka (71').
Referee: Luis Medina Cantalejo (ESP)   Attendance: 80.051

02-06-2007   Tórsvøllur, Tórshavn: Faroe Islands – Italy 1-2 (0-1)
Faroe Islands: Jákup Mikkelsen, Óli Johannesen (C), Marni Djurhuus, Atli Danielsen, Rógvi
Jacobsen, Mikkjal Thomassen, Súni Olsen, Christian Jacobsen, Andrew av Fløtum (56'
Christian Holst), Jákup á Borg (73' Símun Samuelsen), Jón Jacobsen. (Coach: Jógvan Martin
Olsen (FAR)).
Italy: Gianluigi Buffon, Massimo Oddo, Marco Materazzi (66' Andrea Barzagli), Fabio
Cannavaro (C), Gennaro Gattuso (YC51), Andrea Pirlo, Max Tonetto, Aimo Diana, Tommaso
Rocchi (86' Fabio Quagliarella), Filippo Inzaghi (58' Cristiano Lucarelli), Alessandro Del
Piero. (Coach: Roberto Donadoni (ITA)).
Goals: Faroe Islands: 1-2 Rógvi Jacobsen (77').
Italy: 0-1 Filippo Inzaghi (12'), 0-2 Filippo Inzaghi (48').
Referee: Robert Malek (POL)   Attendance: 5.987

06-06-2007   Svangaskard, Toftir: Faroe Islands – Scotland 0-2 (0-2)
Faroe Islands: Jákup Mikkelsen, Óli Johannesen (C) (YC30) (36' Marni Djurhuus, 77' Símun
Samuelsen), Atli Danielsen, Rógvi Jacobsen, Fródi Benjaminsen, Mikkjal Thomassen, Súni
Olsen, Christian Holst, Jón Jacobsen, Christian Jacobsen, Jákup á Borg (82' Andrew av
Fløtum). (Coach: Jógvan Martin Olsen (FAR)).
Scotland: Craig Gordon, Gary Naysmith (YC28), Stephen McManus, Graham Alexander,
David Weir, Paul Hartley, Darren Fletcher (68' Gary Stewart Teale), Barry Ferguson (C)
(YC74), Shaun Maloney (77' Charlie Adam), Garry O'Connor, Kris Boyd (83' Steven
Naismith). (Coach: Alexander (Alex) McLeish (SCO)).
Goals: Scotland: 0-1 Shaun Maloney (31'), 0-2 Garry O'Connor (35').
Referee: Georgios Kasnaferis (GRE)   Attendance: 4.100

06-06-2007   Stade de l'Abbé Deschamps, Auxerre: France – Georgia 1-0 (1-0)
France: Mickaël Landreau, Lilian Thuram (C), William Gallas, François Clerc, Éric Abidal,
Jérémy Toulalan, Franck Ribéry (90'+4' Sidney Govou), Samir Nasri, Florent Malouda (65'
Djibril Cissé), Claude Makéléle, Nicolas Anelka (90'+3' Karim Benzema). (Coach: Raymond
Domenech (FRA)).
Georgia: Georgi Lomaia, Lasha Salukvadze (12' David Mujiri), Dato Kvirkvelia, Zurab
Khizanishvili (YC25), Otar Khizaneishvili, Kakha Kaladze (C), Mate Ghvinianidze, Zaal
Eliava (62' Otar Martsvaladze), Jaba Kankava (YC53) (89' Giorgi Shashiashvili), Vladimer
Burduli, Aleksandre Iashvili. (Coach: Klaus Toppmöller (GER)).
Goal: France: 1-0 Samir Nasri (33').
Referee: Lucílio Cardoso Cortez Batista (POR)   Attendance: 19.345

06-06-2007   S.Darius and S.Girénas, Kaunas: Lithuania – Italy 0-2 (0-2)
Lithuania: Paulius Grybauskas, Tomas Zvirgzdauskas, Marius Stankevicius, Andrius Skerla,
Arūnas Klimavicius, Deividas Semberas, Gediminas Paulauskas (46' Andrius Gedgaudas),
Mindaugas Kalonas, Mantas Savénas (60' Tadas Labukas (YC81)), Tomas Danilevicius (C),
Igoris Morinas (39' Saulius Mikoliūnas). (Coach: Algimantas Liubinskas (LIT)).
Italy: Gianluigi Buffon, Massimo Oddo, Marco Materazzi, Fabio Cannavaro (C), Gianluca
Zambrotta, Simone Perrotta (71' Massimo Ambrosini), Andrea Pirlo (YC35), Daniele De
Rossi (65' Gennaro Gattuso), Fabio Quagliarella, Filippo Inzaghi, Antonio Di Natale (74'
Alessandro Del Piero). (Coach: Roberto Donadoni (ITA)).
Goals: Italy: 0-1 Fabio Quagliarella (31'), 0-2 Fabio Quagliarella (45').
Referee: Pieter Vink (HOL)   Attendance: 7.800

08-09-2007 Hampden Park, Glasgow: Scotland – Lituania 3-1 (1-0)
Scotland: Craig Gordon, James (Jay) McEveley, Stephen McManus, Alan Hutton (YC77), David Weir, Gary Stewart Teale (69' James McFadden), Darren Fletcher (C) (YC87), Scott Brown, Garry O'Connor (YC42) (76' Shaun Maloney), Lee McCulloch (76' Craig Beattie), Kris Boyd. (Coach: Alexander (Alex) McLeish (SCO)).
Lithuania: Zydrūnas Karcemarskas (YC40), Tomas Zvirgzdauskas (YC57), Marius Stankevicius (YC35) (56' Edgaras Jankauskas), Andrius Skerla, Arūnas Klimavicius, Deividas Semberas, Mindaugas Kalonas, Deividas Cesnauskis, Andrius Velicka (YC21) (47' Audrius Ksanavicius (YC64)), Igoris Morinas (47' Saulius Mikoliūnas), Tomas Danilevicius (C). (Coach: Algimantas Liubinskas (LIT)).
Goals: Scotland: 1-0 Kris Boyd (31'), 2-1 Stephen McManus (77'), 3-1 James McFadden (85').
Lithuania: 1-1 Tomas Danilevicius (61' penalty).
Referee: Damir Skomina (SLO)   Attendance: 51.349

08-09-2007 Boris Paichadze Stadium, Tbilisi: Georgia – Ukraine 1-1 (0-1)
Georgia: Georgi Lomaia, Lasha Salukvadze, Kakha Kaladze (C), Mate Ghvinianidze (YC89), Malkhaz Asatiani, Levan Tskitishvili (YC63), Zurab Menteshashvili (79' Dimitri Tatanashvili), Otar Martsvaladze, Lasha Jakobia (62' David Siradze), Aleksandre Iashvili (YC51) (62' Levan Kenia), Georgi Demetradze. (Coach: Klaus Toppmöller (GER)).
Ukraine: Olexandr Shovkovskiy, Volodymyr Yezerskiy, Andriy Rusol, Olexandr Kucher, Oleh Gusev, Oleh Shelayev (88' Olexandr Gladkiy), Ruslan Rotan (YC67) (80' Olexiy Gai), Anatoliy Tymoshchuk, Serhiy Nazarenko, Andriy Voronin (72' Maxym Kalynychenko), Andriy Shevchenko (C) (YC90). (Coach: Oleh Vladimirovich Blokhin (UKR)).
Goals: Georgia: 1-1 David Siradze (89').
Ukraine: 0-1 Oleh Shelayev (7').
Referee: Alain Hamer (LUX)   Attendance: 24.000

08-09-2007 San Siro, Milan: Italy – France 0-0
Italy: Gianluigi Buffon, Massimo Oddo, Fabio Cannavaro (C), Gianluca Zambrotta, Andrea Barzagli, Gennaro Gattuso (YC31), Mauro Camoranesi (58' Simone Perrotta), Andrea Pirlo, Daniele De Rossi (YC86), Filippo Inzaghi (65' Cristiano Lucarelli), Alessandro Del Piero (83' Antonio Di Natale). (Coach: Roberto Donadoni (ITA)).
France: Mickaël Landreau, Lilian Thuram, Julien Escudé, Éric Abidal, Patrick Vieira (C), Franck Ribéry (86' Jérémy Toulalan), Florent Malouda, Claude Makélélé (YC7), Lassana Diarra, Thierry Henry (YC56), Nicolas Anelka. (Coach: Raymond Domenech (FRA)).
Referee: Lubos Michel (SVK)   Attendance: 81.200

12-09-2007 S.Darius and S.Girénas, Kaunas: Lithuania – Faroe Islands 2-1 (1-0)
Lithuania: Zydrūnas Karcemarskas, Andrius Skerla, Arūnas Klimavicius, Vidas Alunderis, Deividas Semberas, Audrius Ksanavicius, Kesturis Ivaskevicius, Saulius Mikoliūnas (32' Andrius Velicka), Deividas Cesnauskis (31' Mindaugas Kalonas), Tomas Danilevicius (C), Edgaras Jankauskas (86' Aurimas Kucys (YC90+1)). (Coach: Algimantas Liubinskas (LIT)).
Faroe Islands: Jákup Mikkelsen (C), Atli Danielsen (YC49), Rógvi Jacobsen, Fródi Benjaminsen, Mikkjal Thomassen, Súni Olsen (YC35) (63' Pauli Hansen), Símun Samuelsen, Christian Holst (74' Hans Pauli Samuelsen), Jón Jacobsen, Christian Jacobsen (84' Andrew av Fløtum), Jákup á Borg. (Coach: Jógvan Martin Olsen (FAR)).
Goals: Lithuania: 1-0 Edgaras Jankauskas (8'), 2-0 Tomas Danilevicius (53').
Faroe Islands: 2-1 Rógvi Jacobsen (90'+3').
Referee: Tsvetan Georgiev (BUL)   Attendance: 5.500

12-09-2007   Olimpiyskiy National Sports Complex, Kiev: Ukraine – Italy 1-2 (0-1)
Ukraine: Olexandr Shovkovskiy, Volodymyr Yezerskiy, Andriy Rusol (YC88), Olexandr Kucher, Oleh Shelayev, Oleh Gusev (88' Artem Milevskiy), Olexiy Gai, Anatoliy Tymoshchuk, Serhiy Nazarenko (69' Olexandr Gladkiy), Maxym Kalynychenko (60' Andriy Voronin), Andriy Shevchenko (C). (Coach: Oleh Vladimirovich Blokhin (UKR)).
Italy: Gianluigi Buffon, Fabio Cannavaro (C) (YC28), Christian Panuccci, Gianluca Zambrotta, Andrea Barzagli, Simone Perrotta (YC47) (68' Alberto Aquilani (YC90)), Mauro Camoranesi (78' Massimo Oddo), Massimo Ambrosini, Andrea Pirlo, Vincenzo Iaquinta (85' Fabio Quagliarella), Antonio Di Natale. (Coach: Roberto Donadoni (ITA)).
Goals: Ukraine: 1-1 Andriy Shevchenko (71').
Italy: 0-1 Antonio Di Natale (41'), 1-2 Antonio Di Natale (77').
Referee: Howard Melton Webb (ENG)   Attendance: 41.500

12-09-2007   Parc des Princes, Paris: France – Scotland 0-1 (0-0)
France: Mickaël Landreau, Lilian Thuram, Julien Escudé, Éric Abidal (77' Karim Benzema), Patrick Vieira (C) (YC22) (69' Samir Nasri (YC74)), Franck Ribéry, Florent Malouda, Claude Makéléle, Lassana Diarra, David Trézéguet, Nicolas Anelka. (Coach: Raymond Domenech (FRA)).
Scotland: Craig Gordon, Stephen McManus, Alan Hutton, Graham Alexander, David Weir, Paul Hartley (YC58), Darren Fletcher (YC24) (26' Stephen Pearson), Barry Ferguson (C), Scott Brown, James McFadden (76' Garry O'Connor), Lee McCulloch. (Coach: Alexander (Alex) McLeish (SCO)).
Goal: Scotland: 0-1 James McFadden (64').
Referee: Konrad Plautz (AUT)   Attendance: 43.342

13-10-2007   Hampden Park, Glasgow: Scotland – Ukraine 3-1 (2-1)
Scotland: Craig Gordon, Gary Naysmith, Stephen McManus, Alan Hutton, David Weir, Stephen Pearson, Barry Ferguson (C) (YC45+4), Scott Brown (76' Shaun Maloney), Kenny Miller (YC72), James McFadden (80' Garry O'Connor (YC89)), Lee McCulloch (YC45+4) (60' Christian Dailly). (Coach: Alexander (Alex) McLeish (SCO)).
Ukraine: Olexandr Shovkovskiy, Volodymyr Yezerskiy, Andriy Nesmachniy (YC3), Olexandr Kucher, Dmytro Chygrynskiy, Oleh Gusev (46' Ruslan Rotan (YC70)), Anatoliy Tymoshchuk (73' Oleh Shelayev), Andriy Vorobey (YC37) (62' Serhiy Nazarenko), Olexandr Gladkiy, Andriy Voronin, Andriy Shevchenko (C) (YC15). (Coach: Oleh Vladimirovich Blokhin (UKR)).
Goals: Scotland: 1-0 Kenny Miller (4'), 2-0 Lee McCulloch (10'), 3-1 James McFadden (68').
Ukraine: 2-1 Andriy Shevchenko (24').
Referee: Pieter Vink (HOL)   Attendance: 50.589

13-10-2007   Tórsvøllur, Tórshavn: Faroe Islands – France 0-6 (0-2)
Faroe Islands: Jákup Mikkelsen (C), Einar Tróndargjógv Hansen, Hjalgrím Elttør (46' Bergur Midjord), Fródi Benjaminsen, Rógvi Jacobsen, Mikkjal Thomassen (78' Rókur av Fløtum Jespersen), Súni Olsen (YC57), Jón Jacobsen, Christian Holst, Símun Samuelsen (86' Andrew av Fløtum), Christian Jacobsen. (Coach: Jógvan Martin Olsen (FAR)).
France: Mickaël Landreau, Bacary Sagna, Lilian Thuram (C), Patrice Evra, Éric Abidal, Jérôme Rothen, Claude Makéléle (73' Lassana Diarra), Franck Ribéry (64' Hatem Ben Arfa), Jérémy Toulalan, Thierry Henry, Nicolas Anelka (46' Karim Benzema). (Coach: Raymond Domenech (FRA)).
Goals: France: 0-1 Nicolas Anelka (6'), 0-2 Thierry Henry (8'), 0-3 Karim Benzema (50'), 0-4 Jérôme Rothen (66'), 0-5 Karim Benzema (81'), 0-6 Hatem Ben Arfa (90'+4').
Referee: Gabriele Rossi (SMR)   Attendance: 1.980

109

13-10-2007   Stadio Luigi Ferraris, Genoa: Italy – Georgia   2-0 (1-0)
Italy: Gianluigi Buffon (C), Massimo Oddo (YC68), Christian Panuccci, Fabio Grosso, Andrea
Barzagli, Gennaro Gattuso, Massimo Ambrosini (88' Stefano Mauri), Andrea Pirlo, Luca Toni,
Fabio Quagliarella (72' Pasquale Foggia), Antonio Di Natale. (Coach: Roberto Donadoni
(ITA)).
Georgia: Georgi Lomaia, Giorgi Shashiashvili (60' Levan Kenia), Lasha Salukvadze, Dato
Kvirkvelia (YC79), Zurab Khizanishvili, Levan Tskitishvili (C), Zurab Menteshashvili, Jaba
Kankava, Malkhaz Asatiani, Georgi Demetradze (YC41) (85' Lasha Jakobia), Levan
Mchedlidze (60' David Siradze). (Coach: Klaus Toppmöller (GER)).
Goals: Italy: 1-0 Andrea Pirlo (44'), 2-0 Fabio Grosso (84').
Referee: Carlos Megía Dávila (ESP)   Attendance: 23.057

17-10-2007   NSC Olympiyskiy Stadium, Kiev: Ukraine – Faroe Islands   5-0 (3-0)
Ukraine: Andriy Pyatov, Andriy Nesmachniy, Andriy Rusol, Dmytro Chygrynskiy, Oleh
Gusev (62' Andriy Vorobey), Olexiy Gai, Anatoliy Tymoshchuk (C) (69' Olexandr Grytsay),
Serhiy Nazarenko, Maxym Kalynychenko, Olexandr Gladkiy (46' Artem Milevskiy), Andriy
Voronin. (Coach: Oleh Vladimirovich Blokhin (UKR)).
Faroe Islands: Jákup Mikkelsen (C), Óli Hansen, Jóhan Davidsen, Einar Tróndargjógv Hansen,
Atli Danielsen, Rógvi Jacobsen, Mikkjal Thomassen (8' Tem Hansen), Símun Samuelsen,
Christian Holst (75' Andrew av Fløtum), Christian Jacobsen (89' Hanus Thorleifsson), Jón
Jacobsen. (Coach: Jógvan Martin Olsen (FAR)).
Goals: Ukraine: 1-0 Maxym Kalynychenko (40'), 2-0 Oleh Gusev (43'), 3-0 Oleh Gusev (45'),
4-0 Maxym Kalynychenko (49'), 5-0 Andriy Vorobey (64').
Referee: Haim Yakov (ISR)   Attendance: 3.000

17-10-2007   Boris Paichadze Stadium, Tbilisi: Georgia – Scotland   2-0 (1-0)
Georgia: Giorgi Makaridze, Giorgi Shashiashvili, Lasha Salukvadze, Dato Kvirkvelia, Zurab
Khizanishvili (C), David Siradze (89' Lasha Jakobia), Zurab Menteshashvili, Levan Kenia (79'
Ilia Kandelaki), Jaba Kankava (YC61), Malkhaz Asatiani (YC90+5), Levan Mchedlidze (85'
Aleksandre (Lekso) Kvakhadze). (Coach: Klaus Toppmöller (GER)).
Scotland: Craig Gordon, Graeme Murty, Stephen McManus (YC61), Graham Alexander,
David Weir, Stephen Pearson (66' Craig Beattie (YC72)), Darren Fletcher, Barry Ferguson
(C), Shaun Maloney, Kenny Miller (66' Kris Boyd), James McFadden. (Coach: Alexander
(Alex) McLeish (SCO)).
Goals: Georgia: 1-0 Levan Mchedlidze (16'), 2-0 David Siradze (64').
Referee: Knut Kircher (GER)   Attendance: 29.377

17-10-2007   Stade de la Beujoire, Nantes: France – Lithuania   2-0 (0-0)
France: Mickaël Landreau, Lilian Thuram (C), William Gallas, Éric Abidal, Jérémy Toulalan,
Franck Ribéry, Florent Malouda, Claude Makélélé, Lassana Diarra (69' Hatem Ben Arfa),
Thierry Henry, Karim Benzema. (Coach: Raymond Domenech (FRA)).
Lithuania: Zydrūnas Karcemarskas, Tomas Zvirgzdauskas, Andrius Skerla, Arūnas
Klimavicius, Ignas Dedura (YC80), Aurimas Kucys (YC53) (84' Andrius Velicka), Audrius
Ksanavicius (YC34) (77' Tadas Labukas), Mindaugas Kalonas (63' Mantas Savénas), Igoris
Morinas, Tomas Danilevicius (C), Edgaras Jankauskas. (Coach: Algimantas Liubinskas (LIT)).
Goals: France: 1-0 Thierry Henry (80'), 2-0 Thierry Henry (81').
Referee: Viktor Kassai (HUN)   Attendance: 36.650

17-11-2007   Hampden Park, Glasgow: Scotland – Italy   1-2 (0-1)
Scotland: Craig Gordon, Alan Hutton, Gary Naysmith (YC34), Stephen McManus, David
Weir, Paul Hartley, Darren Fletcher, Barry Ferguson (C), Scott Brown (74' Kenny Miller), Lee
McCulloch (YC44) (90'+2' Kris Boyd), James McFadden. (Coach: Alexander (Alex) McLeish
(SCO)).
Italy: Gianluigi Buffon, Fabio Cannavaro (C), Andrea Barzagli, Gianluca Zambrotta, Christian
Panuccci, Gennaro Gattuso (87' Daniele De Rossi), Mauro Camoranesi (83' Giorgio Chiellini),
Massimo Ambrosini, Andrea Pirlo, Antonio Di Natale (68' Vincenzo Iaquinta), Luca Toni
(YC45). (Coach: Roberto Donadoni (ITA)).
Goals: Scotland: 1-1 Barry Ferguson (65').
Italy: 0-1 Luca Toni (2'), 1-2 Christian Panuccci (90'+1').
Referee: Manuel Enrique Mejuto González (ESP)   Attendance: 51.301

17-11-2007   S.Darius and S.Girénas, Kaunas: Lithuania – Ukraine   2-0 (1-0)
Lithuania: Zydrūnas Karcemarskas, Arūnas Klimavicius (YC65), Tomas Zvirgzdauskas,
Marius Stankevicius, Andrius Skerla, Gediminas Paulauskas, Ignas Dedura, Tadas Papeckys
(17' Igoris Morinas), Mantas Savénas, Tomas Danilevicius (C) (YC75) (82' Andrius Velicka),
Edgaras Jankauskas (90' Mindaugas Kalonas). (Coach: Algimantas Liubinskas (LIT)).
Ukraine: Olexandr Shovkovskiy (44' Andriy Pyatov), Vladyslav Vashchuk, Volodymyr
Yezerskiy, Dmytro Chygrynskiy, Oleh Shelayev (72' Serhiy Nazarenko), Ruslan Rotan, Oleh
Gusev, Olexiy Gai, Anatoliy Tymoshchuk, Andriy Shevchenko (C) (YC80), Andriy Voronin
(69' Artem Milevskiy). (Coach: Oleh Vladimirovich Blokhin (UKR)).
Goals: Lithuania: 1-0 Mantas Savénas (41'), 2-0 Tomas Danilevicius (67').
Referee: David Malcolm (NIR)   Attendance: 3.000

21-11-2007   Boris Paichadze Stadium, Tbilisi: Georgia – Lithuania   0-2 (0-0)
Georgia: Giorgi Makaridze, Dato Kvirkvelia, Kakha Kaladze (C), Lasha Salukvadze, Levan
Kenia, Jaba Kankava, Malkhaz Asatiani, Levan Tskitishvili, David Siradze (80' Nikoloz
Gelashvili), Zurab Menteshashvili (31' Otar Martsvaladze), Levan Mchedlidze. (Coach: Klaus
Toppmöller (GER)).
Lithuania: Zydrūnas Karcemarskas (YC83), Vidas Alunderis, Tomas Zvirgzdauskas, Marius
Stankevicius, Andrius Skerla (C), Gediminas Paulauskas, Ignas Dedura, Audrius Ksanavicius
(YC90+3), Mantas Savénas (67' Mindaugas Kalonas), Saulius Mikoliūnas (YC76) (76' Igoris
Morinas), Edgaras Jankauskas (YC35) (52' Andrius Velicka). (Coach: Algimantas Liubinskas
(LIT)).
Goals: Lithuania: 0-1 Audrius Ksanavicius (52'), 0-2 Audrius Ksanavicius (90'+6').
Referee: Aleksandar Stavrev (MCD)   Attendance: 21.300

21-11-2007   Stadio Alberto Braglia, Modena: Italy – Faroe Islands   3-1 (3-0)
Italy: Marco Amelia, Massimo Oddo, Fabio Cannavaro (C) (53' Daniele Bonera), Fabio
Grosso, Giorgio Chiellini, Simone Perrotta, Massimo Ambrosini (58' Fabio Quagliarella),
Daniele De Rossi, Raffaele Palladino, Luca Toni (74' Alberto Gilardino), Vincenzo Iaquinta.
(Coach: Roberto Donadoni (ITA)).
Faroe Islands: Jákup Mikkelsen (C), Einar Tróndargjógv Hansen, Jóhan Davidsen, Atli
Danielsen, Rógvi Jacobsen, Fródi Benjaminsen, Súni Olsen, Símun Samuelsen (75' Hanus
Thorleifsson), Christian Holst (86' Andrew av Fløtum), Jón Jacobsen, Christian Jacobsen.
(Coach: Jógvan Martin Olsen (FAR)).
Goals: Italy: 1-0 Fródi Benjaminsen (11' own goal), 2-0 Luca Toni (36'), 3-0 Giorgio Chiellini
(41').
Faroe Islands: 3-1 Rógvi Jacobsen (83').
Referee: Florian Meyer (GER)   Attendance: 16.142

111

21-11-2007   NSC Olympiyskiy, Kiev: Ukraine – France   2-2 (1-2)
Ukraine: Andriy Pyatov, Serhiy Fedorov, Vladyslav Vashchuk, Olexandr Romanchuk (81'
Volodymyr Yezerskiy), Olexandr Grytsay, Ruslan Rotan, Oleh Gusev (90'+1' Artem
Milevskiy), Olexiy Gai (YC84), Anatoliy Tymoshchuk, Andriy Voronin (85' Oleh Shelayev),
Andriy Shevchenko (C). (Coach: Oleh Vladimirovich Blokhin (UKR)).
France: Sébastien Frey, Lilian Thuram (C), William Gallas, François Clerc, Éric Abidal,
Franck Ribéry (89' Hatem Ben Arfa), Claude Makéléle, Lassana Diarra, Thierry Henry, Sidney
Govou (YC53), Karim Benzema (46' Samir Nasri). (Coach: Raymond Domenech (FRA)).
Goals: Ukraine: 1-0 Andriy Voronin (14'), 2-2 Andriy Shevchenko (46').
France: 1-1 Thierry Henry (20'), 1-2 Sidney Govou (34').
Referee: Tom Henning Øvrebø (NOR)   Attendance: 30.000

GROUP   C

02-09-2006	Ta'Qali	Malta – Bosnia and Herzegovina	2-5 (1-3)
02-09-2006	Budapest	Hungary – Norway	1-4 (0-3)
02-09-2006	Chisinau	Moldova – Greece	0-1 (0-0)
06-09-2006	Oslo	Norway – Moldova	2-0 (0-0)
06-09-2006	Frankfurt (GER)	Turkey – Malta	2-0 (0-0)
06-09-2006	Zenica	Bosnia and Herzegovina – Hungary	1-3 (0-1)
07-10-2006	Chisinau	Moldova – Bosnia and Herzegovina	2-2 (2-0)
07-10-2006	Budapest	Hungary – Turkey	0-1 (0-1)
07-10-2006	Athens	Greece – Norway	1-0 (1-0)
11-10-2006	Ta'Qali	Malta – Hungary	2-1 (1-1)
11-10-2006	Frankfurt (GER)	Turkey – Moldova	5-0 (3-0)
11-10-2006	Zenica	Bosnia and Herzegovina – Greece	0-4 (0-1)
24-03-2007	Chisinau	Moldova – Malta	1-1 (0-0)
24-03-2007	Oslo	Norway – Bosnia and Herzegovina	1-2 (0-2)
24-03-2007	Athens	Greece – Turkey	1-4 (1-1)
28-03-2007	Budapest	Hungary – Moldova	2-0 (1-0)
28-03-2007	Ta'Qali	Malta – Greece	0-1 (0-0)
28-03-2007	Frankfurt (GER)	Turkey – Norway	2-2 (0-2)
02-06-2007	Heraklion	Greece – Hungary	2-0 (2-0)
02-06-2007	Sarajevo	Bosnia and Herzegovina – Turkey	3-2 (2-2)
02-06-2007	Oslo	Norway – Malta	4-0 (1-0)
06-06-2007	Oslo	Norway – Hungary	4-0 (1-0)
06-06-2007	Sarajevo	Bosnia and Herzegovian – Malta	1-0 (1-0)
06-06-2007	Heraklion	Greece – Moldova	2-1 (1-0)
08-09-2007	Székesfehérvár	Hungary – Bosnia and Herzegovina	1-0 (1-0)
08-09-2007	Ta'Qali	Malta – Turkey	2-2 (1-1)
08-09-2007	Chisinau	Moldova – Norway	0-1 (0-0)
12-09-2007	Oslo	Norway – Greece	2-2 (2-2)
12-09-2007	Istanbul	Turkey – Hungary	3-0 (0-0)
12-09-2007	Sarajevo	Bosnia and Herzegovina – Moldova	0-1 (0-1)
13-10-2007	Budapest	Hungary – Malta	2-0 (1-0)
13-10-2007	Chisinau	Moldova – Turkey	1-1 (1-0)
13-10-2007	Athens	Greece – Bosnia and Herzegovina	3-2 (1-0)
17-10-2007	Ta'Qali	Malta – Moldova	2-3 (0-3)
17-10-2007	Istanbul	Turkey – Greece	0-1 (0-0)

17-10-2007	Sarajevo	Bosnia and Herzegovina – Norway	0-2 (0-1)
17-11-2007	Chisinau	Moldova – Hungary	3-0 (2-0)
17-11-2007	Oslo	Norway – Turkey	1-2 (1-1)
17-11-2007	Athens	Greece – Malta	5-0 (1-0)
21-11-2007	Ta'Qali	Malta – Norway	1-4 (0-3)
21-11-2007	Istanbul	Turkey – Bosnia and Herzegovina	1-0 (1-0)
21-11-2007	Budapest	Hungary – Greece	1-2 (1-1)

FINAL STANDING

Pos	Team	Pld	W	D	L	GF	GA	GD	Pts
1	Greece	12	10	1	1	25	10	+15	31
2	Turkey	12	7	3	2	25	11	+14	24
3	Norway	12	7	2	3	27	11	+16	23
4	Bosnia and Herzegovina	12	4	1	7	16	22	-6	13
5	Moldova	12	3	3	6	12	19	-7	12
6	Hungary	12	4	0	8	11	22	-11	12
7	Malta	12	1	2	9	10	31	-21	5

Greece and Turkey qualified for the Final Tournament in Austria and Switzerland.

02-09-2006   Ta'Qali Stadium, Ta'Qali: Malta – Bosnia and Herzegovina   2-5 (1-3)
Malta: Justin Haber, Luke Dimech, Ian Ciantar (46' Ivan Woods (YC67)), Ian Azzopardi, Brian Said, Jamie Pace (YC58), Claude Mattocks (66' Peter Pullicino), Michael Mifsud, Gilbert Agius (C) (83' Gareth Sciberras), Kevin Sammut, André Schembri. (Coach: Dusan Fitzel (CZE)).
Bosnia and Herzegovina: Kenan Hasagic, Sasa Papac (62' Ninoslav Milenkovic (YC87)), Dzemal Berberovic, Emir Spahic (YC87), Mirko Hrgovic, Zlatan Bajramovic, Vedin Music, Zvjezdan Misimovic, Mladen Bartolovic (54' Mirsad Beslija), Sergej Barbarez (C) (67' Vladan Grujic), Zlatan Muslimovic. (Coach: Blaz Sliskovic (BOS)).
Goals: Malta: 1-1 Jamie Pace (6'), 2-5 Michael Mifsud (86').
Bosnia and Herzegovina: 0-1 Sergej Barbarez (4'), 1-2 Mirko Hrgovic (10'), 1-3 Mladen Bartolovic (45'+1'), 1-4 Zlatan Muslimovic (49'), 1-5 Zvjezdan Misimovic (51').
Referee: Thomas Vejlgaard (DEN)   Attendance: 2.000

02-09-2006   Szusza Ferenc Stadium, Budapest: Hungary – Norway   1-4 (0-3)
Hungary: Gábor Király, Csaba Fehér, László Éger (YC61), Roland Juhász (65' Vilmos Vanczák), Balász Molnár, Zsolt Löw, András Horváth (61' Zoltán Kiss), Szabolcs Huszti, Pál Dárdai (C), Thomas Sowunmi (80' Sándor Torghelle (YC81)), Zoltán Gera. (Coach: Péter Bozsik (HUN)).
Norway: Thomas Myhre, Marius Johnsen (YC84), Erik Hagen, Brede Hangeland, Fredrik Strømstad (62' Daniel Braaten), Anders Rambekk, Kristofer Hæstad (85' Tommy Svindal Larsen), Martin Andresen (C), Morten Gamst Pedersen, Ole Gunnar Solskjær, John Carew (76' Steffen Iversen). (Coach: Åge Fridtjof Hareide (NOR)).
Goals: Hungary: 1-4 Zoltán Gera (89' penalty).
Norway: 0-1 Ole Gunnar Solskjær (15'), 0-2 Fredrik Strømstad (31'), 0-3 Morten Gamst Pedersen (41'), 0-4 Ole Gunnar Solskjær (54').
Referee: Pieter Vink (HOL)   Attendance: 12.283

113

02-09-2006   Zimbru Stadium, Chisinau: Moldova – Greece   0-1 (0-0)
Moldova: Serghei Pascenco, Ion Testemitanu (YC28), Radu Rebeja (C), Ghenadie Olexic,
Serghei Lascencov, Sergiu Epureanu (64' Serghei Clescenco), Stanislav Ivanov, Serghei
Covalciuc, Andrei Corneencov, Serghei Rogaciov (73' Serghei Dadu), Victor Berco (YC67).
(Coach: Anatol Georgievich Teslev (MOL)).
Greece: Antonis Nikopolidis, Giorgios (Giourkas) Seitaridis, Sotirios Kyrgiakos, Panagiotis
(Takis) Fyssas (YC89), Traianos Dellas (89' Georgios Anatolakis), Theodoros Zagorakis (C)
(46' Nikolaos (Nikos) Lyberopoulos), Konstantinos (Kostas) Katsouranis, Giorgios
Karagounis, Angelos Basinas (YC63), Angelos Charisteas (46' Dimitris Salpingidis), Ioannis
Amanatidis. (Coach: Otto-Heinz Rehhagel (GER)).
Goal: Greece: 0-1 Nikolaos (Nikos) Lyberopoulos (78').
Referee: Matteo Simone Trefoloni (ITA)   Attendance: 8.000
(Angelos Basinas missed a penalty in the 28th minute)

06-09-2006   Ullevaal Stadion, Oslo: Norway – Moldova   2-0 (0-0)
Norway: Thomas Myhre, Marius Johnsen (63' Steffen Iversen), Erik Hagen, Brede Hangeland,
Kristofer Hæstad, Martin Andresen (C) (YC24), Fredrik Strømstad (89' Tommy Svindal
Larsen), Anders Rambekk, Morten Gamst Pedersen, Frode Johnsen (46' Ole Gunnar Solskjær),
John Carew. (Coach: Åge Fridtjof Hareide (NOR)).
Moldova: Serghei Pascenco, Ghenadie Olexic (YC65), Ion Testemitanu, Radu Rebeja (C),
Serghei Lascencov (YC73) (75' Serghei Clescenco), Stanislav Ivanov, Alexandru Epureanu,
Serghei Covalciuc, Andrei Corneencov, Victor Berco (YC11,YC46), Serghei Rogaciov (70'
Serghei Dadu). (Coach: Anatol Georgievich Teslev (MOL)).
Goals: Norway: 1-0 Fredrik Strømstad (73'), 2-0 Steffen Iversen (77').
Referee: Hristo Ristoskov (BUL)   Attendance: 23.848

06-09-2006   Commerzbank-Arena, Frankfurt (GER): Turkey – Malta   2-0 (0-0)
Turkey: Rüstü Reçber, Can Arat, Gökhan Zan (YC65), Ergün Penbe, Tümer Metin, Mehmet
Aurélio, Yildiray Bastürk (46' Arda Turan), Hamit Altintop (YC33), Mehmet Topuz, Fatih
Tekke (46' Nihat Kahveci), Hakan Sükür (C) (85' Nuri Sahin). (Coach: Fatih Terim (TUR)).
Malta: Justin Haber, Luke Dimech, Ian Ciantar (YC77), Stephen (Steve) Wellmann, Brian
Said, Jamie Pace, Michael Mifsud, Gilbert Agius (C) (86' Gareth Sciberras), Ivan Woods
(YC17), Kevin Sammut (80' Peter Pullicino), André Schembri (87' Terence Scerri). (Coach:
Dusan Fitzel (CZE)).
Goals: Turkey: 1-0 Nihat Kahveci (55'), 2-0 Tümer Metin (77').
Referee: Bernardino González Vázquez (ESP)   Attendance: behind closed doors

Turkey were ordered to play their first three home matches at a neutral ground and behind
closed doors following violence in their World Cup Qualifying play-off with Switzerland on
16th November 2005.

06-09-2006   Bilino Polje, Zenica: Bosnia and Herzegovina – Hungary 1-3 (0-1)
Bosnia and Herzegovina: Kenan Hasagic, Sasa Papac, Emir Spahic (YC36,YC38), Vedin
Music (46' Zlatan Muslimovic), Dusan Kerkez, Mirko Hrgovic (73' Mirsad Beslija (YC76)),
Zlatan Bajramovic, Zvjezdan Misimovic, Elvir Bolic (YC51), Sergej Barbarez (C) (YC40),
Mladen Bartolovic (63' Vule Trivunovic). (Coach: Blaz Sliskovic (BOS)).
Hungary: Gábor Király, Csaba Fehér (YC9) (82' Zoltán Kiss), László Éger, Vilmos Vanczák,
Zsolt Löw (65' Roland Juhász), Balász Molnár, Szabolcs Huszti (YC36), Pál Dárdai (C),
Balázs Tóth (YC37), Zoltán Gera, Sándor Torghelle (90' Péter Kabát). (Coach: Péter Bozsik
(HUN)).
Goals: Bosnia and Herzegovina: 1-3 Zvjezdan Misimovic (64' penalty).
Hungary: 0-1 Szabolcs Huszti (35' penalty), 0-2 Zoltán Gera (46'), 0-3 Pál Dárdai (50').
Referee: Costas Kapitanis (CYP)   Attendance: 11.800

07-10-2006   Zimbru Stadium, Chisinau: Moldova – Bosnia and Herzegovina 2-2 (2-0)
Moldova: Serghei Pascenco, Ion Testemitanu, Radu Rebeja (C) (YC25), Ghenadie Olexic,
Valeriu Catînsus (YC54), Serghei Lascencov, Alexandru Epureanu, Stanislav Ivanov, Serghiu
Epureanu (71' Andrei Corneencov), Alexandru Gatcan (90' Serghei Clescenco), Serghei
Rogaciov (69' Serghei Dadu (YC85)). (Coach: Anatol Georgievich Teslev (MOL)).
Bosnia and Herzegovina: Kenan Hasagic, Velimir Vidic (YC19), Vule Trivunovic, Sasa Papac,
Dalibor Silic, Mirko Hrgovic (85' Sulejman Smajic), Dario Damjanovic (46' Ivica Grlic),
Zlatan Bajramovic (77' Vladan Grujic), Zvjezdan Misimovic, Mladen Bartolovic, Sergej
Barbarez (C) (YC25). (Coach: Blaz Sliskovic (BOS)).
Goals: Moldova: 1-0 Serghei Rogaciov (13'), 2-0 Serghei Rogaciov (31' penalty).
Bosnia and Herzegovina: 2-1 Zvjezdan Misimovic (62' penalty), 2-2 Ivica Grlic (69').
Referee: Hervé Piccirillo (FRA)   Attendance: 7.114
(Zvjezdan Misimovic missed a penalty in the 62nd minute)

07-10-2006   Stadium Puskás Ferenc, Budapest: Hungary – Turkey 0-1 (0-1)
Hungary: Gábor Király, Csaba Fehér, László Éger, Roland Juhász, Vilmos Vanczák (YC45),
Szabolcs Huszti, Péter Halmosi (YC36) (46' Péter Kabát, 76' Ádám Komlósi), Pál Dárdai (C)
(YC81), Balázs Tóth, Zoltán Gera, Sándor Torghelle (83' Imre Szabics). (Coach: Péter Bozsik
(HUN)).
Turkey: Rüstü Reçber, Servet Çetin, Gökhan Zan, Sabri Sarioglu, Ibrahim Üzülmez, Mehmet
Aurélio (YC30), Gökdeniz Karadeniz (64' Hüseyin Çimsir), Hamit Altintop, Arda Turan (90'
Mehmet Topuz), Hakan Sükür (C), Tuncay Sanli (90'+2' Can Arat). (Coach: Fatih Terim
(TUR)).
Goal: Turkey: 0-1 Tuncay Sanli (39').
Referee: Alain Hamer (LUX)   Attendance: 6.800

07-10-2006   Karaiskákis Stadium, Athens: Greece – Norway 1-0 (1-0)
Greece: Antonis Nikopolidis, Giorgios (Giourkas) Seitaridis, Sotirios Kyrgiakos, Panagiotis
(Takis) Fyssas, Georgios Anatolakis (YC78), Konstantinos (Kostas) Katsouranis, Giorgios
Karagounis (90' Christos Patsatzoglou), Stylianos Giannakopoulos (46' Angelos Charisteas),
Angelos Basinas, Georgios Samaras (YC44), Nikolaos (Nikos) Lyberopoulos (71' Ioannis
Amanatidis). (Coach: Otto-Heinz Rehhagel (GER)).
Norway: Thomas Myhre, Erik Hagen, John Arne Riise, Brede Hangeland, Fredrik Strømstad
(60' Daniel Braaten), Anders Rambekk (85' Ole Martin Årst), Kristofer Hæstad, Martin
Andresen (C), Morten Gamst Pedersen (YC63), Ole Gunnar Solskjær (YC75), Steffen Iversen.
(Coach: Åge Fridtjof Hareide (NOR)).
Goal: Greece: 1-0 Konstantinos (Kostas) Katsouranis (32').
Referee: Lubos Michel (SVK)   Attendance: 21.189

115

11-10-2006   Ta'Qali Stadium, Ta'Qali: Malta – Hungary 2-1 (1-1)
Malta: Justin Haber, Brian Said, Luke Dimech, Stephen (Steve) Wellmann, Kenneth Scicluna, Jamie Pace, George Mallia (65' Andrew Cohen), Kevin Sammut (YC87), Michael Mifsud, Gilbert Agius (C) (83' Peter Pullicino), André Schembri (73' Terence Scerri). (Coach: Dusan Fitzel (CZE)).
Hungary: Gábor Király, Csaba Fehér (77' Péter Halmosi), Roland Juhász, Vilmos Vanczák (RC38), LEANDRO Marcolini Pedroso de Almeida (46' Zoltán Kiss), Szabolcs Huszti, Pál Dárdai (C), Balázs Tóth, Imre Szabics (60' Péter Czvitkovics), Zoltán Gera, Sándor Torghelle. (Coach: Péter Bozsik (HUN)).
Goals: Malta: 1-0 André Schembri (13'), 2-1 André Schembri (52').
Hungary: 1-1 Sándor Torghelle (19').
Referee: Johny Ver Eecke (BEL)   Attendance: 3.600

11-10-2006   Commerzbank-Arena, Frankfurt (GER): Turkey – Moldova 5-0 (3-0)
Turkey: Rüstü Reçber, Servet Çetin, Gökhan Zan, Ibrahim Üzülmez, Sabri Sarioglu (YC51), Arda Turan (73' Nihat Kahveci), Mehmet Aurélio, Gökdeniz Karadeniz (61' Tümer Metin), Hamit Altintop, Hakan Sükür (C) (82' Halil Antintop), Tuncay Sanli. (Coach: Fatih Terim (TUR)).
Moldova: Serghei Pascenco, Ion Testemitanu, Radu Rebeja (C), Ghenadie Olexic, Valeriu Catînsus (YC32), Alexandru Epureanu (46' Andrei Corneencov), Stanislav Ivanov, Serghiu Epureanu (64' Serghei Dadu), Serghei Covalciuc, Alexandru Gatcan, Serghei Rogaciov. (Coach: Anatol Georgievich Teslev (MOL)).
Goals: Turkey: 1-0 Hakan Sükür (34'), 2-0 Hakan Sükür (37' penalty), 3-0 Hakan Sükür (43'), 4-0 Tuncay Sanli (69'), 5-0 Hakan Sükür (74').
Referee: Nicolai Vollquartz (DEN)   Attendance: behind closed doors

11-10-2006   Bilino Polje, Zenica: Bosnia and Herzegovina – Greece 0-4 (0-1)
Bosnia and Herzegovina: Kenan Hasagic (46' Almir Tolja), Sasa Papac (RC49), Branimir Bajic, Emir Spahic (YC39), Dalibor Silic (YC64) (79' Senijad Ibricic), Mirko Hrgovic, Ivica Grlic (62' Vladan Grujic), Zlatan Bajramovic (C), Zvjezdan Misimovic, Alen Skoro, Mladen Bartolovic. (Coach: Blaz Sliskovic (BOS)).
Greece: Antonis Nikopolidis (C), Giorgios (Giourkas) Seitaridis (57' Christos Patsatzoglou (YC59)), Sotirios Kyrgiakos, Panagiotis (Takis) Fyssas, Georgios Anatolakis, Konstantinos (Kostas) Katsouranis, Giorgios Karagounis (38' Theodoros Zagorakis), Stylianos Giannakopoulos (89' Ioannis Amanatidis), Angelos Basinas, Georgios Samaras, Angelos Charisteas. (Coach: Otto-Heinz Rehhagel (GER)).
Goals: Greece: 0-1 Angelos Charisteas (9' penalty), 0-2 Christos Patsatzoglou (82'), 0-3 Georgios Samaras (85'), 0-4 Konstantinos (Kostas) Katsouranis (90'+3').
Referee: Yuri Valeryevich Baskakov (RUS)   Attendance: 8.000

24-03-2007   Zimbru Stadium, Chisinau: Moldova – Malta 1-1 (0-0)
Moldova: Serghei Pascenco, Radu Rebeja (C) (YC53), Ghenadie Olexic (YC90+3), Victor
Golovatenco, Alexandru Epureanu (YC35), Vitali Bordian, Serghei Namasco (81' Serghei
Dadu (RC84)), Victor Comleonoc, Denis Zmeu (63' Stanislav Ivanov), Viorel Frunza (YC38)
(74' Serghei Alexeev), Igor Bugaev. (Coach: Igor Ivanovich Dobrovolskiy (RUS)).
Malta: Justin Haber, Kenneth Scicluna, Brian Said, Luke Dimech (RC84), Jamie Pace, George
Mallia, Roderick Briffa (YC26), Ivan Woods (77' Kevin Sammut), Michael Mifsud (90'+2'
Gareth Sciberras), Gilbert Agius (C), André Schembri (70' Daniel Bogdanovic). (Coach:
Dusan Fitzel (CZE)).
Goals: Moldova: 1-1 Alexandru Epureanu (85').
Malta: 0-1 George Mallia (73').
Referee: Vusal Aliyev (AZE)   Attendance: 8.033
(Viorel Frunza missed a penalty in the 24th minute)

24-03-2007   Ullevaal Stadion, Oslo: Norway – Bosnia and Herzegovina 1-2 (0-2)
Norway: Thomas Myhre, Erik Hagen (YC39), Jarl André Storbæk (79' Simen Brenne), Brede
Hangeland, John Arne Riise, Kristofer Hæstad, Martin Andresen (C), Fredrik Strømstad (62'
Christian Grindheim), Morten Gamst Pedersen (YC90+3), Frode Johnsen (46' Steffen Iversen),
John Carew. (Coach: Åge Fridtjof Hareide (NOR)).
Bosnia and Herzegovina: Adnan Guso, Branimir Bajic, Safet Nadarevic (47' Ivan Radeljic),
Dzemal Berberovic (58' Vedin Music), Branislav Krunic, Mirko Hrgovic (YC52), Dario
Damjanovic, Zvjezdan Misimovic (C), Adnan Custovic (YC2) (82' Darko Maletic), Zlatan
Muslimovic, Vedad Ibisevic. (Coach: Fuad Muzurovic (BOS)).
Goals: Norway: 1-2 John Carew (50' penalty).
Bosnia and Herzegovina: 0-1 Zvjezdan Misimovic (18'), 0-2 Dario Damjanovic (33').
Referee: Michael (Mike) Riley (ENG)   Attendance: 16.987

24-03-2007   Karaiskákis Stadium, Athens: Greece – Turkey 1-4 (1-1)
Greece: Antonis Nikopolidis (C), Panagiotis (Takis) Fyssas (56' Vasilios Torosidis), Traianos
Dellas, Giorgios (Giourkas) Seitaridis (YC90), Sotirios Kyrgiakos, Konstantinos (Kostas)
Katsouranis, Giorgios Karagounis, Stylianos Giannakopoulos (72' Ioannis Amanatidis),
Angelos Basinas, Angelos Charisteas (63' Theofanis (Fanis) Gekas), Georgios Samaras.
(Coach: Otto-Heinz Rehhagel (GER)).
Turkey: Volkan Demirel (YC83), Servet Çetin, Gökhan Zan (YC36), Sabri Sarioglu, Ibrahim
Üzülmez (19' Volkan Yaman), Tümer Metin (80' Gökdeniz Karadeniz), Mehmet Aurélio,
Hamit Altintop, Tuncay Sanli, Gökhan Ünal (57' Hüseyin Çimsir), Hakan Sükür (C). (Coach:
Fatih Terim (TUR)).
Goals: Greece: 1-0 Sotirios Kyrgiakos (5').
Turkey: 1-1 Tuncay Sanli (27'), 1-2 Gökhan Ünal (55'), 1-3 Tümer Metin (70'), 1-4 Gökdeniz
Karadeniz (81').
Referee: Wolfgang Stark (GER)   Attendance: 31.405

117

28-03-2007   Szusza Ferenc Stadium, Budapest: Hungary – Moldova   2-0 (1-0)
Hungary: Zoltán Végh (C), Csaba Csizmadia, Béla Balogh (36' Tamás Vaskó), Roland Juhász,
Dániel Tözsér, Krisztián Vadócz, Balázs Tóth, Tamás Hajnal (64' Szabolcs Huszti), Boldiszár
Bödör, Tamás Priskin (YC45) (88' Tibor Tisza), Zoltán Gera. (Coach: Péter Várhidi (HUN)).
Moldova: Serghei Pascenco, Ghenadie Olexic, Victor Golovatenco, Alexandru Epureanu,
Andrei Cojocari, Vitali Bordian, Stanislav Ivanov (C) (46' Serghei Namasco), Victor
Comleonoc (66' Denis Zmeu), Andrei Corneencov, Viorel Frunza (46' Serghei Alexeev), Igor
Bugaev (YC71). (Coach: Igor Ivanovich Dobrovolskiy (RUS)).
Goals: Hungary: 1-0 Tamás Priskin (9'), 2-0 Zoltán Gera (63').
Referee: Martin Ingvarsson (SWE)   Attendance: 6.150

28-03-2007   Ta'Qali Stadium, Ta'Qali: Malta – Greece   0-1 (0-0)
Malta: Justin Haber (C), Kenneth Scicluna, Brian Said, Ian Azzopardi (YC56), Jamie Pace,
George Mallia (90'+1' Etienne Barbara), Roderick Briffa (YC40,YC69), Gilbert Agius, Kevin
Sammut, Michael Mifsud, André Schembri (71' Daniel Bogdanovic). (Coach: Dusan Fitzel
(CZE)).
Greece: Konstantinos (Kostas) Chalkias, Loukas Vyntra, Vasilios Torosidis, Sotirios
Kyrgiakos, Michalis Kapsis, Traianos Dellas (83' Georgios Anatolakis), Konstantinos (Kostas)
Katsouranis (YC90+4), Giorgios Karagounis, Angelos Basinas (C), Dimitrios Salpingidis
(YC29) (64' Nikolaos (Nikos) Lyberopoulos), Theofanis (Fanis) Gekas (90'+2' Georgios
Samaras). (Coach: Otto-Heinz Rehhagel (GER)).
Goal: Greece: 0-1 Angelos Basinas (66' penalty).
Referee: Pedro Proença Oliveira Alves Garcia (POR)   Attendance: 8.700

28-03-2007   Commerzbank-Arena, Frankfurt (GER): Turkey – Norway   2-2 (0-2)
Turkey: Volkan Demirel, Emre Asik (YC44), Servet Çetin, Sabri Sarioglu, Emre Belözoglu,
Tümer Metin (46' Volkan Yaman), Mehmet Aurélio, Gökdeniz Karadeniz (79' Mehmet
Yildiz), Hamit Altintop, Hakan Sükür (C) (90'+3' Hüseyin Çimsir), Tuncay Sanli. (Coach:
Fatih Terim (TUR)).
Norway: Thomas Myhre, Jarl André Storbæk, Erik Hagen, John Arne Riise, Brede Hangeland,
Fredrik Strømstad, Kristofer Hæstad (57' Per Ciljan Skjelbred (YC59)), Simen Brenne (YC62)
(85' Erik Nevland), Martin Andresen (C), Thorstein Helstad (63' Daniel Fredheim Holm),
John Carew. (Coach: Åge Fridtjof Hareide (NOR)).
Goals: Turkey: 1-2 Hamit Altintop (72'), 2-2 Hamit Altintop (90').
Norway: 0-1 Simen Brenne (31'), 0-2 Martin Andresen (40').
Referee: Stefano Farina (ITA)   Attendance: behind closed doors

02-06-2007   Pankritio Stadium, Heraklion: Greece – Hungary   2-0 (2-0)
Greece: Konstantinos (Kostas) Chalkias, Vasilios Torosidis, Giorgios (Giourkas) Seitaridis,
Sotirios Kyrgiakos, Georgios Anatolakis (53' Christos Patsatzoglou), Konstantinos (Kostas)
Katsouranis, Giorgios Karagounis, Angelos Basinas (C) (YC33), Angelos Charisteas (79'
Stylianos Giannakopoulos), Ioannis Amanatidis (87' Nikolaos (Nikos) Lyberopoulos),
Theofanis (Fanis) Gekas. (Coach: Otto-Heinz Rehhagel (GER)).
Hungary: Zoltán Végh (C), Béla Balogh, Csaba Csizmadia, Roland Juhász, Dániel Tözsér,
Krisztián Vadócz (73' Zoltán Szélesi), Balázs Tóth, Tamás Hajnal, Boldiszár Bödör (YC34)
(40' Vilmos Vanczák), Tamás Priskin (79' Balász Dzsudzsák), Zoltán Gera. (Coach: Péter
Várhidi (HUN)).
Goals: Greece: 1-0 Theofanis (Fanis) Gekas (16'), 2-0 Giorgios (Giourkas) Seitaridis (29').
Referee: Claus Bo Larsen (DEN)   Attendance: 17.244

*Greece were forced to play away from Athens for two matches following crowd disturbances
in the game against Turkey on 24-03-2007.*

118

02-06-2007   Asim Ferhatovic Hase Stadium, Sarajevo:
              Bosnia and Herzegovina – Turkey 3-2 (2-2)
Bosnia and Herzegovina: Adnan Guso, Branimir Bajic, Ivan Radeljic, Vedin Music, Darko
Maletic (YC19) (84' Adnan Custovic), Mirko Hrgovic, Dario Damjanovic (YC34), Elvir
Rahimic, Zvjezdan Misimovic (C), Zlatan Muslimovic (90'+3' Boris Pandza), Edin Dzeko
(62' Zajko Zeba). (Coach: Fuad Muzurovic (BOS)).
Turkey: Rüstü Reçber, Servet Çetin, Gökhan Zan, Sabri Sarioglu (77' Ümit Karan), Ibrahim
Üzülmez, Mehmet Aurélio (YC11), Gökdeniz Karadeniz (46' Hüseyin Çimsir), Hamit
Altintop, Arda Turan (64' Yildiray Bastürk (YC90+4)), Tuncay Sanli, Hakan Sükür (C).
(Coach: Fatih Terim (TUR)).
Goals: Bosnia and Herzegovina: 1-1 Zlatan Muslimovic (27'), 2-2 Edin Dzeko (45'+2'), 3-2
Adnan Custovic (90').
Turkey: 0-1 Hakan Sükür (13'), 1-2 Sabri Sarioglu (39').
Referee: Peter Fröjdfeldt (SWE)   Attendance: 13.800

02-06-2007   Ullevaal Stadion, Oslo: Norway – Malta 4-0 (1-0)
Norway: Håkon Opdal, Jarl André Storbæk, Erik Hagen, John Arne Riise, Brede Hangeland,
Kristofer Hæstad (82' Daniel Braaten), Martin Andresen (C), Bjørn Helge Riise, Morten
Gamst Pedersen (62' Simen Brenne), John Carew (72' Thorstein Helstad), Steffen Iversen.
(Coach: Åge Fridtjof Hareide (NOR)).
Malta: Mario Muscat, Stephen (Steve) Wellmann, Kenneth Scicluna, Brian Said, Ian
Azzopardi, Jamie Pace, George Mallia (YC48), Gilbert Agius (C), Kevin Sammut (46' Ivan
Woods), Michael Mifsud (83' Etienne Barbara), André Schembri (69' Daniel Bogdanovic).
(Coach: Dusan Fitzel (CZE)).
Goals: Norway: 1-0 Kristofer Hæstad (31'), 2-0 Thorstein Helstad (73'), 3-0 Steffen Iversen
(79'), 4-0 John Arne Riise (90'+1').
Referee: Jacek Granat (POL)   Attendance: 16.364

06-06-2007   Ullevaal Stadion, Oslo: Norway – Hungary 4-0 (1-0)
Norway: Håkon Opdal, Jarl André Storbæk, Erik Hagen (YC29), John Arne Riise, Brede
Hangeland, Martin Andresen (C), Bjørn Helge Riise, Morten Gamst Pedersen (82' Thorstein
Helstad), Christian Grindheim (46' Kristofer Hæstad), John Carew, Steffen Iversen (46' Daniel
Braaten). (Coach: Åge Fridtjof Hareide (NOR)).
Hungary: Zoltán Végh (C), Béla Balogh, Vilmos Vanczák, Zoltán Szélesi, Roland Juhász,
Ákos Buzsáky (83' Krisztián Vadócz), Dániel Tözsér, Balázs Tóth, Tamás Hajnal (YC29),
Tamás Priskin (71' Tibor Tisza), Zoltán Gera. (Coach: Péter Várhidi (HUN)).
Goals: Norway: 1-0 Steffen Iversen (22'), 2-0 Daniel Braaten (57'), 3-0 John Carew (60'), 4-0
John Carew (78').
Referee: Eduardo Iturralde González (ESP)   Attendance: 19.198

06-06-2007   Asim Ferhatovic Hase Stadium, Sarajevo:
              Bosnia and Herzegovina – Malta 1-0 (1-0)
Bosnia and Herzegovina: Adnan Guso, Ivan Radeljic, Boris Pandza, Elvir Rahimic, Vedin
Music (90'+1' Veldin Muharemovic), Darko Maletic (80' Mladen Bartolovic), Mirko Hrgovic,
Dario Damjanovic, Zvjezdan Misimovic (C) (YC54), Zlatan Muslimovic, Edin Dzeko (57'
Zajko Zeba). (Coach: Fuad Muzurovic (BOS)).
Malta: Mario Muscat, Brian Said, Luke Dimech (YC57), Ian Azzopardi, Jamie Pace (82'
Etienne Barbara), Roderick Briffa, Gilbert Agius (C), Ivan Woods (70' George Mallia), Kevin
Sammut, Michael Mifsud, Daniel Bogdanovic (65' André Schembri). (Coach: Dusan Fitzel
(CZE)).
Goal: Bosnia and Herzegovina: 1-0 Zlatan Muslimovic (6').
Referee: David Ceri Richards (WAL)   Attendance: 10.500

06-06-2007   Pankritio Stadium, Heraklion: Greece – Moldova   2-1 (1-0)
Greece: Antonis Nikopolidis (C), Vasilios Torosidis, Giorgios (Giourkas) Seitaridis, Sotirios Kyrgiakos, Christos Patsatzoglou (83' Stylianos Giannakopoulos), Giannis Goumas, Konstantinos (Kostas) Katsouranis, Giorgios Karagounis (YC60), Angelos Charisteas, Ioannis Amanatidis (71' Georgios Samaras), Theofanis (Fanis) Gekas (63' Nikolaos (Nikos) Lyberopoulos). (Coach: Otto-Heinz Rehhagel (GER)).
Moldova: Nicolae Calancea, Valeriu Catînsus (C), Victor Golovatenco, Alexandru Epureanu, Vitali Bordian, Serghei Namasco, Victor Comleonoc (82' Igor Tîgîrlas (YC89)), Nicolae Josan (YC11), Alexandru Gatcan (YC34), Igor Bugaev (50' Denis Zmeu), Serghei Alexeev (64' Viorel Frunza). (Coach: Igor Ivanovich Dobrovolskiy (RUS)).
Goals: Greece: 1-0 Angelos Charisteas (30'), 2-1 Nikolaos (Nikos) Lyberopoulos (90'+3').
Moldova: 1-1 Viorel Frunza (80').
Referee: Jan Willem Wegereef (HOL)   Attendance: 19.000

08-09-2007   Stadion Sóstói, Székesfehérvár: Hungary – Bosnia and Herzegovina   1-0 (1-0)
Hungary: Márton Fülöp, Tamás Vaskó (YC16), Vilmos Vanczák, Zoltán Szélesi, Roland Juhász (YC64), Ádám Vass, Dániel Tözsér, Tamás Hajnal (72' Csaba Csizmadia), Balász Dzsudzsák (90'+3' Péter Halmosi), Róbert Feczesin (89' Attila Filkor), Zoltán Gera. (Coach: Péter Várhidi (HUN)).
Bosnia and Herzegovina: Adnan Guso, Ivan Radeljic, Branimir Bajic (YC38), Dzemal Berberovic, Elvir Rahimic (YC25), Darko Maletic (79' Mario Bozic), Mirko Hrgovic (YC45) (84' Adnan Custovic), Zvjezdan Misimovic (C) (YC19), Zlatan Muslimovic, Dragan Blatnjak, Vedad Ibisevic (67' Edin Dzeko). (Coach: Fuad Muzurovic (BOS)).
Goal: Hungary: 1-0 Zoltán Gera (39' penalty).
Referee: Matteo Simone Trefoloni (ITA)   Attendance: 10.877

08-09-2007   Ta'Qali Stadium, Ta'Qali: Malta – Turkey   2-2 (1-1)
Malta: Justin Haber, Kenneth Scicluna, Brian Said (YC51), Luke Dimech, Ian Azzopardi, Jamie Pace (YC33), Roderick Briffa (88' Kevin Sammut), Ivan Woods (83' George Mallia), Michael Mifsud, Gilbert Agius (C) (YC82), André Schembri (YC37) (90'+1' Terence Scerri). (Coach: Dusan Fitzel (CZE)).
Turkey: Hakan Arikan, Ibrahim Toraman (YC86), Servet Çetin, Ibrahim Üzülmez, Sabri Sarioglu (52' Gökdeniz Karadeniz), Arda Turan (30' Ayhan Akman (YC63)), Emre Belözoglu, Hamit Altintop, Hakan Sükür (C), Tuncay Sanli (66' Deniz Baris), Halil Altintop. (Coach: Fatih Terim (TUR)).
Goals: Malta: 1-0 Brian Said (41'), 2-1 André Schembri (76').
Turkey: 1-1 Hakan Sükür (45'), 2-2 Servet Çetin (78').
Referee: Stefan Messner (AUT)   Attendance: 10.500

08-09-2007   Zimbru Stadium, Chisinau: Moldova – Norway   0-1 (0-0)
Moldova: Serghei Pascenco, Radu Rebeja (C), Ghenadie Olexic (78' Serghei Rogaciov), Serghei Lascencov, Alexandru Epureanu, Vitali Bordian, Victor Comleonoc, Denis Zmeu (65' Alexandru Suvorov), Alexandru Gatcan, Viorel Frunza (YC67), Igor Bugaev. (Coach: Igor Ivanovich Dobrovolskiy (RUS)).
Norway: Håkon Opdal, Jarl André Storbæk, Kjetil Wæhler (66' Vidar Riseth), John Arne Riise, Brede Hangeland, Martin Andresen (C), Bjørn Helge Riise, Morten Gamst Pedersen, Christian Grindheim, John Carew, Steffen Iversen (68' Thorstein Helstad). (Coach: Åge Fridtjof Hareide (NOR)).
Goal: Norway: 0-1 Steffen Iversen (48').
Referee: Robert Malek (POL)   Attendance: 10.173

12-09-2007 Ullevaal Stadion, Oslo: Norway – Greece 2-2 (2-2)
Norway: Håkon Opdal, Jarl André Storbæk, Erik Hagen, John Arne Riise, Brede Hangeland, Jan Gunnar Solli (70' Thorstein Helstad), Martin Andresen (C), Bjørn Helge Riise (90'+3' Frode Kippe), Morten Gamst Pedersen, John Carew (YC67), Steffen Iversen (80' Vidar Riseth). (Coach: Åge Fridtjof Hareide (NOR)).
Greece: Konstantinos (Kostas) Chalkias (YC52), Vasilios Torosidis, Giorgios (Giourkas) Seitaridis (YC35) (64' Paraskevas Antzas), Sotirios Kyrgiakos, Traianos Dellas (YC17), Christos Patsatzoglou, Konstantinos (Kostas) Katsouranis, Giorgios Karagounis, Angelos Basinas (C) (76' Georgios Samaras (YC89)), Dimitrios Salpingidis (46' Nikolaos (Nikos) Lyberopoulos), Theofanis (Fanis) Gekas (YC74). (Coach: Otto-Heinz Rehhagel (GER)).
Goals: Norway: 1-1 John Carew (15'), 2-2 John Arne Riise (39').
Greece: 0-1 Sotirios Kyrgiakos (7'), 1-2 Sotirios Kyrgiakos (30').
Referee: Massimo Busacca (SUI)   Attendance: 24.080

12-09-2007 BJK Inönü Stadium, Istanbul: Turkey – Hungary 3-0 (0-0)
Turkey: Hakan Arikan, Servet Çetin, Emre Asik, Ibrahim Üzülmez, Mehmet Aurélio, Gökdeniz Karadeniz (61' Halil Altintop), Hamit Altintop (YC23), Ayhan Akman (67' Serdar Özkan), Gökhan Ünal, Tuncay Sanli, Nihat Kahveci (C) (46' Emre Belözoglu). (Coach: Fatih Terim (TUR)).
Hungary: Márton Fülöp (71' János Balogh), Tamás Vaskó, Csaba Csizmadia, Vilmos Vanczák (YC39), Zoltán Szélesi, Roland Juhász, Ádám Vass, Tamás Hajnal (YC90), Balász Dzsudzsák (82' Péter Halmosi), Tamás Priskin (YC26) (66' Balázs Tóth), Zoltán Gera (C) (YC19,YC63). (Coach: Péter Várhidi (HUN)).
Goals: Turkey: 1-0 Gökhan Ünal (68'), 2-0 Mehmet Aurélio (72'), 3-0 Halil Altintop (90'+3').
Referee: Stuart Dougal (SCO)   Attendance: 28.020

12-09-2007 Asim Ferhatovic Hase Stadium, Sarajevo:
          Bosnia and Herzegovina – Moldova 0-1 (0-1)
Bosnia and Herzegovina: Adnan Guso (YC10), Ivan Radeljic (46' Vedad Ibisevic), Safet Nadarevic, Branimir Bajic, Dzemal Berberovic (C), Zajko Zeba (47' Dario Damjanovic), Elvir Rahimic, Darko Maletic (78' Adnan Custovic), Zlatan Muslimovic, Dragan Blatnjak, Edin Dzeko. (Coach: Fuad Muzurovic (BOS)).
Moldova: Nicolae Calancea, Radu Rebeja (C), Serghei Lascencov (YC78), Victor Golovatenco, Alexandru Epureanu, Vitali Bordian, Victor Comleonoc (63' Serghei Namasco), Alexandru Gatcan (85' Nicolae Josan), Andrei Corneencov (YC17), Igor Bugaev (YC89), Anatoli Doros (73' Serghei Rogaciov). (Coach: Igor Ivanovich Dobrovolskiy (RUS)).
Goal: Moldova: 0-1 Igor Bugaev (22').
Referee: Jouni Hyytiä (FIN)   Attendance: 2.000

13-10-2007 Szusza Ferenc Stadium, Budapest: Hungary – Malta 2-0 (1-0)
Hungary: Márton Fülöp, Béla Balogh, Tamás Vaskó, Zoltán Szélesi, Roland Juhász (YC52), Ádám Vass, Dániel Tözsér, Attila Filkor (75' Ákos Buzsáky), Balász Dzsudzsák (88' LEANDRO Marcolini Pedroso de Almeida), Róbert Feczesin (83' Péter Rajczi), Zoltán Gera (C). (Coach: Péter Várhidi (HUN)).
Malta: Justin Haber, Luke Dimech, Ian Azzopardi, Kenneth Scicluna, Brian Said (C), Roderick Briffa, George Mallia, Ivan Woods (YC9) (90'+1' Roderick Bajada), Kevin Sammut (66' Udochukwu Nwoko), Michael Mifsud, André Schembri (83' Terence Scerri). (Coach: Dusan Fitzel (CZE)).
Goals: Hungary: 1-0 Róbert Feczesin (34'), 2-0 Dániel Tözsér (78').
Referee: Karen Nalbandyan (ARM)   Attendance: 7.633

121

13-10-2007   Zimbru Stadium, Chisinau: Moldova – Turkey   1-1 (1-0)
Moldova: Nicolae Calancea, Victor Golovatenco, Alexandru Epureanu (YC65), Vitali
Bordian, Victor Comleonoc (C), Alexei Savinov, Denis Zmeu (67' Serghei Namasco), Nicolae
Josan, Alexandru Gatcan (89' Ghenadie Olexic), Andrei Corneencov, Viorel Frunza (86' Denis
Calincov). (Coach: Igor Ivanovich Dobrovolskiy (RUS)).
Turkey: Hakan Arikan (17' Volkan Demirel), Selçuk Inan (46' Ümit Karan), Gökhan Zan
(YC29), Servet Çetin, Ibrahim Üzülmez, Arda Turan (69' Tümer Metin), Mehmet Topuz,
Mehmet Aurélio, Emre Belözoglu (C), Gökhan Ünal, Tuncay Sanli. (Coach: Fatih Terim
(TUR)).
Goals: Moldova: 1-0 Viorel Frunza (11').
Turkey: 1-1 Ümit Karan (63').
Referee: Martin Atkinson (ENG)   Attendance: 9.815

13-10-2007   Olympic Stadium, Athens: Greece – Bosnia and Herzegovina   3-2 (1-0)
Greece: Antonis Nikopolidis (C), Sotirios Kyrgiakos, Traianos Dellas, Vasilios Torosidis,
Christos Patsatzoglou (YC73), Konstantinos (Kostas) Katsouranis (YC49), Giorgios
Karagounis, Angelos Basinas, Angelos Charisteas (69' Nikolaos (Nikos) Lyberopoulos),
Ioannis Amanatidis (70' Stylianos Giannakopoulos), Theofanis (Fanis) Gekas (81' Paraskevas
Antzas). (Coach: Otto-Heinz Rehhagel (GER)).
Bosnia and Herzegovina: Adnan Guso, Safet Nadarevic (YC80), Branimir Bajic, Dzemal
Berberovic, Branislav Krunic (46' Vedad Ibisevic), Mirko Hrgovic (RC56), Elvir Rahimic
(YC29), Zvjezdan Misimovic (C) (82' Sejad Salihovic), Admir Vladavic, Zlatan Muslimovic,
Dragan Blatnjak (62' Samir Merzic). (Coach: Fuad Muzurovic (BOS)).
Goals: Greece: 1-0 Angelos Charisteas (10'), 2-1 Theofanis (Fanis) Gekas (58'), 3-1 Nikolaos
(Nikos) Lyberopoulos (73').
Bosnia and Herzegovina: 1-1 Mirko Hrgovic (54'), 3-2 Vedad Ibisevic (90'+2').
Referee: Grzegorz Gilewski (POL)   Attendance: 30.250

17-10-2007   Ta'Qali Stadium, Ta'Qali: Malta – Moldova   2-3 (0-3)
Malta: Justin Haber, Kenneth Scicluna (YC25) (46' Terence Scerri), Brian Said (C), Luke
Dimech (YC13), Ian Azzopardi (90'+1' Udochukwu Nwoko), Roderick Briffa, Jamie Pace,
George Mallia, Ivan Woods (YC74), Michael Mifsud, André Schembri (46' Andrew Cohen).
(Coach: Dusan Fitzel (CZE)).
Moldova: Serghei Pascenco (YC61), Serghei Stroenco (YC11), Serghei Lascencov, Victor
Golovatenco (YC56,YC88), Vitali Bordian, Victor Comleonoc (C) (69' Serghei Namasco),
Nicolae Josan, Alexandru Gatcan (YC10) (77' Denis Zmeu), Andrei Corneencov (YC86), Igor
Bugaev, Viorel Frunza (83' Anatoli Doros). (Coach: Igor Ivanovich Dobrovolskiy (RUS)).
Goals: Malta: 1-3 Terence Scerri (71'), 2-3 Michael Mifsud (84' penalty).
Moldova: 0-1 Igor Bugaev (24' penalty), 0-2 Viorel Frunza (31'), 0-3 Viorel Frunza (35').
Referee: Igorj Ishchenko (UKR)   Attendance: 7.069

17-10-2007   Ali Sami Yen Stadium, Istanbul: Turkey – Greece 0-1 (0-0)
Turkey: Volkan Demirel, Gökhan Zan, Servet Çetin, Ibrahim Üzülmez, Emre Belözoglu (C) (YC55) (71' Arda Turan), Mehmet Aurélio, Gökdeniz Karadeniz (65' Hakan Sükür), Hamit Altintop, Gökhan Ünal, Tuncay Sanli, Ümit Karan (46' Tümer Metin). (Coach: Fatih Terim (TUR)).
Greece: Konstantinos (Kostas) Chalkias, Vasilios Torosidis (YC64), Giorgios (Giourkas) Seitaridis, Sotirios Kyrgiakos, Traianos Dellas, Paraskevas Antzas, Giorgios Karagounis, Angelos Basinas (C), Angelos Charisteas (59' Georgios Samaras), Ioannis Amanatidis, Theofanis (Fanis) Gekas (56' Nikolaos (Nikos) Lyberopoulos). (Coach: Otto-Heinz Rehhagel (GER)).
Goal: Greece: 0-1 Ioannis Amanatidis (79').
Referee: Manuel Enrique Mejuto González (ESP)   Attendance: 22.818

17-10-2007   Asim Ferhatovic Hase Stadium, Sarajevo:
              Bosnia and Herzegovina – Norway 0-2 (0-1)
Bosnia and Herzegovina: Adnan Guso, Safet Nadarevic, Branimir Bajic, Dzemal Berberovic, Samir Merzic, Darko Maletic (78' Veldin Muharemovic), Branislav Krunic, Sejad Salihovic (YC37), Zvjezdan Misimovic (C) (YC43), Zlatan Muslimovic (46' Edin Dzeko (YC90+3)), Dragan Blatnjak (46' Vedad Ibisevic). (Coach: Fuad Muzurovic (BOS)).
Norway: Håkon Opdal, Jarl André Storbæk, Erik Hagen (YC67), John Arne Riise, Brede Hangeland, Jan Gunnar Solli, Martin Andresen (C), Bjørn Helge Riise (90'+2' John Anders Bjørkøy), Morten Gamst Pedersen, Christian Grindheim (58' Sigurd Rushfeldt (YC73)), Thorstein Helstad (76' Daniel Braaten). (Coach: Åge Fridtjof Hareide (NOR)).
Goals: Norway: 0-1 Erik Hagen (5'), 0-2 Bjørn Helge Riise (74').
Referee: Stéphane Laurent Lannoy (FRA)   Attendance: 1.500

17-11-2007   Zimbru Stadium, Chisinau: Moldova – Hungary 3-0 (2-0)
Moldova: Stanislav Namasco, Radu Bebeja (C), Serghei Lascencov, Alexandru Epureanu (YC84), Vitali Bordian, Serghei Namasco, Eugeniu Cebotaru (50' Simeon Bulgaru), Denis Zmeu (YC75) (90'+3' Ghenadie Olexic), Nicolae Josan (YC80), Igor Bugaev, Denis Calincov (64' Serghei Alexeev). (Coach: Igor Ivanovich Dobrovolskiy (RUS)).
Hungary: Márton Fülöp (YC84), Tamás Vaskó, Csaba Csizmadia, Vilmos Vanczák, Zoltán Szélesi, Dániel Tözsér (38' Ákos Buzsáky), Krisztián Vadócz (39' Béla Balogh), Tamás Hajnal, Zoltán Gera (C) (YC30), Balász Dzsudzsák (71' Róbert Feczesin), Tamás Priskin. (Coach: Péter Várhidi (HUN)).
Goals: Moldova: 1-0 Igor Bugaev (13'), 2-0 Nicolae Josan (23'), 3-0 Serghei Alexeev (86').
Referee: Pavel Královec (CZE)   Attendance: 6.483

17-11-2007   Ullevaal Stadion, Oslo: Norway – Turkey 1-2 (1-1)
Norway: Håkon Opdal, Jarl André Storbæk (88' Sigurd Rushfeldt), Erik Hagen, John Arne Riise, Brede Hangeland, Kristofer Hæstad (YC8) (68' Per Ciljan Skjelbred), Alexander Tettey, Bjørn Helge Riise, Morten Gamst Pedersen, John Carew (C), Steffen Iversen (84' Thorstein Helstad). (Coach: Åge Fridtjof Hareide (NOR)).
Turkey: Volkan Demirel (YC63), Servet Çetin, Emre Asik, Ibrahim Kas (15' Gökhan Gönül), Mehmet Aurélio, Arda Turan (87' Tuncay Sanli), Emre Belözoglu (C), Hamit Altintop, Hakan Balta, Nihat Kahveci, Semih Sentürk (67' Yusuf Simsek (YC90+2)). (Coach: Fatih Terim (TUR)).
Goals: Norway: 1-0 Erik Hagen (12').
Turkey: 1-1 Emre Belözoglu (31'), 1-2 Nihat Kahveci (59').
Referee: Dr.Markus Merk (GER)   Attendance: 23.783

123

17-11-2007   Olympic Stadium, Athens: Greece – Malta   5-0 (1-0)
Greece: Antonis Nikopolidis, Vasilios Torosidis (48' Nikolaos (Nikos) Spyropoulos), Sotirios Kyrgiakos, Traianos Dellas (YC51), Christos Patsatzoglou, Konstantinos (Kostas) Katsouranis, Giorgios Karagounis (70' Alexandros Tziolis), Stylianos Giannakopoulos (46' Nikolaos (Nikos) Lyberopoulos), Angelos Basinas (C), Ioannis Amanatidis, Theofanis (Fanis) Gekas. (Coach: Otto-Heinz Rehhagel (GER)).
Malta: Justin Haber, Brian Said (YC61), John Mifsud (C), Ian Azzopardi, Roderick Briffa, Peter Pullicino, Jamie Pace, Kevin Sammut (61' Andrew Cohen), Udochukwu Nwoko (YC34), Michael Mifsud (78' Gareth Sciberras), André Schembri (68' Terence Scerri). (Coach: Dusan Fitzel (CZE)).
Goals: Greece: 1-0 Theofanis (Fanis) Gekas (32'), 2-0 Angelos Basinas (54'), 3-0 Ioannis Amanatidis (61'), 4-0 Theofanis (Fanis) Gekas (72'), 5-0 Theofanis (Fanis) Gekas (74').
Referee: Sten Kaldma (EST)   Attendance: 31.332

21-11-2007   Ta'Qali Stadium, Ta'Qali: Malta – Norway   1-4 (0-3)
Malta: Justin Haber, Stephen (Steve) Wellmann (YC40), Luke Dimech, Ian Azzopardi, Roderick Briffa, Jamie Pace, Peter Pullicino, Michael Mifsud (C) (YC50) (87' Terence Scerri), Ivan Woods (YC69) (83' Etienne Barbara), Udochukwu Nwoko (86' Andrew Cohen), André Schembri (YC56,YC68). (Coach: Dusan Fitzel (CZE)).
Norway: Håkon Opdal, Erik Hagen (YC12), Jarl André Storbæk, John Arne Riise, Brede Hangeland, Per Ciljan Skjelbred, Morten Gamst Pedersen (YC52), Vidar Riseth (YC37), Bjørn Helge Riise (75' Kristofer Hæstad), John Carew (C) (68' Thorstein Helstad), Steffen Iversen (84' Sigurd Rushfeldt). (Coach: Åge Fridtjof Hareide (NOR)).
Goals: Malta: 1-3 Michael Mifsud (53').
Norway: 0-1 Steffen Iversen (25'), 0-2 Steffen Iversen (27' penalty), 0-3 Steffen Iversen (45'), 1-4 Morten Gamst Pedersen (75').
Referee: Yuri Valeryevich Baskakov (RUS)   Attendance: 6.000

21-11-2007   Ali Sami Yen Stadium, Istanbul: Turkey – Bosnia and Herzegovina   1-0 (1-0)
Turkey: Rüstü Reçber, Servet Çetin, Emre Asik, Gökhan Gönül, Arda Turan (76' Tuncay Sanli), Emre Belözoglu (C), Mehmet Aurélio, Hamit Altintop, Hakan Balta, Nihat Kahveci (90' Gökdeniz Karadeniz), Semih Sentürk (YC48) (61' Sabri Sanoglu). (Coach: Fatih Terim (TUR)).
Bosnia and Herzegovina: Adnan Guso, Branimir Bajic, Safet Nadarevic (YC82), Dzemal Berberovic (YC39), Elvir Rahimic, Darko Maletic, Branislav Krunic, Samir Merzic (89' Veldin Muharemovic), Zvjezdan Misimovic (C), Senijad Ibricic (75' Vedad Ibisevic), Edin Dzeko (83' Sejad Salihovic). (Coach: Fuad Muzurovic (BOS)).
Goal: Turkey: 1-0 Nihat Kahveci (43').
Referee: Eric Frederikus Johannes Braamhaar (HOL)   Attendance: 20.106

124

21-11-2007   Puskás Ferenc Stadium, Budapest: Hungary – Greece 1-2 (1-1)
Hungary: Márton Fülöp, Tamás Vaskó, Vilmos Vanczák (YC90+3), Zoltán Szélesi, Roland
Juhász, Ádám Vass, Dániel Tözsér (YC29) (85' LEANDRO Marcolini Pedroso de Almeida),
Ákos Buzsáky, Péter Halmosi (81' Róbert Feczesin), Tamás Hajnal (C) (76' Attila Filkor),
Tamás Priskin. (Coach: Péter Várhidi (HUN)).
Greece: Konstantinos (Kostas) Chalkias (46' Antonis Nikopolidis), Loukas Vyntra, Sotirios
Kyrgiakos (YC62), Michalis Kapsis, Christos Patsatzoglou (YC70), Alexandros Tziolis (46'
Georgios Samaras), Konstantinos (Kostas) Katsouranis, Giorgios Karagounis, Angelos Basinas
(C), Dimitrios Salpingidis, Theofanis (Fanis) Gekas (82' Ioannis Amanatidis). (Coach: Otto-
Heinz Rehhagel (GER)).
Goals: Hungary: 1-0 Ákos Buzsáky (7').
Greece: 1-1 Vilmos Vanczák (22' *own goal*), 1-2 Angelos Basinas (59' penalty).
Referee: Robert (Rob) Styles (ENG)   Attendance: 32.300

GROUP   D

02-09-2006	Teplice	Czech Republic – Wales	2-1 (0-0)
02-09-2006	Bratislava	Slovakia – Cyprus	6-1 (3-0)
02-09-2006	Stuttgart	Germany – Republic of Ireland	1-0 (0-0)
06-09-2006	Bratislava	Slovakia – Czech Republic	0-3 (0-2)
06-09-2006	Serravalle	San Marino – Germany	0-13 (0-6)
07-10-2006	Cardiff	Wales – Slovakia	1-5 (1-3)
07-10-2006	Liberec	Czech Republic – San Marino	7-0 (4-0)
07-10-2006	Nicosia	Cyprus – Republic of Ireland	5-2 (2-2)
11-10-2006	Dublin	Republic of Ireland – Czech Republic	1-1 (0-0)
11-10-2006	Bratislava	Slovakia – Germany	1-4 (0-3)
11-10-2006	Cardiff	Wales – Cyprus	3-1 (2-0)
15-11-2006	Nicosia	Cyprus – Germany	1-1 (1-1)
15-11-2006	Dublin	Republic of Ireland – San Marino	5-0 (3-0)
07-02-2007	Serrvalle	San Marino – Republic of Ireland	1-2 (0-0)
24-03-2007	Dublin	Republic of Ireland – Wales	1-0 (1-0)
24-03-2007	Nicosia	Cyprus – Slovakia	1-3 (1-0)
24-03-2007	Prague	Czech Republic – Germany	1-2 (0-1)
28-03-2007	Liberec	Czech Republic – Cyprus	1-0 (1-0)
28-03-2007	Dublin	Republic of Ireland – Slovakia	1-0 (1-0)
28-03-2007	Cardiff	Wales – San Marino	3-0 (2-0)
02-06-2007	Cardiff	Wales – Czech Republic	0-0
02-06-2007	Nuremberg	Germany – San Marino	6-0 (1-0)
06-06-2007	Hamburg	Germany – Slovakia	2-1 (2-1)
22-08-2007	Serravalle	San Marino – Cyprus	0-1 (0-0)
08-09-2007	Serravalle	San Marino – Czech Republic	0-3 (0-1)
08-09-2007	Bratislava	Slovakia – Republic of Ireland	2-2 (1-1)
08-09-2007	Cardiff	Wales – Germany	0-2 (0-1)
12-09-2007	Trnava	Slovakia – Wales	2-5 (1-3)
12-09-2007	Nicosia	Cyprus – San Marino	3-0 (2-0)
12-09-2007	Prague	Czech Republic – Republic of Ireland	1-0 (1-0)

13-10-2007	Dubnica nad Váhom	Slovakia – San Marino	7-0 (3-0)
13-10-2007	Nicosia	Cyprus – Wales	3-1 (0-1)
13-10-2007	Dublin	Republic of Ireland – Germany	0-0
17-10-2007	Serravalle	San Marino – Wales	1-2 (0-2)
17-10-2007	Dublin	Republic of Ireland – Cyprus	1-1 (0-0)
12-10-2007	Munich	Germany – Czech Republic	0-3 (0-2)
17-11-2007	Cardiff	Wales – Republic of Ireland	2-2 (1-1)
17-11-2007	Hanover	Germany – Cyprus	4-0 (2-0)
17-11-2007	Prague	Czech Republic – Slovakia	3-1 (1-0)
21-11-2007	Nicosia	Cyprus – Czech Republic	0-2 (0-1)
21-11-2007	Frankfurt	Germany – Wales	0-0
21-11-2007	Serravalle	San Marino – Slovakia	0-5 (0-1)

FINAL STANDING

Pos	Team	Pld	W	D	L	GF	GA	GD	Pts
1	Czech Republic	12	9	2	1	27	5	+22	29
2	Germany	12	8	3	1	35	7	+28	27
3	Republic of Ireland	12	4	5	3	17	14	+3	17
4	Slovakia	12	5	1	6	33	23	+10	16
5	Wales	12	4	3	5	18	18	-1	15
6	Cyprus	12	4	2	6	17	24	-7	14
7	San Marino	12	0	0	12	2	57	-55	0

Czech Republic and Germany qualified for the Final Tournament in Austria and Switzerland.

02-09-2006   Na Stínadlech, Teplice: Czech Republic – Wales   2-1 (0-0)
Czech Republic: Petr Cech, Tomás Ujfalusi, David Rozehnal, Martin Jiránek, Marek Jankulovski, Tomás Rosicky (C), Jaroslav Plasil, Tomás Galásek (88' Radoslav Kovác), Jirí Stajner (46' Libor Sionko), Marek Kulic (75' David Lafata), Jan Koller. (Coach: Karel Brückner (CZE)).
Wales: Paul Jones, Sam Ricketts (79' Robert (Rob) Earnshaw), Lewin Nyatanga, Daniel (Danny) Gabbidon, Mark Delaney (78' David Cotterill), James Collins, Carl Robinson (YC77), Ryan Giggs (C), Carl Fletcher (47' Joe Ledley), Simon Davies, Craig Bellamy. (Coach: John Benjamin Toshack (WAL)).
Goals: Czech Republic: 1-0 David Lafata (76'), 2-1 David Lafata (89').
Wales: 1-1 Martin Jiránek (85' *own goal*).
Referee: Jonas Eriksson (SWE)   Attendance: 16.204

02-09-2006   Tehelné pole, Bratislava: Slovakia – Cyprus 6-1 (3-0)
Slovakia: Kamil Contofalsky, Ján Durica, Marek Cech, Martin Skrtel (YC7), Dusan Svento, Peter Hlinka, Radoslav Zabavník (46' Matej Krajcík), Marek Mintál, Miroslav Karhan (C), Filip Sebo (56' Ivan Hodúr), Szilárd Németh (46' Filip Holosko). (Coach: Dusan Gális (SVK)).
Cyprus: Michalis Morphis, Georgios Theodotou, Loukas Louka (67' Christos Theophilou), Constantinos (Costas) Charalambides, Chrysostomos (Chrysis) Michail, Constantinos Makrides (YC50), Lambros Lambrou, Alexandros Garpozis (46' Marios Elia), Nektarios Alexandrou (46' Asimakis (Simos) Krassas), Yiasoumis Yiasoumi, Ioannis Okkas (C). (Coach: Angelos Anastasiadis (GRE)).
Goals: Slovakia: 1-0 Martin Skrtel (9'), 2-0 Marek Mintál (33'), 3-0 Filip Sebo (43'), 4-0 Filip Sebo (48'), 5-0 Miroslav Karhan (52'), 6-0 Marek Mintál (55').
Cyprus: 6-1 Yiasoumis Yiasoumi (90').
Referee: Oleh Oriekhov (UKR)   Attendance: 4.783

02-09-2006   Gottlieb-Daimler-Stadion, Stuttgart: Germany – Republic of Ireland 1-0 (0-0)
Germany: Jens Lehmann, Philipp Lahm, Marcell Jansen, Manuel Friedrich, Arne Friedrich, Bastian Schweinsteiger (YC49), Bernd Schneider (YC79) (83' Tim Borowski), Torsten Frings, Michael Ballack (C), Lukas Podolski (76' Oliver Neuville), Miroslav Klose (YC60). (Coach: Joachim Löw (GER)).
Republic of Ireland: Shay Given (YC90+2), John O'Shea, Andy O'Brien (YC49), Steve Finnan, Stephen Carr, Richard Dunne (YC90+1), Kevin Kilbane (82' Alan O'Brien), Damien Duff (76' Aiden McGeady), Steven Reid (YC55), Robbie Keane (C) (YC54), Kevin Doyle (78' Stephen Elliott). (Coach: Stephen (Steve) Staunton (IRL)).
Goal: Germany: 1-0 Lukas Podolski (57').
Referee: Luis Medina Cantalejo (ESP)   Attendance: 53.198
(Stephen (Steve) Staunton was sent to the stands in the 75th minute)

06-09-2006   Tehelné pole, Bratislava: Slovakia – Czech Republic 0-3 (0-2)
Slovakia: Kamil Contofalsky, Martin Skrtel (YC49), Ján Durica (YC61), Marek Cech (24' Szilárd Németh), Jozef Valachovic (46' Filip Holosko), Dusan Svento, Matej Krajcík (YC89), Peter Hlinka, Marek Mintál, Miroslav Karhan (C), Filip Sebo (46' Ivan Hodúr). (Coach: Dusan Gális (SVK)).
Czech Republic: Petr Cech, Tomás Ujfalusi, David Rozehnal, Martin Jiránek, Marek Jankulovski, Libor Sionko (78' Jirí Stajner), Tomás Rosicky (C), Jan Polák (73' Radoslav Kovác), Jaroslav Plasil, Tomás Galásek, Jan Koller. (Coach: Karel Brückner (CZE)).
Goals: Czech Republic: 0-1 Libor Sionko (10'), 0-2 Libor Sionko (21'), 0-3 Jan Koller (57').
Referee: Stephen Graham (Steve) Bennett (ENG)   Attendance: 27.683

06-09-2006   Stadio Olimpico, Serravalle: San Marino – Germany   0-13 (0-6)
San Marino: Aldo Simoncini, Alessandro Della Valle, Damiano Vannucci (67' Davide
Simoncini), Carlo Valentini, Simone Bacciocchi, Nicola Albani, Mirko Palazzi (YC78), Marco
Domeniconi (46' Giovanni Bonini), Michele Marani (YC89), Andy Selva (C), Manuel Marani
(76' Mattia Masi). (Coach: Giampaolo Mazza (SMR)).
Germany: Jens Lehmann, Philipp Lahm, Marcell Jansen, Manuel Friedrich, Arne Friedrich,
Bastian Schweinsteiger, Bernd Schneider, Torsten Frings (60' Thomas Hitzlsperger), Michael
Ballack (C) (46' David Odonkor (YC73)), Lukas Podolski, Miroslav Klose (46' Gerald
Asamoah). (Coach: Joachim Löw (GER)).
Goals: Germany: 0-1 Lukas Podolski (11'), 0-2 Bastian Schweinsteiger (28'), 0-3 Miroslav
Klose (29'), 0-4 Michael Ballack (34'), 0-5 Lukas Podolski (43'), 0-6 Miroslav Klose (44'),
0-7 Bastian Schweinsteiger (47'), 0-8 Lukas Podolski (62'), 0-9 Thomas Hitzlsperger (65'),
0-10 Lukas Podolski (70'), 0-11 Thomas Hitzlsperger (72'), 0-12 Manuel Friedrich (88'), 0-13
Bernd Schneider (89' penaldty).
Referee: Selçuk Dereli (TUR)   Attendance: 5.019

07-10-2006   Millennium Stadium, Cardiff: Wales – Slovakia   1-5 (1-3)
Wales: Paul Jones, Lewin Nyatanga, Daniel (Danny) Gabbidon, Robert (Rob) Edwards (58'
Joe Ledley), Richard Duffy, Carl Robinson, Jason Koumas (YC24), Simon Davies (YC68)
(88' David Cotterill), Gareth Bale, Robert (Rob) Earnshaw (46' Paul Perry), Craig Bellamy
(C). (Coach: John Benjamin Toshack (WAL)).
Slovakia: Kamil Contofalsky, Stanislav Varga, Martin Petrás, Roman Kratochvil, Ján Durica,
Peter Petrás, Dusan Svento, Ján Kozák, Marek Mintál (71' Ivan Hodúr), Miroslav Karhan (C)
(67' Matej Krajcík), Róbert Vittek (77' Filip Holosko). (Coach: Dusan Gális (SVK)).
Goals: Wales: 1-2 Gareth Bale (37').
Slovakia: 0-1 Dusan Svento (14'), 0-2 Marek Mintál (32'), 1-3 Marek Mintál (39'), 1-4
Miroslav Karhan (51'), 1-5 Róbert Vittek (59').
Referee: Dick J.H.van Egmond (HOL)   Attendance: 28.493

07-10-2006   U Nisy Stadion, Liberec: Czech Republic – San Marino   7-0 (4-0)
Czech Republic: Petr Cech, Tomás Ujfalusi, David Rozehnal (46' David Lafata), Zdenek
Grygera, Marek Jankulovski, Tomás Rosicky (C) (63' Jaroslav Plasil), Jan Polák, David
Jarolím, Marek Kulic (46' Tomás Zápotocny), Jan Koller, Milan Baros. (Coach: Karel
Brückner (CZE)).
San Marino: Federico Valentini, Alessandro Della Valle, Damiano Vannucci, Carlo Valentini,
Simone Bacciocchi, Matteo Andreini (82' Paolo Mariotti), Nicola Albani, Michele Moretti (55'
Michele Marani), Mattia Masi (69' Federico Crescentini), Marco Domeniconi (YC64), Andy
Selva (C). (Coach: Giampaolo Mazza (SMR)).
Goals: Czech Republic: 1-0 Marek Kulic (15'), 2-0 Jan Polák (22'), 3-0 Milan Baros (28'), 4-0
Jan Koller (43'), 5-0 David Jarolím (49'), 6-0 Jan Koller (52'), 7-0 Milan Baros (68').
Referee: Vusal Aliyev (AZE)   Attendance: 9.514

128

07-10-2006   Neo GSP Stadium, Nicosia: Cyprus – Republic of Ireland 5-2 (2-2)
Cyprus: Michalis Morphis (YC21), Georgios Theodotou (YC79), Loukas Louka, Marinos
Satsias (YC35), Chrysostomos (Chrysis) Michail (46' Constantinos (Costas) Charalambides),
Constantinos Makrides, Lambros Lambrou, Alexandros Garpozis (YC32) (77' Elias
Charalambous), Ioannis Okkas (C) (YC54) (86' Yiasoumis Yiasoumi), Michalis Konstantinou
(YC37), Efstathios (Stathis) Aloneftis (YC56). (Coach: Angelos Anastasiadis (GRE)).
Republic of Ireland: Paddy Kenny, John O'Shea, Andy O'Brien (YC49) (71' Alan Lee), Steve
Finnan, Richard Dunne (YC34,YC77), Kevin Kilbane, Damien Duff, Stephen Ireland (82'
Jonathan Douglas), Clinton Morrison, Aiden McGeady (80' Alan O'Brien), Robbie Keane (C)
(YC54). (Coach: Stephen (Steve) Staunton (IRL)).
Goals: Cyprus: 1-1 Michalis Konstantinou (9'), 2-1 Alexandros Garpozis (15'), 3-2 Michalis
Konstantinou (50' penalty), 4-2 Constantinos (Costas) Charalambides (59'), 5-2 Constantinos
(Costas) Charalambides (84').
Republic of Ireland: 0-1 Stephen Ireland (7'), 2-2 Richard Dunne (43').
Referee: Lucílio Cardoso Cortez Batista (POR)   Attendance: 5.000

11-10-2006   Lansdowne Road, Dublin: Republic of Ireland – Czech Republic 1-1 (0-0)
Republic of Ireland: Wayne Henderson, John O'Shea, Paul McShane, Stephen
Kelly, Andy Reid (70' Alan Quinn), Kevin Kilbane (YC10) (78' Alan O'Brien), Damien Duff,
Jonathan Douglas (YC70), Lee Carsley (YC83), Robbie Keane (C). (Coach: Stephen (Steve)
Staunton (IRL)).
Czech Republic: Petr Cech, Tomás Ujfalusi, David Rozehnal (YC46), Martin Jiránek,
Radoslav Kovác (YC73), Marek Jankulovski, Tomás Rosicky (C), Jan Polák (YC33), Jaroslav
Plasil (84' Zdenek Grygera), Jan Koller, Milan Baros (YC30) (82' David Jarolím). (Coach:
Karel Brückner (CZE)).
Goals: Republic of Ireland: 1-0 Kevin Kilbane (62').
Czech Republic: 1-1 Jan Koller (63').
Referee: Bertrand Layec (FRA)   Attendance: 35.500

11-10-2006   Tehelné pole, Bratislava: Slovakia – Germany 1-4 (0-3)
Slovakia: Kamil Contofalsky, Martin Skrtel, Martin Petrás (YC60), Ján Durica, Stanislav
Varga, Peter Petrás (YC4) (72' Filip Holosko), Dusan Svento, Ján Kozák (65' Ivan Hodúr),
Marek Mintál, Miroslav Karhan (C), Róbert Vittek. (Coach: Dusan Gális (SVK)).
Germany: Jens Lehmann, Philipp Lahm, Clemens Fritz (YC65), Manuel Friedrich, Arne
Friedrich, Torsten Frings, Michael Ballack (C), Bastian Schweinsteiger (76' Piotr
Trochowski), Bernd Schneider (76' David Odonkor), Lukas Podolski (85' Mike Hanke),
Miroslav Klose. (Coach: Joachim Löw (GER)).
Goals: Slovakia: 1-3 Stanislav Varga (58').
Germany: 0-1 Lukas Podolski (13'), 0-2 Michael Ballack (25'), 0-3 Bastian Schweinsteiger
(36'), 1-4 Lukas Podolski (72').
Referee: Terje Hauge (NOR)   Attendance: 21.582

11-10-2006   Millennium Stadium, Cardiff: Wales – Cyprus 3-1 (2-0)
Wales: Lewis Price, Craig Morgan, Lewin Nyatanga, Daniel (Danny) Gabbidon, Richard
Duffy (78' Robert (Rob) Edwards), Carl Robinson, Jason Koumas (YC44) (75' Joe Ledley),
Simon Davies, Gareth Bale, Robert (Rob) Earnshaw, Craig Bellamy (C) (90'+1' Paul Perry).
(Coach: John Benjamin Toshack (WAL)).
Cyprus: Michalis Morphis, Georgios Theodotou, Loukas Louka, Marinos Satsias (YC52) (83'
Yiasoumis Yiasoumi), Chrysostomos (Chrysis) Michail (46' Elias Charalambous),
Constantinos Makrides, Lambros Lambrou, Alexandros Garpozis (YC3) (46' Constantinos
(Costas) Charalambides), Efstathios (Stathis) Aloneftis, Ioannis Okkas (C), Michalis
Konstantinou. (Coach: Angelos Anastasiadis (GRE)).
Goals: Wales: 1-0 Jason Koumas (33'), 2-0 Robert (Rob) Earnshaw (38'), 3-0 Craig Bellamy
(72').
Cyprus: 3-1 Ioannis Okkas (83').
Referee: Jacek Granat (POL)   Attendance: 20.456

15-11-2006   Neo GSP Stadium, Nicosia: Cyprus – Germany 1-1 (1-1)
Cyprus: Antonis Giorgallides, Georgios Theodotou (80' Elias Charalambous), Loukas Louka
(YC45), Marios Elia, Chrysostomos (Chrysis) Michail (68' Asimakis (Simos) Krassas),
Constantinos Makrides, Lambros Lambrou, Constantinos (Costas) Charalambides (YC20),
Michalis Konstantinou, Ioannis Okkas (C) (YC39) (72' Charis Nicolaou), Efstathios (Stathis)
Aloneftis. (Coach: Angelos Anastasiadis (GRE)).
Germany: Timo Hildebrand, Philipp Lahm (YC86), Clemens Fritz (YC78), Manuel Friedrich,
Arne Friedrich, Bastian Schweinsteiger, Torsten Frings, Michael Ballack (C), David Odonkor
(80' Thomas Hitzlsperger), Oliver Neuville (62' Mike Hanke), Miroslav Klose (YC19).
(Coach: Joachim Löw (GER)).
Goals: Cyprus: 1-1 Ioannis Okkas (43').
Germany: 0-1 Michael Ballack (15').
Referee: Peter Fröjdfeldt (SWE)   Attendance: 12.300

15-11-2006   Lansdowne Road, Dublin: Republic of Ireland – San Marino 5-0 (3-0)
Republic of Ireland: Shay Given, John O'Shea, Steve Finnan, Richard Dunne, Paul McShane
(YC83), Andy Reid, Kevin Kilbane (80' Alan Lee), Damien Duff, Lee Carsley (50' Jonathan
Douglas), Robbie Keane (C), Kevin Doyle (64' Aiden McGeady). (Coach: Stephen (Steve)
Staunton (IRL)).
San Marino: Federico Valentini, Damiano Vannucci (73' Federico Crescentini), Carlo
Valentini, Matteo Andreini, Davide Simoncini (81' Giovanni Bonini), Simone Bacciocchi,
Nicola Albani, Paolo Mariotti (59' Michele Marani), Matteo Bugli, Andy Selva (C), Manuel
Marani (YC67). (Coach: Giampaolo Mazza (SMR)).
Goals: Republic of Ireland: 1-0 Andy Reid (6'), 2-0 Kevin Doyle (24'), 3-0 Robbie Keane
(31'), 4-0 Robbie Keane (57' penalty), 5-0 Robbie Keane (85').
Referee: Lassin Isaksen (FAR)   Attendance: 34.018

130

07-02-2007   Stadio Olimpico, Serravalle: San Marino – Republic of Ireland   1-2 (0-0)
San Marino: Aldo Simoncini, Carlo Valentini, Davide Simoncini (YC17), Nicola Albani,
Riccardo Muccioli, Alex Gasperoni (66' Matteo Andreini), Marco Domeniconi (88' Matteo
Bugli), Michele Marani, Giovanni Bonini (76' Damiano Vannucci), Manuel Marani, Andy
Selva (C) (YC35). (Coach: Giampaolo Mazza (SMR)).
Republic of Ireland: Wayne Henderson, Ian Harte (74' Stephen Hunt), John O'Shea (46' Paul
McShane), Steve Finnan, Richard Dunne, Damien Duff, Lee Carsley, Kevin Kilbane, Stephen
Ireland, Shane Long (80' Anthony Stokes), Robbie Keane (C). (Coach: Stephen (Steve)
Staunton (IRL)).
Goals: San marino: 1-1 Manuel Marani (86').
Republic of Ireland: 0-1 Kevin Kilbane (49'), 1-2 Stephen Ireland (90'+4').
Referee: Peter Rasmussen (DEN)   Attendance: 3.294

24-03-2007   Croke Park, Dublin: Republic of Ireland – Wales   1-0 (1-0)
Republic of Ireland: Shay Given, John O'Shea, Steve Finnan, Paul McShane, Richard Dunne,
Kevin Kilbane, Damien Duff, Jonathan Douglas (80' Stephen Hunt), Lee Carsley, Stephen
Ireland (59' Kevin Doyle), Robbie Keane (C) (YC68) (89' Aiden McGeady). (Coach: Stephen
(Steve) Staunton (IRL)).
Wales: Danny Coyne, Sam Ricketts (YC82), Lewin Nyatanga, Steve Evans, James Collins,
Carl Robinson (YC86) (90'+1' Jermaine Easter), Joe Ledley (46' Carl Fletcher), Ryan Giggs
(C), Simon Davies, Gareth Bale (74' Danny Collins), Craig Bellamy. (Coach: John Benjamin
Toshack (WAL)).
Goal: Republic of Ireland: 1-0 Stephen Ireland (39').
Referee: Terje Hauge (NOR)   Attendance: 72.539

24-03-2007   Neo GSP Stadium, Nicosia: Cyprus – Slovakia   1-3 (1-0)
Cyprus: Michalis Morphis (RC42), Georgios Theodotou (C) (43' Antonis Giorgallides
goalkeeper), Loukas Louka, Chrysostomos (Chrysis) Michail, Constantinos Makrides (58'
Marios Elia), Constantinou (Costas) Charalambides, Marinos Satsias, Lambros Lambrou,
Alexandros Garpozis (66' Elias Charalambous), Yiasoumis Yiasoumi (YC72), Efstathios
(Stathis) Aloneftis. (Coach: Angelos Anastasiadis (GRE)).
Slovakia: Kamil Contofalsky, Peter Singlár (46' Igor Zofcák), Ján Durica (YC20), Martin
Skrtel (YC89), Dusan Svento, Matej Krajcík (YC50), Vralislav Gresko (YC27), Marek Sapara
(68' Ján Kozák), Balázs Borbély, Róbert Vittek (C), Martin Jakubko (79' Stanislav Sesták).
(Coach: Ján Kocian (SVK)).
Goals: Cyprus: 1-0 Efstathios (Stathis) Aloneftis (45').
Slovakia: 1-1 Róbert Vittek (54'), 1-2 Martin Skrtel (67'), 1-3 Martin Jakubko (77').
Referee: Gerald Lehner (AUT)   Attendance: 2.696

24-03-2007   Toyota Arena, Prague: Czech Republic – Germany   1-2 (0-1)
Czech Republic: Petr Cech, Tomás Ujfalusi (84' Stanislav Vlcek), David Rozehnal, Martin
Jiránek, Marek Jankulovski (YC82), Libor Sionko (46' Jaroslav Plasil), Tomás Rosicky (C),
Jan Polák, Tomás Galásek (YC53) (62' Marek Kulic), Jan Koller (YC89), Milan Baros.
(Coach: Karel Brückner (CZE)).
Germany: Jens Lehmann (YC85), Christoph Metzelder, Per Mertesacker, Philipp Lahm,
Marcell Jansen (YC84), Bastian Schweinsteiger, Bernd Schneider, Torsten Frings, Michael
Ballack (C), Kevin Kurányi, Lukas Podolski (89' Thomas Hitzlsperger). (Coach: Joachim Löw
(GER)).
Goals: Czech Republic: 1-2 Milan Baros (77').
Germany: 0-1 Kevin Kurányi (42'), 0-2 Kevin Kurányi (62').
Referee: Roberto Rosetti (ITA)   Attendance: 17.821

131

28-03-2007   U Nisy Stadion, Liberec: Czech Republic – Cyprus   1-0 (1-0)
Czech Republic: Petr Cech, Tomás Ujfalusi, David Rozehnal, Zdenek Grygera (12' Radoslav Kovác, 27' Martin Jiránek), Marek Jankulovski, Tomás Rosicky (C), Jan Polák, David Jarolím, Tomás Galásek, Jan Koller, Milan Baros (77' Jaroslav Plasil). (Coach: Karel Brückner (CZE)).
Cyprus: Antonis Giorgallides, Georgios Theodotou, Marios Elia (YC74) (76' Elias Charalambous), Paraskevas Christou, Marinos Satsias, Constantinos Makrides (YC90), Lambros Lambrou, Constantinos (Costas) Charalambides (75' Asimakis (Simos) Krassas), Yiasoumis Yiasoumi (C) (72' Kyriakos Chailis), Ioannis Okkas (YC16), Efstathios (Stathis) Aloneftis. (Coach: Angelos Anastasiadis (GRE)).
Goal: Czech Republic: 1-0 Radoslav Kovác (22').
Referee: Ivan Bebek (CRO)   Attendance: 9.310

28-03-2007   Croke Park, Dublin: Republic of Ireland – Slovakia   1-0 (1-0)
Republic of Ireland: Shay Given (C), Steve Finnan, John O'Shea, Richard Dunne, Paul McShane, Kevin Kilbane, Damien Duff, Lee Carsley, Stephen Ireland (70' Stephen Hunt), Kevin Doyle (74' Shane Long), Aiden McGeady (87' Alan Quinn). (Coach: Stephen (Steve) Staunton (IRL)).
Slovakia: Kamil Contofalsky, Peter Singlár (80' Stanislav Sesták), Maros Klimpl (YC81), Martin Skrtel, Vralislav Gresko, Igor Zofcák, Dusan Svento (86' Lubomír Michalík), Marek Sapara (72' Filip Holosko), Balázs Borbély, Róbert Vittek (C), Martin Jakubko. (Coach: Ján Kocian (SVK)).
Goal: Republic of Ireland: 1-0 Kevin Doyle (12').
Referee: Yuri Valeryevich Baskakov (RUS)   Attendance: 71.297

28-03-2007   Millennium Park, Cardiff: Wales – San Marino   3-0 (2-0)
Wales: Danny Coyne, Sam Ricketts, Steve Evans (63' Lewin Nyatanga), James Collins, Jason Koumas (YC29), Ryan Giggs (C) (73' Paul Parry), Carl Fletcher, Simon Davies, Gareth Bale, Jermaine Easter (46' David Cotterill), Craig Bellamy. (Coach: John Benjamin Toshack (WAL)).
San Marino: Aldo Simoncini, Carlo Valentini (85' Alan Toccaceli), Simone Bacciocchi (YC64), Matteo Andreini, Nicola Albani, Riccardo Muccioli (YC17), Alex Gasperoni, Marco Domeniconi (67' Matteo Bugli), Cristian Negri (79' Federico Nanni), Andy Selva (C), Manuel Marani. (Coach: Giampaolo Mazza (SMR)).
Goals: Wales: 1-0 Ryan Giggs (3'), 2-0 Gareth Bale (20'), 3-0 Jason Koumas (63' penalty).
Referee: Ararat Tshagharyan (ARM)   Attendance: 18.752

02-06-2007   Millennium Stadium, Cardiff: Wales – Czech Republic   0-0
Wales: Wayne Hennessey, Sam Ricketts, Lewin Nyatanga, Daniel (Danny) Gabbidon, James Collins, Simon Davies, Carl Robinson, Joe Ledley, Jason Koumas, Ryan Giggs (C) (89' Robert (Rob) Earnshaw), Craig Bellamy. (Coach: John Benjamin Toshack (WAL)).
Czech Republic: Petr Cech, Tomás Ujfalusi, David Rozehnal, Radoslav Kovác, Marek Jankulovski, Tomás Sivok (83' Marek Matejovsky), Tomás Rosicky (C), Jan Polák (65' David Jarolím), Jaroslav Plasil, Jan Koller, Milan Baros (46' Marek Kulic). (Coach: Karel Brückner (CZE)).
Referee: Paul Allaerts (BEL)   Attendance: 30.714

02-06-2007   Frankenstadion, Nuremberg: Germany – San Marino   6-0 (1-0)
Germany: Jens Lehmann, Christoph Metzelder, Per Mertesacker, Philipp Lahm (70' Patrick Helmes), Marcell Jansen, Bernd Schneider (C), Thomas Hitzlsperger, Roberto Hilbert (59' Clemens Fritz), Torsten Frings, Kevin Kurányi (59' Mario Gómez García), Miroslav Klose. (Coach: Joachim Löw (GER)).
San Marino: Aldo Simoncini, Alessandro Della Valle, Damiano Vannucci, Carlo Valentini, Davide Simoncini (YC14,YC54), Simone Bacciocchi (C), Nicola Albani, Alex Gasperoni, Matteo Bugli (85' Fabio Vitaioli), Cristian Negri (69' Giovanni Bonini), Manuel Marani (76' Marco Domeniconi). (Coach: Giampaolo Mazza (SMR)).
Goals: Germany: 1-0 Kevin Kurányi (45'), 2-0 Marcell Jansen (52'), 3-0 Torsten Frings (56' penalty), 4-0 Mario Gómez García (63'), 5-0 Mario Gómez García (65'), 6-0 Clemens Fritz (67').
Referee: Jouni Hyytiä (FIN)   Attendance: 43.967

06-06-2007   AOL Arena, Hamburg: Germany – Slovakia   2-1 (2-1)
Germany: Jens Lehmann, Christoph Metzelder, Per Mertesacker, Philipp Lahm, Marcell Jansen, Clemens Fritz, Bernd Schneider (C) (YC54) (90'+2' Simon Rolfes), Thomas Hitzlsperger, Torsten Frings, Kevin Kurányi (65' Mario Gómez García), Miroslav Klose (74' Piotr Trochowski). (Coach: Joachim Löw (GER)).
Slovakia: Kamil Contofalsky, Martin Skrtel, Maros Klimpl, Ján Durica, Zdeno Strba (YC40) (83' Tomás Oravec), Marek Hamsík, Dusan Svento, Matej Krajcík, Marek Sapara (65' Igor Zofcák), Róbert Vittek (C), Stanislav Sesták (65' Filip Holosko). (Coach: Ján Kocian (SVK)).
Goals: Germany: 1-0 Ján Durica (10' own goal), 2-1 Thomas Hitzlsperger (43').
Slovakia: 1-1 Christoph Metzelder (20' own goal).
Referee: Olegário Manuel Bártolo Faustino Benquerença (POR)   Attendance: 51.600

22-08-2007   Stadio Olimpico, Serravalle: San Marino – Cyprus   0-1 (0-0)
San Marino: Aldo Simoncini, Alessandro Della Valle (YC59), Gianluca Bollini (77' Nicola Ciacci (YC86)), Damiano Vannucci, Carlo Valentini, Nicola Albani (YC30), Matteo Bugli (YC43), Giovanni Bonini (84' Federico Nanni), Fabio Bollini (YC14) (63' Matteo Andreini), Manuel Marani, Andy Selva (C). (Coach: Giampaolo Mazza (SMR)).
Cyprus: Antonis Giorgallides, Georgios Theodotou, Paraskevas Christou, Chrysostomos (Chrysis) Michail, Lambros Lambrou, Christos Marangos (24' Marios Nikolaou), Alexandros Garpozis (86' Elias Charalambous), Yiasoumis Yiasoumi (C) (55' Constantinos (Costas) Charalambides), Ioannis Okkas (C), Michalis Konstantinou, Efstathios (Stathis) Aloneftis. (Coach: Angelos Anastasiadis (GRE)).
Goal: Cyprus: 0-1 Ioannis Okkas (54').
Referee: Albano Janku (ALB)   Attendance: 552

08-09-2007   Stadio Olimpico, Serravalle: San Marino – Czech Republic   0-3 (0-1)
San Marino: Aldo Simoncini, Alessandro Della Valle (YC31,YC65), Gianluca Bollini (85' Paolo Mariotti), Damiano Vannucci, Carlo Valentini, Davide Simoncini (YC52), Matteo Bugli (67' Fabio Vitaioli), Giovanni Bonini, Fabio Bollini (58' Matteo Andreini), Manuel Marani, Andy Selva (C). (Coach: Giampaolo Mazza (SMR)).
Czech Republic: Petr Cech, Tomás Ujfalusi, David Rozehnal, Radoslav Kovác, Marek Jankulovski, Tomás Rosicky (C), David Jarolím (69' Jan Polák), Tomás Galásek (82' Jaroslav Plasil), Martin Fenin, Marek Kulic (56' Stanislav Vlcek), Jan Koller (YC61). (Coach: Karel Brückner (CZE)).
Goals: Czech Republic: 0-1 Tomás Rosicky (33'), 0-2 Marek Jankulovski (75'), 0-3 Jan Koller (90'+3').
Referee: Dejan Filipovic (SRB)   Attendance: 3.412

133

08-09-2007   Tehelné pole, Bratislava: Slovakia – Republic of Ireland   2-2 (1-1)
Slovakia: Stefan Senecky, Maros Klimpl, Ján Durica (YC88), Marek Cech, Marek Hamsík,
Matej Krajcík (YC69), Vratislav Gresko, Marek Sapara (71' Filip Sebo), Marek Mintál (C),
Stanislav Sesták (65' Branislav Obzera), Filip Holosko. (Coach: Ján Kocian (SVK)).
Republic of Ireland: Shay Given, John O'Shea, Paul McShane, Stephen Kelly, Richard Dunne,
Kevin Kilbane, Lee Carsley, Stephen Ireland (76' Jonathan Douglas), Aiden McGeady (61'
Darron Gibson), Robbie Keane (C), Kevin Doyle (89' Daryl Murphy). (Coach: Stephen (Steve)
Staunton (IRL)).
Goals: Slovakia: 1-1 Maros Klimpl (37'), 2-2 Marek Cech (90'+1').
Republic of Ireland: 0-1 Stephen Ireland (7'), 1-2 Kevin Doyle (57').
Referee: Stefano Farina (ITA)   Attendance: 12.360

08-09-2007   Millennium Stadium, Cardiff: Wales – Germany   0-2 (0-1)
Wales: Wayne Hennessey, Sam Ricketts, Lewin Nyatanga, Daniel (Danny) Gabbidon (C)
(YC38), James Collins (YC41), Carl Robinson, Joe Ledley (46' Robert (Rob) Earnshaw),
Jason Koumas (67' Carl Fletcher), Simon Davies (79' Andrew Crofts), Gareth Bale, Freddy
Eastwood. (Coach: John Benjamin Toshack (WAL)).
Germany: Jens Lehmann, Arne Friedrich, Marcell Jansen, Christoph Metzelder, Per
Mertesacker, Roberto Hilbert, Christian Pander (46' Piotr Trochowski), Bastian
Schweinsteiger, Thomas Hitzlsperger, Kevin Kurányi (72' Lukas Podolski), Miroslav Klose
(C) (87' Patrick Helmes). (Coach: Joachim Löw (GER)).
Goals: Germany: 0-1 Miroslav Klose (6'), 0-2 Miroslav Klose (60').
Referee: Manuel Enrique Mejuto González (ESP)   Attendance: 27.889

12-09-2007   Stadion Antona Malatinského, Trnava: Slovakia – Wales   2-5 (1-3)
Slovakia: Stefan Senecky, Maros Klimpl, Ján Durica, Marek Cech, Peter Petrás, Marek
Hamsík, Vratislav Gresko (64' Igor Zofcák), Marek Sapara, Marek Mintál (C), Stanislav
Sesták (46' Branislav Obzera) (YC89), Filip Holosko. (Coach: Ján Kocian (SVK)).
Wales: Wayne Hennessey, Sam Ricketts, Craig Morgan, Daniel (Danny) Gabbidon, James
Collins, Carl Robinson, Joe Ledley (85' David Vaughan), Simon Davies, Gareth Bale, Freddy
Eastwood (73' Carl Fletcher), Craig Bellamy (C) (YC24). (Coach: John Benjamin Toshack
(WAL)).
Goals: Slovakia: 1-0 Marek Mintál (12'), 2-3 Marek Mintál (57').
Wales: 1-1 Freddy Eastwood (22'), 1-2 Craig Bellamy (34'), 1-3 Craig Bellamy (41'), 2-4 Ján
Durica (78' own goal), 2-5 Simon Davies (90').
Referee: Laurent Duhamel (FRA)   Attendance: 5.486

12-09-2007   Neo GSP Stadium, Nicosia: Cyprus – San Marino   3-0 (2-0)
Cyprus: Antonis Giorgallides, Stelios Okkarides, Marios Elia (76' Georgios Theodotou),
Paraskevas Christou, Marios Nikolaou (YC88), Chrysostomos (Chrysis) Michail, Constantinos
Makrides, Elias Charalambous (65' Alexandros Garpozis (YC78)), Ioannis Okkas (C) (46'
Yiasoumis Yiasoumi), Michalis Konstantinou, Efstathios (Stathis) Aloneftis. (Coach: Angelos
Anastasiadis (GRE)).
San Marino: Federico Valentini, Fabio Bollini, Fabio Vitaioli, Damiano Vannucci, Carlo
Valentini, Matteo Andreini, Nicola Albani (81' Giacomo Benedettini), Manuel Marani (87'
Federico Nanni), Matteo Bugli, Giovanni Bonini (73' Paolo Mariotti), Andy Selva (C) (YC78).
(Coach: Giampaolo Mazza (SMR)).
Goals: Cyprus: 1-0 Constantinos Makrides (15'), 2-0 Efstathios (Stathis) Aloneftis (41'), 3-0
Efstathios (Stathis) Aloneftis (90'+2').
Referee: Aliaksei Kulbakov (BLS)   Attendance: 600

12-09-2007   AXA Arena, Prague: Czech Republic – Republic of Ireland   1-0 (1-0)
Czech Republic: Petr Cech, Tomás Ujfalusi (YC45+3), David Rozehnal, Radoslav Kovác,
Marek Jankulovski (YC90), Libor Sionko (74' Stanislav Vlcek), Tomás Rosicky (C), Jan Polák
(YC45+3), Jaroslav Plasil, Tomás Galásek (46' Tomás Sivok (YC84)), Milan Baros (YC59)
(89' David Jarolím). (Coach: Karel Brückner (CZE)).
Republic of Ireland: Shay Given, John O'Shea (38' Stephen Hunt (RC61)), Paul McShane
(YC29), Stephen Kelly (YC36), Richard Dunne, Andy Reid, Kevin Kilbane, Kevin Doyle, Lee
Carsley (82' Andrew (Andy) Keogh), Aiden McGeady (62' Shane Long (YC90+2)), Robbie
Keane (C) (YC89). (Coach: Stephen (Steve) Staunton (IRL)).
Goal: Czech Republic: 1-0 Marek Jankulovski (15').
Referee: Kyros Vassaras (GRE)   Attendance: 16.648

13-10-2007   Mestsky stadión, Dubnica nad Váhom: Slovakia – San Marino   7-0 (3-0)
Slovakia: Kamil Contofalsky (C), Martin Skrtel, Ján Durica, Marek Cech, Ottó Szabó, Matej
Krajcík, Ján Kozák, Marek Hamsík, Marek Sapara (YC64) (79' Andrej Hesek), Stanislav
Sesták (60' Blazej Vascák), Filip Holosko (71' Filip Sebo). (Coach: Ján Kocian (SVK)).
San Marino: Federico Valentini, Alessandro Della Valle, Gianluca Bollini (YC45) (57'
Giacomo Benedettini), Fabio Vitaioli, Damiano Vannucci (C), Carlo Valentini, Matteo
Andreini, Nicola Albani, Federico Nanni, Matteo Bugli (68' Luca Bonifazi), Manuel Marani
(YC77) (85' Marco De Luigi). (Coach: Giampaolo Mazza (SMR)).
Goals: Slovakia: 1-0 Marek Hamsík (24'), 2-0 Stanislav Sesták (32'), 3-0 Marek Sapara (37'),
4-0 Martin Skrtel (51'), 5-0 Filip Holosko (54'), 6-0 Stanislav Sesták (57'), 7-0 Ján Durica (76'
penalty).
Referee: Luc Wilmes (LUX)   Attendance: 2.576

13-10-2007   Neo GSP Stadium, Nicosia: Cyprus – Wales   3-1 (0-1)
Cyprus: Antonis Giorgallides, Stelios Okkarides, Marios Elia (63' Constantinos (Costas)
Charalambides), Paraskevas Christou, Marinos Satsias (71' Christos Marangos (YC76)),
Chrysostomos (Chrysis) Michail (46' Yiasoumis Yiasoumi), Constantinos Makrides,
Alexandros Garpozis, Ioannis Okkas (C), Marios Nikolaou, Efstathios (Stathis) Aloneftis
(YC90). (Coach: Angelos Anastasiadis (GRE)).
Wales: Danny Coyne, Sam Ricketts (73' Jermaine Easter (YC77)), Lewin Nyatanga, Daniel
(Danny) Gabbidon, James Collins (44' Craig Morgan), Carl Robinson, Joe Ledley, Simon
Davies, Gareth Bale, Freddy Eastwood (YC45) (58' Robert (Rob) Earnshaw), Craig Bellamy
(C). (Coach: John Benjamin Toshack (WAL)).
Goals: Cyprus: 1-1 Ioannis Okkas (59'), 2-1 Ioannis Okkas (68'), 3-1 Constantinos (Costas)
Charalambides (79').
Wales: 0-1 James Collins (21').
Referee: Carlo Bertolini (SUI)   Attendance: 2.852

13-10-2007   Croke Park, Dublin: Republic of Ireland – Germany   0-0
Republic of Ireland: Shay Given, Steve Finnan, Stephen Kelly, Richard Dunne (YC44), Andy
Reid, Lee Carsley (YC36), Joey O'Brien, Kevin Kilbane (90'+2' Daryl Murphy), Robbie
Keane (C), Kevin Doyle (70' Shane Long), Andrew (Andy) Keogh (80' Aiden McGeady).
(Coach: Stephen (Steve) Staunton (IRL)).
Germany: Jens Lehmann (YC52), Arne Friedrich (YC90), Christoph Metzelder, Per
Mertesacker, Marcell Jansen, Clemens Fritz, Piotr Trochowski (90' Gonzalo Castro Randón),
Bastian Schweinsteiger (18' Simon Rolfes), Torsten Frings (C) (YC55), Kevin Kurányi, Mario
Gómez García (64' Lukas Podolski). (Coach: Joachim Löw (GER)).
Referee: Martin Hansson (SWE)   Attendance: 67.495

17-10-2007   Stadio Olimpico, Serravalle: San Marino – Wales   1-2 (0-2)
San Marino: Aldo Simoncini, Alessandro Della Valle, Damiano Vannucci (YC68) (76' Matteo
Bugli), Carlo Valentini (YC40), Davide Simoncini, Matteo Andreini, Nicola Albani
(YC55,YC85), Luca Bonifazi (62' Giovanni Bonini), Riccardo Muccioli, Marco De Luigi (80'
Matteo Vitaioli (YC86)), Andy Selva (C). (Coach: Giampaolo Mazza (SMR)).
Wales: Lewis Price, Lewin Nyatanga, Daniel (Danny) Gabbidon, Neal Eardley, David
Vaughan (62' Sam Ricketts (YC87)), Carl Robinson, Joe Ledley (YC70), Simon Davies,
Gareth Bale (YC42), Robert (Rob) Earnshaw, Craig Bellamy (C). (Coach: John Benjamin
Toshack (WAL)).
Goals: San Marino: 1-2 Andy Selva (73').
Wales: 0-1 Robert (Rob) Earnshaw (13'), 0-2 Joe Ledley (36').
Referee: Anthony Zammit (MLT)   Attendance: 1.182

17-10-2007   Croke Park, Dublin: Republic of Ireland – Cyprus   1-1 (0-0)
Republic of Ireland: Shay Given, Steve Finnan, John O'Shea, Paul McShane, Kevin Kilbane,
Stephen Hunt (74' Jonathan Douglas), Andy Reid, Joey O'Brien (46' Liam Miller (YC67)),
Robbie Keane (C), Kevin Doyle, Andrew (Andy) Keogh (63' Aiden McGeady). (Coach:
Stephen (Steve) Staunton (IRL)).
Cyprus: Antonis Giorgallides, Stelios Okkarides, Marios Elia (RC90+4), Paraskevas Christou,
Constantinos Makrides (86' Christos Theophilou), Constantinos (Costas) Charalambides,
Marinos Satsias (YC68) (69' Christos Marangos), Alexandros Garpozis, Marios Nikolaou,
Yiasoumis Yiasoumi (73' Chrysostomos (Chrysis) Michail), Ioannis Okkas (C). (Coach:
Angelos Anastasiadis (GRE)).
Goals: Republic of Ireland: 1-1 Steve Finnan (90'+2').
Cyprus: 0-1 Stelios Okkarides (80').
Referee: Mikko Vuorela (FIN)   Attendance: 54.861

17-10-2007   Allianz Arena, Munich: Germany – Czech Republic   0-3 (0-2)
Germany: Timo Hildebrand, Christoph Metzelder (46' Simon Rolfes), Per Mertesacker,
Marcell Jansen, Arne Friedrich, Piotr Trochowski (46' Clemens Fritz), Bastian Schweinsteiger
(65' Mario Gómez García), Torsten Frings (C), Lukas Podolski (YC46), David Odonkor,
Kevin Kurányi. (Coach: Joachim Löw (GER)).
Czech Republic: Petr Cech (C), Tomás Ujfalusi, David Rozehnal, Zdenek Pospech, Radoslav
Kovác, Daniel Pudil (73' Marek Kulic), Marek Matejovsky, Libor Sionko (58' Stanislav
Vlcek), Jaroslav Plasil, Tomás Galásek, Jan Koller (79' Martin Fenin). (Coach: Karel Brückner
(CZE)).
Goals: Czech Republic: 0-1 Libor Sionko (2'), 0-2 Marek Matejovsky (23'), 0-3 Jaroslav Plasil
(63').
Referee: Howard Melton Webb (ENG)   Attendance: 66.445

17-11-2007   Millennium Stadium, Cardiff: Wales – Republic of Ireland   2-2 (1-1)
Wales: Wayne Hennessey, Chris Gunter, Daniel (Danny) Gabbidon, Neal Eardley (81' David
Cotterill), James Collins, Carl Robinson (37' David (Dave) Edwards), Joe Ledley, Jason
Koumas (YC57), Carl Fletcher, Simon Davies (C), Freddy Eastwood (60' Jermaine Easter).
(Coach: John Benjamin Toshack (WAL)).
Republic of Ireland: Shay Given, John O'Shea (YC33), Steve Finnan, Paul McShane, Andy
Reid (87' Darren Potter), Liam Miller (60' Stephen Hunt), Kevin Kilbane, Lee Carsley, Aiden
McGeady, Robbie Keane (C), Kevin Doyle. (Coach: Daniel Joseph (Don) Givens (IRL)).
Goals: Wales: 1-0 Jason Koumas (23'), 2-2 Jason Koumas (89' penalty).
Republic of Ireland: 1-1 Robbie Keane (31'), 1-2 Kevin Doyle (60').
Referee: Oleh Oriekhov (UKR)   Attendance: 24.619

17-11-2007   AWD-Arena, Hanover: Germany – Cyprus   4-0 (2-0)
Germany: Jens Lehmann, Christoph Metzelder, Per Mertesacker, Philipp Lahm, Clemens Fritz
(77' Roberto Hilbert), Arne Friedrich, Piotr Trochowski (66' Tim Borowski), Thomas
Hitzlsperger, Lukas Podolski, Miroslav Klose (C), Mario Gómez García (73' Mike Hanke).
(Coach: Joachim Löw (GER)).
Cyprus: Antonis Giorgallides, Georgios Theodotou (27' Marios Nikolaou), Paraskevas
Christou, Marinos Satsias, Constantinos Makrides, Lambros Lambrou, Constantinos (Costas)
Charalambides (46' Christos Theophilou), Alexandros Garpozis, Ioannis Okkas (C), Michalis
Konstantinou (68' Yiasoumis Yiasoumi), Efstathios (Stathis) Aloneftis. (Coach: Angelos
Anastasiadis (GRE)).
Goals: Germany: 1-0 Clemens Fritz (2'), 2-0 Miroslav Klose (20'), 3-0 Lukas Podolski (53'),
4-0 Thomas Hitzlsperger (82').
Referee: Peter Rasmussen (DEN)   Attendance: 45.016

17-11-2007   AXA Arena, Prague: Czech Republic – Slovakia   3-1 (1-0)
Czech Republic: Jaromír Blazek, David Rozehnal, Zdenek Grygera (45' Michal Kadlec),
Zdenek Pospech, Radoslav Kovác, Tomás Rosicky (C), Jan Polák (86' Marek Matejovsky),
Jaroslav Plasil, Tomás Galásek, Jan Koller, Milan Baros (70' Marek Kulic). (Coach: Karel
Brückner (CZE)).
Slovakia: Kamil Contofalsky (C), Martin Skrtel (YC78), Lubomír Michalík, Marek Cech
(YC69), Karol Kisel (88' Juraj Halenár), Zdeno Strba (YC56), Matej Krajcík, Ján Kozák,
Marek Hamsík (58' Filip Holosko), Marek Sapara (YC57), Marek Mintál (C) (67' Stanislav
Sesták). (Coach: Ján Kocian (SVK)).
Goals: Czech Republic: 1-0 Zdenek Grygera (13'), 2-0 Marek Kulic (76'), 3-1 Tomás Rosicky
(83').
Slovakia: 2-1 Michal Kadlec (79' *own goal*).
Referee: Tony Asumaa (FIN)   Attendance: 15.681

21-11-2007   Neo GSP Stadium, Nicosia: Cyprus – Czech Republic   0-2 (0-1)
Cyprus: Antonis Giorgallides, Paraskevas Christou, Marios Nikolaou (56' Elias Charalambous
(YC88)), Marinos Satsias (YC75), Constantinos Makrides (84' Chrysostomos (Chrysis)
Michail), Lambros Lambrou, Constantinos (Costas) Charalambides (62' Yiasoumis Yiasoumi),
Alexandros Garpozis, Ioannis Okkas (C), Michalis Konstantinou, Efstathios (Stathis)
Aloneftis. (Coach: Angelos Anastasiadis (GRE)).
Czech Republic: Daniel Zitka, David Rozehnal (C), Michal Kadlec (YC65), Zdenek Pospech,
Radoslav Kovác, Daniel Pudil, Jaroslav Plasil (87' Jirí Kladrubsky), Marek Matejovsky,
Tomás Galásek, Marek Kulic (57' Milan Baros), Jan Koller (76' Martin Fenin). (Coach: Karel
Brückner (CZE)).
Goals: Czech Republic: 0-1 Daniel Pudil (11'), 0-2 Jan Koller (74').
Referee: Levan Paniashvili (GEO)   Attendance: 5.866

21-11-2007   Commerzbank-Arena, Frankfurt: Germany – Wales   0-0
Germany: Jens Lehmann, Philipp Lahm, Clemens Fritz, Christoph Metzelder, Per Mertesacker,
Thomas Hitzlsperger (46' Simon Rolfes), Gonzalo Castro Randón (56' Roberto Hilbert), Tim
Borowski, Miroslav Klose (C), Mario Gómez García (71' Oliver Neuville), Lukas Podolski.
(Coach: Joachim Löw (GER)).
Wales: Wayne Hennessey (YC89), Daniel (Danny) Gabbidon (YC83), Sam Ricketts, Lewin
Nyatanga, Chris Gunter, James Collins (YC82), Joe Ledley, Carl Fletcher, Simon Davies (C),
David (Dave) Edwards (90'+1' Andrew Crofts), Robert (Rob) Earnshaw (56' Jermaine Easter).
(Coach: John Benjamin Toshack (WAL)).
Referee: Pavel Cristian Balaj (ROM)   Attendance: 49.262

137

21-11-2007   Stadio Olimpico, Serravalle: San Marino – Slovakia   0-5 (0-1)
San Marino: Federico Valentini, Alessandro Della Valle, Gianluca Bollini (61' Maicol
Berretti), Damiano Vannucci (YC52), Carlo Valentini (YC89), Davide Simoncini, Riccardo
Muccioli (YC59), Michele Marani, Mauro Marani (YC81) (84' Matteo Andreini), Andy Selva
(C) (YC44) (50' Marco De Luigi), Manuel Marani. (Coach: Giampaolo Mazza (SMR)).
Slovakia: Stefan Senecky, Marek Cech, Lubomír Michalík (YC29), Tomás Hubocan (YC73),
Matej Krajčík (63' Peter Petrás), Ján Kozák (C), Karol Kisel (46' Ottó Szabó), Marek Hamsík,
Balász Borbély, Stanislav Sesták (75' Juraj Halenár (YC81)), Filip Holosko. (Coach: Ján
Kocian (SVK)).
Goals: Slovakia: 0-1 Lubomír Michalík (42'), 0-2 Filip Holosko (51'), 0-3 Marek Hamsík
(53'), 0-4 Filip Holosko (57'), 0-5 Marek Cech (83').
Referee: Andrejs Sipailo (LAT)   Attendance: 538

GROUP   E

16-08-2006	Tallinn	Estonia – Macedonia	0-1 (0-0)
02-09-2006	Manchester	England – Andorra	5-0 (3-0)
02-09-2006	Tallinn	Estonia – Israel	0-1 (0-1)
06-09-2006	Moscow	Russia – Croatia	0-0
06-09-2006	Nijmegen (HOL)	Israel – Andorra	4-1 (3-0)
06-09-2006	Skopje	Macedonia – England	0-1 (0-0)
07-10-2006	Moscow	Russia – Israel	1-1 (1-0)
07-10-2006	Manchester	England – Macedonia	0-0
07-10-2006	Zagreb	Croatia – Andorra	7-0 (2-0)
11-10-2006	Andorra la Vella	Andorra – Macedonia	0-3 (0-3)
11-10-2006	Saint Petersburg	Russia – Estonia	2-0 (0-0)
11-10-2006	Zagreb	Croatia – England	2-0 (0-0)
15-11-2006	Skopje	Macedonia – Russia	0-2 (0-2)
15-11-2006	Ramat-Gan	Israel – Croatia	3-4 (1-2)
24-03-2007	Tallinn	Estonia – Russia	0-2 (0-0)
24-03-2007	Ramat-Gan	Israel – England	0-0
24-03-2007	Zagreb	Croatia – Macedonia	2-1 (0-1)
28-03-2007	Ramat-Gan	Israel – Estonia	4-0 (2-0)
28-03-2007	Barcelona (ESP)	Andorra – England	0-3 (0-0)
02-06-2007	Tallinn	Estonia – Croatia	0-1 (0-1)
02-06-2007	Saint Petersburg	Russia – Andorra	4-0 (2-0)
02-06-2007	Skopje	Macedonia – Israel	1-2 (1-2)
06-06-2007	Andorra la Vella	Andorra – Israel	0-2 (0-1)
06-06-2007	Zagreb	Croatia – Russia	0-0
06-06-2007	Tallinn	Estonia – England	0-3 (0-1)
22-08-2007	Tallinn	Estonia – Andorra	2-1 (1-0)
08-09-2007	Moscow	Russia – Macedonia	3-0 (1-0)
08-09-2007	London	England – Israel	3-0 (1-0)
08-09-2007	Zagreb	Croatia – Estonia	2-0 (2-0)
12-09-2007	Andorro la Vella	Andorra – Croatia	0-6 (0-3)
12-09-2007	Skopje	Macedonia – Estonia	1-1 (1-1)
12-09-2007	London	England – Russia	3-0 (2-0)
13-10-2007	London	England – Estonia	3-0 (3-0)
13-10-2007	Zagreb	Croatia – Israel	1-0 (0-0)

17-10-2007	Moscow	Russia – England	2-1 (0-1)
17-10-2007	Skopje	Macedonia – Andorra	3-0 (2-0)
17-11-2007	Andorra la Vella	Andorra – Estonia	0-2 (0-1)
17-11-2007	Ramat-Gan	Israel – Russia	2-1 (1-0)
17-11-2007	Skopje	Macedonia – Croatia	2-0 (0-0)
21-11-2007	Ramat-Gan	Israel – Macedonia	1-0 (1-0)
21-11-2007	Andorra la Vella	Andorra – Russia	0-1 (0-1)
21-11-2007	London	England – Croatia	2-3 (0-2)

FINAL STANDING

Pos	Team	Pld	W	D	L	GF	GA	GD	Pts
1	Croatia	12	9	2	1	28	8	+20	29
2	Russia	12	7	3	2	18	7	+11	24
3	England	12	7	2	3	24	7	+17	23
4	Israel	12	7	2	3	20	12	+8	23
5	Macedonia	12	4	2	6	12	12	0	14
6	Estonia	12	2	1	9	5	21	-16	7
7	Andorra	12	0	0	12	2	42	-40	0

Croatia and Russia qualified for the Final Tournament in Austria and Switzerland.

16-08-2006   A.Le Coq Arena, Tallinn: Estonia – Macedonia   0-1 (0-0)
Estonia: Mart Poom (C), Andrei Stepanov, Raio Piiroja, Dmitri Kruglov, Ragnar Klavan, Enar Jääger, Andrei Sidorenkov (67' Ingemar Teever), Joel Lindpere (74' Tarmo Neemelo), Aleksandr Dmitrijev, Kristen Viikmäe (90'+3' Alo Bärengrub), Sergei Terehhov (YC21). (Coach: Jelle Goes (HOL)).
Macedonia: Jane Nikoloski, Goce Sedloski (C) (YC57), Robert Petrov (87' Aleksandar Vasoski), Nikolce Noveski, Igor Mitreski (YC13), Vlade Lazarevski, Igor Jancevski, Velice Sumulikoski, Goran Pandev (82' Darko Tasevski), Ilco Naumoski (71' Aco Stojkov), Goran Maznov. (Coach: Srecko Katanec (SLO)).
Goal: Macedonia: 0-1 Goce Sedloski (73').
Referee: Kristinn Jakobsson (ISL)   Attendance: 7.500

02-09-2006   Old Trafford, Manchester: England – Andorra   5-0 (3-0)
England: Paul Robinson, John Terry (C), Phil Neville (68' Aaron Lennon), Ashley Cole, Wes Brown (YC45), Owen Hargreaves, Stewart Downing (68' Kieran Richardson), Frank Lampard, Steven Gerrard, Jermain Defoe (74' Andrew (Andy) Johnson), Peter Crouch. (Coach: Steve McClaren (ENG)).
Andorra: Jesús Luis Álvarez de Eulate Güergue "Koldo", José Manuel "Txema" García Luena, Andoni Miguel "Toni" Sivera Peris (YC69) (81' Genís García Iscla), Antonio "Toni" Lima Sola (YC47), Márcio Vieira de Vasconcelos, Javier "Javi" Francisco Martin Sánchez (46' Juli Sánchez Soto), Jose Manuel Díaz "Josep" Ayala, Óscar Masand Sonejee, Marc Pujol Pons (48' Manolo "Manel" Jiménez Soria (YC90+1)), Fernando José Silva Garcia, Justo Ruíz González (C). (Coach: David Rodrigo Lo (ESP)).
Goals: England: 1-0 Peter Crouch (4'), 2-0 Steven Gerrard (12'), 3-0 Jermain Defoe (37'), 4-0 Jermain Defoe (46'), 5-0 Peter Crouch (66').
Referee: Bernhard Brugger (AUT)   Attendance: 56.290

02-09-2006   A.Le Coq Arena, Tallinn: Estonia – Israel   0-1 (0-1)
Estonia: Mart Poom (C), Andrei Stepanov, Raio Piiroja (YC45), Dmitri Kruglov, Ragnar Klavan, Enar Jääger, Aleksandr Dmitrijev (86' Ingemar Teever), Kristen Viikmäe (68' Konstantin Vassiljev), Sergei Terehhov, Andres Oper, Aleksander Saharov (86' Alo Bärengrub). (Coach: Jelle Goes (HOL)).
Israel: Dudu Aouate, Shimon Gershon, Tal Ben Haim, Michael Zandberg (59' Amit Ben Shushan), Idan Tal, Walid Badier (YC24), Omri Afek, Yossi Benayoun (C), Yaniv Katan (72' Gal Alberman), Roberto Colautti, Yoav Ziv. (Coach: Dror Kashtan (ISR)).
Goal: Israel: 0-1 Roberto Colautti (6').
Referee: Johan Verbist (BEL)   Attendance: 7.800

06-09-2006   Lokomotiv Stadium, Moscow: Russia – Croatia   0-0
Russia: Igor Akinfeev, Denis Kolodin, Sergei Ignashevich, Aleksei Berezutski, Aleksandr Anyukov, Marat Izmailov, Evgeni Aldonin (C) (YC68), Igor Semshov, Diniyar Bilyaletdinov, Andrey Arshavin, Roman Pavlyuchenko (53' Pavel Pogrebnyak). (Coach: Guus Hiddink (HOL)).
Croatia: Stipe Pletikosa, Goran Sabljic, Anthony Seric, Robert Kovac, Vedran Corluka, Milan Rapaic (58' Mladen Petric), Niko Kranjcar, Niko Kovac (C), Luka Modric, Ivan Klasnic (88' Marko Babic), EDUARDO Alves da Silva (71' Jerko Leko). (Coach: Slaven Bilic (CRO)).
Referee: Manuel Enrique Mejuto González (ESP)   Attendance: 27.500

06-09-2006   Stadion de Goffert, Nijmegen (HOL): Israel – Andorra   4-1 (3-0)
Israel: Dudu Aouate, Shimon Gershon, Tal Ben Haim, Idan Tal (YC12), Walid Badier (76' Gal Alberman), Omri Afek, Yossi Benayoun (C) (YC31) (69' Omer Golan), Yaniv Katan (63' Toto Tamuz), Amit Ben Shushan, Yoav Ziv, Roberto Colautti (YC57). (Coach: Dror Kashtan (ISR)).
Andorra: Jesús Luis Álvarez de Eulate Güergue "Koldo", José Manuel "Txema" García Luena, Antonio "Toni" Lima Sola, Marc Bernaus Cano, Márcio Vieira de Vasconcelos (67' Sergi Moreno Marín (YC90+2)), Jose Manuel Díaz "Josep" Ayala (YC48), Óscar Masand Sonejee (YC15), Manolo "Manel" Jiménez Soria, Marc Pujol Pons (46' Genís García Iscla), Fernando José Silva Garcia (RC78), Justo Ruíz González (C) (54' Julia "Juli" Fernández Ariza (YC82)). (Coach: David Rodrigo Lo (ESP)).
Goals: Israel: 1-0 Yossi Benayoun (9'), 2-0 Amit Ben Shushan (11'), 3-0 Shimon Gershon (43' penalty), 4-0 Toto Tamuz (70').
Andorra: 4-1 Julia "Juli" Fernández Ariza (84').
Referee: Sinisa Zrnic (BOS)   Attendance: 450

Due to the 2006 Israel-Lebanon conflict, UEFA ordered that no matches in its competitions could be held in Israel until further notice. UEFA was scheduled to reconsider its ban on 14th September 2006. On 15th September 2006, UEFA lifted its ban on matches in Israel, returning to its previous policy of restricting Israel home matches to the Tel Aviv area. Israel's national stadium in Ramat-Gan is within the allowed area.

06-09-2006   Skopje City Stadium, Skopje: Macedonia – England   0-1 (0-0)
Macedonia: Jane Nikoloski, Goce Sedloski (C), Robert Petrov, Nikolce Noveski, Igor Mitreski,
Vlade Lazarevski (YC38), Igor Jancevski (53' Darko Tasevski), Velice Sumulikoski, Goran
Pandev (YC67), Ilco Naumoski (YC1) (74' Artim Shakiri), Goran Maznov (56' Aco Stojkov).
(Coach: Srecko Katanec (SLO)).
England: Paul Robinson, John Terry (C), Phil Neville, Ashley Cole (YC89), Rio Ferdinand,
Owen Hargreaves, Stewart Downing, Frank Lampard (84' Michael Carrick), Steven Gerrard
(YC88), Jermain Defoe (76' Aaron Lennon), Peter Crouch (YC60) (88' Andrew (Andy)
Johnson). (Coach: Steve McClaren (ENG)).
Goal: England: 0-1 Peter Crouch (46').
Referee: Bertrand Layec (FRA)   Attendance: 16.500

07-10-2006   Dynamo Stadium, Moscow: Russia – Israel   1-1 (1-0)
Russia: Igor Akinfeev, Aleksei Berezutski, Sergei Ignashevich, Vasili Berezutski, Aleksandr
Anyukov, Aleksei Smertin, Evgeni Aldonin (C), Yuri Zhirkov (76' Igor Semshov (YC87)),
Diniyar Bilyaletdinov (30' Aleksandr Kerzhakov (YC45)), Pavel Pogrebnyak (YC12) (57'
Marat Izmailov), Andrey Arshavin. (Coach: Guus Hiddink (HOL)).
Israel: Dudu Aouate, Adoram Keisi, Shimon Gershon (46' Tomer Ben Yossef), Klemi Saban
(YC19) (46' Amit Ben Shushan (YC78)), Tal Ben Haim, Idan Tal, Walid Badier, Omri Afek,
Yossi Benayoun (C) (75' Toto Tamuz), Gal Alberman, Roberto Colautti. (Coach: Dror
Kashtan (ISR)).
Goals: Russia: 1-0 Andrey Arshavin (5').
Israel: 1-1 Amit Ben Shushan (83').
Referee: Florian Meyer (GER)   Attendance: 22.000

07-10-2006   Old Trafford, Manchester: England – Macedonia   0-0
England: Paul Robinson, Ashley Cole, John Terry (C), Gary Neville, Ledley King, Stewart
Downing (70' Shaun Wright-Phillips), Michael Carrick, Frank Lampard, Steven Gerrard
(YC49), Wayne Rooney (75' Jermain Defoe), Peter Crouch. (Coach: Steve McClaren (ENG)).
Macedonia: Jane Nikoloski, Aleksandar Mitreski, Vlade Lazarevski, Goce Sedloski (C), Robert
Petrov (YC47), Nikolce Noveski, Igor Mitreski, Velice Sumulikoski, Goran Pandev (83' Darko
Tasevski), Ilco Naumoski (46' Aco Stojkov), Goran Maznov. (Coach: Srecko Katanec (SLO)).
Referee: Dr.Markus Merk (GER)   Attendance: 72.062

07-10-2006   Maksimir Stadium, Zagreb: Croatia – Andorra   7-0 (2-0)
Croatia: Stipe Pletikosa, Dario Simic, Robert Kovac, Vedran Corluka, Josip Simunic, Niko
Kranjcar, Luka Modric, Niko Kovac (C) (69' Jerko Leko), Mladen Petric (61' Bosko Balaban),
Ivan Klasnic, EDUARDO Alves da Silva (64' Marko Babic). (Coach: Slaven Bilic (CRO)).
Andorra: Jesús Luis Álvarez de Eulate Güergue "Koldo", Antoni "Toni" Sivera Peris (61' Justo
Ruíz González), Jordi Rubio Gómez, Jordi Escura Aixas, Julia "Juli" Fernández Ariza (YC87),
Genís García Iscla (YC31) (68' Manolo "Manel" Jiménez Soria), Jose Manuel Díaz "Josep"
Ayala, Márcio Vieira de Vasconcelos, Óscar Masand Sonejee (C) (YC54), Juli Sánchez Soto
(53' Juan Carlos Toscano Beltrán (YC65)), Marc Pujol Pons. (Coach: David Rodrigo Lo
(ESP)).
Goals: Croatia: 1-0 Mladen Petric (14'), 2-0 Mladen Petric (38'), 3-0 Mladen Petric (48'), 4-0
Mladen Petric (50'), 5-0 Ivan Klasnic (57'), 6-0 Bosko Balaban (62'), 7-0 Luka Modric (83').
Referee: Anthony Zammit (MLT)   Attendance: 17.618

11-10-2006   Estadio Comunal, Andorra la Vella: Andorra – Macedonia   0-3 (0-3)
Andorra: Jesús Luis Álvarez de Eulate Güergue "Koldo", José Manuel "Txema" García Luena (YC18), Antoni "Toni" Sivera Peris (RC26), Jordi Rubio Gómez, Márcio Vieira de Vasconcelos, Genís García Iscla, Marc Bernaus Cano, Jose Manuel Díaz "Josep" Ayala, Juan Carlos Toscano Beltrán (34' Justo Ruíz González), Óscar Masand Sonejee (C), Marc Pujol Pons (YC31) (87' Manolo "Manel" Jiménez Soria). (Coach: David Rodrigo Lo (ESP)).
Macedonia: Jane Nikoloski, Aleksandar Mitreski, Goce Sedloski (C), Robert Petrov (70' Artim Shakiri), Nikolce Noveski, Igor Mitreski, Vlade Lazarevski, Velice Sumulikoski, Goran Pandev (YC10) (56' Darko Tasevski), Ilco Naumoski (YC21) (32' Aco Stojkov), Goran Maznov. (Coach: Srecko Katanec (SLO)).
Goals: Macedonia: 0-1 Goran Pandev (12'), 0-2 Nikolce Noveski (16'), 0-3 Ilco Naumoski (30').
Referee: Lasha Silagava (GEO)   Attendance: 300

11-10-2006   Petrovsky Stadium, Saint Petersburg: Russia – Estonia   2-0 (0-0)
Russia: Igor Akinfeev, Sergei Ignashevich, Vasili Berezutski, Aleksei Berezutski (YC89), Aleksandr Anyukov, Yegor Titov, Evgeni Aldonin (C) (75' Dmitri Sychev), Vladimir Bystrov, Diniyar Bilyaletdinov (90'+3' Ivan Saenko), Andrey Arshavin (YC64), Aleksandr Kerzhakov (46' Pavel Pogrebnyak). (Coach: Guus Hiddink (HOL)).
Estonia: Mart Poom (C), Andrei Stepanov (YC73), Teet Allas (81' Ats Purje), Raio Piiroja (YC64,YC89), Dmitri Kruglov (YC56), Ragnar Klavan, Enar Jääger (YC45), Aleksandr Dmitrijev, Sergei Terehhov (81' Andrei Sidorenkov), Ingemar Teever (81' Vladislav Gussev), Andres Oper. (Coach: Jelle Goes (HOL)).
Goals: Russia: 1-0 Pavel Pogrebnyak (78'), 2-0 Dmitri Sychev (90'+1').
Referee: Eric Frederikus Johannes Braamhaar (HOL)   Attendance: 21.517

11-10-2006   Maksimir Stadium, Zagreb: Croatia – England   2-0 (0-0)
Croatia: Stipe Pletikosa, Vedran Corluka, Josip Simunic, Dario Simic, Robert Kovac, Milan Rapaic (73' Ivica Olic), Niko Kranjcar (88' Marko Babic), Luka Modric, Niko Kovac (C) (YC63), EDUARDO Alves da Silva (80' Jerko Leko), Mladen Petric. (Coach: Slaven Bilic (CRO)).
England: Paul Robinson, Ashley Cole (YC76), Jamie Carragher (73' Jermain Defoe), John Terry (C), Gary Neville, Rio Ferdinand (YC20), Scott Parker (73' Kieran Richardson), Michael Carrick, Frank Lampard, Wayne Rooney, Peter Crouch (73' Shaun Wright-Phillips). (Coach: Steve McClaren (ENG)).
Goals: Croatia: 1-0 EDUARDO Alves da Silva (59'), 2-0 Gary Neville (65' *own goal*).
Referee: Roberto Rosetti (ITA)   Attendance: 31.991

15-11-2006   Skopje City Stadium, Skopje: Macedonia – Russia   0-2 (0-2)
Macedonia: Jane Nikoloski, Aleksandar Mitreski (46' Igor Jancevski, 72' Vlatko Grozdanoski), Goce Sedloski (C), Igor Mitreski, Vlade Lazarevski, Robert Petrov (YC43), Nikolce Noveski, Artim Shakiri (36' Darko Tasevski), Velice Sumulikoski, Aco Stojkov, Goran Maznov. (Coach: Srecko Katanec (SLO)).
Russia: Igor Akinfeev, Denis Kolodin (YC86), Vasili Berezutski, Aleksei Berezutski, Yegor Titov (C), Igor Semshov, Yuri Zhirkov, Vladimir Bystrov, Diniyar Bilyaletdinov, Pavel Pogrebnyak (YC50) (56' Dmitri Sychev (YC65)), Andrey Arshavin (90' Roman Pavlyuchenko). (Coach: Guus Hiddink (HOL)).
Goals: Russia: 0-1 Vladimir Bystrov (18'), 0-2 Andrey Arshavin (32').
Referee: Paul Allaerts (BEL)   Attendance: 13.000

15-11-2006   Ramat Gan Stadium, Ramat-Gan: Israel – Croatia 3-4 (1-2)
Israel: Dudu Aouate (YC34), Adoram Keisi, Tomer Ben Yossef, Tal Ben Haim, Idan Tal
(YC60), Walid Badier (45'+1' Toto Tamuz), Omri Afek, Yossi Benayoun (C), Gal Alberman,
Michael Zandberg (58' Amit Ben Shushan), Roberto Colautti (YC40). (Coach: Dror Kashtan
(ISR)).
Croatia: Vedran Runje, Vedran Corluka, Josip Simunic, Dario Simic, Robert Kovac, Niko
Kranjcar (67' Marko Babic), Darijo Srna (87' Ivica Olic), Luka Modric, Niko Kovac (C),
Mladen Petric, EDUARDO Alves da Silva (80' Jerko Leko). (Coach: Slaven Bilic (CRO)).
Goals: Israel: 1-0 Roberto Colautti (8'), 2-3 Yossi Benayoun (67'), 3-4 Roberto Colautti (88').
Croatia: 1-1 Darijo Srna (34' penalty), 1-2 EDUARDO Alves da Silva (38'), 1-3 EDUARDO
Alves da Silva (53'), 2-4 EDUARDO Alves da Silva (72').
Referee: Eduardo Iturralde González (ESP)   Attendance: 35.000

24-03-2007   A.Le Coq Arena, Tallinn: Estonia – Russia 0-2 (0-0)
Estonia: Mart Poom (C), Tihhon Sisov (80' Tarmo Neemelo), Marek Lemsalu, Dmitri
Kruglov, Ragnar Klavan, Andrei Stepanov (YC34), Liivo Leetma (69' Tarmo Kink), Joel
Lindpere, Aleksandr Dmitrijev, Sergei Terehhov (52' Gert Kams), Andres Oper. (Coach: Jelle
Goes (HOL)).
Russia: Igor Akinfeev, Roman Shishkin, Sergei Ignashevich, Aleksandr Anyukov, Dmitri
Torbinski, Konstantin Zyryanov (YC25), Vladimir Bystrov (90' Ivan Saenko), Yuri Zhirkov,
Diniyar Bilyaletdinov, Andrey Arshavin (C), Aleksandr Kerzhakov (83' Dmitri Sychev).
(Coach: Guus Hiddink (HOL)).
Goals: Russia: 0-1 Vladimir Bystrov (66'), 0-2 Aleksandr Kerzhakov (78').
Referee: Darko Ceferin (SLO)   Attendance: 8.212

24-03-2007   Ramat Gan Stadium, Ramat-Gan: Israel – England 0-0
Israel: Dudu Aouate, Yuval Shpungin, Shimon Gershon, Arik Benado (YC10), Tal Ben Haim
(YC62), Walid Badier, Yossi Benayoun (C), Toto Tamuz (75' Elyaniv Barda), Amit Ben
Shushan (87' Gal Alberman), Pini Balili (69' Ben Sahar), Yoav Ziv. (Coach: Dror Kashtan
(ISR)).
England: Paul Robinson, John Terry (C), Phil Neville (72' Micah Richards), Jamie Carragher
(YC13), Rio Ferdinand, Owen Hargreaves, Aaron Lennon (83' Stewart Downing), Frank
Lampard, Steven Gerrard, Andrew (Andy) Johnson (80' Jermain Defoe), Wayne Rooney
(YC62). (Coach: Steve McClaren (ENG)).
Referee: Tom Henning Øvrebø (NOR)   Attendance: 38.000

24-03-2007   Maksimir Stadium, Zagreb: Croatia – Macedonia 2-1 (0-1)
Croatia: Stipe Pletikosa, Josip Simunic, Dario Simic, Vedran Corluka, Milan Rapaic (46'
Darijo Srna), Niko Kranjcar, Marko Babic, Luka Modric, Niko Kovac (C), Bosko Balaban (79'
Igor Budan), EDUARDO Alves da Silva. (Coach: Slaven Bilic (CRO)).
Macedonia: Jane Nikoloski, Aleksandar Mitreski (77' Igor Jancevski), Aleksandar Vasoski,
Goce Sedloski (C) (YC8,YC68), Nikolce Noveski, Vlade Lazarevski, Robert Popov, Velice
Sumulikoski (YC46), Goran Pandev (YC67), Ilco Naumoski (YC47) (60' Darko Tasevski),
Goran Maznov (71' Miroslav Vajs). (Coach: Srecko Katanec (SLO)).
Goals: Croatia: 1-1 Darijo Srna (58'), 2-1 EDUARDO Alves da Silva (87').
Macedonia: 0-1 Goce Sedloski (36').
Referee: Konrad Plautz (AUT)   Attendance: 29.969

28-03-2007   Ramat Gan Stadium, Ramat-Gan: Israel – Estonia   4-0 (2-0)
Israel: Dudu Aouate, Yuval Shpungin, Shimon Gershon, Tal Ben Haim (YC27), Idan Tal (87'
Salim Toama), Walid Badier, Yossi Benayoun (C) (YC76), Toto Tamuz (64' Ben Sahar), Amit
Ben Shushan (70' Gal Alberman), Yoav Ziv, Roberto Colautti. (Coach: Dror Kashtan (ISR)).
Estonia: Mart Poom (C), Tihhon Sisov, Marek Lemsalu, Taavi Rähn (YC21) (39' Tarmo
Kink), Dmitri Kruglov, Ragnar Klavan, Alo Bärengrub, Joel Lindpere (80' Gert Kams),
Aleksandr Dmitrijev, Andres Oper, Tarmo Neemelo (61' Oliver Konsa). (Coach: Jelle Goes
(HOL)).
Goals: Israel: 1-0 Idan Tal (19'), 2-0 Roberto Colautti (29'), 3-0 Ben Sahar (77'), 4-0 Ben
Sahar (80').
Referee: Cüneyt Çakir (TUR)   Attendance: 23.658

28-03-2007   Olímpic Lluís Companys, Barcelona (ESP): Andorra – England   0-3 (0-0)
Andorra: Jesús Luis Álvarez de Eulate Güergue "Koldo", Antonio "Toni" Lima Sola (YC11),
Jordi Escura Aixas, Genís García Iscla (YC80), Marc Bernaus Cano, Jose Manuel Díaz "Josep"
Ayala, Márcio Vieira de Vasconcelos, Juan Carlos Toscano Beltrán (YC25) (90'+3' Sergi
Moreno Marín), Óscar Masand Sonejee (YC56), Manolo "Manel" Jiménez Soria (69' Francisc
Jöel Martínez Villar), Justo Ruíz González (C) (88' Julia "Juli" Fernández Ariza). (Coach:
David Rodrigo Lo (ESP)).
England: Paul Robinson, Ashley Cole (YC80), John Terry (C), Micah Richards (61' Jermain
Defoe), Rio Ferdinand, Owen Hargreaves (YC77), Stewart Downing, Aaron Lennon, Steven
Gerrard, Andrew (Andy) Johnson (79' David Nugent), Wayne Rooney (YC56) (61' Kieron
Dyer). (Coach: Steve McClaren (ENG)).
Goals: England: 0-1 Steven Gerrard (54'), 0-2 Steven Gerrard (76'), 0-3 David Nugent
(90'+2').
Referee: Bruno Miguel Duarte Paixão (POR)   Attendance: 12.800

02-06-2007   A.Le Coq Arena, Tallinn: Estonia – Croatia   0-1 (0-1)
Estonia: Mart Poom (C) (YC67), Andrei Stepanov, Raio Piiroja (YC37), Dmitri Kruglov,
Ragnar Klavan (YC90), Enar Jääger, Konstantin Vassiljev, Joel Lindpere (78' Tarmo Kink),
Aleksandr Dmitrijev (YC55), Oliver Konsa (71' Tarmo Neemelo), Vladimir Voskoboinikov.
(Coach: Jelle Goes (HOL)).
Croatia: Stipe Pletikosa, Josip Simunic (YC38), Robert Kovac, Vedran Corluka, Niko Kranjcar
(74' Jerko Leko), Marko Babic, Darijo Srna, Luka Modric, Niko Kovac (C), Mladen Petric
(54' Ivica Olic), EDUARDO Alves da Silva (84' Bosko Balaban). (Coach: Slaven Bilic
(CRO)).
Goal: Croatia: 0-1 EDUARDO Alves da Silva (32').
Referee: Viktor Kassai (HUN)   Attendance: 8.651

02-06-2007   Petrovsky Stadium, Saint Petersburg: Russia – Andorra 4-0 (2-0)
Russia: Vyacheslav Malafeev, Sergei Ignashevich, Vasili Berezutski, Aleksei Berezutski (46'
Aleksandr Anyukov), Dmitri Torbinski, Igor Semshov, Konstantin Zyryanov, Yuri Zhirkov
(57' Viktor Budyanski), Vladimir Bystrov, Andrey Arshavin (C), Aleksandr Kerzhakov (54'
Dmitri Sychev). (Coach: Guus Hiddink (HOL)).
Andorra: Jesús Luis Álvarez de Eulate Güergue "Koldo", José Manuel "Txema" García Luena,
Jordi Escura Aixas, José Óscar Da Cunha Alfonso (57' Juli Sánchez Soto), Jose Manuel Díaz
"Josep" Ayala, Márcio Vieira de Vasconcelos, Marc Bernaus Cano, Manolo "Manel" Jiménez
Soria (YC44) (73' Xavier "Xavi" Andorrà Julià), Marc Pujol Pons (YC18), Justo Ruíz
González (C), Sergi Moreno Marín (88' Álex Somoza Losada). (Coach: David Rodrigo Lo
(ESP)).
Goals: Russia: 1-0 Aleksandr Kerzhakov (8'), 2-0 Aleksandr Kerzhakov (16'), 3-0 Aleksandr
Kerzhakov (49'), 4-0 Dmitri Sychev (71').
Referee: Tommy Skjerven (NOR)   Attendance: 21.520

02-06-2007   Skopje City Stadium, Skopje: Macedonia – Israel 1-2 (1-2)
Macedonia: Jane Nikoloski, Aleksandar Vasoski, Robert Petrov, Nikolce Noveski, Igor
Mitreski (C), Vlade Lazarevski (46' Vlatko Grozdanoski), Darko Tasevski, Velice
Sumulikoski, Goran Pandev (55' Artim Polozani), Ilco Naumoski (46' Stevica Ristic), Aco
Stojkov. (Coach: Srecko Katanec (SLO)).
Israel: Dudu Aouate (C), Yuval Shpungin (YC15), Arik Benado, Dekel Keinan (YC5), Idan
Tal, Walid Badier, Gal Alberman (YC79), Barak Itzhaki (YC45+1) (76' Michael Zandberg),
Pini Balili (61' Ben Sahar), Yoav Ziv (YC63), Roberto Colautti (81' Omer Golan). (Coach:
Dror Kashtan (ISR)).
Goals: Macedonia: 1-1 Aco Stojkov (13').
Israel: 0-1 Barak Itzhaki (11'), 1-2 Roberto Colautti (44').
Referee: Knut Kircher (GER)   Attendance: 12.000

06-06-2007   Estadi Comunal, Andorra la Vella: Andorra – Israel 0-2 (0-1)
Andorra: Jesús Luis Álvarez de Eulate Güergue "Koldo", Antonio "Toni" Lima Sola, Jordi
Escura Aixas (YC60), José Manuel "Txema" García Luena (61' Óscar Masand Sonejee),
Ildefons Lima Solà (YC26), Genís García Iscla, Marc Bernaus Cano, Jose Manuel Díaz
"Josep" Ayala, Márcio Vieira de Vasconcelos (77' Sergi Moreno Marín), Juan Carlos Toscano
Beltrán (77' Juli Sánchez Soto), Justo Ruíz González (C). (Coach: David Rodrigo Lo (ESP)).
Israel: Dudu Aouate, Arik Benado, Avi Yehiel, Dedi Ben Dayan, Idan Tal, Yossi Benayoun
(C), Gal Alberman (71' Walid Badier), Barak Itzhaki, Toto Tamuz (77' Michael Zandberg),
Roberto Colautti (86' Omer Golan), Yoav Ziv. (Coach: Dror Kashtan (ISR)).
Goals: Israel: 0-1 Toto Tamuz (37'), 0-2 Roberto Colautti (53').
Referee: Ian Stokes (IRL)   Attendance: 680
(Juli Sánchez Soto missed a penalty in the 81st minute)

06-06-2007   Maksimir Stadium, Zagreb: Croatia – Russia 0-0
Croatia: Stipe Pletikosa, Vedran Corluka, Josip Simunic, Dario Simic, Robert Kovac, Niko
Kranjcar (66' Mladen Petric), Niko Kovac (C), Darijo Srna (8' Jerko Leko (YC72)), Luka
Modric, EDUARDO Alves da Silva, Ivica Olic (83' Marko Babic). (Coach: Slaven Bilic
(CRO)).
Russia: Vyacheslav Malafeev, Aleksei Berezutski, Aleksandr Anyukov, Sergei Ignashevich,
Vasili Berezutski, Igor Semshov, Viktor Budyanski (46' Dmitri Torbinski (YC69)), Yuri
Zhirkov, Vladimir Bystrov (61' Ivan Saenko (YC71)), Andrey Arshavin (C), Aleksandr
Kerzhakov (73' Dmitri Sychev). (Coach: Guus Hiddink (HOL)).
Referee: Lubos Michel (SVK)   Attendance: 36.194

06-06-2007   A.Le Coq Arena, Tallinn: Estonia – England   0-3 (0-1)
Estonia: Mart Poom (C), Andrei Stepanov, Dmitri Kruglov, Ragnar Klavan, Enar Jääger, Konstantin Vassiljev, Joel Lindpere, Aleksandr Dmitrijev, Sergei Terehhov (64' Tarmo Kink), Oliver Konsa (46' Tarmo Neemelo), Vladimir Voskoboinikov. (Coach: Jelle Goes (HOL)).
England: Paul Robinson, John Terry (C), Wes Brown, Wayne Bridge, Ledley King, Joe Cole (75' Stewart Downing), David Beckham (68' Kieron Dyer), Frank Lampard, Steven Gerrard, Michael Owen (88' Jermaine Jenas), Peter Crouch (YC81). (Coach: Steve McClaren (ENG)).
Goals: England: 0-1 Joe Cole (37'), 0-2 Peter Crouch (54'), 0-3 Michael Owen (62').
Referee: Grzegorz Gilewski (POL)   Attendance: 9.635

22-08-2007   A.Le Coq Arena, Tallinn: Estonia – Andorra   2-1 (1-0)
Estonia: Mart Poom (C), Andrei Stepanov, Raio Piiroja, Dmitri Kruglov, Ragnar Klavan (RC45+1), Enar Jääger (YC42), Martin Reim, Joel Lindpere, Aleksandr Dmitrijev, Indrek Zelinski (YC58,YC90+2), Vladimir Voskoboinikov (46' Tarmo Kink). (Coach: Viggo Biehl Jensen (DEN)).
Andorra: Jesús Luis Álvarez de Eulate Güergue "Koldo", José Manuel "Txema" García Luena, Antoni "Toni" Sivera Peris (53' Juan Carlos Toscano Beltrán (YC69)), Antonio "Toni" Lima Sola (YC73), Jordi Escura Aixas (YC55), Ildefons Lima Solà (YC42), Márcio Vieira de Vasconcelos, Jose Manuel Díaz "Josep" Ayala (90' Genís García Iscla), Óscar Masand Sonejee (C), Marc Pujol Pons (80' Juli Sánchez Soto), Fernando José Silva Garcia (YC61). (Coach: David Rodrigo Lo (ESP)).
Goals: 1-0 Raio Piiroja (34'), 2-1 Indrek Zelinski (90'+2').
Andorra: 1-1 Fernando José Silva Garcia (82').
Referee: Adrian McCourt (NIR)   Attendance: 7.500

08-09-2007   Lokomotiv Stadium, Moscow: Russia – Macedonia   3-0 (1-0)
Russia: Vladimir Gabulov (RC70), Sergei Ignashevich, Vasili Berezutski, Aleksei Berezutski, Igor Semshov, Konstantin Zyryanov, Vladimir Bystrov (89' Aleksandr Anyukov), Diniyar Bilyaletdinov, Dmitri Sychev (70' Vyacheslav Malafeev goalkeeper), Roman Pavlyuchenko (66' Aleksandr Kerzhakov), Andrey Arshavin (C). (Coach: Guus Hiddink (HOL)).
Macedonia: Petar Milosevski, Aleksandar Mitreski (46' Goran Maznov), Aleksandar Vasoski (88' Goce Toleski), Goce Sedloski (C), Igor Mitreski (YC82), Vlade Lazarevski, Darko Tasevski, Velice Sumulikoski, Goran Popov, Goran Pandev (YC46), Aco Stojkov (46' Vanco Trajanov). (Coach: Srecko Katanec (SLO)).
Goals: Russia: 1-0 Vasili Berezutski (6'), 2-0 Andrey Arshavin (83'), 3-0 Aleksandr Kerzhakov (86').
Referee: Tom Henning Øvrebø (NOR)   Attendance: 23.000
(Igor Mitreski missed a penalty in the 72nd minute)

08-09-2007   Wembley Stadium, London: England – Israel   3-0 (1-0)
England: Paul Robinson, Ashley Cole, John Terry (C) (YC67), Micah Richards, Rio Ferdinand, Joe Cole, Shaun Wright-Phillips (82' David Bentley), Gareth Barry, Steven Gerrard (70' Phil Neville), Michael Owen, Emile Heskey (70' Andrew (Andy) Johnson). (Coach: Steve McClaren (ENG)).
Israel: Dudu Aouate (YC66), Yuval Shpungin, Shimon Gershon (YC15), Arik Benado (YC45+1) (57' Omer Golan), Tal Ben Haim, Walid Badier, Idan Tal, Yossi Benayoun (C), Yaniv Katan (73' Michael Zandberg), Barak Itzhaki (46' Toto Tamuz), Yoav Ziv (YC55). (Coach: Dror Kashtan (ISR)).
Goals: England: 1-0 Shaun Wright-Phillips (20'), 2-0 Michael Owen (50'), 3-0 Micah Richards (66').
Referee: Pieter Vink (HOL)   Attendance: 85.372

08-09-2007   Maksimir Stadium, Zagreb: Croatia – Estonia   2-0 (2-0)
Croatia: Stipe Pletikosa, Josip Simunic, Dario Simic, Robert Kovac, Vedran Corluka, Niko Kranjcar (61' Ivan Rakitic), Darijo Srna (82' Marko Babic), Luka Modric, Niko Kovac (C), Mladen Petric (72' Ivica Olic), EDUARDO Alves da Silva. (Coach: Slaven Bilic (CRO)).
Estonia: Pavel Londak, Andrei Stepanov, Urmas Rooba (85' Aivar Anniste), Teet Allas (YC19), Taavi Rähn, Raio Piiroja, Dmitri Kruglov, Joel Lindpere (90'+2' Martin Reim), Aleksandr Dmitrijev, Andres Oper (C), Tarmo Kink (81' Kaimar Saag). (Coach: Viggo Biehl Jensen (DEN)).
Goals: Croatia: 1-0 EDUARDO Alves da Silva (39'), 2-0 EDUARDO Alves da Silva (45'+1').
Referee: Jérôme Laperrière (SUI)   Attendance: 15.102
(Darijo Srna missed a penalty in the 6th minute)

12-09-2007   Estadi Comunal, Andorra la Vella: Andorra – Croatia   0-6 (0-3)
Andorra: Jesús Luis Álvarez de Eulate Güergue "Koldo", José Manuel "Txema" García Luena, Antoni "Toni" Sivera Peris (YC33) (59' Xavier "Xavi" Andorrà Julià), Antonio "Toni" Lima Sola (YC63), Márcio Vieira de Vasconcelos, Genís García Iscla (RC77), Jose Manuel Díaz "Josep" Ayala, Óscar Masand Sonejee, Manolo "Manel" Jiménez Soria, Fernando José Silva Garcia (57' Sergi Moreno Marín), Justo Ruíz González (C) (82' Álex Somoza Losada). (Coach: David Rodrigo Lo (ESP)).
Croatia: Vedran Runje, Robert Kovac (C), Dario Knezevic, Vedran Corluka, Niko Kranjcar, Marko Babic, Darijo Srna, Luka Modric (46' Danijel Pranjic), Jerko Leko, Mladen Petric (46' Bosko Balaban), EDUARDO Alves da Silva (62' Ivan Rakitic). (Coach: Slaven Bilic (CRO)).
Goals: Croatia: 0-1 Darijo Srna (34'), 0-2 Mladen Petric (38'), 0-3 Mladen Petric (44'), 0-4 Niko Kranjcar (49'), 0-5 EDUARDO Alves da Silva (55'), 0-6 Ivan Rakitic (64').
Referee: Olivier Thual (FRA)   Attendance: 925

12-09-2007   Skopje City Stadium, Skopje: Macedonia – Estonia   1-1 (1-1)
Macedonia: Petar Milosevski, Aleksandar Vasoski (YC42), Goce Sedloski (C), Nikolce Noveski, Vlade Lazarevski, Vanco Trajanov (46' Artim Polozani), Darko Tasevski, Velice Sumulikoski, Vlatko Grozdanoski, Aco Stojkov (81' Goce Toleski), Goran Maznov (YC55). (Coach: Srecko Katanec (SLO)).
Estonia: Pavel Londak, Andrei Stepanov, Taavi Rähn (62' Martin Reim), Raio Piiroja, Dmitri Kruglov, Ragnar Klavan, Enar Jääger, Joel Lindpere, Aleksandr Dmitrijev, Kaimar Saag (79' Tarmo Kink (YC83)), Andres Oper (C) (90' Aivar Anniste). (Coach: Viggo Biehl Jensen (DEN)).
Goals: Macedonia: 1-1 Goran Maznov (30').
Estonia: 0-1 Raio Piiroja (17').
Referee: Leontios Trattou (CYP)   Attendance: 5.000

12-09-2007   Wembley Stadium, London: England – Russia   3-0 (2-0)
England: Paul Robinson, John Terry (C), Micah Richards, Ashley Cole, Rio Ferdinand, Shaun Wright-Phillips, Joe Cole (YC78) (88' Phil Neville), Steven Gerrard, Gareth Barry, Michael Owen (90'+1' Stewart Downing), Emile Heskey (80' Peter Crouch). (Coach: Steve McClaren (ENG)).
Russia: Vyacheslav Malafeev, Sergei Ignashevich, Vasili Berezutski, Aleksei Berezutski, Aleksandr Anyukov (80' Aleksandr Kerzhakov), Igor Semshov (40' Vladimir Bystrov), Konstantin Zyryanov, Yuri Zhirkov, Diniyar Bilyaletdinov, Dmitri Sychev (63' Roman Pavlyuchenko), Andrey Arshavin (C). (Coach: Guus Hiddink (HOL)).
Goals: England: 1-0 Michael Owen (7'), 2-0 Michael Owen (31'), 3-0 Rio Ferdinand (84').
Referee: Martin Hansson (SWE)   Attendance: 86.106

13-10-2007   Wembley Stadium, London: England – Estonia   3-0 (3-0)
England: Paul Robinson, Micah Richards, Ashley Cole (49' Phil Neville), Sol Campbell, Rio
Ferdinand (46' Joleon Lescott), Shaun Wright-Phillips, Joe Cole, Steven Gerrard (C), Gareth
Barry, Michael Owen (70' Frank Lampard), Wayne Rooney. (Coach: Steve McClaren (ENG)).
Estonia: Mart Poom (C), Andrei Stepanov, Taavi Rähn (YC12), Raio Piiroja, Dmitri Kruglov,
Ragnar Klavan, Enar Jääger, Joel Lindpere (YC73), Aleksandr Dmitrijev, Kaimar Saag,
Tarmo Kink (62' Kristen Viikmäe). (Coach: Viggo Biehl Jensen (DEN)).
Goals: England: 1-0 Shaun Wright-Phillips (11'), 2-0 Wayne Rooney (32'), 3-0 Taavi Rähn
(33' own goal).
Referee: Nicolai Vollquartz (DEN)   Attendance: 86.665

13-10-2007   Maksimir Stadium, Zagreb: Croatia – Israel   1-0 (0-0)
Croatia: Stipe Pletikosa, Josip Simunic, Dario Simic, Robert Kovac (C), Vedran Corluka, Niko
Kranjcar (46' Danijel Pranjic), Darijo Srna, Luka Modric, Jerko Leko (YC24), Ivica Olic (81'
Ivan Rakitic), EDUARDO Alves da Silva (YC45). (Coach: Slaven Bilic (CRO)).
Israel: Nir Davidovitch, Eyal Meshumar, Shimon Gershon, Ygal Antebi (YC87), Tal Ben
Haim (YC65), Tamir Cohen (YC71), Aviram Baruchyan (58' Omer Golan), Yossi Benayoun
(C), Gal Alberman, Pini Balili (YC62) (67' Toto Tamuz), Elyaniv Barda (76' Moshe Ohayon).
(Coach: Dror Kashtan (ISR)).
Goal: Croatia: 1-0 EDUARDO Alves da Silva (52').
Referee: Wolfgang Stark (GER)   Attendance: 30.084

17-10-2007   Luzhniki Stadium, Moscow: Russia – England   2-1 (0-1)
Russia: Vladimir Gabulov, Sergei Ignashevich, Vasili Berezutski (YC14) (46' Dmitri
Torbinski), Aleksei Berezutski, Aleksandr Anyukov, Igor Semshov, Konstantin Zyryanov,
Yuri Zhirkov, Diniyar Bilyaletdinov, Andrey Arshavin (C) (90' Denis Kolodin), Aleksandr
Kerzhakov (58' Roman Pavlyuchenko (YC74)). (Coach: Guus Hiddink (HOL)).
England: Paul Robinson, Micah Richards, Joleon Lescott (79' Frank Lampard), Rio Ferdinand
(YC58), Sol Campbell, Shaun Wright-Phillips (80' Stewart Downing), Joe Cole (80' Peter
Crouch), Steven Gerrard (C), Gareth Barry, Michael Owen, Wayne Rooney (YC69). (Coach:
Steve McClaren (ENG)).
Goals: Russia: 1-1 Roman Pavlyuchenko (69' penalty), 2-1 Roman Pavlyuchenko (73').
England: 0-1 Wayne Rooney (29').
Referee: Luis Medina Cantalejo (ESP)   Attendance: 84.700

17-10-2007   Skopje City Stadium, Skopje: Macedonia – Andorra   3-0 (2-0)
Macedonia: Tome Pacovski, Goce Sedloski (C), Nikolce Noveski, Igor Mitreski, Vlade
Lazarevski, Darko Tasevski (84' Vanco Trajanov), Velice Sumulikoski, Goran Popov, Goran
Pandev, Ilco Naumoski (75' Artim Polozani), Goran Maznov (62' Stevica Ristic). (Coach:
Srecko Katanec (SLO)).
Andorra: Jesús Luis Álvarez de Eulate Güergue "Koldo" (YC56), Jordi Escura Aixas, Ildefons
Lima Solà (YC26), Julia "Juli" Fernández Ariza, Márcio Vieira de Vasconcelos, Jose Manuel
Díaz "Josep" Ayala, Juan Carlos Toscano Beltrán (82' Gabriel "Gabi" Riera), Óscar Masand
Sonejee (YC77), Manolo "Manel" Jiménez Soria (78' Álex Somoza Losada), Marc Pujol Pons,
Justo Ruíz González (C) (63' Xavier "Xavi" Andorrà Julià). (Coach: David Rodrigo Lo (ESP)).
Goals: Macedonia: 1-0 Ilco Naumoski (30'), 2-0 Goce Sedloski (44'), 3-0 Goran Pandev (59').
Referee: Paulius Malzinskas (LIT)   Attendance: 17.500

17-11-2007   Estadi Comunal, Andorra la Vella: Andorra – Estonia   0-2 (0-1)
Andorra: Jesús Luis Álvarez de Eulate Güergue "Koldo", José Manuel "Txema" García Luena (46' Manolo "Manel" Jiménez Soria), Antonio "Toni" Lima Sola, Antoni "Toni" Sivera Peris, Jordi Rubio Gómez, Ildefons Lima Solà (81' Justo Ruíz González (YC84)), Jose Manuel Díaz "Josep" Ayala (YC65), Márcio Vieira de Vasconcelos (YC16), Óscar Masand Sonejee (C), Marc Pujol Pons (YC45+4), Sergi Moreno Marín (70' Juan Carlos Toscano Beltrán (YC84)). (Coach: David Rodrigo Lo (ESP)).
Estonia: Pavel Londak, Andrei Stepanov, Dmitri Kruglov (YC36) (84' Konstantin Vassiljev), Ragnar Klavan (YC90+2), Enar Jääger, Raio Piiroja, Joel Lindpere, Aleksandr Dmitrijev, Martin Reim (C) (YC40) (68' Taijo Teniste), Andres Oper (46' Tarmo Kink), Kaimar Saag. (Coach: Viggo Biehl Jensen (DEN)).
Goals: Estonia: 0-1 Andres Oper (31'), 0-2 Joel Lindpere (60').
Referee: William (Willie) Collum (SCO)   Attendance: 700

17-11-2007   Ramat Gan Stadium, Ramat-Gan: Israel – Russia   2-1 (1-0)
Israel: Dudu Aouate (C), Yuval Shpungin, Tal Ben Haim, Dekel Keinan, Tamir Cohen, Gal Alberman (YC45+1), Barak Itzhaki (62' Amit Ben Shushan), Elyaniv Barda, Yoav Ziv, Ben Sahar (YC53) (69' Omer Golan), Maor Buzaglo (64' Moshe Ohayon). (Coach: Dror Kashtan (ISR)).
Russia: Vladimir Gabulov, Aleksei Berezutski, Aleksandr Anyukov (YC77), Sergei Ignashevich, Vasili Berezutski (68' Pavel Pogrebnyak), Igor Semshov (30' Dmitri Torbinski), Konstantin Zyryanov, Yuri Zhirkov, Diniyar Bilyaletdinov, Andrey Arshavin (C), Roman Pavlyuchenko (52' Dmitri Sychev). (Coach: Guus Hiddink (HOL)).
Goals: Israel: 1-0 Elyaniv Barda (10'), 2-1 Omer Golan (90'+2').
Russia: 1-1 Diniyar Bilyaletdinov (61').
Referee: Stefano Farina (ITA)   Attendance: 27.563

17-11-2007   Skopje City Stadium, Skopje: Macedonia – Croatia   2-0 (0-0)
Macedonia: Petar Milosevski, Goce Sedloski (C) (88' Boban Grncarov), Nikolce Noveski, Igor Mitreski, Vlade Lazarevski, Darko Tasevski (YC14), Velice Sumulikoski, Goran Popov, Vlatko Grozdanoski, Ilco Naumoski (YC27) (84' Artim Polozani), Goran Maznov. (Coach: Srecko Katanec (SLO)).
Croatia: Stipe Pletikosa, Josip Simunic, Dario Simic, Robert Kovac, Vedran Corluka, Niko Kranjcar (75' Ognjen Vukojevic), Darijo Srna, Luka Modric, Niko Kovac (C), Mladen Petric (42' Mario Mandzukic), EDUARDO Alves da Silva (54' Ivica Olic). (Coach: Slaven Bilic (CRO)).
Goals: Macedonia: 1-0 Goran Maznov (71'), 2-0 Ilco Naumoski (83').
Referee: Frank de Bleeckere (BEL)   Attendance: 14.500

21-11-2007   Ramat Gan Stadium, Ramat-Gan: Israel – Macedonia   1-0 (1-0)
Israel: Dudu Aouate (C), Yuval Shpungin, Dekel Keinan, Tal Ben Haim, Tamir Cohen, Moshe Ohayon, Barak Itzhaki (72' Aviram Baruchyan), Yoav Ziv, Roberto Colautti (55' Ben Sahar), Maor Buzaglo (46' Amit Ben Shushan), Elyaniv Barda (YC43). (Coach: Dror Kashtan (ISR)).
Macedonia: Petar Milosevski, Goce Sedloski (C), Nikolce Noveski, Igor Mitreski, Vlade Lazarevski, Darko Tasevski (46' Artim Polozani), Velice Sumulikoski, Goran Popov, Vlatko Grozdanoski (66' Slavco Georgievski), Aco Stojkov, Goran Maznov (60' Stevica Ristic). (Coach: Srecko Katanec (SLO)).
Goal: Israel: 1-0 Elyaniv Barda (35').
Referee: Tomasz Mikulski (POL)   Attendance: 2.736

149

21-11-2007   Estadi Comunal, Andorra la Vella: Andorra – Russia   0-1 (0-1)
Andorra: Jesús Luis Álvarez de Eulate Güergue "Koldo" (YC45) (46' Josep Antonio Gómes Moreira), Antoni "Toni" Sivera Peris, Antonio "Toni" Lima Sola (YC59), Jordi Escura Aixas (YC76), Ildefons Lima Solà (YC46), Márcio Vieira de Vasconcelos (50' Xavier "Xavi" Andorrà Julià), Marc Bernaus Cano, Óscar Masand Sonejee (C) (83' Gabriel "Gabi" Riera), Manolo "Manel" Jiménez Soria, Sergi Moreno Marín, Justo Ruíz González (YC24). (Coach: David Rodrigo Lo (ESP)).
Russia: Vladimir Gabulov, Denis Kolodin, Vasili Berezutski (38' Dmitri Torbinski), Aleksei Berezutski (YC10), Aleksandr Anyukov, Konstantin Zyryanov, Yuri Zhirkov, Diniyar Bilyaletdinov, Dmitri Sychev, Andrey Arshavin (C) (RC84), Aleksandr Kerzhakov. (Coach: Guus Hiddink (HOL)).
Goal: Russia: 0-1 Dmitri Sychev (38').
Referee: Terje Hauge (NOR)   Attendance: 780
(Denis Kolodin missed a penalty in the 45+1 minute)

21-11-2007   Wembley Stadium, London: England – Croatia   2-3 (0-2)
England: Scott Carson, Micah Richards, Wayne Bridge, Joleon Lescott, Sol Campbell, Shaun Wright-Phillips (46' Jermain Defoe), Joe Cole (80' Darren Bent), Frank Lampard, Steven Gerrard (C), Gareth Barry (46' David Beckham), Peter Crouch. (Coach: Steve McClaren (ENG)).
Croatia: Stipe Pletikosa, Josip Simunic, Dario Simic, Robert Kovac (YC32), Vedran Corluka, Niko Kranjcar (75' Danijel Pranjic), Darijo Srna, Luka Modric, Niko Kovac (C), Ivica Olic (84' Ivan Rakitic), EDUARDO Alves da Silva (YC50) (69' Mladen Petric). (Coach: Slaven Bilic (CRO)).
Goals: England: 1-2 Frank Lampard (56' penalty), 2-2 Peter Crouch (65').
Croatia: 0-1 Niko Kranjcar (8'), 0-2 Ivica Olic (14'), 2-3 Mladen Petric (77').
Referee: Peter Fröjdfeldt (SWE)   Attendance: 88.091

GROUP F

02-09-2006	Belfast	Northern Ireland – Iceland	0-3 (0-3)
02-09-2006	Riga	Latvia – Sweden	0-1 (0-1)
02-09-2006	Badajoz	Spain – Liechtenstein	4-0 (2-0)
06-09-2006	Gothenburg	Sweden – Liechtenstein	3-1 (1-1)
06-09-2006	Reykjavik	Iceland – Denmark	0-2 (0-2)
06-09-2006	Belfast	Northern Ireland – Spain	3-2 (1-1)
07-10-2006	Copenhagen	Denmark – Northern Ireland	0-0
07-10-2006	Riga	Latvia – Iceland	4-0 (3-0)
07-10-2006	Solna	Sweden – Spain	2-0 (1-0)
11-10-2006	Reykjavik	Iceland – Sweden	1-2 (1-1)
11-10-2006	Vaduz	Liechtenstein – Denmark	0-4 (0-2)
11-10-2006	Belfast	Northern Ireland – Latvia	1-0 (1-0)
24-03-2007	Vaduz	Liechtenstein – Northern Ireland	1-4 (0-0)
24-03-2007	Madrid	Spain – Denmark	2-1 (2-0)
28-03-2007	Vaduz	Liechtenstein – Latvia	1-0 (1-0)
28-03-2007	Belfast	Northern Ireland – Sweden	2-1 (1-1)
28-03-2007	Palma de Mallorca	Spain – Iceland	1-0 (0-0)
02-06-2007	Reykjavik	Iceland – Liechtenstein	1-1 (1-0)
02-06-2007	Copenhagen	Denmark – Sweden	0-3
02-06-2007	Riga	Latvia – Spain	0-2 (0-1)

06-06-2007	Solna	Sweden – Iceland	5-0 (3-0)
06-06-2007	Vaduz	Liechtenstein – Spain	0-2 (0-2)
06-06-2007	Riga	Latvia – Denmark	0-2 (0-2)
22-08-2007	Belfast	Northern Ireland – Liechtenstein	3-1 (2-0)
08-09-2007	Riga	Latvia – Northern Ireland	1-0 (0-0)
08-09-2007	Solna	Sweden – Denmark	0-0
08-09-2007	Reykjavik	Iceland – Spain	1-1 (1-0)
12-09-2007	Aarhus	Denmark – Liechtenstein	4-0 (4-0)
12-09-2007	Reykjavik	Iceland – Northern Ireland	2-1 (1-0)
12-09-2007	Oviedo	Spain – Latvia	2-0 (1-0)
13-10-2007	Reykjavik	Iceland – Latvia	2-4 (1-3)
13-10-2007	Vaduz	Liechtenstein – Sweden	0-3 (0-2)
13-10-2007	Aarhus	Denmark – Spain	1-3 (0-2)
17-10-2007	Copenhagen	Denmark – Latvia	3-1 (2-0)
17-10-2007	Vaduz	Liechtenstein – Iceland	3-0 (1-0)
17-10-2007	Solna	Sweden – Northern Ireland	1-1 (1-0)
17-11-2007	Riga	Latvia – Liechtenstein	4-1 (2-1)
17-11-2007	Belfast	Northern Ireland – Denmark	2-1 (0-0)
17-11-2007	Madrid	Spain – Sweden	3-0 (2-0)
21-11-2007	Copenhagen	Denmark – Iceland	3-0 (2-0)
21-11-2007	Las Palmas	Spain – Northern Ireland	1-0 (0-0)
21-11-2007	Solna	Sweden – Latvia	2-1 (1-1)

FINAL STANDING

Pos	Team	Pld	W	D	L	GF	GA	GD	Pts
1	Spain	12	9	1	2	23	8	+15	28
2	Sweden	12	8	2	2	23	9	+14	26
3	Northern Ireland	12	6	2	4	17	14	+3	20
4	Denmark	12	6	2	4	21	11	+10	20
5	Latvia	12	4	0	8	15	17	-2	12
6	Iceland	12	2	2	8	10	27	-17	8
7	Liechtenstein	12	2	1	9	9	32	-23	7

Spain and Sweden qualified for the Final Tournament in Austria and Switzerland.

02-09-2006   Windsor Park, Belfast: Northern Ireland – Iceland   0-3 (0-3)
Northern Ireland: Maik Taylor, Stephen Craigan, Aaron Hughes (C), Chris Baird, Stuart Elliott (64' Kyle Lafferty), Tony Capaldi (77' Michael Duff), Steven Davis, Sammy Clingan, David Healy (YC45+1), Keith Gillespie, James Quinn (83' Warren Feeney). (Coach: Lawrence Philip (Lawrie) Sanchez (NIR)).
Iceland: Árni Arason, Hermann Hreidarsson, Brynjar Gunnarsson (75' Stefán Gíslason), Grétar Steinsson, Indridi Sigurdsson (YC58), Ívar Ingimarsson, Jóhannes Gudjónsson, Kári Árnason (33' Helgi Daníelsson), Hannes Sigurdsson (64' Hjálmar Jónsson), Eidur Gudjohnsen (C), Gunnar Heidar Thorvaldsson. (Coach: Eyjólfur Gjafar Sverrisson (ISL)).
Goals: Iceland: 0-1 Gunnar Heidar Thorvaldsson (13'), 0-2 Hermann Hreidarsson (20'), 0-3 Eidur Gudjohnsen (37').
Referee: Tommy Skjerven (NOR)   Attendance: 13.522

151

02-09-2006   Skonto Stadions, Riga: Latvia – Sweden   0-1 (0-1)
Latvia: Aleksandrs Kolinko, Igors Stepanovs (YC13), Māris Smirnovs, Oskars Klava (YC15), Dzintars Zirnis (83' Girts Karlsons), Andrejs Rubins, Juris Laizāns (86' Aleksejs Visnakovs), Imants Bleidelis, Vitālijs Astafjevs (C) (YC58), Māris Verpakovskis, Andrejs Prohorenkovs (57' Marians Pahars). (Coach: Juris Andrejevs (LAT)).
Sweden: Rami Shaaban, Olof Mellberg, Petter Hansson, Erik Edman, Mikael Nilsson, Fredrik (Freddie) Ljungberg (C), Tobias Linderoth, Kim Källström (73' Anders Svensson), Albin Ekdal, Zlatan Ibrahimovic (YC42), Johan Elmander (81' Christian Wilhelmsson). (Coach: Lars Lagerbäck (SWE)).
Goal: Sweden: 0-1 Kim Källström (38').
Referee: Darko Ceferin (SLO)   Attendance: 7.500

02-09-2006   Estadio Nuevo Vivero, Badajoz: Spain – Liechtenstein   4-0 (2-0)
Spain: IKER CASILLAS Fernández, MARIANO Andrés PERNÍA Molina, PABLO IBÁÑEZ Tebar, SERGIO RAMOS García (YC51), Carles PUYOL Saforcada, David ALBELDA Aliqués (67' BORJA OUBIÑA Meléndez), Xabier "XABI" ALONSO Olano, Francesc "CESC" FÀBREGAS Soler (62' Andrés INIESTA Luján), RAÚL González Blanco (C), DAVID VILLA Sánchez (YC41) (62' LUIS Javier GARCÍA Sanz), FERNANDO José TORRES Sanz. (Coach: LUIS ARAGONÉS Suárez (ESP)).
Liechtenstein: Peter Jehle, Martin Stocklasa, Sandro Maierhofer (YC9), Daniel Hasler (C), Fabio D'Elia, Martin Telser (55' Benjamin Fischer), Marco Ritzberger, Martin Büchel, Franz Burgmeier, Mario Frick (85' Raphael Rohrer), Thomas Beck (67' Roger Beck). (Coach: Martin Andermatt (SUI)).
Goals: Spain: 1-0 FERNANDO José TORRES Sanz (20'), 2-0 DAVID VILLA Sánchez (45'), 3-0 DAVID VILLA Sánchez (61'), 4-0 LUIS Javier GARCÍA Sanz (65').
Referee: Emil Bozinovski (MCD)   Attendance: 14.876

06-09-2006   Nya Ullevi, Gothenburg: Sweden – Liechtenstein   3-1 (1-1)
Sweden: Rami Shaaban, Teddy Lucic, Petter Hansson, Erik Edman (YC26), Mikael Nilsson, Fredrik (Freddie) Ljungberg (C), Tobias Linderoth, Kim Källström (56' Anders Svensson (YC71)), Niclas Alexandersson, Johan Elmander (82' Markus Rosenberg), Marcus Allbäck. (Coach: Lars Lagerbäck (SWE)).
Liechtenstein: Peter Jehle, Martin Stocklasa, Christof Ritter, Sandro Maierhofer (YC42) (88' Fabio D'Elia), Daniel Hasler (C), Marco Ritzberger, Martin Büchel, Mario Frick, Daniel Frick (YC16), Benjamin Fischer (54' Ronny Büchel), Thomas Beck (42' Franz Burgmeier). (Coach: Martin Andermatt (SUI)).
Goals: Sweden: 1-0 Marcus Allbäck (1'), 2-1 Marcus Allbäck (70'), 3-1 Markus Rosenberg (88').
Liechtenstein: 1-1 Mario Frick (27').
Referee: Veaceslav Banari (MOL)   Attendance: 17.735
(Fredrik (Freddie) Ljungberg missed a penalty in the 89th minute)

06-09-2006   Laugardalsvöllur, Reykjavik: Iceland – Denmark   0-2 (0-2)
Iceland: Árni Arason, Hjálmar Jónsson (66' Veigar Gunnarsson), Hermann Hreidarsson, Brynjar Gunnarsson (YC52) (77' Stefán Gíslason), Grétar Steinsson, Indridi Sigurdsson, Ívar Ingimarsson, Jóhannes Gudjónsson (YC3), Kári Árnason (83' Arnar Vidarsson), Eidur Gudjohnsen (C) (YC57), Gunnar Heidar Thorvaldsson. (Coach: Eyjólfur Gjafar Sverrisson (ISL)).
Denmark: Thomas Sørensen, Lars Jacobsen, Michael Gravgaard, Daniel Agger, Christian Poulsen, Jan Kristiansen, Thomas Kahlenberg (83' Claus Jensen), Thomas Gravesen (71' Daniel Jensen), Martin Jørgensen (90' Thomas Helveg), Jon Dahl Tomasson (C), Dennis Rommedahl. (Coach: Morten Per Olsen (DEN)).
Goals: Denmark: 0-1 Dennis Rommedahl (5'), 0-2 Jon Dahl Tomasson (33').
Referee: Nikolay Vladimirovich Ivanov (RUS)   Attendance: 10.007

06-09-2006   Windsor Park, Belfast: Northern Ireland – Spain   3-2 (1-1)
Northern Ireland: Roy Carroll (12' Maik Taylor), Stephen Craigan, Michael Duff (YC78), Chris Baird, Jonny Evans, Aaron Hughes (C), Steven Davis, Sammy Clingan, David Healy (84' Warren Feeney (YC90+1)), Keith Gillespie, Kyle Lafferty (53' James Quinn). (Coach: Lawrence Philip (Lawrie) Sanchez (NIR)).
Spain: IKER CASILLAS Fernández, ANTONIO LÓPEZ Guerrero (YC40), PABLO IBÁÑEZ Tebar, SERGIO RAMOS García (46' Miguel Ángel "MÍCHEL" SALGADO Fernández), Carles PUYOL Saforcada (YC70), David ALBELDA Aliqués (28' Francesc "CESC" FÀBREGAS Soler), Xavier "XAVI" Hernández i Creus, Xabier "XABI" ALONSO Olano, RAÚL González Blanco (C), FERNANDO José TORRES Sanz (62' LUIS Javier GARCÍA Sanz), DAVID VILLA Sánchez. (Coach: LUIS ARAGONÉS Suárez (ESP)).
Goals: Northern Ireland: 1-1 David Healy (20'), 2-2 David Healy (64'), 3-2 David Healy (80').
Spain: 0-1 Xavier "XAVI" Hernández i Creus (14'), 1-2 DAVID VILLA Sánchez (52').
Referee: Frank de Bleeckere (BEL)   Attendance: 13.885

07-10-2006   Parken Stadium, Copenhagen: Denmark – Northern Ireland   0-0
Denmark: Thomas Sørensen (68' Jesper Christiansen), Michael Gravgaard, Daniel Agger, Lars Jacobsen, Niclas Jensen (73' Nicklas Bendtner), Christian Poulsen, Thomas Kahlenberg, Daniel Jensen, Martin Jørgensen, Jon Dahl Tomasson (C), Peter Løvenkrands (54' Claus Jensen). (Coach: Morten Per Olsen (DEN)).
Northern Ireland: Maik Taylor (YC10), Michael Duff (YC44), Stephen Craigan, Aaron Hughes (C), Jonny Evans (YC62), Chris Baird, Steven Davis, Sammy Clingan (56' Damien Johnson), David Healy (83' Warren Feeney), Keith Gillespie (YC65), Kyle Lafferty (63' Stephen (Steve) Jones). (Coach: Lawrence Philip (Lawrie) Sanchez (NIR)).
Referee: Konrad Plautz (AUT)   Attendance: 41.482

07-10-2006   Skonto Stadions, Riga: Latvia – Iceland   4-0 (3-0)
Latvia: Aleksandrs Kolinko, Māris Smirnovs, Oskars Klava (YC78) (84' Deniss Kacanovs), Igors Stepanovs, Dzintars Zirnis, Genādijs Solonicins, Juris Laizāns, Imants Bleidelis (46' Aleksejs Visnakovs), Vitālijs Astafjevs (C), Māris Verpakovskis (59' Marians Pahars), Girts Karlsons. (Coach: Juris Andrejevs (LAT)).
Iceland: Árni Arason, Hermann Hreidarsson, Brynjar Gunnarsson (YC64), Grétar Steinsson, Indridi Sigurdsson, Ívar Ingimarsson (YC90+1), Jóhannes Gudjónsson (46' Veigar Gunnarsson), Stefán Gíslason, Kári Árnason (45' Helgi Daníelsson), Hannes Sigurdsson (74' Emil Hallfredsson), Eidur Gudjohnsen (C). (Coach: Eyjólfur Gjafar Sverrisson (ISL)).
Goals: Latvia: 1-0 Girts Karlsons (17'), 2-0 Māris Verpakovskis (18'), 3-0 Māris Verpakovskis (28'), 4-0 Aleksejs Visnakovs (54').
Referee: Alan Kelly (IRL)   Attendance: 6.800

07-10-2006   Råsunda Stadium, Solna: Sweden – Spain   2-0 (1-0)
Sweden: Rami Shaaban, Olof Mellberg, Petter Hansson, Erik Edman, Fredrik (Freddie)
Ljungberg (C) (56' Christian Wilhelmsson), Tobias Linderoth, Niclas Alexandersson, Mikael
Nilsson (YC81), Anders Svensson (YC45) (75' Kim Källström), Johan Elmander (77' Daniel
Andersson), Marcus Allbäck. (Coach: Lars Lagerbäck (SWE)).
Spain: IKER CASILLAS Fernández (C), Juan Gutierrez Moreno "JUANITO", Joan
CAPDEVILA Méndez (YC) (52' Antonio José PUERTA Pérez), SERGIO RAMOS García
(YC89), Carles PUYOL Saforcada (YC40), David ALBELDA Aliqués, Xavier "XAVI"
Hernández i Creus (YC83), Francesc "CESC" FÀBREGAS Soler (YC35) (46' Andrés
INIESTA Luján (YC65)), Miguel Ángel ANGULO Valderrey (59' LUIS Javier GARCÍA Sanz
(YC90+2)), DAVID VILLA Sánchez, FERNANDO José TORRES Sanz. (Coach: LUIS
ARAGONÉS Suárez (ESP)).
Goals: Sweden: 1-0 Johan Elmander (11'), 2-0 Marcus Allbäck (82').
Referee: Stephen Graham (Steve) Bennett (ENG)   Attendance: 33.056

11-10-2006   Laugardalsvöllur, Reykjavik: Iceland – Sweden   1-2 (1-1)
Iceland: Árni Arason, Hermann Hreidarsson (YC57), Grétar Steinsson (YC38), Indridi
Sigurdsson (51' Hjálmar Jónsson), Kristján Sigurdsson, Ívar Ingimarsson, Jóhannes
Gudjónsson (81' Marel Baldvinsson), Arnar Vidarsson, Emil Hallfredsson, Hannes Sigurdsson
(YC68), Eidur Gudjohnsen (C). (Coach: Eyjólfur Gjafar Sverrisson (ISL)).
Sweden: Rami Shaaban, Petter Hansson, Erik Edman, Mikael Antonsson, Christian
Wilhelmsson (YC90+3), Mikael Nilsson, Kim Källström, Daniel Andersson (YC69), Niclas
Alexandersson (C), Johan Elmander (YC86) (90' Daniel Majstorovic), Marcus Allbäck (79'
Markus Rosenberg). (Coach: Lars Lagerbäck (SWE)).
Goals: Iceland: 1-0 Arnar Vidarsson (6').
Sweden: 1-1 Kim Källström (8'), 1-2 Christian Wilhelmsson (59').
Referee: Grzegorz Gilewski (POL)   Attendance: 8.725

11-10-2006   Rheinpark Stadion. Vaduz: Liechtenstein – Denmark   0-4 (0-2)
Liechtenstein: Peter Jehle, Martin Stocklasa, Christof Ritter, Yves Oehri, Daniel Hasler (C),
Martin Büchel, Franz Burgmeier (63' Daniel Frick), Martin Telser, Mario Frick, Benjamin
Fischer (79' Fabio D'Elia), Thomas Beck (63' Marco Ritzberger). (Coach: Martin Andermatt
(SUI)).
Denmark: Jesper Christiansen, Lars Jacobsen, Michael Gravgaard, Daniel Agger, Christian
Poulsen, Thomas Kahlenberg (64' Claus Jensen), Niclas Jensen, Daniel Jensen (46' Dennis
Sørensen), Martin Jørgensen, Jon Dahl Tomasson (C), Dennis Rommedahl (78' Michael
Krohn-Dehli). (Coach: Morten Per Olsen (DEN)).
Goals: Denmark: 0-1 Daniel Jensen (29'), 0-2 Michael Gravgaard (32'), 0-3 Jon Dahl
Tomasson (51'), 0-4 Jon Dahl Tomasson (64').
Referee: David Ceri Richards (WAL)   Attendance: 2.665

11-10-2006   Windsor Park, Belfast: Northern Ireland – Latvia   1-0 (1-0)
Northern Ireland: Maik Taylor, Stephen Craigan, Aaron Hughes (C), Jonny Evans, Chris Baird,
Damien Johnson, Steven Davis, Sammy Clingan, David Healy (90'+1' Warren Feeney), Keith
Gillespie, Kyle Lafferty (YC48) (89' James Quinn). (Coach: Lawrence Philip (Lawrie)
Sanchez (NIR)).
Latvia: Aleksandrs Kolinko, Igors Stepanovs, Māris Smirnovs (46' Kaspars Gorkss (YC68)),
Dzintars Zirnis, Genādijs Solonicins (86' Aleksejs Visnakovs), Juris Laizāns, Deniss
Kacanovs, Vitālijs Astafjevs (C) (YC86), Māris Verpakovskis (78' Gatis Kalnins), Girts
Karlsons, Marians Pahars. (Coach: Juris Andrejevs (LAT)).
Goal: Northern Ireland: 1-0 David Healy (35').
Referee: Dr.Helmut Fleischer (GER)   Attendance: 13.500

24-03-2007   Rheinpark Stadion, Vaduz: Liechtenstein – Northern Ireland   1-4 (0-0)
Liechtenstein: Peter Jehle, Michael Stocklasa (C), Martin Stocklasa, Christof Ritter, Yves Oehri (68' Martin Telser), Raphael Rohrer (84' Stefan Büchel), Martin Büchel (YC19), Franz Burgmeier (YC85), Mario Frick, Ronny Büchel (88' Daniel Frick), Thomas Beck. (Coach: Hans-Peter Zaugg (SUI)).
Northern Ireland: Maik Taylor, Michael Duff, Stephen Craigan, Aaron Hughes, Jonny Evans, Damien Johnson, Steven Davis, Chris Brunt (68' Grant McCann), David Healy (84' Stephen (Steve) Jones), Keith Gillespie (C) (YC23), Kyle Lafferty (56' Warren Feeney). (Coach: Lawrence Philip (Lawrie) Sanchez (NIR)).
Goals: Liechtenstein: 1-3 Franz Burgmeier (90'+1').
Northern Ireland: 0-1 David Healy (52'), 0-2 David Healy (74'), 0-3 David Healy (83'), 1-4 Grant McCann (90'+2').
Referee: Oleh Oriekhov (UKR)   Attendance: 4.340

24-03-2007   Santiago Bernabéu Stadium, Madrid: Spain – Denmark   2-1 (2-0)
Spain: IKER CASILLAS Fernández (C), Joan CAPDEVILA Méndez, ÁNGEL David LÓPEZ Ruano (YC84), Francisco Javier Vicente "JAVI" NAVARRO, Carlos MARCHENA López, David ALBELDA Aliqués (YC57), DAVID Jiménez SILVA, Xavier "XAVI" Hernández i Creus (60' Xabier "XABI" ALONSO Olano (YC89)), Andrés INIESTA Luján, Fernando MORIENTES Sánchez (64' FERNANDO José TORRES Sanz), DAVID VILLA Sánchez (76' Miguel Ángel ANGULO Valderrey (YC78)). (Coach: LUIS ARAGONÉS Suárez (ESP)).
Denmark: Thomas Sørensen, Daniel Agger, Lars Jacobsen, Michael Gravgaard, Christian Poulsen, Thomas Kahlenberg (60' Jesper Grønkjær), Niclas Jensen (YC17,YC20), Daniel Jensen, Martin Jørgensen (38' Leon Andreasen (YC63), 73' Nicklas Bendtner), Jon Dahl Tomasson (C) (YC70), Dennis Rommedahl. (Coach: Morten Per Olsen (DEN)).
Goals: Spain: 1-0 Fernando MORIENTES Sánchez (34'), 2-0 DAVID VILLA Sánchez (45'+1').
Denmark: 2-1 Michael Gravgaard (49').
Referee: Massimo Busacca (SUI)   Attendance: 73.575

28-03-2007   Rheinpark Stadion, Vaduz: Liechtenstein – Latvia   1-0 (1-0)
Liechtenstein: Peter Jehle, Martin Stocklasa (YC63), Michael Stocklasa, Daniel Hasler (C), Raphael Rohrer (YC42) (90'+1' Stefan Büchel), Martin Büchel, Franz Burgmeier, Martin Telser, Mario Frick, Ronny Büchel, Thomas Beck (76' Benjamin Fischer). (Coach: Hans-Peter Zaugg (SUI)).
Latvia: Aleksandrs Kolinko, Igors Stepanovs (C) (YC42), Viktors Morozs (YC8) (61' Andrejs Pereplotkins), Oskars Klava, Kaspars Gorkss (79' Andrejs Prohorenkovs), Juris Laizāns, Imants Bleidelis, Aleksejs Visnakovs, Deniss Kacanovs (YC73), Māris Verpakovskis (46' Girts Karlsons), Marians Pahars (YC66). (Coach: Juris Andrejevs (LAT)).
Goal: Liechtenstein: 1-0 Mario Frick (17').
Referee: Serge Gumienny (BEL)   Attendance: 1.680

28-03-2007   Windsor Park, Belfast: Northern Ireland – Sweden   2-1 (1-1)
Northern Ireland: Maik Taylor, Michael Duff, Stephen Craigan, Aaron Hughes (C), Jonny
Evans, Grant McCann, Damien Johnson (YC38), Steven Davis, Chris Brunt (90'+2' Ivan
Sproule), David Healy (89' Sean Webb), Warren Feeney (79' Kyle Lafferty). (Coach:
Lawrence Philip (Lawrie) Sanchez (NIR)).
Sweden: Andreas Isaksson, Olof Mellberg (69' Daniel Majstorovic), Petter Hansson, Erik
Edman, Mikael Nilsson, Fredrik (Freddie) Ljungberg (C), Daniel Andersson, Niclas
Alexandersson (61' Christian Wilhelmsson), Anders Svensson (46' Kim Källström), Zlatan
Ibrahimovic, Johan Elmander. (Coach: Lars Lagerbäck (SWE)).
Goals: Northern Ireland: 1-1 David Healy (31'), 2-1 David Healy (58').
Sweden: 0-1 Johan Elmander (26').
Referee: Eric Frederikus Johannes Braamhaar (HOL)   Attendance: 13.500

28-03-2007   ONO Estadi, Palma de Mallorca: Spain – Iceland   1-0 (0-0)
Spain: IKER CASILLAS Fernández (C), Carlos MARCHENA López, Joan CAPDEVILA
Méndez (46' Miguel Ángel ANGULO Valderrey), SERGIO RAMOS García, Carles PUYOL
Saforcada, David ALBELDA Aliqués (78' Xabier "XABI" ALONSO Olano), Xavier "XAVI"
Hernández i Creus, DAVID Jiménez SILVA, Andrés INIESTA Luján, Fernando MORIENTES
Sánchez (43' FERNANDO José TORRES Sanz), DAVID VILLA Sánchez. (Coach: LUIS
ARAGONÉS Suárez (ESP)).
Iceland: Árni Arason, Gunnar Thor Gunnarsson, Brynjar Gunnarsson, Grétar Steinsson,
Kristján Sigurdsson, Ívar Ingimarsson, Ólafur Örn Bjarnason, Arnar Vidarsson (83' Hannes
Sigurdsson), Emil Hallfredsson (74' Indridi Sigurdsson), Veigar Gunnarsson (56' Stefán
Gíslason), Eidur Gudjohnsen (C). (Coach: Eyjólfur Gjafar Sverrisson (ISL)).
Goal: Spain: 1-0 Andrés INIESTA Luján (80').
Referee: Laurent Duhamel (FRA)   Attendance: 18.326

02-06-2007   Laugardalsvöllur, Reykjavik: Iceland – Liechtenstein   1-1 (1-0)
Iceland: Árni Arason, Gunnar Thor Gunnarsson, Brynjar Gunnarsson, Grétar Steinsson,
Kristján Sigurdsson, Ívar Ingimarsson, Stefán Gíslason, Matthías Gudmundsson (70' Birkir
Már Sævarsson), Emil Hallfredsson (YC71) (82' Theodór (Teddy) Elmar Bjarnason), Eidur
Gudjohnsen (C) (YC62), Veigar Gunnarsson (72' Hannes Sigurdsson). (Coach: Eyjólfur Gjafar
Sverrisson (ISL)).
Liechtenstein: Peter Jehle, Martin Stocklasa, Michael Stocklasa, Daniel Hasler (C), Raphael
Rohrer, Marco Ritzberger (YC50), Franz Burgmeier (78' Daniel Frick), Michele Polverino
(85' Wolfgang Kieber), Mario Frick, Ronny Büchel, Thomas Beck (87' Roger Beck). (Coach:
Hans-Peter Zaugg (SUI)).
Goals: Iceland: 1-0 Brynjar Gunnarsson (27').
Liechtenstein: 1-1 Raphael Rohrer (69').
Referee: Sten Kaldma (EST)   Attendance: 5.139

156

02-06-2007   Parken Stadium, Copenhagen: Denmark – Sweden   0-3 (abandoned)
Denmark: Thomas Sørensen, Lars Jacobsen, Michael Gravgaard, Daniel Agger, Christian
Poulsen (RC89), Jan Kristiansen (35' Leon Andreasen (YC77)), Thomas Kahlenberg (46'
Nicklas Bendtner), Daniel Jensen (63' Jesper Grønkjær), Martin Jørgensen, Jon Dahl
Tomasson (C), Dennis Rommedahl. (Coach: Morten Per Olsen (DEN)).
Sweden: Andreas Isaksson, Olof Mellberg, Petter Hansson, Christian Wilhelmsson, Mikael
Nilsson, Fredrik (Freddie) Ljungberg (C), Thobias Linderoth (YC84), Niclas Alexandersson
(YC44), Anders Svensson, Johan Elmander (YC38) (74' Markus Rosenberg), Marcus Allbäck
(80' Kennedy Bakircioglu). (Coach: Lars Lagerbäck (SWE)).
Goals: Denmark: 1-3 Daniel Agger (34'), 2-3 Jon Dahl Tomasson (62'), 3-3 Leon Andreasen
(75').
Sweden: 0-1 Johan Elmander (7'), 0-2 Petter Hansson (23'), 0-3 Johan Elmander (26').
Referee: Herbert Fandel (GER)   Attendance: 42.083
(The goalscorers in this match are not added to the Goalscorers Tournament list!)

*A Danish supporter ran onto the pitch and attacked referee Herbert Fandel after the referee
had awarded Sweden a penalty in the 89th minute of the match, sending-off Danish
midfielder Christian Poulsen for punching Swedish striker Markus Rosenberg in the
stomach. The match was abandoned by the referee following this attack with the scoreline
standing at 3-3. The match was awarded to Sweden with a 3-0 scoreline by UEFA's
disciplinary committee on 8th June 2007.*
*Christian Poulsen was banned for three competitive matches, and Denmark's two
subsequent matches were ordered to be played at least 140 kilometres from Copenhagen.*

02-06-2007   Skonto Stadions, Riga: Latvia – Spain   0-2 (0-1)
Latvia: Aleksandrs Kolinko (YC36), Artūrs Zakresevskis, Oskars Klava (YC27), Deniss
Ivanovs, Dzintars Zirnis, Andrejs Rubins (65' Genādijs Solonicins), Juris Laizāns, Imants
Bleidelis (85' Andrejs Pereplotkins), Vitālijs Astafjevs (C), Māris Verpakovskis, Girts
Karlsons (89' Aleksandrs Cauna). (Coach: Aleksandrs Starkovs (LAT)).
Spain: IKER CASILLAS Fernández (C), Carlos MARCHENA López (YC73), Joan
CAPDEVILA Méndez, SERGIO RAMOS García, Carles PUYOL Saforcada, David
ALBELDA Aliqués (66' Xabier "XABI" ALONSO Olano), Xavier "XAVI" Hernández i Creus
(YC90+2), Andrés INIESTA Luján, Miguel Ángel ANGULO Valderrey (45' JOAQUÍN
Sánchez Rodríguez), LUIS GARCÍA Fernández (56' Roberto SOLDADO Rillo), DAVID
VILLA Sánchez. (Coach: LUIS ARAGONÉS Suárez (ESP)).
Goals: Spain: 0-1 DAVID VILLA Sánchez (45'), 0-2 Xavier "XAVI" Hernández i Creus (60').
Referee: Craig Alexander Thomson (SCO)   Attendance: 10.000

06-06-2007   Råsunda Stadium, Solna: Sweden – Iceland   5-0 (3-0)
Sweden: Andreas Isaksson, Olof Mellberg, Petter Hansson, Christian Wilhelmsson, Mikael
Nilsson (57' Max von Schlebrügge), Fredrik (Freddie) Ljungberg (C), Thobias Linderoth (62'
Daniel Andersson), Niclas Alexandersson, Anders Svensson, Markus Rosenberg, Marcus
Allbäck (73' Zlatan Ibrahimovic). (Coach: Lars Lagerbäck (SWE)).
Iceland: Árni Arason, Gunnar Thor Gunnarsson (YC6), Brynjar Gunnarsson (C), Grétar
Steinsson (90'+2' Kristján Sigurdsson), Birkir Már Sævarsson (65' Matthías Gudmundsson),
Ívar Ingimarsson, Ólafur Örn Bjarnason, Arnar Vidarsson (YC54), Emil Hallfredsson (53'
Hjálmar Jónsson), Theodór (Teddy) Elmar Bjarnason, Hannes Sigurdsson. (Coach: Eyjólfur
Gjafar Sverrisson (ISL)).
Goals: Sweden: 1-0 Marcus Allbäck (11'), 2-0 Anders Svensson (42'), 3-0 Olof Mellberg
(45'), 4-0 Markus Rosenberg (50'), 5-0 Marcus Allbäck (51').
Referee: Alain Hamer (LUX)   Attendance: 33.338

157

06-06-2007   Rheinpark Stadion, Vaduz: Liechtenstein – Spain   0-2 (0-0)
Liechtenstein: Peter Jehle (YC90+2), Michael Stocklasa (29' Martin Telser), Martin Stocklasa,
Daniel Hasler (C) (YC80), Raphael Rohrer (59' Daniel Frick), Marco Ritzberger, Franz
Burgmeier (YC69), Michele Polverino, Mario Frick, Ronny Büchel (YC38), Thomas Beck
(82' Roger Beck). (Coach: Hans-Peter Zaugg (SUI)).
Spain: José Manuel "PEPE" REINA Páez, Carlos MARCHENA López, Francisco Javier
Vicente "JAVI" NAVARRO, Joan CAPDEVILA Méndez (52' ANTONIO LÓPEZ Guerrero),
SERGIO RAMOS García, JOAQUÍN Sánchez Rodríguez (C), Xabier "XABI" ALONSO
Olano, DAVID Jiménez SILVA (77' Roberto SOLDADO Rillo), Andrés INIESTA Luján,
Francesc "CESC" FÀBREGAS Soler (YC6) (67' LUIS GARCÍA Fernández), DAVID VILLA
Sánchez. (Coach: LUIS ARAGONÉS Suárez (ESP)).
Goals: Spain: 0-1 DAVID VILLA Sánchez (8'), 0-2 DAVID VILLA Sánchez (14').
Referee: Nikolay Vladimirovich Ivanov (RUS)   Attendance: 5.739
(DAVID VILLA Sánchez missed a penalty in the 90+3 minute)

06-06-2007   Skonto Stadions, Riga: Latvia – Denmark   0-2 (0-2)
Latvia: Aleksandrs Kolinko, Igors Stepanovs, Oskars Klava, Deniss Ivanovs, Dzintars Zirnis,
Andrejs Rubins (75' Aleksandrs Cauna), Juris Laizāns, Imants Bleidelis (66' Genādijs
Solonicins), Vitālijs Astafjevs (C), Māris Verpakovskis (YC8), Girts Karlsons (61' Marians
Pahars (YC64)). (Coach: Aleksandrs Starkovs (LAT)).
Denmark: Thomas Sørensen, Martin Laursen, Lars Jacobsen, Daniel Agger, Niclas Jensen,
Daniel Jensen (YC68), Jesper Grønkjær, Martin Jørgensen, Jon Dahl Tomasson (C), Dennis
Rommedahl (YC16) (46' Thomas Kahlenberg), Nicklas Bendtner (60' Rasmus Würtz).
(Coach: Morten Per Olsen (DEN)).
Goals: Denmark: 0-1 Dennis Rommedahl (15'), 0-2 Dennis Rommedahl (17').
Referee: Matteo Simone Trefoloni (ITA)   Attendance: 3.900

22-08-2007   Windsor Park, Belfast: Northern Ireland – Liechtenstein   3-1 (2-0)
Northern Ireland: Maik Taylor, George McCartney, Michael Duff (YC44), Stephen Craigan,
Chris Baird (C), Steven Davis, Sammy Clingan, Chris Brunt (62' Stuart Elliott), David Healy,
Keith Gillespie (85' Stephen (Steve) Jones), Kyle Lafferty (75' Warren Feeney). (Coach: Nigel
Worthington (NIR)).
Liechtenstein: Peter Jehle, Michael Stocklasa (YC25) (38' Yves Oehri), Martin Stocklasa,
Fabio D'Elia (YC66), Martin Telser, Raphael Rohrer (74' Roger Beck), Christoph Biedermann
(62' Stefan Büchel), Michele Polverino, Mario Frick (C), Daniel Frick, Ronny Büchel. (Coach:
Hans-Peter Zaugg (SUI)).
Goals: Northern Ireland: 1-0 David Healy (5'), 2-0 David Healy (35'), 3-0 Kyle Lafferty (56').
Liechtenstein: 3-1 Mario Frick (89').
Referee: Radek Matejek (CZE)   Attendance: 13.544

08-09-2007   Skonto Stadions, Riga: Latvia – Northern Ireland   1-0 (0-0)
Latvia: Andris Vanins, Oskars Klava, Deniss Ivanovs, Kaspars Gorkss, Dzintars Zirnis
(YC64), Andrejs Rubins, Juris Laizāns, Imants Bleidelis, Vitālijs Astafjevs (C), Māris
Verpakovskis (90' Kristaps Blanks), Girts Karlsons (71' Vits Rimkus (YC74)). (Coach:
Aleksandrs Starkovs (LAT)).
Northern Ireland: Maik Taylor, George McCartney, Michael Duff, Jonny Evans, Chris Baird
(YC48), Stuart Elliott (66' Chris Brunt), Steven Davis, Sammy Clingan, David Healy (C),
Keith Gillespie (YC90+2), Kyle Lafferty (71' Warren Feeney). (Coach: Nigel Worthington
(NIR)).
Goal: Latvia: 1-0 Chris Baird (69' *own goal*).
Referee: Pedro Proença Oliveira Alves Garcia (POR)   Attendance: 7.500

08-09-2007   Råsunda Stadium, Solna: Sweden – Denmark   0-0
Sweden: Andreas Isaksson, Olof Mellberg (YC27), Petter Hansson, Erik Edman, Christian
Wilhelmsson (57' Kennedy Bakircioglu), Mikael Nilsson, Thobias Linderoth (C), Niclas
Alexandersson, Anders Svensson (69' Kim Källström), Zlatan Ibrahimovic (YC80) (89' Rade
Prica), Johan Elmander (YC56). (Coach: Lars Lagerbäck (SWE)).
Denmark: Thomas Sørensen, Martin Laursen, Thomas Helveg, Leon Andreasen (81' Peter
Løvenkrands), Daniel Agger (YC21), Thomas Kahlenberg (54' Nicklas Bendtner), Niclas
Jensen, Daniel Jensen (YC8), Jesper Grønkjær (YC80), Jon Dahl Tomasson (C) (90'+1'
Michael Gravgaard), Dennis Rommedahl. (Coach: Morten Per Olsen (DEN)).
Referee: Frank de Bleeckere (BEL)   Attendance: 33.082

08-09-2007   Laugardalsvöllur, Reykjavik: Iceland – Spain   1-1 (1-0)
Iceland: Árni Arason, Hermann Hreidarsson (C), Ragnar Sigurdsson (YC61), Grétar Steinsson,
Jóhannes Gudjónsson (YC36) (79' Baldur Adalsteinsson), Kristján Sigurdsson, Ívar
Ingimarsson, Kári Árnason, Arnar Vidarsson (69' Ólafur Skúlason), Emil Hallfredsson,
Gunnar Heidar Thorvaldsson (88' Ármann Björnsson). (Coach: Eyjólfur Gjafar Sverrisson
(ISL)).
Spain: IKER CASILLAS Fernández (C), MARIANO Andrés PERNÍA Molina (YC8) (26'
David ALBELDA Aliqués), Carlos MARCHENA López, Juan Gutierrez Moreno "JUANITO",
SERGIO RAMOS García, JOAQUÍN Sánchez Rodríguez (C) (69' LUIS GARCÍA Fernández),
Xavier "XAVI" Hernández i Creus, Xabier "XABI" ALONSO Olano (RC21), DAVID Jiménez
SILVA, FERNANDO José TORRES Sanz (57' Andrés INIESTA Luján), DAVID VILLA
Sánchez. (Coach: LUIS ARAGONÉS Suárez (ESP)).
Goals: Iceland: 1-0 Emil Hallfredsson (40').
Spain: 1-1 Andrés INIESTA Luján (86').
Referee: Wolfgang Stark (GER)   Attendance: 9.483

12-09-2007   NRGi Park, Aarhus: Denmark – Liechtenstein   4-0 (4-0)
Denmark: Thomas Sørensen, Leon Andreasen, Martin Laursen, Thomas Helveg, Daniel Agger
(28' Michael Gravgaard), Niclas Jensen, Jesper Grønkjær (46' Thomas Kahlenberg), Esben
Hansen, Jon Dahl Tomasson (C) (68' Peter Løvenkrands), Dennis Rommedahl, Morten
Nordstrand. (Coach: Morten Per Olsen (DEN)).
Liechtenstein: Peter Jehle, Martin Stocklasa (YC87), Yves Oehri (46' Daniel Frick), Fabio
D'Elia (YC62), Martin Telser, Raphael Rohrer, Marco Ritzberger (46' Thomas Beck (YC47)),
Franz Burgmeier, Michele Polverino, Mario Frick (C) (84' Roger Beck), Ronny Büchel.
(Coach: Hans-Peter Zaugg (SUI)).
Goals: Denmark: 1-0 Morten Nordstrand (3'), 2-0 Martin Laursen (12'), 3-0 Jon Dahl
Tomasson (18'), 4-0 Morten Nordstrand (36').
Referee: Mark Clattenburg (ENG)   Attendance: 20.005

159

12-09-2007   Laugardalsvöllur, Reykjavik: Iceland – Northern Ireland   2-1 (1-0)
Iceland: Árni Arason, Hermann Hreidarsson (C) (YC65), Ármann Björnsson (YC19) (53'
Eidur Gudjohnsen), Grétar Steinsson, Ragnar Sigurdsson, Kristján Sigurdsson, Ívar
Ingimarsson, Emil Hallfredsson, Kári Árnason (88' Ásgeir Ásgeirsson), Arnar Vidarsson,
Gunnar Heidar Thorvaldsson (79' Ólafur Skúlason). (Coach: Eyjólfur Gjafar Sverrisson (ISL)).
Northern Ireland: Maik Taylor, Michael Duff, George McCartney, Jonny Evans, Chris Baird
(C) (YC86), Steven Davis (79' Grant McCann), Sammy Clingan, Chris Brunt (YC68) (83'
Stephen (Steve) Jones), David Healy, Keith Gillespie, Warren Feeney (YC41). (Coach: Nigel
Worthington (NIR)).
Goals: Iceland: 1-0 Ármann Björnsson (6'), 2-1 Keith Gillespie (90'+1' own goal).
Northern Ireland: 1-1 David Healy (72' penalty).
Referee: Yuri Valeryevich Baskakov (RUS)   Attendance: 7.727

12-09-2007   Estadio Carlos Tartiere, Oviedo: Spain – Latvia   2-0 (1-0)
Spain: IKER CASILLAS Fernández (C), MARIANO Andrés PERNÍA Molina, Carlos
MARCHENA López, Juan Gutierrez Moreno "JUANITO", SERGIO RAMOS García,
JOAQUÍN Sánchez Rodríguez (77' Miguel Ángel ANGULO Valderrey), David ALBELDA
Aliqués, Xavier "XAVI" Hernández i Creus, DAVID Jiménez SILVA (69' Francesc "CESC"
FÀBREGAS Soler), DAVID VILLA Sánchez (48' Andrés INIESTA Luján), FERNANDO
José TORRES Sanz. (Coach: LUIS ARAGONÉS Suárez (ESP)).
Latvia: Andris Vanins, Oskars Klava, Deniss Ivanovs (YC60), Kaspars Gorkss, Dzintars
Zirnis, Andrejs Rubins, Juris Laizāns, Imants Bleidelis (74' Aleksejs Visnakovs), Vitālijs
Astafjevs (C) (YC51), Māris Verpakovskis (88' Kristaps Blanks), Girts Karlsons (63' Marians
Pahars). (Coach: Aleksandrs Starkovs (LAT)).
Goals: Spain: 1-0 Xavier "XAVI" Hernández i Creus (13'), 2-0 FERNANDO José TORRES
Sanz (85').
Referee: Alon Yefet (ISR)   Attendance: 22.560

13-10-2007   Laugardalsvöllur, Reykjavik: Iceland – Latvia   2-4 (1-3)
Iceland: Árni Arason, Hjálmar Jónsson, Brynjar Gunnarsson (YC86), Ragnar Sigurdsson,
Grétar Steinsson (25' Kári Árnason), Kristján Sigurdsson (YC48) (88' Ármann Björnsson),
Ívar Ingimarsson, Jóhannes Gudjónsson, Emil Hallfredsson, Eidur Gudjohnsen (C), Gunnar
Heidar Thorvaldsson (65' Hannes Sigurdsson). (Coach: Eyjólfur Gjafar Sverrisson (ISL)).
Latvia: Andris Vanins, Oskars Klava, Deniss Ivanovs, Kaspars Gorkss, Dzintars Zirnis,
Aleksejs Visnakovs (90'+2' Jurijs Zigajevs), Genādijs Solonicins, Juris Laizāns, Vitālijs
Astafjevs (C), Māris Verpakovskis (YC22) (78' Marians Pahars), Girts Karlsons (59' Vits
Rimkus). (Coach: Aleksandrs Starkovs (LAT)).
Goals: Iceland: 1-0 Eidur Gudjohnsen (4'), 2-4 Eidur Gudjohnsen (52').
Latvia: 1-1 Oskars Klava (27'), 1-2 Juris Laizāns (31'), 1-3 Māris Verpakovskis (37'), 1-4
Māris Verpakovskis (46').
Referee: Michael Leslie (Mike) Dean (ENG)   Attendance: 5.865

13-10-2007   Rheinpark Stadion, Vaduz: Liechtenstein – Sweden   0-3 (0-2)
Liechtenstein: Peter Jehle, Yves Oehri, Daniel Hasler (C), Martin Büchel (61' Andreas Gerster), Martin Telser (YC67), Raphael Rohrer, Franz Burgmeier, Ronny Büchel, Thomas Beck, Mario Frick (74' Roger Beck), Daniel Frick (60' Benjamin Fischer). (Coach: Hans-Peter Zaugg (SUI)).
Sweden: Andreas Isaksson, Erik Edman, Hernán Matías Arsenio Concha, Daniel Majstorovic, Petter Hansson, Christian Wilhelmsson, Fredrik (Freddie) Ljungberg (C) (39' Kim Källström), Thobias Linderoth (70' Daniel Andersson (YC88)), Anders Svensson, Johan Elmander (60' Markus Rosenberg), Marcus Allbäck. (Coach: Lars Lagerbäck (SWE)).
Goals: Sweden: 0-1 Fredrik (Freddie) Ljungberg (19'), 0-2 Christian Wilhelmsson (29'), 0-3 Anders Svensson (56').
Referee: Paolo Dondarini (ITA)   Attendance: 4.131

13-10-2007   NRGi Park, Aarhus: Denmark – Spain   1-3 (0-2)
Denmark: Thomas Sørensen, Ulrik Laursen, Martin Laursen, Thomas Helveg, Leon Andreasen (46' Nicklas Bendtner (YC77)), Niclas Jensen (79' Kenneth Perez), Daniel Jensen (YC2), Christian Poulsen, Jesper Grønkjær (65' Thomas Kahlenberg), Jon Dahl Tomasson (C), Dennis Rommedahl. (Coach: Morten Per Olsen (DEN)).
Spain: IKER CASILLAS Fernández (C), Carlos MARCHENA López, Joan CAPDEVILA Méndez (YC18), Raúl ALBIOL Tortajada, SERGIO RAMOS García, JOAQUÍN Sánchez Rodríguez (69' Albert RIERA Ortega), David ALBELDA Aliqués (64' PABLO IBÁÑEZ Tébar), Xavier "XAVI" Hernández i Creus, Andrés INIESTA Luján, Francesc "CESC" FÀBREGAS Soler (78' LUIS GARCÍA Fernández), RAÚL TAMUDO Montero. (Coach: LUIS ARAGONÉS Suárez (ESP)).
Goals: Denmark: 1-2 Jon Dahl Tomasson (87').
Spain: 0-1 RAÚL TAMUDO Montero (14'), 0-2 SERGIO RAMOS García (40'), 1-3 Albert RIERA Ortega (89').
Referee: Lubos Michel (SVK)   Attendance: 19.849

17-10-2007   Parken Stadium, Copenhagen: Denmark – Latvia   3-1 (2-0)
Denmark: Thomas Sørensen, Chris Sørensen, Ulrik Laursen (32' Leon Andreasen), Martin Laursen, Thomas Helveg, Daniel Jensen (YC32), Christian Poulsen (71' Jesper Grønkjær), Thomas Kahlenberg, Jon Dahl Tomasson (C), Dennis Rommedahl, Nicklas Bendtner. (Coach: Morten Per Olsen (DEN)).
Latvia: Andris Vanins, Oskars Klava, Deniss Ivanovs, Kaspars Gorkss, Dzintars Zirnis, Aleksejs Visnakovs (78' Jurijs Zigajevs), Genādijs Solonicins, Juris Laizāns, Vitālijs Astafjevs (C), Vits Rimkus (63' Andrejs Butriks), Marians Pahars (90'+1' Deniss Kacanovs). (Coach: Aleksandrs Starkovs (LAT)).
Goals: Denmark: 1-0 Jon Dahl Tomasson (7' penalty), 2-0 Ulrik Laursen (27'), 3-1 Dennis Rommedahl (90').
Latvia: 2-1 Kaspars Gorkss (80').
Referee: Cüneyt Çakir (TUR)   Attendance: 19.004

17-10-2007   Rheinpark Stadion, Vaduz: Liechtenstein – Iceland   3-0 (1-0)
Liechtenstein: Peter Jehle, Martin Stocklasa (YC64), Yves Oehri, Daniel Hasler (C), Martin
Telser (YC87), Raphael Rohrer (68' Roger Beck), Andreas Gerster, Franz Burgmeier, Mario
Frick (90'+1' Fabio D'Elia), Benjamin Fischer (62' Thomas Beck), Ronny Büchel. (Coach:
Hans-Peter Zaugg (SUI)).
Iceland: Árni Arason, Hermann Hreidarsson, Brynjar Gunnarsson (85' Ásgeir Ásgeirsson),
Ragnar Sigurdsson, Kristján Sigurdsson, Ívar Ingimarsson, Jóhannes Gudjónsson (58' Ármann
Björnsson), Arnar Vidarsson, Emil Hallfredsson, Eidur Gudjohnsen (C) (YC75), Gunnar
Heidar Thorvaldsson (71' Helgi Sigurdsson). (Coach: Eyjólfur Gjafar Sverrisson (ISL)).
Goals: Liechtenstein: 1-0 Mario Frick (28'), 2-0 Thomas Beck (80'), 3-0 Thomas Beck (82').
Referee: Christoforos Zografos (GRE)   Attendance: 2.589

17-10-2007   Råsunda Stadium, Solna: Sweden – Northern Ireland   1-1 (1-0)
Sweden: Andreas Isaksson, Erik Edman, Hernán Matías Arsenio Concha (YC45+2), Olof
Mellberg, Petter Hansson (YC82), Kim Källström (85' Andreas Johansson), Christian
Wilhelmsson (45' Mikael Nilsson), Thobias Linderoth (C), Anders Svensson, Johan Elmander
(73' Marcus Allbäck), Zlatan Ibrahimovic. (Coach: Lars Lagerbäck (SWE)).
Northern Ireland: Maik Taylor, Stephen Craigan, George McCartney (87' Tony Capaldi),
Gareth McAuley, Aaron Hughes (C), Ivan Sproule, Sammy Clingan, Chris Brunt, Steven
Davis, David Healy, Kyle Lafferty (YC19). (Coach: Nigel Worthington (NIR)).
Goals: Sweden: 1-0 Olof Mellberg (15').
Northern Ireland: 1-1 Kyle Lafferty (72').
Referee: Bertrand Layec (FRA)   Attendance: 33.112

17-11-2007   Skonto Stadions, Riga: Latvia – Liechtenstein   4-1 (2-1)
Latvia: Andris Vanins, Oskars Klava (YC66), Deniss Ivanovs, Kaspars Gorkss, Dzintars
Zirnis, Andrejs Rubins, Juris Laizāns, Imants Bleidelis (82' Aleksejs Visnakovs), Vitālijs
Astafjevs (C), Māris Verpakovskis (77' Vits Rimkus), Girts Karlsons (YC40) (71' Marians
Pahars). (Coach: Aleksandrs Starkovs (LAT)).
Liechtenstein: Peter Jehle, Martin Stocklasa, Daniel Hasler (C), Fabio D'Elia, Raphael Rohrer
(72' Daniel Frick (YC76)), Marco Ritzberger, Andreas Gerster (YC81), Franz Burgmeier,
Mario Frick, Benjamin Fischer (71' Roger Beck), Ronny Büchel (YC59) (80' Martin Büchel).
(Coach: Hans-Peter Zaugg (SUI)).
Goals: Latvia: 1-1 Girts Karlsons (14'), 2-1 Māris Verpakovskis (30'), 3-1 Juris Laizāns (63'),
4-1 Aleksejs Visnakovs (87').
Liechtenstein: 0-1 Dzintars Zirnis (13' own goal).
Referee: Svein Oddvar Moen (NOR)   Attendance: 4.800

17-11-2007   Windsor Park, Belfast: Northern Ireland – Denmark   2-1 (0-0)
Northern Ireland: Maik Taylor, Stephen Craigan, Gareth McAuley, Aaron Hughes (C), Jonny
Evans (YC82), Steven Davis, Sammy Clingan, Chris Brunt, David Healy, Keith Gillespie
(YC21) (74' Ivan Sproule), Warren Feeney (85' Chris Baird). (Coach: Nigel Worthington
(NIR)).
Denmark: Thomas Sørensen, Chris Sørensen, Brian Priske (72' Rasmus Würtz), Martin
Laursen, Per Krøldrup, Leon Andreasen (YC52), Christian Poulsen, Thomas Kahlenberg (46'
Dennis Sørensen), Martin Jørgensen (C) (79' Simon Poulsen), Dennis Rommedahl, Nicklas
Bendtner. (Coach: Morten Per Olsen (DEN)).
Goals: Northern Ireland: 1-1 Warren Feeney (62'), 2-1 David Healy (80').
Denmark: 0-1 Nicklas Bendtner (51').
Referee: Pieter Vink (HOL)   Attendance: 12.997

17-11-2007   Santiago Bernabéu Stadium, Madrid: Spain – Sweden   3-0 (2-0)
Spain: IKER CASILLAS Fernández (C), Joan CAPDEVILA Méndez, Carlos MARCHENA
López, SERGIO RAMOS García, Carles PUYOL Saforcada (YC88), David ALBELDA
Aliqués, Francesc "CESC" FÀBREGAS Soler, Xavier "XAVI" Hernández i Creus, DAVID
Jiménez SILVA (66' Albert RIERA Ortega), Andrés INIESTA Luján (52' JOAQUÍN Sánchez
Rodríguez), DAVID VILLA Sánchez (52' RAÚL TAMUDO Montero). (Coach: LUIS
ARAGONÉS Suárez (ESP)).
Sweden: Andreas Isaksson, Petter Hansson (YC76), Erik Edman, Olof Mellberg, Daniel
Andersson (46' Kim Källström), Christian Wilhelmsson (79' Kennedy Bakircioglu), Mikael
Nilsson, Fredrik (Freddie) Ljungberg (C), Anders Svensson, Markus Rosenberg (60' Marcus
Allbäck), Zlatan Ibrahimovic. (Coach: Lars Lagerbäck (SWE)).
Goals: Spain: 1-0 Joan CAPDEVILA Méndez (14'), 2-0 Andrés INIESTA Luján (39'), 3-0
SERGIO RAMOS García (65').
Referee: Roberto Rosetti (ITA)   Attendance: 67.055

21-11-2007   Parken Stadium, Copenhagen: Denmark – Iceland   3-0 (2-0)
Denmark: Thomas Sørensen, Chris Sørensen, Per Krøldrup (YC77), Ulrik Laursen, William
Kvist, Christian Poulsen, Daniel Jensen, Martin Jørgensen (53' Thomas Kahlenberg), Jon Dahl
Tomasson (C), Nicklas Bendtner (84' Søren Larsen), Dennis Rommedahl (73' Simon Poulsen).
(Coach: Morten Per Olsen (DEN)). (Not used sub: Leon Andreasen YC68)).
Iceland: Árni Arason, Brynjar Gunnarsson, Hermann Hreidarsson (C), Grétar Steinsson
(YC40), Ragnar Sigurdsson, Stéfan Gíslason (YC79), Kristján Sigurdsson (7' Sverrir
Gardarsson (YC68)), Emil Hallfredsson (73' Eggert Jónsson), Theodór (Teddy) Elmar
Bjarnason (YC68), Veigar Gunnarsson (84' Ásgeir Ásgeirsson), Gunnar Heidar Thorvaldsson.
(Coach: Ólafur David Jóhannesson (ISL)).
Goals: Denmark: 1-0 Nicklas Bendtner (34'), 2-0 Jon Dahl Tomasson (44'), 3-0 Thomas
Kahlenberg (59').
Referee: Olegário Manuel Bártolo Faustino Benquerença (POR)   Attendance: 15.393

21-11-2007   Estadio Gran Canaria, Las Palmas: Spain – Northern Ireland   1-0 (0-0)
Spain: José Manuel "PEPE" REINA Páez, MARIANO Andrés PERNÍA Molina, PABLO
IBÁÑEZ Tébar, Raúl ALBIOL Tortajada, SERGIO RAMOS García, MARCOS Antonio
SENNA Da Silva, DAVID Jiménez SILVA, Francesc "CESC" FÀBREGAS Soler (47'
JOAQUÍN Sánchez Rodríguez), Xavier "XAVI" Hernández i Creus (C) (67' DAVID VILLA
Sánchez), Andrés INIESTA Luján, Daniel González GÜIZA (57' RAÚL TAMUDO Montero).
(Coach: LUIS ARAGONÉS Suárez (ESP)).
Northern Ireland: Maik Taylor, Stephen Craigan, Chris Baird, Aaron Hughes (C), Gareth
McAuley, Ivan Sproule (46' Stephen Robinson), Chris Brunt (59' Kyle Lafferty (YC76)),
Steven Davis, Sammy Clingan, Warren Feeney (72' Martin Paterson), David Healy (YC74).
(Coach: Nigel Worthington (NIR)).
Goal: Spain: 1-0 Xavier "XAVI" Hernández i Creus (52').
Referee: Herbert Fandel (GER)   Attendance: 30.339

21-11-2007   Råsunda Stadium, Solna: Sweden – Latvia 2-1 (1-1)
Sweden: Andreas Isaksson, Erik Edman, Daniel Majstorovic, Olof Mellberg, Fredrik (Freddie)
Ljungberg (C), Kim Källström, Christian Wilhelmsson, Mikael Nilsson, Anders Svensson,
Marcus Allbäck, Zlatan Ibrahimovic. (Coach: Lars Lagerbäck (SWE)).
Latvia: Aleksandrs Kolinko, Deniss Ivanovs, Igors Stepanovs, Kaspars Gorkss, Dzintars Zirnis
(YC58), Imants Bleidelis (43' Aleksejs Visnakovs), Juris Laizāns, Andrejs Rubins, Vitālijs
Astafjevs (C) (49' Genādijs Solonicins (YC77)), Māris Verpakovskis, Girts Karlsons (62'
Marians Pahars). (Coach: Aleksandrs Starkovs (LAT)).
Goals: Sweden: 1-0 Marcus Allbäck (1'), 2-1 Kim Källström (57').
Latvia: 1-1 Juris Laizāns (26').
Referee: Wolfgang Stark (GER)   Attendance: 26.128

GROUP   G

02-09-2006	Minsk	Belarus – Albania	2-2 (2-1)
02-09-2006	Constanta	Romania – Bulgaria	2-2 (1-0)
02-09-2006	Luxembourg	Luxembourg – Netherlands	0-1 (0-1)
06-09-2006	Sofia	Bulgaria – Slovenia	3-0 (0-0)
06-09-2006	Tirana	Albania – Romania	0-2 (0-0)
06-09-2006	Eindhoven	Netherlands – Belarus	3-0 (1-0)
07-10-2006	Bucharest	Romania – Belarus	3-1 (2-1)
07-10-2006	Sofia	Bulgaria – Netherlands	1-1 (1-0)
07-10-2006	Celje	Slovenia – Luxembourg	2-0 (2-0)
11-10-2006	Minsk	Belarus – Slovenia	4-2 (1-2)
11-10-2006	Luxembourg	Luxembourg – Bulgaria	0-1 (0-1)
11-10-2006	Amsterdam	Netherlands – Albania	2-1 (2-0)
24-03-2007	Luxembourg	Luxembourg – Belarus	1-2 (0-1)
24-03-2007	Shkodër	Albania – Slovenia	0-0
24-03-2007	Netherlands	Netherlands – Romania	0-0
28-03-2007	Sofia	Bulgaria – Albania	0-0
28-03-2007	Piatra Neamt	Romania – Luxembourg	3-0 (1-0)
28-03-2007	Celje	Slovenia – Netherlands	0-1 (0-0)
02-06-2007	Tirana	Albania – Luxembourg	2-0 (1-0)
02-06-2007	Celje	Slovenia – Romania	1-2 (0-0)
02-06-2007	Minsk	Belarus – Bulgaria	0-2 (0-1)
06-06-2007	Sofia	Bulgaria – Belarus	2-1 (2-1)
06-06-2007	Luxembourg	Luxembourg – Albania	0-3 (0-2)
06-06-2007	Timisoara	Romania – Slovenia	2-0 (1-0)
08-09-2007	Luxembourg	Luxembourg – Slovenia	0-3 (0-2)
08-09-2007	Minsk	Belarus – Romania	1-3 (1-2)
08-09-2007	Amsterdam	Netherlands – Bulgaria	2-0 (1-0)
12-09-2007	Sofia	Bulgaria – Luxembourg	3-0 (2-0)
12-09-2007	Celje	Slovenia – Belarus	1-0 (1-0)
12-09-2007	Tirana	Albania – Netherlands	0-1 (0-0)
13-10-2007	Gomel	Belarus – Luxembourg	0-1 (0-0)
13-10-2007	Constanta	Romania – Netherlands	1-0 (0-0)
13-10-2007	Celje	Slovenia – Albania	0-0
17-10-2007	Luxembourg	Luxembourg – Romania	0-2 (0-1)
17-10-2007	Eindhoven	Netherlands – Slovenia	2-0 (1-0)

17-10-2007	Tirana	Albania – Bulgaria	1-1 (1-0)
17-11-2007	Sofia	Bulgaria – Romania	1-0 (1-0)
17-11-2007	Tirana	Albania – Belarus	2-4 (2-2)
17-11-2007	Rotterdam	Netherlands – Luxembourg	1-0 (1-0)
21-11-2007	Bucharest	Romania – Albania	6-1 (1-0)
21-11-2007	Minsk	Belarus – Netherlands	2-1 (0-0)
21-11-2007	Celje	Slovenia – Bulgaria	0-2 (0-0)

FINAL STANDING

Pos	Team	Pld	W	D	L	GF	GA	GD	Pts
1	Romania	12	9	2	1	26	7	+19	29
2	Netherlands	12	8	2	2	15	5	+10	26
3	Bulgaria	12	7	4	1	18	7	+11	25
4	Belarus	12	4	1	7	17	23	-6	13
5	Albania	12	2	5	5	12	18	-6	11
6	Slovenia	12	3	2	7	9	16	-7	11
7	Luxembourg	12	1	0	11	2	23	-21	3

Romania and Netherlands qualified for the Final Tournament in Austria and Switzerland.

02-09-2006   Dinamo Stadium, Minsk: Belarus – Albania 2-2 (2-1)
Belarus: Vasili Khomutovski, Sergei Shtaniuk (C), Sergei Omelyanchuk, Maksim Romashchenko (YC86), Denis Kovba, Aleksandr Kulchiy, Vladimir Korytko, Timofei Kalachev (85' Vitali Lanko), Aleksandr Hleb, Vitali Kutuzov, Vyacheslav Hleb (64' Vitali Bulyga). (Coach: Yuri Puntus (BLS)).
Albania: Ilion Lika, Armend Dallku, Adrian Aliaj (46' Debatik Çurri), Elvin Beqiri (YC90+1), Ervin Skela (74' Edmond Kapllani), Altin Haxhi, Besnik Hasi, Lorik Cana (YC29), Altin Lala (83' Devis Mukaj), Igli Tar (C), Erjon Bogdani. (Coach: Otto Baric (CRO)).
Goals: Belarus: 1-0 Timofei Kalachev (2'), 2-1 Maksim Romashchenko (24').
Albania: 1-1 Ervin Skela (7' penalty), 2-2 Besnik Hasi (86').
Referee: Tony Asumaa (FIN)   Attendance: 23.000

02-09-2006   Gheorghe Hagi Stadium, Constanta: Romania – Bulgaria 2-2 (1-0)
Romania: Bogdan Lobont, Cristian Chivu (C), Gabriel Tamas (YC62,YC90+3), Razvan Rat, Cosmin Contra (YC23), Paul Codrea (YC58), Florentin Petre (71' Banel Nicolita), Nicolae Dica (YC37) (58' Razvan Cocis), Laurentiu Rosu (79' Vasile Maftei), Adrian Mutu, Ciprian Marica. (Coach: Victor Piturca (ROM)).
Bulgaria: Georgi Petkov, Aleksandar Tunchev (YC90), Elin Topuzakov, Lucio Wagner Freitas do Souza, Radostin Kishishev (46' Blagoy Georgiev), Stiliyan Petrov (C), Martin Petrov, Georgi Peev (YC39) (46' Chavdar Yankov (YC75)), Stanislav Angelov, Dimitar Berbatov (62' Valeri Bozhinov), Zoran Jankovic. (Coach: Hristo Stoichkov (BUL)).
Goals: Romania: 1-0 Laurentiu Rosu (40'), 2-0 Ciprian Marica (54').
Bulgaria: 2-1 Martin Petrov (82'), 2-2 Martin Petrov (83').
Referee: Stefano Farina (ITA)   Attendance: 12.620

02-09-2006   Stade Josy Barthel, Luxembourg: Luxembourg – Netherlands   0-1 (0-1)
Luxembourg: Jonathan Joubert, Claude Reiter, Kim Kintziger (YC90+3), Eric Hoffmann
(YC12), Jeff Strasser (C), Sébastien Remy, Claudio Lombardelli (83' Ben Federspiel), Joao
Carlos Ferreira Capela (87' Daniel Huss), Gilles Bettmer, Mario Mutsch (YC19), Aurélien
Joachim. (Coach: Guy Hellers (LUX)).
Netherlands: Edwin van der Sar (C), Joris Mathijsen, Tim de Cler, André Ooijer (46' Jan
Vennegoor of Hesselink), John Heitinga, Stijn Schaars (46' Urby Emanuelson), Denny
Landzaat (YC70), Theo Janssen, Robin van Persie (74' Ryan Babel), Dirk Kuyt, Klaas-Jan
Huntelaar (YC64). (Coach: Marcel (Marco) van Basten (HOL)).
Goal: Netherlands: 0-1 Joris Mathijsen (16').
Referee: João Francisco Lopes Ferreira dos Santos (POR)   Attendance: 8.055

06-09-2006   Vasil Levski National Stadium, Sofia: Bulgaria – Slovenia   3-0 (0-0)
Bulgaria: Dimitar Ivankov, Aleksandar Tunchev (YC55), Elin Topuzakov (YC12), Lucio
Wagner Freitas do Souza, Chavdar Yankov (68' Radostin Kishishev), Stiliyan Petrov (C),
Martin Petrov (YC52), Blagoy Georgiev (53' Dimitar Telkiyski), Stanislav Angelov, Zoran
Jankovic, Valeri Bozhinov (YC45) (58' Hristo Yovov). (Coach: Hristo Stoichkov (BUL)).
Slovenia: Borut Mavric, Aleksander Knavs (C), Branko Ilic, Bostjan Cesar, Anton Zlogar,
Robert Koren (YC56) (75' Klemen Lavric), Andrej Komac, Bojan Jokic (YC56), Milenko
Acimovic (YC14), Valter Birsa (79' Borut Semler), Milivoje Novakovic. (Coach: Branko
Oblak (SLO)).
Goals: Bulgaria: 1-0 Valeri Bozhinov (58'), 2-0 Martin Petrov (73'), 3-0 Dimitar Telkiyski
(80').
Referee: Claus Bo Larsen (DEN)   Attendance: 14.491

06-09-2006   Qemal Stafa, Tirana: Albania – Romania   0-2 (0-0)
Albania: Arjan Beqaj, Armend Dallku, Debatik Çurri (YC73), Elvin Beqiri (YC82), Ervin
Skela (68' Adrian Aliaj), Altin Haxhi, Besnik Hasi (YC45+1), Lorik Cana (YC83), Altin Lala
(78' Devis Mukaj), Igli Tar (C) (YC20), Erjon Bogdani (YC40) (63' Bekim Kastrati). (Coach:
Otto Baric (CRO)).
Romania: Bogdan Lobont, Razvan Rat, Sorin Ghionea, Cristian Chivu (C), Cosmin Contra
(YC70), Florentin Petre, Paul Codrea, Nicolae Dica, Laurentiu Rosu (YC69) (89' Andrei
Silviu Margaritescu), Adrian Mutu (85' Banel Nicolita), Ciprian Marica (78' Ioan Ganea).
(Coach: Victor Piturca (ROM)).
Goals: Romania: 0-1 Nicolae Dica (64'), 0-2 Adrian Mutu (74' penalty).
Referee: Olegário Manuel Bártolo Faustino Benquerença (POR)   Attendance: 9.001

06-09-2006   Philips Stadion, Eindhoven: Netherlands – Belarus   3-0 (1-0)
Netherlands: Edwin van der Sar (C), Joris Mathijsen (YC45), John Heitinga (68' Khalid
Boulahrouz), André Ooijer, Giovanni van Bronckhorst, Denny Landzaat (68' Stijn Schaars),
Nigel de Jong, Wesley Sneijder, Klaas-Jan Huntelaar (76' Ryan Babel), Robin van Persie
(YC28), Dirk Kuyt. (Coach: Marcel (Marco) van Basten (HOL)).
Belarus: Vasili Khomutovski, Aleksandr Yurevich, Sergei Shtaniuk (C), Dmitri Lentsevich
(YC90), Sergei Omelyanchuk, Maksim Romashchenko (70' Artyom Kontsevoi), Denis Kovba,
Timofei Kalachev (74' Vitali Lanko), Aleksandr Hleb, Vladimir Korytko (46' Oleg
Strakhanovich), Sergei Kornilenko. (Coach: Yuri Puntus (BLS)).
Goals: Netherlands: 1-0 Robin van Persie (32'), 2-0 Robin van Persie (78'), 3-0 Dirk Kuyt
(90'+1').
Referee: Howard Melton Webb (ENG)   Attendance: 30.089

166

07-10-2006   Ghencea Stadium, Bucharest: Romania – Belarus 3-1 (2-1)
Romania: Danut Coman, Gabriel Tamas (YC30), Razvan Rat, Petre Marin, Dorin Goian,
Cristian Chivu (C), Florentin Petre, Nicolae Dica (88' Razvan Cocis), Laurentiu Rosu, Adrian
Mutu (72' Mugurel Buga), Ciprian Marica (90'+2' Claudiu Niculescu). (Coach: Victor Piturca
(ROM)).
Belarus: Vladimir Gaev, Aleksandr Yurevich, Sergei Shtaniuk (C), Dmitri Lentsevich, Sergei
Gurenko, Sergei Omelyanchuk (YC64), Maksim Romashchenko, Aleksandr Kulchiy (66' Oleg
Strakhanovich), Timofei Kalachev (51' Vyacheslav Hleb), Aleksandr Hleb, Sergei Kornilenko
(65' Vladimir Korytko). (Coach: Yuri Puntus (BLS)).
Goals: Romania: 1-0 Adrian Mutu (7'), 1-0 Ciprian Marica (10'), 3-1 Dorin Goian (76').
Belarus: 2-1 Sergei Kornilenko (20').
Referee: Alberto Undiano Mallenco (ESP)   Attendance: 12.000

07-10-2006   Vasil Levski National Stadium, Sofia: Bulgaria – Netherlands 1-1 (1-0)
Bulgaria: Dimitar Ivankov, Lucio Wagner Freitas do Souza, Radostin Kishishev, Valentin
Iliev, Chavdar Yankov (83' Zoran Jankovic), Stiliyan Petrov (C), Martin Petrov (YC53) (62'
Valeri Bozhinov), Elin Topuzakov, Stanislav Angelov (YC80), Hristo Yovov (55' Dimitar
Telkiyski), Dimitar Berbatov. (Coach: Hristo Stoichkov (BUL)).
Netherlands: Edwin van der Sar (C), Joris Mathijsen, André Ooijer, Khalid Boulahrouz,
Giovanni van Bronckhorst, Denny Landzaat, Wesley Sneijder (YC80) (90'+2' Stijn Schaars),
Nigel de Jong, Robin van Persie, Arjen Robben, Dirk Kuyt (14' Ryan Babel). (Coach: Marcel
(Marco) van Basten (HOL)).
Goals: Bulgaria: 1-0 Martin Petrov (12').
Netherlands: 1-1 Robin van Persie (62').
Referee: Tom Henning Øvrebø (NOR)   Attendance: 30.547

07-10-2006   Arena Petrol, Celje: Slovenia – Luxembourg 2-0 (2-0)
Slovenia: Borut Mavric, Matej Mavric, Bostjan Cesar, Branko Ilic (YC90+1), Robert Koren,
Bojan Jokic, Nastja Ceh, Milenko Acimovic (C) (75' Andrej Komac), Klemen Lavric (84'
Miran Burgic), Valter Birsa, Milivoje Novakovic. (Coach: Branko Oblak (SLO)).
Luxembourg: Jonathan Joubert (72' Stéphane Gillet), Claude Reiter, Kim Kintziger, Eric
Hoffmann (YC53), Jeff Strasser (C), Sébastien Remy, René Peters, Claudio Lombardelli (42'
Charles Leweck), Gilles Bettmer, Mario Mutsch, Aurélien Joachim (62' Daniel Huss). (Coach:
Guy Hellers (LUX)).
Goals: Slovenia: 1-0 Milivoje Novakovic (30'), 2-0 Robert Koren (44').
Referee: Panicos Kailis (CYP)   Attendance: 3.800

11-10-2006   Dinamo Stadium, Minsk: Belarus – Slovenia 4-2 (1-2)
Belarus: Vladimir Gaev, Sergei Shtaniuk (C), Sergei Gurenko (YC86), Sergei Omelyanchuk,
Maksim Romashchenko (51' Vladimir Korytko), Denis Kovba, Aleksandr Hleb, Aleksandr
Kulchiy, Timofei Kalachev, Sergei Kornilenko (90' Artyom Kontsevoi), Vyacheslav Hleb (69'
Oleg Strakhanovich). (Coach: Yuri Puntus (BLS)).
Slovenia: Borut Mavric, Matej Mavric, Branko Ilic, Bostjan Cesar, Milenko Acimovic (C) (70'
Andrej Komac (YC83)), Anton Zlogar (YC61), Robert Koren, Bojan Jokic, Valter Birsa,
Klemen Lavric, Milivoje Novakovic (83' Miran Burgic). (Coach: Branko Oblak (SLO)).
Goals: Belarus: 1-0 Denis Kovba (17'), 2-2 Sergei Kornilenko (52'), 3-2 Sergei Kornilenko
(59'), 4-2 Vladimir Korytko (85').
Slovenia: 1-1 Bostjan Cesar (18'), 1-2 Klemen Lavric (44').
Referee: Viktor Kassai (HUN)   Attendance: 21.150

11-10-2006   Stade Josy Barthel, Luxembourg: Luxembourg – Bulgaria 0-1 (0-1)
Luxembourg: Stéphane Gillet, Claude Reiter, Kim Kintziger, Jeff Strasser (C), Sébastien Remy (YC87), René Peters (61' Ben Payal), Claudio Lombardelli (YC48) (67' Charles Leweck), Joao Carlos Ferreira Capela, Gilles Bettmer, Mario Mutsch (YC30), Aurélien Joachim (53' Daniel Huss). (Coach: Guy Hellers (LUX)).
Bulgaria: Dimitar Ivankov (YC90+3), Aleksandar Tunchev, Elin Topuzakov, Lucio Wagner Freitas do Souza, Chavdar Yankov (76' Radostin Kishishev), Dimitar Telkiyski, Stiliyan Petrov (C) (YC76), Stanislav Angelov (YC62), Zdravko Lazarov (46' Hristo Yovov), Valeri Bozhinov (67' Zoran Jankovic), Dimitar Berbatov. (Coach: Hristo Stoichkov (BUL)).
Goal: Bulgaria: 0-1 Aleksandar Tunchev (26').
Referee: Novo Panic (BOS)   Attendance: 3.156

11-10-2006   Amsterdam ArenA, Amsterdam: Netherlands – Albania 2-1 (2-0)
Netherlands: Edwin van der Sar (C), Joris Mathijsen, André Ooijer, Khalid Boulahrouz, Giovanni van Bronckhorst (67' Urby Emanuelson), Denny Landzaat, Wesley Sneijder (80' Tim de Cler), Nigel de Jong (YC44) (50' Stijn Schaars), Ryan Babel, Robin van Persie, Arjen Robben. (Coach: Marcel (Marco) van Basten (HOL)).
Albania: Arjan Beqaj, Nevil Dede, Armend Dallku, Debatik Çurri (YC76), Adrian Aliaj (64' Edvin Murati), Ervin Skela, Altin Haxhi, Besnik Hasi, Altin Lala (YC44) (45' Devis Mukaj), Igli Tar (C), Erjon Bogdani (79' Besart Berisha). (Coach: Otto Baric (CRO)).
Goals: Netherlands: 1-0 Robin van Persie (15'), 2-0 Arjan Beqaj (41' own goal).
Albania: 2-1 Debatik Çurri (76').
Referee: Alon Yefet (ISR)   Attendance: 40.085

24-03-2007   Stade Josy Barthel, Luxembourg: Luxembourg – Belarus 1-2 (0-1)
Luxembourg: Jonathan Joubert, Kim Kintziger (YC59), Eric Hoffmann, Claude Reiter, Dan Collette (64' Chris Sagramola), Ben Payal (67' Joao Carlos Ferreira Capela), Claudio Lombardelli (58' Jérôme Bigard), Gilles Bettmer, Jeff Strasser (C), Sébastien Remy, René Peters. (Coach: Guy Hellers (LUX)).
Belarus: Yuri Zhevnov, Aleksandr Yurevich, Sergei Shtaniuk (C), Aleksandr Kulchiy (YC9), Vladimir Korytko (YC30), Timofei Kalachev, Aleksandr Hleb, Oleg Strakhanovich (58' Artyom Chelyadinski), Vitali Kutuzov (80' Artyom Radkov), Sergei Kornilenko (74' Gennadi Bliznyuk (YC84)), Vyacheslav Hleb. (Coach: Yuri Puntus (BLS)).
Goals: Luxembourg: 1-2 Chris Sagramola (68').
Belarus: 0-1 Timofei Kalachev (25'), 0-2 Vitali Kutuzov (54').
Referee: Mark Steven Whitby (WAL)   Attendance: 2.021

24-03-2007   Loro-Boriçi Stadium, Shkodër: Albania – Slovenia 0-0
Albania: Arjan Beqaj, Nevil Dede (YC31), Armend Dallku (YC90+3), Elvin Beqiri, Devis Mukaj (86' Besart Berisha), Altin Haxhi, Klodian Duro, Lorik Cana, Altin Lala (C), Edmond Kapllani (58' Alban Bushi), Erjon Bogdani (89' Hamdi Salihi). (Coach: Otto Baric (CRO)).
Slovenia: Samir Handanovic, Matej Mavric, Branko Ilic, Bostjan Cesar, Anton Zlogar (YC52), Robert Koren, Andrej Komac (90' Fabijan Cipot), Bojan Jokic, Nastja Ceh (C) (80' Milenko Acimovic), Ermin Rakovic (63' Valter Birsa), Klemen Lavric. (Coach: Matjaz Kek (SLO)).
Referee: Joseph Attard (MLT)   Attendance: 7.000

168

24-03-2007   De Kuip, Rotterdam: Netherlands – Romania   0-0
Netherlands: Maarten Stekelenburg, Wilfred Bouma, Kew Jaliens (YC69), Joris Mathijsen, Rafael van der Vaart (YC64) (86' Clarence Seedorf), Giovanni van Bronckhorst (C), Denny Landzaat (79' Urby Emanuelson), Wesley Sneijder, Ryan Babel, Klaas-Jan Huntelaar, Arjen Robben. (Coach: Marcel (Marco) van Basten (HOL)).
Romania: Bogdan Lobont (YC35), Dorin Goian (YC55), Gabriel Tamas, Razvan Rat (78' Stefan Radu), Cosmin Contra, Paul Codrea (YC83) (87' Laurentiu Rosu), Banel Nicolita, Razvan Cocis, Mirel Radoi, Adrian Mutu (C), Ciprian Marica (64' Daniel Niculae). (Coach: Victor Piturca (ROM)).
Referee: Dr.Markus Merk (GER)   Attendance: 47.000

28-03-2007   Vasil Levski National Stadium, Sofia: Bulgaria – Albania   0-0
Bulgaria: Dimitar Ivankov, Aleksandar Tunchev, Igor Tomasic, Lucio Wagner Freitas do Souza, Radostin Kishishev, Chavdar Yankov (YC6), Stiliyan Petrov, Georgi Peev (65' Valeri Bozhinov), Hristo Yovov (46' Svetoslav Todorov), Zoran Jankovic (YC31) (46' Dimitar Telkiyski), Dimitar Berbatov (C). (Coach: Hristo Stoichkov (BUL)).
Albania: Arjan Beqaj (YC31), Nevil Dede, Armend Dallku, Debatik Çurri, Elvin Beqiri, Altin Haxhi (54' Edmond Kapllani (YC71)), Klodian Duro (C) (68' Ervin Bulku (YC90)), Lorik Cana (YC17), Altin Lala, Besart Berisha (79' Alban Bushi), Erjon Bogdani. (Coach: Otto Baric (CRO)).
Referee: Jonas Eriksson (SWE)   Attendance: 19.800

28-03-2007   Caehlaul Stadium, Piatra Neamt: Romania – Luxembourg   3-0 (1-0)
Romania: Bogdan Lobont, Gabriel Tamas (87' Dorel Stoica), Stefan Radu, Dorin Goian (YC44), Cosmin Contra, Ianis Zicu, Mirel Radoi, Razvan Cocis, Laurentiu Rosu (53' Adrian Cristea), Daniel Niculae (65' Ciprian Marica), Adrian Mutu (C). (Coach: Victor Piturca (ROM)).
Luxembourg: Jonathan Joubert, Claude Reiter, Eric Hoffmann, Jérôme Bigard, Dan Collette (49' Chris Sagramola), Jeff Strasser (C), Sébastien Remy, René Peters, Claudio Lombardelli (YC63) (81' Joao Carlos Ferreira Capela), Gilles Bettmer (50' Ben Payal (YC68)), Mario Mutsch. (Coach: Guy Hellers (LUX)).
Goals: Romania: 1-0 Adrian Mutu (26'), 2-0 Cosmin Contra (56'), 3-0 Ciprian Marica (90').
Referee: Romans Lajuks (LAT)   Attendance: 9.120

28-03-2007   Arena Petrol, Celje: Slovenia – Netherlands   0-1 (0-0)
Slovenia: Samir Handanovic, Branko Ilic, Bostjan Cesar (YC76), Matej Mavric, Robert Koren, Andrej Komac, Bojan Jokic, Nastja Ceh, Milenko Acimovic (C) (61' Goran Sukalo), Klemen Lavric (83' Valter Birsa), Ermin Rakovic (65' Milivoje Novakovic). (Coach: Matjaz Kek (SLO)).
Netherlands: Edwin van der Sar (C), Joris Mathijsen, Wilfred Bouma, John Heitinga (74' Demy de Zeeuw), Giovanni van Bronckhorst (YC68), Wesley Sneijder, Urby Emanuelson, Ibrahim Afellay (85' Clarence Seedorf (YC90+1)), Ryan Babel (73' Danny Koevermans), Arjen Robben, Dirk Kuyt. (Coach: Marcel (Marco) van Basten (HOL)).
Goal: Netherlands: 0-1 Giovanni van Bronckhorst (86').
Referee: Manuel Enrique Mejuto González (ESP)   Attendance: 9.500

02-06-2007   Qemal Stafa, Tirana: Albania – Luxembourg   2-0 (1-0)
Albania: Arjan Beqaj, Debatik Çurri, Nevil Dede, Armend Dallku, Ervin Skela (YC39), Altin
Haxhi (C) (74' Kristi Vangjeli), Klodian Duro, Lorik Cana, Edmond Kapllani, Alban Bushi
(76' Hamdi Salihi), Besart Berisha (45' Devis Mukaj). (Coach: Otto Baric (CRO)).
Luxembourg: Jonathan Joubert, Kim Kintziger, Eric Hoffmann (YC58), Jérôme Bigard (60'
Daniël Alves Da Mota), Dan Collette (70' Chris Sagramola), Jeff Strasser (C), Sébastien
Remy, René Peters, Ben Payal (82' Joao Carlos Ferreira Capela), Gilles Bettmer, Mario
Mutsch. (Coach: Guy Hellers (LUX)).
Goals: Albania: 1-0 Edmond Kapllani (38'), 2-0 Altin Haxhi (57').
Referee: Lasha Silagava (GEO)   Attendance: 3.500

02-06-2007   Arena Petrol, Celje: Slovenia – Romania   1-2 (0-0)
Slovenia: Samir Handanovic, Matej Mavric (YC26), Branko Ilic, Bostjan Cesar (YC34,RC80),
Goran Sukalo (YC18), Robert Koren (YC43) (53' Valter Birsa), Andrej Komac, Bojan Jokic,
Nastja Ceh (C) (83' Dare Vrsic), Ermin Rakovic (YC40) (61' Milivoje Novakovic), Klemen
Lavric. (Coach: Matjaz Kek (SLO)).
Romania: Bogdan Lobont, Cristian Chivu (C), Gabriel Tamas, Dorel Stoica (77' Gabriel
Stelian Muresan), Razvan Rat, Cosmin Contra, Paul Codrea, Banel Nicolita (YC81), Laurentiu
Rosu (63' Ianis Zicu), Adrian Mutu (YC38), Ciprian Marica (74' Daniel Niculae (RC80)).
(Coach: Victor Piturca (ROM)).
Goals: Slovenia: 1-2 Dare Vrsic (90'+4').
Romania: 0-1 Gabriel Tamas (52'), 0-2 Banel Nicolita (69').
Referee: Stuart Dougal (SCO)   Attendance: 6.500

02-06-2007   Dinamo Stadium, Minsk: Belarus – Bulgaria   0-2 (0-1)
Belarus: Yuri Zhevnov, Yan Tigorev, Sergei Shtaniuk (C), Sergei Omelyanchuk (YC18) (71'
Oleg Strakhanovich), Denis Kovba, Aleksandr Kulchiy (YC42), Vladimir Korytko, Timofei
Kalachev, Aleksandr Hleb, Vitali Kutuzov (46' Vyacheslav Hleb), Sergei Kornilenko (59'
Roman Vasilyuk). (Coach: Yuri Puntus (BLS)).
Bulgaria: Dimitar Ivankov, Aleksandar Tunchev, Igor Tomasic, Lucio Wagner Freitas do
Souza, Radostin Kishishev, Dimitar Telkiyski, Stiliyan Petrov, Martin Petrov (90'+1' Tsvetan
Genkov), Stanislav Angelov (90'+3' Valeri Domovchiyski), Hristo Yovov (79' Vladimir
Manchev), Dimitar Berbatov (C). (Coach: Stanimir Kolev Stoilov (BUL)).
Goals: Bulgaria: 0-1 Dimitar Berbatov (28'), 0-2 Dimitar Berbatov (46').
Referee: Jaroslav Jára (CZE)   Attendance: 25.962

06-06-2007   Vasil Levski National Stadium, Sofia: Bulgaria – Belarus   2-1 (2-1)
Bulgaria: Dimitar Ivankov, Aleksandar Tunchev, Igor Tomasic, Lucio Wagner Freitas do
Souza, Radostin Kishishev, Chavdar Yankov (90'+3' Zahari Sirakov), Dimitar Telkiyski,
Stiliyan Petrov, Martin Petrov (84' Vladimir Manchev), Hristo Yovov (68' Stanislav Angelov),
Dimitar Berbatov (C). (Coach: Stanimir Kolev Stoilov (BUL)).
Belarus: Yuri Zhevnov, Aleksandr Yurevich, Yan Tigorev (YC66), Sergei Shtaniuk (C),
Artyom Radkov, Denis Kovba, Oleg Strakhanovich (64' Vyacheslav Hleb), Vladimir Korytko,
Timofei Kalachev (YC42) (43' Vitali Kutuzov), Aleksandr Hleb, Roman Vasilyuk (55' Sergei
Kornilenko (YC83)). (Coach: Yuri Puntus (BLS)).
Goals: Bulgaria: 1-1 Martin Petrov (10'), 2-1 Chavdar Yankov (40').
Belarus: 0-1 Roman Vasilyuk (5' penalty).
Referee: Kristinn Jakobsson (ISL)   Attendance: 10.227

06-06-2007   Stade Josy Barthel, Luxembourg: Luxembourg – Albania   0-3 (0-2)
Luxembourg: Jonathan Joubert, Kim Kintziger, Eric Hoffmann, Jérôme Bigard (46' Claudio
Lombardelli), Dan Collette (79' Chris Sagramola), Jeff Strasser (C), Sébastien Remy (YC63),
René Peters, Ben Payal (64' Daniël Alves Da Mota), Gilles Bettmer, Mario Mutsch. (Coach:
Guy Hellers (LUX)).
Albania: Arjan Beqaj, Nevil Dede, Armend Dallku, Debatik Çurri, Ervin Skela (YC13) (60'
Klodian Duro), Devis Mukaj (77' Daniel Xhafaj), Altin Haxhi (C), Lorik Cana, Alban Bushi
(YC54) (67' Besart Berisha), Edmond Kapllani, Erjon Bogdani. (Coach: Otto Baric (CRO)).
Goals: Albania: 0-1 Ervin Skela (25'), 0-2 Edmond Kapllani (36'), 0-3 Edmond Kapllani (72').
Referee: Paulius Malzinskas (LIT)   Attendance: 4.325

06-06-2007   Dan Paltinisanu, Timisoara: Romania – Slovenia   2-0 (1-0)
Romania: Bogdan Lobont, Cristian Chivu (C), Gabriel Tamas (YC61), Razvan Rat, Dorin
Goian, Cosmin Contra (YC27), Paul Codrea (78' Mihaita Plesan), Ianis Zicu (60' Laurentiu
Rosu), Florentin Petre (75' Banel Nicolita), Adrian Mutu, Ciprian Marica. (Coach: Victor
Piturca (ROM)).
Slovenia: Samir Handanovic, Mitja Mörec, Matej Mavric (YC24), Branko Ilic (YC82), Nastja
Ceh (C), Anton Zlogar (YC73) (77' Goran Sukalo), Andrej Komac, Bojan Jokic (YC17) (84'
Suad Filekovic), Dare Vrsic (YC47), Valter Birsa (54' Milivoje Novakovic (YC88)), Klemen
Lavric. (Coach: Matjaz Kek (SLO)).
Goals: Romania: 1-0 Adrian Mutu (40'), 2-0 Cosmin Contra (70').
Referee: Alon Yefet (ISR)   Attendance: 23.172

08-09-2007   Stade Josy Barthel, Luxembourg: Luxembourg – Slovenia   0-3 (0-2)
Luxembourg: Jonathan Joubert, Eric Hoffmann, Jérôme Bigard, René Peters, Claudio
Lombardelli (46' Ben Payal), Joao Carlos Ferreira Capela, Gilles Bettmer, Jeff Strasser (C),
Mario Mutsch, Daniel Huss (63' Joël Kitenge), Jérémie Peiffer (52' Daniël Alves Da Mota).
(Coach: Guy Hellers (LUX)).
Slovenia: Samir Handanovic, Ales Kokot, Miso Brecko, Mitja Mörec, Robert Koren, Anton
Zlogar (82' Fabijan Cipot), Dalibor Stevanovic, Dare Vrsic (78' Rene Mihelic (YC86)),
Andraz Kirm (64' Andrej Komac), Klemen Lavric (C), Milivoje Novakovic. (Coach: Matjaz
Kek (SLO)).
Goals: Slovenia: 0-1 Klemen Lavric (7'), 0-2 Milivoje Novakovic (37'), 0-3 Klemen Lavric
(47').
Referee: Sergiy Berezka (UKR)   Attendance: 2.012

08-09-2007   Dinamo Stadium, Minsk: Belarus – Romania   1-3 (1-2)
Belarus: Vasili Khomutovski (YC75), Yan Tigorev, Pavel Plaskonny, Artyom Radkov,
Maksim Romashchenko, Igor Stasevich, Timofei Kalachev (77' Aleksei Skvernyuk),
Aleksandr Hleb (C), Vladimir Korytko, Vitali Rodionov (61' Roman Vasilyuk), Sergei
Kornilenko. (Coach: Bernd Stange (GER)).
Romania: Bogdan Lobont, Petre Marin, Dorin Goian, Cristian Chivu (C) (YC83), Razvan Rat
(YC61), Banel Nicolita, Paul Codrea (YC56) (90' Eugen Trica), Ovidiu Petre (YC81), Nicolae
Dica (67' Dorinel Munteanu), Adrian Mutu, Sergiu Radu (56' Florentin Petre). (Coach: Victor
Piturca (ROM)).
Goals: Belarus: 1-1 Maksim Romashchenko (20').
Romania: 0-1 Adrian Mutu (16'), 1-2 Nicolae Dica (42'), 1-3 Adrian Mutu (77' penalty).
Referee: Peter Fröjdfeldt (SWE)   Attendance: 19.320

08-09-2007   Amsterdam ArenA, Amsterdam: Netherlands – Bulgaria   2-0 (1-0)
Netherlands: Edwin van der Sar (C), Mario Melchiot (YC14) (66' Khalid Boulahrouz), Joris
Mathijsen, Wilfred Bouma, John Heitinga, Giovanni van Bronckhorst, Wesley Sneijder (73'
Clarence Seedorf), Demy de Zeeuw (81' Nigel de Jong), Ryan Babel, Ruud van Nistelrooy,
Robin van Persie. (Coach: Marcel (Marco) van Basten (HOL)).
Bulgaria: Dimitar Ivankov, Aleksandar Tunchev, Igor Tomasic, Lucio Wagner Freitas do
Souza (YC25) (79' Chavdar Yankov), Radostin Kishishev, Dimitar Telkiyski (68' Velizar
Dimitrov), Stiliyan Petrov, Martin Petrov, Georgi Peev (59' Ivelin Popov), Stanislav Angelov,
Dimitar Berbatov (C). (Coach: Dimitar Penev (BUL)).
Goals: Netherlands: 1-0 Wesley Sneijder (22'), 2-0 Ruud van Nistelrooy (58').
Referee: Luis Medina Cantalejo (ESP)   Attendance: 49.500

12-09-2007   Vasil Levski National Stadium, Sofia: Bulgaria – Luxembourg   3-0 (2-0)
Bulgaria: Georgi Petkov, Petar Zanev (YC39), Aleksandar Tunchev, Igor Tomasic, Radostin
Kishishev, Stiliyan Petrov (60' Chavdar Yankov), Martin Petrov (66' Hristo Yovov), Velizar
Dimitrov, Stanislav Angelov (YC82), Dimitar Berbatov (C), Ivelin Popov (74' Martin
Kushev). (Coach: Dimitar Penev (BUL)).
Luxembourg: Jonathan Joubert, Kim Kintziger, Eric Hoffmann (YC54), Jérôme Bigard, Jeff
Strasser (C) (YC83), Sébastien Remy (YC30), René Peters, Gilles Bettmer (83' Daniël Alves
Da Mota), Mario Mutsch, Jérémie Peiffer (46' Dan Collette), Daniel Huss (46' Ben Payal).
(Coach: Guy Hellers (LUX)).
Goals: Bulgaria: 1-0 Dimitar Berbatov (27'), 2-0 Dimitar Berbatov (28'), 3-0 Martin Petrov
(54' penalty).
Referee: Bülent Demirlek (TUR)   Attendance: 4.674

12-09-2007   Arena Petrol, Celje: Slovenia – Belarus   1-0 (1-0)
Slovenia: Samir Handanovic, Mitja Mörec (YC72), Branco Ilic (82' Miso Brecko), Fabijan
Cipot, Dalibor Stevanovic (75' Luka Zinko), Robert Koren, Bojan Jokic, Andraz Kirm,
Klemen Lavric (C) (YC89), Valter Birsa (67' Dare Vrsic (YC87)), Milivoje Novakovic.
(Coach: Matjaz Kek (SLO)).
Belarus: Vladimir Gaev, Yan Tigorev, Artyom Radkov (YC69,YC70), Pavel Plaskonny, Igor
Stasevich, Maksim Romashchenko, Vladimir Korytko (89' Nikolai Kashevski), Timofei
Kalachev, Aleksandr Hleb (C), Gennadi Bliznyuk (74' Yegor Filipenko), Sergei Kornilenko
(46' Vitali Rodionov). (Coach: Bernd Stange (GER)).
Goal: Slovenia: 1-0 Klemen Lavric (3' penalty).
Referee: Veaceslav Banari (MOL)   Attendance: 3.500

12-09-2007   Qemal Stafa, Tirana: Albania – Netherlands   0-1 (0-0)
Albania: Arjan Beqaj, Nevil Dede, Armend Dallku (YC45+1), Debatik Çurri, Kristi Vangjeli,
Devis Mukaj, Klodian Duro (YC65) (69' Altin Haxhi), Lorik Cana (RC87), Altin Lala (C),
Edmond Kapllani (YC31) (46' Alban Bushi), Erjon Bogdani (83' Ervin Bulku). (Coach: Otto
Baric (CRO)).
Netherlands: Edwin van der Sar (C), Mario Melchiot (YC71), Joris Mathijsen, Wilfred Bouma
(63' Urby Emanuelson), André Ooijer, Giovanni van Bronckhorst, Wesley Sneijder (YC87),
Demy de Zeeuw, Ryan Babel (75' Dirk Kuyt), Robin van Persie (YC37) (46' Rafael van der
Vaart), Ruud van Nistelrooy (YC87). (Coach: Marcel (Marco) van Basten (HOL)).
Goal: Netherlands: 0-1 Ruud van Nistelrooy (90'+1').
Referee: Michael (Mike) Riley (ENG)   Attendance: 19.600

172

13-10-2007   Central Stadion, Gomel: Belarus – Luxembourg   0-1 (0-0)
Belarus: Yuri Zhevnov (69' Vasili Khomutovski), Pavel Plaskonny, Sergei Omelyanchuk, Yegor Filipenko, Igor Stasevich (62' Timofei Kalachev), Maksim Romashchenko, Aleksei Skvernyuk, Vladimir Korytko, Aleksandr Hleb (C), Andrei Voronkov (80' Vitali Rodioov), Sergei Kornilenko. (Coach: Bernd Stange (GER)).
Luxembourg: Jonathan Joubert (YC82), Jean Wagner, Benoît Lang (YC71), Kim Kintziger, Sébastien Remy (C), René Peters (YC46), Ben Payal (79' Joao Carlos Ferreira Capela), Claudio Lombardelli (YC28) (45'+2' Fons Leweck (YC78)), Gilles Bettmer, Mario Mutsch, Joël Kitenge (61' Daniël Alves Da Mota (YC85)). (Coach: Guy Hellers (LUX)).
Goal: Luxembourg: 0-1 Fons Leweck (90'+5').
Referee: Michael Svendsen (DEN)   Attendance: 14.000

13-10-2007   Gheorghe Hagi Stadium, Constanta: Romania – Netherlands   1-0 (0-0)
Romania: Bogdan Lobont, George Ogararu (YC76), Gabriel Tamas (YC81), Razvan Rat, Dorin Goian, Cristian Chivu (C), Ovidiu Petre, Banel Nicolita (YC90+1), Paul Codrea (YC90+2), Adrian Mutu (YC86), Ciprian Marica (70' Daniel Niculae). (Coach: Victor Piturca (ROM)).
Netherlands: Maarten Stekelenburg, Joris Mathijsen (YC66), Wilfred Bouma, André Ooijer (84' Danny Koevermans), John Heitinga (68' Kew Jaliens), Rafael van der Vaart, Giovanni van Bronckhorst (C) (YC75), Clarence Seedorf, Demy de Zeeuw, Ruud van Nistelrooy (YC64), Arjen Robben (78' Ryan Babel). (Coach: Marcel (Marco) van Basten (HOL)).
Goal: Romania: 1-0 Dorin Goian (71').
Referee: Kyros Vassaras (GRE)   Attendance: 12.595

13-10-2007   Arena Petrol, Celje: Slovenia – Albania   0-0
Slovenia: Samir Handanovic, Mitja Mörec, Fabijan Cipot, Miso Brecko (YC90+4), Anton Zlogar, Robert Koren, Bojan Jokic (77' Branco Ilic), Andraz Kirm (YC75), Klemen Lavric (C), Valter Birsa (82' Rene Mihelic), Milivoje Novakovic (61' Dejan Rusic (YC74)). (Coach: Matjaz Kek (SLO)).
Albania: Arjan Beqaj, Blerim Rrustemi, Nevil Dede, Debatik Çurri (YC22), Kristi Vangjeli, Ervin Skela (90'+1' Jahmir Hyka), Altin Haxhi (60' Devis Mukaj), Klodian Duro (77' Alban Bushaj), Altin Lala (C), Ervin Bulku, Erjon Bogdani. (Coach: Otto Baric (CRO)).
Referee: Duarte Nuno Pereira Gomes (POR)   Attendance: 4.625

17-10-2007   Stade Josy Barthel, Luxembourg: Luxembourg – Romania   0-2 (0-1)
Luxembourg: Stéphane Gillet, Jean Wagner, Benoît Lang, Kim Kintziger, Eric Hoffmann, Sébastien Remy (C), René Peters, Ben Payal (68' Fons Leweck), Gilles Bettmer (49' Joao Carlos Ferreira Capela), Mario Mutsch, Joël Kitenge (57' Daniël Alves Da Mota). (Coach: Guy Hellers (LUX)).
Romania: Bogdan Lobont, Gabriel Tamas, Razvan Rat, George Ogararu, Dorin Goian, Cristian Chivu (C) (87' Ovidiu Petre), Florentin Petre (YC72), Silviu Andrei Margaritescu, Nicolae Dica (68' Adrian Cristea), Daniel Niculae (76' Florin Bratu), Ciprian Marica (YC61). (Coach: Victor Piturca (ROM)).
Goals: Romania: 0-1 Florentin Petre (42'), 0-2 Ciprian Marica (61').
Referee: Dr.Felix Brych (GER)   Attendance: 3.584

173

17-10-2007   Philips Stadion, Eindhoven: Netherlands – Slovenia   2-0 (1-0)
Netherlands: Maarten Stekelenburg, Kew Jaliens, Wilfred Bouma (YC75), John Heitinga,
Rafael van der Vaart (C) (29' Arjen Robben, 62' Ryan Babel), Clarence Seedorf, Wesley
Sneijder, Urby Emanuelson, Demy de Zeeuw, Robin van Persie (59' André Ooijer), Klaas-Jan
Huntelaar. (Coach: Marcel (Marco) van Basten (HOL)).
Slovenia: Samir Handanovic, Mitja Mörec, Branko Ilic, Bostjan Cesar (YC89), Miso Brecko,
Anton Zlogar, Robert Koren, Andrej Komac (85' Zlatan Ljubijankic), Andraz Kirm (81' Bojan
Jokic), Klemen Lavric (C), Valter Birsa (67' Milivoje Novakovic). (Coach: Matjaz Kek
(SLO)).
Goals: Netherlands: 1-0 Wesley Sneijder (14'), 2-0 Klaas-Jan Huntelaar (86').
Referee: Nicola Rizzoli (ITA)   Attendance: 32.500

17-10-2007   Qemal Stafa, Tirana: Albania – Bulgaria   1-1 (1-0)
Albania: Arjan Beqaj (YC85), Nevil Dede, Armend Dallku (YC35), Debatik Çurri, Kristi
Vangjeli, Ervin Skela, Altin Haxhi (46' Devis Mukaj), Klodian Duro, Altin Lala (C), Hamdi
Salihi (YC63) (73' Ervin Bulku), Erjon Bogdani. (Coach: Otto Baric (CRO)).
Bulgaria: Georgi Petkov, Igor Tomasic, Lucio Wagner Freitas do Souza (YC83), Radostin
Kishishev, Valentin Iliev, Dimitar Telkiyski (46' Blagoy Georgiev), Stiliyan Petrov (46'
Chavdar Yankov), Martin Petrov, Stanislav Angelov (YC28), Dimitar Berbatov (C), Ivelin
Popov (72' Hristo Yovov). (Coach: Dimitar Penev (BUL)).
Goals: Albania: 1-0 Klodian Duro (25').
Bulgaria: 1-1 Dimitar Berbatov (87').
Referee: Fritz Stuchlik (AUT)   Attendance: 3.000
(Ervin Skela missed a penalty in the 90th minute)
(Otto Baric was sent to the stands in the 24th minute)

17-11-2007   Vasil Levski National Stadium, Sofia: Bulgaria – Romania   1-0 (1-0)
Bulgaria: Dimitar Ivankov, Zhivko Milanov (YC90), Petar Zanev, Aleksandar Tunchev, Igor
Tomasic, Stiliyan Petrov, Martin Petrov (90' Zdravko Lazarov), Blagoy Georgiev, Velizar
Dimitrov, Hristo Yovov (83' Dimitar Telkiyski), Dimitar Berbatov (C). (Coach: Dimitar Penev
(BUL)).
Romania: Bogdan Lobont, Gabriel Tamas (58' Razvan Cocis), Razvan Rat, George Ogararu,
Dorin Goian, Cristian Chivu (C), Ovidiu Petre, Banel Nicolita, Paul Codrea (YC49) (82'
Eugen Trica (YC85)), Daniel Niculae, Ionut Mazilu (65' Ciprian Marica). (Coach: Victor
Piturca (ROM)).
Goal: Bulgaria: 1-0 Velizar Dimitrov (6').
Referee: Konrad Plautz (AUT)   Attendance: 6.000

17-11-2007   Qemal Stafa, Tirana: Albania – Belarus   2-4 (2-2)
Albania: Arjan Beqaj, Blemir Rrustemi (38' Kristi Vangjeli), Nevil Dede, Armend Dallku
(YC62), Debatik Çurri, Ervin Skela (YC53), Klodian Duro, Lorik Cana (YC86), Altin Lala (C)
(75' Alban Bushi), Edmond Kapllani (74' Hamdi Salihi), Erjon Bogdani. (Coach: Slavko
Kovacic (CRO)).
Belarus: Yuri Zhevnov, Roman Kirenkin (YC8), Pavel Plaskonny (YC3) (65' Aleksei
Skvernyuk), Sergei Omelyanchuk, Yegor Filipenko (YC90), Maksim Romashchenko,
Aleksandr Kulchiy, Timofei Kalachev (YC49) (75' Vladimir Korytko), Aleksandr Hleb (C),
Vitali Kutuzov (90' Sergei Kornilenko), Vitali Bulyga. (Coach: Bernd Stange (GER)).
Goals: Albania: 1-1 Erjon Bogdani (43'), 2-1 Edmond Kapllani (44').
Belarus: 0-1 Maksim Romashchenko (32'), 2-2 Vitali Kutuzov (45'+1'), 2-3 Vitali Kutuzov
(54'), 2-4 Maksim Romashchenko (63' penalty).
Referee: Bülent Demirlek (TUR)   Attendance: 2.064

174

17-11-2007   De Kuip, Rotterdam: Netherlands – Luxembourg   1-0 (1-0)
Netherlands: Edwin van der Sar (C), Mario Melchiot, Joris Mathijsen, Wilfred Bouma, Rafael
van der Vaart, Giovanni van Bronckhorst, Clarence Seedorf (77' Urby Emanuelson), Wesley
Sneijder, Demy de Zeeuw, Danny Koevermans (84' Ryan Babel), Ruud van Nistelrooy (46'
Dirk Kuyt). (Coach: Marcel (Marco) van Basten (HOL)).
Luxembourg: Jonathan Joubert, Jean Wagner, Kim Kintziger, Eric Hoffmann, Jeff Strasser (C)
(YC80), Sébastien Remy, René Peters, Ben Payal, Gilles Bettmer (66' Fons Leweck), Mario
Mutsch, Joël Kitenge (50' Aurélien Joachim, 85' Daniël Alves Da Mota). (Coach: Guy Hellers
(LUX)).
Goal: Netherlands: 1-0 Danny Koevermans (43').
Referee: Martin Hansson (SWE)   Attendance: 45.000

21-11-2007   Lia Manoliu Stadium, Bucharest: Romania – Albania   6-1 (1-0)
Romania: Bogdan Lobont (C), Gabriel Tamas (78' Marius Constantin), Razvan Rat, George
Ogararu, Dorin Goian, Florentin Petre (65' Gheorghe Bucur), Silviu Andrei Margaritescu,
Nicolae Dica, Razvan Cocis, Daniel Niculae, Ciprian Marica (YC30) (73' Ionut Mazilu).
(Coach: Victor Piturca (ROM)).
Albania: Arjan Beqaj, Nevil Dede (YC47,YC70), Debatik Çurri (YC29,YC61), Andi Lila,
Kristi Vangjeli (YC37) (41' Edmond Kapllani), Ervin Skela, Altin Haxhi, Klodian Duro (78'
Jahmir Hyka), Altin Lala (C), Ervin Bulku, Erjon Bogdani (83' Elis Bakaj). (Coach: Slavko
Kovacic (CRO)).
Goals: Romania: 1-0 Nicolae Dica (22'), 2-0 Gabriel Tamas (53'), 3-0 Daniel Niculae (62'),
4-1 Daniel Niculae (65'), 5-1 Ciprian Marica (69' penalty), 6-1 Nicolae Dica (71' penalty).
Albania: 3-1 Edmond Kapllani (64').
Referee: Edo Trickovic (CRO)   Attendance: 23.427

21-11-2007   Dinamo Stadium, Minsk: Belarus – Netherlands   2-1 (0-0)
Belarus: Yuri Zhevnov, Roman Kirenkin, Sergei Omelyanchuk (YC9) (90'+1' Igor Stasevich),
Yegor Filipenko, Maksim Romashchenko (YC40), Aleksei Skvernyuk, Aleksandr Kulchiy,
Vladimir Korytko, Aleksandr Hleb (C) (46' Nikolai Kashevski), Vitali Kutuzov, Vitali Bulyga
(86' Sergei Kornilenko). (Coach: Bernd Stange (GER)).
Netherlands: Maarten Stekelenburg, Mario Melchiot, Joris Mathijsen, Wilfred Bouma, André
Ooijer, Rafael van der Vaart, Giovanni van Bronckhorst (C) (66' Orlando Engelaar), Wesley
Sneijder (46' Dirk Kuyt), Demy de Zeeuw (69' Nigel de Jong), Danny Koevermans, Ryan
Babel (YC57). (Coach: Marcel (Marco) van Basten (HOL)).
Goals: Belarus: 1-0 Vitali Bulyga (49'), 2-0 Vladimir Korytko (65').
Netherlands: 2-1 Rafael van der Vaart (89').
Referee: Bertrand Layec (FRA)   Attendance: 11.900

21-11-2007   Arena Petrol, Celje: Slovenia – Bulgaria   0-2 (0-0)
Slovenia: Samir Handanovic, Mitja Mörec, Bostjan Cesar, Miso Brecko, Anton Zlogar
(YC35), Dalibor Stevanovic (56' Andrej Komac (YC75)), Robert Koren, Bojan Jokic (RC45),
Andraz Kirm, Klemen Lavric (C) (65' Milivoje Novakovic), Valter Birsa (48' Branko Ilic
(YC53)). (Coach: Matjaz Kek (SLO)).
Bulgaria: Dimitar Ivankov, Aleksandar Tunchev, Igor Tomasic, Zhivko Milanov (46' Yordan
Todorov), Stiliyan Petrov (YC38) (46' Dimitar Telkiyski), Martin Petrov, Blagoy Georgiev
(YC82), Velizar Dimitrov, Stanislav Angelov, Hristo Yovov (75' Zdravko Lazarov), Dimitar
Berbatov (C). (Coach: Dimitar Penev (BUL)).
Goals: Bulgaria: 0-1 Blagoy Georgiev (82'), 0-2 Dimitar Berbatov (84').
Referee: Howard Melton Webb (ENG)   Attendance: 3.700

FINAL TOURNAMENT IN AUSTRIA-SWITZERLAND

Austria and Switzerland automatically qualified for the Final Tournament as the host nations.

GROUP STAGE

GROUP A

07-06-2008   St.Jakob-Park, Basel: Switzerland – Czech Republic   0-1 (0-0)
Switzerland: Diego Benaglio, Stephan Lichtsteiner (75' Johan Vonlanthen (YC76)), Patrick Müller, Philippe Senderos, Ludovic Magrin (YC59), Gökhan Inler, Gélson da Conceição Tavares Fernandes, Valon Behrami (84' Eren Derdiyok), Tranquillo Barnetta (YC90+3), Alexander Frei (C) (46' Hakan Yakin), Marco Streller. (Coach: Jakob (Köbi) Kuhn (SUI)).
Czech Republic: Petr Cech, Zdenek Grygera, Tomás Ujfalusi (C), David Rozehnal, Marek Jankulovski, Tomás Galásek, David Jarolím (87' Radoslav Kovác), Jan Polák, Libor Sionko (83' Stanislav Vlcek), Jaroslav Plasil, Jan Koller (56' Václav Sverkos). (Coach: Karel Brückner (CZE)).
Goal: Czech Republic: 0-1 Václav Sverkos (71').
Referee: Roberto Rosetti (ITA)   Attendance: 39.730

07-06-2008   Stade de Genève, Geneva: Portugal – Turkey   2-0 (0-0)
Portugal: RICARDO Alexandre Martins Soares Pereira, JOSÉ José BOSINGWA da Silva, Képler Laveran Lima Ferreira "PEPE", RICARDO Alberto Silveira de CARVALHO, PAULO Renato Rebocho FERREIRA, Armando Gonçalves Teixeira PETIT, JOÃO Filipe Iria Santos MOUTINHO, CRISTIANO RONALDO dos Santos Aveiro, Anderson Luís de Souza "DECO" (90'+2' FERNANDO José da Silva Freitas MEIRA), SIMÃO Pedro Fonseca Sabrosa (83' RAÚL José Trindade MEIRELES), NUNO "GOMES" Miguel Soares Pereira Ribeiro (C) (69' Luís Carlos Almeida da Cunha "NANI"). (Coach: Luiz Felipe Scolari (BRA)).
Turkey: Volkan Demirel, Hamit Altintop (76' Semih Sentürk), Servet Çetin, Gökhan Zan (YC51) (55' Emre Asik), Hakan Balta, Colin Kazim-Richards (YC4), Emre Belözoglu (C), Mehmet Aurélio, Mevlüt Erdinç (46' Sabri Sarioglu (YC73)), Tuncay Sanli, Nihat Kahveci. (Coach: Fatih Terim (TUR)).
Goals: Portugal: 1-0 Képler Laveran Lima Ferreira "PEPE" (61'), 2-0 RAÚL José Trindade MEIRELES (90'+3').
Referee: Herbert Fandel (GER)   Attendance: 29.016

11-06-2008   Stade de Genève, Geneva: Czech Rupublic – Portugal 1-3 (1-1)
Czech Republic: Petr Cech, Zdenek Grygera, Tomás Ujfalusi (C), David Rozehnal, Marek
Jankulovski, Tomás Galásek (73' Jan Koller), Marek Matejovsky (68' Stanislav Vlcek), Jan
Polák (YC22), Libor Sionko, Jaroslav Plasil (84' David Jarolím), Milan Baros. (Coach: Karel
Brückner (CZE)).
Portugal: RICARDO Alexandre Martins Soares Pereira, JOSÉ José BOSINGWA da Silva
(YC31), Képler Laveran Lima Ferreira "PEPE", RICARDO Alberto Silveira de CARVALHO,
PAULO Renato Rebocho FERREIRA, Armando Gonçalves Teixeira PETIT, JOÃO Filipe Iria
Santos MOUTINHO (75' FERNANDO José da Silva Freitas MEIRA), CRISTIANO
RONALDO dos Santos Aveiro, Anderson Luís de Souza "DECO", SIMÃO Pedro Fonseca
Sabrosa (80' RICARDO Andrade QUARESMA Bernardo), NUNO "GOMES" Miguel Soares
Pereira Ribeiro (C) (79' HUGO Miguel Pereira de ALMEIDA). (Coach: Luiz Felipe Scolari
(BRA)).
Goals: Czech Republic: 1-1 Libor Sionko (17').
Portugal: 0-1 Anderson Luís de Souza "DECO" (8'), 1-2 CRISTIANO RONALDO dos Santos
Aveiro (63'), 1-3 RICARDO Andrade QUARESMA Bernardo (90'+1').
Referee: Kyros Vassaras (GRE)   Attendance: 29.016

11-06-2008   St.Jakob-Park, Basel: Switzerland – Turkey 1-2 (1-0)
Switzerland: Diego Benaglio, Stephan Lichtsteiner, Patrick Müller, Philippe Senderos, Ludovic
Magrin (C), Valon Behrami, Gökhan Inler, Gélson da Conceição Tavares Fernandes (76'
Ricardo Cabanas), Tranquillo Barnetta (66' Johan Vonlanthen), Hakan Yakin (85' Daniel
Gygax), Eren Derdiyok (YC55). (Coach: Jakob (Köbi) Kuhn (SUI)).
Turkey: Volkan Demirel, Hamit Altintop, Emre Asik, Servet Çetin, Hakan Balta (YC48),
Mehmet Aurélio (YC41), Gökdeniz Karadeniz (46' Mehmet Topal), Arda Turan, Tümer Metin
(46' Semih Sentürk), Nihat Kahveci (C) (85' Colin Kazim-Richards), Tuncay Sanli (YC31).
(Coach: Fatih Terim (TUR)).
Goals: Switzerland: 1-0 Hakan Yakin (32').
Turkey: 1-1 Semih Sentürk (57'), 1-2 Arda Turan (90'+2').
Referee: Lubos Michel (SVK)   Attendance: 39.730

15-06-2008   St.Jakob-Park, Basel: Switzerland – Portugal 2-0 (0-0)
Switzerland: Pascal Zuberbühler, Stephan Lichtsteiner (83' Stéphane Grichting), Patrick
Müller, Philippe Senderos, Ludovic Magrin (C), Valon Behrami, Gélson da Conceição Tavares
Fernandes (YC90+2), Gökhan Inler, Johan Vonlanthen (YC37) (61' Tranquillo Barnetta
(YC81)), Hakan Yakin (YC27) (86' Ricardo Cabanas), Eren Derdiyok. (Coach: Jakob (Köbi)
Kuhn (SUI)).
Portugal: RICARDO Alexandre Martins Soares Pereira, Luís MIGUEL Brito Garcia Monteiro
(YC81), Képler Laveran Lima Ferreira "PEPE", BRUNO Eduardo Regufe ALVES, PAULO
Renato Rebocho FERREIRA (YC30) (41' JORGE Miguel de Oliveira RIBEIRO (YC64)),
FERNANDO José da Silva Freitas MEIRA (C) (YC78), MIGUEL Luís Pinto VELOSO (71'
JOÃO Filipe Iria Santos MOUTINHO), RAÚL José Trindade MEIRELES, RICARDO
Andrade QUARESMA Bernardo, Luís Carlos Almeida da Cunha "NANI", HÉLDER Manuel
Marques POSTIGA (74' HUGO Miguel Pereira de ALMEIDA). (Coach: Luiz Felipe Scolari
(BRA)).
Goals: Switzerland: 1-0 Hakan Yakin (71'), 2-0 Hakan Yakin (83' penalty).
Referee: Konrad Plautz (AUT)   Attendance: 39.730

177

15-06-2008   Stade de Genève, Geneva: Turkey – Czech Republic 3-2 (0-1)
Turkey: Volkan Demirel (RC90+6), Hamit Altintop, Emre Güngör (63' Emre Asik (YC73)),
Servet Çetin, Hakan Balta, Mehmet Topal (YC6) (57' Colin Kazim-Richards), Mehmet
Aurélio (YC10), Arda Turan (YC90+5), Tuncay Sanli, Nihat Kahveci (C), Semih Sentürk (46'
Sabri Sarioglu). (Coach: Fatih Terim (TUR)).
Czech Republic: Petr Cech, Zdenek Grygera, Tomás Ujfalusi (C) (YC90+4), David Rozehnal,
Marek Jankulovski, Tomás Galásek (YC80), Marek Matejovsky (39' David Jarolím), Jan
Polák, Libor Sionko (85' Stanislav Vlcek), Jaroslav Plasil (80' Michal Kadlec), Jan Koller.
(Coach: Karel Brückner (CZE)). (Not used sub: Milan Baros (YC90+5)).
Goals: Turkey: 1-2 Arda Turan (75'), 2-2 Nihat Kahveci (87'), 3-2 Nihat Kahveci (89').
Czech Republic: 0-1 Jan Koller (34'), 0-2 Jaroslav Plasil (62').
Referee: Peter Fröjdfeldt (SWE)   Attendance: 29.016

STANDINGS

Pos	Team	Pld	W	D	L	GF	GA	GD	Pts
1	Portugal	3	2	0	1	5	3	+2	6
2	Turkey	3	2	0	1	5	5	0	6
3	Czech Republic	3	1	0	2	4	6	-2	3
4	Switzerland	3	1	0	2	3	3	0	3

Portugal and Turkey qualified for the Quarter-finals.

GROUP B

08-06-2008   Ernst-Happel-Stadion, Vienna: Austria – Croatia 0-1 (0-0)
Austria: Jürgen Macho, Sebastian Prödl (YC68), Martin Stranzl, Emanuel Pogatetz (YC3),
René Aufhauser, Jürgen Säumel (YC21) (61' Ivica Vastic), Joachim Standfest, Ronald
Gërçaliu (69' Ümit Korkmaz), Andreas Ivanschitz (C), Martin Harnik, Roland Linz (73'
Roman Kienast). (Coach: Josef Hickersberger (AUT)).
Croatia: Stipe Pletikosa, Vedran Corluka, Robert Kovac (YC51), Josip Simunic, Danijel
Pranjic, Darijo Srna, Niko Kovac (C), Luka Modric, Niko Kranjcar (61' Dario Knezevic), Ivica
Olic (83' Ognjen Vukojevic), Mladen Petric (72' Igor Budan). (Coach: Slaven Bilic (CRO)).
Goal: Croatia: 0-1 Luka Modric (4' penalty).
Referee: Pieter Vink (HOL)   Attendance: 51.428

08-06-2008   Hypo-Arena, Klagenfurt: Germany – Poland 2-0 (1-0)
Germany: Jens Lehmann, Philipp Lahm, Christoph Metzelder, Per Mertesacker, Marcell
Jansen, Clemens Fritz (56' Bastian Schweinsteiger (YC64)), Torsten Frings, Michael Ballack
(C), Lukas Podolski, Mario Gómez García (75' Thomas Hitzlsperger), Miroslav Klose (90'+1'
Kevin Kurányi). (Coach: Joachim Löw (GER)).
Poland: Artur Boruc, Marcin Wasilewski, Michal Zewlakow, Jacek Bak, Pawel Golanski (75'
Marek Saganowski), Dariusz Dudka, Mariusz Lewandowski (YC60), Wojciech Lobodzinksi
(65' Lukasz Piszczek), Maciej Zurawski (C) (46' Roger Guerreiro), Jacek Krzynówek,
Euzebiusz (Ebi) Smolarek (YC40). (Coach: Leo Beenhakker (HOL)).
Goals: Germany: 1-0 Lukas Podolski (20'), 2-0 Lukas Podolski (72').
Referee: Tom Henning Øvrebø (NOR)   Attendance: 30.461

178

12-06-2008   Hypo-Arena, Klagenfurt: Croatia – Germany   2-1 (1-0)
Croatia: Stipe Pletikosa, Vedran Corluka, Robert Kovac, Josip Simunic (YC45+1), Danijel Pranjic, Darijo Srna (YC27) (80' Jerko Leko (YC90+2)), Luka Modric (YC90+3), Niko Kovac (C), Ivan Rakitic, Niko Kranjcar (85' Dario Knezevic), Ivica Olic (72' Mladen Petric). (Coach: Slaven Bilic (CRO)).
Germany: Jens Lehmann (YC90+2), Philipp Lahm, Christoph Metzelder, Per Mertesacker, Marcell Jansen (46' David Odonkor), Clemens Fritz (82' Kevin Kurányi), Torsten Frings, Michael Ballack (C) (YC75), Lukas Podolski, Mario Gómez García (66' Bastian Schweinsteiger (RC90+2)), Miroslav Klose. (Coach: Joachim Löw (GER)).
Goals: Croatia: 1-0 Darijo Srna (24'), 2-0 Ivica Olic (62').
Germany: 2-1 Lukas Podolski (79').
Referee: Frank de Bleeckere (BEL)   Attendance: 30.461

12-06-2008   Ernst-Happel-Stadion, Vienna: Austria – Poland   1-1 (0-1)
Austria: Jürgen Macho, György Garics, Sebastian Prödl (YC68), Martin Stranzl, Emanuel Pogatetz, René Aufhauser (74' Jürgen Säumel), Christoph Leitgeb, Andreas Ivanschitz (C) (64' Ivica Vastic), Ümit Korkmaz (YC56), Martin Harnik, Roland Linz (64' Roman Kienast). (Coach: Josef Hickersberger (AUT)).
Poland: Artur Boruc, Marcin Wasilewski (YC58), Mariusz Jop (46' Pawel Golanski), Jacek Bak (C) (YC90), Michal Zewlakow, Dariusz Dudka, Mariusz Lewandowski, Jacek Krzynówek (YC61), Roger Guerreiro (85' Rafal Murawski), Marek Saganowski (83' Wojciech Lobodzinksi), Euzebiusz (Ebi) Smolarek. (Coach: Leo Beenhakker (HOL)).
Goals: Austria: 1-1 Ivica Vastic (90'+3' penalty).
Poland: 0-1 Roger Guerreiro (30').
Referee: Howard Melton Webb (ENG)   Attendance: 51.428

16-06-2008   Hypo-Arena, Klagenfurt: Poland – Croatia   0-1 (0-0)
Poland: Artur Boruc, Marcin Wasilewski, Michal Zewlakow (C), Dariusz Dudka, Jakub Wawrzyniak, Rafal Murawski, Mariusz Lewandowski (YC38) (46' Adam Kokoszka), Wojciech Lobodzinksi (55' Euzebiusz (Ebi) Smolarek), Roger Guerreiro, Jacek Krzynówek, Marek Saganowski (69' Tomasz Zahorski (YC84)). (Coach: Leo Beenhakker (HOL)).
Croatia: Vedran Runje, Dario Simic (C), Hrvoje Vejic (YC45), Dario Knezevic (27' Vedran Corluka), Danijel Pranjic, Jerko Leko, Ognjen Vukojevic (YC85), Nikola Pokrivac, Ivan Rakitic, Ivan Klasnic (74' Nikola Kalinic), Mladen Petric (75' Niko Kranjcar). (Coach: Slaven Bilic (CRO)).
Goal: Croatia: 0-1 Ivan Klasnic (53').
Referee: Kyros Vassaras (GRE)   Attendance: 30.461

16-06-2008   Ernst-Happel-Stadion, Vienna: Austria – Germany   0-1 (0-0)
Austria: Jürgen Macho, György Garics, Martin Stranzl (YC13), Martin Hiden (55' Christoph Leitgeb), Emanuel Pogatetz, René Aufhauser (63' Jürgen Säumel), Christian Fuchs, Andreas Ivanschitz (C) (YC48), Martin Harnik (67' Roman Kienast), Ümit Korkmaz, Erwin Hoffer (YC31). (Coach: Josef Hickersberger (AUT)).
Germany: Jens Lehmann, Arne Friedrich, Per Mertesacker, Christoph Metzelder, Philipp Lahm, Clemens Fritz (90'+3' Tim Borowski), Torsten Frings, Michael Ballack (C), Lukas Podolski (83' Oliver Neuville), Mario Gómez García (60' Thomas Hitzlsperger), Miroslav Klose. (Coach: Joachim Löw (GER)).
Goal: Germany: 0-1 Michael Ballack (49').
Referee: Manuel Enrique Mejuto González (ESP)   Attendance: 51.428
(Josef Hickersberger and Joachim Löw were sent to the stands in the 41st minute)

STANDINGS

Pos	Team	Pld	W	D	L	GF	GA	GD	Pts
1	Croatia	3	3	0	0	4	1	+3	9
2	Germany	3	2	0	1	4	2	+2	6
3	Austria	3	0	1	2	1	3	-2	1
4	Poland	3	0	1	2	1	4	-3	1

Croatia and Germany qualified for the Quarter-finals.

GROUP C

09-06-2008   Letzigrund, Zürich: Romania – France   0-0
Romania: Bogdan Lobont, Cosmin Contra (YC40), Gabriel Tamas, Dorin Gioan (YC43), Razvan Rat, Razvan Cocis (64' Paul Codrea), Mirel Radoi (90'+3' Nicolae Dica), Cristian Chivu (C), Banel Nicolita, Daniel Niculae (YC27), Adrian Mutu (78' Marius Niculae). (Coach: Victor Piturca (ROM)).
France: Grégory Coupet, Willy Sagnol (YC51), Lilian Thuram (C), William Gallas, Éric Abidal, Jérémy Toulalan, Claude Makélélé, Franck Ribéry, Florent Malouda, Nicolas Anelka (72' Bafétimbi Gomis), Karim Benzema (78' Samir Nasri). (Coach: Raymond Domenech (FRA)).
Referee: Manuel Enrique Mejuto González (ESP)   Attendance: 30.585

09-06-2008   Stade de Suisse, Bern: Netherlands – Italy   3-0 (2-0)
Netherlands: Edwin van der Sar (C), André Ooijer, Khalid Boulahrouz (77' John Heitinga), Joris Mathijsen, Giovanni van Bronckhorst, Nigel de Jong (YC58), Orlando Engelaar, Dirk Kuyt (81' Ibrahim Afellay), Rafael van der Vaart, Wesley Sneijder, Ruud van Nistelrooy (70' Robin van Persie). (Coach: Marcel (Marco) van Basten (HOL)).
Italy: Gianluigi Buffon (C), Christian Panucci, Andrea Barzagli, Marco Materazzi (54' Fabio Grosso), Gianluca Zambrotta (YC35), Massimo Ambrosini, Andrea Pirlo, Gennaro Gattuso (YC51), Mauro Camoranesi (75' Antonio Cassano), Antonio Di Natale (64' Alessandro Del Piero), Luca Toni (YC27). (Coach: Roberto Donadoni (ITA)).
Goals: Netherlands: 1-0 Ruud van Nistelrooy (26'), 2-0 Wesley Sneijder (31'), 3-0 Giovanni van Bronckhorst (79').
Referee: Peter Fröjdfeldt (SWE)   Attendance: 30.777

13-06-2008   Letzigrund, Zürich: Italy – Romania   1-1 (0-0)
Italy: Gianluigi Buffon, Gianluca Zambrotta, Christian Panucci, Giorgio Chiellini, Fabio Grosso, Andrea Pirlo (YC61), Daniele De Rossi (YC90+2), Mauro Camoranesi (85' Massimo Ambrosini), Simone Perrotta (57' Antonio Cassano), Alessandro Del Piero (C) (77' Fabio Quagliarella), Luca Toni. (Coach: Roberto Donadoni (ITA)).
Romania: Bogdan Lobont, Cosmin Contra, Gabriel Tamas, Dorin Gioan (YC73), Razvan Rat, Mirel Radoi (25' Nicolae Dica), Florentin Petre (60' Banel Nicolita), Paul Codrea, Cristian Chivu (C) (YC58), Adrian Mutu (YC43) (88' Razvan Cocis), Daniel Niculae. (Coach: Victor Piturca (ROM)).
Goals: Italy: 1-1 Christian Panucci (56').
Romania: 0-1 Adrian Mutu (55').
Referee: Tom Henning Øvrebø (NOR)   Attendance: 30.585

180

13-06-2008   Stade de Suisse, Bern: Netherlands – France   4-1 (1-0)
Netherlands: Edwin van der Sar (C), Khalid Boulahrouz, André Ooijer (YC51), Joris
Mathijsen, Giovanni van Bronckhorst, Nigel de Jong, Orlando Engelaar (46' Arjen Robben),
Dirk Kuyt (55' Robin van Persie), Rafael van der Vaart (78' Wilfred Bouma), Wesley
Sneijder, Ruud van Nistelrooy. (Coach: Marcel (Marco) van Basten (HOL)).
France: Grégory Coupet, Willy Sagnol, Lilian Thuram (C), William Gallas, Patrice Evra,
Jérémy Toulalan (YC82), Claude Makélélé (YC32), Sidney Govou (75' Nicolas Anelka),
Florent Malouda (60' Bafétimbi Gomis), Franck Ribéry, Thierry Henry. (Coach: Raymond
Domenech (FRA)).
Goals: Netherlands: 1-0 Dirk Kuyt (9'), 2-0 Robin van Persie (59'), 3-1 Arjen Robben (72'),
4-1 Wesley Sneijder (90'+2').
France: 2-1 Thierry Henry (71').
Referee: Herbert Fandel (GER)   Attendance: 30.777

17-06-2008   Stade de Suisse, Bern: Netherlands – Romania   2-0 (0-0)
Netherlands: Maarten Stekelenburg, Khalid Boulahrouz (58' Mario Melchiot), John Heitinga
(C), Wilfred Bouma, Tim de Cler, Demy de Zeeuw, Orlando Engelaar, Ibrahim Afellay, Robin
van Persie, Arjen Robben (61' Dirk Kuyt), Klaas-Jan Huntelaar (83' Jan Vennegoor of
Hesselink). (Coach: Marcel (Marco) van Basten (HOL)).
Romania: Bogdan Lobont, Cosmin Contra, Gabriel Tamas, Sorin Ghionea, Razvan Rat, Paul
Codrea (72' Nicolae Dica), Razvan Cocis, Cristian Chivu (C) (YC78), Banel Nicolita (82'
Florentin Petre), Adrian Mutu, Daniel Niculae (59' Daniel Niculae). (Coach: Victor Piturca
(ROM)).
Goals: Netherlands: 1-0 Klaas-Jan Huntelaar (54'), 2-0 Robin van Persie (87').
Referee: Massimo Busacca (SUI)   Attendance: 30.777

17-06-2008   Letzigrund, Zürich: France – Italy   0-2 (0-1)
France: Grégory Coupet, François Clerc, William Gallas, Éric Abidal (RC24), Patrice Evra
(YC18), Jérémy Toulalan, Claude Makélélé, Sidney Govou (YC47) (66' Nicolas Anelka),
Franck Ribéry (10' Samir Nasri, 26' Jean-Alain Boumsong), Karim Benzema, Thierry Henry
(C) (YC85). (Coach: Raymond Domenech (FRA)).
Italy: Gianluigi Buffon (C), Gianluca Zambrotta, Christian Panucci, Giorgio Chiellini
(YC45+4), Fabio Grosso, Andrea Pirlo (YC44) (55' Massimo Ambrosini), Daniele De Rossi,
Gennaro Gattuso (YC54) (82' Alberto Aquilani), Simone Perrotta (64' Mauro Camoranesi),
Luca Toni, Antonio Cassano. (Coach: Roberto Donadoni (ITA)).
Goals: Italy: 0-1 Andrea Pirlo (25' penalty), 0-2 Daniele De Rossi (62').
Referee: Lubos Michel (SVK)   Attendance: 30.585

STANDINGS

Pos	Team	Pld	W	D	L	GF	GA	GD	Pts
1	Netherlands	3	3	0	0	9	1	+8	9
2	Italy	3	1	1	1	3	4	-1	4
3	Romania	3	0	2	1	1	3	-2	2
4	France	3	0	1	2	1	6	-5	1

Netherlands and Italy qualified for the Quarter-finals.

181

GROUP   D

10-06-2008   Tivoli-Neu, Innsbruck: Spain – Russia   4-1 (2-0)
Spain: IKER CASILLAS Fernández (C), SERGIO RAMOS García, Carles PUYOL Saforcada,
Carlos MARCHENA López, Joan CAPDEVILA Méndez, DAVID Jiménez SILVA (77'
Xabier "XABI" ALONSO Olano), MARCOS Antonio SENNA Da Silva, Xavier "XAVI"
Hernández i Creus, Andrés INIESTA Luján (63' Santiago "SANTI" CAZORLA González),
DAVID VILLA Sánchez, FERNANDO José TORRES Sanz (54' Francesc "CESC"
FÀBREGAS Soler). (Coach: LUIS ARAGONÉS Suárez (ESP)).
Russia: Igor Akinfeev, Aleksandr Anyukov, Roman Shirokov, Denis Kolodin, Yuri Zhirkov,
Sergei Semak (C), Konstantin Zyryanov, Igor Semshov (58' Dmitri Torbinski), Dmitri Sychev
(46' Vladimir Bystrov, 70' Roman Adamov), Diniyar Bilyaletdinov, Roman Pavlyuchenko.
(Coach: Guus Hiddink (HOL)).
Goals: Spain: 1-0 DAVID VILLA Sánchez (20'), 2-0 DAVID VILLA Sánchez (44'), 3-0
DAVID VILLA Sánchez (75'), 4-1 Francesc "CESC" FÀBREGAS Soler (90'+1').
Russia: 3-1 Roman Pavlyuchenko (86').
Referee: Konrad Plautz (AUT)   Attendance: 30.772

10-06-2008   Wals-Siezenheim Stadium, Salzburg: Greece – Sweden   0-2 (0-0)
Greece: Antonis Nikopolidis, Giorgios (Giourkas) Seitaridis (YC51), Sotirios Kyrgiakos,
Paraskevas Antzas, Traianos Dellas (70' Ioannis Amanatidis), Vasilios Torosidis (YC61),
Angelos Charisteas (YC1), Angelos Basinas (C), Konstantinos (Kostas) Katsouranis, Giorgios
Karagounis, Theofanis (Fanis) Gekas (46' Georgios Samaras). (Coach: Otto-Heinz Rehhagel
(GER)).
Sweden: Andreas Isaksson, Niclas Alexandersson (74' Fredrik Stoor), Olof Mellberg, Petter
Hansson, Mikael Nilsson, Anders Svensson, Christian Wilhelmsson (78' Markus Rosenberg),
Fredrik (Freddie) Ljungberg (C), Daniel Andersson, Zlatan Ibrahimovic (71' Johan Elmander),
Henrik Larsson. (Coach: Lars Lagerbäck (SWE)).
Goals: Sweden: 0-1 Zlatan Ibrahimovic (67'), 0-2 Petter Hansson (72').
Referee: Massimo Busacca (SUI)   Attendance: 31.063

14-06-2008   Tivoli-Neu, Innsbruck: Sweden – Spain   1-2 (1-1)
Sweden: Andreas Isaksson, Fredrik Stoor, Olof Mellberg, Petter Hansson, Mikael Nilsson,
Johan Elmander (79' Sebastian Larsson), Daniel Andersson, Anders Svensson (YC55), Fredrik
(Freddie) Ljungberg (C), Henrik Larsson (87' Kim Källström), Zlatan Ibrahimovic (46'
Markus Rosenberg). (Coach: Lars Lagerbäck (SWE)).
Spain: IKER CASILLAS Fernández (C), SERGIO RAMOS García, Carlos MARCHENA
López (YC53), Carles PUYOL Saforcada (24' Raúl ALBIOL Tortajada), Joan CAPDEVILA
Méndez, Andrés INIESTA Luján (59' Santiago "SANTI" CAZORLA González), MARCOS
Antonio SENNA Da Silva, Xavier "XAVI" Hernández i Creus (58' Francesc "CESC"
FÀBREGAS Soler), DAVID Jiménez SILVA, DAVID VILLA Sánchez, FERNANDO José
TORRES Sanz. (Coach: LUIS ARAGONÉS Suárez (ESP)).
Goals: Sweden: 1-1 Zlatan Ibrahimovic (34').
Spain: 0-1 FERNANDO José TORRES Sanz (15'), 1-2 DAVID VILLA Sánchez (90'+2').
Referee: Pieter Vink (HOL)   Attendance: 30.772

182

14-06-2008   Wals-Siezenheim Stadium, Salzburg: Greece – Russia   0-1 (0-1)
Greece: Antonis Nikopolidis, Giorgios (Giourkas) Seitaridis (40' Giorgios Karagounis (YC42)), Traianos Dellas, Sotirios Kyrgiakos, Vasilios Torosidis, Konstantinos (Kostas) Katsouranis, Angelos Basinas (C), Christos Patsatzoglou, Angelos Charisteas, Ioannis Amanatidis (80' Stylianos Giannakopoulos), Nikolaos (Nikos) Liberopoulos (YC58) (61' Theofanis (Fanis) Gekas). (Coach: Otto-Heinz Rehhagel (GER)).
Russia: Igor Akinfeev, Aleksandr Anyukov, Denis Kolodin, Sergei Ignashevich, Yuri Zhirkov (87' Vasili Berezutski), Sergei Semak (C), Dmitri Torbinski (YC84), Konstantin Zyryanov, Igor Semshov, Diniyar Bilyaletdinov (70' Ivan Saenko (YC77)), Roman Pavlyuchenko. (Coach: Guus Hiddink (HOL)).
Goal: Russia: 0-1 Konstantin Zyryanov (33').
Referee: Roberto Rosetti (ITA)   Attendance: 31.063

18-06-2008   Wals-Siezenheim Stadium, Salzburg: Greece – Spain   1-2 (1-0)
Greece: Antonis Nikopolidis (C), Loukas Vyntra (YC90+1), Sotirios Kyrgiakos (62' Paraskevas Antzas), Traianos Dellas, Nikolaos (Nikos) Spyropoulos, Angelos Basinas (YC72), Konstantinos (Kostas) Katsouranis, Dimitrios Salpingidis (86' Stylianos Giannakopoulos), Giorgios Karagounis (YC34) (74' Alexandros Tziolis), Ioannis Amanatidis, Angelos Charisteas. (Coach: Otto-Heinz Rehhagel (GER)).
Spain: José Manuel "PEPE" REINA Páez, Álvaro ARBELOA Coca (YC45), Raúl ALBIOL Tortajada, "JUANITO" Juan Gutierrez Moreno, FERNANDO NAVARRO Corbacho, Rubén DE LA RED Gutiérrez, Xabier "XABI" ALONSO Olano (C), SERGIO GARCÍA de la Fuente, Francesc "CESC" FÀBREGAS Soler, Andrés INIESTA Luján (58' Santiago "SANTI" CAZORLA González), Daniel González GÜIZA (YC41). (Coach: LUIS ARAGONÉS Suárez (ESP)).
Goals: Greece: 1-0 Angelos Charisteas (42').
Spain: 1-1 Rubén DE LA RED Gutiérrez (61'), 1-2 Daniel González GÜIZA (88').
Referee: Howard Melton Webb (ENG)   Attendance: 30.883

18-06-2008   Tivoli-Neu, Innsbruck: Russia – Sweden   2-0 (1-0)
Russia: Igor Akinfeev, Aleksandr Anyukov, Sergei Ignashevich, Denis Kolodin (YC76), Yuri Zhirkov, Sergei Semak (C) (YC57), Konstantin Zyryanov, Igor Semshov, Diniyar Bilyaletdinov (66' Ivan Saenko), Andrey Arshavin (YC65), Roman Pavlyuchenko (90' Vladimir Bystrov). (Coach: Guus Hiddink (HOL)).
Sweden: Andreas Isaksson (YC10), Fredrik Stoor, Olof Mellberg, Petter Hansson, Mikael Nilsson (79' Marcus Allbäck), Johan Elmander (YC49), Daniel Andersson (56' Kim Källström), Anders Svensson, Fredrik (Freddie) Ljungberg (C), Henrik Larsson, Zlatan Ibrahimovic. (Coach: Lars Lagerbäck (SWE)).
Goals: Russia: 1-0 Roman Pavlyuchenko (24'), 2-0 Andrey Arshavin (50').
Referee: Frank de Bleeckere (BEL)   Attendance: 30.772

STANDINGS

Pos	Team	Pld	W	D	L	GF	GA	GD	Pts
1	Spain	3	3	0	0	8	3	+5	9
2	Russia	3	2	0	1	4	4	0	6
3	Sweden	3	1	0	2	3	4	-1	3
4	Greece	3	0	0	3	1	5	-4	0

Spain and Russia qualified for the Quarter-finals.

19-06-2008   St.Jakob-Park, Basel: Portugal – Germany 2-3 (1-2)
Portugal: RICARDO Alexandre Martins Soares Pereira, JOSÉ José BOSINGWA da Silva,
Képler Laveran Lima Ferreira "PEPE" (YC60), RICARDO Alberto Silveira de CARVALHO,
PAULO Renato Rebocho FERREIRA, Armando Gonçalves Teixeira PETIT (YC26) (73'
HÉLDER Manuel Marques POSTIGA (YC90)), JOÃO Filipe Iria Santos MOUTINHO (31'
RAÚL José Trindade MEIRELES), CRISTIANO RONALDO dos Santos Aveiro, Anderson
Luís de Souza "DECO", SIMÃO Pedro Fonseca Sabrosa, NUNO "GOMES" Miguel Soares
Pereira Ribeiro (67' Luís Carlos Almeida da Cunha "NANI"). (Coach: Luiz Felipe Scolari
(BRA)).
Germany: Jens Lehmann, Arne Friedrich (YC48), Per Mertesacker, Christoph Metzelder,
Philipp Lahm (YC49), Simon Rolfes, Michael Ballack (C), Bastian Schweinsteiger (83'
Clemens Fritz), Thomas Hitzlsperger (73' Tim Borowski), Miroslav Klose (89' Marcell
Jansen), Lukas Podolski. (Coach: Hans-Dieter Flick (GER)).
Goals: Portugal: 1-1 NUNO "GOMES" Miguel Soares Pereira Ribeiro (40'), 2-3 HÉLDER
Manuel Marques POSTIGA (87').
Germany: 0-1 Bastian Schweinsteiger (22'), 0-2 Miroslav Klose (26'), 1-3 Michael Ballack
(61').
Referee: Peter Fröjdfeldt (SWE)   Attendance: 39.374

20-06-2008   Ernst-Happel-Stadion, Vienna: Croatia – Turkey 1-1 (0-0) (0-0) (AET)
Croatia: Stipe Pletikosa, Vedran Corluka, Robert Kovac, Josip Simunic, Danijel Pranjic, Luka
Modric, Niko Kovac (C), Darijo Srna, Ivan Rakitic, Niko Kranjcar (65' Mladen Petric), Ivica
Olic (97' Ivan Klasnic). (Coach: Slaven Bilic (CRO)).
Turkey: Rüstü Reçber, Hamit Altintop, Gökhan Zan, Emre Asik (YC107), Hakan Balta,
Mehmet Topal (76' Semih Sentürk), Sabri Sarioglu, Tuncay Sanli (YC27), Arda Turan
(YC49), Colin Kazim-Richards (61' Ugur Boral (YC89)), Nihat Kahveci (C) (117' Gökdeniz
Karadeniz). (Coach: Fatih Terim (TUR)).
Goals: Croatia: 1-0 Ivan Klasnic (119').
Turkey: 1-1 Semih Sentürk (120'+2').
Referee: Roberto Rosetti (ITA)   Attendance: 51.428
Penalties: * Luka Modric   1 Arda Turan
                  1 Darijo Srna   2 Semih Sentürk
                  * Ivan Rakitic   3 Hamit Altintop
                  * Mladen Petric

21-06-2008   St.Jakob-Park, Basel: Netherlands – Russia 1-3 (0-0) (1-1) (AET)
Netherlands: Edwin van der Sar (C), Khalid Boulahrouz (YC50) (54' John Heitinga), André
Ooijer, Joris Mathijsen, Giovanni van Bronckhorst, Nigel de Jong, Orlando Engelaar (62'
Ibrahim Afellay), Dirk Kuyt (46' Robin van Persie (YC55)), Rafael van der Vaart (YC60),
Wesley Sneijder, Ruud van Nistelrooy. (Coach: Marcel (Marco) van Basten (HOL)).
Russia: Igor Akinfeev, Aleksandr Anyukov, Sergei Ignashevich, Denis Kolodin (YC71), Yuri
Zhirkov (YC103), Sergei Semak (C), Konstantin Zyryanov, Igor Semshov (69' Diniyar
Bilyaletdinov), Ivan Saenko (81' Dmitri Torbinski (YC111)), Andrey Arshavin, Roman
Pavlyuchenko (115' Dmitri Sychev). (Coach: Guus Hiddink (HOL)).
Goals: Netherlands: 1-1 Ruud van Nistelrooy (86').
Russia: 0-1 Roman Pavlyuchenko (56'), 1-2 Dmitri Torbinski (112'), 1-3 Andrey Arshavin
(116').
Referee: Lubos Michel (SVK)   Attendance: 38.374

22-06-2008   Ernst-Happel-Stadion, Vienna: Spain – Italy   0-0 (AET)
Spain: IKER CASILLAS Fernández (C), SERGIO RAMOS García, Carlos MARCHENA López, Carles PUYOL Saforcada, Joan CAPDEVILA Méndez, Andrés INIESTA Luján (YC11) (59' Santiago "SANTI" CAZORLA González (YC113)), MARCOS Antonio SENNA Da Silva, Xavier "XAVI" Hernández i Creus (60' Francesc "CESC" FÀBREGAS Soler), DAVID Jiménez SILVA, DAVID VILLA Sánchez (YC72), FERNANDO José TORRES Sanz (85' Daniel González GÜIZA). (Coach: LUIS ARAGONÉS Suárez (ESP)).
Italy: Gianluigi Buffon (C), Gianluca Zambrotta, Christian Panucci, Giorgio Chiellini, Fabio Grosso, Alberto Aquilani (108' Alessandro Del Piero), Daniele De Rossi, Massimo Ambrosini (YC31), Simone Perrotta (58' Mauro Camoranesi), Luca Toni, Antonio Cassano (75' Antonio Di Natale). (Coach: Roberto Donadoni (ITA)).

Referee: Herbert Fandel (GER)	Attendance: 51.178

Penalties:

1 DAVID VILLA Sánchez	1 Fabio Grosso
2 Santiago "SANTI" CAZORLA González	* Daniele De Rossi
3 MARCOS Antonio SENNA Da Silva	2 Mauro Camoranesi
* Daniel González GÜIZA	* Antonio Di Natale
4 Francesc "CESC" FÀBREGAS Soler	

SEMI-FINALS

25-06-2008   St.Jakob-Park, Basel: Germany – Turkey   3-2 (1-1)
Germany: Jens Lehmann, Arne Friedrich, Per Mertesacker, Christoph Metzelder, Philipp Lahm, Thomas Hitzlsperger, Simon Rolfes (46' Torsten Frings), Bastian Schweinsteiger, Michael Ballack (C), Lukas Podolski, Miroslav Klose (90'+2' Marcell Jansen). (Coach: Joachim Löw (GER)).
Turkey: Rüstü Reçber (C), Sabri Sarioglu (YC90+4), Mehmet Topal, Gökhan Zan, Hakan Balta, Mehmet Aurélio, Colin Kazim-Richards (90'+2' Tümer Metin), Hamit Altintop, Ayhan Akman (81' Mevlüt Erdinç), Ugur Boral (84' Gökdeniz Karadeniz), Semih Sentürk (YC53). (Coach: Fatih Terim (TUR)).
Goals: Germany: 1-1 Bastian Schweinsteiger (26'), 2-1 Miroslav Klose (79'), 3-2 Philipp Lahm (90').
Turkey: 0-1 Ugur Boral (22'), 2-2 Semih Sentürk (86').

Referee: Massimo Busacca (SUI)	Attendance: 39.374

26-06-2008   Ernst-Happel-Stadion, Vienna: Russia – Spain   0-3 (0-0)
Russia: Igor Akinfeev, Aleksandr Anyukov, Vasili Berezutski, Sergei Ignashevich, Yuri Zhirkov (YC56), Sergei Semak (C), Konstantin Zyryanov, Igor Semshov (56' Diniyar Bilyaletdinov (YC60)), Ivan Saenko (57' Dmitri Sychev), Andrey Arshavin, Roman Pavlyuchenko. (Coach: Guus Hiddink (HOL)).
Spain: IKER CASILLAS Fernández (C), SERGIO RAMOS García, Carlos MARCHENA López, Carles PUYOL Saforcada, Joan CAPDEVILA Méndez, Andrés INIESTA Luján, MARCOS Antonio SENNA Da Silva, Xavier "XAVI" Hernández i Creus (69' Xabier "XABI" ALONSO Olano), DAVID Jiménez SILVA, DAVID VILLA Sánchez (34' Francesc "CESC" FÀBREGAS Soler), FERNANDO José TORRES Sanz (69' Daniel González GÜIZA). (Coach: LUIS ARAGONÉS Suárez (ESP)).
Goals: Spain: 0-1 Xavier "XAVI" Hernández i Creus (50'), 0-2 Daniel González GÜIZA (73'), 0-3 DAVID Jiménez SILVA (82').

Referee: Frank de Bleeckere (BEL)	Attendance: 51.428

185

FINAL

29-06-2008   Ernst-Happel-Stadion, Vienna: Germany – Spain   0-1 (0-1)
Germany: Jens Lehmann, Arne Friedrich, Per Mertesacker, Christoph Metzelder, Philipp Lahm
(46' Marcell Jansen), Torsten Frings, Thomas Hitzlsperger (58' Kevin Kurányi (YC88)),
Bastian Schweinsteiger, Michael Ballack (C) (YC43), Lukas Podolski, Miroslav Klose (79'
Mario Gómez García). (Coach: Joachim Löw (GER)).
Spain: IKER CASILLAS Fernández (C) (YC43), SERGIO RAMOS García, Carlos
MARCHENA López, Carles PUYOL Saforcada, Joan CAPDEVILA Méndez, MARCOS
Antonio SENNA Da Silva, Andrés INIESTA Luján, Xavier "XAVI" Hernández i Creus,
Francesc "CESC" FÀBREGAS Soler (63' Xabier "XABI" ALONSO Olano), DAVID Jiménez
SILVA (66' Santiago "SANTI" CAZORLA González), FERNANDO José TORRES Sanz
(YC74) (78' Daniel González GÜIZA). (Coach: LUIS ARAGONÉS Suárez (ESP)).
Goal: Spain: 0-1 FERNANDO José TORRES Sanz (33').
Referee: Roberto Rosetti (ITA)   Attendance: 51.428

*** Spain were European Champions ***

GOALSCORERS TOURNAMENT 2006-2008:

Goals	Players
13	David Healy (NIR)
11	DAVID VILLA Sánchez (ESP), Lukas Podolski (GER)
10	EDUARDO Alves da Silva (CRO)
9	Euzebiusz (Ebi) Smolarek (POL), CRISTIANO RONALDO dos Santos Aveiro (POR)
7	Mladen Petric (CRO), Jan Koller (CZE), Jon Dahl Tomasson (DEN), Thierry Henry (FRA), Miroslav Klose (GER), Steffen Iversen (NOR), Adrian Mutu (ROM), Nikola Zigic (SRB)
6	Dimitar Berbatov (BUL), Martin Petrov (BUL), Robin van Persie (HOL), Roberto Colautti (ISR), Marek Mintál (SVK), Marcus Allbäck (SWE), Hakan Sükür (TUR)
5	Edmond Kapllani (ALB), Ioannis Okkas (CYP), Peter Crouch (ENG), Xavier "XAVI" Hernández i Creus (ESP), Shota Arveladze (GEO), Michael Ballack (GER), Bastian Schweinsteiger (GER), Theofanis (Fanis) Gekas (GRE), Luca Toni (ITA), Dmitriy Byakov (KAZ), Māris Verpakovskis (LAT), Ciprian Marica (ROM), Andrey Arshavin (RUS), Aleksandr Kerzhakov (RUS), Roman Pavlyuchenko (RUS), Nihat Kahveci (TUR), Andriy Shevchenko (UKR)
4	Mousa Dembélé (BEL), Maksim Romashchenko (BLS), Zvjezdan Misimovic (BOS), Darijo Srna (CRO), Libor Sionko (CZE), Dennis Rommedahl (DEN), Michael Owen (ENG), FERNANDO José TORRES Sanz (ESP), Rógvi Jacobsen (FAR), Nicolas Anelka (FRA), Thomas Hitzlsperger (GER), Angelos Charisteas (GRE), Ruud van Nistelrooy (HOL), Wesley Sneijder (HOL), Zoltán Gera (HUN), Kevin Doyle (IRL), Stephen Ireland (IRL), Robbie Keane (IRL), Mario Frick (LIE), Tomas Danilevicius (LIT), Viorel Frunza (MOL), John Carew (NOR), Jacek Krzynówek (POL), NUNO "GOMES" Miguel Soares Pereira Ribeiro

186

	(POR), Nicolae Dica (ROM), Kris Boyd (SCO), James McFadden (SCO), Klemen Lavric (SLO), Danko Lazovic (SRB), Oleh Gusev (UKR), Jason Koumas (WAL)
3	Sergei Kornilenko (BLS), Vitali Kutuzov (BLS), Zlatan Muslimovic (BOS), Ivan Klasnic (CRO), Efstathios Aloneftis (CYP), Constantino (Costas) Charalambidis (CYP), Milan Baros (CZE), Steven Gerrard (ENG), Andrés INIESTA Luján (ESP), Jari Litmanen (FIN), Sidney Govou (FRA), Alexander Iashvili (GEO), David Siradze (GEO), Kevin Kurányi (GER), Angelos Basinas (GRE), Sotirios Kyrgiakos (GRE), Nikolaos (Nikos) Lyberopoulos (GRE), Eidur Gudjohnsen (ISL), Filippo Inzaghi (ITA), Juris Laizāns (LAT), Ilco Naumoski (MCD), Goce Sedloski (MCD), Michael Mifsud (MLT), André Schembri (MLT), Igor Bugaev (MOL), Radoslaw Matusiak (POL), SIMÃO Pedro Fonseca Sabrosa (POR), Dmitri Sychev (RUS), Kenny Miller (SCO), Bosko Jankovic (SRB), Hakan Yakin (SUI), Filip Holosko (SVK), Martin Skrtel (SVK), Kim Källström (SWE), Tuncay Sanli (TUR), Semih Sentürk (TUR), Craig Bellamy (WAL)
2	Ervin Skela (ALB), Robert Arzumanyan (ARM), Karel Geraerts (BEL), Kevin Mirallas (BEL), Timofei Kalachev (BLS), Vladimir Korytko (BLS), Mirko Hrgovic (BOS), Niko Kranjcar (CRO), Luka Modric (CRO), Ivica Olic (CRO), Michalis Konstantinou (CYP), Marek Jankulovski (CZE), Marek Kulic (CZE), David Lafata (CZE), Jaroslav Plasil (CZE), Tomás Rosicky (CZE), Nicklas Bendtner (DEN), Michael Gravgaard (DEN), Morten Nordstrand (DEN), Jermain Defoe (ENG), Wayne Rooney (ENG), Shaun Wright-Phillips (ENG), Daniel González GÜIZA (ESP), SERGIO RAMOS García (ESP), Raio Piiroja (EST), Alexei Eremenko (FIN), Jonathan Johansson (FIN), Karim Benzema (FRA), Louis Saha (FRA), David Trézéguet (FRA), Clemens Fritz (GER), Mario Gómez García (GER), Ioannis Amanatidis (GRE), Giovanni van Bronckhorst (HOL), Klaas-Jan Huntelaar (HOL), Dirk Kuyt (HOL), Kevin Kilbane (IRL), Elyaniv Barda (ISR), Yossi Benayoun (ISR), Amit Ben-Shushan (ISR), Ben Sahar (ISR), Toto Tamuz (ISR), Daniele De Rossi (ITA), Antonio Di Natale (ITA), Christian Panucci (ITA), Andrea Pirlo (ITA), Fabio Quagliarella (ITA), Ruslan Baltiev (KAZ), Girts Karlsons (LAT), Aleksejs Visnakovs (LAT), Thomas Beck (LIE), Audrius Ksanavicius (LIT), Goran Maznov (MCD), Goran Pandev (MCD), Sergei Rogaciov (MOL), Kyle Lafferty (NIR), Erik Hagen (NOR), Morten Gamst Pedersen (NOR), John Arne Riise (NOR), Ole Gunnar Solskjær (NOR), Fredrik Strømstad (NOR), HÉLDER Manuel Marques POSTIGA (POR), HUGO Miguel Pereira de ALMEIDA (POR), RICARDO Andrade QUARESMA Bernardo (POR), Cosmin Contra (ROM), Dorin Goian (ROM), Daniel Niculae (ROM), Gabriel Tamas (ROM), Vladimir Bystrov (RUS), Garry O'Connor (SCO), Milivoje Novakovic (SLO), Milan Jovanovic (SRB), Zdravko Kuzmanovic (SRB), Marek Cech (SVK), Marek Hamsik (SVK), Miroslav Karhan (SVK), Filip Sebo (SVK), Stanislav Sesták (SVK), Róbert Vittek (SVK), Johan Elmander (SWE), Zlatan Ibrahimovic (SWE), Olof Mellberg (SWE), Markus Rosenberg (SWE), Christian Wilhelmsson (SWE), Anders Svensson (SWE), Halil Altintop (TUR), Tümer Metin (TUR), Arda Turan (TUR), Gökhan Ünal (TUR), Maxym Kalynychenko (UKR), Gareth Bale (WAL), Robert Earnshaw (WAL)
1	Erjon Bogdani (ALB), Debatik Curri (ALB), Klodian Duro (ALB), Besnik Hasi (ALB), Altin Haxhi (ALB), Julia "Juli" Fernández Ariza (AND), Fernando José Silva Garcia (AND), Sarkis Hovsepyan (ARM), Hamlet

Mkhitaryan (ARM), Ivica Vastic (AUT), Samir Aliyev (AZE), Mahmud Gurbanov (AZE), Emin Imamaliev (AZE), André Luiz Ladaga (AZE), Vügar Nadirov (AZE), Branimir Subasic (AZE), Daniel van Buyten (BEL), Marouane Fellaini (BEL), Luigi Pieroni (BEL), Timmy Simons (BEL), Wesley Sonck (BEL), Kevin Vandenbergh (BEL), Vital Bulyga (BLS), Denis Kovba (BLS), Roman Vasilyuk (BLS), Sergej Barbarez (BOS), Mladen Bartolovic (BOS), Adnan Custovic (BOS), Dario Damjanovic (BOS), Edin Dzeko (BOS), Ivica Grlic (BOS), Vedad Ibisevic (BOS), Valeri Bojinov (BUL), Velizar Dimitrov (BUL), Blagoy Georgiev (BUL), Dimitar Telkiyski (BUL), Aleksandar Tunchev (BUL), Chavdar Yankov (BUL), Bosko Balaban (CRO), Ivan Rakitic (CRO), Alexandros Garpozis (CYP), Constantinos Makrides (CYP), Stelios Okkarides (CYP), Yiasoumis Yiasoumi (CYP), Zdenek Grygera (CZE), David Jarolím (CZE), Radoslav Kovác (CZE), Marek Matejovsky (CZE), Jan Polák (CZE), Daniel Pudil (CZE), Václav Sverkos (CZE), Daniel Jensen (DEN), Thomas Kahlenberg (DEN), Martin Laursen (DEN), Ulrik Laursen (DEN), Joe Cole (ENG), Rio Ferdinand (ENG), Frank Lampard (ENG), David Nugent (ENG), Micah Richards (ENG), Joan CAPDEVILA Méndez (ESP), Francesc "CESC" FÀBREGAS Soler (ESP), DAVID Jiménez SILVA (ESP), Rubén DE LA RED Gutiérrez (ESP), LUIS Javier GARCÍA Sanz (ESP), Fernando MORIENTES Sánchez (ESP), RAÚL TAMUDO Montero (ESP), Albert RIERA Ortega (ESP), Joel Lindpere (EST), Andres Oper (EST), Indrek Zelinski (EST), Mikael Forssell (FIN), Sami Hyypiä (FIN), Shefki Kuqi (FIN), Mika Nurmela (FIN), Teemu Tainio (FIN), Mika Väyrynen (FIN), Hatem Ben Arfa (FRA), Florent Malouda (FRA), Samir Nasri (FRA), Franck Ribéry (FRA), Jérôme Rothen (FRA), Georgi Demetradze (GEO), Levan Kobiashvili (GEO), Levan Mchedlidze (GEO), Davit Mujiri (GEO), Georgi Shashiashvili (GEO), Manuel Friedrich (GER), Torsten Frings (GER), Marcell Jansen (GER), Philipp Lahm (GER), Bernd Schneider (GER), Christos Patsatzoglou (GRE), Georgios Samaras (GRE), Giorgios (Giourkas) Seitaridis (GRE), Danny Koevermans (HOL), Joris Mathijsen (HOL), Arjen Robben (HOL), Rafael van der Vaart (HOL), Ákos Buzsáky (HUN), Pál Dárdai (HUN), Róbert Feczesin (HUN), Szabolcs Huszti (HUN), Tamás Priskin (HUN), Sándor Torghelle (HUN), Dániel Tözsér (HUN), Richard Dunne (IRL), Steve Finnan (IRL), Andy Reid (IRL), Ármann Smári Björnsson (ISL), Brynjar Gunnarsson (ISL), Emil Hallfredsson (ISL), Hermann Hreidarsson (ISL), Gunnar Heidar Thorvaldsson (ISL), Arnar Vidarsson (ISL), Shimon Gershon (ISR), Omer Golan (ISR), Idan Tal (ISR), Barak Yitzhaki (ISR), Mauro Camoranesi (ITA), Giorgio Chiellini (ITA), Alberto Gilardino (ITA), Fabio Grosso (ITA), Massimo Oddo (ITA), Simone Perrotta (ITA), Kairat Ashirbekov (KAZ), Sergei Ostapenko (KAZ), Samat Smakov (KAZ), Nurbol Zhumaskaliyev (KAZ), Kaspars Gorkss (LAT), Oskars Klava (LAT), Franz Burgmeier (LIE), Raphael Rohrer (LIE), Edgaras Jankauskas (LIT), Darius Miceika (LIT), Saulius Mikoliūnas (LIT), Mantas Savénas (LIT), Andrius Skerla (LIT), Alphonse Leweck (LUX), Chris Sagramola (LUX), Nikolce Noveski (MCD), Aco Stojkov (MCD), George Mallia (MLT), Jamie Pace (MLT), Brian Said (MLT), Terence Scerri (MLT), Serghei Alexeev (MOL), Alexandru Epureanu (MOL), Nicolae Josan (MOL), Warren Feeney (NIR), Grant McCann (NIR), Martin Andresen (NOR), Daniel Braaten (NOR), Simen Brenne (NOR), Kristofer Hæstad (NOR), Thorstein Helstad (NOR), Bjørn Helge Riise (NOR), Jacek Bak (POL), Dariusz Dudka (POL), Lukasz

	Gargula (POL), Roger Guerreiro (POL), Przemyslaw Kazmierczak (POL), Mariusz Lewandowski (POL), Wojciech Lobodzinski (POL), Rafal Murawski (POL), Maciej Zurawski (POL), BRUNO Eduardo Regufe ALVES (POR), Anderson Luís de Souza "DECO" (POR), Ariza Makukula (POR), Nuno Ricardo de Oliveira Ribeiro "MANICHE" (POR), Luis Carlos Almeida da Cunha "NANI" (POR), Képler Laveran Lima Ferreira "PEPE" (POR), RAÚL José Trindade MEIRELES (POR), RICARDO Alberto Silveira de CARVALHO (POR), TIAGO Cardoso Mendes (POR), Banel Nicolita (ROM), Florentin Petre (ROM), Laurentiu Rosu (ROM), Vasili Berezutski (RUS), Diniyar Bilyaletdinov (RUS), Pavel Pogrebnyak (RUS), Dmitri Torbinski (RUS), Konstantin Zyryanov (RUS), Craig Beattie (SCO), Gary Caldwell (SCO), Christian Dailly (SCO), Barry Ferguson (SCO), Darren Fletcher (SCO), Shaun Maloney (SCO), Lee McCulloch (SCO), Stephen McManus (SCO), Bostjan Cesar (SLO), Robert Koren (SLO), Dare Vrsic (SLO), Branislav Ivanovic (SRB), Dejan Stankovic (SRB), Dusko Tosic (SRB), Manuel Marani (SMR), Andy Selva (SMR), Ján Durica (SVK), Martin Jakubko (SVK), Maros Klimpl (SVK), Lubomir Michalík (SVK), Marek Sapara (SVK), Dusan Svento (SVK), Stanislav Varga (SVK), Petter Hansson (SWE), Fredrik (Freddie) Ljungberg (SWE), Hamit Altintop (TUR), Mehmet Aurélio (TUR), Emre Belözoglu (TUR), Ugur Boral (TUR), Servet Çetin (TUR), Gökdeniz Karadeniz (TUR), Ümit Karan (TUR), Sabri Sarioglu (TUR), Olexandr Kucher (UKR), Ruslan Rotan (UKR), Andriy Rusol (UKR), Oleh Shelayev (UKR), Andriy Vorobey (UKR), Andriy Voronin (UKR), Volodymyr Yezerskiy (UKR), James Collins (WAL), Simon Davies (WAL), Freddy Eastwood (WAL), Ryan Giggs (WAL), Joe Ledley (WAL)
1 own goal	Arjan Beqaj (ALB) for Netherlands, Martin Jiránet (CZE) for Wales, Gary Neville (ENG) for Croatia, Taavi Rähn (EST) for England, Fródi Benjaminsen (FAR) for Italy, Malkhaz Asatiani (GEO) for France, Christoph Metzelder (GER for Slovakia, Vilmos Vanczák (HUN) for Greece, Sergei Ostapenko (KAZ) for Serbia, Dzintars Zirnis (LAT) for Liechtenstein, Chris Baird (NIR) for Latvia, Keith Gillespie (NIR) for Iceland, Michal Kadlec (SVK) for Slovakia
2 own goals	Ján Durica (SVK) for Germany and for Wales

Goals scored in the Denmark vs Sweden match are not included in goalscoring totals as the match was abandoned in the 89th minute and the score annulled up to that point.

UEFA Euro 2012

QUALIFYING ROUND

GROUP A

03-09-2010	Astana	Kazakhstan – Turkey	0-3 (0-2)
03-09-2010	Brussels	Belgium – Germany	0-1 (0-0)
07-09-2010	Istanbul	Turkey – Belgium	3-2 (0-1)
07-09-2010	Salzburg	Austria – Kazakhstan	2-0 (0-0)
07-09-2010	Cologne	Germany – Azerbaijan	6-1 (3-0)
08-10-2010	Astana	Kazakhstan – Belgium	0-2 (0-0)
08-10-2010	Vienna	Austria – Azerbaijan	3-0 (1-0)
08-10-2010	Berlin	Germany – Turkey	3-0 (1-0)
12-10-2010	Baku	Azerbaijan – Turkey	1-0 (1-0)
12-10-2010	Astana	Kazakhstan – Germany	0-3 (0-0)
12-10-2010	Brussels	Belgium – Austria	4-4 (1-2)
25-03-2011	Vienna	Austria – Belgium	0-2 (0-1)
26-03-2011	Kaiserslautern	Germany – Kazakhstan	4-0 (3-0)
29-03-2011	Istanbul	Turkey – Austria	2-0 (1-0)
29-03-2011	Brussels	Belgium – Azerbaijan	4-1 (3-1)
03-06-2011	Astana	Kazakhstan – Azerbaijan	2-1 (0-0)
03-06-2011	Vienna	Austria – Germany	1-2 (0-1)
03-06-2011	Brussels	Belgium – Turkey	1-1 (1-1)
07-06-2011	Baku	Azerbaijan – Germany	1-3 (0-2)
02-09-2011	Baku	Azerbaijan – Belgium	1-1 (0-0)
02-09-2011	Istanbul	Turkey – Kazakhstan	2-1 (1-0)
02-09-2011	Gelsenkirchen	Germany – Austria	6-2 (3-1)
06-09-2011	Baku	Azerbaijan – Kazakhstan	3-2 (0-1)
06-09-2011	Vienna	Austria – Turkey	0-0
07-10-2011	Baku	Azerbaijan – Austria	1-4 (0-1)
07-10-2011	Istanbul	Turkey – Germany	1-3 (0-1)
07-10-2011	Brussels	Belgium – Kazakhstan	4-1 (2-0)
11-10-2011	Astana	Kazakhstan – Austria	0-0
11-10-2011	Düsseldorf	Germany – Belgium	3-1 (2-0)
11-10-2011	Istanbul	Turkey – Azerbaijan	1-0 (0-0)

FINAL STANDING

Pos	Team	Pld	W	D	L	GF	GA	GD	Pts
1	Germany	10	10	0	0	34	7	+27	30
2	Turkey	10	5	2	3	13	11	+2	17
3	Belgium	10	4	3	3	21	15	+6	15
4	Austria	10	3	4	4	16	17	-1	12
5	Azerbaijan	10	2	1	7	10	26	-16	7
6	Kazakhstan	10	1	1	8	6	24	-18	4

Germany qualified for the Final Tournament in Poland and Ukraine.
Turkey qualified for the play-offs

03-09-2010   Astana Arena, Astana: Kazakhstan – Turkey   0-3 (0-2)
Kazakhstan: Andrei Sidelnikov, Aleksei Popov, Aleksandr Kislitsyn (85' Mikhail Rozhkov),
Aleksandr Kirov, Renat Abdulin, Nurbol Zhumaskaliyev (YC62), Heinrich Schmidtgal, Azat
Nurgaliyev, Andrei Karpovich (C) (YC58) (64' Denis Rodionov), Sergei Ostapenko (72' Gleb
Maltsev), Maksim Azovski. (Coach: Bernd Storck (GER)).
Turkey: Onur Kivrak, Sabri Sarioglu, Ömer Erdogan, Servet Çetin, Hakan Balta (C), Arda
Turan, Emre Belözoglu, Mehmet Aurélio (89' Colin Kazim-Richards), Hamit Altintop, Tuncay
Sanli (80' Halil Altintop), Nihat Kahveci (82' Selçuk Inan). (Coach: Guus Hiddink (HOL)).
Goals: Turkey: 0-1 Arda Turan (24'), 0-2 Hamit Altintop (26'), 0-3 Nihat Kahveci (76').
Referee: István Vad II (HUN)   Attendance: 15.800

03-09-2010   King Baudouin Stadium, Brussels: Belgium – Germany   0-1 (0-0)
Belgium: Logan Bailly, Thomas Vermaelen (C), Daniel van Buyten, Vincent Kompany
(YC12), Toby Alderweireld, Timmy Simons (83' Jelle Vossen), Jan Vertonghen, Eden Hazard
(73' Steven Defour), Marouane Fellaini, Romelu Lukaku (73' Christian Benteke), Mousa
Dembélé. (Coach: Georges Leekens (BEL)).
Germany: Manuel Neuer, Per Mertesacker, Philipp Lahm (C), Marcell Jansen (46' Heiko
Westermann), Holger Badstuber, Bastian Schweinsteiger (YC45+1), Mesut Özil (88' Jeronimo
Maria Barreto Claudemir da Silva "CACAU" (YC90+1)), Thomas Müller, Sami Khedira,
Lukas Podolski (70' Toni Kroos), Miroslav Klose. (Coach: Joachim Löw (GER)).
Goal: Germany: 0-1 Miroslav Klose (51').
Referee: Terje Hauge (NOR)   Attendance: 41.126

07-09-2010   Sükrü Saracoglu Stadium, Istanbul: Turkey – Belgium   3-2 (0-1)
Turkey: Onur Kivrak, Sabri Sarioglu (73' Gökhan Gönül), Ismail Köybasi, Ömer Erdogan,
Servet Çetin, Arda Turan, Selçuk Inan (46' Semih Sentürk), Emre Belözoglu (C) (YC32),
Mehmet Aurélio, Hamit Altintop, Tuncay Sanli (82' Selçuk Sahin (YC90+1)). (Coach: Guus
Hiddink (HOL)).
Belgium: Logan Bailly, Daniel van Buyten (YC45+2), Thomas Vermaelen (C), Vincent
Kompany (YC40,YC64), Toby Alderweireld (YC90+3), Timmy Simons, Jan Vertonghen,
Guillaume Gillet (82' Eden Hazard), Marouane Fellaini, Romelu Lukaku (76' Axel Witsel),
Mousa Dembélé (64' Kevin Mirallas). (Coach: Georges Leekens (BEL)).
Goals: Turkey: 1-1 Hamit Altintop (48'), 2-1 Semih Sentürk (66'), 3-2 Arda Turan (78').
Belgium: 0-1 Daniel van Buyten (28'), 2-2 Daniel van Buyten (69').
Referee: Damir Skomina (SLO)   Attendance: 43.538

07-09-2010   Red Bull Arena, Wals-Siezenheim: Austria – Kazakhstan   2-0 (0-0)
Austria: Jürgen Macho, Ekrem Dag, Franz Schiemer, Sebastian Prödl, Emanuel Pogatetz,
Christian Fuchs, Veli Kavlak, Jakob Jantscher (YC60) (66' David Alaba), Martin Harnik (66'
Erwin Hoffer), Roland Linz, Marc Janko (C) (78' Stefan Maierhofer). (Coach: Dietmar
Constantini (AUT)).
Kazakhstan: Andrei Sidelnikov, Renat Abdulin, Aleksei Popov, Aleksandr Kislitsyn (YC53)
(75' Mikhail Rozhkov (YC80)), Aleksandr Kirov, Evgeni Averchenko, Nurbol Zhumaskaliyev,
Azat Nurgaliyev (YC45+1) (59' Maksim Azovski), Andrei Karpovich (C), Kazbek Geteriyev,
Gleb Maltsev (46' Sergei Khizhnichenko). (Coach: Bernd Storck (GER)).
Goals: Austria: 1-0 Roland Linz (90'+1'), 2-0 Erwin Hoffer (90'+2').
Referee: Marijo Strahonja (CRO)   Attendance: 22.500

191

07-09-2010   RheinEnergieStadion, Cologne: Germany – Azerbaijan   6-1 (3-0)
Germany: Manuel Neuer, Per Mertesacker (11' Heiko Westermann), Philipp Lahm (C), Holger
Badstuber, Bastian Schweinsteiger (78' Jeronimo Maria Barreto Claudemir da Silva
"CACAU"), Sascha Riether, Mesut Özil, Thomas Müller (61' Marko Marin), Sami Khedira,
Lukas Podolski, Miroslav Klose. (Coach: Joachim Löw (GER)).
Azerbaijan: Kamran Agayev, Samir Abbasov, Sasa Yunisoglu (56' Vurgun Hüseynov), Mahir
Shukurov, Maksim Medvedev, Elnur Allahverdiyev, Rail Malikov, Rashad Farhad oglu
Sadygov (C), Aleksandr Chertoganov (64' Rashad Abulfaz oglu Sadiqov), Vüqar Nadirov (85'
Araz Abdullayev), Vagif Javadov. (Coach: Hans-Hubert (Berti) Vogts (GER)).
Goals: Germany: 1-0 Heiko Westermann (28'), 2-0 Lukas Podolski (45'+1'), 3-0 Miroslav
Klose (45'+2'), 4-0 Rashad Farhad oglu Sadygov (53' *own goal*), 5-1 Holger Badstuber (86'),
6-1 Miroslav Klose (90'+2').
Azerbaijan: 4-1 Vagif Javadov (57').
Referee: Markus Strömbergsson (SWE)   Attendance: 43.751

08-10-2010   Astana Arena, Astana: Kazakhstan – Belgium   0-2 (0-0)
Kazakhstan: Andrei Sidelnikov, Aleksei Popov, Aleksandr Kislitsyn (YC51,YC68), Aleksandr
Kirov, Renat Abdulin, Nurbol Zhumaskaliyev (87' Evgeni Averchenko), Heinrich Schmidtgal,
Azat Nurgaliyev (74' Mikhail Rozhkov), Andrei Karpovich (C) (YC55), Kazbek Geteriyev,
Sergei Khizhnichenko. (Coach: Bernd Storck (GER)).
Belgium: Logan Bailly, Jelle van Damme (79' Jonathan Legear), Olivier Deschacht, Daniel
van Buyten (C), Nicolas Lombaerts, Toby Alderweireld, Timmy Simons, Axel Witsel,
Marouane Fellaini (YC26), Jelle Vossen (YC19), Romelu Lukaku (46' Marvin Ogunjimi).
(Coach: Georges Leekens (BEL)).
Goals: Belgium: 0-1 Marcin Ogunjimi (52'), 0-2 Marvin Ogunjimi (70').
Referee: Marcin Borski (POL)   Attendance: 8.500

08-10-2010   Ernst Happel Stadion, Vienna: Austria – Azerbaijan   3-0 (1-0)
Austria: Jürgen Macho, Franz Schiemer, Paul Scharner, Sebastian Prödl (YC10), Florian Klein,
Christian Fuchs (C), Zlatko Junuzovic (78' Julian Baumgartlinger), Martin Harnik (55' Veli
Kavlak), Marko Arnautovic, Stefan Maierhofer, Roland Linz (59' Erwin Hoffer). (Coach:
Dietmar Constantini (AUT)).
Azerbaijan: Kamran Agayev, Sasa Yunisoglu (YC36), Mahir Shukurov, Elnur Allahverdiyev
(YC7), Samir Abbasov, Rail Malikov, Rashad Farhad oglu Sadygov (C), Elvin Mammadov
(59' Vüqar Nadirov), Rahid Amirguliyev, Vagif Javadov (74' Rashad Abulfaz oglu Sadiqov),
Rauf Aliyev (YC73). (Coach: Hans-Hubert (Berti) Vogts (GER)).
Goals: Austria: 1-0 Sebastian Prödl (3'), 2-0 Marko Arnautovic (53'), 3-0 Marko Arnautovic
(90'+2').
Referee: Nicolai Vollquartz (DEN)   Attendance: 26.500

08-10-2010   Olympiastadion, Berlin: Germany – Turkey   3-0 (1-0)
Germany: Manuel Neuer, Heiko Westermann, Per Mertesacker, Philipp Lahm (C), Holger
Badstuber, Mesut Özil (90' Marko Marin), Thomas Müller, Toni Kroos, Sami Khedira, Lukas
Podolski (86' Christian Träsch), Miroslav Klose (90' Jeronimo Maria Barreto Claudemir da
Silva "CACAU"). (Coach: Joachim Löw (GER)).
Turkey: Volkan Demirel, Sabri Sarioglu, Gökhan Gönül, Ömer Erdogan, Servet Çetin
(YC45+5), Nuri Sahin (78' Sercan Yildirim), Mehmet Aurélio (24' Tuncay Sanli), Özer
Hurmaci, Emre Belözoglu (C), Hamit Altintop, Halil Altintop (63' Semih Sentürk). (Coach:
Guus Hiddink (HOL)).
Goals: Germany: 1-0 Miroslav Klose (42'), 2-0 Mesut Özil (79'), 3-0 Miroslav Klose (87').
Referee: Howard Melton Webb (ENG)   Attendance: 74.244

12-10-2010   Tofiq Bakhramov Stadium, Baku: Azerbaijan – Turkey   1-0 (1-0)
Azerbaijan: Kamran Agayev (YC80), Sasa Yunisoglu, Mahir Shukurov (YC58), Elnur
Allahverdiyev, Rail Malikov (45'+2' Aleksandr Chertoganov (YC87)), Rashad Farhad oglu
Sadygov (C), Rahid Amirguliyev (YC60), Ruslan Abisov, Farid Guliyev (71' Rauf Aliyev),
Vüqar Nadirov, Vagif Javadov (85' Vurgun Hüseynov). (Coach: Hans-Hubert (Berti) Vogts
(GER)).
Turkey: Volkan Demirel, Ibrahim Toraman, Gökhan Gönül, Servet Çetin, Hakan Balta
(YC58), Selçuk Inan (82' Halil Altintop), Özer Hurmaci (46' Nihat Kahveci), Emre Belözoglu
(C), Hamit Altintop, Tuncay Sanli (62' Sercan Yildirim), Semih Sentürk. (Coach: Guus
Hiddink (HOL)).
Goal: Azerbaijan: 1-0 Rashad Farhad oglu Sadygov (38').
Referee: Alexandru Deaconu (ROM)   Attendance: 29.500

12-10-2010   Astana Arena, Astana: Kazakhstan – Germany   0-3 (0-0)
Kazakhstan: Andrei Sidelnikov, Aleksandr Kirov, Renat Abdulin (YC37), Farkhadbek
Irismetov (YC60) (68' Mikhail Rozhkov), Aleksei Popov, Kazbek Geteriyev, Nurbol
Zhumaskaliyev (C), Heinrich Schmidtgal, Azat Nurgaliyev (63' Evgeni Averchenko), Sergei
Khizhnichenko (79' Andrei Finonchenko), Maksim Azovski. (Coach: Bernd Storck (GER)).
Germany: Manuel Neuer, Philipp Lahm (C), Holger Badstuber, Heiko Westermann, Per
Mertesacker, Toni Kroos, Sami Khedira, Mesut Özil (79' Jeronimo Maria Barreto Claudemir
da Silva "CACAU"), Thomas Müller (71' Marko Marin), Miroslav Klose (55' Mario Gómez
García), Lukas Podolski. (Coach: Joachim Löw (GER)).
Goals: Germany: 0-1 Miroslav Klose (48'), 0-2 Mario Gómez García (76'), 0-3 Lukas Podolski
(85').
Referee: Alexandru Dan Tudor (ROM)   Attendance: 18.000

12-10-2010   King Baudouin Stadium, Brussels: Belgium – Austria   4-4 (1-2)
Belgium: Logan Bailly, Nicolas Lombaerts (YC45+1), Vincent Kompany (C), Toby
Alderweireld (46' Dedryck Boyata), Timmy Simons (YC64) (73' Romelu Lukaku), Jonathan
Legear, Axel Witsel, Jan Vertonghen, Marouane Fellaini (81' Eden Hazard), Jelle Vossen,
Marvin Ogunjimi. (Coach: Georges Leekens (BEL)).
Austria: Jürgen Macho, Franz Schiemer (YC36), Paul Scharner (RC68), Sebastian Prödl,
Florian Klein (YC83), Christian Fuchs (C), Veli Kavlak (56' Erwin Hoffer), Zlatko Junuzovic
(72' Yasin Pehlivan), Julian Baumgartlinger, Marko Arnautovic (88' Martin Harnik), Stefan
Maierhofer (YC28). (Coach: Dietmar Constantini (AUT)).
Goals: Belgium: 1-0 Jelle Vossen (11'), 2-2 Marouane Fellaini (47'), 3-3 Marvin Ogunjimi
(87'), 4-3 Nicolas Lombaerts (90').
Austria: 1-1 Franz Schiemer (14'), 1-2 Marko Arnautovic (29'), 2-3 Franz Schiemer (62'), 4-4
Martin Harnik (90'+3').
Referee: Michael Leslie (Mike) Dean (ENG)   Attendance: 24.231

25-03-2011   Ernst Happel Stadion, Vienna: Austria – Belgium   0-2 (0-1)
Austria: Jürgen Macho, Emanuel Pogatez, Christian Fuchs (C), Aleksandar Dragovic, Ekrem
Dag, Zlatko Junuzovic (69' Ümit Korkmaz), Martin Harnik, Julian Baumgartlinger, Marko
Arnautovic, David Alaba (54' Yasin Pehlivan), Marc Janko (C) (54' Stefan Maierhofer).
(Coach: Dietmar Constantini (AUT)).
Belgium: Simon Mignolet, Daniel van Buyten (C), Vincent Kompany (YC41), Laurent Ciman,
Timmy Simons, Axel Witsel, Jan Vertonghen, Steven Defour, Nacer Chadli, Marvin Ogunjimi
(80' Kevin Mirallas), Mousa Dembélé. (Coach: Georges Leekens (BEL)).
Goals: Belgium: 0-1 Axel Witsel (6'), 0-2 Axel Witsel (50').
Referee: Vladislav Yuryevich Bezborodov (RUS)   Attendance: 45.000

26-03-2011   Fritz-Walter-Stadion, Kaiserslautern: Germany – Kazakhstan 4-0 (3-0)
Germany: Manuel Neuer, Per Mertesacker, Philipp Lahm (C), Holger Badstuber, Dennis Aogo,
Bastian Schweinsteiger (77' Toni Kroos), Mesut Özil, Thomas Müller (78' Mario Götze), Sami
Khedira, Lukas Podolski (65' Mario Gómez García), Miroslav Klose. (Coach: Joachim Löw
(GER)).
Kazakhstan: David Loria, Farkhadbek Irismetov (YC25), Vladislav Chernyshov, Renat
Abdulin, Kairat Nurdauletov (C), Anton Chichulin, Nurbol Zhumaskaliyev (C) (46' Maksat
Bayzhanov), Azat Nurgaliyev (60' Zhambyl Kukeyev), Kazbek Geteriyev (81' Sergei
Ostapenko), Ulan Konysbayev, Sergei Khizhnichenko. (Coach: Miroslav Beránek (CZE)).
Goals: Germany: 1-0 Miroslav Klose (3'), 2-0 Thomas Müller (25'), 3-0 Thomas Müller (43'),
4-0 Miroslav Klose (88').
Referee: Aleksandar Stavrev (MCD)   Attendance: 47.849

29-03-2011   Sükrü Saracoglu Stadium, Istanbul: Turkey – Austria 2-0 (1-0)
Turkey: Volkan Demirel, Serdar Kesimal, Gökhan Gönül, Servet Çetin, Hakan Balta, Hamit
Altintop (C), Arda Turan (89' Mehmet Topal), Nuri Sahin, Selçuk Inan, Mehmet Ekici (63'
Mehmet Topuz (YC83)), Burak Yilmaz (72' Semih Sentürk). (Coach: Guus Hiddink (HOL)).
Austria: Jürgen Macho, Paul Scharner (YC90+2), Emanuel Pogatetz (YC13), Christian Fuchs
(C) (YC73), Aleksandar Dragovic, Ekrem Dag, Yasin Pehlivan (57' Ümit Korkmaz), Martin
Harnik (69' Marko Arnautovic), Julian Baumgartlinger (46' Erwin Hoffer), David Alaba,
Stefan Maierhofer. (Coach: Dietmar Constantini (AUT)).
Goals: Turkey: 1-0 Arda Turan (28'), 2-0 Gökhan Gönül (78').
Referee: Pavel Královec (CZE)   Attendance: 40.420
(Stefan Maierhofer missed a penalty in the 85th minute)

29-03-2011   King Baudouin Stadium, Brussels: Belgium – Azerbaijan 4-1 (3-1)
Belgium: Simon Mignolet, Nicolas Lombaerts, Laurent Ciman, Daniel van Buyten (C) (80'
Jelle van Damme), Timmy Simons, Jan Vertonghen, Steven Defour (90' Vadis Odjidja-Ofoe),
Nacer Chadli, Axel Witsel, Jelle Vossen, Mousa Dembélé (64' Eden Hazard). (Coach: Georges
Leekens (BEL)).
Azerbaijan: Kamran Agayev, Vladimir Levin, Mahir Shukurov, Rail Malikov (YC30), Elvin
Mammadov (78' Javid Hüseynov), Aleksandr Chertoganov, Rahid Amirguliyev, Ruslan
Abisov, Rashad Farhad oglu Sadygov (C), Vagif Javadov (76' Vüqar Nadirov), Rauf Aliyev.
(Coach: Hans-Hubert (Berti) Vogts (GER)).
Goals: Belgium: 1-0 Jan Vertonghen (12'), 2-1 Timmy Simons (32' penalty), 3-1 Nacer Chadli
(45'+1'), 4-1 Jelle Vossen (74').
Azerbaijan: 1-1 Ruslan Abisov (16').
Referee: Daniel Stalhammar (SWE)   Attendance: 34.985

03-06-2011   Astana Arena, Astana: Kazakhstan – Azerbaijan 2-1 (0-0)
Kazakhstan: Roman Nesterenko, Mukhtar Mukhtarov, Yuri Logvinenko (65' Mikhail
Rozhkov), Kairat Nurdauletov (C), Heinrich Schmidtgal (YC77), Kazbek Geteriyev, Samat
Smakov, Marat Khayrullin (82' Aleksandr Kirov), Sergei Ostapenko (79' Sergei
Khizhnichenko), Ulan Konysbayev, Sergei Gridin. (Coach: Miroslav Beránek (CZE)).
Azerbaijan: Kamran Agayev, Maksim Medvedev, Vladimir Levin, Rail Malikov, Rashad
Farhad oglu Sadygov (C), Rashad Abulfaz oglu Sadiqov, Afran Ismayilov, Ruslan Abisov,
Javid Hüseynov (61' Vüqar Nadirov), Vagif Javadov, Rauf Aliyev (79' Murad Hüseynov).
(Coach: Hans-Hubert (Berti) Vogts (GER)).
Goals: Kazakhstan: 1-0 Sergei Gridin (57'), 2-1 Sergei Gridin (68').
Azerbaijan: 1-1 Vüqar Nadirov (63').
Referee: Euan Norris (SCO)   Attendance: 6.500

03-06-2011   Ernst Happel Stadion, Vienna: Austria – Germany   1-2 (0-1)
Austria: Christian Gratzei, Paul Scharner (YC80), Emanuel Pogatetz, Florian Klein, Christian
Fuchs (C), Ekrem Dag (66' Zlatko Junuzovic), Stefan Kulovits, Martin Harnik (81' Daniel
Royer), Julian Baumgartlinger (YC29), David Alaba, Erwin Hoffer (88' Marc Janko). (Coach:
Dietmar Constantini (AUT)).
Germany: Manuel Neuer, Marcel Schmelzer, Philipp Lahm (C), Mats Hummels, Arne
Friedrich, Mesut Özil (YC86), Thomas Müller, Toni Kroos (90'+3' Dennis Aogo), Sami
Khedira (69' Holger Badstuber), Lukas Podolski (67' André Schürrle), Mario Gómez García
(YC90+1). (Coach: Joachim Löw (GER)).
Goals: Austria: 1-1 Arne Friedrich (50' own goal).
Germany: 0-1 Mario Gómez García (44'), 1-2 Mario Gómez García (90').
Referee: Massimo Busacca (SUI)   Attendance: 47.500

03-06-2011   King Baudouin Stadium, Brussels: Belgium – Turkey   1-1 (1-1)
Belgium: Simon Mignolet, Nicolas Lombaerts, Vincent Kompany (C), Toby Alderweireld,
Timmy Simons, Axel Witsel, Jan Vertonghen (46' Thomas Vermaelen), Eden Hazard (60'
Dries Mertens), Steven Defour (YC37) (88' Jelle Vossen), Nacer Chadli, Marvin Ogunjimi.
(Coach: Georges Leekens (BEL)).
Turkey: Volkan Demirel, Sabri Sarioglu, Serdar Kesimal, Servet Çetin, Çaglar Birinci, Arda
Turan (85' Semih Sentürk), Selçuk Sahin, Colin Kazim-Richards (YC37), Selçuk Inan (78'
Mehmet Topal), Emre Belözoglu (C), Burak Yilmaz (76' Mehmet Ekici). (Coach: Guus
Hiddink (HOL)).
Goals: Belgium: 1-0 Marvin Ogunjimi (4').
Turkey: 1-1 Burak Yilmaz (22').
Referee: Nicola Rizzoli (ITA)   Attendance: 44.185
(Axel Witsel missed a penalty in the 75th minute)

07-06-2011   Tofiq Bakhramov Stadium, Baku: Azerbaijan – Germany   1-3 (0-2)
Azerbaijan: Kamran Agayev, Vurgun Hüseynov, Elnur Allahverdiyev, Rail Malikov, Rashad
Farhad oglu Sadygov (C), Afran Ismayilov (57' Arif Isayev), Aleksandr Chertoganov (86'
Rashad Abulfaz oglu Sadiqov), Rahid Amirguliyev, Ruslan Abisov, Vüqar Nadirov (YC64),
Vagif Javadov (71' Murad Hüseynov). (Coach: Hans-Hubert (Berti) Vogts (GER)).
Germany: Manuel Neuer, Philipp Lahm (C), Mats Hummels, Benedikt Höwedes (YC22),
Holger Badstuber, Dennis Aogo, Mesut Özil (81' Mario Götze), Thomas Müller (88' Lewis
Holtby), Toni Kroos, Lukas Podolski (75' André Schürrle), Mario Gómez García. (Coach:
Joachim Löw (GER)).
Goals: Azerbaijan: 1-2 Murad Hüseynov (89').
Germany: 0-1 Mesut Özil (29'), 0-2 Mario Gómez García (40'), 1-3 André Schürrle (90'+3').
Referee: Michail Koukoulakis (GRE)   Attendance: 29.858

195

02-09-2011   Tofiq Bakhramov Stadium, Baku: Azerbaijan – Belgium 1-1 (0-0)
Azerbaijan: Kamran Agayev, Vurgun Hüseynov, Elnur Allahverdiyev (YC70), Mahir
Shukurov, Rashad Farhad oglu Sadygov (C), Agil Nabiyev (YC55), Afran Ismayilov (58'
Elvin Mammadov (YC82)), Aleksandr Chertoganov (83' Branimir Subasic), Ruslan Abisov
(63' Rahid Amirguliyev), Vagif Javadov, Rauf Aliyev. (Coach: Hans-Hubert (Berti) Vogts
(GER)).
Belgium: Simon Mignolet, Nicolas Lombaerts (YC77), Vincent Kompany (C) (YC30), Toby
Alderweireld, Timmy Simons, Dries Mertens, Eden Hazard, Marouane Fellaini (YC41), Axel
Witsel, Jan Vertonghen, Romelu Lukaku (61' Igor de Camargo). (Coach: Georges Leekens
(BEL)).
Goals: Azerbaijan: 1-1 Rauf Aliyev (86').
Belgium: 0-1 Timmy Simons (55' penalty).
Referee: Lee William Probert (ENG)   Attendance: 9.300

02-09-2011   Türk Telekom Arena, Istanbul: Turkey – Kazakhstan 2-1 (1-0)
Turkey: Volkan Demirel, Sabri Sarioglu (YC29), Egemen Korkmaz, Serdar Kesimal, Hakan
Balta, Arda Turan (YC79), Colin Kazim-Richards (82' Umut Bulut), Selçuk Inan (RC90+2),
Mehmet Ekici (51' Selçuk Sahin), Emre Belözoglu (C) (60' Gökhan Töre), Burak Yilmaz.
(Coach: Guus Hiddink (HOL)).
Kazakhstan: Aleksandr Mokin (YC90+1), Mukhtar Mukhtarov, Yuri Logvinenko (YC76),
Aleksandr Kirov, Kairat Nurdauletov (C), Mark Gorman, Marat Shakhmetov (82' Maksat
Bayzhanov), Heinrich Schmidtgal, Marat Khayrullin (67' Sergei Ostapenko), Ulan
Konysbayev (86' Tanat Nuserbayev (YC90+6)), Sergei Gridin. (Coach: Miroslav Beránek
(CZE)).
Goals: Turkey: 1-0 Burak Yilmaz (31'), 2-1 Arda Turan (90'+6').
Kazakhstan: 1-1 Ulan Konysbayev (55').
Referee: Clément Turpin (FRA)   Attendance: 47.756
(Burak Yilmaz missed a penalty in the 62nd minute)

02-09-2011   Arena AufSchalke, Gelsenkirchen: Germany – Austria 6-2 (3-1)
Germany: Manuel Neuer, Philipp Lahm (C), Mats Hummels, Benedikt Höwedes (46' Jérôme
Boateng), Holger Badstuber, Mesut Özil, Thomas Müller, Toni Kroos (85' Mario Götze),
Bastian Schweinsteiger, Lukas Podolski (73' André Schürrle), Miroslav Klose. (Coach:
Joachim Löw (GER)).
Austria: Christian Gratzei, Franz Schiemer, Emanuel Pogatez, Florian Klein, Christian Fuchs
(C), Ekrem Dag, Daniel Royer (73' Erwin Hoffer), Martin Harnik, Julian Baumgartlinger,
Marko Arnautovic, David Alaba. (Coach: Dietmar Constantini (AUT)).
Goals: Germany: 1-0 Miroslav Klose (8'), 2-0 Mesut Özil (23'), 3-0 Lukas Podolski (28'), 4-1
Mesut Özil (47'), 5-2 André Schürrle (83'), 6-2 Mario Götze (88').
Austria: 3-1 Marko Arnautovic (42'), 4-2 Martin Harnik (51').
Referee: Paolo Tagliavento (ITA)   Attendance: 53.313

06-09-2011   Tofiq Bakhramor Stadium, Baku: Azerbaijan – Kazakhstan   3-2 (0-1)
Azerbaijan: Kamran Agayev, Mahir Shukurov (YC88), Vurgun Hüseynov, Rahid Amirguliyev,
Rashad Farhad oglu Sadygov (C), Agil Nabiyev (13' Sasa Yunisoglu), Afran Ismayilov (87'
Ruslan Abisov), Aleksandr Chertoganov (46' Branimir Subasic), Ufuk Budak, Rauf Aliyev,
Vagif Javadov. (Coach: Hans-Hubert (Berti) Vogts (GER)).
Kazakhstan: Aleksandr Mokin, Aleksandr Kirov, Mikhail Rozhkov (77' Vitali Yevstigneyev),
Yuri Logvinenko (YC50), Mark Gorman (YC78), Kairat Nurdauletov (C), Marat Shakhmetov
(70' Serikzhan Muzhikov), Zhambyl Kukeyev (59' Marat Khayrullin), Sergei Gridin, Sergei
Ostapenko, Ulan Konysbayev. (Coach: Miroslav Beránek (CZE)).
Goals: Azerbaijan: 1-1 Rauf Aliyev (53'), 2-1 Mahir Shukurov (62' penalty), 3-1 Vagif
Javadov (68').
Kazakhstan: 0-1 Sergei Ostapenko (20'), 3-2 Vitali Yevstigneyev (77').
Referee: Anders Hermansen (DEN)   Attendance: 9.112

06-09-2011   Ernst Happel Stadion, Vienna: Austria – Turkey   0-0
Austria: Pascal Grünwald (YC90), Christian Fuchs (C), Ekrem Dag, Franz Schiemer, Paul
Scharner, Emanuel Pogatetz, Daniel Royer (67' Erwin Hoffer), Julian Baumgartlinger, Marko
Arnautovic (90'+3' Stefan Maierhofer), David Alaba, Martin Harnik. (Coach: Dietmar
Constantini (AUT)).
Turkey: Volkan Demirel, Servet Çetin (C), Hakan Balta, Sabri Sarioglu, Egemen Korkmaz,
Arda Turan, Mehmet Topal, Selçuk Sahin, Yekta Kurtulus (YC51), Umut Bulut, Burak Yilmaz
(YC77) (90'+3' Gökhan Töre). (Coach: Guus Hiddink (HOL)).
Referee: Alberto Undiano Mallenco (ESP)   Attendance: 47.500
(Arda Turan missed a penalty in the 90+1 minute)

07-10-2011   Dalga Stadium, Baku: Azerbaijan – Austria   1-4 (0-1)
Azerbaijan: Kamran Agayev, Elnur Allahverdiyev, Sasa Yunisoglu (RC27), Vurgun
Hüseynov, Ruslan Abisov, Rashad Abulfaz oglu Sadiqov (46' Rahid Amirguliyev), Rashad
Farhad oglu Sadygov (C), Afran Ismayilov, Ufuk Budak, Rauf Aliyev (YC78), Vagif Javadov
(57' Vüqar Nadirov). (Coach: Hans-Hubert (Berti) Vogts (GER)).
Austria: Pascal Grünwald, Ekrem Dag, Paul Scharner, Sebastian Prödl, Christian Fuchs,
Aleksandar Dragovic, Andreas Ivanschitz (73' Daniel Royer), Julian Baumgartlinger (YC22),
Marko Arnautovic (66' Zlatko Juzunovic), David Alaba (YC86), Marc Janko (C) (88' Philipp
Hosiner). (Coach: Willibald (Willi) Ruttensteiner (AUT)).
Goals: Azerbaijan: 1-3 Vüqar Nadirov (74').
Austria: 0-1 Andreas Ivanschitz (34'), 0-2 Marc Janko (52'), 0-3 Marc Janko (62'), 1-4 Zlatko
Juzunovic (90'+1').
Referee: Stéphan Studer (SUI)   Attendance: 6.000

07-10-2011   Türk Telekom Arena, Istanbul: Turkey – Germany   1-3 (0-1)
Turkey: Volkan Demirel, Sabri Sarioglu, Egemen Korkmaz, Gökhan Gönül, Servet Çetin,
Hakan Balta, Arda Turan (70' Colin Kazim-Richards), Mehmet Aurélio (86' Umut Bulut),
Selçuk Inan (46' Gökhan Töre), Hamit Altintop (C) (YC61), Burak Yilmaz. (Coach: Guus
Hiddink (HOL)).
Germany: Manuel Neuer, Per Mertesacker, Philipp Lahm (C), Jérôme Boateng (73' Benedikt
Höwedes), Holger Badstuber (YC55), Bastian Schweinsteiger, Thomas Müller, Sami Khedira,
Mario Götze (90' Marco Reus), Lukas Podolski (62' André Schürrle), Mario Gómez García.
(Coach: Joachim Löw (GER)).
Goals: Turkey: 1-2 Hakan Balta (79').
Germany: 0-1 Mario Gómez García (35'), 0-2 Thomas Müller (66'), 1-3 Bastian
Schweinsteiger (86' penalty).
Referee: Martin Atkinson (ENG)   Attendance: 49.532

07-10-2011   King Baudouin Stadium, Brussels: Belgium – Kazakhstan   4-1 (2-0)
Belgium: Simon Mignolet, Vincent Kompany (C), Laurent Ciman, Daniel van Buyten (YC67), Timmy Simons (75' Steven Defour), Jan Vertonghen, Axel Witsel, Dries Mertens, Eden Hazard (63' Vadis Odjidja-Ofoe), Igor de Camargo (73' Marvin Ogunjimi), Mousa Dembélé. (Coach: Georges Leekens (BEL)).
Kazakhstan: Vladimir Loginovski, Mikhail Rozhkov, Mukhtar Mukhtarov, Nurtas Kurgulin (RC59), Aleksandr Kirov, Vitali Yevstigneyev, Zhambyl Kukeyev (61' Kairat Nurdauletov), Andrei Karpovich (C) (YC40) (75' Marat Shakhmetov), Serikzhan Muzhikov, Daurenbek Tazhimbetov (57' Sergei Ostapenko), Sergei Khizhnichenko. (Coach: Miroslav Beránek (CZE)).
Goals: Belgium: 1-0 Timmy Simons (40' penalty), 2-0 Eden Hazard (43'), 3-0 Vincent Kompany (49'), 4-0 Marvin Ogunjimi (84').
Kazakhstan: 4-1 Kairat Nurdauletov (86' penalty).
Referee: Milorad Mazic (SRB)   Attendance: 29.758

11-10-2011   Astana Arena, Astana: Kazakhstan – Austria   0-0
Kazakhstan: Andrei Sidelnikov, Mikhail Rozhkov, Mukhtar Mukhtarov, Aleksandr Kirov, Kairat Nurdauletov (C), Mark Gorman (YC35) (77' Vitali Yevstigneyev), Heinrich Schmidtgal (YC90+1), Azat Nurgaliyev (46' Serikzhan Muzhikov), Marat Khayrullin, Sergei Ostapenko (YC86), Sergei Gridin. (Coach: Miroslav Beránek (CZE)).
Austria: Pascal Grünwald, Paul Scharner, Sebastian Prödl, Christian Fuchs, Aleksandar Dragovic, Ekrem Dag, Stefan Kulovits (74' Veli Kavlak), Andreas Ivanschitz (66' Zlatko Juzunovic), Marko Arnautovic (83' Stefan Maierhofer), David Alaba, Marc Janko (C). (Coach: Willibald (Willi) Ruttensteiner (AUT)).
Referee: Hannes Kaasik (EST)   Attendance: 11.000

11-10-2011   Esprit Arena, Düsseldorf: Germany – Belgium   3-1 (2-0)
Germany: Manuel Neuer, Per Mertesacker, Philipp Lahm (C) (84' Ilkay Gündogan), Mats Hummels, Benedikt Höwedes, Mesut Özil, Thomas Müller (71' Marco Reus), Toni Kroos, Sami Khedira (YC76), André Schürrle, Mario Gómez García (76' Jeronimo Maria Barreto Claudemir da Silva "CACAU"). (Coach: Joachim Löw (GER)).
Belgium: Simon Mignolet, Nicolas Lombaerts, Vincent Kompany (C), Laurent Ciman, Timmy Simons, Axel Witsel (YC84), Jan Vertonghen, Eden Hazard, Marouane Fellaini, Marvin Ogunjimi (46' Romelu Lukaku), Mousa Dembélé (65' Dries Mertens). (Coach: Georges Leekens (BEL)).
Goals: Germany: 1-0 Mesut Özil (30'), 2-0 André Schürrle (33'), 3-0 Mario Gómez García (48').
Belgium: 3-1 Marouane Fellaini (86').
Referee: Svein Oddvar Moen (NOR)   Attendance: 48.483

11-10-2011   Türk Telekom Arena, Istanbul: Turkey – Azerbaijan   1-0 (0-0)
Turkey: Sinan Bolat, Gökhan Zan, Sabri Sarioglu, Egemen Korkmaz, Hakan Balta, Arda Turan, Mehmet Topal, Colin Kazim-Richards (58' Selçuk Inan), Emre Belözoglu (C) (78' Gökhan Töre), Hamit Altintop, Burak Yilmaz (88' Umut Bulut). (Coach: Guus Hiddink (HOL)).
Azerbaijan: Kamran Agayev, Mahir Shukurov, Vladimir Levin, Vurgun Hüseynov, Rashad Farhad oglu Sadygov (C), Afran Ismayilov (46' Elvin Mammadov, 85' Arif Isayev), Aleksandr Chertoganov, Ufuk Budak (90'+3' Rahid Amirguliyev), Ruslan Abisov, Branimir Subasic, Vüqar Nadirov. (Coach: Hans-Hubert (Berti) Vogts (GER)).
Goal: Turkey: 1-0 Burak Yilmaz (60').
Referee: Peter Rasmussen (DEN)   Attendance: 32.174

198

GROUP B

03-09-2010	Yerevan	Armenia – Republic of Ireland	0-1 (0-0)
03-09-2010	Andorra la Vella	Andorra – Russia	0-2 (0-1)
03-09-2010	Bratislava	Slovakia – Macedonia	1-0 (0-0)
07-09-2010	Moscow	Russia – Slovakia	0-1 (0-1)
07-09-2010	Skopje	Macedonia – Armenia	2-2 (1-1)
07-09-2010	Dublin	Republic of Ireland – Andorra	3-1 (2-1)
08-10-2010	Yerevan	Armenia – Slovakia	3-1 (1-1)
08-10-2010	Andorra la Vella	Andorra – Macedonia	0-2 (0-1)
08-10-2010	Dublin	Republic of Ireland – Russia	2-3 (0-2)
12-10-2010	Yerevan	Armenia – Andorra	4-0 (3-0)
12-10-2010	Skopje	Macedonia – Russia	0-1 (0-1)
12-10-2010	Zilina	Slovakia – Republic of Ireland	1-1 (1-1)
26-03-2011	Yerevan	Armenia – Russia	0-0
26-03-2011	Andorra la Vella	Andorra – Slovakia	0-1 (0-1)
26-03-2011	Dublin	Republic of Ireland – Macedonia	2-1 (2-1)
04-06-2011	Saint Petersburg	Russia – Armenia	3-1 (1-1)
04-06-2011	Bratislava	Slovakia – Andorra	1-0 (0-0)
04-06-2011	Skopje	Macedonia – Republic of Ireland	0-2 (0-2)
02-09-2011	Andorra la Vella	Andorra – Armenia	0-3 (0-1)
02-09-2011	Moscow	Russia – Macedonia	1-0 (1-0)
02-09-2011	Dublin	Republic of Ireland – Slovakia	0-0
06-09-2011	Moscow	Russia – Republic of Ireland	0-0
06-09-2011	Skopje	Macedonia – Andorra	1-0 (0-0)
06-09-2011	Zilina	Slovakia – Armenia	0-4 (0-0)
07-10-2011	Yerevan	Armenia – Macedonia	4-1 (2-0)
07-10-2011	Zilina	Slovakia – Russia	0-1 (0-0)
07-10-2011	Andorra la Vella	Andorra – Republic of Ireland	0-2 (0-2)
11-10-2011	Moscow	Russia – Andorra	6-0 (4-0)
11-10-2011	Dublin	Republic of Ireland – Armenia	2-1 (1-0)
11-10-2011	Skopje	Macedonia – Slovakia	1-1 (0-0)

FINAL STANDING

Pos	Team	Pld	W	D	L	GF	GA	GD	Pts
1	Russia	10	7	2	1	17	4	+13	23
2	Republic of Ireland	10	6	3	1	15	7	+8	21
3	Armenia	10	5	2	3	22	10	+12	17
4	Slovakia	10	4	3	3	7	10	-3	15
5	Macedonia	10	2	2	6	8	14	-6	8
6	Andorra	10	0	0	10	1	25	-24	0

Russia qualified for the Final Tournament in Poland and Ukraine.

Republic of Ireland qualified for the play-offs

03-09-2010   Hanrapetakan Stadium, Yerevan: Armenia – Republic of Ireland   0-1 (0-0)
Armenia: Roman Berezovski, Artak Yedigaryan (YC62) (71' Hovhannes Hambardzumyan),
Robert Arzumanyan, Ararat Arakelyan, Artur Yedigaryan (68' Davit Manoyan), Sargis
Hovsepyan (C), Levon Pachajyan, Karlen Mkrtchyan, Henrikh Mkhitaryan, Edgar Malakyan
(79' Edgar Manucharyan), Yura Movsisyan. (Coach: Vardan Razmik Minasyan (ARM)).
Republic of Ireland: Shay Given, Sean St Ledger, John O'Shea, Richard Dunne, Glenn Whelan
(YC88), Liam Lawrence, Kevin Kilbane, Paul Green, Aiden McGeady (68' Keith Fahey),
Robbie Keane (C) (85' Andrew (Andy) Keogh), Kevin Doyle. (Coach: Giovanni Luciano
Giuseppe Trapattoni (ITA)).
Goal: Republic of Ireland: 0-1 Keith Fahey (76').
Referee: Zsolt Szabó (HUN)   Attendance: 8.600

03-09-2010   Estadi Comunal, Andorra la Vella: Andorra – Russia   0-2 (0-1)
Andorra: Josep Antonio Gómes Moreira, Jordi Rubio Gómez (57' Iván Lorenzo Roncero),
Cristian Martínez Alejo (YC66), Marc Bernaus Cano, Ildefons Lima Solà (C) (YC26), Márcio
Vieira de Vasconcelos, Marc Pujol Pons (YC28) (88' Daniel Mejías Hurtado), Jose Manuel
Díaz "Josep" Ayala (YC20), Fernando José Silva Garcia, Sergi Moreno Marín (76' Manolo
"Manel" Jiménez Soria), Sebastián Gómez Pérez. (Coach: Jesús Luis Álvarez de Eulate
Güergue "Koldo" (AND)).
Russia: Igor Akinfeev, Sergei Ignashevich, Vasili Berezutski, Aleksandr Anyukov, Igor
Semshov, Konstantin Zyryanov, Roman Shirokov, Vladimir Bystrov (60' Alan Dzagoev),
Diniyar Bilyaletdinov (YC75), Pavel Pogrebnyak (85' Roman Pavlyuchenko), Andrey
Arshavin (C). (Coach: Dick Nicolaas Advocaat (HOL)).
Goal: Russia: 0-1 Pavel Pogrebnyak (14'), 0-2 Pavel Pogrebnyak (64' penalty).
Referee: Marco Borg (MLT)   Attendance: 1.100

03-09-2010   Stadión Pasienky, Bratislava: Slovakia – Macedonia   1-0 (0-0)
Slovakia: Ján Mucha, Martin Skrtel (YC81), Peter Pekarík (90' Jakub Sylvestr), Tomás
Hubocan, Kornel Saláta (76' Juraj Kucka), Vladimír Weiss (61' Erik Jendrisek), Zdeno Strba,
Marek Sapara, Marek Hamsík (C), Miroslav Stoch (YC86), Filip Holosko. (Coach: Vladimír
Weiss (SVK)).
Macedonia: Edin Nuredinovski (YC77), Nikolce Noveski, Igor Mitreski, Vance Sikov
(YC66,YC85), Velice Sumulikoski, Goran Popov, Slavco Georgievski, Filip Despotovski
(YC54) (73' Aleksandar Lazevski), Ivan Trickovski (80' Boban Grncarov), Goran Pandev (C)
(YC86), Ilco Naumoski (61' Stevica Ristic). (Coach: Mirsad Jonuz (MCD)).
Goal: Slovakia: 1-0 Filip Holosko (90'+1').
Referee: Claudio Circhetta (SUI)   Attendance: 5.980

07-09-2010   Lokomotiv Stadium, Moscow: Russia – Slovakia   0-1 (0-1)
Russia: Igor Akinfeev, Sergei Ignashevich (81' Diniyar Bilyaletdinov), Vasili Berezutski,
Aleksandr Anyukov, Igor Semshov (61' Vladimir Bystrov), Konstantin Zyryanov, Yuri
Zhirkov (YC33), Roman Shirokov, Alan Dzagoev, Pavel Pogrebnyak (71' Roman
Pavlyuchenko), Andrey Arshavin (C). (Coach: Dick Nicolaas Advocaat (HOL)).
Slovakia: Ján Mucha, Radoslav Zabavník, Martin Skrtel, Tomás Hubocan, Kornel Saláta,
Zdeno Strba, Juraj Kucka (YC38) (58' Erik Jendrisek), Miroslav Karhan (73' Marek Sapara),
Marek Hamsík (C), Miroslav Stoch (90'+2' Mário Pecalka), Filip Holosko. (Coach: Vladimír
Weiss (SVK)).
Goal: Slovakia: 0-1 Miroslav Stoch (27').
Referee: Frank de Bleeckere (BEL)   Attendance: 27.052

200

07-09-2010   Philip II Arena, Skopje: Macedonia – Armenia   2-2 (1-1)
Macedonia: Edin Nuredinovski, Aleksandar Todorovski, Nikolce Noveski, Igor Mitreski, Velice Sumulikoski, Goran Popov, Mario Gjurovski (YC42) (75' Baze Ilijoski), Slavco Georgievski (67' Filip Despotovski), Ivan Trickovski, Stevica Ristic (62' Ilco Naumoski (YC67)), Goran Pandev (C). (Coach: Mirsad Jonuz (MCD)).
Armenia: Roman Berezovski, Artak Yedigaryan, Robert Arzumanyan, Ararat Arakelyan (YC67), Sargis Hovsepyan (C), Levon Pachajyan (70' Artur Yedigaryan), Karlen Mkrtchyan (YC63) (90'+2' Hrayr Mkoyan), Henrikh Mkhitaryan, Davit Manoyan, Edgar Malakyan (60' Edgar Manucharyan), Yura Movsisyan (YC77). (Coach: Vardan Razmik Minasyan (ARM)).
Goals: Macedonia: 1-1 Mario Gjurovski (42'), 2-2 Ilco Naumoski (90'+6' penalty).
Armenia: 0-1 Yura Movsisyan (41'), 1-2 Edgar Manucharyan (90'+1').
Referee: Espen Berntsen (NOR)   Attendance: 9.000

07-09-2010   Lansdowne Road, Dublin: Republic of Ireland – Andorra   3-1 (2-1)
Republic of Ireland: Shay Given, Sean St Ledger, John O'Shea (75' Stephen Kelly), Richard Dunne (YC62), Glenn Whelan (61' Darron Gibson), Liam Lawrence, Kevin Kilbane, Paul Green, Aiden McGeady, Robbie Keane (C), Kevin Doyle (82' Andrew (Andy) Keogh). (Coach: Giovanni Luciano Giuseppe Trapattoni (ITA)).
Andorra: Josep Antonio Gómes Moreira, Cristian Martínez Alejo, Jordi Escura Aixas, Marc Bernaus Cano, Ildefons Lima Solà (C) (YC34), Márcio Vieira de Vasconcelos, Marc Pujol Pons (86' Óscar Masand Sonejee), Jose Manuel Díaz "Josep" Ayala (71' Xavier "Xavi" Andorrà Julià), Fernando José Silva Garcia (YC31), Sergi Moreno Marín (YC58) (59' Manolo "Manel" Jiménez Soria), Sebastián Gómez Pérez. (Coach: Jesús Luis Álvarez de Eulate Güergue "Koldo" (AND)).
Goals: Republic of Ireland: 1-0 Kevin Kilbane (15'), 2-0 Kevin Doyle (41'), 3-1 Robbie Keane (54').
Andorra: 2-1 Cristian Martínez Alejo (45').
Referee: Leontios Trattou (CYP)   Attendance: 40.283

08-10-2010   Hanrapetakan Stadium, Yerevan: Armenia – Slovakia   3-1 (1-1)
Armenia: Roman Berezovski, Artak Yedigaryan, Robert Arzumanyan (79' Ararat Arakelyan), Sargis Hovsepyan (C), Levon Pachajyan (46' Edgar Manucharyan), Karlen Mkrtchyan (YC19), Henrikh Mkhitaryan, Hrayr Mkoyan, Gevorg Ghazaryan, Yura Movsisyan, Marcos Piñeiro Pizzelli (72' Artur Yedigaryan). (Coach: Vardan Razmik Minasyan (ARM)).
Slovakia: Ján Mucha, Radoslav Zabavník (YC68) (81' Filip Sebo), Martin Skrtel (YC18), Peter Pekarík, Kornel Saláta, Vladimír Weiss, Kamil Kopúnek (YC48) (57' Juraj Kucka), Miroslav Karhan, Marek Hamsík (C), Miroslav Stoch (57' Filip Holosko), Stanislav Sesták. (Coach: Vladimír Weiss (SVK)).
Goals: Armenia: 1-0 Yura Movsisyan (23'), 2-1 Gevorg Ghazaryan (50'), 3-1 Henrikh Mkhitaryan (89').
Slovakia: 1-1 Vladimír Weiss (37').
Referee: Daniele Orsato (ITA)   Attendance: 7.500

08-10-2010   Estadi Comunal, Andorra la Vella: Andorra – Macedonia   0-2 (0-1)
Andorra: Josep Antonio Gómes Moreira, Cristian Martínez Alejo (74' Manolo "Manel" Jiménez Soria), Jordi Escura Aixas (C) (YC44), Marc Bernaus Cano, Márcio Vieira de Vasconcelos, Marc Vales González, Daniel Mejías Hurtado (62' Iván Lorenzo Roncero), Jose Manuel Díaz "Josep" Ayala (86' Samir Bousenine el Mourabit), Sebastián Gómez Pérez, Fernando José Silva Garcia, Sergi Moreno Marín. (Coach: Jesús Luis Álvarez de Eulate Güergue "Koldo" (AND)).
Macedonia: Edin Nuredinovski, Nikolce Noveski, Igor Mitreski, Vlade Lazarevski, Vance Sikov, Velice Sumulikoski (C) (83' Boban Grncarov), Slavco Georgievski (34' Mario Gjurovski), Filip Despotovski, Ivan Trickovski, Stevica Ristic, Ilco Naumoski (73' Agim Ibraimi). (Coach: Mirsad Jonuz (MCD)).
Goals: Macedonia: 0-1 Ilco Naumoski (42'), 0-2 Vance Sikov (60').
Referee: Gediminas Mazeika (LIT)   Attendance: 550

08-10-2010   Aviva Stadium, Dublin: Republic of Ireland – Russia   2-3 (0-2)
Republic of Ireland: Shay Given, Sean St Ledger (YC32), John O'Shea, Richard Dunne, Glenn Whelan (66' Darron Gibson), Liam Lawrence (62' Shane Long), Kevin Kilbane, Paul Green, Aiden McGeady, Robbie Keane (C), Kevin Doyle (YC57) (71' Keith Fahey). (Coach: Giovanni Luciano Giuseppe Trapattoni (ITA)).
Russia: Igor Akinfeev, Sergei Ignashevich, Vasili Berezutski, Aleksandr Anyukov (YC60), Konstantin Zyryanov (68' Igor Semshov), Yuri Zhirkov, Roman Shirokov, Alan Dzagoev (85' Aleksei Berezutski (YC89)), Andrey Arshavin (C), Aleksandr Kerzhakov (80' Pavel Pogrebnyak), Igor Denisov (YC27). (Coach: Dick Nicolaas Advocaat (HOL)).
Goals: Republic of Ireland:1-3 Robbie Keane (72' penalty), 2-3 Shane Long (78').
Russia: 0-1 Aleksandr Kerzhakov (11'), 0-2 Alan Dzagoev (29'), 0-3 Roman Shirokov (50').
Referee: Kevin Bernie Raymond Blom (HOL)   Attendance: 50.411

12-10-2010   Hanrapetakan Stadium, Yerevan: Armenia – Andorra   4-0 (3-0)
Armenia: Roman Berezovski, Artak Yedigaryan, Robert Arzumanyan, Sargis Hovsepyan (C), Artur Yedigaryan, Henrikh Mkhitaryan, Hrayr Mkoyan, Edgar Manucharyan, Gevorg Ghazaryan (67' Edgar Malakyan), Yura Movsisyan (53' Hovhannes Goharyan), Marcos Piñeiro Pizzelli (83' Artur Yuspashyan). (Coach: Vardan Razmik Minasyan (ARM)).
Andorra: Josep Antonio Gómes Moreira, Jordi Escura Aixas, Marc Bernaus Cano, Cristian Martínez Alejo (87' Jordi Rubio Gómez), Ildefons Lima Solà (C) (YC61), Jose Manuel Díaz "Josep" Ayala, Márcio Vieira de Vasconcelos (YC68), Marc Vales González (64' Xavier "Xavi" Andorrà Julià (YC74)), Sebastián Gómez Pérez, Fernando José Silva Garcia (YC58), Sergi Moreno Marín (51' Manolo "Manel" Jiménez Soria). (Coach: Jesús Luis Álvarez de Eulate Güergue "Koldo" (AND)).
Goals: Armenia: 1-0 Gevorg Ghazaryan (4'), 2-0 Henrikh Mkhitaryan (16'), 3-0 Yura Movsisyan (33'), 4-0 Marcos Piñeiro Pizzelli (52').
Referee: Tomasz Mikulski (POL)   Attendance: 11.000

202

12-10-2010   Philip II Arena, Skopje: Macedonia – Russia 0-1 (0-1)
Macedonia: Edin Nuredinovski, Nikolce Noveski (YC22), Igor Mitreski, Aleksandar Lazevski, Vance Sikov (YC36), Velice Sumulikoski (C), Agim Ibraimi (49' Stevica Ristic), Mario Gjurovski (79' Armend Alimi), Filip Despotovski (78' Slavco Georgievski), Ivan Trickovski, Ilco Naumoski. (Coach: Mirsad Jonuz (MCD)).
Russia: Igor Akinfeev, Sergei Ignashevich (YC72), Vasili Berezutski, Aleksandr Anyukov (YC57), Konstantin Zyryanov (YC50), Yuri Zhirkov, Roman Shirokov, Alan Dzagoev (61' Aleksei Berezutski), Andrey Arshavin (C) (81' Vladimir Bystrov), Aleksandr Kerzhakov (79' Pavel Pogrebnyak), Igor Denisov. (Coach: Dick Nicolaas Advocaat (HOL)).
Goal: Russia: 0-1 Aleksandr Kerzhakov (8').
Referee: Stefan Johannesson (SWE)   Attendance: 10.500
(Ilco Naumoski missed a penalty in the 73rd minute)

12-10-2010   Stadium Pod Dubnom, Zilina: Slovakia – Republic of Ireland 1-1 (1-1)
Slovakia: Ján Mucha (YC45+1), Radoslav Zabavník, Tomás Hubocan (YC18), Ján Durica, Kornel Saláta, Vladimír Weiss (70' Filip Holosko), Juraj Kucka, Miroslav Karhan (YC90+1), Marek Hamsík (C), Stanislav Sesták (YC32) (70' Miroslav Stoch), Erik Jendrisek (84' Tomás Oravec). (Coach: Vladimír Weiss (SVK)).
Republic of Ireland: Shay Given, Sean St Ledger, John O'Shea, Richard Dunne, Glenn Whelan, Kevin Kilbane, Paul Green (42' Darron Gibson), Keith Fahey (71' Andrew (Andy) Keogh), Aiden McGeady, Shane Long, Robbie Keane (C). (Coach: Giovanni Luciano Giuseppe Trapattoni (ITA)).
Goals: Slovakia: 1-1 Ján Durica (36').
Republic of Ireland: 0-1 Sean St Ledger (16').
Referee: Alberto Undiano Mallenco (ESP)   Attendance: 10.892
(Robbie Keane missed a penalty in the 45+2 minute)

26-03-2011   Hanrapetakan Stdium, Yerevan: Armenia – Russia 0-0
Armenia: Roman Berezovski, Robert Arzumanyan, Sargis Hovsepyan (C), Karlen Mkrtchyan, Henrikh Mkhitaryan, Edgar Malakyan (49' Edgar Manucharyan (YC87)), Hrayr Mkoyan, Levon Hayrapetyan (YC33) (67' Artak Yedigaryan), Gevorg Ghazaryan, Marcos Piñeiro Pizzelli (57' Artur Yedigaryan), Yura Movsisyan. (Coach: Vardan Razmik Minasyan (ARM)).
Russia: Igor Akinfeev, Roman Shishkin (YC63), Sergei Ignashevich, Vasili Berezutski, Konstantin Zyryanov, Yuri Zhirkov, Roman Shirokov, Alan Dzagoev, Andrey Arshavin (C) (90' Diniyar Bilyaletdinov), Aleksandr Kerzhakov (78' Pavel Pogrebnyak), Igor Denisov. (Coach: Dick Nicolaas Advocaat (HOL)).
Referee: Craig Alexander Thomson (SCO)   Attendance: 14.400

26-03-2011   Estadi Comunal, Andorra la Vella: Andorra – Slovakia 0-1 (0-1)
Andorra: Josep Antonio Gómes Moreira, Jordi Rubio Gómez, Cristian Martínez Alejo, Emili Josep García Miramontes, Marc Bernaus Cano, Ildefons Lima Solà, Marc Vales González, Manolo "Manel" Jiménez Soria (C) (YC58) (87' Óscar Masand Sonejee), Jose Manuel Díaz "Josep" Ayala (81' Juli Sánchez Soto), Sebastián Gómez Pérez (72' Márcio Vieira de Vasconcelos), Sergi Moreno Marín (YC35). (Coach: Jesús Luis Álvarez de Eulate Güergue "Koldo" (AND)).
Slovakia: Ján Mucha (YC65), Martin Skrtel, Peter Pekarík, Ján Durica, Filip Luksík, Marek Hamsík (C), Tomás Kóna, Róbert Vittek (78' Juraj Piroska), Miroslav Stoch (YC54) (90' Kornel Saláta), Filip Sebo, Erik Jendrisek (87' Filip Holosko). (Coach: Vladimír Weiss (SVK)).
Goal: Slovakia: 0-1 Filip Sebo (21').
Referee: Menashe Masiah (ISR)   Attendance: 850

203

26-03-2011   Aviva Stadium, Dublin: Republic of Ireland – Macedonia   2-1 (2-1)
Republic of Ireland: Keiren Westwood (YC48), Darren O'Dea, Kevin Foley, Richard Dunne
(YC67), Kevin Kilbane, Darron Gibson (YC70) (77' Keith Fahey), Damien Duff, Glenn
Whelan, Aiden McGeady, Robbie Keane (C) (87' James McCarthy), Kevin Doyle (20' Shane
Long). (Coach: Giovanni Luciano Giuseppe Trapattoni (ITA)).
Macedonia: Edin Nuredinovski, Nikolce Noveski, Boban Grncarov (YC50), Vance Sikov,
Velice Sumulikoski, Goran Popov (YC57), Muhamed Demiri (YC80) (84' Slavco
Georgievski), Darko Tasevski (61' Mario Gjurovski), Goran Pandev (C), Ilco Naumoski (68'
Stevica Ristic), Ivan Trickovski. (Coach: Mirsad Jonuz (MCD)).
Goals: Republic of Ireland: 1-0 Aiden McGeady (2'), 2-0 Robbie Keane (21')
Macedonia: 2-1 Ivan Trickovski (45').
Referee: István Vad II (HUN)   Attendance: 33.200

04-06-2011   Petrovsky Stadium, Saint Petersburg: Russia – Armenia   3-1 (1-1)
Russia: Igor Akinfeev, Vasili Berezutski (YC90+3), Aleksandr Anyukov (75' Renat
Yanbayev), Sergei Ignashevich (YC37), Dmitri Torbinski, Igor Semshov (69' Denis
Glushakov), Konstantin Zyryanov (82' Alan Dzagoev), Yuri Zhirkov, Andrey Arshavin (C),
Roman Pavlyuchenko, Igor Denisov. (Coach: Dick Nicolaas Advocaat (HOL)).
Armenia: Roman Berezovski, Robert Arzumanyan (YC76), Sargis Hovsepyan (C), Henrikh
Mkhitaryan, Levon Pachajyan (YC55) (57' Edgar Manucharyan), Karlen Mkrtchyan (90'
Artak Yedigaryan), Gevorg Ghazaryan, Levon Hayrapetyan, Hrayr Mkoyan (YC87), Marcos
Piñeiro Pizzelli (67' Artur Yedigaryan (YC71)), Yura Movsisyan (YC21). (Coach: Vardan
Razmik Minasyan (ARM)).
Goals: Russia: 1-1 Roman Pavlyuchenko (26'), 2-1 Roman Pavlyuchenko (59'), 3-1 Roman
Pavlyuchenko (73' penalty).
Armenia: 0-1 Marcos Piñeiro Pizzelli (25').
Referee: Stéphane Lannoy (FRA)   Attendance: 18.000

04-06-2011   Stadión Pasienky, Bratislava: Slovakia – Andorra   1-0 (0-0)
Slovakia: Marián Kello, Tomáš Hubocan, Ján Durica, Marek Cech (83' Kornel Saláta), Juraj
Kucka (46' Stanislav Sesták), Miroslav Karhan, Róbert Jez (YC13), Marek Hamsík (C),
Róbert Vittek, Filip Sebo, Filip Holosko (74' Igor Zofcák). (Coach: Vladimír Weiss (SVK)).
Andorra: Josep Antonio Gómes Moreira, Cristian Martínez Alejo, Jordi Rubio Gómez, Emili
Josep García Miramontes, Marc Bernaus Cano, Ildefons Lima Solà, Márcio Vieira de
Vasconcelos, Marc Vales González (YC32), Manolo "Manel" Jiménez Soria (C) (86' Joaquim
Salvat Besora), Jose Manuel Díaz "Josep" Ayala (16' Xavier "Xavi" Andorrà Julià (YC76)),
Fernando José Silva Garcia (63' Sebastián Gómez Pérez). (Coach: Jesús Luis Álvarez de
Eulate Güergue "Koldo" (AND)).
Goal: Slovakia: 1-0 Miroslav Karhan (63').
Referee: Lorenc Jemini (ALB)   Attendance: 4.300

04-06-2011 Philip II Arena, Skopje: Macedonia – Republic of Ireland 0-2 (0-2)
Macedonia: Martin Bogatinov, Nikolce Noveski, Boban Grncarov, Vance Sikov, Velice Sumulikoski, Goran Popov, Filip Despotovski (57' Mario Gjurovski), Muhamed Demiri (72' Dusan Savic), Ivan Trickovski, Goran Pandev (C), Ilco Naumoski (10' Ferhan Hasani). (Coach: Mirsad Jonuz (MCD)).
Republic of Ireland: Shay Given, John O'Shea, Darren O'Dea, Stephen Kelly, Glenn Whelan, Kevin Kilbane, Stephen Hunt, Keith Andrews, Aiden McGeady, Robbie Keane (C), Simon Cox (YC16) (65' Shane Long). (Coach: Giovanni Luciano Giuseppe Trapattoni (ITA)).
Goals: Republic of Ireland: 0-1 Robbie Keane (8'), 0-2 Robbie Keane (37').
Referee: Florian Meyer (GER)   Attendance: 29.500
(Ivan Trickovski missed a penalty in the 41st minute)

02-09-2011 Estadi Comunal, Andorra la Vella: Andorra – Armenia 0-3 (0-1)
Andorra: Josep Antonio Gómes Moreira, Cristian Martínez Alejo, Jordi Rubio Gómez, Emili Josep García Miramontes, Marc Bernaus Cano, Ildefons Lima Solà (C) (RC90+1), Marc Vales González, Marc Pujol Pons (YC27), Jose Manuel Díaz "Josep" Ayala (87' Juli Sánchez Soto), Fernando José Silva Garcia (72' Sebastián Gómez Pérez), Sergi Moreno Marín (81' Márcio Vieira de Vasconcelos). (Coach: Jesús Luis Álvarez de Eulate Güergue "Koldo" (AND)).
Armenia: Roman Berezovski, Sargis Hovsepyan (C), Karlen Mkrtchyan, Henrikh Mkhitaryan, Valeri Aleksanyan, Hrayr Mkoyan, Edgar Manucharyan (78' Edgar Malakyan), Levon Hayrapetyan, Gevorg Ghazaryan (89' Zaven Badoyan), Artur Sarkisov (YC43), Marcos Piñeiro Pizzelli (83' Artur Yedigaryan). (Coach: Vardan Razmik Minasyan (ARM)).
Goals: Armenia: 0-1 Marcos Piñeiro Pizzelli (35'), 0-2 Gevorg Ghazaryan (75'), 0-3 Henrikh Mkhitaryan (90'+2' penalty).
Referee: Aleksandar Kostadinov (BUL)   Attendance: 750

02-09-2011 Luzhniki Stadium, Moscow: Russia – Macedonia 1-0 (1-0)
Russia: Vyacheslav Malafeev, Vasili Berezutski, Aleksei Berezutski, Aleksandr Anyukov, Igor Semshov (46' Roman Pavlyuchenko), Konstantin Zyryanov (60' Dmitri Torbinski), Yuri Zhirkov, Roman Shirokov (YC71), Andrey Arshavin (C), Aleksandr Kerzhakov (YC61) (88' Denis Glushakov), Igor Denisov (YC56). (Coach: Dick Nicolaas Advocaat (HOL)).
Macedonia: Martin Bogatinov, Nikolce Noveski (YC90), Vance Sikov, Daniel Georgievski (66' Ferhan Hasani), Velice Sumulikoski (YC76) (85' Muarem Muarem), Goran Popov, Muhamed Demiri (YC61), Ivan Trickovski, Goran Pandev (C) (YC42,YC90+5), Mirko Ivanovski (75' Aleksandar Trajkovski), Agim Ibraimi. (Coach: John Benjamin Toshack (WAL)).
Goal: Russia: 1-0 Igor Semshov (41').
Referee: Bülent Yildirim (TUR)   Attendance: 31.028

02-09-2011 Aviva Stadium, Dublin: Republic of Ireland – Slovakia 0-0
Republic of Ireland: Shay Given, Stephen Ward, Sean St Ledger (YC87), John O'Shea, Richard Dunne (YC67), Glenn Whelan, Damien Duff, Keith Andrews, Aiden McGeady (85' Stephen Hunt), Robbie Keane (C), Kevin Doyle (64' Simon Cox). (Coach: Giovanni Luciano Giuseppe Trapattoni (ITA)).
Slovakia: Ján Mucha (YC75), Martin Skrtel, Peter Pekarík, Ján Durica, Marek Cech, Vladimír Weiss (86' Erik Jendrisek), Juraj Kucka (YC66) (77' Karim Abdul-Jabbar Guédé), Miroslav Karhan, Marek Hamsík (C), Miroslav Stoch, Filip Holosko (88' Róbert Vittek). (Coach: Vladimír Weiss (SVK)).
Referee: Pedro Proença Oliveira Alves Garcia (POR) Attendance: 35.480

205

06-09-2011   Luzhniki Stadium, Moscow: Russia – Republic of Ireland   0-0
Russia: Vyacheslav Malafeev, Sergei Ignashevich, Vasili Berezutski, Aleksei Berezutski,
Aleksandr Anyukov (YC47), Igor Semshov, Konstantin Zyryanov, Yuri Zhirkov (76' Diniyar
Bilyaletdinov), Roman Shirokov, Andrey Arshavin (C), Aleksandr Kerzhakov (54' Roman
Pavlyuchenko). (Coach: Dick Nicolaas Advocaat (HOL)).
Republic of Ireland: Shay Given, Stephen Ward (YC90), Darren O'Dea, Stephen Kelly,
Richard Dunne (YC74), Glenn Whelan, Damien Duff (67' Stephen Hunt (YC78)), Keith
Andrews, Aiden McGeady, Robbie Keane (C), Kevin Doyle (59' Simon Cox). (Coach:
Giovanni Luciano Giuseppe Trapattoni (ITA)).
Referee: Dr.Felix Brych (GER)   Attendance: 49.515

06-09-2011   Philip II Arena, Skopje: Macedonia – Andorra   1-0 (0-0)
Macedonia: Martin Bogatinov, Daniel Mojsov, Vance Sikov, Daniel Georgievski, Velice
Sumulikoski (C), Goran Popov, Ferhan Hasani (68' Samir Fazli), Ivan Trickovski, Muarem
Muarem (YC17) (77' Muhamedin Huseini (YC90+1)), Mirko Ivanovski (YC24), Agim Ibraimi
(46' Aleksandar Trajkovski). (Coach: John Benjamin Toshack (WAL)).
Andorra: Josep Antonio Gómes Moreira, Cristian Martínez Alejo, Jordi Rubio Gómez (YC17)
(26' Alexandre Ruben Martínez Gutiérrez (YC45+2)), Emili Josep García Miramontes
(YC66), Marc Bernaus Cano, Márcio Vieira de Vasconcelos (83' Marc García Renom), Marc
Vales González (YC89), Jose Manuel Díaz "Josep" Ayala, Óscar Masand Sonejee (C)
(YC45+2), Fernando José Silva Garcia (74' Sebastián Gómez Pérez), Sergi Moreno Marín.
(Coach: Jesús Luis Álvarez de Eulate Güergue "Koldo" (AND)).
Goal: Macedonia: 1-0 Mirko Ivanovski (59').
Referee: Mark Steven Whitby (WAL)   Attendance: 5.000

06-09-2011   Stadium Pod Dubnom, Zilina: Slovakia – Armenia   0-4 (0-0)
Slovakia: Ján Mucha, Martin Skrtel, Peter Pekarík, Ján Durica (YC86), Marek Cech (YC45+4)
(78' Erik Jendrisek), Karim Abdul-Jabbar Guédé (YC52) (55' Róbert Jez), Vladimír Weiss
(71' Stanislav Sesták (YC72)), Miroslav Karhan, Marek Hamsík (C) (YC75), Miroslav Stoch
(YC90+3), Filip Holosko. (Coach: Vladimír Weiss (SVK)).
Armenia: Roman Berezovski, Sargis Hovsepyan (C), Artur Yedigaryan (90'+2' Artur
Yuspashyan), Karlen Mkrtchyan, Henrikh Mkhitaryan, Valeri Aleksanyan, Hrayr Mkoyan
(YC37), Levon Hayrapetyan, Gevorg Ghazaryan, Marcos Piñeiro Pizzelli (YC43) (73' Edgar
Manucharyan), Yura Movsisyan (85' Artur Sarkisov). (Coach: Vardan Razmik Minasyan
(ARM)).
Goals: Armenia: 0-1 Yura Movsisyan (57'), 0-2 Henrikh Mkhitaryan (70'), 0-3 Gevorg
Ghazaryan (80'), 0-4 Artur Sarkisov (90'+1').
Referee: Marcin Borski (POL)   Attendance: 7.238

07-10-2011 Hanrapetakan Stadium, Yerevan: Armenia – Macedonia 4-1 (2-0)
Armenia: Roman Berezovski, Sargis Hovsepyan (C), Artur Yedigaryan, Artur Yuspashyan, Henrikh Mkhitaryan, Valeri Aleksanyan, Karlen Mkrtchyan (YC66) (75' Artur Sarkisov), Levon Hayrapetyan, Gevorg Ghazaryan (83' Edgar Malakyan), Marcos Piñeiro Pizzelli (63' Edgar Manucharyan), Yura Movsisyan. (Coach: Vardan Razmik Minasyan (ARM)).
Macedonia: Martin Bogatinov, Nikolce Noveski, Daniel Georgievski (51' Vlade Lazarevski), Vance Sikov, Muhamed Demiri, Velice Sumulikoski (C) (YC40,YC53), Goran Popov (YC28), Muarem Muarem (46' Mario Gjurovski), Mirko Ivanovski (YC31), Filip Ivanovski (60' Igor Mitreski), Ivan Trickovski. (Coach: John Benjamin Toshack (WAL)).
Goals: Armenia: 1-0 Marcos Piñeiro Pizzelli (28'), 2-0 Henrikh Mkhitaryan (34'), 3-0 Gevorg Ghazaryan (69'), 4-1 Artur Sarkisov (90'+1').
Macedonia: 3-1 Vance Sikov (86').
Referee: Robert Schörgenhofer (AUT)   Attendance: 14.403

07-10-2011 Stadium Pod Dubnom, Zilina: Slovakia – Russia 0-1 (0-0)
Slovakia: Ján Mucha, Peter Pekarík, Tomás Hubocan, Ján Durica, Martin Skrtel (YC83), Juraj Kucka (73' Karim Abdul-Jabbar Guédé), Miroslav Karhan (86' Filip Sebo), Marek Hamsík (C), Filip Holosko (73' Vladimír Weiss), Miroslav Stoch (YC52), Erik Jendrisek. (Coach: Vladimír Weiss (SVK)).
Russia: Vyacheslav Malafeev, Sergei Ignashevich, Vasili Berezutski, Aleksandr Anyukov (YC60), Roman Shirokov, Alan Dzagoev (90'+3' Aleksandr Samedov), Konstantin Zyryanov (YC57), Yuri Zhirkov (90'+4' Aleksei Berezutski), Roman Pavlyuchenko (87' Pavel Pogrebnyak), Andrey Arshavin (C), Igor Denisov. (Coach: Dick Nicolaas Advocaat (HOL)).
Goal: Russia: 0-1 Alan Dzagoev (71').
Referee: Jonas Eriksson (SWE)   Attendance: 10.087

07-10-2011 Estadi Comunal, Andorra la Vella: Andorra – Republic of Ireland 0-2 (0-2)
Andorra: Josep Antonio Gómes Moreira, Alexandre Ruben Martínez Gutiérrez (78' Iván Lorenzo Roncero), Cristian Martínez Alejo (YC19), Emili Josep García Miramontes, Marc Bernaus Cano, Ildefons Lima Solà (C) (81' Óscar Masand Sonejee), Márcio Vieira de Vasconcelos, Marc Pujol Pons (60' Carlos Eduardo "Edu" Peppe Britos), Jose Manuel Díaz "Josep" Ayala (YC67), Fernando José Silva Garcia, Sergi Moreno Marín. (Coach: Jesús Luis Álvarez de Eulate Güergue "Koldo" (AND)).
Republic of Ireland: Shay Given, Stephen Ward (YC31), Sean St Ledger, John O'Shea, Darren O'Dea, Glenn Whelan (65' Keith Fahey), Damien Duff (75' Stephen Hunt), Keith Andrews, Aiden McGeady, Robbie Keane (C), Kevin Doyle (71' Shane Long). (Coach: Giovanni Luciano Giuseppe Trapattoni (ITA)).
Goals: Republic of Ireland: 0-1 Kevin Doyle (8'), 0-2 Aiden McGeady (20').
Referee: Libor Kovarík (CZE)   Attendance: 860

11-10-2011   Luzhniki Stadium, Moscow: Russia – Andorra   6-0 (4-0)
Russia: Vyacheslav Malafeev, Roman Shishkin, Sergei Ignashevich, Vasili Berezutski, Aleksei
Berezutski, Igor Semshov (72' Diniyar Bilyaletdinov), Denis Glushakov (80' Aleksandr
Samedov), Alan Dzagoev, Roman Pavlyuchenko (YC62) (73' Pavel Pogrebnyak), Andrey
Arshavin (C), Igor Denisov (YC74). (Coach: Dick Nicolaas Advocaat (HOL)).
Andorra: Josep Antonio Gómes Moreira, Alexandre Ruben Martínez Gutiérrez, Emili Josep
García Miramontes, Marc Bernaus Cano, Ildefons Lima Solà (C) (YC62), Marc Vales
González, Marc Pujol Pons (YC45+2) (85' Juli Sánchez Soto), Márcio Vieira de Vasconcelos,
Carlos Eduardo "Edu" Peppe Britos (79' Iván Lorenzo Roncero), Sergi Moreno Marín,
Sebastián Gómez Pérez (70' Fernando José Silva Garcia (YC73)). (Coach: Jesús Luis Álvarez
de Eulate Güergue "Koldo" (AND)).
Goals: Russia: 1-0 Alan Dzagoev (5'), 2-0 Sergei Ignashevich (26'), 3-0 Roman Pavlyuchenko
(30'), 4-0 Alan Dzagoev (44'), 5-0 Denis Glushakov (59'), 6-0 Diniyar Bilyaletdinov (78').
Referee: Eli Hacmon (ISR)   Attendance: 38.790

11-10-2011   Aviva Stadium, Dublin: Republic of Ireland – Armenia   2-1 (1-0)
Republic of Ireland: Shay Given (C), Sean St Ledger (YC61), John O'Shea, Stephen Kelly
(YC13), Richard Dunne, Glenn Whelan (76' Keith Fahey), Damien Duff, Keith Andrews,
Aiden McGeady (YC66) (67' Stephen Hunt), Kevin Doyle (YC69,YC81), Simon Cox (80'
Jonathan (Jon) Walters). (Coach: Giovanni Luciano Giuseppe Trapattoni (ITA)).
Armenia: Roman Berezovski (RC26), Sargis Hovsepyan (C), Karlen Mkrtchyan, Henrikh
Mkhitaryan, Edgar Malakyan (28' Arsen Petrosyan (YC44) goalkeeper), Valeri Aleksanyan
(YC64), Hrayr Mkoyan (YC84), Levon Hayrapetyan, Gevorg Ghazaryan (62' Artur Sarkisov),
Marcos Piñeiro Pizzelli (53' Edgar Manucharyan), Yura Movsisyan. (Coach: Vardan Razmik
Minasyan (ARM)).
Goals: Republic of Ireland: 1-0 Valeri Aleksanyan (43' own goal), 2-0 Richard Dunne (59').
Armenia: 2-1 Henrikh Mkhitaryan (62').
Referee: Eduardo Iturralde González (ESP)   Attendance: 45.200

11-10-2011   Philip II Arena, Skopje: Macedonia – Slovakia   1-1 (0-0)
Macedonia: Martin Bogatinov, Nikolce Noveski (C), Daniel Mojsov (YC9), Aleksandar
Lazevski (64' Filip Ivanovski), Vlade Lazarevski, Vance Sikov, Vlatko Gorzdanoski (46'
Robert Petrov), Mario Gjurovski, Muhamed Demiri, Ivan Trickovski, Samir Fazli (84'
Aleksandar Trajkovski). (Coach: John Benjamin Toshack (WAL)).
Slovakia: Ján Mucha, Peter Pekarík, Lubomír Michalík, Tomás Hubocan (46' Marek Cech),
Kornel Saláta, Vladimír Weiss, Juraj Kucka, Róbert Jez (88' Peter Grajciar), Marek Hamsík
(C), Juraj Piroska (87' Filip Holosko), Erik Jendrisek (YC81). (Coach: Vladimír Weiss
(SVK)).
Goals: Macedonia: 1-1 Nikolce Noveski (79').
Slovakia: 0-1 Juraj Piroska (54').
Referee: Tony Chapron (FRA)   Attendance: 4.100

GROUP C

11-08-2010	Tallinn	Estonia – Faroe Islands	2-1 (0-1)
03-09-2010	Tórshavn	Faroe Islands – Serbia	0-3 (0-2)
03-09-2010	Tallinn	Estonia – Italy	1-2 (1-0)
03-09-2010	Maribor	Slovenia – Northern Ireland	0-1 (0-0)
07-09-2010	Belgrade	Serbia – Slovenia	1-1 (0-0)
07-09-2010	Florence	Italy – Faroe Islands	5-0 (3-0)
08-10-2010	Belgrade	Serbia – Estonia	1-3 (0-0)
08-10-2010	Belfast	Northern Ireland – Italy	0-0
08-10-2010	Ljubljana	Slovenia – Faroe Islands	5-1 (2-0)
12-10-2010	Toftir	Faroe Islands – Northern Ireland	1-1 (0-0)
12-10-2010	Tallinn	Estonia – Slovenia	0-1 (0-0)
12-10-2010	Genoa	Italy – Serbia	3-0
25-03-2011	Belgrade	Serbia – Northern Ireland	2-1 (0-1)
25-03-2011	Ljubljana	Slovenia – Italy	0-1 (0-0)
29-03-2011	Tallinn	Estonia – Serbia	1-1 (0-1)
29-03-2011	Belfast	Northern Ireland – Slovenia	0-0
03-06-2011	Toftir	Faroe Islands – Slovenia	0-2 (0-1)
03-06-2011	Modena	Italy – Estonia	3-0 (2-0)
07-06-2011	Toftir	Faroe Islands – Estonia	2-0 (1-0)
10-08-2011	Belfast	Northern Ireland – Faroe Islands	4-0 (1-0)
02-09-2011	Tórshavn	Faroe Islands – Italy	0-1 (0-1)
02-09-2011	Ljubljana	Slovenia – Estonia	1-2 (0-1)
02-09-2011	Belfast	Northern Ireland – Serbia	0-1 (0-0)
06-09-2011	Belgrade	Serbia – Faroe Islands	3-1 (2-1)
06-09-2011	Tallinn	Estonia – Northern Ireland	4-1 (2-1)
06-09-2011	Florence	Italy – Slovenia	1-0 (0-0)
07-10-2011	Belfast	Northern Ireland – Estonia	1-2 (1-0)
07-10-2011	Belgrade	Serbia – Italy	1-1 (1-1)
11-10-2011	Pescara	Italy – Northern Ireland	3-0 (1-0)
11-10-2011	Maribor	Slovenia – Serbia	1-0 (1-0)

FINAL STANDING

Pos	Team	Pld	W	D	L	GF	GA	GD	Pts
1	Italy	10	8	2	0	20	2	+18	26
2	Estonia	10	5	1	4	15	14	+1	16
3	Serbia	10	4	3	3	13	12	+1	15
4	Slovenia	10	4	2	4	11	7	+4	14
5	Northern Ireland	10	2	3	5	9	13	-4	9
6	Faroe Islands	10	1	1	8	6	26	-20	4

Italy qualified for the Final Tournament in Poland and Ukraine.

Estonia qualified for the play-offs

11-08-2010   A.Le Coq Arena, Tallinn: Estonia – Faroe Islands   2-1 (0-1)
Estonia: Sergei Pareiko, Enar Jääger, Alo Bärengrub, Raio Piiroja (C), Dmitri Kruglov (70'
Sander Post), Ragnar Klavan, Aleksandr Dmitrijev, Sander Puri (76' Ats Purje), Konstantin
Vassiljev, Andres Oper (62' Kaimar Saag), Tarmo Kink. (Coach: Tarmo Rüütli (EST)).
Faroe Islands: Gunnar Nielsen (YC40), Jóhan Davidsen, Hendrik Rubeksen, Jónas Tór Næs,
Atli Gregersen, Fródi Benjaminsen (C), Jann Ingi Petersen (85' Bogi Løkin), Christian Holst
(YC21), Jóan Edmundsson (YC36), Jákup á Borg (YC52) (67' Rógvi Poulsen), Símun
Samuelsen (74' Jústinus Hansen). (Coach: Brian Kerr (IRL)).
Goals: Estonia: 1-1 Kaimar Saag (90'+1'), 2-1 Raio Piiroja (90'+3').
Faroe Islands: 0-1 Jóan Edmundsson (28').
Referee: Ante Vucemilovic-Simunovic Jr. (CRO)   Attendance: 5.470

03-09-2010   Tórsvøllur, Tórshavn: Faroe Islands – Serbia   0-3 (0-2)
Faroe Islands: Gunnar Nielsen, Hendrik Rubeksen, Jónas Tór Næs, Atli Gregersen, Jóhan
Davidsen, Jann Ingi Petersen (73' Jústinus Hansen), Christian Holst (79' Arnbjørn Hansen),
Jóan Edmundsson, Fródi Benjaminsen (C), Daniel Udsen (46' Christian Mouritsen), Símun
Samuelsen. (Coach: Brian Kerr (IRL)).
Serbia: Andjelko Djuricic, Nemanja Vidic, Neven Subotic, Antonio Rukavina (YC86), Ivan
Obradovic (YC32) (46' Aleksandar Lukovic), Dejan Stankovic (C) (58' Radosav Petrovic),
Zdravko Kuzmanovic, Milos Krasic, Nikola Zigic, Danko Lazovic (83' Milos Ninkovic),
Milan Jovanovic. (Coach: Radomir Antic (SRB)).
Goals: Serbia: 0-1 Danko Lazovic (14'), 0-2 Dejan Stankovic (18'), 0-3 Nikola Zigic (90'+1').
Referee: Albert (Abby) Toussaint (LUX)   Attendance: 1.847

03-09-2010   A.Le coq Arena, Tallinn: Estonia – Italy   1-2 (1-0)
Estonia: Sergei Pareiko, Taavi Rähn, Raio Piiroja (C) (YC90+7), Dmitri Kruglov (82' Tarmo
Kink), Enar Jääger, Ragnar Klavan (YC85), Martin Vunk (YC56), Sander Puri (77' Ats Purje),
Aleksandr Dmitrijev, Konstantin Vassiljev, Sergei Zenjov (63' Kaimar Saag). (Coach: Tarmo
Rüütli (EST)).
Italy: Salvatore Sirigu, Cristian Molinaro, Mattia Cassani, Giorgio Chiellini, Leonardo
Bonucci, Simone Pepe (60' Fabio Quagliarella), Riccardo Montolivo (75' Angelo Palombo),
Andrea Pirlo (C), Daniele De Rossi, Giampaolo Pazzini, Antonio Cassano (80' Luca
Antonelli). (Coach: Cesare Claudio Prandelli (ITA)).
Goals: Estonia: 1-0 Sergei Zenjov (31').
Italy: 1-1 Antonio Cassano (60'), 1-2 Leonardo Bonucci (63').
Referee: Carlos Velasco Carballo (ESP)   Attendance: 8.600

03-09-2010   Ljudski vrt, Maribor: Slovenia – Northern Ireland   0-1 (0-0)
Slovenia: Samir Handanovic, Miso Brecko, Bostjan Cesar, Matej Mavric, Bojan Jokic,
Aleksandar Radosavljevic, Robert Koren (C), Andraz Kirm (74' Josip Ilicic), Valter Birsa,
Zlatan Ljubijankic (88' Tim Matavz), Milivoje Novakovic (74' Zlatko Dedic). (Coach: Matjaz
Kek (SLO)).
Northern Ireland: Maik Taylor, Craig Cathcart, Chris Baird, Gareth McAuley, Aaron Hughes,
Stephen Craigan (C), Chris Brunt (YC47) (89' Johnny Gorman), Grant McCann (67' Kyle
Lafferty (YC83)), Steven Davis, David Healy (YC26) (67' Corry Evans), Warren Feeney.
(Coach: Nigel Worthington (NIR)).
Goal: Northern Ireland: 0-1 Corry Evans (70').
Referee: Pavel Cristian Balaj (ROM)   Attendance: 12.000

210

07-09-2010   Stadion Crvena Zvezda, Belgrade: Serbia – Slovenia   1-1 (0-0)
Serbia: Andjelko Djuricic, Nemanja Vidic (YC88), Neven Subotic, Antonio Rukavina,
Aleksandar Lukovic (YC58), Zoran Tosic (46' Milos Krasic), Dejan Stankovic (C) (YC14)
(71' Gojko Kacar), Zdravko Kuzmanovic (YC90+4), Nikola Zigic (YC42), Danko Lazovic,
Milan Jovanovic (YC37) (64' Milos Ninkovic). (Coach: Radomir Antic (SRB)).
Slovenia: Samir Handanovic (YC16), Matej Mavric (YC90+2), Bojan Jokic, Miso Brecko,
Bostjan Cesar, Aleksandar Radosavljevic (YC14), Robert Koren (C), Andraz Kirm (YC32)
(89' Dalibor Stevanovic), Valter Birsa (78' Josip Ilicic), Milivoje Novakovic, Zlatko Dedic
(77' Zlatan Ljubijankic). (Coach: Matjaz Kek (SLO)).
Goals: Serbia: 1-1 Nikola Zigic (86').
Slovenia: 0-1 Milivoje Novakovic (63').
Referee: Olegário Manuel Bártolo Faustino Benquerença (POR)   Attendance: 24.028

07-09-2010   Stadio Artemio Franchi, Florence: Italy – Faroe Islands   5-0 (3-0)
Italy: Emiliano Viviano, Lorenzo De Silvestri, Giorgio Chiellini, Leonardo Bonucci, Luca
Antonelli, Riccardo Montolivo, Andrea Pirlo (C), Daniele De Rossi (76' Angelo Palombo),
Alberto Gilardino (59' Giampaolo Pazzini), Giuseppe Rossi (59' Fabio Quagliarella), Antonio
Cassano. (Coach: Cesare Claudio Prandelli (ITA)).
Faroe Islands: Gunnar Nielsen, Atli Gregersen, Jóhan Davidsen (YC7), Egil á Bø, Hendrik
Rubeksen, Jann Ingi Petersen, Bogi Løkin (74' Jónas Tór Næs), Jóan Edmundsson (89' Daniel
Udsen), Fródi Benjaminsen (C), Christian Mouritsen (74' Christian Holst), Símun Samuelsen.
(Coach: Brian Kerr (IRL)).
Goals: Italy: 1-0 Alberto Gilardino (11'), 2-0 Daniele De Rossi (22'), 3-0 Antonio Cassano
(27'), 4-0 Fabio Quagliarella (81'), 5-0 Andrea Pirlo (90').
Referee: Aliaksei Kulbakov (BLS)   Attendance: 19.266

08-10-2010   Stadion FK Partizan, Belgrade: Serbia – Estonia   1-3 (0-0)
Serbia: Vladimir Stojkovic, Nemanja Vidic (YC87), Aleksandar Lukovic, Branislav Ivanovic,
Marko Lomic, Dejan Stankovic (C), Zdravko Kuzmanovic (79' Danko Lazovic (YC90)), Milos
Krasic (YC80), Gojko Kacar (46' Milos Ninkovic), Nikola Zigic, Milan Jovanovic (46' Zoran
Tosic). (Coach: Vladimir Petrovic (SRB)).
Estonia: Sergei Pareiko, Taavi Rähn, Raio Piiroja (C) (YC10), Dmitri Kruglov, Enar Jääger,
Ragnar Klavan, Sander Puri (70' Ats Purje), Aleksandr Dmitrijev (YC53), Konstantin
Vassiljev (YC80), Tarmo Kink (64' Kaimar Saag), Sergei Zenjov (87' Martin Vunk). (Coach:
Tarmo Rüütli (EST)).
Goals: Serbia: 1-0 Nikola Zigic (60').
Estonia: 1-1 Tarmo Kink (63'), 1-2 Konstantin Vassiljev (73'), 1-3 Aleksandar Lukovic
(90'+1' own goal).
Referee: Maxim Viktorovich Layushkin (RUS)   Attendance: 12.000

08-10-2010   Windsor Park, Belfast: Northern Ireland – Italy   0-0
Northern Ireland: Maik Taylor, Gareth McAuley, Aaron Hughes (C), Jonny Evans, Stephen
Craigan, Chris Baird, Grant McCann (80' Corry Evans), Steven Davis, Chris Brunt (71' Niall
McGinn), David Healy (66' Kyle Lafferty), Warren Feeney. (Coach: Nigel Worthington
(NIR)).
Italy: Emiliano Viviano, Domenico Criscito, Mattia Cassani, Giorgio Chiellini, Leonardo
Bonucci, Simone Pepe (84' Giuseppe Rossi), Stefano Mauri (79' Claudio Marchisio), Andrea
Pirlo (C), Daniele De Rossi, Marco Borriello (74' Giampaolo Pazzini), Antonio Cassano.
(Coach: Cesare Claudio Prandelli (ITA)).
Referee: Tony Chapron (FRA)   Attendance: 15.200

211

08-10-2010   Stozice Stadium, Ljubljana: Slovenia – Faroe Islands   5-1 (2-0)
Slovenia: Samir Handanovic, Marko Suler, Bojan Jokic, Miso Brecko, Bostjan Cesar (YC29),
Aleksandar Radosavljevic (59' Armin Bacinovic), Robert Koren (C), Josip Ilicic, Tim Matavz,
Valter Birsa (51' Andraz Kirm), Milivoje Novakovic (73' Zlatko Dedic). (Coach: Matjaz Kek
(SLO)).
Faroe Islands: Jákup Mikkelsen, Hendrik Rubeksen (YC70), Jónas Tór Næs, Atli Gregersen
(YC26), Egil á Bø, Bogi Løkin (41' Hjalgrím Elttør), Christian Holst (81' Christian
Mouritsen), Jústinus Hansen (YC17), Jóan Edmundsson, Fródi Benjaminsen (C) (YC52),
Daniel Udsen (81' Jann Ingi Petersen). (Coach: Brian Kerr (IRL)).
Goals: Slovenia: 1-0 Tim Matavz (25'), 2-0 Tim Matavz (36'), 3-0 Tim Matavz (65'), 4-0
Milivoje Novakovic (72' penalty), 5-0 Zlatko Dedic (84').
Faroe Islands: 5-1 Christian Mouritsen (90'+3').
Referee: Stanislav Todorov (BUL)   Attendance: 15.750

12-10-2010   Svangaskard, Toftir: Faroe Islands – Northern Ireland   1-1 (0-0)
Faroe Islands: Jákup Mikkelsen, Erling Jacobsen, Jónas Tór Næs (YC38), Atli Gregersen
(YC72), Jóhan Davidsen, Christian Holst (85' Jústinus Hansen), Hjalgrím Elttør, Jóan
Edmundsson, Fródi Benjaminsen (C), Daniel Udsen (68' Jann Ingi Petersen), Símun
Samuelsen (78' Arnbjørn Hansen (YC84)). (Coach: Brian Kerr (IRL)).
Northern Ireland: Maik Taylor, Gareth McAuley, Aaron Hughes (C), Jonny Evans, Stephen
Craigan, Chris Baird, Niall McGinn (83' Corry Evans), Steven Davis (YC87), Chris Brunt,
Kyle Lafferty, Warren Feeney (50' David Healy). (Coach: Nigel Worthington (NIR)).
Goals: Faroe Islands: 1-0 Christian Holst (60').
Northern Ireland: 1-1 Kyle Lafferty (76').
Referee: Cyril Zimmermann (SUI)   Attendance: 1.921

12-10-2010   A.Le Coq Arena, Tallinn: Estonia – Slovenia   0-1 (0-0)
Estonia: Sergei Pareiko, Enar Jääger, Taavi Rähn (55' Karl Palatu), Dmitri Kruglov (YC34),
Ragnar Klavan, Aleksandr Dmitrijev, Andrei Sidorenkov, Sander Puri (69' Ats Purje),
Konstantin Vassiljev (C), Tarmo Kink (59' Sergei Zenjov), Kaimar Saag. (Coach: Tarmo
Rüütli (EST)).
Slovenia: Samir Handanovic, Miso Brecko, Bostjan Cesar, Marko Suler, Bojan Jokic,
Aleksandar Radosavljevic, Robert Koren (C), Josip Ilicic (67' Andraz Kirm), Valter Birsa
(YC83) (90'+1' Zlatan Ljubijankic), Tim Matavz (53' Zlatko Dedic), Milivoje Novakovic.
(Coach: Matjaz Kek (SLO)).
Goal: Slovenia: 0-1 Andrei Sidorenkov (67' own goal).
Referee: Tommy Skjerven (NOR)   Attendance: 5.722

12-10-2010   Stadio Luigi Ferraris, Genoa: Italy – Serbia   3-0 (awarded)
Italy: Emiliano Viviano, Gianluca Zambrotta, Domenico Criscito, Giorgio Chiellini, Leonardo
Bonucci, Angelo Palombo, Stefano Mauri, Andrea Pirlo (C), Claudio Marchisio, Giampaolo
Pazzini, Antonio Cassano. (Coach: Cesare Claudio Prandelli (ITA)).
Serbia: Zeljko Brkic, Neven Subotic, Slobodan Rajkovic (YC3), Aleksandar Lukovic,
Branislav Ivanovic, Zoran Tosic, Dejan Stankovic (C), Zdravko Kuzmanovic, Milos Krasic,
Gojko Kacar, Dragan Mrdja. (Coach: Vladimir Petrovic (SRB)).
Referee: Craig Alexander Thomson (SCO)   Attendance: 22.013

The match was abandoned due to crowd trouble. Only six minutes of play were possible at
the Stadio Luigi Ferraris and kick-off of the game had already been delayed by 35 minutes
due to crowd disturbances. It was subsequently decided to abandon the match in order to
ensure the safety and security of all parties involved due to the disturbances and flares

thrown by the Serbian fans. The UEFA Control and Disciplinary Body awarded the match as a 3-0 forfeit win to Italy.

As punishment for the crowd trouble, Serbia was ordered to play its next home match against Northern Ireland behind closed doors, with another one-match crowd ban deferred for a probationary period of two years. Italy received a one-match crowd ban deferred for a probationary period of two years. However, the Irish Football Association objected and as a result, UEFA decreed that 200 Northern Irish fans would be allowed to attend the game against Serbia. Serbian fans were not allowed to visit the away game against Estonia.

25-03-2011   Stadion Crvena Zvezda, Belgrade: Serbia – Northern Ireland   2-1 (0-1)
Serbia: Zeljko Brkic, Branislav Ivanovic, Milan Bisevac, Neven Subotic, Aleksandar Kolarov, Zoran Tosic, Dejan Stankovic (C) (YC37), Nenad Milijas (46' Milos Ninkovic), Adem Ljajic (46' Milan Jovanovic), Milos Krasic (YC55) (86' Radosav Petrovic), Marko Pantelic (YC45+2). (Coach: Vladimir Petrovic (SRB)).
Northern Ireland: Lee Camp, Chris Baird (C), Gareth McAuley, Aaron Hughes, Jonny Evans (YC27) (86' Patrick James (Paddy) McCourt), Craig Cathcart, Chris Brunt, Johnny Gorman (78' Warren Feeney), Corry Evans, Sammy Clingan, Kyle Lafferty (46' David Healy (YC62)). (Coach: Nigel Worthington (NIR)).
Goals: Serbia: 1-1 Marko Pantelic (65'), 2-1 Zoran Tosic (74').
Northern Ireland: 0-1 Gareth McAuley (40').
Referee: Serge Gumienny (BEL)   Attendance: 350

25-03-2011   Stozice Stadium, Ljubljana: Slovenia – Italy   0-1 (0-0)
Slovenia: Samir Handanovic, Marko Suler, Bojan Jokic, Miso Brecko (70' Sinisa Andjelkovic), Bostjan Cesar (C) (YC80), Aleksandar Radosavljevic, Robert Koren, Andraz Kirm, Valter Birsa (74' Josip Ilicic), Milivoje Novakovic, Zlatko Dedic (56' Zlatan Ljubijankic). (Coach: Matjaz Kek (SLO)).
Italy: Gianluigi Buffon (C), Christian Maggio, Federico Balzaretti, Giorgio Chiellini, Leonardo Bonucci, Riccardo Montolivo (YC55) (87' Claudio Marchisio), Stefano Mauri (63' Antonio Nocerino), Thiago Motta (YC90+1), Alberto Aquilani, Giampaolo Pazzini, Antonio Cassano (74' Giuseppe Rossi). (Coach: Cesare Claudio Prandelli (ITA)).
Goal: Italy: 0-1 Thiago Motta (73').
Referee: Dr.Felix Brych (GER)   Attendance: 15.790

29-03-2011   A.Le Coq Arena, Tallinn: Estonia – Serbia   1-1 (0-1)
Estonia: Sergei Pareiko, Taavi Rähn (YC90+1), Raio Piiroja (C) (YC16), Dmitri Kruglov, Enar Jääger, Ragnar Klavan, Sander Puri (29' Ats Purje (YC52)), Aleksandr Dmitrijev, Konstantin Vassiljev (C) (YC46), Kaimar Saag (66' Tarmo Kink), Jarmo Ahjupera (55' Andres Oper). (Coach: Tarmo Rüütli (EST)).
Serbia: Zeljko Brkic, Nemanja Vidic (C), Aleksandar Kolarov, Branislav Ivanovic, Milan Bisevac (YC83), Zoran Tosic, Radosav Petrovic, Milos Ninkovic (14' Veseljko (Vesko) Trivunovic), Nenad Milijas (YC66), Marko Pantelic, Milan Jovanovic (74' Nikola Zigic). (Coach: Vladimir Petrovic (SRB)).
Goals: Estonia: 1-1 Konstantin Vassiljev (84').
Serbia: 0-1 Marko Pantelic (38').
Referee: Hendrikus Sebastiaan Hermanus (Bas) Nijhuis (HOL)   Attendance: 5.185

29-03-2011   Windsor Park, Belfast: Northern Ireland – Slovenia   0-0
Northern Ireland: Lee Camp, Chris Baird (YC43), Gareth McAuley (C), Jonny Evans, Stephen
Craigan, Craig Cathcart, Chris Brunt (YC89), Grant McCann (72' Josh McQuoid), Corry
Evans (YC53) (90'+1' Liam Boyce), Sammy Clingan, Warren Feeney (82' Patrick James
(Paddy) McCourt). (Coach: Nigel Worthington (NIR)).
Slovenia: Samir Handanovic, Miso Brecko, Marko Suler, Matej Mavric, Bojan Jokic, Armin
Bacinovic (YC38) (90' Goran Sukalo), Robert Koren (C) (YC34), Andraz Kirm, Josip Ilicic
(29' Zlatan Ljubijankic), Valter Birsa, Milivoje Novakovic (84' Zlatko Dedic). (Coach: Matjaz
Kek (SLO)).
Referee: Björn Kuipers (HOL)   Attendance: 14.200

03-06-2011   Svangaskard, Toftir: Faroe Islands – Slovenia   0-2 (0-1)
Faroe Islands: Jákup Mikkelsen, Jónas Tór Næs (81' Súni Olsen), Pól Jóhannus Justinussen,
Einar Tróndargjógv Hansen, Jóhan Davidsen (YC62), Christian Holst (75' Christian
Mouritsen), Hjalgrím Elttør, Jóan Edmundsson (YC39), Fródi Benjaminsen (C), Daniel Udsen
(45'+2' Atli Danielsen), Rógvi Baldvinsson. (Coach: Brian Kerr (IRL)).
Slovenia: Samir Handanovic, Marko Suler (RC25), Bojan Jokic, Miso Brecko, Bostjan Cesar,
Robert Koren (C), Josip Ilicic, Armin Bacinovic, Tim Matavz (76' Andraz Kirm), Valter Birsa
(47' Matej Mavric), Milivoje Novakovic (55' Zlatan Ljubijankic). (Coach: Matjaz Kek (SLO)).
Goals: Slovenia: 0-1 Tim Matavz (29'), 0-2 Rógvi Baldvinsson (47' own goal).
Referee: Oliver Drachta (AUT)   Attendance: 974

03-06-2011   Stadio Alberto Braglia, Modena: Italy – Estonia   3-0 (2-0)
Italy: Gianluigi Buffon (C), Andrea Ranocchia, Christian Maggio, Federico Balzaretti, Giorgio
Chiellini, Riccardo Montolivo, Andrea Pirlo, Claudio Marchisio, Alberto Aquilani (YC8) (24'
Antonio Nocerino), Giuseppe Rossi (79' Sebastian Giovinco), Antonio Cassano (65'
Giampaolo Pazzini). (Coach: Cesare Claudio Prandelli (ITA)).
Estonia: Sergei Pareiko, Taavi Rähn, Raio Piiroja (C), Dmitri Kruglov, Enar Jääger, Ragnar
Klavan (YC42), Martin Vunk (YC54), Sander Puri, Taijo Teniste (58' Kaimar Saag), Tarmo
Kink (79' Gert Kams), Sergei Zenjov (58' Jarmo Ahjupera). (Coach: Tarmo Rüütli (EST)).
Goals: Italy: 1-0 Giuseppe Rossi (21'), 2-0 Antonio Cassano (39'), 3-0 Giampaolo Pazzini
(68').
Referee: Alexandru Dan Tudor (ROM)   Attendance: 19.434

07-06-2011   Svangaskard, Toftir: Faroe Islands – Estonia   2-0 (1-0)
Faroe Islands: Jákup Mikkelsen, Jónas Tór Næs, Pól Jóhannus Justinussen (YC75,YC89),
Einar Tróndargjógv Hansen, Atli Gregersen, Atli Danielsen, Christian Holst (85' Christian
Mouritsen), Hjalgrím Elttør (90'+1' Súni Olsen), Fródi Benjaminsen (C), Rógvi Baldvinsson,
Arnbjørn Hansen (69' Símun Samuelsen). (Coach: Brian Kerr (IRL)).
Estonia: Sergei Pareiko (YC75), Taavi Rähn, Raio Piiroja (C), Dmitri Kruglov, Enar Jääger,
Sander Puri (YC42,YC57), Konstantin Vassiljev, Kaimar Saag (82' Sergei Mosnikov), Tarmo
Kink, Jarmo Ahjupera (66' Gert Kams), Sergei Zenjov (YC46). (Coach: Tarmo Rüütli (EST)).
Goals: Faroe Islands: 1-0 Fródi Benjaminsen (43' penalty), 2-0 Arnbjørn Hansen (47').
Referee: Antti Munukka (FIN)   Attendance: 1.715
(Fródi Benjaminsen missed a penalty in the 47th minute)

10-08-2011   Windsor Park, Belfast: Northern Ireland – Faroe Islands   4-0 (1-0)
Northern Ireland: Lee Camp, Jonny Evans, Chris Baird, Gareth McAuley (46' Craig Cathcart),
Aaron Hughes (C), Corry Evans (59' Niall McGinn), Steven Davis, Sammy Clingan, Patrick
James (Paddy) McCourt (YC33), Grant McCann, David Healy (83' Jamie Ward). (Coach:
Nigel Worthington (NIR)).
Faroe Islands: Jákup Mikkelsen, Atli Gregersen, Jóhan Davidsen, Jónas Tór Næs, Christian
Holst (68' Arnbjørn Hansen), Hjalgrím Elttør (75' Christian Mouritsen), Jóan Edmundsson,
Fródi Benjaminsen (C), Súni Olsen (75' Atli Danielsen), Rógvi Baldvinsson, Daniel Udsen.
(Coach: Brian Kerr (IRL)).
Goals: Northern Ireland: 1-0 Aaron Hughes (5'), 2-0 Steven Davis (66'), 3-0 Patrick James
(Paddy) McCourt (71'), 4-0 Patrick James (Paddy) McCourt (88').
Referee: Emir Aleckovic (BOS)   Attendance: 13.183

02-09-2011   Tórsvøllur, Tórshavn: Faroe Islands – Italy   0-1 (0-1)
Faroe Islands: René Tórgard, Jónas Tór Næs, Pól Jóhannus Justinussen (87' Símun
Samuelsen), Atli Gregersen, Jóhan Davidsen, Súni Olsen (YC56) (76' Atli Danielsen),
Christian Holst (87' Christian Mouritsen), Hjalgrím Elttør, Jóan Edmundsson, Fródi
Benjaminsen (C), Rógvi Baldvinsson. (Coach: Brian Kerr (IRL)).
Italy: Gianluigi Buffon (C), Andrea Ranocchia, Christian Maggio, Domenico Criscito, Giorgio
Chiellini, Riccardo Montolivo, Andrea Pirlo, Thiago Motta (73' Alberto Aquilani), Daniele De
Rossi, Giuseppe Rossi (59' Giampaolo Pazzini), Antonio Cassano (85' Mario Balotelli).
(Coach: Cesare Claudio Prandelli (ITA)).
Goal: Italy: 0-1 Antonio Cassano (11').
Referee: Tamás Bognár (HUN)   Attendance: 5.654

02-09-2011   Stozice Stadium, Ljubljana: Slovenia – Estonia   1-2 (0-1)
Slovenia: Samir Handanovic (YC27), Bojan Jokic, Brank Ilic, Miso Brecko, Bostjan Cesar,
Aleksandar Radosavljevic (56' Dare Vrsic), Robert Koren (C), Josip Ilicic (81' Nejc Pecnik),
Tim Matavz, Valter Birsa, Milivoje Novakovic (56' Zlatan Ljubijankic). (Coach: Matjaz Kek
(SLO)).
Estonia: Sergei Pareiko, Taavi Rähn, Raio Piiroja (C) (74' Andrei Stepanov), Dmitri Kruglov
(69' Ats Purje), Enar Jääger, Ragnar Klavan, Martin Vunk, Aleksandr Dmitrijev (YC85),
Konstantin Vassiljev, Taijo Teniste, Sergei Zenjov (61' Jarmo Ahjupera). (Coach: Tarmo
Rüütli (EST)).
Goals: Slovenia: 1-1 Tim Matavz (78').
Estonia: 0-1 Konstantin Vassiljev (29' penalty), 1-2 Ats Purje (81').
Referee: Stephan Studer (SUI)   Attendance: 15.480

02-09-2011   Windsor Park, Belfast: Northern Ireland – Serbia   0-1 (0-0)
Northern Ireland: Lee Camp, Gareth McAuley, Aaron Hughes (C), Jonny Evans (YC90+2),
Craig Cathcart, Chris Baird, Grant McCann (YC30) (71' Warren Feeney), Corry Evans (YC57)
(59' Niall McGinn), Steven Davis, Chris Brunt, David Healy (84' Josh McQuoid). (Coach:
Nigel Worthington (NIR)).
Serbia: Bojan Jorgacevic, Neven Subotic, Slobodan Rajkovic (YC45), Aleksandar Kolarov,
Branislav Ivanovic, Zoran Tosic (78' Adem Ljajic), Dejan Stankovic (C), Milos Ninkovic
(YC41) (74' Radosav Petrovic (YC90+3)), Zdravko Kuzmanovic (90' Ljubomir Fejsa), Marko
Pantelic, Milan Jovanovic. (Coach: Vladimir Petrovic (SRB)).
Goal: Serbia: 0-1 Marko Pantelic (67').
Referee: Thomas Einwaller (AUT)   Attendance: 15.148

215

06-09-2011   Stadion FK Partizan, Belgrade: Serbia – Faroe Islands 3-1 (2-1)
Serbia: Bojan Jorgacevic, Neven Subotic, Aleksandar Kolarov, Branislav Ivanovic, Milan Bisevac (45' Nenad Tomovic), Zoran Tosic, Dejan Stankovic (C) (46' Radosav Petrovic), Milos Ninkovic (82' Ljubomir Fejsa), Zdravko Kuzmanovic, Marko Pantelic, Milan Jovanovic. (Coach: Vladimir Petrovic (SRB)).
Faroe Islands: René Tórgard, Jónas Tór Næs, Atli Gregersen, Jóhan Davidsen, Atli Danielsen, Christian Holst (YC42) (78' Christian Mouritsen), Hjalgrím Elttør (YC79), Jóan Edmundsson, Fródi Benjaminsen (C), Rógvi Baldvinsson, Símun Samuelsen (73' Pól Jóhannus Justinussen). (Coach: Brian Kerr (IRL)).
Goals: Serbia: 1-0 Milan Jovanovic (6'), 2-0 Zoran Tosic (22'), 3-1 Zdravko Kuzmanovic (69').
Faroe Islands: 2-1 Fródi Benjaminsen (37').
Referee: Arman Amirkhanyan (ARM)   Attendance: 7.500

06-09-2011   A.Le Coq Arena, Tallinn: Estonia – Northern Ireland 4-1 (2-1)
Estonia: Sergei Pareiko, Taavi Rähn (YC39), Raio Piiroja (C), Dmitri Kruglov, Enar Jääger, Ragnar Klavan, Martin Vunk, Sander Puri (63' Ats Purje), Konstantin Vassiljev, Tarmo Kink (88' Kaimar Saag), Jarmo Ahjupera (53' Sergei Zenjov). (Coach: Tarmo Rüütli (EST)).
Northern Ireland: Lee Camp, Gareth McAuley, Aaron Hughes (C), Craig Cathcart, Chris Baird, Niall McGinn (65' Warren Feeney), Grant McCann, Steven Davis, Sammy Clingan, Chris Brunt, David Healy (65' Josh McQuoid). (Coach: Nigel Worthington (NIR)).
Goals: Estonia: 1-0 Martin Vunk (28'), 2-0 Tarmo Kink (32'), 3-1 Sergei Zenjov (60'), 4-1 Kaimar Saag (90'+3').
Northern Ireland: 2-1 Raio Piiroja (40' own goal).
Referee: Daniel Stålhammar (SWE)   Attendance: 8.660

06-09-2011   Stadio Artemio Franchi, Florence: Italy – Slovenia 1-0 (0-0)
Italy: Gianluigi Buffon (C), Andrea Ranocchia, Mattia Cassani, Federico Balzaretti (YC64), Giorgio Chiellini, Riccardo Montolivo (76' Mario Balotelli), Andrea Pirlo, Thiago Motta (46' Claudio Marchisio), Daniele De Rossi, Giuseppe Rossi, Antonio Cassano (61' Giampaolo Pazzini). (Coach: Cesare Claudio Prandelli (ITA)).
Slovenia: Jasmin Handanovic, Marko Suler, Bojan Jokic, Miso Brecko (YC64), Bostjan Cesar (YC85), Dare Vrsic (75' Nejc Pecnik), Aleksandar Radosavljevic, Robert Koren (C) (YC24), Andraz Kirm (87' Zlatko Dedic), Valter Birsa (56' Josip Ilicic (YC90+2)), Milivoje Novakovic. (Coach: Matjaz Kek (SLO)).
Goal: Italy: 1-0 Giampaolo Pazzini (85').
Referee: Svein Oddvar Moen (NOR)   Attendance: 18.000

07-10-2011   Windsor Park, Belfast: Northern Ireland – Estonia 1-2 (1-0)
Northern Ireland: Lee Camp (YC75), Gareth McAuley (YC90+2), Lee Hodson, Craig Cathcart (YC76), Chris Baird, Patrick James (Paddy) McCourt, Grant McCann (83' David Healy), Steven Davis (C), Sammy Clingan (32' Corry Evans), Chris Brunt, Kyle Lafferty (YC53) (69' Warren Feeney). (Coach: Nigel Worthington (NIR)).
Estonia: Sergei Pareiko, Andrei Stepanov, Raio Piiroja (C), Dmitri Kruglov, Enar Jääger, Ragnar Klavan, Martin Vunk, Sander Puri (57' Ats Purje), Aleksandr Dmitrijev, Tarmo Kink (65' Konstantin Vassiljev), Jarmo Ahjupera (46' Sergei Zenjov (YC48)). (Coach: Tarmo Rüütli (EST)).
Goals: Northern Ireland: 1-0 Steven Davis (22').
Estonia: 1-1 Konstantin Vassiljev (77' penalty), 1-2 Konstantin Vassiljev (84').
Referee: Manuel Gräfe (GER)   Attendance: 12.604

216

07-10-2011   Stadion Crvena Zvezda, Belgrade: Serbia – Italy   1-1 (1-1)
Serbia: Bojan Jorgacevic, Neven Subotic, Slobodan Rajkovic, Aleksandar Kolarov, Branislav Ivanovic (YC55), Zoran Tosic (YC88), Dejan Stankovic (C) (YC80) (87' Milan Jovanovic), Milos Ninkovic, Milos Krasic (76' Nikola Zigic (YC90)), Ljubomir Fejsa (46' Radosav Petrovic), Marko Pantelic. (Coach: Vladimir Petrovic (SRB)).
Italy: Gianluigi Buffon (C), Christian Maggio (YC28), Giorgio Chiellini, Leonardo Bonucci, Andrea Barzagli, Riccardo Montolivo (82' Alberto Aquilani), Andrea Pirlo, Claudio Marchisio (70' Antonio Nocerino), Daniele De Rossi, Giuseppe Rossi, Antonio Cassano (67' Sebastian Giovinco). (Coach: Cesare Claudio Prandelli (ITA)).
Goals: Serbia: 1-1 Branislav Ivanovic (26').
Italy: 0-1 Claudio Marchisio (2').
Referee: Pedro Proença Oliveira Alves Garcia (POR)   Attendance: 30.000

11-10-2011   Stadio Adriatico, Pescara: Italy – Northern Ireland   3-0 (1-0)
Italy: Gianluigi Buffon (C) (76' Morgan De Sanctis), Mattia Cassani, Federico Balzaretti, Giorgio Chiellini, Andrea Barzagli, Riccardo Montolivo, Daniele De Rossi, Alberto Aquilani (68' Antonio Nocerino), Andrea Pirlo, Sebastian Giovinco, Antonio Cassano (56' Pablo Daniel Osvaldo). (Coach: Cesare Claudio Prandelli (ITA)).
Northern Ireland: Maik Taylor (C), Ryan McGivern, Gareth McAuley, Lee Hodson, Chris Baird, Jonny Gorman (77' Niall McGinn), Corry Evans, Steven Davis, Oliver Norwood (73' Conor McLaughlin), Andrew (Andy) Little, David Healy (65' Warren Feeney). (Coach: Nigel Worthington (NIR)).
Goals: Italy: 1-0 Antonio Cassano (21'), 2-0 Antonio Cassano (53'), 3-0 Gareth McAuley (74' own goal).
Referee: Antonio Mateu Lahoz (ESP)   Attendance: 19.480

11-10-2011   Ljudski vrt, Maribor: Slovenia – Serbia   1-0 (1-0)
Slovenia: Samir Handanovic, Marko Suler (YC64), Bojan Jokic, Bostjan Cesar (C), Miso Brecko (65' Branko Ilic), Dare Vrsic (76' Valter Birsa), Aleksandar Radosavljevic, Andraz Kirm, Armin Bacinovic (YC50) (69' René Krhin), Tim Matavz (YC22), Zlatan Ljubijankic. (Coach: Matjaz Kek (SLO)).
Serbia: Bojan Jorgacevic, Nemanja Vidic, Neven Subotic, Aleksandar Kolarov, Branislav Ivanovic, Zoran Tosic, Dejan Stankovic (C), Radosav Petrovic (51' Marko Pantelic), Milos Ninkovic (72' Nenad Milijas), Dragan Mrdja, Milan Jovanovic (YC39) (57' Milos Krasic). (Coach: Vladimir Petrovic (SRB)).
Goal: Slovenia: 1-0 Dare Vrsic (45'+1').
Referee: Frank de Bleeckere (BEL)   Attendance: 9.848
(Nemanja Vidic missed a penalty in the 64th minute)

217

GROUP D

03-09-2010	Piatra Neamt	Romania – Albania	1-1 (0-0)
03-09-2010	Luxembourg	Luxembourg – Bosnia and Herzegovina	0-3 (0-3)
03-09-2010	Saint-Denis	France – Belarus	0-1 (0-0)
07-09-2010	Minsk	Belarus – Romania	0-0
07-09-2010	Tirana	Albania – Luxembourg	1-0 (1-0)
07-09-2010	Sarajevo	Bosnia and Herzegovina – France	0-2 (0-0)
08-10-2010	Luxembourg	Luxembourg – Belarus	0-0
08-10-2010	Tirana	Albania – Bosnia and Herzegovina	1-1 (1-1)
09-10-2010	Saint-Denis	France – Romania	2-0 (0-0)
12-10-2010	Minsk	Belarus – Albania	2-0 (1-0)
12-10-2010	Metz	France – Luxembourg	2-0 (1-0)
25-03-2011	Luxembourg	Luxembourg – France	0-2 (0-1)
26-03-2011	Zenica	Bosnia and Herzegovina	2-1 (0-1)
26-03-2011	Tirana	Albania – Belarus	1-0 (0-0)
29-03-2011	Piatra Neamt	Romania – Luxembourg	3-1 (1-1)
03-06-2011	Bucharest	Romania – Bosnia and Herzegovina	3-0 (2-0)
03-06-2011	Minsk	Belarus – France	1-1 (1-1)
07-06-2011	Minsk	Belarus – Luxembourg	2-0 (0-0)
07-06-2011	Zenica	Bosnia and Herzegovina – Albania	2-0 (0-0)
02-09-2011	Luxembourg	Luxembourg – Romania	0-2 (0-2)
02-09-2011	Minsk	Belarus – Bosnia and Herzegovina	0-2 (0-2)
02-09-2011	Tirana	Albania – France	1-2 (0-2)
06-09-2011	Zenica	Bosnia and Herzegovina – Belarus	1-0 (0-0)
06-09-2011	Luxembourg	Luxembourg – Albania	2-1 (1-0)
06-09-2011	Bucharest	Romania – France	0-0
07-10-2011	Zenica	Bosnia and Herzegovina – Luxembourg	5-0 (4-0)
07-10-2011	Bucharest	Romania – Belarus	2-2 (1-1)
07-10-2011	Saint-Denis	France – Albania	3-0 (2-0)
11-10-2011	Tirana	Albania – Romania	1-1 (1-0)
11-10-2011	Saint-Denis	France – Bosnia and Herzegovina	1-1 (0-1)

FINAL STANDING

Pos	Team	Pld	W	D	L	GF	GA	GD	Pts
1	France	10	6	3	1	15	4	+11	21
2	Bosnia and Herzegovina	10	6	2	2	17	8	+9	20
3	Romania	10	3	5	2	13	9	+4	14
4	Belarus	10	3	4	3	8	7	+1	13
5	Albania	10	2	3	5	7	14	-7	9
6	Luxembourg	10	1	1	8	3	21	-18	4

France qualified for the Final Tournament in Poland and Ukraine.

Bosnia and Herzegovina qualified for the play-offs

03-09-2010   Stadionul Ceahlaul, PiatraNeamt: Romania – Albania 1-1 (0-0)
Romania: Bogdan Lobont, Gabriel Tamas, Razvan Rat (YC40), Mirel Radoi (C), Cosmin
Contra (56' Gabriel Muresan), Gabriel Torje, George Florescu, Ciprian Deac, Razvan Cocis
(77' Ovidiu Herea (YC87)), Daniel Niculae (64' Bogdan Stancu), Ciprian Marica. (Coach:
Razvan Lucescu (ROM)).
Albania: Arjan Beqaj, Kristi Vangjeli (YC50), Andi Lila, Armend Dallku, Debatik Çurri, Ervin
Skela (C) (79' Gilman Lika), Klodian Duro (81' Gjergj Muzaka), Lorik Cana, Ansi Agolli,
Ervin Bulku, Erjon Bogdani (57' Hamdi Salihi). (Coach: Josip Kuze (CRO)).
Goals: Romania: 1-0 Bogdan Stancu (80').
Albania: 1-1 Gjergj Muzaka (87').
Referee: Robert Schörgenhofer (AUT)   Attendance: 13.400

03-09-2010   Stade Josy Barthel, Luxembourg:
                Luxembourg – Bosnia and Herzegovina 0-3 (0-3)
Luxembourg: Jonathan Joubert, Tom Schnell, Kim Kintziger, Mathias Jänisch, Eric Hoffmann
(YC12), Dan Collette (76' Daniël Alves Da Mota), Gilles Bettmer (86' Tom Laterza), René
Peters, Lars Christian Krogh Gerson, Mario Mutsch, Stefan Bensi (YC38) (46' Joël Kitenge).
(Coach: Luc Holtz (LUX)).
Bosnia and Herzegovina: Kenan Hasagic, Safet Nadarevic, Emir Spahic, Mensur Mujdza, Elvir
Rahimic (67' Sanel Jahic), Miralem Pjanic (78' Ermin Zec), Zvjezdan Misimovic (C), Senad
Lulic, Senijad Ibricic (72' Haris Medunjanin), Vedad Ibisevic, Edin Dzeko. (Coach: Safet
Susic (BOS)).
Goals: Bosnia and Herzegovina: 0-1 Senijad Ibricic (6'), 0-2 Miralem Pjanic (12'), 0-3 Edin
Dzeko (16').
Referee: Veaceslav Banari (MOL)   Attendance: 7.327

03-09-2010   Stade de France, Saint-Denis: France – Belarus 0-1 (0-0)
France: Hugo Lloris, Adil Rami, Philippe Mexès, Gaël Clichy, Bacary Sagna, Florent Malouda
(C), Yann M'Vila, Abou Diaby, Jérémy Ménez (69' Louis Saha, 80' Kevin Gameiro),
Guillaume Hoarau, Loïc Rémy (34' Mathieu Valbuena). (Coach: Laurent Robert Blanc
(FRA)).
Belarus: Yuri Zhevnov (C), Aleksandr Yurevich, Igor Shitov, Sergei Omelyanchuk, Aleksandr
Martynovich, Yan Tigorev (YC14), Aleksandr Kulchiy, Aleksandr Hleb, Vitali Rodionov
(YC49) (85' Sergei Kornilenko), Vitali Kutuzov (75' Sergei Kislyak), Vyacheslav Hleb (89'
Anton Putsila). (Coach: Bernd Stange (GER)).
Goal: Belarus: 0-1 Sergei Kislyak (86').
Referee: William (Willie) Collum (SCO)   Attendance: 76.395

07-09-2010   Dinamo Stadium, Minsk: Belarus – Romania 0-0
Belarus: Yuri Zhevnov (C), Aleksandr Yurevich, Igor Shitov, Sergei Omelyanchuk, Aleksandr
Martynovich, Aleksandr Kulchiy, Sergei Kislyak, Aleksandr Hleb (73' Anton Putsila), Vitali
Kutuzov (87' Sergei Krivets), Sergei Kornilenko (76' Vitali Rodionov), Vyacheslav Hleb.
(Coach: Bernd Stange (GER)).
Romania: Costel Pantilimon, Gabriel Tamas, Razvan Rat, Mirel Radoi (YC88), Vasile Maftei
(YC90+1), Cristian Chivu (C), Gabriel Torje (46' Razvan Cocis), George Florescu, Ciprian
Deac (YC72) (83' Ciprian Marica), Bogdan Stancu (73' Daniel Niculae), Marius Bilasco.
(Coach: Razvan Lucescu (ROM)).
Referee: Pavel Královec (CZE)   Attendance: 26.354

07-09-2010   Qemal Stafa, Tirana: Albania – Luxembourg   1-0 (1-0)
Albania: Arjan Beqaj, Armend Dallku, Debatik Çurri, Ervin Skela (C), Gjergj Muzaka (80'
Jahmir Hyka), Klodian Duro (90'+1' Andi Lila), Lorik Cana, Ansi Agolli, Ervin Bulku
(YC86), Hamdi Salihi, Erjon Bogdani (YC85). (Coach: Josip Kuze (CRO)).
Luxembourg: Jonathan Joubert, Tom Schnell, Kim Kintziger, Eric Hoffmann, Guy Blaise,
René Peters (C) (YC28), Ben Payal, Gilles Bettmer (90'+1' Dan Collette), Mario Mutsch
(YC23,YC58), Tom Laterza (81' Massimo Martino), Daniël Alves Da Mota. (Coach: Luc
Holtz (LUX)).
Goal: Albania: 1-0 Hamdi Salihi (37').
Referee: Richard Trutz (SVK)   Attendance: 11.800

07-09-2010   Asim Ferhatovic Hase Stadium, Sarajevo:
              Bosnia and Herzegovina – France   0-2 (0-0)
Bosnia and Herzegovina: Kenan Hasagic, Safet Nadarevic, Emir Spahic (C), Mensur Mujdza,
Elvir Rahimic (74' Ermin Zec), Zvjezdan Misimovic, Miralem Pjanic (YC45), Senad Lulic,
Senijad Ibricic (YC71), Vedad Ibisevic (74' Sanel Jahic), Edin Dzeko. (Coach: Safet Susic
(BOS)).
France: Hugo Lloris, Adil Rami, Philippe Mexès, Gaël Clichy, Bacary Sagna, Florent Malouda
(80' Blaise Matuidi), Yann M'Vila, Alou Diarra (C), Abou Diaby, Mathieu Valbuena (YC40),
Karim Benzema. (Coach: Laurent Robert Blanc (FRA)).
Goals: France: 0-1 Karim Benzema (72'), 0-2 Florent Malouda (78').
Referee: Dr.Felix Brych (GER)   Attendance: 28.000

08-10-2010   Stade Josy Barthel, Luxembourg: Luxembourg – Belarus   0-0
Luxembourg: Jonathan Joubert, Tom Schnell, Kim Kintziger (YC74), Eric Hoffmann, Guy
Blaise, René Peters (C), Ben Payal (77' Michel Kettenmeyer), Gilles Bettmer (62' Lars
Christian Krogh Gerson), Tom Laterza, Charles Leweck, Aurélien Joachim (66' Daniël Alves
Da Mota). (Coach: Luc Holtz (LUX)).
Belarus: Yuri Zhevnov (C), Aleksandr Yurevich (87' Dmitri Molosh), Igor Shitov, Sergei
Omelyanchuk, Aleksandr Martynovich, Yan Tigorev (67' Vitali Rodionov), Aleksandr
Kulchiy (YC59), Sergei Kislyak, Timofei Kalachev (YC74), Sergei Kornilenko (RC69),
Vyacheslav Hleb (67' Anton Putsila). (Coach: Bernd Stange (GER)).
Referee: Aleksandar Stavrev (MCD)   Attendance: 1.857

08-10-2010   Qemal Stafa, Tirana: Albania – Bosnia and Herzegovina   1-1 (1-1)
Albania: Arjan Beqaj, Kristi Vangjeli, Andi Lila, Armend Dallku (YC38), Gjergj Muzaka (65'
Gilman Lika), Klodian Duro, Lorik Cana (C), Ansi Agolli, Ervin Bulku, Hamdi Salihi (85'
Jahmir Hyka), Erjon Bogdani (YC9) (46' Ervin Skela). (Coach: Dzemal Mustedanagic (BOS)).
Bosnia and Herzegovina: Kenan Hasagic (46' Asmir Begovic), Adnan Mravac (YC45) (46'
Boris Pandza), Emir Spahic (C) (YC53), Mensur Mujdza, Elvir Rahimic, Miralem Pjanic,
Zvjezdan Misimovic, Haris Medunjanin, Senad Lulic (YC39), Vedad Ibisevic, Edin Dzeko
(89' Senijad Ibricic). (Coach: Safet Susic (BOS)).
Goals: Albania: 1-1 Klodian Duro (45'+2').
Bosnia and Herzegovina: 0-1 Vedad Ibisevic (21').
Referee: Kristinn Jakobsson (ISL)   Attendance: 14.220

09-10-2010   Stade de France, Saint-Denis: France – Romania   2-0 (0-0)
France: Hugo Lloris, Gaël Clichy, Anthony Réveillère, Adil Rami, Philippe Mexès (YC82), Yann M'Vila, Alou Diarra (C) (YC45), Samir Nasri (74' Yoann Gourcuff), Florent Malouda, Mathieu Valbuena (68' Loïc Rémy), Karim Benzema (86' Dimitri Payet). (Coach: Laurent Robert Blanc (FRA)).
Romania: Costel Pantilimon, Cristian Chivu (C), Gabriel Tamas, Cristian Sapunaru (YC30), Razvan Rat, Mirel Radoi, George Florescu (YC86), Razvan Cocis (87' Mihai Roman), Ianis Zicu (46' Ciprian Deac), Daniel Niculae (63' Ciprian Marica), Bogdan Stancu. (Coach: Razvan Lucescu (ROM)).
Goals: France: 1-0 Loïc Rémy (83'), 2-0 Yoann Gourcuff (90'+3').
Referee: Pedro Proença Oliveira Alves Garcia (POR)   Attendance: 79.299

12-10-2010   Dinamo Stadium, Minsk: Belarus – Albania   2-0 (1-0)
Belarus: Yuri Zhevnov (C), Igor Shitov, Sergei Omelyanchuk, Dmitri Molosh (YC47) (87' Aleksandr Yurevich), Aleksandr Martynovich, Yan Tigorev, Anton Putsila (YC79) (83' Vyacheslav Hleb), Aleksandr Kulchiy (75' Sergei Krivets), Sergei Kislyak, Timofei Kalachev (YC52), Vitali Rodionov. (Coach: Bernd Stange (GER)).
Albania: Arjan Beqaj, Kristi Vangjeli, Andi Lila, Armend Dallku (YC10,YC90+1), Admir Teli, Ervin Skela (C) (YC42) (81' Edmond Kapllani), Gilman Lika (YC28) (76' Elis Bakaj), Klodian Duro, Ansi Agolli, Ervin Bulku (59' Gjergj Muzaka), Hamdi Salihi. (Coach: Dzemal Mustedanagic (BOS)).
Goals: Belarus: 1-0 Vitali Rodionov (10'), 2-0 Sergei Krivets (77').
Referee: Peter Rasmussen (DEN)   Attendance: 7.000

12-10-2010   Stade Saint-Symphorien, Metz: France – Luxembourg   2-0 (1-0)
France: Hugo Lloris, Gaël Clichy, Philippe Mexès, Adil Rami (YC42), Anthony Réveillère, Yoann Gourcuff, Florent Malouda (63' Samir Nasri), Abou Diaby, Alou Diarra (C), Guillaume Hoarau (73' Loïc Rémy), Karim Benzema (63' Dimitri Payet). (Coach: Laurent Robert Blanc (FRA)).
Luxembourg: Jonathan Joubert, Tom Schnell, Eric Hoffmann, Guy Blaise, Ben Payal, Gilles Bettmer (84' Daniël Alves Da Mota), René Peters (C) (YC29,YC54), Mario Mutsch, Tom Laterza (69' Jeff Strasser), Aurélien Joachim (53' Joël Kitenge), Charles Leweck. (Coach: Luc Holtz (LUX)).
Goals: France: 1-0 Karim Benzema (22'), 2-0 Yoann Gourcuff (76').
Referee: Matej Jug (SLO)   Attendance: 24.710

25-03-2011   Stade Josy Barthel, Luxembourg: Luxembourg – France   0-2 (0-1)
Luxembourg: Jonathan Joubert, Eric Hoffmann (C), Guy Blaise, Tom Schnell, Lars Christian Krogh Gerson (71' Daniël Alves Da Mota), Gilles Bettmer, Ben Payal, Mario Mutsch (YC83), Tom Laterza (54' Massimo Martino), Aurélien Joachim, Charles Leweck (90' Jacques Plein). (Coach: Luc Holtz (LUX)).
France: Hugo Lloris, Adil Rami, Philippe Mexès, Patrice Evra, Bacary Sagna, Yann M'Vila, Yoann Gourcuff, Franck Ribéry, Samir Nasri (C), Florent Malouda, Karim Benzema. (Coach: Laurent Robert Blanc (FRA)).
Goals: France: 0-1 Philippe Mexès (28'), 0-2 Yoann Gourcuff (72').
Referee: Tom Harald Hagen (NOR)   Attendance: 8.052

26-03-2011   Bilino Polje, Zenica: Bosnia and Herzegovina – Romania   2-1 (0-1)
Bosnia and Herzegovina: Kenan Hasagic, Adnan Mravac, Emir Spahic (C), Mensur Mujdza, Elvir Rahimic (YC78), Miralem Pjanic, Zvjezdan Misimovic (81' Senijad Ibricic), Haris Medunjanin (70' Darko Maletic), Senad Lulic, Vedad Ibisevic (YC54) (76' Zlatan Muslimovic), Edin Dzeko. (Coach: Safet Susic (BOS)).
Romania: Costel Pantilimon, Gabriel Tamas, Razvan Rat, Cornel Rapa, Dorin Goian, Gabriel Torje (71' Razvan Cocis), George Florescu (76' Adrian Ropotan), Ciprian Deac (85' Ianis Zicu), Dan Alexa, Adrian Mutu, Ciprian Marica. (Coach: Razvan Lucescu (ROM)).
Goals: Bosnia and Herzegovina: 1-1 Vedad Ibisevic (63'), 2-1 Edin Dzeko (83').
Romania: 0-1 Ciprian Marica (29').
Referee: Fernando Teixeira Vitienes (ESP)   Attendance: 13.000

26-03-2011   Qemal Stafa, Tirana: Albania – Belarus   1-0 (0-0)
Albania: Samir Ujkani, Kristi Vangjeli, Andi Lila, Admir Teli, Ervin Skela (81' Klodian Duro), Lorik Cana (YC38), Ansi Agolli, Altin Lala (C) (YC18), Ervin Bulku, Hamdi Salihi (YC17) (90'+3' Gjergj Muzaka), Erjon Bogdani (75' Elis Bakaj). (Coach: Josip Kuze (CRO)).
Belarus: Sergei Veremko, Igor Shitov (YC32), Sergei Omelyanchuk (C), Dmitri Molosh (YC53), Aleksandr Martynovich, Yan Tigorev, Anton Putsila (82' Pavel Sitko), Aleksandr Kulchiy (YC21) (62' Aleksandr Bychenok), Sergei Krivets (46' Leonid Kovel), Sergei Kislyak, Vyacheslav Hleb (YC49). (Coach: Bernd Stange (GER)).
Goal: Albania: 1-0 Hamdi Salihi (62').
Referee: Markus Strömbergsson (SWE)   Attendance: 13.826

29-03-2011   Ceahlaul Stadium, Piatra Neamt: Romania – Luxembourg   3-1 (1-1)
Romania: Cirpian Tatarusanu, Gabriel Tamas (C) (YC36) (65' Dorin Goian), Cristian Sapunaru, Razvan Rat, Florin Gardos, Ianis Zicu, Adrian Ropotan (YC87), Gabriel Muresan, Bogdan Stancu (46' Gabriel Torje), Adrian Mutu (84' Marius Alexe), Ciprian Marica. (Coach: Razvan Lucescu (ROM)).
Luxembourg: Jonathan Joubert, Tom Schnell (90' Massimo Martino), Eric Hoffmann, Guy Blaise (YC18), René Peters (C), Ben Payal, Lars Christian Krogh Gerson (58' Daniël Alves Da Mota), Gilles Bettmer (81' Tom Laterza), Mario Mutsch (YC82), Charles Leweck, Aurélien Joachim. (Coach: Luc Holtz (LUX)).
Goals: Romania: 1-1 Adrian Mutu (24'), 2-1 Adrian Mutu (68'), 3-1 Ianis Zicu (78').
Luxembourg: 0-1 Lars Christian Krogh Gerson (22').
Referee: Hüseyin Göçek (TUR)   Attendance: 13.500

03-06-2011   Stadionul Giulesti-Valentin Stanescu, Bucharest:
               Romania – Bosnia and Herzegovina   3-0 (2-0)
Romania: Cirpian Tatarusanu, Gabriel Tamas, Cristian Sapunaru (YC72), Razvan Rat, Paul Papp, Gabriel Torje (YC68), Lucian Sanmartean (63' Cristian Tanase), Gabriel Muresan, Alexandru Bourceanu, Adrian Mutu (C) (83' Romeo Surdu (YC90+1)), Ciprian Marica (87' Marius Alexe). (Coach: Razvan Lucescu (ROM)).
Bosnia and Herzegovina: Kenan Hasagic, Adnan Mravac, Emir Spahic (C), Mensur Mujdza, Elvir Rahimic, Miralem Pjanic, Zvjezdan Misimovic, Haris Medunjanin (46' Vedad Ibisevic), Senad Lulic, Senijad Ibricic (64' Semir Stilic (YC77)), Edin Dzeko (64' Zlatan Muslimovic). (Coach: Safet Susic (BOS)).
Goals: Romania: 1-0 Adrian Mutu (37'), 2-0 Ciprian Marica (41'), 3-0 Ciprian Marica (55').
Referee: Jonas Eriksson (SWE)   Attendance: 8.200
(Cristian Sapunaru missed a penalty in the 90+5 minute)

03-06-2011   Dinamo Stadium, Minsk: Belarus – France   1-1 (1-1)
Belarus: Sergei Veremko (YC86), Dmitri Verkhovtsov, Vitali Trubilo, Igor Shitov, Sergei Omelyanchuk (C), Aleksandr Martynovich, Maksim Bordachev, Yan Tigorev, Anton Putsila (86' Sergei Kislyak), Timofei Kalachev (YC33) (90' Vyacheslav Hleb), Andrei Voronkov. (Coach: Bernd Stange (GER)).
France: Hugo Lloris, Éric Abidal, Adil Rami (YC19), Mamadou Sakho, Bacary Sagna (YC25), Franck Ribéry, Samir Nasri, Florent Malouda, Alou Diarra (C), Abou Diaby (73' Loïc Rémy), Karim Benzema. (Coach: Laurent Robert Blanc (FRA)).
Goals: Belarus: 1-0 Éric Abidal (20' *own goal*).
France: 1-1 Florent Malouda (22').
Referee: David Fernández Borbalán (ESP)   Attendance: 26.500

07-06-2011   Dinamo Stadium, Minsk: Belarus – Luxembourg   2-0 (0-0)
Belarus: Yuri Zhevnov (C), Dmitri Verkhovtsov, Vitali Trubilo (62' Vyacheslav Hleb), Igor Shitov, Sergei Omelyanchuk, Maksim Bordachev, Yan Tigorev, Anton Putsila, Aleksandr Kulchiy (87' Sergei Kislyak), Timofei Kalachev, Andrei Voronkov (YC38) (46' Sergei Kornilenko). (Coach: Bernd Stange (GER)).
Luxembourg: Jonathan Joubert, Tom Schnell, Massimo Martino, Kevin Malget (60' Joël Kitenge), Eric Hoffmann, Guy Blaise, René Peters (C), Ben Payal (YC46), Lars Christian Krogh Gerson, Charles Leweck (84' Dan Collette), Daniël Alves Da Mota (77' Tom Laterza). (Coach: Luc Holtz (LUX)).
Goals: Belarus: 1-0 Sergei Kornilenko (48' penalty), 2-0 Anton Putsila (73').
Referee: Anar Salmanov (AZE)   Attendance: 9.500

07-06-2011   Bilino Polje, Zenica: Bosnia and Herzegovina – Albania   2-0 (0-0)
Bosnia and Herzegovina: Kenan Hasagic, Boris Pandza, Emir Spahic (C), Mensur Mujdza (73' Darko Maletic (YC77)), Elvir Rahimic, Miralem Pjanic (77' Muhamed Besic), Zvjezdan Misimovic, Haris Medunjanin, Senad Lulic, Vedad Ibisevic (61' Zlatan Muslimovic), Edin Dzeko. (Coach: Safet Susic (BOS)).
Albania: Samir Ujkani, Kristi Vangjeli, Armend Dallku, Debatik Çurri, Ervin Skela, Lorik Cana, Ansi Agolli (60' Andi Lila (RC87)), Altin Lala (C) (73' Gjergj Muzaka), Ervin Bulku, Hamdi Salihi, Erjon Bogdani (46' Klodian Duro (YC78)). (Coach: Josip Kuze (CRO)).
Goals: Bosnia and Herzegovina: 1-0 Haris Medunjanin (67'), 2-0 Darko Maletic (90'+1').
Referee: Kevin Bernie Raymond Blom (HOL)   Attendance: 9.000

02-09-2011   Stade Josy Barthel, Luxembourg: Luxembourg – Romania   0-2 (0-2)
Luxembourg: Jonathan Joubert, Tom Schnell, Eric Hoffmann (C) (76' Ante Bukvic), Guy Blaise, Ben Payal, Lars Christian Krogh Gerson, Gilles Bettmer, Mario Mutsch, Charles Leweck, Aurélien Joachim (46' Joël Kitenge), Daniël Alves Da Mota (61' Mathias Jänisch). (Coach: Luc Holtz (LUX)).
Romania: Cirpian Tatarusanu, Razvan Rat (C), Alexandru Matel, Dorin Goian (YC66), George Galamaz (62' Vlad Chiriches), Gabriel Torje (YC19) (76' Banel Nicolita (YC90+3)), Cristian Tanase, Costin Lazar, Razvan Cocis, Gheorghe Bucur, Ciprian Marica (87' Bogdan Stancu). (Coach: Victor Piturca (ROM)).
Goals: Romania: 0-1 Gabriel Torje (34'), 0-2 Gabriel Torje (45').
Referee: Sergey Gennadyevich Karasev (RUS)   Attendance: 2.812

02-09-2011   Dinamo Stadium, Minsk: Belarus – Bosnia and Herzegovina   0-2 (0-2)
Belarus: Yuri Zhevnov (C), Dmitri Verkhovtsov, Vitali Trubilo (YC40), Igor Shitov, Aleksandr Martynovich, Anton Putsila, Aleksandr Kulchiy, Sergei Kislyak, Maksim Zhavnerchik (63' Pavel Sitko), Timofei Kalachev, Sergei Kornilenko (63' Andrei Voronkov). (Coach: Bernd Stange (GER)).
Bosnia and Herzegovina: Kenan Hasagic, Sasa Papac (YC86), Boris Pandza, Emir Spahic (C) (YC34), Adnan Zahirovic, Elvir Rahimic, Sejad Salihovic (72' Darko Maletic (YC83)), Miralem Pjanic (YC79), Haris Medunjanin (88' Zlatan Muslimovic), Senad Lulic, Edin Dzeko (80' Zvjezdan Misimovic). (Coach: Safet Susic (BOS)).
Goals: Bosnia and Herzegovina: 0-1 Sejad Salihovic (22' penalty), 0-2 Haris Medunjanin (24').
Referee: Viktor Kassai (HUN)   Attendance: 25.365

02-09-2011   Qemal Stafa, Tirana: Albania – France   1-2 (0-2)
Albania: Samir Ujkani, Kristi Vangjeli, Armend Dallku (YC49), Debatik Çurri (24' Altin Lala), Admir Teli (YC36), Ervin Skela (46' Jahmir Hyka), Lorik Cana (C) (YC65), Ansi Agolli, Ervin Bulku (70' Elis Bakaj), Hamdi Salihi, Erjon Bogdani. (Coach: Josip Kuze (CRO)).
France: Hugo Lloris, Anthony Réveillère, Younès Kaboul, Éric Abidal, Patrice Evra, Franck Ribéry, Samir Nasri, Florent Malouda (82' Marvin Martin), Yann M'Vila, Alou Diarra (C), Karim Benzema. (Coach: Laurent Robert Blanc (FRA)).
Goals: Albania: 1-2 Erjon Bogdani (46').
France: 0-1 Karim Benzema (11'), 0-2 Yann M'Vila (18').
Referee: Alexey Nikolaev (RUS)   Attendance: 15.600

06-09-2011   Bilino Polje, Zenica: Bosnia and Herzegovina – Belarus   1-0 (0-0)
Bosnia and Herzegovina: Asmir Begovic, Sasa Papac, Boris Pandza (YC33) (46' Zvjezdan Misimovic), Mensur Mujdza, Adnan Zahirovic (YC90), Elvir Rahimic, Senijad Ibricic (64' Ermin Zec), Sejad Salihovic (YC9) (19' Semir Stilic), Haris Medunjanin, Senad Lulic, Edin Dzeko (C). (Coach: Safet Susic (BOS)).
Belarus: Yuri Zhevnov (C), Dmitri Verkhovtsov, Vitali Trubilo (YC15), Igor Shitov (YC22), Aleksandr Martynovich (YC79,YC85), Sergei Kislyak, Pavel Sitko (77' Andrei Voronkov), Anton Putsila (YC88), Aleksandr Kulchiy, Timofei Kalachev (YC27,YC34), Sergei Kornilenko (YC55) (72' Stanislav Dragun (YC90)). (Coach: Bernd Stange (GER)).
Goal: Bosnia and Herzegovina: 1-0 Zvjezdan Misimovic (87').
Referee: Martin Atkinson (ENG)   Attendance: 12.000

06-09-2011   Stade Josy Barthel, Luxembourg: Luxembourg – Albania   2-1 (1-0)
Luxembourg: Jonathan Joubert, Ante Bukvic, Guy Blaise, Tom Schnell (YC40), Mathias Jänisch, Gilles Bettmer, Ben Payal (88' Joël Pedro de Almeida), Lars Christian Krogh Gerson, Mario Mutsch (C), Charles Leweck (68' Aurélien Joachim), Daniël Alves Da Mota (70' Stefano Bensi). (Coach: Luc Holtz (LUX)).
Albania: Samir Ujkani, Franc Veliu (62' Ervin Bulku), Kristi Vangjeli, Admir Teli (YC35), Klodian Duro (46' Elis Bakaj), Ansi Agolli (RC53), Ervin Skela, Altin Lala (C) (YC50), Hamdi Salihi, Edmond Kapllani (46' Gjergj Muzaka), Erjon Bogdani (YC85,YC85). (Coach: Josip Kuze (CRO)).
Goals: Luxembourg: 1-0 Gilles Bettmer (27'), 2-1 Aurélien Joachim (78').
Albania: 1-1 Erjon Bogdani (64').
Referee: Petteri Kari (FIN)   Attendance: 2.132

224

06-09-2011   Stadionul National, Bucharest: Romania – France   0-0
Romania: Cirpian Tatarusanu, Srdjan Luchin, Razvan Rat (C), Dorin Goian (YC69), Vlad
Chiriches, Banel Nicolita (YC84), Cristian Tanase (YC14), Costin Lazar (43' Bogdan Stancu),
Razvan Cocis (YC54), Alexandru Bourceanu, Ciprian Marica (90' Gheorghe Bucur). (Coach:
Victor Piturca (ROM)).
France: Hugo Lloris (C), Adil Rami, Éric Abidal, Bacary Sagna, Patrice Evra, Franck Ribéry,
Marvin Martin, Yann M'Vila (YC26), Mathieu Valbuena (71' Loïc Rémy), Yohan Cabaye
(75' Samir Nasri), Karim Benzema. (Coach: Laurent Robert Blanc (FRA)).
Referee: Howard Melton Webb (ENG)   Attendance: 49.137

07-10-2011   Bilino Polje, Zenica: Bosnia and Herzegovina – Luxembourg 5-0 (4-0)
Bosnia and Herzegovina: Asmir Begovic, Sasa Papac, Emir Spahic (C), Mensur Mujdza, Elvir
Rahimic (59' Adnan Zahirovic), Miralem Pjanic, Zvjezdan Misimovic, Haris Medunjanin (64'
Senijad Ibricic), Senad Lulic (66' Darko Maletic), Vedad Ibisevic, Edin Dzeko. (Coach: Safet
Susic (BOS)).
Luxembourg: Jonathan Joubert, Ante Bukvic (YC22), Guy Blaise, Tom Schnell, Gilles
Bettmer, Ben Payal, Lars Christian Krogh Gerson, Mario Mutsch (C) (YC50), Tom Laterza
(83' Mathias Jänisch), Charles Leweck, Daniël Alves Da Mota (44' Aurélien Joachim).
(Coach: Luc Holtz (LUX)).
Goals: Bosnia and Herzegovina: 1-0 Edin Dzeko (12'), 2-0 Zvjezdan Misimovic (15'), 3-0
Zvjezdan Misimovic (22' penalty), 4-0 Miralem Pjanic (36'), 5-0 Haris Medunjanin (51').
Referee: Simon Lee Evans (WAL)   Attendance: 10.000

07-10-2011   Stadionul National, Bucharest: Romania – Belarus   2-2 (1-1)
Romania: Costel Pantilimon, Gabriel Tamas, Razvan Rat (C) (YC47), Cosmin Moti (YC85),
Alexandru Matel, Gabriel Torje, Lucian Sanmartean (28' Adrian Cristea), Costin Lazar (70'
Razvan Cocis), Alexandru Bourceanu, Adrian Mutu, Ciprian Marica (80' Bogdan Stancu).
(Coach: Victor Piturca (ROM)).
Belarus: Yuri Zhevnov (C), Dmitri Verkhovtsov (YC51), Sergei Omelyanchuk, Egor Filipenko
(19' Pavel Plaskonny), Maksim Bordachev (90'+2' Oleg Veretilo), Aleksandr Kulchiy, Sergei
Krivets (60' Filipp Rudik), Sergei Kislyak, Pavel Nekhaychik, Stanislav Dragun, Sergei
Kornilenko (YC23). (Coach: Bernd Stange (GER)).
Goals: Romania: 1-0 Adrian Mutu (19'), 2-1 Adrian Mutu (51' penalty).
Belarus: 1-1 Sergei Kornilenko (45'), 2-2 Stanislav Dragun (82').
Referee: Alan Kelly (IRL)   Attendance: 29.486

07-10-2011   Stade de France, Saint-Denis: France – Albania   3-0 (2-0)
France: Hugo Lloris (C), Adil Rami (YC75), Younès Kaboul, Patrice Evra (46' Anthony
Réveillère), Mathieu Debuchy (YC90+1), Samir Nasri, Florent Malouda, Yann M'Vila, Yohan
Cabaye (47' Marvin Martin), Bafétimbi Gomis (80' Djibril Cissé), Loïc Rémy (YC52).
(Coach: Laurent Robert Blanc (FRA)).
Albania: Samir Ujkani, Kristi Vangjeli (YC49), Andi Lila (YC71), Armend Dallku, Gjergj
Muzaka (74' Ahmed Januzi), Gilman Lika (81' Sabien Lilaj), Jahmir Hyka (63' Elis Bakaj),
Klodian Duro (YC61), Lorik Cana (C) (YC36), Odise Roshi, Hamdi Salihi. (Coach: Josip
Kuze (CRO)).
Goals: France: 1-0 Florent Malouda (11'), 2-0 Loïc Rémy (38'), 3-0 Anthony Réveillère (67').
Referee: Michail Koukoulakis (GRE)   Attendance: 65.239

11-10-2011   Qemal Stafa, Tirana: Albania – Romania 1-1 (1-0)
Albania: Samir Ujkani, Andi Lila, Armend Dallku, Admir Teli, Sabien Lilaj, Lorik Cana,
Odise Roshi (77' Gjergj Muzaka), Altin Lala (C), Hamdi Salihi, Erjon Bogdani (46' Ahmed
Januzi (YC75)), Elis Bakaj (67' Jahmir Hyka). (Coach: Josip Kuze (CRO)).
Romania: Silviu Lung Jr., Gabriel Tamas (YC70), Srdjan Luchin, Iasmin Latovlevici, Dorin
Goian, Banel Nicolita (YC56) (63' Gabriel Torje), Costin Lazar (87' Gheorghe Bucur), Razvan
Cocis, Alexandru Bourceanu, Adrian Mutu (C), Ciprian Marica (49' Bogdan Stancu). (Coach:
Victor Piturca (ROM)).
Goals: Albania: 1-0 Hamdi Salihi (24').
Romania: 1-1 Srdjan Luchin (77').
Referee: Gediminas Mazeika (LIT)   Attendance: 3.000

11-10-2011   Stade de France, Dainst-Denis: France – Bosnia and Herzegovina 1-1 (0-1)
France: Hugo Lloris (C), Anthony Réveillère, Adil Rami, Éric Abidal, Patrice Evra (YC67),
Samir Nasri, Florent Malouda (61' Marvin Martin), Yann M'Vila, Yohan Cabaye (YC33) (61'
Kevin Gameiro), Jérémy Ménez, Loïc Rémy (82' Alou Diarra (YC88)). (Coach: Laurent
Robert Blanc (FRA)).
Bosnia and Herzegovina: Kenan Hasagic (46' Asmir Begovic), Sasa Papac (YC32), Boris
Pandza (YC68), Emir Spahic (C) (YC54), Mensur Mujdza (YC61) (61' Darko Maletic), Elvir
Rahimic, Miralem Pjanic, Zvjezdan Misimovic, Haris Medunjanin (71' Adnan Zahirovic),
Senad Lulic, Edin Dzeko. (Coach: Safet Susic (BOS)).
Goals: France: 1-1 Samir Nasri (78' penalty).
Bosnia and Herzegovina: 0-1 Edin Dzeko (40').
Referee: Craig Alexander Thomson (SCO)   Attendance: 78.467

GROUP   E

03-09-2010	Chisinau	Moldova – Finland	2-0 (0-0)
03-09-2010	Solna	Sweden – Hungary	2-0 (0-0)
03-09-2010	Serravalle	San Marino – Netherlands	0-5 (0-2)
07-09-2010	Malmö	Sweden – San Marino	6-0 (3-0)
07-09-2010	Budapest	Hungary – Moldova	2-1 (0-0)
07-09-2010	Rotterdam	Netherlands – Finland	2-1 (2-1)
08-10-2010	Budapest	Hungary – San Marino	8-0 (4-0)
08-10-2010	Chisinau	Moldova – Netherlands	0-1 (0-1)
12-10-2010	Helsinki	Finland – Hungary	1-2 (0-0)
12-10-2010	Amsterdam	Netherlands – Sweden	4-1 (2-0)
12-10-2010	Serravalle	San Marino – Moldova	0-2 (0-1)
17-11-2010	Helsinki	Finland – San Marino	8-0 (1-0)
25-03-2011	Budapest	Hungary – Netherlands	0-4 (0-2)
29-03-2011	Solna	Sweden – Moldova	2-1 (1-0)
29-03-2011	Amsterdam	Netherlands – Hungary	5-3 (1-0)
03-06-2011	Serravalle	San Marino – Finland	0-1 (0-1)
03-06-2011	Chisinau	Moldova – Sweden	1-4 (0-2)
07-06-2011	Solna	Sweden – Finland	5-0 (3-0)
07-06-2011	Serravalle	San Marino – Hungary	0-3 (0-1)
02-09-2011	Helsinki	Finland – Moldova	4-1 (2-0)
02-09-2011	Budapest	Hungary – Sweden	2-1 (1-0)
02-09-2011	Eindhoven	Netherlands – San Marino	11-0 (3-0)

06-09-2011	Helsinki	Finland – Netherlands	0-2 (0-1)
06-09-2011	Chisinau	Moldova – Hungary	0-2 (0-1)
06-09-2011	Serravalle	San Marino – Sweden	0-5 (0-0)
07-10-2011	Helsinki	Finland – Sweden	1-2 (0-1)
07-10-2011	Rotterdam	Netherlands – Moldova	1-0 (1-0)
11-10-2011	Budapest	Hungary – Finland	0-0
11-10-2011	Chisinau	Moldova – San Marino	4-0 (1-0)
11-10-2011	Solna	Sweden – Netherlands	3-2 (1-1)

FINAL STANDING

Pos	Team	Pld	W	D	L	GF	GA	GD	Pts
1	Netherlands	10	9	0	1	37	8	+29	27
2	Sweden	10	8	0	2	31	11	+20	24
3	Hungary	10	6	1	3	22	14	+8	19
4	Finland	10	3	1	6	16	16	0	10
5	Moldova	10	3	0	7	12	16	-4	9
6	San Marino	10	0	0	10	0	53	-53	0

Netherlands and Sweden qualified for the Final Tournament in Poland and Ukraine.

03-09-2010   Zimbru Stadium, Chisinau: Moldova – Finland   2-0 (0-0)
Moldova: Stanislav Namasco, Simeon Bulgaru, Vitali Bordian, Alexandru Epureanu (C), Igor Tîgîrlas (YC68) (68' Igor Bugaev), Alexei Savinov, Nicolae Josan (58' Alexandru Suvorov), Vadim Boret, Eugeniu (Eugen) Cebotaru, Viorel Frunza, Anatoli Doros (75' Valeriu Andronic (YC87)). (Coach: Gavril Pelé Balint (ROM)).
Finland: Otto Fredrikson, Petri Pasanen, Niklas Moisander, Sami Hyypiä (C) (RC36), Tim Sparv, Markus Heikkinen, Roman Eremenko, Alexei Eremenko (81' Mikael Forssell), Roni Porokara (75' Mika Väyrynen), Jari Litmanen (C) (46' Kasper Hämäläinen), Jonathan Johansson. (Coach: Stuart Baxter (ENG)).
Goals: Moldova: 1-0 Alexandru Suvorov (69'), 2-0 Anatoli Doros (74').
Referee: Robert Malek (POL)   Attendance: 10.300

03-09-2010   Råsunda Stadium, Solna: Sweden – Hungary   2-0 (0-0)
Sweden: Andreas Isaksson (46' Johan Wiland), Behrang Safari, Olof Mellberg, Daniel Majstorovic, Mikael Lustig, Pontus Wernbloom, Anders Svensson (33' Kim Källström), Emir Bajrami, Ola Toivonen (YC75), Zlatan Ibrahimovic (C), Johan Elmander (49' Sebastian Larsson). (Coach: Erik Hamrén (SWE)).
Hungary: Gábor Király (YC86), Zoltán Lipták (YC66), Pál Lázár (YC90+3), Roland Juhász, Krisztián Vadócz, Zsolt Laczkó (YC90+1), Vladimir Koman, Ákos Elek (59' Tamás Priskin), Balázs Dzsudzsák (46' Szabolcs Huszti), Zoltán Gera (C), Gergely Rudolf (82' Tamás Hajnal). (Coach: Sándor Egervári (HUN)).
Goals: Sweden: 1-0 Pontus Wernbloom (51'), 2-0 Pontus Wernbloom (73').
Referee: Martin Atkinson (ENG)   Attendance: 32.304

03-09-2010   Stadio Olimpico, Serravalle: San Marino – Netherlands   0-5 (0-2)
San Marino: Aldo Simoncini, Fabio Vitaioli, Carlo Valentini, Davide Simoncini (YC15) (61'
Simone Bacciocchi (YC64)), Alessandro Della Valle (YC45), Maicol Berretti (YC45+1),
Damiano Vannucci, Pier Filippo Mazza, Andy Selva (C), Manuel Marani (76' Alex
Gasperoni), Matteo Vitaioli (82' Nicola Ciacci). (Coach: Giampaolo Mazza (SMR)).
Netherlands: Maarten Stekelenburg, Gregory van der Wiel, Erik Pieters, Joris Mathijsen,
Hedwiges Maduro (YC35), Mark van Bommel (C), Nigel de Jong (46' Rafael van der Vaart),
Wesley Sneijder, Eljero Elia (59' Ibrahim Afellay), Dirk Kuyt (67' Ruud van Nistelrooy),
Klaas-Jan Huntelaar. (Coach: Lambertus (Bert) van Marwijk (HOL)).
Goals: Netherlands: 0-1 Dirk Kuyt (16' penalty), 0-2 Klaas-Jan Huntelaar (38'), 0-3 Klaas-Jan
Huntelaar (48'), 0-4 Klaas-Jan Huntelaar (66'), 0-5 Ruud van Nistelrooy (90').
Referee: Simon Lee Evans (WAL)   Attendance: 4.127

07-09-2010   Swedbank Stadion, Malmö: Sweden – San Marino   6-0 (3-0)
Sweden: Johan Wiland, Behrang Safari, Olof Mellberg (RC33), Daniel Majstorovic, Mikael
Lustig, Emir Bajrami, Pontus Wernbloom (69' Johan Elmander), Sebastian Larsson, Kim
Källström, Ola Toivonen (46' Andreas Granqvist), Zlatan Ibrahimovic (C) (82' Marcus Berg).
(Coach: Erik Hamrén (SWE)).
San Marino: Aldo Simoncini, Simone Bacciocchi (79' Carlo Valentini), Fabio Vitaioli (YC59),
Davide Simoncini, Alessandro Della Valle, Nicola Chiaruzzi (72' Alex Gasperoni), Damiano
Vannucci, Pier Filippo Mazza, Andy Selva (C), Manuel Marani (YC26) (56' Maicol Berretti),
Matteo Vitaioli. (Coach: Giampaolo Mazza (SMR)).
Goals: Sweden: 1-0 Zlatan Ibrahimovic (7'), 2-0 Davide Simoncini (12' own goal), 3-0 Aldo
Simoncini (26' own goal), 4-0 Andreas Granqvist (51'), 5-0 Zlatan Ibrahimovic (77'), 6-0
Marcus Berg (90'+2').
Referee: David McKeon (IRL)   Attendance: 21.083

07-10-2010   Szusza Ferenc Stadium, Budapest: Hungary – Moldova   2-1 (0-0)
Hungary: Gábor Király, Zoltán Lipták (YC11), Pál Lázár (YC33), Roland Juhász, Zsolt
Laczkó, Vladimir Koman (88' Krisztián Vadócz), Ákos Elek, Balázs Dzsudzsák, Péter
Czvitkovics (46' Ádám Szalai), Zoltán Gera (C), Gergely Rudolf (64' Vilmos Vanczák).
(Coach: Sándor Egervári (HUN)).
Moldova: Stanislav Namasco, Simeon Bulgaru, Vitali Bordian, Vadim Bolohan, Alexandru
Epureanu (C), Igor Tîgîrlas, Nicolae Josan (59' Anatoli Doros), Alexandru Suvorov, Petru
Racu, Eugeniu (Eugen) Cebotaru (71' Andrei Cojocari), Viorel Frunza (YC28) (84' Igor
Bugaev). (Coach: Gavril Pelé Balint (ROM)).
Goals: Hungary: 1-0 Gergely Rudolf (50'), 2-0 Vladimir Koman (66').
Moldova: 2-1 Alexandru Suvorov (79').
Referee: Libor Kovarík (CZE)   Attendance: 9.209

07-10-2010   De Kuip, Rotterdam: Netherlands – Finland   2-1 (2-1)
Netherlands: Maarten Stekelenburg, Gregory van der Wiel, Joris Mathijsen, John Heitinga,
Ibrahim Afellay (74' Jeremain Lens), Rafael van der Vaart (64' Eljero Elia), Mark van
Bommel (C), Nigel de Jong, Wesley Sneijder, Vurnon Anita, Klaas-Jan Huntelaar (82' Ruud
van Nistelrooy). (Coach: Lambertus (Bert) van Marwijk (HOL)).
Finland: Otto Fredrikson, Petri Pasanen (C), Niklas Moisander, Veli Lampi, Roman Eremenko
(YC33), Mika Väyrynen, Tim Sparv (YC60), Daniel Sjölund (68' Jonathan Johansson),
Markus Heikkinen (YC16), Kasper Hämäläinen (46' Roni Porokara), Mikael Forssell (80'
Alexei Eremenko). (Coach: Stuart Baxter (ENG)).
Goals: Netherlands: 1-0 Klaas-Jan Huntelaar (7'), 2-0 Klaas-Jan Huntelaar (16' penalty).
Finland: 2-1 Mikael Forssell (18').
Referee: Alexey Nikolaev (RUS)   Attendance: 25.000

08-10-2010   Stadium Puskás Ferenc, Budapest: Hungary – San Marino   8-0 (4-0)
Hungary: Gábor Király, Krisztián Vermes, Vilmos Vanczák, Roland Juhász, Zsolt Laczkó, Vladimir Koman (79' Péter Czvitkovics), Ákos Elek (64' Krisztián Vadócz), Balázs Dzsudzsák, Zoltán Gera (C), Ádám Szalai (64' Tamás Priskin), Gergely Rudolf. (Coach: Sándor Egervári (HUN)).
San Marino: Aldo Simoncini, Fabio Vitaioli, Carlo Valentini (YC38,YC90+2), Alessandro Della Valle (YC43), Simone Bacciocchi (52' Nicola Albani), Maicol Berretti, Damiano Vannucci (C), Fabio Bollini (84' Michele Cervellini), Paolo Montagna, Manuel Marani, Matteo Vitaioli (77' Matteo Bugli). (Coach: Giampaolo Mazza (SMR)).
Goals: Hungary: 1-0 Gergely Rudolf (11'), 2-0 Ádám Szalai (18'), 3-0 Gergely Rudolf (25'), 4-0 Ádám Szalai (27'), 5-0 Ádám Szalai (48'), 6-0 Vladimir Koman (60'), 7-0 Balázs Dzsudzsák (89'), 8-0 Zoltán Gera (90'+3' penalty).
Referee: Hannes Kaasik (EST)   Attendance: 10.596

08-10-2010   Zimbru Stadium, Chisinau: Moldova – Netherlands   0-1 (0-1)
Moldova: Stanislav Namasco, Simeon Bulgaru, Vitali Bordian, Vadim Bolohan, Victor Golovatenco, Alexandru Epureanu (C), Alexandru Suvorov, Petru Racu, Eugeniu (Eugen) Cebotaru (69' Valeriu Andronic), Viorel Frunza (46' Igor Bugaev), Anatoli Doros (78' Nicolae Josan). (Coach: Gavril Pelé Balint (ROM)).
Netherlands: Maarten Stekelenburg, Gregory van der Wiel, Erik Pieters, Joris Mathijsen, John Heitinga, Rafael van der Vaart, Mark van Bommel (C), Ibrahim Afellay (90' Urby Emanuelson), Wesley Sneijder, Dirk Kuyt, Klaas-Jan Huntelaar. (Coach: Lambertus (Bert) van Marwijk (HOL)).
Goal: Netherlands: 0-1 Klaas-Jan Huntelaar (37').
Referee: Florian Meyer (GER)   Attendance: 10.500

12-10-2010   Olympic Stadium, Helsinki: Finland – Hungary   1-2 (0-0)
Finland: Jussi Jääskeläinen, Petri Pasanen, Niklas Moisander, Sami Hyypiä (C), Mika Väyrynen (YC41), Tim Sparv (72' Jari Litmanen), Daniel Sjölund (81' Shefki Kuqi), Markus Heikkinen, Roman Eremenko, Roni Porokara (71' Alexei Eremenko), Mikael Forssell. (Coach: Stuart Baxter (ENG)).
Hungary: Gábor Király, Krisztián Vermes, Zoltán Lipták (YC37), Roland Juhász, Krisztián Vadócz (75' Ádám Pintér), Zsolt Laczkó (86' Vilmos Vanczák), Ákos Elek (YC88), Balázs Dzsudzsák, Zoltán Gera (C), Ádám Szalai, Gergely Rudolf (46' Vladimir Koman). (Coach: Sándor Egervári (HUN)).
Goals: Finland: 1-1 Mikael Forssell (86').
Hungary: 0-1 Ádám Szalai (50'), 1-2 Balázs Dzsudzsák (90'+4').
Referee: Alan Kelly (IRL)   Attendance: 18.532

12-10-2010   Amsterdam ArenA, Amsterdam: Netherlands – Sweden   4-1 (2-0)
Netherlands: Maarten Stekelenburg, Gregory van der Wiel, Erik Pieters, Joris Mathijsen, John Heitinga, Rafael van der Vaart, Mark van Bommel (C) (72' Wout Brama), Ibrahim Afellay, Wesley Sneijder, Dirk Kuyt (29' Jeremain Lens), Klaas-Jan Huntelaar (85' Ruud van Nistelrooy). (Coach: Lambertus (Bert) van Marwijk (HOL)).
Sweden: Andreas Isaksson, Behrang Safari (46' Oscar Wendt), Daniel Majstorovic, Mikael Lustig, Andreas Granqvist, Pontus Wernbloom (54' Kim Källström), Anders Svensson, Sebastian Larsson (YC49), Ola Toivonen (YC66) (79' Marcus Berg), Zlatan Ibrahimovic (C), Johan Elmander. (Coach: Erik Hamrén (SWE)).
Goals: Netherlands: 1-0 Klaas-Jan Huntelaar (4'), 2-0 Ibrahim Afellay (37'), 3-0 Klaas-Jan Huntelaar (55'), 4-0 Ibrahim Afellay (59').
Sweden: 4-1 Andreas Granqvist (69').
Referee: Stéphane Lannoy (FRA)   Attendance: 46.000

229

12-10-2010   Stadio Olimpico, Serravalle: San Marino – Moldova   0-2 (0-1)
San Marino: Aldo Simoncini, Fabio Vitaioli, Davide Simoncini, Simone Bacciocchi (YC86), Damiano Vannucci (C), Michele Cervellini (60' Maicol Berretti), Fabio Bollini (67' Nicola Ciacci (YC90+3)), Pier Filippo Mazza, Paolo Montagna (81' Matteo Coppini), Manuel Marani, Matteo Vitaioli (YC27). (Coach: Giampaolo Mazza (SMR)).
Moldova: Stanislav Namasco, Vitali Bordian, Victor Golovatenco, Alexandru Epureanu (C), Nicolae Josan (69' Denis Zmeu), Andrei Cojocari (YC42) (81' Alexei Savinov), Vadim Boret, Valeriu Andronic, Alexandru Suvorov, Viorel Frunza, Igor Bugaev (62' Anatoli Doros). (Coach: Gavril Pelé Balint (ROM)).
Goals: Moldova: 0-1 Nicolae Josan (20'), 0-2 Anatoli Doros (86' penalty).
Referee: Mark Courtney (NIR)   Attendance: 714

17-11-2010   Olympic Stadium, Helsinki: Finland – San Marino   8-0 (1-0)
Finland: Otto Fredrikson, Petri Pasanen (C), Niklas Moisander, Veli Lampi, Markus Heikkinen, Kasper Hämäläinen (70' Roni Porokara), Roman Eremenko (YC89), Alexei Eremenko (80' Shefki Kuqi), Mika Väyrynen, Daniel Sjölund (46' Jari Litmanen), Mikael Forssell. (Coach: Olavi (Olli) Huttunen (FIN)).
San Marino: Aldo Simoncini, Alessandro Della Valle, Fabio Vitaioli (72' Damiano Vannucci), Maicol Berretti (67' Alex Della Valle), Michele Cervellini, Matteo Bugli, Matteo Coppini, Andy Selva (C) (YC83), Paolo Montagna (79' Manuel Marani), Nicola Albani (YC70), Matteo Vitaioli. (Coach: Giampaolo Mazza (SMR)).
Goals: Finland: 1-0 Mika Väyrynen (39'), 2-0 Kasper Hämäläinen (49'), 3-0 Mikael Forssell (51'), 4-0 Mikael Forssell (59'), 5-0 Kasper Hämäläinen (67'), 6-0 Jari Litmanen (71' penalty), 7-0 Roni Porokara (73'), 8-0 Mikael Forssell (78').
Referee: Radek Matejek (CZE)   Attendance: 8.192

25-03-2011   Stadium Puskás Ferenc, Budapest: Hungary – Netherlands   0-4 (0-2)
Hungary: Gábor Király, Zoltán Lipták (YC67), Roland Juhász, Vilmos Vanczák (YC61), Zsolt Laczkó, Vladimir Koman (YC44) (46' Péter Czvitkovics), Ákos Elek (YC59) (79' Tamás Priskin), Balázs Dzsudzsák, József Varga (46' Krisztián Vadócz), Zoltán Gera (C), Gergely Rudolf. (Coach: Sándor Egervári (HUN)).
Netherlands: Michel Vorm, Erik Pieters, Joris Mathijsen, Gregory van der Wiel, John Heitinga, Ibrahim Afellay (63' Eljero Elia), Rafael van der Vaart (C) (82' Kevin Strootman), Wesley Sneijder, Nigel de Jong, Dirk Kuyt (82' Ruud van Nistelrooy), Robin van Persie (YC18). (Coach: Lambertus (Bert) van Marwijk (HOL)).
Goals: Netherlands: 0-1 Rafael van der Vaart (8'), 0-2 Ibrahim Afellay (45'), 0-3 Dirk Kuyt (54'), 0-4 Robin van Persie (62').
Referee: Carlos Velasco Carballo (ESP)   Attendance: 23.817

29-03-2011   Råsunda Stadium, Solna: Sweden – Moldova   2-1 (1-0)
Sweden: Andreas Isaksson, Oscar Wendt, Mikael Lustig, Andreas Granqvist, Mikael Antonsson, Pontus Wernbloom (YC17) (65' Rasmus Elm), Sebastian Larsson, Kim Källström (YC88), Emir Bajrami (73' Martin Olsson), Zlatan Ibrahimovic (C), Johan Elmander (89' Alexander Gerndt). (Coach: Erik Hamrén (SWE)).
Moldova: Stanislav Namasco, Vadim Bolohan, Victor Golovatenco, Igor Armas, Vadim Boret, Alexandru Suvorov, Petru Racu, Alexandru Gatcan (83' Valeriu Andronic), Eugeniu (Eugen) Cebotaru, Viorel Frunza (C) (46' Igor Bugaev), Anatoli Doros (72' Anatoli Cheptine). (Coach: Gavril Pelé Balint (ROM)).
Goals: Sweden: 1-0 Mikael Lustig (30'), 2-0 Sebastian Larsson (82').
Moldova: 2-1 Alexandru Suvorov (90'+2').
Referee: Knut Kircher (GER)   Attendance: 25.544
(Zlatan Ibrahimovic missed a penalty in the 43rd minute)

230

29-03-2011   Amsterdam ArenA, Amsterdam: Netherlands – Hungary 5-3 (1-0)
Netherlands: Michel Vorm, Erik Pieters (64' Urby Emanuelson), Joris Mathijsen, Gregory van der Wiel, John Heitinga, Ibrahim Afellay, Rafael van der Vaart (C), Wesley Sneijder, Nigel de Jong, Dirk Kuyt (90' Eljero Elia), Robin van Persie (46' Ruud van Nistelrooy). (Coach: Lambertus (Bert) van Marwijk (HOL)).
Hungary: Márton Fülöp, Ádám Pintér (YC39) (46' Vladimir Koman), Pál Lázár (YC23), Roland Juhásh (YC59), Vilmos Vanczák, Zsolt Laczkó, Balázs Dzsudzsák, Krisztián Vadócz (90' Péter Czvitkovic), Zoltán Gera (C), Gergely Rudolf, Tamás Priskin (73' Attila Tököli). (Coach: Sándor Egervári (HUN)).
Goals: Netherlands: 1-0 Robin van Persie (13'), 2-2 Wesley Sneijder (61'), 3-2 Ruud van Nistelrooy (73'), 4-3 Dirk Kuyt (78'), 5-3 Dirk Kuyt (81').
Hungary: 1-1 Gergely Rudolf (46'), 1-2 Zoltán Gera (50'), 3-3 Zoltán Gera (75').
Referee: Svein Oddvar Moen (NOR)   Attendance: 51.774

03-06-2011   Stadio Olimpico, Serravalle: San Marino – Finland 0-1 (0-1)
San Marino: Aldo Simoncini, Fabio Vitaioli (88' Simone Bacciocchi), Davide Simoncini (YC80), Alessandro Della Valle (YC49), Damiano Vannucci, Michele Cervellini, Fabio Bollini, Pier Filippo Mazza (77' Maicol Berretti), Andy Selva (C), Manuel Marani, Matteo Vitaioli (81' Paolo Montagna). (Coach: Giampaolo Mazza (SMR)).
Finland: Lukás Hrádecky, Jukka Raitala, Petri Pasanen (C), Niklas Moisander, Veli Lampi, Mika Väyrynen, Përparim Hetemaj (84' Daniel Sjölund), Markus Heikkinen, Kasper Hämäläinen, Alexei Eremenko (68' Riku Riski), Mikael Forssell (90' Berat Sadik). (Coach: Mika-Matti (Mixu) Petteri Paatelainen (FIN)).
Goal: Finland: 0-1 Mikael Forssell (41').
Referee: Andrejs Sipailo (LAT)   Attendance: 1.218

03-06-2011   Zimbru Stadium, Chisinau: Moldova – Sweden 1-4 (0-2)
Moldova: Stanislav Namasco, Vadim Bolohan, Victor Golovatenco, Igor Armas, Stanislav Ivanov (C), Alexandru Suvorov, Petru Racu, Alexandru Gatcan (46' Igor Tîgîrlas), Eugeniu (Eugen) Cebotaru (78' Artur Patras), Igor Bugaev, Anatoli Doros (63' Gheorghe Boghiu). (Coach: Gavril Pelé Balint (ROM)).
Sweden: Andreas Isaksson, Oscar Wendt, Olof Mellberg, Daniel Majstorovic, Mikael Lustig, Anders Svensson (C), Sebastian Larsson, Kim Källström, Tobias Hysén (41' Emir Bajrami), Ola Toivonen (69' Pontus Wernbloom), Johan Elmander (76' Alexander Gerndt). (Coach: Erik Hamrén (SWE)).
Goals: Moldova: 1-3 Igor Bugaev (61').
Sweden: 0-1 Ola Toivonen (11'), 0-2 Johan Elmander (30'), 0-3 Johan Elmander (58'), 1-4 Alexander Gerndt (88').
Referee: Andre Marriner (ENG)   Attendance: 10.500

07-06-2011   Råsunda Stadium, Solna: Sweden – Finland 5-0 (3-0)
Sweden: Andreas Isaksson, Oscar Wendt, Olof Mellberg, Daniel Majstorovic, Mikael Lustig, Anders Svensson (C), Sebastian Larsson (89' Christian Wilhelmsson), Kim Källström, Emir Bajrami, Ola Toivonen (25' Zlatan Ibrahimovic), Johan Elmander (81' Pontus Wernbloom). (Coach: Erik Hamrén (SWE)).
Finland: Anssi Jaakkola, Joona Toivio, Petri Pasanen (C), Niklas Moisander, Mika Väyrynen, Përparim Hetemaj, Markus Heikkinen (46' Markus Halsti), Kasper Hämäläinen (46' Mika Ääritalo), Roman Eremenko, Alexei Eremenko (YC11) (80' Alexander Ring), Mikael Forssell. (Coach: Mika-Matti (Mixu) Petteri Paatelainen (FIN)).
Goals: Sweden: 1-0 Kim Källström (11'), 2-0 Zlatan Ibrahimovic (31'), 3-0 Zlatan Ibrahimovic (35'), 4-0 Zlatan Ibrahimovic (53'), 5-0 Emir Bajrami (83').
Referee: Antony Gautier (FRA)   Attendance: 32.128

07-06-2011   Stadio Olimpico, Serravalle: San Marino – Hungary   0-3 (0-1)
San Marino: Aldo Simoncini (YC41), Fabio Vitaioli (46' Alex Della Valle), Alessandro Della
Valle (YC73), Giacomo Benedettini, Damiano Vannucci, Michele Cervellini (YC29), Fabio
Bollini (79' Simone Bacciocchi), Pier Filippo Mazza, Andy Selva (C), Manuel Marani (64'
Maicol Berretti (YC75)), Matteo Vitaioli. (Coach: Giampaolo Mazza (SMR)).
Hungary: Gábor Király, Vilmos Vanczák (YC64), Zoltán Lipták (87' Ádám Pintér), Roland
Juhász (C) (YC17), Zsolt Laczkó, Vladimir Koman, Tamás Hajnal (71' Péter Czvitkovic),
Ákos Elek, Balázs Dzsudzsák, Krisztián Németh, Imre Szabics (83' Tamás Koltai). (Coach:
Sándor Egervári (HUN)).
Goals: Hungary: 0-1 Zoltán Lipták (40'), 0-2 Imre Szabics (49'), 0-3 Vladimir Koman (83').
Referee: Pavle Radovanovic (MNE)   Attendance: 1.915

02-09-2011   Olympic Stadium, Helsinki: Finland – Moldova   4-1 (2-0)
Finland: Lukás Hrádecky, Joona Toivio, Jukka Raitala, Niklas Moisander (C), Roman
Eremenko, Kari Arkivuo, Daniel Sjölund (61' Teemu Pukki), Përparim Hetemaj (YC83),
Kasper Hämäläinen (77' Timo Furuholm), Alexander Ring (72' Mika Väyrynen), Mikael
Forssell. (Coach: Mika-Matti (Mixu) Petteri Paatelainen (FIN)).
Moldova: Nicolae Calancea, Igor Armas, Victor Golovatenco, Alexandru Epureanu (C)
(YC67), Vadim Boret, Denis Zmeu, Alexei Savinov, Alexandru Suvorov (YC47) (55' Vitali
Bordian), Eugeniu (Eugen) Cebotaru (YC68), Gheorghe Ovsyannikov (69' Serghei Alexeev),
Anatoli Doros (YC51) (55' Anatoli Cheptine). (Coach: Gavril Pelé Balint (ROM)).
Goals: Finland: 1-0 Kasper Hämäläinen (11'), 2-0 Kasper Hämäläinen (43'), 3-0 Mikael
Forssell (52' penalty), 4-0 Igor Armas (70' own goal).
Moldova: 4-1 Serghei Alexeev (85').
Referee: Anastassios Kakos (GRE)   Attendance: 9.056

02-09-2011   Stadium Puskás Ferenc, Budapest: Hungary – Sweden   2-1 (1-0)
Hungary: Gábor Király, Ádám Pintér, Zoltán Lipták (YC48) (74' György Sándor), Zsolt
Korcsmár, József Varga, Zsolt Laczkó, Vladimir Koman, Tamás Hajnal (C) (66' Zoltán
Stieber), Ákos Elek, Gergely Rudolf, Imre Szabics (YC50) (80' Tamás Priskin). (Coach:
Sándor Egervári (HUN)).
Sweden: Andreas Isaksson, Oscar Wendt (YC19), Daniel Majstorovic, Mikael Lustig, Andreas
Granqvist, Christian Wilhelmsson (YC49), Anders Svensson (53' Rasmus Elm), Sebastian
Larsson (68' Ola Toivonen), Kim Källström (88' Pontus Wernbloom), Zlatan Ibrahimovic (C)
(YC35), Johan Elmander. (Coach: Erik Hamrén (SWE)).
Goals: Hungary: 1-0 Imre Szabics (44'), 2-1 Gergely Rudolf (90').
Sweden: 1-1 Christian Wilhelmsson (60').
Referee: Damir Skomina (SLO)   Attendance: 23.500
(Tamás Hajnal missed a penalty in the 19th minute)

02-09-2011   Philips Stadion, Eindhoven: Netherlands – San Marino   11-0 (3-0)
Netherlands: Maarten Stekelenburg, Gregory van der Wiel, Erik Pieters, Joris Mathijsen, John
Heitinga, Mark van Bommel (C) (74' Hedwiges Maduro), Kevin Strootman (86' Georginio
Wijnaldum), Wesley Sneijder, Dirk Kuyt (74' Eljero Elia), Klaas-Jan Huntelaar, Robin van
Persie. (Coach: Lambertus (Bert) van Marwijk (HOL)).
San Marino: Aldo Simoncini, Giacomo Benedettini, Matteo Andreini, Fabio Vitaioli, Davide
Simoncini (YC45+1) (82' Simone Bacciocchi), Fabio Bollini (68' Alex Gasperoni (YC75)),
Damiano Vannucci, Michele Cervellini, Pier Filippo Mazza (54' Matteo Coppini), Andy Selva
(C), Matteo Vitaioli. (Coach: Giampaolo Mazza (SMR)).
Goals: Netherlands: 1-0 Robin van Persie (7'), 2-0 Wesley Sneijder (12'), 3-0 John Heitinga
(17'), 4-0 Dirk Kuyt (49'), 5-0 Klaas-Jan Huntelaar (56'), 6-0 Robin van Persie (65'), 7-0
Robin van Persie (67'), 8-0 Klaas-Jan Huntelaar (77'), 9-0 Robin van Persie (79'), 10-0
Wesley Sneijder (87'), 11-0 Georginio Wijnaldum (90').
Referee: Liran Liany (ISR)   Attendance: 35.000

06-09-2011   Olympic Stadium, Helsinki: Finland – Netherlands   0-2 (0-1)
Finland: Lukás Hrádecky, Petri Pasanen (78' Jukka Raitala), Niklas Moisander (C), Joona
Toivio, Përparim Hetemaj (YC28,YC60), Kasper Hämäläinen, Roman Eremenko, Kari
Arkivuo, Alexander Ring, Mikael Forssell (86' Daniel Sjölund), Teemu Pukki (61' Mika
Väyrynen). (Coach: Mika-Matti (Mixu) Petteri Paatelainen (FIN)).
Netherlands: Maarten Stekelenburg, Erik Pieters, Joris Mathijsen, Gregory van der Wiel, John
Heitinga, Mark van Bommel (C), Kevin Strootman, Wesley Sneijder, Dirk Kuyt, Klaas-Jan
Huntelaar (68' Luuk de Jong), Robin van Persie (68' Eljero Elia). (Coach: Lambertus (Bert)
van Marwijk (HOL)).
Goals: Netherlands: 0-1 Kevin Strootman (29'), 0-2 Luuk de Jong (90'+3').
Referee: Manuel Gräfe (GER)   Attendance: 21.580

06-09-2011   Zimbru Stadium, Chisinau: Moldova – Hungary   0-2 (0-1)
Moldova: Artiom Gaiduchevici, Victor Golovatenco, Alexandru Epureanu (C), Igor Armas,
Alexei Savinov, Anatoli Cheptine (62' Anatoli Doros), Vadim Boret, Denis Zmeu (46' Igor
Bugaev), Eugeniu (Eugen) Cebotaru, Alexandru Suvorov, Serghei Alexeev (YC42) (73' Igor
Tigîrlas). (Coach: Gavril Pelé Balint (ROM)).
Hungary: Gábor Király, Ádám Pintér (64' György Sándor), Zsolt Korcsmár (69' Zsolt Laczkó
(YC75)), Roland Juhász (C) (YC78), Vilmos Vanczák, Vladimir Koman, Tamás Hajnal, Ákos
Elek, József Varga, Gergely Rudolf, Imre Szabics (82' Krisztián Vadócz). (Coach: Sándor
Egervári (HUN)).
Goals: Hungary: 0-1 Vilmos Vanczák (7'), 0-2 Gergely Rudolf (83').
Referee: Ivan Bebek (CRO)   Attendance: 10.500

06-09-2011   Stadio Olimpico, Serravalle: San Marino – Sweden   0-5 (0-0)
San Marino: Federico Valentini (YC73), Fabio Vitaioli (YC12), Davide Simoncini
(YC33,YC53), Simone Bacciocchi (YC51), Damiano Vannucci, Michele Cervellini, Fabio
Bollini (YC62) (84' Alex Gasperoni), Matteo Coppini (71' Matteo Andreini), Andy Selva (C),
Manuel Marani (YC20) (56' Giacomo Benedettini), Matteo Vitaioli. (Coach: Giampaolo
Mazza (SMR)).
Sweden: Andreas Isaksson, Martin Olsson, Daniel Majstorovic, Mikael Lustig, Andreas
Granqvist, Christian Wilhelmsson, Kim Källström, Rasmus Elm (YC20) (65' Anders
Svensson), Ola Toivonen (57' Sebastian Larsson), Zlatan Ibrahimovic (C), Johan Elmander
(67' Tobias Hysén). (Coach: Erik Hamrén (SWE)).
Goals: Sweden: 0-1 Kim Källström (64'), 0-2 Christian Wilhelmsson (70'), 0-3 Martin Olsson
(81'), 0-4 Tobias Hysén (89'), 0-5 Christian Wilhelmsson (90'+3').
Referee: Steven McLean (SCO)   Attendance: 2.946

07-10-2011   Olympic Stadium, Helsinki: Finland – Sweden 1-2 (0-1)
Finland: Lukás Hrádecky, Joona Toivio, Jukka Raitala (YC37), Niklas Moisander (C), Mika
Väyrynen (70' Timo Furuholm), Tim Sparv, Kasper Hämäläinen, Roman Eremenko, Kari
Arkivuo (YC45), Alexander Ring, Teemu Pukki (60' Mikael Forssell). (Coach: Mika-Matti
(Mixu) Petteri Paatelainen (FIN)).
Sweden: Andreas Isaksson, Martin Olsson, Olof Mellberg, Daniel Majstorovic (YC55), Mikael
Lustig, Christian Wilhelmsson (54' Anders Svensson), Sebastian Larsson (68' Ola Toivonen),
Kim Källström (87' Emir Bajrami), Rasmus Elm, Zlatan Ibrahimovic (C) (YC43), Johan
Elmander (YC55). (Coach: Erik Hamrén (SWE)).
Goals: Finland: 1-2 Joona Toivio (73').
Sweden: 0-1 Sebastian Larsson (8'), 0-2 Martin Olsson (52').
Referee: Mark Clattenburg (ENG)   Attendance: 23.257

07-10-2011   De Kuip, Rotterdam: Netherlands – Moldova 1-0 (1-0)
Netherlands: Michel Vorm, Erik Pieters, Joris Mathijsen, Jeffrey Bruma, Gregory van der
Wiel, Rafael van der Vaart (78' Eljero Elia), Mark van Bommel (C), Kevin Strootman
(YC90+2), Dirk Kuyt, Klaas-Jan Huntelaar, Robin van Persie. (Coach: Lambertus (Bert) van
Marwijk (HOL)).
Moldova: Stanislav Namasco, Simeon Bulgaru, Igor Armas, Victor Golovatenco, Alexandru
Epureanu (C), Anatoli Cheptine (84' Gheorghe Ovsyannikov), Stanislav Ivanov, Eugeniu
(Eugen) Cebotaru, Alexandru Suvorov (58' Denis Zmeu), Petru Racu, Serghei Alexeev (69'
Igor Bugaev). (Coach: Gavril Pelé Balint (ROM)).
Goal: Netherlands: 1-0 Klaas-Jan Huntelaar (40').
Referee: Matej Jug (SLO)   Attendance: 47.226

11-10-2011   Stadium, Puskás Ferenc, Budapest: Hungary – Finland 0-0
Hungary: Gábor Király, Vilmos Vanczák, Zsolt Korcsmár, Roland Juhász (C), József Varga,
Vladimir Koman, Tamás Hajnal (88' Zoltán Stieber), Ákos Elek, György Sándor (60' Krisztián
Vadócz), Tamás Priskin (59' Balázs Dzsudzsák), Imre Szabics. (Coach: Sándor Egervári
(HUN)).
Finland: Otto Fredrikson, Joona Toivio, Jukka Raitala, Niklas Moisander (C) (YC82), Mika
Väyrynen, Tim Sparv, Kasper Hämäläinen (85' Teemu Pukki), Roman Eremenko, Kari
Arkivuo (55' Veli Lampi), Alexander Ring, Mikael Forssell (66' Timo Furuholm). (Coach:
Mika-Matti (Mixu) Petteri Paatelainen (FIN)).
Referee: Alberto Undiano Mallenco (ESP)   Attendance: 25.169

11-10-2011   Zimbru Stadium, Chisinau: Moldova – San Marino 4-0 (1-0)
Moldova: Artiom Gaiduchevici, Victor Golovatenco, Alexandru Epureanu (C), Igor Armas,
Denis Zmeu, Anatoli Cheptine, Alexandru Suvorov, Petru Racu (70' Gheorghe Andronic),
Eugeniu (Eugen) Cebotaru (78' Igor Tîgîrls (RC84)), Anatoli Doros, Serghei Alexeev (61' Igor
Bugaev). (Coach: Gavril Pelé Balint (ROM)).
San Marino: Aldo Simoncini, Alessandro Della Valle, Giacomo Benedettini, Simone
Bacciocchi (89' Nicola Albani), Maicol Berretti (67' Matteo Bugli), Damiano Vannucci, Alex
Gasperoni (76' Paolo Montagna), Michele Cervellini, Matteo Coppini, Andy Selva (C), Matteo
Vitaioli (YC84). (Coach: Giampaolo Mazza (SMR)).
Goals: Moldova: 1-0 Denis Zmeu (30'), 2-0 Simone Bacciocchi (62' own goal), 3-0 Alexandru
Suvorov (66'), 4-0 Gheorghe Andronic (87').
Referee: Petur Reinert (FAR)   Attendance: 6.534

11-10-2011   Råsunda Stadium, Solna: Sweden – Netherlands   3-2 (1-1)
Sweden: Andreas Isaksson, Martin Olsson, Olof Mellberg, Daniel Majstorovic, Mikael Lustig, Anders Svensson (C), Sebastian Larsson, Kim Källström, Rasmus Elm, Ola Toivonen (74' Pontus Wernbloom), Johan Elmander. (Coach: Erik Hamrén (SWE)).
Netherlands: Michel Vorm, Jeffrey Bruma, Gregory van der Wiel, Erik Pieters, Joris Mathijsen, Rafael van der Vaart (YC90+3), Mark van Bommel (C), Kevin Strootman (81' Luuk de Jong), Robin van Persie, Dirk Kuyt (73' Eljero Elia), Klaas-Jan Huntelaar. (Coach: Lambertus (Bert) van Marwijk (HOL)).
Goals: Sweden: 1-1 Kim Källström (14'), 2-2 Sebastian Larsson (52' penalty), 3-2 Ola Toivonen (53').
Netherlands: 1-1 Klaas-Jan Huntelaar (23'), 1-2 Dirk Kuyt (50').
Referee: Cüneyt Çakir (TUR)   Attendance: 33.066

GROUP F

02-09-2010	Ramat Gan	Israel – Malta	3-1 (1-1)
03-09-2010	Riga	Latvia – Croatia	0-3 (0-1)
03-09-2010	Piraeus	Greece – Georgia	1-1 (0-1)
07-09-2010	Tbilisi	Georgia – Israel	0-0
07-09-2010	Ta'Qali	Malta – Latvia	0-2 (0-1)
07-09-2010	Zagreb	Croatia – Greece	0-0
08-10-2010	Tbilisi	Georgia – Malta	1-0 (0-0)
08-10-2010	Piraeus	Greece – Latvia	1-0 (0-0)
09-10-2010	Ramat Gan	Israel – Croatia	1-2 (0-2)
12-10-2010	Riga	Latvia – Georgia	1-1 (0-0)
12-10-2010	Piraeus	Greece – Israel	2-1 (1-0)
17-11-2010	Zagreb	Croatia – Malta	3-0 (2-0)
26-03-2011	Tbilisi	Georgia – Croatia	1-0 (0-0)
26-03-2011	Tel Aviv	Israel – Latvia	2-1 (1-0)
26-03-2011	Ta'Qali	Malta – Greece	0-1 (0-0)
29-03-2011	Tel Aviv	Israel – Georgia	1-0 (0-0)
03-06-2011	Split	Croatia – Georgia	2-1 (0-1)
04-06-2011	Riga	Latvia – Israel	1-2 (0-2)
04-06-2011	Piraeus	Greece – Malta	3-1 (2-0)
02-09-2011	Tel Aviv	Israel – Greece	0-1 (0-0)
02-09-2011	Tbilisi	Georgia – Latvia	0-1 (0-0)
02-09-2011	Ta'Qali	Malta – Coatia	1-3 (1-2)
06-09-2011	Zagreb	Croatia – Israel	3-1 (0-1)
06-09-2011	Ta'Qali	Malta – Georgia	1-1 (1-1)
06-09-2011	Riga	Latvia – Greece	1-1 (1-0)
07-10-2011	Riga	Latvia – Malta	2-0 (1-0)
07-10-2011	Piraeus	Greece – Croatia	2-0 (0-0)
11-10-2011	Tbilisi	Georgia – Greece	1-2 (1-0)
11-10-2011	Ta'Qali	Malta – Israel	0-2 (0-1)
11-10-2011	Rijeka	Croatia – Latvia	2-0 (0-0)

FINAL STANDING

Pos	Team	Pld	W	D	L	GF	GA	GD	Pts
1	Greece	10	7	3	0	14	5	+9	24
2	Croatia	10	7	1	2	18	7	+11	22
3	Israel	10	5	1	4	13	11	+2	16
4	Latvia	10	3	2	5	9	12	-3	11
5	Georgia	10	2	4	4	7	9	-2	10
6	Malta	10	0	1	9	4	21	-17	1

Greece qualified for the Final Tournament in Poland and Ukraine.

Croatia qualified for the play-offs.

02-09-2010   Ramat Gan Stadium, Ramat Gan: Israel – Malta   3-1 (1-1)
Israel: Dudu Aouate, Dani Bondarv, Dedi Ben Dayan, Tal Ben Haim (I), Lior Refaelov, Biram Kayal (86' Eyal Golasa), Tamir Cohen, Almog Cohen, Yossi Benayoun (C) (YC40), Eran Zahavi (51' Gil Vermouth), Ben Sahar (73' Shlomi Arbeitman). (Coach: Luis Miguel Fernández Toledo (FRA)).
Malta: Andrew Hogg, Carlo Mamo, Jonathan Caruana, Gareth Sciberras, Jamie Pace (YC90), Roderick Briffa (82' Clayton Failla), Shaun Bajada, Andrei Agius, Michael Mifsud (C), Edward Herrera (80' Emmanuel (Manny) Muscat), Daniel Bogdanovic (YC34) (57' Andrew Cohen (YC61)). (Coach: John Buttigieg (MLT)).
Goals: Israel: 1-0 Yossi Benayoun (7'), 2-1 Yossi Benayoun (64' penalty), 3-1 Yossi Benayoun (75').
Malta: 1-1 Jamie Pace (38').
Referee: Saïd Ennjimi (FRA)   Attendance: 17.365

03-09-2010   Skonto Stadium, Riga: Latvia – Croatia   0-3 (0-1)
Latvia: Andris Vanins, Oskars Klava, Deniss Ivanovs, Kaspars Gorkss (C), Andrejs Rubins (85' Jurijs Zigajevs), Maksims Rafalskis, Pāvels Mihadjuks (YC76), Juris Laizāns (87' Vitālijs Astafjevs), Aleksandrs Cauna, Māris Verpakovskis (YC76), Girts Karlsons (63' Artjoms Rudnevs). (Coach: Aleksandrs Starkovs (LAT)).
Croatia: Vedran Runje, Ivan Strinic, Josip Simunic, Vedran Corluka, Niko Kranjcar, Ognjen Vukojevic (YC37) (70' Danijel Pranjic), Darijo Srna (C) (YC90), Ivan Rakitic, Mladen Petric (84' Mario Mandzukic), Ivica Olic, Eduardo Alves da Silva (62' Nikica Jelavic). (Coach: Slaven Bilic (CRO)).
Goals: Croatia: 0-1 Mladen Petric (43'), 0-2 Ivica Olic (51'), 0-3 Darijo Srna (82').
Referee: Björn Kuipers (HOL)   Attendance: 7.600

03-09-2010   Karaiskakis Stadium, Piraeus: Greece – Georgia   1-1 (0-1)
Greece: Michalis Sifakis, Vasilios Torosidis, Giorgios (Giourkas) Seitaridis (71' Konstantinos (Kostas) Mitroglou), Nikolaos (Nikos) Spyropoulos, Sokratis Papastathopoulos, Avraam Papadopoulos (YC83), Konstantinos (Kostas) Katsouranis (YC74), Giorgios Karagounis (C), Georgios Samaras (YC37) (59' Sotiris Ninis), Dimitrios Salpingidis, Theofanis (Fanis) Gekas. (Coach: FERNANDO Manuel Fernandes da Costa SANTOS (POR)).
Georgia: Nukri Revishvili, Ucha Lobzhanidze (YC44), Dato Kvirkvelia, Zurab Khizanishvili (YC81), Kakha Kaladze (C), Aleksandr Amisulashvili, Levan Kobiashvili, Gogita Gogua (87' Giorgi Merebashvili), Malkhaz Asatiani, Aleksandr Iashvili (54' Jano Ananidze), Vladimir Dvalishvili (60' Nikoloz Gelashvili). (Coach: Temur Ketsbaia (GEO)).
Goals: Greece: 1-1 Nikolaos (Nikos) Spyropoulos (72').
Georgia: 0-1 Aleksandr Iashvili (3').
Referee: Carlos Clos Gómez (ESP)   Attendance: 14.794

07-09-2010   Boris Paichadze Stadium, Tbilisi: Georgia – Israel   0-0
Georgia: Nukri Revishvili, Ucha Lobzhanidze (YC29), Zurab Khizanishvili, Kakha Kaladze (C), Aleksandr Amisulashvili, Levan Kobiashvili (YC42), Gogita Gogua (75' Tornike Aptisauri), Malkhaz Asatiani, Jano Ananidze, Aleksandr Iashvili (46' David Siradze), Vladimir Dvalishvili (63' Giorgi Merebashvili). (Coach: Temur Ketsbaia (GEO)).
Israel: Dudu Aouate, Dekel Keinan, Dani Bondarv (YC69), Dedi Ben Dayan, Tal Ben Haim (I) (YC21), Lior Refaelov (75' Gil Vermouth), Biram Kayal, Tamir Cohen (61' Eran Zahavi), Almog Cohen, Yossi Benayoun (C), Ben Sahar (53' Shlomi Arbeitman). (Coach: Luis Miguel Fernández Toledo (FRA)).
Referee: Sascha Kever (SUI)   Attendance: 45.000

07-09-2010   Ta'Qali Stadium, Ta'Qali: Malta – Latvia   0-2 (0-1)
Malta: Andrew Hogg, Emmanuel (Manny) Muscat (59' Daniel Bogdanovic (YC65)), Carlo Mamo (77' Ryan Fenech), Jonathan Caruana, Gareth Sciberras (77' Clayton Failla), Jamie Pace, Roderick Briffa, Shaun Bajada, Andrei Agius (YC39), Andrew Cohen, Michael Mifsud (C) (YC58). (Coach: John Buttigieg (MLT)).
Latvia: Andris Vanins, Oskars Klava (YC34), Deniss Ivanovs, Kaspars Gorkss (C), Andrejs Rubins, Maksims Rafalskis (YC61) (82' Vitālijs Astafjevs), Pāvels Mihadjuks, Juris Laizāns, Aleksandrs Cauna, Māris Verpakovskis (90'+2' Andrejs Pereplotkins), Artjoms Rudnevs (70' Girts Karlsons). (Coach: Aleksandrs Starkovs (LAT)).
Goals: Latvia: 0-1 Kaspars Gorkss (43'), 0-2 Māris Verpakovskis (85').
Referee: Tony Asumaa (FIN)   Attendance: 6.255

07-09-2010   Maksimir Stadium, Zagreb: Croatia – Greece   0-0
Croatia: Vedran Runje, Ivan Strinic, Josip Simunic, Vedran Corluka, Niko Kranjcar, Ognjen Vukojevic (57' Ivan Rakitic (YC62)), Darijo Srna (C) (YC68), Danijel Pranjic, Luka Modric, Mladen Petric (46' Nikica Jelavic), Ivica Olic (73' Eduardo Alves da Silva). (Coach: Slaven Bilic (CRO)).
Greece: Michalis Sifakis, Loukas Vyntra, Giorgos Tzavellas (YC46), Vasilios Torosidis (YC16) (90'+2' Giorgios (Giourkas) Seitaridis), Sokratis Papastathopoulos (YC79), Avraam Papadopoulos, Alexandros Tziolis, Konstantinos (Kostas) Katsouranis, Giorgios Karagounis (C) (70' Sotiris Ninis), Georgios Samaras, Dimitrios Salpingidis (59' Theofanis (Fanis) Gekas). (Coach: FERNANDO Manuel Fernandes da Costa SANTOS (POR)).
Referee: Claus Bo Larsen (DEN)   Attendance: 24.399

08-10-2010   Boris Paichadze Stadium, Tbilisi: Georgia – Malta   1-0 (0-0)
Georgia: Nukri Revishvili, Lasha Salukvadze, Zurab Khizanishvili (YC31), Kakha Kaladze
(C), Aleksandr Amisulashvili, Giorgi Merebashvili (46' Aleksandr Iashvili), Levan
Kobiashvili, Gogita Gogua, Malkhaz Asatiani, Jano Ananidze (73' Murtaz Daushvili),
Vladimir Dvalishvili (46' David Siradze). (Coach: Temur Ketsbaia (GEO)).
Malta: Justin Haber, Carlo Mamo, Jonathan Caruana, Gareth Sciberras (69' Ryan Fenech),
Jamie Pace, Roderick Briffa, Shaun Bajada, Andrei Agius (YC65), Andrew Cohen (YC56)
(90' Massimo Grima), André Schembri (YC59) (80' Paul Fenech), Michael Mifsud (C).
(Coach: John Buttigieg (MLT)).
Goal: Georgia: 1-0 David Siradze (90'+1').
Referee: Alan Black (NIR)   Attendance: 38.000

08-10-2010   Karaiskakis Stadium, Piraeus: Greece – Latvia   1-0 (0-0)
Greece: Michalis Sifakis, Giorgos Tzavellas, Vasilios Torosidis (YC27), Sokratis
Papastathopoulos, Avraam Papadopoulos, Alexandros Tziolis (YC90+1), Sotiris Ninis (82'
Ioannis (Giannis) Fetfatzidis), Konstantinos (Kostas) Katsouranis, Giorgios Karagounis (C)
(90' Pantelis Kafes), Georgios Samaras, Konstantinos (Kostas) Mitroglou (77' Dimitrios
Salpingidis). (Coach: FERNANDO Manuel Fernandes da Costa SANTOS (POR)).
Latvia: Andris Vanins, Oskars Klava, Deniss Ivanovs, Kaspars Gorkss (C), Dzintars Zirnis
(YC82), Andrejs Rubins (65' Jurijs Zigajevs (YC75)), Juris Laizāns (82' Andrejs
Pereplotkins), Aleksandrs Cauna, Vitālijs Astafjevs, Māris Verpakovskis (YC45+1), Artjoms
Rudnevs (73' Girts Karlsons). (Coach: Aleksandrs Starkovs (LAT)).
Goal: Greece: 1-0 Vasilios Torosidis (58').
Referee: Antonio Damato (ITA)   Attendance: 13.520

09-10-2010   Ramat Gan Stadium, Ramat Gan: Israel – Croatia   1-2 (0-2)
Israel: Dudu Aouate (C), Yoav Ziv, Dekel Keinan (YC35), Tal Ben Haim (I) (YC65), Gil
Vermouth, Bibras Natcho, Tamir Cohen (51' Roberto Colautti), Almog Cohen, Elroy Cohen
(69' Eyal Golasa (YC88)), Itay Shechter (YC36), Elyaniv Barda (56' Lior Refaelov). (Coach:
Luis Miguel Fernández Toledo (FRA)).
Croatia: Vedran Runje, Vedran Corluka, Ivan Strinic, Josip Simunic (C), Gordon Schildenfeld,
Niko Kranjcar (YC59), Ivan Rakitic (77' Ognjen Vukojevic (YC90+3)), Danijel Pranjic, Luka
Modric, Ivica Olic (72' Mate Bilic), Eduardo Alves da Silva (57' Mario Mandzukic). (Coach:
Slaven Bilic (CRO)).
Goals: Israel: 1-2 Itay Shechter (81').
Croatia: 0-1 Niko Kranjcar (36' penalty), 0-2 Niko Kranjcar (41').
Referee: Wolfgang Stark (GER)   Attendance: 33.421

12-10-2010   Skonto Stadium, Riga: Latvia – Georgia   1-1 (0-0)
Latvia: Andris Vanins, Oskars Klava (YC48), Deniss Ivanovs, Kaspars Gorkss (C) (YC64),
Dzintars Zirnis, Jurijs Zigajevs (86' Andrejs Pereplotkins), Andrejs Rubins, Juris Laizāns (82'
Kristaps Grebis), Aleksandrs Cauna, Vitālijs Astafjevs, Artjoms Rudnevs. (Coach: Aleksandrs
Starkovs (LAT)).
Georgia: Nukri Revishvili (YC88), Ucha Lobzhanidze, Dato Kvirkvelia (69' Gogita Gogua
(YC82)), Kakha Kaladze (C), Aleksandr Amisulashvili, David Siradze (YC75), Levan
Kobiashvili, Murtaz Daushvili, Malkhaz Asatiani, Jano Ananidze (79' Lasha Salukvadze),
Aleksandr Iashvili (88' Aleksandr Koshkadze). (Coach: Temur Ketsbaia (GEO)).
Goals: Latvia: 1-1 Aleksandrs Cauna (90'+1').
Georgia: 0-1 David Siradze (74').
Referee: Manuel Jorge Neves Moreira De Sousa (POR)   Attendance: 4.330

238

12-10-2010   Karaiskakis Stadium, Piraeus: Greece – Israel   2-1 (1-0)
Greece: Michalis Sifakis, Loukas Vyntra, Nikolaos (Nikos) Spyropoulos, Sokratis
Papastathopoulos, Avraam Papadopoulos, Sotiris Ninis (15' Ioannis (Giannis) Fetfatzidis
(YC85)), Konstantinos (Kostas) Katsouranis, Giorgios Karagounis (C), Pantelis Kafes,
Dimitrios Salpingidis (87' Ioannis (Giannis) Maniatis), Georgios Samaras (81' Konstantinos
(Kostas) Mitroglou). (Coach: FERNANDO Manuel Fernandes da Costa SANTOS (POR)).
Israel: Dudu Aouate (C), Dekel Keinan, Rami Gershon, Dani Bondarv, Tamir Cohen (69'
Elroy Cohen (YC75)), Bibras Natcho (63' Gil Vermouth), Lior Refaelov, Eyal Golasa, Almog
Cohen, Itay Shechter (YC45+1), Roberto Colautti (75' Elyaniv Barda). (Coach: Luis Miguel
Fernández Toledo (FRA)).
Goals: Greece: 1-0 Dimitrios Salpingidis (22'), 2-1 Giorgios Karagounis (63' penalty).
Israel: 1-1 Nikolaos (Nikos) Spyropoulos (59' *own goal*).
Referee: Martin Hansson (SWE)   Attendance: 16.935

17-11-2010   Stadion Maksimir, Zagreb: Croatia – Malta   3-0 (2-0)
Croatia: Vedran Runje, Vedran Corluka, Gordon Schildenfeld, Niko Kranjcar, Tomislav
Dujmovic, Luka Modric, Darijo Srna (C) (YC74), Ivan Rakitic (69' Ivo Ilicevic), Danijel
Pranjic, Mladen Petric (61' Nikola Kalinic), Eduardo Alves da Silva (78' Mario Mandzukic).
(Coach: Slaven Bilic (CRO)).
Malta: Andrew Hogg, Jonathan Caruana, Massimo Grima (YC84), Roderick Briffa, Shaun
Bajada, Gareth Sciberras (C) (88' Paul Fenech), Jamie Pace, John Hutchinson, Daniel
Bogdanovic (82' Kevin Sammut), André Schembri (70' Ryan Fenech), Michael Mifsud.
(Coach: John Buttigieg (MLT)).
Goals: Croatia: 1-0 Niko Kranjcar (18'), 2-0 Niko Kranjcar (42'), 3-0 Nikola Kalinic (81').
Referee: Duarte Nuno Pereira Gomes (POR)   Attendance: 9.000

26-03-2011   Boris Paichadze Stadium, Tbilisi: Georgia – Croatia   1-0 (0-0)
Georgia: Nukri Revishvili, Lasha Salukvadze, Akaki Khubutia, Zurab Khizanishvili, Kakha
Kaladze (C), Aleksandr Amisulashvili, Levan Kobiashvili, Jaba Kankava, Murtaz Daushvili
(73' Gogita Gogua), Aleksandr Iashvili (62' Otar Martsvaladze (YC71)), Vladimir Dvalishvili
(46' David Siradze). (Coach: Temur Ketsbaia (GEO)).
Croatia: Vedran Runje, Ivan Strinic, Dejan Lovren, Vedran Corluka, Niko Kranjcar (YC66)
(70' Nikica Jelavic), Tomislav Dujmovic (YC52), Darijo Srna (C), Ivan Rakitic (61' Ivan
Perisic), Luka Modric, Mladen Petric (84' Danijel Pranjic), Nikola Kalinic. (Coach: Slaven
Bilic (CRO)).
Goal: Georgia: 1-0 Levan Kobiashvili (90').
Referee: Paolo Tagliavento (ITA)   Attendance; 54.500

26-03-2011   Bloomfield Stadium, Tel Aviv: Israel – Latvia   2-1 (1-0)
Israel: Dudu Aouate (C), Itzhak Cohen, Yoav Ziv (66' Ben Sahar), Rami Gershon, Tal Ben
Haim (I), Omer Damari, Taleb Twatha (YC90), Lior Refaelov (84' Gil Vermouth), Bibras
Natcho (YC86), Biram Kayal, Elyaniv Barda (69' Maor Buzaglo). (Coach: Luis Miguel
Fernández Toledo (FRA)).
Latvia: Andris Vanins, Ritus Krjauklis, Deniss Ivanovs, Kaspars Gorkss (C), Deniss Kacanovs
(YC54), Artis Lazdins, Andrejs Rubins (57' Andrejs Pereplotkins), Maksims Rafalskis (58'
Jurijs Zigajevs), Ivans Lukjanovs, Māris Verpakovskis (73' Daniils Turkovs), Artjoms
Rudnevs. (Coach: Aleksandrs Starkovs (LAT)).
Goals: Israel: 1-0 Elyaniv Barda (16'), 2-1 Biram Kayal (81').
Latvia: 1-1 Kaspars Gorkss (62').
Referee: Milorad Mazic (CRO)   Attendance: 10.801

239

26-03-2011   Ta'Qali Stadium, Ta'Qali: Malta – Greece   0-1 (0-0)
Malta: Justin Haber, Carlo Mamo, Jonathan Caruana (46' Jamie Pace), Gareth Sciberras, John
Hutchinson, Roderick Briffa, Shaun Bajada (78' Ryan Fenech), Andrei Agius, André Schembri
(90'+1' Andrew Cohen (YC90+2)), Michael Mifsud (C), Daniel Bogdanovic. (Coach: John
Buttigieg (MLT)).
Greece: Alexandros Tzorvas, Giorgos Tzavellas (YC57), Vasilios Torosidis (YC88), Sokratis
Papastathopoulos (RC84), Avraam Papadopoulos, Sotiris Ninis (81' Panagiotis Kone),
Konstantinos (Kostas) Katsouranis, Giorgios Karagounis (C), Georgios Samaras, Dimitrios
Salpingidis (61' Ioannis (Giannis) Fetfatzidis), Nikolaos (Nikos) Lyberopoulos (70'
Konstantinos (Kostas) Mitroglou). (Coach: FERNANDO Manuel Fernandes da Costa
SANTOS (POR)).
Goal: Greece: 0-1 Vasilios Torosidis (90'+4').
Referee: Michael Weiner (GER)   Attendance: 10.605

29-03-2011   Bloomfield Stadium, Tel Aviv: Israel – Georgia   1-0 (0-0)
Israel: Dudu Aouate (C), Dekel Keinan, Rami Gershon, Dani Bondarv (YC76), Tal Ben Haim
(I), Lior Refaelov (63' Gil Vermouth), Bibras Natcho (52' Tal Ben Haim (II)), Biram Kayal,
Almog Cohen (YC62), Maor Buzaglo, Elyaniv Barda (71' Yossi Benayoun). (Coach: Luis
Miguel Fernández Toledo (FRA)).
Georgia: Nukri Revishvili, Lasha Salukvadze, Akaki Khubutia, Zurab Khizanishvili, Kakha
Kaladze (C), Aleksandr Amisulashvili (YC44), Levan Kobiashvili (YC89), Jaba Kankava,
Murtaz Daushvili (46' Dato Kvirkvelia), Otar Martsvaladze (YC45) (73' David Siradze),
Aleksandr Iashvili (63' Vladimir Dvalishvili). (Coach: Temur Ketsbaia (GEO)).
Goal: Israel: 1-0 Tal Ben Haim (II) (59').
Referee: Fredy Fautrel (FRA)   Attendance: 13.716

03-06-2011   Stadion Poljud, Split: Croatia – Georgia   2-1 (0-1)
Croatia: Vedran Runje, Josip Simunic, Vedran Corluka, Darijo Srna (C), Danijel Pranjic, Luka
Modric, Ivan Perisic (71' Ivan Klasnic), Ognjen Vukojevic (71' Tomislav Dujmovic), Mario
Mandzukic, Nikica Jelavic (46' Nikola Kalinic (YC78)), Eduardo Alves da Silva. (Coach:
Slaven Bilic (CRO)).
Georgia: Giorgi Loria, Dato Kvirkvelia, Akaki Khubutia (YC75), Zurab Khizanishvili, Guram
Kashia (80' Jano Ananidze), Kakha Kaladze (C), Gia Grigalava, Lasha Salukvadze, Jaba
Kankava, David Siradze (56' Vladimir Dvalishvili), Aleksandr Iashvili (YC26) (62' Murtaz
Daushvili). (Coach: Temur Ketsbaia (GEO)).
Goals: Croatia: 1-1 Mario Mandzukic (76'), 2-1 Nikola Kalinic (78').
Georgia: 0-1 Jaba Kankava (17').
Referee: Stefan Johannesson (SWE)   Attendance: 28.000

04-06-2011   Skonto Stadium, Riga: Latvia – Israel   1-2 (0-2)
Latvia: Andris Vanins, Ritus Krjauklis, Oskars Klava (YC82), Deniss Ivanovs (YC45+1),
Kaspars Gorkss (C), Artis Lazdins, Aleksandrs Cauna, Aleksejs Visnakovs (71' Ritvars
Rugins), Maksims Rafalskis (28' Jurijs Zigajevs (YC76)), Artjoms Rudnevs, Andrejs
Pereplotkins (60' Edgars Gauracs). (Coach: Aleksandrs Starkovs (LAT)).
Israel: Dudu Aouate, Rami Gershon, Yuval Shpungin, Dekel Keinan, Tal Ben Haim (I), Almog
Cohen, Yossi Benayoun (C), Lior Refaelov (79' Tal Ben Haim (II) (YC90+1)), Tomer Hemed,
Maor Buzaglo (69' Bibras Natcho), Eran Zahavi (89' Eyal Golasa). (Coach: Luis Miguel
Fernández Toledo (FRA)).
Goals: Latvia: 1-2 Aleksandrs Cauna (62' penalty).
Israel: 0-1 Yossi Benayoun (19'), 0-2 Tal Ben Haim (I) (43' penalty).
Referee: Alan Kelly (IRL)   Attendance: 6.147

240

04-06-2011   Karaiskakis Stadium, Piraeus: Greece – Malta 3-1 (2-0)
Greece: Dimitrios Konstantopoulos, Vasilios Torosidis, Nikolaos (Nikos) Spyropoulos, Vangelis Moras, Kyriakos Papadopoulos (YC15), Alexandros Tziolis, Sotiris Ninis (80' Lazaros Christodoulopoulos), Konstantinos (Kostas) Katsouranis, Giorgios Karagounis (C) (70' Pantelis Kafes), Ioannis (Giannis) Fetfatzidis, Dimitrios Salpingidis (89' Konstantinos (Kostas) Mitroglou). (Coach: FERNANDO Manuel Fernandes da Costa SANTOS (POR)).
Malta: Andrew Hogg, Jonathan Caruana, Gareth Sciberras, John Hutchinson (87' Paul Fenech), Ryan Fenech, Roderick Briffa, Shaun Bajada (80' Clayton Failla), Andrei Agius, André Schembri, Michael Mifsud (C), Daniel Bogdanovic (60' Andrew Cohen). (Coach: John Buttigieg (MLT)).
Goals: 1-0 Ioannis (Giannis) Fetfatzidis (7'), 2-0 Kyriakos Papadopoulos (26'), 3-1 Ioannis (Giannis) Fetfatzidis (63').
Malta: 2-1 Michael Mifsud (54').
Referee: Pawel Gil (POL)   Attendance: 14.746

02-09-2011   Bloomfield Stadium, Tel Aviv: Israel – Greece 0-1 (0-0)
Israel: Dudu Aouate, Yuval Shpungin, Rami Gershon, Omri Ben Harush (YC61), Tal Ben Haim (I), Lior Refaelov, Biram Kayal (YC44), Almog Cohen (YC38) (61' Bibras Natcho (YC76)), Yossi Benayoun (C), Eran Zahavi (YC4) (55' Tomer Hemed), Itay Shecher (55' Omer Damari). (Coach: Luis Miguel Fernández Toledo (FRA)).
Greece: Michalis Sifakis, Giannis Zaradoukas, Vasilios Torosidis (YC75), Kyriakos Papadopoulos, Avraam Papadopoulos, Sotiris Ninis (77' Ioannis (Giannis) Fetfatzidis), Konstantinos (Kostas) Katsouranis (YC54), Giorgios Karagounis (C), Pantelis Kafes (YC35) (42' Grigoris Makos), Georgios Samaras, Dimitrios Salpingidis (YC75) (84' Ioannis (Giannis) Maniatis (YC90+4)). (Coach: FERNANDO Manuel Fernandes da Costa SANTOS (POR)).
Goal: Greece: 0-1 Sotiris Ninis (60').
Referee: Craig Alexander Thomson (SCO)   Attendance: 13.245

02-09-2011   Mikheil Meskhi Stadium, Tbilisi: Georgia – Latvia 0-1 (0-0)
Georgia: Giorgi Loria, Zurab Khizanishvili, Guram Kashia, Kakha Kaladze (C), Aleksandr Amisulashvili (71' Vladimir Dvalishvili), David Targamadze, Levan Kobiashvili, Jaba Kankava (YC11), Jano Ananidze (54' Shota Grigalashvili), Otar Martsvaladze, Aleksandr Iashvili (54' David Siradze). (Coach: Temur Ketsbaia (GEO)).
Latvia: Andris Vanins, Ritus Krjauklis (YC86), Oskars Klava, Deniss Ivanovs, Kaspars Gorkss (C) (YC50), Aleksandrs Fertovs (YC21), Aleksejs Visnakovs, Artis Lazdins (88' Olegs Laizāns), Aleksandrs Cauna, Ivans Lukjanovs, Māris Verpakovskis (YC39) (77' Edgars Gauracs). (Coach: Aleksandrs Starkovs (LAT)).
Goal: Latvia: 0-1 Aleksandrs Cauna (64').
Referee: Leontios Trattou (CYP)   Attendance:15.422

02-09-2011   Ta'Qali Stadium, Ta'Qali: Malta – Croatia 1-3 (1-2)
Malta: Andrew Hogg, Emmanuel (Manny) Muscat, Gareth Sciberras, John Hutchinson, Ryan Fenech (YC25) (88' Carlo Mamo), Roderick Briffa (74' Jamie Pace), Andrei Agius, Andrew Cohen, André Schembri, Michael Mifsud (C) (82' Ivan Woods), Clayton Failla (YC66). (Coach: John Buttigieg (MLT)).
Croatia: Stipe Pletikosa, Sime Vrsaljko, Ivan Strinic, Dejan Lovren, Vedran Corluka (YC51), Ognjen Vukojevic, Darijo Srna (C), Ivan Perisic (68' Tomislav Dujmovic), Milan Badelj (82' Eduardo Alves da Silva), Ivan Klasnic (46' Nikola Kalinic), Mario Mandzukic (YC35). (Coach: Slaven Bilic (CRO)).
Goals: Malta: 1-2 Michael Mifsud (38').
Croatia: 0-1 Ognjen Vukojevic (11'), 0-2 Milan Badelj (32'), 1-3 Dejan Lovren (68').
Referee: Tony Chapron (FRA)   Attendance: 6.150

241

06-09-2011   Stadion Maksimir, Zagreb: Croatia – Israel   3-1 (0-1)
Croatia: Stipe Pletikosa, Vedran Corluka (46' Eduardo Alves da Silva), Ivan Strinic (YC76),
Josip Simunic, Dejan Lovren, Niko Kranjcar, Ognjen Vukojevic (46' Tomislav Dujmovic),
Darijo Srna (C) (YC62), Luka Modric, Nikica Jelavic (87' Nikola Kalinic), Mario Mandzukic.
(Coach: Slaven Bilic (CRO)).
Israel: Dudu Aouate (46' Guy Haimov), Omri Ben Harush (YC38), Iyad Khutaba, Rami
Gershon, Tal Ben Haim (I) (RC51), Yossi Benayoun (C), Taleb Twatha, Biram Kayal, Tamir
Cohen (57' Eyal Golasa), Eran Zahavi (YC45+2) (68' Itay Shecher), Tomer Hemed. (Coach:
Luis Miguel Fernández Toledo (FRA)).
Goals: Croatia: 1-1 Luka Modric (47'), 2-1 Eduardo Alves da Silva (55'), 3-1 Eduardo Alves
da Silva (57').
Israel: 0-1 Tomer Hemed (44').
Referee: Carlos Velasco Carballo (ESP)   Attendance: 13.688

06-09-2011   Ta'Qali Stadium, Ta'Qali: Malta – Georgia   1-1 (1-1)
Malta: Andrew Hogg (YC90+4), Jonathan Caruana, Roderick Briffa, Andrei Agius, Gareth
Sciberras, John Hutchinson, Ryan Fenech (59' Daniel Bogdanovic), Andrew Cohen (90'+1'
Ivan Woods), André Schembri (76' Jamie Pace), Michael Mifsud (C), Clayton Failla. (Coach:
John Buttigieg (MLT)).
Georgia: Nukri Revishvili, Gia Grigalava, Zurab Khizanishvili (YC11), Guram Kashia
(YC58), Kakha Kaladze (C), Jano Ananidze (77' Aleksandr Kobakhidze), David Targamadze,
Levan Kobiashvili, Jaba Kankava, Aleksandr Iashvili (61' Vladimir Dvalishvili), Otar
Martsvaladze (66' Shota Grigalashvili). (Coach: Temur Ketsbaia (GEO)).
Goals: Malta: 1-1 Michael Mifsud (25').
Georgia: 0-1 Jaba Kankava (15').
Referee: Paulus Hendrikus Martinus (Pol) van Boekel (HOL)   Attendance: 2.000

06-09-2011   Skonto Stadium, Riga: Latvia – Greece   1-1 (1-0)
Latvia: Andris Vanins (YC64), Ritus Krjauklis (YC57), Oskars Klava, Deniss Ivanovs (C),
Aleksandrs Fertovs, Aleksandrs Cauna, Aleksejs Visnakovs (83' Jurijs Zigajevs), Pāvels
Mihadjuks, Olegs Laizāns (YC42), Ivans Lukjanovs, Māris Verpakovskis (68' Artjoms
Rudnevs (YC87)). (Coach: Aleksandrs Starkovs (LAT)).
Greece: Michalis Sifakis, Giannis Zaradoukas (YC45+1), Loukas Vyntra (72' Ioannis
(Giannis) Maniatis (YC89)), Sokratis Papastathopoulos, Kyriakos Papadopoulos (YC56),
Grigoris Makos (81' Giorgos Georgiadis), Giorgios Karagounis (C), Ioannis (Giannis)
Fetfatzidis (46' Alexandros Tziolis), Georgios Samaras, Dimitrios Salpingidis, Nikolaos
(Nikos) Lyberopoulos. (Coach: FERNANDO Manuel Fernandes da Costa SANTOS (POR)).
Goals: Latvia : 1-0 Aleksandrs Cauna (19').
Greece: 1-1 Kyriakos Papadopoulos (84').
Referee: Stanislav Todorov (BUL)   Attendance: 5.415

07-10-2011   Skonto Stadium, Riga: Latvia – Malta   2-0 (1-0)
Latvia: Andris Vanins, Oskars Klava, Deniss Ivanovs, Kaspars Gorkss (C), Aleksejs
Visnakovs, Pāvels Mihadjuks, Olegs Laizāns (76' Ritvars Rugins), Aleksandrs Cauna, Ivans
Lukjanovs (YC90+2), Māris Verpakovskis (YC90+1) (90'+1' Andrejs Rubins), Artjoms
Rudnevs (88' Edgars Gauracs). (Coach: Aleksandrs Starkovs (LAT)).
Malta: Andrew Hogg, Steve Borg, Gareth Sciberras (83' Paul Fenech), Jamie Pace (70' Ivan
Woods), John Hutchinson, Ryan Fenech (82' Carlo Mamo), Roderick Briffa (C), Andrei Agius
(YC90+1), Andrew Cohen (YC48), André Schembri, Clayton Failla (YC64). (Coach: John
Buttigieg (MLT)).
Goals: Latvia: 1-0 Aleksejs Visnakovs (33'), 2-0 Artjoms Rudnevs (83').
Referee: Richard Trutz (SVK)   Attendance: 4.315

07-10-2011   Karaiskakis Stadium, Piraeus: Greece – Croatia   2-0 (0-0)
Greece: Alexandros Tzorvas (YC60), Giannis Zaradoukas (YC45+5), Vasilios Torosidis (43'
Loukas Vyntra), Sokratis Papastathopoulos, (YC81), Sokratis Papastathopoulos, Konstantinos
(Kostas) Katsouranis, Giorgios Karagounis (C) (YC40) (87' Grigoris Makos), Alexandros
Tziolis (62' Georgios Fotakis), Georgios Samaras (YC64), Dimitrios Salpingidis, Theofanis
(Fanis) Gekas. (Coach: FERNANDO Manuel Fernandes da Costa SANTOS (POR)).
Croatia: Stipe Pletikosa, Dejan Lovren (YC90+1), Vedran Corluka (75' Domagoj Vida), Ivan
Strinic, Josip Simunic (C), Niko Kranjcar, Ognjen Vukojevic, Luka Modric, Mario Mandzukic,
Nikica Jelavic (YC60) (61' Nikola Kalinic (YC77)), Eduardo Alves da Silva (YC45+2) (52'
Ivan Perisic). (Coach: Slaven Bilic (CRO)).
Goals: Greece: 1-0 Georgios Samaras (71'), 2-0 Theofanis (Fanis) Gekas (79').
Referee: Howard Melton Webb (ENG)   Attendance: 27.316

11-10-2011   Mikheil Meskhi Stadium, Tbilisi: Georgia – Greece   1-2 (1-0)
Georgia: Nukri Revishvili, Kakha Kaladze (C), Aleksandr Amisulashvili, Zurab Khizanishvili,
Guram Kashia, Shota Grigalashvili (51' Aleksandr Iashvili), David Targamadze (YC61),
Levan Kobiashvili, Jaba Kankava (YC16) (42' Ucha Lobzhanidze), Otar Martsvaladze, Levan
Mchedlidze (YC22) (65' Aleksandr Guruli). (Coach: Temur Ketsbaia (GEO)).
Greece: Alexandros Tzorvas, Loukas Vyntra, Nikolaos (Nikos) Spyropoulos (YC43), Sokratis
Papastathopoulos, Kyriakos Papadopoulos, Giorgios Karagounis (C), Alexandros Tziolis (56'
Georgios Fotakis), Konstantinos (Kostas) Katsouranis, Angelos Charisteas, Dimitrios
Salpingidis (68' Stefanos Athanasiadis (YC74)), Theofanis (Fanis) Gekas (90'+1' Panagiotis
Kone). (Coach: FERNANDO Manuel Fernandes da Costa SANTOS (POR)).
Goals: Georgia: 1-0 David Targamadze (19').
Greece: 1-1 Georgios Fotakis (79'), 1-2 Angelos Charisteas (85').
Referee: Daniele Orsato (ITA)   Attendance: 7.824

11-10-2011   Ta'Qali Stadium, Ta'Qali: Malta – Israel   0-2 (0-1)
Malta: Andrew Hogg, Carlo Mamo, Jonathan Caruana (83' Steve Borg), Gareth Sciberras,
John Hutchinson, Ryan Fenech, Paul Fenech (64' Edward Herrera), Roderick Briffa, Andrei
Agius (YC90+2), Ivan Woods (YC66) (81' Christian Caruana), Michael Mifsud (C). (Coach:
John Buttigieg (MLT)).
Israel: Dudu Aouate (C), Rami Gershon, Dani Bondarv (57' Gil Vermouth), Taleb Twatha,
Lior Refaelov (49' Almog Cohen), Bibras Natcho, Eyal Golasa, Ben Sahar (78' Tal Ben Haim
(II)), Tomer Hemed, Maor Buzaglo, Nir Bitton. (Coach: Luis Miguel Fernández Toledo
(FRA)).
Goals: Israel: 0-1 Lior Refaelov (11'), 0-2 Rami Gershon (90'+3').
Referee: Bruno Miguel Duarte Paixão (POR)   Attendance: 2.614

11-10-2011   Stadion Kantrida, Rijeka: Croatia – Latvia   2-0 (0-0)
Croatia: Stipe Pletikosa, Ivan Strinic, Josip Simunic, Dejan Lovren, Vedran Corluka (34'
Domagoj Vida), Niko Kranjcar (59' Ivan Perisic), Darijo Srna (C), Ivan Rakitic, Luka Modric,
Mario Mandzukic (84' Nikica Jelavic), Eduardo Alves da Silva. (Coach: Slaven Bilic (CRO)).
Latvia: Andris Vanins, Oskars Klava (YC35), Deniss Ivanovs, Kaspars Gorkss (C), Ritvars
Rugins (YC38) (81' Igors Tarasovs), Aleksejs Visnakovs (88' Andrejs Rubins), Pāvels
Mihadjuks, Olegs Laizāns, Aleksandrs Cauna, Artjoms Rudnevs, Andrejs Pereplotkins (71'
Edgars Gauracs). (Coach: Aleksandrs Starkovs (LAT)).
Goals: Croatia: 1-0 Eduardo Alves da Silva (66'), 2-0 Mario Mandzukic (72').
Referee: Antony Gautier (FRA)   Attendance: 8.370

GROUP G

03-09-2010	Podgorica	Montenegro – Wales	1-0 (1-0)
03-09-2010	London	England – Bulgaria	4-0 (1-0)
07-09-2010	Sofia	Bulgaria – Montenegro	0-1 (0-1)
07-09-2010	Basel	Swtizerland – England	1-3 (0-1)
08-10-2010	Podgorica	Montenegro – Swtizerland	1-0 (0-0)
08-10-2010	Cardiff	Wales – Bulgaria	0-1 (0-0)
12-10-2010	Basel	Switzerland – Wales	4-1 (2-1)
12-10-2010	London	England – Montenegro	0-0
26-03-2011	Cardiff	Wales – England	0-2 (0-2)
26-03-2011	Sofia	Bulgaria – Switzerland	0-0
04-06-2011	London	England – Switzerland	2-2 (1-2)
04-06-2011	Podgorica	Montenegro – Bulgaria	1-1 (0-0)
02-09-2011	Sofia	Bulgaria – England	0-3 (0-3)
02-09-2011	Cardiff	Wales – Montenegro	2-1 (1-0)
06-09-2011	Basel	Switzerland – Bulgaria	3-1 (1-1)
06-09-2011	London	England – Wales	1-0 (1-0)
07-10-2011	Swansea	Wales – Switzerland	2-0 (0-0)
07-10-2011	Podgorica	Montenegro – England	2-2 (1-2)
11-10-2011	Sofia	Bulgaria – Wales	0-1 (0-1)
11-10-2011	Basel	Switzerland – Montenegro	2-0 (0-0)

FINAL STANDING

Pos	Team	Pld	W	D	L	GF	GA	GD	Pts
1	England	8	5	3	0	17	5	+12	18
2	Montenegro	8	3	3	2	7	7	0	12
3	Switzerland	8	3	2	3	12	10	+2	11
4	Wales	8	3	0	5	6	10	-4	9
5	Bulgaria	8	1	2	5	3	13	-10	5

England qualified for the Final Tournament in Poland and Ukraine.

Montenegro qualified for the play-offs.

03-09-2010   Podgorica City Stadium, Podgorica: Montenegro – Wales   1-0 (1-0)
Montenegro: Mladen Bozovic, Elsad Zverotic, Savo Pavicevic (YC8), Milan Jovanovic, Marko Basa, Miodrag Dzudovic (YC53), Simon Vukcevic (87' Fatos Beciraj), Milorad Pekovic (YC70), Branko Boskovic (74' Vladimir Bozovic), Mirko Vucinic (C), Radomir Djalovic (83' Mitar Novakovic). (Coach: Zlatko Kranjcar (CRO)).
Wales: Wayne Hennessey, Ashley Williams, Sam Ricketts (YC49), Chris Gunter, James Collins (75' Craig Morgan), David Vaughan, Joe Ledley, David (Dave) Edwards (68' Robert (Rob) Earnshaw), Gareth Bale (YC57), Steve Morison (YC45) (78' Simon Church), Craig Bellamy (C). (Coach: John Benjamin Toshack (WAL)).
Goal: Montenegro: 1-0 Mirko Vucinic (30').
Referee: Anastasios Kakos (GRE)   Attendance: 7.442

03-09-2010   Wembley Stadium, London: England – Bulgaria   4-0 (1-0)
England: Joe Hart, Michael Dawson (57' Gary Cahill), Ashley Cole, Glen Johnson, Phil Jagielka, Gareth Barry, Steven Gerrard (C), James Milner (YC90), Jermain Defoe (87' Ashley Young), Theo Walcott (74' Adam Johnson), Wayne Rooney. (Coach: Fabio Capello (ITA)).
Bulgaria: Nikolay Mihaylov, Zhivko Milanov, Stanislav Manolev (66' Veselin Minev), Ilian Stoyanov, Ivan Ivanov, Stanislav Angelov, Chavdar Yankov, Stiliyan Petrov (C), Martin Petrov, Valeri Bozhinov (63' Dimitar Rangelov), Ivelin Popov (YC62) (79' Georgi Peev). (Coach: Stanimir Kolev Stoilov (BUL)).
Goals: England: 1-0 Jermain Defoe (3'), 2-0 Jermain Defoe (61'), 3-0 Adam Johnson (83'), 4-0 Jermain Defoe (86').
Referee: Viktor Kassai (HUN)   Attendance: 73.426

07-09-2010   Vasil Levski National Stadium, Sofia: Bulgaria – Montenegro   0-1 (0-1)
Bulgaria: Nikolay Mihaylov, Ilian Stoyanov, Veselin Minev, Zhivko Milanov (46' Stanislav Genchev), Ivan Ivanov, Stiliyan Petrov (C) (YC53), Martin Petrov (YC79), Georgi Peev (67' Valeri Domovchiyski), Stanislav Angelov (YC64), Dimitar Rangelov (46' Valeri Bozhinov), Ivelin Popov. (Coach: Stanimir Kolev Stoilov (BUL)).
Montenegro: Mladen Bozovic, Elsad Zverotic (68' Mitar Novakovic), Savo Pavicevic, Milan Jovanovic, Marko Basa, Miodrag Dzudovic, Simon Vukcevic, Milorad Pekovic (YC45), Branko Boskovic (YC55) (64' Vladimir Bozovic), Mirko Vucinic (C), Radomir Djalovic (77' Mladen Kascelan). (Coach: Zlatko Kranjcar (CRO)).
Goal: Montenegro: 0-1 Elsad Zverotic (36').
Referee: Vladislav Yuryevich Bezborodov (RUS)   Attendance: 9.470

07-09-2010   St.Jakob Park, Basel: Switzerland – England   1-3 (0-1)
Switzerland: Diego Benaglio, Stéphane Grichting (YC81), Reto Ziegler, Steve von Bergen, Stephan Lichtsteiner (YC57,YC65), Gökhan Inler, David Degen (64' Marco Streller), Pirmin Schwegler (83' Moreno Costanzo), Xavier Margairaz (46' Xherdan Shaqiri), Alexander Frei (C), Eren Derdiyok. (Coach: Ottmar Hitzfeld (GER)).
England: Joe Hart, Ashley Cole (YC76), Joleon Lescott, Glen Johnson, Phil Jagielka, Gareth Barry, Steven Gerrard (C), James Milner (YC60), Jermain Defoe (73' Darren Bent), Theo Walcott (13' Adam Johnson), Wayne Rooney (79' Shaun Wright-Phillips). (Coach: Fabio Capello (ITA)).
Goals: Switzerland: 1-2 Xherdan Shaqiri (71').
England: 0-1 Wayne Rooney (10'), 0-2 Adam Johnson (69'), 1-3 Darren Bent (88').
Referee: Nicola Rizzoli (ITA)   Attendance: 37.500

08-10-2010   Podgorica City Stadium, Podgorica: Montenegro – Switzerland   1-0 (0-0)
Montenegro: Mladen Bozovic, Marko Basa, Elsad Zverotic, Stefan Savic, Milan Jovanovic, Miodrag Dzudovic, Simon Vukcevic (YC65) (84' Fatos Beciraj), Mitar Novakovic, Branko Boskovic (46' Mladen Kascelan), Mirko Vucinic (C) (YC68), Radomir Djalovic (90'+2' Radoslav Batak). (Coach: Zlatko Kranjcar (CRO)).
Switzerland: Marco Wölfli, Reto Ziegler, Steve von Bergen, Scott Sutter, Stéphane Grichting, Valentin Stocker (76' Hakan Yakin), Xherdan Shaqiri (67' Tranquillo Barnetta), Pirmin Schwegler, Gökhan Inler, Marco Streller (67' Eren Derdiyok), Alexander Frei (C). (Coach: Ottmar Hitzfeld (GER)).
Goal: Montenegro: 1-0 Mirko Vucinic (68').
Referee: Eduardo Iturralde González (ESP)   Attendance: 10.750

245

08-10-2010   Cardiff City Stadium, Cardiff: Wales – Bulgaria   0-1 (0-0)
Wales: Wayne Hennessey, Chris Gunter (RC90+3), James Collins, Danny Collins, Ashley Williams (C), Sam Ricketts (YC41), Joe Ledley (59' Andy King), David (Dave) Edwards (68' Simon Church), David Vaughan, Gareth Bale, Steve Morison (82' Hal Robson-Kanu). (Coach: Brian Flynn (WAL)).
Bulgaria: Nikolay Mihaylov, Petar Zanev (YC90+3), Ivan Ivanov, Valentin Iliev (37' Pavel Vidanov), Nikolaj Bodurov (YC80), Georgi Peev (72' Dimitar Rangelov), Stiliyan Petrov (C), Martin Petrov (YC90+1), Blagoy Georgiev (YC50), Dimitar Makriev (87' Chavdar Yankov), Ivelin Popov. (Coach: Lothar Herbert Matthäus (GER)).
Goal: Bulgaria: 0-1 Ivelin Popov (48').
Referee: Jonas Eriksson (SWE)   Attendance: 14.061

12-10-2010   St.Jakob Park, Basel: Switzerland – Wales   4-1 (2-1)
Switzerland: Diego Benaglio (8' Marco Wölfli), Reto Ziegler, Steve von Bergen, Stephan Lichtsteiner (YC18), Stéphane Grichting, Valentin Stocker, Pirmin Schwegler (90'+1' Gélson da Conceição Tavares Fernandes), Gökhan Inler, Tranquillo Barnetta (YC35), Marco Streller, Alexander Frei (C) (79' Eren Derdiyok). (Coach: Ottmar Hitzfeld (GER)).
Wales: Wayne Hennessey, Danny Collins, Andrew Crofts, Ashley Williams (C), James Collins (YC71), Andy King (YC7), David Vaughan (89' Shaun MacDonald), David (Dave) Edwards (77' Steve Morison), Darcy Blake (54' Christian Ribeiro), Gareth Bale, Simon Church. (Coach: Brian Flynn (WAL)).
Goals: Switzerland: 1-0 Valentin Stocker (8'), 2-1 Marco Streller (21'), 3-1 Gökhan Inler (82' penalty), 4-1 Valentin Stocker (89').
Wales: 1-1 Gareth Bale (13').
Referee: Alain Hamer (LUX)   Attendance: 26.000

12-10-2010   Wembley Stadium, London: England – Montenegro   0-0
England: Joe Hart, Joleon Lescott, Rio Ferdinand (C), Ashley Cole, Glen Johnson, Adam Johnson, Gareth Barry (YC63), Ashley Young (YC60) (74' Shaun Wright-Phillips), Steven Gerrard, Peter Crouch (70' Kevin Davies (YC86)), Wayne Rooney (YC53). (Coach: Fabio Capello (ITA)).
Montenegro: Mladen Bozovic, Stefan Savic (YC52), Milan Jovanovic, Marko Basa (YC57), Elsad Zverotic, Miodrag Dzudovic (YC25), Simon Vukcevic (YC90+4), Milorad Pekovic, Mitar Novakovic (62' Mladen Kascelan (YC64)), Branko Boskovic (C) (83' Fatos Beciraj), Radomir Djalovic (77' Andrija Delibasic). (Coach: Zlatko Kranjcar (CRO)).
Referee: Manuel Gräfe (GER)   Attendance: 73.451

26-03-2011   Millennium Stadium, Cardiff: Wales – England   0-2 (0-2)
Wales: Wayne Hennessey, Chris Gunter, Andrew Crofts (YC56), James Collins (YC86), Danny Collins, Ashley Williams, Aaron Ramsey (C), Joe Ledley (YC70), Andy King (65' David Vaughan (YC81)), Craig Bellamy (YC83), Steve Morison (65' Ched Evans). (Coach: Gary Andrew Speed (WAL)).
England: Joe Hart, Michael Dawson, Ashley Cole, John Terry (C), Glen Johnson (YC84), Ashley Young, Scott Parker (88' Phil Jagielka), Frank Lampard, Jack Wilshere (82' Stewart Downing), Darren Bent, Wayne Rooney (YC37) (70' James Milner) (Coach: Fabio Capello (ITA)).
Goals: England: 0-1 Frank Lampard (7' penalty), 0-2 Darren Bent (15').
Referee: Olegário Manuel Bártolo Faustino Benquerença (POR)   Attendance: 68.959

26-03-2011   Vasil Levski National Stadium, Sofia: Bulgaria – Switzerland   0-0
Bulgaria: Nikolay Mihaylov, Petar Zanev, Kostadin Stoyanov (YC16), Stanislav Manolev (YC87), Ivan Bandalovski, Ivan Ivanov, Stiliyan Petrov (C), Blagoy Georgiev (YC68), Spas Delev (81' Zdravko Lazarov), Ivelin Popov (85' Stanislav Angelov), Dimitar Makriev (52' Tsvetan Genkov). (Coach: Lothar Herbert Matthäus (GER)).
Switzerland: Marco Wölfli, Reto Ziegler, Steve von Bergen, Stephan Lichtsteiner, Stéphane Grichting, Valentin Stocker (67' Eren Derdiyok (YC76)), Gökhan Inler, Blerim Dzemaili, Valon Behrami (YC14) (17' Gélson da Conceição Tavares Fernandes), Marco Streller (77' Mario Gavranovic), Alexander Frei (C). (Coach: Ottmar Hitzfeld (GER)).
Referee: William (Willie) Collum (SCO)   Attendance: 9.600

04-06-2011   Wembley Stadium, London: England – Switzerland   2-2 (1-2)
England: Joe Hart, John Terry (C), Rio Ferdinand (YC88), Ashley Cole (31' Leighton Baines), Glen Johnson, Scott Parker, Jack Wilshere (YC64), James Milner, Frank Lampard (46' Ashley Young), Theo Walcott (78' Stewart Downing), Darren Bent. (Coach: Fabio Capello (ITA)).
Switzerland: Diego Benaglio, Johan Djourou (YC36), Reto Ziegler, Philippe Senderos, Stephan Lichtsteiner, Granit Xhaka, Xherdan Shaqiri, Gökhan Inler (C), Valon Behrami (YC45) (59' Blerim Dzemaili), Tranquillo Barnetta (90' Innocent Nkasiobi Emeghara), Eren Derdiyok (75' Admir Mehmedi). (Coach: Ottmar Hitzfeld (GER)).
Goals: England: 1-2 Frank Lampard (37' penalty), 2-2 Ashley Young (51').
Switzerland: 0-1 Tranquillo Barnetta (32'), 0-2 Tranquillo Barnetta (35').
Referee: Damir Skomina (SLO)   Attendance: 84.459

04-06-2011   Podgorica City Stadium, Podgorica: Montenegro – Bulgaria   1-1 (0-0)
Montenegro: Mladen Bozovic, Elsad Zverotic (72' Stevan Jovetic), Stefan Savic, Luka Pejovic, Savo Pavicevic (YC71) (82' Mladen Kascelan), Marko Basa, Milorad Pekovic (YC78), Nikola Drincic, Vladimir Bozovic (YC54) (76' Ivan Fatic), Mirko Vucinic (C), Radomir Djalovic. (Coach: Zlatko Kranjcar (CRO)).
Bulgaria: Nikolay Mihaylov, Petar Zanev, Stanislav Manolev, Ivan Bandalovski, Ivan Ivanov, Nikolaj Bodurov, Hristo Yanev (84' Tsvetan Genkov), Stiliyan Petrov (C) (46' Chavdar Yankov), Martin Petrov (88' Spas Delev), Marcos Antônio Malachias Júnior "Marquinhos" (YC54), Ivelin Popov. (Coach: Lothar Herbert Matthäus (GER)).
Goals: Montenegro: 1-0 Radomir Djalovic (53').
Bulgaria: 1-1 Ivelin Popov (66').
Referee: Alon Yefet (ISR)   Attendance: 11.500

02-09-2011   Vasil Levski National Stadium, Sofia: Bulgaria – England   0-3 (0-3)
Bulgaria: Nikolay Mihaylov, Zhivko Milanov (YC84), Ivan Bandalovski (46' Georgi Sarmov (YC59)), Petar Zanev, Ivan Ivanov, Nikolaj Bodurov, Stiliyan Petrov (C), Martin Petrov, Blagoy Georgiev, Tsvetan Genkov (61' Georgi Bozhilov), Ivelin Popov (81' Marcos Antônio Malachias Júnior "Marquinhos"). (Coach: Lothar Herbert Matthäus (GER)).
England: Joe Hart, John Terry (C), Ashley Cole, Chris Smalling, Gary Cahill, Scott Parker (YC35), Stewart Downing, Gareth Barry (80' Frank Lampard), Ashley Young (61' James Milner), Theo Walcott (83' Adam Johnson), Wayne Rooney. (Coach: Fabio Capello (ITA)).
Goals: England: 0-1 Gary Cahill (13'), 0-2 Wayne Rooney (21'), 0-3 Wayne Rooney (45'+1').
Referee: Frank de Bleeckere (BEL)   Attendance: 27.230

247

02-09-2011   Cardiff City Stadium, Cardiff: Wales – Montenegro   2-1 (1-0)
Wales: Wayne Hennessey, Ashley Williams (YC23), Neil Taylor, Chris Gunter, David
Vaughan (YC36), Aaron Ramsey (C) (64' Andrew Crofts), Joe Ledley, Darcy Blake, Gareth
Bale (90'+4' Robert (Rob) Earnshaw), Steve Morison (83' Hal Robson-Kanu), Craig Bellamy
(YC44). (Coach: Gary Andrew Speed (WAL)).
Montenegro: Mladen Bozovic, Elsad Zverotic, Stefan Savic, Radoslav Batak, Sasa Balic
(YC27) (83' Milan Jovanovic), Simon Vukcevic (YC78), Milorad Pekovic, Nikola Drincic
(YC38), Mirko Vucinic (C) (79' Andrija Delibasic), Stevan Jovetic, Radomir Djalovic (57'
Dejan Damjanovic). (Coach: Zlatko Kranjcar (CRO)).
Goals: Wales: 1-0 Steve Morison (29'), 2-0 Aaron Ramsey (50').
Montenegro: 2-1 Stevan Jovetic (71').
Referee: Luca Banti (ITA)   Attendance: 8.194

06-09-2011   St.Jakob Park, Basel: Switzerland – Bulgaria   3-1 (1-1)
Switzerland: Diego Benaglio, Johan Djourou (YC60), Reto Ziegler, Philippe Senderos,
Stephan Lichtsteiner, Granit Xhaka (88' Gélson da Conceição Tavares Fernandes), Xherdan
Shaqiri (YC62) (90'+1' Nassim Ben Khalifa), Gökhan Inler (C), Blerim Dzemaili, Eren
Derdiyok, Admir Mehmedi (83' Innocent Nkasiobi Emeghara). (Coach: Ottmar Hitzfeld
(GER)).
Bulgaria: Nikolay Mihaylov, Zhivko Milanov (YC32,YC65), Petar Zanev, Ivan Ivanov,
Valentin Iliev, Georgi Sarmov, Stiliyan Petrov (C), Martin Petrov (60' Vladimir Gadzhev
(YC89)), Blagoy Georgiev (YC30), Tsvetan Genkov (70' Nikolaj Bodurov), Ivelin Popov.
(Coach: Lothar Herbert Matthäus (GER)).
Goals: Switzerland: 1-1 Xherdan Shaqiri (45'+2'), 2-1 Xherdan Shaqiri (62'), 3-1 Xherdan
Shaqiri (90').
Bulgaria: 0-1 Ivan Ivanov (9').
Referee: Pavel Královec (CZE)   Attendance: 16.880

06-09-2011   Wembley Stadium, London: England – Wales   1-0 (1-0)
England: Joe Hart, John Terry (C), Ashley Cole, Chris Smalling, Gary Cahill, Ashley Young,
Stewart Downing (79' Adam Johnson), Gareth Barry, James Milner (YC20), Frank Lampard
(73' Scott Parker), Wayne Rooney (89' Andy Carroll). (Coach: Fabio Capello (ITA)).
Wales: Wayne Hennessey, Ashley Williams, Neil Taylor, Chris Gunter, Andrew Crofts, Aaron
Ramsey (C), Joe Ledley, Jack Collison (85' Andy King), Darcy Blake, Gareth Bale, Steve
Morison (67' Robert (Rob) Earnshaw). (Coach: Gary Andrew Speed (WAL)).
Goal: England: 1-0 Ashley Young (35').
Referee: Robert Schörgenhofer (AUT)   Attendance: 77.128

07-10-2011   Liberty Stadium, Swansea: Wales – Switzerland   2-0 (0-0)
Wales: Wayne Hennessey, Chris Gunter, Andrew Crofts (81' David Vaughan), Ashley
Williams, Neil Taylor, Aaron Ramsey (C), Darcy Blake (YC82), Joe Allen, Gareth Bale, Steve
Morison (81' Simon Church), Craig Bellamy. (Coach: Gary Andrew Speed (WAL)).
Switzerland: Diego Benaglio, Timm Klose (YC59), Stephan Lichtsteiner, Steve von Bergen
(YC3), Reto Ziegler (RC55), Granit Xhaka (81' Admir Mehmedi), Fabian Frei (71' Innocent
Nkasiobi Emeghara), Xherdan Shaqiri (62' Ricardo Ivan Rodríguez Araya), Gökhan Inler (C),
Valon Behrami, Eren Derdiyok. (Coach: Ottmar Hitzfeld (GER)).
Goals: Wales: 1-0 Aaron Ramsey (60' penalty), 2-0 Gareth Bale (71').
Referee: Björn Kuipers (HOL)   Attendance: 12.317

07-10-2011   Podgorica City Stadium, Podgorica: Montenegro – England   2-2 (1-2)
Montenegro: Mladen Bozovic, Elsad Zverotic, Stefan Savic, Miodrag Dzudovic, Vladimir
Bozovic (79' Andrija Delibasic (YC90+2)), Simon Vukcevic, Milorad Pekovic (YC90+1),
Mladen Kascelan (46' Milan Jovanovic (YC60)), Stevan Jovetic (YC89), Fatos Beciraj (64'
Dejan Damjanovic), Mirko Vucinic (C) (YC90+2). (Coach: Branko Brnovic (MNE)).
England: Joe Hart, Ashley Cole, John Terry (C), Gary Cahill, Phil Jones, Gareth Barry, Ashley
Young (60' Stewart Downing), Scott Parker, Darren Bent (64' Frank Lampard), Theo Walcott
(76' Danny Welbeck), Wayne Rooney (RC74). (Coach: Fabio Capello (ITA)).
Goals: Montenegro: 1-2 Elsad Zverotic (45'), 2-2 Andrija Delibasic (90'+1').
England: 0-1 Ashley Young (11'), 0-2 Darren Bent (31').
Referee: Wolfgang Stark (GER)   Attendance: 11.340

11-10-2011   Vasil Levski National Stadium, Sofia: Bulgaria – Wales   0-1 (0-1)
Bulgaria: Nikolay Mihaylov, Petar Zanev, Georgi Terziev, Yordan Miliev, Stanislav Manolev
(52' Spas Delev), Ivan Ivanov (YC52), Aleksandar Tonev, Stiliyan Petrov (C) (YC90+3),
Vladimir Gadzhev (YC47), Valeri Domovchiyski (62' Valeri Bozhinov), Ivelin Popov (70'
Dimitar Rangelov). (Coach: Mihail Madanski (BUL)).
Wales: Wayne Hennessey, Ashley Williams, Neil Taylor, Chris Gunter, Andrew Crofts, Aaron
Ramsey (C), Darcy Blake (41' Adam Matthews), Joe Allen (YC56), Gareth Bale, Steve
Morison (70' Simon Church), Craig Bellamy. (Coach: Gary Andrew Speed (WAL)).
Goal: Wales: 0-1 Gareth Bale (45').
Referee: Pawel Gil (POL)   Attendance: 1.672

11-10-2011   St.Jakob Park, Basel: Switzerland – Montenegro   2-0 (0-0)
Switzerland: Diego Benaglio, Ricardo Ivan Rodríguez Araya, Johan Djourou, Steve von
Bergen, Stephan Lichtsteiner (YC14), Granit Xhaka (85' Gélson da Conceição Tavares
Fernandes), Xherdan Shaqiri (79' David Degen), Gökhan Inler (C), Valon Behrami (YC22),
Admir Mehmedi, Eren Derdiyok (69' Innocent Nkasiobi Emeghara). (Coach: Ottmar Hitzfeld
(GER)).
Montenegro: Mladen Bozovic, Marko Cetkovic (YC90+1), Elsad Zverotic, Stefan Savic, Luka
Pejovic (46' Vladimir Bozovic), Radoslav Batak, Nikola Drincic (C) (72' Petar Grbic), Drasko
Bozovic, Radomir Djalovic (YC42) (66' Andrija Delibasic), Dejan Damjanovic, Fatos Beciraj
(YC40). (Coach: Branko Brnovic (MNE)).
Goals: Switzerland: 1-0 Eren Derdiyok (51'), 2-0 Stephan Lichtsteiner (65').
Referee: Olegário Manuel Bártolo Faustino Benquerença (POR)   Attendance: 19.997

GROUP   H

03-09-2010	Reykjavik	Iceland – Norway	1-2 (1-0)
03-09-2010	Guimarães	Portugal – Cyprus	4-4 (2-2)
07-09-2010	Copenhagen	Denmark – Iceland	1-0 (0-0)
07-09-2010	Oslo	Norway – Portugal	1-0 (1-0)
08-10-2010	Larnaca	Cyprus – Norway	1-2 (0-2)
08-10-2010	Porto	Portugal – Denmark	3-1 (2-0)
12-10-2010	Copenhagen	Denmark – Cyprus	2-0 (0-0)
12-10-2010	Reykjavik	Iceland –Portugal	1-3 (1-2)
26-03-2011	Nicosia	Cyprus – Iceland	0-0

249

26-03-2011	Oslo	Norway – Denmark	1-1 (0-1)
04-06-2011	Reykjavik	Iceland – Denmark	0-2 (0-0)
04-06-2011	Lisbon	Portugal – Norway	1-0 (0-0)
02-09-2011	Oslo	Norway – Iceland	1-0 (0-0)
02-09-2011	Nicosia	Cyprus – Portugal	0-4 (0-1)
06-09-2011	Copenhagen	Denmark – Norway	2-0 (2-0)
06-09-2011	Reykjavik	Iceland – Cyprus	1-0 (1-0)
07-10-2011	Nicosia	Cyprus – Denmark	1-4 (1-4)
07-10-2011	Porto	Portugal – Iceland	5-3 (3-0)
11-10-2011	Oslo	Norway – Cyprus	3-1 (2-1)
11-10-2011	Copenhagen	Denmark – Portugal	2-1 (1-0)

FINAL STANDING

Pos	Team	Pld	W	D	L	GF	GA	GD	Pts
1	Denmark	8	6	1	1	15	6	+9	19
2	Portugal	8	5	1	2	21	12	+9	16
3	Norway	8	5	1	2	10	7	+3	16
4	Iceland	8	1	1	6	6	14	-8	4
5	Cyprus	8	0	2	6	7	20	-13	2

Denmark qualified for the Final Tournament in Poland and Ukraine.

Portugal qualified for the play-offs.

03-09-2010   Laugardalsvöllur, Reykjavik: Iceland – Norway   1-2 (1-0)
Iceland: Gunnleifur Gunnleifsson, Grétar Steinsson (76' Arnór Adalsteinsson), Indridi
Sigurdsson, Sölvi Ottesen (C), Kristján Sigurdsson, Gylfi Sigurdsson, Eggert Jónsson, Aron
Gunnarsson (YC32), Heidar Helguson, Veigar Gunnarsson (76' Birkir Bjarnason), Jóhann
Gudmundsson (87' Rúrik Gíslason). (Coach: Ólafur David Jóhannesson (ISL)).
Norway: Jon Knudsen, Kjetil Wæhler, John Arne Riise, Tom Høgli, Brede Hangeland (C)
(YC83), Bjørn Helge Riise (57' Steffen Iversen), Morten Gamst Pedersen, Erik Huseklepp (76'
Espen Ruud), Henning Hauger, Christian Grindheim, Mohammed Abdellaoue (88' Jan Gunnar
Solli). (Coach: Egil Roger Olsen (NOR)).
Goals: Iceland: 1-0 Heidar Helguson (38').
Norway: 1-1 Brede Hangeland (58'), 1-2 Mohammed Abdellaoue (75').
Referee: Luca Banti (ITA)   Attendance: 6.137

03-09-2010   Estádio Dom Afonso Henriques, Guimarães: Portugal – Cyprus 4-4 (2-2)
Portugal: EDUARDO dos Reis Carvalho, Luis MIGUEL Brito Garcia Monteiro, RICARDO
Alberto Silveira de CARVALHO (C), BRUNO Eduardo Regufe ALVES, RAÚL José
Trindade MEIRELES, MANUEL Henriques Tavares FERNANDES (79' JOÃO Filipe Iria
Santos MOUTINHO), FÁBIO Alexandre da Silva COENTRÃO, DANNY Miguel Alves
Gomes (61' LIÉDSON da Silva Muniz), HUGO Miguel Pereira de ALMEIDA (84'
YANNICK dos Santos DJALÓ), RICARDO Andrade QUARESMA Bernardo, Luís Carlos
Almeida da Cunha "NANI". (Coach: AGOSTINHO Vieira de OLIVEIRA (POR)).
Cyprus: Antonis Giorgallides, Giorgios Merkis, Marios Elia (66' Savvas Poursaitidis), Marinos
Satsias, Constantinos Makrides, Sinisa Dobrasinovic, Elias Charalambous (YC67),
Constantinos (Costas) Charalambides (76' Marios Nikolaou), Efstathios (Stathis) Aloneftis
(56' Ioannis Okkas), Michalis Konstantinou (C), Andreas Avraam. (Coach: Angelos
Anastasiadis (GRE)).
Goals: Portugal: 1-1 HUGO Miguel Pereira de ALMEIDA (8'), 2-2 RAÚL José Trindade
MEIRELES (29'), 3-2 DANNY Miguel Alves Gomes (50'), 4-3 MANUEL Henriques Tavares
FERNANDES (60').
Cyprus: 0-1 Efstathios (Stathis) Aloneftis (3'), 1-2 Michalis Konstantinou (11'), 3-3 Ioannis
Okkas (57'), 4-4 Andreas Avraam (89').
Referee: Mark Clattenburg (ENG)   Attendance: 9.100

07-09-2010   Parken Stadium, Copenhagen: Denmark – Iceland 1-0 (0-0)
Denmark: Anders Lindegaard, Simon Kjær, Leon Jessen, Lars Jacobsen, Daniel Agger,
Christian Poulsen (C), Thomas Kahlenberg, Christian Eriksen (56' Mads Junker), Michael
Krohn-Dehli (76' Martin Vingaard), Dennis Rommedahl, Nicklas Pedersen (71' Morten
Skoubo (YC89)). (Coach: Morten Per Olsen (DEN)).
Iceland: Gunnleifur Gunnleifsson, Birkir Sævarsson, Indridi Sigurdsson, Sölvi Ottesen (C),
Kristján Sigurdsson, Gylfi Sigurdsson (YC61), Eggert Jónsson (YC57), Aron Gunnarsson,
Rúrik Gíslason (YC82), Heidar Helguson (77' Kolbeinn Sigthórsson), Jóhann Gudmundsson
(90'+2' Birkir Bjarnason). (Coach: Ólafur David Jóhannesson (ISL)).
Goal: Denmark: 1-0 Thomas Kahlenberg (90'+1').
Referee: Douglas (Dougie) McDonald (SCO)   Attendance: 18.908

07-09-2010   Ullevaal Stadion, Oslo: Norway – Portugal 1-0 (1-0)
Norway: Jon Knudsen, Kjetil Wæhler (28' Vadim Demidov), Espen Ruud, Tom Høgli, Brede
Hangeland (C), Bjørn Helge Riise (YC65), Morten Gamst Pedersen, Erik Huseklepp, Henning
Hauger, Christian Grindheim (86' Ruben Yttergård Jenssen), John Carew (38' Mohammed
Abdellaoue). (Coach: Egil Roger Olsen (NOR)).
Portugal: EDUARDO dos Reis Carvalho, SÍLVIO Manuel de Azevedo Ferreira Sa Pereira,
RICARDO Alberto Silveira de CARVALHO (C), BRUNO Eduardo Regufe ALVES, TIAGO
Cardoso Mendes (71' DANNY Miguel Alves Gomes), RAÚL José Trindade MEIRELES
(YC62), MIGUEL Luis Pinto VELOSO, MANUEL Henriques Tavares FERNANDES,
RICARDO Andrade QUARESMA Bernardo (83' LIÉDSON da Silva Muniz), Luís Carlos
Almeida da Cunha "NANI", HUGO Miguel Pereira de ALMEIDA (YC90+1). (Coach:
AGOSTINHO Vieira de OLIVEIRA (POR)).
Goal: Norway: 1-0 Erik Huseklepp (21').
Referee: Laurent Duhamel (FRA)   Attendance: 24.535

251

08-10-2010   Antonis Papadopoulos Stadium, Larnaca: Cyprus – Norway 1-2 (0-2)
Cyprus: Antonis Giorgallides, Giorgios Merkis (81' Dimitris Christofi), Sinisa Dobrasinovic, Elias Charalambous (86' Georgios Efrem), Constantinos (Costas) Charalambides (46' Marinos Satsias (YC76)), Savvas Poursaitidis (YC6), Constantinos Makrides, Michalis Konstantinou, Efstathios (Stathis) Aloneftis, Ioannis Okkas (C), Andreas Avraam. (Coach: Angelos Anastasiadis (GRE)).
Norway: Jon Knudsen, Tom Høgli, Brede Hangeland (C), Kjetil Wæhler, John Arne Riise (YC13), Erik Huseklepp (80' Espen Ruud), Henning Hauger, Christian Grindheim, Bjørn Helge Riise (74' Petter Vaagan Moen), Morten Gamst Pedersen, John Carew (YC71) (83' Mohammed Abdellaoue). (Coach: Egil Roger Olsen (NOR)).
Goals: Cyprus: 1-2 Ioannis Okkas (58').
Norway: 0-1 John Arne Riise (2'), 0-2 John Carew (42').
Referee: Serge Gumienny (BEL)   Attendance: 7.648

08-10-2010   Estádio do Dragão, Porto: Portugal – Denmark 3-1 (2-0)
Portugal: EDUARDO dos Reis Carvalho, JOÃO Pedro da Silva PEREIRA, RICARDO Alberto Silveira de CARVALHO, Képler Laveran Lima Ferreira "PEPE", CARLOS Jorge Neto MARTINS (75' TIAGO Cardoso Mendes), RAÚL José Trindade MEIRELES, JOÃO Filipe Iria Santos MOUTINHO, FÁBIO Alexandre da Silva COENTRÃO, CRISTIANO RONALDO dos Santos Aveiro (C), Luís Carlos Almeida da Cunha "NANI" (88' Silvestre Manuel Gonçalves VARELA), HUGO Miguel Pereira de ALMEIDA (69' HÉLDER Manuel Marques POSTIGA). (Coach: PAULO Jorge Gomes BENTO (POR)).
Denmark: Thomas Sørensen (32' Anders Lindegaard), William Kvist (72' Peter Løvenkrands), Per Krøldrup, Simon Kjær, Lars Jacobsen, Daniel Jensen (58' Christian Eriksen), Martin Vingaard, Michael Silberbauer (YC2), Christian Poulsen (C), Dennis Rommedahl, Nicklas Pedersen. (Coach: Morten Per Olsen (DEN)).
Goals: Portugal: 1-0 Luís Carlos Almeida da Cunha "NANI" (29'), 2-0 Luís Carlos Almeida da Cunha "NANI" (30'), 3-1 CRISTIANO RONALDO dos Santos Aveiro (85').
Denmark: 2-1 RICARDO Alberto Silveira de CARVALHO (79' own goal).
Referee: Eric Frederikus Johannes Braamhaar (HOL)   Attendance: 27.117

12-10-2010   Parken Stadium, Copenhagen: Denmark – Cyprus 2-0 (0-0)
Denmark: Anders Lindegaard, Simon Kjær, Leon Jessen, Lars Jacobsen, Daniel Agger (39' Per Krøldrup), Christian Poulsen (C), Kasper Lorentzen, Michael Krohn-Dehli (65' Christian Eriksen), Dennis Rommedahl, Nicklas Pedersen (YC88), Mads Junker (46' Morten Rasmussen). (Coach: Morten Per Olsen (DEN)).
Cyprus: Antonis Giorgallides, Giorgios Merkis, Marinos Satsias (YC77), Savvas Poursaitidis, Constantinos Makrides, Sinisa Dobrasinovic, Elias Charalambous (28' Paraskevas Christou), Ioannis Okkas (C), Michalis Konstantinou, Efstathios (Stathis) Aloneftis (54' Constantinos (Costas) Charalambides), Andreas Avraam (63' Alexandros Garpozis). (Coach: Angelos Anastasiadis (GRE)).
Goals: Denmark: 1-0 Morten Rasmussen (47'), 2-0 Kasper Lorentzen (81').
Referee: César Muñiz Fernández (ESP)   Attendance: 15.544

12-10-2010   Laugardalsvöllur, Reykjavik: Iceland – Portugal 1-3 (1-2)
Iceland: Gunnleifur Gunnleifsson, Grétar Steinsson, Ragnar Sigurdsson, Indridi Sigurdsson (86' Arnór Adalsteinsson), Birkir Sævarsson (85' Veigar Gunnarsson), Ólafur Skúlason (YC36), Kristján Sigurdsson (C), Helgi Danielsson, Birkir Bjarnason (68' Gunnar Heidar Thorvaldsson), Heidar Helguson, Eidur Gudjohnsen (YC79). (Coach: Ólafur David Jóhannesson (ISL)).
Portugal: EDUARDO dos Reis Carvalho (YC17), JOÃO Pedro da Silva PEREIRA, Képler Laveran Lima Ferreira "PEPE", RICARDO Alberto Silveira de CARVALHO, JOÃO Filipe Iria Santos MOUTINHO, RAÚL José Trindade MEIRELES, CARLOS Jorge Neto MARTINS (77' TIAGO Cardoso Mendes (YC79)), FÁBIO Alexandre da Silva COENTRÃO, CRISTIANO RONALDO dos Santos Aveiro (C), Luís Carlos Almeida da Cunha "NANI" (87' DANNY Miguel Alves Gomes), HUGO Miguel Pereira de ALMEIDA (66' HÉLDER Manuel Marques POSTIGA). (Coach: PAULO Jorge Gomes BENTO (POR)).
Goals: Iceland: 1-1 Heidar Helguson (17').
Portugal: 0-1 CRISTIANO RONALDO dos Santos Aveiro (3'), 1-2 RAÚL José Trindade MEIRELES (27'), 1-3 HÉLDER Manuel Marques POSTIGA (72').
Referee: Thomas Einwaller (AUT)   Attendance: 9.767

26-03-2011   GSP Stadium, Nicosia: Cyprus – Iceland 0-0
Cyprus: Antonis Giorgallides, Valentinos Sielis (46' Jason Demetriou), Giorgios Merkis (YC42), Savvas Poursaitidis (61' Marios Elia), Chrysostomos (Chrysis) Michail, Constantinos Makrides, Sinisa Dobrasinovic, Constantinos (Costas) Charalambides, Efstathios (Stathis) Aloneftis, Andreas Avraam, Dimitris Christofi (73' Nektarios Alexandrou). (Coach: Angelos Anastasiadis (GRE)).
Iceland: Stefán Magnússon (YC88), Indridi Sigurdsson, Birkir Sævarsson, Hermann Hreidarsson (C), Kristján Sigurdsson (YC21), Gylfi Sigurdsson (90'+1' Birkir Bjarnason), Eggert Jónsson (YC72), Aron Gunnarsson, Rúrik Gíslason (63' Alfred Finnbogason), Heidar Helguson, Jóhann Gudmundsson (59' Arnór Smárason). (Coach: Ólafur David Jóhannesson (ISL)).
Referee: Darko Ceferin (SLO)   Attendance: 2.088
(Chrysostomos (Chrysis) Michail missed a penalty in the 21st minute)

26-03-2011   Ullevaal Stadion, Oslo: Norway – Denmark 1-1 (0-1)
Norway: Rune Jarstein, Kjetil Wæhler (YC37), Espen Ruud (78' Daniel Braaten), John Arne Riise, Brede Hangeland (C), Bjørn Helge Riise, Morten Gamst Pedersen, Erik Huseklepp (89' Steffen Iversen), Henning Hauger, Christian Grindheim, Mohammed Abdellaoue. (Coach: Egil Roger Olsen (NOR)).
Denmark: Thomas Sørensen, William Kvist, Mathias Jørgensen, Lars Jacobsen (YC34), Daniel Agger, Michael Silberbauer, Christian Poulsen (C) (69' Jakob Poulsen), Christian Eriksen, Michael Krohn-Dehli (82' Thomas Enevoldsen), Dennis Rommedahl (90'+3' Daniel Wass), Nicklas Bendtner. (Coach: Morten Per Olsen (DEN)).
Goals: Norway: 1-1 Erik Huseklepp (81').
Denmark: 0-1 Dennis Rommedahl (27').
Referee: Gianluca Rocchi (ITA)   Attendance: 24.828

04-06-2011   Laugardalsvöllur, Reykjavik: Iceland – Denmark   0-2 (0-0)
Iceland: Stefán Magnússon, Birkir Sævarsson, Hermann Hreidarsson (C), Bjarni Eiríksson, Ólafur Skúlason (YC66) (67' Alfred Finnbogason), Kristján Sigurdsson (YC22), Gylfi Sigurdsson, Aron Gunnarsson, Kolbeinn Sigthórsson, Heidar Helguson (77' Jóhann Gudmundsson), Eidur Gudjohnsen. (Coach: Ólafur David Jóhannesson (ISL)).
Denmark: Thomas Sørensen (C), Bo Svensson, Simon Poulsen, William Kvist (60' Christian Poulsen), Simon Kjær, Lars Jacobsen, Niki Zimling, Christian Eriksen, Michael Krohn-Dehli (46' Lasse Schöne), Dennis Rommedahl, Nicklas Bendtner. (Coach: Morten Per Olsen (DEN)).
Goals: Denmark: 0-1 Lasse Schöne (60'), 0-2 Christian Eriksen (75').
Referee: Firat Aydinus (TUR)   Attendance: 7.629

04-06-2011   Estádio da Luz, Lisbon: Portugal – Norway   1-0 (0-0)
Portugal: EDUARDO dos Reis Carvalho, BRUNO Eduardo Regufe ALVES, Képler Laveran Lima Ferreira "PEPE", JOÃO Pedro da Silva PEREIRA (73' SÍLVIO Manuel de Azevedo Ferreira Sa Pereira), JOÃO Filipe Iria Santos MOUTINHO, CARLOS Jorge Neto MARTINS (69' RÚBEN MICAEL Freitas da Ressureição), RAÚL José Trindade MEIRELES, FÁBIO Alexandre da Silva COENTRÃO, HÉLDER Manuel Marques POSTIGA, CRISTIANO RONALDO dos Santos Aveiro (C), Luís Carlos Almeida da Cunha "NANI" (86' Silvestre Manuel Gonçalves VARELA). (Coach: PAULO Jorge Gomes BENTO (POR)).
Norway: Rune Jarstein, Tom Høgli, Brede Hangeland (C), Vadim Demidov, John Arne Riise, Erik Huseklepp (75' Daniel Braaten), Henning Hauger, Christian Grindheim (83' Markus Henriksen), Bjørn Helge Riise, Morten Gamst Pedersen, John Carew (60' Mohammed Abdellaoue). (Coach: Egil Roger Olsen (NOR)).
Goal: Portugal; 1-0 HÉLDER Manuel Marques POSTIGA (53').
Referee: Cüneyt Çakir (TUR)   Attendance: 47.829

02-09-2011   Ullevaal Stadion, Oslo: Norway – Iceland   1-0 (0-0)
Norway: Rune Jarstein, Kjetil Wæhler, Espen Ruud, Tom Høgli, Brede Hangeland (C), Alexander Tettey, Jonathan Parr (68' Daniel Braaten (YC73)), Erik Huseklepp (87' Simen Brenne), Henning Hauger, Christian Grindheim (80' John Carew), Mohammed Abdellaoue. (Coach: Egil Roger Olsen (NOR)).
Iceland: Stefán Magnússon (YC79), Indridi Sigurdsson (YC66), Birkir Sævarsson, Sölvi Ottesen, Hjörtur Valgardsson, Eggert Jónsson, Rúrik Gíslason (YC27), Helgi Danielsson (90' Birkir Bjarnason), Kolbeinn Sigthórsson (78' Veigar Gunnarsson), Jóhann Gudmundsson (80' Steinthór Thorsteinsson), Eidur Gudjohnsen (C). (Coach: Ólafur David Jóhannesson (ISL)).
Goal: Norway: 1-0 Mohammed Abdellaoue (88' penalty).
Referee: Ovidiu Alin Hategan (ROM)   Attendance: 22.381

02-09-2011   GSP Stadium, Nicosia: Cyprus – Portugal   0-4 (0-1)
Cyprus: Antonis Giorgallides, Giorgios Merkis, Jason Demetriou, Paraskevas Christou, Savvas
Poursaitidis, Constantinos Makrides (YC35) (38' Marios Nikolaou), Sinisa Dobrasinovic
(YC17,YC34), Constantinos (Costas) Charalambides (63' Nektarios Alexandrou), Ioannis
Okkas (C), Dimitris Christofi (80' Georgios Efrem), Andreas Avraam. (Coach: Nikolaos
(Nikos) Nioplias (GRE)).
Portugal: RUI Pedro dos Santos PATRÍCIO, JOÃO Pedro da Silva PEREIRA, Képler Laveran
Lima Ferreira "PEPE", BRUNO Eduardo Regufe ALVES, RÚBEN MICAEL Freitas da
Ressureição (YC37) (63' MIGUEL Luis Pinto VELOSO), JOÃO Filipe Iria Santos
MOUTINHO, RAÚL José Trindade MEIRELES, FÁBIO Alexandre da Silva COENTRÃO,
HÉLDER Manuel Marques POSTIGA (76' HUGO Miguel Pereira de ALMEIDA),
CRISTIANO RONALDO dos Santos Aveiro (C) (YC83'), Luís Carlos Almeida da Cunha
"NANI" (86' DANNY Miguel Alves Gomes). (Coach: PAULO Jorge Gomes BENTO (POR)).
Goals: Portugal: 0-1 CRISTIANO RONALDO dos Santos Aveiro (35' penalty), 0-2
CRISTIANO RONALDO dos Santos Aveiro (82'), 0-3 HUGO Miguel Pereira de ALMEIDA
(84'), 0-4 DANNY Miguel Alves Gomes (90'+2').
Referee: Gianluca Rocchi (ITA)   Attendance: 15.444

06-09-2011   Parken Stadium, Copenhagen: Denmark – Norway   2-0 (2-0)
Denmark: Thomas Sørensen, Lars Jacobsen, Nicolai Boilesen, Daniel Agger (C), William
Kvist, Simon Kjær (YC18), Christian Eriksen, Niki Zimling, Michael Krohn-Dehli (69' Lasse
Schöne), Nicklas Bendtner (89' Nicklas Pedersen), Dennis Rommedahl (65' Michael
Silberbauer). (Coach: Morten Per Olsen (DEN)).
Norway: Rune Jarstein, Tom Høgli (YC88), Brede Hangeland (C) (YC67), Kjetil Wæhler (46'
Vadim Demidov), Espen Ruud, John Arne Riise (61' Daniel Braaten (YC83)), Håvard
Nordtveit (YC73), Erik Huseklepp (69' John Carew), Christian Grindheim (YC81), Alexander
Tettey, Mohammed Abdellaoue. (Coach: Egil Roger Olsen (NOR)).
Goals: Denmark: 1-0 Nicklas Bendtner (24'), 2-0 Nicklas Bendtner (44').
Referee: Stéphane Lannoy (FRA)   Attendance: 37.167

06-09-2011   Laugardalsvöllur, Reykjavik: Iceland – Cyprus   1-0 (1-0)
Iceland: Hannes Halldórsson, Birkir Sævarsson, Hallgrímur Jónasson, Helgi Danielsson, Birkir
Bjarnason (YC17) (84' Björn Sigurdarsson), Hjörtur Valgardsson, Kristján Sigurdsson, Eggert
Jónsson (YC34), Jóhann Gudmundsson (88' Matthías Vilhjálmsson), Eidur Gudjohnsen (C),
Kolbeinn Sigthórsson (84' Alfred Finnbogason). (Coach: Ólafur David Jóhannesson (ISL)).
Cyprus: Antonis Giorgallides, Paraskevas Christou, Giorgios Merkis, Jason Demetriou
(YC34), Constantinos (Costas) Charalambides (83' Kyriakos Pavlou), Marinos Satsias, Savvas
Poursaitidis, Nektarios Alexandrou (61' Georgios Efrem), Ioannis Okkas (C) (YC22) (46'
Constantinos Makrides (YC47)), Dimitris Christofi, Andreas Avraam. (Coach: Nikolaos
(Nikos) Nioplias (GRE)).
Goal: Iceland: 1-0 Kolbeinn Sigthórsson (5').
Referee: Bosko Jovanetic (SRB)   Attendance: 5.267

07-10-2011   GSP Stadium, Nicosia: Cyprus – Denmark   1-4 (1-4)
Cyprus: Antonis Giorgallides, Giorgos Pelagias, Giorgios Merkis, Jason Demetriou (71'
Marinos Satsias), Constantinos (Costas) Charalambides, Savvas Poursaitidis (YC35) (46'
Athos Solomou), Georgios Efrem, Sinisa Dobrasinovic (YC75), Nektarios Alexandrou,
Michalis Konstantinou (C) (62' Dimitris Christofi), Andreas Avraam (YC64). (Coach:
Nikolaos (Nikos) Nioplias (GRE)).
Denmark: Thomas Sørensen, Simon Poulsen, William Kvist, Simon Kjær, Lars Jacobsen (82'
Michael Silberbauer), Andreas Bjelland (YC24), Christian Eriksen, Niki Zimling (YC39) (68'
Martin Jørgensen), Michael Krohn-Dehli, Nicklas Bendtner, Dennis Rommedahl (71' Christian
Poulsen). (Coach: Morten Per Olsen (DEN)).
Goals: Cyprus: 1-4 Andreas Avraam (45'+1').
Denmark: 0-1 Lars Jacobsen (7'), 0-2 Dennis Rommedahl (11'), 0-3 Michael Krohn-Dehli
(20'), 0-4 Dennis Rommedahl (22').
Referee: Marijo Strahonja (CRO)   Attendance: 2.408

07-10-2011   Estádio do Dragão, Porto: Portugal – Iceland   5-3 (3-0)
Portugal: RUI Pedro dos Santos PATRÍCIO, ROLANDO Jorge Pires da Fonseca (YC90+4),
JOÃO Pedro da Silva PEREIRA, BRUNO Eduardo Regufe ALVES, ELISEU Pereira dos
Santos, JOÃO Filipe Iria Santos MOUTINHO, RAÚL José Trindade MEIRELES (60'
MIGUEL Luis Pinto VELOSO), CARLOS Jorge Neto MARTINS (YC60) (72' RÚBEN
MICAEL Freitas da Ressureição), HÉLDER Manuel Marques POSTIGA (88' NUNO
"GOMES" Miguel Soares Pereira Ribeiro), CRISTIANO RONALDO dos Santos Aveiro (C),
Luís Carlos Almeida da Cunha "NANI". (Coach: PAULO Jorge Gomes BENTO (POR)).
Iceland: Stefán Magnússon, Birkir Sævarsson (YC36), Sölvi Ottesen (C), Hallgrímur Jónasson
(89' Matthías Vilhjálmsson), Hjörtur Valgardsson, Kristján Sigurdsson, Gylfi Sigurdsson,
Aron Gunnarsson, Jóhann Gudmundsson (81' Kjartan Henry Finnbogason), Rúrik Gíslason
(89' Arnór Smárason), Birkir Bjarnason. (Coach: Ólafur David Jóhannesson (ISL)).
Goals: Portugal: 1-0 Luís Carlos Almeida da Cunha "NANI" (13'), 2-0 Luís Carlos Almeida da
Cunha "NANI" (21'), 3-0 HÉLDER Manuel Marques POSTIGA (44'), 4-2 JOÃO Filipe Iria
Santos MOUTINHO (81'), 5-2 ELISEU Pereira dos Santos (87').
Iceland: 3-1 Hallgrímur Jónasson (48'), 3-2 Hallgrímur Jónasson (68'), 5-3 Gylfi Sigurdsson
(90'+4' penalty).
Referee: Hendrikus Sebastiaan Hermanus (Bas) Nijhuis (HOL)   Attendance: 35.715

11-10-2011   Ullevaal Stadion, Oslo: Norway – Cyprus   3-1 (2-1)
Norway: Rune Jarstein, Kjetil Wæhler (C), Espen Ruud (YC26) (63' Simen Brenne), John
Arne Riise, Tom Høgli, Vadim Demidov, Alexander Tettey (82' Ruben Yttergård Jenssen),
Morten Gamst Pedersen (46' Jonathan Parr), Erik Huseklepp, Christian Grindheim, John
Carew. (Coach: Egil Roger Olsen (NOR)).
Cyprus: Anastasios (Tasos) Kissas, Giorgos Pelagias (6' Stelios Parpas), Giorgios Merkis
(YC68), Jason Demetriou, Marinos Satsias, Sinisa Dobrasinovic, Elias Charalambous,
Constantinos (Costas) Charalambides (62' Dimitris Christofi), Athos Solomou, Ioannis Okkas
(C) (82' Andreas Stavrou), Andreas Avraam. (Coach: Nikolaos (Nikos) Nioplias (GRE)).
Goals: Norway: 1-0 Morten Gamst Pedersen (25'), 2-0 John Carew (34'), 3-1 Tom Høgli (65').
Cyprus: 2-1 Ioannis Okkas (42').
Referee: William (Willie) Collum (SCO)   Attendance: 13.490

11-10-2011   Parken Stadium, Copenhagen: Denmark – Portugal 2-1 (1-0)
Denmark: Thomas Sørensen (C), William Kvist, Simon Kjær, Lars Jacobsen, Andreas Bjelland, Niki Zimling (70' Christian Poulsen), Michael Silberbauer (YC75) (76' Simon Poulsen), Christian Eriksen, Michael Krohn-Dehli, Dennis Rommedahl (YC45) (87' Jakob Poulsen), Nicklas Bendtner. (Coach: Morten Per Olsen (DEN)).
Portugal: RUI Pedro dos Santos PATRÍCIO, BRUNO Eduardo Regufe ALVES, ROLANDO Jorge Pires da Fonseca, JOÃO Pedro da Silva PEREIRA, ELISEU Pereira dos Santos (65' RICARDO Andrade QUARESMA Bernardo), RAÚL José Trindade MEIRELES, JOÃO Filipe Iria Santos MOUTINHO, CARLOS Jorge Neto MARTINS (65' MIGUEL Luis Pinto VELOSO), HÉLDER Manuel Marques POSTIGA (78' NUNO "GOMES" Miguel Soares Pereira Ribeiro), CRISTIANO RONALDO dos Santos Aveiro (C), Luís Carlos Almeida da Cunha "NANI". (Coach: PAULO Jorge Gomes BENTO (POR)).
Goals: Denmark: 1-0 Michael Krohn-Dehli (13'), 2-0 Nicklas Bendtner (63').
Portugal: 2-1 CRISTIANO RONALDO dos Santos Aveiro (90'+2').
Referee: Nicola Rizzoli (ITA)   Attendance: 37.012

GROUP   I

03-09-2010	Kaunas	Lithuania – Scotland	0-0
03-09-2010	Vaduz	Liechtenstein – Spain	0-4 (0-2)
07-09-2010	Olomouc	Czech Republic – Lithuania	0-1 (0-1)
07-09-2010	Glasgow	Scotland – Liechtenstein	2-1 (0-0)
08-10-2010	Prague	Czech Republic – Scotland	1-0 (0-0)
08-10-2010	Salamanca	Spain – Lithuania	3-1 (0-0)
12-10-2010	Vaduz	Liechtenstein – Czech Republic	0-2 (0-2)
12-10-2010	Glasgow	Scotland – Spain	2-3 (0-1)
25-03-2011	Granada	Spain – Czech Republic	2-1 (0-1)
29-03-2011	Ceske Budejovice	Czech Republic – Liechtenstein	2-0 (1-0)
29-03-2011	Kaunas	Lithuania – Spain	1-3 (0-1)
03-06-2011	Vaduz	Liechtenstein – Lithuania	2-0 (2-0)
02-09-2011	Kaunas	Lithuania – Liechtenstein	0-0
03-09-2011	Glasgow	Scotland – Czech Republic	2-2 (1-0)
06-09-2011	Glasgow	Scotland – Lithuania	1-0 (0-0)
06-09-2011	Logroño	Spain – Liechtenstein	6-0 (3-0)
07-10-2011	Prague	Czech Republic – Spain	0-2 (0-2)
08-10-2011	Vaduz	Liechtenstein – Scotland	0-1 (0-1)
11-10-2011	Alicante	Spain – Scotland	3-1 (2-0)
11-10-2011	Kaunas	Lithuania – Czech Republic	1-4 (0-3)

FINAL STANDING

Pos	Team	Pld	W	D	L	GF	GA	GD	Pts
1	Spain	8	8	0	0	26	6	+20	24
2	Czech Republic	8	4	1	3	12	8	+4	13
3	Scotland	8	3	2	3	9	10	-1	11
4	Lithuania	8	1	2	5	4	13	-9	5
5	Liechtenstein	8	1	1	6	3	17	-14	4

Spain qualified for the Final Tournament in Poland and Ukraine.

Czech Republic qualified for the play-offs.

03-09-2010   S.Darius and S.Girénas Stadium, Kaunas: Lithuania – Scotland   0-0
Lithuania: Zydrūnas Karcemarskas, Marius Stankevicius, Andrius Skerla (YC67), Deividas Semberas, Tadas Kijanskas (YC15), Darvydas Sernas (80' Vytautas Luksa), Ramūnas Radavicius (YC18), Mindaugas Panka, Saulius Mikoliūnas (71' Robertas Poskus), Edgaras Cesnauskis, Tomas Danilevicius (C) (90' Kestutis Ivaskevicius (YC90+3)). (Coach: Raimondas Zutautas (LIT)).
Scotland: Allan McGregor, Steven Whittaker (90' Christophe Berra), David Weir, Stephen McManus, Alan Hutton, Barry Robson (69' James McFadden), Steven Naismith, Darren Fletcher (C), Scott Brown (YC42) (76' James Morrison), Kenny Miller, Lee McCulloch (YC72). (Coach: Craig Levein (SCO)).
Referee: Cüneyt Çakir (TUR)   Attendance: 5.248

03-09-2010   Rheinpark Stadion, Vaduz: Liechtenstein – Spain   0-4 (0-2)
Liechtenstein: Peter Jehle, Michael Stocklasa, Martin Stocklasa, Yves Oehri (46' Franz-Josef Vogt), Michele Polverino, Lucas Eberle (45' Martin Rechsteiner), Franz Burgmeier, Sandro Wieser (82' Ronny Büchel), Daniel Hasler (YC40), Mario Frick (C), Philippe Erne. (Coach: Hans-Peter Zaugg (SUI)).
Spain: IKER CASILLAS Fernández (C), Carlos MARCHENA López, Joan CAPDEVILA Méndez, SERGIO RAMOS García, Gerard PIQUÉ i Bernabéu, Xavier "XAVI" Hernández i Creus (46' Francesc "CESC" FÀBREGAS Soler), Andrés INIESTA Luján (65' PEDRO Eliezer Rodríguez Ledesma), Sergio BUSQUETS Burgos, Xabier "XABI" ALONSO Olano, DAVID VILLA Sánchez, FERNANDO José TORRES Sanz (57' DAVID Jiménez SILVA). (Coach: VICENTE DEL BOSQUE González (ESP)).
Goals: Spain: 0-1 FERNANDO José TORRES Sanz (18'), 0-2 DAVID VILLA Sánchez (26'), 0-3 FERNANDO José TORRES Sanz (54'), 0-4 DAVID Jiménez SILVA (62').
Referee: Bülent Yildirim (TUR)   Attendance: 6.127

07-09-2010   Andruv stadion, Olomouc: Czech Republic – Lithuania   0-1 (0-1)
Czech Republic: Petr Cech, Zdenek Pospech, Michal Kadlec, Tomás Hübschman, Roman Hubník (YC90+2), Tomás Rosicky (C), Daniel Pudil (84' Roman Bednár), Jan Polák (69' Jirí Stajner), Jaroslav Plasil, Martin Fenin (59' Tomás Necid), Milan Baros. (Coach: Michal Bílek (CZE)).
Lithuania: Zydrūnas Karcemarskas, Marius Stankevicius, Andrius Skerla, Deividas Semberas (YC74), Tadas Kijanskas, Darvydas Sernas (C) (YC19) (61' Robertas Poskus), Ramūnas Radavicius, Mindaugas Panka, Saulius Mikoliūnas (79' Vytautas Luksa), Edgaras Cesnauskis (YC42), Tomas Danilevicius (90' Kestutis Ivaskevicius). (Coach: Raimondas Zutautas (LIT)).
Goal: Lithuania: 0-1 Darvydas Sernas (27').
Referee: Alon Yefet (ISR)   Attendance: 12.038
(Milan Baros missed a penalty in the 40th minute)

07-09-2010   Hampden Park, Glasgow: Scotland – Liechtenstein   2-1 (0-0)
Scotland: Allan McGregor (YC88), David Weir, Lee Wallace (54' Barry Robson (YC57)), Stephen McManus, Alan Hutton (YC90+4), Darren Fletcher (C), Scott Brown, Kenny Miller, James McFadden (46' James Morrison), Lee McCulloch (YC86), Kris Boyd (66' Steven Naismith). (Coach: Craig Levein (SCO)).
Liechtenstein: Peter Jehle, Michael Stocklasa, Martin Stocklasa (YC51), Martin Rechsteiner (YC68), Yves Oehri, Michele Polverino (YC90+4), Franz Burgmeier (YC9), Sandro Wieser (YC31) (71' Ronny Büchel), Daniel Hasler (90'+2' Nicolas Hasler), Mario Frick (C) (YC67) (79' Fabio D'Elia (YC90+1)), Philippe Erne. (Coach: Hans-Peter Zaugg (SUI)).
Goals: Scotland: 1-1 Kenny Miller (63'), 2-1 Stephen McManus (90'+7').
Liechtenstein: 0-1 Mario Frick (47').
Referee: Viktor Borysovych Shvetsov (UKR)   Attendance: 37.050

08-10-2010   Synot Tip Arena, Prague: Czech Republic – Scotland   1-0 (0-0)
Czech Republic: Petr Cech, Zdenek Pospech, Michal Kadlec, Tomás Hübschman (YC33), Roman Hubník, Marek Suchy, Tomás Rosicky (C), Jan Polák, Jaroslav Plasil (90'+4' Jan Rajnoch), Tomás Necid (YC15) (84' Mario Holek), Lukás Magera (59' Roman Bednár). (Coach: Michal Bílek (CZE)).
Scotland: Allan McGregor, Steven Whittaker (YC13), David Weir (YC82), Stephen McManus, Alan Hutton, Gary Caldwell (76' Chris Iwelumo), Steven Naismith, James Morrison (84' Barry Robson (YC86)), Darren Fletcher (C), Graham Dorrans, Jamie Mackie (76' Kenny Miller). (Coach: Craig Levein (SCO)).
Goal: Czech Republic: 1-0 Roman Hubník (69').
Referee: Ivan Bebek (CRO)   Attendance: 14.922

08-10-2010   Estadio El Helmántico, Salamanca: Spain – Lithuania   3-1 (0-0)
Spain: IKER CASILLAS Fernández (C), Joan CAPDEVILA Méndez, SERGIO RAMOS
García (82' Álvaro ARBELOA Coca), Carles PUYOL Saforcada, Gerard PIQUÉ i Bernabéu,
Sergio BUSQUETS Burgos, DAVID Jiménez SILVA, Andrés INIESTA Luján, Santiago
"SANTI" CAZORLA González, Fernando Javier LLORENTE Torres (77' Aritz ADURIZ
Zubeldia), DAVID VILLA Sánchez (76' PABLO HERNÁNDEZ Domínguez). (Coach:
VICENTE DEL BOSQUE González (ESP)).
Lithuania: Zydrūnas Karcemarskas, Marius Stankevicius, Andrius Skerla, Deividas Semberas,
Tadas Kijanskas, Edgaras Cesnauskis (84' Robertas Poskus), Darvydas Sernas, Ramūnas
Radavicius, Mindaugas Panka, Saulius Mikoliūnas (59' Deividas Cesnauskis), Tomas
Danilevicius (C) (82' Kestutis Ivaskevicius). (Coach: Raimondas Zutautas (LIT)).
Goals: Spain: 1-0 Fernando Javier LLORENTE Torres (47'), 2-1 Fernando Javier LLORENTE
Torres (56'), 3-1 DAVID Jiménez SILVA (79').
Lithuania: 1-1 Darvydas Sernas (54').
Referee: Gianluca Rocchi (ITA)   Attendance: 17.340

12-10-2010   Rheinpark Stadion, Vaduz: Liechtenstein – Czech Republic   0-2 (0-2)
Liechtenstein: Peter Jehle, Michael Stocklasa (YC65), Martin Stocklasa, Martin Rechsteiner,
Yves Oehri, Franz Burgmeier, Michele Polverino (YC47), Sandro Wieser (YC57) (84' Ronny
Büchel), Mario Frick (C), Thomas Beck (66' Nicolas Hasler), Philippe Erne (78' Rony
Hanselmann). (Coach: Hans-Peter Zaugg (SUI)).
Czech Republic: Petr Cech, Michal Kadlec, Tomás Hübschman, Roman Hubník, Zdenek
Pospech, Marek Suchy, Tomás Rosicky (C), Jan Polák (59' Jirí Stajner (YC72)), Jaroslav
Plasil, Tomás Necid (89' Milan Petrzela), Václav Kadlec (64' Roman Bednár). (Coach: Michal
Bílek (CZE)).
Goals: Czech Republic: 0-1 Tomás Necid (12'), 0-2 Václav Kadlec (29').
Referee: Stanislav Valeryevich Sukhina (RUS)   Attendance: 2.555

12-10-2010   Hampden Park, Glasgow: Scotland – Spain   2-3 (0-1)
Scotland: Allan McGregor, Steven Whittaker (YC44,YC89), David Weir, Stephen McManus,
Phil Bardsley, Steven Naismith, James Morrison (88' Shaun Malony), Darren Fletcher (C),
Graham Dorrans (80' Jamie Mackie), Kenny Miller (YC73), Lee McCulloch (46' Charlie
Adam). (Coach: Craig Levein (SCO)).
Spain: IKER CASILLAS Fernández (C), Joan CAPDEVILA Méndez, SERGIO RAMOS
García, Carles PUYOL Saforcada, Gerard PIQUÉ i Bernabéu, Xabier "XABI" ALONSO
Olano, Andrés INIESTA Luján, DAVID Jiménez SILVA (76' Fernando Javier LLORENTE
Torres), Santiago "SANTI" CAZORLA González (71' PABLO HERNÁNDEZ Domínguez),
Sergio BUSQUETS Burgos (90' Carlos MARCHENA López), DAVID VILLA Sánchez.
(Coach: VICENTE DEL BOSQUE González (ESP)).
Goals: Scotland: 1-2 Steven Naismith (58'), 2-2 Gerard PIQUÉ i Bernabéu (66' own goal).
Spain: 0-1 DAVID VILLA Sánchez (44' penalty), 0-2 Andrés INIESTA Luján (55'), 2-3
Fernando Javier LLORENTE Torres (79').
Referee: Massimo Busacca (SUI)   Attendance: 51.322

25-03-2011   Estadio Nuevo Los Cármenes, Granada: Spain – Czech Republic   2-1 (0-1)
Spain: IKER CASILLAS Fernández (C), Joan CAPDEVILA Méndez (58' Santiago "SANTI" CAZORLA González), Álvaro ARBELOA Coca (YC84), SERGIO RAMOS García, Gerard PIQUÉ i Bernabéu, Jesús NAVAS González (86' Carlos MARCHENA López), Xavier "XAVI" Hernández i Creus, Xabier "XABI" ALONSO Olano (YC39) (46' FERNANDO José TORRES Sanz), Andrés INIESTA Luján, Sergio BUSQUETS Burgos; DAVID VILLA Sánchez. (Coach: VICENTE DEL BOSQUE González (ESP)).
Czech Republic: Petr Cech, Zdenek Pospech (YC46), Michal Kadlec, Tomás Hübschman, Roman Hubník, Tomás Sivok, Tomás Rosicky (C), Daniel Pudil (78' Adam Hlousek), Jaroslav Plasil, Jan Rezek (YC60) (84' Tomás Necid), Milan Baros. (Coach: Michal Bílek (CZE)).
Goals: Spain: 1-1 DAVID VILLA Sánchez (69'), 2-1 DAVID VILLA Sánchez (72' penalty).
Czech Republic: 0-1 Jaroslav Plasil (29').
Referee: Viktor Kassai (HUN)   Attendance: 16.301

29-03-2011   Stadion Strelecky ostrov, Ceske Budejovice:
              Czech Republic – Liechtenstein   2-0 (1-0)
Czech Republic: Petr Cech, Zdenek Pospech, Michal Kadlec, Tomás Hübschman, Roman Hubník, Tomás Sivok, Tomás Rosicky (C) (84' Jan Polák), Jaroslav Plasil (YC81), Jan Morávek (56' Adam Hlousek), David Lafata (59' Tomás Necid), Milan Baros. (Coach: Michal Bílek (CZE)).
Liechtenstein: Peter Jehle, Michael Stocklasa (YC38), Martin Stocklasa, Martin Rechsteiner (YC56), Nicolas Hasler, Franz Burgmeier, Martin Büchel (10' Wolfgang Kieber, 81' Andreas Christen), David Hasler, Mario Frick (C) (YC57), Thomas Beck (YC71), Philippe Erne. (Coach: Hans-Peter Zaugg (SUI)).
Goals: Czech Republic: 1-0 Milan Baros (3'), 2-0 Michal Kadlec (70').
Referee: Ovidiu Alin Hategan (ROM)   Attendance: 6.600

29-03-2011   S.Darius and S.Girénas Stadium, Kaunas: Lithuania – Spain   1-3 (0-1)
Lithuania: Zydrūnas Karcemarskas, Marius Stankevicius, Andrius Skerla, Deividas Semberas, Tadas Kijanskas, Marius Zaliūkas, Darvydas Sernas (74' Tadas Labukas), Mindaugas Panka, Saulius Mikoliūnas (71' Ramūnas Radavicius), Edgaras Cesnauskis, Tomas Danilevicius (C) (85' Dominykas Galkevicius). (Coach: Raimondas Zutautas (LIT)).
Spain: IKER CASILLAS Fernández (C), Andoni IRAOLA Sagama, Álvaro ARBELOA Coca, Gerard PIQUÉ i Bernabéu (89' SERGIO RAMOS García), Raúl ALBIOL Tortajada, Xavier "XAVI" Hernández i Creus, Javier "JAVI" MARTÍNEZ Aginaga, Santiago "SANTI" CAZORLA González (67' Juan Manuel MATA García), Xabier "XABI" ALONSO Olano, Fernando Javier LLORENTE Torres, DAVID VILLA Sánchez (54' DAVID Jiménez SILVA). (Coach: VICENTE DEL BOSQUE González (ESP)).
Goals: Lithuania: 1-1 Marius Stankevicius (57').
Spain: 0-1 Xavier "XAVI" Hernández i Creus (19'), 1-2 Tadas Kijanskas (70' own goal), 1-3 Juan Manuel MATA García (83').
Referee: Laurent Duhamel (FRA)   Attendance: 9.180

03-06-2011   Rheinpark Stadion, Vaduz: Liechtenstein – Lithuania   2-0 (2-0)
Liechtenstein: Benjamin Büchel, Martin Stocklasa (C), Marco Ritzberger, Daniel Kaufmann
(YC81), Michele Polverino, Nicolas Hasler, Franz Burgmeier, Martin Büchel, Benjamin
Fischer (72' Mathias Christen), Thomas Beck (YC78) (84' Andreas Christen), Philippe Erne
(87' Rony Hanselmann). (Coach: Hans-Peter Zaugg (SUI)).
Lithuania: Ernestas Setkus, Marius Stankevicius (46' Deividas Cesnauskis), Andrius Skerla,
Deividas Semberas, Tadas Kijanskas, Darvydas Sernas (YC8), Ramūnas Radavicius (YC77),
Mindaugas Panka, Saulius Mikoliūnas, Edgaras Cesnauskis (68' Mantas Savénas), Tomas
Danilevicius (C) (YC14) (46' Tadas Labukas). (Coach: Raimondas Zutautas (LIT)).
Goals: Liechtenstein: 1-0 Philippe Erne (7'), 2-0 Michele Polverino (36').
Referee: Artyom Kuchin (KAZ)   Attendance: 1.886

02-09-2011   S.Darius and S.Girénas Stadium, Kaunas: Lithuania – Liechtenstein   0-0
Lithuania: Zydrūnas Karcemarskas, Arūnas Klimavicius (YC68), Tadas Kijanskas, Deividas
Semberas, Marius Zaliūkas, Saulius Mikoliūnas (64' Marius Papsys), Edgaras Cesnauskis
(RC74), Mindaugas Panka (88' Mantas Savénas), Deividas Cesnauskis, Tomas Danilevicius
(C), Arvydas Novikovas (YC42) (46' Tadas Labukas). (Coach: Raimondas Zutautas (LIT)).
Liechtenstein: Peter Jehle, Martin Rechsteiner, Yves Oehri (YC50) (52' Daniel Kaufmann),
Michael Stocklasa, Martin Stocklasa, Marco Ritzberger, Franz Burgmeier, Martin Büchel (90'
Wolfgang Kieber), Sandro Wieser (YC14) (46' Nicolas Hasler), David Hasler, Mario Frick (C)
(YC86). (Coach: Hans-Peter Zaugg (SUI)).
Referee: Ken Henry Johnsen (NOR)   Attendance: 3.500

03-09-2011   Hampden Park, Glasgow: Scotland – Czech Republic   2-2 (1-0)
Scotland: Allan McGregor, Alan Hutton, Christophe Berra (YC90), Gary Caldwell, Phil
Bardsley (76' Danny Wilson (YC90)), Steven Naismith (86' Barry Robson), James Morrison,
Scott Brown (YC18), Charlie Adam (79' Don Cowie), Kenny Miller (YC49), Darren Fletcher
(C). (Coach: Craig Levein (SCO)).
Czech Republic: Jan Lastuvka, Jan Rajnoch, Michal Kadlec, Tomás Hübschman, Roman
Hubník, Petr Jirácek (YC24) (78' Tomás Pekhart (YC90+3)), Tomás Sivok, Tomás Rosicky
(C), Jaroslav Plasil (YC60), Milan Petrzela (56' Jan Rezek (YC63)), Milan Baros (YC90+1)
(90'+2' Kamil Vacek). (Coach: Michal Bílek (CZE)).
Goals: Scotland: 1-0 Kenny Miller (44'), 2-1 Darren Fletcher (82').
Czech Republic: 1-1 Jaroslav Plasil (78'), 2-2 Michal Kadlec (90' penalty).
Referee: Kevin Bernie Raymond Blom (HOL)   Attendance: 51.564

06-09-2011   Hampden Park, Glasgow: Scotland – Lithuania   1-0 (0-0)
Scotland: Allan McGregor, Christophe Berra, Steven Whittaker, Gary Caldwell, Phil Bardsley
(70' Stephen Crainey), James Morrison (79' Graham Dorrans (YC82)), Darren Fletcher (C),
Don Cowie, Barry Bannan (84' Robert Snodgrass), Steven Naismith, David Goodwillie.
(Coach: Craig Levein (SCO)).
Lithuania: Zydrūnas Karcemarskas, Deividas Semberas (C) (YC65), Arūnas Klimavicius,
Tadas Kijanskas (61' Tomas Danilevicius), Marius Zaliūkas, Darvydas Sernas, Ramūnas
Radavicius, Linas Pilibaitis, Saulius Mikoliūnas (77' Ricardas Beniusis), Deividas Cesnauskis,
Tadas Labukas (YC44) (46' Arvydas Novikovas). (Coach: Raimondas Zutautas (LIT)).
Goal: Scotland: 1-0 Steven Naismith (50').
Referee: Kristinn Jakobsson (ISL)   Attendance: 34.071
(Darren Fletcher missed a penalty in the 45th minute)

06-09-2011   Estadio Las Gaunas, Logroño: Spain – Liechtenstein   6-0 (3-0)
Spain: IKER CASILLAS Fernández (C), Álvaro ARBELOA Coca, SERGIO RAMOS García
(54' THIAGO Alcântara do Nascimento), Raúl ALBIOL Tortajada, Andrés INIESTA Luján,
Xavier "XAVI" Hernández i Creus (46' Francesc "CESC" FÀBREGAS Soler), Sergio
BUSQUETS Burgos, Xabier "XABI" ALONSO Olano, Álvaro NEGREDO Sánchez (61'
Fernando Javier LLORENTE Torres), DAVID VILLA Sánchez, Juan Manuel MATA García.
(Coach: VICENTE DEL BOSQUE González (ESP)).
Liechtenstein: Peter Jehle, Michael Stocklasa, Martin Stocklasa, Marco Ritzberger, Martin
Rechsteiner, Franz Burgmeier (YC78), Martin Büchel (81' Wolfgang Kieber), Sandro Wieser
(71' Nicolas Hasler (YC89)), David Hasler, Mario Frick (C), Thomas Beck (88' Rony
Hanselmann). (Coach: Hans-Peter Zaugg (SUI)).
Goals: Spain: 1-0 Álvaro NEGREDO Sánchez (33'), 2-0 Álvaro NEGREDO Sánchez (37'),
3-0 Xavier "XAVI" Hernández i Creus (44'), 4-0 SERGIO RAMOS García (52'), 5-0 DAVID
VILLA Sánchez (59'), 6-0 DAVID VILLA Sánchez (79').
Referee: Harald Lechner (AUT)   Attendance: 15.660

07-10-2011   Generali Arena, Prague: Czech Republic – Spain   0-2 (0-2)
Czech Republic: Petr Cech, Theodor Gebre Selassie, Tomás Hübschman (RC69), Roman
Hubník, Daniel Kolár (77' Kamil Vacek), Tomás Sivok, Tomás Rosicky (C), Daniel Pudil,
Petr Jirácek, Milan Baros (62' Tomás Pekhart), Michal Kadlec. (Coach: Michal Bílek (CZE)).
Spain: IKER CASILLAS Fernández (C), Álvaro ARBELOA Coca, SERGIO RAMOS García
(46' Carles PUYOL Saforcada), Raúl ALBIOL Tortajada, Gerard PIQUÉ i Bernabéu, Xavier
"XAVI" Hernández i Creus, Xabier "XABI" ALONSO Olano (71' Javier "JAVI" MARTÍNEZ
Aginaga), DAVID Jiménez SILVA, Sergio BUSQUETS Burgos, Juan Manuel MATA García,
FERNANDO José TORRES Sanz (61' DAVID VILLA Sánchez). (Coach: VICENTE DEL
BOSQUE González (ESP)).
Goals: Spain: 0-1 Juan Manuel MATA García (7'), 0-2 Xabier "XABI" ALONSO Olano (23').
Referee: Paolo Tagliavento (ITA)   Attendance: 17.873

08-10-2011   Rheinpark Stadion, Vaduz: Liechtenstein – Scotland   0-1 (0-1)
Liechtenstein: Peter Jehle, Martin Stocklasa (YC64), Marco Ritzberger, Martin Rechsteiner,
Daniel Kaufmann, Martin Büchel (71' Wolfgang Kieber), Michele Polverino (YC43), Nicolas
Hasler, Rony Hanselmann (75' Lucas Eberle), Mario Frick (C), Thomas Beck (YC85). (Coach:
Hans-Peter Zaugg (SUI)).
Scotland: Allan McGregor, Alan Hutton, Christophe Berra, Phil Bardsley, Gary Caldwell,
Barry Bannan (73' James Forrest), Charlie Adam (76' Don Cowie), Steven Naismith, James
Morrison, Darren Fletcher (C), Craig Mackail-Smith (YC33). (Coach: Craig Levein (SCO)).
Goal: Scotland: 0-1 Craig Mackail-Smith (32').
Referee: Tom Harald Hagen (NOR)   Attendance; 5.636

11-10-2011   Estadio Jose1 Rico Pérez, Alicante: Spain – Scotland 3-1 (2-0)
Spain: VÍCTOR VALDÉS Arribas, Jordi ALBA Ramos, SERGIO RAMOS García (YC37),
Carles PUYOL Saforcada (46' Álvaro ARBELOA Coca), Gerard PIQUÉ i Bernabéu, Xavier
"XAVI" Hernández i Creus (C) (62' Fernando Javier LLORENTE Torres), DAVID Jiménez
SILVA (55' THIAGO Alcântara do Nascimento), Santiago "SANTI" CAZORLA González,
Sergio BUSQUETS Burgos, PEDRO Eliezer Rodríguez Ledesma, DAVID VILLA Sánchez.
(Coach: VICENTE DEL BOSQUE González (ESP)).
Scotland: Allan McGregor, Alan Hutton, Christophe Berra, Gary Caldwell, Phil Bardsley,
Steven Naismith, James Morrison (YC80), Darren Fletcher (C) (YC70) (85' Don Cowie),
Barry Bannan (63' David Goodwillie (YC74)), Charlie Adam (63' James Forrest), Craig
Mackail-Smith. (Coach: Craig Levein (SCO)).
Goals: Spain: 1-0 DAVID Jiménez SILVA (6'), 2-0 DAVID Jiménez SILVA (44'), 3-0
DAVID VILLA Sánchez (54').
Scotland: 3-1 David Goodwillie (66' penalty).
Referee: Stefan Johannesson (SWE)   Attendance: 27.559

11-10-2011   S.Darius and S.Girénas Stadium, Kaunas:
              Lithuania – Czech Republic 1-4 (0-3)
Lithuania: Zydrūnas Karcemarskas, Marius Stankevicius, Andrius Skerla (C) (YC1), Marius
Zaliūkas, Darvydas Sernas, Ramūnas Radavicius (YC84), Linas Pilibaitis (74' Ricardas
Beniusis), Saulius Mikoliūnas, Kestutis Ivaskevicius (46' Arvydas Novikovas), Gediminas
Vicius, Robertas Poskus (57' Mindaugas Panka (YC79)). (Coach: Raimondas Zutautas (LIT)).
Czech Republic: Petr Cech (C), Michal Kadlec, Roman Hubník (RC67), Theodor Gebre
Selassie, Jaroslav Plasil, Petr Jirácek, Daniel Kolár, Tomás Sivok, Václav Pilar (70' Daniel
Pudil), Milan Baros (59' Tomás Pekhart), Jan Rezek (82' Zdenek Pospech). (Coach: Michal
Bílek (CZE)).
Goals: Lithuania: 1-3 Darvydas Sernas (68' penalty).
Czech Republic: 0-1 Michal Kadlec (2' penalty), 0-2 Jan Rezek (16'), 0-3 Jan Rezek (45'), 1-4
Michal Kadlec (85' penalty).
Referee: David Fernández Borbalán (ESP)   Attendance: 2.000

QUALIFICATION PLAY-OFFS

11-11-2011   Bilino Polje, Zenica: Bosnia and Herzegovina – Portugal 0-0
Bosnia and Herzegovina: Asmir Begovic, Sanel Jahic (YC42), Emir Spahic (C), Adnan
Zahirovic, Elvir Rahimic, Sejad Salihovic (YC18) (68' Vedad Ibisevic), Miralem Pjanic,
Zvjezdan Misimovic (86' Senijad Ibricic), Haris Medunjanin (67' Darko Maletic), Senad Lulic,
Edin Dzeko. (Coach: Safet Susic (BOS)).
Portugal: RUI Pedro dos Santos PATRÍCIO, BRUNO Eduardo Regufe ALVES, Képler
Laveran Lima Ferreira "PEPE", JOÃO Pedro da Silva PEREIRA, RAÚL José Trindade
MEIRELES (81' RÚBEN MICAEL Freitas da Ressureição), MIGUEL Luis Pinto VELOSO,
JOÃO Filipe Iria Santos MOUTINHO, FÁBIO Alexandre da Silva COENTRÃO, HÉLDER
Manuel Marques POSTIGA (YC42) (65' HUGO Miguel Pereira de ALMEIDA), CRISTIANO
RONALDO dos Santos Aveiro (C), Luís Carlos Almeida da Cunha "NANI". (Coach: PAULO
Jorge Gomes BENTO (POR)).
Referee: Howard Melton Webb (ENG)   Attendance: 12.352

11-11-2011   Türk Telekom Arena, Istanbul: Turkey – Croatia   0-3 (0-2)
Turkey: Volkan Demirel, Remzi Giray Kaçar, Sabri Sarioglu (YC71), Egemen Korkmaz, Gökhan Gönül (46' Gökhan Töre), Hakan Balta (YC64), Hamit Altintop, Arda Turan (YC87), Selçuk Inan (69' Mehmet Topal), Emre Belözoglu (C) (YC66), Burak Yilmaz (81' Umut Bulut). (Coach: Guus Hiddink (HOL)).
Croatia: Stipe Pletikosa, Domagoj Vida, Josip Simunic, Gordon Schildenfeld, Vedran Corluka (YC35), Tomislav Dujmovic (YC41), Darijo Srna (C), Ivan Rakitic (83' Danijel Pranjic), Luka Modric, Ivica Olic (YC69) (85' Nikica Jelavic), Mario Mandzukic (90' Eduardo Alves da Silva). (Coach: Slaven Bilic (CRO)).
Goals: Croatia: 0-1 Ivica Olic (2'), 0-2 Mario Mandzukic (32'), 0-3 Vedran Corluka (51').
Referee: Dr.Felix Brych (GER)   Attendance: 42.863

11-11-2011   Generali Arena, Prague: Czech Republic – Montenegro   2-0 (0-0)
Czech Republic: Petr Cech, Michal Kadlec, Theodor Gebre Selassie, Tomás Sivok, Jaroslav Plasil, Petr Jirácek, Tomás Rosicky (C), Daniel Pudil, Václav Pilar (YC45+2) (90' Daniel Kolár), Tomás Pekhart (90'+3' David Lafata), Jan Rezek (YC64) (81' Zdenek Pospech). (Coach: Michal Bílek (CZE)).
Montenegro: Mladen Bozovic, Milan Jovanovic (YC68), Stefan Savic, Savo Pavicevic (YC15), Miodrag Dzudovic (YC35), Nikola Drincic, Simon Vukcevic (88' Andrija Delibasic), Milorad Pekovic (YC78) (80' Elsad Zverotic), Stevan Jovetic, Dejan Damjanovic (61' Vladimir Bozovic), Mirko Vucinic (C). (Coach: Branko Brnovic (MNE)).
Goals: Czech Republic: 1-0 Václav Pilar (63'), 2-0 Tomás Sivok (90'+2').
Referee: Martin Atkinson (ENG)   Attendance: 14.560

11-11-2011   A.Le Cow Arena, Tallinn: Estonia – Republic of Ireland   0-4 (0-1)
Estonia: Sergei Pareiko (YC88), Andrei Stepanov (YC17,YC35), Raio Piiroja (C) (YC70,YC76), Dmitri Kruglov, Enar Jääger, Ragnar Klavan, Martin Vunk (61' Joel Lindpere), Aleksandr Dmitrijev, Konstantin Vassiljev, Tarmo Kink (67' Ats Purje), Jarmo Ahjupera (YC41) (55' Vladimir Voskoboinikov). (Coach: Tarmo Rüütli (EST)).
Republic of Ireland: Shay Given, Stephen Ward, Sean St Ledger, Stephen Kelly, Richard Dunne, Glenn Whelan (78' Keith Fahey), Damien Duff (73' Stephen Hunt), Keith Andrews, Jonathan (Jon) Walters (83' Simon Cox), Aiden McGeady, Robbie Keane (C). (Coach: Giovanni Luciano Giuseppe Trapattoni (ITA)).
Goals: Republic of Ireland: 0-1 Keith Andrews (13'), 0-2 Jonathan (Jon) Walters (67'), 0-3 Robbie Keane (71'), 0-4 Robbie Keane (88' penalty).
Referee: Viktor Kassai (HUN)   Attendance: 9.692

15-11-2011   Maksimir Stadium, Zagreb: Croatia – Turkey   0-0
Croatia: Stipe Pletikosa, Domagoj Vida (YC18), Josip Simunic, Gordon Schildenfeld, Ognjen Vukojevic (88' Eduardo Alves da Silva), Darijo Srna (C), Ivan Rakitic, Danijel Pranjic, Luka Modric, Mario Mandzukic (YC45+2) (77' Nikica Jelavic), Ivica Olic (62' Ivan Perisic). (Coach: Slaven Bilic (CRO)).
Turkey: Sinan Bolat, Ömer Toprak, Ismail Köybasi, Egemen Korkmaz (YC45+2), Selçuk Inan (YC81), Hamit Altintop (C) (YC59), Serkan Balci (YC22), Selçuk Sahin, Colin Kazim-Richards, Caner Erkin (YC6) (36' Gökhan Töre), Umut Bulut (71' Halil Altintop). (Coach: Guus Hiddink (HOL)).
Referee: Pedro Proença Oliveira Alves Garcia (POR)   Attendance: 26.371

265

15-11-2011   Podgorica City Stadium, Podgorica: Montenegro – Czech Republic   0-1 (0-0)
Montenegro: Mladen Bozovic, Elsad Zverotic, Stefan Savic (YC72), Savo Pavicevic (YC45+2), Miodrag Dzudovic, Nikola Drincic (YC66), Vladimir Bozovic (79' Radomir Djalovic), Mirko Vucinic (C) (YC63), Stevan Jovetic, Dejan Damjanovic (YC42) (76' Simon Vukcevic), Fatos Beciraj (57' Andrija Delibasic). (Coach: Branko Brnovic (MNE)).
Czech Republic: Petr Cech (C), Michal Kadlec, Roman Hubník, Theodor Gebre Selassie, Tomás Sivok (YC66), Tomás Rosicky (C), Jaroslav Plasil, Petr Jirácek, Jan Rezek (60' Zdenek Pospech), Václav Pilar (69' Daniel Kolár), Tomás Pekhart (84' Milan Baros (YC54)). (Coach: Michal Bílek (CZE)).
Goal: Czech Republic: 0-1 Petr Jirácek (81').
Referee: Nicola Rizzoli (ITA)   Attendance: 10.100

15-11-2011   Aviva Stadium, Dublin: Republic of Ireland – Estonia   1-1 (1-0)
Republic of Ireland: Shay Given, Stephen Ward, Sean St Ledger, John O'Shea, Richard Dunne, Glenn Whelan, Stephen Hunt (59' Aiden McGeady), Damien Duff (79' Keith Fahey), Keith Andrews, Robbie Keane (C) (67' Simon Cox), Kevin Doyle. (Coach: Giovanni Luciano Giuseppe Trapattoni (ITA)).
Estonia: Pavel Pondak, Taavi Rähn (YC10), Dmitri Kruglov (18' Sander Puri), Enar Jääger, Ragnar Klavan, Martin Vunk (YC66), Joel Lindpere (54' Tarmo Kink), Konstantin Vassiljev (C), Taijo Teniste, Vladimir Voskoboinikov (73' Ats Purje), Kaimar Saag. (Coach: Tarmo Rüütli (EST)).
Goals: Republic of Ireland: 1-0 Stephen Ward (32').
Estonia: 1-1 Konstantin Vassiljev (57').
Referee: Björn Kuipers (HOL)   Attendance: 51.151

15-11-2011   Estádio da Luz, Lisbon: Portugal – Bosnia and Herzegovina   6-2 (2-1)
Portugal: RUI Pedro dos Santos PATRÍCIO, BRUNO Eduardo Regufe ALVES, Képler Laveran Lima Ferreira "PEPE", JOÃO Pedro da Silva PEREIRA, RAÚL José Trindade MEIRELES (63' RÚBEN MICAEL Freitas da Ressureição (YC77)), MIGUEL Luis Pinto VELOSO, JOÃO Filipe Iria Santos MOUTINHO, FÁBIO Alexandre da Silva COENTRÃO (YC40), HÉLDER Manuel Marques POSTIGA (YC36) (84' CARLOS Jorge Neto MARTINS), CRISTIANO RONALDO dos Santos Aveiro (C), Luís Carlos Almeida da Cunha "NANI" (83' RICARDO Andrade QUARESMA Bernardo). (Coach: PAULO Jorge Gomes BENTO (POR)).
Bosnia and Herzegovina: Asmir Begovic, Sanel Jahic, Sasa Papac (YC79), Emir Spahic (C) (YC22), Adnan Zahirovic, Elvir Rahimic (YC43) (57' Darko Maletic), Miralem Pjanic (64' Muhamed Besic), Zvjezdan Misimovic, Haris Medunjanin (YC51), Senad Lulic (YC53,YC54), Edin Dzeko (YC68). (Coach: Safet Susic (BOS)).
Goals: Portugal: 1-0 CRISTIANO RONALDO dos Santos Aveiro (8'), 2-0 Luís Carlos Almeida da Cunha "NANI" (24'), 3-1 CRISTIANO RONALDO dos Santos Aveiro (53'), 4-2 HÉLDER Manuel Marques POSTIGA (72'), 5-2 MIGUEL Luis Pinto VELOSO (80'), 6-2 HÉLDER Manuel Marques POSTIGA (82').
Bosnia and Herzegovina: 2-1 Zvjezdan Misimovic (41' penalty), 3-2 Emir Spahic (65').
Referee: Wolfgang Stark (GER)   Attendance: 47.728

266

FINAL TOURNAMENT IN POLAND-UKRAINE

Poland and Ukraine automatically qualified for the Final Tournament as hosts.

GROUP STAGE

GROUP A

08-06-2012   National Stadium, Warsaw: Poland – Greece   1-1 (1-0)
Poland: Wojciech Szczesny (RC68), Lukasz Piszczek, Marcin Wasilewski, Damien Perquis, Sebastian Boenisch, Rafal Murawski, Eugen Polanski, Jakub Blaszczykowski (C), Ludovic Obraniak, Maciej Rybus (70' Przemyslaw Tyton *goalkeeper*), Robert Lewandowski. (Coach: Franciszek Smuda (POL)).
Greece: Konstantinos (Kostas) Chalkias, Vasilios Torosidis, Sokratis Papastathopoulos (YC35,YC44), Avraam Papadopoulos (37' Kyriakos Papadopoulos), José Lloyd Holebas (YC45+2), Ioannis (Giannis) Maniatis, Konstantinos (Kostas) Katsouranis, Giorgios Karagounis (C) (YC54), Sotiris Ninis (46' Dimitrios Salpingidis), Theofanis (Fanis) Gekas (68' Konstantinos (Kostas) Fortounis), Georgios Samaras. (Coach: FERNANDO Manuel Fernandes da Costa SANTOS (POR)).
Goals: Poland: 1-0 Robert Lewandowski (17').
Greece: 1-1 Dimitrios Salpingidis (51').
Referee: Carlos Velasco Carballo (ESP)   Attendance: 56.070
(*José Lloyd Holebas* also known as *Iosif Cholevas*)

08-06-2012   Municipal Stadium, Wroclaw: Russia – Czech Republic   4-1 (2-0)
Russia: Vyacheslav Malafeev, Aleksandr Anyukov, Aleksei Berezutski, Sergei Ignashevich, Yuri Zhirkov, Roman Shirokov, Igor Denisov, Konstantin Zyryanov, Alan Dzagoev (84' Aleksandr Kokorin), Andrey Arshavin (C), Aleksandr Kerzhakov (73' Roman Pavlyuchenko). (Coach: Dick Nicolaas Advocaat (HOL)).
Czech Republic: Petr Cech (C), Theodor Gebre Selassie, Roman Hubník, Tomás Sivok, Michal Kadlec, Jaroslav Plasil, Petr Jirácek (76' Milan Petrzela), Václav Pilar, Tomás Rosicky (C), Jan Rezek (46' Tomás Hübschman), Milan Baros (85' David Lafata). (Coach: Michal Bílek (CZE)).
Goals: Russia: 1-0 Alan Dzagoev (15'), 2-0 Roman Shirokov (24'), 3-1 Alan Dzagoev (79'), 4-1 Roman Pavlyuchenko (82').
Czech Republic: 2-1 Václav Pilar (52').
Referee: Howard Melton Webb (ENG)   Attendance: 40.803

12-06-2012   Municipal Stadium, Wroclaw: Greece – Czech Republic   1-2 (0-2)
Greece: Konstantinos (Kostas) Chalkias (23' Michalis Sifakis), Vasilios Torosidis (YC34),
Kyriakos Papadopoulos (YC56), Konstantinos (Kostas) Katsouranis, José Lloyd Holebas,
Georgios Fotakis (46' Theofanis (Fanis) Gekas), Ioannis (Giannis) Maniatis, Giorgios
Karagounis (C), Dimitrios Salpingidis (YC57), Georgios Samaras, Konstantinos (Kostas)
Fortounis (71' Konstantinos (Kostas) Mitroglou). (Coach: FERNANDO Manuel Fernandes da
Costa SANTOS (POR)).
Czech Republic: Petr Cech (C), Theodor Gebre Selassie, Tomás Sivok, Michal Kadlec, David
Limbersky, Tomás Hübschman, Jaroslav Plasil, Petr Jirácek (YC36), Tomás Rosicky (C)
(YC27) (46' Daniel Kolár (YC65), 90' Frantisek Rajtoral), Václav Pilar, Milan Baros (64'
Tomás Pekhart). (Coach: Michal Bílek (CZE)).
Goals: Greece: 1-2 Theofanis (Fanis) Gekas (53').
Czech Republic: 0-1 Petr Jirácek (3'), 0-2 Václav Pilar (6').
Referee: Stéphane Lannoy (FRA)   Attendance: 41.105

12-06-2012   National Stadium, Warsaw: Poland – Russia   1-1 (0-1)
Poland: Przemyslaw Tyton, Lukasz Piszczek, Marcin Wasilewski, Damien Perquis, Sebastian
Boenisch, Dariusz Dudka (73' Adrian Mierzejewski), Eugen Polanski (YC79) (85' Adam
Matuszczyk), Jakub Blaszczykowski (C), Rafal Murawski, Ludovic Obraniak (90'+3' Pawel
Brozek), Robert Lewandowski (YC60). (Coach: Franciszek Smuda (POL)).
Russia: Vyacheslav Malafeev, Aleksandr Anyukov, Aleksei Berezutski, Sergei Ignashevich,
Yuri Zhirkov, Roman Shirokov, Igor Denisov (YC60), Konstantin Zyryanov, Alan Dzagoev
(YC75) (79' Marat Izmailov), Andrey Arshavin (C), Aleksandr Kerzhakov (70' Roman
Pavlyuchenko). (Coach: Dick Nicolaas Advocaat (HOL)).
Goals: Poland: 1-1 Jakub Blaszczykowski (57').
Russia: 0-1 Alan Dzagoev (37').
Referee: Wolfgang Stark (GER)   Attendance: 55.920

16-06-2012   Municipal Stadium, Wroclaw: Czech Republic – Poland   1-0 (0-0)
Czech Republic: Petr Cech (C), Theodor Gebre Selassie, Tomás Sivok, Michal Kadlec, David
Limbersky (YC12), Tomás Hübschman, Jaroslav Plasil (YC87), Petr Jirácek (84' Frantisek
Rajtoral), Daniel Kolár, Václav Pilar (88' Jan Rezek), Milan Baros (90'+1' Tomás Pekhart
(YC90+4)). (Coach: Michal Bílek (CZE)).
Poland: Przemyslaw Tyton, Lukasz Piszczek, Marcin Wasilewski (YC61), Damien Perquis
(YC90), Sebastian Boenisch, Dariusz Dudka, Eugen Polanski (YC48) (56' Kamil Grosicki),
Jakub Blaszczykowski (C) (YC87), Rafal Murawski (YC22) (73' Adrian Mierzejewski),
Ludovic Obraniak (73' Pawel Brozek), Robert Lewandowski. (Coach: Franciszek Smuda
(POL)).
Goal: Czech Republic: 1-0 Petr Jirácek (72').
Referee: Craig Alexander Thomson (SCO)   Attendance: 41.480

268

16-06-2012   National Stadium, Warsaw: Greece – Russia   1-0 (1-0)
Greece: Michalis Sifakis, Vasilios Torosidis, Sokratis Papastathopoulos, Kyriakos Papadopoulos, Georgios Tzavelas, Konstantinos (Kostas) Katsouranis, Ioannis (Giannis) Maniatis, Dimitrios Salpingidis (83' Sotiris Ninis), Giorgios Karagounis (C) (YC61) (67' Grigoris Makos), Georgios Samaras, Theofanis (Fanis) Gekas (64' José Lloyd Holebas (YC90+4)). (Coach: FERNANDO Manuel Fernandes da Costa SANTOS (POR)).
Russia: Vyacheslav Malafeev, Aleksandr Anyukov (YC61) (81' Marat Izmailov), Aleksei Berezutski, Sergei Ignashevich, Yuri Zhirkov (YC69), Roman Shirokov, Igor Denisov, Denis Glushakov (72' Pavel Pogrebnyak (YC90+3)), Alan Dzagoev (YC70), Aleksandr Kerzhakov (46' Roman Pavlyuchenko), Andrey Arshavin (C). (Coach: Dick Nicolaas Advocaat (HOL)).
Goal: Greece: 1-0 Giorgios Karagounis (45'+2').
Referee: Jonas Eriksson (SWE)   Attendance: 55.614

STANDINGS

Pos	Team	Pld	W	D	L	GF	GA	GD	Pts
1	Czech Republic	3	2	0	1	4	5	-1	6
2	Greece	3	1	1	1	3	3	0	4
3	Russia	3	1	1	1	5	3	+2	4
4	Poland	3	0	2	1	2	3	-1	2

Czech Republic and Greece qualified for the Quarter-finals.

Greece finished second ahead of Russia based on their head-to-head record (1-0).

GROUP B

09-06-2012   Metalist Stadium, Kharkiv: Netherlands – Denmark   0-1 (0-1)
Netherlands: Maarten Stekelenburg, Gregory van der Wiel (85' Dirk Kuyt), John Heitinga, Ron Vlaar, Jetro Willems, Nigel de Jong (71' Rafael van der Vaart), Mark van Bommel (C) (YC67), Arjen Robben, Wesley Sneijder, Ibrahim Afellay (71' Klaas-Jan Huntelaar), Robin van Persie. (Coach: Lambertus (Bert) van Marwijk (HOL)).
Denmark: Stephan Andersen, Lars Jacobsen, Simon Kjær, Daniel Agger (C), Simon Poulsen (YC78), William Kvist (YC81), Niki Zimling, Dennis Rommedahl (84' Tobias Mikkelsen), Christian Eriksen (74' Lasse Schøne), Michael Krohn-Dehli, Nicklas Bendtner. (Coach: Morten Per Olsen (DEN)).
Goal: Denmark: 0-1 Michael Krohn-Dehli (24').
Referee: Damir Skomina (SLO)   Attendance: 35.923

09-06-2012   Arena Lviv, Lviv: Germany – Portugal   1-0 (0-0)
Germany: Manuel Neuer, Jérôme Boateng (YC69), Mats Hummels, Holger Badstuber (YC43),
Philipp Lahm (C), Sami Khedira, Bastian Schweinsteiger, Thomas Müller (90'+4' Lars
Bender), Mesut Özil (87' Toni Kroos), Lukas Podolski, Mario Gómez García (80' Miroslav
Klose). (Coach: Joachim Löw (GER)).
Portugal: RUI Pedro dos Santos PATRÍCIO, JOÃO Pedro da Silva PEREIRA, BRUNO
Eduardo Regufe ALVES, Képler Laveran Lima Ferreira "PEPE", FÁBIO Alexandre da Silva
COENTRÃO (YC60), RAÚL José Trindade MEIRELES (80' Silvestre Manuel Gonçalves
VARELA), MIGUEL Luis Pinto VELOSO, JOÃO Filipe Iria Santos MOUTINHO, Luís
Carlos Almeida da Cunha "NANI", HÉLDER Manuel Marques POSTIGA (YC13) (70'
NÉLSON Miguel Castro OLIVEIRA), CRISTIANO RONALDO dos Santos Aveiro (C).
(Coach: PAULO Jorge Gomes BENTO (POR)).
Goal: Germany: 1-0 Mario Gómez García (72').
Referee: Stéphane Lannoy (FRA)   Attendance: 32.990

13-06-2012   Arena Lviv, Lviv: Denmark – Portugal   2-3 (1-2)
Denmark: Stephan Andersen, Lars Jacobsen (YC81), Simon Kjær, Daniel Agger (C), Simon
Poulsen, William Kvist, Niki Zimling (16' Jakob Poulsen (YC56)), Dennis Rommedahl (60'
Tobias Mikkelsen), Christian Eriksen, Michael Krohn-Dehli (90'+2' Lasse Schøne), Nicklas
Bendtner. (Coach: Morten Per Olsen (DEN)).
Portugal: RUI Pedro dos Santos PATRÍCIO, JOÃO Pedro da Silva PEREIRA, BRUNO
Eduardo Regufe ALVES, Képler Laveran Lima Ferreira "PEPE", FÁBIO Alexandre da Silva
COENTRÃO, RAÚL José Trindade MEIRELES (YC29) (84' Silvestre Manuel Gonçalves
VARELA), MIGUEL Luis Pinto VELOSO, JOÃO Filipe Iria Santos MOUTINHO, Luís
Carlos Almeida da Cunha "NANI" (89' ROLANDO Jorge Pires da Fonseca), HÉLDER
Manuel Marques POSTIGA (64' NÉLSON Miguel Castro OLIVEIRA), CRISTIANO
RONALDO dos Santos Aveiro (C) (YC90+2). (Coach: PAULO Jorge Gomes BENTO (POR)).
Goals: Denmark: 1-2 Nicklas Bendtner (41'), 2-2 Nicklas Bendtner (80').
Portugal: 0-1 Képler Laveran Lima Ferreira "PEPE" (24'), 0-2 HÉLDER Manuel Marques
POSTIGA (36'), 2-3 Silvestre Manuel Gonçalves VARELA (87').
Referee: Craig Alexander Thomson (SCO)   Attendance: 31.840

13-06-2012   Metalist Stadium, Kharkiv: Netherlands – Germany   1-2 (0-2)
Netherlands: Maarten Stekelenburg, Gregory van der Wiel, John Heitinga, Joris Mathijsen,
Jetro Willems (YC90), Nigel de Jong (YC80), Mark van Bommel (C) (46' Rafael van der
Vaart), Arjen Robben (83' Dirk Kuyt), Wesley Sneijder, Ibrahim Afellay (46' Klaas-Jan
Huntelaar), Robin van Persie. (Coach: Lambertus (Bert) van Marwijk (HOL)).
Germany: Manuel Neuer, Jérôme Boateng (YC87), Mats Hummels, Holger Badstuber, Philipp
Lahm (C), Sami Khedira, Bastian Schweinsteiger, Thomas Müller (90'+2' Lars Bender),
Mesut Özil (81' Toni Kroos), Lukas Podolski, Mario Gómez García (72' Miroslav Klose).
(Coach: Joachim Löw (GER)).
Goals: Netherlands: 1-2 Robin van Persie (73').
Germany: 0-1 Mario Gómez García (24'), 0-2 Mario Gómez García (38').
Referee: Jonas Eriksson (SWE)   Attendance: 37.750

17-06-2012   Metalist Stadium, Kharkiv: Portugal – Netherlands   2-1 (0-1)
Portugal: RUI Pedro dos Santos PATRÍCIO, JOÃO Pedro da Silva PEREIRA (YC90+2),
BRUNO Eduardo Regufe ALVES, Képler Laveran Lima Ferreira "PEPE", FÁBIO Alexandre
da Silva COENTRÃO, RAÚL José Trindade MEIRELES (72' CUSTÓDIO Miguel Dias de
Castro), MIGUEL Luis Pinto VELOSO, JOÃO Filipe Iria Santos MOUTINHO, Luís Carlos
Almeida da Cunha "NANI" (87' ROLANDO Jorge Pires da Fonseca), HÉLDER Manuel
Marques POSTIGA (64' NÉLSON Miguel Castro OLIVEIRA), CRISTIANO RONALDO dos
Santos Aveiro (C). (Coach: PAULO Jorge Gomes BENTO (POR)).
Netherlands: Maarten Stekelenburg, Gregory van der Wiel, Ron Vlaar, Joris Mathijsen, Jetro
Willems (YC51) (67' Ibrahim Afellay), Nigel de Jong, Rafael van der Vaart (C), Arjen
Robben, Robin van Persie (YC69), Wesley Sneijder, Klaas-Jan Huntelaar. (Coach: Lambertus
(Bert) van Marwijk (HOL)).
Goals: Portugal: 1-1 CRISTIANO RONALDO dos Santos Aveiro (28'), 2-1 CRISTIANO
RONALDO dos Santos Aveiro (74').
Netherlands: 0-1 Rafael van der Vaart (11').
Referee: Nicola Rizzoli (ITA)   Attendance: 37.445

17-06-2012   Arena Lviv, Lviv: Denmark – Germany   1-2 (1-1)
Denmark: Stephan Andersen, Lars Jacobsen, Simon Kjær, Daniel Agger (C), Simon Poulsen,
William Kvist, Jakob Poulsen (82' Tobias Mikkelsen), Niki Zimling (78' Christian Poulsen),
Christian Eriksen, Michael Krohn-Dehli, Nicklas Bendtner. (Coach: Morten Per Olsen (DEN)).
Germany: Manuel Neuer, Lars Bender, Mats Hummels, Holger Badstuber, Philipp Lahm (C),
Sami Khedira, Bastian Schweinsteiger, Thomas Müller (84' Toni Kroos), Mesut Özil, Lukas
Podolski (64' André Schürrle), Mario Gómez García (74' Miroslav Klose). (Coach: Joachim
Löw (GER)).
Goals: Denmark: 1-1 Michael Krohn-Dehli (24').
Germany: 0-1 Lukas Podolski (19'), 1-2 Lars Bender (80').
Referee: Carlos Velasco Carballo (ESP)   Attendance: 32.990

STANDINGS

Pos	Team	Pld	W	D	L	GF	GA	GD	Pts
1	Germany	3	3	0	0	5	2	+3	9
2	Portugal	3	2	0	1	5	4	+1	6
3	Denmark	3	1	0	2	4	5	-1	3
4	Netherlands	3	0	0	3	2	5	-3	0

Germany and Portugal qualified for the Quarter-finals.

GROUP   C

10-06-2012   PGE Arena, Gdansk: Spain – Italy   1-1 (0-0)
Spain: IKER CASILLAS Fernández (C), Álvaro ARBELOA Coca (YC84), Gerard PIQUÉ i Bernabéu, SERGIO RAMOS García, Jordi ALBA Ramos (YC66), Xavier "XAVI" Hernández i Creus, Sergio BUSQUETS Burgos, Xabier "XABI" ALONSO Olano, DAVID Jiménez SILVA (64' Jesús NAVAS González), Francesc "CESC" FÀBREGAS Soler (74' FERNANDO José TORRES Sanz (YC84)), Andrés INIESTA Luján. (Coach: VICENTE DEL BOSQUE González (ESP)).
Italy: Gianluigi Buffon (C), Giorgio Chiellini (YC79), Daniele De Rossi, Leonardo Bonucci (YC66), Emanuele Giaccherini, Claudio Marchisio, Andrea Pirlo, Thiago Motta (90' Antonio Nocerino), Christian Maggio (YC89), Antonio Cassano (65' Sebastian Giovinco), Mario Balotelli (YC37) (56' Antonio Di Natale). (Coach: Cesare Claudio Prandelli (ITA)).
Goals: Spain: 1-1 Francesc "CESC" FÀBREGAS Soler (64').
Italy: 0-1 Antonio Di Natale (61').
Referee: Viktor Kassai (HUN)   Attendance: 38.869

10-06-2012   Municipal Stadium, Poznan: Republic of Ireland – Croatia   1-3 (1-2)
Republic of Ireland: Shay Given, John O'Shea, Sean St Ledger, Richard Dunne, Stephen Ward, Glenn Whelan, Keith Andrews (YC45+1), Aiden McGeady (54' Simon Cox), Damien Duff, Kevin Doyle (53' Jonathan (Jon) Walters), Robbie Keane (C) (75' Shane Long). (Coach: Giovanni Luciano Giuseppe Trapattoni (ITA)).
Croatia: Stipe Pletikosa, Darijo Srna (C), Vedran Corluka, Gordon Schildenfeld, Ivan Strinic, Ognjen Vukojevic, Ivan Rakitic (90'+2' Tomislav Dujmovic), Luka Modric (YC53), Ivan Perisic (89' Eduardo Alves da Silva), Mario Mandzukic, Nikica Jelavic (72' Niko Kranjcar (YC84)). (Coach: Slaven Bilic (CRO)).
Goals: Republic of Ireland: 1-1 Sean St Ledger (19').
Croatia: 0-1 Mario Mandzukic (3'), 1-2 Nikica Jelavic (43'), 1-3 Mario Mandzukic (49').
Referee: Björn Kuipers (HOL)   Attendance: 39.550

14-06-2012   Municipal Stadium, Poznan: Italy – Croatia   1-1 (1-0)
Italy: Gianluigi Buffon (C), Leonardo Bonucci, Daniele De Rossi, Giorgio Chiellini, Andrea Pirlo, Claudio Marchisio, Thiago Motta (YC56) (62' Riccardo Montolivo (YC80)), Christian Maggio, Emanuele Giaccherini, Mario Balotelli (69' Antonio Di Natale), Antonio Cassano (83' Sebastian Giovinco). (Coach: Cesare Claudio Prandelli (ITA)).
Croatia: Stipe Pletikosa, Darijo Srna (C), Vedran Corluka, Gordon Schildenfeld (YC86), Ivan Strinic, Ognjen Vukojevic, Luka Modric, Ivan Rakitic, Ivan Perisic (68' Danijel Pranjic), Nikica Jelavic (83' Eduardo Alves da Silva), Mario Mandzukic (90'+4' Niko Kranjcar). (Coach: Slaven Bilic (CRO)).
Goals: Italy: 1-0 Andrea Pirlo (39').
Croatia: 1-1 Mario Mandzukic (72').
Referee: Howard Melton Webb (ENG)   Attendance: 37.096

14-06-2012   PGE Arena, Gdansk: Spain – Republic of Ireland 4-0 (1-0)
Spain: IKER CASILLAS Fernández (C), Álvaro ARBELOA Coca, Gerard PIQUÉ i Bernabéu, SERGIO RAMOS García, Jordi ALBA Ramos, Xavier "XAVI" Hernández i Creus, Sergio BUSQUETS Burgos, Xabier "XABI" ALONSO Olano (YC54) (65' Javier "JAVI" MARTÍNEZ Aginaga (YC76)), DAVID Jiménez SILVA, FERNANDO José TORRES Sanz (74' Francesc "CESC" FÀBREGAS Soler), Andrés INIESTA Luján (80' Santiago "SANTI" CAZORLA González). (Coach: VICENTE DEL BOSQUE González (ESP)).
Republic of Ireland: Shay Given, John O'Shea, Sean St Ledger (YC84), Richard Dunne, Stephen Ward, Damien Duff (76' James McClean), Keith Andrews, Glenn Whelan (YC45+1) (80' Paul Green), Aiden McGeady, Simon Cox (46' Jonathan (Jon) Walters), Robbie Keane (C) (YC36). (Coach: Giovanni Luciano Giuseppe Trapattoni (ITA)).
Goals: Spain: 1-0 FERNANDO José TORRES Sanz (4'), 2-0 DAVID Jiménez SILVA (49'), 3-0 FERNANDO José TORRES Sanz (70'), 4-0 Francesc "CESC" FÀBREGAS Soler (83').
Referee: Pedro Proença Oliveira Alves Garcia (POR)   Attendance: 39.150

18-06-2012   PGE Arena, Gdansk: Croatia – Spain 0-1 (0-0)
Croatia: Stipe Pletikosa, Domagoj Vida (66' Nikica Jelavic (YC90+1)), Vedran Corluka (YC27), Gordon Schildenfeld, Ivan Strinic (YC53), Ognjen Vukojevic (81' Eduardo Alves da Silva), Ivan Rakitic (YC90+3), Darijo Srna (C) (YC44), Luka Modric, Danijel Pranjic (66' Ivan Perisic), Mario Mandzukic (YC90). (Coach: Slaven Bilic (CRO)).
Spain: IKER CASILLAS Fernández (C), Álvaro ARBELOA Coca, Gerard PIQUÉ i Bernabéu, SERGIO RAMOS García, Jordi ALBA Ramos, Xavier "XAVI" Hernández i Creus (89' Álvaro NEGREDO Sánchez), Sergio BUSQUETS Burgos, Xabier "XABI" ALONSO Olano, DAVID Jiménez SILVA (73' Francesc "CESC" FÀBREGAS Soler), FERNANDO José TORRES Sanz (61' Jesús NAVAS González), Andrés INIESTA Luján. (Coach: VICENTE DEL BOSQUE González (ESP)).
Goal: Spain: 0-1 Jesús NAVAS González (88').
Referee: Wolfgang Stark (GER)   Attendance: 39.076

18-06-2012   Municipal Stadium, Poznan: Italy – Republic of Ireland 2-0 (1-0)
Italy: Gianluigi Buffon (C) (YC73), Ignazio Abate, Andrea Barzagli, Giorgio Chiellini (57' Leonardo Bonucci), Federico Balzaretti (YC28), Andrea Pirlo, Claudio Marchisio, Thiago Motta, Daniele De Rossi (YC71), Antonio Di Natale (74' Mario Balotelli), Antonio Cassano (63' Alessandro Diamanti). (Coach: Cesare Claudio Prandelli (ITA)).
Republic of Ireland: Shay Given, John O'Shea (YC39), Richard Dunne, Sean St Ledger (YC84), Stephen Ward, Aiden McGeady (65' Shane Long), Glenn Whelan, Keith Andrews (YC37,YC89), Damien Duff (C), Robbie Keane (86' Simon Cox), Kevin Doyle (76' Jonathan (Jon) Walters). (Coach: Giovanni Luciano Giuseppe Trapattoni (ITA)).
Goals: Italy: 1-0 Antonio Cassano (35'), 2-0 Mario Balotelli (90').
Referee: Cüneyt Çakir (TUR)   Attendance: 38.794

STANDINGS

Pos	Team	Pld	W	D	L	GF	GA	GD	Pts
1	*Spain*	3	2	1	0	6	1	+5	7
2	*Italy*	3	1	2	0	4	2	+2	5
3	Croatia	3	1	1	1	4	3	+1	4
4	Republic of Ireland	3	0	0	3	1	9	-8	0

Spain and Italy qualified for the Quarter-finals.

273

GROUP   D

11-06-2012   Donbass Arena, Donetsk: France – England   1-1 (1-1)
France: Hugo Lloris (C), Mathieu Debuchy, Adil Rami, Philippe Mexès, Patrice Evra, Alou Diarra, Yohan Cabaye (84' Hatem Ben Arfa), Florent Malouda (85' Marvin Martin), Samir Nasri, Franck Ribéry, Karim Benzema. (Coach: Laurent Robert Blanc (FRA)).
England: Joe Hart, Glen Johnson, John Terry, Joleon Lescott, Ashley Cole, James Milner, Steven Gerrard (C), Scott Parker (78' Jordan Henderson), Alex Oxlade-Chamberlain (YC34) (77' Jermain Defoe), Ashley Young (YC71), Danny Welbeck (90'+1' Theo Walcott). (Coach: Roy Hodgson (ENG)).
Goals: France: 1-1 Samir Nasri (39').
England: 0-1 Joleon Lescott (30').
Referee: Nicola Rizzoli (ITA)   Attendance: 47.400

11-06-2012   Olympic Stadium, Kiev: Ukraine – Sweden   2-1 (0-0)
Ukraine: Andriy Pyatov, Oleh Gusev, Taras Mykhalyk, Yevhen Khacheridi, Yevhen Selin, Andriy Yarmolenko, Anatoliy Tymoshchuk, Yevhen Konoplyanka (90'+3' Marko Devic), Serhiy Nazarenko, Andriy Voronin (85' Ruslan Rotan), Andriy Shevchenko (C) (81' Artem Milevskiy). (Coach: Oleh Vladimirovich Blokhin (UKR)).
Sweden: Andreas Isaksson, Mikael Lustig, Olof Mellberg, Andreas Granqvist, Martin Olsson, Rasmus Elm (YC83), Kim Källström (YC11), Sebastian Larsson (68' Christian Wilhelmsson), Zlatan Ibrahimovic (C), Ola Toivonen (62' Anders Svensson), Markus Rosenberg (71' Johan Elmander). (Coach: Erik Hamrén (SWE)).
Goals: Ukraine: 1-1 Andriy Shevchenko (55'), 2-1 Andriy Shevchenko (62').
Swedene: 0-1 Zlatan Ibrahimovic (52').
Referee: Cüneyt Çakir (TUR)   Attendance: 64.290

15-06-2012   Donbass Arena, Donetsk: Ukraine – France   0-2 (0-0)
Ukraine: Andriy Pyatov, Oleh Gusev, Taras Mykhalyk, Yevhen Khacheridi, Yevhen Selin (YC55), Anatoliy Tymoshchuk (YC87), Andriy Voronin (46' Marko Devic), Andriy Yarmolenko (68' Oleksandr Aliyev), Serhiy Nazarenko (60' Artem Milevskiy), Yevhen Konoplyanka, Andriy Shevchenko (C). (Coach: Oleh Vladimirovich Blokhin (UKR)).
France: Hugo Lloris (C), Mathieu Debuchy (YC79), Adil Rami, Philippe Mexès (YC81), Gaël Clichy, Alou Diarra, Samir Nasri, Yohan Cabaye (68' Yann M'Vila), Jérémy Ménez (YC40) (73' Marvin Martin), Franck Ribéry, Karim Benzema (76' Olivier Giroud). (Coach: Laurent Robert Blanc (FRA)).
Goals: France: 0-1 Jérémy Ménez (53'), 0-2 Yohan Cabaye (56').
Referee: Björn Kuipers (HOL)   Attendance: 48.000

15-06-2012   Olympic Stadium, Kiev: Sweden – England   2-3 (0-1)
Sweden: Andreas Isaksson, Andreas Granqvist (66' Mikael Lustig), Olof Mellberg (YC63),
Jonas Olsson (YC72), Martin Olsson, Sebastian Larsson, Anders Svensson (YC90+1), Kim
Källström, Rasmus Elm (81' Christian Wilhelmsson), Zlatan Ibrahimovic (C), Johan Elmander
(79' Markus Rosenberg). (Coach: Erik Hamrén (SWE)).
England: Joe Hart, Glen Johnson, John Terry, Joleon Lescott, Ashley Cole, James Milner
(YC58) (61' Theo Walcott), Steven Gerrard (C), Scott Parker, Ashley Young, Danny Welbeck
(90' Alex Oxlade-Chamberlain), Andy Carroll. (Coach: Roy Hodgson (ENG)).
Goals: Sweden: 1-1 Glen Johnson (49' own goal), 2-1 Olof Mellberg (59').
England: 0-1 Andy Carroll (23'), 2-2 Theo Walcott (64'), 2-3 Danny Welbeck (78').
Referee: Damir Skomina (SLO)   Attendance: 64.640

19-06-2012   Donbass Arena, Donetsk: England – Ukraine   1-0 (0-0)
England: Joe Hart, Glen Johnson, John Terry, Joleon Lescott, Ashley Cole (YC78), James
Milner (70' Theo Walcott), Steven Gerrard (C) (YC73), Scott Parker, Ashley Young, Wayne
Rooney (87' Alex Oxlade-Chamberlain), Danny Welbeck (82' Andy Carroll). (Coach: Roy
Hodgson (ENG)).
Ukraine: Andriy Pyatov, Oleh Gusev, Yevhen Khacheridi, Yaroslav Rakitskiy (YC74),
Yevhen Selin, Anatoliy Tymoshchuk (C) (YC63), Andriy Yarmolenko, Yevhen Konoplyanka,
Denys Harmash (78' Serhiy Nazarenko), Artem Milevskiy (77' Bohdan Butko), Marko Devic
(70' Andriy Shevchenko (YC86)). (Coach: Oleh Vladimirovich Blokhin (UKR)).
Goal: England: 1-0 Wayne Rooney (48').
Referee: Viktor Kassai (HUN)   Attendance: 48.700

19-06-2012   Olympic Stadium, Kiev: Sweden – France   2-0 (0-0)
Sweden: Andreas Isaksson, Andreas Granqvist, Olof Mellberg, Jonas Olsson, Martin Olsson,
Anders Svensson (YC70) (79' Samuel Holmén (YC81)), Kim Källström, Sebastian Larsson,
Zlatan Ibrahimovic (C), Emir Bajrami (46' Christian Wilhelmsson), Ola Toivonen (78' Pontus
Wernbloom). (Coach: Erik Hamrén (SWE)).
France: Hugo Lloris (C), Mathieu Debuchy, Adil Rami, Philippe Mexès (YC68), Gaël Clichy,
Alou Diarra, Samir Nasri (77' Jérémy Ménez), Yann M'Vila (83' Olivier Giroud), Hatem Ben
Arfa (59' Florent Malouda), Franck Ribéry, Karim Benzema. (Coach: Laurent Robert Blanc
(FRA)).
Goals: Sweden: 1-0 Zlatan Ibrahimovic (54'), 2-0 Sebastian Larsson (90'+1').
Referee: Pedro Proença Oliveira Alves Garcia (POR)   Attendance: 63.010

STANDINGS

Pos	Team	Pld	W	D	L	GF	GA	GD	Pts
1	England	3	2	1	0	5	3	+2	7
2	France	3	1	1	1	3	3	0	4
3	Ukraine	3	1	0	2	2	4	-2	3
4	Sweden	3	1	0	2	5	5	0	3

England and France qualified for the Quarter-finals.

QUARTER-FINALS

21-06-2012   National Stadium, Warsaw: Czech Republic – Portugal 0-1 (0-0)
Czech Republic: Petr Cech (C), Theodor Gebre Selassie, Tomás Sivok, Michal Kadlec, David
Limbersky (YC90), Tomás Hübschman (86' Tomás Pekhart), Jaroslav Plasil, Petr Jirácek,
Vladimír Darida (61' Jan Rezek), Václav Pilar, Milan Baros. (Coach: Michal Bílek (CZE)).
Portugal: RUI Pedro dos Santos PATRÍCIO, JOÃO Pedro da Silva PEREIRA, Képler Laveran
Lima Ferreira "PEPE", BRUNO Eduardo Regufe ALVES, FÁBIO Alexandre da Silva
COENTRÃO, RAÚL José Trindade MEIRELES (88' ROLANDO Jorge Pires da Fonseca),
MIGUEL Luis Pinto VELOSO (YC27), JOÃO Filipe Iria Santos MOUTINHO, Luís Carlos
Almeida da Cunha "NANI" (YC26) (84' CUSTÓDIO Miguel Dias de Castro), HÉLDER
Manuel Marques POSTIGA (40' HUGO Miguel Pereira de ALMEIDA), CRISTIANO
RONALDO dos Santos Aveiro (C). (Coach: PAULO Jorge Gomes BENTO (POR)).
Goal: Portugal: 0-1 CRISTIANO RONALDO dos Santos Aveiro (79').
Referee: Howard Melton Webb (ENG)   Attendance: 55.590

22-06-2012   PGE Arena, Gdansk: Germany – Greece 4-2 (1-0)
Germany: Manuel Neuer, Jérôme Boateng, Mats Hummels, Holger Badstuber, Philipp Lahm
(C), Sami Khedira, Bastian Schweinsteiger, Marco Reus (80' Mario Götze), Mesut Özil, André
Schürrle (67' Thomas Müller), Miroslav Klose (80' Mario Gómez García). (Coach: Joachim
Löw (GER)).
Greece: Michalis Sifakis, Vasilios Torosidis, Sokratis Papastathopoulos (YC75), Kyriakos
Papadopoulos, Georgios Tzavelas (46' Theofanis (Fanis) Gekas), Grigoris Makos (72'
Nikolaos (Nikos) Lyberopoulos), Ioannis (Giannis) Maniatis, Sotiris Ninis (46' Georgios
Fotakis), Konstantinos (Kostas) Katsouranis (C), Georgios Samaras (YC14), Dimitrios
Salpingidis. (Coach: FERNANDO Manuel Fernandes da Costa SANTOS (POR)).
Goals: Germany: 1-0 Philipp Lahm (39'), 2-1 Sami Khedira (61'), 3-1 Miroslav Klose (68'),
4-1 Marco Reus (74').
Greece: 1-1 Georgios Samaras (55'), 4-2 Dimitrios Salpingidis (89' penalty).
Referee: Damir Skomina (SLO)   Attendance: 38.751

23-06-2012   Donbass Arena, Donetsk: Spain – France 2-0 (1-0)
Spain: IKER CASILLAS Fernández (C), Álvaro ARBELOA Coca, Gerard PIQUÉ i Bernabéu,
SERGIO RAMOS García (YC31), Jordi ALBA Ramos, Xavier "XAVI" Hernández i Creus,
Sergio BUSQUETS Burgos, Xabier "XABI" ALONSO Olano, DAVID Jiménez SILVA (65'
PEDRO Eliezer Rodríguez Ledesma), Francesc "CESC" FÀBREGAS Soler (67' FERNANDO
José TORRES Sanz), Andrés INIESTA Luján (84' Santiago "SANTI" CAZORLA González).
(Coach: VICENTE DEL BOSQUE González (ESP)).
France: Hugo Lloris (C), Anthony Réveillère, Adil Rami, Laurent Koscielny, Gaël Clichy,
Yann M'Vila (79' Olivier Giroud), Yohan Cabaye (YC42), Florent Malouda (65' Samir Nasri),
Mathieu Debuchy (64' Jérémy Ménez (YC76)), Franck Ribéry, Karim Benzema. (Coach:
Laurent Robert Blanc (FRA)).
Goals: Spain: 1-0 Xabier "XABI" ALONSO Olano (19'), 2-0 Xabier "XABI" ALONSO Olano
(90'+1' penalty).
Referee: Nicola Rizzoli (ITA)   Attendance: 47.000

24-06-2012   Olympic Stadium, Kiev: England – Italy   0-0 (AET)
England: Joe Hart, Glen Johnson, John Terry, Joleon Lescott, Ashley Cole, Steven Gerrard (C), Scott Parker (94' Jordan Henderson), James Milner (61' Theo Walcott), Ashley Young, Wayne Rooney, Danny Welbeck (60' Andy Carroll). (Coach: Roy Hodgson (ENG)).
Italy: Gianluigi Buffon (C), Ignazio Abate (90'+1' Christian Maggio (YC94)), Andrea Barzagli (YC82), Leonardo Bonucci, Federico Balzaretti, Andrea Pirlo, Claudio Marchisio, Riccardo Montolivo, Daniele De Rossi (80' Antonio Nocerino), Mario Balotelli, Antonio Cassano (78' Alessandro Diamanti). (Coach: Cesare Claudio Prandelli (ITA)).
Referee: Pedro Proença Oliveira Alves Garcia (POR)   Attendance: 64.340
Penalties: 1 Mario Balotelli   1 Steven Gerrard
              * Riccardo Montolivo   2 Wayne Rooney
              2 Andrea Pirlo   * Ashley Young
              3 Antonio Nocerino   * Ashley Cole
              4 Alessandro Diamanti

SEMI-FINALS

27-06-2012   Donbass Arena, Donetsk: Portugal – Spain   0-0 (AET)
Portugal: RUI Pedro dos Santos PATRÍCIO, JOÃO Pedro da Silva PEREIRA (YC64), Képler Laveran Lima Ferreira "PEPE" (YC61), BRUNO Eduardo Regufe ALVES (YC86), FÁBIO Alexandre da Silva COENTRÃO (YC45), RAÚL José Trindade MEIRELES (113' Silvestre Manuel Gonçalves VARELA), MIGUEL Luis Pinto VELOSO (YC90+3) (106' CUSTÓDIO Miguel Dias de Castro), JOÃO Filipe Iria Santos MOUTINHO, Luís Carlos Almeida da Cunha "NANI", HUGO Miguel Pereira de ALMEIDA (81' NÉLSON Miguel Castro OLIVEIRA), CRISTIANO RONALDO dos Santos Aveiro (C). (Coach: PAULO Jorge Gomes BENTO (POR)).
Spain: IKER CASILLAS Fernández (C), Álvaro ARBELOA Coca (YC84), Gerard PIQUÉ i Bernabéu, SERGIO RAMOS García (YC40), Jordi ALBA Ramos, Xavier "XAVI" Hernández i Creus (87' PEDRO Eliezer Rodríguez Ledesma), Sergio BUSQUETS Burgos (YC60), Xabier "XABI" ALONSO Olano (YC113), DAVID Jiménez SILVA (60' Jesús NAVAS González), Álvaro NEGREDO Sánchez (54' Francesc "CESC" FÀBREGAS Soler), Andrés INIESTA Luján. (Coach: VICENTE DEL BOSQUE González (ESP)).
Referee: Cüneyt Çakir (TUR)   Attendance: 48.000
Penalties:
* Xabier "XABI" ALONSO Olano   * JOÃO Filipe Iria Santos MOUTINHO
1 Andrés INIESTA Luján   1 Képler Laveran Lima Ferreira "PEPE"
2 Gerard PIQUÉ i Bernabéu   2 Luís Carlos Almeida da Cunha "NANI"
3 SERGIO RAMOS García   * BRUNO Eduardo Regufe ALVES
4 Francesc "CESC" FÀBREGAS Soler

28-06-2012   National Stadium, Warsaw: Germany – Italy   1-2 (0-2)
Germany: Manuel Neuer, Jérôme Boateng (71' Thomas Müller), Mats Hummels (YC90+4), Holger Badstuber, Philipp Lahm (C), Bastian Schweinsteiger, Sami Khedira, Toni Kroos, Mesut Özil, Lukas Podolski (46' Marco Reus), Mario Gómez García (46' Miroslav Klose). (Coach: Joachim Löw (GER)).
Italy: Gianluigi Buffon (C), Federico Balzaretti, Andrea Barzagli, Leonardo Bonucci (YC61), Giorgio Chiellini, Andrea Pirlo, Claudio Marchisio, Riccardo Montolivo (64' Thiago Motta (YC89)), Daniele De Rossi (YC84), Mario Balotelli (YC37) (70' Antonio Di Natale), Antonio Cassano (58' Alessandro Diamanti). (Coach: Cesare Claudio Prandelli (ITA)).
Goals: Germany: 1-2 Mesut Özil (90'+2').
Italy: 0-1 Mario Balotelli (20'), 0-2 Mario Balotelli (36').
Referee: Stéphane Lannoy (FRA)   Attendance: 55.540

277

FINAL

01-07-2012   Olympic Stadium, Kiev: Spain – Italy 4-0 (2-0)
Spain: IKER CASILLAS Fernández (C), Álvaro ARBELOA Coca, Gerard PIQUÉ i Bernabéu
(YC25), SERGIO RAMOS García, Jordi ALBA Ramos, Xavier "XAVI" Hernández i Creus,
Sergio BUSQUETS Burgos, Xabier "XABI" ALONSO Olano, Francesc "CESC" FÀBREGAS
Soler (75' FERNANDO José TORRES Sanz), DAVID Jiménez SILVA (59' PEDRO Eliezer
Rodríguez Ledesma), Andrés INIESTA Luján (87' Juan Manuel MATA García). (Coach:
VICENTE DEL BOSQUE González (ESP)).
Italy: Gianluigi Buffon (C), Ignazio Abate, Andrea Barzagli (YC45), Leonardo Bonucci,
Giorgio Chiellini (21' Federico Balzaretti), Andrea Pirlo, Claudio Marchisio, Riccardo
Montolivo (57' Thiago Motta), Daniele De Rossi, Mario Balotelli, Antonio Cassano (46'
Antonio Di Natale). (Coach: Cesare Claudio Prandelli (ITA)).
Goals: Spain: 1-0 DAVID Jiménez SILVA (14'), 2-0 Jordi ALBA Ramos (41'), 3-0
FERNANDO José TORRES Sanz (84'), 4-0 Juan Manuel MATA García (88').
Referee: Pedro Proença Oliveira Alves Garcia (POR)   Attendance: 63.170

*** Spain were European Champions ***

GOALSCORERS TOURNAMENT 2010-2012:

Goals	Players
12	Klaas-Jan Huntelaar (HOL)
10	Miroslav Klose (GER), CRISTIANO RONALDO dos Santos Aveiro (POR)
9	Mario Gómez García (GER)
7	DAVID VILLA Sánchez (ESP), Mikael Forssell (FIN), Robin van Persie (HOL), Robbie Keane (IRL), Antonio Cassano (ITA), Alan Dzagoev (RUS), Zlatan Ibrahimovic (SWE)
6	Henrikh Mkhitaryan (ARM), Mario Mandzukic (CRO), DAVID Josué Jiménez SILVA (ESP), Konstantin Vassiljev (EST), Mesut Özil (GER), Dirk Kuyt (HOL), Gergely Rudolf (HUN), HÉLDER Manuel Marques POSTIGA (POR)
5	Gevorg Ghazaryan (ARM), Marvin Ogunjimi (BEL), Nicklas Bendtner (DEN), FERNANDO José TORRES Sanz (ESP), Luís Carlos Almeida da Cunha "NANI" (POR), Adrian Mutu (ROM), Roman Pavlyuchenko (RUS), Tim Matavz (SLO)
4	Yura Movsisyan (ARM), Marcos Piñeiro Pizzelli (ARM), Marko Arnautovic (AUT), Edin Dzeko (BOS), Zvjezdan Misimovic (BOS), Niko Kranjcar (CRO), Michal Kadlec (CZE), Michael Krohn-Dehli (DEN), Wayne Rooney (ENG), Kasper Hämäläinen (FIN), Lukas Podolski (GER), Ádám Szalai (HUN), Yossi Benayoun (ISR), Aleksandrs Cauna (LAT), Alexandr Suvorov (MOL), Xherdan Shaqiri (SUI), Sebastian Larsson (SWE), Arda Turan (TUR)
3	Hamdi Salihi (ALB), Timmy Simons (BEL), Haris Medunjanin (BOS), Eduardo Alves da Silva (CRO), Ioannis Okkas (CYP), Petr Jirácek (CZE), Václav Pilar (CZE), Dennis Rommedahl (DEN), Darren Bent (ENG), Jermain Defoe (ENG), Ashley Young (ENG), JUAN Manuel MATA García (ESP), Fernando Javier LLORENTE Torrs (ESP), Xabier "XABI" ALONSO Olano (ESP), Karim Benzema (FRA), Yoann Gourcuff (FRA),

	Florent Malouda (FRA), Thomas Müller (GER), André Schürrle (GER), Dimitris Salpingidis (GRE), Ibrahim Afellay (HOL), Wesley Sneijder (HOL), Zoltán Gera (HUN), Vladimir Koman (HUN), Mario Balotelli (ITA), Darvydas Sernas (LIT), Michael Mifsud (MLT), Ciprian Marica (ROM), Marko Pantelic (SRB), Nikola Zigic (SRB), Kim Källström (SWE), Christian Wilhelmsson (SWE), Burak Yilmaz (TUR), Gareth Bale (WAL)
2	Erjon Bogdani (ALB), Artur Sarkisov (ARM), Martin Harnik (AUT), Marc Janko (AUT), Franz Schiemer (AUT), Rauf Aliyev (AZE), Vagif Javadov (AZE), Vügar Nadirov (AZE), Daniel van Buyten (BEL), Marouane Fellaini (BEL), Jello Vossen (BEL), Axel Witsel (BEL), Sergei Kornilenko (BLS), Vedad Ibisevic (BOS), Miralem Pjanic (BOS), Ivelin Popov (BUL), Nikola Kalinic (CRO), Ivica Olic (CRO), Andreas Avraam (CYP), Jaroslav Plasil (CZE), Jan Rezek (CZE), Adam Johnson (ENG), Frank Lampard (ENG), ÁLVARO NEGREDO Sánchez (ESP), Francesc "CESC" FÀBREGAS Soler (ESP), Xavier "XAVI" Hernández i Creus (ESP), Tarmo Kink (EST), Kaimar Saag (EST), Sergei Zenjov (EST), Fródi Benjaminsen (FAR), Samir Nasri (FRA), Loïc Rémy (FRA), Jaba Kankava (GEO), David Siradze (GEO), Ioannis Fetfatzidis (GRE), Theofanis (Fanis) Gekas (GRE), Geogios Karagounis (GRE), Kyriakos Papadopoulos (GRE), Georgios Samaras (GRE), Vasilis Torosidis (GRE), Ruud van Nistelrooy (HOL), Rafael van der Vaart (HOL), Balázs Dzsudzsák (HUN), Imre Szabics (HUN), Kevin Doyle (IRL), Aiden McGeady (IRL), Sean St Ledger (IRL), Heidar Helguson (ISL), Hallgrímur Jónasson (ISL), Giampaolo Pazzini (ITA), Andrea Pirlo (ITA), Sergey Gridin (KAZ), Kaspars Grokss (LAT), Ilco Naumoski (MCD), Vance Sikov (MCD), Mirko Vucinic (MNE), Elsad Zverotic (MNE), Anatolie Doros (MOL), Steven Davis (NIR), Paddy McCourt (NIR), Mohammed Abdellaoue (NOR), John Carew (NOR), Erik Huseklepp (NOR), Daniel Miguel Alves Gomes "DANNY" (POR), HUGO Miguel Pereira de ALMEIDA (POR), RAÚL José Trindade MEIRELES (POR), Gabriel Torje (ROM), Aleksandr Kerzhakov (RUS), Pavel Pogrebnyak (RUS), Roman Shirokov (RUS), Kenny Miller (SCO), Steven Naismith (SCO), Milivoje Novakovic (SLO), Zoran Tosic (SRB), Tranquillo Barnetta (SUI), Valentin Stocker (SUI), Johan Elmander (SWE), Andreas Granqvist (SWE), Martin Olsson (SWE), Ola Toivonen (SWE), Hamir Altintop (TUR), Andriy Shevchenko (UKR), Aaron Ramsey (WAL)
1	Klorian Duro (ALB), Gjergji Muzaka (ALB), Cristian Martínez (AND), Edgar Manucharyan (ARM), Erwin Hoffer (AUT), Andreas Ivanschitz (AUT), Zlatko Junuzovic (AUT), Roland Linz (AUT), Sebastian Prödl (AUT), Ruslan Abishov (AZE), Murad Hüseynov (AZE), Rashad Farhad oglu Sadygov (AZE), Mahir Shukurov (AZE), Nacer Chadli (BEL), Eden Hazard (BEL), Vincent Kompany (BEL), Nicolas Lombaerts (BEL), Jan Vertonghen (BEL), Stanislaw Drahun (BLS), Sergei Kislyak (BLS), Sergey Krivets (BLS), Anton Putsila (BLS), Vitali Rodionov (BLS), Senijad Ibricic (BOS), Darko Maletic (BOS), Sejad Salihovic (BOS), Emir Spahic (BOS), Ivan Ivanov (BUL), Milan Badelj (CRO), Vedran Corluka (CRO), Nikica Jelavic (CRO), Dejan Lovren (CRO), Luka Modric (CRO), Mladen Petric (CRO), Darijo Srna (CRO), Ognjen Vukojevic (CRO), Efstathios (Stathis) Aloneftis (CYP), Michalis Konstantinou (CYP), Milan Baros (CZE), Roman Hubník (CZE), Václav Kadlec (CZE), Tomás Necid (CZE), Tomás Sivok (CZE), Christian Eriksen (DEN), Lars Jacobsen (DEN), Thomas Kahlenberg (DEN), Kasper Lorentzen (DEN), Morten Rasmussen (DEN), Lasse Schøne (DEN), Gary Cahill (ENG), Andy Carroll (ENG), Joleon

Lescott (ENG), Theo Walcott (ENG), Danny Welbeck (ENG), Jordi ALBA Ramos (ESP), Andrés INIESTA Luján (ESP), Jesús NAVAS González (ESP), SERGIO RAMOS García (ESP), Raio Piiroja (EST), Ats Purje (EST), Martin Vunk (EST), Jóan Símun Edmundsson (FAR), Arnbjørn Hansen (FAR), Christian Holst (FAR), Christian Mouritsen (FAR), Jari Litmanen (FIN), Roni Porokara (FIN), Joona Toivio (FIN), Mika Väyrynen (FIN), Yohan Cabaye (FRA), Jérémy Ménez (FRA), Philippe Mexès (FRA), Yann M'Vila (FRA), Anthony Réveillère (FRA), Alexander Iashvili (GEO), Levan Kobiashvili (GEO), David Targamadze (GEO), Holger Badstuber (GER), Lars Bender (GER), Mario Götze (GER), Sami Khedira (GER), Philipp Lahm (GER), Marco Reus (GER), Bastian Schweinsteiger (GER), Heiko Westermann (GER), Angelos Charisteas (GRE), Georgios Fotakis (GRE), Sotiris Ninis (GRE), Nikolaos (Nikos) Spyropoulos (GRE), John Heitinga (HOL), Luuk de Jong (HOL), Kevin Strootman (HOL), Georginio Wijnaldum (HOL), Zoltán Lipták (HUN), Vilmos Vanczák (HUN), Keith Andrews (IRL), Richard Dunne (IRL), Keith Fahey (IRL), Kevin Kilbane (IRL), Shane Long (IRL), Jonathan (Jon) Walters (IRL), Stephen Ward (IRL), Kolbeinn Sigthórsson (ISL), Gylfi Sigurdsson (ISL), Elyaniv Barda (ISR), Tal Ben Haim (I) (ISR), Tal Ben Haim (II) (ISR), Rami Gershon (ISR), Tomer Hemed (ISR), Biram Kayal (ISR), Lior Refaelov (ISR), Itay Shechter (ISR), Leonardo Bonucci (ITA), Daniele De Rossi (ITA), Antonio Di Natale (ITA), Alberto Gilardino (ITA), Claudio Marchisio (ITA), thiago Motta (ITA), Fabio Quagliarella (ITA), Giuseppe Rossi (ITA), Ulan Konysbayev (KAZ), Kairat Nurdauletov (KAZ), Sergei Ostapenko (KAZ), Vitali Yevstigneyev (KAZ), Artjoms Rudnevs (LAT), Māris Verpakovskis (LAT), Aleksejs Visnakovs (LAT), Philippe Erne (LIE), Mario Frick (LIE), Michele Polverino (LIE), Marius Stankevicius (LIT), Gilles Bettmer (LUX), Aurélien Joachim (LUX), Larsd Christian Krogh Gerson (LUX), Mario Gjurovski (MCD), Mirko Ivanovski (MCD), Nikolce Noveski (MCD), Ivan Trickovski (MCD), Jamie Pace (MLT), Radomir Djalovic (MNE), Andrija Delibasic (MNE), Stevan Jovetic (MNE), Serghei Alexeev (MOL), Gheorghe Andronic (MOL), Igor Bugaiov (MOL), Nicolae Josan (MOL), Denis Zmeu (MOL), Corry Evans (NIR), Aaron Hughes (NIR), Kyle Lafferty (NIR), Gareth McAuley (NIR), Brede Hangeland (NOR), Tom Høgli (NOR), Morten Gamst Pedersen (NOR), John Arne Riise (NOR), Jakub Blaszczykowski (POL), Robert Lewandowski (POL), ELISEU Pereira dos Santos (POR), JOÃO Filipe Iria Santos MOUTINHO (POR), MANUEL Henrique Tavares FERNANDES (POR), MIGUEL Luis Pinto VELOSO (POR), Képler Laveran Lima Ferreira "PEPE" (POR), Silvestre Manuel Gonçalves VARELA (POR), Srdjan Luchin (ROM), Bogdan Stancu (ROM), Ianis Zicu (ROM), Diniyar Bulyaletdinov (RUS), Denis Glushakov (RUS), Sergei Ignashevich (RUS), Igor Semshov (RUS), Darren Fletcher (SCO), David Goodwillie (SCO), Craig Mackail-Smith (SCO), Stephen McManus (SCO), Zlatko Dedic (SLO), Dare Vrsic (SLO), Branislav Ivanovic (SRB), Milan Jovanovic (SRB), Zdravko Kuzmanovic (SRB), Danko Lazovic (SRB), Dejan Stankovic (SRB), Eren Derdiyok (SUI), Gökhan Inler (SUI), Stephan Lichsteiner (SUI), Marco Streller (SUI), Ján Durica (SVK), Filip Holosko (SVK), Miroslav Karhan (SVK), Juraj Piroska (SVK), Filip Sebo (SVK), Miroslav Stoch (SVK), Vladimír Weiss (SVK), Emir Bajrami (SWE), Marcus Berg (SWE), Alexander Gerndt (SWE), Tobias Hysén (SWE), Mikael Lustig (SWE), Olof Mellberg (SWE), Hakan Balta (TUR), Gökhan Gönül (TUR), Nihat Kahveci (TUR), Semih Sentürk

	(TUR), Steve Morison (WAL)
1 own goal	Valeri Aleksanyan (ARM) for Republic of Ireland, Rashad Farhad oglu Sadygov (AZE) for Germany, Glen Johnson (ENG) for Sweden, Gerard PIQUÉ i Bernabéu (ESP) for Scotland, Raio Piiroja (EST) for Northern Ireland, Andrei Sidorenkov (EST) for Slovenia, Rógvi Baldvinsson (FAR) for Slovenia, Éric Abidal (FRA) for Belarus, Arne Friedrich (GER) for Austria, Nikolaos (Nikos) Spyropoulos (GRE) for Israel, Tadas Kijanskas (LIT) for Spain, Igor Armas (MOL) for Finland, Gareth McAuley (NIR) for Italy, RICARDO Alberto Silveira de CARVALHO (POR) for Denmark, Simone Bacchiocchi (SMR) for Moldova, Aldo Simoncini (SMR) for Sweden, Davide Simoncini (SMR) for Sweden, Aleksandar Lukovic (SRB) for Estonia

UEFA Euro 2016

QUALIFYING ROUND

GROUP A

09-09-2014	Astana	Kazakhstan- Latvia	0-0
09-09-2014	Prague	Czech Republic – Netherlands	2-1 (1-0)
09-09-2014	Reykjavik	Iceland – Turkey	3-0 (1-0)
10-10-2014	Riga	Latvia – Iceland	0-3 (0-0)
10-10-2014	Amsterdam	Netherlands – Kazakhstan	3-1 (0-1)
10-10-2014	Istanbul	Turkey – Czech Republic	1-2 (1-1)
13-10-2014	Astana	Kazakhstan – Czech Republic	2-4 (0-2)
13-10-2014	Reykjavik	Iceland – Netherlands	2-0 (2-0)
13-10-2014	Riga	Latvia – Turkey	1-1 (0-0)
16-11-2014	Amsterdam	Netherlands – Latvia	6-0 (3-0)
16-11-2014	Plzen	Czech Republic – Iceland	2-1 (1-1)
16-11-2014	Istanbul	Turkey – Kazakhstan	3-1 (2-0)
28-03-2015	Astana	Kazakhstan – Iceland	0-3 (0-2)
28-03-2015	Prague	Czech Republic – Latvia	1-1 (0-1)
28-03-2015	Amsterdam	Netherlands – Turkey	1-1 (0-1)
12-06-2015	Almaty	Kazakhstan – Turkey	0-1 (0-0)
12-06-2015	Reykjavik	Iceland – Czech Republic	2-1 (0-0)
12-06-2015	Riga	Latvia – Netherlands	0-2 (0-0)
03-09-2015	Plzen	Czech Republic – Kazakhstan	2-1 (0-1)
03-09-2015	Amsterdam	Netherlands – Iceland	0-1 (0-0)
03-09-2015	Konya	Turkey – Latvia	1-1 (0-0)
06-09-2015	Riga	Latvia – Czech Republic	1-2 (0-2)
06-09-2015	Konya	Turkey – Netherlands	3-0 (2-0)
06-09-2015	Reykjavik	Iceland – Kazakhstan	0-0
10-10-2015	Reykjavik	Iceland- Latvia	2-2 (2-0)
10-10-2015	Astanan	Kazakhstan – Netherlands	1-2 (0-1)
10-10-2015	Prague	Czech Republic – Turkey	0-2 (0-0)
13-10-2015	Riga	Latvia – Kazakhstan	0-1 (0-0)
13-10-2015	Amsterdam	Netherlands – Czech Republic	2-3 (0-2)
13-10-2015	Konya	Turkey – Iceland	1-0 (0-0)

FINAL STANDING

Pos	Team	Pld	W	D	L	GF	GA	GD	Pts
1	Czech Republic	10	7	1	2	19	14	+5	22
2	Iceland	10	6	2	2	17	6	+11	20
3	Turkey	10	5	3	2	14	9	+5	18
4	Netherlands	10	4	1	5	17	14	+3	13
5	Kazakhstan	10	1	2	7	7	18	-11	5
6	Latvia	10	0	5	5	6	19	-13	5

Czech Republic, Iceland and Turkey qualified for the Final Tournament in France.

09-09-2014   Astana Arena, Astana: Kazakhstan – Latvia   0-0
Kazakhstan: Andrey Sidelnikov, Samat Smakov, Renat Abdulin, Ilya Vorotnikov, Yuriy
Logvinenko, Tanat Nuserbayev (C) (73' Bauyrzhan Dzholchiyev), Dmitry Miroshnichenko,
Anatoliy Bogdanov, Dmitriy Shomko, Bauyrzhan Islamkhan (82' Azat Nurgaliyev), Sergey
Khizhnichenko. (Coach: Yuri Krasnozhan (RUS)).
Latvia: Aleksandrs Kolinko, Kaspars Gorkss (C) (YC29), Vladislavs Gabovs, Nauris Bulvitis,
Vitalijs Maksimenko, Artis Lazdins (27' Aleksandrs Fertovs), Arturs Zjuzins (YC90+3),
Andrejs Kovalovs, Artjoms Rudnevs (79' Eduards Visnakovs), Valerijs Sabala (YC23), Olegs
Laizans. (Coach: Marians Pahars (LAT)).
Referee: Ivan Kruzliak (SVK)   Attendance: 10.200

09-09-2014   Generali Arena, Prague: Czech Republic – Netherlands   2-1 (1-0)
Czech Republic: Petr Cech, Václav Procházka (YC7), David Limbersky (YC90+2), Michal
Kadlec, Lukás Vácha (81' Daniel Kolár), Tomás Rosicky (C), Ladislav Krejcí (66' Václav
Pilar), Pavel Kaderábek, Borek Dockal, Vladimír Darida, David Lafata (72' Matej Vydra).
(Coach: Pavel Vrba (CZE)).
Netherlands: Jasper Cillessen, Joël Veltman (39' Luciano Narsingh), Bruno Martins Indi
(YC70), Daryl Janmaat, Stefan de Vrij, Daley Blind, Georginio Wijnaldum, Wesley Sneijder,
Nigel de Jong, Robin van Persie (C), Memphis Depay. (Coach: Guus Hiddink (HOL)).
Goals: Czech Republic: 1-0 Borek Dockal (22'), 2-1 Václav Pilar (90'+1').
Netherlands: 1-1 Stefan de Vrij (55').
Referee: Gianluca Rocchi (ITA)   Attendance: 17.946

09-09-2014   Laugardalsvöllur, Reykjavik: Iceland – Turkey   3-0 (1-0)
Iceland: Hannes Halldórsson, Ragnar Sigurdsson, Ari Skúlason (YC36), Gylfi Sigurdsson
(YC50) (89' Ólafur Skúlason), Emil Hallfredsson, Aron Gunnarsson (C), Theodór (Teddy)
Elmar Bjarnason, Birkir Bjarnason (70' Rúrik Gíslason), Kári Árnason, Kolbeinn Sigthórsson,
Jón Dadi Bödvarsson (90'+2' Vidar Kjartansson). (Coach: Lars Lagerbäck (SWE)).
Turkey: Onur Kivrak, Ömer Toprak (YC55,YC59), Ersan Gülüm, Gökhan Gönül (YC44),
Caner Erkin, Arda Turan (YC60), Mehmet Topal (77' Hakan Çalhanoglu), Selçuk Inan (65'
Ozan Tufan), Emre Belözoglu (C), Olcan Adin (65' Mustafa Pektemek), Burak Yilmaz.
(Coach: Fatih Terim (TUR)).
Goals: Iceland: 1-0 Jón Dadi Bödvarsson (19'), 2-0 Gylfi Sigurdssson (76'), 3-0 Kolbeinn
Sigthórsson (77').
Referee: Ivan Bebek (CRO)   Attendance: 8.811

10-10-2014   Skonto Stadium, Riga: Latvia – Iceland   0-3 (0-0)
Latvia: Aleksandrs Kolinko, Kaspars Gorkss (C), Vladislavs Gabovs, Kaspars Dubra, Nauris
Bulvitis (YC89), Ritvars Rugins (63' Gints Freimanis), Viktors Morozs, Andrejs Kovalovs
(81' Aleksejs Visnakovs), Aleksandrs Fertovs (YC90+8), Valerijs Sabala (81' Eduards
Visnakovs), Artjoms Rudnevs (YC43,YC55). (Coach: Marians Pahars (LAT)).
Iceland: Hannes Halldörsson, Ragnar Sigurdsson, Ari Skúlason, Gylfi Sigurdsson (80' Ólafur
Skúlason), Emil Hallfredsson (87' Rúrik Gíslason), Aron Gunnarsson (C), Theodór (Teddy)
Elmar Bjarnason, Birkir Bjarnason, Kári Árnason, Kolbeinn Sigthórsson, Jón Dadi
Bödvarsson (77' Alfred Finnbogason). (Coach: Lars Lagerbäck (SWE)).
Goals: Iceland: 0-1 Gylfi Sigurdsson (66'), 0-2 Aron Gunnarsson (77'), 0-3 Rúrik Gíslason
(90').
Referee: Robert Schörgenhofer (AUT)   Attendance: 6.354

10-10-2014   Amsterdam ArenA, Amsterdam: Netherlands – Kazakhstan   3-1 (0-1)
Netherlands: Jasper Cillessen, Gregory van der Wiel, Bruno Martins Indi (81' Leroy Fer),
Stefan de Vrij, Daley Blind, Wesley Sneijder, Nigel de Jong (56' Klaas Jan Huntelaar),
Ibrahim Afellay, Robin van Persie (C), Arjen Robben, Jeremain Lens. (Coach: Guus Hiddink
(HOL)).
Kazakhstan: Aleksandr Mokin, Ilya Vorotnikov, Gafurzhan Suyumbayev, Dmitry
Miroshnichenko, Viktor Dmitrenko (YC55) (72' Mark Gurman), Renat Abdulin (YC33),
Dmitriy Shomko (YC89), Andrey Karpovich (C) (79' Valeriy Korobkin), Anatoliy Bogdanov,
Bauyrzhan Dzholchiyev (RC64), Sergey Khizhnichenko (90' Azat Nurgaliyev). (Coach: Yuri
Krasnozhan (RUS)).
Goals: Netherlands: 1-1 Klaas Jan Huntelaar (62'), 2-1 Ibrahim Afellay (82'), 3-1 Robin van
Persie (89' penalty).
Kazakhstan: 0-1 Renat Abdulin (17').
Referee: Matej Jug (SLO)   Attendance: 47.500

10-10-2014   Sükrü Saracoglu Stadium, Istanbul: Turkey – Czech Republic   1-2 (1-1)
Turkey: Tolga Zengin, Ozan Tufan, Semih Kaya, Gökhan Gönül, Caner Erkin, Arda Turan (C),
Gökhan Töre (68' Olcan Adin), Mehmet Topal, Olcay Sahan (66' Muhammed Demir), Selçuk
Inan (79' Oguzhan Özyakup (YC85)), Umut Bulut. (Coach: Fatih Terim (TUR)).
Czech Republic: Petr Cech, Michal Kadlec, David Limbersky, Pavel Kaderábek, Borek Dockal
(90'+2' Jaroslav Plasil), Vladimír Darida, Lukás Vácha, Tomás Sivok, Tomás Rosicky (C),
Ladislav Krejcí (68' Václav Pilar), David Lafata (84' Matej Vydra). (Coach: Pavel Vrba
(CZE)).
Goals: Turkey: 1-0 Umut Bulut (8').
Czech Republic: 1-1 Tomás Sivok (15'), 1-2 BorekDockal (58'0.
Referee: Jonas Eriksson (SWE)   Attendance: 24.007

13-10-2014   Astana Arena, Astana: Kazakhstan – Czech Republic   2-4 (0-2)
Kazakhstan: Andrey Sidelnikov, Ilya Vorotnikov, Dmitry Miroshnichenko (83' Abzal
Beysebekov), Yuriy Logvinenko, Renat Abdulin, Askhat Tagybergen (YC27), Dmitriy
Shomko, Andrey Karpovich (58' Ulan Konysbayev), Bauyrzhan Islamkhan, Tanat Nuserbayev
(C) (YC53), Sergey Khizhnichenko (70' Azat Nurgaliyev). (Coach: Yuri Krasnozhan (RUS)).
Czech Republic: Petr Cech (C), David Limbersky, Michal Kadlec, Lukás Vácha, Tomás Sivok
(81' Václav Procházka), Ladislav Krejcí (69' Václav Pilar), Daniel Kolár (YC31), Pavel
Kaderábek, Borek Dockal, Vladimír Darida (YC76), David Lafata (79' Tomás Necid). (Coach:
Pavel Vrba (CZE)).
Goals: Kazakhstan: 1-3 Yuriy Logvinenko (84'), 2-4 Yuriy Logvinenko (90'+1').
Czech Republic: 0-1 Borek Dockal (13'), 0-2 David Lafata (44'), 0-3 Ladislav Krejcí (56'), 1-4
Tomás Necid (88').
Referee: Mattias Gestranius (FIN)   Attendance: 13.752

13-10-2014   Laugardalsvöllur, Reykjavik: Iceland – Netherlands   2-0 (2-0)
Iceland: Hannes Halldórsson, Ragnar Sigurdsson, Ari Skúlason (46' Birkir Már Sævarsson),
Gylfi Sigurdsson, Emil Hallfredsson, Aron Gunnarsson (C), Theodór (Teddy) Elmar
Bjarnason, Birkir Bjarnason, Kári Árnason, Kolbeinn Sigthórsson, Jón Dadi Bödvarsson (89'
Rúrik Gíslason). (Coach: Lars Lagerbäck (SWE)).
Netherlands: Jasper Cillessen, Gregory van der Wiel, Bruno Martins Indi, Stefan de Vrij, Daley
Blind, Wesley Sneijder (46' Klaas Jan Huntelaar), Nigel de Jong (YC83), Ibrahim Afellay (78'
Leroy Fer), Robin van Persie (C), Arjen Robben, Jeremain Lens (68' Quincy Promes). (Coach:
Guus Hiddink (HOL)).
Goals: Iceland: 1-0 Gylfi Sigurdsson (10' penalty), 2-0 Gylfi Sigurdsson (42').
Referee: Carlos Velasco Carballo (ESP)   Attendance: 9.760

13-10-2014   Skonto Stadium, Riga: Latvia – Turkey   1-1 (0-0)
Latvia: Aleksandrs Kolinko, Antons Kurakins, Kaspars Gorkss (C) (38' Gints Freimanis (YC52,YC90+1)), Vladislavs Gabovs, Kaspars Dubra, Arturs Zjuzins (83' Viktors Morozs), Aleksejs Visnakovs, Janis Ikaunieks (YC45), Aleksandrs Fertovs, Eduards Visnakovs (YC45+2) (80' Deniss Rakels), Valerijs Sabala. (Coach: Marians Pahars (LAT)).
Turkey: Volkan Babacan, Ozan Tufan, Semih Kaya, Gökhan Gönül, Caner Erkin, Arda Turan (C) (YC52), Gökhan Töre (YC53) (70' Hamit Altintop (YC90+2)), Mehmet Topal, Olcay Sahan (59' Adem Büyük), Oguzhan Özyakup (40' Bilal Kisa (YC65)), Umut Bulut. (Coach: Fatih Terim (TUR)).
Goals: Latvia: 1-1 Valerijs Sabala (54' penalty).
Turkey: 0-1 Bilal Kisa (47').
Referee: Bobby Madden (SCO)   Attendance: 6.442

16-11-2014   Amsterdam ArenA, Amsterdam: Netherlands – Latvia   6-0 (3-0)
Netherlands: Jasper Cillessen, Jetro Willems, Gregory van der Wiel, Stefan de Vrij (YC71), Jeffey Bruma, Daley Blind (20' Jordy Clasie), Wesley Sneijder, Ibrahim Afellay (69' Memphis Depay), Robin van Persie (C) (79' Georginio Wijnaldum), Arjen Robben, Klaas Jan Huntelaar. (Coach: Guus Hiddink (HOL)).
Latvia: Aleksandrs Kolinko, Antons Kurakins (YC26), Kaspars Gorkss (C), Vladislavs Gabovs, Kaspars Dubra, Arturs Zjuzins (YC24) (54' Aleksandrs Cauna), Aleksejs Visnakovs, Janis Ikaunieks (46' Olegs Laizans (YC57)), Aleksandrs Fertovs, Eduards Visnakovs (70' Artjoms Rudnevs), Valerijs Sabala. (Coach: Marians Pahars (LAT)).
Goals: Netherlands: 1-0 Robin van Persie (6'), 2-0 Arjen Robben (35'), 3-0 Klaas Jan Huntelaar (42'), 4-0 Jeffey Bruma (78'), 5-0 Arjen Robben (82'), 6-0 Klaas Jan Huntelaar (89').
Referee: Liran Liany (ISR)   Attendance: 47.500

16-11-2014   Doosan Arena, Plzen: Czech Republic – Iceland   2-1 (1-1)
Czech Republic: Petr Cech, Michal Kadlec, Tomás Sivok, Tomás Rosicky (C) (90'+2' Václav Procházka), Daniel Pudil, Jaroslav Plasil, Ladislav Krejcí (65' Václav Pilar), Pavel Kaderábek, Borek Dockal (YC86), Vladimír Darida, David Lafata (82' Tomás Necid). (Coach: Pavel Vrba (CZE)).
Iceland: Hannes Halldórsson, Ragnar Sigurdsson (YC12), Ari Skúlason, Gylfi Sigurdsson, Emil Hallfredsson (YC53) (62' Rúrik Gíslason (YC68)), Aron Gunnarsson (C), Theodór (Teddy) Elmar Bjarnason (62' Birkir Már Sævarsson), Birkir Bjarnason (77' Jóhann Gudmundsson), Kári Árnason, Kolbeinn Sigthórsson (YC70), Jón Dadi Bödvarsson. (Coach: Lars Lagerbäck (SWE)).
Goals: Czech Republic: 1-1 Pavel Kaderábek (45'+1'), 2-1 Jón Dadi Bödvarsson (61' own goal).
Iceland: 0-1 Ragnar Sigurdsson (9').
Referee: Wolfgang Stark (GER)   Attendance: 11.533

285

16-11-2014   Türk Telekom Arena, Istanbul: Turkey – Kazakhstan   3-1 (2-0)
Turkey: Volkan Babacan, Ozan Tufan, Semih Kaya, Serdar Aziz, Caner Erkin, Arda Turan (C)
(YC90), Volkan Sen (81' Gökhan Töre), Olcay Sahan (85' Mehmet Ekici), Selçuk Inan, Burak
Yilmaz (YC7), Umut Bulut (74' Mehmet Topal (YC87)). (Coach: Fatih Terim (TUR)).
Kazakhstan: Aleksandr Mokin, Renat Abdulin (76' Sergiy Maliy), Samat Smakov (C), Yuriy
Logvinenko, Mark Gurman, Askhat Tagybergen, Dmitriy Shomko, Ulan Konysbayev,
Bauyrzhan Islamkhan, Stanislav Lunin (73' Aleksey Shchetkin), Sergey Khizhnichenko (82'
Azat Nurgaliyev (YC90+6)). (Coach: Yuri Krasnozhan (RUS)).
Goals: Turkey: 1-0 Burak Yilmaz (26' penalty), 2-0 Burak Yilmaz (29'), 3-0 Serdar Aziz (83').
Kazakhstan: 3-1 Samat Smakov (87' penalty).
Referee: Aleksei Eskov (RUS)   Attendance: 27.549

28-03-2015   Astana Arena, Astana: Kazakhstan – Iceland   0-3 (0-2)
Kazakhstan: Andrey Sidelnikov, Ilya Vorotnikov, Gafurzhan Suyombayev, Samat Smakov (C),
Yuriy Logvinenko, Mark Gurman (67' Ermek Kuantayev (YC70)), Renat Abdulin (80'
Aleksey Shchetkin), Askhat Tagybergen, Azat Nurgaliyev (YC55) (56' Ulan Konysbayev),
Bauyrzhan Islamkhan, Daurenbek Tazhimbetov. (Coach: Yuri Krasnozhan (RUS)).
Iceland: Hannes Halldórsson, Ragnar Sigurdsson, Birkir Már Sævarsson, Ari Skúlason
(YC63), Gylfi Sigurdsson, Aron Gunnarsson (C) (72' Emil Hallfredsson), Birkir Bjarnason,
Kári Árnason, Kolbeinn Sigthórsson (70' Jón Dadi Bödvarsson), Jóhann Gudmundsson, Eidur
Gudjohnsen (83' Alfred Finnbogason). (Coach: Lars Lagerbäck (SWE)).
Goals: Iceland: 0-1 Eidur Gudjohnsen (20'), 0-2 Birkir Bjarnason (32'), 0-3 Birkir Bjarnason
(90'+1').
Referee: Anastasios (Tasos) Sidiropoulos (GRE)   Attendance: 13.182

28-03-2015   Eden Arena, Prague: Czech Republic – Latvia   1-1 (0-1)
Czech Republic: Petr Cech, Václav Procházka, David Limbersky (YC47), Michal Kadlec,
Theodor Gebre Selassie, Tomás Rosicky (C), Jaroslav Plasil (46' Václav Pilar), Ladislav
Krejcí (57' Tomás Necid), Borek Dockal (YC90+1), Vladimír Darida, David Lafata (81'
Václav Kadlec). (Coach: Pavel Vrba (CZE)).
Latvia: Andris Vanins, Vitalijs Maksimenko, Kaspars Gorkss (C) (YC29), Kaspars Dubra,
Arturs Zjuzins (87' Jurijs Zigajevs), Aleksejs Visnakovs (82' Aleksandrs Fertovs), Igors
Tarasovs, Olegs Laizans (66' Janis Ikaunieks), Gints Freimanis (YC71), Valerijs Sabala,
Deniss Rakels. (Coach: Marians Pahars (LAT)).
Goals: Czech Republic: 1-1 Václav Pilar (90').
Latvia: 0-1 Aleksejs Visnakovs (30').
Referee: Javier Estrada Fernández (ESP)   Attendance: 13.722

28-03-2015   Amsterdam ArenA, Amsterdam: Netherlands – Turkey   1-1 (0-1)
Netherlands: Jasper Cillessen, Stefan de Vrij, Gregory van der Wiel (YC68), Bruno Martins
Indi (77' Jetro Willems), Daley Blind, Nigel de Jong (63' Bas Drost), Ibrahim Afellay,
Georginio Wijnaldum (46' Luciano Narsingh), Wesley Sneijder (C), Klaas Jan Huntelaar,
Memphis Depay. (Coach: Guus Hiddink (HOL)).
Turkey: Volkan Babacan, Gökhan Gönül (C), Hakan Balta, Serdar Aziz (69' Ersan Gülüm),
Ozan Tufan, Caner Erkin, Gökhan Töre (YC42), Mehmet Topal, Volkan Sen (61' Hakan
Çalhanoglu), Selçuk Inan, Burak Yilmaz (79' Colin Kâzim-Richards). (Coach: Fatih Terim
(TUR)).
Goals: Netherlands: 1-1 Klaas Jan Huntelaar (90'+2').
Turkey: 0-1 Burak Yilmaz (37').
Referee: Felix Brych (GER)   Attendance: 49.500

12-06-2015   Central Stadium, Almaty: Kazakhstan – Turkey   0-1 (0-0)
Kazakhstan: Stas Pokatilov, Samat Smakov (C) (67' Abzal Beysebekov), Heinrich Schmidtgal
(YC77), Sergiy Maliy, Yuriy Logvinenko, Mark Gurman (78' Askhat Tagybergen), Renat
Abdulin (YC88), Dmitriy Shomko (YC90+3), Ulan Konysbayev, Bauyrzhan Islamkhan (85'
Zhambyl Kukeyev), Sergey Khizhnichenko. (Coach: Yuri Krasnozhan (RUS)).
Turkey: Volkan Babacan, Ozan Tufan (64' Umut Bulut), Semih Kaya (75' Emre Tasdemir),
Gökhan Gönül, Hakan Balta, Serdar Aziz, Arda Turan (C), Mehmet Topal (46' Volkan Sen),
Selçuk Inan, Hakan Çalhanoglu, Burak Yilmaz. (Coach: Fatih Terim (TUR)).
Goal: Turkey: 0-1 Arda Turan (83').
Referee: Michael Oliver (ENG)   Attendance: 25.125

12-06-2015   Laugardalsvöllur, Reykjavik: Iceland – Czech Republic   2-1 (0-0)
Iceland: Hannes Halldórsson, Ragnar Sigurdsson, Birkir Már Sævarsson, Ari Skúlason, Gylfi
Sigurdsson, Emil Hallfredsson (63' Jón Dadi Bödvarsson), Aron Gunnarsson (C), Birkir
Bjarnason, Kári Árnason, Kolbeinn Sigthórsson (90'+3' Rúrik Gíslason), Jóhann
Gudmundsson. (Coach: Lars Lagerbäck (SWE)).
Czech Republic: Petr Cech, Václav Procházka, David Limbersky, Lukás Vácha (79' Milan
Skoda), Tomás Sivok, Tomás Rosicky (C) (YC28), Jaroslav Plasil, Václav Pilar (67' Ladislav
Krejcí (YC72)), Pavel Kaderábek, Borek Dockal (84' Vladimír Darida), Tomás Necid. (Coach:
Pavel Vrba (CZE)).
Goals: Iceland: 1-1 Aron Gunnarsson (60'), 2-1 Kolbeinn Sigthórsson (76').
Czech Republic: 0-1 Borek Dockal (55').
Referee: William (Willie) Collum (SCO)   Attendance: 9.767

12-06-2015   Skonto Stadium, Riga: Latvia – Netherlands   0-2 (0-0)
Latvia: Andris Vanins, Vitalijs Maksimenko, Vitalijs Jagodinskis, Kaspars Gorkss (C), Arturs
Zjuzins, Aleksejs Visnakovs (75' Arturs Karasausks), Igors Tarasovs, Janis Ikaunieks, Gints
Freimanis (37' Vladislavs Gabovs), Valerijs Sabala (62' Eduards Visnakovs), Deniss Rakels
(YC13). (Coach: Marians Pahars (LAT)).
Netherlands: Jasper Cillessen, Jetro Willems (77' Daryl Janmaat), Gregory van der Wiel,
Bruno Martins Indi (YC65), Stefan de Vrij, Daley Blind, Wesley Sneijder, Robin van Persie
(C) (63' Georginio Wijnaldum), Luciano Narsingh, Klaas Jan Huntelaar, Memphis Depay (87'
Jeremain Lens). (Coach: Guus Hiddink (HOL)).
Goals: Netherlands: 0-1 Georginio Wijnaldum (67'), 0-2 Luciano Narsingh (71').
Referee: Svein Oddvar Moen (NOR)   Attendance: 8.067

03-09-2015   Doosan Arena, Plzen: Czech Republic – Kazakhstan   2-1 (0-1)
Czech Republic: Petr Cech (C), Marek Suchy, Václav Procházka, David Limbersky, David
Pavelka, Ladislav Krejcí (84' Jan Kopic), Pavel Kaderábek, Borek Dockal, Vladimír Darida
(68' Josef Sural), Jirí Skalák (46' Milan Skoda), David Lafata. (Coach: Pavel Vrba (CZE)).
Kazakhstan: Stas Pokatilov, Samat Smakov (C), Sergiy Maliy, Yuriy Logvinenko, Mark
Gurman, Dmitriy Shomko (YC42), Islambek Kuat, Ulan Konysbayev (88' Zhambyl Kukeyev),
Bauyrzhan Islamkhan (78' Gafurzhan Suyumbayev), Tanat Nuserbayev (72' Sergey
Khizhnichenko), Bauyrzhan Dzholchiyev. (Coach: Yuri Krasnozhan (RUS)).
Goals: Czech Republic: 1-1 Milan Skoda (74'), 2-1 Milan Skoda (86').
Kazakhstan: 0-1 Yuriy Logvinenko (21').
Referee: Martin Strömbergsson (SWE)   Attendance: 10.572

287

03-09-2015   Amsterdam ArenA, Amsterdam: Netherlands – Iceland   0-1 (0-0)
Netherlands: Jasper Cillessen, Gregory van der Wiel (YC50), Bruno Martins Indi (RC33),
Stefan de Vrij, Daley Blind, Georginio Wijnaldum (80' Quincy Promes), Wesley Sneijder
(YC90+3), Davy Klaassen, Arjen Robben (C) (31' Luciano Narsingh), Klaas Jan Huntelaar
(40' Jeffrey Bruma), Memphis Depay. (Coach: Danny Blind (HOL)).
Iceland: Hannes Halldórsson, Ragnar Sigurdsson, Birkir Már Sævarsson (YC80), Ari
Skúlason, Gylfi Sigurdsson, Aron Gunnarsson (C) (86' Ólafur Skúlason), Birkir Bjarnason,
Kári Árnason (YC59), Kolbeinn Sigthórsson (YC33) (64' Eidur Gudjohnsen), Jóhann
Gudmundsson, Jón Dadi Bödvarsson (78' Alfred Finnbogason). (Coach: Lars Lagerbäck
(SWE)).
Goal: Iceland: 0-1 Gylfi Sigurdsson (51' penalty).
Referee: Milorad Mazic (SRB)   Attendance: 50.275

03-09-2015   Torku Arena, Konya: Turkey – Latvia   1-1 (0-0)
Turkey: Volkan Babacan, Ozan Tufan (YC32), Hakan Balta, Serdar Aziz, Caner Erkin, Arda
Turan (C), Gökhan Töre (58' Sener Özbayrakli), Volkan Sen (56' Umut Bulut), Selçuk Inan,
Hakan Çalhanoglu, Burak Yilmaz (84' Mehmet Topal). (Coach: Fatih Terim (TUR)).
Latvia: Andris Vanins (C) (YC34), Vitalijs Maksimenko, Vitalijs Jagodinskis, Vladislavs
Gabovs, Kaspars Dubra, Aleksejs Visnakovs, Igors Tarasovs (YC9), Igors Laizans (82'
Eduards Visnakovs (YC90+1)), Aleksandrs Cauna (60' Arturs Zjuzins), Deniss Rakels, Arturs
Karasausks (85' Valerijs Sabala (YC90+1)). (Coach: Marians Pahars (LAT)).
Goals: Turkey: 1-0 Selçuk Inan (77').
Latvia: 1-1 Valerijs Sabala (90'+1').
Referee: Stefan Johannesson (SWE)   Attendance: 35.900

06-09-2015   Skonto Stadium, Riga: Latvia – Czech Republic   1-2 (0-2)
Latvia: Andris Vanins, Vitalijs Maksimenko (YC45+1), Kaspars Gorkss (C), Kaspars Dubra
(YC55), Arturs Zjuzins, Igors Tarasovs, Gints Freimanis (33' Vladislavs Gabovs), Aleksandrs
Fertovs, Deniss Rakels, Arturs Karasausks (66' Aleksandrs Cauna), Vladimir Kamess (29'
Aleksejs Visnakovs). (Coach: Marians Pahars (LAT)).
Czech Republic: Petr Cech (C), Marek Suchy, Václav Procházka, David Limbersky, David
Pavelka, Daniel Kolár (54' Ladislav Krejcí), Pavel Kaderábek, Borek Dockal (90' Theodor
Gebre Selassie), Vladimír Darida, Josef Sural (77' Ondrej Vanek), Milan Skoda. (Coach: Pavel
Vrba (CZE)).
Goals: Latvia: 1-2 Arturs Zjuzins (73').
Czech Republic: 0-1 David Limbersky (13'), 0-2 Vladimír Darida (25').
Referee: Deniz Aytekin (GER)   Attendance: 7.913

06-09-2015   Torku Arena, Konya: Turkey – Netherlands   3-0 (2-0)
Turkey: Volkan Babacan, Ozan Tufan (YC87), Sener Özbayrakli (YC69), Hakan Balta
(YC74), Serdar Aziz, Caner Erkin, Selçuk Inan, Hakan Çalhanoglu (65' Mehmet Topal),
Oguzhan Özyakup (YC75) (83' Olcay Sahan), Arda Turan (C) (YC25) (56'), Burak Yilmaz.
(Coach: Fatih Terim (TUR)).
Netherlands: Jasper Cillessen, Gregory van der Wiel (YC62), Jaïro Riedewald, Stefan de Vrij
(46' Georginio Wijnaldum), Jeffrey Bruma, Daley Blind (74' Luuk de Jong), Wesley Sneijder,
Davy Klaassen, Robin van Persie (C) (YC36), Luciano Narsingh (69' Quincy Promes),
Memphis Depay. (Coach: Danny Blind (HOL)).
Goals: Turkey: 1-0 Oguzhan Özyakup (8'), 2-0 Arda Turan (26'), 3-0 Burak Yilmaz (86').
Referee: Antonio Mateu Lahoz (ESP)   Attendance: 41.007

06-09-2015   Laugardalsvöllur, Reykjavik: Iceland – Kazakhstan   0-0
Iceland: Hannes Halldórsson, Ragnar Sigurdsson, Birkir Már Sævarsson, Ari Skúlason, Gylfi
Sigurdsson, Aron Gunnarsson (C) (YC80,YC89), Birkir Bjarnason, Kári Árnason, Kolbeinn
Sigthórsson, Jóhann Gudmundsson (YC20), Jón Dadi Bödvarsson (85' Vidar Kjartansson).
(Coach: Lars Lagerbäck (SWE)).
Kazakhstan: Stas Pokatilov, Gafurzhan Suyumbayev (YC64), Samat Smakov (C), Sergiy
Maliy, Yuriy Logvinenko (YC71), Mark Gurman, Islambek Kuat, Ulan Konysbayev,
Bauyrzhan Islamkhan, Tanat Nuserbayev (YC40) (76' Aleksey Shchetkin), Bauyrzhan
Dzholchiyev (YC30) (46' Alexander Merkel (YC74)). (Coach: Yuri Krasnozhan (RUS)).
Referee: Yevhen Aranovsky (UKR)   Attendance: 9.767

10-10-2015   Laugardalsvöllur, Reykjavik: Iceland – Latvia   2-2 (2-0)
Iceland: Hannes Halldórsson, Ragnar Sigurdsson (YC78), Birkir Már Sævarsson, Ari
Skúlason, Gylfi Sigurdsson, Emil Hallfredsson, Birkir Bjarnason, Kári Árnason (18' Sölvi
Ottesen), Kolbeinn Sigthórsson (C), Jóhann Gudmundsson, Alfred Finnbogason (YC23) (65'
Eidur Gudjohnsen). (Coach: Lars Lagerbäck (SWE)).
Latvia: Andris Vanins, Vitalijs Maksimenko (YC75), Kaspars Gorkss (C), Vladislavs Gabovs,
Kaspars Dubra, Arturs Zjuzins (85' Janis Ikaunieks), Aleksejs Visnakovs (65' Arturs
Karasausks), Igors Tarasovs (YC57) (77' Olegs Laizans), Aleksandrs Cauna, Valerijs Sabala,
Deniss Rakels. (Coach: Marians Pahars (LAT)).
Goals: Iceland: 1-0 Kolbeinn Sigthórsson (5'), 2-0 Gylfi Sigurdsson (27').
Latvia: 2-1 Aleksandrs Cauna (49'), 2-2 Valerijs Sabala (68').
Referee: Aleksei Eskov (RUS)   Attendance: 9.767

10-10-2015   Astana Arena, Astana: Kazakhstan – Netherlands   1-2 (0-1)
Kazakhstan: Stas Pokatilov, Yuriy Logvinenko (YC1), Konstantin Engel, Gafurzhan
Suyumbayev, Samat Smakov (C), Sergiy Maliy, Islambek Kuat, Ulan Konysbayev, Bauyrzhan
Islamkhan (16' Kazbek Geteriyev), Timur Dosmagambetov (81' Azat Nurgaliyev), Aleksey
Shchetkin (63' Sergey Khizhnichenko). (Coach: Yuri Krasnozhan (RUS)).
Netherlands: Tim Krul (81' Jeroen Zoet), Jeffrey Bruma (YC31), Virgil van Dijk, Kenny Tete,
Jaïro Riedewald, Daley Blind (YC5), Georginio Wijnaldum, Wesley Sneijder (C) (80' Ibrahim
Afellay), Klaas Jan Huntelaar (87' Robin van Persie), Anwar El Ghazi (YC72), Memphis
Depay. (Coach: Danny Blind (HOL)).
Goals: Kazakhstan: 1-2 Islambek Kuat (90'+6').
Netherlands: 0-1 Georginio Wijnaldum (33'), 0-2 Wesley Sneijder (50').
Referee: Clément Turpin (FRA)   Attendance: 20.716

10-10-2015   Generali Arena, Prague: Czech Republic – Turkey   0-2 (0-0)
Czech Republic: Tomás Vaclík, Marek Suchy (C), Václav Procházka, David Pavelka (YC46),
Filip Novák (YC61), Ladislav Krejcí (YC32) (54' Jirí Skalák), Pavel Kaderábek, Borek Dockal
(YC34) (78' Milan Petrzela), Vladimír Darida, David Lafata, Josef Sural (67' Milan Skoda).
(Coach: Pavel Vrba (CZE)).
Turkey: Volkan Babacan, Sener Özbayrakli (YC50), Hakan Balta, Serdar Aziz, Ozan Tufan,
Caner Erkin, Oguzhan Özyakup (87' Mehmet Topal), Selçuk Inan, Hakan Çalhanoglu, Arda
Turan (C) (86' Gökhan Töre), Cenk Tosun (64' Volkan Sen (YC83)). (Coach: Fatih Terim
(TUR)).
Goals: Turkey: 0-1 Selçuk Inan (62' penalty), 0-2 Hakan Çalhanoglu (79').
Referee: Martin Atkinson (ENG)   Attendance: 17.190

13-10-2015   Skonto Stadium, Riga: Latvia – Kazakhstan   0-1 (0-0)
Latvia: Andris Vanins, Vitalijs Maksimenko, Kaspars Gorkss (C), Vladislavs Gabovs, Kaspars
Dubra, Olegs Laizans, Aleksandrs Cauna (72' Eduards Visnakovs), Arturs Zjuzins (83' Janis
Ikaunieks), Aleksejs Visnakovs (57' Arturs Karasausks (YC73)), Deniss Rakels, Valerijs
Sabala. (Coach: Marians Pahars (LAT)).
Kazakhstan: Stas Pokatilov, Sergiy Maliy, Yuriy Logvinenko, Konstantin Engel, Gafurzhan
Suyumbayev, Samat Smakov (C), Islambek Kuat (YC84), Timur Dosmagambetov (68' Ulan
Konysbayev), Dmitriy Shomko, Tanat Nuserbayev (82' Mark Gurman), Sergey Khizhnichenko
(90' Aleksey Shchetkin). (Coach: Yuri Krasnozhan (RUS)).
Goal: Kazakhstan: 0-1 Islambek Kuat (65').
Referee: Steven McLean (SCO)   Attendance: 7.027

13-10-2015   Amsterdam ArenA, Amsterdam: Netherlands – Czech Republic   2-3 (0-2)
Netherlands: Jeroen Zoet, Virgil van Dijk (64' Bas Dost), Kenny Tete, Jaïro Riedewald (39'
Robin van Persie (YC84)), Jeffrey Bruma, Daley Blind (YC29), Georginio Wijnaldum, Wesley
Sneijder (C) (YC88), Klaas Jan Huntelaar (YC21), Anwar El Ghazi (69' Jeremain Lens),
Memphis Depay. (Coach: Danny Blind (HOL)).
Czech Republic: Petr Cech (C), Theodor Gebre Selassie (YC90+2), Marek Suchy (C) (RC43),
Michal Kadlec, Jaroslav Plasil (86' Milan Skoda), David Pavelka, Pavel Kaderábek, Vladimír
Darida, Tomás Necid (46' Václav Procházka), Josef Sural (71' Tomás Kalas), Jirí Skalák
(YC42). (Coach: Pavel Vrba (CZE)).
Goals: Netherlands: 1-3 Klaas Jan Huntelaar (70'), 2-3 Robin van Persie (83').
Czech Republic: 0-1 Pavel Kaderábek (24'), 0-2 Josef Sural (35'), 0-3 Robin van Persie (66'
own goal).
Referee: Damir Skomina (SLO)   Attendance: 48.000

13-10-2015   Torku Arena, Konya: Turkey – Iceland   1-0 (0-0)
Turkey: Volkan Babacan, Sener Özbayrakli, Hakan Balta, Serdar Aziz, Ozan Tufan, Caner
Erkin, Volkan Sen (75' Umut Bulut), Oguzhan Özyakup (62' Gökhan Töre (RC78)), Selçuk
Inan, Hakan Çalhanoglu (72' Cenk Tosun (YC86)), Arda Turan (C). (Coach: Fatih Terim
(TUR)).
Iceland: Ögmundur Kristinsson, Ragnar Sigurdsson, Birkir Már Sævarsson, Gylfi Sigurdsson,
Aron Gunnarsson (C), Birkir Bjarnason, Ari Skúlason, Kári Árnason, Jóhann Gudmundsson
(YC23), Jón Dadi Bödvarsson (82' Vidar Kjartansson), Kolbeinn Sigthórsson (88' Alfred
Finnbogason). (Coach: Lars Lagerbäck (SWE)).
Goal: Turkey: 1-0 Selçuk Inan (89').
Referee: Gianluca Rocchi (ITA)   Attendance: 39.404

GROUP   B

09-09-2014	Andorra la Vella	Andorra – Wales	1-2 (1-1)
09-09-2014	Zenica	Bosnia and Herzegovina – Cyprus	1-2 (1-1)
10-10-2014	Brussels	Belgium – Andorra	6-0 (3-0)
10-10-2014	Nicosia	Cyprus – Israel	1-2 (0-2)
10-10-2014	Cardiff	Wales – Bosnia and Herzegovina	0-0
13-10-2014	Andorra la Vella	Andorra – Israel	1-4 (1-2)
13-10-2014	Zenica	Bosnia and Herzegovina – Belgium	1-1 (1-0)
13-10-2014	Cardiff	Wales – Cyprus	2-1 (2-1)
16-11-2014	Brussels	Belgium – Wales	0-0
16-11-2014	Nicosia	Cyprus – Andorra	5-0 (3-0)

16-11-2014	Haifa	Israel – Bosnia and Herzegovina	3-0 (2-0)
28-03-2015	Haifa	Israel – Wales	0-3 (0-1)
28-03-2015	Andorra la Vella	Andorra – Bosnia and Herzegovina	0-3 (0-1)
28-03-2015	Brussels	Belgium – Cyprus	5-0 (2-0)
31-03-2015	Jerusalem	Israel – Belgium	0-1 (0-1)
12-06-2015	Andorra la Vella	Andorra – Cyprus	1-3 (1-2)
12-06-2015	Zenica	Bosnia and Herzegovina – Israel	3-1 (2-1)
12-06-2015	Cardiff	Wales – Belgium	1-0 (1-0)
03-09-2015	Brussels	Belgium – Bosnia and Herzegovina	3-1 (2-1)
03-09-2015	Nicosia	Cyprus – Wales	0-1 (0-0)
03-09-2015	Haifa	Israel – Andorra	4-0 (4-0)
06-09-2015	Cardiff	Wales – Israel	0-0
06-09-2015	Zenica	Bosnia and Herzegovina – Andorra	3-0 (3-0)
06-09-2015	Nicosia	Cyprus – Belgium	0-1 (0-0)
10-10-2015	Andorra la Vella	Andorra – Belgium	1-4 (0-2)
10-10-2015	Zenica	Bosnia and Herzegovina – Wales	2-0 (0-0)
10-10-2015	Jerusalem	Israel – Cyprus	1-2 (0-0)
13-10-2015	Brussels	Belgium – Israel	3-1 (0-0)
13-10-2015	Nicosia	Cyprus – Bosnia and Herzegovina	2-3 (2-2)
13-10-2015	Cardiff	Wales – Andorra	2-0 (0-0)

FINAL STANDING

Pos	Team	Pld	W	D	L	GF	GA	GD	Pts
1	Belgium	10	7	2	1	24	5	+19	23
2	Wales	10	6	3	1	11	4	+7	21
3	Bosnia and Herzegovina	10	5	2	3	17	12	+5	17
4	Israel	10	4	1	5	16	14	+2	13
5	Cyprus	10	4	0	6	16	17	-1	12
6	Andorra	10	0	0	10	4	36	-32	0

Belgium and Wales qualified for the Final Tournament in France.

Bosnia and Herzegovina qualified for the play-offs

09-09-2014   Estadio Nacional, Andorra la Vella: Andorra – Wales 1-2 (1-1)
Andorra: Ferran Pol Pérez, Jordi Rubio Gómez, David Maneiro Ton (YC69), Emili Josep García Miramontes, Ildefons Lima Solà (C), Jose Manuel "Josep" Díaz Ayala (86' Juli Sánchez Soto), Marc Vales González (YC90+5), Gabriel "Gabi" Riera Lancha (YC81), Carlos Eduardo "Edu" Peppe Britos (YC45) (53' Márcio Vieira de Vasconcelos (YC76)), Cristian Martínez Alejo (83' Óscar Sonejee Masand), Iván Lorenzo Roncero (YC68). (Coach: Jesús Luis Álvarez de Eulate Güergue "Koldo" (AND)).
Wales: Wayne Hennessey, Ashley Williams (C), Neil Taylor, Chris Gunter, Benjamin (Ben) Davies, James Chester, Joe Allen (YC45), Aaron Ramsey (90'+4' Emyr Huws), Andy King (76' George Williams), Simon Church (YC59) (62' Joseph (Joe) Ledley), Gareth Bale. (Coach: Chris Coleman (WAL)).
Goals: Andorra: 1-0 Ildefons Lima Solà (6' penalty).
Wales: 1-1 Gareth Bale (22'), 1-2 Gareth Bale (81').
Referee: Slavko Vincic (SLO)   Attendance: 3.150

09-09-2014   Bilino Polje, Zenica: Bosnia and Herzegovina – Cyprus   1-2 (1-1)
Bosnia and Herzegovina: Asmir Begovic, Ermin Bicakcic, Muhamed Besic, Toni Sunjic, Avdija Vrsajevic, Tino-Sven Susic (62' Haris Medunjanin), Sanjin Prcic (YC28) (61' Izet Hajrovic), Miralem Pjanic, Senad Lulic, Vedad Ibisevic, Edin Dzeko (C) (YC76). (Coach: Safet Susic (BOS)).
Cyprus: Antonis Giorgallides, Marios Antoniades, Giorgios Merkis, DOSSA Momad Omar Hassamo JÚNIOR, Georgios Efrem (YC58) (71' Nektarios Alexandrou), Dimitris Christofi, Marios Nikolaou, Constantinos Makrides (C) (83' Valentinos Sielis), Vincent Laban (YC66), Charalampos (Charis) Kyriakou, Efstathios (Stathis) Aloneftis (46' Constantinos (Costas) Charalambides). (Coach: Charalambos (Pambos) Christodoulou (CYP)).
Goals: Bosnia and Herzegovina: 1-0 Vedad Ibisevic (6').
Cyprus: 1-1 Dimitris Christofi (45'), 1-2 Dimitris Christofi (73').
Referee: Yevhen Anatoliyovich Aranovskiy (UKR)   Attendance: 12.100
(Miralem Pjanic missed a penalty in the 89th minute)

10-10-2014   King Baudouin Stadium, Brussels: Belgium – Andorra   6-0 (3-0)
Belgium: Thibaut Courtois, Jan Vertonghen, Nicolas Lombaerts, Vincent Kompany (C) (56' Sébastien Pocognoli), Toby Alderweireld, Radja Nainggolan, Steven Defour, Kevin De Bruyne, Divock Okoth Origi (66' Romelu Lukaku Menama), Dries Mertens, Nacer Chadli (61' Marouane Fellaini). (Coach: Marc Wilmots (BEL)).
Andorra: Ferran Pol Pérez, Moisés San Nicolás (YC89), Jordi Rubio Gómez (61' Iván Lorenzo Roncero (YC75)), David Maneiro Ton, Emili Josep García Miramontes, Ildefons Lima Solà (C), Márcio Vieira de Vasconcelos (YC20), Marc Vales González, Gabriel "Gabi" Riera Lancha (72' Marc Garcia Renom), Cristian Martínez Alejo (78' Sergi Moreno Marín), Jose Manuel "Josep" Díaz Ayala (YC30). (Coach: Jesús Luis Álvarez de Eulate Güergue "Koldo" (AND)).
Goals: Belgium: 1-0 Kevin De Bruyne (31' penalty), 2-0 Kevin de Bruyne (34'), 3-0 Nacer Chadli (37'), 4-0 Divock Okoth Origi (59'), 5-0 Dries Mertens (65'), 6-0 Dries Mertens (68').
Referee: Serhiy Mykolayovych Boyko (UKR)   Attendance: 45.459

10-10-2014   GSP Stadium, Nicosia: Cyprus – Israel   1-2 (0-2)
Cyprus: Antonis Giorgallides, Marios Antoniades, Giorgios Merkis, DOSSA Momad Omar Hassamo JÚNIOR, Dimitris Christofi, Constantinos (Costas) Charalambides (45'+1' Pieros Sotiriou), Marios Stylianou (45'+1' Charalampos (Charis) Kyriakou), Marios Nikolaou, Andreas Makris (69' Nektarios Alexandrou), Constantinos Makrides (C), Vincent Laban (YC54). (Coach: Charalambos (Pambos) Christodoulou (CYP)).
Israel: Ofir Marciano (YC65), Eyal Meshumar (YC61), Omri Ben Harush, Tal Ben Haim (I) (C), Eitan Tibi, Gil Vermouth (82' Nir Bitton), Shiran Yeini, Bibras Natcho, Omer Damari (70' Itay Shechter), Tal Ben Haim (II) (YC74) (73' Lior Refaelov (YC83)), Eran Zahavy. (Coach: Eli Guttmann (ISR)).
Goals: Cyprus: 1-2 Constantinos Makrides (67').
Israel: 0-1 Omer Damari (38'), 0-2 Tal Ben Haim (II) (45').
Referee: Daniele Orsato (ITA)   Attendance: 19.164

10-10-2014   Cardiff City Stadium, Cardiff: Wales – Bosnia and Herzegovina   0-0
Wales: Wayne Hennessey, James Chester (YC70), Ashley Williams (C) (YC71), Neil Taylor
(YC57), Chris Gunter, Benjamin (Ben) Davies, Jonathan Williams (83' George Williams),
Joseph (Joe) Ledley, Andy King, Simon Church (65' Hal Robson-Kanu), Gareth Bale. (Coach:
Chris Coleman (WAL)).
Bosnia and Herzegovina: Asmir Begovic, Muhamed Besic, Toni Sunjic, Mensur Mujdza, Tino-
Sven Susic, Miralem Pjanic (YC34), Haris Medunjanin, Senad Lulic, Anel Hadzic (YC16),
Edin Dzeko (C) (YC72), Vedad Ibisevic (83' Izet Hajrovic). (Coach: Safet Susic (BOS)).
Referee: Vladislav Yuryevich Bezborodov (RUS)   Attendance: 30.741

13-10-2014   Estadi Nacional, Andorra la Vella: Andorra – Israel   1-4 (1-2)
Andorra: Ferran Pol Pérez, Jordi Rubio Gómez (YC45+2) (70' Marc Pujol Pons), David
Maneiro Ton, Emili Josep García Miramontes, Ildefons Lima Solà (C) (40' Jose Manuel
"Josep" Díaz Ayala), Gabriel "Gabi" Riera Lancha, Carlos Eduardo "Edu" Peppe Britos (83'
Juan Carlos Toscano Beltrán), Cristian Martínez Alejo (YC83), Márcio Vieira de Vasconcelos,
Marc Vales González, Iván Lorenzo Roncero. (Coach: Jesús Luis Álvarez de Eulate Güergue
"Koldo" (AND)).
Israel: Ofir Marciano, Eitan Tibi, Taleb Twatha, Eyal Meshumar, Tal Ben Haim (I) (C), Gil
Vermouth (YC45+2) (65' Itay Shechter), Bibras Natcho, Nir Bitton, Omer Damari (84' Tomer
Hemed), Tal Ben Haim (II), Eran Zahavy (70' Lior Refaelov). (Coach: Eli Guttmann (ISR)).
Goals: Andorra: 1-1 Ildefons Lima Solà (15' penalty).
Israel: 0-1 Omer Damari (3'), 1-2 Omer Damari (41'), 1-3 Omer Damari (82'), 1-4 Tomer
Hemed (90'+6' penalty).
Referee: Pavel Cristian Balaj (ROM)   Attendance: 2.032

13-10-2014   Bilino Polje, Zenica: Bosnia and Herzegovina – Belgium   1-1 (1-0)
Bosnia and Herzegovina: Asmir Begovic, Toni Sunjic, Mensur Mujdza, Muhamed Besic, Tino-
Sven Susic (71' Edin Visca), Miralem Pjanic, Haris Medunjanin, Senad Lulic, Anel Hadzic,
Vedad Ibisevic, Edin Dzeko (C). (Coach: Safet Susic (BOS)).
Belgium: Thibaut Courtois, Jan Vertonghen, Nicolas Lombaerts, Vincent Kompany (C)
(YC87), Toby Alderweireld, Radja Nainggolan, Eden Hazard, Steven Defour (78' Marouane
Fellaini), Kevin De Bruyne, Divock Okoth Origi, Romelu Lukaku Menama (57' Dries
Mertens). (Coach: Marc Wilmots (BEL)).
Goals: Bosnia and Herzegovina: 1-0 Edin Dzeko (28').
Belgium: 1-1 Radja Nainggolan (51').
Referee: Luca Banti (ITA)   Attendance: 12.070

13-10-2014   Cardiff City Stadium, Cardiff: Wales – Cyprus   2-1 (2-1)
Wales: Wayne Hennessey, Ashley Williams (C), Neil Taylor, Chris Gunter, James Chester,
Hal Robson-Kanu (84' Jake Taylor), Joseph (Joe) Ledley (YC5), Andy King (RC47), George
Williams (58' David (Dave) Edwards (YC90+1)), Simon Church (6' David Cotterill (YC34)),
Gareth Bale (YC48). (Coach: Chris Coleman (WAL)).
Cyprus: Anastasios (Tasos) Kissas, Giorgios Merkis (YC90+4), DOSSA Momad Omar
Hassamo JÚNIOR (29' Angelis Angeli (YC39), 85' Andreas Papathanasiou), Marios
Antoniades, Marios Nikolaou (YC5) (68' Nektarios Alexandrou), Constantinos Makrides (C),
Vincent Laban, Charalampos (Charis) Kyriakou (YC85), Georgios Efrem, Dimitris Christofi,
Pieros Sotiriou (YC64). (Coach: Charalambos (Pambos) Christodoulou (CYP)).
Goals: Wales: 1-0 David Cotterill (13'), 2-0 Hal Robson-Kanu (23').
Cyprus: 2-1 Vincent Laban (36').
Referee: Manuel Gräfe (GER)   Attendance: 21.273
(*Angelis Angeli* also known as *Angelis Charalambous*)

16-11-2014   King Baudouin Stadium, Brussels: Belgium – Wales   0-0
Belgium: Thibaut Courtois, Jan Vertonghen (C), Anthony Vanden Borre, Nicolas Lombaerts, Toby Alderweireld, Axel Witsel, Eden Hazard, Marouane Fellaini, Kevin De Bruyne, Divock Okoth Origi (73' Dries Mertens, 89' Adnan Januzaj), Nacer Chadli (62' Christian Benteke). (Coach: Marc Wilmots (BEL)).
Wales: Wayne Hennessey (YC90+4), Ashley Williams (C), Neil Taylor, Chris Gunter, James Chester, Hal Robson-Kanu (90'+5' Emyr Huws), Aaron Ramsey, Joseph (Joe) Ledley (YC33), David Cotterill (46' George Williams (YC85)), Joe Allen (YC73), Gareth Bale. (Coach: Chris Coleman (WAL)).
Referee: Pavel Královec (CZE)   Attendance: 41.535

16-11-2014   GSP Stadium, Nicosia: Cyprus – Andorra   5-0 (3-0)
Cyprus: Antonis Giorgallides, Giorgios Merkis, Jason Demetriou, Marios Antoniades, Angelis Angeli, Marios Nikolaou, Vincent Laban, Georgios Efrem (78' Konstantinos (Kostas) Laifis), Dimitris Christofi, Nestoras Mitidis (63' Giorgos Kolokoudias), Efstathios (Stathis) Aloneftis (C) (46' Andreas Makris). (Coach: Charalambos (Pambos) Christodoulou (CYP)).
Andorra: Ferran Pol Pérez, Jordi Rubio Gómez (73' Adrián Rodrígues Gonçalves), Emili Josep García Miramontes, Ildefons Lima Solà (C) (49' Victor Rodríguez Soria), Márcio Vieira de Vasconcelos (46' Jose Manuel "Josep" Díaz Ayala), Marc Vales González, Gabriel "Gabi" Riera Lancha, Marc Pujol Pons (YC83), Cristian Martínez Alejo (YC43), Marc Garcia Renom, Iván Lorenzo Roncero. (Coach: Jesús Luis Álvarez de Eulate Güergue "Koldo" (AND)).
Goals: Cyprus: 1-0 Giorgios Merkis (9'), 2-0 Georgios Efrem (31'), 3-0 Georgios Efrem (42'), 4-0 Georgios Efrem (60'), 5-0 Dimitris Christofi (87' penalty).
Referee: Mark Clattenburg (ENG)   Attendance: 6.078

16-11-2014   Sammy Ofer Stadium, Haifa: Israel – Bosnia and Herzegovina   3-0 (2-0)
Israel: Ofir Marciano, Eitan Tibi, Eyal Meshumar, Omri Ben Harush (78' Ofir Davidadze), Tal Ben Haim (I) (C) (YC17), Shiran Yeini (YC27), Gil Vermouth (70' Lior Refaelov), Bibras Natcho (74' Nir Bitton (YC84)), Tal Ben Haim (II), Eran Zahavy, Omer Damari. (Coach: Eli Guttmann (ISR)).
Bosnia and Herzegovina: Asmir Begovic (C), Toni Sunjic (RC47), Emir Spahic (YC87), Mensur Mujdza (46' Edin Visca), Muhamed Besic (46' Sanjin Prcic), Miralem Pjanic (61' Gojko Cimirot), Haris Medunjanin, Senad Lulic, Zoran Kvzic (YC90), Izet Hajrovic, Anel Hadzic. (Coach: Safet Susic (BOS)).
Goals: Israel: 1-0 Gil Vermouth (36'), 2-0 Omer Damari (45'), 3-0 Eran Zahavy (70').
Referee: Antonio Mateu Lahoz (ESP)   Attendance: 28.300

28-03-2015   Sammy Ofer Stadium, Haifa: Israel – Wales   0-3 (0-1)
Israel: Ofir Marciano, Orel Dgani, Omri Ben Harush, Tal Ben Haim (I) (C), Eitan Tibi (YC48,YC51), Shiran Yeini, Lior Refaelov (YC44), Bibras Natcho, Omer Damari (43' Tomer Hemed), Tal Ben Haim (II) (60' Nir Bitton), Eran Zahavy (70' Ben Sahar). (Coach: Eli Guttmann (ISR)).
Wales: Wayne Hennessey, Chris Gunter, Benjamin (Ben) Davies, James Collins, Ashley Williams (C), Neil Taylor, Joe Allen, Hal Robson-Kanu (68' Samuel Michael (Sam) Vokes), Aaron Ramsey (85' Shaun MacDonald), Joseph (Joe) Ledley (47' David Vaughan), Gareth Bale. (Coach: Chris Coleman (WAL)).
Goals: Wales: 0-1 Aaron Ramsey (45'+1'), 0-2 Gareth Bale (50'), 0-3 Gareth Bale (77').
Referee: Milorad Mazic (SRB)   Attendance: 30.200

28-03-2015   Estadi Nacional, Andorra la Vella:
                Andorra – Bosnia and Herzegovina   0-3 (0-1)
Andorra: Ferran Pol Pérez, Moisés San Nicolás, Victor Rodríguez Soria, Ildefons Lima Solà, Márcio Vieira de Vasconcelos (YC9), Marc Vales González, Óscar Sonejee Masand (C), Marc Garcia Renom, Iván Lorenzo Roncero (85' Jordi Rubio Gómez), Ludovic Clemente Garces (YC25) (54' Cristian Martínez Alejo), Sebastián Gómez Pérez (59' Gabriel "Gabi" Riera Lancha). (Coach: Jesús Luis Álvarez de Eulate Güergue "Koldo" (AND)).
Bosnia and Herzegovina: Asmir Begovic, Ervin Zukanovic, Ognjen Vranjes (YC9) (73' Edin Cocalic), Emir Spahic, Mensur Mujdza, Muhamed Besic, Edin Visca, Miralem Pjanic, Senad Lulic (77' Haris Medunjanin), Vedad Ibisevic (67' Milan Djuric), Edin Dzeko (C). (Coach: Mehmed Bazdarevic (BOS)).
Goals: Bosnia and Herzegovina: 0-1 Edin Dzeko (13'), 0-2 Edin Dzeko (49'), 0-3 Edin Dzeko (62').
Referee: István Vad (II) (HUN)   Attendance: 2.498

28-03-2015   King Baudouin Stadium, Brussels: Belgium – Cyprus 5-0 (2-0)
Belgium: Thibaut Courtois, Jan Vertonghen, Nicolas Lombaerts, Vincent Kompany (C), Toby Alderweireld, Axel Witsel, Radja Nainggolan, Eden Hazard (69' Dries Mertens), Marouane Fellaini (69' Yannick Ferreira-Carrasco), Kevin De Bruyne, Christian Benteke (77' Michy Batshuayi). (Coach: Marc Wilmots (BEL)).
Cyprus: Anastasios (Tasos) Kissas, Giorgios Merkis, Konstantinos (Kostas) Laifis, Marios Antoniades, Marios Nikolaou, Andreas Makris (71' Giorgos Eleftheriou), Constantinos Makrides (C) (84' Grigoris Kastanos), Vincent Laban (57' Giorgos Ecomomides), Charalampos (Charis) Kyriakou, Pieros Sotiriou, Nestoras Mitidis. (Coach: Charalambos (Pambos) Christodoulou (CYP)).
Goals: Belgium: 1-0 Marouane Fellaini (21'), 2-0 Christian Benteke (35'), 3-0 Marouane Fellaini (66'), 4-0 Eden Hazard (67'), 5-0 Michy Batshuayi (80').
Referee: Ovidiu Alin Hategan (ROM)   Attendance: 45.213

31-03-2015   Teddy Stadium, Jerusalem: Israel – Belgium   0-1 (0-1)
Israel: Ofir Marciano, Tal Ben Haim (I) (C), Rami Gershon, Orel Dgani (YC17), Omri Ben Harush (84' Elyaniv Barda), Shiran Yeini (YC54) (66' Lior Refaelov (YC87)), Bibras Natcho, Nir Bitton, Eran Zahavy, Ben Sahar, Tomer Hemed (46' Tal Ben Haim (II)). (Coach: Eli Guttmann (ISR)).
Belgium: Thibaut Courtois, Toby Alderweireld (YC19), Jan Vertonghen, Nicolas Lombaerts (YC75), Vincent Kompany (C) (YC11,YC64), Axel Witsel, Radja Nainggolan (86' Divock Okoth Origi), Eden Hazard (63' Nacer Chadli), Marouane Fellaini, Kevin De Bruyne, Christian Benteke (66' Jason Denayer). (Coach: Marc Wilmots (BEL)).
Goal: Belgium: 0-1 Marouane Fellaini (9').
Referee: Mark Clattenburg (ENG)   Attendance: 29.750

295

12-06-2015   Estadi Nacional, Andorra la Vella: Andorra – Cyprus 1-3 (1-2)
Andorra: Ferran Pol Pérez, Jordi Rubio Gómez (YC6), Adrián Rodrígues Gonçalves, Victor Rodríguez Soria, Marc Vales González, Marc Rebés Ruiz (YC50) (79' Carlos Eduardo "Edu" Peppe Britos), Cristian Martínez Alejo, Marc Garcia Renom (YC56), Jose Manuel "Josep" Díaz Ayala (C) (YC37) (60' Óscar Sonejee Masand), Aarón Sánchez Alburquerque, Sergi Moreno Marín (67' Ildefons Lima Solà). (Coach: Jesús Luis Álvarez de Eulate Güergue "Koldo" (AND)).
Cyprus: Antonis Giorgallides, Valentinos Sielis, DOSSA Momad Omar Hassamo JÚNIOR, Jason Demetriou, Marios Antoniades, Marios Nikolaou, Constantinos Makrides (C) (88' Grigoris Kastanos), Vincent Laban (YC26) (76' Giorgos Ecomomides), Georgios Efrem, Dimitris Christofi (82' Nektarios Alexandrou), Nestoras Mitidis. (Coach: Charalambos (Pambos) Christodoulou (CYP)).
Goals: Andorra: 1-0 DOSSA Momad Omar Hassamo JÚNIOR (2' *own goal*).
Cyprus: 1-1 Nestoras Mitidis (13'), 1-2 Nestoras Mitidis (45'), 1-3 Nestoras Mitidis (53').
Referee: Tobias Welz (GER)   Attendance: 1.054
(DOSSA Momad Omar Hassamo JÚNIOR missed a penalty in the 51st minute)

12-06-2015   Bilino Polje, Zenica: Bosnia and Herzegovina – Israel 3-1 (2-1)
Bosnia and Herzegovina: Asmir Begovic, Ognjen Vranjes, Emir Spahic, Mensur Mujdza, Sead Kolasinac, Muhamed Besic, Edin Visca (80' Izet Hajrovic), Miralem Pjanic (88' Vedad Ibisevic), Haris Medunjanin (YC50), Senad Lulic (85' Anel Hadzic), Edin Dzeko (C). (Coach: Mehmed Bazdarevic (BOS)).
Israel: Ofir Marciano, Rami Gershon, Orel Dgani, Omri Ben Harush (YC72), Tal Ben Haim (I) (C) (YC82), Shiran Yeini (YC45+1) (46' Omer Damari), Bibras Natcho, Nir Bitton (80' Roi Kehat), Eran Zahavy, Ben Sahar (62' Maor Buzaglo), Tal Ben Haim (II). (Coach: Eli Guttmann (ISR)).
Goals: Bosnia and Herzegovina: 1-1 Edin Visca (42'), 2-1 Edin Dzeko (45'+2' penalty), 3-1 Edin Visca (75').
Israel: 0-1 Tal Ben Haim (II) (41').
Referee: Ruddy Buquet (FRA)   Attendance: 12.100

12-06-2015   Cardiff City Stadium, Cardiff: Wales – Belgium 1-0 (1-0)
Wales: Wayne Hennessey, Ashley Williams (C), Neil Taylor, Chris Gunter, James Chester, Hal Robson-Kanu (90'+3' Andy King), Jazz Richards, Aaron Ramsey, Joseph (Joe) Ledley, Joe Allen (YC28), Gareth Bale (87' Samuel Michael (Sam) Vokes). (Coach: Chris Coleman (WAL)).
Belgium: Thibaut Courtois, Jan Vertonghen, Nicolas Lombaerts (YC59), Jason Denayer, Toby Alderweireld (77' Yannick Ferreira-Carrasco), Axel Witsel, Radja Nainggolan, Eden Hazard (C), Kevin De Bruyne, Dries Mertens (46' Romelu Lukaku Menama), Christian Benteke. (Coach: Marc Wilmots (BEL)).
Goal: Wales: 1-0 Gareth Bale (25').
Referee: Dr.Felix Brych (GER)   Attendance: 33.280

03-09-2015   King Baudouin Stadium, Brussels:
Belgium – Bosnia and Herzegovina   3-1 (2-1)
Belgium: Thibaut Courtois, Thomas Vermaelen, Vincent Kompany (C), Toby Alderweireld, Jan Vertonghen, Radja Nainggolan, Eden Hazard, Marouane Fellaini, Kevin De Bruyne (89' Dries Mertens), Axel Witsel, Romelu Lukaku Menama (82' Divock Okoth Origi). (Coach: Marc Wilmots (BEL)).
Bosnia and Herzegovina: Asmir Begovic, Emir Spahic (56' Toni Sunjic (YC77)), Mensur Mujdza, Sead Kolasinac (YC54) (72' Izet Hajrovic), Muhamed Besic, Ognjen Vranjes, Miralem Pjanic, Haris Medunjanin (80' Vedad Ibisevic), Senad Lulic (YC87), Edin Visca, Edin Dzeko (C). (Coach: Mehmed Bazdarevic (BOS)).
Goals: Belgium: 1-1 Marouane Fellaini (23'), 2-1 Kevin De Bruyne (44'), 3-1 Eden Hazard (78' penalty).
Bosnia and Herzegovina: 0-1 Edin Dzeko (15').
Referee: Manuel Jorge Neves Moreira de Sousa (POR)   Attendance: 42.975

03-09-2015   GSP Stadium, Nicosia: Cyprus – Wales   0-1 (0-0)
Cyprus: Antonis Giorgallides, Konstantinos (Kostas) Laifis, DOSSA Momad Omar Hassamo JÚNIOR, Jason Demetriou, Marios Antoniades, Marios Nikolaou, Andreas Makris (84' Pieros Sotiriou), Constantinos Makrides, Giorgos Ecomomides, Constantinos (Costas) Charalambides (C) (74' Nikos Englezou), Nestoras Mitidis (65' Giorgos Kolokoudias). (Coach: Charalambos (Pambos) Christodoulou (CYP)).
Wales: Wayne Hennessey, Ashley Williams (C), Neil Taylor, Chris Gunter, Benjamin (Ben) Davies, Hal Robson-Kanu (68' Samuel Michael (Sam) Vokes), Jazz Richards, Aaron Ramsey (90'+3' Shaun MacDonald), Andy King, David (Dave) Edwards, Gareth Bale (90' Simon Church). (Coach: Chris Coleman (WAL)).
Goal: Wales: 0-1 Gareth Bale (82').
Referee: Szymon Marciniak (POL)   Attendance: 14.492

03-09-2015   Sammy Ofer Stadium, Haifa: Israel – Andorra   4-0 (4-0)
Israel: Ofir Marciano, Eitan Tibi, Elazar (Eli) Dasa, Tal Ben Haim (I) (C) (46' Maor Melikson), Avraham (Avi) Rikan, Bibras Natcho, Nir Bitton, Eran Zahavy (46' Maor Buzaglo), Tomer Hemed (YC46) (75' Beram Kayal), Munas Dabbur, Tal Ben Haim (II). (Coach: Eli Guttmann (ISR)).
Andorra: Ferran Pol Pérez, Moisés San Nicolás (YC59), Victor Rodríguez Soria (54' Óscar Sonejee Masand), Emili Josep García Miramontes, Ildefons Lima Solà (C), Márcio Vieira de Vasconcelos (YC47), Marc Rebés Ruiz (81' Max Llovera González-Adrio), Cristian Martínez Alejo, Marc Garcia Renom, Aarón Sánchez Alburquerque, Sergi Moreno Marín (72' Jordi Rubio Gómez (YC88)). (Coach: Jesús Luis Álvarez de Eulate Güergue "Koldo" (AND)).
Goals: Israel: 1-0 Eran Zahavy (3'), 2-0 Nir Bitton (22'), 3-0 Tomer Hemed (26' penalty), 4-0 Munas Dabbur (38').
Referee: Tamás Bognár (HUN)   Attendance: 22.650

06-09-2015   Cardiff City Stadium, Cardiff: Wales – Israel   0-0
Wales: Wayne Hennessey, Ashley Williams (C), Neil Taylor, Chris Gunter, Benjamin (Ben) Davies, Hal Robson-Kanu (YC79) (79' Simon Church), Jazz Richards (YC59), Aaron Ramsey, Andy King (86' Samuel Michael (Sam) Vokes), David (Dave) Edwards, Gareth Bale. (Coach: Chris Coleman (WAL)).
Israel: Ofir Marciano, Eitan Tibi, Orel Dgani (YC56), Elazar (Eli) Dasa (YC45+1), Omri Ben Harush, Tal Ben Haim (I) (C), Bibras Natcho (YC56), Beram Kayal (46' Tal Ben Haim (II)), Nir Bitton (YC61), Eran Zahavy (90'+3' Ben Sahar), Munas Dabbur (YC18) (46' Tomer Hemed). (Coach: Eli Guttmann (ISR)).
Referee: Ivan Bebek (CRO)   Attendance: 32.653

297

06-09-2015   Bilino Polje, Zenica: Bosnia and Herzegovina – Andorra   3-0 (3-0)
Bosnia and Herzegovina: Asmir Begovic, Toni Sunjic, Emir Spahic, Sead Kolasinac (79'
Mario Vrancic), Ermin Bicakcic, Muhamed Besic (RC63), Miralem Pjanic (45' Anel Hadzic
(YC66)), Senad Lulic, Ermin Zec, Vedad Ibisevic (YC21), Edin Dzeko (C) (68' Milan Djuric).
(Coach: Mehmed Bazdarevic (BOS)).
Andorra: Ferran Pol Pérez, Moisés San Nicolás, Victor Rodríguez Soria (RC64), Ildefons Lima
Solà, Márcio Vieira de Vasconcelos, Óscar Sonejee Masand (C), Gabriel "Gabi" Riera Lancha
(87' Leonel Felipe "Leo" Alves Alves), Marc Rebés Ruiz (YC71), Cristian Martínez Alejo
(YC53) (76' Aarón Sánchez Alburquerque), Marc Garcia Renom, Jose Manuel "Josep" Díaz
Ayala (YC63) (81' Carlos Eduardo "Edu" Peppe Britos). (Coach: Jesús Luis Álvarez de Eulate
Güergue "Koldo" (AND)).
Goals: Bosnia and Herzegovina: 1-0 Ermin Bicakcic (14'), 2-0 Edin Dzeko (30'), 3-0 Senad
Lulic (45').
Referee: Arnold Hunter (NIR)   Attendance: 6.830

06-09-2015   GSP Stadium, Nicosia: Cyprus – Belgium   0-1 (0-0)
Cyprus: Antonis Giorgallides, Konstantinos (Kostas) Laifis, DOSSA Momad Omar Hassamo
JÚNIOR, Jason Demetriou (YC61), Marios Antoniades (YC47), Marios Nikolaou (84'
Kostakis Artymatas), Andreas Makris, Constantinos Makrides, Giorgos Ecomomides (YC73),
Constantinos (Costas) Charalambides (C) (53' Vincent Laban), Nestoras Mitidis (11' Pieros
Sotiriou). (Coach: Charalambos (Pambos) Christodoulou (CYP)).
Belgium: Thibaut Courtois, Jan Vertonghen, Thomas Vermaelen, Vincent Kompany (C)
(YC90+2), Toby Alderweireld, Axel Witsel, Radja Nainggolan, Eden Hazard, Marouane
Fellaini (64' Dries Mertens), Kevin De Bruyne, Christian Benteke (46' Divock Okoth Origi).
(Coach: Marc Wilmots (BEL)).
Goal: Belgium: 0-1 Eden Hazard (86').
Referee: Vladislav Yuryevich Bezborodov (RUS)   Attendance: 11.866

10-10-2015   Estadi Nacional, Andorra la Vella: Andorra – Belgium   1-4 (0-2)
Andorra: Ferran Pol Pérez, Moisés San Nicolás, Max Llovera González-Adrio, Ildefons Lima
Solà, Márcio Vieira de Vasconcelos (86' Carlos Eduardo "Edu" Peppe Britos), Óscar Sonejee
Masand (C) (YC41) (62' Adrián Rodrígues Gonçalves), Jordi Rubio Gómez, Marc Rebés Ruiz
(YC12), Marc Garcia Renom (YC83), Aarón Sánchez Alburquerque, Victor Hugo Moreira
Teixeira (73' Gabriel "Gabi" Riera Lancha (YC77)). (Coach: Jesús Luis Álvarez de Eulate
Güergue "Koldo" (AND)).
Belgium: Simon Mignolet, Jan Vertonghen (YC50), Jordan Zacharie Lukaku Menama
Mokelenge (YC28), Toby Alderweireld, Thomas Meunier (81' Luis Pedro Cavanda), Axel
Witsel, Radja Nainggolan, Eden Hazard (79' Zakaria Bakkali), Kevin De Bruyne, Dries
Mertens (72' Nacer Chadli), Laurent Depoitre (YC72). (Coach: Marc Wilmots (BEL)).
Goals: Andorra: 1-2 Ildefons Lima Solà (51' penalty).
Belgium: 0-1 Radja Nainggolan (19'), 0-2 Kevin De Bruyne (42'), 1-3 Eden Hazard (56'
penalty), 1-4 Laurent Depoitre (64').
Referee: Pawel Gil (POL)   Attendance: 3.032
(Eden Hazard missed a penalty in the 78th minute)

298

10-10-2015   Bilino Polje, Zenica: Bosnia and Herzegovina – Wales   2-0 (0-0)
Bosnia and Herzegovina: Asmir Begovic (C) (YC85), Ervin Zukanovic, Toni Sunjic (YC85),
Emir Spahic (YC42) (46' Edin Cocalic), Mensur Mujdza, Edin Visca (61' Milan Djuric), Sejad
Salihovic, Miralem Pjanic, Senad Lulic, Anel Hadzic (89' Ermin Bicakcic), Vedad Ibisevic.
(Coach: Mehmed Bazdarevic (BOS)).
Wales: Wayne Hennessey, Ashley Williams (C), Neil Taylor (YC84), Chris Gunter, Benjamin
(Ben) Davies, Hal Robson-Kanu (84' Simon Church), Jazz Richards, Aaron Ramsey, Joseph
(Joe) Ledley (75' Samuel Michael (Sam) Vokes), Joe Allen (85' David (Dave) Edwards),
Gareth Bale. (Coach: Chris Coleman (WAL)).
Goals: Bosnia and Herzegovina: 1-0 Milan Djuric (71'), 2-0 Vedad Ibisevic (90').
Referee: Alberto Undiano Mallenco (ESP)   Attendance: 10.250

10-10-2015   Teddy Stadium, Jerusalem: Israel – Cyprus   1-2 (0-0)
Israel: Ofir Marciano, Eitan Tibi, Elazar (Eli) Dasa (54' Orel Dgani), Omri Ben Harush (71'
Maor Melikson), Tal Ben Haim (I) (C), Beram Kayal, Nir Bitton (YC45+1), Gil Vermouth
(65' Tomer Hemed), Munas Dabbur, Tal Ben Haim (II) (YC90+3), Eran Zahavy. (Coach: Eli
Guttmann (ISR)).
Cyprus: Antonis Giorgallides, Konstantinos (Kostas) Laifis, DOSSA Momad Omar Hassamo
JÚNIOR (YC59), Jason Demetriou, Marios Antoniades (YC51), Andreas Makris (46'
Constantinos (Costas) Charalambides), Constantinos Makrides (C) (84' Giorgos Ecomomides),
Vincent Laban, Georgios Efrem (86' Giorgios Merkis), Marios Nikolaou, Nestoras Mitidis.
(Coach: Charalambos (Pambos) Christodoulou (CYP)).
Goals: Israel: 1-1 Nir Bitton (76').
Cyprus: 0-1 DOSSA Momad Omar Hassamo JÚNIOR (58'), 1-2 Jason Demetriou (80').
Referee: Manuel Jorge Neves Moreira de Sousa (POR)   Attendance: 25.300

13-10-2015   King Baudouin Stadium, Brussels: Belgium – Israel   3-1 (0-0)
Belgium: Simon Mignolet, Nicolas Lombaerts, Vincent Kompany (C) (58' Thomas Meunier),
Toby Alderweireld, Jan Vertonghen (YC45+2), Eden Hazard, Marouane Fellaini (66' Axel
Witsel), Kevin De Bruyne (YC33), Radja Nainggolan, Romelu Lukaku Menama (65' Divock
Okoth Origi), Dries Mertens. (Coach: Marc Wilmots (BEL)).
Israel: Ofir Marciano, Orel Dgani, Omri Ben Harush, Tal Ben Haim (I) (C), Eitan Tibi, Beram
Kayal (66' Omer Damari), Shiran Yeini (77' Gil Vermouth), Dor Peretz, Tomer Hemed, Tal
Ben Haim (II) (59' Avraham (Avi) Rikan (YC76)), Eran Zahavy. (Coach: Eli Guttmann (ISR)).
Goals: Belgium: 1-0 Dries Mertens (64'), 2-0 Kevin De Bruyne (78'), 3-0 Eden Hazard (84').
Israel: 3-1 Tomer Hemed (88').
Referee: Anastasios (Tasos) Sidiropoulos (GRE)   Attendance: 39.773

13-10-2015   GSP Stadium, Nicosia: Cyprus – Bosnia and Herzegovina   2-3 (2-2)
Cyprus: Antonis Giorgallides, Konstantinos (Kostas) Laifis, DOSSA Momad Omar Hassamo
JÚNIOR (YC81), Jason Demetriou, Marios Antoniades, Marios Nikolaou (YC36) (65' Giorgos
Ecomomides), Constantinos Makrides, Vincent Laban (75' Efstathios (Stathis) Aloneftis),
Georgios Efrem, Constantinos (Costas) Charalambides (C) (83' Giorgos Kolokoudias),
Nestoras Mitidis. (Coach: Charalambos (Pambos) Christodoulou (CYP)).
Bosnia and Herzegovina: Asmir Begovic (C) (YC51), Ervin Zukanovic (60' Milan Djuric
(YC70)), Ognjen Vranjes, Toni Sunjic, Emir Spahic, Mensur Mujdza (YC80), Edin Visca (79'
Ermin Bicakcic), Miralem Pjanic (YC65) (85' Sejad Salihovic), Haris Medunjanin, Senad
Lulic, Vedad Ibisevic. (Coach: Mehmed Bazdarevic (BOS)).
Goals: Cyprus: 1-1 Constantinos (Costas) Charalambides (32'), 2-1 Nestoras Mitidis (41').
Bosnia and Herzegovina: 0-1 Haris Medunjanin (13'), 2-2 Haris Medunjanin (44'), 2-3 Milan
Djuric (67').
Referee: Anthony Taylor (ENG)   Attendance: 17.687

13-10-2015   Cardiff City Stadium, Cardiff: Wales – Andorra 2-0 (0-0)
Wales: Wayne Hennessey, Ashley Williams (C) (YC57), Chris Gunter (YC57), Benjamin
(Ben) Davies, James Chester, David Vaughan (YC33), Hal Robson-Kanu (23' David (Dave)
Edwards, 46' Tom Lawrence), Aaron Ramsey, Samuel Michael (Sam) Vokes, Gareth Bale,
Jonathan Williams (86' Simon Church). (Coach: Chris Coleman (WAL)).
Andorra: Ferran Pol Pérez (YC65), Moisés San Nicolás, Jordi Rubio Gómez, Adrián Rodrígues
Gonçalves (YC78), Max Llovera González-Adrio, Ildefons Lima Solà (YC15), Márcio Vieira
de Vasconcelos (YC57), Óscar Sonejee Masand (C) (70' Jose Manuel "Josep" Díaz Ayala
(YC82)), Aarón Sánchez Alburquerque (YC51), Victor Hugo Moreira Teixeira (12' Gabriel
"Gabi" Riera Lancha), Iván Lorenzo Roncero (YC49) (81' Marc Garcia Renom). (Coach: Jesús
Luis Álvarez de Eulate Güergue "Koldo" (AND)).
Goals: Wales: 1-0 Aaron Ramsey (50'), 2-0 Gareth Bale (86').
Referee: Kevin Bernie Raymond Blom (HOL)   Attendance: 33.280

GROUP   C

08-09-2014	Luxembourg	Luxembourg – Belarus	1-1 (1-0)
08-09-2014	Valencia	Spain – Macedonia	5-1 (3-1)
08-09-2014	Kiev	Ukraine – Slovakia	0-1 (0-1)
09-10-2014	Barysaw	Belarus – Ukraine	0-2 (0-0)
09-10-2014	Skopje	Macedonia – Luxembourg	3-2 (1-2)
09-10-2014	Zilina	Slovakia – Spain	2-1 (1-0)
12-10-2014	Lviv	Ukraine – Macedonia	1-0 (1-0)
12-10-2014	Barysaw	Belarus – Slovakia	1-3 (0-0)
12-10-2014	Luxembourg	Luxembourg – Spain	0-4 (0-2)
15-11-2014	Luxembourg	Luxembourg – Ukraine	0-3 (0-1)
15-11-2014	Skopje	Macedonia – Slovakia	0-2 (0-2)
15-11-2014	Huelva	Spain – Belarus	3-0 (2-0)
27-03-2015	Skopje	Macedonia – Belarus	1-2 (1-1)
27-03-2015	Zilina	Slovakia – Luxembourg	3-0 (3-0)
27-03-2015	Seville	Spain – Ukraine	1-0 (1-0)
14-06-2015	Lviv	Ukraine – Luxembourg	3-0 (0-0)
14-06-2015	Barysaw	Belarus – Spain	0-1 (0-1)
14-06-2015	Zilina	Slovakia – Macedonia	2-1 (2-0)
05-09-2015	Luxembourg	Luxembourg – Macedonia	1-0 (0-0)
05-09-2015	Lviv	Ukraine – Belarus	3-1 (3-0)
05-09-2015	Oviedo	Spain – Slovakia	2-0 (2-0)
08-09-2015	Barysaw	Belarus – Luxembourg	2-0 (1-0)
08-09-2015	Skopje	Macedonia – Spain	0-1 (0-1)
08-09-2015	Zilina	Slovakia – Ukraine	0-0
09-10-2015	Skopje	Macedonia – Ukraine	0-2 (0-0)
09-10-2015	Zilina	Slovakia – Belarus	0-1 (0-1)
09-10-2015	Logroño	Spain – Luxembourg	4-0 (1-0)
12-10-2015	Barysaw	Belarus – Macedonia	0-0
12-10-2015	Luxembourg	Luxembourg – Slovakia	2-4 (0-3)
12-10-2015	Kiev	Ukraine – Spain	0-1 (0-1)

FINAL STANDING

Pos	Team	Pld	W	D	L	GF	GA	GD	Pts
1	Spain	10	9	0	1	23	3	+20	27
2	Slovakia	10	7	1	2	17	8	+9	22
3	Ukraine	10	6	1	3	14	2	+10	19
4	Belarus	10	3	2	5	8	14	-6	11
5	Luxembourg	10	1	1	8	6	27	-21	4
6	Macedonia	10	1	1	8	6	18	-12	4

Spain and Slovakia qualified for the Final Tournament in France.

Ukraine qualified for the play-offs

08-09-2014   Stade Josy Barthel, Luxembourg: Luxembourg – Belarus 1-1 (1-0)
Luxembourg: Jonathan Joubert, Tom Schnell (C), Chris Philipps (YC28), Mathias Jänisch, Christopher Martins Pereira (YC5), Laurent Jans, Dwayn Holter (77' Ben Payal (YC81)), Lars Christian Krogh Gerson (YC34), Daniël Alves Da Mota (YC45) (67' Tom Laterza), David Turpel (63' Antonio Luisi), Stefano Bensi. (Coach: Luc Holtz (LUX)).
Belarus: Aleksandr Gutor, Oleg Veretilo (62' Igor Stasevich), Igor Shitov, Edgar Olekhnovich (YC68) (77' Ilya Aleksievich), Aleksandr Martynovich (YC81), Egor Filipenko, Sergei Krivets, Sergei Kislyak (73' Sergei Kornilenko), Timofei Kalachev (C), Stanislav Dragun, Sergei Balanovich. (Coach: Georgiy Petrovich Kondratiev (BLS)).
Goals: Luxembourg: 1-0 Lars Christian Krogh Gerson (42').
Belarus: 1-1 Stanislav Dragun (78').
Referee: Gediminas Mazeika (LIT)   Attendance: 3.265

08-09-2014   Ciutat de Valènvia, Valencia: Spain – Macedonia 5-1 (3-1)
Spain: IKER CASILLAS Fernández (C), SERGIO RAMOS García (68' Marc BARTRA Aregall), Raúl ALBIOL Tortajada, Jordi ALBA Ramos, Juan Francisco Torres Belén "JUANFRAN", DAVID Jiménez SILVA, Francesc "CESC" FÀBREGAS Soler (YC83), Sergio BUSQUETS Burgos, Jorge Resurrección Merodio "KOKE" (YC36) (77' MUNIR El Haddadi Mohamed), Francisco "PACO" ALCÁCER García (57' Francisco Román Alarcón Suárez "ISCO"), PEDRO Eliezer Rodríguez Ledesma. (Coach: VICENTE DEL BOSQUE González (ESP)).
Macedonia: Tome Pacovski (C), Ardijan Cuculi, Ezgjan Alioski (46' Muhamed Demiri), Vance Sikov, Daniel Mojsov, Stefan Ristovski (YC14), Stefan Spirovski (64' Marjan Radeski), Besart Abdurahimi (YC26) (74' Krste Velkoski), Aleksandar Trajkovski, Adis Jahovic, Agim Ibraimi. (Coach: Bosko Djurovski (MCD)).
Goals: Spain: 1-0 SERGIO RAMOS García (16' penalty), 2-0 Francisco "PACO" ALCÁCER García (17'), 3-1 Sergio BUSQUETS Burgos (45'+3'), 4-1 DAVID Jiménez SILVA (50'), 5-1 PEDRO Eliezer Rodríguez Ledesma (90'+1').
Macedonia: 2-1 Agim Ibraimi (28' penalty).
Referee: Anastasios (Tasos) Sidiropoulos (GRE)   Attendance: 18.553

08-09-2014   Olympic Stadium, Kiev: Ukraine – Slovakia   0-1 (0-1)
Ukraine: Andriy Pyatov, Vyacheslav Shevchuk, Yaroslav Rakitskiy (YC37), Olexandr Kucher (C), Artem Fedetskiy (YC77), Taras Stepanenko (YC27), Kyrylo Kovalchuk (66' Roman Bezus (YC72)), Oleh Gusev (81' Artem Gromov), EDMAR Golovski de Lacerda Aparecida (YC82), Roman Zozulya, Andriy Yarmolenko. (Coach: Mikhail Ivanovich Fomenko (UKR)).
Slovakia: Matús Kozácik, Peter Pekarík, Tomás Hubocan, Norbert Gyömbér, Ján Durica (YC37), Vladimír Weiss (67' Miroslav Stoch), Viktor Pecovsky, Róbert Mak (90'+2' Michal Duris), Juraj Kucka (YC35), Marek Hamsík (C), Adam Nemec (YC63) (63' Filip Kiss (YC86)). (Coach: Ján Kozák (SVK)).
Goal: Slovakia: 0-1 Róbert Mak (17').
Referee: Craig Alexander Thomson (SCO)   Attendance: 38.454

09-10-2014   Borisov Arena, Barysaw: Belarus – Ukraine   0-2 (0-0)
Belarus: Yuri Zhevnov, Dmitri Verkhovtsov, Denis Polyakov (YC88), Aleksandr Martynovich (87' Pavel Savitskiy), Egor Filipenko, Igor Stasevich (46' Sergei Kislyak), Sergei Krivets, Timofei Kalachev (C), Mikhail Gordeychuk (79' Sergei Kornilenko), Stanislav Dragun, Sergei Balanovich. (Coach: Georgiy Petrovich Kondratiev (BLS)).
Ukraine: Andriy Pyatov, Vyacheslav Shevchuk, Olexandr Kucher (YC74), Yevhen Khacheridi, Artem Fedetskiy, Taras Stepanenko, Ruslan Rotan (C) (64' Sergei Sydorchuk), Yevhen Konoplyanka, EDMAR Golovski de Lacerda Aparecida (79' Pylyp Budkovsky), Roman Zozulya (YC89) (90'+1' Anatoliy Tymoshchuk), Andriy Yarmolenko. (Coach: Mikhail Ivanovich Fomenko (UKR)).
Goals: Ukraine: 0-1 Aleksandr Martynovich (82' own goal), 0-2 Sergei Sydorchuk (90'+3').
Referee: Paulus Hendrikus Martinus (Pol) van Boekel (HOL)   Attendance: 10.512

09-10-2014   Philip II Arena, Skopje: Macedonia – Luxembourg   3-2 (1-2)
Macedonia: Tome Pacovski (C), Stefan Ristovski (YC26), Daniel Mojsov (YC22), Ardijan Cuculi (46' Ezgjan Alioski), Vance Sikov (YC75), Muhamed Demiri, Arijan Ademi, Muarem Muarem (60' Adis Jahovic), Jovan Kostovski, Agim Ibraimi (46' Besart Abdurahimi), Aleksandar Trajkovski. (Coach: Bosko Djurovski (MCD)).
Luxembourg: Jonathan Joubert, Chris Philipps (YC90+1), Mathias Jänisch (YC70), Maxime Chanot, Mario Mutsch (C) (YC62), Christopher Martins Pereira, Laurent Jans, Lars Christian Krogh Gerson, Stefano Bensi (75' Tom Laterza (YC90)), Daniël Alves Da Mota (63' Dwayn Holter), David Turpel (YC51) (70' Maurice Deville). (Coach: Luc Holtz (LUX)).
Goals: Macedonia: 1-0 Aleksandar Trajkovski (20'), 2-2 Adis Jahovic (66' penalty), 3-2 Besart Abdurahimi (90'+2').
Luxembourg: 1-1 Stefano Bensi (39'), 1-2 David Turpel (44').
Referee: Paolo Mazzoleni (ITA)   Attendance: 11.500

09-10-2014   Stadión pod Dubnom, Zilina: Slovakia – Spain 2-1 (1-0)
Slovakia: Matús Kozácik, Martin Skrtel (C), Peter Pekarík, Tomás Hubocan (YC37), Norbert
Gyömbér (YC90+1), Ján Durica, Vladimír Weiss (54' Michal Duris), Viktor Pecovsky, Róbert
Mak (61' Miroslav Stoch (YC87)), Juraj Kucka (YC4) (83' Filip Kiss), Marek Hamsík.
(Coach: Ján Kozák (SVK)).
Spain: IKER CASILLAS Fernández (C), Raúl ALBIOL Tortajada (58' PEDRO Eliezer
Rodríguez Ledesma), Jordi ALBA Ramos, Gerard PIQUÉ i Bernabéu, Juan Francisco Torres
Belén "JUANFRAN" (81' Santiago "SANTI" CAZORLA González (YC90+3)), Jorge
Resurrección Merodio "KOKE", Andrés INIESTA Luján, DAVID Jiménez SILVA (YC44)
(71' Francisco "PACO" ALCÁCER García), Francesc "CESC" FÀBREGAS Soler, Sergio
BUSQUETS Burgos, Diego da Silva COSTA (YC90+1). (Coach: VICENTE DEL BOSQUE
González (ESP)).
Goals: Slovakia: 1-0 Juraj Kucka (17'), 2-1 Miroslav Stoch (87').
Spain: 1-1 Francisco "PACO" ALCÁCER García (82').
Referee: Björn Kuipers (HOL)   Attendance: 9.478

12-10-2014   Arena Lviv, Lviv: Ukraine – Macedonia 1-0 (1-0)
Ukraine: Andriy Pyatov, Vyacheslav Shevchuk, Olexandr Kucher, Yevhen Khacheridi, Artem
Fedetskiy (YC42), Taras Stepanenko, Sergei Sydorchuk (YC45) (90'+5' EDMAR Golovski de
Lacerda Aparecida), Ruslan Rotan (C) (YC72) (90'+2' Anatoliy Tymoshchuk), Yevhen
Konoplyanka, Roman Zozulya (77' Pylyp Budkovsky (YC86)), Andriy Yarmolenko. (Coach:
Mikhail Ivanovich Fomenko (UKR)).
Macedonia: Tome Pacovski (C), Vance Sikov, Stefan Ristovski, Aleksandar Damcevski
(YC39), Ezgjan Alioski, Nikola Gligorov (86' Aco Stojkov), Arijan Ademi, Aleksandar
Trajkovski (YC60), Adis Jahovic (YC30) (62' KrsteVelkoski (YC90+3)), Mirko Ivanovski
(70' Jovan Kostovski), Besart Abdurahimi (YC63). (Coach: Bosko Djurovski (MCD)).
Goal: Ukraine: 1-0 Sergei Sydorchuk (45'+2').
Referee: Sébastien Delferière (BEL)   Attendance: 33.978
(Andriy Yarmolenko missed a penalty in the 47th minute)

12-10-2014   Borisov Arena, Barysaw: Belarus – Slovakia 1-3 (0-0)
Belarus: Yuri Zhevnov, Dmitri Verkhovtsov (YC49), Igor Shitov (YC58) (76' Igor Stasevich),
Aleksandr Martynovich, Egor Filipenko (55' Denis Polyakov), Maksim Bordachev, Renan
Bressan (46' Mikhail Gordeychuk), Sergei Krivets, Timofei Kalachev (C), Stanislav Dragun,
Sergei Balanovich. (Coach: Georgiy Petrovich Kondratiev (BLS)).
Slovakia: Matús Kozácik, Martin Skrtel (C), Peter Pekarík, Norbert Gyömbér (YC87), Ján
Durica, Vladimír Weiss (80' Miroslav Stoch), Viktor Pecovsky, Róbert Mak (62' Stanislav
Sesták), Juraj Kucka (86' Filip Kiss), Marek Hamsík, Adam Nemec. (Coach: Ján Kozák
(SVK)).
Goals: Belarus: 1-1 Timofei Kalachev (79').
Slovakia: 0-1 Marek Hamsík (65'), 1-2 Marek Hamsík (84'), 1-3 Stanislav Sesták (90'+1').
Referee: Serge Gumienny (BEL)   Attendance: 3.684

303

12-10-2014   Stade Josy Barthel, Luxembourg: Luxembourg – Spain   0-4 (0-2)
Luxembourg: Jonathan Joubert, Chris Philipps, Mathias Jänisch, Maxime Chanot, Christopher Martins Pereira (61' David Turpel), Mario Mutsch (C) (86' Maurice Deville), Laurent Jans (YC68), Dwayn Holter (YC43), Lars Christian Krogh Gerson, Daniël Alves Da Mota (75' Ben Payal), Stefano Bensi. (Coach: Luc Holtz (LUX)).
Spain: David DE GEA Quintana, Gerard PIQUÉ i Bernabéu (YC75), Jordi ALBA Ramos, Daniel "DANI" CARVAJAL Ramos, Marc BARTRA Aregall, Jorge Resurrección Merodio "KOKE", Andrés INIESTA Luján (C) (70' Juan BERNAT Velasco), DAVID Jiménez SILVA (70' PEDRO Eliezer Rodríguez Ledesma), Sergio BUSQUETS Burgos, Francisco "PACO" ALCÁCER García, Diego da Silva COSTA (YC63) (82' RODRIGO Moreno Machado). (Coach: VICENTE DEL BOSQUE González (ESP)).
Goals: Spain: 0-1 DAVID Jiménez SILVA (27'), 0-2 Francisco "PACO" ALCÁCER García (42'), 0-3 Diego da Silva COSTA (69'), 0-4 Juan BERNAT Velasco (88').
Referee: Pawel Gil (POL)   Attendance: 8.125

15-11-2014   Stade Josy Barthel, Luxembourg: Luxembourg – Ukraine   0-3 (0-1)
Luxembourg: Jonathan Joubert, Tom Schnell, Mathias Jänisch, Maxime Chanot, Mario Mutsch (C), Christopher Martins Pereira (YC11) (53' Daniël Alves Da Mota), Laurent Jans, Dwayn Holter, Lars Christian Krogh Gerson, David Turpel (76' Maurice Deville), Stefano Bensi (63' Aurélien Joachim). (Coach: Luc Holtz (LUX)).
Ukraine: Andriy Pyatov, Vyacheslav Shevchuk, Yaroslav Rakitskiy, Yevhen Khacheridi (YC34), Artem Fedetskiy, Anatoliy Tymoshchuk (C), Sergei Sydorchuk (YC14), Denys Oliynyk (85' Kyrylo Kovalchuk), Yevhen Konoplyanka (76' Mykola Morozyuk), Roman Zozulya (72' Pylyp Budkovsky), Andriy Yarmolenko. (Coach: Mikhail Ivanovich Fomenko (UKR)).
Goals: Ukraine: 0-1 Andriy Yarmolenko (33'), 0-2 Andriy Yarmolenko (53'), 0-3 Andriy Yarmolenko (56').
Referee: Kristinn Jakobsson (ISL)   Attendance: 4.379

15-11-2014   Philip II Arena, Skopje: Macedonia – Slovakia   0-2 (0-2)
Macedonia: Tome Pacovski (C), Vance Sikov, Stefan Ristovski, Daniel Mojsov, Ezgjan Alioski, Muhamed Demiri (74' David Badunski), Arijan Ademi, Aco Stojkov (46' Jovan Kostovski (YC90+1)), Besart Abdurahimi, KrsteVelkoski (70' Mirko Ivanovski), Aleksandar Trajkovski. (Coach: Bosko Djurovski (MCD)).
Slovakia: Matús Kozácik, Martin Skrtel (C) (YC73), Peter Pekarík (46' Dusan Svento), Tomás Hubocan, Ján Durica, Viktor Pecovsky, Juraj Kucka (55' Filip Kiss), Marek Hamsík, Vladimír Weiss (78' Michal Duris), Adam Nemec, Miroslav Stoch. (Coach: Ján Kozák (SVK)).
Goals: Slovakia: 0-1 Juraj Kucka (25'), 0-2 Adam Nemec (38').
Referee: Pedro Proença Oliveira Alves Garcia (POR)   Attendance: 11.322

15-11-2014   Nuevo Colombino, Huelva: Spain – Belarus   3-0 (2-0)
Spain: IKER CASILLAS Fernández (C), SERGIO RAMOS García, Gerard PIQUÉ i
Bernabéu, Jordi ALBA Ramos, Juan Francisco Torres Belén "JUANFRAN", Santiago
"SANTI" CAZORLA González (69' JOSÉ María CALLEJÓN Bueno), Jorge Resurrección
Merodio "KOKE", Francisco Román Alarcón Suárez "ISCO" (80' Álvaro Borja MORATA
Martín), Sergio BUSQUETS Burgos (YC26) (46' BRUNO Soriano Llido), Francisco "PACO"
ALCÁCER García, PEDRO Eliezer Rodríguez Ledesma. (Coach: VICENTE DEL BOSQUE
González (ESP)).
Belarus: Yuri Zhevnov, Aleksei Yanushkevich, Sergei Politevich, Aleksandr Martynovich (31'
Maksim Bordachev YC90+3)), Sergei Balanovich (YC45+2), Pavel Nekhaychik, Sergei
Matveichyk, Sergei Krivets (80' Sergei Kislyak), Timofei Kalachev (C) (YC45+2), Stanislav
Dragun, Sergei Kornilenko (67' Nikolai Signevich). (Coach: Andrey Vikentyevich
Zygmantovich (BLS)).
Goals: Spain: 1-0 Francisco Román Alarcón Suárez "ISCO" (18'), 2-0 Sergio BUSQUETS
Burgos (19'), 3-0 PEDRO Eliezer Rodríguez Ledesma (55').
Referee: Kenn Pii Hansen (DEN)   Attendance: 19.249

27-03-2015   Philip II Arena, Skopje: Macedonia – Belarus   1-2 (1-1)
Macedonia: Tome Pacovski (C), Vance Sikov (YC20), Stefan Ristovski, Bojan Markoski
(YC53), Daniel Georgievski (YC60), Artim Polozhani (31' Enis Bardhi), Ferhan Hasani, Krste
Velkoski (63' Blagoja (Blaze) Todorovski (YC66)), Aleksandar Trajkovski (YC68), Agim
Ibraimi, Besart Abdurahimi (75' Dejan Blazevski). (Coach: Bosko Djurovski (MCD)).
Belarus: Yuri Zhevnov, Igor Shitov (YC89), Aleksandr Martynovich (C) (YC10), Egor
Filipenko, Maksim Bordachev (YC90), Igor Stasevich (YC90+1) (90'+3' Pavel Nekhaychik),
Ivan Maevski (80' Anton Putsila, Sergei Kislyak, Timofei Kalachev (YC36), Aleksandr Hleb
(87' Stanislav Dragun), Sergei Kornilenko. (Coach: Aleksandr Khatskevich (BLS)).
Goals: Macedonia: 1-0 Aleksandar Trajkovski (9').
Belarus: 1-1 Timofei Kalachev (44'), 1-2 Sergei Kornilenko (82').
Referee: Anthony Taylor (ENG)   Attendance: 3.447

27-03-2015   Stadión pod Dubnom, Zilina: Slovakia – Luxembourg   3-0 (3-0)
Slovakia: Matús Kozácik, Martin Skrtel (C) (YC86), Peter Pekarík (YC30), Tomás Hubocan,
Ján Durica, Vladimír Weiss (71' Róbert Mak), Viktor Pecovsky, Juraj Kucka (59' Patrik
Hrosovsky), Marek Hamsík, Miroslav Stoch (80' Stanislav Sesták), Adam Nemec. (Coach: Ján
Kozák (SVK)).
Luxembourg: Jonathan Joubert, Tom Schnell, Chris Philipps, Maxime Chanot, Mario Mutsch
(C) (YC62), Laurent Jans, Dwayn Holter (YC47) (51' Daniël Alves Da Mota), Lars Christian
Krogh Gerson, Aurélien Joachim, Maurice Deville (YC36) (64' Ben Payal), Stefano Bensi (78'
Tom Laterza). (Coach: Luc Holtz (LUX)).
Goals: Slovakia: 1-0 Adam Nemec (10'), 2-0 Vladimír Weiss (21'), 3-0 Peter Pekarík (40').
Referee: Stéphan Studer (SUI)   Attendance: 9.524

27-03-2015   Ramón Sánchez-Pizjuán, Seville: Spain – Ukraine   1-0 (1-0)
Spain: IKER CASILLAS Fernández (C), Jordi ALBA Ramos (78' Juan BERNAT Velasco),
SERGIO RAMOS García (YC50), Gerard PIQUÉ i Bernabéu, Juan Francisco Torres Belén
"JUANFRAN", Francisco Román Alarcón Suárez "ISCO", Andrés INIESTA Luján (74'
Santiago "SANTI" CAZORLA González), DAVID Jiménez SILVA, Sergio BUSQUETS
Burgos, Jorge Resurrección Merodio "KOKE", Álvaro Borja MORATA Martín (65' PEDRO
Eliezer Rodríguez Ledesma). (Coach: VICENTE DEL BOSQUE González (ESP)).
Ukraine: Andriy Pyatov, Olexandr Kucher (YC72), Yevhen Khacheridi, Artem Fedetskiy
(YC16), Vyacheslav Shevchuk, Yevhen Konoplyanka, Anatoliy Tymoshchuk (C), Taras
Stepanenko (76' Denys Harmash), Ruslan Rotan, Roman Zozulya (32' Artem Kravets (YC54),
90'+1' Pylyp Budkovsky), Andriy Yarmolenko. (Coach: Mikhail Ivanovich Fomenko (UKR)).
Goal: Spain: 1-0 Álvaro Borja MORATA Martín (28').
Referee: Cüneyt Çakir (TUR)   Attendance: 33.775

14-06-2015   Arena Lviv, Lviv: Ukraine – Luxembourg   3-0 (0-0)
Ukraine: Andriy Pyatov, Vyacheslav Shevchuk, Yaroslav Rakitskiy (77' Olexandr Kucher),
Yevhen Khacheridi, Taras Stepanenko, Sergei Sydorchuk, Ruslan Rotan (C) (46' Denys
Harmash), Mykola Morozyuk, Yevhen Konoplyanka, Andriy Yarmolenko, Artem Kravets (69'
Yevhen Seleznyov). (Coach: Mikhail Ivanovich Fomenko (UKR)).
Luxembourg: Jonathan Joubert, Tom Schnell, Kevin Malget, Maxime Chanot, Ben Payal
(YC84), Mario Mutsch (C) (YC47), Laurent Jans, Dwayn Holter (77' Chris Philipps), Lars
Christian Krogh Gerson, Daniël Alves Da Mota (YC17) (71' Maurice Deville), David Turpel
(52' Stefano Bensi (YC62)). (Coach: Luc Holtz (LUX)).
Goals: Ukraine: 1-0 Artem Kravets (49'), 2-0 Denys Harmash (57'), 3-0 Yevhen Konoplyanka
(86').
Referee: Arnold Hunter (NIR)   Attendance: 21.635

14-06-2015   Borisov Arena, Barysaw: Belarus – Spain   0-1 (0-1)
Belarus: Andrei Gorbunov, Igor Shitov, Aleksandr Martynovich (C), Egor Filipenko, Maksim
Bordachev (YC7), Maksim Volodko (81' Igor Stasevich), Pavel Nekhaychik (YC21), Ivan
Maevski, Sergei Kislyak (78' Stanislav Dragun), Aleksandr Hleb (89' Anton Putsila), Sergei
Kornilenko. (Coach: Aleksandr Khatskevich (BLS)).
Spain: IKER CASILLAS Fernández (C), SERGIO RAMOS García, Gerard PIQUÉ i
Bernabéu, Jordi ALBA Ramos, Juan Francisco Torres Belén "JUANFRAN", Santiago
"SANTI" CAZORLA González, DAVID Jiménez SILVA (YC85) (85' Juan BERNAT
Velasco), Francesc "CESC" FÀBREGAS Soler (75' Víctor Machín Pérez "VITOLO"), Sergio
BUSQUETS Burgos, Álvaro Borja MORATA Martín (YC54) (65'), PEDRO Eliezer
Rodríguez Ledesma (YC59) (65' Francisco Román Alarcón Suárez "ISCO"). (Coach:
VICENTE DEL BOSQUE González (ESP)).
Goal: Spain: 0-1 DAVID Jiménez SILVA (45').
Referee: Robert Schörgenhofer (AUT)   Attendance: 13.121

306

14-06-2015   Stadión pod Dubnom, Zilina: Slovakia – Macedonia   2-1 (2-0)
Slovakia: Matús Kozácik, Martin Skrtel (C) (YC28), Kornel Saláta, Peter Pekarík, Tomás
Hubocan, Vladimír Weiss (YC86), Viktor Pecovsky, Róbert Mak, Juraj Kucka (YC26) (73'
Patrik Hrosovsky), Marek Hamsík (80' Ondrej Duda), Adam Nemec (84' Filip Holosko).
(Coach: Ján Kozák (SVK)).
Macedonia: Tome Pacovski (C), Leonard Zhuta, Aleksandar Todorovski, Daniel Mojsov,
Vladimir Dimitrovski, Dusko Trajcevski, Ferhan Hasani (YC23,YC84), Arijan Ademi,
Aleksandar Trajkovski (56' Mirko Ivanovski), Muarem Muarem (82' Krste Velkoski), Agim
Ibraimi (89' Besart Abdurahimi). (Coach: Ljubinko Drulovic (SRB)).
Goals: Slovakia: 1-0 Kornel Saláta (8'), 2-0 Marek Hamsík (38').
Macedonia: 2-1 Arijan Ademi (69').
Referee: Kenn Pii Hansen (DEN)   Attendance: 10.765

05-09-2015   Stade Josy Barthel, Luxembourg: Luxembourg – Macedonia   1-0 (0-0)
Luxembourg: Jonathan Joubert, Chris Philipps, Ricardo Antonio Delgado, Maxime Chanot,
Ben Payal, Christopher Martins Pereira (YC43) (72' Sébastien Thill), Laurent Jans, Lars
Christian Krogh Gerson, Daniël Alves Da Mota, Aurélien Joachim (C), Maurice Deville (64'
Stefano Bensi). (Coach: Luc Holtz (LUX)).
Macedonia: Tome Pacovski (C), Leonard Zhuta (YC31), Vance Sikov, Stefan Ristovski
(YC40), Milovan Petrovic, Daniel Mojsov (37' Kire Ristevski (YC90+2)), Nikola Gligorov,
Aleksandar Trajkovski (74' Baze Ilijoski), Mirko Ivanovski, Agim Ibraimi (80' Stefan
Askovski), Besart Abdurahimi (YC55). (Coach: Ljubinko Drulovic (SRB)).
Goal: Luxembourg: 1-0 Sébastien Thill (90'+2').
Referee: Simon Lee Evans (WAL)   Attendance: 1.657
(Besart Abdurahimi missed a penalty in the 85th minute)

05-09-2015   Arena Lviv, Lviv: Ukraine – Belarus   3-1 (3-0)
Ukraine: Andriy Pyatov, Vyacheslav Shevchuk, Yaroslav Rakitskiy, Yevhen Khacheridi
(YC61), Artem Fedetskiy, Taras Stepanenko, Ruslan Rotan (C) (YC64) (75' Serhiy Rybalka),
Yevhen Konoplyanka, Denys Harmash (YC14,YC90+2), Andriy Yarmolenko (69' Oleh
Gusev), Artem Kravets (85' Olexandr Gladkiy). (Coach: Mikhail Ivanovich Fomenko (UKR)).
Belarus: Andrei Gorbunov, Igor Shitov, Aleksandr Martynovich (C) (YC79), Egor Filipenko,
Maksim Volodko, Igor Stasevich, Mikhail Sivakov (YC40) (46' Mikhail Gordeychuk), Ivan
Maevski, Timofei Kalachev (72' Nikolai Signevich), Aleksandr Hleb (86' Renan Bressan),
Sergei Kornilenko. (Coach: Aleksandr Khatskevich (BLS)).
Goals: Ukraine: 1-0 Artem Kravets (7'), 2-0 Andriy Yarmolenko (30'), 3-0 Yevhen
Konoplyanka (40' penalty).
Belarus: 3-1 Sergei Kornilenko (62' penalty).
Referee: Liran Liany (ISR)   Attendance: 32.648

307

05-09-2015   Carlos Tartiere, Oviedo: Spain – Slovakia   2-0 (2-0)
Spain: IKER CASILLAS Fernández (C), SERGIO RAMOS García, Gerard PIQUÉ i
Bernabéu, Jordi ALBA Ramos, Juan Francisco Torres Belén "JUANFRAN", Andrés INIESTA
Luján (85' Jorge Resurrección Merodio "KOKE"), DAVID Jiménez SILVA, Francesc "CESC"
FÀBREGAS Soler (67' Santiago "SANTI" CAZORLA González), Sergio BUSQUETS
Burgos, Diego da Silva COSTA (75' Francisco "PACO" ALCÁCER García), PEDRO Eliezer
Rodríguez Ledesma. (Coach: VICENTE DEL BOSQUE González (ESP)).
Slovakia: Matús Kozácik (YC30), Lukás Tesák (YC83), Kornel Saláta, Peter Pekarík, Tomás
Hubocan, Norbert Gyömbér, Dusan Svento, Róbert Mak (46' Michal Duris), Patrik Hrosovsky
(73' Erik Sabo), Marek Hamsík (C) (61' Ondrej Duda), Ján Gregus. (Coach: Ján Kozák
(SVK)).
Goals: Spain: 1-0 Jordi ALBA Ramos (5'), 2-0 Andrés INIESTA Luján (30' penalty).
Referee: Damir Skomina (SLO)   Attendance: 19.874

08-09-2015   Borisov Arena, Barysaw: Belarus – Luxembourg   2-0 (1-0)
Belarus: Yuri Zhevnov, Igor Shitov, Egor Filipenko, Maksim Bordachev, Mikhail Sivakov,
Renan Bressan, Pavel Nekhaychik, Aleksandr Hleb (58' Sergei Kislyak), Mikhail Gordeychuk
(75' Timofei Kalachev), Stanislav Dragun, Sergei Kornilenko (C) (84' Nikolai Signevich).
(Coach: Aleksandr Khatskevich (BLS)).
Luxembourg: Jonathan Joubert, Tom Schnell, Chris Philipps (YC77), Mathias Jänisch,
Maxime Chanot, Ben Payal (46' Daniël Alves Da Mota), Mario Mutsch (C), Laurent Jans, Lars
Christian Krogh Gerson, Aurélien Joachim (46' Stefano Bensi), Maurice Deville (69' David
Turpel). (Coach: Luc Holtz (LUX)).
Goals: Belarus: 1-0 Mikhail Gordeychuk (34'), 2-0 Mikhail Gordeychuk (62').
Referee: Slavko Vincic (SLO)   Attendance: 3.482

08-09-2015   Philip II Arena, Skopje: Macedonia – Spain   0-1 (0-1)
Macedonia: Tome Pacovski (C), Leonard Zhuta, Vance Sikov, Kire Ristevski, Milovan
Petrovic (YC33), Vladica Brdarovski, Stefan Askovski (76' Enis Bardhi), Ferhan Hasani,
Nikola Gligorov, Marjan Radeski (84' Agim Ibraimi), Mirko Ivanovski (68' Aleksandar
Trajkovski). (Coach: Ljubinko Drulovic (SRB)).
Spain: David DE GEA Quintana, SERGIO RAMOS García (C), Gerard PIQUÉ i Bernabéu,
Juan BERNAT Velasco, Daniel "DANI" CARVAJAL Ramos, Santiago "SANTI" CAZORLA
González (68' Jorge Resurrección Merodio "KOKE"), JUAN Manuel MATA García,
Francisco Román Alarcón Suárez "ISCO" (78' Andrés INIESTA Luján), DAVID Jiménez
SILVA, Sergio BUSQUETS Burgos (YC47), Diego da Silva COSTA (YC30) (61' Francisco
"PACO" ALCÁCER García). (Coach: VICENTE DEL BOSQUE González (ESP)).
Goal: Spain: 0-1 Tome Pacovski (8' own goal).
Referee: Paolo Tagliavento (ITA)   Attendance: 28.843

08-09-2015   Stadión pod Dubnom, Zilina: Slovakia – Ukraine   0-0
Slovakia: Matús Kozácik, Martin Skrtel (C), Peter Pekarík (51' Kornel Saláta), Tomás
Hubocan, Norbert Gyömbér (YC47), Viktor Pecovsky, Róbert Mak (84' Miroslav Stoch), Juraj
Kucka, Marek Hamsík (YC11), Róbert Vittek (66' Martin Jakubko), Michal Duris. (Coach: Ján
Kozák (SVK)).
Ukraine: Andriy Pyatov, Vyacheslav Shevchuk, Yaroslav Rakitskiy, Yevhen Khacheridi,
Artem Fedetskiy, Taras Stepanenko (YC90+2), Serhiy Rybalka (YC21), Ruslan Rotan (C),
Yevhen Konoplyanka (YC79), Andriy Yarmolenko, Artem Kravets (90'+1' Olexandr
Gladkiy). (Coach: Mikhail Ivanovich Fomenko (UKR)).
Referee: Martin Atkinson (ENG)   Attendance: 10.648

09-10-2015   Philip II Arena, Skopje: Macedonia – Ukraine   0-2 (0-0)
Macedonia: Tome Pacovski (C), Leonard Zhuta (YC58), Vance Sikov, Kire Ristevski, Milovan
Petrovic, Vladica Brdarovski (YC45+1), Stefan Askovski (78' Ilija Nestorovski), Ferhan
Hasani (22' Besart Abdurahimi), Armend Alimi, Baze Ilijoski (64' Mirko Ivanovski), Agim
Ibraimi. (Coach: Ljubinko Drulovic (SRB)).
Ukraine: Andriy Pyatov, Vyacheslav Shevchuk, Yaroslav Rakitskiy, Yevhen Khacheridi
(YC9), Artem Fedetskiy, Sergei Sydorchuk (YC37), Serhiy Rybalka, Ruslan Rotan (C) (90'
Ruslan Malinovskiy), Yevhen Konoplyanka, Andriy Yarmolenko (86' Olexandr Karavaev),
Yevhen Seleznyov (74' Artem Kravets). (Coach: Mikhail Ivanovich Fomenko (UKR)).
Goals: Ukraine: 0-1 Yevhen Seleznyov (59' penalty), 0-2 Artem Kravets (87').
Referee: Ovidiu Alin Hategan (ROM)   Attendance: 4.821

09-10-2015   Stadión pod Dubnom, Zilina: Slovakia – Belarus   0-1 (0-1)
Slovakia: Matús Kozácik, Martin Skrtel (C) (YC11), Kornel Saláta, Tomás Hubocan, Dusan
Svento, Vladimír Weiss (YC36) (71' Miroslav Stoch), Viktor Pecovsky (60' Adam Nemec),
Róbert Mak (79' Ondrej Duda), Juraj Kucka, Marek Hamsík, Michal Duris. (Coach: Ján Kozák
(SVK)).
Belarus: Andrei Gorbunov, Denis Polyakov (YC90+4), Aleksandr Martynovich (C)
(YC57,YC65), Maksim Bordachev (40' Maksim Volodko), Igor Stasevich (YC49), Mikhail
Sivakov, Renan Bressan, Pavel Nekhaychik (69' Sergei Politevich), Mikhail Gordeychuk
(YC83), Stanislav Dragun, Nikolai Signevich (72' Sergei Kislyak). (Coach: Aleksandr
Khatskevich (BLS)).
Goal: Belarus: 0-1 Stanislav Dragun (34').
Referee: Hüseyin Göçek (TUR)   Attendance: 9.859

09-10-2015   Las Gaunas, Logroño: Spain – Luxembourg   4-0 (1-0)
Spain: IKER CASILLAS Fernández (C), Jordi ALBA Ramos, Marc BARTRA Aregall, Gerard
PIQUÉ i Bernabéu, Juan Francisco Torres Belén "JUANFRAN", DAVID Jiménez SILVA (11'
JUAN Manuel MATA García), Francesc "CESC" FÀBREGAS Soler, Sergio BUSQUETS
Burgos, Santiago "SANTI" CAZORLA González, Álvaro Borja MORATA Martín (33'
Francisco "PACO" ALCÁCER García), PEDRO Eliezer Rodríguez Ledesma (YC55) (77'
Manuel Agudo Durán "NOLITO"). (Coach: VICENTE DEL BOSQUE González (ESP)).
Luxembourg: Jonathan Joubert, Kevin Malget (YC54), Ricardo Antonio Delgado, Maxime
Chanot, Christopher Martins Pereira (79' Daniël Alves Da Mota (YC88)), Laurent Jans, Lars
Christian Krogh Gerson, Ben Payal, Mario Mutsch (C), Aurélien Joachim (89' David Turpel),
Stefano Bensi (YC20) (64' Maurice Deville). (Coach: Luc Holtz (LUX)).
Goals: Spain: 1-0 Santiago "SANTI" CAZORLA González (42'), 2-0 Francisco "PACO"
ALCÁCER García (67'), 3-0 Francisco "PACO" ALCÁCER García (80'), 4-0 Santiago
"SANTI" CAZORLA González (85').
Referee: Sébastien Delferière (BEL)   Attendance: 14.472

12-10-2015   Borisov Arena, Barysaw: Belarus – Macedonia   0-0
Belarus: Andrei Gorbunov, Denis Polyakov, Sergei Politevich, Maksim Volodko, Igor
Stasevich, Mikhail Sivakov, Renan Bressan, Pavel Nekhaychik (61' Sergei Kislyak (YC75)),
Mikhail Gordeychuk, Stanislav Dragun (C) (YC63) (73' Anton Putsila), Nikolai Signevich.
(Coach: Aleksandr Khatskevich (BLS)).
Macedonia: David Mitov Nilsson, Leonard Zhuta (YC49), Vance Sikov (C), Stefan Ristovski,
Milovan Petrovic, Daniel Mojsov, Vladica Brdarovski (73' Besart Abdurahimi), Ostoja
Stjepanovic (84' Armend Alimi), Ivan Trickovski, Aleksandar Trajkovski, Agim Ibraimi (86'
Ilija Nestorovski). (Coach: Ljubinko Drulovic (SRB)).
Referee: Christian Dingert (GER)   Attendance: 1.545

12-10-2015   Stade Josy Barthel, Luxembourg: Luxembourg – Slovakia   2-4 (0-3)
Luxembourg: Jonathan Joubert, Chris Philipps (YC20), Ricardo Antonio Delgado (81' David Turpel), Maxime Chanot, Ben Payal (YC49) (57' Kevin Malget), Mario Mutsch (C) (YC9), Christopher Martins Pereira, Laurent Jans (YC63), Lars Christian Krogh Gerson, Aurélien Joachim, Stefano Bensi (66' Sébastien Thill). (Coach: Luc Holtz (LUX)).
Slovakia: Matús Kozácik, Martin Skrtel (C) (YC90+4), Tomás Hubocan, Norbert Gyömbér, Dusan Svento, Vladimír Weiss (72' Stanislav Sesták (YC84)), Viktor Pecovsky, Róbert Mak (87' Erik Sabo), Juraj Kucka (YC65), Marek Hamsík, Adam Nemec (79' Martin Jakubko). (Coach: Ján Kozák (SVK)).
Goals: Luxembourg: 1-3 Mario Mutsch (61'), 2-3 Lars Christian Krogh Gerson (65' penalty). Slovakia: 0-1 Marek Hamsík (24'), 0-2 Adam Nemec (29'), 0-3 Róbert Mak (30'), 2-4 Marek Hamsík (90'+1').
Referee: Oliver Drachta (AUT)   Attendance: 2.512

12-10-2015   Olympic Stadium, Kiev: Ukraine – Spain   0-1 (0-1)
Ukraine: Andriy Pyatov, Vyacheslav Shevchuk, Yaroslav Rakitskiy, Olexandr Kucher (YC23), Artem Fedetskiy (YC77), Taras Stepanenko (YC61), Ruslan Rotan (C) (87' Olexandr Zinchenko), Yevhen Konoplyanka, Denys Harmash (58' Serhiy Rybalka), Andriy Yarmolenko, Artem Kravets (87' Yevhen Seleznyov). (Coach: Mikhail Ivanovich Fomenko (UKR)).
Spain: David DE GEA Quintana (YC88), Mikel SAN JOSÉ Domínguez (YC53), José Ignacio Fernández Iglesias "NACHO", MARIO Gaspar Pérez Martínez, Xabier ETXEITA Gorritxategi, César AZPILICUETA Tanco, THIAGO Alcântara do Nascimento (YC36), Francisco Román Alarcón Suárez "ISCO", Francesc "CESC" FÀBREGAS Soler (C) (64' JUAN Manuel MATA García), Francisco "PACO" ALCÁCER García (85' Sergio BUSQUETS Burgos), Manuel Agudo Durán "NOLITO" (75' Jordi ALBA Ramos). (Coach: VICENTE DEL BOSQUE González (ESP)).
Goal: Spain: 0-1 MARIO Gaspar Pérez Martínez (22').
Referee: Milorad Mazic (SRB)   Attendance: 61.248
(Francesc "CESC" FÀBREGAS Soler missed a penalty in the 25th minute)

GROUP   D

07-09-2014	Tbilisis	Georgia – Republic of Ireland	1-2 (1-1)
07-09-2014	Dortmund	Germany – Scotland	2-1 (1-0)
07-09-2014	Faro/Loulé (POR)	Gibraltar – Poland	0-7 (0-1)
11-10-2014	Dublin	Republic of Ireland – Gibraltar	7-0 (3-0)
11-10-2014	Glasgow	Scotland – Georgia	1-0 (1-0)
11-10-2014	Warsaw	Poland – Germany	2-0 (0-0)
14-10-2014	Gelsenkirchen	Germany – Republic of Ireland	1-1 (0-0)
14-10-2014	Faro/Loulé (POR)	Gibraltar – Georgia	0-3 (0-2)
14-10-2014	Warsaw	Poland – Scotland	2-2 (1-1)
14-11-2014	Tbilisi	Georgia – Poland	0-4 (0-0)
14-11-2014	Nuremberg	Germany – Gibraltar	4-0 (3-0)
14-11-2014	Glasgow	Scotland – Republic of Ireland	1-0 (1-0)
29-03-2015	Tbilisi	Georgia – Germany	0-2 (0-2)
29-03-2015	Glasgow	Scotland – Gibraltar	6-1 (4-1)
29-03-2015	Dublin	Republic of Ireland – Poland	1-1 (0-1)

13-06-2015	Warsaw	Poland – Georgia	4-0 (0-0)
13-06-2015	Dublin	Republic of Ireland – Scotland	1-1 (1-0)
13-06-2015	Faro/Loulé (POR)	Gibraltar – Germany	0-7 (0-1)
04-09-2015	Tbilisi	Georgia – Scotland	1-0 (1-0)
04-09-2015	Frankfurt am Main	Germany – Poland	3-1 (2-1)
04-09-2015	Faro/Loulé (POR)	Gibraltar – Republic of Ireland	0-4 (0-1)
07-09-2015	Warsaw	Poland – Gibraltar	8-1 (4-0)
07-09-2015	Dublin	Republic of Ireland – Georgia	1-0 (0-0)
07-09-2015	Glasgow	Scotland – Germany	2-3 (2-2)
08-10-2015	Tbilisi	Georgia – Gibraltar	4-0 (3-0)
08-10-2015	Dublin	Republic of Ireland – Germany	1-0 (0-0)
08-10-2015	Glasgow	Scotland – Poland	2-2 (1-1)
11-10-2015	Leipzig	Germany – Georgia	2-1 (0-0)
11-10-2015	Faro/Loulé (POR)	Gibraltar – Scotland	0-6 (0-2)
11-10-2015	Warsaw	Poland – Republic of Ireland	2-1 (2-1)

FINAL STANDING

Pos	Team	Pld	W	D	L	GF	GA	GD	Pts
1	Germany	10	7	1	2	24	9	+15	22
2	Poland	10	6	3	1	33	10	+23	21
3	Republic of Ireland	10	5	3	2	19	7	+12	18
4	Scotland	10	4	3	3	22	12	+10	15
5	Georgia	10	3	0	7	10	16	-6	9
6	Gibraltar	10	0	0	10	2	56	-54	0

Germany and Poland qualified for the Final Tournament in France.

Republic of Ireland qualified for the play-offs

07-09-2014   Boris Paichadze Dinamo Arena, Tbilisi:
        Georgia – Republic of Ireland   1-2 (1-1)
Georgia: Giorgi Loria (46' Roin Kvaskhvadze), Ucha Lobzhanidze, Dato Kvirkvelia (YC36), Solomon Kverkvelia, Akaki Khubutia (YC48), Guram Kashia, Jaba Kankava (C), Murtaz Daushvili (YC83), Jano Ananidze (63' David Targamadze), Tornike Okriashvili (88' Levan Mchedlidze), Nikoloz Gelashvili. (Coach: Temur Ketsbaia (GEO)).
Republic of Ireland: David Forde, Marc Wilson, Stephen Ward, John O'Shea, Séamus Coleman, Glenn Whelan, Stephen Quinn (76' Robert (Robbie) Brady), Aiden McGeady, James McCarthy (90'+1' David Meyler), Jonathan (Jon) Walters (YC36), Robbie Keane (C) (76' Shane Long). (Coach: Martin Hugh Michael O'Neill (NIR)).
Goals: Georgia: 1-1 Tornike Okriashvili (38').
Republic of Ireland: 0-1 Aiden McGeady (24'), 1-2 Aiden McGeady (90').
Referee: Kevin Bernie Raymond Blom (HOL)   Attendance: 22.000

07-09-2014   Signal Iduna Park, Dortmund: Germany – Scotland   2-1 (1-0)
Germany: Manuel Neuer (C), Benedikt Höwedes, Erik Durm (YC72), Jérôme Boateng,
Sebastian Rudy, Marco Reus (90'+2' Matthias Ginter), Toni Kroos, Christoph Kramer, Mario
Götze, André Schürrle (84' Lukas Podolski), Thomas Müller (YC90+5). (Coach: Joachim Löw
(GER)).
Scotland: David Marshall, Alan Hutton, Grant Hanley (YC50), Steven Whittaker, Charles
(Charlie) Mulgrew (YC90+1,YC90+4), Russell Martin, Darren Fletcher (C) (58' James
McArthur), Barry Bannan (58' Steven Fletcher), Ikechi Anya, Steven Naismith (82' Shaun
Maloney), James Morrison (YC76). (Coach: Gordon David Strachan (SCO)).
Goals: Germany: 1-0 Thomas Müller (18'), 2-1 Thomas Müller (70').
Scotland: 1-1 Ikechi Anya (66').
Referee: Svein Oddvar Moen (NOR)   Attendance: 60.209

07-09-2014   Estádio Algarve, Faro/Loulé (POR): Gibraltar – Poland   0-7 (0-1)
Gibraltar: Jordan Perez, Scott Wiseman, Roy Chipolina (C), Joseph Chipolina, Ryan Casciaro,
David Artell (YC68) (88' Aaron Payas), Brian Perez, Liam Walker, Kyle Casciaro (63' Adam
Priestley), Rafael (Rafa) Bado Blanco (46' Jake Gosling), Lee Casciaro. (Coach: Allen Bula
(GIB)).
Poland: Wojciech Szczesny, Lukasz Szukala, Pawel Olkowski, Jakub Wawrzyniak, Grzegorz
Krychowiak, Kamil Glik (YC41), Maciej Rybus, Mateusz Klich (YC17) (71' Krzysztof
Maczynski), Arkadiusz Milik (71' Waldemar Sobota), Robert Lewandowski (C), Kamil
Grosicki (78' Filip Starzynski). (Coach: Adam Nawalka (POL)).
Goals: Poland: 0-1 Kamil Grosicki (11'), 0-2 Kamil Grosicki (48'), 0-3 Robert Lewandowski
(50'), 0-4 Robert Lewandowski (53'), 0-5 Lukasz Szukala (58'), 0-6 Robert Lewandowski
(86'), 0-7 Robert Lewandowski (90'+2').
Referee: Stefan Johnanesson (SWE)   Attendance: 1.620

11-10-2014   Aviva Stadium, Dublin: Republic of Ireland – Gibraltar   7-0 (3-0)
Republic of Ireland: David Forde, Marc Wilson, Stephen Ward (70' Robert (Robbie) Brady),
John O'Shea, David Meyler, Aiden McGeady, Wesley (Wes) Hoolahan (64' Kevin Doyle),
Jeffrey (Jeff) Hendrick, Darron Gibson, James McClean, Robbie Keane (C) (63' Daryl
Murphy). (Coach: Martin Hugh Michael O'Neill (NIR)).
Gibraltar: Jordan Perez (60' Jamie Robba), Scott Wiseman, Roy Chipolina (C) (57' Yogan
Santos), Joseph Chipolina, Ryan Casciaro, Liam Walker, Brian Perez, Aaron Payas, Jake
Gosling, Rafael (Rafa) Bado Blanco (46' Robert Guilling), Lee Casciaro. (Coach: Allen Bula
(GIB)).
Goals: Republic of Ireland: 1-0 Robbie Keane (6'), 2-0 Robbie Keane (14'), 3-0 Robbie Keane
(18' penalty), 4-0 James McClean (46'), 5-0 Jordan Perez (52' own goal), 6-0 James McClean
(53'), 7-0 Wesley (Wes) Hoolahan (56').
Referee: Leontios Trattou (CYP)   Attendance: 35.123

11-10-2014   Ibrox Stadium, Glasgow: Scotland – Georgia   1-0 (1-0)
Scotland: David Marshall, Andrew Robertson, Alan Hutton, Grant Hanley, Steven Naismith
(80' James McArthur), James Morrison (YC33), Russell Martin, Shaun Maloney (YC68), Scott
Brown (C), Ikechi Anya, Steven Fletcher (90' Chris Martin). (Coach: Gordon David Strachan
(SCO)).
Georgia: Giorgi Loria, Ucha Lobzhanidze, Dato Kvirkvelia (46' Tornike Okriashvili),
Solomon Kverkvelia, Akaki Khubutia, Gia Grigalava (YC49), Valeri (Vako) Qazaishvili (80'
Giorgi Chanturia), Giorgi Papava (70' Irakli Dzaria), Jaba Kankava (C), Murtaz Daushvili
(YC53), Nikoloz Gelashvili. (Coach: Temur Ketsbaia (GEO)).
Goal: Scotland: 1-0 Akaki Khubutia (28' own goal).
Referee: Miroslav Zelinka (CZE)   Attendance: 34.719

11-10-2014   Stadion Narodowy, Warsaw: Poland – Germany 2-0 (0-0)
Poland: Wojciech Szczesny, Lukasz Szukala (YC20), Jakub Wawrzyniak (84' Artur Jedrzejczyk), Grzegorz Krychowiak, Kamil Glik, Maciej Rybus, Lukasz Piszczek (YC90+3), Tomasz Jodlowiec, Arkadiusz Milik (77' Sebastian Mila), Robert Lewandowski (C) (YC56), Kamil Grosicki (71' Waldemar Sobota). (Coach: Adam Nawalka (POL)).
Germany: Manuel Neuer (C), Antonio Rüdiger (83' Max Kruse), Mats Hummels, Erik Durm, Jérôme Boateng (YC25), Toni Kroos, Christoph Kramer (71' Julian Draxler), Mario Götze, Karim Bellarabi (YC86), André Schürrle (77' Lukas Podolski), Thomas Müller. (Coach: Joachim Löw (GER)).
Goals: Poland: 1-0 Arkadiusz Milik (51'), 2-0 Sebastian Mila (88').
Referee: Pedro Proença Oliveira Alves Garcia (POR)   Attendance: 56.934

14-10-2014   Veltins-Arena, Gelsenkirchen: Germany – Republic of Ireland 1-1 (0-0)
Germany: Manuel Neuer (C), Antonio Rüdiger, Mats Hummels (YC85), Matthias Ginter (46' Lukas Podolski), Erik Durm, Jérôme Boateng, Toni Kroos, Mario Götze, Julian Draxler (70' Max Kruse), Karim Bellarabi (86' Sebastian Rudy), Thomas Müller. (Coach: Joachim Löw (GER)).
Republic of Ireland: David Forde, Marc Wilson (YC67), Stephen Ward, John O'Shea, Glenn Whelan (YC41) (53' Jeffrey (Jef) Hendrick), Stephen Quinn (76' Wesley (Wes) Hoolahan), David Meyler, Aiden McGeady, Jonathan (Jon) Walters, James McClean, Robbie Keane (C) (63' Darron Gibson). (Coach: Martin Hugh Michael O'Neill (NIR)).
Goals: Germany: 1-0 Toni Kroos (71').
Republic of Ireland: 1-1 John O'Shea (90'+4').
Referee: Damir Skomina (SLO)   Attendance: 51.204

14-10-2014   Estádio Algarve, Faro/Loulé (POR): Gibraltar – Georgia 0-3 (0-2)
Gibraltar: Jamie Robba, Scott Wiseman, Yogan Santos (76' Roy Chipolina), Juan Carlos (Jean) Garcia (YC18), Joseph Chipolina (C) (YC71), Ryan Casciaro (YC33), Liam Walker, Brian Perez, Robert Guilling (75' Jake Gosling), Kyle Casciaro (46' Adam Priestley), Lee Casciaro. (Coach: Allen Bula (GIB)).
Georgia: Giorgi Loria, Ucha Lobzhanidze, Solomon Kverkvelia, Akaki Khubutia, Gia Grigalava, Jaba Kankava (C), Irakli Dzaria (YC47), Jano Ananidze (80' Avtandil Ebralidze), Tornike Okriashvili, Nikoloz Gelashvili (67' Giorgi Papunashvili (YC87)), Giorgi Chanturia (76' Vladimer Dvalishvili). (Coach: Temur Ketsbaia (GEO)).
Goals: Georgia: 0-1 Nikoloz Gelashvili (9'), 0-2 Tornike Okriashvili (19'), 0-3 Jaba Kankava (69').
Referee: Harald Lechner (AUT)   Attendance: 281

14-10-2014   Stadion Narodowy, Warsaw: Poland – Scotland 2-2 (1-1)
Poland: Wojciech Szczesny, Lukasz Szukala, Grzegorz Krychowiak (YC60), Artur Jedrzejczyk, Kamil Glik, Waldemar Sobota (63' Sebastian Mila (YC83)), Lukasz Piszczek, Krzysztof Maczynski, Arkadiusz Milik, Robert Lewandowski (C), Kamil Grosicki (89' Michal Zyro). (Coach: Adam Nawalka (POL)).
Scotland: David Marshall, Steven Whittaker, Alan Hutton, Gordon Greer (YC85), Steven Naismith (71' Darren Fletcher), James Morrison, Russell Martin, Shaun Maloney, Scott Brown (C), Ikechi Anya, Steven Fletcher (71' Chris Martin). (Coach: Gordon David Strachan (SCO)).
Goals: Poland: 1-0 Krzysztof Maczynski (11'), 2-2 Arkadiusz Milik (76').
Scotland: 1-1 Shaun Maloney (18'), 1-2 Steven Naismith (57').
Referee: Alberto Undiano Mallenco (ESP)   Attendance: 55.197

14-11-2014   Boris Paichadze Dinamo Arena, Tbilisi: Georgia – Poland   0-4 (0-0)
Georgia: Giorgi Loria, Ucha Lobzhanidze (YC56), Solomon Kverkvelia, Akaki Khubutia, Guram Kashia, Gia Grigalava, Aleksandr Kobakhidze (88' Nika Dzalamidze), Jaba Kankava (C) (YC52), Murtaz Daushvili, Jano Ananidze (59' Tornike Okriashvili), Levan Mchedlidze (68' Giorgi Chanturia). (Coach: Temur Ketsbaia (GEO)).
Poland: Wojciech Szczesny, Lukasz Szukala, Grzegorz Krychowiak, Artur Jedrzejczyk, Kamil Glik (YC79), Sebastian Mila (86' Karol Linetty (YC90+1)), Lukasz Piszczek, Krzysztof Maczynski (66' Tomasz Jodlowiec (YC83)), Robert Lewandowski (C), Kamil Grosicki (69' Maciej Rybus), Arkadiusz Milik. (Coach: Adam Nawalka (POL)).
Goals: Poland: 0-1 Kamil Glik (51'), 0-2 Grzegorz Krychowiak (71'), 0-3 Sebastian Mila (73'), 0-4 Arkadiusz Milik (90'+2').
Referee: Paolo Tagliavento (ITA)   Attendance: 25.635

14-11-2014   Grundig-Stadion, Nuremberg: Germany – Gibraltar   4-0 (3-0)
Germany: Manuel Neuer (C), Erik Durm (72' Jonas Hector), Jérôme Boateng, Shkodran Mustafi, Karim Bellarabi, Toni Kroos (79' Lars Bender), Sami Khedira (60' Kevin Volland), Mario Götze, Lukas Podolski, Thomas Müller, Max Kruse. (Coach: Joachim Löw (GER)).
Gibraltar: Jamie Robba, Ryan Casciaro, David Artell, Scott Wiseman, Juan Carlos (Jean) Garcia, Roy Chipolina (C), Joseph Chipolina, Liam Walker, John Iain Stephen (Jack) Sergeant (58' Yogan Santos), Brian Perez (90'+1' Adam Priestley), Lee Casciaro (71' Kyle Casciaro). (Coach: Allen Bula (GIB)).
Goals: Germany: 1-0 Thomas Müller (12'), 2-0 Thomas Müller (29'), 3-0 Mario Götze (38'), 4-0 Yogan Santos (67' own goal).
Referee: Alexandru Dan Tudor (ROM)   Attendance: 43.520

14-11-2014   Celtic Park, Glasgow: Scotland – Republic of Ireland   1-0 (0-0)
Scotland: David Marshall, Steven Whittaker, Andrew Robertson (YC82), Charles (Charlie) Mulgrew, Grant Hanley (YC12), Steven Naismith, Russell Martin, Shaun Maloney, Scott Brown (C), Ikechi Anya (88' Darren Fletcher), Steven Fletcher (56' Chris Martin). (Coach: Gordon David Strachan (SCO)).
Republic of Ireland: David Forde, Stephen Ward, John O'Shea (C), Richard Keogh, Séamus Coleman (YC59), Aiden McGeady (YC15), Jeffrey (Jeff) Hendrick (YC30) (78' Robbie Keane), Darron Gibson (68' Stephen Quinn (YC90)), Jonathan (Jon) Walters, James McClean (YC78), Shane Long (68' Robert (Robbie) Brady). (Coach: Martin Hugh Michael O'Neill (NIR)).
Goal: Scotland: 1-0 Shaun Maloney (75').
Referee: Milorad Mazic (SRB)   Attendance: 59.239

29-03-2015   Boris Paichadze Dinamo Arena, Tbilisi: Georgia – Germany   0-2 (0-2)
Georgia: Giorgi Loria, Ucha Lobzhanidze, Solomon Kverkvelia, Guram Kashia, Aleksandr Amisulashvili (4' Lasha Dvali), Giorgi Navalovski, Kakha Makharadze (YC32) (63' Levan Kenia), Aleksandr Kobakhidze, Jaba Kankava (C) (YC74), Tornike Okriashvili (46' Giorgi Chanturia (YC82)), Levan Mchedlidze. (Coach: Kakhaber Dzhumberovich Tskhadadze (GEO)).
Germany: Manuel Neuer, Mats Hummels, Jonas Hector, Jérôme Boateng, Bastian Schweinsteiger (C) (YC74), Sebastian Rudy, Marco Reus, Mesut Özil, Toni Kroos, Mario Götze (87' Lukas Podolski), Thomas Müller (86' André Schürrle). (Coach: Joachim Löw (GER)).
Goals: Germany: 0-1 Marco Reus (39'), 0-2 Thomas Müller (44').
Referee: Clément Turpin (FRA)   Attendance: 54.549

29-03-2015   Hampden Park, Glasgow: Scotland – Gibraltar 6-1 (4-1)
Scotland: David Marshall, Andrew Robertson, Alan Hutton, Ikechi Anya (74' Barry Bannan),
Matthew (Matt) Ritchie (46' Gordon Greer), Steven Naismith (67' Jordan Rhodes), James
Morrison, Russell Martin, Shaun Maloney, Scott Brown (C), Steven Fletcher. (Coach: Gordon
David Strachan (SCO)).
Gibraltar: Jamie Robba, David Artell (53' Juan Carlos (Jean) Garcia), Scott Wiseman, Roy
Chipolina (C) (74' Jake Gosling), Joseph Chipolina, Ryan Casciaro, Liam Walker, Aaron
Payas, Anthony Bardon (82' Daniel Duarte), Adam Priestley, Lee Casciaro. (Coach: David
James (Dave) Wilson (SCO)).
Goals: Scotland: 1-0 Shaun Maloney (18' penalty), 2-1 Steven Fletcher (29'), 3-1 Shaun
Maloney (34' penalty), 4-1 Steven Naismith (39'), 5-1 Steven Fletcher (77'), 6-1 Steven
Fletcher (90').
Gibraltar: 1-1 Lee Casciaro (19').
Referee: Mattias Gestranius (FIN)   Attendance: 34.255

29-03-2015   Aviva Stadium, Dublin: Republic of Ireland – Poland 1-1 (0-1)
Republic of Ireland: Shay Given, Marc Wilson (YC70), John O'Shea (YC32), Séamus
Coleman (YC45), Robert (Robbie) Brady, Glenn Whelan (84' Shane Long), Aiden McGeady
(68' James McClean), James McCarthy (YC86), Wesley (Wes) Hoolahan (YC25), Jonathan
(Jon) Walters, Robbie Keane (C). (Coach: Martin Hugh Michael O'Neill (NIR)).
Poland: Lukasz Fabianski, Lukasz Szukala (YC60), Pawel Olkowski, Jakub Wawrzyniak,
Grzegorz Krychowiak, Kamil Glik (YC50), Maciej Rybus, Slawomir Peszko (YC86) (88'
Michal Kucharczyk), Tomasz Jodlowiec, Arkadiusz Milik (84' Sebastian Mila), Robert
Lewandowski (C). (Coach: Adam Nawalka (POL)).
Goals: Republic of Ireland: 1-1 Shane Long (90'+1').
Poland: 0-1 Slawomir Peszko (26').
Referee: Jonas Eriksson (SWE)   Attendance: 50.500

13-06-2015   Stadion Narodowy, Warsaw: Poland – Georgia 4-0 (0-0)
Poland: Lukasz Fabianski, Lukasz Szukala, Michal Pazdan (90' Marcin Komorowski),
Grzegorz Krychowiak, Maciej Rybus, Lukasz Piszczek, Slawomir Peszko (64' Jakub
Blaszczykowski), Krzysztof Maczynski, Arkadiusz Milik, Robert Lewandowski (C), Kamil
Grosicki (80' Tomasz Jodlowiec). (Coach: Adam Nawalka (POL)).
Georgia: Giorgi Loria, Ucha Lobzhanidze, Guram Kashia, Lasha Dvali, Aleksandr
Amisulashvili (C), Aleksandr Kobakhidze (76' Bachana Tskhadadze), Valeri Qazaishvili, Jano
Ananidze, Giorgi Navalovski, Tornike Okriashvili (46' Murtaz Daushvili), Mate Vatsadze (63'
Giorgi Chanturia). (Coach: Kakhaber Dzhumberovich Tskhadadze (GEO)).
Goals: Poland: 1-0 Arkadiusz Milik (62'), 2-0 Robert Lewandowski (89'), 3-0 Robert
Lewandowski (90'+2'), 4-0 Robert Lewandowski (90'+3').
Referee: Aliaksei Kulbakov (BLS)   Attendance: 56.512

315

13-06-2015   Aviva Stadium, Dublin: Republic of Ireland – Scotland   1-1 (1-0)
Republic of Ireland: Shay Given, Séamus Coleman, Marc Wilson, John O'Shea (C), Robert
(Robbie) Brady, James McCarthy (YC30), Wesley (Wes) Hoolahan (73' Robbie Keane),
Jeffrey (Jeff) Hendrick, Glenn Whelan (YC20) (68' James McClean (YC88)), Jonathan (Jon)
Walters, Daryl Murphy (80' Shane Long). (Coach: Martin Hugh Michael O'Neill (NIR)).
Scotland: David Marshall, Alan Hutton, Craig Forsyth, Charles (Charlie) Mulgrew, Shaun
Maloney, Scott Brown (C) (85' James McArthur), Matthew (Matt) Ritchie (46' Ikechi Anya),
Steven Naismith (YC88) (90'+2' Christophe Berra), James Morrison, Russell Martin, Steven
Fletcher. (Coach: Gordon David Strachan (SCO)).
Goals: Republic of Ireland: 1-0 Jonathan (Jon) Walters (38').
Scotland: 1-1 John O'Shea (47' own goal).
Referee: Nicola Rizzoli (ITA)   Attendance: 49.063

13-06-2015   Estádio Algarve, Faro/Loulé (POR): Gibraltar – Germany   0-7 (0-1)
Gibraltar: Jordan Perez, Juan Carlos (Jean) Garcia, Roy Chipolina (C), Joseph Chipolina
(YC54), Ryan Casciaro, Liam Walker, Aaron Payas (82' John Iain Stephen (Jack) Sergeant),
Jake Gosling, Kyle Casciaro (78' James (Jamie) Bosio), Adam Priestley (61' James Coombes),
Lee Casciaro (YC90+2). (Coach: David James (Dave) Wilson (SCO)).
Germany: Roman Weidenfeller, Jonas Hector, Jérôme Boateng, Bastian Schweinsteiger (C),
Patrick Herrmann (56' Lukas Podolski), Ilkay Gündogan (67' Sami Khedira), Sebastian Rudy,
Mesut Özil, Mario Götze (36' Max Kruse), Karim Bellarabi, André Schürrle. (Coach: Joachim
Löw (GER)).
Goals: Germany: 0-1 André Schürrle (28'), 0-2 Max Kruse (47'), 0-3 Ilkay Gündogan (51'),
0-4 Karim Bellarabi (57'), 0-5 André Schürrle (65'), 0-6 André Schürrle (71'), 0-7 Max Kruse
(81').
Referee: Clayton Pisani (MLT)   Attendance: 7.467
(Bastian Schweinsteiger missed a penalty in the 10th minute)

04-09-2015   Boris Paichadze Dinamo Arena, Tbilisi: Georgia – Scotland   1-0 (1-0)
Georgia: Nukri Revishvili, Ucha Lobzhanidze, Solomon Kverkvelia, Guram Kashia (YC10),
Aleksandr Amisulashvili, Valeri Qazaishvili, Giorgi Navalovski (YC78), Jaba Kankava (C),
Jano Ananidze (YC44) (82' Murtaz Daushvili), Tornike Okriashvili (71' Giorgi Merebashvili),
Levan Mchedlidze (90'+3' Mate Vatsadze). (Coach: Kakhaber Dzhumberovich Tskhadadze
(GEO)).
Scotland: David Marshall, Andrew Robertson (59' Grant Hanley), Charles (Charlie) Mulgrew,
Alan Hutton, Steven Naismith (59' James Forrest), James Morrison, Russell Martin, Shaun
Maloney, Scott Brown (C), Ikechi Anya (75' Leigh Griffiths), Steven Fletcher. (Coach:
Gordon David Strachan (SCO)).
Goal: Georgia: 1-0 Valeri Qazaishvili (38').
Referee: Ovidiu Alin Hategan (ROM)   Attendance: 23.000

04-09-2015   Commerzbank-Arena, Frankfurt am Main: Germany – Poland   3-1 (2-1)
Germany: Manuel Neuer, Mats Hummels, Jonas Hector, Jérôme Boateng, Bastian
Schweinsteiger (C) (YC79), Mesut Özil, Toni Kroos (YC61), Mario Götze (90'+1' Lukas
Podolski), Emre Can, Karim Bellarabi (53' Ilkay Gündogan), Thomas Müller. (Coach: Joachim
Löw (GER)).
Poland: Lukasz Fabianski, Lukasz Szukala, Grzegorz Krychowiak, Kamil Glik, Maciej Rybus
(YC8), Lukasz Piszczek (43' Pawel Olkowski), Krzysztof Maczynski (63' Jakub
Blaszczykowski), Tomasz Jodlowiec, Arkadiusz Milik, Robert Lewandowski (C), Kamil
Grosicki (YC67) (83' Slawomir Peszko). (Coach: Adam Nawalka (POL)).
Goals: Germany: 1-0 Thomas Müller (12'), 2-0 Mario Götze (19'), 3-1 Mario Götze (82').
Poland: 2-1 Robert Lewandowski (37').
Referee: Nicola Rizzoli (ITA)   Attendance: 48.500

04-09-2015   Estádio Algarve, Faro/Loulé (POR): Gibraltar – Republic of Ireland   0-4 (0-1)
Gibraltar: Jordan Perez, Juan Carlos (Jean) Garcia, Roy Chipolina (C), Joseph Chipolina, Erin
Barnett (YC48), Kyle Casciaro (YC9) (61' Jake Gosling), Anthony Bardon, Liam Walker,
John Iain Stephen (Jack) Sergeant (85' Robert Guilling), John-Paul Duarte (73' Michael
Yome), Lee Casciaro. (Coach: Jeffrey Reginald (Jeff) Wood (ENG)).
Republic of Ireland: Shay Given, John O'Shea, Ciaran Clark, Cyrus Christie, Robert (Robbie)
Brady, James McCarthy (70' Stephen Quinn), Wesley (Wes) Hoolahan (77' Aiden McGeady),
Jeffrey (Jeff) Hendrick, Glenn Whelan, Robbie Keane (C) (71' Shane Long), Jonathan (Jon)
Walters (YC42). (Coach: Martin Hugh Michael O'Neill (NIR)).
Goals: Republic of Ireland: 0-1 Cyrus Christie (26'), 0-2 Robbie Keane (49'), 0-3 Robbie
Keane (51' penalty), 0-4 Shane Long (79').
Referee: Marijo Strahonja (CRO)   Attendance: 5.393

07-09-2015   Stadion Narodowy, Warsaw: Poland – Gibraltar   8-1 (4-0)
Poland: Lukasz Fabianski, Lukasz Szukala, Pawel Olkowski (87' Sebastian Mila), Grzegorz
Krychowiak, Kamil Glik, Maciej Rybus, Krzysztof Maczynski, Jakub Blaszczykowski (62'
Bartosz Kapustka), Arkadiusz Milik, Robert Lewandowski (C) (66' Piotr Zielinski), Kamil
Grosicki. (Coach: Adam Nawalka (POL)).
Gibraltar: Jordan Perez, Juan Carlos (Jean) Garcia, Roy Chipolina (C), Joseph Chipolina, Erin
Barnett, Liam Walker, Jake Gosling, James Coombes (46' Kyle Casciaro), Anthony Bardon,
John-Paul Duarte (68' James (Jamie) Bosio), Lee Casciaro (79' Jeremy Lopez). (Coach:
Jeffrey Reginald (Jeff) Wood (ENG)).
Goals: Poland: 1-0 Kamil Grosicki (8'), 2-0 Kamil Grosicki (15'), 3-0 Robert Lewandowski
(18'), 4-0 Robert Lewandowski (29'), 5-0 Arkadiusz Milik (56'), 6-0 Jakub Blaszczykowski
(59' penalty), 7-0 Arkadiusz Milik (72'), 8-0 Bartosz Kapustka (73').
Gibraltar: 8-1 Jake Gosling (87').
Referee: Gediminas Mazeika (LIT)   Attendance: 27.763

07-09-2015   Aviva Stadium, Dublin: Republic of Ireland – Georgia   1-0 (0-0)
Republic of Ireland: Shay Given, John O'Shea, Séamus Coleman, Ciaran Clark, Robert
(Robbie) Brady, Glenn Whelan (YC74), James McCarthy, Wesley (Wes) Hoolahan (75' James
McClean (YC76)), Jeffrey (Jeff) Hendrick, Jonathan (Jon) Walters, Robbie Keane (C) (46'
Shane Long). (Coach: Martin Hugh Michael O'Neill (NIR)).
Georgia: Nukri Revishvili, Ucha Lobzhanidze, Solomon Kverkvelia, Zurab Khizanishvili (81'
Levan Kenia), Guram Kashia (76' Mate Tsintsadze), Aleksandr Amisulashvili, Giorgi
Navalovski, Valeri Qazaishvili (64' Giorgi Papunashvili), Jaba Kankava (C), Tornike
Okriashvili, Levan Mchedlidze. (Coach: Kakhaber Dzhumberovich Tskhadadze (GEO)).
Goal: Republic of Ireland: 1-0 Jonathan (Jon) Walters (69').
Referee: István Vad II (HUN)   Attendance: 27.200

07-09-2015   Hampden Park, Glasgow: Scotland – Germany   2-3 (2-2)
Scotland: David Marshall, Charles (Charlie) Mulgrew, Alan Hutton, Grant Hanley, James
Morrison (YC56), James McArthur, Russell Martin, Shaun Maloney (YC58) (60' Ikechi
Anya), James Forrest (81' Matthew (Matt) Ritchie), Scott Brown (C) (81' Chris Martin),
Steven Fletcher. (Coach: Gordon David Strachan (SCO)).
Germany: Manuel Neuer, Mats Hummels, Jonas Hector, Jérôme Boateng, Bastian
Schweinsteiger (C), Ilkay Gündogan, Mesut Özil (90'+2' Christoph Kramer), Toni Kroos,
Mario Götze (86' André Schürrle), Emre Can, Thomas Müller. (Coach: Joachim Löw (GER)).
Goals: Scotland: 1-1 Mats Hummels (28' own goal), 2-2 James McArthur (43').
Germany: 0-1 Thomas Müller (18'), 1-2 Thomas Müller (34'), 2-3 Ilkay Gündogan (54').
Referee: Björn Kuipers (HOL)   Attendance: 50.753

08-10-2015   Boris Paichadze Dinamo Arena, Tbilisi: Georgia – Gibraltar   4-0 (3-0)
Georgia: Nukri Revishvili, Nika Kvekveskiri, Guram Kashia, Otar Kakabadze, Gia Grigalava,
Aleksandr Amisulashvili, Aleksandr Kobakhidze, Valeri Qazaishvili, Jaba Kankava (C) (58'
Guga Phalavandishvili), Tornike Okriashvili (YC31) (58' Nika Dzalamidze), Mate Vatsadze
(73' Bachana Tskhadadze). (Coach: Kakhaber Dzhumberovich Tskhadadze (GEO)).
Gibraltar: Jordan Perez, Juan Carlos (Jean) Garcia, Roy Chipolina (C), Joseph Chipolina, Ryan
Casciaro, Liam Walker, Jake Gosling, Kyle Casciaro (85' Michael Yome), Anthony Bardon,
Lee Casciaro (76' John-Paul Duarte), George Cabrera (YC15) (46' Brian Perez). (Coach:
Jeffrey Reginald (Jeff) Wood (ENG)).
Goals: Georgia: 1-0 Mate Vatsadze (30'), 2-0 Tornike Okriashvili (35' penalty), 3-0 Mate
Vatsadze (45'), 4-0 Valeri Qazaishvili (87').
Referee: Serhiy Mykolayovych Boyko (UKR)   Attendance: 11.330

08-10-2015   Aviva Stadium, Dublin: Republic of Ireland – Germany   1-0 (0-0)
Republic of Ireland: Shay Given (43' Darren Randolph), Richard Keogh, Cyrus Christie,
Stephen Ward (69' David Meyler), John O'Shea (C), Robert (Robbie) Brady, James McCarthy,
Wesley (Wes) Hoolahan (YC89), Jeffrey (Jeff) Hendrick, Jonathan (Jon) Walters, Daryl
Murphy (66' Shane Long). (Coach: Martin Hugh Michael O'Neill (NIR)).
Germany: Manuel Neuer (C), Mats Hummels (YC86), Jonas Hector, Matthias Ginter (77'
Karim Bellarabi), Jérôme Boateng, Ilkay Gündogan (84' Kevin Volland), Marco Reus, Mesut
Özil, Toni Kroos, Mario Götze (35' André Schürrle), Thomas Müller. (Coach: Joachim Löw
(GER)).
Goal: Republic of Ireland: 1-0 Shane Long (70').
Referee: Carlos Velasco Carballo (ESP)   Attendance: 50.604

318

08-10-2015   Hampden Park, Glasgow: Scotland – Poland   2-2 (1-1)
Scotland: David Marshall, Steven Whittaker, Alan Hutton (YC68), Grant Hanley, Matthew (Matt) Ritchie, Steven Naismith (69' Shaun Maloney), Russell Martin, James Forrest (84' Graham Dorrans), Darren Fletcher (74' James McArthur), Scott Brown (C) (YC56), Steven Fletcher. (Coach: Gordon David Strachan (SCO)).
Poland: Lukasz Fabianski, Michal Pazdan, Grzegorz Krychowiak (YC84), Kamil Glik, Maciej Rybus (YC22) (71' Jakub Wawrzyniak), Lukasz Piszczek, Krzysztof Maczynski, Jakub Blaszczykowski (83' Pawel Olkowski), Arkadiusz Milik (63' Tomasz Jodlowiec), Robert Lewandowski (C), Kamil Grosicki. (Coach: Adam Nawalka (POL)).
Goals: Scotland: 1-1 Matthew (Matt) Ritchie (45'), 2-1 Steven Fletcher (62').
Poland: 0-1 Robert Lewandowski (3'), 2-2 Robert Lewandowski (90'+4').
Referee: Viktor Kassai (HUN)   Attendance: 49.359

11-10-2015   Red Bull Arena, Leipzig: Germany – Georgia   2-1 (0-0)
Germany: Manuel Neuer (C), Mats Hummels (YC90+2), Jonas Hector, Matthias Ginter, Jérôme Boateng, Ilkay Gündogan, Marco Reus (90' Karim Bellarabi), Mesut Özil, Toni Kroos, André Schürrle (76' Max Kruse), Thomas Müller. (Coach: Joachim Löw (GER)).
Georgia: Nukri Revishvili (YC49), Ucha Lobzhanidze, Solomon Kverkvelia, Nika Kvekveskiri (78' Zurab Khizanishvili), Guram Kashia, Aleksandr Amisulashvili, Valeri Qazaishvili (90' Aleksandr Kobakhidze), Giorgi Navalovski (YC33), Jaba Kankava (C), Tornike Okriashvili (YC71), Nikoloz Gelashvili (46' Mate Vatsadze). (Coach: Kakhaber Dzhumberovich Tskhadadze (GEO)).
Goals: Germany: 1-0 Thomas Müller (50' penalty), 2-1 Max Kruse (79').
Georgia: 1-1 Jaba Kankava (53').
Referee: Pavel Královec (CZE)   Attendance: 43.630

11-10-2015   Estádio Algarve, Faro/Loulé (POR): Gibraltar – Scotland   0-6 (0-2)
Gibraltar: Jamie Robba, Juan Carlos (Jean) Garcia, Roy Chipolina (C), Joseph Chipolina, Ryan Casciaro, Erin Barnett, Liam Walker, Daniel Duarte (57' Brian Perez), Kyle Casciaro (89' Michael Yome), Anthony Bardon, Lee Casciaro (82' John-Paul Duarte). (Coach: Jeffrey Reginald (Jeff) Wood (ENG)).
Scotland: Allan McGregor, Andrew Robertson, Alan Hutton, Gordon Greer, Christophe Berra, Matthew (Matt) Ritchie (64' Johnathon (Johnny) Russell), Shaun Maloney, Graham Dorrans, Scott Brown (C) (63' Darren Fletcher), Chris Martin (76' Steven Naismith), Steven Fletcher. (Coach: Gordon David Strachan (SCO)).
Goals: Scotland: 0-1 Chris Martin (25'), 0-2 Shaun Maloney (39'), 0-3 Steven Fletcher (52'), 0-4 Steven Fletcher (56'), 0-5 Steven Fletcher (85'), 0-6 Steven Naismith (90'+1').
Referee: Aliaksei Kulbakov (BLS)   Attendance: 12.401

11-10-2015   Stadion Narodowy, Warsaw: Poland – Republic of Ireland   2-1 (2-1)
Poland: Lukasz Fabianski, Pawel Olkowski (63' Jakub Blaszczykowski), Grzegorz Krychowiak, Kamil Glik (YC74), Jakub Wawrzyniak, Michal Pazdan, Krzysztof Maczynski (78' Lukasz Szukala), Karol Linetty, Lukasz Piszczek, Robert Lewandowski (C), Kamil Grosicki (85' Slawomir Peszko (YC87)). (Coach: Adam Nawalka (POL)).
Republic of Ireland: Darren Randolph, Richard Keogh, Séamus Coleman, John O'Shea (C) (YC19,YC90+2), Robert (Robbie) Brady, James McCarthy, Jeffrey (Jeff) Hendrick, Glenn Whelan (YC45+1) (58' Aiden McGeady), James McClean (73' Wesley (Wes) Hoolahan), Shane Long (55' Robbie Keane), Jonathan (Jon) Walters (YC90+5). (Coach: Martin Hugh Michael O'Neill (NIR)).
Goals: Poland: 1-0 Grzegorz Krychowiak (13'), 2-1 Robert Lewandowski (42').
Republic of Ireland: 1-1 Jonathan (Jon) Walters (16' penalty).
Referee: Cüneyt Çakir (TUR)   Attendance: 57.497

GROUP E

08-09-2014	Tallinn	Estonia – Slovenia	1-0 (0-0)
08-09-2014	Serravalle	San Marino – Lithuania	0-2 (0-2)
08-09-2014	Basel	Switzerland – England	0-2 (0-0)
09-10-2014	London	England – San Marino	5-0 (2-0)
09-10-2014	Vilnius	Lithuania – Estonia	1-0 (0-0)
09-10-2014	Maribor	Slovenia – Switzerland	1-0 (0-0)
12-10-2014	Tallinn	Estonia – England	0-1 (0-0)
12-10-2014	Vilnius	Lithuania – Slovenia	0-2 (0-2)
14-10-2014	Serravalle	San Marino – Switzerland	0-4 (0-3)
15-11-2014	London	England – Slovenia	3-1 (0-0)
15-11-2014	Serravalle	San Marino – Estonia	0-0
15-11-2014	St.Gallen	Switzerland – Lithuania	4-0 (0-0)
27-03-2015	London	England – Lithuania	4-0 (2-0)
27-03-2015	Ljubljana	Slovenia – San Marino	6-0 (1-0)
27-03-2015	Lucerne	Switzerland – Estonia	3-0 (2-0)
14-06-2015	Tallinn	Estonia – San Marino	2-0 (1-0)
14-06-2015	Ljubljana	Slovenia – England	2-3 (1-0)
14-06-2015	Vilnius	Lithuania – Switzerland	1-2 (0-0)
05-09-2015	Tallinn	Estonia – Lithuania	1-0 (0-0)
05-09-2015	Serravalle	San Marino – England	0-6 (0-2)
05-09-2015	Basel	Switzerland – Slovenia	3-2 (0-1)
08-09-2015	London	England – Switzerland	2-0 (0-0)
08-09-2015	Vilnius	Lithuania – San Marino	2-1 (1-0)
08-09-2015	Maribor	Slovenia – Estonia	1-0 (0-0)
09-10-2015	London	England – Estonia	2-0 (1-0)
09-10-2015	Ljubljana	Slovenia – Lithuania	1-1 (1-0)
09-10-2015	St.Gallen	Switzerland – San Marino	7-0 (1-0)
12-10-2015	Tallinn	Estonia – Switzerland	0-1 (0-0)
12-10-2015	Vilnius	Lithuania – England	0-3 (0-2)
12-10-2015	Serravalle	San Marino – Slovenia	0-2 (0-0)

FINAL STANDING

Pos	Team	Pld	W	D	L	GF	GA	GD	Pts
1	England	10	10	0	0	31	3	+28	30
2	Switzerland	10	7	0	3	24	8	+16	21
3	Slovenia	10	5	1	4	18	11	+7	16
4	Estonia	10	3	1	6	4	9	-5	10
5	Lithuania	10	3	1	6	7	18	-11	10
6	San Marino	10	0	1	9	1	36	-35	1

England and Switzerland qualified for the Final Tournament in France.

Slovenia qualified for the play-offs

08-09-2014   A.Le Coq Arena, Tallinn: Estonia – Slovenia   1-0 (0-0)
Estonia: Sergei Pareiko, Igor Morozov, Ragnar Klavan (C), Ken Kallaste, Taijo Teniste (71'
Enar Jääger), Martin Vunk, Ilja Antonov (YC36) (67' Gert Kams), Karol Mets, Sergei Zenjov,
Joel Lindpere (85' Ats Purje), Henri Anier. (Coach: Magnus Pehrsson (SWE)).
Slovenia: Samir Handanovic, Miral Samardzic, Bostjan Cesar (C), Miso Brecko, Andraz
Struna, Dalibor Stevanovic (YC63,YC79), Rajko Rotman (89' Dejan Lazarevic), Jasmin
Kurtic, Josip Ilicic (62' Valter Birsa), Kevin Kampl, Milivoje Novakovic. (Coach: Srecko
Katanec (SLO)).
Goal: Estonia: 1-0 Ats Purje (86').
Referee: Szymon Marciniak (POL)   Attendance: 6.561

08-09-2014   San Marino Stadium, Serravalle: San Marino – Lithuania   0-2 (0-2)
San Marino: Aldo Simoncini, Fabio Vitaioli, Davide Simoncini, Cristian Brolli, Giovanni
Bonini (87' Lorenzo Buscarini), Luca Tosi (56' Michele Cervellini (YC85)), Alex Gasperoni
(YC45+1), Manuel Battistini (YC72), Matteo Vitaioli, Andy Selva (C), Adolfo José Hirsch
(76' Mattia Stefanelli). (Coach: Pierangelo Manzaroli (SMR)).
Lithuania: Giedrius Arlauskis, Marius Zaliūkas, Tadas Kijanskas (C), Georgas Freidgeimas
(YC89), Vaidas Slavickas, Mindaugas Panka (66' Gediminas Vicius (YC90)), Arvydas
Novikovas, Mindaugas Kalonas, Karolis Chvedukas, Fiodor Cernych (90' Mantas Kuklys),
Deivydas Matulevicius (86' Simonas Stankevicius). (Coach: Igoris Pankratjevas (LIT)).
Goals: Lithuania: 0-1 Deivydas Matulevicius (5'), 0-2 Arvydas Novikovas (36').
Referee: Libor Kovarik (CZE)   Attendance: 986

08-09-2014   St.Jakob-Park, Basel: Switzerland – England   0-2 (0-0)
Switzerland: Yann Sommer, Ricardo Ivan Rodríguez Araya, Stephan Lichtsteiner, Johan
Djourou, Steve von Bergen, Gökhan Inler (C), Valon Behrami, Granit Xhaka (74' Blerim
Dzemaili), Xherdan Shaqiri, Admir Mehmedi (64' Josip Drmic), Haris Seferovic. (Coach:
Vladimir Petkovic (SUI)).
England: Joe Hart, Philip (Phil) Jones (77' Philip (Phil) Jagielka), Leighton Baines, Gary
Cahill, John Stones, Fabian Delph (YC9), Raheem Sterling, Jordan Henderson, Jack Wilshere
(73' James Milner), Danny Welbeck, Wayne Rooney (C) (90' Richard (Rickie) Lambert
(YC90+1)). (Coach: Roy Hodgson (ENG)).
Goals: England: 0-1 Danny Welbeck (58'), 0-2 Danny Welbeck (90'+4').
Referee: Cünet Çakir (TUR)   Attendance: 35.500

09-10-2014   Wembley Stadium, London: England – San Marino   5-0 (2-0)
England: Joe Hart, Philip (Phil) Jagielka, Kieran Gibbs, Gary Cahill, Calum Chambers, Jack
Wilshere, Raheem Sterling (46' Adam Lallana), James Milner (YC38), Jordan Henderson (46'
Alex Oxlade-Chamberlain), Danny Welbeck (66' Andros Townsend), Wayne Rooney (C).
(Coach: Roy Hodgson (ENG)).
San Marino: Aldo Simoncini, Fabio Vitaioli, Nicola Chiaruzzi, Cristian Brolli, Alessandro
Della Valle, Luca Tosi (63' Lorenzo Gasperoni), Mirko Palazzi (74' Lorenzo Buscarini),
Manuel Battistini, Matteo Vitaioli, Andy Selva (C) (YC43) (87' Danilo Rinaldi (YC90)),
Adolfo José Hirsch. (Coach: Pierangelo Manzaroli (SMR)).
Goals: England: 1-0 Philip (Phil) Jagielka (25'), 2-0 Wayne Rooney (43' penalty), 3-0 Danny
Welbeck (49'), 4-0 Andros Townsend (72'), 5-0 Alessandro Della Valle (78' own goal).
Referee: Marcin Borski (POL)   Attendance: 55.990

321

09-10-2014   LFF Stadium, Vilnius: Lithuania – Estonia   1-0 (0-0)
Lithuania: Giedrius Arlauskis, Egidijus Vaitkūnas (YC87), Tadas Kijanskas (C), Georgas
Freidgeimas, Vytautas Andriuskevicius (YC61), Gediminas Vicius, Mindaugas Panka,
Arvydas Novikovas, Mindaugas Kalonas (63' Saulius Mikoliūnas), Fiodor Cernych, Deivydas
Matulevicius (90' Ricardas Beniusis). (Coach: Igoris Pankratjevas (LIT)).
Estonia: Sergei Pareiko, Ragnar Klavan (C), Ken Kallaste (YC64,YC86), Enar Jääger, Alo
Bärengrub, Martin Vunk (80' Ats Purje), Ilja Antonov, Karol Mets, Sergei Zenjov (YC33) (64'
Henrik Ojamaa), Joel Lindpere (76' Konstantin Vassiljev), Henri Anier. (Coach: Magnus
Pehrsson (SWE)).
Goal: Lithuania: 1-0 Saulius Mikoliūnas (76').
Referee: Carlos Clos Gómez (ESP)   Attendance: 4.780

09-10-2014   Ljudski vrt, Maribor: Slovenia – Switzerland   1-0 (0-0)
Slovenia: Samir Handanovic, Branko Ilic, Bostjan Cesar (C), Miso Brecko, Andraz Struna,
Ales Mertelj, Andraz Kirm (72' Nejc Pecnik), Valter Birsa (56' Dejan Lazarevic (YC90+4)),
Kevin Kampl, Milivoje Novakovic, Zlatan Ljubijankic (YC36) (46' Jasmin Kurtic). (Coach:
Srecko Katanec (SLO)).
Switzerland: Yann Sommer, Philippe Senderos (70' Steve von Bergen), Ricardo Ivan
Rodríguez Araya, Stephan Lichtsteiner, Johan Djourou (YC79), Granit Xhaka, Xherdan
Shaqiri, Gökhan Inler (C) (82' Pajtim Kasami), Valon Behrami, Haris Seferovic, Josip Drmic
(74' Admir Mehmedi). (Coach: Vladimir Petkovic (SUI)).
Goal: Slovenia: 1-0 Milivoje Novakovic (79' penalty).
Referee: Wolfgang Stark (GER)   Attendance: 8.500

12-10-2014   A.Le Coq Arena, Tallinn: Estonia – England   0-1 (0-0)
Estonia: Sergei Pareiko, Artur Pikk, Igor Morozov, Ragnar Klavan (C) (YC29,YC48), Enar
Jääger, Martin Vunk (83' Dmitri Kruglov), Konstantin Vassiljev (46' Joel Lindpere), Ilja
Antonov, Karol Mets, Sergei Zenjov (80' Henrik Ojamaa), Henri Anier. (Coach: Magnus
Pehrsson (SWE)).
England: Joe Hart, Philip (Phil) Jagielka, Leighton Baines (YC45+1), Gary Cahill, Fabian
Delph (61' Alex Oxlade-Chamberlain), Calum Chambers, Jack Wilshere (YC87), Adam
Lallana, Jordan Henderson (YC53) (64' Raheem Sterling), Danny Welbeck (80' Richard
(Rickie) Lambert), Wayne Rooney (C). (Coach: Roy Hodgson (ENG)).
Goal: England: 0-1 Wayne Rooney (74').
Referee: Marijo Strahonja (CRO)   Attendance: 10.195

12-10-2014   LFF Stadium, Vilnius: Lithuania – Slovenia   0-2 (0-2)
Lithuania: Giedrius Arlauskis, Egidijus Vaitkūnas, Tadas Kijanskas (C) (YC90+3), Georgas
Freidgeimas, Vytautas Andriuskevicius, Artūras Zulpa, Mindaugas Panka (32' Gediminas
Vicius), Arvydas Novikovas (YC45+3), Karolis Chvedukas (YC56) (75' Saulius Mikoliūnas),
Fiodor Cernych, Deivydas Matulevicius (YC45+3). (Coach: Igoris Pankratjevas (LIT)).
Slovenia: Samir Handanovic, Branko Ilic, Bostjan Cesar (C), Miso Brecko, Andraz Struna,
Dalibor Stevanovic (YC23) (46' Ales Mertelj), Nejc Pecnik (66' Valter Birsa), Jasmin Kurtic,
Andraz Kirm (86' Dejan Lazarevic), Kevin Kampl, Milivoje Novakovic. (Coach: Srecko
Katanec (SLO)).
Goals: Slovenia: 0-1 Milivoje Novakovic (33'), 0-2 Milivoje Novakovic (37').
Referee: Michail Koukoulakis (GRE)   Attendance: 4.250

14-10-2014   San Marino Stadium, Serravalle: San Marino – Switzerland   0-4 (0-3)
San Marino: Aldo Simoncini, Fabio Vitaioli (17' Michele Cervellini), Nicola Chiaruzzi, Cristian Brolli, Alessandro Della Valle (C), Giovanni Bonini (YC89), Mirko Palazzi, Alex Gasperoni (YC59) (69' Lorenzo Gasperoni), Manuel Battistini, Matteo Vitaioli (61' Adolfo José Hirsch), Mattia Stefanelli. (Coach: Pierangelo Manzaroli (SMR)).
Switzerland: Yann Sommer, Steve von Bergen, Ricardo Ivan Rodríguez Araya, Stephan Lichtsteiner (C) (59' Silvan Widmer), Johan Djourou, Granit Xhaka, Xherdan Shaqiri, Pajtim Kasami (71' Tranquillo Barnetta), Blerim Dzemaili (YC27), Haris Seferovic, Josip Drmic (46' Admir Mehmedi). (Coach: Vladimir Petkovic (SUI)).
Goals: Switzerland: 0-1 Haris Seferovic (10'), 0-2 Haris Seferovic (23'), 0-3 Blerim Dzemaili (30'), 0-4 Xherdan Shaqiri (79').
Referee: Tony Chapron (FRA)   Attendance: 2.289
(Ricardo Ivan Rodríguez Araya missed a penalty in the 90th minute)

15-11-2014   Wembley Stadium, London: England – Slovenia   3-1 (0-0)
England: Joe Hart, Kieran Gibbs (YC52), Philip (Phil) Jagielka (YC88) (89' Chris Smalling), Nathaniel Clyne (YC79), Gary Cahill, Jack Wilshere, Adam Lallana (80' James Milner), Jordan Henderson, Raheem Sterling (YC82) (85' Alex Oxlade-Chamberlain), Danny Welbeck, Wayne Rooney (C). (Coach: Roy Hodgson (ENG)).
Slovenia: Samir Handanovic, Branko Ilic, Bostjan Cesar (C) (YC59), Miso Brecko, Andraz Struna, Ales Mertelj, Valter Birsa (63' Dejan Lazarevic), Jasmin Kurtic (75' Rajko Rotman), Andraz Kirm (78' Zlatan Ljubijankic), Kevin Kampl, Milivoje Novakovic. (Coach: Srecko Katanec (SLO)).
Goals: England: 1-1 Wayne Rooney (59' penalty), 2-1 Danny Welbeck (66'), 3-1 Danny Welbeck (72').
Slovenia: 0-1 Jordan Henderson (58' own goal).
Referee: Olegário Manuel Bártolo Faustino Benquerença (POR)   Attendance: 82.309

15-11-2014   San Marino Stadium, Serravalle: San Marino – Estonia   0-0
San Marino: Aldo Simoncini, Fabio Vitaioli, Davide Simoncini (YC11), Nicola Chiaruzzi, Cristian Brolli, Giovanni Bonini, Luca Tosi, Mirko Palazzi (YC57), Matteo Vitaioli (77' Enrico Golinucci), Andy Selva (C) (83' Danilo Rinaldi), Adolfo José Hirsch (60' Manuel Battistini). (Coach: Pierangelo Manzaroli (SMR)).
Estonia: Mihkel Aksalu, Igor Morozov (YC68), Dmitri Kruglov, Taijo Teniste, Konstantin Vassiljev (C), Aleksandr Dmitrijev (YC1) (46' Joel Lindpere), Artjom Artjunin (74' Ingemar Teever), Ilja Antonov, Karol Mets (YC90+2), Sergei Zenjov, Henrik Ojamaa (62' Henri Anier). (Coach: Magnus Pehrsson (SWE)).
Referee: Dr.Felix Brych (GER)   Attendance: 759

15-11-2014   AFG Arena, St.Gallen: Switzerland – Lithuania   4-0 (0-0)
Switzerland: Yann Sommer, Fabian Schär, François Moubandje (YC24) (75' Gélson da Conceição Tavares Fernandes), Stephan Lichtsteiner, Johan Djourou, Xherdan Shaqiri, Gökhan Inler (C), Blerim Dzemaili, Valon Behrami, Haris Seferovic (83' Marco Schönbächler), Admir Mehmedi (63' Josip Drmic (YC66)). (Coach: Vladimir Petkovic (SUI)).
Lithuania: Giedrius Arlauskis, Tadas Kijanskas (C), Georgas Freidgeimas (YC35), Vytautas Andriuskevicius, Egidijus Vaitkūnas (64' Valdemars Borovskis), Arvydas Novikovas (87' Donatas Kazlauskas), Karolis Chvedukas, Artūras Zulpa, Gediminas Vicius (82' Tautvydas Eliosius), Fiodor Cernych, Deivydas Matulevicius. (Coach: Igoris Pankratjevas (LIT)).
Goals: Switzerland: 1-0 Giedrius Arlauskis (66' own goal), 2-0 Fabian Schär (68'), 3-0 Xherdan Shaqiri (80'), 4-0 Xherdan Shaqiri (90').
Referee: Svein Oddvar Moen (NOR)   Attendance: 17.300

323

27-03-2015   Wembley Stadium, London: England – Lithuania   4-0 (2-0)
England: Joe Hart, Leighton Baines, Philip (Phil) Jones, Nathaniel Clyne, Gary Cahill, Michael Carrick, Fabian Delph, Raheem Sterling (YC80), Jordan Henderson (71' Ross Barkley), Danny Welbeck (77' Theo Walcott), Wayne Rooney (C) (71' Harry Kane). (Coach: Roy Hodgson (ENG)).
Lithuania: Giedrius Arlauskis, Tadas Kijanskas (C), Georgas Freidgeimas, Vytautas Andriuskevicius (83' Vaidas Slavickas), Marius Zaliūkas (YC41), Tomas Mikuckis (66' Simonas Stankevicius), Saulius Mikoliūnas (88' Donatas Kazlauskas (YC90+1)), Karolis Chvedukas, Artūras Zulpa, Fiodor Cernych, Deivydas Matulevicius. (Coach: Igoris Pankratjevas (LIT)).
Goals: England: 1-0 Wayne Rooney (6'), 2-0 Danny Welbeck (45'), 3-0 Raheem Sterling (58'), 4-0 Harry Kane (73').
Referee: Pavel Královec (CZE)   Attendance: 83.671

27-03-2015   Stozice Stadium, Ljubljana: Slovenia – San Marino   6-0 (1-0)
Slovenia: Samir Handanovic, Branko Ilic, Bostjan Cesar (C), Miso Brecko (76' Petar Stojanovic), Andraz Struna, Jasmin Kurtic, Andraz Kirm (60' Dejan Lazarevic), Josip Ilicic (72' Robert Beric), Valter Birsa, Kevin Kampl, Milivoje Novakovic. (Coach: Srecko Katanec (SLO)).
San Marino: Elia Benedettini, Davide Simoncini (YC40), Alessandro Della Valle (78' Fabio Vitaioli), Cristian Brolli, Giovanni Bonini, Luca Tosi (56' Manuel Battistini), Mirko Palazzi (YC56), Pier Filippo Mazza, Matteo Vitaioli, Andy Selva (C) (YC75), Adolfo José Hirsch (84' Alessandro Golinucci). (Coach: Pierangelo Manzaroli (SMR)).
Goals: Slovenia: 1-0 Josip Ilicic (10'), 2-0 Kevin Kampl (49'), 3-0 Andraz Struna (50'), 4-0 Milivoje Novakovic (52'), 5-0 Dejan Lazarevic (73'), 6-0 Branko Ilic (88').
Referee: Oliver Drachta (AUT)   Attendance: 8.325

27-03-2015   Swissporarena, Lucerne: Switzerland – Estonia   3-0 (2-0)
Switzerland: Yann Sommer, Johan Djourou, Fabian Schär, Ricardo Ivan Rodríguez Araya, Stephan Lichtsteiner (78' Silvan Widmer), Gökhan Inler (C), Valon Behrami, Granit Xhaka (YC56) (87' Fabian Frei (YC90+2)), Xherdan Shaqiri, Josip Drmic (62' Valentin Stocker), Haris Seferovic. (Coach: Vladimir Petkovic (SUI)).
Estonia: Sergei Pareiko, Ken Kallaste, Enar Jääger, Ragnar Klavan (C), Taijo Teniste, Aleksandr Dmitrijev (YC51) (63' Dmitri Kruglov), Ilja Antonov, Konstantin Vassiljev, Karol Mets, Henri Anier (56' Henrik Ojamaa), Sergei Zenjov (YC44) (87' Rauno Alliku). (Coach: Magnus Pehrsson (SWE)).
Goals: Switzerland: 1-0 Fabian Schär (17'), 2-0 Granit Xhaka (27'), 3-0 Haris Seferovic (80').
Referee: Danny Desmond Makkelie (HOL)   Attendance: 14.500

14-06-2015   A.Le Coq Arena, Tallinn: Estonia – San Marino   2-0 (1-0)
Estonia: Mihkel Aksalu, Ragnar Klavan (C), Ken Kallaste, Taijo Teniste, Konstantin Vassiljev (79' Ilja Antonov), Ats Purje, Aleksandr Dmitrijev, Karol Mets, Sergei Zenjov (89' Ingemar Teever), Joel Lindpere (84' Dmitri Kruglov), Rauno Alliku. (Coach: Magnus Pehrsson (SWE)).
San Marino: Aldo Simoncini, Alessandro Della Valle (C), Cristian Brolli, Giovanni Bonini, Luca Tosi (71' Michele Cervellini), Mirko Palazzi, Lorenzo Gasperoni, Manuel Battistini (YC58), Matteo Vitaioli (89' Alessandro Bianchi), Danilo Rinaldi (79' Mattia Stefanelli), Adolfo José Hirsch. (Coach: Pierangelo Manzaroli (SMR)).
Goals: Estonia: 1-0 Sergei Zenjov (35'), 2-0 Sergei Zenjov (63').
Referee: Ivan Kruzliak (SVK)   Attendance: 6.131

14-06-2015   Stozice Stadium, Ljubljana: Slovenia – England   2-3 (1-0)
Slovenia: Samir Handanovic, Bojan Jokic, Branko Ilic, Bostjan Cesar (C), Miso Brecko
(YC57), Ales Mertelj, Jasmin Kurtic (79' Dejan Lazarevic), Andraz Kirm (72' Nejc Pecnik),
Josip Ilicic (61' Valter Birsa), Kevin Kampl (YC90+2), Milivoje Novakovic. (Coach: Srecko
Katanec (SLO)).
England: Joe Hart, Philip (Phil) Jones (46' Adam Lallana), Kieran Gibbs, Chris Smalling, Gary
Cahill, Andros Townsend (74' Theo Walcott), Fabian Delph (85' Nathaniel Clyne), Jack
Wilshere, Raheem Sterling, Jordan Henderson, Wayne Rooney (C). (Coach: Roy Hodgson
(ENG)).
Goals: Slovenia: 1-0 Milivoje Novakovic (37'), 2-2 Nejc Pecnik (84').
England: 1-1 Jack Wilshere (57'), 1-2 Jack Wilshere (73'), 2-3 Wayne Rooney (86').
Referee: Alberto Undiano Mallenco (ESP)   Attendance: 15.796

14-06-2015   LFF Stadium, Vilnius: Lithuania – Switzerland   1-2 (0-0)
Lithuania: Emilius Zubas, Egidijus Vaitkūnas, Tomas Mikuckis (YC90+2), Linas Klimavicius,
Vytautas Andriuskevicius, Deividas Cesnauskis (YC83) (86' Vytautas Luksa), Artūras Zulpa
(61' Karolis Chvedukas (YC89)), Vykintas Slivka (76' Gediminas Vicius), Mindaugas Panka
(YC44), Fiodor Cernych, Deivydas Matulevicius (C). (Coach: Igoris Pankratjevas (LIT)).
Switzerland: Yann Sommer, Fabian Schär, Ricardo Ivan Rodríguez Araya, Stephan
Lichtsteiner, Johan Djourou, Granit Xhaka (YC44), Xherdan Shaqiri, Gökhan Inler (C) (57'
Blerim Dzemaili), Valon Behrami, Haris Seferovic (57' Admir Mehmedi), Josip Drmic (81'
Breel-Donald Embolo). (Coach: Vladimir Petkovic (SUI)).
Goals: Lithuania: 1-0 Fiodor Cernych (64').
Switzerland: 1-1 Josip Drmic (69'), 1-2 Xherdan Shaqiri (84').
Referee: Craig Alexander Thomson (SCO)   Attendance: 4.786

05-09-2015   A.Le Coq Arena, Tallinn: Estonia – Lithuania   1-0 (0-0)
Estonia: Mihkel Aksalu, Ragnar Klavan (C), Enar Jääger, Artur Pikk, Taijo Teniste, Aleksandr
Dmitrijev (YC87), Konstantin Vassiljev (90'+3' Siim Luts), Ats Purje (YC79) (86' Sander
Puri), Karol Mets, Joel Lindpere (67' Ken Kallaste), Sergei Zenjov. (Coach: Magnus Pehrsson
(SWE)).
Lithuania: Giedrius Arlauskas (C), Linas Klimavicius, Marius Zaliūkas (YC65), Egidijus
Vaitkūnas, Deividas Cesnauskis (YC69) (79' Georgas Freidgeimas), Artūras Zulpa, Vykintas
Slivka, Mindaugas Panka (78' Deimantas Petravicius), Arvydas Novikovas, Fiodor Cernych,
Deivydas Matulevicius (YC30) (63' Lukas Spalvis). (Coach: Igoris Pankratjevas (LIT)).
Goal: Estonia: 1-0 Konstantin Vassiljev (71').
Referee: Oliver Drachta (AUT)   Attendance: 6.621

05-09-2015   San Marino Stadium, Serravalle: San Marino – England   0-6 (0-2)
San Marino: Aldo Simoncini, Davide Simoncini (81' Alessandro Della Valle), Nicola
Chiaruzzi, Cristian Brolli, Marco Berardi (YC12), Giovanni Bonini (72' Luca Tosi), Mirko
Palazzi, Manuel Battistini, Matteo Vitaioli, Andy Selva (C) (75' Danilo Rinaldi), Adolfo José
Hirsch. (Coach: Pierangelo Manzaroli (SMR)).
England: Joe Hart, Luke Shaw, Philip (Phil) Jagielka, John Stones, Nathaniel Clyne, Jonjo
Shelvey, James Milner (58' Fabian Delph), Ross Barkley, Alex Oxlade-Chamberlain (67' Theo
Walcott), Jamie Vardy, Wayne Rooney (C) (58' Harry Kane). (Coach: Roy Hodgson (ENG)).
Goals: England: 0-1 Wayne Rooney (13' penalty), 0-2 Cristian Brolli (30' *own goal*), 0-3 Ross
Barkley (46'), 0-4 Theo Walcott (68'), 0-5 Harry Kane (77'), 0-6 Theo Walcott (78').
Referee: Leontios Trattou (CYP)   Attendance: 4.378

05-09-2015   St.Jakob-Park, Basel: Switzerland – Slovenia   3-2 (0-1)
Switzerland: Yann Sommer, Fabian Schär (YC56), Ricardo Ivan Rodríguez Araya, Stephan
Lichtsteiner (C) (YC63), Timm Klose, Granit Xhaka, Xherdan Shaqiri, Blerim Dzemaili
(YC63) (64' Josip Drmic), Valon Behrami (YC64), Haris Seferovic (80' Valentin Stocker),
Admir Mehmedi (56' Breel-Donald Embolo). (Coach: Vladimir Petkovic (SUI)).
Slovenia: Samir Handanovic (YC64), Bojan Jokic, Branko Ilic, Bostjan Cesar (C), Andraz
Struna, Dalibor Stevanovic, Jasmin Kurtic, Josip Ilicic (YC88) (90' Miral Samardzic), Valter
Birsa (83' René Krhin), Kevin Kampl (YC24), Milivoje Novakovic (YC34) (58' Nejc Pecnik
(YC64)). (Coach: Srecko Katanec (SLO)).
Goals: Switzerland: 1-2 Josip Drmic (80'), 2-2 Valentin Stocker (84'), 3-2 Josip Drmic
(90'+4').
Slovenia: 0-1 Milivoje Novakovic (45'), 0-2 Bostjan Cesar (48').
Referee: Pavel Královec (CZE)   Attendance: 25.750

08-09-2015   Wembley Stadium, London: England – Switzerland   2-0 (0-0)
England: Joe Hart, Luke Shaw, Chris Smalling (YC71), Nathaniel Clyne (68' John Stones),
Gary Cahill, Jonjo Shelvey (58' Harry Kane), Fabian Delph (3' Ross Barkley), Raheem
Sterling, James Milner (YC28), Alex Oxlade-Chamberlain, Wayne Rooney (C). (Coach: Roy
Hodgson (ENG)).
Switzerland: Yann Sommer, Fabian Schär, Ricardo Ivan Rodríguez Araya, Stephan
Lichtsteiner, Timm Klose, Xherdan Shaqiri, Gökhan Ilner (C), Valon Behrami (79' Blerim
Dzemaili), Granit Xhaka, Valentin Stocker (71' Haris Seferovic), Josip Drmic (63' Breel-
Donald Embolo). (Coach: Vladimir Petkovic (SUI)).
Goals: England: 1-0 Harry Kane (67'), 2-0 Wayne Rooney (84' penalty).
Referee: Gianluca Rocchi (ITA)   Attendance: 75.751

08-09-2015   LFF Stadium, Vilnius: Lithuania – San Marino   2-1 (1-0)
Lithuania: Giedrius Arlauskas (C) (RC50), Linas Klimavicius, Georgas Freidgeimas, Marius
Zaliūkas, Vaidas Slavickas (73' Deivydas Matulevicius), Linas Pilibaitis (82' Karolis
Chvedukas), Arvydas Novikovas (YC60), Artūras Zulpa, Vykintas Slivka (53' Vytautas
Cerniauskas goalkeeper), Fiodor Cernych, Lukas Spalvis (YC83). (Coach: Igoris Pankratjevas
(LIT)).
San Marino: Elia Benedettini, Alessandro Della Valle (C), Nicola Chiaruzzi (YC67,YC88),
Cristian Brolli (YC66), Fabio Vitaioli, Mirko Palazzi, Lorenzo Gasperoni (68' Maicol
Berretti), Manuel Battistini (YC26), Matteo Vitaioli (80' Andy Selva), Mattia Stefanelli
(YC40) (73' Adolfo José Hirsch), Danilo Rinaldi. (Coach: Pierangelo Manzaroli (SMR)).
Goals: Lithuania: 1-0 Fiodor Cernych (7'), 2-1 Lukas Spalvis (90'+2').
San Marino: 1-1 Matteo Vitaioli (55').
Referee: Clayton Pisani (MLT)   Attendance: 2.856

08-09-2015   Ljudski vrt, Maribor: Slovenia – Estonia   1-0 (0-0)
Slovenia: Samir Handanovic, Bojan Jokic, Branko Ilic, Bostjan Cesar (C), Andraz Struna,
Jasmin Kurtic, René Krhin (88' Rajko Rotman), Josip Ilicic (55' Zlatan Ljubijankic), Valter
Birsa, Kevin Kampl (YC52), Robert Beric (77' Dejan Lazarevic). (Coach: Srecko Katanec
(SLO)).
Estonia: Mihkel Aksalu, Artur Pikk, Ragnar Klavan (C), Ken Kallaste (88' Siim Luts), Enar
Jääger, Taijo Teniste, Konstantin Vassiljev, Ats Purje, Karol Mets (YC53), Sergei Zenjov (46'
Sander Puri), Joel Lindpere (YC21) (84' Ingemar Teever). (Coach: Magnus Pehrsson (SWE)).
Goal: Slovenia: 1-0 Robert Beric (63').
Referee: Anastasios (Tasos) Sidiropoulos (GRE)   Attendance: 6.868

09-10-2015   Wembley Stadium, London: England – Estonia   2-0 (1-0)
England: Joe Hart, Chris Smalling, Nathaniel Clyne, Gary Cahill (C), Ryan Bertrand, Raheem
Sterling, James Milner, Adam Lallana (73' Alex Oxlade-Chamberlain), Ross Barkley (88' Dele
Alli), Theo Walcott (82' Jamie Vardy), Harry Kane. (Coach: Roy Hodgson (ENG)).
Estonia: Mihkel Aksalu, Artur Pikk (YC73), Ragnar Klavan (C), Ken Kallaste (88' Siim Luts),
Enar Jääger, Taijo Teniste, Konstantin Vassiljev, Ats Purje (69' Sander Puri), Aleksandr
Dmitrijev (70' Joel Lindpere), Karol Mets, Sergei Zenjov. (Coach: Magnus Pehrsson (SWE)).
Goals: England: 1-0 Theo Walcott (45'), 2-0 Raheem Sterling (85').
Referee: István Vad II (HUN)   Attendance: 75.427

09-10-2015   Stozice Stadium, Ljubljana: Slovenia – Lithuania   1-1 (1-0)
Slovenia: Samir Handanovic, Bojan Jokic, Branko Ilic, Bostjan Cesar (C), Andraz Struna
(YC19), Dejan Lazarevic (YC30) (73' Nejc Pecnik), Jasmin Kurtic, René Krhin, Josip Ilicic
(90'+1' Tim Matavz), Valter Birsa, Robert Beric (62' Zlatan Ljubijankic). (Coach: Srecko
Katanec (SLO)).
Lithuania: Emilius Zubas, Marius Zaliūkas (YC45+1) (89' Tomas Mikuckis), Linas
Klimavicius, Georgas Freidgeimas, Artūras Zulpa, Vykintas Slivka (69' Deimantas Petravicius
(YC90+3)), Vaidas Slavickas, Mindaugas Panka (YC60), Arvydas Novikovas, Fiodor Cernych
(YC15) (63' Deividas Cesnauskis), Lukas Spalvis. (Coach: Igoris Pankratjevas (LIT)).
Goals: Slovenia: 1-0 Valter Birsa (45'+1' penalty).
Lithuania: 1-1 Arvydas Novikovas (79' penalty).
Referee: Björn Kuipers (HOL)   Attendance: 10.498

09-10-2015   AFG Arena, St.Gallen: Switzerland – San Marino   7-0 (1-0)
Switzerland: Roman Bürki, Fabian Schär, Ricardo Ivan Rodríguez Araya (62' François
Moubandje), Michael Lang, Johan Djourou, Pajtim Kasami, Gökhan Ilner (C), Luca Zuffi,
Admir Mehmedi (68' Eren Derdiyok), Breel-Donald Embolo, Josip Drmic (78' Renato
Steffen). (Coach: Vladimir Petkovic (SUI)).
San Marino: Aldo Simoncini, Davide Simoncini, Alessandro Della Valle (C) (YC80), Davide
Cesarini (78' Fabio Vitaioli), Marco Berardi, Mirko Palazzi, Enrico Golinucci (83' Adolfo José
Hirsch), Lorenzo Gasperoni (64' Matteo Copponi), Luca Tosi (YC81), Matteo Vitaioli, Mattia
Stefanelli. (Coach: Pierangelo Manzaroli (SMR)).
Goals: Switzerland: 1-0 Michael Lang (17'), 2-0 Gökhan Ilner (55' penalty), 3-0 Admir
Mehmedi (65'), 4-0 Johan Djourou (72' penalty), 5-0 Pajtim Kasami (75'), 6-0 Breel-Donald
Embolo (80' penalty), 7-0 Eren Derdiyok (89').
Referee: Mattias Gestranius (FIN)   Attendance: 16.200

12-10-2015   A.Le Coq Arena, Tallinn: Estonia – Switzerland   0-1 (0-0)
Estonia: Mihkel Aksalu, Ragnar Klavan (C), Ken Kallaste (80' Siim Luts), Enar Jääger, Artur
Pikk, Taijo Teniste, Ilja Antonov, Konstantin Vassiljev, Sander Puri (67' Joel Lindpere), Karol
Mets (YC78), Sergei Zenjov (61' Ats Purje). (Coach: Magnus Pehrsson (SWE)).
Switzerland: Marwin Hitz, Johan Djourou, François Moubandje, Michael Lang, Gökhan Ilner
(C), Blerim Dzemaili, Granit Xhaka (80' Pajtim Kasami), Xherdan Shaqiri (46' Breel-Donald
Embolo), Fabian Lustenberger, Eren Derdiyok, Admir Mehmedi (71' Renato Steffen). (Coach:
Vladimir Petkovic (SUI)).
Goal: Switzerland: 0-1 Ragnar Klavan (90'+4' own goal).
Referee: Paulus Hendrikus Martinus (Pol) van Boekel (HOL)   Attendance: 7.304

327

12-10-2015   LFF Stadium, Vilnius: Lithuania – England   0-3 (0-2)
Lithuania: Giedrius Arlauskis, Vytautas Andriuskevicius (82' Egidijus Vaitkūnas (YC89)),
Tomas Mikuckis, Linas Klimavicius, Georgas Freidgeimas, Artūras Zulpa, Vykintas Slivka,
Mindaugas Panka (C), Arvydas Novikovas (63' Deimantas Petravicius), Fiodor Cernych,
Lukas Spalvis (YC84) (86' Deivydas Matulevicius). (Coach: Igoris Pankratjevas (LIT)).
England: Jack Butland, Philip (Phil) Jones, Philip (Phil) Jagielka (C), Kieran Gibbs, Kyle
Walker, Jonjo Shelvey (YC79), Ross Barkley (73' Andros Townsend), Adam Lallana (67'
Dele Alli), Alex Oxlade-Chamberlain, Jamie Vardy (YC79), Harry Kane (59' Daniel (Danny)
Ings). (Coach: Roy Hodgson (ENG)).
Goals: England: 0-1 Ross Barkley (29'), 0-2 Giedrius Arlauskis (35' *own goal*), 0-3 Alex
Oxlade-Chamberlain (62').
Referee: Kenn Pii Hansen (DEN)   Attendance: 5.051

12-10-2015   San Marino Stadium, Serravalle: San Marino – Slovenia   0-2 (0-0)
San Marino: Aldo Simoncini, Carlo Valentini (73' Alessandro Della Valle), Davide Simoncini,
Nicola Chiaruzzi, Cristian Brolli (YC73), Mirko Palazzi, Alex Gasperoni (YC12), Manuel
Battistini, Matteo Vitaioli (90' Pier Filippo Mazza), Andy Selva (C) (71' Danilo Rinaldi),
Adolfo José Hirsch. (Coach: Pierangelo Manzaroli (SMR)).
Slovenia: Jan Oblak, Miral Samardzic, Bojan Jokic, Bostjan Cesar (C), Andraz Struna, Jasmin
Kurtic (YC48), René Krhin, Andraz Kirm (70' Dejan Lazarevic), Josip Ilicic (YC34) (46' Nejc
Pecnik), Valter Birsa, Robert Beric (46' Tim Matavz). (Coach: Srecko Katanec (SLO)).
Goals: Slovenia: 0-1 Bostjan Cesar (54'), 0-2 Nejc Pecnik (75').
Referee: Aleksandar Stavrev (MCD)   Attendance: 781

GROUP   F

07-09-2014	Budapest	Hungary – Northern Ireland	1-2 (0-0)
07-09-2014	Tórshavn	Faroe Islands – Finland	1-3 (1-0)
07-09-2014	Piraeus	Greece – Romania	0-1 (0-1)
11-10-2014	Bucharest	Romania – Hungary	1-1 (1-0)
11-10-2014	Helsinki	Finland – Greece	1-1 (0-1)
11-10-2014	Belfast	Northern Ireland – Faroe Islands	2-0 (2-0)
14-10-2014	Tórshavn	Faroe Islands – Hungary	0-1 (0-1)
14-10-2014	Helsinki	Finland – Romania	0-2 (0-0)
14-10-2014	Piraeus	Greece – Northern Ireland	0-2 (0-1)
14-11-2014	Piraeus	Greece – Faroe Islands	0-1 (0-0)
14-11-2014	Budapest	Hungary – Finland	1-0 (0-0)
14-11-2014	Bucharest	Romania – Northern Ireland	2-0 (0-0)
29-03-2015	Belfast	Northern Ireland – Finland	2-1 (2-0)
29-03-2015	Ploiesti	Romania – Faroe Islands	1-0 (1-0)
29-03-2015	Budapest	Hungary – Greece	0-0
13-06-2015	Helsinki	Finland – Hungary	0-1 (0-0)
13-06-2015	Tórshavn	Faroe Islands – Greece	2-1 (1-0)
13-06-2015	Belfast	Northern Ireland – Romania	0-0
04-09-2015	Tórshavn	Faroe Islands – Northern Ireland	1-3 (1-1)
04-09-2015	Piraeus	Greece – Finland	0-1 (0-0)
04-09-2015	Budapest	Hungary – Romania	0-0
07-09-2015	Helsinki	Finland – Faroe Islands	1-0 (1-0)
07-09-2015	Belfast	Northern Ireland – Hungary	1-1 (0-0)

07-09-2015	Bucharest	Romania – Greece	0-0
08-10-2015	Budapest	Hungary – Faroe Islands	2-1 (0-1)
08-10-2015	Belfast	Northern Ireland – Greece	3-1 (1-0)
08-10-2015	Bucharest	Romania – Finland	1-1 (0-0)
11-10-2015	Tórshavn	Faroe Islands – Romania	0-3 (0-2)
11-10-2015	Helsinki	Finland – Northern Ireland	1-1 (0-1)
11-10-2015	Piraeus	Greece – Hungary	4-3 (1-1)

FINAL STANDING

Pos	Team	Pld	W	D	L	GF	GA	GD	Pts
1	Northern Ireland	10	6	3	1	16	8	+8	21
2	Romania	10	5	5	0	11	2	+9	20
3	Hungary	10	4	4	2	11	9	+2	16
4	Finland	10	3	3	4	9	10	-1	12
5	Faroe Islands	10	2	0	8	6	17	-11	6
6	Greece	10	1	3	6	7	14	-7	6

Northern Ireland and Romania qualified for the Final Tournament in France.

Hungary qualified for the play-offs

07-09-2014   Groupama Arena, Budapest: Hungary – Northern Ireland   1-2 (0-0)
Hungary: Péter Gulácsi, Zoltán Lipták, Roland Juhász, Vilmos Vanczák (YC35), Balász Balogh, József Varga, Dániel Tözsér, Nemanja Nikolic (46' Tamás Priskin), Gergely Rudolf (70' István Kovács), Ádám Gyurcsó (58' Gergö Lovrencsics), Balázs Dzsudzsák (C). (Coach: Atilla Pintér (HUN)).
Northern Ireland: Roy Carroll, Aaron Hughes, Conor McLaughlin, Gareth McAuley (72' Craig Cathcart), Corry Evans, Steven Davis (C), Chris Brunt, Oliver Norwood (YC44) (79' Billy McKay), Chris Baird, Jamie Ward (66' Niall McGinn), Kyle Lafferty. (Coach: Michael Andrew Martin O'Neill (NIR)).
Goals: Hungary: 1-0 Tamás Priskin (75').
Northern Ireland: 1-1 Niall McGinn (81'), 1-2 Kyle Lafferty (88').
Referee: Deniz Aytekin (GER)   Attendance: 20.672

07-09-2014   Tórsvøllur, Tórshavn: Faroe Islands – Finland   1-3 (1-0)
Faroe Islands: Gunnar Nielsen, Sonni Ragnar Nattestad (YC80), Jónas Tór Næs, Odmar Færø, Viljormur Davidsen, Róaldur Jacobsen (YC51) (55' Rógvi Baldvinsson), Christian Holst, Hallur Hansson (YC49), Fródi Benjaminsen (C), Páll Klettskard (46' Jóan Edmundsson (YC81)), Gilli Rólantsson Sørensen (76' Ári Jónsson). (Coach: Lars Christian Olsen (DEN)).
Finland: Niki Mäenpää, Niklas Moisander (C), Jere Uronen (75' Eero Markkanen), Joona Toivio, Përparim Hetemaj (YC37), Roman Eremenko, Kari Arkivuo, Riku Riski, Tim Sparv, Alexander Ring, Teemu Pukki (88' Joel Pohjanpalo). (Coach: Mika-Matti (Mixu) Petteri Paatelainen (FIN)).
Goals: Faroe Islands: 1-0 Christian Holst (41').
Finland: 1-1 Riku Riski (53'), 1-2 Riku Riski (78'), 1-3 Roman Eremenko (82').
Referee: Simon Lee Evans (WAL)   Attendance: 3.300

07-09-2014   Karaiskakis Stadium, Piraeus: Greece – Romania   0-1 (0-1)
Greece: Orestis Karnezis, Konstantinos (Kostas) Manolas (YC25), José Lloyd Holebas, Vasilis
Torosidis (YC45+2), Sokratis Papastathopoulos, Petros Mantalos (65' Lazaros
Christodoulopoulos), Panagiotis Tachtsidis, Andreas Samaris (YC17) (65' Panagiotis Kone
(YC90+4)), Dimitrios Salpingidis (C), Konstantinos (Kostas) Mitroglou, Georgios Samaras
(46' Dimitriso Diamantakos (YC58)). (Coach: Claudio Ranieri (ITA)).
Romania: Ciprian Tatarusanu (YC90+4), Dragos Grigore, Vlad Chiriches, Gabriel Tamas,
Razvan Rat, Ovidiu Hoban (84' Andrei Prepelita), Alexandru Chipciu (90' Gabriel Torje),
Mihai Pintilii (YC30), Alexandru Maxim (68' Gabriel Enache), Ciprian Marica (C)
(YC45+2,YC53), Bogdan Stancu. (Coach: Victor Piturca (ROM)).
Goal: Romania: 0-1 Ciprian Marica (10' penalty).
Referee: Mark Clattenburg (ENG)   Attendance: 173 (behind closed doors)
(José Lloyd Holebas also known as Iosif Cholevas)

11-10-2014   Arena Nationala, Bucharest: Romania – Hungary   1-1 (1-0)
Romania: Ciprian Tatarusanu, Dragos Grigore (YC80), Dorin Goian (5' Florin Gardos
(YC31)), Vlad Chiriches, Razvan Rat (C) (YC90+2), Ovidiu Hoban (YC18), Alexandru
Chipciu (YC90), Lucian Sanmartean (67' Cristian Tanase), Mihai Pintilii, Alexandru Maxim
(84' Bogdan Stancu), Raul Rusescu. (Coach: Victor Piturca (ROM)).
Hungary: Gábor Király (YC86), Tamás Kádár, Roland Juhász (YC69), Zsolt Korcsmár
(YC90+1), Ákos Elek (YC75), József Varga (YC51), Zoltán Stieber (46' Nemanja Nikolic),
Zoltán Gera (YC26) (77' Dániel Tözsér (YC90+2)), Gergö Lovrencsics (63' Krisztián Simon),
Ádám Szalai, Balázs Dzsudzsák (C). (Coach: Pál Dárdai (HUN)).
Goals: Romania: 1-0 Raul Rusescu (45').
Hungary: 1-1 Balázs Dzsudzsák (82').
Referee: William (Willie) Collum (SCO)   Attendance: 52.000

11-10-2014   Olympiastadion, Helsinki: Finland – Greece   1-1 (0-1)
Finland: Niki Mäenpää (YC84), Joona Toivio, Niklas Moisander (C), Jarkko Hurme, Tim
Sparv (YC74), Riku Riski (88' Teemu Tainio), Alexander Ring, Përparim Hetemaj (YC13)
(46' Kasper Hämäläinen), Roman Eremenko, Kari Arkivuo, Teemu Pukki (70' Joel
Pohjanpalo). (Coach: Mika-Matti (Mixu) Petteri Paatelainen (FIN)).
Greece: Orestis Karnezis, Loukas Vyntra, Vasilis Torosidis (C) (YC22), Sokratis
Papastathopoulos, Konstantinos (Kostas) Manolas, Panagiotis Tachtsidis, Andreas Samaris,
Charalampos (Charis) Mavrias (70' Vangelis Moras), Ioannis (Giannis) Maniatis (YC84),
Nikolaos (Nikos) Karelis (YC29) (81' Georgios Samaras), Stefanos Athanasiadis (84'
Konstantinos (Kostas) Mitroglou). (Coach: Claudio Ranieri (ITA)).
Goals: Finland: 1-1 Jarkko Hurme (55').
Greece: 0-1 Nikolaos (Nikos) Karelis (24').
Referee: David Fernández Borbalán (ESP)   Attendance: 26.548

11-10-2014   Windsor Park, Belfast: Northern Ireland – Faroe Islands   2-0 (2-0)
Northern Ireland: Roy Carroll, Conor McLaughlin, Gareth McAuley (56' Luke McCullough),
Aaron Hughes, Shane Ferguson (YC36), Oliver Norwood, Steven Davis (C), Jamie Ward,
Niall McGinn (67' Patrick (Paddy) McCourt), Chris Baird, Kyle Lafferty (84' Josh Magennis).
(Coach: Michael Andrew Martin O'Neill (NIR)).
Faroe Islands: Gunnar Nielsen, Sonni Ragnar Nattestad, Jónas Tór Næs (YC15), Pól Jóhannus
Justinussen (90'+1' Kaj Leo í Bartalsstovu), Atli Gregersen, Viljormur Davidsen, Christian
Holst (82' Brandur Hendriksson Olsen), Hallur Hansson, Jóan Edmundsson, Fródi
Benjaminsen (C), Páll Klettskard (75' Arnbjørn Hansen). (Coach: Lars Christian Olsen
(DEN)).
Goals: Northern Ireland: 1-0 Gareth McAuley (6'), 2-0 Kyle Lafferty (20').
Referee: Alon Yefet (ISR)   Attendance: 10.049
(Fródi Benjaminsen missed a penalty in the 37th minute)

14-10-2014   Tórsvøllur, Tórshavn: Faroe Islands – Hungary   0-1 (0-1)
Faroe Islands: Gunnar Nielsen, Sonni Ragnar Nattestad, Jónas Tór Næs, Atli Gregersen
(YC20), Viljormur Davidsen, Sølvi Vatnhamar (81' Gilli Rólantsson Sørensen), Brandur
Hendriksson Olsen, Christian Holst (69' Kaj Leo í Bartalsstovu), Hallur Hansson (YC32), Jóan
Edmundsson (76' Arnbjørn Hansen), Fródi Benjaminsen (C) (YC56). (Coach: Lars Christian
Olsen (DEN)).
Hungary: Dénes Dibusz, Mihály Korhut, Tamás Kádár, Roland Juhász, József Varga, Dániel
Tözsér (73' Zsolt Kalmár), Zoltán Gera (YC48), Ádám Szalai (84' Tamás Priskin), Krisztián
Simon, Nemanja Nikolic (46' Attila Fiola), Balázs Dzsudzsák (C). (Coach: Pál Dárdai (HUN)).
Goal: Hungary: 0-1 Ádám Szalai (21').
Referee: Aliaksei Kulbakov (BLS)   Attendance: 2.000

14-10-2014   Olympiastadion, Helsinki: Finland – Romania   0-2 (0-0)
Finland: Niki Mäenpää, Joona Toivio, Niklas Moisander (C), Jarkko Hurme, Tim Sparv,
Alexander Ring (YC52,YC56), Përparim Hetemaj (64' Joel Pohjanpalo), Kasper Hämäläinen
(74' Eero Markkanen), Roman Eremenko, Kari Arkivuo, Teemu Pukki (46' Riku Riski).
(Coach: Mika-Matti (Mixu) Petteri Paatelainen (FIN)).
Romania: Ciprian Tatarusanu, Razvan Rat (C), Srdjan Luchin, Dragos Grigore, Vlad Chiriches,
Gabriel Torje, Cristian Tanase (YC8) (84' Gabriel Enache), Mihai Pintilii, Ovidiu Hoban,
Alexandru Chipciu (49' Lucian Sanmartean), Bogdan Stancu (YC44) (86' Raul Rusescu).
(Coach: Victor Piturca (ROM)).
Goals: Romania: 0-1 Bogdan Stancu (54'), 0-2 Bogdan Stancu (83').
Referee: Paolo Tagliavento (ITA)   Attendance: 19.408

14-10-2014   Karaiskakis Stadium, Piraeus: Greece – Northern Ireland   0-2 (0-1)
Greece: Orestis Karnezis, Loukas Vyntra (16' Konstantinos (Kostas) Stafylidis), Vasilis
Torosidis (C), Sokratis Papastathopoulos, Konstantinos (Kostas) Manolas, Panagiotis
Tachtsidis, Ioannis (Giannis) Maniatis (YC59), Georgios Samaras (YC33) (67' Dimitrios
Salpingidis), Konstantinos (Kostas) Mitroglou, Nikolaos (Nikos) Karelis, Stefanos
Athanasiadis (46' Andreas Samaris (YC90)). (Coach: Claudio Ranieri (ITA)).
Northern Ireland: Roy Carroll, Conor McLaughlin, Gareth McAuley, Aaron Hughes, Shane
Ferguson (78' Benjamin (Ben) Reeves), Oliver Norwood, Corry Evans, Steven Davis (C),
Jamie Ward (59' Ryan McGivern), Chris Baird, Kyle Lafferty (YC28) (72' Josh Magennis).
(Coach: Michael Andrew Martin O'Neill (NIR)).
Goals: Northern Ireland: 0-1 Jamie Ward (9'), 0-2 Kyle Lafferty (51').
Referee: Stéphane Lannoy (FRA)   Attendance: 18.726

331

14-11-2014   Karaiskakis Stadium, Piraeus: Greece – Faroe Islands   0-1 (0-0)
Greece: Orestis Karnezis, Vangelis Moras, Konstantinos (Kostas) Manolas (YC88), Nikolaos (Nikos) Karabelas (78' Petros Mantalos), Vasilis Torosidis (C), Ioannis (Giannis) Maniatis, Panagiotis Kone, Andreas Samaris, Nikolaos (Nikos) Karelis (62' Charalampos (Charis) Mavrias), Theofanis (Fanis) Gekas (46' Stefanos Athanasiadis), Lazaros Christodoulopoulos. (Coach: Claudio Ranieri (ITA)).
Faroe Islands: Gunnar Nielsen, Jónas Tór Næs, Sonni Ragnar Nattestad, Atli Gregersen (YC57), Viljormur Davidsen, Sølvi Vatnhamar, Brandur Hendriksson Olsen (YC33) (88' Klæmint Olsen), Christian Holst (76' Pól Jóhannus Justinussen), Hallur Hansson (YC49), Jóan Edmundsson (86' Odmar Færø), Fródi Benjaminsen (C). (Coach: Lars Christian Olsen (DEN)).
Goal: Faroe Islands: 0-1 Jóan Edmundsson (61').
Referee: Nicola Rizzoli (ITA)   Attendance: 16.821

14-11-2014   Groupama Arena, Budapest: Hungary – Finland   1-0 (0-0)
Hungary: Gábor Király, Tamás Kádár, Roland Juhász (57' Gyula Forró), Attila Fiola, Ádám Lang, Ákos Elek (YC58), Dániel Tözsér (YC35), Zoltán Gera, Ádám Szalai (63' Nemanja Nikolic), Krisztián Simon (77' Gergö Lovrencsics), Balázs Dzsudzsák (C) (YC76). (Coach: Pál Dárdai (HUN)).
Finland: Lukás Hrádecky, Niklas Moisander (C), Jarkko Hurme (YC54), Markus Halsti (85' Fero Markkanen), Jere Uronen, Joona Toivio, Përparim Hetemaj, Kasper Hämäläinen (82' Riku Riski), Roman Eremenko, Tim Sparv, Teemu Pukki (65' Joel Pohjanpalo). (Coach: Mika-Matti (Mixu) Petteri Paatelainen (FIN)).
Goal: Hungary: 1-0 Zoltán Gera (84').
Referee: Clément Turpin (FRA)   Attendance: 19.600

14-11-2014   Arena Nationala, Bucharest: Romania – Northern Ireland   2-0 (0-0)
Romania: Ciprian Tatarusanu, Razvan Rat (C), Paul Papp, Dragos Grigore, Vlad Chiriches, Gabriel Torje (80' Ovidiu Hoban), Cristian Tanase (58' Alexandru Maxim (YC77)), Lucian Sanmartean, Mihai Pintilii (YC47), Alexandru Chipciu (YC76), Bogdan Stancu (46' Claudiu Keserü). (Coach: Anghel Iordanescu (ROM)).
Northern Ireland: Roy Carroll, Conor McLaughlin (YC45+1), Ryan McGivern, Gareth McAuley (C), Aaron Hughes, Oliver Norwood, Corry Evans (78' Billy McKay), Chris Brunt, Niall McGinn (63' Sammy Clingan), Chris Baird, Kyle Lafferty (YC52). (Coach: Michael Andrew Martin O'Neill (NIR)).
Goals: Romania: 1-0 Paul Papp (74'), 2-0 Paul Papp (79').
Referee: Jonas Eriksson (SWE)   Attendance: 28.892

29-03-2015   Windsor Park, Belfast: Northern Ireland – Finland   2-1 (2-0)
Northern Ireland: Roy Carroll, Gareth McAuley, Jonathan (Jonny) Evans, Conor McLaughlin, Steven Davis (C) (46' Corry Evans), Chris Brunt (YC67), Oliver Norwood, Chris Baird (YC63), Jamie Ward, Niall McGinn (64' Stuart Dallas), Kyle Lafferty (79' Josh Magennis). (Coach: Michael Andrew Martin O'Neill (NIR)).
Finland: Lukás Hrádecky, Niklas Moisander (C), Jere Uronen, Joona Toivio (46' Paulus Arajuuri (YC79)), Alexander Ring, Sakari Mattila, Kasper Hämäläinen (43' Joel Pohjanpalo (YC70)), Roman Eremenko, Tim Sparv, Sebastian Sorsa, Teemu Pukki (70' Berat Sadik). (Coach: Mika-Matti (Mixu) Petteri Paatelainen (FIN)).
Goals: Northern Ireland: 1-0 Kyle Lafferty (33'), 2-0 Kyle Lafferty (38').
Finland: 2-1 Berat Sadik (90'+1').
Referee: Szymon Marciniak (POL)   Attendance: 10.264

29-03-2015   Ilie Oana Stadium, Ploiesti: Romania – Faroe Islands 1-0 (1-0)
Romania: Costel Pantilimon, Razvan Rat (C), Paul Papp, Dragos Grigore, Vlad Chiriches,
Lucian Sanmartean (86' Andrei Prepelita), Adrian Popa (I) (71' Gabriel Torje (YC84)), Mihai
Pintilii, Alexandru Maxim, Raul Rusescu (60' Cristian Tanase), Claudiu Keserü (YC90+4).
(Coach: Anghel Iordanescu (ROM)).
Faroe Islands: Gunnar Nielsen, Sonni Ragnar Nattestad, Róaldur Jakobsen (80' René Joensen),
Atli Gregersen (C), Odmar Færø (74' Andreas Lave Olsen), Viljormur Davidsen, Jóhan
Davidsen, Sølvi Vatnhamar (YC63), Brandur Hendriksson Olsen (80' Gilli Rólantsson
Sørensen), Christian Holst, Jóan Edmundsson. (Coach: Lars Christian Olsen (DEN)).
Goal: Romania: 1-0 Claudiu Keserü (21').
Referee: Artur Manuel Ribeiro Soares Dias (POR)   Attendance: 13.898

29-03-2015   Groupama Arena, Budapest: Hungary – Greece 0-0
Hungary: Gábor Király, Tamás Kádár, Roland Juhász, Attila Fiola, Dániel Tözsér, Zoltán
Stieber, LEANDRO Marcolini Pedroso de Almeida (YC10), Ákos Elek (YC55) (70' Ádám
Pintér (YC79)), Zoltán Gera, Ádám Szalai (68' Nemanja Nikolic), Balázs Dzsudzsák (C).
(Coach: Pál Dárdai (HUN)).
Greece: Orestis Karnezis, Vasilis Torosidis (C), Konstantinos (Kostas) Stafylidis, Sokratis
Papastathopoulos, Kyriakos Papadopoulos, Konstantinos (Kostas) Manolas, Andreas Samaris,
Panagiotis Kone (YC64) (77' Konstantinos (Kostas) Katsouranis), Ioannis Fetfatzidis (YC65)
(77' Giannis Gianniotas), Lazaros Christodoulopoulos (69' Konstantinos (Kostas) Fortounis),
Stefanos Athanasiadis. (Coach: Sergio Apraham Markarián Abrahamian (URU)).
Referee: Sergey Gennadyevich Karasev (RUS)   Attendance: 22.000

13-06-2015   Olympiastadion, Helsinki: Finland – Hungary 0-1 (0-0)
Finland: Lukás Hrádecky, Markus Halsti (YC81), Jukka Raitala, Niklas Moisander (C), Sakari
Mattila (85' Joel Pohjanpalo), Përparim Hetemaj, Kasper Hämäläinen, Roman Eremenko, Kari
Arkivuo, Tim Sparv (YC80), Teemu Pukki (46' Riku Riski (YC55)). (Coach: Mika-Matti
(Mixu) Petteri Paatelainen (FIN)).
Hungary: Gábor Király, Ádám Lang (YC56), Tamás Kádár, Roland Juhász (YC82), Attila
Fiola, Dániel Tözsér, Zoltán Stieber (YC82), Zoltán Gera (YC64), Ádám Szalai (77' Nemanja
Nikolic), Tamás Priskin (46' Krisztián Németh), Balázs Dzsudzsák (C) (YC81) (88' Ádám
Simon). (Coach: Pál Dárdai (HUN)).
Goal: Hungary: 0-1 Zoltán Stieber (82').
Referee: Matej Jug (SLO)   Attendance: 20.434

13-06-2015   Tórsvøllur, Tórshavn: Faroe Islands – Greece 2-1 (1-0)
Faroe Islands: Gunnar Nielsen, Sonni Ragnar Nattestad, Atli Gregersen (YC76), Sølvi
Vatnhamar, Brandur Hendriksson Olsen (YC84), Christian Holst (74' Odmar Færø), Hallur
Hansson, Bárdur Jógvanson Hansen (YC55), Jóan Edmundsson (90'+2' René Joensen), Fródi
Benjaminsen (C) (YC27), Gilli Rólantsson Sørensen (13' Jóhan Davidsen). (Coach: Lars
Christian Olsen (DEN)).
Greece: Orestis Karnezis, Vasilis Torosidis (C) (YC57), Konstantinos (Kostas) Stafylidis,
Sokratis Papastathopoulos, Konstantinos (Kostas) Manolas, Andreas Samaris, Panagiotis Kone
(81' Taxiarchis Fountas), Ioannis Fetfatzidis (71' Dimitris Kolovos), Konstantinos (Kostas)
Mitroglou, Nikolaos (Nikos) Karelis (YC90), Lazaros Christodoulopoulos (46' Sotiris Ninis).
(Coach: Sergio Apraham Markarián Abrahamian (URU)).
Goals: Faroe Islands: 1-0 Hallur Hansson (32'), 2-0 Brandur Hendriksson Olsen (70').
Greece: 2-1 Sokratis Papastathopoulos (84').
Referee: Tom Harald Hagen (NOR)   Attendance: 4.731

333

13-06-2015   Windsor Park, Belfast: Northern Ireland – Romania 0-0
Northern Ireland: Michael McGovern, Conor McLaughlin, Gareth McAuley, Jonathan (Jonny) Evans (79' Craig Cathcart), Oliver Norwood, Steven Davis (C), Stuart Dallas, Chris Brunt (YC50), Jamie Ward (79' Corry Evans), Chris Baird, Kyle Lafferty. (Coach: Michael Andrew Martin O'Neill (NIR)).
Romania: Ciprian Tatarusanu, László Sepsi (YC47), Paul Papp, Dragos Grigore, Vlad Chiriches (C), Gabriel Torje (YC78), Andrei Prepelita, Mihai Pintilii (YC29), Alexandru Maxim (90' Gabriel Tamas), Alexandru Chipciu (61' Bogdan Stancu), Claudiu Keserü (72' Florin Andone). (Coach: Anghel Iordanescu (ROM)).
Referee: Carlos Velasco Carballo (ESP)   Attendance: 10.000

04-09-2015   Tórsvøllur, Tórshavn: Faroe Islands – Northern Ireland 1-3 (1-1)
Faroe Islands: Gunnar Nielsen, Odmar Færø, Jónas Tór Næs, Sonni Ragnar Nattestad, Christian Holst (76' Pól Jóhannus Justinussen), Brandur Hendriksson Olsen (83' Klæmint Olsen), Hallur Hansson (YC70), Jóan Edmundsson (YC6,YC65), Fródi Benjaminsen (C) (87' Rógvi Baldvinsson), Sølvi Vatnhamar, Gilli Rólantsson Sørensen. (Coach: Lars Christian Olsen (DEN)).
Northern Ireland: Michael McGovern, Conor McLaughlin (YC22) (70' Josh Magennis (YC73)), Gareth McAuley, Jonathan (Jonny) Evans, Oliver Norwood, Steven Davis (C), Stuart Dallas, Chris Brunt (83' Shane Ferguson), Niall McGinn, Chris Baird, Kyle Lafferty (78' Patrick (Paddy) McNair). (Coach: Michael Andrew Martin O'Neill (NIR)).
Goals: Faroe Islands: 1-1 Jóan Edmundsson (36').
Northern Ireland: 0-1 Gareth McAuley (12'), 1-2 Gareth McAuley (71'), 1-3 Kyle Lafferty (75').
Referee: Felix Zwayer (GER)   Attendance: 4.513

04-09-2015   Karaiskakis Stadium, Piraeus: Greece – Finland 0-1 (0-0)
Greece: Orestis Karnezis, José Lloyd Holebas, Loukas Vyntra, Sokratis Papastathopoulos (C) (YC90+4), Kyriakos Papadopoulos, Konstantinos (Kostas) Fortounis, Christos Aravidis (YC52) (68' Panagiotis Kone), Alexandros Tziolis, Andreas Samaris (86' Panagiotis Tachtsidis), Nikolaos (Nikos) Karelis (77' Taxiarchis Fountas), Konstantinos (Kostas) Mitroglou. (Coach: Konstantinos (Kostas) Tsanas (GRE)).
Finland: Lukás Hrádecky, Markus Halsti, Paulus Arajuuri (YC48), Jere Uronen, Joona Toivio, Përparim Hetemaj, Kasper Hämäläinen (46' Berat Sadik, 81' Sakari Mattila), Kari Arkivuo, Tim Sparv (C), Alexander Ring, Teemu Pukki (67' Joel Pohjanpalo). (Coach: Markku Kanerva (FIN)).
Goal: Finland: 0-1 Joel Pohjanpalo (75').
Referee: Serhiy Mykolayovych Boyko (UKR)   Attendance: 17.358

04-09-2015   Groupama Arena, Budapest: Hungary – Romania 0-0
Hungary: Gábor Király, Tamás Kádár, Roland Juhász (24' Richárd Guzmics), Attila Fiola, Ákos Elek, Dániel Tözsér (YC48), Zoltán Stieber (88' Tamás Priskin), LEANDRO Marcolini Pedroso de Almeida (YC67), Ádám Szalai (YC62), Nemanja Nikolic (70' Krisztián Németh), Balázs Dzsudzsák (C). (Coach: Bernd Storck (GER)).
Romania: Ciprian Tatarusanu, Paul Papp, Dragos Grigore, Vlad Chiriches (YC50), Razvan Rat (C), Ovidiu Hoban, Gabriel Torje (90' Alexandru Maxim), Lucian Sanmartean (78' Constantin Budescu), Andrei Prepelita, Adrian Popa (I) (YC21) (68' Alexandru Chipciu (YC73)), Claudiu Keserü (YC62). (Coach: Anghel Iordanescu (ROM)).
Referee: Dr.Felix Brych (GER)   Attendance: 22.060

07-09-2015   Olympiastadion, Helsinki: Finland – Faroe Islands   1-0 (1-0)
Finland: Lukás Hrádecky, Jere Uronen, Thomas Lam (YC65) (84' Sakari Mattila), Markus
Halsti (YC16), Paulus Arajuuri, Tim Sparv (C) (YC80), Riku Riski (74' Tim Väyrynen),
Alexander Ring, Joel Pohjanpalo (90'+3' Kasper Hämäläinen), Përparim Hetemaj, Kari
Arkivuo. (Coach: Markku Kanerva (FIN)).
Faroe Islands: Gunnar Nielsen, Sonni Ragnar Nattestad, Jónas Tór Næs (YC47), Atli
Gregersen, Sølvi Vatnhamar, Christian Holst (57' Kaj Leo í Bartalsstovu (YC89)), Brandur
Hendriksson Olsen (YC50), Hallur Hansson (YC65), Fródi Benjaminsen (C) (YC33) (84'
Rógvi Baldvinsson), Gilli Rólantsson Sørensen, Klæmint Olsen (75' Finnur Justinussen).
(Coach: Lars Christian Olsen (DEN)).
Goal: Finland: 1-0 Joel Pohjanpalo (23').
Referee: Marcin Borski (POL)   Attendance: 9.477

07-09-2015   Windsor Park, Belfast: Northern Ireland – Hungary   1-1 (0-0)
Northern Ireland: Michael McGovern, Gareth McAuley, Jonathan (Jonny) Evans, Conor
McLaughlin (YC72), Corry Evans (56' Niall McGinn), Steven Davis (C), Stuart Dallas (84'
Shane Ferguson), Chris Brunt, Oliver Norwood (75' Josh Magennis), Chris Baird
(YC81,YC81), Kyle Lafferty (YC10). (Coach: Michael Andrew Martin O'Neill (NIR)).
Hungary: Gábor Király, Tamás Kádár, Richárd Guzmics (YC19), Attila Fiola, LEANDRO
Marcolini Pedroso de Almeida (YC41), Zsolt Kalmár, Ákos Elek (22' Ádám Nagy), Zoltán
Gera, Ádám Szalai (68' Tamás Priskin (YC85)), Krisztián Németh (YC89) (89' Vilmos
Vanczák), Balázs Dzsudzsák (C). (Coach: Bernd Storck (GER)).
Goals: Northern Ireland: 1-1 Kyle Lafferty (90'+3').
Hungary: 0-1 Richárd Guzmics (74').
Referee: Cüneyt Çakir (TUR)   Attendance: 10.200

07-09-2015   Arena Nationala, Bucharest: Romania – Greece   0-0
Romania: Ciprian Tatarusanu, Dragos Grigore, Vlad Chiriches, Razvan Rat (C), Paul Papp
(YC78), Ovidiu Hoban (80' Florin Andone), Gabriel Torje, Mihai Pintilii, Alexandru Maxim
(64' Adrian Popa (I)), Claudiu Keserü, Constantin Budescu (64' Lucian Sanmartean). (Coach:
Anghel Iordanescu (ROM)).
Greece: Orestis Karnezis, José Lloyd Holebas (YC68), Sokratis Papastathopoulos (C),
Konstantinos (Kostas) Manolas (YC90), Konstantinos (Kostas) Fortounis (54' Panagiotis
Kone), Ioannis Fetfatzidis (46' Loukas Vyntra), Christos Aravidis, Alexandros Tziolis,
Andreas Samaris, Stelios Kitsiou, Konstantinos (Kostas) Mitroglou (87' Nikolaos (Nikos)
Karelis). (Coach: Konstantinos (Kostas) Tsanas (GRE)).
Referee: Aliaksei Kulbakov (BLS)   Attendance: 38.153

08-10-2015   Groupama Arena, Budapest: Hungary – Faroe Islands   2-1 (0-1)
Hungary: Gábor Király, Tamás Kádár, Roland Juhász, Richárd Guzmics, Attila Fiola, Dániel
Tözsér (46' Krisztián Németh), Ádám Nagy, Ádám Bódi (46' Dániel Böde), Zoltán Gera
(YC36), Nemanja Nikolic (75' Tamás Priskin), Balázs Dzsudzsák (C). (Coach: Bernd Storck
(GER)).
Faroe Islands: Gunnar Nielsen, Sonni Ragnar Nattestad (84' Odmar Færø), Jónas Tór Næs,
René Joensen (78' Gilli Rólantsson Sørensen), Atli Gregersen (C) (YC43,YC90+4), Viljormur
Davidsen, Rógvi Baldvinsson (YC18), Sølvi Vatnhamar, Róaldur Jakobsen (62' Pól Jóhannus
Justinussen), Jóan Edmundsson, Kaj Leo í Bartalsstovu. (Coach: Lars Christian Olsen (DEN)).
Goals: Hungary: 1-1 Dániel Böde (63'), 2-1 Dániel Böde (71').
Faroe Islands: 0-1 Róaldur Jakobsen (11').
Referee: Robert Schörgenhofer (AUT)   Attendance: 16.500

335

08-10-2015   Windsor Park, Belfast: Northern Ireland – Greece   3-1 (1-0)
Northern Ireland: Michael McGovern, Gareth McAuley, Craig Cathcart, Oliver Norwood, Corry Evans, Steven Davis (C), Stuart Dallas, Chris Brunt, Jamie Ward (81' Niall McGinn), Patrick (Paddy) McNair (85' Luke McCullough), Josh Magennis (78' Liam Boyce). (Coach: Michael Andrew Martin O'Neill (NIR)).
Greece: Orestis Karnezis, Vasilis Torosidis (C), Vangelis Moras, José Lloyd Holebas, Sokratis Papastathopoulos, Alexandros Tziolis, Andreas Samaris, Panagiotis Kone (71' Dimitris Pelkas), Christos Aravidis, Konstantinos (Kostas) Mitroglou (76' Stefanos Athanasiadis), Nikolaos (Nikos) Karelis (65' Petros Mantalos). (Coach: Konstantinos (Kostas) Tsanas (GRE)).
Goals: Northern Ireland: 1-0 Steven Davis (35'), 2-0 Josh Magennis (49'), 3-0 Steven Davis (58').
Greece: 3-1 Christos Aravidis (87').
Referee: Hendrikus Sebastiaan Hermanus (Bas) Nijhuis (HOL)   Attendance: 11.700

08-10-2015   Arena Nationala, Bucharest: Romania – Finland   1-1 (0-0)
Romania: Ciprian Tatarusanu, Razvan Rat (C), Paul Papp, Dragos Grigore, Vlad Chiriches, Gabriel Torje (87' Adrian Popa (I)), Lucian Sanmartean, Ovidiu Hoban (YC71), Alexandru Chipciu (60' Alexandru Maxim), Bogdan Stancu (69' Florin Andone), Claudiu Keserü. (Coach: Anghel Iordanescu (ROM)).
Finland: Lukás Hrádecky, Jere Uronen, Niklas Moisander (C), Markus Halsti (YC54), Paulus Arajuuri (62' Joona Toivio (YC74)), Rasmus Schüller, Alexander Ring, Joel Pohjanpalo (YC49) (77' Kasper Hämäläinen), Përparim Hetemaj (YC82), Kari Arkivuo (64' Ville Jalasto), Teemu Pukki. (Coach: Markku Kanerva (FIN)).
Goals: Romania: 1-1 Ovidiu Hoban (90'+1').
Finland: 0-1 Joel Pohjanpalo (67').
Referee: Craig Alexander Thomson (SCO)   Attendance: 47.987

11-10-2015   Tórsvøllur, Tórshavn: Faroe Islands – Romania   0-3 (0-2)
Faroe Islands: Gunnar Nielsen, Sonni Ragnar Nattestad (YC7) (84' Rógvi Baldvinsson), Jónas Tór Næs (C), Odmar Færø (YC79), Sølvi Vatnhamar (69' Árni Frederiksberg), Christian Holst (69' Andreas Lave Olsen), Brandur Hendriksson Olsen, Hallur Hansson (YC71), Jóan Edmundsson, Kaj Leo í Bartalsstovu, Gilli Rólantsson Sørensen. (Coach: Lars Christian Olsen (DEN)).
Romania: Ciprian Tatarusanu, Razvan Rat (C), Alexandru Matel, Dragos Grigore, Vlad Chiriches, Gabriel Torje (YC18) (78' Alexandru Maxim), Adrian Popa (I), Mihai Pintilii, Ovidiu Hoban, Bogdan Stancu (90' Denis Alibec), Constantin Budescu (88' Andrei Prepelita). (Coach: Anghel Iordanescu (ROM)).
Goals: Romania: 0-1 Constantin Budescu (4'), 0-2 Constantin Budescu (45'+1'), 0-3 Alexandru Maxim (83').
Referee: Ivan Kruzliak (SVK)   Attendance: 3.941

336

11-10-2015   Olympiastadion, Helsinki: Finland – Northern Ireland 1-1 (0-1)
Finland: Lukás Hrádecky, Paulus Arajuuri, Jere Uronen, Juhani Ojala, Ville Jalasto, Tim Sparv
(C), Rasmus Schüller (79' Kasper Hämäläinen), Alexander Ring (44' Robin Lod), Joel
Pohjanpalo, Sakari Mattila, Berat Sadik (66' Teemu Pukki). (Coach: Markku Kanerva (FIN)).
Northern Ireland: Michael McGovern, Gareth McAuley, Craig Cathcart, Oliver Norwood,
Steven Davis (C), Stuart Dallas, Chris Brunt, Chris Baird, Patrick (Paddy) McNair (51' Conor
McLaughlin), Niall McGinn (71' Shane Ferguson), Kyle Lafferty (79' Josh Magennis).
(Coach: Michael Andrew Martin O'Neill (NIR)).
Goals: Finland: 1-1 Paulus Arajuuri (87').
Northern Ireland: 0-1 Craig Cathcart (31').
Referee: Sergey Gennadyevich Karasev (RUS)   Attendance: 14.550

11-10-2015   Karaiskakis Stadium, Piraeus: Greece – Hungary 4-3 (1-1)
Greece: Orestis Karnezis, Sokratis Papastathopoulos (C) (64' Adam Tzanetopoulos), Vangelis
Moras (YC44), Konstantinos (Kostas) Stafylidis (35' José Lloyd Holebas (YC43)), Andreas
Samaris, Dimitris Pelkas, Petros Mantalos (72' Panagiotis Kone), Stelios Kitsiou, Konstantinos
(Kostas) Fortounis, Panagiotis Tachtsidis, Konstantinos (Kostas) Mitroglou. (Coach:
Konstantinos (Kostas) Tsanas (GRE)).
Hungary: Gábor Király, Tamás Kádár, Roland Juhász (YC36), Attila Fiola (YC89),
LEANDRO Marcolini Pedroso de Almeida, Ákos Elek (YC42), Zoltán Gera (71' Ádám Nagy),
Gergö Lovrencsics (62' Nemanja Nikolic), Krisztián Németh (YC45+2), Balázs Dzsudzsák (C)
(71' Zsolt Kalmár), Dániel Böde (YC78). (Coach: Bernd Storck (GER)).
Goals: Greece: 1-0 Konstantinos (Kostas) Stafylidis (5'), 2-2 Panagiotis Tachtsidis (57'), 3-3
Konstantinos (Kostas) Mitroglou (79'), 4-3 Panagiotis Kone (86').
Hungary: 1-1 Gergö Lovrencsics (26'), 1-2 Krisztián Németh (55'), 2-3 Krisztián Németh
(75').
Referee: Ivan Bebek (CRO)   Attendance: 9.500

GROUP   G

08-09-2014	Khimki	Russia – Liechtenstein	4-0 (1-0)
08-09-2014	Vienna	Austria – Sweden	1-1 (1-1)
08-09-2014	Podgorica	Montenegro – Moldova	2-0 (1-0)
09-10-2014	Vaduz	Liechtenstein – Montenegro	0-0
09-10-2014	Chisinau	Moldova – Austria	1-2 (1-1)
09-10-2014	Solna	Sweden – Russia	1-1 (0-1)
12-10-2014	Vienna	Austria – Montenegro	1-0 (1-0)
12-10-2014	Moscow	Russia – Moldova	1-1 (0-0)
12-10-2014	Solna	Sweden – Liechtenstein	2-0 (1-0)
15-11-2014	Vienna	Austria – Russia	1-0 (0-0)
15-11-2014	Chisinau	Moldova – Liechtenstein	0-1 (0-0)
15-11-2014	Podgorica	Montenegro – Sweden	1-1 (0-1)
27-03-2015	Vaduz	Liechtenstein – Austria	0-5 (0-2)
27-03-2015	Chisinau	Moldova – Sweden	0-2 (0-0)
27-03-2015	Podgorica	Montenegro – Russia	0-3
14-06-2015	Vaduz	Liechtenstein – Moldova	1-1 (1-1)
14-06-2015	Moscow	Russia – Austria	0-1 (0-1)
14-06-2015	Solna	Sweden – Montenegro	3-1 (3-0)
05-09-2015	Moscow	Russia – Sweden	1-0 (1-0)

337

05-09-2015	Vienna	Austria – Moldova	1-0 (0-0)
05-09-2015	Podgorica	Montenegro – Liechtenstein	2-0 (1-0)
08-09-2015	Vaduz	Liechtenstein – Russia	0-7 (0-3)
08-09-2015	Chisinau	Moldova – Montenegro	0-2 (0-1)
08-09-2015	Solna	Sweden – Austria	1-4 (0-2)
09-10-2015	Vaduz	Liechtenstein – Sweden	0-2 (0-1)
09-10-2015	Chisinau	Moldova – Russia	1-2 (0-0)
09-10-2015	Podgorica	Montenegro – Austria	2-3 (1-0)
12-10-2015	Vienna	Austria – Liechtenstein	3-0 (1-0)
12-10-2015	Moscow	Russia – Montenegro	2-0 (2-0)
12-10-2015	Solna	Sweden – Moldova	2-0 (1-0)

FINAL STANDING

Pos	Team	Pld	W	D	L	GF	GA	GD	Pts
1	Austria	10	9	1	0	22	5	+17	28
2	Russia	10	6	2	2	21	5	+16	20
3	Sweden	10	5	3	2	15	9	+6	18
4	Montenegro	10	3	2	5	10	13	-3	11
5	Liechtenstein	10	1	2	7	2	26	-24	5
6	Moldova	10	0	2	8	4	16	-12	2

**Austria and Russia qualified for the Final Tournament in France.
Sweden qualified for the play-offs**

08-09-2014   Arena Khimki, Khimki: Russia – Liechtenstein 4-0 (1-0)
Russia: Igor Akinfeev (72' Yuri Lodygin), Igor Smolnikov, Sergei Ignashevich, Vasili Berezutski (C), Dmitri Kombarov, Denis Glushakov, Alan Dzagoev (64' Magomed Ozdoev), Aleksandr Kokorin, Aleksandr Kerzhakov (46' Artem Dzyuba), Denis Cheryshev, Aleksandr Samedov. (Coach: Fabio Capello (ITA)).
Liechtenstein: Peter Jehle, Ivan Quintans (87' Sandro Wolfinger), Mario Frick (C) (YC27), Franz Burgmeier, Michele Polverino (73' Robin Gubser), Nicolas Hasler, Andreas Christen (64' Daniel Brändle), Martin Büchel, Seyhan Yildiz, Sandro Wieser (YC19), Dennis Salanovic. (Coach: René Pauritsch (AUT)).
Goals: Russia: 1-0 Martin Büchel (4' own goal), 2-0 Franz Burgmeier (50' own goal), 3-0 Dmitri Kombarov (54' penalty), 4-0 Artem Dzyuba (65').
Referee: Sébastien Delferière (BEL)   Attendance: 11.236

08-09-2014   Ernst-Happel-Stadion Vienna: Austria – Sweden 1-1 (1-1)
Austria: Robert Almer, Martin Hinteregger, Christian Fuchs (C), Aleksandar Dragovic (YC74), Florian Klein, Zlatko Juzunovic (76' Christoph Leitgeb), David Alaba, Julian Baumgartlinger, Marc Janko (68' Rubin Rafael Okotie), Martin Harnik (86' Valentino Lazaro), Marko Arnautovic. (Coach: Marcel Koller (SUI)).
Sweden: Andreas Isaksson, Pierre Bengtsson, Mikael Antonsson, Andreas Granqvist, Martin Olsson, Sebastian Larsson (YC59), Kim Källström (YC80) (85' Pontus Wernbloom), Albin Ekdal, Zlatan Ibrahimovic (C) (YC22), Jimmy Durmaz (72' Johan Elmander), Erkan Zengin. (Coach: Erik Hamrén (SWE)).
Goals: Austria: 1-0 David Alaba (7' penalty).
Sweden: 1-1 Erkan Zengin (12').
Referee: Pavel Královec (CZE)   Attendance: 48.500

08-09-2014   Stadion pod Goricom, Podgorica: Montenegro – Moldova   2-0 (1-0)
Montenegro: Vukasin Poleksic, Vladimir Volkov (YC27) (46' Sasa Balic), Zarko Tomasevic, Marko Simic, Stefan Savic, Elsad Zverotic, Nemanja Nikolic, Vladimir Bozovic, Mirko Vucinic (C) (YC60), Dejan Damjanovic (81' Nikola Vuksevic), Fatos Beciraj (66' Vladimir Jovovic). (Coach: Branko Brnovic (MNE)).
Moldova: Ilie Cebanu, Petru Racu, Victor Golovatenco, Alexandru Epureanu (C), Igor Armas (YC41), Artur Ionita, Serghei Gheorghiev (YC62) (81' Eugeniu (Eugen) Cebotaru), Alexandru Antoniuc (54' Maxim Antoniuc), Alexandru Dedov, Serghei Alexeev, Eugeniu Sidorenco (68' Veaceslav Posmac). (Coach: Ion Caras (MOL)).
Goals: Montenegro: 1-0 Mirko Vucinic (45'+2'), 2-0 Zarko Tomasevic (73').
Referee: Aliaksei Kulbakov (BLS)   Attendance: 8.759

09-10-2014   Rheinpark Stadion, Vaduz: Liechtenstein – Montenegro   0-0
Liechtenstein: Peter Jehle (62' Cengiz Biçer (YC90+5)), Daniel Kaufmann, Mario Frick (C) (YC88), Franz Burgmeier, Ivan Quintans (80' Simon Kühne), Nicolas Hasler, Martin Büchel (YC87), Michele Polverino, Seyhan Yildiz, Sandro Wieser (44' Andreas Christen), Dennis Salanovic. (Coach: René Pauritsch (AUT)).
Montenegro: Vukasin Poleksic, Savo Pavicevic, Milan Jovanovic, Zarko Tomasevic, Marko Simic (YC84), Vladimir Jovovic, Elsad Zverotic, Simon Vukcevic (57' Nemanja Nikolic), Stevan Jovetic (C) (74' Petar Grbic), Dejan Damjanovic, Fatos Beciraj (46' Mirko Vucinic). (Coach: Branko Brnovic (MNE)).
Referee: Simon Lee Evans (WAL)   Attendance: 2.790

09-10-2014   Zimbru Stadium, Chisinau: Moldova – Austria   1-2 (1-1)
Moldova: Ilie Cebanu, Victor Golovatenco, Iulian Erhan (87' Artur Patras), Alexandru Epureanu (C), Igor Armas, Ion Jardan (YC11), Artur Ionita, Alexandru Gatcan, Andrei Cojocari (65' Alexandru Antoniuc), Alexandru Dedov (YC82), Igor Picusceac (46' Eugeniu Sidorenco). (Coach: Alexandru Curtianu (MOL)).
Austria: Robert Almer, Sebastian Prödl (YC26), Christian Fuchs (C), Aleksandar Dragovic (YC90+2), Florian Klein, Zlatko Juzunovic (86' Stefan Ilsanker), David Alaba, Julian Baumgartlinger (YC33), Marc Janko (RC82), Marcel Sabitzer (46' Martin Harnik), Marko Arnautovic (79' Christoph Leitgeb). (Coach: Marcel Koller (SUI)).
Goals: Moldova: 1-1 Alexandru Dedov (27' penalty).
Austria: 0-1 David Alaba (12' penalty), 1-2 Marc Janko (51').
Referee: Manuel Jorge Neves Moreira de Sousa (POR)   Attendance: 9.381

09-10-2014   Friends Arena, Solna: Sweden – Russia   1-1 (0-1)
Sweden: Andreas Isaksson (C), Pierre Bengtsson, Mikael Antonsson, Andreas Granqvist, Martin Olsson, Kim Källström (86' Pontus Wernbloom (YC90+6)), Sebastian Larsson, Nabil Bahoui (79' Alexander Kacaniklic), Ola Toivonen (57' Johan Elmander (YC80)), Jimmy Durmaz, Erkan Zengin (YC32). (Coach: Erik Hamrén (SWE)).
Russia: Igor Akinfeev, Sergei Ignashevich, Vasili Berezutski (C), Igor Smolnikov (YC13), Dmitri Kombarov (88' Vladimir Granat), Denis Glushakov (YC51), Viktor Fayzulin (87' Alan Dzagoev), Oleg Shatov, Artem Dzyuba, Aleksandr Kokorin, Aleksandr Samedov (73' Maksim Grigoryev). (Coach: Fabio Capello (ITA)).
Goals: Sweden: 1-1 Ola Toivonen (49').
Russia: 0-1 Aleksandr Kokorin (10').
Referee: Nicola Rizzoli (ITA)   Attendance: 49.023
(Sebastian Larsson missed a penalty in the 13th minute)

339

12-10-2014   Ernst-Happel-Stadion, Vienna: Austria – Montenegro 1-0 (1-0)
Austria: Robert Almer, Martin Hinteregger, Christian Fuchs (C), Aleksandar Dragovic, Florian
Klein, Zlatko Juzunovic (YC56) (77' Stefan Ilsanker), David Alaba, Julian Baumgartlinger
(YC68), Rubin Rafael Okotie (83' Valentino Lazaro), Martin Harnik, Marko Arnautovic (62'
Lukas Hinterseer). (Coach: Marcel Koller (SUI)).
Montenegro: Vukasin Poleksic, Vladimir Volkov, Marko Simic (YC69), Stefan Savic, Marko
Basa, Elsad Zverotic (YC13) (70' Vladimir Jovovic), Simon Vukcevic (46' Stevan Jovetic),
Nemanja Nikolic, Vladimir Bozovic (YC54) (76' Dejan Damjanovic), Mirko Vucinic (C),
Fatos Beciraj. (Coach: Branko Brnovic (MNE)).
Goal: Austria: 1-0 Rubin Rafael Okotie (24').
Referee: Hendrikus Sebastiaan Hermanus (Bas) Nijhuis (HOL)   Attendance: 44.200

12-10-2014   Otkrytiye Arena, Moscow: Russia – Moldova 1-1 (0-0)
Russia: Igor Akinfeev, Sergei Parshivlyuk, Sergei Ignashevich, Vladimir Granat, Vasili
Berezutski (C), Denis Glushakov, Alan Dzagoev, Aleksandr Kerzhakov (46' Magomed
Ozdoev), Artem Dzyuba, Denis Cheryshev (62' Dmitri Poloz), Aleksei Ionov (75' Georgi
Schennikov). (Coach: Fabio Capello (ITA)).
Moldova: Ilie Cebanu, Ion Jardan, Victor Golovatenco (YC72), Iulian Erhan (YC33),
Alexandru Epureanu (C), Igor Armas, Artur Ionita, Alexandru Gatcan, Andrei Cojocari (73'
Petru Racu), Alexandru Dedov (82' Eugeniu Sidorenco (YC90+2)), Igor Picusceac (46' Artur
Patras). (Coach: Alexandru Curtianu (MOL)).
Goals: Russia: 1-0 Artem Dzyuba (73' penalty).
Moldova: 1-1 Alexandru Epureanu (74').
Referee: Kristinn Jakobsson (ISL)   Attendance: 30.017

12-10-2014   Friends Arena, Solna: Sweden – Liechtenstein 2-0 (1-0)
Sweden: Andreas Isaksson (C), Pierre Bengtsson, Mikael Antonsson, Martin Olsson, Andreas
Granqvist, Kim Källström, Emil Forsberg (66' Branimir Hrgota), Albin Ekdal (74' Nabil
Bahoui), Johan Elmander (79' Pontus Wernbloom), Erkan Zengin, Jimmy Durmaz. (Coach:
Erik Hamrén (SWE)).
Liechtenstein: Cengiz Biçer, Ivan Quintans (YC64), Daniel Kaufmann, Mario Frick (C)
(YC49), Franz Burgmeier, Michele Polverino, Nicolas Hasler, Andreas Christen (78' Simon
Kühne), Martin Büchel (83' Sandro Wolfinger), Seyhan Yildiz (27' Daniel Brändle), Dennis
Salanovic. (Coach: René Pauritsch (AUT)).
Goals: Sweden: 1-0 Erkan Zengin (34'), 2-0 Jimmy Durmaz (46').
Referee: Gediminas Mazeika (LIT)   Attendance: 22.528

15-11-2014   Ernsy-Happel-Stadion, Vienna: Austria – Russia 1-0 (0-0)
Austria: Robert Almer, Martin Hinteregger (YC65), Christian Fuchs (C), Aleksandar Dragovic
(86' Sebastian Prödl), Florian Klein, Christoph Leitgeb, Zlatko Juzunovic, Stefan Ilsanker,
Marc Janko (59' Rubin Rafael Okotie), Martin Harnik, Marko Arnautovic (90'+1' Marcel
Sabitzer). (Coach: Marcel Koller (SUI)).
Russia: Igor Akinfeev, Sergei Parshivlyuk (YC71), Sergei Ignashevich, Vasili Berezutski,
Dmitri Kombarov, Roman Shirokov (C), Oleg Shatov (81' Alan Dzagoev), Denis Glushakov
(YC10), Viktor Fayzulin (75' Artem Dzyuba), Aleksandr Kokorin, Denis Cheryshev (56'
Aleksei Ionov). (Coach: Fabio Capello (ITA)).
Goal: Austria: 1-0 Rubin Rafael Okotie (73').
Referee: Martin Atkinson (ENG)   Attendance: 47.500

15-11-2014   Zimbru Stadium, Chisinau: Moldova – Liechtenstein   0-1 (0-0)
Moldova: Ilie Cebanu, Petru Racu, Victor Golovatenco, Alexandru Epureanu (C), Igor Armas, Artur Patras (75' Alexandru Suvorov), Artur Ionita, Alexandru Gatcan, Andrei Cojocari (56' Dan Spataru), Alexandru Dedov, Radu Gînsari. (Coach: Alexandru Curtianu (MOL)).
Liechtenstein: Benjamin Büchel, Ivan Quintans (90' Niklas Kieber), Daniel Kaufmann, Franz Burgmeier (C), Daniel Brändle (YC55) (63' Simon Kühne), Michele Polverino, Nicolas Hasler, Andreas Christen, Martin Büchel (88' Robin Gubser), Sandro Wieser, Dennis Salanovic (YC79). (Coach: René Pauritsch (AUT)).
Goal: Liechtenstein: 0-1 Franz Burgmeier (74').
Referee: Mattias Gestranius (FIN)   Attendance: 6.843

15-11-2014   Stadion pod Goricom, Podgorica: Montenegro – Sweden   1-1 (0-1)
Montenegro: Mladen Bozovic, Marko Basa (YC73), Vladimir Volkov, Zarko Tomasevic (77' Branislav Jankovic), Stefan Savic, Elsad Zverotic, Nikola Vuksevic, Vladimir Jovovic, Vladimir Bozovic (46' Marko Bakic (YC50)), Stevan Jovetic (C), Dejan Damjanovic (67' Fatos Beciraj). (Coach: Branko Brnovic (MNE)).
Sweden: Andreas Isaksson, Mikael Antonsson, Pierre Bengtsson, Mikael Lustig (46' Oscar Wendt), Andreas Granqvist, Kim Källström (YC87), Emil Forsberg (63' Sebastian Larsson), Albin Ekdal (YC68), Erkan Zengin (86' Isaac Kiese Thelin), Zlatan Ibrahimovic (C), Jimmy Durmaz. (Coach: Erik Hamrén (SWE)).
Goals: Montenegro: 1-1 Stevan Jovetic (80' penalty).
Sweden: 0-1 Zlatan Ibrahimovic (9').
Referee: William (Willie) Collum (SCO)   Attendance: 10.538

27-03-2015   Rheinpark Stadion, Vaduz: Liechtenstein – Austria   0-5 (0-2)
Liechtenstein: Peter Jehle (YC32), Ivan Quintans (55' Dennis Salanovic), Yves Oehri, Daniel Kaufmann, Mario Frick (C), Franz Burgmeier, Michele Polverino, Nicolas Hasler, Andreas Christen (83' Simon Kühne), Martin Büchel (88' Robin Gubser), Sandro Wieser. (Coach: René Pauritsch (AUT)).
Austria: Robert Almer, Martin Hinteregger, Christian Fuchs (C), Aleksandar Dragovic, Florian Klein (YC38), Zlatko Juzunovic (82' Lukas Hinterseer), David Alaba, Julian Baumgartlinger, Marc Janko (77' Marco Djuricin), Martin Harnik (72' Marcel Sabitzer), Marko Arnautovic. (Coach: Marcel Koller (SUI)).
Goals: Austria: 0-1 Martin Harnik (14'), 0-2 Marc Janko (16'), 0-3 David Alaba (59'), 0-4 Zlatko Juzunovic (74'), 0-5 Marko Arnautovic (90'+3').
Referee: Felix Zwayer (GER)   Attendance: 5.864
(David Alaba missed a penalty in the 33rd minute)

27-03-2015   Zimbru Stadium, Chisinau: Moldova – Sweden   0-2 (0-0)
Moldova: Ilie Cebanu, Victor Golovatenco (YC28), Alexandru Epureanu (C), Vadim Bolohan, Igor Armas, Petru Racu (YC45), Alexandru Gatcan (YC90+4), Gheorghe Andronic (70' Viorel Frunza), Artur Ionita (36' Andrei Cojocari), Alexandru Dedov, Gheorghe Boghiu (86' Serghei Gheorghiev (YC87)). (Coach: Alexandru Curtianu (MOL)).
Sweden: Andreas Isaksson, Pierre Bengtsson, Martin Olsson (YC54), Erik Johansson, Andreas Granqvist (YC4,YC90+3), Sebastian Larsson (80' Emil Forsberg), Kim Källström, Albin Ekdal, Isaac Kiese Thelin (70' Marcus Berg), Zlatan Ibrahimovic (C) (YC65), Erkan Zengin (85' Pontus Wernbloom). (Coach: Erik Hamrén (SWE)).
Goals: Sweden: 0-1 Zlatan Ibrahimovic (46'), 0-2 Zlatan Ibrahimovic (84' penalty).
Referee: Ivan Bebek (CRO)   Attendance: 10.375

341

27-03-2015   Stadion pod Goricom, Podgorica: Montenegro – Russia   0-3 (Awarded)
Montenegro: Vukasin Poleksic, Vladimir Volkov, Marko Simic, Marko Basa, Sasa Balic (46'
Marko Bakic), Elsad Zverotic, Nikola Vuksevic, Adam Marusic, Mladen Kascelan (YC52),
Mirko Vucinic (YC66), Stevan Jovetic (C). (Coach: Branko Brnovic (MNE)).
Russia: Igor Akinfeev (2' Yuri Lodygin), Igor Smolnikov, Sergei Ignashevich, Vasili
Berezutski, Dmitri Kombarov, Yuri Zhirkov, Roman Shirokov (C), Oleg Shatov (YC17), Alan
Dzagoev (46' Dmitri Torbinskiy), Igor Denisov (YC32), Aleksandr Kokorin. (Coach: Fabio
Capello (ITA)).
Referee: Deniz Aytekin (GER)   Attendance: 16.000

*(This match was awarded as a 3-0 win to Russia after the match was abandoned on 67 minutes
due to crowd violence and a scuffle between the players caused by Dmitri Kombarov being hit
by an object thrown from the Montenegran section of the ground. The scoreline at the time was
0-0 and Russia had missed a penalty moments before the match was abandoned (the penalty
was missed by Roman Shirokov). This was the second delay of the match as, in the first minute,
Russian goalkeeper Igor Akinfeev was hit by a flare, an incident which caused a 33-minute
delay. The Montenegro FA was fined €50.000 and the Russian FA was also fined €25.000 by
UEFA. Montenegro were ordered to play their next home match behind closed doors)*

14-06-2015   Rheinpark Stadion, Vaduz: Liechtenstein – Moldova   1-1 (1-1)
Liechtenstein: Peter Jehle, Yves Oehri (42' Simon Kühne), Daniel Kaufmann, Mario Frick (C),
Franz Burgmeier, Michele Polverino, Andreas Christen, Martin Büchel (69' Robin Gubser),
Seyhan Yildiz, Sandro Wieser (YC50), Philippe Erne (YC76) (83' Daniel Brändle). (Coach:
René Pauritsch (AUT)).
Moldova: Ilie Cebanu, Petru Racu, Iulian Erhan, Alexandru Epureanu (C) (46' Catalin Carp),
Igor Armas, Artur Patras (89' Maxim Antoniuc), Alexandru Gatcan (YC50), Andrei Cojocari,
Anatoli Cheptine (37' Nicolae Milinceanu), Alexandru Dedov, Gheorghe Boghiu. (Coach:
Alexandru Curtianu (MOL)).
Goals: Liechtenstein: 1-0 Sandro Wieser (20').
Moldova: 1-1 Gheorghe Boghiu (43').
Referee: Libor Kovarík (CZE)   Attendance: 2.080

14-06-2015   Otkrytiye Arena, Moscow: Russia – Austria   0-1 (0-1)
Russia: Igor Akinfeev, Igor Smolnikov, Ivan Novoseltsev, Vasili Berezutski (12' Nikita
Chernov), Dmitri Kombarov (71' Aleksandr Kerzhakov), Yuri Zhirkov, Roman Shirokov (C),
Oleg Shatov, Oleg Ivanov (46' Aleksei Miranchuk), Denis Glushakov, Aleksandr Kokorin
(YC80). (Coach: Fabio Capello (ITA)).
Austria: Robert Almer, Martin Hinteregger, Christian Fuchs (C), Aleksandar Dragovic, Florian
Klein (YC87), Zlatko Juzunovic (86' Sebastian Prödl), Stefan Ilsanker, Julian Baumgartlinger,
Marc Janko (75' Rubin Rafael Okotie), Martin Harnik (65' Marcel Sabitzer), Marko
Arnautovic. (Coach: Marcel Koller (SUI)).
Goal: Austria: 0-1 Marc Janko (33').
Referee: Milorad Mazic (SRB)   Attendance: 33.750

14-06-2015   Friends Arena, Solna: Sweden – Montenegro   3-1 (3-0)
Sweden: Andreas Isaksson, Alexander Milosevic, Pierre Bengtsson, Oscar Wendt, Erik
Johansson, Sebastian Larsson, Kim Källström (YC67) (72' Pontus Wernbloom), Albin Ekdal
(YC80), Zlatan Ibrahimovic (C) (90'+1' Ola Toivonen), Marcus Berg, Erkan Zengin (64' Emil
Forsberg). (Coach: Erik Hamrén (SWE)).
Montenegro: Vukasin Poleksic (C), Zarko Tomasevic (YC54), Marko Simic (YC48) (74' Sasa
Balic), Stefan Savic, Elsad Zverotic (58' Esteban Saveljic), Nikola Vuksevic (YC88), Adam
Marusic, Mladen Kascelan (46' Vladimir Boljevic (YC55)), Stefan Mugosa, Dejan
Damjanovic, Fatos Beciraj. (Coach: Branko Brnovic (MNE)).
Goals: Sweden: 1-0 Marcus Berg (37'), 2-0 Zlatan Ibrahimovic (40'), 3-0 Zlatan Ibrahimovic
(44').
Montenegro: 3-1 Dejan Damjanovic (64' penalty).
Referee: Hüseyin Göçek (TUR)   Attendance: 32.224

05-09-2015   Otkrytiye Arena, Moscow: Russia – Sweden   1-0 (1-0)
Russia: Igor Akinfeev, Sergei Ignashevich, Vasili Berezutski, Igor Smolnikov, Alan Dzagoev
(YC34), Igor Denisov, Yuri Zhirkov (71' Oleg Kuzmin (YC82)), Roman Shirokov (C) (83'
Aleksei Berezutski), Oleg Shatov, Aleksandr Kokorin, Artem Dzyuba (79' Aleksei Ionov).
(Coach: Leonid Viktorovich Slutski (RUS)).
Sweden: Andreas Isaksson, Pierre Bengtsson (60' Marcus Berg), Mikael Antonsson, Andreas
Granqvist, Martin Olsson, Sebastian Larsson, Emil Forsberg (YC90+1), Albin Ekdal (82' Isaac
Kiese Thelin), Pontus Wernbloom (YC52), Zlatan Ibrahimovic (C) (46' Ola Toivonen), Jimmy
Durmaz. (Coach: Erik Hamrén (SWE)).
Goal: Russia: 1-0 Artem Dzyuba (38').
Referee: Mark Clattenburg (ENG)   Attendance: 43.768

05-09-2015   Ernst-Happel-Stadion, Vienna: Austria – Moldova   1-0 (0-0)
Austria: Robert Almer, Sebastian Prödl (YC37), Christian Fuchs (C), Aleksandar Dragovic,
Florian Klein, David Alaba (90'+2' Stefan Ilsanker), Zlatko Juzunovic, Julian Baumgartlinger,
Marc Janko (84' Rubin Rafael Okotie), Martin Harnik (76' Jakob Jantscher), Marko
Arnautovic. (Coach: Marcel Koller (SUI)).
Moldova: Ilie Cebanu (C) (YC39), Ion Jardan, Victor Golovatenco, Iulian Erhan, Igor Armas,
Artur Patras, Andrei Cojocari, Eugeniu (Eugen) Cebotaru (YC25) (79' Radu Gînsari),
Gheorghe Andronic (55' Petru Racu), Alexandru Dedov, Nicolae Milinceanu (87' Catalin
Carp). (Coach: Alexandru Curtianu (MOL)).
Goal: Austria: 1-0 Zlatko Juzunovic (52').
Referee: Aleksandar Stavrev (MCD)   Attendance: 48.500

05-09-2015   Stadion pod Goricon, Podgorica: Montenegro – Liechtenstein   2-0 (1-0)
Montenegro: Vukasin Poleksic (C), Vladimir Volkov, Zarko Tomasevic, Stefan Savic, Marko
Basa, Nikola Vukcevic, Adam Marusic (YC47) (68' Elsad Zverotic), Vladimir Boljevic, Mirko
Vucinic (59' Dejan Damjanovic), Stevan Jovetic (69' Stefan Mugosa), Fatos Beciraj. (Coach:
Branko Brnovic (MNE)).
Liechtenstein: Peter Jehle, Martin Rechsteiner, Daniel Kaufmann, Mario Frick (C) (YC22),
Franz Burgmeier (76' Niklas Kieber), Michele Polverino, Nicolas Hasler, Andreas Christen,
Martin Büchel (85' Robin Gubser), Seyhan Yildiz, Sandro Wieser (YC32) (66' Dennis
Salanovic). (Coach: René Pauritsch (AUT)).
Goals: Montenegro: 1-0 Fatos Beciraj (38'), 2-0 Stevan Jovetic (56').
Referee: Javier Estrada Fernández (ESP)   Attendance: behind closed doors

343

08-09-2015   Rheinpark Stadion, Vaduz: Liechtenstein – Russia   0-7 (0-3)
Liechtenstein: Peter Jehle, Martin Rechsteiner, Daniel Kaufmann (RC40), Mario Frick (C),
Franz Burgmeier, Martin Büchel (84' Robin Gubser), Michele Polverino (YC62), Nicolas
Hasler, Seyhan Yildiz, Dennis Salanovic (88' Andreas Christen), Niklas Kieber (YC59) (77'
Mathias Sele). (Coach: René Pauritsch (AUT)).
Russia: Igor Akinfeev, Igor Smolnikov, Sergei Ignashevich, Vasili Berezutski, Dmitri
Kombarov, Oleg Shatov (65' Pavel Mamaev), Igor Denisov (46' Denis Glushakov), Roman
Shirokov (C) (75' Fedor Smolov), Alan Dzagoev, Aleksandr Kokorin, Artem Dzyuba. (Coach:
Leonid Viktorovich Slutski (RUS)).
Goals: Russia: 0-1 Artem Dzyuba (21'), 0-2 Aleksandr Kokorin (40' penalty), 0-3 Artem
Dzyuba (45'), 0-4 Artem Dzyuba (73'), 0-5 Fedor Smolov (77'), 0-6 Alan Dzagoev (85'), 0-7
Artem Dzyuba (90').
Referee: Bobby Madden (SCO)   Attendance: 2.874

08-09-2015   Zimbru Stadium, Chisinau: Moldova – Montenegro   0-2 (0-1)
Moldova: Ilie Cebanu, Igor Armas, Ion Jardan, Victor Golovatenco (YC61), Iulian Erhan,
Artur Patras (71' Radu Gînsari), Alexandru Gatcan (C) (YC45), Andrei Cojocari (YC89),
Eugeniu (Eugen) Cebotaru (36' Petru Racu), Alexandru Dedov (YC46), Nicolae Milinceanu.
(Coach: Alexandru Curtianu (MOL)).
Montenegro: Vukasin Poleksic, Marko Basa (YC40), Zarko Tomasevic, Marko Simic, Stefan
Savic (YC49), Nikola Vukcevic (YC56), Adam Marusic (69' Stanisa Mandic), Vladimir
Boljevic, Stevan Jovetic (C) (88' Mladen Kascelan), Dejan Damjanovic (46' Stefan Mugosa),
Fatos Beciraj. (Coach: Branko Brnovic (MNE)).
Goals: Montenegro: 0-1 Stefan Savic (9'), 0-2 Petru Racu (65' own goal).
Referee: Sébastien Delferière (BEL)   Attendance: 6.243

08-09-2015   Friends Arena, Solna: Sweden – Austria   1-4 (0-2)
Sweden: Andreas Isaksson, Mikael Antonsson, Martin Olsson (82' Jimmy Durmaz), Andreas
Granqvist (YC15), Sebastian Larsson, Kim Källström, Emil Forsberg, Albin Ekdal (86' Abdul
Rahman Khalili), Zlatan Ibrahimovic (C), Marcus Berg, Erkan Zengin (62' Isaac Kiese
Thelin). (Coach: Erik Hamrén (SWE)).
Austria: Robert Almer, Sebastian Prödl, Christian Fuchs (C), Aleksandar Dragovic, Florian
Klein, Zlatko Juzunovic (YC24) (80' Marcel Sabitzer), David Alaba, Julian Baumgartlinger,
Marc Janko (YC30) (84' Stefan Ilsanker (YC90+1)), Martin Harnik, Marko Arnautovic (88'
Jakob Jantscher). (Coach: Marcel Koller (SUI)).
Goals: Sweden: 1-4 Zlatan Ibrahimovic (90'+1').
Austria: 0-1 David Alaba (9' penalty), 0-2 Martin Harnik (38'), 0-3 Marc Janko (77'), 0-4
Martin Harnik (88').
Referee: Carlos Velasco Carballo (ESP)   Attendance: 48.355

09-10-2015   Rheinpark Stadion, Vaduz: Liechtenstein – Sweden   0-2 (0-1)
Liechtenstein: Peter Jehle, Martin Rechsteiner (YC90+1), Yves Oehri, Mario Frick (C), Franz
Burgmeier, Michele Polverino (59' Robin Gubser), Andreas Christen (83' Niklas Kieber),
Martin Büchel, Sandro Wieser, Simon Kühne (72' Seyhan Yildiz), Marcel Büchel. (Coach:
René Pauritsch (AUT)).
Sweden: Andreas Isaksson, Mikael Antonsson, Martin Olsson, Mikael Lustig (YC60), Andreas
Granqvist, Kim Källström (YC48), Albin Ekdal (66' Oscar Lewicki), Erkan Zengin, Zlatan
Ibrahimovic (C), Jimmy Durmaz (69' Sebastian Larsson), Marcus Berg (62' John Guidetti).
(Coach: Erik Hamrén (SWE)).
Goals: Sweden: 0-1 Marcus Berg (18'), 0-2 Zlatan Ibrahimovic (55').
Referee: Liran Liany (ISR)   Attendance: 4.740
(Zlatan Ibrahimovic missed a penalty in the 40th minute)

344

09-10-2015   Zimbru Stadium, Chisinau: Moldova – Russia 1-2 (0-0)
Moldova: Alexei Koselev, Ion Jardan, Vitali Bordian, Igor Armas (C), Stefan Burghiu, Alexandru Onica (79' Vladimir Ambros), Eugeniu (Eugen) Cebotaru, Catalin Carp (70' Alexandru Vremea), Alexandru Antoniuc (YC57), Dan Spataru, Nicolae Milinceanu (88' Sergiu Istrati). (Coach: Stefan Stoica (ROM)).
Russia: Igor Akinfeev, Igor Smolnikov (27' Oleg Kuzmin), Sergei Ignashevich, Aleksei Berezutski, Dmitri Kombarov (YC42), Roman Shirokov (C) (76' Denis Glushakov), Oleg Shatov, Pavel Mamaev (YC75), Igor Denisov, Aleksandr Kokorin, Artem Dzyuba (88' Fedor Smolov). (Coach: Leonid Viktorovich Slutski (RUS)).
Goals: Moldova: 1-2 Eugeniu (Eugen) Cebotaru (85').
Russia: 0-1 Sergei Ignashevich (58'), 0-2 Artem Dzyuba (78').
Referee: Michail Koukoulakis (GRE)   Attendance: 10.244

09-10-2015   Stadion pod Goricom, Podgorica: Montenegro – Austria 2-3 (1-0)
Montenegro: Vukasin Poleksic (YC79), Zarko Tomasevic (74' Sasa Balic), Marko Simic, Stefan Savic, Nikola Vukcevic, Adam Marusic, Vladimir Boljevic (56' Elsad Zverotic), Vladimir Rodic, Fatos Beciraj, Mirko Vucinic (C) (YC87,RC87), Stefan Mugosa (64' Stanisa Mandic). (Coach: Branko Brnovic (MNE)).
Austria: Robert Almer, Sebastian Prödl, Christian Fuchs (C), Aleksandar Dragovic, Florian Klein, David Alaba (82' Marcel Sabitzer), Zlatko Juzunovic (82' Jakob Jantscher), Julian Baumgartlinger, Marc Janko (82' Rubin Rafael Okotie), Marko Arnautovic, Martin Harnik. (Coach: Marcel Koller (SUI)).
Goals: Montenegro: 1-0 Mirko Vucinic (32'), 2-1 Fatos Beciraj (68').
Austria: 1-1 Marc Janko (55'), 2-2 Marko Arnautovic (81'), 2-3 Marcel Sabitzer (90'+2').
Referee: Daniele Orsato (ITA)   Attendance: 7.107
(Branko Brnovic was sent to the stands in the 87th minute)

12-10-2015   Ernst-Happel-Stadion, Vienna: Austria – Liechtenstein 3-0 (1-0)
Austria: Robert Almer, Christian Fuchs (C), Aleksandar Dragovic, Sebastian Prödl, Florian Klein, Zlatko Juzunovic, David Alaba (64' Marcel Sabitzer), Julian Baumgartlinger (71' Stefan Ilsanker), Marc Janko (64' Rubin Rafael Okotie (YC69)), Martin Harnik, Marko Arnautovic. (Coach: Marcel Koller (SUI)).
Liechtenstein: Peter Jehle, Mario Frick (C) (90'+1' Simon Kühne), Franz Burgmeier (YC57), Martin Rechsteiner, Yves Oehri (46' Daniel Brändle), Daniel Kaufmann, Martin Büchel, Michele Polverino (YC90+2), Sandro Wieser, Niklas Kieber (62' Seyhan Yildiz), Marcel Büchel. (Coach: René Pauritsch (AUT)).
Goals: Austria: 1-0 Marko Arnautovic (12'), 2-0 Marc Janko (54'), 3-0 Marc Janko (57').
Referee: Miroslav Zelinka (CZE)   Attendance: 48.500

12-10-2015   Otkrytiye Arena, Moscow: Russia – Montenegro 2-0 (2-0)
Russia: Igor Akinfeev, Aleksei Berezutski, Oleg Kuzmin, Sergei Ignashevich, Dmitri Kombarov, Igor Denisov, Roman Shirokov (C), Oleg Shatov (69' Pavel Mamaev), Alan Dzagoev (86' Denis Cheryshev), Aleksandr Kokorin, Artem Dzyuba (84' Fedor Smolov). (Coach: Leonid Viktorovich Slutski (RUS)).
Montenegro: Milan Mijatovic, Sasa Balic, Marko Simic, Stefan Savic (C), Esteban Saveljic, Mladen Kascelan, Nikola Vukcevic (85' Vladimir Boljevic), Nemanja Nikolic (46' Stefan Mugosa), Vladimir Rodic (YC36) (67' Adam Marusic), Fatos Beciraj, Stanisa Mandic. (Coach: Radislav Dragicevic (MNE)).
Goals: Russia: 1-0 Oleg Kuzmin (33'), 2-0 Aleksandr Kokorin (37' penalty).
Referee: Svein Oddvar Moen (NOR)   Attendance: 35.604

12-10-2015   Friends Arena, Solna: Sweden – Moldova   2-0 (1-0)
Sweden: Andreas Isaksson, Mikael Antonsson, Martin Olsson, Mikael Lustig (83' Anton Tinnerholm), Andreas Granqvist, Oscar Lewicki, Sebastian Larsson, Kim Källström (57' Gustav Svensson), Erkan Zengin, Zlatan Ibrahimovic (C) (57' Ola Toivonen), John Guidetti. (Coach: Erik Hamrén (SWE)).
Moldova: Ilie Cebanu, Maxim Potîrniche, Ion Jardan (80' Dan Spataru), Victor Golovatenco, Iulian Erhan (63' Igor Armas), Vitali Bordian, Stefan Burghiu, Alexandru Vremea, Artur Patras (61' Alexandru Antoniuc), Sergiu Istrati, Eugeniu (Eugen) Cebotaru (C). (Coach: Stefan Stoica (ROM)).
Goals: Sweden: 1-0 Zlatan Ibrahimovic (23'), 2-0 Erkan Zengin (47').
Referee: Luca Banti (ITA)   Attendance: 25.351

GROUP   H

09-09-2014	Baku	Azerbaijan – Bulgaria	1-2 (0-1)
09-09-2014	Zagreb	Croatia – Malta	2-0 (0-0)
09-09-2014	Oslo	Norway – Italy	0-2 (0-1)
10-10-2014	Sofia	Bulgaria – Croatia	0-1 (0-1)
10-10-2014	Palermo	Italy – Azerbaijan	2-1 (1-0)
10-10-2014	Ta'Qali	Malta – Norway	0-3 (0-2)
13-10-2014	Osijek	Croatia – Azerbaijan	6-0 (4-0)
13-10-2014	Ta'Qali	Malta – Italy	0-1 (0-1)
13-10-2014	Oslo	Norway – Bulgaria	2-1 (1-1)
16-11-2014	Baku	Azerbaijan – Norway	0-1 (0-1)
16-11-2014	Sofia	Bulgaria – Malta	1-1 (1-0)
16-11-2014	Milan	Italy – Croatia	1-1 (1-1)
28-03-2015	Baku	Azerbaijan – Malta	2-0 (1-0)
28-03-2015	Zagreb	Croatia – Norway	5-1 (1-0)
28-03-2015	Sofia	Bulgaria – Italy	2-2 (2-1)
12-06-2015	Split	Croatia – Italy	1-1 (1-1)
12-06-2015	Ta'Qali	Malta – Bulgaria	0-1 (0-0)
12-06-2015	Oslo	Norway – Azerbaijan	0-0
03-09-2015	Baku	Azerbaijan – Croatia	0-0
03-09-2015	Sofia	Bulgaria – Norway	0-1 (0-0)
03-09-2015	Florence	Italy – Malta	1-0 (0-0)
06-09-2015	Ta'Qali	Malta – Azerbaijan	2-2 (0-1)
06-09-2015	Oslo	Norway – Croatia	2-0 (0-0)
06-09-2015	Palermo	Italy – Bulgaria	1-0 (1-0)
10-10-2015	Baku	Azerbaijan – Italy	1-3 (1-2)
10-10-2015	Oslo	Norway – Malta	2-0 (1-0)
10-10-2015	Zagreb	Croatia – Bulgaria	3-0 (2-0)
13-10-2015	Sofia	Bulgaria – Azerbaijan	2-0 (1-0)
13-10-2015	Rome	Italy – Norway	2-1 (0-1)
13-10-2015	Ta'Qali	Malta – Croatia	0-1 (0-1)

FINAL STANDING

Pos	Team	Pld	W	D	L	GF	GA	GD	Pts
1	Italy	10	7	3	0	16	7	+9	24
2	Croatia	10	6	3	1	20	5	+15	20
3	Norway	10	6	1	3	13	10	+3	19
4	Bulgaria	10	3	2	5	9	12	-3	11
5	Azerbaijan	10	1	3	6	7	18	-11	6
6	Malta	10	0	2	8	3	16	-13	2

Croatia had one point deducted following charges of racist behaviour in the match against Italy at Stadion Poljud. In addition, the Croatian Football Federation were ordered to play their next two home matches of UEFA competition behind closed doors and not to play any of its remaining qualifying games at Poljud. A fine of €100.000 was also imposed. The Croatian Football Federation appealed against the decision but, in a hearing on 17th September 2015, Croatia's appeal was rejected.

Italy and Croatia qualified for the Final Tournament in France.

Norway qualified for the play-offs

09-09-2014   Bakcell Arena, Baku: Azerbaijan – Bulgaria 1-2 (0-1)
Azerbaijan: Kamran Agayev, Mahir Shukurov, Rashad Farhad oglu Sadygov (C), Badavi Hüseynov, Gara Garayev, Ufuk Budak (90' Vüqar Nadirov), Dmitri Nazarov, Ruslan Abisov (YC23) (74' Tarlan Guliyev), Vagif Javadov (YC35) (46' Azar Abdullayev (YC90)), Rüfat Dadasov, Rauf Aliyev. (Coach: Hans-Hubert (Berti) Vogts (GER)).
Bulgaria: Vladislav Stoyanov, Apostol Popov, Veselin Minev, Stanislav Manolev, Nikolay Bodurov (C), Georgi Milanov, Georgi Iliev (74' Todor Nedelev), Vladimir Gadzhev (YC63), Svetoslav Dyakov, Mihail Alexandrov (83' Ventsislav Hristov), Ilian Mitsanski (58' Andrey Galabinov). (Coach: Luboslav Mladenov Penev (BUL)).
Goals: Azerbaijan: 1-1 Dmitri Nazarov (54').
Bulgaria: 0-1 Ilian Mitsanski (14'), 1-2 Ventsislav Hristov (87').
Referee: Alon Yefet (ISR)   Attendance: 11.000

09-09-2014   Stadion Maksimir, Zagreb: Croatia – Malta 2-0 (0-0)
Croatia: Danijel Subasic, Vedran Corluka, Darijo Srna (C), Dejan Lovren, Alen Halilovic (67' Andrej Kramaric), Marcelo Brozovic, Ivan Rakitic, Luka Modric, Hrvoje Milic, Mateo Kovacic (46' Nikica Jelavic), Mario Mandzukic (YC31) (79' Ivica Olic). (Coach: Niko Kovac (CRO)).
Malta: Andrew Hogg, Ryan Camilleri, Steve Borg (RC31), Andrei Agius, Zach Muscat, Rowen Muscat (76' Bjorn Kristensen), Ryan Fenech (YC59), Paul Fenech (87' Ryan Scicluna), André Schembri, Michael Mifsud (C) (33' Steven Bezzina), Clayton Failla. (Coach: Pietro Ghedin (ITA)).
Goals: Croatia: 1-0 Luka Modric (46'), 2-0 Andrej Kramaric (81').
Referee: Vladislav Yuryevich Bezborodov (RUS)   Attendance: 8.333

09-09-2014   Ullevaal Stadion, Oslo: Norway – Italy   0-2 (0-1)
Norway: Ørjan Nyland, Håvard Nordtveit (YC83), Vegard Forren (YC90), Per-Egil Flo, Omar
Elabdellaoui, Mats Møller Dæhli, Ruben Yttergård Jenssen (70' Alexander Tettey), Per Ciljan
Skjelbred (C) (75' Morten Gamst Pedersen), Joshua King, Stefan Johansen, Håvard Nielsen
(50' Tarik Elyounoussi). (Coach: Per-Mathias Høgmo (NOR)).
Italy: Gianluigi Buffon (C), Leonardo Bonucci, Davide Astori (YC66), Andrea Ranocchia,
Mattia De Sciglio, Matteo Darmian (61' Manuel Pasqual), Alessandro Florenzi (YC41) (87'
Andrea Poli), Daniele De Rossi, Emanuele Giaccherini, Ciro Immobile, Simone Zaza (83'
Mattia Destro). (Coach: Antonio Conte (ITA)).
Goals: Italy: 0-1 Simone Zaza (16'), 0-2 Leonardo Bonucci (62').
Referee: Milorad Mazic (SRB)   Attendance: 26.265

10-10-2014   Vasil Levski National Stadium, Sofia: Bulgaria – Croatia   0-1 (0-1)
Bulgaria: Vladislav Stoyanov, Petar Zanev (YC15) (46' Georgi Iliev), Apostol Popov, Yordan
Minev, Stanislav Manolev, Nikolay Bodurov, Georgi Milanov, Vladimir Gadzhev (68'
Aleksandar Tonev), Svetoslav Dyakov, Ivelin Popov (C), Ilian Mitsanski (46' Andrey
Galabinov). (Coach: Luboslav Mladenov Penev (BUL)).
Croatia: Danijel Subasic, Domagoj Vida (YC51), Darijo Srna (C), Vedran Corluka, Ivan
Rakitic (80' Mateo Kovacic), Danijel Pranjic, Ivan Perisic, Luka Modric, Marcelo Brozovic
(YC23), Ivica Olic (YC84), Mario Mandzukic. (Coach: Niko Kovac (CRO)).
Goal: Croatia: 0-1 Nikolay Bodurov (36' own goal).
Referee: Antonio Mateu Lahoz (ESP)   Attendance: 29.733

10-10-2014   Stadio Renzo Barbera, Palermo: Italy – Azerbaijan   2-1 (1-0)
Italy: Gianluigi Buffon (C), Andrea Ranocchia, Giorgio Chiellini, Leonardo Bonucci, Mattia
De Sciglio, Matteo Darmian (81' Antonio Candreva), Andrea Pirlo (YC33) (73' Alberto
Aquilani), Claudio Marchisio, Alessandro Florenzi (77' Sebastian Giovinco), Simone Zaza
(YC87), Ciro Immobile. (Coach: Antonio Conte (ITA)).
Azerbaijan: Kamran Agayev, Rashad Farhad oglu Sadygov (C) (YC84), Ilkin Qirtimov (46'
Rasim Ramaldanov), Gara Garayev, Badavi Hüseynov, Elnur Allahverdiyev, Dmitri Nazarov,
Rahid Amirguliyev (86' Vüqar Nadirov), Azar Abdullayev, Rüfat Dadasov (YC12) (59' Javid
Hüseynov), Rauf Aliyev. (Coach: Hans-Hubert (Berti) Vogts (GER)).
Goals: Italy: 1-0 Giorgio Chiellini (44'), 2-1 Giorgio Chiellini (82').
Azerbaijan: 1-1 Giorgio Chiellini (76' own goal).
Referee: Hüseyin Göçek (TUR)   Attendance: 33.000

10-10-2014   National Stadium, Ta'Qali: Malta – Norway   0-3 (0-2)
Malta: Andrew Hogg, Ryan Camilleri, Andrei Agius (YC71), Zach Muscat, Rowen Muscat,
Ryan Fenech (72' Bjorn Kristensen), Paul Fenech, Roderick Briffa (72' Justin Grioli), Michael
Mifsud (C), Clayton Failla, André Schembri (85' Terence Vella). (Coach: Pietro Ghedin
(ITA)).
Norway: Ørjan Nyland, Håvard Nordtveit, Vegard Forren, Omar Elabdellaoui, Martin Linnes,
Tarik Elyounoussi, Mats Møller Dæhli, Alexander Tettey (78' Harmeet Singh), Per Ciljan
Skjelbred (C) (62' Jone Samuelsen), Joshua King (75' Håvard Nielsen), Stefan Johansen.
(Coach: Per-Mathias Høgmo (NOR)).
Goals: Norway: 0-1 Mats Møller Dæhli (22'), 0-2 Joshua King (26'), 0-3 Joshua King (49').
Referee: Antony Gautier (FRA)   Attendance: 8.067

348

13-10-2014   Stadion Gradski vrt, Osijek: Croatia – Azerbaijan   6-0 (4-0)
Croatia: Danijel Subasic, Darijo Srna (C), Vedran Corluka, Domagoj Vida, Ivan Rakitic,
Danijel Pranjic, Luka Modric (60' Alen Halilovic), Marcelo Brozovic, Mateo Kovacic (24'
Ivan Perisic), Mario Mandzukic, Andrej Kramaric (76' Ivica Olic). (Coach: Niko Kovac
(CRO)).
Azerbaijan: Kamran Agayev, Maksim Medvedev, Badavi Hüseynov, Gara Garayev (30'
Agabala Ramazanov (YC36), 41' Javid Hüseynov), Elnur Allahverdiyev (YC55) (66' Tarlan
Guliyev), Rashad Farhad oglu Sadygov (C), Rasim Ramaldanov (YC16), Dmitri Nazarov,
Rahid Amirguliyev, Azar Abdullayev, Rauf Aliyev. (Coach: Hans-Hubert (Berti) Vogts
(GER)).
Goals: Croatia: 1-0 Andrej Kramaric (11'), 2-0 Ivan Perisic (34'), 3-0 Ivan Perisic (45'), 4-0
Marcelo Brozovic (45'+1'), 5-0 Luka Modric (57' penalty), 6-0 Rashad Farhad oglu Sadygov
(61' own goal).
Referee: Stéphan Studer (SUI)   Attendance: 16.021

13-10-2014   National Stadium, Ta'Qali: Malta – Italy   0-1 (0-1)
Malta: Andrew Hogg, Ryan Camilleri, Andrei Agius, Zach Muscat, Paul Fenech, Roderick
Briffa (YC42), Rowen Muscat, John Mintoff (72' Clifford Gatt Baldacchino), Clayton Failla
(90'+3' Steven Bezzina), André Schembri (85' Andrew Cohen), Michael Mifsud (C) (RC28).
(Coach: Pietro Ghedin (ITA)).
Italy: Gianluigi Buffon (C), Giorgio Chiellini, Leonardo Bonucci (RC73), Manuel Pasqual,
Matteo Darmian (YC44), Claudio Marchisio, Alessandro Florenzi (59' Alberto Aquilani),
Antonio Candreva, Marco Verratti, Ciro Immobile (65' Sebastian Giovinco), Graziano Pellè
(75' Angelo Ogbonna). (Coach: Antonio Conte (ITA)).
Goal: Italy: 0-1 Graziano Pellè (24').
Referee: Ovidiu Alin Hategan (ROM)   Attendance: 16.942

13-10-2014   Ullevaal Stadion, Oslo: Norway – Bulgaria   2-1 (1-1)
Norway: Ørjan Nyland, Håvard Nordtveit, Vegard Forren, Omar Elabdellaoui, Alexander
Tettey, Per Ciljan Skjelbred (C), Martin Linnes, Tarik Elyounoussi (YC59) (83' Jone
Samuelsen), Mats Møller Dæhli (63' Martin Ødegaard), Joshua King (58' Håvard Nielsen),
Stefan Johansen (YC90+2). (Coach: Per-Mathias Høgmo (NOR)).
Bulgaria: Nikolay Mihaylov, Apostol Popov, Veselin Minev (YC87), Stanislav Manolev (69'
Yordan Minev (YC90+2)), Nikolay Bodurov, Aleksandar Tonev, Georgi Milanov, Georgi Iliev
(76' Mihail Aleksandrov), Svetoslav Dyakov, Ivelin Popov (C) (YC88), Ventsislav Hristov
(56' Andrey Galabinov). (Coach: Luboslav Mladenov Penev (BUL)).
Goals: Norway: 1-0 Tarik Elyounoussi (13'), 2-1 Håvard Nielsen (72').
Bulgaria: 1-1 Nikolay Bodurov (43').
Referee: Olegário Manuel Bártolo Faustino Benquerença (POR)   Attendance: 18.990

16-10-2014   Bakcell Arena, Baku: Azerbaijan – Norway   0-1 (0-1)
Azerbaijan: Salahat Agayev, Rashad Farhad oglu Sadygov (C), Maksim Medvedev, Elvin
Yunuszade (YC52), Mahir Shukurov, Javid Imamverdiyev (69' Dmitri Nazarov (YC84)),
Rahid Amirguliyev, Ruslan Abisov (65' Gara Garayev), Azar Abdullayev, Vagif Javadov,
Rauf Aliyev. (Coach: Makhmud Gurbanov (AZE)).
Norway: Ørjan Nyland, Håvard Nordtveit, Tom Høgli, Vegard Forren, Omar Elabdellaoui,
Tarik Elyounoussi (YC16) (90'+1' Fredrik Gulbrandsen), Mats Møller Dæhli (57' Jone
Samuelsen (YC61)), Alexander Tettey, Per Ciljan Skjelbred (C), Håvard Nielsen (72'
Alexander Søderlund (YC75)), Stefan Johansen. (Coach: Per-Mathias Høgmo (NOR)).
Goal: Norway: 0-1 Håvard Nordtveit (25').
Referee: Yevhen Anatoliyovich Aranovskiy (UKR)   Attendance: 9.200

16-11-2014   Vasil Levski National Stadium, Sofia: Bulgaria – Malta   1-1 (1-0)
Bulgaria: Vladislav Stoyanov, Georgi Terziev, Veselin Minev (YC86), Stanislav Manolev,
Nikolay Bodurov, Georgi Milanov (58' Marcos Antônio Malachias Júnior "MARQUINHOS"),
Georgi Iliev (71' Aleksandar Tonev), Svetoslav Dyakov, Mihail Aleksandrov, Ivelin Popov
(C), Andrey Galabinov (58' Ilian Mitsanski). (Coach: Luboslav Mladenov Penev (BUL)).
Malta: Andrew Hogg, Jonathan Caruana (YC89), Ryan Camilleri, Andrei Agius, Zach Muscat,
Rowen Muscat, Roderick Briffa (C), Paul Fenech (YC90+4), André Schembri (78' Ryan
Fenech), Clayton Failla (YC77) (81' Steven Bezzina), Jean Paul Farrugia (YC43) (90'+3'
Terence Vella). (Coach: Pietro Ghedin (ITA)).
Goals: Bulgaria: 1-0 Andrey Galabinov (6').
Malta: 1-1 Clayton Failla (49' penalty).
Referee: Martin Strömbergsson (SWE)   Attendance: 3.300
(Ivelin Popov missed a penalty in the 76th minute)

16-11-2014   Stadio Giuseppe Meazza, Milan: Italy – Croatia   1-1 (1-1)
Italy: Gianluigi Buffon (C), Andrea Ranocchia, Manuel Pasqual (28' Roberto Soriano),
Giorgio Chiellini, Mattia De Sciglio, Matteo Darmian, Claudio Marchisio, Daniele De Rossi,
Antonio Candreva, Simone Zaza (63' Graziano Pellè), Ciro Immobile (YC46) (52' Stephan El
Shaarawy). (Coach: Antonio Conte (ITA)).
Croatia: Danijel Subasic, Domagoj Vida, Darijo Srna (C), Vedran Corluka, Ivan Rakitic,
Danijel Pranjic, Ivan Perisic (YC65), Luka Modric (28' Mateo Kovacic (YC37)), Marcelo
Brozovic (83' Milan Badelj), Ivica Olic (68' Andrej Kramaric), Mario Mandzukic. (Coach:
Niko Kovac (CRO)).
Goals: Italy: 1-0 Antonio Candreva (11').
Croatia: 1-1 Ivan Perisic (15').
Referee: Björn Kuipers (HOL)   Attendance: 63.222

28-03-2015   Tofiq Bakhramov Republican Stadium, Baku: Azerbaijan – Malta   2-0 (1-0)
Azerbaijan: Kamran Agayev, Rashad Farhad oglu Sadygov (C), Maksim Medvedev, Badavi
Hüseynov, Gara Garayev, Afran Ismayilov (70' Dmitri Nazarov (YC80)), Arif Dashdemirov,
Rahid Amirguliyev (YC56), Namig Alasgarov (22' Ruslan Gurbanov), Vüqar Nadirov (81'
Eddy Silvestre Pascual Israfilov), Javid Hüseynov. (Coach: Robert Prosinecki (CRO)).
Malta: Andrew Hogg, Ryan Camilleri (36' Zach Muscat), Steve Borg, Steven Bezzina (46'
Stephen Pisani), Andrei Agius, Jonathan Caruana (YC89), Rowen Muscat, Paul Fenech,
Roderick Briffa (C), André Schembri (81' Ryan Fenech), Alfred Effiong. (Coach: Pietro
Ghedin (ITA)).
Goals: Azerbaijan: 1-0 Javid Hüseynov (4'), 2-0 Dmitri Nazarov (90'+2').
Referee: Halis Özkahya (TUR)   Attendance: 14.600

28-03-2015   Stadion Maksimir, Zagreb: Croatia – Norway 5-1 (1-0)
Croatia: Danijel Subasic, Vedran Corluka (YC68,YC74), Domagoj Vida, Darijo Srna (C),
Danijel Pranjic, Ivan Perisic, Luka Modric, Marcelo Brozovic, Ivan Rakitic (75' Gordon
Schildenfeld), Ivica Olic (70' Andrej Kramaric), Mario Mandzukic (87' Milan Badelj). (Coach:
Niko Kovac (CRO)).
Norway: Ørjan Nyland (YC66), Håvard Nordtveit (YC35), Tom Høgli, Vegard Forren, Mats
Møller Dæhli (61' Håvard Nielsen), Martin Linnes (YC31), Tarik Elyounoussi (YC35) (79'
Mohammed Abdellaoue), Alexander Tettey, Per Ciljan Skjelbred (C) (19' Jone Samuelsen
(YC81)), Martin Ødegaard, Stefan Johansen. (Coach: Per-Mathias Høgmo (NOR)).
Goals: Croatia: 1-0 Marcelo Brozovic (30'), 2-0 Ivan Perisic (53'), 3-0 Ivica Olic (65'), 4-1
Gordon Schildenfeld (87'), 5-1 Danijel Pranjic (90'+4').
Norway: 3-1 Alexander Tettey (80').
Referee: Carlos Velasco Carballo (ESP)   Attendance: 23.920
(Tarik Elyounoussi missed a penalty in the 69th minute)

28-03-2015   Vasil Levski National Stadium, Sofia: Bulgaria – Italy 2-2 (2-1)
Bulgaria: Nikolay Mihaylov, Yordan Minev, Stanislav Manolev, Nikolay Bodurov, Aleksander
Dragomirov Aleksandrov, Georgi Milanov (88' Ventislav Vasilev), Vladimir Gadzhev,
Svetoslav Dyakov (C) (YC56), Mihail Aleksandrov, Ivelin Popov (85' Simeon Slavchev), Ilian
Mitsanski (73' Valeri Bozhinov). (Coach: Ivaylo Bogdanov Petev (BUL)).
Italy: Salvatore Sirigu, Giorgio Chiellini (C), Leonardo Bonucci, Andrea Barzagli, Luca
Antonelli (77' Manolo Gabbiadini), Matteo Darmian (YC90+1), Marco Verratti, Antonio
Candreva, Andrea Bertolacci (72' Roberto Soriano (YC88)), Simone Zaza (58' ÉDER Citalin
Martins), Ciro Immobile (YC82). (Coach: Antonio Conte (ITA)).
Goals: Bulgaria: 1-1 Ivelin Popov (11'), 2-1 Ilian Mitsanski (17').
Italy: 0-1 Yordan Minev (4' *own goal*), 2-2 ÉDER Citalin Martins (84').
Referee: Damir Skomina (SLO)   Attendance: 10.359

12-06-2015   Stadion Poljud, Split: Croatia – Italy 1-1 (1-1)
Croatia: Danijel Subasic, Gordon Schildenfeld, Domagoj Vida, Darijo Srna (C) (YC54,YC90),
Ivan Rakitic, Danijel Pranjic (72' Sime Vrsaljko), Ivan Perisic, Marcelo Brozovic, Mateo
Kovacic (YC87) (90'+2' Marin Leovac), Ivica Olic (YC43) (46' Ante Rebic (YC82)), Mario
Mandzukic (YC35). (Coach: Niko Kovac (CRO)).
Italy: Gianluigi Buffon (C) (YC11) (46' Salvatore Sirigu), Lorenzo De Silvestri (27' Mattia De
Sciglio), Leonardo Bonucci, Davide Astori, Matteo Darmian, Marco Parolo (YC53), Claudio
Marchisio (YC71), Antonio Candreva, Andrea Pirlo, Stephan El Shaarawy (80' Andrea
Ranocchia), Graziano Pellè. (Coach: Antonio Conte (ITA)).
Goals: Croatia: 1-0 Mario Mandzukic (11').
Italy: 1-1 Antonio Candreva (36' penalty).
Referee: Martin Atkinson (ENG)   Attendance: behind closed doors
(Mario Mandzukic missed a penalty in the 7th minute)

12-06-2015   National Stadium, Ta'Qali: Malta – Bulgaria   0-1 (0-0)
Malta: Justin Haber, Zach Muscat (YC45+1), Alex Muscat (63' Edward Herrera), Ryan
Camilleri (YC45+1), Andrei Agius (YC11), Rowen Muscat, Paul Fenech (YC59), Roderick
Briffa (76' André Schembri), Michael Mifsud (C) (84' Andrew Cohen), Clayton Failla, Alfred
Effiong. (Coach: Pietro Ghedin (ITA)).
Bulgaria: Bozhidar Mitrev, Yordan Minev, Stanislav Manolev, Nikolay Bodurov, Ivan
Bandalovski, Aleksander Dragomirov Aleksandrov, Vladimir Gadzhev, Svetoslav Dyakov (C)
(YC62), Mihail Aleksandrov (YC58) (75' Georgi Milanov), Ivelin Popov (81' Ivaylo
Chochev), Ilian Mitsanski (89' Radoslav Vasilev). (Coach: Ivaylo Bogdanov Petev (BUL)).
Goal: Bulgaria: 0-1 Ivelin Popov (56').
Referee: Aleksandar Stavrev (MCD)   Attendance: 3.924
(Ilian Mitsanski missed a penalty in the 45+2nd minute)

12-06-2015   Ullevaal Stadion, Oslo: Norway – Azerbaijan   0-0
Norway: Ørjan Nyland, Håvard Nordtveit, Even Hovland, Tom Høgli, Vegard Forren, Omar
Elabdellaoui, Per Ciljan Skjelbred (C) (52' Pål André Helland), Martin Ødegaard, Alexander
Søderlund (68' Magnus Wolff Eikrem), Joshua King (79' Adama Diomandé), Stefan Johansen.
(Coach: Per-Mathias Høgmo (NOR)).
Azerbaijan: Kamran Agayev, Rashad Farhad oglu Sadygov (C), Maksim Medvedev, Badavi
Hüseynov, Gara Garayev, Afran Ismayilov, Arif Dashdemirov (YC45), Dmitri Nazarov
(90'+3' Magomed Kurbanov), Rahid Amirguliyev, Ruslan Gurbanov (81' Vüqar Nadirov),
Javid Hüseynov. (Coach: Robert Prosinecki (CRO)).
Referee: Pawel Gil (POL)   Attendance: 21.228

03-09-2015   Bakcell Arena, Baku: Azerbaijan – Croatia   0-0
Azerbaijan: Kamran Agayev (YC82), Badavi Hüseynov, Gara Garayev (YC90+3), Rashad
Farhad oglu Sadygov (C), Afran Ismayilov, Arif Dashdemirov, Dmitri Nazarov (90' Eddy
Silvestre Pascual Israfilov), Magodem Mirzabekov, Magomed Kurbanov (63' Rashad Abulfaz
oglu Sadiqov), Rahid Amirguliyev, Ruslan Gurbanov (YC79) (79' Vüqar Nadirov). (Coach:
Robert Prosinecki (CRO)).
Croatia: Danijel Subasic, Sime Vrsaljko, Domagoj Vida (YC44), Vedran Corluka, Ivan Rakitic
(YC77), Danijel Pranjic, Ivan Perisic (83' Nikola Kalinic), Luka Modric (C) (71' Marcelo
Brozovic), Milan Badelj (59' Mateo Kovacic (YC90+1)), Mario Mandzukic, Marko Pjaca.
(Coach: Niko Kovac (CRO)).
Referee: Ruddy Buquet (FRA)   Attendance: 10.000

03-09-2015   Vasil Levski National Stadium, Sofia: Bulgaria – Norway   0-1 (0-0)
Bulgaria: Bozhidar Mitrev, Yordan Minev (YC89), Stanislav Manolev (61' Aleksandar
Tonev), Nikolay Bodurov, Ivan Bandalovski, Aleksander Dragomirov Aleksandrov, Georgi
Milanov (78' Todor Nedelev), Svetoslav Dyakov (C), Ivaylo Chochev, Ivelin Popov (YC45),
Ilian Mitsanski (68' Dimitar Rangelov). (Coach: Ivaylo Bogdanov Petev (BUL)).
Norway: Ørjan Nyland, Even Hovland, Tom Høgli (C) (YC20), Vegard Forren (75' Håvard
Nordtveit), Omar Elabdellaoui, Alexander Tettey (YC40), Jone Samuelsen (64' Per Ciljan
Skjelbred (YC89)), Markus Henriksen, Alexander Søderlund, Stefan Johansen (87' Stefan
Strandberg), Jo Inge Berget. (Coach: Per-Mathias Høgmo (NOR)).
Goal: Norway: 0-1 Vegard Forren (57').
Referee: Hendrikus Sebastiaan Hermanus (Bas) Nijhuis (HOL)   Attendance: 12.913

05-09-2015   Stadio Artemio Franchi, Florence: Italy – Malta   1-0 (0-0)
Italy: Gianluigi Buffon (C), Manuel Pasqual, Giorgio Chiellini, Leonardo Bonucci, Matteo Darmian, Marco Verratti (77' Roberto Soriano), Andrea Pirlo, Andrea Bertolacci (55' Marco Parolo), Graziano Pellè, Manolo Gabbiadini (64' Antonio Candreva (YC88)), ÉDER Citalin Martins. (Coach: Antonio Conte (ITA)).
Malta: Andrew Hogg, Zach Muscat, Alex Muscat, Steve Borg, Andrei Agius, Rowen Muscat, Paul Fenech (YC35), Roderick Briffa (C) (90'+1' Gareth Sciberras), André Schembri (73' Bjorn Kristensen), Clayton Failla, Alfred Effiong (YC69) (90'+3' Michael Mifsud). (Coach: Pietro Ghedin (ITA)).
Goal: Italy: 1-0 Graziano Pellè (69').
Referee: Ivan Kruzliak (SVK)   Attendance: 12.551

06-09-2015   National Stadium, Ta'Qali: Malta – Azerbaijan   2-2 (0-1)
Malta: Andrew Hogg, Ryan Camilleri (79' Joseph Zerafa), Steve Borg, Andrei Agius, Alex Muscat, Roderick Briffa, Rowen Muscat, Alfred Effiong (YC45+1), André Schembri, Michael Mifsud (C) (62' Andrew Cohen), Clayton Failla (85' Stephen Pisani). (Coach: Pietro Ghedin (ITA)).
Azerbaijan: Kamran Agayev, Badavi Hüseynov, Gara Garayev, Rashad Farhad oglu Sadygov (C), Arif Dashdemirov, Javid Taghiyev, Afran Ismayilov (72' Araz Abdullayev), Rahid Amirguliyev, Dmitri Nazarov (70' Rashad Abulfaz oglu Sadiqov), Magodem Mirzabekov, Ruslan Gurbanov (81' Rauf Aliyev). (Coach: Robert Prosinecki (CRO)).
Goals: Malta: 1-1 Michael Mifsud (55'), 2-1 Alfred Effiong (71').
Azerbaijan: 0-1 Rahid Amirguliyev (36'), 2-2 Rahid Amirguliyev (80').
Referee: Harald Lechner (AUT)   Attendance: 5.266

06-09-2015   Ullevaal Stadion, Oslo: Norway – Croatia   2-0 (0-0)
Norway: Ørjan Nyland, Even Hovland, Vegard Forren (YC38), Tom Høgli (YC75), Omar Elabdellaoui, Markus Henriksen, Alexander Tettey, Per Ciljan Skjelbred (C) (90'+1' Håvard Nielsen), Stefan Johansen (90'+2' Håvard Nordtveit), Jo Inge Berget, Alexander Søderlund (YC59) (90'+4' Valon Berisha). (Coach: Per-Mathias Høgmo (NOR)).
Croatia: Danijel Subasic, Vedran Corluka, Sime Vrsaljko (YC36), Domagoj Vida, Darijo Srna (C), Ivan Perisic, Luka Modric, Marcelo Brozovic (YC50), Ivan Rakitic (72' Nikola Kalinic), Mario Mandzukic, Marko Pjaca (63' Ivica Olic (YC72)). (Coach: Niko Kovac (CRO)).
Goals: Norway: 1-0 Jo Inge Berget (51'), 2-0 Vedran Corluka (69' own goal).
Referee: Viktor Kassai (HUN)   Attendance: 26.751

06-09-2015   Stadio Renzo Barbera, Palermo: Italy – Bulgaria   1-0 (1-0)
Italy: Gianluigi Buffon (C), Giorgio Chiellini, Leonardo Bonucci, Mattia De Sciglio, Matteo Darmian, Marco Verratti, Marco Parolo, Daniele De Rossi (RC55), Antonio Candreva (86' ÉDER Citalin Martins), Graziano Pellè (73' Simone Zaza), Stephan El Shaarawy (72' Alessandro Florenzi). (Coach: Antonio Conte (ITA)).
Bulgaria: Bozhidar Mitrev, Veselin Minev, Yordan Minev (YC58) (64' Ivan Bandalovski), Nikolay Bodurov, Aleksander Dragomirov Aleksandrov, Todor Nedelev (67' Mihail Aleksandrov), Georgi Milanov, Svetoslav Dyakov (C) (YC85), Ivaylo Chochev, Ivelin Popov (71' Dimitar Rangelov (YC80)), Ilian Mitsanski (RC55). (Coach: Ivaylo Bogdanov Petev (BUL)).
Goal: Italy: 1-0 Daniele De Rossi (6' penalty).
Referee: Sergey Gennadyevich Karasev (RUS)   Attendance: 21.000

353

10-10-2015   National Stadium, Baku: Azerbaijan – Italy   1-3 (1-2)
Azerbaijan: Kamran Agayev, Rashad Farhad oglu Sadygov (C), Maksim Medvedev (YC90+3), Badavi Hüseynov (RC88), Gara Garayev, Afran Ismayilov (90'+1' Magodem Mirzabekov), Arif Dashdemirov, Dmitri Nazarov, Eddy Silvestre Pascual Israfilov (66' Rashad Abulfaz oglu Sadiqov), Rahid Amirguliyev, Ruslan Gurbanov (74' Tugrul Erat). (Coach: Robert Prosinecki (CRO)).
Italy: Gianluigi Buffon (C), Giorgio Chiellini, Leonardo Bonucci, Mattia De Sciglio, Matteo Darmian, Marco Verratti, Marco Parolo, Antonio Candreva (88' Riccardo Montolivo), Graziano Pellè, Stephan El Shaarawy (74' Alessandro Florenzi), ÉDER Citalin Martins (79' Sebastian Giovinco). (Coach: Antonio Conte (ITA)).
Goals: Azerbaijan: 1-1 Dmitri Nazarov (31').
Italy: 0-1 ÉDER Citalin Martins (11'), 1-2 Stephan El Shaarawy (43'), 1-3 Matteo Darmian (65').
Referee: William (Willie) Collum (SCO)   Attendance: 48.000

10-10-2015   Ullevaal Stadion, Oslo: Norway – Malta   2-0 (1-0)
Norway: Ørjan Nyland, Even Hovland, Vegard Forren, Haitam Aleesami, Omar Elabdellaoui, Alexander Tettey, Per Ciljan Skjelbred (C) (53' Martin Ødegaard), Markus Henriksen, Alexander Søderlund (77' Joshua King), Stefan Johansen, Jo Inge Berget (84' Valon Berisha). (Coach: Per-Mathias Høgmo (NOR)).
Malta: Andrew Hogg, Zach Muscat, Alex Muscat (56' Joseph Zerafa), Steve Borg (83' Ryan Camilleri), Andrei Agius, Rowen Muscat, Paul Fenech, Roderick Briffa (C) (YC12), André Schembri (81' Bjorn Kristensen), Clayton Failla, Alfred Effiong. (Coach: Pietro Ghedin (ITA)).
Goals: Norway: 1-0 Alexander Tettey (19'), 2-0 Alexander Søderlund (52').
Referee: Arnold Hunter (NIR)   Attendance: 27.120

10-10-2015   Stadion Maksimir, Zagreb: Croatia – Bulgaria   3-0 (2-0)
Croatia: Danijel Subasic, Domagoj Vida, Darijo Srna (C), Josip Pivaric, Vedran Corluka, Ivan Rakitic, Ivan Perisic (YC87), Luka Modric (46' Milan Badelj), Mateo Kovacic, Nikola Kalinic (85' Andrej Kramaric), Marko Pjaca (60' Duje Cop (RC89)). (Coach: Ante Cacic (CRO)).
Bulgaria: Bozhidar Mitrev, Georgi Terziev (46' Ivo Ivanov), Zhivko Milanov, Aleksander Dragomirov Aleksandrov, Hristo Zlatinski, Aleksandar Tonev, Simeon Slavchev, Strahil Popov, Todor Nedelev (46' Georgi Milanov), Dimitar Rangelov, Ivelin Popov (C) (71' Mihail Aleksandrov). (Coach: Ivaylo Bogdanov Petev (BUL)).
Goals: Croatia: 1-0 Ivan Perisic (2'), 2-0 Ivan Rakitic (42'), 3-0 Nikola Kalinic (81').
Referee: Artur Manuel Ribeiro Soares Dias (POR)   Attendance: behind closed doors

13-10-2015   Vasil Levski National Stadium, Sofia: Bulgaria – Azerbaijan   2-0 (1-0)
Bulgaria: Bozhidar Mitrev, Yordan Minev, Zhivko Milanov, Ivo Ivanov (YC15), Aleksander Dragomirov Aleksandrov, Hristo Zlatinski, Georgi Milanov (YC90), Svetoslav Dyakov (C) (YC79), Mihail Aleksandrov (80' Simeon Slavchev), Dimitar Rangelov (88' Todor Nedelev), Ivelin Popov (65' Ventsislav Hristov). (Coach: Ivaylo Bogdanov Petev (BUL)).
Azerbaijan: Kamran Agayev, Rashad Farhad oglu Sadygov (C) (YC48), Maksim Medvedev (63' Arif Dashdemirov), Gara Garayev (YC79) (82' Eddy Silvestre Pascual Israfilov), Afran Ismayilov, Dmitri Nazarov, Magodem Mirzabekov, Rahid Amirguliyev (YC77), Ruslan Abisov, Elnur Jafarov (67' Tugrul Erat), Ruslan Gurbanov. (Coach: Robert Prosinecki (CRO)).
Goals: Bulgaria: 1-0 Mihail Aleksandrov (20'), 2-0 Dimitar Rangelov (56').
Referee: Tamás Bognár (HUN)   Attendance: 2.500

13-10-2015   Stadio Olimpico, Rome: Italy – Norway   2-1 (0-1)
Italy: Gianluigi Buffon (C), Giorgio Chiellini, Leonardo Bonucci, Andrea Barzagli (72'
Antonio Candreva), Mattia De Sciglio, Matteo Darmian, Roberto Soriano, Riccardo Montolivo
(68' Andrea Bertolacci), Alessandro Florenzi, Graziano Pellè, ÉDER Citalin Martins (62'
Sebastian Giovinco). (Coach: Antonio Conte (ITA)).
Norway: Ørjan Nyland, Even Hovland, Vegard Forren, Haitam Aleesami, Omar Elabdellaoui,
Alexander Tettey, Per Ciljan Skjelbred (C) (51' Jone Samuelsen), Markus Henriksen,
Alexander Søderlund (60' Joshua King), Stefan Johansen, Jo Inge Berget (78' Valon Berisha).
(Coach: Per-Mathias Høgmo (NOR)).
Goals: Italy: 1-1 Alessandro Florenzi (73'), 2-1 Graziano Pellè (82').
Norway: 0-1 Alexander Tettey (23').
Referee: Dr.Felix Brych (GER)   Attendance: 30.000

13-10-2015   Nationa Stadium, Ta'Qali: Malta – Croatia   0-1 (0-1)
Malta: Andrew Hogg, Joseph Zerafa, Zach Muscat, Steve Borg, Andrei Agius, Rowen Muscat,
Bjorn Kristensen, Roderick Briffa (C) (79' Paul Fenech), André Schembri (90'+2' Andrew
Cohen), Clayton Failla (YC69), Alfred Effiong (75' Michael Mifsud). (Coach: Pietro Ghedin
(ITA)).
Croatia: Danijel Subasic, Domagoj Vida, Darijo Srna (C), Josip Pivaric, Vedran Corluka, Ivan
Rakitic (77' Marcelo Brozovic), Ivan Perisic (YC90+2), Milan Badelj (YC39), Mateo Kovacic,
Nikola Kalinic (60' Andrej Kramaric), Marko Pjaca (83' Ivica Olic). (Coach: Ante Cacic
(CRO)).
Goal: Croatia: 0-1 Ivan Perisic (25').
Referee: Mark Clattenburg (ENG)   Attendance: 5.835

GROUP I

07-09-2014	Copenhagen	Denmark – Armenia	2-1 (0-0)
07-09-2014	Aveiro	Portugal – Albania	0-1 (0-0)
11-10-2014	Yerevan	Armenia – Serbia	1-1 (0-0)
11-10-2014	Elbassan	Albania – Denmark	1-1 (1-0)
14-10-2014	Copenhagen	Denmark – Portugal	0-1 (0-0)
14-10-2014	Belgrade	Serbia – Albania	0-3
14-11-2014	Faro/Loulé	Portugal – Armenia	1-0 (0-0)
14-11-2014	Belgrade	Serbia – Denmark	1-3 (1-0)
29-03-2015	Elbasan	Albania – Armenia	2-1 (0-1)
29-03-2015	Lisbon	Portugal- Serbia	2-1 (1-0)
13-06-2015	Yerevan	Armenia – Portugal	2-3 (1-1)
13-06-2015	Copenhagen	Denmark – Serbia	2-0 (1-0)
04-09-2015	Copenhagen	Denmark – Albania	0-0
04-09-2015	Novi Sad	Serbia – Armenia	2-0 (1-0)
07-09-2015	Yerevan	Armenia – Denmark	0-0
07-09-2015	Elbasan	Albania – Portugal	0-1 (0-0)
08-10-2015	Elbasan	Albania – Serbia	0-2 (0-0)
08-10-2015	Braga	Portugal – Denmark	1-0 (0-0
11-10-2015	Yerevan	Armenia – Albania	0-3 (0-2)
11-10-2015	Belgrade	Serbia – Portugal	1-2 (0-1)

FINAL STANDING

Pos	Team	Pld	W	D	L	GF	GA	GD	Pts
1	*Portugal*	8	7	0	1	11	5	+6	21
2	*Albania*	8	4	2	2	10	5	+5	14
3	*Denmark*	8	3	3	2	8	5	+3	12
4	Serbia	8	2	1	5	8	13	-5	4
5	Armenia	8	0	2	6	5	14	-9	2

The match between Serbia and Albania on 14th October 2014 was abandoned after 41 minutes when Serbian fans and officials invaded the pitch and attacked Albania players as a drone carrying a pro-Albania flag was flown over the stadium. UEFA initially awarded the game as a 3-0 win to Serbia who also received a three point deduction and were ordered to play two matches behind closed doors. Both teams received a €100.000 fine.

This decision was appealed by both Serbia and Albania, but was upheld by UEFA and the two associations then filed further appeals to the Court of Arbitration for Sport. On 10th July 2015, the Court of Arbitration for Sport rejected the appeal filed by the Serbian FA, and partially upheld the appeal filed by the Albanian FA, meaning the match was deemed to have been forfeited by Serbia 3-0 so they were still deducted three points and Albania were duly awarded three points, though they were still required to pay the fine.

Portugal and Albania qualified for the Final Tournament in France.
Denmark qualified for the play-offs

07-09-2014   Telia Parken, Copenhagen: Denmark – Armenia   2-1 (0-0)
Denmark: Kasper Schmeichel, Simon Kjær (57' Jores Okore), Nicolai Boilesen, Andreas Bjelland, Peter Ankersen, Lasse Schöne (56' Lasse Vibe), William Kvist (C) (74' Thomas Kahlenberg), Michael Krohn-Dehli, Pierre-Emile Højbjerg (YC54), Christian Eriksen, Nicklas Bendtner. (Coach: Morten Per Olsen (DEN)).
Armenia: Roman Berezovski (C), Artur Yedigaryan (YC75), Varazdat Haroyan, Robert Arzumanyan (66' Taron Voskanyan), Hrayr Mkoyan, Henrikh Mkhitaryan (71' Marcos Piñeiro Pizzelli), Edgar Manucharyan (84' Artak Dashyan), Rumyan Hovsepyan, Kamo Hovhannisyan, Levon Hayrapetyan, Gevorg Ghazaryan. (Coach: Bernard Challandes (SUI)).
Goals: Denmark: 1-1 Pierre-Emile Højbjerg (65'), 2-1 Thomas Kahlenberg (80').
Armenia: 0-1 Henrikh Mkhitaryan (50').
Referee: Alexandru Dan Tudor (ROM)   Attendance: 20.141

07-09-2014   Estádio Municipal, Aveiro: Portugal – Albania   0-1 (0-0)
Portugal: RUI Pedro dos Santos PATRÍCIO, JOÃO Pedro da Silva PEREIRA, Képler Laveran Lima Ferreira "PEPE", RICARDO Miguel Moreira da COSTA (73' MIGUEL Luis Pinto VELOSO), Adelino André Vieira de Freitas "VIEIRINHA" (46' IVAN Ricardo Neves Abreu CAVALEIRO), JOÃO Filipe Iria Santos MOUTINHO, ANDRÉ Filipe Tavares GOMES, FÁBIO Alexandre da Silva COENTRÃO, WILLIAM Silva de CARVALHO (56' RICARDO Jorge Luz HORTA), "ÉDER" Éderzito António Macedo Lopes, Luís Carlos Almeida da Cunha "NANI" (C) (YC69). (Coach: PAULO Jorge Gomes BENTO (POR)).
Albania: Etrit Berisha (YC70), Mërgim Mavraj (YC67), Ermir Lenjani (75' Andi Lila), Elseid Hysaj, Odise Roshi (YC4), Burim Kukeli (66' Ergys Kaçe (YC69)), Lorik Cana (C), Ansi Agolli, Taulant Xhaka (YC34), Amir Abrashi (YC21), Bekim Balaj (82' Sokol Çikalleshi). (Coach: Giovanni De Biasi (ITA)).
Goal: Albania: 0-1 Bekim Balaj (52').
Referee: Ruddy Buquet (FRA)   Attendance: 23.205

11-10-2014   Vazgen Sargsyan Republican Stadium, Yerevan: Armenia – Serbia 1-1 (0-0)
Armenia: Roman Berezovski (C), Artur Yedigaryan, Varazdat Haroyan (YC90+1), Robert
Arzumanyan, Taron Voskanyan, Karlen Mkrtchyan (52' Rumyan Hovsepyan), Edgar
Manucharyan (66' Artak Dashyan), Kamo Hovhannisyan, Levon Hayrapetyan, Artur Sarkisov,
Marcos Piñeiro Pizzelli (84' Alexander Karapetyan). (Coach: Bernard Challandes (SUI)).
Serbia: Vladimir Stojkovic, Matija Nastasic (YC45), Stefan Mitrovic (YC82), Aleksandar
Kolarov, Branislav Ivanovic (C), Zoran Tosic, Nemanja Matic, Lazar Markovic (26' Zdravko
Kuzmanovic), Nemanja Gudelj (74' Aleksandar Mitrovic), Dusan Tadic, Filip Djordjevic (69'
Danko Lazovic). (Coach: Dick Nicolaas Advocaat (HOL)).
Goals: Armenia: 1-0 Robert Arzumanyan (73').
Serbia: 1-1 Zoran Tosic (89').
Referee: Tom Harald Hagen (NOR)   Attendance: 8.500
(Marcos Piñeiro Pizzelli missed a penalty in the 83th minute)

11-10-2014   Elbasan Arena, Elbasan: Albania – Denmark 1-1 (1-0)
Albania: Etrit Berisha, Mërgim Mavraj, Andi Lila (87' Debatik Çurri), Ermir Lenjani, Elseid
Hysaj, Burim Kukeli, Lorik Cana (C), Ansi Agolli, Taulant Xhaka (82' Valdet Rama), Amir
Abrashi, Bekim Balaj (69' Sokol Çikalleshi). (Coach: Giovanni De Biasi (ITA)).
Denmark: Kasper Schmeichel, Simon Kjær, Nicolai Boilesen, Andreas Bjelland, Peter
Ankersen (71' Uffe Bech), William Kvist (C), Michael Krohn-Dehli, Pierre-Emile Højbjerg
(79' Thomas Kahlenberg), Christian Eriksen, Yussuf Poulsen (46' Lasse Vibe), Nicklas
Bendtner. (Coach: Morten Per Olsen (DEN)).
Goals: Albania: 1-0 Ermir Lenjani (38').
Denmark: 1-1 Lasse Vibe (81').
Referee: Viktor Kassai (HUN)   Attendance: 11.330

14-10-2014   Telia Parken, Copenhagen: Denmark – Portugal 0-1 (0-0)
Denmark: Kasper Schmeichel, Daniel Agger (C), Simon Kjær, Lars Jacobsen, Nicolai Boilesen
(58' Simon Poulsen), Lasse Vibe (46' Uffe Bech), William Kvist, Michael Krohn-Dehli,
Pierre-Emile Højbjerg, Christian Eriksen (84' Thomas Kahlenberg), Nicklas Bendtner. (Coach:
Morten Per Olsen (DEN)).
Portugal: RUI Pedro dos Santos PATRÍCIO, CÉDRIC Ricardo Alves SOARES, RICARDO
Alberto Silveira CARVALHO, Képler Laveran Lima Ferreira "PEPE", ELISEU Pereira dos
Santos, WILLIAM Silva de CARVALHO, TIAGO Cardoso Mendes (84' RICARDO Andrade
QUARESMA Bernardo), JOÃO Filipe Iria Santos MOUTINHO, DANNY Miguel Alves
Gomes (77' "ÉDER" Éderzito António Macedo Lopes), CRISTIANO RONALDO dos Santos
Aveiro (C) (YC90+2), Luís Carlos Almeida da Cunha "NANI" (68' JOÃO MÁRIO Naval da
Costa Eduardo). (Coach: FERNANDO Manuel Fernandes da Costa SANTOS (POR)).
Goal: Portugal: 0-1 CRISTIANO RONALDO dos Santos Aveiro (90'+5').
Referee: Dr.Felix Brych (GER)   Attendance: 36.562

14-10-2014   Partizan Stadium, Belgrade: Serbia – Albania 0-3 (Awarded)
Serbia: Vladimir Stojkovic, Matija Nastasic, Stefan Mitrovic, Aleksandar Kolarov, Branislav
Ivanovic (C) (YC35), Filip Djuricic, Zoran Tosic, Nemanja Matic, Nemanja Gudelj, Dusan
Tadic, Danko Lazovic. (Coach: Dick Nicolaas Advocaat (HOL)).
Albania: Etrit Berisha, Mërgim Mavraj, Andi Lila, Ermir Lenjani, Elseid Hysaj, Burim Kukeli,
Lorik Cana (C), Ansi Agolli (YC34), Taulant Xhaka, Amir Abrashi, Bekim Balaj. (Coach:
Giovanni De Biasi (ITA)).
Referee: Martin Atkinson (ENG)   Attendance: 25.200
(The match was suspended in the 41th minute following a pitch invasion and fighting. Further
details of the incident are listed opposite).

357

14-11-2014   Estádio Algarve, Faro/Loulé: Portugal – Armenia   1-0 (0-0)
Portugal: RUI Pedro dos Santos PATRÍCIO, Képler Laveran Lima Ferreira "PEPE" (YC42),
RICARDO Alberto Silveira CARVALHO (YC14), JOSÉ José BOSINGWA da Silva,
RAPHAËL Adelino José GUERREIRO, TIAGO Cardoso Mendes (YC36), JOÃO Filipe Iria
Santos MOUTINHO, HÉLDER Manuel Marques POSTIGA (56' "ÉDER" Éderzito António
Macedo Lopes), DANNY Miguel Alves Gomes (YC69) (70' RICARDO Andrade
QUARESMA Bernardo), CRISTIANO RONALDO dos Santos Aveiro (C), Luís Carlos
Almeida da Cunha "NANI" (88' WILLIAM Silva de CARVALHO (YC90+1)). (Coach:
FERNANDO Manuel Fernandes da Costa SANTOS (POR)).
Armenia: Roman Berezovski (C), Artur Yedigaryan (YC34) (77' Artur Sarkisov), Varazdat
Haroyan, Robert Arzumanyan (YC90+4), Taron Voskanyan, Karlen Mkrtchyan (84' Marcos
Piñeiro Pizzelli), Henrikh Mkhitaryan, Kamo Hovhannisyan, Levon Hayrapetyan, Yura
Movsisyan, Gevorg Ghazaryan (62' Edgar Manucharyan). (Coach: Bernard Challandes (SUI)).
Goal: Portugal: 1-0 CRISTIANO RONALDO dos Santos Aveiro (72').
Referee: Anastasios (Tasos) Sidiropoulos (GRE)   Attendance: 21.042

14-11-2014   Partizan Stadium, Belgrade: Serbia – Denmark   1-3 (1-0)
Serbia: Vladimir Stojkovic, Dusko Tosic, Stefan Mitrovic, Branislav Ivanovic (C), Milan
Bisevac, Zoran Tosic, Nemanja Matic, Nemanja Gudelj (66' Aleksandar Mitrovic), Filip
Djuricic (46' Zdravko Kuzmanovic), Dusan Tadic (71' Lazar Markovic), Danko Lazovic.
(Coach: Dick Nicolaas Advocaat (HOL)).
Denmark: Kasper Schmeichel, Simon Kjær, Nicolai Boilesen, Andreas Bjelland, Peter
Ankersen (70' Lars Jacobsen (YC87)), Lasse Vibe, William Kvist (C) (YC78), Michael Krohn-
Dehli (YC78), Thomas Kahlenberg (88' Rasmus Würtz), Christian Eriksen, Nicklas Bendtner
(88' Yussuf Yurary Poulsen). (Coach: Morten Per Olsen (DEN)).
Goals: Serbia: 1-0 Zoran Tosic (4').
Denmark: 1-1 Nicklas Bendtner (60'), 1-2 Simon Kjær (62'), 1-3 Nicklas Bendtner (85').
Referee: Cüneyt Çakir (TUR)   Attendance: behind closed doors

29-03-2015   Elbasan Arena, Elbasan: Albania – Armenia   2-1 (0-1)
Albania: Etrit Berisha, Mërgim Mavraj, Elseid Hysaj, Lorik Cana (C) (YC19), Ansi Agolli,
Odise Roshi (69' Hamdi Salihi), Ledian Memushaj (46' Shkëlzen Gashi), Burim Kukeli
(YC84), Amir Abrashi (46' Ermir Lenjani), Taulant Xhaka, Sokol Çikalleshi (YC90+2).
(Coach: Giovanni De Biasi (ITA)).
Armenia: Roman Berezovski (C), Hovhannes Hambardzumyan (YC51,YC70), Robert
Arzumanyan (YC86), Gaël Andonian, Artur Yedigaryan (84' Ruslan Koryan), Henrikh
Mkhitaryan, Edgar Manucharyan (67' Kamo Hovhannisyan), Levon Hayrapetyan, Gevorg
Ghazaryan, Marcos Piñeiro Pizzelli (YC38), Yura Movsisyan. (Coach: Bernard Challandes
(SUI)).
Goals: Albania: 1-1 Mërgim Mavraj (77'), 2-1 Shkëlzen Gashi (81').
Armenia: 0-1 Mërgim Mavraj (4' *own goal*).
Referee: David Fernández Borbalán (ESP)   Attendance: 12.300

358

29-03-2015   Estádio da Luz, Lisbon: Portugal – Serbia 2-1 (1-0)
Portugal: RUI Pedro dos Santos PATRÍCIO, RICARDO Alberto Silveira CARVALHO (17'
JOSÉ Miguel da Rocha FONTE), BRUNO Eduardo Regufe ALVES, JOSÉ José BOSINGWA
da Silva, ELISEU Pereira dos Santos, TIAGO Cardoso Mendes, JOÃO Filipe Iria Santos
MOUTINHO (YC90+2), FÁBIO Alexandre da Silva COENTRÃO (YC41) (78' RICARDO
Andrade QUARESMA Bernardo), DANNY Miguel Alves Gomes (86' WILLIAM Silva de
CARVALHO), CRISTIANO RONALDO dos Santos Aveiro (C), Luís Carlos Almeida da
Cunha "NANI". (Coach: ILÍDIO Fernando Torres do VALE (POR)).
Serbia: Vladimir Stojkovic, Matija Nastasic, Aleksandar Kolarov (YC47), Branislav Ivanovic
(C), Dusan Basta, Radosav Petrovic, Nemanja Matic (YC25), Lazar Markovic (65' Filip
Djuricic (YC90+1)), Dusan Tadic (78' Zoran Tosic (YC82)), Aleksandar Mitrovic, Adem
Ljajic (YC41) (85' Petar Skuletic). (Coach: Radovan Curcic (SRB)).
Goals: Portugal: 1-0 RICARDO Alberto Silveira CARVALHO (10'), 2-1 FÁBIO Alexandre
da Silva COENTRÃO (63').
Serbia: 1-1 Nemanja Matic (61').
Referee: Gianluca Rocchi (ITA)   Attendance: 58.430

13-06-2015   Vazgen Sargsyan Republican Stadium, Yerevan: Armenia – Portugal 2-3 (1-1)
Armenia: Roman Berezovski (C), Robert Arzumanyan, Gaël Andonian, Karlen Mkrtchyan (29'
Rumyan Hovsepyan (YC85)), Hrayr Mkoyan, Henrikh Mkhitaryan, Kamo Hovhannisyan (61'
Aras Özbiliz), Levon Hayrapetyan, Artur Sarkisov (72' Ruslan Koryan), Marcos Piñeiro
Pizzelli, Gevorg Ghazaryan. (Coach: Sargis Hovsepyan (ARM)).
Portugal: RUI Pedro dos Santos PATRÍCIO (YC90), RICARDO Alberto Silveira
CARVALHO (78' JOSÉ Miguel da Rocha FONTE), BRUNO Eduardo Regufe ALVES,
Adelino André Vieira de Freitas "VIEIRINHA", ELISEU Pereira dos Santos, FÁBIO
Alexandre da Silva COENTRÃO (72' ADRIEN Sebastian Perruchet SILVA), TIAGO Cardoso
Mendes (YC33,YC62), JOÃO Filipe Iria Santos MOUTINHO, DANNY Miguel Alves Gomes
(63' WILLIAM Silva de CARVALHO), CRISTIANO RONALDO dos Santos Aveiro (C),
Luís Carlos Almeida da Cunha "NANI". (Coach: ILÍDIO Fernando Torres do VALE (POR)).
Goals: Armenia: 1-0 Marcos Piñeiro Pizzelli (14'), 2-3 Hrayr Mkoyan (72').
Portugal: 1-1 CRISTIANO RONALDO dos Santos Aveiro (29' penalty), 1-2 CRISTIANO
RONALDO dos Santos Aveiro (55'), 1-3 CRISTIANO RONALDO dos Santos Aveiro (58').
Referee: Serge Gumienny (BEL)   Attendance: 14.527

13-06-2015   Telia Parken, Copenhagen: Denmark – Serbia 2-0 (1-0)
Denmark: Kasper Schmeichel, Simon Poulsen, Simon Kjær (YC46), Lars Jacobsen, Daniel
Agger (C), William Kvist (YC58) (77' Andreas Christensen), Michael Krohn-Dehli (61' Jakob
Poulsen), Pierre-Emile Højbjerg, Christian Eriksen, Nicklas Bendtner, Yussuf Yurary Poulsen
(73' Lasse Vibe). (Coach: Morten Per Olsen (DEN)).
Serbia: Vladimir Stojkovic, Matija Nastasic, Nikola Maksimovic, Aleksandar Kolarov (YC63),
Branislav Ivanovic (C), Nemanja Matic, Lazar Markovic, Ljubomir Fejsa, Zoran Tosic (65'
Filip Kostic), Aleksandar Mitrovic (90' Petar Skuletic), Adem Ljajic (81' Filip Djuricic).
(Coach: Radovan Curcic (SRB)).
Goals: Denmark: 1-0 Yussuf Yurary Poulsen (13'), 2-0 Jakob Poulsen (87').
Referee: Björn Kuipers (HOL)   Attendance: 30.887
(Daniel Agger missed a penalty in the 34th minute)

04-09-2015   Telia Parken, Copenhagen: Denmark – Albania   0-0
Denmark: Kasper Schmeichel, Daniel Agger (C), Simon Kjær (YC86), Lars Jacobsen (YC32),
Riza Durmisi, Pione Sisto Ifolo Emirmija (46' Yussuf Yurary Poulsen), William Kvist (46'
Jakob Poulsen), Michael Krohn-Dehli, Pierre-Emile Højbjerg, Nicolai Jørgensen, Nicklas
Bendtner. (Coach: Morten Per Olsen (DEN)).
Albania: Etrit Berisha, Ermir Lenjani (64' Armando Sadiku), Berat Xhimshiti, Arlind Ajeti
(YC75), Burim Kukeli (YC77), Shkëlzen Gashi (83' Odise Roshi), Lorik Cana (C), Ansi
Agolli (YC32), Amir Abrashi (64' Migjen Basha), Taulant Xhaka (YC86), Sokol Çikalleshi.
(Coach: Giovanni De Biasi (ITA)).
Referee: William (Willie) Collum (SCO)   Attendance: 35.648

04-09-2015   Karadjordje Stadium, Novi Sad: Serbia – Armenia   2-0 (1-0)
Serbia: Vladimir Stojkovic, Uros Spajic, Nenad Tomovic, Aleksandar Kolarov, Branislav
Ivanovic (C) (YC45), Darko Brasanac, Andrija Zivkovic (59' Zoran Tosic), Nemanja Matic,
Filip Kostic (84' Dusan Tadic), Aleksandar Mitrovic (YC55), Adem Ljajic (73' Ljubomir
Fejsa). (Coach: Radovan Curcic (SRB)).
Armenia: Gevorg Kasparov, Gaël Andonian, Robert Arzumanyan, Karlen Mkrtchyan, Hrayr
Mkoyan, Henrikh Mkhitaryan (C), Levon Hayrapetyan, Marcos Piñeiro Pizzelli (65' Ruslan
Koryan), Aras Özbiliz (59' Kamo Hovhannisyan), Yura Movsisyan, Gevorg Ghazaryan
(YC43) (82' Artem Simonyan). (Coach: Sargis Hovsepyan (ARM)).
Goals: Serbia: 1-0 Levon Hayrapetyan (22' own goal), 2-0 Adem Ljajic (53').
Referee: Miroslav Zelinka (CZE)   Attendance: behind closed doors

07-09-2015   Vazgen Sargsyan Republican Stadium, Yerevan: Armenia – Denmark   0-0
Armenia: Gevorg Kasparov, Varazdat Haroyan, Robert Arzumanyan, Gaël Andonian, Karlen
Mkrtchyan (YC44), Hrayr Mkoyan, Henrikh Mkhitaryan (C), Kamo Hovhannisyan (87' Artem
Simonyan), Marcos Piñeiro Pizzelli (62' Ruslan Koryan), Yura Movsisyan (YC77) (83' Aras
Özbiliz), Gevorg Ghazaryan (YC10). (Coach: Sargis Hovsepyan (ARM)).
Denmark: Kasper Schmeichel, Simon Kjær (80' Erik Sviatchenko), Lars Jacobsen, Riza
Durmisi, Daniel Agger (C), Jakob Poulsen, Michael Krohn-Dehli (56' Thomas Delaney),
Pierre-Emile Højbjerg, Yussuf Yurary Poulsen, Nicolai Jørgensen (YC63) (64' Martin
Braithwaite), Nicklas Bendtner. (Coach: Morten Per Olsen (DEN)).
Referee: Svein Oddvar Moen (NOR)   Attendance: 7.500

07-09-2015   Elbasan Arena, Elbasan: Albania – Portugal   0-1 (0-0)
Albania: Etrit Berisha, Arlind Ajeti, Ermir Lenjani, Berat Xhimshiti (YC23), Lorik Cana (C),
Ansi Agolli, Burim Kukeli, Shkëlzen Gashi (70' Odise Roshi), Amir Abrashi (YC44) (54'
Migjen Basha), Taulant Xhaka, Sokol Çikalleshi (86' Bekim Balaj). (Coach: Giovanni De
Biasi (ITA)).
Portugal: RUI Pedro dos Santos PATRÍCIO, RICARDO Alberto Silveira CARVALHO,
Képler Laveran Lima Ferreira "PEPE", Adelino André Vieira de Freitas "VIEIRINHA" (54'
CÉDRIC Ricardo Alves SOARES), ELISEU Pereira dos Santos, BERNARDO Mota Veiga de
Carvalho e SILVA (65' RICARDO Andrade QUARESMA Bernardo), MIGUEL Luis Pinto
VELOSO, DANILO Luís Hélio Pereira, CRISTIANO RONALDO dos Santos Aveiro (C),
DANNY Miguel Alves Gomes (76' "ÉDER" Éderzito António Macedo Lopes), Luís Carlos
Almeida da Cunha "NANI" (YC82). (Coach: FERNANDO Manuel Fernandes da Costa
SANTOS (POR)).
Goal: Portugal: 0-1 MIGUEL Luis Pinto VELOSO (90'+2').
Referee: Jonas Eriksson (SWE)   Attendance: 12.121

08-10-2015   Elbasan Arena, Elbasan: Albania – Serbia   0-2 (0-0)
Albania: Etrit Berisha, Andi Lila (46' Ergys Kaçe), Ermir Lenjani (83' Alban Meha), Berat
Xhimshiti, Elseid Hysaj, Ledian Menushaj, Lorik Cana (C) (YC16), Migjen Basha, Ansi Agolli
(YC79), Taulant Xhaka, Bekim Balaj (69' Sokol Çikalleshi). (Coach: Giovanni De Biasi
(ITA)).
Serbia: Vladimir Stojkovic, Nenad Tomovic (YC68), Stefan Mitrovic, Aleksandar Kolarov,
Branislav Ivanovic (C) (65' Dusko Tosic), Zoran Tosic, Luka Milivojevic (YC3), Nemanja
Matic (73' Ljubomir Fejsa), Dusan Tadic (54' Miralem Sulejmani), Aleksandar Mitrovic
(YC90+3), Adem Ljajic. (Coach: Radovan Curcic (SRB)).
Goals: Serbia: 0-1 Aleksandar Kolarov (90'+1'), 0-2 Adem Ljajic (90'+4').
Referee: Nicola Rizzoli (ITA)   Attendance: 12.330

08-10-2015   Estádio Municipal, Braga: Portugal – Denmark   1-0 (0-0)
Portugal: RUI Pedro dos Santos PATRÍCIO (YC82), CÉDRIC Ricardo Alves SOARES,
BRUNO Eduardo Regufe ALVES, RICARDO Alberto Silveira CARVALHO, BERNARDO
Mota Veiga de Carvalho e SILVA (76' DANNY Miguel Alves Gomes), TIAGO Cardoso
Mendes, JOÃO Filipe Iria Santos MOUTINHO (90'+1' JOSÉ Miguel da Rocha FONTE),
FÁBIO Alexandre da Silva COENTRÃO, DANILO Luís Hélio Pereira (YC88), CRISTIANO
RONALDO dos Santos Aveiro (C), Luís Carlos Almeida da Cunha "NANI" (82' RICARDO
Andrade QUARESMA Bernardo). (Coach: FERNANDO Manuel Fernandes da Costa
SANTOS (POR)).
Denmark: Kasper Schmeichel, Riza Durmisi, Daniel Agger (C), Daniel Wass (YC69) (69'
Nicolai Jørgensen), Simon Kjær, Lars Jacobsen, Michael Krohn-Dehli, Pierre-Emile Højbjerg
(YC25) (46' William Kvist), Christian Eriksen (YC43) (82' Yussuf Yurary Poulsen), Martin
Braithwaite, Nicklas Bendtner. (Coach: Morten Per Olsen (DEN)).
Goal: Portugal: 1-0 JOÃO Filipe Iria Santos MOUTINHO (66').
Referee: Mark Clattenburg (ENG)   Attendance: 29.860

11-10-2015   Vazgen Sargsyan Republican Stadium, Yerevan: Armenia – Albania   0-3 (0-2)
Armenia: Gevorg Kasparov, Varazdat Haroyan, Robert Arzumanyan (YC17), Gaël Andonian
(YC82), Henrikh Mkhitaryan (C), Kamo Hovhannisyan, Karlen Mkrtchyan, Gevorg Ghazaryan
(83' Vardan Pogosyan), Artur Yuspashyan (YC27) (46' Aras Özbiliz), Marcos Piñeiro Pizzelli,
Yura Movsisyan (59' Artur Sarkisov). (Coach: Sargis Hovsepyan (ARM)).
Albania: Etrit Berisha, Berat Xhimshiti (YC64), Naser Aliji (YC52), Elseid Hysaj, Shkëlzen
Gashi, Lorik Cana (C), Migjen Basha (YC81) (87' Amir Abrashi), Odise Roshi, Ledian
Memushaj (72' Burim Kukeli), Taulant Xhaka, Sokol Çikalleshi (58' Armando Sadiku).
(Coach: Giovanni De Biasi (ITA)).
Goals: Albania: 0-1 Kamo Hovhannisyan (9' own goal), 0-2 Berat Xhimshiti (23'), 0-3
Armando Sadiku (76').
Referee: Szymon Marciniak (POL)   Attendance: 4.700

11-10-2015   Partizan Stadium, Belgrade: Serbia – Portugal   1-2 (0-1)
Serbia: Vladimir Stojkovic, Nenad Tomovic, Stefan Mitrovic, Aleksandar Kolarov (C)
(YC79,YC80) (77' Ivan Obradovic), Dusko Tosic (YC78), Luka Milivojevic, Nemanja Matic
(RC81), Zoran Tosic (84' Miralem Sulejmani), Dusan Tadic, Aleksandar Mitrovic (YC50) (85'
Petar Skuletic), Adem Ljajic. (Coach: Radovan Curcic (SRB)).
Portugal: RUI Pedro dos Santos PATRÍCIO, JOSÉ Miguel da Rocha FONTE, BRUNO
Eduardo Regufe ALVES (46' Luís Carlos Novo NETO), ELISEU Pereira dos Santos,
DANILO Luís Hélio Pereira (YC50), Nélson Cabral Semedo "NELSINHO" (YC28), ANDRÉ
Filipe Brás ANDRÉ (YC82), MIGUEL Luis Pinto VELOSO (70' JOÃO Filipe Iria Santos
MOUTINHO), DANNY Miguel Alves Gomes (YC42) (57' "ÉDER" Éderzito António Macedo
Lopes), Luís Carlos Almeida da Cunha "NANI" (C) (YC42), RICARDO Andrade
QUARESMA Bernardo. (Coach: FERNANDO Manuel Fernandes da Costa SANTOS (POR)).
Goals: Serbia: 1-1 Zoran Tosic (65').
Portugal: 0-1 Luís Carlos Almeida da Cunha "NANI" (5'), 1-2 JOÃO Filipe Iria Santos
MOUTINHO (78').
Referee: David Fernández Borbalán (ESP)   Attendance: 7.485

QUALIFICATION   PLAY-OFFS

12-11-2015   Ullevaal Stadion, Oslo: Norway – Hungary   0-1 (0-1)
Norway: Ørjan Nyland, Tom Høgli, Even Hovland, Vegard Forren, Omar Elabdellaoui
(YC65), Markus Henriksen, Alexander Tettey (YC20), Per Ciljan Skjelbred (C) (86' Pål André
Helland), Jo Inge Berget (74' Mohamed Elyounoussi), Alexander Søderlund (61' Marcus
Pedersen), Stefan Johansen. (Coach: Per-Mathias Høgmo (NOR)).
Hungary: Gábor Király, Tamás Kádár (YC34), Richárd Guzmics (YC39), Attila Fiola, Ádám
Lang, László Kleinheisler (72' Ádám Nagy), Ákos Elek, Zoltán Gera (YC23), Ádám Szalai
(90'+2' Tamás Priskin), Krisztián Németh, Balázs Dzsudzsák (C) (76' Gergö Lovrencsics).
(Coach: Bernd Storck (GER)).
Goal: Hungary: 0-1 László Kleinheisler (26').
Referee: Mark Clattenburg (ENG)   Attendance: 27.182

13-11-2015   Bilino Polje, Zenica: Bosnia and Herzegovina – Republic of Ireland   1-1 (0-0)
Bosnia and Herzegovina: Asmir Begovic, Toni Sunjic, Emir Spahic, Mensur Mujdza (51'
Ognjen Vranjes), Edin Cocalic, Ervin Zukanovic, Edin Visca (73' Milan Djuric), Miralem
Pjanic, Senad Lulic (88' Izet Hajrovic), Vedad Ibisevic, Edin Dzeko (C). (Coach: Mehmed
Bazdarevic (BOS)).
Republic of Ireland: Darren Randolph, Richard Keogh, Séamus Coleman, Ciaran Clark,
Stephen Ward (YC26) (67' Marc Wilson), Robert (Robbie) Brady (86' Aiden McGeady),
James McCarthy, Wesley (Wes) Hoolahan (60' James McClean), Jeffrey (Jeff) Hendrick,
Glenn Whelan (C), Daryl Murphy. (Coach: Martin Hugh Michael O'Neill (NIR)).
Goals: Bosnia and Heregovina: 1-1 Edin Dzeko (85').
Republic of Ireland: 0-1 Robert (Robbie) Brady (82').
Referee: Dr.Felix Brych (GER)   Attendance: 15.260

14-11-2015   Arena Lviv, Lviv: Ukraine – Slovenia   2-0 (1-0)
Ukraine: Andriy Pyatov, Yevhen Khacheridi (YC35), Artem Fedetskiy, Vyacheslav Shevchuk, Yaroslav Rakitskiy (YC84), Yevhen Konoplyanka (C), Denys Harmash (79' Ruslan Malinovskiy), Sergei Sydorchuk, Serhiy Rybalka, Andriy Yarmolenko (90'+1' Oleksandr Karavayev), Yevhen Seleznyov (YC19) (84' Artem Kravets). (Coach: Mikhail Ivanovich Fomenko (UKR)).
Slovenia: Samir Handanovic, Bojan Jokic, Branko Ilic, Bostjan Cesar (C), Miso Brecko, Josip Ilicic (63' Roman Bezjak), Valter Birsa (73' Nejc Pecnik), Jasmin Kurtic, René Krhin (YC44), Kevin Kampl, Milivoje Novakovic (YC35) (90' Zlatan Ljubijankic). (Coach: Srecko Katanec (SLO)).
Goals: Ukraine: 1-0 Andriy Yarmolenko (22'), 2-0 Yevhen Seleznyov (54').
Referee: Jonas Eriksson (SWE)   Attendance: 32.592

14-11-2015   Friend Arena, Solna: Sweden – Denmark   2-1 (1-0)
Sweden: Andreas Isaksson, Mikael Antonsson (29' Erik Johansson), Andreas Granqvist, Martin Olsson, Mikael Lustig, Emil Forsberg (YC47), Oscar Lewicki, Kim Källström, Zlatan Ibrahimovic (C) (82' John Guidetti), Jimmy Durmaz (68' Sebastian Larsson), Marcus Berg. (Coach: Erik Hamrén (SWE)).
Denmark: Kasper Schmeichel, Riza Durmisi, Daniel Agger (C) (YC45+2), Simon Kjær, Lars Jacobsen, William Kvist, Thomas Kahlenberg (54' Nicolai Jørgensen), Christian Eriksen, Martin Braithwaite (71' Yussuf Yurary Poulsen), Nicklas Bendtner, Viktor Fischer (54' Pierre-Emile Højbjerg). (Coach: Morten Per Olsen (DEN)).
Goals: Sweden: 1-0 Emil Forsberg (45'), 2-0 Zlatan Ibrahimovic (50' penalty).
Denmark: 2-1 Nicolai Jørgensen (80').
Referee: Nicola Rizzoli (ITA)   Attendance: 49.053

15-11-2015   Groupama Arena, Budapest: Hungary – Norway   2-1 (1-0)
Hungary: Gábor Király, Ádám Lang, Tamás Kádár, Richárd Guzmics, Attila Fiola, László Kleinheisler (75' Krisztián Németh), Ákos Elek (46' Ádám Pintér), Ádám Nagy (YC72), Gergö Lovrencsics, Tamás Priskin (62' Dániel Böde (YC81)), Balázs Dzsudzsák (C). (Coach: Bernd Storck (GER)).
Norway: Ørjan Nyland, Even Hovland, Vegard Forren (YC65), Haitam Aleesami, Omar Elabdellaoui, Markus Henriksen, Mohamed Elyounoussi (46' Marcus Pedersen), Alexander Tettey, Per Ciljan Skjelbred (C) (80' Jo Inge Berget), Martin Ødegaard (46' Pål André Helland), Stefan Johansen (YC11). (Coach: Per-Mathias Høgmo (NOR)).
Goals: Hungary: 1-0 Tamás Priskin (14'), 2-0 Markus Henriksen (83' own goal).
Norway: 2-1 Markus Henriksen (87').
Referee: Carlos Velasco Carballo (ESP)   Attendance: 22.189

16-11-2015   Aviva Stadium, Dublin:
            Republic of Ireland – Bosnia and Herzegovina   2-0 (1-0)
Republic of Ireland: Darren Randolph, Richard Keogh, Séamus Coleman, Ciaran Clark, Robert (Robbie) Brady, Glenn Whelan (C) (90'+1' John O'Shea), James McCarthy, Wesley (Wes) Hoolahan (54' James McClean (YC59)), Jeffrey (Jeff) Hendrick, Jonathan (Jon) Walters, Daryl Murphy (55' Shane Long (YC84)). (Coach: Martin Hugh Michael O'Neill (NIR)).
Bosnia and Herzegovina: Asmir Begovic, Ervin Zukanovic (YC83), Ognjen Vranjes, Emir Spahic (YC20), Sead Kolasinac, Edin Cocalic (46' Muhamed Besic), Edin Visca, Miralem Pjanic, Haris Medunjanin (69' Milan Djuric (YC90+3)), Senad Lulic (YC23) (80' Vedad Ibisevic), Edin Dzeko (C) (YC90+3). (Coach: Mehmed Bazdarevic (BOS)).
Goals: Republic of Ireland: 1-0 Jonathan (Jon) Walters (24' penalty), 2-0 Jonathan (Jon) Walters (70').
Referee: Björn Kuipers (HOL)   Attendance: 50.500

17-11-2015   Ljudski vrt, Maribor: Slovenia – Ukraine 1-1 (1-0)
Slovenia: Samir Handanovic, Bojan Jokic (YC25), Branko Ilic, Bostjan Cesar (C) (YC1), Miso
Brecko (RC90+3), Valter Birsa (80' Dejan Lazarevic (YC90+4)), Nejc Pecnik (YC38) (67'
Josip Ilicic), René Krhin, Kevin Kampl, Roman Bezjak (68' Zlatan Ljubijankic), Milivoje
Novakovic. (Coach: Srecko Katanec (SLO)).
Ukraine: Andriy Pyatov, Yevhen Khacheridi, Artem Fedetskiy, Vyacheslav Shevchuk,
Yaroslav Rakitskiy, Yevhen Konoplyanka (C) (YC4) (90'+6' Anatoliy Tymoshchuk), Taras
Stepanenko, Sergei Sydorchuk (61' Denys Harmash), Serhiy Rybalka (YC32), Andriy
Yarmolenko, Yevhen Seleznyov (80' Artem Kravets). (Coach: Mikhail Ivanovich Fomenko
(UKR)).
Goals: Slovenia: 1-0 Bostjan Cesar (11').
Ukraine: 1-1 Andriy Yarmolenko (90'+7').
Referee: Cüneyt Çakir (TUR)   Attendance: 12.702

17-11-2015   Telia Parken, Copenhagen: Denmark – Sweden 2-2 (0-1)
Denmark: Kasper Schmeichel, Lars Jacobsen, Riza Durmisi (YC50) (84' Jannik Vestergaard),
Daniel Agger (C), Simon Kjær, Pierre-Emile Højbjerg (YC77), Christian Eriksen, Thomas
Delaney (46' Michael Krohn-Dehli), Nicklas Bendtner (60' Morten Rasmussen), Yussuf
Yurary Poulsen (YC59), Nicolai Jørgensen. (Coach: Morten Per Olsen (DEN)).
Sweden: Andreas Isaksson, Pierre Bengtsson (YC11) (86' Martin Olsson), Andreas Granqvist,
Mikael Lustig, Erik Johansson, Emil Forsberg, Oscar Lewicki, Sebastian Larsson (YC70) (81'
Oscar Hiljemark), Kim Källström (69' Gustav Svensson), Zlatan Ibrahimovic (C), Marcus
Berg. (Coach: Erik Hamrén (SWE)).
Goals: Denmark: 1-2 Yussuf Yurary Poulsen (82'), 2-2 Jannik Vestergaard (90'+1').
Sweden: 0-1 Zlatan Ibrahimovic (19'), 0-2 Zlatan Ibrahimovic (76').
Referee: Martin Atkinson (ENG)   Attendance: 36.051

FINAL   TOURNAMENT   IN   FRANCE

France automatically qualified for the Final Tournament as hosts.

GROUP   STAGE

GROUP   A

10-06-2016   Stade de France, Saint-Denis: France – Romania 2-1 (0-0)
France: Hugo Lloris (C), Patrice Evra, Adil Rami, Bacary Sagna, Laurent Koscielny, N'Golo
Kanté, Dimitri Payet (90'+2' Moussa Sissoko), Blaise Matuidi, Paul Pogba (77' Anthony
Martial), Antoine Griezmann (66' Kingsley Coman), Olivier Giroud (YC69). (Coach: Didier
Deschamps (FRA)).
Romania: Ciprian Tatarusanu, Razvan Rat (YC45), Vlad Chiriches (C) (YC32), Dragos
Grigore, Cristian Sapunaru, Ovidiu Hoban, Mihai Pintilii, Nicolae Stanciu (72' Alexandru
Chipciu), Adrian Popa (I) (YC78) (82' Gabriel Torje), Florin Andone (61' Denis Alibec),
Bogdan Stancu. (Coach: Anghel Iordanescu (ROM)).
Goals: France: 1-0 Olivier Giroud (57'), 2-1 Dimitri Payet (89').
Romania: 1-1 Bogdan Stancu (65' penalty).
Referee: Viktor Kassai (HUN)   Attendance: 75.113

11-06-2016   Stade Bollaert-Delelis, Lens: Albania – Switzerland   0-1 (0-1)
Albania: Etrit Berisha, Ermir Lenjani, Elseid Hysaj, Lorik Cana (C) (YC23,YC36), Ansi
Agolli, Mërgim Mavraj (YC90+2), Burim Kukeli (YC89), Taulant Xhaka (61' Ergys Kaçe
(YC63)), Odise Roshi (73' Sokol Çikalleshi), Amir Abrashi, Armando Sadiku (82' Shkëlzen
Gashi). (Coach: Giovanni De Biasi (ITA)).
Switzerland: Yann Sommer, Stephan Lichtsteiner (C), Ricardo Ivan Rodríguez Araya, Johan
Djourou, Fabian Schär (YC14), Granit Xhaka, Valon Behrami (YC66), Blerim Dzemaili (75'
Fabian Frei), Xherdan Shaqiri (88' Gélson da Conceição Tavares Fernandes), Haris Seferovic,
Admir Mehmedi (61' Breel-Donald Embolo). (Coach: Vladimir Petkovic (SUI)).
Goal: Switzerland: 0-1 Fabian Schär (5').
Referee: Carlos Velasco Carballo (ESP)   Attendance: 33.805

15-06-2016   Parc des Princes, Paris: Romania – Switzerland   1-1 (1-0)
Romania: Ciprian Tatarusanu, Razvan Rat (62' Steliano Filip), Vlad Chiriches (C), Dragos
Grigore (YC76), Cristian Sapunaru, Alexandru Chipciu (YC24), Mihai Pintilii (46' Ovidiu
Hoban), Gabriel Torje, Andrei Prepelita (YC22), Claudiu Keserü (YC37), Bogdan Stancu (84'
Florin Andone). (Coach: Anghel Iordanescu (ROM)).
Switzerland: Yann Sommer, Stephan Lichtsteiner (C), Ricardo Ivan Rodríguez Araya, Johan
Djourou, Fabian Schär, Granit Xhaka (YC50), Valon Behrami, Blerim Dzemaili (83' Michael
Lang), Xherdan Shaqiri (90'+1' Shani Tarashaj), Haris Seferovic (63' Breel-Donald Embolo
(YC90+4)), Admir Mehmedi. (Coach: Vladimir Petkovic (SUI)).
Goals: Romania: 1-0 Bogdan Stancu (18' penalty).
Switzerland: 1-1 Admir Mehmedi (57').
Referee: Sergey Gennadyevich Karasev (RUS)   Attendance: 43.576

15-06-2016   Stade Vélodrome, Marseille: France – Albania   2-0 (0-0)
France: Hugo Lloris (C), Patrice Evra, Adil Rami, Bacary Sagna, Laurent Koscielny, N'Golo
Kanté (YC88), Dimitri Payet, Blaise Matuidi, Olivier Giroud (77' André-Pierre Gignac),
Anthony Martial (46' Paul Pogba), Kingsley Coman (68' Antoine Griezmann). (Coach: Didier
Deschamps (FRA)).
Albania: Etrit Berisha, Andi Lila (71' Odise Roshi), Ermir Lenjani, Elseid Hysaj, Ansi Agolli
(C), Mërgim Mavraj, Arlind Ajeti (85' Frédéric (Freddie) Veseli), Ledian Memushaj, Burim
Kukeli (YC55) (74' Taulant Xhaka), Amir Abrashi (YC81), Armando Sadiku. (Coach:
Giovanni De Biasi (ITA)).
Goals: France: 1-0 Antoine Griezmann (90'), 2-0 Dimitri Payet (90'+6').
Referee: William (Willie) Collum (SCO)   Attendance: 63.670

19-06-2016   Parc Olympique Lyonnais, Lyon: Romania – Albania   0-1 (0-1)
Romania: Ciprian Tatarusanu, Alexandru Matel (YC54), Vlad Chiriches (C), Dragos Grigore,
Cristian Sapunaru (YC85), Ovidiu Hoban, Nicolae Stanciu, Andrei Prepelita (46' Lucian
Sanmartean), Adrian Popa (I) (68' Florin Andone), Denis Alibec (57' Gabriel Torje
(YC90+3)), Bogdan Stancu. (Coach: Anghel Iordanescu (ROM)).
Albania: Etrit Berisha, Andi Lila, Ermir Lenjani (77' Odise Roshi), Elseid Hysaj (YC90+4),
Ansi Agolli (C), Mërgim Mavraj, Arlind Ajeti, Migjen Basha (YC6) (83' Lorik Cana), Ledian
Memushaj (YC85), Amir Abrashi, Armando Sadiku (59' Bekim Balaj). (Coach: Giovanni De
Biasi (ITA)).
Goal: Albania: 0-1 Armando Sadiku (43').
Referee: Pavel Královec (CZE)   Attendance: 49.752

19-06-2016   Stade Pierre-Mauroy, Villeneuve-d'Ascq: Switzerland – France   0-0
Switzerland: Yann Sommer, Stephan Lichtsteiner (C), Ricardo Ivan Rodríguez Araya, Johan
Djourou, Fabian Schär, Granit Xhaka, Valon Behrami, Blerim Dzemaili, Xherdan Shaqiri (79'
Gélson da Conceição Tavares Fernandes), Breel-Donald Embolo (74' Haris Seferovic), Admir
Mehmedi (86' Michael Lang). (Coach: Vladimir Petkovic (SUI)).
France: Hugo Lloris (C), Patrice Evra, Adil Rami (YC25), Bacary Sagna, Laurent Koscielny
(YC83), Yohan Cabaye, Paul Pogba, Moussa Sissoko, Antoine Griezmann (77' Blaise
Matuidi), André-Pierre Gignac, Kingsley Coman (63' Dimitri Payet). (Coach: Didier
Deschamps (FRA)).
Referee: Damir Skomina (SLO)   Attendance: 45.616

STANDINGS

Pos	Team	Pld	W	D	L	GF	GA	GD	Pts
1	France	3	2	1	0	4	1	+3	7
2	Switzerland	3	1	2	0	2	1	+1	5
3	Albania	3	1	0	2	1	3	-2	3
4	Romania	3	0	1	2	2	4	-2	1

France and Switzerland qualified for the knockout phase.

GROUP   B

11-06-2016   Nouveau Stade de Bordeaux, Bordeaux: Wales – Slovakia   2-1 (1-0)
Wales: Daniel (Danny) Ward, Chris Gunter, Neil Taylor, Benjamin (Ben) Davies, James
Chester, Ashley Williams (C), Joe Allen, Aaron Ramsey (88' Jazz Richards), David (Dave)
Edwards (69' Joseph (Joe) Ledley), Gareth Bale, Jonathan Williams (71' Hal Robson-Kanu).
(Coach: Chris Coleman (WAL)).
Slovakia: Matús Kozácik, Peter Pekarík, Martin Skrtel (C) (YC90+2), Ján Durica, Dusan
Svento, Vladimir Weiss (YC80) (83' Miroslav Stoch), Patrik Hrosovsky (YC31) (60' Ondrej
Duda), Marek Hamsík, Juraj Kucka (YC83), Róbert Mak (YC78), Michal Duris (59' Adam
Nemec). (Coach: Ján Kozák (SVK)).
Goals: Wales: 1-0 Gareth Bale (10'), 2-1 Hal Robson-Kanu (81').
Slovakia: 1-1 Ondrej Duda (61').
Referee: Svein Oddvar Moen (NOR)   Attendance: 37.831

11-06-2016   Stade Vélodrome, Marseille: England – Russia   1-1 (0-0)
England: Joe Hart, Kyle Walker, Danny Rose, Gary Cahill (YC62), Chris Smalling, Raheem
Sterling (87' James Milner), Adam Lallana, Wayne Rooney (C) (78' Jack Wilshere), Eric Dier,
Dele Alli, Harry Kane. (Coach: Roy Hodgson (ENG)).
Russia: Igor Akinfeev, Igor Smolnikov, Sergei Ignashevich, Vasili Berezutski (C), Georgi
Schennikov (YC72), Roman Neustädter (80' Denis Glushakov), Aleksandr Golovin (77'
Roman Shirokov), Oleg Shatov, Aleksandr Kokorin, Fedor Smolov (85' Pavel Mamaev),
Artem Dzyuba. (Coach: Leonid Viktorovich Slutski (RUS)).
Goals: England: 1-0 Eric Dier (73').
Russia: 1-1 Vasili Berezutski (90'+2').
Referee: Nicola Rizzoli (ITA)   Attendance: 62.343

15-06-2016   Stade Pierre-Mauroy, Villeneuve-d'Ascq: Russia – Slovakia 1-2 (0-2)
Russia: Igor Akinfeev, Igor Smolnikov, Sergei Ignashevich, Vasili Berezutski (C), Georgi Schennikov, Roman Neustädter (46' Denis Glushakov), Aleksandr Golovin (46' Pavel Mamaev), Oleg Shatov, Aleksandr Kokorin (75' Roman Shirokov), Fedor Smolov, Artem Dzyuba. (Coach: Leonid Viktorovich Slutski (RUS)).
Slovakia: Matús Kozácik, Peter Pekarík, Martin Skrtel (C), Ján Durica (YC46), Tomás Hubocan, Vladimír Weiss (72' Dusan Svento), Marek Hamsík, Juraj Kucka, Róbert Mak (80' Michal Duris), Viktor Pecovsky, Ondrej Duda (67' Adam Nemec). (Coach: Ján Kozák (SVK)).
Goals: Russia: 1-2 Denis Glushakov (80').
Slovakia: 0-1 Vladimír Weiss (32'), 0-2 Marek Hamsík (45').
Referee: Damir Skomina (SLO)   Attendance: 38.989

16-06-2016   Stade Bollaert-Delelis, Lens: England – Wales 2-1 (0-1)
England: Joe Hart, Kyle Walker, Danny Rose, Gary Cahill, Chris Smalling, Raheem Sterling (46' Daniel Sturridge), Adam Lallana (73' Marcus Rashford), Wayne Rooney (C), Eric Dier, Dele Alli, Harry Kane (46' Jamie Vardy). (Coach: Roy Hodgson (ENG)).
Wales: Wayne Hennessey, Chris Gunter, Neil Taylor, Benjamin (Ben) Davies (YC61), James Chester, Ashley Williams (C), Joe Allen, Aaron Ramsey, Joseph (Joe) Ledley (67' David (Dave) Edwards), Hal Robson-Kanu (72' Jonathan Williams), Gareth Bale. (Coach: Chris Coleman (WAL)).
Goals: England: 1-0 Jamie Vardy (56'), 2-1 Daniel Sturridge (90'+2').
Wales: 0-1 Gareth Bale (42').
Referee: Dr.Felix Brych (GER)   Attendance: 34.033

20-06-2016   Stadium Municipal, Toulouse: Russia – Wales 0-3 (0-2)
Russia: Igor Akinfeev, Igor Smolnikov, Sergei Ignashevich, Vasili Berezutski (46' Aleksei Berezutski), Denis Glushakov, Pavel Mamaev (YC64), Roman Shirokov (C) (52' Aleksandr Golovin), Dmitri Kombarov, Aleksandr Kokorin, Fedor Smolov (70' Aleksandr Samedov), Artem Dzyuba. (Coach: Leonid Viktorovich Slutski (RUS)).
Wales: Wayne Hennessey, Chris Gunter, Neil Taylor, Benjamin (Ben) Davies, James Chester, Ashley Williams (C), Joe Allen (74' David (Dave) Edwards), Aaron Ramsey, Joseph (Joe) Ledley (76' Andy King), Gareth Bale (83' Simon Church), Samuel Michael (Sam) Vokes (YC16). (Coach: Chris Coleman (WAL)).
Goals: Wales: 0-1 Aaron Ramsey (11'), 0-2 Neil Taylor (20'), 0-3 Gareth Bale (67').
Referee: Jonas Eriksson (SWE)   Attendance: 28.840

20-06-2016   Stade Geoffroy-Guichard, Saint-Étienne: Slovakia – England 0-0
Slovakia: Matús Kozácik, Peter Pekarík, Martin Skrtel (C), Ján Durica, Tomás Hubocan, Vladimír Weiss (78' Milan Skriniar), Marek Hamsík, Juraj Kucka, Róbert Mak, Viktor Pecovsky (YC23) (66' Norbert Gyömbér), Ondrej Duda (57' Dusan Svento). (Coach: Ján Kozák (SVK)).
England: Joe Hart, Gary Cahill (C), Chris Smalling, Nathaniel Clyne, Ryan Bertrand (YC51), Adam Lallana (60' Dele Alli), Jordan Henderson, Eric Dier, Jack Wilshere (55' Wayne Rooney), Jamie Vardy, Daniel Sturridge (75' Harry Kane). (Coach: Roy Hodgson (ENG)).
Referee: Carlos Velasco Carballo (ESP)   Attendance: 39.051

STANDINGS

Pos	Team	Pld	W	D	L	GF	GA	GD	Pts
1	Wales	3	2	0	1	6	3	+3	6
2	England	3	1	2	0	3	2	+1	5
3	Slovakia	3	1	1	1	3	3	0	4
4	Russia	3	0	1	2	2	6	-4	1

Wales, England and Slovakia qualified for the knockout phase.

GROUP C

12-06-2016   Stade de Nice, Nice: Poland – Northern Ireland   1-0 (0-0)
Poland: Wojciech Szczesny, Michal Pazdan, Artur Jedrzejczyk, Kamil Glik, Lukasz Piszczek (YC89), Krzysztof Maczynski (78' Tomasz Jodlowiec), Grzegorz Krychowiak, Jakub Blaszczykowski (80' Kamil Grosicki), Bartosz Kapustka (YC65) (88' Slawomir Peszko), Arkadiusz Milik, Robert Lewandowski (C). (Coach: Adam Nawalka (POL)).
Northern Ireland: Michael McGovern, Conor McLaughlin, Shane Ferguson (66' Conor Washington), Gareth McAuley, Jonathan (Jonny) Evans, Craig Cathcart (YC69), Chris Baird (76' Jamie Ward), Steven Davis (C), Oliver Norwood, Patrick (Paddy) McNair (46' Stuart Dallas), Kyle Lafferty. (Coach: Michael Andrew Martin O'Neill (NIR)).
Goal: Poland: 1-0 Arkadiusz Milik (51').
Referee: Ovidiu Alin Hategan (ROM)   Attendance: 33.742

12-06-2016   Stade Pierre-Mauroy, Villeneuce-d'Ascq: Germany – Ukraine   2-0 (1-0)
Germany: Manuel Neuer (C), Shkodran Mustafi, Jonas Hector, Benedikt Höwedes, Jérôme Boateng, Sami Khedira, Mesut Özil, Julian Draxler (78' André Schürrle), Thomas Müller, Toni Kroos, Mario Götze (90' Bastian Schweinsteiger). (Coach: Joachim Löw (GER)).
Ukraine: Andriy Pyatov, Yevhen Khacheridi, Vyacheslav Shevchuk, Artem Fedetskiy, Yaroslav Rakitskiy, Taras Stepanenko, Viktor Kovalenko (73' Olexandr Zinchenko), Sergei Sydorchuk, Andriy Yarmolenko, Roman Zozulya (66' Yevhen Seleznyov), Yevhen Konoplyanka (YC68). (Coach: Mikhail Ivanovich Fomenko (UKR)).
Goals: Germany: 1-0 Shkodran Mustafi (19'), 2-0 Bastian Schweinsteiger (90'+2').
Referee: Martin Atkinson (ENG)   Attendance: 43.035

16-06-2016   Parc Olympique Lyonnais, Lyon: Ukraine – Northern Ireland   0-2 (0-0)
Ukraine: Andriy Pyatov, Yevhen Khacheridi, Vyacheslav Shevchuk (C), Artem Fedetskiy, Yaroslav Rakitskiy, Taras Stepanenko, Viktor Kovalenko (83' Olexandr Zinchenko), Sergei Sydorchuk (YC67) (76' Denys Harmash), Andriy Yarmolenko, Yevhen Konoplyanka, Yevhen Seleznyov (YC40) (71' Roman Zozulya). (Coach: Mikhail Ivanovich Fomenko (UKR)).
Northern Ireland: Michael McGovern, Gareth McAuley, Jonathan (Jonny) Evans (YC90+5), Aaron Hughes, Craig Cathcart, Steven Davis (C), Corry Evans (90'+3' Patrick (Paddy) McNair), Stuart Dallas (YC87), Oliver Norwood, Conor Washington (84' Josh Magennis), Jamie Ward (YC63) (69' Niall McGinn). (Coach: Michael Andrew Martin O'Neill (NIR)).
Goals: Northern Ireland: 0-1 Gareth McAuley (49'), 0-2 Niall McGinn (90'+6').
Referee: Pavel Královec (CZE)   Attendance: 51.043

16-06-2016   Stade de France, Saint-Denis: Germany – Poland   0-0
Germany: Manuel Neuer (C), Jonas Hector, Benedikt Höwedes, Mats Hummels, Jérôme
Boateng (YC67), Sami Khedira (YC3), Mesut Özil (YC34), Julian Draxler (71' Mario Gómez
García), Thomas Müller, Toni Kroos, Mario Götze (66' André Schürrle). (Coach: Joachim
Löw (GER)).
Poland: Lukasz Fabianski, Michal Pazdan, Artur Jedrzejczyk, Kamil Glik, Lukasz Piszczek,
Krzysztof Maczynski (YC45) (76' Tomasz Jodlowiec), Grzegorz Krychowiak, Kamil Grosicki
(YC55) (87' Slawomir Peszko (YC90+3)), Jakub Blaszczykowski (80' Bartosz Kapustka),
Arkadiusz Milik, Robert Lewandowski (C). (Coach: Adam Nawalka (POL)).
Referee: Björn Kuipers (HOL)   Attendance: 73.648

21-06-2016   Stade Vélodrome, Marseille: Ukraine – Poland   0-1 (0-0)
Ukraine: Andriy Pyatov, Bohdan Butko, Yevhen Khacheridi, Olexandr Kucher (YC38), Artem
Fedetskiy, Taras Stepanenko, Ruslan Rotan (C) (YC25), Olexandr Zinchenko (73' Viktor
Kovalenko), Andriy Yarmolenko, Roman Zozulya (90'+2' Anatoliy Tymoshchuk), Yevhen
Konoplyanka. (Coach: Mikhail Ivanovich Fomenko (UKR)).
Poland: Lukasz Fabianski, Michal Pazdan, Artur Jedrzejczyk, Thiago Rangel Cionek, Kamil
Glik, Tomasz Jodlowiec, Grzegorz Krychowiak, Piotr Zielinski (46' Jakub Blaszczykowski),
Bartosz Kapustka (YC60) (71' Kamil Grosicki), Arkadiusz Milik (90'+3' Filip Starzynski),
Robert Lewandowski (C). (Coach: Adam Nawalka (POL)).
Goal: Poland: 0-1 Jakub Blaszczykowski (54').
Referee: Svein Oddvar Moen (NOR)   Attendance: 58.874

21-06-2016   Parc des Princes, Paris: Northern Ireland – Germany   0-1 (0-1)
Northern Ireland: Michael McGovern, Gareth McAuley, Jonathan (Jonny) Evans, Aaron
Hughes, Craig Cathcart, Steven Davis (C), Corry Evans (84' Niall McGinn), Stuart Dallas,
Oliver Norwood, Conor Washington (59' Kyle Lafferty), Jamie Ward (70' Josh Magennis).
(Coach: Michael Andrew Martin O'Neill (NIR)).
Germany: Manuel Neuer (C), Jonas Hector, Mats Hummels, Jérôme Boateng (76' Benedikt
Höwedes), Sami Khedira (69' Bastian Schweinsteiger), Mesut Özil, Thomas Müller, Toni
Kroos, Joshua Kimmich, Mario Götze (55' André Schürrle), Mario Gómez García. (Coach:
Joachim Löw (GER)).
Goal: Germany: 0-1 Mario Gómez García (30').
Referee: Clément Turpin (FRA)   Attendance: 44.125

STANDINGS

Pos	Team	Pld	W	D	L	GF	GA	GD	Pts
1	Germany	3	2	1	0	3	0	+3	7
2	Poland	3	2	1	0	2	0	+2	7
3	Northern Ireland	3	1	0	2	2	2	0	3
4	Ukraine	3	0	0	3	0	5	-5	0

Germany, Poland and Northern Ireland qualified for the knockout phase.

12-06-2016   Parc des Princes, Paris: Turkey – Croatia 0-1 (0-1)
Turkey: Volkan Babacan, Hakan Balta (YC48), Gökhan Gönül, Mehmet Topal, Caner Erkin, Hakan Çalhanoglu, Selçuk Inan, Arda Turan (C) (65' Burak Yilmaz), Oguzhan Özyakup (46' Volkan Sen (YC90+1)), Ozan Tufan, Cenk Tosun (YC31) (69' Emre Mor). (Coach: Fatih Terim (TUR)).
Croatia: Danijel Subasic, Ivan Strinic (YC80), Vedran Corluka, Darijo Srna (C), Domagoj Vida, Ivan Perisic (87' Andrej Kramaric), Ivan Rakitic (90' Gordon Schildenfeld), Luka Modric, Marcelo Brozovic, Milan Badelj, Mario Mandzukic (90'+3' Marko Pjaca). (Coach: Ante Cacic (CRO)).
Goal: Croatia: 0-1 Luka Modric (41').
Referee: Jonas Eriksson (SWE)   Attendance: 43.842

13-06-2016   Stadium Municipal, Toulouse: Spain – Czech Republic 1-0 (0-0)
Spain: David DE GEA Quintana, Gerard PIQUÉ i Bernabéu, SERGIO RAMOS García (C), Juan Francisco Torres Belén "JUANFRAN", Jordi ALBA Ramos, Sergio BUSQUETS Burgos, Andrés INIESTA Luján, Francesc "CESC" FÀBREGAS Soler (70' THIAGO Alcântara do Nascimento), DAVID Jiménez SILVA, Álvaro Borja MORATA Martín (62' Aritz ADURIZ Zubeldia), Manuel Agudo Durán "NOLITO" (82' PEDRO Eliezer Rodríguez Ledesma). (Coach: VICENTE DEL BOSQUE González (ESP)).
Czech Republic: Petr Cech, Pavel Kaderábek, Theodor Gebre Selassie (86' Josef Sural), Roman Hubník, Tomás Sivok, David Limbersky (YC61), Tomás Rosicky (C) (88' David Pavelka), Jaroslav Plasil, Ladislav Krejcí, Vladimír Darida, Tomás Necid (75' David Lafata). (Coach: Pavel Vrba (CZE)).
Goal: Spain: 1-0 Gerard PIQUÉ i Bernabéu (87').
Referee: Szymon Marciniak (POL)   Attendance: 29.400

17-06-2016   Stade Geoffroy-Guichard, Saint-Étienne: Czech Republic – Croatia 2-2 (0-1)
Czech Republic: Petr Cech, Pavel Kaderábek, Roman Hubník, Tomás Sivok (YC72), David Limbersky, Tomás Rosicky (C), Jaroslav Plasil (86' Tomás Necid), Ladislav Krejcí, Jirí Skalák (67' Josef Sural), Vladimír Darida, David Lafata (67' Milan Skoda). (Coach: Pavel Vrba (CZE)).
Croatia: Danijel Subasic, Ivan Strinic (90'+1' Sime Vrsaljko), Vedran Corluka, Darijo Srna (C), Domagoj Vida (YC88), Ivan Perisic, Ivan Rakitic (90'+2' Gordon Schildenfeld), Luka Modric (62' Mateo Kovacic), Marcelo Brozovic (YC74), Milan Badelj (YC14), Mario Mandzukic. (Coach: Ante Cacic (CRO)).
Goals: Czech Republic: 1-2 Milan Skoda (76'), 2-2 Tomás Necid (89' penalty).
Croatia: 0-1 Ivan Perisic (37'), 0-2 Ivan Rakitic (59').
Referee: Mark Clattenburg (ENG)   Attendance: 38.376

17-06-2016   Stade de Nice, Nice: Spain – Turkey   3-0 (2-0)
Spain: David DE GEA Quintana, Gerard PIQUÉ i Bernabéu, SERGIO RAMOS García (C)
(YC2), Juan Francisco Torres Belén "JUANFRAN", Jordi ALBA Ramos (81' César
AZPILICUETA Tanco), Sergio BUSQUETS Burgos, Andrés INIESTA Luján, Francesc
"CESC" FÀBREGAS Soler (71' Jorge Resurrección Merodio "KOKE"), DAVID Jiménez
SILVA (64' BRUNO SORIANO Llido), Álvaro Borja MORATA Martín, Manuel Agudo
Durán "NOLITO". (Coach: VICENTE DEL BOSQUE González (ESP)).
Turkey: Volkan Babacan, Hakan Balta, Gökhan Gönül, Mehmet Topal, Caner Erkin, Hakan
Çalhanoglu (46' Nuri Sahin), Selçuk Inan (70' Yunus Malli), Arda Turan (C), Oguzhan
Özyakup (62' Olcay Sahan), Ozan Tufan (YC41), Burak Yilmaz (YC9). (Coach: Fatih Terim
(TUR)).
Goals: Spain: 1-0 Álvaro Borja MORATA Martín (34'), 2-0 Manuel Agudo Durán "NOLITO"
(37'), 3-0 Álvaro Borja MORATA Martín (48').
Referee: Milorad Mazic (SRB)   Attendance: 33.409

21-06-2016   Stade Bollaert-Delelis, Lens: Czech Republic – Turkey   0-2 (0-1)
Czech Republic: Petr Cech (C), Pavel Kaderábek, Roman Hubník, Tomás Sivok, Daniel Pudil,
Borek Dockal (71' Josef Sural (YC87)), Jaroslav Plasil (YC36) (90' Daniel Kolár), David
Pavelka (YC39) (57' Milan Skoda), Ladislav Krejcí, Vladimír Darida, Tomás Necid. (Coach:
Pavel Vrba (CZE)).
Turkey: Volkan Babacan, Hakan Balta (YC50), Gökhan Gönül, Ismail Köybasi (YC35),
Mehmet Topal, Selçuk Inan, Arda Turan (C), Ozan Tufan, Burak Yilmaz (90' Cenk Tosun),
Volkan Sen (61' Oguzhan Özyakup), Emre Mor (69' Olcay Sahan). (Coach: Fatih Terim
(TUR)).
Goals: Turkey: 0-1 Burak Yilmaz (10'), 0-2 Ozan Tufan (65').
Referee: William (Willie) Collum (SCO)   Attendance: 32.836

21-06-2016   Nouveau Stade de Bordeaux, Bordeaux: Croatia – Spain   2-1 (1-1)
Croatia: Danijel Subasic, Sime Vrsaljko (YC70), Vedran Corluka, Tin Jedvaj, Darijo Srna (C)
(YC70), Ivan Perisic (YC88) (90'+4' Andrej Kramaric), Ivan Rakitic, Marko Rog (YC29) (82'
Mateo Kovacic), Milan Badelj, Nikola Kalinic, Marko Pjaca (90'+2' Duje Cop). (Coach: Ante
Cacic (CRO)).
Spain: David DE GEA Quintana, Gerard PIQUÉ i Bernabéu, SERGIO RAMOS García (C),
Juan Francisco Torres Belén "JUANFRAN", Jordi ALBA Ramos, Sergio BUSQUETS Burgos,
Andrés INIESTA Luján, Francesc "CESC" FÀBREGAS Soler (84' THIAGO Alcântara do
Nascimento), DAVID Jiménez SILVA, Álvaro Borja MORATA Martín (67' Aritz ADURIZ
Zubeldia), Manuel Agudo Durán "NOLITO" (60' BRUNO SORIANO Llido). (Coach:
VICENTE DEL BOSQUE González (ESP)).
Goals: Croatia: 1-1 Nikola Kalinic (45'), 2-1 Ivan Perisic (87').
Spain: 0-1 Álvaro Borja MORATA Martín (7').
Referee: Björn Kuipers (HOL)   Attendance: 37.245
(SERGIO RAMOS García missed a penalty in the 72nd minute)

STANDINGS

Pos	Team	Pld	W	D	L	GF	GA	GD	Pts
1	Croatia	3	2	1	0	5	3	+2	7
2	Spain	3	2	0	1	5	2	+3	6
3	Turkey	3	1	0	2	2	4	-2	3
4	Czech Republic	3	0	1	2	2	5	-3	1

Croatia and Spain qualified for the knockout phase.

GROUP E

13-06-2016   Stade de France, Saint-Denis: Republic of Ireland – Sweden   1-1 (0-0)
Republic of Ireland: Darren Randolph, Séamus Coleman, Ciaran Clark, John O'Shea (C), Robert (Robbie) Brady, Glenn Whelan (YC77), James McCarthy (YC43) (85' Aiden McGeady), Jeffrey (Jeff) Hendrick, Wesley (Wes) Hoolahan (78' Robbie Keane), Shane Long, Jonathan (Jon) Walters (64' James McClean). (Coach: Martin Hugh Michael O'Neill (NIR)).
Sweden: Andreas Isaksson, Mikael Lustig (45' Erik Johansson), Andreas Granqvist, Martin Olsson, Victor Lindelöf (YC61), Emil Forsberg, Sebastian Larsson, Kim Källström, Oscar Lewicki (86' Albin Ekdal), Zlatan Ibrahimovic (C), Marcus Berg (59' John Guidetti). (Coach: Erik Hamrén (SWE)).
Goals: Republic of Ireland: 1-0 Wesley (Wes) Hoolahan (48').
Sweden: 1-1 Ciaran Clark (71' *own goal*).
Referee: Milorad Mazic (SRB)   Attendance: 73.419

13-06-2016   Parc Olympique Lyonnais, Lyon: Belgium – Italy   0-2 (0-1)
Belgium: Thibaut Courtois, Toby Alderweireld, Thomas Vermaelen, Jan Vertonghen (YC90+2), Laurent Ciman (76' Yannick Ferreira-Carrasco), Radja Nainggolan (62' Dries Mertens), Axel Witsel, Kevin De Bruyne, Marouane Fellaini, Eden Hazard (C), Romelu Lukaku Menama (73' Divock Okoth Origi). (Coach: Marc Wilmots (BEL)).
Italy: Gianluigi Buffon (C), Giorgio Chiellini (YC65), Matteo Darmian (58' Mattia De Sciglio), Andrea Barzagli, Leonardo Bonucci (YC78), Antonio Candreva, Daniele De Rossi (78' Thiago Motta (YC84)), Marco Parolo, Emanuele Giaccherini, Graziano Pellè, ÉDER Citalin Martins (YC75) (75' Ciro Immobile). (Coach: Antonio Conte (ITA)).
Goals: Italy: 0-1 Emanuele Giaccherini (32'), 0-2 Graziano Pellè (90'+3').
Referee: Mark Clattenburg (ENG)   Attendance: 55.408

17-06-2016   Stadium Municipal, Toulouse: Italy – Sweden   1-0 (0-0)
Italy: Gianluigi Buffon (C) (YC90+3), Giorgio Chiellini, Andrea Barzagli, Leonardo Bonucci, Antonio Candreva, Alessandro Florenzi (85' Stefano Sturaro), Daniele De Rossi (YC69) (74' Thiago Motta), Marco Parolo, Emanuele Giaccherini, Graziano Pellè (60' Simone Zaza), ÉDER Citalin Martins. (Coach: Antonio Conte (ITA)).
Sweden: Andreas Isaksson, Erik Johansson, Andreas Granqvist, Martin Olsson (YC89), Victor Lindelöf, Emil Forsberg (79' Jimmy Durmaz), Sebastian Larsson, Albin Ekdal (79' Oscar Lewicki), Kim Källström, Zlatan Ibrahimovic (C), John Guidetti (85' Marcus Berg). (Coach: Erik Hamrén (SWE)).
Goal: Italy: 1-0 ÉDER Citalin Martins (88').
Referee: Viktor Kassai (HUN)   Attendance: 35.472

18-06-2016   Nouveau Stade de Bordeaux, Bordeaux:
Belgium – Republic of Ireland 3-0 (0-0)
Belgium: Thibaut Courtois, Toby Alderweireld, Thomas Vermaelen (YC49), Jan Vertonghen, Thomas Meunier, Axel Witsel, Kevin De Bruyne, Eden Hazard (C), Yannick Ferreira-Carrasco (64' Dries Mertens, Mousa Dembéle (57' Radja Nainggolan), Romelu Lukaku Menama (83' Christian Benteke). (Coach: Marc Wilmots (BEL)).
Republic of Ireland: Darren Randolph, Séamus Coleman, Ciaran Clark, John O'Shea (C), Stephen Ward, Robert (Robbie) Brady, Glenn Whelan, James McCarthy (62' James McClean), Jeffrey (Jeff) Hendrick (YC42), Wesley (Wes) Hoolahan (71' Aiden McGeady), Shane Long (79' Robbie Keane). (Coach: Martin Hugh Michael O'Neill (NIR)).
Goals: Belgium: 1-0 Romelu Lukaku Menama (48'), 2-0 Axel Witsel (61'), 3-0 Romelu Lukaku Menama (70').
Referee: Cüneyt Çakir (TUR)   Attendance: 39.493

22-06-2016   Stade Pierre-Mauroy, Villeneuve-d'Ascq: Italy – Republic of Ireland   0-1 (0-0)
Italy: Salvatore Sirigu (YC39), Mattia De Sciglio (81' Stephan El Shaarawy), Angelo Ogbonna, Andrea Barzagli (YC78), Leonardo Bonucci (C), Alessandro Florenzi, Thiago Motta, Stefano Sturaro, Simone Zaza (YC87), Ciro Immobile (74' Lorenzo Insigne (YC90+1)), Federico Bernardeschi (60' Matteo Darmian). (Coach: Antonio Conte (ITA)).
Republic of Ireland: Darren Randolph, Séamus Coleman (C), Richard Keogh, Shane Duffy, Stephen Ward (YC73), Robert (Robbie) Brady, James McCarthy (77' Wesley (Wes) Hoolahan), Jeffrey (Jeff) Hendrick, Shane Long (YC39) (90' Stephen Quinn), James McClean, Daryl Murphy (70' Aiden McGeady). (Coach: Martin Hugh Michael O'Neill (NIR)).
Goal: Republic of Ireland: 0-1 Robert (Robbie) Brady (85').
Referee: Ovidiu Alin Hategan (ROM)   Attendance: 44.268

22-06-2016   Stade de Nice, Nice: Sweden – Belgium 0-1 (0-0)
Sweden: Andreas Isaksson, Erik Johansson (YC36), Andreas Granqvist, Martin Olsson, Victor Lindelöf, Emil Forsberg (82' Erkan Zengin), Sebastian Larsson (70' Jimmy Durmaz), Albin Ekdal (YC33), Kim Källström, Zlatan Ibrahimovic (C), Marcus Berg (63' John Guidetti). (Coach: Erik Hamrén (SWE)).
Belgium: Thibaut Courtois, Toby Alderweireld, Thomas Vermaelen, Jan Vertonghen, Thomas Meunier (YC30), Radja Nainggolan, Axel Witsel (YC45+1), Kevin De Bruyne, Eden Hazard (C) (90'+3' Divock Okoth Origi), Yannick Ferreira-Carrasco (71' Dries Mertens), Romelu Lukaku Menama (87' Christian Benteke). (Coach: Marc Wilmots (BEL)).
Goal: Belgium: 0-1 Radja Nainggolan (84').
Referee: Dr.Felix Brych (GER)   Attendance: 34.011

STANDINGS

Pos	Team	Pld	W	D	L	GF	GA	GD	Pts
1	Italy	3	2	0	1	3	1	+2	6
2	Belgium	3	2	0	1	4	2	+2	6
3	Republic of Ireland	3	1	1	1	2	4	-2	4
4	Sweden	3	0	1	2	1	3	-2	1

Italy, Belgium and Republic of Ireland qualified for the knockout phase.

GROUP F

14-06-2016   Nouveau Stade de Bordeaux, Bordeaux: Austria – Hungary   0-2 (0-0)
Austria: Robert Almer, Aleksandar Dragovic (YC33,YC66), Martin Hinteregger, Christian
Fuchs (C), Florian Klein, David Alaba, Zlatko Juzunovic (59' Marcel Sabitzer), Julian
Baumgartlinger, Marko Arnautovic, Martin Harnik (77' Alessandro Schöpf), Marc Janko (65'
Rubin Rafael Okotie). (Coach: Marcel Koller (SUI)).
Hungary: Gábor Király, Ádám Lang, Tamás Kádár, Attila Fiola, Richárd Guzmics, Ádám
Nagy, Zoltán Gera, László Kleinheisler (80' Zoltán Stieber), Balázs Dzsudzsák (C), Ádám
Szalai (69' Tamás Priskin), Krisztián Németh (YC80) (89' Ádám Pintér). (Coach: Bernd
Storck (GER)).
Goals: Hungary: 0-1 Ádám Szalai (62'), 0-2 Zoltán Stieber (87').
Referee: Clément Turpin (FRA)   Attendance: 34.424

14-06-2016   Stade Geoffroy-Guichard, Saint-Étienne: Portugal – Iceland   1-1 (1-0)
Portugal: RUI Pedro dos Santos PATRÍCIO, Képler Laveran Lima Ferreira "PEPE",
RAPHAËL Adelino José GUERREIRO, RICARDO Alberto Silveira CARVALHO, Adelino
André Vieira de Freitas "VIEIRINHA", JOÃO Filipe Iria Santos MOUTINHO (71' RENATO
Júnior Luz SANCHES), JOÃO MÁRIO Naval da Costa Eduardo (76' RICARDO Andrade
QUARESMA Bernardo), DANILO Luís Hélio Pereira, ANDRÉ Filipe Tavares GOMES (84'
"ÉDER" Éderzito António Macedo Lopes), CRISTIANO RONALDO dos Santos Aveiro (C),
Luís Carlos Almeida da Cunha "NANI". (Coach: FERNANDO Manuel Fernandes da Costa
SANTOS (POR)).
Iceland: Hannes Halldórsson, Birkir Már Sævarsson, Ragnar Sigurdsson, Kári Árnason, Ari
Skúlason, Jóhann Gudmundsson (90' Theodór (Teddy) Elmar Bjarnason), Birkir Bjarnason
(YC55), Gylfi Sigurdsson, Aron Gunnarsson (C), Kolbeinn Sigthórsson (81' Alfred
Finnbogason (YC90+4)), Jón Dadi Bödvarsson. (Coaches: Lars Lagerbäck (SWE) & Heimir
Hallgrímsson (ISL)).
Goals: Portugal: 1-0 Luís Carlos Almeida da Cunha "NANI" (31').
Iceland: 1-1 Birkir Bjarnason (50').
Referee: Cüneyt Çakir (TUR)   Attendance: 38.742

18-06-2016   Stade Vélodrome, Marseille: Iceland – Hungary   1-1 (1-0)
Iceland: Hannes Halldórsson, Birkir Már Sævarsson (YC77), Ragnar Sigurdsson, Kári
Árnason, Ari Skúlason, Jóhann Gudmundsson (YC42), Birkir Bjarnason, Gylfi Sigurdsson,
Aron Gunnarsson (C) (65' Emil Hallfredsson), Kolbeinn Sigthórsson (84' Eidur Gudjohnsen),
Jón Dadi Bödvarsson (69' Alfred Finnbogason (YC75)). (Coaches: Lars Lagerbäck (SWE) &
Heimir Hallgrímsson (ISL)).
Hungary: Gábor Király, Ádám Lang, Tamás Kádár (YC81), Richárd Guzmics, Roland Juhász
(84' Ádám Szalai), Ádám Nagy (YC90+1), Zoltán Gera, László Kleinheisler (YC83), Zoltán
Stieber (66' Nemanja Nikolic), Balázs Dzsudzsák (C), Tamás Priskin (66' Dániel Böde).
(Coach: Bernd Storck (GER)).
Goals: Iceland: Gylfi Sigurdsson (40' penalty).
Hungary: 1-1 Birkir Már Sævarsson (88' own goal).
Referee: Sergey Gennadyevich Karasev (RUS)   Attendance: 60.842

18-06-2016   Parc des Princes, Paris: Portugal – Austria   0-0
Portugal: RUI Pedro dos Santos PATRÍCIO, Képler Laveran Lima Ferreira "PEPE" (YC40),
RAPHAËL Adelino José GUERREIRO, RICARDO Alberto Silveira CARVALHO, Adelino
André Vieira de Freitas "VIEIRINHA", JOÃO Filipe Iria Santos MOUTINHO, WILLIAM
Silva de CARVALHO, ANDRÉ Filipe Tavares GOMES (83' "ÉDER" Éderzito António
Macedo Lopes), CRISTIANO RONALDO dos Santos Aveiro (C), Luís Carlos Almeida da
Cunha "NANI" (89' "RAFA" Rafael Alexandre Fernandes Ferreira da SILVA), RICARDO
Andrade QUARESMA Bernardo (YC31) (71' JOÃO MÁRIO Naval da Costa Eduardo).
(Coach: FERNANDO Manuel Fernandes da Costa SANTOS (POR)).
Austria: Robert Almer, Martin Hinteregger (YC78), Christian Fuchs (C) (YC60), Sebastian
Prödl, Florian Klein, Stefan Ilsanker (87' Kevin Wimmer), David Alaba (65' Alessandro
Schöpf (YC86)), Julian Baumgartlinger, Marko Arnautovic, Martin Harnik (YC47), Marcel
Sabitzer (85' Lukas Hinterseer). (Coach: Marcel Koller (SUI)).
Referee: Nicola Rizzoli (ITA)   Attendance: 44.291
(CRISTIANO RONALDO dos Santos Aveiro missed a penalty in the 79th minute)

22-06-2016   Stade de France, Saint-Denis: Iceland – Austria   2-1 (1-0)
Iceland: Hannes Halldórsson (YC82), Birkir Már Sævarsson, Ragnar Sigurdsson, Kári Árnason
(YC78), Ari Skúlason (YC36), Jóhann Gudmundsson (86' Sverrir Ingason), Birkir Bjarnason,
Gylfi Sigurdsson, Aron Gunnarsson (C), Kolbeinn Sigthórsson (YC51) (80' Arnór Ingvi
Traustason), Jón Dadi Bödvarsson (71' Theodór (Teddy) Elmar Bjarnason). (Coaches: Lars
Lagerbäck (SWE) & Heimir Hallgrímsson (ISL)).
Austria: Robert Almer, Aleksandar Dragovic, Martin Hinteregger, Christian Fuchs (C),
Sebastian Prödl (46' Alessandro Schöpf), Florian Klein, Stefan Ilsanker (46' Marc Janko
(YC70)), David Alaba, Julian Baumgartlinger, Marko Arnautovic, Marcel Sabitzer (78' Jakob
Jantscher). (Coach: Marcel Koller (SUI)).
Goals: Iceland: 1-0 Jón Dadi Bödvarsson (18'), 2-1 Arnór Ingvi Traustason (90'+4').
Austria: 1-1 Alessandro Schöpf (60').
Referee: Szymon Marciniak (POL)   Attendance: 68.714
(Aleksandar Dragovic missed a penalty in the 37th minute)

22-06-2016   Parc Olympique Lyonnais, Lyon: Hungary – Portugal   3-3 (1-1)
Hungary: Gábor Király, Ádám Lang, Mihály Korhut, Richárd Guzmics (YC13), Roland Juhász
(YC28), Ákos Elek, Zoltán Gera (YC34) (46' Barnabás Bese), Gergö Lovrencsics (83' Zoltán
Stieber), Ádam Pintér, Balázs Dzsudzsák (C) (YC56), Ádám Szalai (71' Krisztián Németh).
(Coach: Bernd Storck (GER)).
Portugal: RUI Pedro dos Santos PATRÍCIO, Képler Laveran Lima Ferreira "PEPE",
RICARDO Alberto Silveira CARVALHO, Adelino André Vieira de Freitas "VIEIRINHA",
ELISEU Pereira dos Santos, JOÃO Filipe Iria Santos MOUTINHO (46' RENATO Júnior Luz
SANCHES), JOÃO MÁRIO Naval da Costa Eduardo, WILLIAM Silva de CARVALHO,
ANDRÉ Filipe Tavares GOMES (61' RICARDO Andrade QUARESMA Bernardo),
CRISTIANO RONALDO dos Santos Aveiro (C), Luís Carlos Almeida da Cunha "NANI" (81'
DANILO Luís Hélio Pereira). (Coach: FERNANDO Manuel Fernandes da Costa SANTOS
(POR)).
Goals: Hungary: 1-0 Zoltán Gera (19'), 2-1 Balázs Dzsudzsák (47'), 3-2 Balázs Dzsudzsák
(55').
Portugal: 1-1 Luís Carlos Almeida da Cunha "NANI" (42'), 2-2 CRISTIANO RONALDO dos
Santos Aveiro (50'), 3-3 CRISTIANO RONALDO dos Santos Aveiro (62').
Referee: Martin Atkinson (ENG)   Attendance: 55.514

STANDINGS

Pos	Team	Pld	W	D	L	GF	GA	GD	Pts
1	Hungary	3	1	2	0	6	4	+2	5
2	Iceland	3	1	2	0	4	3	+1	5
3	Portugal	3	0	3	0	4	4	0	3
4	Austria	3	0	1	2	1	4	-3	1

Hungary, Iceland and Portugal qualified for the knockout phase.

KNOCKOUT PHASE

ROUND OF 16

25-06-2016   Stade Geoffroy-Guichard, Saint-Étienne:
Switzerland – Poland   1-1 (0-1) (AET)
Switzerland: Yann Sommer, Stephan Lichtsteiner (C), Ricardo Ivan Rodríguez Araya, Johan Djourou (YC117), Fabian Schär (YC55), Granit Xhaka, Valon Behrami (77' Gélson da Conceição Tavares Fernandes), Blerim Dzemaili (58' Breel-Donald Embolo), Xherdan Shaqiri, Haris Seferovic, Admir Mehmedi (70' Eren Derdiyok). (Coach: Vladimir Petkovic (SUI)).
Poland: Lukasz Fabianski, Michal Pazdan (YC111), Artur Jedrzejczyk (YC58), Kamil Glik, Lukasz Piszczek, Krzysztof Maczynski (101' Tomasz Jodlowiec), Grzegorz Krychowiak, Kamil Grosicki (104' Slawomir Peszko), Jakub Blaszczykowski, Arkadiusz Milik, Robert Lewandowski (C). (Coach: Adam Nawalka (POL)).
Goals: Switzerland: 1-1 Xherdan Shaqiri (82').
Poland: 0-1 Jakub Blaszczykowski (39').
Referee: Mark Clattenburg (ENG)   Attendance: 38.842
Penalties: 1 Stephan Lichtsteiner   1 Robert Lewandowski
              * Granit Xhaka   2 Arkadiusz Milik
              2 Xherdan Shaqiri   3 Kamil Glik
              3 Fabian Schär   4 Jakub Blaszczykowski
              4 Ricardo Ivan Rodríguez Araya   5 Grzegorz Krychowiak

25-06-2016   Parc des Princes, Paris: Wales – Northern Ireland   1-0 (0-0)
Wales: Wayne Hennessey, Chris Gunter, Neil Taylor (YC58), Benjamin (Ben) Davies, James Chester, Ashley Williams (C), Joe Allen, Aaron Ramsey (YC90+4), Joseph (Joe) Ledley (63' Jonathan Williams), Gareth Bale, Samuel Michael (Sam) Vokes (55' Hal Robson-Kanu). (Coach: Chris Coleman (WAL)).
Northern Ireland: Michael McGovern, Gareth McAuley (84' Josh Magennis), Jonathan (Jonny) Evans, Aaron Hughes, Craig Cathcart, Steven Davis (C) (YC67), Corry Evans, Stuart Dallas (YC44), Oliver Norwood (79' Niall McGinn), Kyle Lafferty, Jamie Ward (69' Conor Washington). (Coach: Michael Andrew Martin O'Neill (NIR)).
Goal: Wales: 1-0 Gareth McAuley (75' *own goal*).
Referee: Martin Atkinson (ENG)   Attendance: 44.342

25-06-2016   Stade Bollaert-Delelis, Lens: Croatia – Portugal   0-1 (0-0) (AET)
Croatia: Danijel Subasic, Ivan Strinic, Vedran Corluka (120'+1' Andrej Kramaric), Darijo Srna
(C), Domagoj Vida, Ivan Perisic, Ivan Rakitic (110' Marko Pjaca), Luka Modric, Marcelo
Brozovic, Milan Badelj, Mario Mandzukic (88' Nikola Kalinic). (Coach: Ante Cacic (CRO)).
Portugal: RUI Pedro dos Santos PATRÍCIO, Képler Laveran Lima Ferreira "PEPE", JOSÉ
Miguel da Rocha FONTE, RAPHAËL Adelino José GUERREIRO, CÉDRIC Ricardo Alves
SOARES, JOÃO MÁRIO Naval da Costa Eduardo (87' RICARDO Andrade QUARESMA
Bernardo), WILLIAM Silva de CARVALHO (YC78), ANDRÉ Filipe Tavares GOMES (50'
RENATO Júnior Luz SANCHES), ADRIEN Sebastian Perruchet SILVA (108' DANILO Luís
Hélio Pereira), CRISTIANO RONALDO dos Santos Aveiro (C), Luís Carlos Almeida da
Cunha "NANI". (Coach: FERNANDO Manuel Fernandes da Costa SANTOS (POR)).
Goal: Portugal: 0-1 RICARDO Andrade QUARESMA Bernardo (117').
Referee: Carlos Velasco Carballo (ESP)   Attendance: 33.523

26-06-2016   Parc Olympique Lyonnais, Lyon: France – Republic of Ireland   2-1 (0-1)
France: Hugo Lloris (C), Patrice Evra, Adil Rami (YC44), Bacary Sagna, Laurent Koscielny,
N'Golo Kanté (YC27) (46' Kingsley Coman, 90'+3' Moussa Sissoko), Dimitri Payet, Blaise
Matuidi, Paul Pogba, Antoine Griezmann, Olivier Giroud (73' André-Pierre Gignac). (Coach:
Didier Deschamps (FRA)).
Republic of Ireland: Darren Randolph, Séamus Coleman (C) (YC25), Richard Keogh, Shane
Duffy (RC66), Stephen Ward, Robert (Robbie) Brady, James McCarthy (71' Wesley (Wes)
Hoolahan), Jeffrey (Jeff) Hendrick (YC41), Shane Long (YC72), James McClean (68' John
O'Shea), Daryl Murphy (65' Jonathan (Jon) Walters). (Coach: Martin Hugh Michael O'Neill
(NIR)).
Goals: France: 1-1 Antoine Griezmann (58'), 2-1 Antoine Griezmann (61').
Republic of Ireland: 0-1 Robert (Robbie) Brady (2' penalty).
Referee: Nicola Rizzoli (ITA)   Attendance: 56.279

26-06-2016   Stade Pierre-Mauroy, Villeneuve-d'Ascq: Germany – Slovakia   3-0 (2-0)
Germany: Manuel Neuer (C), Jonas Hector, Mats Hummels (YC67), Jérôme Boateng (71'
Benedikt Höwedes), Sami Khedira (76' Bastian Schweinsteiger), Mesut Özil, Julian Draxler
(72' Lukas Podolski), Thomas Müller, Toni Kroos, Joshua Kimmich (YC46), Mario Gómez
García. (Coach: Joachim Löw (GER)).
Slovakia: Matús Kozácik, Peter Pekarík, Martin Skrtel (C) (YC13), Ján Durica, Norbert
Gyömbér (84' Kornel Saláta), Milan Skriniar, Vladimír Weiss (46' Ján Gregus), Patrik
Hrosovsky, Marek Hamsík, Juraj Kucka (YC90+1), Michal Duris (64' Stanislav Sesták).
(Coach: Ján Kozák (SVK)).
Goals: Germany: 1-0 Jérôme Boateng (8'), 2-0 Mario Gómez García (43'), 3-0 Julian Draxler
(63').
Referee: Szymon Marciniak (POL)   Attendance: 44.312
(Mesut Özil missed a penalty in the 13th minute)

26-06-2016   Stadium Municipal, Toulouse: Hungary – Belgium   0-4 (0-1)
Hungary: Gábor Király, Ádám Lang (YC47), Tamás Kádár (YC34), Richárd Guzmics, Roland
Juhász (79' Dániel Böde), Ádám Nagy, Zoltán Gera (46' Ákos Elek (YC61)), Gergö
Lovrencsics, Ádam Pintér (75' Nemanja Nikolic), Balázs Dzsudzsák (C), Ádám Szalai
(YC90+2). (Coach: Bernd Storck (GER)).
Belgium: Thibaut Courtois, Toby Alderweireld, Thomas Vermaelen (YC67), Jan Vertonghen,
Thomas Meunier, Radja Nainggolan, Axel Witsel, Kevin De Bruyne, Eden Hazard (C) (81'
Marouane Fellaini (YC90+2)), Romelu Lukaku Menama (76' Michy Batshuayi (YC89)), Dries
Mertens (70' Yannick Ferreira-Carrasco). (Coach: Marc Wilmots (BEL)).
Goals: Belgium: 0-1 Toby Alderweireld (10'), 0-2 Michy Batshuayi (78'), 0-3 Eden Hazard
(80'), 0-4 Yannick Ferreira-Carrasco (90'+1').
Referee: Milorad Mazic (SRB)   Attendance: 28.921

27-06-2016   Stade de France, Saint-Denis: Italy – Spain   2-0 (1-0)
Italy: Gianluigi Buffon (C), Mattia De Sciglio (YC24), Giorgio Chiellini, Andrea Barzagli,
Leonardo Bonucci, Alessandro Florenzi (84' Matteo Darmian), Daniele De Rossi (54' Thiago
Motta (YC89)), Marco Parolo, Emanuele Giaccherini, Graziano Pellè (YC54), ÉDER Citalin
Martins (82' Lorenzo Insigne). (Coach: Antonio Conte (ITA)).
Spain: David DE GEA Quintana, Gerard PIQUÉ i Bernabéu, SERGIO RAMOS García (C),
Juan Francisco Torres Belén "JUANFRAN", Jordi ALBA Ramos (YC89), Sergio BUSQUETS
Burgos (YC89), Andrés INIESTA Luján, Francesc "CESC" FÀBREGAS Soler, DAVID
Jiménez SILVA (YC90+4), Álvaro Borja MORATA Martín (70' LUCAS VÁZQUEZ
Iglesias), Manuel Agudo Durán "NOLITO" (YC41) (46' Aritz ADURIZ Zubeldia, 81' PEDRO
Eliezer Rodríguez Ledesma). (Coach: VICENTE DEL BOSQUE González (ESP)).
Goals: Italy: 1-0 Giorgio Chiellini (33'), 2-0 Graziano Pellè (90'+1').
Referee: Cüneyt Çakir (TUR)   Attendance: 76.165

27-06-2016   Stade de Nice, Nice: England – Iceland   1-2 (1-2)
England: Joe Hart, Kyle Walker, Danny Rose, Gary Cahill, Chris Smalling, Raheem Sterling
(60' Jamie Vardy), Wayne Rooney (C) (87' Marcus Rashford), Eric Dier (46' Jack Wilshere),
Dele Alli, Harry Kane, Daniel Sturridge (YC47). (Coach: Roy Hodgson (ENG)).
Iceland: Hannes Halldórsson, Birkir Már Sævarsson, Ragnar Sigurdsson, Kári Árnason, Ari
Skúlason, Jóhann Gudmundsson, Birkir Bjarnason, Gylfi Sigurdsson (YC38), Aron
Gunnarsson (C) (YC65), Kolbeinn Sigthórsson (76' Theodór (Teddy) Elmar Bjarnason), Jón
Dadi Bödvarsson (89' Arnór Ingvi Traustason). (Coaches: Lars Lagerbäck (SWE) & Heimir
Hallgrímsson (ISL)).
Goals: England: 1-0 Wayne Rooney (4' penalty).
Iceland: 1-1 Ragnar Sigurdsson (6'), 1-2 Kolbeinn Sigthórsson (18').
Referee: Damir Skomina (SLO)   Attendance: 33.901

QUARTER-FINALS

30-06-2016   Stade Vélodrome, Marseille: Poland – Portugal 1-1 (1-1) (AET)
Poland: Lukasz Fabianski, Michal Pazdan, Artur Jedrzejczyk (YC42), Kamil Glik (YC66),
Lukasz Piszcek, Krzysztof Maczynski (98' Tomasz Jodlowiec), Grzegorz Krychowiak, Kamil
Grosicki (82' Bartosz Kapustka (YC89)), Jakub Blaszczykowski, Arkadiusz Milik, Robert
Lewandowski (C). (Coach: Adam Nawalka (POL)).
Portugal: RUI Pedro dos Santos PATRÍCIO, Képler Laveran Lima Ferreira "PEPE", JOSÉ
Miguel da Rocha FONTE, ELISEU Pereira dos Santos, CÉDRIC Ricardo Alves SOARES,
JOÃO MÁRIO Naval da Costa Eduardo (80' RICARDO Andrade QUARESMA Bernardo),
WILLIAM Silva de CARVALHO (YC90+2) (96' DANILO Luís Hélio Pereira), RENATO
Júnior Luz SANCHES, ADRIEN Sebastian Perruchet SILVA (YC70) (73' JOÃO Filipe Iria
Santos MOUTINHO), CRISTIANO RONALDO dos Santos Aveiro (C), Luís Carlos Almeida
da Cunha "NANI". (Coach: FERNANDO Manuel Fernandes da Costa SANTOS (POR)).
Goals: Poland: 1-0 Robert Lewandowski (2').
Portugal: 1-1 RENATO Júnior Luz SANCHES (33').
Referee: Dr.Felix Brych (GER)   Attendance: 62.940
Penalties:
1 CRISTIANO RONALDO dos Santos Aveiro   1 Robert Lewandowski
2 RENATO Júnior Luz SANCHES   2 Arkadiusz Milik
3 JOÃO Filipe Iria Santos MOUTINHO   3 Kamil Glik
4 Luís Carlos Almeida da Cunha "NANI"   * Jakub Blaszczykowski
5 RICARDO Andrade QUARESMA Bernardo

01-07-2016   Stade Pierre-Mauroy, Villeneuve-d'Ascq: Wales – Belgium 3-1 (1-1)
Wales: Wayne Hennessey, Chris Gunter (YC24), Neil Taylor, Benjamin (Ben) Davies (YC5),
James Chester (YC16), Ashley Williams (C), Joe Allen, Aaron Ramsey (YC75) (90' James
Collins), Joseph (Joe) Ledley (78' Andy King), Hal Robson-Kanu (80' Samuel Michael (Sam)
Vokes), Gareth Bale. (Coach: Chris Coleman (WAL)).
Belgium: Thibaut Courtois, Toby Alderweireld (YC85), Jason Denayer, Thomas Meunier,
Jordan Lukaku Menama (75' Dries Mertens), Radja Nainggolan, Axel Witsel, Kevin De
Bruyne, Eden Hazard (C), Yannick Ferreira-Carrasco (46' Marouane Fellaini (YC59)), Romelu
Lukaku Menama (83' Michy Batshuayi). (Coach: Marc Wilmots (BEL)).
Goals: Wales: 1-1 Ashley Williams (31'), 2-1 Hal Robson-Kanu (55'), 3-1 Samuel Michael
(Sam) Vokes (86').
Belgium: 0-1 Radja Nainggolan (13').
Referee: Damir Skomina (SLO)   Attendance: 45.936

02-07-2016   Nouveau Stade de Bordeaux, Bordeaux: Germany – Italy   1-1 (0-0) (AET)
Germany: Manuel Neuer (C), Jonas Hector, Benedikt Höwedes, Mats Hummels (YC90),
Jérôme Boateng, Sami Khedira (16' Bastian Schweinsteiger (YC112)), Mesut Özil, Thomas
Müller, Toni Kroos, Joshua Kimmich, Mario Gómez García (72' Julian Draxler). (Coach:
Joachim Löw (GER)).
Italy: Gianluigi Buffon (C), Mattia De Sciglio (YC57), Giorgio Chiellini (120'+1' Simone
Zaza), Andrea Barzagli, Leonardo Bonucci, Alessandro Florenzi (86' Matteo Darmian),
Stefano Sturaro (YC56), Marco Parolo (YC59), Emanuele Giaccherini (YC103), Graziano
Pellè (YC91), ÉDER Citalin Martins (108' Lorenzo Insigne). (Coach: Antonio Conte (ITA)).
Goals: Germany: 1-0 Mesut Özil (65').
Italy: 1-1 Leonardo Bonucci (78' penalty).
Referee: Viktor Kassai (HUN)   Attendance: 38.764
Penalties: 1 Lorenzo Insigne   1 Toni Kroos
                  * Simone Zaza   * Thomas Müller
                  2 Andrea Barzagli   * Mesut Özil
                  * Graziano Pellè   2 Julian Draxler
                  * Leonardo Bonucci   * Bastian Schweinsteiger
                  3 Emanuele Giaccherini   3 Mats Hummels
                  4 Marco Parolo   4 Joshua Kimmich
                  5 Mattia De Sciglio   5 Jérôme Boateng
                  * Matteo Darmian   6 Jonas Hector

03-07-2016   Stade de France, Saint-Denis: France – Iceland   5-2 (4-0)
France: Hugo Lloris (C), Patrice Evra, Bacary Sagna, Laurent Koscielny (72' Eliaquim
Mangala), Samuel Umtiti (YC75), Dimitri Payet (80' Kingsley Coman), Blaise Matuidi, Paul
Pogba, Moussa Sissoko, Antoine Griezmann, Olivier Giroud (60' André-Pierre Gignac).
(Coach: Didier Deschamps (FRA)).
Iceland: Hannes Halldórsson, Birkir Már Sævarsson, Ragnar Sigurdsson, Kári Árnason (46'
Sverrir Ingason), Ari Skúlason, Jóhann Gudmundsson, Birkir Bjarnason (YC58), Gylfi
Sigurdsson, Aron Gunnarsson (C), Kolbeinn Sigthórsson (83' Eidur Gudjohnsen), Jón Dadi
Bödvarsson (46' Alfred Finnbogason). (Coaches: Lars Lagerbäck (SWE) & Heimir
Hallgrímsson (ISL)).
Goals: France: 1-0 Olivier Giroud (12'), 2-0 Paul Pogba (20'), 3-0 Dimitri Payet (43'), 4-0
Antoine Griezmann (45'), 5-1 Olivier Giroud (59').
Iceland: 4-1 Kolbeinn Sigthórsson (56'), 5-2 Birkir Bjarnason (84').
Referee: Björn Kuipers (HOL)   Attendance: 76.833

380

06-07-2016   Parc Olympique Lyonnais, Lyon: Portugal – Wales   2-0 (0-0)
Portugal: RUI Pedro dos Santos PATRÍCIO, BRUNO Eduardo Regufe ALVES (YC71), JOSÉ Miguel da Rocha FONTE, RAPHAËL Adelino José GUERREIRO, CÉDRIC Ricardo Alves SOARES, JOÃO MÁRIO Naval da Costa Eduardo, DANILO Luís Hélio Pereira, RENATO Júnior Luz SANCHES (74' ANDRÉ Filipe Tavares GOMES), ADRIEN Sebastian Perruchet SILVA (79' JOÃO Filipe Iria Santos MOUTINHO), CRISTIANO RONALDO dos Santos Aveiro (C) (YC72), Luís Carlos Almeida da Cunha "NANI" (86' RICARDO Andrade QUARESMA Bernardo). (Coach: FERNANDO Manuel Fernandes da Costa SANTOS (POR)).
Wales: Wayne Hennessey, Chris Gunter, Neil Taylor, James Chester (YC62), Ashley Williams (C), James Collins (66' Jonathan Williams), Joe Allen (YC8), Andy King, Joseph (Joe) Ledley (58' Samuel Michael (Sam) Vokes), Hal Robson-Kanu (63' Simon Church), Gareth Bale (YC88). (Coach: Chris Coleman (WAL)).
Goals: Portugal: 1-0 CRISTIANO RONALDO dos Santos Aveiro (50'), 2-0 Luís Carlos Almeida da Cunha "NANI" (53').
Referee: Jonas Eriksson (SWE)   Attendance: 55.679

07-07-2016   Stade Vélodrome, Marseille: Germany – France   0-2 (0-1)
Germany: Manuel Neuer (C), Jonas Hector, Benedikt Höwedes, Emre Can (YC36) (67' Mario Götze), Jérôme Boateng (61' Shkodran Mustafi), Bastian Schweinsteiger (YC45+1) (79' Leroy Sané), Mesut Özil (YC45+1), Julian Draxler (YC50), Thomas Müller, Toni Kroos, Joshua Kimmich. (Coach: Joachim Löw (GER)).
France: Hugo Lloris (C), Patrice Evra (YC43), Bacary Sagna, Laurent Koscielny, Samuel Umtiti, Dimitri Payet (71' N'Golo Kanté (YC75)), Blaise Matuidi, Paul Pogba, Moussa Sissoko, Antoine Griezmann (90'+2' Yohan Cabaye), Olivier Giroud (78' André-Pierre Gignac). (Coach: Didier Deschamps (FRA)).
Goals: France: 0-1 Antoine Griezmann (45'+2' penalty), 0-2 Antoine Griezmann (72').
Referee: Nicola Rizzoli (ITA)   Attendance: 64.078

FINAL

10-07-2016   Stade de France: Portugal – France   1-0 (0-0) (AET)
Portugal: RUI Pedro dos Santos PATRÍCIO (YC120+3), Képler Laveran Lima Ferreira "PEPE", JOSÉ Miguel da Rocha FONTE (YC119), RAPHAËL Adelino José GUERREIRO (YC95), CÉDRIC Ricardo Alves SOARES (YC34), JOÃO MÁRIO Naval da Costa Eduardo (YC62), WILLIAM Silva de CARVALHO (YC98), RENATO Júnior Luz SANCHES (79' "ÉDER" Éderzito António Macedo Lopes), ADRIEN Sebastian Perruchet SILVA (66' JOÃO Filipe Iria Santos MOUTINHO), CRISTIANO RONALDO dos Santos Aveiro (C) (25' RICARDO Andrade QUARESMA Bernardo), Luís Carlos Almeida da Cunha "NANI".(Coach: FERNANDO Manuel Fernandes da Costa SANTOS (POR)).
France: Hugo Lloris (C), Patrice Evra, Bacary Sagna, Laurent Koscielny (YC107), Samuel Umtiti (YC80), Dimitri Payet (58' Kingsley Coman), Blaise Matuidi (YC97), Paul Pogba (YC115), Moussa Sissoko (110' Anthony Martial), Antoine Griezmann, Olivier Giroud (78' André-Pierre Gignac). (Coach: Didier Deschamps (FRA)).
Goal: Portugal: 1-0 "ÉDER" Éderzito António Macedo Lopes (109').
Referee: Mark Clattenburg (ENG)   Attendance: 75.868

*** **Portugal were European Champions** ***

GOALSCORERS TOURNAMENT 2014-2016:

Goals	Players
14	Robert Lewandowski (POL)
11	Zlatan Ibrahimovic (SWE)
10	Gareth Bale (WAL)
9	Thomas Müller (GER)
8	Edin Dzeko (BOS), Ivan Perisic (CRO), Wayne Rooney (ENG), CRISTIANO RONALDO dos Santos Aveiro (POR), Artyom Dzyuba (RUS)
7	Marc Janko (AUT), Gylfi Sigurdsson (ISL), Kyle Lafferty (NIR), Arkadiusz Milik (POL), Steven Fletcher (SCO)
6	Eden Hazard (BEL), Danny Welbeck (ENG), Antoine Griezmann (FRA), Milivoje Novakovic (SLO), Marek Hamsik (SVK), Andriy Yarmolenko (UKR)
5	Kevin De Bruyne (BEL), Francisco "PACO" ALCÁCER Garcia (ESP), Klaas-Jan Huntelaar (HOL), Robbie Keane (IRL), Jonathan (Jon) Walters (IRL), Kolbeinn Sigthórsson (ISL), Omer Damari (ISR), Graziano Pellè (ITA), Shaun Maloney (SCO), Xherdan Shaqiri (SUI), Burak Yilmaz (TUR)
4	David Alaba (AUT), Marouane Fellaini (BEL), Radja Nainggolan (BEL), Nestoras Mitidis (CYP), Borek Dockal (CZE), Álvaro Borja MORATA Martín (ESP), Birkir Bjarnason (ISL), Gareth McAuley (NIR), Kamil Grosicki (POL), Luís Carlos Almeida da Cunha "NANI" (POR), Bogdan Stancu (ROM)
3	Ildefons Lima Solà (AND), Marko Arnautovic (AUT), Martin Harnik (AUT), Dmitri Nazarov (AZE), Dries Mertens (BEL), Luka Modric (CRO), Demetris Christofi (CYP), Georgios Efrem (CYP), Harry Kane (ENG), Theo Walcott (ENG), DAVID Josué Jiménez SILVA (ESP), Joal Pohjanpalo (FIN), Olivier Giroud (FRA), Dimitri Payet (FRA), Tornike Okriashvili (GEO), Mario Götze (GER), Max Kruse (GER), André Schürrle (GER), Robin van Persie (HOL), Balász Dzsudzsák (HUN), Robert (Robbie) Brady (IRL), Shane Long (IRL), Tomer Hemed (ISR), Giorgio Chiellini (ITA), ÉDER Citadin Martins (ITA), Yuriy Logvinenko (KAZ), Valerijs Sabala (LAT), Alexander Tettey (NOR), Jakub Blaszczykowski (POL), Aleksandr Kokorin (RUS), Steven Naismith (SCO), Bostjan Cesar (SLO), Zoran Tosic (SRB), Josip Drmic (SUI), Fabian Schär (SUI), Haris Seferovic (SUI), Adam Nemec (SVK), Erkand Zengin (SWE), Selçuk Inan (TUR), Artem Kravets (UKR), Aaron Ramsey (WAL), Hal Robson-Kanu (WAL)
2	Armando Sadiku (ALB), Zlatko Junuzovic (AUT), Rubin Okotie (AUT), Rahid Amirguliyev (AZE), Michy Batshuayi (BEL), Romelu Lukaku Menama (BEL), Stanislav Dragun (BLS), Mikhail Gordeichuk (BLS), Timofei Kalachev (BLS), Sergei Kornilenko (BLS), Milan Djuric (BOS), Vedad Ibisevic (BOS), Haris Medunjanin (BOS), Edin Visca (BOS),Iliyan Mitsanski (BUL), Ivelin Popov (BUL), Marcelo Brozovic (CRO), Nikola Kalinic (CRO), Andrej Kramaric (CRO), Ivan Rakitic (CRO), Pavel Kaderábek (CZE), Tomás Necid (CZE), Václav Pilar (CZE), Nicklas Bendtner (DEN), Yussuf Yurary Poulsen (DEN), Ross Barkley (ENG), Raheem Sterling (ENG), Jack Wilshere (ENG), Sergio BUSQUETS Burgos (ESP), PEDRO Eliezer Rodríguez Ledesma (ESP), Santiago "SANTI" CAZORLA González (ESP), Sergei Zenjov (EST), Jóan Símun

	Edmundsson (FAR), Riku Riski (FIN), Jaba Kankava (GEO), Valeri Kazaishvili (GEO), Mate Vatsadze (GEO), Mario Gómez García (GER), Arjen Robben (HOL), Georginio Wijnaldum (HOL), Dániel Böde (HUN), Zoltán Gera (HUN), Krisztián Németh (HUN), Tamás Priskin (HUN), Zoltán Stieber (HUN), Ádám Szalai (HUN), Wesley (Wes) Hoolahan (IRL), James McClean (IRL), Aiden McGeady (IRL), Jón Dadi Bödvarsson (ISL), Aron Gunnarsson (ISL), Ragnar Sigurdsson (ISL), Nir Bitton (ISR), Tal Ben Haim (II) (ISR), Eran Zahavy (ISR), Leonardo Bonucci (ITA), Antonio Candreva (ITA), Islambek Kuat (KAZ), Fiodor Cernych (LIT), Arvydas Novikovas (LIT), Lars Christian Krogh Gerson (LUX), Aleksandar Trajkovski (MCD), Fatos Beciraj (MNE), Stevan Jovetic (MNE), Mirko Vucinic (MNE), Steven Davis (NIR), Niall McGinn (NIR), Joshua King (NOR), Grzegorz Krychowiak (POL), Sebastian Mila (POL), JOÃO Filipe Iria Santos MOUTINHO (POR), RICARDO Alberto Silveira de CARVALHO (POR), Constantin Budescu (ROM), Paul Papp (ROM), Nejc Pecnik (SLO), Adem Ljajic (SRB), Admir Mehmedi (SUI), Juraj Kucka (SVK), Róbert Mak (SVK), Vladimír Weiss (SVK), Marcus Berg (SWE), Arda Turan (TUR), Yevhen Konoplyanka (UKR), Yevhen Seleznyov (UKR), Serhiy Sydorchuk (UKR)
1	Bekim Balaj (ALB), Shkélzen Gashi (ALB), Ermir Lenjani (ALB), Mërgim Mavraj (ALB), Berat Xhimshiti (ALB), Robert Arzumanyan (ARM), Henrikh Mkhitaryan (ARM), Hrayr Mkoyan (ARM), Marcos Piñeiro Pizzelli (ARM), Marcel Sabitzer (AUT), Alessandro Schöpf (AUT), Javid Huseynov (AZE), Toby Alderweireld (BEL), Christian Benteke (BEL), Yannick Ferreira Carrasco (BEL), Nacer Chadli (BEL), Laurent Depoitre (BEL), Divock Okoth Origi (BEL), Axel Witsel (BEL), Ermin Bicakcic (BOS), Senad Lulic (BOS), Mihail Aleksandrov (BUL), Nikolay Bodurov (BUL), Andrey Galabinov (BUL), Ventsislav Hristov (BUL), Dimitar Rangelov (BUL), Mario Mandzukic (CRO), Ivica Olic (CRO), Danijel Pranjic (CRO), Gordon Schildenfeld (CRO), Constantinos Charalambidis (CYP), Jason Demetriou (CYP), DOSSA Momad Omar Hassamo JÚNIOR (CYP), Vincent Laban (CYP), Constantinos Makrides (CYP), Giorgios Merkis (CYP), Vladimír Darida (CZE), Ladislav Krejci (CZE), David Lafata (CZE), David Limbersky (CZE), Tomás Sivok (CZE), Milan Skoda (CZE), Josef Sural (CZE), Pierre-Emile Højbjerg (DEN), Nicolai Jørgensen (DEN), Thomas Kahlenberg (DEN), Simon Kjær (DEN), Jakob Poulsen (DEN), Jannik Vestergaard (DEN), Lasse Vibe (DEN), Eric Dier (ENG), Philip (Phil) Jagielka (ENG), Alex Oxlade-Chamberlain (ENG), Daniel Sturridge (ENG), Andros Townsend (ENG), Jamie Vardy (ENG), Jordi ALBA Ramos (ESP), Juan BERNAT Velasco (ESP), Diego da Silva COSTA (ESP), Andrés INIESTA Luján (ESP), Francisco Román Alarcón Suárez "ISCO" (ESP), MARIO Gaspar Pérez Martínez (ESP), Manuel Agudo Durán "NOLITO" (ESP), Gerard PIQUÉ i Bernabéu (ESP), SERGIO RAMOS García (ESP), Ats Purje (EST), Konstantin Vassiljev (EST), Hallur Hansson (FAR), Christian Holst (FAR), Róaldur Jakobsen (FAR), Brandur Olsen (FAR), Paulus Arajuuri (FIN), Roman Eremenko (FIN), Jarkko Hurme (FIN), Berat Sadik (FIN), Paul Pogba (FRA), Nikoloz Gelashvili (GEO), Karim Bellarabi (GER), Jérôme Boateng (GER), Julian Draxler (GER), Toni Kroos (GER), Shkodran Mustafi (GER), Mesut Özil (GER), Marco Reus (GER), Bastian Schweinsteiger (GER), Lee Casciaro (GIB), Jake Gosling (GIB), Christos Aravidis (GRE), Nikolaos Karelis (GRE), Panagiotis Kone (GRE), Konstantinos (Kostas) Mitroglou (GRE),

	Sokratis Papastathopoulos (GRE), Konstantinos (Kostas) Stafylidis (GRE), Panagiotis Tachsidis (GRE), Ibrahim Afellay (HOL), Jeffrey Bruma (HOL), Luciano Narsingh (HOL), Wesley Sneijder (HOL), Stefan de Vrij (HOL), Richárd Guzmics (HUN), László Kleinheister (HUN), Gergö Lovrencsics (HUN), Cyrus Christie (IRL), John O'Shea (IRL), Rúrik Gíslason (ISL), Eidur Gudjohnsen (ISL), Arnór Ingvi Traustason (ISL), Moanes Dabour (ISR), Gil Vermouth (ISR), Matteo Darmian (ITA), Daniele De Rossi (ITA), Stephan El Shaarawy (ITA), Alessandro Florenzi (ITA), Emanuele Giaccherini (ITA), Simone Zaza (ITA), Rinat Abdulin (KAZ), Samat Smakov (KAZ), Aleksandrs Cauna (LAT), Aleksejs Visnakovs (LAT), Artūrs Zjuzins (LAT), Franz Burgmeier (LIE), Sandro Wieser (LIE), Deivydas Matulevicius (LIT), Saulius Mikoliūnas (LIT), Lukas Spalvis (LIT), Stefano Bensi (LUX), Mario Mutsch (LUX), Sébastien Thill (LUX), David Turpel (LUX), Besart Abdurahimi (MCD), Arijan Ademi (MCD), Agim Ibraimi (MCD), Adis Jahovic (MCD), Alfred Effiong (MLT), Clayton Failla (MLT), Michael Mifsud (MLT), Dejan Damjanovic (MNE), Stefan Savic (MNE), Zarko Tomasevic (MNE), Gheorghe Boghiu (MOL), Eugeniu Cebotaru (MOL), Alexandru Dedov (MOL), Alexandru Epureanu (MOL), Craig Cathcart (NIR), Josh Magennis (NIR), Jamie Ward (NIR), Jo Inge Berget (NOR), Mats Møller Dæhli (NOR), Tarik Elyounoussi (NOR), Vegard Forren (NOR), Markus Henriksen (NOR), Håvard Nielsen (NOR), Håvard Nordtveit (NOR), Alexander Søderlund (NOR), Kamil Glik (POL), Bartosz Kapustka (POL), Krzysztof Maczynski (POL), Slawomir Peszko (POL), Lukasz Szukala (POL), "ÉDER" Éderzito António Macedo Lopes (POR), FÁBIO Alexandre da Silva COENTRÃO (POR), MIGUEL Luís Pinto VELOSO (POR), RENATO Júnior Luz SANCHES (POR), Ovidiu Hoban (ROM), Claudiu Keserü (ROM), Ciprian Marica (ROM), Alexandru Maxim (ROM), Raul Rusescu (ROM), Vasili Berezutski (RUS), Alan Dzagoev (RUS), Denis Glushakov (RUS), Sergei Ignashevich (RUS), Dmitri Kombarov (RUS), Oleg Kuzmin (RUS), Fyodor Smolov (RUS), Ikechi Anya (SCO), Chris Martin (SCO), James McArthur (SCO), Matt Ritchie (SCO), Robert Beric (SLO), Valter Birsa (SLO), Branko Ilic (SLO), Josip Ilicic (SLO), Kevin Kampl (SLO), Dejan Lazarevic (SLO), Andraz Struna (SLO), Matteo Vitaioli (SMR), Aleksandar Kolarov (SRB), Nemanja Matic (SRB), Eren Derdiyok (SUI), Johan Djourou (SUI), Blerim Dzemaili (SUI), Breel-Donald Embolo (SUI), Gökhan Inler (SUI), Pajtim Kasami (SUI), Michael Lang (SUI), Valentin Stocker (SUI), Granit Xhaka (SUI), Ondrej Duda (SVK), Peter Pekarík (SVK), Kornel Saláta (SVK), Stanislav Sesták (SVK), Miroslav Stoch (SVK), Jimmy Durmaz (SWE), Emil Forsberg (SWE), Ola Toivonen (SWE), Serdar Aziz (TUR), Umut Bulut (TUR), Hakan Calhanoglu (TUR), Bilal Kisa (TUR), Oguzhan Özyakup (TUR), Ozan Tufan (TUR), Denys Harmash (UKR), David Cotterill (WAL), Neil Taylor (WAL), Samuel Michael (Sam) Vokes (WAL), Ashley Williams (WAL)
1 own goal	Mërgim Mavraj (ALB) for Armenia, Levon Hayrapetyan (ARM) for Serbia, Kamo Hovhannisyan (ARM) for Albania, Rashad Farhad oglu Sadygov (AZE) for Croatia, Aleksandr Martynovich (BLS) for Ukraine, Nikolay Bodurov (BUL) for Croatia, Yordan Minev (BUL) for Italy, Vedran Corluka (CRO) for Norway,

	DOSSA Momad Omar Hassamo JÚNIOR (CYP) for Andorra, Jordan Henderson (ENG) for Slovenia, Ragnar Klavan (EST) for Switzerland, Akaki Khubutia (GEO) for Scotland, Mats Hummels (GER) for Scotland, Jordan Perez (GIB) for Republic of Ireland, Yogan Santos (GIB) for Germany, Robin van Persie (HOL) for Czech Republic, Ciaran Clark (IRL) for Sweden, John O'Shea (IRL) for Scotland, Jón Dadi Bödvarsson (ISL) for Czech Republic, Birkir Már Sævarsson (ISL) for Hungary, Giorgio Chiellini (ITA) for Azerbaijan, Martin Büchel (LIE) for Russia, Franz Burgmeier (LIE) for Russia, Tome Pacovski (MCD) for Spain, Petru Racu (MOL) for Montenegro, Gareth McAuley (NIR) for Wales, Markus Henriksen (NOR) for Hungary, Cristian Brolli (SMR) for England, Alessandro Della Valle (SMR) for England
2 own goals	Giedrius Arlauskas (LIT) for Switzerland & England

UEFA Euro 2020

GROUP   A

22-03-2019	Sofia	Bulgaria – Montenegro	1-1 (0-0)
22-03-2019	London	England – Czech Republic	5-0 (2-0)
25-03-2019	Pristina	Kosovo – Bulgaria	1-1 (0-1)
25-03-2019	Podgorica	Montenegro – England	1-5 (1-2)
07-06-2019	Prague	Czech Republic – Bulgaria	2-1 (1-1)
07-06-2019	Podgorica	Montenegro – Kosovo	1-1 (0-1)
10-06-2019	Sofia	Bulgaria – Kosovo	2-3 (1-1)
10-06-2019	Olomouc	Czech Republic – Montenegro	3-0 (1-0)
07-09-2019	Pristina	Kosovo – Czech Republic	2-1 (1-1)
07-09-2019	London	England – Bulgaria	4-0 (1-0)
10-09-2019	Southampton	England – Kosovo	5-3 (5-1)
10-09-2019	Podgorica	Montenegro – Czech Republic	0-3 (0-0)
11-10-2019	Prague	Czech Republic – England	2-1 (1-1)
11-10-2019	Podgorica	Montenegro – Bulgaria	0-0
14-10-2019	Sofia	Bulgaria – England	0-6 (0-4)
14-10-2019	Pristina	Kosovo – Montenegro	2-0 (2-0)
14-11-2019	Plzen	Czech Republic – Kosovo	2-1 (0-0)
14-11-2019	London	England – Montenegro	7-0 (5-0)
17-11-2019	Sofia	Bulgaria – Czech Republic	1-0 (0-0)
17-11-2019	Pristina	Kosovo – England	0-4 (0-1)

FINAL STANDING

Pos	Team	Pld	W	D	L	GF	GA	GD	Pts
1	England	8	7	0	1	37	6	+31	21
2	Czech Republic	8	5	0	3	13	11	+2	15
3	Kosovo	8	3	2	3	13	16	-3	11
4	Bulgaria	8	1	3	4	6	17	-11	6
5	Montenegro	8	0	3	5	3	22	-19	3

England and Czech Republic qualified for final tournament.

386

22-03-2019   Vasil Levski National Stadium, Sofia: Bulgaria – Montenegro 1-1 (0-0)
Bulgaria: Nikolay Mihaylov, Nikolaj Bodurov, Petar Zanev, Strahil Popov, Vasil Bozhikov, Ivelin Popov (YC34), Galin Ivanov (51' Stanislav Kostov), Georgi Kostadinov, Ivaylo Chochev (YC68) (68' Simeon Slavchev), Todor Nedelev, Spas Delev (82' Martin Minchev). (Coach: Petar Hubchev (BUL)).
Montenegro: Danijel Petkovic, Zarko Tomasevic, Marko Simic (YC25), Filip Stojkovic, Adam Marusic, Marko Vesovic (78' Vladimir Jovovic (YC81)), Nikola Vukcevic, Marko Jankovic (64' Aleksandar Boljevic (YC89)), Mirko Ivanic, Fatos Beciraj (YC25), Stefan Mugosa (89' Nebojsa Kosovic). (Coach: Ljubisa Tumbakovic (SRB)).
Goals: Bulgaria: 1-1 Todor Nedelev (82' penalty).
Montenegro: 0-1 Stefan Mugosa (50').
Referee: Ruddy Buquet (FRA)   Attendance: 5.652

22-03-2019   Wembley Stadium, London: England – Czech Republic 5-0 (2-0)
England: Jordan Pickford, Kyle Walker, Harry Maguire, Ben Chilwell, Jordan Henderson, Dele Alli (63' Declan Rice), Eric Dier (17' Ross Barkley), Jadon Sancho, Harry Kane, Raheem Sterling (70' Callum Hudson-Odoi). (Coach: Gareth Southgate (ENG)).
Czech Republic: Jirí Pavlenka, Ondrej Celustka, Theodor Gebre Selassie, Filip Novák, Pavel Kaderábek (YC45+1), Tomás Kalas, David Pavelka, Vladimír Darida (67' Lukás Masopust), Tomás Soucek, Jakub Jankto (46' Matej Vydra), Patrik Schick (YC53) (82' Milan Skoda). (Coach: Jaroslav Silhavy (CZE)).
Goals: England: 1-0 Raheem Sterling (24'), 2-0 Harry Kane (45+2' penalty), 3-0 Raheem Sterling (62'), 4-0 Raheem Sterling (68'), 5-0 Tomás Kalas (84' *own goal*).
Referee: Artur Soares Dias (POR)   Attendance: 82.575

25-03-2019   Stadiumi Fadil Vokrri, Pristina: Kosovo – Bulgaria 1-1 (0-1)
Kosovo: Aro Muric, Fidan Aliti, Amir Rrahmani, Mergim Vojvoda (YC19), Herolind Shala (59' Edon Zhegrova), Hekuran Kryeziu (YC71), Benjamin Kololli (78' Leart Paqarada), Milot Rashica, Arber Zeneli, Bersant Celina (58' Besar Halimi (YC90+2)), Vedat Muriqi. (Coach: Bernard Challandes (SUI)).
Bulgaria: Nikolay Mihaylov, Nikolaj Bodurov, Strahil Popov (YC53), Vasil Bozhikov, Kristiyan Malinov (76' Martin Minchev), Anton Nedyalkov (YC19), Ivelin Popov (YC41), Georgi Kostadinov (80' Valentin Antov (YC86)), Simeon Slavchev (YC36), Todor Nedelev, Spas Delev (68' Petar Zanev). (Coach: Petar Hubchev (BUL)).
Goals: Kosovo: 1-1 Arber Zeneli (61').
Bulgaria: 0-1 Vasil Bozhikov (39').
Referee: Gediminas Mazeika (LTU)   Attendance: 12.580

25-03-2019   Stadion Pod Goricom, Podgorica: Montenegro – England 1-5 (1-2)
Montenegro: Danijel Petkovic, Zarko Tomasevic, Stefan Savic, Marko Simic (74' Vladimir Jovovic), Filip Stojkovic, Adam Marusic, Marko Vesovic (70' Aleksandar Boljevic (YC90+2)), Nikola Vukcevic, Mirko Ivanic, Fatos Beciraj (61' Marko Jankovic), Stefan Mugosa. (Coach: Ljubisa Tumbakovic (SRB)).
England: Jordan Pickford, Danny Rose (YC90+3), Kyle Walker, Harry Maguire, Michael Keane, Ross Barkley (YC52) (82' James Ward-Prowse), Dele Alli (64' Jordan Henderson (YC90+2)), Declan Rice, Harry Kane (83' Callum Wilson), Raheem Sterling, Callum Hudson-Odoi. (Coach: Gareth Southgate (ENG)).
Goals: Montenegro: 1-0 Marko Vesovic (17').
England: 1-1 Michael Keane (30'), 1-2 Ross Barkley (39'), 1-3 Ross Barkley (59'), 1-4 Harry Kane (71'), 1-5 Raheem Sterling (81').
Referee: Aleksei Kulbakov (BLS)   Attendance: 8.329

07-06-2019   Generali Arena, Prague: Czech Republic – Bulgaria 2-1 (1-1)
Czech Republic: Tomás Vaclík, Marek Suchy, Ondrej Celustka, Filip Novák, Pavel Kaderábek (YC13), David Pavelka (YC49), Lukás Masopust (66' Jan Kopic), Tomás Soucek, Alex Král, Jakub Jankto (83' Ladislav Krejcí), Patrik Schick (78' Martin Dolezal). (Coach: Jaroslav Silhavy (CZE)).
Bulgaria: Nikolay Mihaylov, Strahil Popov, Vasil Bozhikov, Kristiyan Malinov (YC35) (64' Yanis Karabelyov), Anton Nedyalkov, Kristian Dimitrov (YC74), Georgi Sarmov, Ivelin Popov, Todor Nedelev (82' Tsvetelin Chunchukov (YC90+3)), Martin Minchev (46' Kiril Despodov (YC90+3)), Ismail Isa. (Coach: Krassimir Balakov (BUL)).
Goals: Czech Republic: 1-1 Patrik Schick (19'), 2-1 Patrik Schick (50').
Bulgaria: 0-1 Ismail Isa (3').
Referee: Tamás Bognár (HUN)   Attendance: 13.482

07-06-2019   Stadion Pod Goricom, Podgorica: Montenegro – Kosovo 1-1 (0-1)
Montenegro: Milan Mijatovic, Zarko Tomasevic (71' Aleksandar Boljevic), Marko Simic (YC83), Igor Vujacic, Adam Marusic, Marko Vesovic (YC51), Aleksandar Scekic (59' Marko Bakic), Nebojsa Kosovic, Marko Jankovic (85' Vladimir Jovovic), Fatos Beciraj, Stefan Mugosa. (Coach: Ljubisa Tumbakovic (SRB)).
Kosovo: Aro Muric (YC76), Fidan Aliti, Leart Paqarada (YC57) (70' Benjamin Kololli), Amir Rrahmani, Mergim Vojvoda, Idriz Voca, Besar Halimi, Milot Rashica (YC82), Arber Zeneli (38' Edon Zhegrova), Bersant Celina (78' Elbasan Rashani), Vedat Muriqi. (Coach: Bernard Challandes (SUI)).
Goals: Montenegro: 1-1 Stefan Mugosa (69').
Kosovo: 0-1 Milot Rashica (24').
Referee: Daniele Orsato (ITA)   Attendance: 100

Montenegro were sanctioned by UEFA to play one home match without spectators for racist behaviour in their home match against England.

10-06-2019   Vasil Levski National Stadium, Sofia: Bulgaria – Kosovo 2-3 (1-1)
Bulgaria: Nikolay Mihaylov, Strahil Popov, Vasil Bozhikov (46' Kristian Dimitrov), Ivan Goranov, Anton Nedyalkov, Ivelin Popov, Galin Ivanov, Georgi Kostadinov (YC85), Todor Nedelev (70' Georgi Iliev), Ismail Isa (79' Tsvetelin Chunchukov), Kiril Despodov. (Coach: Krassimir Balakov (BUL)).
Kosovo: Aro Muric, Fidan Aliti, Amir Rrahmani, Mergim Vojvoda (62' Florent Hadërglonaj), Idriz Voca (62' Anel Rashkaj), Besar Halimi (YC78), Benjamin Kololli, Milot Rashica, Edon Zhegrova (76' Elbasan Rashani), Bersant Celina, Vedat Muriqi. (Coach: Bernard Challandes (SUI)).
Goals: Bulgaria: 1-1 Ivelin Popov (43'), 2-1 Kristian Dimitrov (55').
Kosovo: 0-1 Milot Rashica (14'), 2-2 Vedat Muriqi (64'), 2-3 Elbasan Rashani (90+3').
Referee: Mads-Kristoffer Kristoffersen (DEN)   Attendance: 4.994

10-06-2019   Andruv stadion, Olomouc: Czech Republic – Montenegro 3-0 (1-0)
Czech Republic: Tomás Vaclík, Marek Suchy (YC21), Ondrej Celustka, Filip Novák (YC14), Pavel Kaderábek, David Pavelka, Lukás Masopust (39' Jan Kopic), Tomás Soucek, Alex Král, Jakub Jankto (74' Ladislav Krejcí), Patrik Schick (YC23) (88' Libor Kozák). (Coach: Jaroslav Silhavy (CZE)).
Montenegro: Milan Mijatovic, Risto Radunovic, Boris Kopitovic, Igor Vujacic (YC62), Adam Marusic (60' Marko Jankovic), Marko Vesovic (YC80), Nebojsa Kosovic, Nikola Vukcevic (67' Vukan Savicevic), Marko Bakic (YC15), Stefan Mugosa (85' Fatos Beciraj), Vladimir Jovovic. (Coach: Miodrag Dzudovic (MNE)).
Goals: Czech Republic: 1-0 Jakub Jankto (18'), 2-0 Boris Kopitovic (49' *own goal*), 3-0 Patrik Schick (82' penalty).
Referee: Vladislav Bezborodov (RUS)   Attendance: 11.565

07-09-2019   Stadiumi Fadil Vokrri, Pristina: Kosovo – Czech Republic 2-1 (1-1)
Kosovo: Aro Muric, Fidan Aliti, Amir Rrahmani, Florent Hadërglonaj, Mergim Vojvoda, Idriz Voca, Elbasan Rashani (51' Valon Berisha), Besar Halimi (87' Anel Rashkaj), Edon Zhegrova (56' Florent Muslija), Bersant Celina, Vedat Muriqi (YC15). (Coach: Bernard Challandes (SUI)).
Czech Republic: Tomás Vaclík, Marek Suchy, Ondrej Celustka (YC18), Jan Boríl, Pavel Kaderábek, Vladimír Darida, Lukás Masopust (YC77) (80' Martin Dolezal), Tomás Soucek, Alex Král (72' Josef Husbauer), Jakub Jankto, Patrik Schick (61' Michal Krmencík). (Coach: Jaroslav Silhavy (CZE)).
Goals: Kosovo: 1-1 Vedat Muriqi (20'), 2-1 Mergim Vojvoda (67').
Czech Republic: 0-1 Patrik Schick (16').
Referee: Danny Makkelie (HOL)   Attendance: 12.678

07-09-2019   Wembley Stadium, London: England – Bulgaria 4-0 (1-0)
England: Jordan Pickford, Danny Rose (YC90+2), Kieran Trippier, Harry Maguire, Michael Keane (YC30), Jordan Henderson (67' Mason Mount), Ross Barkley, Declan Rice, Harry Kane (77' Alex Oxlade-Chamberlain), Raheem Sterling (71' Jadon Sancho), Marcus Rashford. (Coach: Gareth Southgate (ENG)).
Bulgaria: Plamen Iliev, Nikolaj Bodurov (YC36) (65' Kristian Dimitrov), Strahil Popov, Vasil Bozhikov, Kristian Malinov, Anton Nedyalkov, Georgi Sarmov, Ivelin Popov, Galin Ivanov (82' Daniel Mladenov), Wanderson, Marcelinho (67' Kiril Despodov). (Coach: Krassimir Balakov (BUL)).
Goals: England: 1-0 Harry Kane (24'), 2-0 Harry Kane (50' penalty), 3-0 Raheem Sterling (55'), 4-0 Harry Kane (73' penalty).
Referee: Marco Guida (ITA)   Attendance: 82.605

10-09-2019   St. Mary's Stadium, Southampton: England – Kosovo 5-3 (5-1)
England: Jordan Pickford, Harry Maguire, Michael Keane, Trent Alexander-Arnold, Ben Chilwell, Jordan Henderson, Ross Barkley (83' Mason Mount), Declan Rice, Jadon Sancho (85' Marcus Rashford), Harry Kane, Raheem Sterling. (Coach: Gareth Southgate (ENG)).
Kosovo: Aro Muric, Fidan Aliti (YC70), Amir Rrahmani, Florent Hadërglonaj, Mergim Vojvoda, Idriz Voca (59' Anel Rashkaj (YC86)), Valon Berisha (YC83) (85' Florent Hasani), Besar Halimi, Florent Muslija (46' Leart Paqarada (YC65)), Bersant Celina, Vedat Muriqi. (Coach: Bernard Challandes (SUI)).
Goals: England: 1-1 Raheem Sterling (8'), 2-1 Harry Kane (19'), 3-1 Mergim Vojvoda (38' own goal), 4-1 Jadon Sancho (44'), 5-1 Jadon Sancho (45+1').
Kosovo: 0-1 Valon Berisha (1'), 5-2 Valon Berisha (49'), 5-3 Vedat Muriqi (55' penalty).
Referee: Felix Zwayer (GER)   Attendance: 30.155
(Harry Kane missed a penalty kick in the 65th minute)

10-09-2019   Stadion Pod Goricom, Podgorica: Montenegro – Czech Republic 0-3 (0-0)
Montenegro: Danijel Petkovic, Zarko Tomasevic, Risto Radunovic (YC53) (73' Fatos Beciraj), Adam Marusic (YC74), Marko Vesovic, Nebojsa Kosovic (73' Vukan Savicevic), Deni Hocko, Nikola Vukcevic (68' Marko Bakic), Aleksandar Boljevic, Dusan Lagator, Stefan Mugosa. (Coach: Faruk Hadzibegic (BIH)).
Czech Republic: Tomás Vaclík, Marek Suchy (46' Jakub Brabec), Ondrej Celustka, Jan Boríl, Vladimír Coufal, Vladimír Darida, Lukás Masopust (77' Jan Kopic), Tomás Soucek (YC82), Alex Král, Jakub Jankto (YC75), Patrik Schick (90+2' Michal Krmencík). (Coach: Jaroslav Silhavy (CZE)).
Goals: Czech Republic: 0-1 Tomás Soucek (54'), 0-2 Lukás Masopust (58'), 0-3 Vladimír Darida (90+4' penalty).
Referee: Ali Palabiyik (TUR)   Attendance: 5.951

11-10-2019   Sinobo Stadium, Prague: Czech Republic – England 2-1 (1-1)
Czech Republic: Tomás Vaclík, Ondrej Celustka, Jakub Brabec, Jan Boríl, Vladimír Coufal, Vladimír Darida, Lukás Masopust (90' Jarolím Zmrhal), Tomás Soucek, Alex Král, Jakub Jankto (YC8) (83' Jan Kopic), Patrik Schick (65' Zdenek Ondrásek). (Coach: Jaroslav Silhavy (CZE)).
England: Jordan Pickford, Danny Rose (YC10), Kieran Trippier, Harry Maguire, Michael Keane, Jordan Henderson (YC90+2), Mason Mount (72' Ross Barkley), Declan Rice (88' Tammy Abraham), Jadon Sancho (73' Marcus Rashford), Harry Kane, Raheem Sterling (YC68). (Coach: Gareth Southgate (ENG)).
Goals: Czech Republic: 1-1 Jakub Brabec (9'), 2-1 Zdenek Ondrásek (85').
England: 0-1 Harry Kane (5' penalty).
Referee: Damir Skomina (SLO)   Attendance: 18.651

11-10-2019   Stadion Pod Goricom, Podgorica: Montenegro – Bulgaria 0-0
Montenegro: Danijel Petkovic, Stefan Savic (39' Nebojsa Kosovic), Marko Simic, Adam Marusic, Nemanja Sekulic, Nikola Vukcevic, Aleksandar Boljevic, Dusan Lagator (YC30), Sead Haksabanovic (82' Luka Mirkovic), Fatos Beciraj, Vladimír Jovovic (67' Marko Jankovic (YC90+5)). (Coach: Faruk Hadzibegic (BIH)).
Bulgaria: Plamen Iliev, Petar Zanev, Strahil Popov (63' Georgi Kostadinov), Kristiyan Malinov (YC90), Anton Nedyalkov, Kristian Dimitrov, Galin Ivanov, Georgi Pashov (YC20), Wanderson (77' Birsent Karagaren), Bozhidar Kraev, Marcelinho (70' Ismail Isa). (Coach: Krassimir Balakov (BUL)).
Referee: Andreas Ekberg (SWE)   Attendance: 2.743

390

14-10-2019   Vasil Levski National Stadium, Sofia: Bulgaria – England 0-6 (0-4)
Bulgaria: Plamen Iliev, Petar Zanev, Georgi Terziev, Kamen Hadzhiev, Georgi Sarmov (46'
Bozhidar Kraev), Ivelin Popov, Georgi Pashov, Georgi Kostadinov, Wanderson (76' Kristiyan
Malinov), Ismail Isa (68' Galin Ivanov), Kiril Despodov. (Coach: Krassimir Balakov (BUL)).
England: Jordan Pickford, Kieran Trippier, Harry Maguire, Tyrone Mings, Ben Chilwell,
Jordan Henderson (YC4), Ross Barkley (73' Mason Mount), Harry Winks, Harry Kane,
Raheem Sterling (73' Jadon Sancho), Marcus Rashford (76' Callum Wilson). (Coach: Gareth
Southgate (ENG)).
Goals: England: 0-1 Marcus Rashford (7'), 0-2 Ross Barkley (20'), 0-3 Ross Barkley (32'), 0-4
Raheem Sterling (45+3'), 0-5 Raheem Sterling (69'), 0-6 Harry Kane (85').
Referee: Ivan Bebek (CRO)   Attendance: 17.481

14-10-2019   Stadiumi Fadil Vokrri, Pristina: Kosovo – Montenegro 2-0 (2-0)
Kosovo: Aro Muric, Fidan Aliti, Amir Rrahmani, Florent Hadërglonaj, Mergim Vojvoda
(YC85) (89' Edon Zhegrova), Herolind Shala (82' Anel Rashkaj), Valon Berisha, Benjamin
Kololli (YC90+1), Milot Rashica, Bersant Celina (90+3' Florent Hasani), Vedat Muriqi (YC7).
(Coach: Bernard Challandes (SUI)).
Montenegro: Danijel Petkovic (15' Milan Mijatovic), Darko Bulatovic, Marko Simic, Adam
Marusic, Aleksandar Scekic (YC16), Nebojsa Kosovic (46' Fatos Beciraj), Nikola Vukcevic
(YC85), Aleksandar Boljevic, Dusan Lagator, Stefan Mugosa, Vladimír Jovovic (YC7) (74'
Marko Jankovic (YC90)). (Coach: Faruk Hadzibegic (BIH)).
Goals: 1-0 Amir Rrahmani (10'), 2-0 Vedat Muriqi (35').
Referee: Artur Soares Dias (POR)   Attendance: 12.600

14-11-2019   Doosan Aréna, Plzen: Czech Republic – Kosovo 2-1 (0-0)
Czech Republic: Tomás Vaclík, Ondrej Celustka, Jakub Brabec, Jan Boríl (YC31), Vladimír
Coufal, Vladimír Darida, Lukás Masopust (76' Petr Sevcík), Tomás Soucek (YC55), Alex
Král, Jakub Jankto (90+1' Pavel Kaderábek), Michal Krmencík (61' Zdenek Ondrásek).
(Coach: Jaroslav Silhavy (CZE)).
Kosovo: Aro Muric, Fidan Aliti (YC23), Amir Rrahmani, Florent Hadërglonaj (77' Edon
Zhegrova (YC90+2)), Mergim Vojvoda, Anel Rashkaj (YC15) (46' Besar Halimi), Valon
Berisha, Benjamin Kololli, Milot Rashica, Atdhe Nuhiu (YC32), Bersant Celina (85' Elbasan
Rashani). (Coach: Bernard Challandes (SUI)).
Goals: Czech Republic: 1-1 Alex Král (71'), 2-1 Ondrej Celustka (79').
Kosovo: 0-1 Atdhe Nuhiu (50').
Referee: Gianluca Rocchi (ITA)   Attendance: 10.986

14-11-2019   Wembley Stadium, London: England – Montenegro 7-0 (5-0)
England: Jordan Pickford, Harry Maguire, John Stones, Trent Alexander-Arnold, Ben
Chilwell, Alex Oxlade-Chamberlain (56' James Maddison), Harry Winks, Mason Mount (70'
Joe Gomez), Jadon Sancho, Harry Kane (57' Tammy Abraham), Marcus Rashford. (Coach:
Gareth Southgate (ENG)).
Montenegro: Milan Mijatovic, Risto Radunovic (46' Momcilo Raspopovic), Marko Simic,
Aleksandar Sofranac, Marko Vesovic (YC33), Deni Hocko, Nikola Vukcevic, Dusan Lagator,
Sead Haksabanovic (74' Aleksandar Boljevic), Fatos Beciraj, Vladimír Jovovic (65' Branislav
Jankovic). (Coach: Faruk Hadzibegic (BIH)).
Goals: England: 1-0 Alex Oxlade-Chamberlain (11'), 2-0 Harry Kane (19'), 3-0 Harry Kane
(24'), 4-0 Marcus Rashford (30'), 5-0 Harry Kane (37'), 6-0 Aleksandar Sofranac (66' *own
goal*), 7-0 Tammy Abraham (84').
Referee: ANTONIO MATEU Lahoz (ESP)   Attendance: 77.277

17-11-2019   Vasil Levski National Stadium, Sofia: Bulgaria – Czech Republic 1-0 (0-0)
Bulgaria: Georgi Georgiev (YC90+2), Petar Zanev, Strahil Popov, Vasil Bozhikov, Georgi
Terziev, Kristiyan Malinov (89' Aleksandar Tsvetkov), Ivelin Popov, Georgi Kostadinov
(YC50), Wanderson (72' Todor Nedelev), Marcelinho, Kiril Despodov (69' Bozhidar Kraev).
(Coach: Georgi Dermendzhiev (BUL)).
Czech Republic: Ondrej Kolár, Ondrej Kúdela (YC64), Ondrej Celustka, Jan Boríl, Pavel
Kaderábek, Vladimír Darida, Petr Sevcík (65' Lukás Masopust), Tomás Soucek, Alex Král
(71' Josef Husbauer), Jakub Jankto (YC90+3), Zdenek Ondrásek (80' Martin Dolezal).
(Coach: Jaroslav Silhavy (CZE)).
Goal: Bulgaria: 1-0 Vasil Bozhikov (56').
Referee: Sergei Karasev (RUS)   Attendance: 0

*Bulgaria played the match against Czech Republic behind closed doors due to a UEFA
punishment for racist behaviour in their home match played on 14-10-2019 against England.*

17-11-2019   Stadiumi Fadil Vokrri, Pristina: Kosovo – England 0-4 (0-1)
Kosovo: Aro Muric, Fidan Aliti, Amir Rrahmani, Florent Hadërglonaj (73' Edon Zhegrova),
Mergim Vojvoda, Ibrahim Dresevic, Valon Berisha (65' Besar Halimi), Benjamin Kololli
(YC48), Milot Rashica, Atdhe Nuhiu (82' Elbasan Rashani), Bersant Celina. (Coach: Bernard
Challandes (SUI)).
England: Nick Pope, Harry Maguire, Tyrone Mings, Trent Alexander-Arnold (84' Fikayo
Tomori), Ben Chilwell, Alex Oxlade-Chamberlain (72' Mason Mount), Harry Winks, Declan
Rice, Harry Kane, Raheem Sterling, Callum Hudson-Odoi (59' Marcus Rashford). (Coach:
Gareth Southgate (ENG)).
Goals: England: 0-1 Harry Winks (32'), 0-2 Harry Kane (79'), 0-3 Marcus Rashford (83'), 0-4
Mason Mount (90+1').
Referee: Pawel Gil (POL)   Attendance: 12.326

GROUP   B

22-03-2019	Luxembourg	Luxembourg – Lithuania	2-1 (1-1)
22-03-2019	Lisbon	Portugal – Ukraine	0-0
25-03-2019	Luxembourg	Luxembourg – Ukraine	1-2 (1-1)
25-03-2019	Lisbon	Portugal – Serbia	1-1 (1-1)
07-06-2019	Vilnius	Lithuania – Luxembourg	1-1 (0-1)
07-06-2019	Lviv	Ukraine – Serbia	5-0 (2-0)
10-06-2019	Belgrade	Serbia – Lithuania	4-1 (3-0)
10-06-2019	Lviv	Ukraine – Luxembourg	1-0 (1-0)
07-09-2019	Vilnius	Lithuania – Ukraine	0-3 (0-2)
07-09-2019	Belgrade	Serbia – Portugal	2-4 (0-1)
10-09-2019	Vilnius	Lithuania – Portugal	1-5 (1-1)
10-09-2019	Luxembourg	Luxembourg – Serbia	1-3 (0-1)
11-10-2019	Lisbon	Portugal – Luxembourg	3-0 (1-0)
11-10-2019	Kharkiv	Ukraine – Lithuania	2-0 (1-0)
14-10-2019	Vilnius	Lithuania – Serbia	1-2 (0-0)
14-10-2019	Kiev	Ukraine – Portugal	2-1 (2-0)
14-11-2019	Faro/Loulé	Portugal – Lithuania	6-0 (2-0)
14-11-2019	Belgrade	Serbia – Luxembourg	3-2 (2-0)
17-11-2019	Luxembourg	Luxembourg – Portugal	0-2 (0-1)
17-11-2019	Belgrade	Serbia – Ukraine	2-2 (1-1)

FINAL STANDING

Pos	Team	Pld	W	D	L	GF	GA	GD	Pts
1	*Ukraine*	*8*	*6*	*2*	*0*	*17*	*4*	*+13*	*20*
2	*Portugal*	*8*	*5*	*2*	*1*	*22*	*6*	*+16*	*17*
3	Serbia	8	4	2	2	17	17	0	14
4	Luxembourg	8	1	1	6	7	16	-9	4
5	Lithuania	8	0	1	7	5	25	-20	1

Ukraine and Portugal qualified for final tournament.

22-03-2019   Stade Josy Barthel, Luxembourg: Luxembourg – Lithuania 2-1 (1-1)
Luxembourg: Anthony Moris, Lars Gerson, Maxime Chanot, Laurent Jans, Dirk Carlson (YC70), Christopher Martins Pereira (YC30), Oliver Thill, Vincent Thill (78' David Turpel), Leandro Barreiro (67' Danel Sinani (YC86)), Daniël Alves da Mota (59' Stefano Bensi), Gerson Rodrigues. (Coach: Luc Holtz (LUX)).
Lithuania: Ernestas Setkus, Vaidas Slavickas, Algis Jankauskas, Linas Klimavicius, Rolandas Baravykas, Saulius Mikoliūnas (YC45+1) (76' Justinas Marazas), Mantas Kuklys, Arvydas Novikovas (56' Artūras Zulpa), Fiodor Cernych, Deimantas Petravicius (61' Nerijus Valskis (YC86)), Vykintas Slivka. (Coach: Valdas Urbonas (LTU)).
Goals: Luxembourg: 1-1 Leandro Barreiro (45'), 2-1 Gerson Rodrigues (55').
Lithuania: 0-1 Fiodor Cernych (14').
Referee: Roi Reinshreiber (ISR)   Attendance: 3.353

22-03-2019   Estádio do Sport Lisboa e Benfica, Lisbon: Portugal – Ukraine 0-0
Portugal: RUI Pedro dos Santos PATRÍCIO, Képler Laveran Lima Ferreira "PEPE", JOÃO Pedro Cavaco CANCELO, RAPHAËL Adelino José GUERREIRO, RÚBEN Santos Gato Alves DIAS, JOÃO Filipe Iria Santos MOUTINHO (87' JOÃO MÁRIO Naval da Costa Eduardo), WILLIAM Silva de CARVALHO, RÚBEN Diogo da Silva NEVES (62' Rafael Alexandre Fernandes Ferreira "RAFA" da SILVA), BERNARDO Mota Veiga de Carvalho e SILVA, CRISTIANO RONALDO dos Santos Aveiro, ANDRÉ Miguel Valente da SILVA (73' DYEGO Wilverson Ferreira SOUSA). (Coach: FERNANDO Manuel Fernandes da Costa SANTOS (POR)).
Ukraine: Andriy Pyatov, Sergiy Krivtsov, Oleksandr Zinchenko, Mykola Matvienko, Vitali Mykolenko, Marlos (67' Viktor Tsygankov), Taras Stepanenko (YC86), Yevhen Konoplyanka (87' Vitaliy Buyalskiy), Ruslan Malinovskiy, Oleksandr Karavaev, Roman Yaremchuk (76' Júnior Moraes). (Coach: Andriy Shevchenko (UKR)).
Referee: Clément Turpin (FRA)   Attendance: 58.355

25-03-2019   Stade Josy Barthel, Luxembourg: Luxembourg – Ukraine 1-2 (1-1)
Luxembourg: Anthony Moris, Kevin Malget (YC62), Maxime Chanot (YC51), Laurent Jans, Dirk Carlson (YC90+2), Christopher Martins Pereira, Oliver Thill (90+1' Mario Mutsch), Vincent Thill (74' Stefano Bensi), Leandro Barreiro (YC45), David Turpel, Gerson Rodrigues. (Coach: Luc Holtz (LUX)).
Ukraine: Andriy Pyatov, Bogdan Butko (YC63) (79' Oleksandr Karavaev, 87' Vitaliy Buyalskiy), Mykyta Burda (YC48), Oleksandr Zinchenko, Mykola Matvienko, Vitali Mykolenko, Yevhen Konoplyanka, Roman Bezus (64' Roman Yaremchuk), Ruslan Malinovskiy, Viktor Tsygankov, Júnior Moraes. (Coach: Andriy Shevchenko (UKR)).
Goals: Luxembourg: 1-0 David Turpel (34').
Ukraine: 1-1 Viktor Tsygankov (40'), 1-2 Gerson Rodrigues (90+3' *own goal*).
Referee: Mattias Gestranius (FIN)   Attendance: 4.653

25-03-2019   Estádio do Sport Lisboa e Benfica, Lisbon: Portugal – Serbia 1-1 (1-1)
Portugal: RUI Pedro dos Santos PATRÍCIO, Képler Laveran Lima Ferreira "PEPE" (YC45+1), JOÃO Pedro Cavaco CANCELO, RAPHAËL Adelino José GUERREIRO, RÚBEN Santos Gato Alves DIAS, DANILO Luís Hélio PEREIRA, WILLIAM Silva de CARVALHO, Rafael Alexandre Fernandes Ferreira "RAFA" da SILVA (84' GONÇALO Manuel Gabchinho GUEDES), BERNARDO Mota Veiga de Carvalho e SILVA, CRISTIANO RONALDO dos Santos Aveiro (30' Luís Miguel Afonso Fernandes "PIZZI"), DYEGO Wilverson Ferreira SOUSA (58' ANDRÉ Miguel Valente da SILVA). (Coach: FERNANDO Manuel Fernandes da Costa SANTOS (POR)).
Serbia: Marko Dmitrovic, Antonio Rukavina, Filip Mladenovic (YC77), Uros Spajic (YC79), Nikola Milenkovic, Darko Lazovic (69' Andrija Zivkovic), Adem Ljajic (87' Sergej Milinkovic-Savic), Mijat Gacinovic (21' Nemanja Radonjic), Nemanja Maksimovic, Dusan Tadic (YC86), Aleksandar Mitrovic. (Coach: Mladen Krstajic (SRB)).
Goals: Portugal: 1-1 DANILO Luís Hélio PEREIRA (42').
Serbia: 0-1 Dusan Tadic (7' penalty).
Referee: Szymon Marciniak (POL)   Attendance: 50.342

07-06-2019   Vilniaus LFF stadionas, Vilnius: Lithuania – Luxembourg 1-1 (0-1)
Lithuania: Dziugas Bartkus, Linas Klimavicius (YC85), Markus Palionis, Vytautas Andriuskevicius, Saulius Mikoliūnas (YC5,YC42), Arvydas Novikovas (YC28), Fiodor Cernych (89' Donatas Kazlauskas), Vykintas Slivka, Modestas Vorobjovas (YC57,YC90+4), Paulius Golubickas (YC39) (52' Domantas Simkus), Nerijus Valskis (55' Karolis Laukzemis (YC71)). (Coach: Valdas Urbonas (LTU)).
Luxembourg: Anthony Moris, Lars Gerson, Laurent Jans, Dirk Carlson (YC27) (61' Kevin Malget (YC85)), Vahid Selimovic, Christopher Martins Pereira, Oliver Thill (YC76) (80' Danel Sinani), Vincent Thill, Leandro Barreiro, David Turpel (67' Stefano Bensi), Gerson Rodrigues. (Coach: Luc Holtz (LUX)).
Goals: Lithuania: 1-1 Arvydas Novikovas (74').
Luxembourg: 0-1 Gerson Rodrigues (21').
Referee: Ádám Farkas (HUN)   Attendance: 3.263

07-06-2019   Arena Lviv, Lviv: Ukraine – Serbia 5-0 (2-0)
Ukraine: Andriy Pyatov, Sergiy Krivtsov, Oleksandr Zinchenko, Mykola Matvienko, Vitali Mykolenko, Taras Stepanenko (72' Volodymyr Shepeliev), Yevhen Konoplyanka (76' Viktor Kovalenko), Ruslan Malinovskiy, Oleksandr Karavaev, Viktor Tsygankov, Roman Yaremchuk (67' Artem Kravets). (Coach: Andriy Shevchenko (UKR)).
Serbia: Marko Dmitrovic, Aleksandar Kolarov, Uros Spajic (YC32), Nikola Milenkovic (YC22), Adem Ljajic (59' Ljubomir Fejsa), Filip Kostic, Mijat Gacinovic, Nemanja Maksimovic, Aleksandar Prijovic (53' Aleksandar Mitrovic), Dusan Tadic, Luka Jovic (72' Darko Lazovic). (Coach: Mladen Krstajic (SRB)).
Goals: Ukraine: 1-0 Viktor Tsygankov (26'), 2-0 Viktor Tsygankov (27'), 3-0 Yevhen Konoplyanka (46'), 4-0 Roman Yaremchuk (58'), 5-0 Yevhen Konoplyanka (75').
Referee: ANTONIO MATEU Lahoz (ESP)   Attendance: 34.700

10-06-2019   Stadion Rajko Mitic, Belgrade: Serbia – Lithuania 4-1 (3-0)
Serbia: Marko Dmitrovic, Aleksandar Kolarov, Antonio Rukavina, Uros Spajic, Nikola Milenkovic, Filip Kostic (71' Andrija Zivkovic), Sasa Lukic, Nemanja Maksimovic, Dusan Tadic (81' Adem Ljajic), Aleksandar Mitrovic (YC70), Luka Jovic (88' Aleksandar Katai). (Coach: Mladen Krstajic (SRB)).
Lithuania: Dziugas Bartkus, Algis Jankauskas (46' Karolis Chvedukas (YC83)), Linas Klimavicius, Markus Palionis, Vytautas Andriuskevicius, Rolandas Baravykas, Arvydas Novikovas (YC39), Fiodor Cernych (69' Deimantas Petravicius), Vykintas Slivka, Domantas Simkus (YC59), Karolis Laukzemis (77' Nerijus Valskis). (Coach: Valdas Urbonas (LTU)).
Goals: Serbia: 1-0 Aleksandar Mitrovic (20'), 2-0 Aleksandar Mitrovic (34'), 3-0 Luka Jovic (35'), 4-1 Adem Ljajic (90+2').
Lithuania: 3-1 Arvydas Novikovas (71' penalty).
Referee: Adrien Jaccottet (SUI)   Attendance: 52

Serbia were ordered by UEFA to play this matche behind closed doors following racist behaviour by the crowd during their home match against Montenegro.

10-06-2019   Arena Lviv, Lviv: Ukraine – Luxembourg 1-0 (1-0)
Ukraine: Andriy Pyatov, Sergiy Krivtsov, Oleksandr Zinchenko (YC81), Mykola Matvienko, Vitali Mykolenko (YC56), Taras Stepanenko, Yevhen Konoplyanka (80' Viktor Kovalenko), Ruslan Malinovskiy, Oleksandr Karavaev (YC67), Viktor Tsygankov (88' Eduard Sobol), Roman Yaremchuk. (Coach: Andriy Shevchenko (UKR)).
Luxembourg: Anthony Moris, Lars Gerson, Maxime Chanot, Laurent Jans, Marvin Martins Santos da Graça, Christopher Martins Pereira, Oliver Thill (YC29) (77' David Turpel), Vincent Thill (YC90+4), Leandro Barreiro, Daniël Alves da Mota (YC30) (52' Stefano Bensi), Gerson Rodrigues (YC51). (Coach: Luc Holtz (LUX)).
Goal: Ukraine: 1-0 Roman Yaremchuk (6').
Referee: Peter Kralovic (SVK)   Attendance: 35.264

07-09-2019   Vilniaus LFF stadionas, Vilnius: Lithuania – Ukraine 0-3 (0-2)
Lithuania: Emilius Zubas, Markus Palionis, Edvinas Girdvainis, Saulius Mikoliūnas, Artūras Zulpa, Fiodor Cernych (68' Karolis Laukzemis), Ovidijus Verbickas, Domantas Simkus, Modestas Vorobjovas, Giedrius Matulevicius (63' Mantas Kuklys), Paulius Golubickas (52' Vykintas Slivka). (Coach: Valdas Urbonas (LTU)).
Ukraine: Andriy Pyatov, Sergiy Krivtsov, Oleksandr Zinchenko, Mykola Matvienko, Vitali Mykolenko (YC73), Marlos, Taras Stepanenko, Ruslan Malinovskiy (80' Roman Bezus), Sergiy Bolbat, Andrey Yarmolenko (60' Viktor Tsygankov), Roman Yaremchuk (65' Júnior Moraes). (Coach: Andriy Shevchenko (UKR)).
Goals: 0-1 Oleksandr Zinchenko (7'), 0-2 Marlos (27'), 0-3 Ruslan Malinovskiy (62').
Referee: Irfan Peljto (BIH)   Attendance: 5.067

07-09-2019   Stadion Rajko Mitic, Belgrade: Serbia – Portugal 2-4 (0-1)
Serbia: Marko Dmitrovic, Aleksandar Kolarov (YC64), Nikola Maksimovic (YC10), Matija
Nastasic, Nikola Milenkovic, Nemanja Matic, Darko Lazovic (59' Adem Ljajic), Luka
Milivojevic (87' Luka Jovic), Filip Kostic (83' Aleksandar Katai), Dusan Tadic, Aleksandar
Mitrovic. (Coach: Ljubisa Tumbakovic (SRB)).
Portugal: RUI Pedro dos Santos PATRÍCIO, JOSÉ Miguel da Rocha FONTE, RAPHAËL
Adelino José GUERREIRO, NÉLSON Cabral SEMEDO (65' JOÃO Pedro Cavaco
CANCELO), RÚBEN Santos Gato Alves DIAS (YC39), DANILO Luís Hélio PEREIRA,
WILLIAM Silva de CARVALHO (YC89), GONÇALO Manuel Gabchinho GUEDES (70'
JOÃO FÉLIX Sequeira), BRUNO Miguel Borges FERNANDES (85' JOÃO Filipe Iria Santos
MOUTINHO), BERNARDO Mota Veiga de Carvalho e SILVA, CRISTIANO RONALDO
dos Santos Aveiro. (Coach: FERNANDO Manuel Fernandes da Costa SANTOS (POR)).
Goals: Serbia: 1-2 Nikola Milenkovic (68'), 2-3 Aleksandar Mitrovic (85').
Portugal: 0-1 WILLIAM Silva de CARVALHO (42'), 0-2 GONÇALO Manuel Gabchinho
GUEDES (58'), 1-3 CRISTIANO RONALDO dos Santos Aveiro (80'), 2-4 BERNARDO
Mota Veiga de Carvalho e SILVA (86').
Referee: Cüneyt Çakir (TUR)   Attendance: 39.839

10-09-2019   Vilniaus LFF stadionas, Vilnius: Lithuania – Portugal 1-5 (1-1)
Lithuania: Ernestas Setkus, Markus Palionis, Vytautas Andriuskevicius, Edvinas Girdvainis,
Saulius Mikoliūnas, Mantas Kuklys (69' Artūras Zulpa), Vykintas Slivka, Ovidijus Verbickas
(77' Donatas Kazlauskas), Domantas Simkus, Modestas Vorobjovas, Karolis Laukzemis (66'
Deimantas Petravicius). (Coach: Valdas Urbonas (LTU)).
Portugal: RUI Pedro dos Santos PATRÍCIO, JOSÉ Miguel da Rocha FONTE, JOÃO Pedro
Cavaco CANCELO, RAPHAËL Adelino José GUERREIRO, RÚBEN Santos Gato Alves
DIAS, WILLIAM Silva de CARVALHO, RÚBEN Diogo da Silva NEVES, BRUNO Miguel
Borges FERNANDES (56' Rafael Alexandre Fernandes Ferreira "RAFA" da SILVA),
BERNARDO Mota Veiga de Carvalho e SILVA (89' Luís Miguel Afonso Fernandes "PIZZI"),
CRISTIANO RONALDO dos Santos Aveiro (79' GONÇALO Manuel Gabchinho GUEDES),
JOÃO FÉLIX Sequeira. (Coach: FERNANDO Manuel Fernandes da Costa SANTOS (POR)).
Goals: Lithuania: 1-1 Vytautas Andriuskevicius (28').
Portugal: 0-1 CRISTIANO RONALDO dos Santos Aveiro (7' penalty), 1-2 CRISTIANO
RONALDO dos Santos Aveiro (62'), 1-3 CRISTIANO RONALDO dos Santos Aveiro (65'),
1-4 CRISTIANO RONALDO dos Santos Aveiro (76'), 1-5 WILLIAM Silva de CARVALHO
(90+2').
Referee: Bas Nijhuis (HOL)   Attendance: 5.067

10-09-2019   Stade Josy Barthel, Luxembourg: Luxembourg – Serbia 1-3 (0-1)
Luxembourg: Anthony Moris, Lars Gerson, Maxime Chanot, Laurent Jans, Dirk Carlson,
Oliver Thill, Danel Sinani (62' Daniël Alves da Mota), Vincent Thill (86' Aurélien Joachim),
Leandro Barreiro (YC36), Maurice Deville (YC32) (61' David Turpel), Gerson Rodrigues.
(Coach: Luc Holtz (LUX)).
Serbia: Marko Dmitrovic, Aleksandar Kolarov (YC53), Antonio Rukavina, Nikola
Maksimovic, Uros Spajic (YC56), Adem Ljajic, Luka Milivojevic, Aleksandar Katai (46'
Nemanja Radonjic), Sasa Lukic (61' Mijat Gacinovic), Sergej Milinkovic-Savic (79' Nemanja
Matic), Aleksandar Mitrovic (YC29). (Coach: Ljubisa Tumbakovic (SRB)).
Goals: Luxembourg: 1-2 David Turpel (66').
Serbia: 0-1 Aleksandar Mitrovic (36'), 0-2 Nemanja Radonjic (55'), 1-3 Aleksandar Mitrovic
(78').
Referee: Orel Grinfeld (ISR)   Attendance: 6.373

11-10-2019   Estádio José Alvalade, Lisbon: Portugal – Luxembourg 3-0 (1-0)
Portugal: RUI Pedro dos Santos PATRÍCIO, Képler Laveran Lima Ferreira "PEPE",
RAPHAËL Adelino José GUERREIRO, NÉLSON Cabral SEMEDO, RÚBEN Santos Gato
Alves DIAS, JOÃO Filipe Iria Santos MOUTINHO (90' RÚBEN Diogo da Silva NEVES),
DANILO Luís Hélio PEREIRA, BRUNO Miguel Borges FERNANDES, BERNARDO Mota
Veiga de Carvalho e SILVA (77' GONÇALO Manuel Gabchinho GUEDES), CRISTIANO
RONALDO dos Santos Aveiro, JOÃO FÉLIX Sequeira (88' JOÃO MÁRIO Naval da Costa
Eduardo). (Coach: FERNANDO Manuel Fernandes da Costa SANTOS (POR)).
Luxembourg: Anthony Moris, Lars Gerson, Maxime Chanot, Laurent Jans, Dirk Carlson,
Oliver Thill, Vincent Thill (88' Stefano Bensi), Leandro Barreiro (YC9), David Turpel (59'
Daniël Alves da Mota), Florian Bohnert (46' Danel Sinani), Gerson Rodrigues (YC71).
(Coach: Luc Holtz (LUX)).
Goals: Portugal: 1-0 BERNARDO Mota Veiga de Carvalho e SILVA (16'), 2-0 CRISTIANO
RONALDO dos Santos Aveiro (65'), 3-0 GONÇALO Manuel Gabchinho GUEDES (89').
Referee: Daniel Stefanski (POL)   Attendance: 47.305

11-10-2019   Oblasny SportKomplex Metalist, Kharkiv: Ukraine – Lithuania 2-0 (1-0)
Ukraine: Andriy Pyatov, Sergiy Krivtsov, Eduard Sobol, Oleksandr Zinchenko, Mykola
Matvienko, Marlos (59' Yevhen Konoplyanka), Taras Stepanenko (YC55) (73' Sergiy
Sydorchuk), Ruslan Malinovskiy, Sergiy Bolbat, Júnior Moraes, Andrey Yarmolenko (65'
Viktor Tsygankov). (Coach: Andriy Shevchenko (UKR)).
Lithuania: Vytautas Cerniauskas, Linas Klimavicius, Vytautas Andriuskevicius (62' Domantas
Simkus), Edvinas Girdvainis, Saulius Mikoliūnas, Artūras Zulpa (YC57), Arvydas Novikovas
(YC54), Ovidijus Verbickas, Modestas Vorobjovas, Paulius Golubickas (73' Justas Lasickas),
Karolis Laukzemis (77' Deivydas Matulevicius). (Coach: Valdas Urbonas (LTU)).
Goals: Ukraine: 1-0 Ruslan Malinovskiy (29'), 2-0 Ruslan Malinovskiy (58').
Referee: Harald Lechner (AUT)   Attendance: 32.500

14-10-2019   Vilniaus LFF stadionas, Vilnius: Lithuania –Serbia 1-2 (0-0)
Lithuania: Vytautas Cerniauskas, Linas Klimavicius, Edvinas Girdvainis, Rolandas Baravykas,
Saulius Mikoliūnas, Ovidijus Verbickas (56' Artūras Zulpa), Domantas Simkus, Modestas
Vorobjovas, Justas Lasickas, Paulius Golubickas (73' Donatas Kazlauskas (YC90+2)),
Deivydas Matulevicius (64' Karolis Laukzemis (YC90)). (Coach: Valdas Urbonas (LTU)).
Serbia: Marko Dmitrovic, Aleksandar Kolarov, Filip Mladenovic, Nemanja Miletic (I), Nikola
Milenkovic, Adem Ljajic (YC80) (85' Nemanja Gudelj), Luka Milivojevic (72' Sasa Lukic),
Filip Kostic (46' Mijat Gacinovic), Nemanja Radonjic, Nemanja Maksimovic, Aleksandar
Mitrovic. (Coach: Ljubisa Tumbakovic (SRB)).
Goals: Lithuania: 1-2 Donatas Kazlauskas (79').
Serbia: 0-1 Aleksandar Mitrovic (49'), 0-2 Aleksandar Mitrovic (53').
Referee: Pawel Raczkowski (POL)   Attendance: 2.787

14-10-2019   NSK Olimpiyskiy Stadium, Kiev: Ukraine – Portugal 2-1 (2-0)
Ukraine: Andriy Pyatov, Sergiy Krivtsov, Oleksandr Zinchenko (YC90+4), Mykola
Matvienko, Vitali Mykolenko (90+4' Igor Plastun), Marlos (63' Yevhen Konoplyanka), Taras
Stepanenko (YC26,YC72), Ruslan Malinovskiy, Oleksandr Karavaev, Andrey Yarmolenko
(YC47), Roman Yaremchuk (73' Viktor Kovalenko (YC90+5)). (Coach: Andriy Shevchenko
(UKR)).
Portugal: RUI Pedro dos Santos PATRÍCIO, Képler Laveran Lima Ferreira "PEPE" (YC26),
RAPHAËL Adelino José GUERREIRO, NÉLSON Cabral SEMEDO, RÚBEN Santos Gato
Alves DIAS (YC63), JOÃO Filipe Iria Santos MOUTINHO (56' BRUNO Miguel Borges
FERNANDES), DANILO Luís Hélio PEREIRA, JOÃO MÁRIO Naval da Costa Eduardo (68'
Armindo Tué Na Bangna "BRUMA"), GONÇALO Manuel Gabchinho GUEDES (46' JOÃO
FÉLIX Sequeira), BERNARDO Mota Veiga de Carvalho e SILVA, CRISTIANO RONALDO
dos Santos Aveiro. (Coach: FERNANDO Manuel Fernandes da Costa SANTOS (POR)).
Goals: Ukraine: 1-0 Roman Yaremchuk (6'), 2-0 Andrey Yarmolenko (27').
Portugal: 2-1 CRISTIANO RONALDO dos Santos Aveiro (72' penalty).
Referee: Anthony Taylor (ENG)   Attendance: 65.883

14-11-2019   Estádio Do Algarve, Faro/Loulé: Portugal – Lithuania 6-0 (2-0)
Portugal: RUI Pedro dos Santos PATRÍCIO, JOSÉ Miguel da Rocha FONTE, MÁRIO RUI
Silva Duarte, RICARDO Domingos Barbosa PEREIRA, RÚBEN Santos Gato Alves DIAS,
Luís Miguel Afonso Fernandes "PIZZI", RÚBEN Diogo da Silva NEVES, BRUNO Miguel
Borges FERNANDES (72' JOÃO Filipe Iria Santos MOUTINHO), BERNARDO Mota Veiga
de Carvalho e SILVA (66' Armindo Tué Na Bangna "BRUMA"), CRISTIANO RONALDO
dos Santos Aveiro (83' DIOGO "JOTA" José Teixeira da Silva), GONÇALO Mendes
PACIÊNCIA. (Coach: FERNANDO Manuel Fernandes da Costa SANTOS (POR)).
Lithuania: Ernestas Setkus, Markus Palionis (YC27), Vytautas Andriuskevicius, Edvinas
Girdvainis, Saulius Mikoliūnas (YC80), Mantas Kuklys (57' Deivydas Matulevicius), Arvydas
Novikovas, Fiodor Cernych (81' Donatas Kazlauskas), Vykintas Slivka, Domantas Simkus,
Paulius Golubickas (72' Justas Lasickas). (Coach: Valdas Urbonas (LTU)).
Goals: Portugal: 1-0 CRISTIANO RONALDO dos Santos Aveiro (7' penalty), 2-0
CRISTIANO RONALDO dos Santos Aveiro (22'), 3-0 Luís Miguel Afonso Fernandes
"PIZZI" (52'), 4-0 GONÇALO Mendes PACIÊNCIA (56'), 5-0 BERNARDO Mota Veiga de
Carvalho e SILVA (63'), 6-0 CRISTIANO RONALDO dos Santos Aveiro (65').
Referee: Ruddy Buquet (FRA)   Attendance: 18.534

14-11-2019   Stadion Rajko Mitic, Belgrade: Serbia – Luxembourg 3-2 (2-0)
Serbia: Marko Dmitrovic, Aleksandar Kolarov, Nikola Maksimovic, Filip Mladenovic, Nikola
Milenkovic, Adem Ljajic (79' Filip Djuricic), Luka Milivojevic, Sergej Milinkovic-Savic (62'
Nemanja Radonjic), Nemanja Maksimovic, Dusan Tadic (90+2' Sasa Lukic), Aleksandar
Mitrovic. (Coach: Ljubisa Tumbakovic (SRB)).
Luxembourg: Anthony Moris, Lars Gerson, Maxime Chanot, Laurent Jans, Tim Hall, Dirk
Carlson (YC51), Chris Philipps (46' Aldin Skenderovic), Oliver Thill (62' David Turpel),
Vincent Thill (YC38) (79' Danel Sinani), Maurice Deville, Gerson Rodrigues. (Coach: Luc
Holtz (LUX)).
Goals: Serbia: 1-0 Aleksandar Mitrovic (11'), 2-0 Aleksandar Mitrovic (43'), 3-1 Nemanja
Radonjic (70').
Luxembourg: 2-1 Gerson Rodrigues (54'), 3-2 David Turpel (75').
Referee: Serdar Gözübüyük (HOL)   Attendance: 1.560

*Serbia were ordered by UEFA to play this matche behind closed doors following racist
behaviour by the crowd during their home match against Montenegro.*

17-11-2019   Stade Josy Barthel, Luxembourg: Luxembourg – Portugal 0-2 (0-1)
Luxembourg: Anthony Moris, Lars Gerson, Maxime Chanot (YC16), Laurent Jans, Aldin
Skenderovic, Dirk Carlson, Vincent Thill (82' Aurélien Joachim), Leandro Barreiro (74' Danel
Sinani), Maurice Deville (YC7), David Turpel (59' Oliver Thill), Gerson Rodrigues. (Coach:
Luc Holtz (LUX)).
Portugal: RUI Pedro dos Santos PATRÍCIO, JOSÉ Miguel da Rocha FONTE, RAPHAËL
Adelino José GUERREIRO, RICARDO Domingos Barbosa PEREIRA, RÚBEN Santos Gato
Alves DIAS, Luís Miguel Afonso Fernandes "PIZZI" (62' JOÃO Filipe Iria Santos
MOUTINHO), DANILO Luís Hélio PEREIRA, BRUNO Miguel Borges FERNANDES (90'
RÚBEN Diogo da Silva NEVES), BERNARDO Mota Veiga de Carvalho e SILVA (YC70),
CRISTIANO RONALDO dos Santos Aveiro, ANDRÉ Miguel Valente da SILVA (71'
DIOGO "JOTA" José Teixeira da Silva). (Coach: FERNANDO Manuel Fernandes da Costa
SANTOS (POR)).
Goals: Portugal: 0-1 BRUNO Miguel Borges FERNANDES (39'), 0-2 CRISTIANO
RONALDO dos Santos Aveiro (86').
Referee: JESÚS GIL Manzano (ESP)   Attendance: 8.000

17-11-2019   Stadion Rajko Mitic, Belgrade: Serbia – Ukraine 2-2 (1-1)
Serbia: Predrag Rajkovic, Aleksandar Kolarov (YC84), Nikola Maksimovic, Milan Rodic,
Nikola Milenkovic, Adem Ljajic (69' Mijat Gacinovic), Nemanja Gudelj, Nemanja Radonjic
(YC34) (82' Sergej Milinkovic-Savic), Nemanja Maksimovic (76' Luka Milivojevic), Dusan
Tadic, Aleksandar Mitrovic. (Coach: Ljubisa Tumbakovic (SRB)).
Ukraine: Andriy Pyatov, Sergiy Krivtsov, Mykola Matvienko (YC8), Vitali Mykolenko, Sergiy
Sydorchuk, Ruslan Malinovskiy (88' Yevhen Shakhov), Oleksandr Karavaev, Viktor
Kovalenko (77' Volodymyr Shepeliev), Viktor Tsygankov (77' Artem Besedin), Andrey
Yarmolenko, Roman Yaremchuk (YC88). (Coach: Andriy Shevchenko (UKR)).
Goals: Serbia: 1-0 Dusan Tadic (9' penalty), 2-1 Aleksandar Mitrovic (56').
Ukraine: 1-1 Roman Yaremchuk (32'), 2-2 Artem Besedin (90+3').
Referee: Bobby Madden (SCO)   Attendance: 4.457

GROUP   C

21-03-2019	Rotterdam	Netherlands – Belarus	4-0 (2-0)
21-03-2019	Belfast	Northern Ireland – Estonia	2-0 (0-0)
24-03-2019	Amsterdam	Netherlands – Germany	2-3 (0-2)
24-03-2019	Belfast	Northern Ireland – Belarus	2-1 (1-1)
08-06-2019	Tallinn	Estonia – Northern Ireland	1-2 (1-0)
08-06-2019	Borosov	Belarus – Germany	0-2 (0-1)
11-06-2019	Borisov	Belarus – Northern Ireland	0-1 (0-0)
11-06-2019	Mainz	Germany – Estonia	8-0 (5-0)
06-09-2019	Tallinn	Estonia – Belarus	1-2 (0-0)
06-09-2019	Hamburg	Germany – Netherlands	2-4 (1-0)
09-09-2019	Tallinn	Estonia – Netherlands	0-4 (0-1)
09-09-2019	Belfast	Northern Ireland – Germany	0-2 (0-0)
10-10-2019	Minsk	Belarus – Estonia	0-0
10-10-2019	Rotterdam	Netherlands – Northern Ireland	3-1 (0-0)
13-10-2019	Minsk	Belarus – Netherlands	1-2 (0-2)
13-10-2019	Tallinn	Estonia – Germany	0-3 (0-0)
16-11-2019	Mönchengladbach	Germany – Belarus	4-0 (1-0)
16-11-2019	Belfast	Northern Ireland – Netherlands	0-0

| 19-11-2019 | Frankfurt | Germany – Northern Ireland | 6-1 (2-1) |
| 19-11-2019 | Amsterdam | Netherlands – Estonia | 5-0 (2-0) |

FINAL STANDING

Pos	Team	Pld	W	D	L	GF	GA	GD	Pts
1	Germany	8	7	0	1	30	7	+23	21
2	Netherlands	8	6	1	1	24	7	+17	19
3	Northern Ireland	8	4	1	3	9	13	-4	13
4	Belarus	8	1	1	6	4	16	-12	4
5	Estonia	8	0	1	7	2	26	-24	1

Germany and Netherlands qualified for final tournament.

21-03-2019   De Kuip, Rotterdam: Netherlands – Belarus 4-0 (2-0)
Netherlands: Jasper Cillessen, Daley Blind, Virgil van Dijk, Denzel Dumfries (68' Kenny Tete), Matthijs de Ligt, Georginio Wijnaldum, Marten de Roon (YC34) (46' Davy Pröpper), Frenkie de Jong, Ryan Babel (59' Quincy Promes), Memphis Depay, Steven Bergwijn. (Coach: Ronald Koeman (HOL)).
Belarus: Andrey Gorbunov, Denis Polyakov, Mikhail Sivakov, Igor Shitov, Aleksandr Martinovich, Anton Putilo (YC32), Igor Stasevich, Stanislav Dragun (YC30) (87' Denis Laptev), Ivan Maevski, Yuri Kovalev (79' Pavel Savitskiy), Nikolay Signevich (63' Anton Saroka). (Coach: Igor Kriushenko (BLS)).
Goals: Netherlands: 1-0 Menphis Depay (1'), 2-0 Georginio Wijnaldum (21'), 3-0 Memphis Depay (55' penalty), 4-0 Virgil van Dijk (86').
Referee: Davide Massa (ITA)   Attendance: 38.604

21-03-2019   Windsor Park, Belfast: Northern Ireland – Estonia 2-0 (0-0)
Northern Ireland: Bailey Peacock-Farrell, Jonny Evans, Craig Cathcart, Jamal Lewis, Steven Davis, Niall McGinn (84' Conor McLaughlin), Stuart Dallas, Paddy McNair, George Saville, Kyle Lafferty (76' Josh Magennis), Jordan Jones (81' Shane Ferguson). (Coach: Michael O'Neill (NIR)).
Estonia: Sergei Lepmets, Gert Kams, Joonas Tamm (YC35), Nikita Baranov, Karol Mets, Artur Pikk, Madis Vihmann, Artjom Dmitrijev (85' Rauno Sappinen), Mattias Käit, Henri Anier (76' Sergei Zenjov), Henrik Ojamaa (68' Konstantin Vassiljev). (Coach: Martin Reim (EST)).
Goals: Northern Ireland: 1-0 Niall McGinn (56'), 2-0 Steven Davis (75' penalty).
Referee: Ivan Bebek (CRO)   Attendance: 18.176

24-03-2019   Johan Cruijff ArenA, Amsterdam: Netherlands – Germany 2-3 (0-2)
Netherlands: Jasper Cillessen, Daley Blind (YC38), Virgil van Dijk, Denzel Dumfries, Matthijs de Ligt, Georginio Wijnaldum, Marten de Roon (90+1' Luuk de Jong), Frenkie de Jong, Ryan Babel (46' Steven Bergwijn), Memphis Depay, Quincy Promes. (Coach: Ronald Koeman (HOL)).
Germany: Manuel Neuer, Antonio Rüdiger, Niklas Süle, Matthias Ginter, Joshua Kimmich, Thilo Kehrer, Toni Kroos, Nico Schulz, Leon Goretzka (70' Ilkay Gündogan), Serge Gnabry (88' Marco Reus), Leroy Sané. (Coach: Joachim Löw (GER)).
Goals: Netherlands: 1-2 Matthijs de Ligt (48'), 2-2 Memphis Depay (63').
Germany: 0-1 Leroy Sané (15'), 0-2 Serge Gnabry (34'), 2-3 Nico Schulz (90').
Referee: JESÚS GIL Manzano (ESP)   Attendance: 51.694

24-03-2019   Windsor Park, Belfast: Northern Ireland – Belarus 2-1 (1-1)
Northern Ireland: Bailey Peacock-Farrell, Jonny Evans, Craig Cathcart, Jamal Lewis, Steven Davis, Niall McGinn (68' Josh Magennis), Stuart Dallas, Paddy McNair, George Saville, Kyle Lafferty (79' Liam Boyce), Jordan Jones (85' Shane Ferguson). (Coach: Michael O'Neill (NIR)).
Belarus: Andrey Klimovich, Mikhail Sivakov, Igor Shitov (73' Denis Polyakov), Aleksandr Martinovich, Maksim Volodko, Aliaksandr Hleb (66' Anton Putilo), Igor Stasevich, Stanislav Dragun, Ivan Maevski, Pavel Savitskiy (85' Pavel Nekhaychik), Denis Laptev (YC82). (Coach: Igor Kriushenko (BLS)).
Goals: Northern Ireland: 1-0 Jonny Evans (30'), 2-1 Josh Magennis (87').
Belarus: 1-1 Igor Stasevich (33').
Referee: Pawel Raczkowski (POL)   Attendance: 18.188

08-06-2019   A. Le Coq Arena, Tallinn: Estonia – Northern Ireland 1-2 (1-0)
Estonia: Sergei Lepmets (YC64), Taijo Teniste (85' Gert Kams), Karol Mets, Artur Pikk, Madis Vihmann, Artjom Dmitrijev, Konstantin Vassiljev, Vlasiy Sinyavskiy, Mattias Käit (84' Joonas Tamm), Sergei Zenjov, Rauno Sappinen (61' Erik Sorga). (Coach: Martin Reim (EST)).
Northern Ireland: Bailey Peacock-Farrell, Jonny Evans, Craig Cathcart, Michael Smith (64' Jordan Jones), Jamal Lewis, Steven Davis, Stuart Dallas, Paddy McNair, George Saville (YC60) (69' Josh Magennis), Liam Boyce (46' Conor Washington), Gavin Whyte. (Coach: Michael O'Neill (NIR)).
Goals: Estonia: 1-0 Konstantin Vassiljev (25').
Northern Ireland: 1-1 Conor Washington (77'), 1-2 Josh Magennis (80').
Referee: FÁBIO José Costa VERÍSSIMO (POR)   Attendance: 8.378

08-06-2019   Borisov Arena, Borisov: Belarus – Germany 0-2 (0-1)
Belarus: Alyaksandr Hutor, Denis Polyakov, Igor Shitov (YC77), Aleksandr Martinovich, Nikita Naumov, Maksim Volodko, Stanislav Dragun, Ivan Maevski, Yuri Kovalev (69' Mikhail Gordeychuk), Valeriy Gromyko (57' Nikita Korzun (YC90+4)), Denis Laptev (63' Maksim Skavysh). (Coach: Igor Kriushenko (BLS)).
Germany: Manuel Neuer, Niklas Süle, Matthias Ginter, Joshua Kimmich, Jonathan Tah, Lukas Klostermann, Ilkay Gündogan (81' Leon Goretzka), Nico Schulz, Serge Gnabry (71' Julian Draxler), Marco Reus (76' Julian Brandt), Leroy Sané. (Coach: Joachim Löw (GER)).
Goals: Germany: 0-1 Leroy Sané (13'), 0-2 Marco Reus (62').
Referee: Srdjan Jovanovic (SRB)   Attendance: 12.510

11-06-2019   Borisov Arena, Borisov: Belarus – Northern Ireland 0-1 (0-0)
Belarus: Alyaksandr Hutor, Denis Polyakov, Igor Shitov (71' Oleg Veretilo), Aleksandr Martinovich, Nikita Naumov, Pavel Nekhaychik, Igor Stasevich, Ivan Maevski, Nikita Korzun (YC35) (46' Sergey Kislyak), Yuri Kovalev, Yevgeniy Shikavka (58' Denis Laptev). (Coach: Igor Kriushenko (BLS)).
Northern Ireland: Bailey Peacock-Farrell, Jonny Evans (YC69), Craig Cathcart, Michael Smith, Jamal Lewis (YC57), Steven Davis, Corry Evans (69' George Saville), Paddy McNair, Josh Magennis (56' Stuart Dallas (YC90+2)), Conor Washington (72' Kyle Lafferty (YC83)), Jordan Jones. (Coach: Michael O'Neill (NIR)).
Goal: Northern Ireland: 0-1 Paddy McNair (86').
Referee: Harald Lechner (AUT)   Attendance: 5.250

401

11-06-2019   OPEL ARENA, Mainz: Germany – Estonia 8-0 (5-0)
Germany: Manuel Neuer, Niklas Süle, Matthias Ginter, Joshua Kimmich, Thilo Kehrer, Ilkay Gündogan (53' Julian Draxler), Nico Schulz (46' Marcel Halstenberg), Leon Goretzka, Serge Gnabry, Marco Reus (66' Timo Werner), Leroy Sané. (Coach: Joachim Löw (GER)).
Estonia: Sergei Lepmets, Taijo Teniste, Gert Kams, Joonas Tamm (YC25), Karol Mets, Artur Pikk, Madis Vihmann, Sander Puri, Artjom Dmitrijev (59' Mattias Käit), Konstantin Vassiljev (82' Vladislavs Kreida), Sergei Zenjov (71' Henrik Ojamaa). (Coach: Martin Reim (EST)).
Goals: Germany: 1-0 Marco Reus (10'), 2-0 Serge Gnabry (17'), 3-0 Leon Goretzka (20'), 4-0 Ilkay Gündogan (26' penalty), 5-0 Marco Reus (37'), 6-0 Serge Gnabry (62'), 7-0 Timo Werner (79'), 8-0 Leroy Sané (88').
Referee: Ali Palabiyik (TUR)   Attendance: 26.050

06-09-2019   A. Le Coq Arena, Tallinn: Estonia – Belarus 1-2 (0-0)
Estonia: Sergei Lepmets, Ragnar Klavan, Taijo Teniste, Joonas Tamm, Karol Mets, Artur Pikk, Konstantin Vassiljev (77' Artjom Dmitrijev), Mattias Käit, Sergei Zenjov, Henrik Ojamaa (86' Vlasiy Sinyavskiy), Erik Sorga (83' Rauno Sappinen). (Coach: Karel Voolaid (EST)).
Belarus: Alyaksandr Hutor, Sergey Politevich, Denis Polyakov, Sergey Matvejchik, Nikita Naumov (YC65), Igor Stasevich, Stanislav Dragun, Ivan Maevski, Yuri Kovalev (77' Maksim Skavysh), Evgeni Yablonski, Nikolay Signevich (64' Ivan Bakhar (YC66)). (Coach: Mikhail Markhel (BLS)).
Goals: Estonia: 1-1 Erik Sorga (54').
Belarus: 0-1 Nikita Naumov (48'), 1-2 Maksim Skavysh (90+2').
Referee: Alain Durieux (LUX)   Attendance: 7.314

06-09-2019   Volksparkstadion, Hamburg: Germany – Netherlands 2-4 (1-0)
Germany: Manuel Neuer, Niklas Süle, Matthias Ginter (84' Julian Brandt), Joshua Kimmich (YC35), Jonathan Tah, Lukas Klostermann, Toni Kroos, Nico Schulz, Serge Gnabry, Marco Reus (61' Ilkay Gündogan), Timo Werner (61' Kai Havertz). (Coach: Joachim Löw (GER)).
Netherlands: Jasper Cillessen, Daley Blind, Virgil van Dijk, Denzel Dumfries (58' Davy Pröpper), Matthijs de Ligt, Georginio Wijnaldum, Marten de Roon (YC49) (58' Donyell Malen), Frenkie de Jong (YC72), Ryan Babel (81' Nathan Aké), Memphis Depay (YC35), Quincy Promes. (Coach: Ronald Koeman (HOL)).
Goals: Germany: 1-0 Serge Gnabry (9'), 2-2 Toni Kroos (73' penalty).
Netherlands: 1-1 Frenkie de Jong (59'), 1-2 Jonathan Tah (66' *own goal*), 2-3 Donyell Malen (79'), 2-4 Georginio Wijnaldum (90+1).
Referee: Artur Soares Dias (POR)   Attendance: 51.299

09-09-2019   A. Le Coq Arena, Tallinn: Estonia – Netherlands 0-4 (0-1)
Estonia: Sergei Lepmets, Ragnar Klavan, Taijo Teniste (YC53), Ken Kallaste, Joonas Tamm (YC70), Karol Mets (YC86), Mihkel Ainsalu (87' Artjom Dmitrijev), Mattias Käit, Sergei Zenjov (60' Frank Liivak), Henrik Ojamaa (85' Rauno Sappinen), Erik Sorga. (Coach: Karel Voolaid (EST)).
Netherlands: Jasper Cillessen, Daley Blind, Joël Veltman (YC73),Virgil van Dijk, Matthijs de Ligt, Georginio Wijnaldum, Davy Pröpper, Frenkie de Jong (71' Luuk de Jong), Ryan Babel (84' Kevin Strootman), Memphis Depay, Donyell Malen (63' Steven Berghuis). (Coach: Ronald Koeman (HOL)).
Goals: Netherlands: 0-1 Ryan Babel (17'), 0-2 Ryan Babel (47'), 0-3 Memphis Depay (76'), 0-4 Georginio Wijnaldum (87').
Referee: Serhiy Mykolayovych Boyko (UKR)   Attendance: 11.006

402

09-09-2019   Windsor Park, Belfast: Northern Ireland – Germany 0-2 (0-0)
Northern Ireland: Bailey Peacock-Farrell, Jonny Evans, Craig Cathcart, Jamal Lewis, Steven
Davis, Niall McGinn (59' Gavin Whyte), Corry Evans, Stuart Dallas, Paddy McNair (YC43),
George Saville (YC55) (70' Josh Magennis), Conor Washington (83' Shayne Lavery). (Coach:
Michael O'Neill (NIR)).
Germany: Manuel Neuer, Marcel Halstenberg, Niklas Süle, Matthias Ginter (40' Jonathan
Tah), Joshua Kimmich, Lukas Klostermann, Toni Kroos, Serge Gnabry (YC67), Marco Reus
(85' Emre Can), Julian Brandt, Timo Werner (68' Kai Havertz). (Coach: Joachim Löw (GER)).
Goals: Germany: 0-1 Marcel Halstenberg (48'), 0-2 Serge Gnabry (90+3').
Referee: Daniele Orsato (ITA)   Attendance: 18.326

10-10-2019   Stadyen Dynama, Minsk: Belarus – Estonia 0-0
Belarus: Alyaksandr Hutor, Sergey Politevich (YC41), Denis Polyakov, Sergey Matvejchik,
Aleksandr Martinovich, Igor Stasevich, Stanislav Dragun, Ivan Maevski, Pavel Savitskiy (59'
Ivan Bakhar), Evgeni Yablonski (83' Vitaly Lisakovich), Maksim Skavysh (64' Denis Laptev).
(Coach: Mikhail Markhel (BLS)).
Estonia: Sergei Lepmets, Taijo Teniste, Ken Kallaste, Nikita Baranov, Karol Mets, Konstantin
Vassiljev, Mattias Käit, Vladislavs Kreida, Sergei Zenjov (59' Frank Liivak (YC82)), Henrik
Ojamaa (89' Martin Miller), Erik Sorga (80' Rauno Sappinen). (Coach: Karel Voolaid (EST)).
Referee: RICARDO DE BURGOS Bengoetxea (ESP) Attendance: 11.300

10-10-2019   De Kuip, Rotterdam: Netherlands – Northern Ireland 3-1 (0-0)
Netherlands: Jasper Cillessen, Daley Blind, Virgil van Dijk, Denzel Dumfries (78' Luuk de
Jong), Matthijs de Ligt, Georginio Wijnaldum, Marten de Roon (66' Donny van de Beek),
Frenkie de Jong, Ryan Babel (66' Donyell Malen), Memphis Depay, Steven Bergwijn. (Coach:
Ronald Koeman (HOL)).
Northern Ireland: Bailey Peacock-Farrell (YC53), Jonny Evans (YC60), Craig Cathcart,
Michael Smith (YC67), Steven Davis, Corry Evans (87' Tom Flanagan), Shane Ferguson,
Stuart Dallas, Paddy McNair, George Saville (83' Jordan Thompson), Kyle Lafferty (66' Josh
Magennis). (Coach: Michael O'Neill (NIR)).
Goals: Netherlands: 1-1 Memphis Depay (80'), 2-1 Luuk de Jong (90+1'), 3-1 Memphis Depay
(90+4').
Northern Ireland: 0-1 Josh Magennis (75').
Referee: Benoît Bastien (FRA)   Attendance: 41.348

13-10-2019   Stadyen Dynama, Minsk: Belarus – Netherlands 1-2 (0-2)
Belarus: Alyaksandr Hutor, Denis Polyakov, Oleg Veretilo, Aleksandr Martinovich (YC62),
Nikita Naumov (YC90+1), Igor Stasevich (YC57), Stanislav Dragun, Yuri Kovalev (60'
Maksim Skavysh), Evgeni Yablonski (YC69), Ivan Bakhar (YC50) (70' Max Ebong Ngome),
Denis Laptev (Evgeni Shevchenko). (Coach: Mikhail Markhel (BLS)).
Netherlands: Jasper Cillessen, Daley Blind, Joël Veltman, Virgil van Dijk, Matthijs de Ligt,
Georginio Wijnaldum, Donny van de Beek (67' Marten de Roon), Frenkie de Jong, Quincy
Promes (67' Luuk de Jong), Steven Bergwijn (89' Ryan Babel), Donyell Malen. (Coach:
Ronald Koeman (HOL)).
Goals: Belarus: 1-2 Stanislav Dragun (53').
Netherlands: 0-1 Georginio Wijnaldum (32), 0-2 Georginio Wijnaldum (41').
Referee: Anastasios Sidiropoulos (GRE)   Attendance: 21.639

13-10-2019   A. Le Coq Arena, Tallinn: Estonia – Germany 0-3 (0-0)
Estonia: Sergei Lepmets (YC30), Gert Kams, Joonas Tamm, Nikita Baranov (YC38), Karol
Mets, Artur Pikk, Konstantin Vassiljev (61' Mattias Käit), Ilja Antonov, Mihkel Ainsalu,
Rauno Sappinen (56' Sergei Zenjov), Frank Liivak (77' Henrik Ojamaa). (Coach: Karel
Voolaid (EST)).
Germany: Manuel Neuer, Marcel Halstenberg, Niklas Süle, Joshua Kimmich, Lukas
Klostermann, Ilkay Gündogan, Emre Can (RC14), Kai Havertz, Marco Reus (77' Suat Serdar),
Julian Brandt (86' Nadiem Amiri), Luca Waldschmidt (66' Timo Werner). (Coach: Joachim
Löw (GER)).
Goals: Germany: 0-1 Ilkay Gündogan (51'), 0-2 Ilkay Gündogan (57'), 0-3 Timo Werner (71').
Referee: Georgi Kabakov (BUL)   Attendance: 12.062

16-11-2019   Stadion im BORUSSIA-PARK, Mönchengladbach:
               Germany – Belarus 4-0 (1-0)
Germany: Manuel Neuer, Matthias Ginter, Joshua Kimmich, Lukas Klostermann, Robin Koch
(YC75), Toni Kroos, Ilkay Gündogan, Nico Schulz, Leon Goretzka, Serge Gnabry (84' Luca
Waldschmidt, 90+1' Sebastian Rudy), Timo Werner (68' Julian Brandt). (Coach: Joachim Löw
(GER)).
Belarus: Alyaksandr Hutor, Denis Polyakov, Sergey Matvejchik, Aleksandr Martinovich,
Nikita Naumov, Pavel Nekhaychik (84' Dmitry Bessmertny), Igor Stasevich, Stanislav
Dragun, Ivan Maevski, Yuri Kovalev (78' Maksim Skavysh), Denis Laptev (68' Vitaly
Lisakovich). (Coach: Mikhail Markhel (BLS)).
Goals: Germany: 1-0 Matthias Ginter (41'), 2-0 Leon Goretzka (49'), 3-0 Toni Kroos (55'),
4-0 Toni Kroos (83).
Referee: Orel Grinfeld (ISR)   Attendance: 33.164
(Igor Stasevich missed a penalty kick in the 75th minute)

16-11-2019   Windsor Park, Belfast: Northern Ireland – Netherlands 0-0
Northern Ireland: Bailey Peacock-Farrell, Jonny Evans, Craig Cathcart, Jamal Lewis (81'
Jordan Thompson), Steven Davis (YC40), Corry Evans (70' Niall McGinn), Stuart Dallas
(YC84), Paddy McNair, George Saville (58' Michael Smith), Josh Magennis, Gavin Whyte.
(Coach: Michael O'Neill (NIR)).
Netherlands: Jasper Cillessen, Daley Blind, Joël Veltman (YC30), Virgil van Dijk, Matthijs de
Ligt, Marten de Roon (YC11) (36' Davy Pröpper), Donny van de Beek, Frenkie de Jong, Ryan
Babel (90' Nathan Aké), Steven Berghuis (65' Luuk de Jong), Quincy Promes. (Coach: Ronald
Koeman (HOL)).
Referee: Szymon Marciniak (POL)   Attendance: 18.404
(Steven Davis missed a penalty kick in the 32nd minute)

19-11-2019   Commerzbank-Arena, Frankfurt am Main:
Germany – Northern Ireland 6-1 (2-1)
Germany: Marc-André ter Stegen, Joshua Kimmich, Jonathan Tah, Lukas Klostermann (65'
Niklas Stark), Toni Kroos, Ilkay Gündogan, Jonas Hector, Emre Can, Leon Goretzka (73' Suat
Serdar), Serge Gnabry (80' Nadiem Amiri), Julian Brandt. (Coach: Joachim Löw (GER)).
Northern Ireland: Bailey Peacock-Farrell, Craig Cathcart, Michael Smith, Tom Flanagan,
Steven Davis, Corry Evans (65' Conor McLaughlin), Shane Ferguson, Paddy McNair (77'
Liam Boyce), George Saville, Jordan Thompson, Josh Magennis (83' Shayne Lavery). (Coach:
Michael O'Neill (NIR)).
Goals: Germany: 1-1 Serge Gnabry (19'), 2-1 Leon Goretzka (43'), 3-1 Serge Gnabry (47'),
4-1 Serge Gnabry (60'), 5-1 Leon Goretzka (73'), 6-1 Julian Brandt (90+1').
Northern Ireland: 0-1 Michael Smith (7').
Referee: CARLOS DEL CERRO Grande (ESP)   Attendance: 42.855

19-11-2019   Johan Cruijff ArenA, Amsterdam: Netherlands – Estonia 5-0 (2-0)
Netherlands: Jasper Cillessen, Patrick van Aanholt, Nathan Aké, Matthijs de Ligt, Georginio
Wijnaldum, Davy Pröpper, Frenkie de Jong (75' Kevin Strootman), Luuk de Jong (63' Wout
Weghorst), Memphis Depay (46' Myron Boadu), Quincy Promes, Calvin Stengs. (Coach:
Ronald Koeman (HOL)).
Estonia: Sergei Lepmets, Taijo Teniste (61' Nikita Baranov), Ken Kallaste, Joonas Tamm,
Karol Mets, Konstantin Vassiljev, Ilja Antonov, Mihkel Ainsalu, Sergei Zenjov (76' Frank
Liivak), Henrik Ojamaa (83' Mattias Käit), Erik Sorga. (Coach: Karel Voolaid (EST)).
Goals: Netherlands: 1-0 Georginio Wijnaldum (6'), 2-0 Nathan Aké (19'), 3-0 Georginio
Wijnaldum (66'), 4-0 Georginio Wijnaldum (79'), 5-0 Myron Boadu (87').
Referee: Davide Massa (ITA)   Attendance: 50.386

GROUP   D

23-03-2019	Tbilisi	Georgia – Switzerland	0-2 (0-0)
23-03-2019	Gibraltar	Gibraltar – Republic of Ireland	0-1 (0-0)
26-03-2019	Dublin	Republic of Ireland – Georgia	1-0 (1-0)
26-03-2019	Basel	Switzerland – Denmark	3-3 (1-0)
07-06-2019	Tbilisi	Georgia – Gibraltar	3-0 (1-0)
07-06-2019	Copenhagen	Denmark – Republic of Ireland	1-1 (0-0)
10-06-2019	Copenhagen	Denmark – Georgia	5-1 (2-1)
10-06-2019	Dublin	Republic of Ireland – Gibraltar	2-0 (1-0)
05-09-2019	Gibraltar	Gibraltar – Denmark	0-6 (0-2)
05-09-2019	Dublin	Republic of Ireland – Switzerland	1-1 (0-0)
08-09-2019	Tbilisi	Georgia – Denmark	0-0
08-09-2019	Sion	Switzerland – Gibraltar	4-0 (3-0)
12-10-2019	Tbilisi	Georgia – Republic of Ireland	0-0
12-10-2019	Copenhagen	Denmark – Switzerland	1-0 (0-0)
15-10-2019	Gibraltar	Gibraltar – Georgia	2-3 (0-2)
15-10-2019	Geneva	Switzerland – Republic of Ireland	2-0 (1-0)
15-11-2019	Copenhagen	Denmark – Gibraltar	6-0 (1-0)
15-11-2019	St. Gallen	Switzerland – Georgia	1-0 (0-0)
18-11-2019	Gibraltar	Gibraltar – Switzerland	1-6 (0-1)
18-11-2019	Dublin	Republic of Ireland – Denmark	1-1 (0-0)

405

FINAL STANDING

Pos	Team	Pld	W	D	L	GF	GA	GD	Pts
1	Switzerland	8	5	2	1	19	6	+13	17
2	Denmark	8	4	4	0	23	6	+17	16
3	Republic of Ireland	8	3	4	1	7	5	+2	13
4	Georgia	8	2	2	4	7	11	-4	8
5	Gibraltar	8	0	0	8	3	31	-28	0

Switzerland and Denmark qualified for final tournament.

23-03-2019   Boris Paichadze Dinamo Arena, Tbilisi: Georgia – Switzerland 0-2 (0-0)
Georgia: Giorgi Loria, Guram Kashia, Davit Khocholava (YC76), Otar Kakabadze, Jemal
Tabidze (62' Solomon Kverkvelia), Jaba Kankava, Jano Ananidze (83' Nika Kacharava), Nika
Kvekveskiri (YC70), Valeri Qazaishvili, Valeriane Gvilia (YC90+2), Giorgi Kvilitaia (73'
Saba Lobzhanidze) (Coach: Vladimir Weiss (SVK)).
Switzerland: Yann Sommer, Stephan Lichtsteiner, Ricardo Rodríguez, Fabian Schär, Manuel
Akanji, Steven Zuber, Granit Xhaka (YC89), Remo Freuler (89' Djibril Sow), Denis Zakaria,
Mario Gavranovic (61' Albian Ajeti), Breel Embolo (84' Renato Steffen). (Coach: Vladimir
Petkovic (BIH)).
Goals: Switzerland: 0-1 Steven Zuber (56'), 0-2 Denis Zakaria (80').
Referee: Craig Pawson (ENG)   Attendance: 49.207

23-03-2019   Victoria Stadium, Gibraltar: Gibraltar – Republic of Ireland 0-1 (0-0)
Gibraltar: Kyle Goldwin, Joseph Chipolina, Jayce Mascarenhas-Olivero, Roy Chipolina, Louie
Annesley (64' Adam Priestley), Liam Walker, Jack Sergeant, Anthony Bardon, Anthony
Hernandez (78' Alain Pons), Lee Casciaro (YC41), Tlay De Barr (YC90+2). (Coach: JULIO
César RIBAS Vlahovic (URU)).
Republic of Ireland: Darren Randolph, Séamus Coleman, Richard Keogh, Enda Stevens
(YC67), Shane Duffy, Matt Doherty (56' Robbie Brady), Conor Hourihane, James McClean
(YC45+1), Jeff Hendrick, David McGoldrick, Seán Maguire (73' Harry Arter). (Coach: Mick
McCarthy (IRL)).
Goal: Republic of Ireland: 0-1 Jeff Hendrick (49').
Referee: Anastasios Papapetrou (GRE)   Attendance: 2.000

26-03-2019   Aviva Stadium, Dublin: Republic of Ireland – Georgia 1-0 (1-0)
Republic of Ireland: Darren Randolph, Séamus Coleman, Richard Keogh, Enda Stevens, Shane
Duffy, Glenn Whelan, Conor Hourihane, James McClean, Robbie Brady (74' Aiden O'Brien),
Jeff Hendrick, David McGoldrick (82' Matt Doherty). (Coach: Mick McCarthy (IRL)).
Georgia: Giorgi Loria, Guram Kashia (YC33), Solomon Kverkvelia, Davit Khocholava (65'
Levan Kharabadze), Otar Kakabadze (85' Tornike Okriashvili), Jaba Kankava (YC14), Nika
Kvekveskiri, Vato Arveladze (73' Valeri Qazaishvili), Otar Kiteishvili, Valeriane Gvilia,
Giorgi Kvilitaia. (Coach: Vladimir Weiss (SVK)).
Goal: Republic of Ireland: 1-0 Conor Hourihane (36').
Referee: Serdar Gözübüyük (HOL)   Attendance: 40.317

26-03-2019   St. Jakob-Park, Basel: Switzerland – Denmark 3-3 (1-0)
Switzerland: Yann Sommer, Ricardo Rodríguez (46' Loris Benito), Kevin Mbabu, Nico
Elvedi, Manuel Akanji (YC90+1), Steven Zuber, Granit Xhaka (79' Djibril Sow), Remo
Freuler, Denis Zakaria (YC59), Albian Ajeti (71' Admir Mehmedi), Breel Embolo (YC90+4).
(Coach: Vladimir Petkovic (BIH)).
Denmark: Kasper Schmeichel, S Kjær, Mathias Jørgensen "Zanka", Henrik Dalsgaard, Jens
Stryger Larsen, Lasse Schöne (70' Pierre-Emile Højbjerg), Thomas Delaney, Christian
Eriksen, Nicolai Jørgensen (YC38) (70' Christian Gytkjær), Martin Braithwaite, Yussuf
Poulsen. (Coach: Åge Hareide (NOR)).
Goals: Switzerland: 1-0 Remo Freuler (19'), 2-0 Granit Xhaka (66'), 3-0 Breel Embolo (76').
Denmark: 3-1 Mathias Jørgensen "Zanka" (84'), 3-2 Christian Gytkjær (88'), 3-3 Henrik
Dalsgaard (90+3).
Referee: Damir Skomina (SLO)   Attendance: 18.352

07-06-2019   Boris Paichadze Dinamo Arena, Tbilisi: Georgia – Gibraltar 3-0 (1-0)
Georgia: Giorgi Loria, Gia Grigalava, Guram Kashia, Otar Kakabadze, Levan Kharabadze,
Jaba Kankava (YC45) (77' Levan Mchedlidze), Giorgi Merebashvili (72' Otar Kiteishvili),
Nika Kvekveskiri, Vato Arveladze, Valeriane Gvilia, Khvicha Kvaratskhelia (47' Giorgi
Papunashvili). (Coach: Vladimir Weiss (SVK)).
Gibraltar: Kyle Goldwin, Joseph Chipolina, Jayce Mascarenhas-Olivero (YC62), Roy
Chipolina (YC75), Louie Annesley (86' Erin Barnett), Liam Walker, Jack Sergeant (YC50),
Anthony Bardon (77' James Coombes), Anthony Hernandez, Lee Casciaro (65' Alain Pons),
Tlay De Barr. (Coach: JULIO César RIBAS Vlahovic (URU)).
Goals: Goergia: 1-0 Valeriane Gvilia (30'), 2-0 Giorgi Papunashvili (59'), 3-0 Vato Arveladze
(76' penalty).
Referee: Antti Munukka (FIN)   Attendance: 18.631

07-06-2019   Telia Parken, Copenhagen: Denmark – Republic of Ireland 1-1 (0-0)
Denmark: Kasper Schmeichel, Simon Kjær, Henrik Dalsgaard, Jens Stryger Larsen, Andreas
Christensen, Lasse Schöne (72' Pierre-Emile Højbjerg), Thomas Delaney, Christian Eriksen,
Nicolai Jørgensen, Martin Braithwaite (65' Kasper Dolberg), Yussuf Poulsen. (Coach: Åge
Hareide (NOR)).
Republic of Ireland: Darren Randolph, Séamus Coleman, Richard Keogh, Enda Stevens, Shane
Duffy, Glenn Whelan, Conor Hourihane (YC30) (82' Scott Hogan), James McClean, Robbie
Brady (66' Alan Judge), Jeff Hendrick, David McGoldrick (88' Callum Robinson). (Coach:
Mick McCarthy (IRL)).
Goals: Denmark: 1-0 Pierre-Emile Højbjerg (76').
Republic of Ireland: 1-1 Shane Duffy (85').
Referee: Cüneyt Çakir (TUR)   Attendance: 34.610

10-06-2019   Telia Parken, Copenhagen: Denmark – Georgia 5-1 (2-1)
Denmark: Kasper Schmeichel, Simon Kjær (36' Mathias Jørgensen "Zanka"), Jens Stryger Larsen, Peter Ankersen, Andreas Christensen, Thomas Delaney, Christian Eriksen, Pierre-Emile Højbjerg, Robert Skov (62' Daniel Wass), Yussuf Poulsen (75' Martin Braithwaite), Kasper Dolberg. (Coach: Åge Hareide (NOR)).
Georgia: Giorgi Loria, Giorgi Navalovski (79' Lasha Dvali), Gia Grigalava, Guram Kashia, Otar Kakabadze, Jaba Kankava (YC29), Nika Kvekveskiri (YC51), Lasha Parunashvili (58' Giorgi Papunashvili (YC65)), Saba Lobzhanidze, Otar Kiteishvili (74' Elguja Lobjanidze), Valeriane Gvilia (YC54). (Coach: Vladimir Weiss (SVK)).
Goals: Denmark: 1-0 Kasper Dolberg (13'), 2-1 Christian Eriksen (30' penalty), 3-1 Kasper Dolberg (63'), 4-1 Yussuf Poulsen (73'), 5-1 Martin Braithwaite (90+3').
Georgia: 1-1 Saba Lobzhanidze (25').
Referee: Robert Schörgenhofer (AUT)   Attendance: 15.387

10-06-2019   Aviva Stadium, Dublin: Republic of Ireland – Gibraltar 2-0 (1-0)
Republic of Ireland: Darren Randolph, Séamus Coleman, Richard Keogh, Enda Stevens (YC68), Shane Duffy, Conor Hourihane, James McClean, Jeff Hendrick, David McGoldrick, Scott Hogan (66' Seán Maguire), Callum Robinson (73' Robbie Brady). (Coach: Mick McCarthy (IRL)).
Gibraltar: Kyle Goldwin, Joseph Chipolina, Jayce Mascarenhas-Olivero (YC25), Roy Chipolina, Louie Annesley, Liam Walker, Alain Pons (64' Ethan Britto), Jack Sergeant, Andrew Hernandez (77' Ethan Jolley), Lee Casciaro (10' Anthony Bardon), Tlay De Barr. (Coach: JULIO César RIBAS Vlahovic (URU)).
Goals: Republic of Ireland: 1-0 Joseph Chipolina (29' own goal), 2-0 Robbie Brady (90+3').
Referee: Radu Petrescu (ROM)   Attendance: 36.281

05-09-2019   Victoria Stadium, Gibraltar: Gibraltar – Denmark 0-6 (0-2)
Gibraltar: Dayle Coleing, Joseph Chipolina, Jayce Mascarenhas-Olivero, Roy Chipolina, Ethan Britto (46' Alain Pons), Louie Annesley (46' Erin Barnett), Liam Walker, Jack Sergeant (83' Ethan Jolley), Andrew Hernandez (YC49), Anthony Hernandez, Tlay De Barr. (Coach: JULIO César RIBAS Vlahovic (URU)).
Denmark: Kasper Schmeichel, Simon Kjær (YC42) (63' Mathias Jørgensen "Zanka"), Jens Stryger Larsen, Andreas Christensen, Daniel Wass, Thomas Delaney (77' Lasse Schöne), Christian Eriksen, Pierre-Emile Højbjerg, Robert Skov, Christian Gytkjær, Yussuf Poulsen (64' Martin Braithwaite). (Coach: Åge Hareide (NOR)).
Goals: Denmark: 0-1 Robert Skov (6'), 0-2 Christian Eriksen (34' penalty), 0-3 Christian Eriksen (50' penalty), 0-4 Thomas Delaney (69'), 0-5 Christian Gytkjær (73'), 0-6 Christian Gytkjær (78').
Referee: Jonathan Lardot (BEL)   Attendance: 2.076

05-09-2019   Aviva Stadium, Dublin: Republic of Ireland – Switzerland 1-1 (0-0)
Republic of Ireland: Darren Randolph, Séamus Coleman, Richard Keogh, Enda Stevens (YC15), Shane Duffy (YC90+6), Glenn Whelan, Conor Hourihane (82' Scott Hogan), James McClean, Jeff Hendrick, David McGoldrick (90+2' Alan Browne), Callum Robinson (58' Alan Judge (YC90+1)). (Coach: Mick McCarthy (IRL)).
Switzerland: Yann Sommer, Ricardo Rodríguez, Fabian Schär (YC90+6), Kevin Mbabu (YC76) (90+4' Edimilson Fernandes), Nico Elvedi, Manuel Akanji, Granit Xhaka, Remo Freuler (90' Admir Mehmedi), Denis Zakaria, Haris Seferovic, Breel Embolo (86' Albian Ajeti). (Coach: Vladimir Petkovic (BIH)).
Goals: Republic of Ireland: 1-1 David McGoldrick (85').
Switzerland: 0-1 Fabian Schär (74').

Referee: CARLOS DEL CERRO Grande (ESP)   Attendance: 44.111
08-09-2019   Boris Paichadze Dinamo Arena, Tbilisi: Georgia – Denmark 0-0
Georgia: Giorgi Loria, Gia Grigalava (YC42), Guram Kashia, Otar Kakabadze (YC89), Jemal Tabidze, Jano Ananidze, Tornike Okriashvili, Valeri Qazaishvili, Giorgi Aburjania (86' Valeriane Gvilia), Otar Kiteishvili, Giorgi Kvilitaia (90' Murtaz Daushvili). (Coach: Vladimir Weiss (SVK)).
Denmark: Kasper Schmeichel, Simon Kjær, Henrik Dalsgaard, Jens Stryger Larsen, Andreas Christensen, Thomas Delaney, Christian Eriksen, Pierre-Emile Højbjerg (73' Lasse Schöne (YC87)), Martin Braithwaite, Yussuf Poulsen, Kasper Dolberg (67' Christian Gytkjær). (Coach: Åge Hareide (NOR)).
Referee: François Letexier (FRA)   Attendance: 21.456

08-09-2019   Stade de Tourbillon, Sion: Switzerland – Gibraltar 4-0 (3-0)
Switzerland: Yann Sommer, Ricardo Rodríguez, Fabian Schär, Loris Benito (65' Renato Steffen), Nico Elvedi, Admir Mehmedi, Granit Xhaka (74' Ruben Vargas), Edimilson Fernandes, Denis Zakaria, Albian Ajeti, Breel Embolo (55' Mario Gavranovic). (Coach: Vladimir Petkovic (BIH)).
Gibraltar: Dayle Coleing (25' Kyle Goldwin), Joseph Chipolina (YC69), Jayce Mascarenhas-Olivero, Roy Chipolina, Ethan Britto (67' Alain Pons), Louie Annesley, Liam Walker, Jack Sergeant, Andrew Hernandez (58' James Coombes), Anthony Hernandez, Tlay De Barr. (Coach: JULIO César RIBAS Vlahovic (URU)).
Goals: Switzerland: 1-0 Denis Zakaria (37'), 2-0 Admir Mehmedi (43'), 3-0 Ricardo Rodríguez (45+4'), 4-0 Mario Gavranovic (87').
Referee: Pavel Orel (CZE)   Attendance: 8.318

12-10-2019   Boris Paichadze Dinamo Arena, Tbilisi: Georgia – Republic of Ireland 0-0
Georgia: Giorgi Loria, Gia Grigalava (YC87), Guram Kashia, Otar Kakabadze, Jemal Tabidze, Jaba Kankava, Jano Ananidze, Tornike Okriashvili (79' Elguja Lobjanidze), Valeri Qazaishvili, Otar Kiteishvili (90' Giorgi Aburjania), Giorgi Kvilitaia (73' Levan Shengelia). (Coach: Vladimir Weiss (SVK)).
Republic of Ireland: Darren Randolph, Séamus Coleman, Shane Duffy, John Egan, Matt Doherty, Glenn Whelan (YC65), Conor Hourihane (90+3' Derrick Williams), James McClean, Jeff Hendrick, James Collins (79' Aaron Connolly), Callum Robinson (73' Alan Browne). (Coach: Mick McCarthy (IRL)).
Referee: Marco Guida (ITA)   Attendance: 24.385

12-10-2019   Telia Parken, Copenhagen: Denmark – Switzerland 1-0 (0-0)
Denmark: Kasper Schmeichel, Simon Kjær, Henrik Dalsgaard (YC90+2), Jens Stryger Larsen (80' Peter Ankersen), Andreas Christensen (87' Mathias Jørgensen "Zanka"), Lasse Schöne (65' Pierre-Emile Højbjerg), Thomas Delaney, Christian Eriksen, Martin Braithwaite, Yussuf Poulsen (YC6), Andreas Cornelius. (Coach: Åge Hareide (NOR)).
Switzerland: Yann Sommer, Stephan Lichtsteiner (YC2) (68' Kevin Mbabu), Ricardo Rodríguez (YC76) (88' Josip Drmic), Fabian Schär, Nico Elvedi, Manuel Akanji, Admir Mehmedi (83' Remo Freuler), Granit Xhaka, Denis Zakaria (YC36), Haris Seferovic, Breel Embolo. (Coach: Vladimir Petkovic (BIH)).
Goal: Denmark: 1-0 Yussuf Poulsen (84').
Referee: Aleksei Kulbakov (BLS)   Attendance: 35.964

15-10-2019   Victoria Stadium, Gibraltar: Gibraltar – Georgia 2-3 (0-2)
Gibraltar: Kyle Goldwin, Joseph Chipolina (82' Erin Barnett), Aymen Mouelhi, Jayce
Mascarenhas-Olivero, Roy Chipolina, Ethan Britto, Liam Walker (90' Alain Pons), Jack
Sergeant (YC56), Mohamed Badr Hassan (YC45+1) (81' Andrew Hernandez), Lee Casciaro,
Tlay De Barr. (Coach: JULIO César RIBAS Vlahovic (URU)).
Georgia: Giorgi Loria, Giorgi Navalovski (90+3' Solomon Kverkvelia), Gia Grigalava, Davit
Khocholava (YC49), Otar Kakabadze, Jaba Kankava, Jano Ananidze, Valeri Qazaishvili,
Levan Shengelia, Elguja Lobjanidze (68' Giorgi Kvilitaia), Giorgi Kharaishvili (61' Otar
Kiteishvili). (Coach: Vladimir Weiss (SVK)).
iorgiGoals: Gibraltar: 1-2 Lee Casciaro (66'), 2-2 Roy Chipolina (74').
Georgia: 0-1 G Kharaishvili (10'), 0-2 Jaba Kankava (21'), 2-3 Giorgi Kvilitaia (84').
Referee: Paolo Valeri (ITA)   Attendance: 1.455

15-10-2019   Stade de Genève, Geneva: Switzerland – Republic of Ireland 2-0 (1-0)
Switzerland: Yann Sommer, Stephan Lichtsteiner (70' Remo Freuler), Ricardo Rodríguez,
Fabian Schär, Nico Elvedi, Manuel Akanji (YC46), Admir Mehmedi (28' Edimilson
Fernandes), Granit Xhaka (YC32), Denis Zakaria, Haris Seferovic, Breel Embolo (88' Renato
Steffen). (Coach: Vladimir Petkovic (BIH)).
Republic of Ireland: Darren Randolph, Séamus Coleman (YC32,YC76), Enda Stevens, Shane
Duffy (YC66), John Egan, Glenn Whelan, James McClean, Jeff Hendrick (YC55), Alan
Browne (YC34), James Collins (46' Callum O'Dowda), Aaron Connolly (69' Scott Hogan).
(Coach: Mick McCarthy (IRL)).
Goals: Switzerland: 1-0 Haris Seferovic (16'), 2-0 Edimilson Fernandes (90+3').
Referee: Szymon Marciniak (POL)   Attendance: 24.766
(Ricardo Rodríguez missed a penalty kick in the 77th minute)

15-11-2019   Telia Parken, Copenhagen: Denmark – Gilbraltar 6-0 (1-0)
Denmark: Kasper Schmeichel, Simon Kjær, Mathias Jørgensen "Zanka", Jens Stryger Larsen
(78' Andreas Christensen), Lasse Schöne (54' Pierre-Emile Højbjerg), Daniel Wass, Thomas
Delaney, Christian Eriksen, Robert Skov, Christian Gytkjær, Martin Braithwaite (55' Kasper
Dolberg). (Coach: Åge Hareide (NOR)).
Gibraltar: Kyle Goldwin, Joseph Chipolina (YC26), Aymen Mouelhi (66' Erin Barnett), Jayce
Mascarenhas-Olivero (YC14), Roy Chipolina, Ethan Britto, Liam Walker, Jack Sergeant,
Mohamed Badr Hassan (66' Andrew Hernandez), Lee Casciaro, Tlay De Barr (72' Reece
Styche). (Coach: JULIO César RIBAS Vlahovic (URU)).
Goals: Denmark: 1-0 Robert Skov (12'), 2-0 Christian Gytkjær (47'), 3-0 Martin Braithwaite
(51'), 4-0 Robert Skov (64'), 5-0 Christian Eriksen (85'), 6-0 Christian Eriksen (90+3').
Referee: István Vad (II) (HUN)   Attendance: 24.033

15-11-2019   Kybunpark, St. Gallen: Switzerland – Georgia 1-0 (0-0)
Switzerland: Yann Sommer, Stephan Lichtsteiner, Ricardo Rodríguez, Nico Elvedi, Manuel
Akanji, Granit Xhaka, Renato Steffen (YC74), Edimilson Fernandes (84' Djibril Sow), Denis
Zakaria, Albian Ajeti (71' Cedric Itten), Ruben Vargas (78' Christian Fassnacht). (Coach:
Vladimir Petkovic (BIH)).
Georgia: Giorgi Loria, Gia Grigalava, Guram Kashia, Davit Khocholava (YC29), Otar
Kakabadze, Jaba Kankava (YC31), Valeri Qazaishvili, Levan Shengelia, Otar Kiteishvili (85'
Giorgi Papunashvili), Zuriko Davitashvili (85' Valeriane Gvilia), Giorgi Kvilitaia (83' Elguja
Lobjanidze). (Coach: Vladimir Weiss (SVK)).
Goal: Switzerland: 1-0 Cedric Itten (77').
Referee: Danny Makkelie (HOL)   Attendance: 16.400

410

18-11-2019   Victoria Stadium, Gibraltar: Gibraltar – Switzerland 1-6 (0-1)
Gibraltar: Dayle Coleing, Joseph Chipolina, Aymen Mouelhi, Erin Barnett, Roy Chipolina, Ethan Britto (YC78), Liam Walker (YC29), Jack Sergeant, Mohamed Badr Hassan (85' Alain Pons), Lee Casciaro (62' Reece Styche (YC90+2)), Tlay De Barr (62' James Coombes). (Coach: JULIO César RIBAS Vlahovic (URU)).
Switzerland: Yann Sommer, Michael Lang, Ricardo Rodríguez (YC18), Loris Benito, Nico Elvedi (YC49), Manuel Akanji (65' Eray Cömert), Granit Xhaka, Denis Zakaria (60' Djibril Sow), Christian Fassnacht, Cedric Itten, Ruben Vargas (85' Michael Aebischer). (Coach: Vladimir Petkovic (BIH)).
Goals: Gibraltar: 1-3 Reece Styche (74').
Switzerland: 0-1 Cedric Itten (10'), 0-2 Ruben Vargas (50'), 0-3 Christian Fassnacht (57'), 1-4 Loris Benito (75'), 1-5 Cedric Itten (84'), 1-6 Granit Xhaka (86').
Referee: Benoît Millot (FRA)   Attendance: 2.079

18-11-2019   Aviva Stadium, Dublin: Republic of Ireland – Denmark 1-1 (0-0)
Republic of Ireland: Darren Randolph, Enda Stevens, Shane Duffy, John Egan (46' Ciaran Clark), Matt Doherty, Glenn Whelan (YC55) (81' Seán Maguire), Conor Hourihane (68' Callum Robinson), James McClean (YC78), Jeff Hendrick, Alan Browne, David McGoldrick. (Coach: Mick McCarthy (IRL)).
Denmark: Kasper Schmeichel (YC90+3), Simon Kjær, Mathias Jørgensen "Zanka", Henrik Dalsgaard, Jens Stryger Larsen, Lasse Schöne (YC33) (84' Andreas Christensen), Thomas Delaney (13' Pierre-Emile Højbjerg), Christian Eriksen, Martin Braithwaite, Yussuf Poulsen, Andreas Cornelius (33' Kasper Dolberg). (Coach: Åge Hareide (NOR)).
Goals: Republic of Ireland: 1-1 Matt Doherty (85').
Denmark: 0-1 Martin Braithwaite (73').
Referee: Dr. Felix Brych (GER)   Attendance: 50.000

GROUP   E

21-03-2019	Zagreb	Croatia – Azerbaijan	2-1 (1-1)
21-03-2019	Trnava	Slovakia – Hungary	2-0 (1-0)
24-03-2019	Cardiff	Wales – Slovakia	1-0 (1-0)
24-03-2019	Budapest	Hungary – Croatia	2-1 (1-1)
08-06-2019	Osijek	Croatia – Wales	2-1 (1-0)
08-06-2019	Baku	Azerbaijan – Hungary	1-3 (0-1)
11-06-2019	Baku	Azerbaijan – Slovakia	1-5 (1-3)
11-06-2019	Budapest	Hungary – Wales	1-0 (0-0)
06-09-2019	Trnava	Slovakia – Croatia	0-4 (0-1)
06-09-2019	Cardiff	Wales – Azerbaijan	2-1 (1-0)
09-09-2019	Baku	Azerbaijan – Croatia	1-1 (0-1)
09-09-2019	Budapest	Hungary – Slovakia	1-2 (0-1)
10-10-2019	Split	Croatia – Hungary	3-0 (3-0)
10-10-2019	Trnava	Slovakia – Wales	1-1 (0-1)
13-10-2019	Budapest	Hungary – Azerbaijan	1-0 (1-0)
13-10-2019	Cardiff	Wales – Croatia	1-1 (1-1)
16-11-2019	Baku	Azerbaijan – Wales	0-2 (0-2)
16-11-2019	Rijeka	Croatia – Slovakia	3-1 (0-1)
19-11-2019	Trnava	Slovakia – Azerbaijan	2-0 (1-0)
19-11-2019	Cardiff	Wales – Hungary	2-0 (1-0)

FINAL STANDING

Pos	Team	Pld	W	D	L	GF	GA	GD	Pts
1	Croatia	8	5	2	1	17	7	+10	17
2	Wales	8	4	2	2	10	6	+4	14
3	Slovakia	8	4	1	3	13	11	+2	13
4	Hungary	8	4	0	4	8	11	-3	12
5	Azerbaijan	8	0	1	7	5	18	-13	1

Croatia and Wales qualified for final tournament.

21-03-2019   Stadion Maksimir, Zagreb: Croatia – Azerbaijan 2-1 (1-1)
Croatia: Lovre Kalinic, Domagoj Vida, Duje Caleta-Car, Borna Barisic, Luka Modric (90+2'
Milan Badelj), Ivan Rakitic, Ivan Perisic, Mateo Kovacic (73' Nikola Vlasic), Josip Brekalo,
Andrej Kramaric, Bruno Petkovic (69' Ante Rebic). (Coach: Zlatko Dalic (CRO)).
Azerbaijan: Salahat Agayev, Maksim Medvedev (YC67), Qara Qarayev (88' Rufat Dadashov),
Badavi Hüseynov, Rahil Mammadov, Shahriyar Rahimov, Richard Almeyda de Oliveira (73'
Emin Makhmudov), Eddy Silvestre Pascual Israfilov, Dimitrij Nazarov (58' Araz Abdullayev),
Ramil Sheydaev, Mahir Emreli. (Coach: Nikola Jurcevic (CRO)).
Goals: Croatia: 1-1 Borna Barisic (44'), 2-1 Andrej Kramaric (79').
Azerbaijan: 0-1 Ramil Sheydaev (19').
Referee: Georgi Kabakov (BUL)   Attendance: 23.146

21-03-2019   City Arena - Anton Malatinsky Stadium, Trnava: Slovakia – Hungary 2-0 (1-0)
Slovakia: Martin Dúbravka, Peter Pekarík, Milan Skriniar (YC89), Denis Vavro (YC21),
Dávid Hancko, Marek Hamsík (YC77), Juraj Kucka (YC50), Róbert Mak (79' Miroslav
Stoch), Albert Rusnák (90+3' Jaroslav Mihalík), Stanislav Lobotka, Ondrej Duda (88' Pavol
Safranko). (Coach: Pavel Hapal (CZE)).
Hungary: Péter Gulácsi, Mihály Korhut (YC59), Tamás Kádár, Ádám Lang (81' Filip
Holender), Willi Orban, István Kovács, Gergö Lovrencsics, László Kleinheisler (55' Dominik
Szoboszlai), Zsolt Kalmár (YC10) (61' Balász Dzsudzsák), Ádám Nagy (YC88), Ádám Szalai.
(Coach: Marco Rossi (ITA)).
Goals: Slovakia: 1-0 Ondrej Duda (42'), 2-0 Albert Rusnák (85').
Referee: Vladislav Bezborodov (RUS)   Attendance: 14.235

24-03-2019   Cardiff City Stadium, Cardiff: Wales – Slovakia 1-0 (1-0)
Wales: Wayne Hennessey, Ben Davies, Jamie Lawrence, Chris Mepham, Joe Allen (YC53),
Daniel James (73' Ashley Williams), Harry Wilson (87' Will Vaulks), David Brooks (YC60)
(60' Tyler Roberts), Matt Smith, Connor Roberts, Gareth Bale. (Coach: Ryan Giggs (WAL)).
Slovakia: Martin Dúbravka, Peter Pekarík (90' Pavol Safranko), Milan Skriniar, Denis Vavro
(YC31), Dávid Hancko, Marek Hamsík (YC86), Juraj Kucka (YC90+6), Róbert Mak (YC15)
(69' Miroslav Stoch (YC90+3)), Albert Rusnák, Stanislav Lobotka (YC41), Ondrej Duda (65'
Michal Duris (YC69)). (Coach: Pavel Hapal (CZE)).
Goal: Wales: 1-0 Daniel James (5').
Referee: Felix Zwayer (GER)   Attendance: 31.617

24-03-2019   Groupama Aréna, Budapest: Hungary – Croatia 2-1 (1-1)
Hungary: Péter Gulácsi, Tamás Kádár, Botond Baráth, Willi Orban, Balász Dzsudzsák (YC63)
(85' Barnabás Bese), Máté Pátkai, Gergö Lovrencsics, Ádám Nagy, Dominik Szoboszlai (65'
Zsolt Kalmár), Ádám Szalai, Dominik Nagy (40' Roland Varga). (Coach: Marco Rossi (ITA)).
Croatia: Lovre Kalinic, Domagoj Vida, Dejan Lovren (YC82), Tin Jedvaj (77' Bruno
Petkovic), Borna Barisic (30' Marin Leovac), Luka Modric, Ivan Rakitic, Ivan Perisic, Marcelo
Brozovic, Andrej Kramaric, Ante Rebic (67' Josip Brekalo). (Coach: Zlatko Dalic (CRO)).
Goals: Hungary: 1-1 Ádám Szalai (34'), 2-1 Máté Pátkai (76').
Croatia: 0-1 Ante Rebic (13').
Referee: William Collum (SCO)   Attendance: 19.400

08-06-2019   Stadion Gradski vrt, Osijek: Croatia – Wales 2-1 (1-0)
Croatia: Dominik Livakovic, Domagoj Vida (YC69), Dejan Lovren (YC54), Tin Jedvaj
(YC50), Borna Barisic, Luka Modric, Ivan Perisic (90+3' Mile Skoric), Marcelo Brozovic
(YC90+2), Mateo Kovacic (76' Milan Badelj), Josip Brekalo (YC28) (66' Mario Pasalic),
Andrej Kramaric. (Coach: Zlatko Dalic (CRO)).
Wales: Wayne Hennessey, Ben Davies, Jamie Lawrence, Chris Mepham, Joe Allen, Will
Vaulks (66' Ethan Ampadu), Daniel James (79' Rabbi Matondo), Harry Wilson, Matt Smith
(65' David Brooks), Connor Roberts, Gareth Bale (YC48). (Coach: Ryan Giggs (WAL)).
Goals: Croatia: 1-0 Jamie Lawrence (17' own goal), 2-0 Ivan Perisic (48').
Wales: 2-1 David Brooks (77').
Referee: István Kovács (ROM)   Attendance: 17.061

08-06-2019   Bakcell Arena, Baku: Azerbaijan – Hungary 1-3 (0-1)
Azerbaijan: Salahat Agayev, Maksim Medvedev (YC60), Qara Qarayev, Badavi Hüseynov
(YC38), Rahil Mammadov, Anton Krivotsyuk, Richard Almeyda de Oliveira, Dimitrij Nazarov
(YC50) (86' Rufat Dadashov), Ramil Sheydaev, Mahir Emreli (74' Araz Abdullayev), Renat
Dadashov (59' Agabala Ramazanov). (Coach: Nikola Jurcevic (CRO)).
Hungary: Péter Gulácsi, Mihály Korhut, Botond Baráth, Willi Orban, Balász Dzsudzsák (86'
Krisztián Németh (YC87)), Gergö Lovrencsics, László Kleinheisler (YC67) (72' Máté Pátkai),
Ádám Nagy, Dominik Szoboszlai (YC28) (58' Dávid Holman), Ádám Szalai, Dominik Nagy.
(Coach: Marco Rossi (ITA)).
Goals: Azerbaijan: 1-2 Mahir Emreli (69').
Hunagry: 0-1 Willi Orban (18'), 0-2 Willi Orban (53'), 1-3 Dávid Holman (71').
Referee: Kevin Blom (HOL)   Attendance: 10.450

11-06-2019   Bakcell Arena, Baku: Azerbaijan – Slovakia 1-5 (1-3)
Azerbaijan: Salahat Agayev, Maksim Medvedev, Qara Qarayev, Badavi Hüseynov, Anton
Krivotsyuk (YC70), Shahriyar Rahimov, Araz Abdullayev (89' Renat Dadashov), Richard
Almeyda de Oliveira, Rashad Eyubov (79' Emin Makhmudov), Agabala Ramazanov (61'
Mahir Emreli), Ramil Sheydaev. (Coach: Nikola Jurcevic (CRO)).
Slovakia: Martin Dúbravka, Peter Pekarík, Milan Skriniar, Denis Vavro, Dávid Hancko, Marek
Hamsík (86' Lukás Haraslín), Juraj Kucka, Róbert Mak, Albert Rusnák, Stanislav Lobotka
(84' Ján Gregus), Róbert Bozeník (71' Ondrej Duda). (Coach: Pavel Hapal (CZE)).
Goals: Azerbaijan: 1-2 Ramil Sheydaev (29').
Slovakia: 0-1 Stanislav Lobotka (8'), 0-2 Juraj Kucka (27'), 1-3 Marek Hamsík (30'), 1-4
Marek Hamsík (57'), 1-5 Dávid Hancko (85').
Referee: John Beaton (SCO)   Attendance: 8.200

413

11-06-2019   Groupama Aréna, Budapest: Hungary – Wales 1-0 (0-0)
Hungary: Péter Gulácsi, Mihály Korhut (YC90), Botond Baráth, Willi Orban, Balász
Dzsudzsák (70' László Kleinheisler), Máté Pátkai (YC39), Gergö Lovrencsics, Ádám Nagy
(YC49), Dominik Szoboszlai (83' Barnabás Bese), Ádám Szalai, Filip Holender (59' Roland
Varga). (Coach: Marco Rossi (ITA)).
Wales: Wayne Hennessy, Chris Gunter (YC2), Ashley Williams, Ben Davies (YC87), Jamie
Lawrence (YC82), Ethan Ampadu (54' Matt Smith), Joe Allen, Tom Lawrence (79' Sam
Vokes), Daniel James, David Brooks (73' Harry Wilson), Gareth Bale. (Coach: Ryan Giggs
(WAL)).
Goal: Hungary: 1-0 Máté Pátkai (80').
Referee: Matej Jug (SLO)   Attendance: 18.350

06-09-2019   City Arena - Anton Malatinsky Stadium, Trnava: Slovakia – Croatia 0-4 (0-1)
Slovakia: Martin Dúbravka, Milan Skriniar, Denis Vavro, Martin Valjent, Dávid Hancko,
Marek Hamsík, Juraj Kucka (63' Lukás Haraslín), Róbert Mak (79' Michal Duris), Albert
Rusnák (46' Róbert Bozeník), Stanislav Lobotka, Ondrej Duda. (Coach: Pavel Hapal (CZE)).
Croatia: Dominik Livakovic, Domagoj Vida, Dejan Lovren, Borna Barisic, Karlo Bartolec,
Luka Modric, Ivan Perisic, Marcelo Brozovic, Nikola Vlasic (82' Milan Badelj), Ante Rebic
(70' Josip Brekalo), Bruno Petkovic (83' Mario Pasalic). (Coach: Zlatko Dalic (CRO)).
Goals: Croatia: 0-1 Nikola Vlasic (45'), 0-2 Ivan Perisic (46'), 0-3 Bruno Petkovic (72'), 0-4
Dejan Lovren (89').
Referee: Dr. Felix Brych (GER)   Attendance: 18.098

06-09-2019   Cardiff City Stadium, Cardiff: Wales – Azerbaijan 2-1 (1-0)
Wales: Wayne Hennessey, Neil Taylor (80' Ben Davies), Joe Rodon, Ethan Ampadu (75' Sam
Vokes), Chris Mepham (YC52), Joe Allen (YC90), Tom Lawrence, Daniel James, Harry
Wilson (63' Jonathan Williams), Connor Roberts, Gareth Bale. (Coach: Ryan Giggs (WAL)).
Azerbaijan: Salahat Agayev, Pavlo Pashaev, Maksim Medvedev, Qara Qarayev, Bahlul
Mustafazade, Anton Krivotsyuk (YC81), Shahriyar Rahimov (73' Tamkin Khalilzade),
Richard Almeyda de Oliveira (YC66) (69' Rashad Eyubov), Dimitrij Nazarov (YC42) (86'
Agabala Ramazanov), Ramil Sheydaev, Mahir Emreli. (Coach: Nikola Jurcevic (CRO)).
Goals: Wales: 1-0 Pavlo Pashaev (26' own goal), 2-1 Gareth Bale (84').
Azerbaijan: 1-1 Mahir Emreli (59').
Referee: Trustin Farrugia Cann (MLT)   Attendance: 28.385

09-09-2019   Bakcell Arena, Baku: Azerbaijan – Croatia 1-1 (0-1)
Azerbaijan: Emil Balayev, Pavlo Pashaev (46' Tamkin Khalilzade (YC68)), Maksim
Medvedev (YC90+3), Qara Qarayev, Bahlul Mustafazade, Anton Krivotsyuk (YC62), Dzhavid
Hüseynov (60' Emin Makhmudov), Shahriyar Rahimov, Dimitrij Nazarov (YC67) (90' Rashad
Eyubov), Ramil Sheydaev, Mahir Emreli. (Coach: Nikola Jurcevic (CRO)).
Croatia: Dominik Livakovic, Domagoj Vida, Dejan Lovren, Borna Barisic (YC70), Karlo
Bartolec (76' Josip Brekalo), Luka Modric, Ivan Perisic, Marcelo Brozovic (YC21), Nikola
Vlasic, Ante Rebic (86' Mislav Orsic), Bruno Petkovic. (Coach: Zlatko Dalic (CRO)).
Goals: Azerbaijan: 1-1 Tamkin Khalilzade (72').
Croatie: 0-1 Luka Modric (11' penalty).
Referee: Sandro Schárer (SUI)   Attendance: 9.150

414

09-09-2019   Groupama Aréna, Budapest: Hungary – Slovakia 1-2 (0-1)
Hungary: Péter Gulácsi, Tamás Kádár, Botond Baráth (YC54,YC90+5), Willi Orban, Balász
Dzsudzsák (YC19), Gergö Lovrencsics (30' Barnabás Bese), László Kleinheisler (85' Filip
Holender), Ádám Nagy (YC59) (65' Máté Pátkai (YC69)), Dominik Szoboszlai (YC6), Ádám
Szalai (YC53), Roland Sallai. (Coach: Marco Rossi (ITA)).
Slovakia: Martin Dúbravka, Lubomír Satka (YC12), Milan Skriniar, Denis Vavro (YC41),
Dávid Hancko, Marek Hamsík, Juraj Kucka (85' Ján Gregus), Róbert Mak (86' Lukás
Haraslín), Albert Rusnák, Stanislav Lobotka, Róbert Bozeník (77' Michal Duris). (Coach:
Pavel Hapal (CZE)).
Goals: Hungary: 1-1 Dominik Szoboszlai (50').
Slovakia: 0-1 Róbert Mak (40'), 1-2 Róbert Bozeník (56').
Referee: ANTONIO MATEU Lahoz (ESP)   Attendance: 21.700

10-10-2019   Stadion Poljud, Split: Croatia – Hungary 3-0 (3-0)
Croatia: Dominik Livakovic, Domagoj Vida (YC31), Dejan Lovren, Tin Jedvaj, Borna Barisic,
Luka Modric (67' Mateo Kovacic), Ivan Rakitic (74' Nikola Vlasic), Ivan Perisic (61' Josip
Brekalo), Marcelo Brozovic (YC44), Ante Rebic, Bruno Petkovic. (Coach: Zlatko Dalic
(CRO)).
Hungary: Péter Gulácsi, Mihály Korhut, Tamás Kádár (46' Ádám Lang), Willi Orban, Balász
Dzsudzsák (60' Dominik Nagy), Gergö Lovrencsics (YC82), László Kleinheisler
(YC18,YC56), Dávid Holman, Máté Vida, Ádám Szalai, Roland Sallai (76' Roland Varga).
(Coach: Marco Rossi (ITA)).
Goals: Croatia: 1-0 Luka Modric (5'), 2-0 Bruno Petkovic (24'), 3-0 Bruno Petkovic (42').
Referee: Daniele Orsato (ITA)   Attendance: 32.110
(Ivan Perisic missed a penalty kick in the 55th minute)

10-10-2019   City Arena - Anton Malatinsky Stadium, Trnava: Slovakia – Wales 1-1 (0-1)
Slovakia: Martin Dúbravka, Peter Pekarík, Norbert Gyömbér (YC51,YC88), Milan Skriniar,
Dávid Hancko, Marek Hamsík, Juraj Kucka, Róbert Mak (79' Lukás Haraslín), Albert Rusnák,
Stanislav Lobotka, Róbert Bozeník (86' Pavol Safranko). (Coach: Pavel Hapal (CZE)).
Wales: Wayne Hennessey, Ben Davies, Tom Lockyer, Joe Rodon, Ethan Ampadu (YC33) (58'
Joe Morrell), Joe Allen, Jonathan Williams (YC50) (66' Harry Wilson), Daniel James
(YC90+4), Connor Roberts, Gareth Bale (YC15), Kieffer Moore. (Coach: Ryan Giggs
(WAL)).
Goals: Slovakia: 1-1 Juraj Kucka (53').
Wales: 0-1 Kieffer Moore (25').
Referee: CARLOS DEL CERRO Grande (ESP)   Attendance: 18.071

13-10-2019   Groupama Aréna, Budapest: Hungary – Azerbaijan 1-0 (1-0)
Hungary: Péter Gulácsi, Mihály Korhut (YC73), Botond Baráth, Willi Orban, Balász
Dzsudzsák (71' Dominik Nagy), István Kovács (86' Dávid Siger), Gergö Lovrencsics (YC25),
Máté Vida, Dominik Szoboszlai (76' Dávid Holman), Ádám Szalai, Roland Sallai. (Coach:
Marco Rossi (ITA)).
Azerbaijan: Emil Balayev, Pavlo Pashaev, Qara Qarayev (YC90+3), Badavi Hüseynov, Bahlul
Mustafazade (YC90+3), Shahriyar Rahimov (YC12), Richard Almeyda de Oliveira (58' Araz
Abdullayev), Eddy Silvestre Pascual Israfilov (YC67), Tamkin Khalilzade (66' Dzhavid
Hüseynov (YC90+5)), Agabala Ramazanov (85' Renat Dadashov), Ramil Sheydaev. (Coach:
Nikola Jurcevic (CRO)).
Goal: Hungary: 1-0 Mihály Korhut (10').
Referee: Dennis Higler (HOL)   Attendance: 11.300

415

13-10-2019   Cardiff City Stadium, Cardiff: Wales – Croatia 1-1 (1-1)
Wales: Wayne Hennessey, Ben Davies, Tom Lockyer, Joe Rodon, Ethan Ampadu (50' Joe Morrell), Joe Allen (YC86), Jonathan Williams (68' Harry Wilson), Daniel James (YC90+6), Connor Roberts, Gareth Bale, Kieffer Moore (YC57) (86' Tyler Roberts). (Coach: Ryan Giggs (WAL)).
Croatia: Dominik Livakovic, Domagoj Vida (YC14), Dejan Lovren (YC45+4), Tin Jedvaj, Borna Barisic, Luka Modric (YC89) (90' Milan Badelj), Ivan Perisic, Mateo Kovacic (46' Ivan Rakitic (YC85)), Nikola Vlasic, Josip Brekalo, Bruno Petkovic (YC46) (64' Ante Rebic). (Coach: Zlatko Dalic (CRO)).
Goals: Wales: 1-1 Gareth Bale (45+3').
Croatia: 0-1 Nikola Vlasic (9').
Referee: Björn Kuipers (HOL)   Attendance: 31.745

16-11-2019   Bakcell Arena, Baku: Azerbaijan – Wales 0-2 (0-2)
Azerbaijan: Emil Balayev, Pavlo Pashaev, Qara Qarayev, Badavi Hüseynov, Bahlul Mustafazade, Anton Krivotsyuk (46' Tamkin Khalilzade), Shahriyar Rahimov (YC89), Araz Abdullayev (64' Agabala Ramazanov), Richard Almeyda de Oliveira, Dimitrij Nazarov (YC40) (82' Dzhavid Hüseynov (YC89)), Ramil Sheydaev (YC68). (Coach: Nikola Jurcevic (CRO)).
Wales: Wayne Hennessey, Ben Davies, Tom Lockyer, Ethan Ampadu (YC14) (87' Will Vaulks), Chris Mepham, Daniel James (82' Rabbi Matondo (YC90+5)), Joe Morrell (YC81), Harry Wilson (YC89), Connor Roberts, Gareth Bale (60' Aaron Ramsey), Kieffer Moore. (Coach: Ryan Giggs (WAL)).
Goals: Wales: 0-1 Kieffer Moore (10'), 0-2 Harry Wilson (34').
Referee: Deniz Aytekin (GER)   Attendance: 8.622

16-11-2019   Stadion HNK Rijeka, Rijeka: Croatia – Slovakia 3-1 (0-1)
Croatia: Dominik Livakovic, Tin Jedvaj, Duje Caleta-Car (YC13), Dino Peric, Borna Barisic, Luka Modric, Ivan Perisic (82' Mislav Orsic), Marcelo Brozovic, Nikola Vlasic (75' Mateo Kovacic), Ante Rebic (YC43) (54' Josip Brekalo), Bruno Petkovic. (Coach: Zlatko Dalic (CRO)).
Slovakia: Martin Dúbravka (YC79), Peter Pekarík, Milan Skriniar, Denis Vavro, Dávid Hancko, Marek Hamsík, Juraj Kucka (79' Patrik Hrosovsky), Róbert Mak (YC23,YC66), Albert Rusnák (63' Lukás Haraslín), Stanislav Lobotka, Róbert Bozeník (72' Michal Duris). (Coach: Pavel Hapal (CZE)).
Goals: Croatia: 1-1 Nikola Vlasic (56'), 2-1 Bruno Petkovic (60'), 3-1 Ivan Perisic (74').
Slovakia: 0-1 Róbert Bozeník (32').
Referee: Clément Turpin (FRA)   Attendance: 8.212

19-11-2019   City Arena - Anton Malatinsky Stadium, Trnava:
              Slovakia – Azerbaijan 2-0 (1-0)
Slovakia: Martin Dúbravka, Peter Pekarík, Norbert Gyömbér, Milan Skriniar (YC82), Dávid Hancko, Marek Hamsík, Juraj Kucka (85' Ondrej Duda), Matús Bero, Stanislav Lobotka, Lukás Haraslín (YC62) (71' Michal Duris), Róbert Bozeník (77' Samuel Mráz). (Coach: Pavel Hapal (CZE)).
Azerbaijan: Emil Balayev, Qara Qarayev, Badavi Hüseynov, Bahlul Mustafazade, Abbas Hüseynov, Anton Krivotsyuk (73' Tamkin Khalilzade (YC88)), Dzhavid Hüseynov (YC45+1) (79' Renat Dadashov), Shahriyar Rahimov, Eddy Silvestre Pascual Israfilov (YC45) (46' Elvin Dzhamalov), Vüsal Isgandarli, Ramil Sheydaev. (Coach: Nikola Jurcevic (CRO)).
Goals: Slovakia: 1-0 Róbert Bozeník (19'), 2-0 Marek Hamsík (86').
Referee: Serhiy Mykolayovych Boyko (UKR)   Attendance: 7.825

416

19-09-2019   Cardiff City Stadium, Cardiff: Wales – Hungary 2-0 (1-0)
Wales: Wayne Hennessey, Ben Davies, Tom Lockyer (YC72), Chris Mepham, Joe Allen, Aaron Ramsey, Daniel James (YC88), Joe Morrell (50' Ethan Ampadu), Connor Roberts, Gareth Bale (88' Harry Wilson), Kieffer Moore. (Coach: Ryan Giggs (WAL)).
Hungary: Péter Gulácsi, Botond Baráth, Ádám Lang, Zsolt Nagy, Balász Dzsudzsák (72' Roland Varga), Máté Pátkai (YC66), Gergö Lovrencsics, Ádám Nagy (60' István Kovács (YC71)), Dominik Szoboszlai, Ádám Szalai, Roland Sallai (83' Filip Holender). (Coach: Marco Rossi (ITA)).
Goals: Wales: 1-0 Aaron Ramsey (15'), 2-0 Aaron Ramsey (47').
Referee: Ovidiu Hategan (ROM)   Attendance: 31.762

GROUP   F

23-03-2019	Ta'Qali	Malta – Faroe Islands	2-1 (1-0)
23-03-2019	Solna	Sweden – Romania	2-1 (2-0)
23-03-2019	Valencia	Spain – Norway	2-1 (1-0)
26-03-2019	Ta'Qali	Malta – Spain	0-2 (0-1)
26-03-2019	Oslo	Norway – Sweden	3-3 (1-0)
26-03-2019	Cluj-Napoca	Romania – Faroe Islands	4-1 (3-1)
07-06-2019	Tórshavn	Faroe Islands – Spain	1-4 (1-3)
07-06-2019	Oslo	Norway – Romania	2-2 (0-0)
07-06-2019	Solna	Sweden – Malta	3-0 (1-0)
10-06-2019	Tórshavn	Faroe Islands – Norway	0-2 (0-0)
10-06-2019	Ta'Qali	Malta – Romania	0-4 (0-3)
10-06-2019	Madrid	Spain – Sweden	3-0 (1-0)
05-09-2019	Tórshavn	Faroe Islands – Sweden	0-4 (0-4)
05-09-2019	Oslo	Norway – Malta	2-0 (2-0)
05-09-2019	Bucharest	Romania – Spain	1-2 (0-1)
08-09-2019	Ploiesti	Romania – Malta	1-0 (0-0)
08-09-2019	Gijón	Spain – Faroe Islands	4-0 (1-0)
08-09-2019	Solna	Sweden – Norway	1-1 (0-1)
12-10-2019	Tórshavn	Faroe Islands – Romania	0-3 (0-0)
12-10-2019	Ta'Qali	Malta – Sweden	0-4 (0-1)
12-10-2019	Oslo	Norway – Spain	1-1 (0-0)
15-10-2019	Tórshavn	Faroe Islands – Malta	1-0 (0-0)
15-10-2019	Bucharest	Romania – Norway	1-1 (0-0)
15-10-2019	Solna	Sweden – Spain	1-1 (0-0)
15-11-2019	Oslo	Norway – Faroe Islands	4-0 (2-0)
15-11-2019	Bucharest	Romania – Sweden	0-2 (0-2)
15-11-2019	Cádiz	Spain – Malta	7-0 (2-0)
18-11-2019	Ta'Qali	Malta – Norway	1-2 (1-1)
18-11-2019	Madrid	Spain- Romania	5-0 (4-0)
18-11-2019	Solna	Sweden – Faroe Islands	3-0 (1-0)

FINAL STANDING

Pos	Team	Pld	W	D	L	GF	GA	GD	Pts
1	*Spain*	*10*	*8*	*2*	*0*	*31*	*5*	*+26*	*26*
2	*Sweden*	*10*	*6*	*3*	*1*	*23*	*9*	*+14*	*21*
3	Norway	10	4	5	1	19	11	+8	17
4	Romania	10	4	2	4	17	15	+2	14
5	Faroe Islands	10	1	0	9	4	30	-26	3
6	Malta	10	1	0	9	3	27	-24	3

Spain and Sweden qualified for final tournament.

23-03-2019   Ta'Qali Stadium, Ta'Qali: Malta – Faroe Islands 2-1 (1-0)
Malta: Henry Bonello (YC90+8), Jonathan Caruana, Andrei Agius (RC62), Steve Borg (YC61), Paul Fenech, Rowen Muscat (85' John Mintoff), Juan Corbalan (63' Zach Muscat), Kyrian Nwoko (YC36), Matthew Guillaumier, Michael Mifsud (72' Joseph Zerafa), Joseph Mbong. (Coach: Ray Farrugia (MLT)).
Faroe Islands: Gunnar Nielsen, Odmar Færø, Atli Gregersen, Viljormur Davidsen, Rógvi Baldvinsson (79' Árni Frederiksberg), Sølvi Vatnhamar (68' Kaj Leo í Bartalsstovu (YC86)), Hallur Hansson (YC90+9), Brandur Olsen, René Joensen (YC33) (72' Klæmint Olsen), Gilli Rólantsson (YC90+9), Jákup Thomsen. (Coach: Lars Christian Olsen (DEN)).
Goals: Malta: 1-0 Kyrian Nwoko (13'), 2-0 Steve Borg (77' penalty).
Faroe Islands: 2-1 Jákup Thomsen (90+8).
Referee: Vilhjálmur Alvar Thórarinsson (ISL)   Attendance: 7.531
(Brandur Olsen missed a penalty kick in the 64th minute)

23-03-2019   Friends Arena, Solna: Sweden – Romania 2-1 (2-0)
Sweden: Robin Olsen, Andreas Granqvist, Mikael Lustig (24' Emil Krafth (YC90+4)), Ludwig Augustinsson, Filip Helander, Sebastian Larsson, Emil Forsberg (68' Gustav Svensson (YC90+3)), Victor Claesson, Kristoffer Olsson, Marcus Berg, Robin Quaison (89' Alexander Isak). (Coach: Janne Andersson (SWE)).
Romania: Ciprian Tatarusanu, Cristian Sapunaru (YC82), Dragos Grigore (YC72), Nicusor Bancu, Cristian Manea, Tudor Baluta (78' Andrei Ivan), Alexandru Chipciu, Nicolae Stanciu, Razvan Marin, Alexandru Mitrita (46' Claudiu Keserü), George Puscas (64' Ianis Hagi (YC79)). (Coach: Cosmin Contra (ROM)).
Goals: Sweden: 1-0 Robin Quaison (33'), 4-0 Victor Claesson (40').
Romania: 2-1 Claudiu Keserü (58').
Referee: Michael Oliver (ENG)   Attendance: 30.115

23-03-2019   Estadio de Mestalla, Valencia: Spain – Norway 2-1 (1-0)
Spain: David DE GEA Quintana, SERGIO RAMOS García, Jesús NAVAS González, JORDI ALBA Ramos, ÍÑIGO MARTÍNEZ Berridi (YC64), Daniel "DANI" PAREJO Muñoz (77' Rodrigo Hernández Cascante "RODRI"), Sergio BUSQUETS Burgos, Daniel "DANI" CEBALLOS Fernández (YC53) (74' Sergio CANALES Madrazo), Álvaro Borja MORATA Martín (89' Jaime MATA Arnáiz), RODRIGO Moreno Machado, Marco ASENCIO Willemsen. (Coach: LUIS ENRIQUE Martínez García (ESP)).
Norway: Rune Jarstein, Håvard Nordtveit, Omar Elabdellaoui, Haitam Aleesami, Kristoffer Ajer (YC35), Stefan Johansen (YC53) (77' Ola Kamara), Markus Henriksen, Ole Selnæs, Martin Ødegaard (56' Mohamed Elyounoussi), Tarik Elyounoussi (YC51) (55' Bjørn Maars Johnsen (YC74)), Joshua King. (Coach: Lars Lagerbäck (SWE)).
Goals: Spain: 1-0 RODRIGO Moreno Machado (16'), 2-1 SERGIO RAMOS García (71' penalty).
Norway: 1-1 Joshua King (65' penalty).
Referee: Andris Treimanis (LAT)   Attendance: 39.752

26-03-2019   Ta'Qali Stadium, Ta'Qali: Malta – Spain 0-2 (0-1)
Malta: Henry Bonello, Jonathan Caruana (85' Karl Micallef), Joseph Zerafa, Steve Borg, Zach Muscat, Paul Fenech, John Mintoff (70' Michael Mifsud), Juan Corbalan (YC72), Kyrian Nwoko, Matthew Guillaumier, Joseph Mbong (65' Rowen Muscat). (Coach: Ray Farrugia (MLT)).
Spain: KEPA Arrizabalaga Revuelta, SERGIO RAMOS García, SERGI ROBERTO Carnicer, JUAN BERNAT Velasco (56' Iker MUNIAIN Goñi), José Luis GAYÀ Peña, Mario HERMOSO Canseco, Sergio CANALES Madrazo, SAÚL Ñíguez Esclapez (65' Jesús NAVAS González), Rodrigo "RODRI" Hernández Cascante, Álvaro Borja MORATA Martín (79' RODRIGO Moreno Machado), Marco ASENCIO Willemsen. (Coach: LUIS ENRIQUE Martínez García (ESP)).
Goals: Spain: 0-1 Álvaro Borja MORATA Martín (31'), 0-2 Álvaro Borja MORATA Martín (73').
Referee: Andrew Dallas (SCO)   Attendance: 16.542

26-03-2019   Ullevaal Stadion, Oslo: Norway – Sweden 3-3 (1-0)
Norway: Rune Jarstein, Håvard Nordtveit (YC52), Omar Elabdellaoui, Haitam Aleesami, Kristoffer Ajer (YC69), Markus Henriksen, Ole Selnæs (YC28), Mohamed Elyounoussi (72' Ola Kamara), Martin Ødegaard, Joshua King, Bjørn Maars Johnsen (YC62) (87' Alexander Sørloth). (Coach: Lars Lagerbäck (SWE)).
Sweden: Robin Olsen, Andreas Granqvist, Ludwig Augustinsson, Emil Krafth, Filip Helander (YC72), Sebastian Larsson (62' Alexander Isak), Albin Ekdal (66' Gustav Svensson), Victor Claesson (YC55), Kristoffer Olsson (YC29) (90+5' Sebastian Andersson), Marcus Berg, Robin Quaison. (Coach: Janne Andersson (SWE)).
Goals: Norway: 1-0 Bjørn Maars Johnsen (41'), 2-0 Joshua King (59'), 3-3 Ola Kamara (90+7').
Sweden: 2-1 Victor Claesson (70'), 2-2 Håvard Nordtveit (86' own goal), 2-3 Robin Quaison (90+1').
Referee: Gianluca Rocchi (ITA)   Attendance: 23.459
(Andreas Granqvist missed a penalty kick in the 70th minute)

26-03-2019   Stadionul Dr. Constantin Radulescu, Cluj-Napoca:
Romania – Faroe Islands 4-1 (3-1)
Romania: Ciprian Tatarusanu, Cosmin Moti (YC39), Dragos Grigore (YC85), Romario Benzar (46' Ianis Hagi), Nicusor Bancu, Ciprian Deac, Alexandru Chipciu (YC47), Nicolae Stanciu (YC16) (78' Dennis Man), Razvan Marin, Claudiu Keserü (69' Alexandru Cicâldau), George Puscas. (Coach: Cosmin Contra (ROM)).
Faroe Islands: Gunnar Nielsen, Odmar Færø, Atli Gregersen, Heini Vatnsdal (29' Rógvi Baldvinsson), Viljormur Davidsen, Kaj Leo í Bartalsstovu (67' Árni Frederiksberg (YC82)), Hallur Hansson (77' Sølvi Vatnhamar), Brandur Olsen, René Joensen (YC15), Klæmint Olsen (YC86), Gilli Rólantsson. (Coach: Lars Christian Olsen (DEN)).
Goals: Romania: 1-0 Ciprian Deac (26'), 2-0 Claudiu Keserü (29'), 3-0 Claudiu Keserü (33'), 4-1 George Puscas (63').
Faroe Islands: 3-1 Viljormur Davidsen (40' penalty).
Referee: Halil Unut Meler (TUR)   Attendance: 10.502

07-06-2019   Tórsvøllur, Tórshavn: Faroe Islands – Spain 1-4 (1-3)
Faroe Islands: Teitur Gestsson, Odmar Færø, Atli Gregersen, Heini Vatnsdal (74' Rógvi Baldvinsson), Viljormur Davidsen, Sølvi Vatnhamar, Hallur Hansson, Árni Frederiksberg (86' Meinhard Olsen), Brandur Olsen, Klæmint Olsen (68' Patrik Johannesen), Gilli Rólantsson. (Coach: Lars Christian Olsen (DEN)).
Spain: KEPA Arrizabalaga Revuelta, SERGIO RAMOS García (46' Diego Javier LLORENTE Ríos), Jesús NAVAS González (YC46), SERGI ROBERTO Carnicer, José Luis GAYÀ Peña, Mario HERMOSO Canseco, Santiago "SANTI" CAZORLA González, Francisco Román Alarcón Suárez "ISCO" (74' FABIÁN Ruiz Peña), Rodrigo "RODRI" Hernández Cascante, IAGO ASPAS Juncal (56' Marco ASENCIO Willemsen), Álvaro Borja MORATA Martín. (Coach: LUIS ENRIQUE Martínez García (ESP)).
Goals: Faroe Islands: 1-2 Klæmint Olsen (30').
Spain: 0-1 SERGIO RAMOS García (6'), 0-2 Jesús NAVAS González (19'), 1-3 Teitur Gestsson (34' own goal), 1-4 José Luis GAYÀ Peña (71').
Referee: Enea Jorgji (ALB)   Attendance: 3.226

07-06-2019   Ullevaal Stadion, Oslo: Norway – Romania 2-2 (0-0)
Norway: Sten Grytebust, Håvard Nordtveit, Omar Elabdellaoui, Haitam Aleesami, Kristoffer Ajer, Markus Henriksen, Ole Selnæs, Martin Ødegaard, Sander Berge (YC22), Tarik Elyounoussi (84' Ola Kamara), Joshua King. (Coach: Lars Lagerbäck (SWE)).
Romania: Ciprian Tatarusanu, Cristian Sapunaru, Dragos Grigore (YC80), Alin Tosca, Ciprian Deac, Alexandru Chipciu, Paul Anton (YC17), Nicolae Stanciu (72' Alexandru Maxim), Claudiu Keserü, Gheorghe Grozav (60' Ianis Hagi), George Puscas (60' George Tucudean). (Coach: Cosmin Contra (ROM)).
Goals: Norway: 1-0 Tarik Elyounoussi (56'), 2-0 Martin Ødegaard (70').
Romania: 2-1 Claudiu Keserü (77'), 2-2 Claudiu Keserü (90+2').
Referee: Sergei Karasev (RUS)   Attendance: 17.664

07-06-2019   Friends Arena, Solna: Sweden – Malta 3-0 (1-0)
Sweden: Robin Olsen, Mikael Lustig, Pontus Jansson, Ludwig Augustinsson, Filip Helander,
Albin Ekdal (77' Sebastian Larsson), Emil Forsberg, Victor Claesson, Kristoffer Olsson,
Marcus Berg (69' Alexander Isak), Robin Quaison (85' John Guidetti). (Coach: Janne
Andersson (SWE)).
Malta: Henry Bonello, Andrei Agius, Steve Borg (80' Ferdinando Apap), Zach Muscat, Rowen
Muscat, Luke Gambin, Juan Corbalan, Jake Grech (64' Paul Fenech), Alfred Effiong, Luke
Montebello (YC35) (71' Kyrian Nwoko), Joseph Mbong. (Coach: Ray Farrugia (MLT)).
Goals: Sweden: 1-0 Robin Quaison (2'), 2-0 Victor Claesson (50'), 3-0 Alexander Isak (81').
Referee: Robert Harvey (IRL)   Attendance: 26.421

10-06-2019   Tórsvøllur, Tórshavn: Faroe Islands – Norway 0-2 (0-0)
Faroe Islands: Teitur Gestsson, Odmar Færø, Atli Gregersen, Viljormur Davidsen, Rógvi
Baldvinsson (YC61), Sølvi Vatnhamar (69' Árni Frederiksberg), Hallur Hansson, Brandur
Olsen, René Joensen (84' Heini Vatnsdal), Klæmint Olsen (89' Patrik Johannesen), Gilli
Rólantsson (YC88). (Coach: Lars Christian Olsen (DEN)).
Norway: André Hansen, Håvard Nordtveit, Omar Elabdellaoui, Haitam Aleesami, Kristoffer
Ajer, Markus Henriksen (72' Stefan Johansen), Ole Selnæs (81' Fredrik Midtsjø), Martin
Ødegaard, Sander Berge, Tarik Elyounoussi (58' Ola Kamara), Bjørn Maars Johnsen. (Coach:
Lars Lagerbäck (SWE)).
Goals: Norway: 0-1 Bjørn Maars Johnsen (49'), 0-2 Bjørn Maars Johnsen (83').
Referee: Donatas Rumsas (LTU)   Attendance: 3.083

10-06-2019   Ta'Qali Stadium, Ta'Qali: Malta – Romania 0-4 (0-3)
Malta: Henry Bonello, Joseph Zerafa, Andrei Agius, Steve Borg (YC60), Zach Muscat, Paul
Fenech (59' Jake Grech), Rowen Muscat, Luke Gambin (68' Michael Mifsud), Juan Corbalan
(84' Luke Montebello), Alfred Effiong, Joseph Mbong. (Coach: Ray Farrugia (MLT)).
Romania: Ciprian Tatarusanu, Nicusor Bancu, Ionut Nedelcearu (35' Cristian Sapunaru), Iulian
Cristea, Tudor Baluta, Alexandru Chipciu (YC45+2,YC81), Alexandru Maxim (75' Dorin
Rotariu), Razvan Marin, Ianis Hagi, Claudiu Keserü (65' Dennis Man), George Puscas.
(Coach: Cosmin Contra (ROM)).
Goals: Romania: 0-1 George Puscas (7'), 0-2 George Puscas (29'), 0-3 Alexandru Chipciu
(34'), 0-4 Dennis Man (90+1').
Referee: Dennis Higler (HOL)   Attendance: 6.471

10-06-2019   Estadio Santiago Bernabéu, Madrid: Spain – Sweden 3-0 (0-0)
Spain: KEPA Arrizabalaga Revuelta, SERGIO RAMOS García, JORDI ALBA Ramos
(YC24), Daniel "DANI" CARVAJAL Ramos, ÍÑIGO MARTÍNEZ Berridi (88' Diego Javier
LLORENTE Ríos), Daniel "DANI" PAREJO Muñoz, Sergio BUSQUETS Burgos, Francisco
Román Alarcón Suárez "ISCO", FABIÁN Ruiz Peña, RODRIGO Moreno Machado (72'
MIKEL OYARZABAL Ugarte), Marco ASENCIO Willemsen (64' Álvaro Borja MORATA
Martín). (Coach: LUIS ENRIQUE Martínez García (ESP)).
Sweden: Robin Olsen, Mikael Lustig, Pontus Jansson, Ludwig Augustinsson, Filip Helander,
Sebastian Larsson (82' Alexander Isak), Albin Ekdal (86' Kristoffer Olsson), Emil Forsberg,
Victor Claesson (27' Jakob Johansson), Marcus Berg, Robin Quaison. (Coach: Janne
Andersson (SWE)).
Goals: Spain: 1-0 SERGIO RAMOS García (64' penalty), 2-0 Álvaro Borja MORATA Martín
(85' penalty), 3-0 MIKEL OYARZABAL Ugarte (87').
Referee: William Collum (SCO)   Attendance: 72.205

05-09-2019   Tórsvøllur, Tórshavn: Faroe Islands – Sweden 0-4 (0-4)
Faroe Islands: Gunnar Nielsen, Atli Gregersen (YC28), Viljormur Davidsen, Rógvi Baldvinsson, Jóan Edmundsson, Sølvi Vatnhamar, Hallur Hansson, Árni Frederiksberg (63' Jóannes Bjartalíd), Brandur Olsen (76' Meinhard Olsen), René Joensen (46' Heini Vatnsdal), Hørdur Askham. (Coach: Lars Christian Olsen (DEN)).
Sweden: Robin Olsen, Andreas Granqvist, Pierre Bengtsson, Mikael Lustig (46' Emil Krafth), Victor Lindelöf, Sebastian Larsson (73' Jimmy Durmaz), Albin Ekdal (63' Gustav Svensson), Kristoffer Olsson, Marcus Berg, Robin Quaison, Alexander Isak. (Coach: Janne Andersson (SWE)).
Goals: Sweden: 0-1 Alexander Isak (12'), 0-2 Alexander Isak (15'), 0-3 Victor Lindelöf (23'), 0-4 Robin Quaison (41').
Referee: TIAGO Bruno Lopes MARTINS (POR)   Attendance: 3.108

05-09-2019   Ullevaal Stadion, Oslo: Norway – Malta 2-0 (2-0)
Norway: Rune Jarstein, Håvard Nordtveit, Even Hovland, Omar Elabdellaoui, Haitam Aleesami, Stefan Johansen (76' Mathias Normann), Ole Selnæs, Martin Ødegaard, Sander Berge, Joshua King (YC32) (58' Bjørn Maars Johnsen), Erling Håland (66' Tarik Elyounoussi). (Coach: Lars Lagerbäck (SWE)).
Malta: Henry Bonello, Andrei Agius, Steve Borg, Zach Muscat (20' Ferdinando Apap), Paul Fenech (64' Jean Farrugia), Rowen Muscat, Dunstan Vella, Juan Corbalan, Kyrian Nwoko (YC45), Jake Grech (77' Alfred Effiong), Joseph Mbong. (Coach: Ray Farrugia (MLT)).
Goals: Norway: 1-0 Sander Berge (34'), 2-0 Joshua King (45+1' penalty).
Referee: Dumitri Muntean (MOL)   Attendance: 11.269

05-09-2019   Arena Nationala, Bucharest: Romania – Spain 1-2 (0-1)
Romania: Ciprian Tatarusanu, Vlad Chiriches, Dragos Grigore, Alin Tosca, Romario Benzar, Ionut Nedelcearu, Ciprean Deac (72' Alexandru Maxim), Nicolae Stanciu (63' Ianis Hagi), Razvan Marin (YC31), Claudiu Keserü (56' Florin Andone), George Puscas. (Coach: Cosmin Contra (ROM)).
Spain: KEPA Arrizabalaga Revuelta (YC90+2), SERGIO RAMOS García (YC29), Jesús NAVAS González, JORDI ALBA Ramos, Diego Javier LLORENTE Ríos (RC79), Sergio BUSQUETS Burgos, SAÚL Ñíguez Esclapez (YC76), Daniel "DANI" CEBALLOS Fernández (77' PABLO SARABIA García), FABIÁN Ruiz Peña, RODRIGO Moreno Machado (71' MIKEL OYARZABAL Ugarte), Francisco "PACO" ALCÁCER Garcia (85' Mario HERMOSO Canseco). (Coach: ROBERT MORENO González (ESP)).
Goals: Romania: 1-2 Florin Andone (59').
Spain: 0-1 SERGIO RAMOS García (29' penalty), 0-2 Francisco "PACO" ALCÁCER Garcia (47').
Referee: Deniz Aytekin (GER)   Attendance: 50.024

08-09-2019   Stadionul Ilie Oana, Ploiesti: Romania – Malta 1-0 (0-0)
Romania: Ciprian Tatarusanu, Vlad Chiriches, Florin Stefan, Adrián Rus, Alexandru Chipciu, Mihai Bordeianu, Razvan Marin (59' Nicolae Stanciu), Alexandru Cicâldau, Ianis Hagi (72' Gheorghe Grozav), Florin Andone, George Puscas (77' Claudiu Keserü). (Coach: Cosmin Contra (ROM)).
Malta: Henry Bonello (YC42), Andrei Agius, Steve Borg, Zach Muscat, Rowen Muscat, Luke Gambin (81' Joseph Zerafa), Dunstan Vella (86' Jake Grech), Juan Corbalan, Kyrian Nwoko (72' Alfred Effiong), Jean Farrugia, Joseph Mbong. (Coach: Ray Farrugia (MLT)).
Goal: Romania: 1-0 George Puscas (47').
Referee: Duje Strukan (CRO)   Attendance: 13.376

08-09-2019   Estadio Municipal El Molinón, Gijón: Spain – Faroe Islands 4-0 (1-0)
Spain: David DE GEA Quintana, SERGIO RAMOS García (YC72) (84' Unai NÚÑEZ
Gestoso), Daniel "DANI" CARVAJAL Ramos, José Luis GAYÀ Peña, Mario HERMOSO
Canseco, Daniel "DANI" PAREJO Muñoz, THIAGO Alcântara do Nascimento (YC44), Jesús
Joaquín Fernández Sáez de la Torre "SUSO" (68' PABLO SARABIA García), Rodrigo
"RODRI" Hernández Cascante, RODRIGO Moreno Machado, MIKEL OYARZABAL Ugarte
(61' Francisco "PACO" ALCÁCER Garcia). (Coach: ROBERT MORENO González (ESP)).
Faroe Islands: Gunnar Nielsen, Atli Gregersen, Heini Vatnsdal, Viljormur Davidsen, Rógvi
Baldvinsson (55' Andrias Eriksen), Jóan Edmundsson (66' Kaj Leo í Bartalsstovu), Sølvi
Vatnhamar, Hallur Hansson, Brandur Olsen, Jóannes Bjartalíd, Klæmint Olsen (87' Magnus
Egilsson). (Coach: Lars Christian Olsen (DEN)).
Goals: Spain: 1-0 RODRIGO Moreno Machado (13'), 2-0 RODRIGO Moreno Machado (50'),
3-0 Francisco "PACO" ALCÁCER Garcia (90'), 4-0 Francisco "PACO" ALCÁCER Garcia
(90+3').
Referee: Krzysztof Jakubik (POL)   Attendance: 23.644

08-09-2019   Friends Arena, Solna: Sweden – Norway 1-1 (0-1)
Sweden: Robin Olsen, Andreas Granqvist, Pierre Bengtsson, Mikael Lustig, Victor Lindelöf,
Sebastian Larsson (YC70), Albin Ekdal (YC66) (84' Gustav Svensson), Emil Forsberg,
Kristoffer Olsson, Robin Quaison (77' Sebastian Andersson), Alexander Isak (77' Marcus
Berg). (Coach: Janne Andersson (SWE)).
Norway: Rune Jarstein, Tore Reginiussen, Håvard Nordtveit, Omar Elabdellaoui, Haitam
Aleesami, Stefan Johansen (76' Erling Håland), Markus Henriksen (YC44) (64' Tarik
Elyounoussi), Ole Selnæs, Martin Ødegaard, Sander Berge, Joshua King. (Coach: Lars
Lagerbäck (SWE)).
Goals: Sweden: 1-1 Emil Forsberg (60').
Norway: 0-1 Stefan Johansen (45').
Referee: Slavko Vincic (SLO)   Attendance: 38.372

12-10-2019   Tórsvøllur, Tórshavn: Faroe Islands – Romania 0-3 (0-0)
Faroe Islands: Gunnar Nielsen, Atli Gregersen, Heini Vatnsdal, Viljormur Davidsen, Rógvi
Baldvinsson (78' Eli Nielsen (YC82)), Sølvi Vatnhamar, Hallur Hansson (YC46), Brandur
Olsen (YC45) (71' Andrias Eriksen), Jóannes Bjartalíd, Klæmint Olsen (75' Jóan
Edmundsson), Gilli Rólantsson (YC71). (Coach: Lars Christian Olsen (DEN)).
Romania: Ciprian Tatarusanu, Vlad Chiriches (38' Adrián Rus), Romario Benzar, Nicusor
Bancu (YC79), Ionut Nedelceanu (YC18), Paul Anton (YC76), Nicolae Stanciu, Ianis Hagi,
Florin Andone (65' Claudiu Keserü, George Puscas, Florinel Coman (69' Alexandru Mitrita).
(Coach: Cosmin Contra (ROM)).
Goals: Romania: 0-1 George Puscas (74'), 0-2 Alexandru Mitrita (83'), 0-3 Claudiu Keserü
(90+4').
Referee: Aliyar Aghayev (AZE)   Attendance: 2.381

12-10-2019   Ta'Qali Stadium, Ta'Qali: Malta – Sweden 0-4 (0-1)
Malta: Henry Bonello, Joseph Zerafa, Andrei Agius, Zach Muscat (YC47) (66' Jonathan Caruana), Rowen Muscat (68' Paul Fenech), Luke Gambin, Dunstan Vella, Kyrian Nwoko, Kurt Shaw (YC39), Alfred Effiong (76' Michael Mifsud), Joseph Mbong (YC57). (Coach: Ray Farrugia (MLT)).
Sweden: Robin Olsen, Andreas Granqvist, Pierre Bengtsson, Mikael Lustig, Marcus Danielsson, Sebastian Larsson, Albin Ekdal (64' Gustav Svensson), Emil Forsberg, Kristoffer Olsson, Marcus Berg (79' Sebastian Andersson), Robin Quaison (YC62) (71' Alexander Isak). (Coach: Janne Andersson (SWE)).
Goals: Sweden: 0-1 Marcus Danielsson (11'), 0-2 Sebastian Larsson (58' penalty), 0-3 Andrei Agius (66' own goal), 0-4 Sebastian Larsson (71' penalty).
Referee: Sergey Ivanov (RUS)   Attendance: 10.702

12-10-2019   Ullevaal Stadion, Oslo: Norway – Spain 1-1 (0-0)
Norway: Rune Jarstein, Håvard Nordtveit (30' Even Hovland), Omar Elabdellaoui, Haitam Aleesami, Kristoffer Ajer, Stefan Johansen (63' Alexander Sørloth), Markus Henriksen (83' Bjørn Maars Johnsen), Ole Selnæs, Martin Ødegaard, Sander Berge, Joshua King (YC42). (Coach: Lars Lagerbäck (SWE)).
Spain: KEPA Arrizabalaga Revuelta (YC90+2), SERGIO RAMOS García (YC80), Raúl ALBIOL Tortajada, Jesús NAVAS González, JUAN BERNAT Velasco (88' ÍÑIGO MARTÍNEZ Berridi), Sergio BUSQUETS Burgos (YC60), SAÚL Ñíguez Esclapez, Daniel "DANI" CEBALLOS Fernández (64' Santiago "SANTI" CAZORLA González), FABIÁN Ruiz Peña (YC81), RODRIGO Moreno Machado (YC35), MIKEL OYARZABAL Ugarte (78' Rodrigo "RODRI" Hernández Cascante). (Coach: ROBERT MORENO González (ESP)).
Goals: Norway: 1-1 Joshua King (90+4' penalty).
Spain: 0-1 SAÚL Ñíguez Esclapez (47').
Referee: Michael Oliver (ENG)   Attendance: 25.572

15-10-2019   Tórsvøllur, Tórshavn: Faroe Islands – Malta 1-0 (0-0)
Faroe Islands: Gunnar Nielsen, Atli Gregersen, Heini Vatnsdal, Viljormur Davidsen (85' Árni Frederiksberg), Rógvi Baldvinsson, Jóan Edmundsson (90+4' Magnus Egilsson), Sølvi Vatnhamar, Hallur Hansson, Brandur Olsen, Jóannes Bjartalíd (65' Klæmint Olsen), Jóannes Danielsen. (Coach: Lars Christian Olsen (DEN)).
Malta: Henry Bonello, Andrei Agius, Steve Borg (YC75), Zach Muscat, Paul Fenech (71' Luke Gambin), Rowen Muscat (80' Joseph Zerafa), Dunstan Vella, Kyrian Nwoko, Jake Grech, Michael Mifsud (71' Alfred Effiong), Joseph Mbong (YC22). (Coach: Ray Farrugia (MLT)).
Goal: Faroe Islands: 1-0 Rógvi Baldvinsson (71').
Referee: JOSÉ María SÁNCHEZ Martínez (ESP)   Attendance: 2.677

15-10-2019   Arena Nationala, Bucharest: Romania – Norway 1-1 (0-0)
Romania: Ciprian Tatarusanu, Romario Benzar (YC42), Nicusor Bancu, Ionut Nedelcearu,
Adrián Rus, Ciprian Deac, Paul Anton (84' Mihai Bordeianu), Nicolae Stanciu, Razvan Marin,
Alexandru Mitrita (79' Dan Nistor (YC80)), George Puscas (63' Florin Andone). (Coach:
Cosmin Contra (ROM)).
Norway: Rune Jarstein, Even Hovland, Omar Elabdellaoui, Haitam Aleesami, Kristoffer Ajer,
Stefan Johansen (46' Alexander Sørloth), Markus Henriksen (81' Mathias Normann), Ole
Selnæs (67' Bjørn Maars Johnsen), Martin Ødegaard, Sander Berge, Joshua King. (Coach:
Lars Lagerbäck (SWE)).
Goals: Romania: 1-0 Alexandru Mitrita (62').
Norway: 1-1 Alexander Sørloth (90+2').
Referee: Bobby Madden (SCO)   Attendance: 29.854
(*George Puscas missed a penalty kick in the 52nd minute*)

15-10-2019   Friends Arena, Solna: Sweden – Spain 1-1 (0-0)
Sweden: Robin Olsen, Andreas Granqvist, Pierre Bengtsson, Mikael Lustig, Victor Lindelöf,
Sebastian Larsson (YC90+2), Albin Ekdal (83' Gustav Svensson), Emil Forsberg, Kristoffer
Olsson (YC81), Marcus Berg (YC89) (90+3' Sebastian Andersson), Robin Quaison (77'
Alexander Isak). (Coach: Janne Andersson (SWE)).
Spain: David DE GEA Quintana (60' KEPA Arrizabalaga Revuelta), Raúl ALBIOL Tortajada,
Daniel "DANI" CARVAJAL Ramos (81' Jesús NAVAS González), ÍÑIGO MARTÍNEZ
Berridi, JUAN BERNAT Velasco, THIAGO Alcântara do Nascimento (66' RODRIGO
Moreno Machado), Daniel "DANI" CEBALLOS Fernández (YC69), FABIÁN Ruiz Peña
(YC80), Rodrigo "RODRI" Hernández Cascante (YC89), GERARD Moreno Balaguero,
MIKEL OYARZABAL Ugarte. (Coach: ROBERT MORENO González (ESP)).
Goals: Sweden: 1-0 Marcus Berg (50').
Spain: 1-1 RODRIGO Moreno Machado (90+2').
Referee: Clément Turpin (FRA)   Attendance: 49.712

15-11-2019   Ullevaal Stadion, Oslo: Norway – Faroe Islands 4-0 (2-0)
Norway: Rune Jarstein, Tore Reginiussen, Omar Elabdellaoui, Haitam Aleesami, Kristoffer
Ajer, Markus Henriksen (71' Mats Møller Dæhli), Ole Selnæs, Iver Fossum, Sander Berge (84'
Fredrik Ulvestad), Joshua King (78' Tarik Elyounoussi), Alexander Sørloth. (Coach: Lars
Lagerbäck (SWE)).
Faroe Islands: Gunnar Nielsen, Odmar Færø, Atli Gregersen, Heini Vatnsdal, Rógvi
Baldvinsson (YC42), Ári Jónsson, Jóan Edmundsson (71' Klæmint Olsen (YC86)), Sølvi
Vatnhamar (78' Kaj Leo í Bartalsstovu), Brandur Olsen, Jóannes Bjartalíd (71' Árni
Frederiksberg), Gilli Rólantsson. (Coach: Lars Christian Olsen (DEN)).
Goals: Norway: 1-0 Tore Reginiussen (4'), 2-0 Iver Fossum (8'), 3-0 Alexander Sørloth (62'),
4-0 Alexander Sørloth (65').
Referee: Fran Jovic (CRO)   Attendance: 10.400

15-11-2019   Arena Nationala, Bucharest: Romania – Sweden 0-2 (0-2)
Romania: Ciprian Tatarusanu, Nicusor Bancu (YC55), Ionut Nedelcearu, Vasile Mogos, Tudor Baluta, Adrián Rus, Ciprian Deac (46' Ianis Hagi), Nicolae Stanciu (YC23) (73' Denis Alibec), Claudiu Keserü (57' Florinel Coman), Alexandru Mitrita, George Puscas. (Coach: Cosmin Contra (ROM)).
Sweden: Robin Olsen, Andreas Granqvist, Pierre Bengtsson, Mikael Lustig, Victor Lindelöf (YC50), Sebastian Larsson (69' Gustav Svensson), Albin Ekdal, Emil Forsberg, Kristoffer Olsson, Marcus Berg (78' Alexander Isak), Robin Quaison. (Coach: Janne Andersson (SWE)).
Goals: Sweden: 0-1 Marcus Berg (18'), 0-2 Robin Quaison (34').
Referee: Daniele Orsato (ITA)   Attendance: 49.678

15-11-2019   Estadio Ramón de Carranza, Cádiz: Spain – Malta 7-0 (2-0)
Spain: PAU LÓPEZ Sabata, SERGIO RAMOS García (61' Pau Francisco TORRES), Raúl ALBIOL Tortajada, Jesús NAVAS González, JUAN BERNAT Velasco, Santiago "SANTI" CAZORLA González (53' Francisco "PACO" ALCÁCER Garcia), THIAGO Alcântara do Nascimento, PABLO SARABIA García, Rodrigo "RODRI" Hernández Cascante, Álvaro Borja MORATA Martín (66' Daniel "DANI" OLMO Carvajal), GERARD Moreno Balagueró. (Coach: ROBERT MORENO González (ESP)).
Malta: Henry Bonello, Jonathan Caruana, Andrei Agius, Zach Muscat, Rowen Muscat (63' Tristan Caruana), Jurgen Pisani (76' Jake Grech), Dunstan Vella, Juan Corbalan (33' Karl Micallef), Kyrian Nwoko, Brandon Paiber, Joseph Mbong. (Coach: Ray Farrugia (MLT)).
Goals: Spain: 1-0 Álvaro Borja MORATA Martín (23'), 2-0 Santiago "SANTI" CAZORLA González (41'), 3-0 Pau Francisco TORRES (62'), 4-0 PABLO SARABIA García (63'), 5-0 Daniel "DANI" OLMO Carvajal (69'), 6-0 GERARD Moreno Balagueró (71'), 7-0 Jesús NAVAS González (85').
Referee: Viktor Kassai (HUN)   Attendance: 19.773

18-11-2019   Ta'Qali Stadium, Ta'Qali: Malta – Norway 1-2 (1-1)
Malta: Henry Bonello, Joseph Zerafa, Andrei Agius, Steve Borg (YC55) (75' Ferdinando Apap), Zach Muscat (YC66), Paul Fenech, Rowen Muscat (70' Nicky Muscat), Dunstan Vella (61' Alfred Effiong), Kyrian Nwoko, Michael Mifsud, Joseph Mbong. (Coach: Ray Farrugia (MLT)).
Norway: Ørjan Nyland, Tore Reginiussen, Jonas Svensson (65' Tarik Elyounoussi), Birger Meling, Kristoffer Ajer, Markus Henriksen, Mats Møller Dæhli (46' Omar Elabdellaoui), Iver Fossum, Sander Berge, Joshua King (89' Fredrik Ulvestad), Alexander Sørloth. (Coach: Lars Lagerbäck (SWE)).
Goals: Malta: 1-1 Paul Fenech (40').
Norway: 0-1 Joshua King (7'), 1-2 Alexander Sørloth (62').
Referee: Aliyar Aghayev (AZE)   Attendance: 2.708
(Joshua King missed a penalty kick in the 67th minute)

18-11-2019   Estadio Wanda Metropolitano, Madrid: Spain – Romania 5-0 (4-0)
Spain: KEPA Arrizabalaga Revuelta, SERGIO RAMOS García (63' Raúl ALBIOL Tortajada), Daniel "DANI" CARVAJAL Ramos, ÍÑIGO MARTÍNEZ Berridi, José Luis GAYÀ Peña, Santiago "SANTI" CAZORLA González (68' Francisco "PACO" ALCÁCER Garcia), Sergio BUSQUETS Burgos (YC25), SAÚL Ñíguez Esclapez, FABIÁN Ruiz Peña, Álvaro Borja MORATA Martín, GERARD Moreno Balagueró (57' MIKEL OYARZABAL Ugarte). (Coach: ROBERT MORENO González (ESP)).
Romania: Ciprian Tatarusanu, Alin Tosca, Romario Benzar, Ionut Nedelcearu (YC36), Tudor Baluta, Adrián Rus, Nicolae Stanciu, Razvan Marin (65' Alexandru Cicâldau), Ianis Hagi (73' Dan Nistor), George Puscas, Florinel Coman (56' Alexandru Mitrita). (Coach: Cosmin Contra (ROM)).
Goals: Spain: 1-0 FABIÁN Ruiz Peña (8'), 2-0 GERARD Moreno Balagueró (33'), 3-0 GERARD Moreno Balagueró (43'), 4-0 Adrián Rus (45+1' own goal), 5-0 MIKEL OYARZABAL Ugarte (90+2').
Referee: Aleksei Kulbakov (BLS)   Attendance: 36.198

18-11-2019   Friends Arena, Solna: Sweden – Faroe Islands 3-0 (1-0)
Sweden: Kristoffer Nordfeldt, Pontus Jansson (YC90), Marcus Danielsson, Filip Helander, Riccardo Gagliolo, Kristoffer Olsson, Ken Sema (65' Dejan Kulusevski), Mattias Svanberg (YC45), Sebastian Andersson (65' John Guidetti), Muamer Tankovic, Alexander Isak. (Coach: Janne Andersson (SWE)). (Not used sub: Victor Lindelöf (YC45+1)).
Faroe Islands: Gunnar Nielsen, Atli Gregersen (YC45+1), Heini Vatnsdal, Viljormur Davidsen, Rógvi Baldvinsson, Jóan Edmundsson (YC87) (89' Árni Frederiksberg), Sølvi Vatnhamar, Brandur Olsen, Jóannes Bjartalíd (46' Kaj Leo í Bartalsstovu), Klæmint Olsen (74' Patrik Johannesen), Gilli Rólantsson. (Coach: Lars Christian Olsen (DEN)).
Goals: Sweden: 1-0 Sebastian Andersson (29'), 2-0 Mattias Svanberg (72'), 3-0 John Guidetti (80').
Referee: Matej Jug (SLO)   Attendance: 19.737

GROUP   G

21-03-2019	Vienna	Austria – Poland	0-1 (0-0)
21-03-2019	Skopje	North Macedonia – Latvia	3-1 (2-0)
21-03-2019	Haifa	Israel – Slovenia	1-1 (0-0)
24-03-2019	Haifa	Israel – Austria	4-2 (2-1)
24-03-2019	Warsaw	Poland – Latvia	2-0 (0-0)
24-03-2019	Ljubljana	Slovenia – North Macedonia	1-1 (1-0)
07-06-2019	Klagenfurt	Austria – Slovenia	1-0 (0-0)
07-06-2019	Skopje	North Macedonia – Poland	0-1 (0-0)
07-06-2019	Riga	Latvia – Israel	0-3 (0-1)
10-06-2019	Skopje	North Macedonia – Austria	1-4 (1-1)
10-06-2019	Riga	Latvia – Slovenia	0-5 (0-4)
10-06-2019	Warsaw	Poland – Israel	4-0 (1-0)
05-09-2019	Beersheba	Israel – North Macedonia	1-1 (0-0)
06-09-2019	Wals-Siezenheim	Austria – Latvia	6-0 (2-0)
06-09-2019	Ljubljana	Slovenia – Poland	2-0 (1-0)
09-09-2019	Riga	Latvia – North Macedonia	0-2 (0-2)
09-09-2019	Warsaw	Poland – Austria	0-0
09-09-2019	Ljubljana	Slovenia – Israel	3-2 (1-0)
10-10-2019	Vienna	Austria – Israel	3-1 (1-1)

427

10-10-2019	Skopje	North Macedonia – Slovenia	2-1 (0-0)
10-10-2019	Riga	Latvia – Poland	0-3 (0-2)
13-10-2019	Warsaw	Poland – North Macedonia	2-0 (0-0)
13-10-2019	Ljubljana	Slovenia – Austria	0-1 (0-1)
15-10-2019	Beersheba	Israel – Latvia	3-1 (3-1)
16-11-2019	Ljubljana	Slovenia – Latvia	1-0 (0-0)
16-11-2019	Vienna	Austria – North Macedonia	2-1 (1-0)
16-11-2019	Jerusalem	Israel – Poland	1-2 (0-1)
19-11-2019	Skopje	North Macedonia – Israel	1-0 (1-0)
19-11-2019	Riga	Latvia – Austria	1-0 (0-0)
19-11-2019	Warsaw	Poland – Slovenia	3-2 (1-1)

FINAL STANDING

Pos	Team	Pld	W	D	L	GF	GA	GD	Pts
1	Poland	10	8	1	1	18	5	+13	25
2	Austria	10	6	1	3	19	9	+10	19
3	North Macedonia	10	4	2	4	12	13	-1	14
4	Slovenia	10	4	2	4	16	11	+5	14
5	Israel	10	3	2	5	16	18	-2	11
6	Latvia	10	1	0	9	3	28	-25	3

Poland and Austria qualified for final tournament.

21-03-2019   Ernst-Happel-Stadion, Vienna: Austria – Poland 0-1 (0-0)
Austria: Heinz Lindner, Aleksandar Dragovic (YC51), David Alaba (YC81), Stefan Lainer, Martin Hinteregger, Max Wöber, Julian Baumgartlinger, Marcel Sabitzer, Florian Grillitsch (84' Karim Onisiwo), Valentino Lazaro (81' Marc Janko), Marko Arnautovic. (Coach: Franco Foda (GER)).
Poland: Wojciech Szczesny, Kamil Glik, Bartosz Bereszynski (YC54), Tomasz Kedziora, Jan Bednarek, Mateusz Klich, Grzegorz Krychowiak, Piotr Zielinski (59' Krzysztof Piatek), Kamil Grosicki (90+2' Michal Pazdan), Robert Lewandowski, Arkadiusz Milik (46' Przemyslaw Frankowski). (Coach: Jerzy Brzeczek (POL)).
Goal: Poland: 0-1 Krzysztof Piatek (69').
Referee: Anastasios Sidiropoulos (GRE)   Attendance: 40.4000

21-03-2019   Philip II National Arena, Skopje: North Macedonia – Latvia 3-1 (2-0)
North Macedonia: Stole Dimitrievski, Stefan Ristovski, Visar Musliu, Darko Velkovski, Boban Nikolov, Enis Bardhi, Goran Pandev (71' Kire Ristevski), Ilija Nestorovski, Aleksandar Trajkovski (84' Kire Markoski), Ferhan Hasani (23' Eljif Elmas), Ezgjan Alioski. (Coach: Igor Angelovski (MKD)).
Latvia: Andris Vanins (33' Pāvels Steinbors), Vladislavs Gabovs, Igors Tarasovs, Kaspars Dubra, Vitālijs Maksimenko, Vjaceskavs Isajevs, Mārcis Oss, Andrejs Ciganiks (YC60,YC90+1), Deniss Rakels, Valērijs Sabala (79' Roberts Uldrikis), Artūrs Karasausks (69' Kristers Tobers). (Coach: Slavisa Stojanovic (SRB)).
Goals: North Macedonia: 1-0 Ezgjan Alioski (11'), 2-0 Eljif Elmas (29'), 3-1 Eljif Elmas (90+3').
Latvia: 2-1 Darko Velkovski (87' *own goal*).
Referee: Halis Özkahya (TUR)   Attendance: 7.043

21-03-2019   Sammy Ofer Stadium, Haifa: Israel – Slovenia 1-1 (0-0)
Israel: Ariel Harush, Sheran Yeini, Taleb Tawatha (77' Yonatan Cohen), Omri Ben Harush,
Loai Taha, Eli Dasa, Bibras Natcho (YC29) (79' Almog Cohen), Biram Kayal (63' Manor
Solomon), Don Peretz (YC86), Eran Zahavi, Moanas Dabour (YC50). (Coach: Andreas
Herzog (AUT)).
Slovenia: Jan Oblak, Bojan Jokic (YC87), Aljaz Struna, Miha Mevlja, Petar Stojanovic, Josip
Ilicic, Rene Krhin, Jasmin Kurtic, Miha Zajc (62' Domen Crnigoj), Benjamin Verbic (90' Jaka
Bijol), Andraz Sporar (85' Damjan Bohar). (Coach: Matjaz Kek (SVN)).
Goals: Israel: 1-1 Eran Zahavi (55').
Slovenia: 0-1 Andraz Sporar (48').
Referee: TIAGO Bruno Lopes MARTINS (POR)   Attendance: 12.430

24-03-2019   Sammy Ofer Stadium, Haifa: Israel – Austria 4-2 (2-1)
Israel: Ariel Harush, Orel Dgani (YC52), Sheran Yeini, Omri Ben Harush, Loai Taha (YC30)
(77' Ayed Habashi), Eli Dasa, Bibras Natcho, Biram Kayal (72' Almog Cohen), Don Peretz,
Eran Zahavi (YC55), Moanas Dabour (80' Tomer Hemed). (Coach: Andreas Herzog (AUT)).
Austria: Heinz Lindner, Andreas Ulmer, Aleksandar Dragovic (YC60), Martin Hinteregger,
Max Wöber (60' Marc Janko), Julian Baumgartlinger, Marcel Sabitzer, Peter Zulj (YC58) (85'
Florian Kainz), Valentino Lazaro (YC44), Xaver Schlager (61' Karim Onisiwo (YC89)),
Marko Arnautovic (YC65). (Coach: Franco Foda (GER)).
Goals: Israel: 1-1 Eran Zahavi (34'), 2-1 Eran Zahavi (45'), 3-1 Eran Zahavi (55'), 4-1 Moanas
Dabour (66').
Austria: 0-1 Marko Arnautovic (8'), 4-2 Marko Arnautovic (75').
Referee: Yevhen Aranovsky (UKR)   Attendance: 16.180

24-03-2019   PGE Narodowy, Warsaw: Poland – Latvia 2-0 (0-0)
Poland: Wojciech Szczesny, Michal Pazdan, Kamil Glik, Tomasz Kedziora (YC69), Mateusz
Klich (62' Jakub Blaszczykowski), Grzegorz Krychowiak, Piotr Zielinski, Arkadiusz Reca,
Kamil Grosicki (83' Przemyslaw Frankowski), Robert Lewandowski, Krzysztof Piatek (YC25)
(87' Arkadiusz Milik). (Coach: Jerzy Brzeczek (POL)).
Latvia: Pāvels Steinbors, Kaspars Dubra (YC18), Vitālijs Maksimenko (YC53), Vjaceskavs
Isajevs, Mārcis Oss, Olegs Laizāns, Jānis Ikaunieks (YC73), Deniss Rakels, Roberts
Savalnieks (80' Vladislavs Gabovs), Artūrs Karasausks (85' Kristers Tobers), Vladislavs
Gutkovskis (70' Roberts Uldrikis). (Coach: Slavisa Stojanovic (SRB)).
Goals: Poland: 1-0 Robert Lewandowski (76'), 2-0 Kamil Glik (84').
Referee: Aliyar Aghayev (AZE)   Attendance: 51.112

24-03-2019   Stadion Stozice, Ljubljana: Slovenia – North Macedonia 1-1 (1-0)
Slovenia: Jan Oblak, Bojan Jokic (YC56), Aljaz Struna, Miha Mevlja, Petar Stojanovic, Josip
Ilicic (YC19), Rene Krhin, Jasmin Kurtic, Miha Zajc (90+1' Luka Zahovic), Benjamin Verbic
(84' Domen Crnigoj), Andraz Sporar (71' Robert Beric). (Coach: Matjaz Kek (SVN)).
North Macedonia: Stole Dimitrievski, Stefan Ristovski, Visar Musliu (YC18), Darko
Velkovski, Egzon Bejtulai (YC14), Boban Nikolov (YC19), Enis Bardhi, Eljif Elmas, Goran
Pandev (76' Aleksandar Trajkovski), Ilija Nestorovski (YC18) (88' Kire Markoski), Ezgjan
Alioski (90+3' Kire Ristevski). (Coach: Igor Angelovski (MKD)).
Goals: Slovenia: 1-0 Miha Zajc (34').
North Macedonia: 1-1 Enis Bardhi (47').
Referee: XAVIER ESTRADA Fernández (ESP)   Attendance: 9.872

07-06-2019 Wörthersee Stadion, Klagenfurt am Wörthersee: Austria – Slovenia 1-0 (0-0)
Austria: Heinz Lindner, Andreas Ulmer, Aleksandar Dragovic, David Alaba (90' Florian Kainz), Stefan Lainer, Martin Hinteregger, Marcel Sabitzer (71' Guido Burgstaller (YC90+3)), Valentino Lazaro (YC80), Konrad Laimer (82' Stefan Ilsanker), Xaver Schlager, Marko Arnautovic. (Coach: Franco Foda (GER)).
Slovenia: Jan Oblak, Bojan Jokic, Aljaz Struna, Miha Mevlja, Petar Stojanovic, Josip Ilicic, Jasmin Kurtic, Miha Zajc (69' Damjan Bohar), Domen Crnigoj (YC62) (78' Robert Beric), Jaka Bijol (63' Denis Popovic), Andraz Sporar. (Coach: Matjaz Kek (SVN)).
Goal: Austria: 1-0 Guido Burgstaller (74').
Referee: Aleksei Kulbakov (BLS)   Attendance: 19.200

07-06-2019 Philip II National Arena, Skopje: North Macedonia – Poland 0-1 (0-0)
North Macedonia: Stole Dimitrievski, Stefan Ristovski (76' Arijan Ademi), Visar Musliu (YC66,YC85), Darko Velkovski, Egzon Bejtulai, Boban Nikolov (62' Aleksandar Trajkovski), Enis Bardhi, Eljif Elmas, Goran Pandev (85' Ferhan Hasani), Ilija Nestorovski (YC86), Ezgjan Alioski. (Coach: Igor Angelovski (MKD)).
Poland: Lukas Fabianski, Kamil Glik (YC28), Bartosz Bereszynski, Tomasz Kedziora, Jan Bednarek (YC41), Mateusz Klich (90' Jacek Góralski), Grzegorz Krychowiak, Piotr Zielinski, Przemyslaw Frankowski (46' Krzysztof Piatek), Kamil Grosicki (70' Maciej Rybus), Robert Lewandowski. (Coach: Jerzy Brzeczek (POL)).
Goal: Poland: 0-1 Krzysztof Piatek (47').
Referee: Gianluca Rocchi (ITA)   Attendance: 22.000

07-06-2019 Daugavas Stadionā, Riga: Latvia – Israel 0-3 (0-1)
Latvia: Pāvels Steinbors, Kaspars Dubra, Vitālijs Maksimenko, Mārcis Oss, Olegs Laizāns (79' Ritvars Rugins), Jānis Ikaunieks (58' Andrejs Ciganiks), Kristers Tobers (YC19), Deniss Rakels, Roberts Savalnieks, Artūrs Karasausks (YC64) (67' Vladimir Kamess), Vladislavs Gutkovskis. (Coach: Slavisa Stojanovic (SRB)).
Israel: Ariel Harush, Sheran Yeini, Omri Ben Harush (81' Yonatan Cohen), Loai Taha, Eli Dasa, Bibras Natcho, Biram Kayal (73' Dan Glazer), Nir Bitton, Dia Saba (66' Ben Sahar), Don Peretz (YC89), Eran Zahavi. (Coach: Andreas Herzog (AUT)).
Goals: Israel: 0-1 Eran Zahavi (10'), 0-2 Eran Zahavi (60'), 0-3 Eran Zahavi (81').
Referee: Sergey Ivanov (RUS)   Attendance: 5.508

10-06-2019 Philip II National Arena, Skopje: North Macedonia – Austria 1-4 (1-1)
North Macedonia: Stole Dimitrievski, Stefan Ristovski, Darko Velkovski (YC76), Egzon Bejtulai (YC61), Arijan Ademi, Boban Nikolov (67' Ferhan Hasani), Enis Bardhi (YC84), Eljif Elmas (YC26) (56' Kire Ristevski), Goran Pandev, Ilija Nestorovski (56' Marjan Radeski), Ezgjan Alioski. (Coach: Igor Angelovski (MKD)).
Austria: Heinz Lindner, Andreas Ulmer, Aleksandar Dragovic (46' Stefan Posch), Stefan Lainer, Martin Hinteregger, Stefan Ilsanker, Marcel Sabitzer (90+3' Louis Schaub), Valentino Lazaro, Konrad Laimer, Xaver Schlager, Marko Arnautovic (89' Guido Burgstaller). (Coach: Franco Foda (GER)).
Goals: North Macedonia: 1-0 Martin Hinteregger (18' *own goal*).
Austria: 1-1 Valentino Lazaro (39'), 1-2 Marko Arnautovic (62' penalty), 1-3 Marko Arnautovic (82'), 1-4 Egzon Bejtulai (86' *own goal*).
Referee: Aleksei Eskov (RUS)   Attendance: 10.501

10-06-2019   Daugavas Stadionā, Riga: Latvia – Slovenia 0-5 (0-4)
Latvia: Pāvels Steinbors, Aleksandrs Solovjovs, Kaspars Dubra, Vitālijs Maksimenko (16'
Vitālijs Jagodinskis), Mārcis Oss, Vladimir Kamess (YC35), Olegs Laizāns, Kristers Tobers
(YC29) (69' Ritvars Rugins), Deniss Rakels (78' Daniels Ontuzāns), Roberts Savalnieks,
Vladislavs Gutkovskis. (Coach: Slavisa Stojanovic (SRB)).
Slovenia: Jan Oblak, Bojan Jokic (YC41), Aljaz Struna, Miha Mevlja, Petar Stojanovic, Josip
Ilicic, Denis Popovic (77' Luka Zahovic), Jasmin Kurtic, Miha Zajc (64' Jaka Bijol), Domen
Crnigoj (83' Zan Majer), Robert Beric. (Coach: Matjaz Kek (SVN)).
Goals: Slovenia: 0-1 Domen Crnigoj (24'), 0-2 Domen Crnigoj (27'), 0-3 Josip Ilicic (29'
penalty), 0-4 Josip Ilicic (44'), 0-5 Miha Zajc (47').
Referee: Kevin Clancy (SCO)   Attendance: 4.011

10-06-2019   PGE Narodowy, Warsaw: Poland – Israel 4-0 (1-0)
Poland: Lukas Fabianski, Kamil Glik, Bartosz Bereszynski, Tomasz Kedziora, Jan Bednarek,
Mateusz Klich (75' Jacek Góralski), Grzegorz Krychowiak (YC26), Piotr Zielinski, Kamil
Grosicki (77' Damian Kadzior), Robert Lewandowski, Krzysztof Piatek (73' Arkadiusz Milik).
(Coach: Jerzy Brzeczek (POL)).
Israel: Ariel Harush, Sheran Yeini, Omri Ben Harush, Loai Taha, Eli Dasa, Bibras Natcho,
Biram Kayal (56' Yonatan Cohen), Nir Bitton (82' Hatem Abd Elhamed), Don Peretz, Manor
Solomon (72' Dia Saba), Eran Zahavi (YC40). (Coach: Andreas Herzog (AUT)).
Goals: Poland: 1-0 Krzysztof Piatek (35'), 2-0 Robert Lewandowski (56' penalty), 3-0 Kamil
Grosicki (59'), 4-0 Damian Kadzior (84').
Referee: Tobias Stieler (GER)   Attendance: 57.229

05-09-2019   Yaakov Turner Toto Stadium, Beer Sheva: Israel – North Macedonia 1-1 (0-0)
Israel: Ofir Marciano, Orel Dgani, Omri Ben Harush (60' Biram Kayal), Hatem Abd Elhamed
(YC90+3), Loai Taha, Eli Dasa, Bibras Natcho, Don Peretz, Manor Solomon (YC89), Eran
Zahavi, Mounas Dabour (75' Tomer Hemed). (Coach: Andreas Herzog (AUT)).
North Macedonia: Stole Dimitrievski, Kire Ristevski, Visar Musliu, Darko Velkovski, Egzon
Bejtulai, Arijan Ademi, Boban Nikolov (YC7) (75' Aleksandar Trajkovski), Enis Bardhi (83'
Stefan Spirovski), Eljif Elmas, Ilija Nestorovski (69' Goran Pandev), Ezgjan Alioski. (Coach:
Igor Angelovski (MKD)).
Goals: Israel: 1-0 Eran Zahavi (55').
North Macedonia: 1-1 Arijan Ademi (64').
Referee: Andreas Ekberg (SWE)   Attendance: 15.200

06-09-2019   Red Bull Arena, Wals-Siezenheim: Austria – Latvia 6-0 (2-0)
Austria: Cican Stankovic, Andreas Ulmer, Aleksandar Dragovic (82' Florian Grillitsch), David
Alaba, Stefan Lainer, Martin Hinteregger, Julian Baumgartlinger (75' Stefan Ilsanker), Marcel
Sabitzer, Valentino Lazaro (69' Michael Gregoritsch), Konrad Laimer, Marko Arnautovic.
(Coach: Franco Foda (GER)).
Latvia: Pāvels Steinbors, Boriss Bogdaskins (YC52), Kaspars Dubra, Vitālijs Maksimenko,
Antonijs Cernomordijs, Vladimir Kamess, Olegs Laizāns (YC80) (82' Roberts Uldrikis),
Andrejs Ciganiks (67' Roberts Savalnieks (YC87)), Kristers Tobers (77' Ritvars Rugins
(YC81)), Armands Pētersons (YC4), Vladislavs Gutkovskis. (Coach: Slavisa Stojanovic
(SRB)).
Goals: Austria: 1-0 Marko Arnautovic (7'), 2-0 Marcel Sabitzer (13'), 3-0 Marko Arnautovic
(53' penalty), 4-0 Pāvels Steinbors (76' own goal), 5-0 Konrad Laimer (80'), 6-0 Michael
Gregoritsch (85').
Referee: Robert Hennessey (IRL)   Attendance: 16.300

431

06-09-2019   Stadion Stozice, Ljubljana: Slovenia – Poland 2-0 (1-0)
Slovenia: Jan Oblak, Aljaz Struna (YC4), Miha Mevlja, Jure Balkovec, Petar Stojanovic (YC74), Josip Ilicic, Rene Krhin, Jasmin Kurtic, Benjamin Verbic (62' Domen Crnigoj, 90+1' Robert Beric), Roman Bezjak, Andraz Sporar (85' Denis Popovic). (Coach: Matjaz Kek (SVN)).
Poland: Lukas Fabianski, Michal Pazdan, Bartosz Bereszynski (YC90+2), Tomasz Kedziora, Jan Bednarek, Mateusz Klich (YC37) (70' Krystian Bielik), Grzegorz Krychowiak (YC80), Piotr Zielinski, Kamil Grosicki (70' Jakub Blaszczykowski), Robert Lewandowski, Krzysztof Piatek (76' Dawid Kownacki). (Coach: Jerzy Brzeczek (POL)).
Goals: Slovenia: 1-0 Aljaz Struna (35'), 2-0 Andraz Sporar (65').
Referee: Sergei Karasev (RUS)   Attendance: 15.231

09-09-2019   Daugavas Stadionā, Riga: Latvia – North Macedonia 0-2 (0-2)
Latvia: Andris Vanins, Vitālijs Maksimenko (YC47), Antonijs Cernomordijs, Vladimir Kamess (YC43) (84' Valērijs Sabala), Olegs Laizāns, Ritvars Rugins (YC67), Jānis Ikaunieks (YC53), Mārtins Kigurs (76' Ēriks Punculs), Armands Pētersons, Vladislavs Gutkovskis, Roberts Uldrikis (46' Roberts Savalnieks). (Coach: Slavisa Stojanovic (SRB)).
North Macedonia: Stole Dimitrievski, Visar Musliu, Darko Velkovski, Egzon Bejtulai (YC37), Arijan Ademi (YC85), Ivan Trickovski, Enis Bardhi (YC69), Eljif Elmas (88' Marjan Radeski), Goran Pandev (75' Boban Nikolov), Aleksandar Trajkovski (65' Ilija Nestorovski), Ezgjan Alioski. (Coach: Igor Angelovski (MKD)).
Goals: North Macedonia: 0-1 Goran Pandev (14'), 0-2 Enis Bardhi (17').
Referee: Espen Eskås (NOR)   Attendance: 2.724

09-09-2019   PGE Narodowy, Warsaw: Poland – Austria 0-0
Poland: Lukas Fabianski, Kamil Glik, Bartosz Bereszynski, Tomasz Kedziora, Jan Bednarek, Grzegorz Krychowiak, Piotr Zielinski, Krystian Bielik (YC90+3), Kamil Grosicki (70' Sebastian Szymanski), Robert Lewandowski, Dawid Kownacki (58' Jakub Blaszczykowski, 77' Mateusz Klich (YC85)). (Coach: Jerzy Brzeczek (POL)).
Austria: Cican Stankovic, Andreas Ulmer, Aleksandar Dragovic, David Alaba, Stefan Lainer, Stefan Posch, Julian Baumgartlinger, Marcel Sabitzer (YC33), Valentino Lazaro (77' Stefan Ilsanker), Konrad Laimer (YC46) (89' Michael Gregoritsch), Marko Arnautovic (YC8). (Coach: Franco Foda (GER)).
Referee: Viktor Kassai (HUN)   Attendance: 56.788

09-09-2019   Stadion Stozice, Ljubljana: Slovenia – Israel 3-2 (1-0)
Slovenia: Jan Oblak, Bojan Jokic (46' Jure Balkovec), Aljaz Struna (54' Miha Blazic), Miha Mevlja, Petar Stojanovic, Josip Ilicic (YC58), Rene Krhin (81' Denis Popovic), Jasmin Kurtic, Benjamin Verbic (YC90+1), Roman Bezjak (YC57), Andraz Sporar. (Coach: Matjaz Kek (SVN)).
Israel: Ofir Marciano, Orel Dgani, Omri Ben Harush (46' Biram Kayal), Hatem Abd Elhamed, Loai Taha (YC6), Eli Dasa, Bibras Natcho, Don Peretz (YC45+1) (77' Dan Glazer), Manor Solomon, Eran Zahavi, Shon Weissman (61' Mounas Dabour). (Coach: Andreas Herzog (AUT)).
Goals: Slovenia: 1-0 Benjamin Verbic (43'), 2-2 Roman Bezjak (66'), 3-2 Benjamin Verbic (90').
Israel: 1-1 Bibras Natcho (50), 1-2 Eran Zahavi (63').
Referee: Anthony Taylor (ENG)   Attendance: 10.669

10-10-2019   Ernst-Happel-Stadion, Vienna: Austria – Israel 3-1 (1-1)
Austria: Cican Stankovic, Andreas Ulmer, Aleksandar Dragovic, Martin Hinteregger, Stefan
Posch (YC47) (63' Christopher Trimmel), Julian Baumgartlinger (YC31), Stefan Ilsanker,
Marcel Sabitzer, Valentino Lazaro, Konrad Laimer (59' Louis Schaub), Marko Arnautovic (82'
Michael Gregoritsch). (Coach: Franco Foda (GER)).
Israel: Ofir Marciano, Taleb Tawatha (54' Omri Ben Harush), Eitan Tibi, Hatem Abd
Elhamed, Loai Taha (76' Yonatan Cohen), Eli Dasa, Bibras Natcho, Nir Bitton (YC55), Manor
Solomon, Eran Zahavi, Mounas Dabour (YC47) (70' Shon Weissman). (Coach: Andreas
Herzog (AUT)).
Goals: Austria: 1-1 Valentino Lazaro (41'), 2-1 Martin Hinteregger (56'), 3-1 Marcel Sabitzer
(88').
Israel: 0-1 Eran Zahavi (34').
Referee: William Collum (SCO)   Attendance: 26.200

10-10-2019   Philip II National Arena, Skopje: North Macedonia – Slovenia 2-1 (0-0)
North Macedonia: Stole Dimitrievski, Stefan Ristovski (YC43) (82' Gjoko Zajkov (YC90+4)),
Kire Ristevski, Visar Musliu (YC42), Arijan Ademi (78' Kristijan Tosevski), Stefan Spirovski,
Boban Nikolov, Eljif Elmas, Goran Pandev (YC27) (66' Ivan Trickovski), Ilija Nestorovski,
Ezgjan Alioski. (Coach: Igor Angelovski (MKD)).
Slovenia: Jan Oblak, Aljaz Struna, Miha Mevlja, Jure Balkovec, Petar Stojanovic, Josip Ilicic,
Rene Krhin (48' Denis Popovic), Jasmin Kurtic (YC43), Benjamin Verbic (65' Miha Zajc),
Roman Bezjak (79' Robert Beric), Andraz Sporar. (Coach: Matjaz Kek (SVN)).
Goals: North Macedonia: 1-0 Eljif Elmas (50'), 2-0 Eljif Elmas (68').
Slovenia: 2-1 Josip Ilicic (90+5' penalty).
Referee: Danny Makkelie (HOL)   Attendance: 16.500

10-10-2019   Daugavas Stadionā, Riga: Latvia – Poland 0-3 (0-2)
Latvia: Andris Vanins, Kaspars Dubra, Vitālijs Maksimenko (YC52), Vitālijs Jagodinskis,
Mārcis Oss, Olegs Laizāns (72' Kristers Tobers), Ritvars Rugins, Jānis Ikaunieks, Mārtins
Kigurs (86' Andrejs Ciganiks), Deniss Rakels (72' Artūrs Karasausks), Vladislavs Gutkovskis.
(Coach: Slavisa Stojanovic (SRB)).
Poland: Wojciech Szczesny, Kamil Glik, Tomasz Kedziora, Jan Bednarek, Maciej Rybus (80'
Arkadiusz Reca), Mateusz Klich (60' Krzysztof Piatek), Grzegorz Krychowiak, Piotr Zielinski,
Sebastian Szymanski, Kamil Grosicki (77' Przemyslaw Frankowski), Robert Lewandowski.
(Coach: Jerzy Brzeczek (POL)).
Goals: Poland: 0-1 Robert Lewandowski (9'), 0-2 Robert Lewandowski (13'), 0-3 Robert
Lewandowski (76').
Referee: Halis Özkahya (TUR)   Attendance: 7.107

13-10-2019   PGE Narodowy, Warsaw: Poland – North Macedonia 2-0 (0-0)
Poland: Wojciech Szczesny, Kamil Glik, Bartosz Bereszynski, Jan Bednarek (YC35), Grzegorz
Krychowiak, Piotr Zielinski (90+2' Krzysztof Piatek), Jacek Góralski, Arkadiusz Reca
(YC66), Sebastian Szymanski (YC39) (68' Arkadiusz Milik), Kamil Grosicki (73' Przemyslaw
Frankowski), Robert Lewandowski. (Coach: Jerzy Brzeczek (POL)).
North Macedonia: Stole Dimitrievski, Stefan Ristovski (82' Marjan Radeski), Kire Ristevski,
Visar Musliu (YC80), Egzon Bejtulai, Stefan Spirovski (YC62), Boban Nikolov (YC19) (88'
Georgi Stoilov), Eljif Elmas, Goran Pandev (YC13), Ilija Nestorovski (YC33) (73' Aleksandar
Trajkovski), Ezgjan Alioski (YC67). (Coach: Igor Angelovski (MKD)).
Goals: Poland: 1-0 Przemyslaw Frankowski (74'), 2-0 Arkadiusz Milik (80').
Referee: ANTONIO MATEU Lahoz (ESP)   Attendance: 52.894

433

13-10-2019   Stadion Stozice, Ljubljana: Slovenia – Austria 0-1 (0-1)
Slovenia: Jan Oblak, Aljaz Struna (YC16), Miha Mevlja, Jure Balkovec, Petar Stojanovic, Josip Ilicic, Rene Krhin (79' Denis Popovic (RC89)), Jasmin Kurtic, Benjamin Verbic (69' Robert Beric), Roman Bezjak (YC57) (61' Miha Zajc), Andraz Sporar. (Coach: Matjaz Kek (SVN)).
Austria: Cican Stankovic, Andreas Ulmer (YC36), Aleksandar Dragovic, Martin Hinteregger (YC64), Stefan Posch, Julian Baumgartlinger, Stefan Ilsanker, Michael Gregoritsch (83' Karim Onisiwo), Marcel Sabitzer (YC90) (90+2' Florian Kainz), Valentino Lazaro (88' Christopher Trimmel), Konrad Laimer (YC87). (Coach: Franco Foda (GER)).
Goal: Austria: 0-1 Stefan Posch (21').
Referee: Cüneyt Çakir (TUR)   Attendance: 15.108

15-10-2019   Yaakov Turner Toto Stadium, Beer Sheva: Israel – Latvia 3-1 (3-1)
Israel: Ofir Marciano, Taleb Tawatha (78' Sun Menachem), Hatem Abd Elhamed, Loai Taha, Eli Dasa, Bibras Natcho, Nir Bitton, Dia Saba (76' Ilay Elmkies), Dan Glazer (YC56), Eran Zahavi, Mounas Dabour (84' Shon Weissman). (Coach: Andreas Herzog (AUT)).
Latvia: Pavels Steinbors, Igors Tarasovs, Vitālijs Jagodinskis, Mārcis Oss (YC19), Antonijs Cernomordijs (YC87), Vladimir Kamess (78' Dāvis Ikaunieks), Jānis Ikaunieks (YC64) (86' Daniels Ontuzāns), Raivis Jurkovskis, Mārtiņs Kigurs (68' Olegs Laizāns), Roberts Savalnieks, Vladislavs Gutkovskis. (Coach: Slavisa Stojanovic (SRB)).
Goals: Israel: 1-0 Mounas Dabour (16'), 2-0 Eran Zahavi (26'), 3-1 Mounas Dabour (42').
Latvia: 2-1 Vladimir Kamess (40').
Referee: Arnold Hunter (NIR)   Attendance: 9.150

16-11-2019   Stadion Stozice, Ljubljana: Slovenia – Latvia 1-0 (0-0)
Slovenia: Jan Oblak, Bojan Jokic, Aljaz Struna (YC14), Miha Mevlja, Petar Stojanovic, Josip Ilicic, Rene Krhin (74' Jaka Bijol), Haris Vuckic (62' Miha Zajc), Jasmin Kurtic, Benjamin Verbic (YC70) (90+1' Roman Bezjak)), Andraz Sporar. (Coach: Matjaz Kek (SVN)).
Latvia: Pavels Steinbors, Igors Tarasovs, Kaspars Dubra, Vitālijs Maksimenko, Mārcis Oss (YC58), Vladimir Kamess (88' Ēriks Punculs), Dāvis Ikaunieks (72' Roberts Uldrikis), Raivis Jurkovskis, Roberts Savalnieks (YC59), Vladislavs Gutkovskis (YC23) (85' Olegs Laizāns), Vladislavs Flodorovs (YC47). (Coach: Slavisa Stojanovic (SRB)).
Goal: Slovenia: 1-0 Igors Tarasovs (53' own goal).
Referee: Radu Petrescu (ROM)   Attendance: 11.224

16-11-2019   Ernst-Happel-Stadion, Vienna: Austria – North Macedonia 2-1 (1-0)
Austria: Alexander Schlager, Andreas Ulmer, Aleksandar Dragovic, David Alaba (90+2' Michael Gregoritsch), Stefan Lainer, Martin Hinteregger, Julian Baumgartlinger, Marcel Sabitzer, Valentino Lazaro (79' Christopher Trimmel), Konrad Laimer (90' Stefan Ilsanker), Marko Arnautovic. (Coach: Franco Foda (GER)).
North Macedonia: Stole Dimitrievski, Stefan Ristovski, Kire Ristevski, Darko Velkovski, Kristijan Tosevski (62' Daniel Avramovski), Mario Mladenovski (46' Gjoko Zajkov), Stefan Spirovski, Tihomir Kostadinov, Enis Bardhi, Eljif Elmas, Aleksandar Trajkovski (13' Vlatko Stojanovski). (Coach: Igor Angelovski (MKD)).
Goals: Austria: 1-0 David Alaba (7'), 2-0 Stefan Lainer (48').
North Macedonia: 2-1 Vlatko Stojanovski (90+3').
Referee: Michael Oliver (ENG)   Attendance: 41.100

16-11-2019   Teddi Malcha Stadium, Jerusalem: Israel – Poland 1-2 (0-1)
Israel: Ofir Marciano, Omri Ben Harush (65' Sun Menachem), Eitan Tibi, Loai Taha (43'
Dolev Haziza), Eli Dasa, Bibras Natcho, Biram Kayal (79' Ilay Elmkies), Nir Bitton (YC53),
Dan Glazer, Eran Zahavi, Mounas Dabour. (Coach: Andreas Herzog (AUT)).
Poland: Wojciech Szczesny, Kamil Glik, Tomasz Kedziora, Jan Bednarek, Grzegorz
Krychowiak (84' Dominik Furman), Piotr Zielinski, Arkadiusz Reca, Przemyslaw Frankowski,
Krystian Bielik (YC57), Sebastian Szymanski (63' Robert Lewandowski), Krzysztof Piatek
(70' Mateusz Klich). (Coach: Jerzy Brzeczek (POL)).
Goals: Israel: 1-2 Mounas Dabour (88').
Poland: 0-1 Grzegorz Krychowiak (4'), 0-2 Krzysztof Piatek (54').
Referee: Mattias Gestranius (FIN)   Attendance: 16.700

19-11-2019   Philip II National Arena, Skopje: North Macedonia – Israel 1-0 (1-0)
North Macedonia: Stole Dimitrievski, Stefan Ristovski, Kire Ristevski, Visar Musliu, Darko
Velkovski (72' Gjoko Zajkov), Boban Nikolov (YC60), Tihomir Kostadinov, Enis Bardhi
(YC29), Eljif Elmas, Goran Pandev (79' Daniel Avramovski), Vlatko Stojanovski (61' Ilija
Nestorovski). (Coach: Igor Angelovski (MKD)).
Israel: Ariel Harush, Eitan Tibi, Eli Dasa (41' Orel Dgani), Sun Menachem (YC82), Bibras
Natcho, Nir Bitton, Dia Saba (YC35) (68' Shon Weissman), Dan Glazer (YC35), Ilay Elmkies
(59' Dolev Haziza), Eran Zahavi, Mounas Dabour (YC88). (Coach: Andreas Herzog (AUT)).
Goal: North Macedonia: 1-0 Boban Nikolov (45+2').
Referee: Paolo Valeri (ITA)   Attendance: 5.573

19-11-2019   Daugavas Stadionā, Riga: Latvia – Austria 1-0 (0-0)
Latvia: Pavels Steinbors (YC72), Kaspars Dubra, Vitālijs Maksimenko, Mārcis Oss, Vladimir
Kamess, Dāvis Ikaunieks (YC25) (89' Igors Tarasovs), Aleksejs Grjaznovs (90+2' Antonijs
Cernomordijs), Raivis Jurkovskis, Roberts Savalnieks, Vladislavs Flodorovs, Roberts Uldrikis
(70' Vladislavs Gutkovskis). (Coach: Slavisa Stojanovic (SRB)).
Austria: Pavao Pervan, Aleksandar Dragovic, Christopher Trimmel, Stefan Posch, Max Wöber,
Julian Baumgartlinger (46' Karim Onisiwo), Stefan Ilsanker (YC55) (77' Reinhold Ranftl),
Michael Gregoritsch, Louis Schaub, Thomas Goiginger (69' Lukas Hinterseer), Florian
Grillitsch. (Coach: Franco Foda (GER)).
Goal: Latvia: 1-0 Mārcis Oss (65').
Referee: ALEJANDRO HERNÁNDEZ Hernández (ESP)   Attendance: 2.781

19-11-2019   PGE Narodowy, Warsaw: Poland – Slovenia 3-2 (1-1)
Poland: Wojciech Szczesny, Lukas Piszczek (45+4' Tomasz Kedziora (YC85)), Kamil Glik (7'
Artur Jedrzejczyk), Jan Bednarek, Grzegorz Krychowiak (YC70), Piotr Zielinski, Jacek
Góralski, Arkadiusz Reca (YC32), Sebastian Szymanski (86' Kamil Józwiak), Kamil Grosicki,
Robert Lewandowski. (Coach: Jerzy Brzeczek (POL)).
Slovenia: Jan Oblak, Miha Mevlja, Miha Blazic, Jure Balkovec, Petar Stojanovic, Josip Ilicic,
Rene Krhin, Jasmin Kurtic (YC2,YC86), Benjamin Verbic (86' Rajko Rep), Jaka Bijol (72'
Miha Zajc), Tim Matavz (89' Haris Vuckic). (Coach: Matjaz Kek (SVN)).
Goals: Poland: 1-0 Sebastian Szymanski (3'), 2-1 Robert Lewandowski (54'), 3-2 Jacek
Góralski (81').
Slovenia: 1-1 Tim Matavz (14'), 2-2 Josip Ilicic (61').
Referee: Daniel Siebert (GER)   Attendance: 53.946

435

GROUP   H

22-03-2019	Shkodër	Albania – Turkey	0-2 (0-1)
22-03-2019	Andorra la Vella	Andorra – Iceland	0-2 (0-1)
22-03-2019	Chisinau	Moldova – France	1-4 (0-3)
25-03-2019	Eskisehir	Turkey – Moldova	4-0 (2-0)
25-03-2019	Andorra la Vella	Andorra – Albania	0-3 (0-1)
25-03-2019	Saint-Denis	France – Iceland	4-0 (1-0)
08-06-2019	Reykjavik	Iceland – Albania	1-0 (1-0)
08-06-2019	Chisinau	Moldova – Andorra	1-0 (1-0)
08-06-2019	Konya	Turkey – France	2-0 (2-0)
11-06-2019	Elbasan	Albania – Moldova	2-0 (0-0)
11-06-2019	Andorra la Vella	Andorra – France	0-4 (0-3)
11-06-2019	Reykjavik	Iceland – Turkey	2-1 (2-1)
07-09-2019	Reykjavik	Iceland – Moldova	3-0 (1-0)
07-09-2019	Saint-Denis	France – Albania	4-1 (2-0)
07-09-2019	Istanbul	Turkey – Andorra	1-0 (0-0)
10-09-2019	Elbasan	Albania – Iceland	4-2 (1-0)
10-09-2019	Sain-Denis	France – Andorra	3-0 (1-0)
10-09-2019	Chisinau	Moldova – Turkey	0-4 (0-1)
11-10-2019	Andorra la Vella	Andorra – Moldova	1-0 (0-0)
11-10-2019	Reykjavik	Iceland – France	0-1 (0-0)
11-10-2019	Istanbul	Turkey – Albania	1-0 (0-0)
14-10-2019	Saint-Denis	France – Turkey	1-1 (0-0)
14-10-2019	Reykjavik	Iceland – Andorra	2-0 (1-0)
14-10-2019	Chisinau	Moldova – Albania	0-4 (0-3)
14-11-2019	Istanbul	Turkey – Iceland	0-0
14-11-2019	Elbasan	Albania – Andorra	2-2 (1-1)
14-11-2019	Saint-Denis	France – Moldova	2-1 (1-1)
17-11-2019	Tirana	Albania – France	0-2 (0-2)
17-11-2019	Andorra la Vella	Andorra – Turkey	0-2 (0-2)
17-11-2019	Chisinau	Moldova – Iceland	1-2 (0-1)

FINAL STANDING

Pos	Team	Pld	W	D	L	GF	GA	GD	Pts
1	France	10	8	1	1	25	6	+19	25
2	Turkey	10	7	2	1	18	3	+15	23
3	Iceland	10	6	1	3	14	11	+3	19
4	Albania	10	4	1	5	16	14	+2	13
5	Andorra	10	1	1	8	3	20	-17	4
6	Moldova	10	1	0	9	4	26	-22	3

France and Turkey qualified for final tournament.

22-03-2019   Stadiumi Loro Boriçi, Shkodёr: Albania – Turkey 0-2 (0-1)
Albania: Etrit Berisha, Freddie Veseli, Elseid Hysaj, Berat Djimsiti, Ivan Balliu Campeny (YC39) (58' Armando Sadiku), Ardian Ismajli (YC45+2), Amir Abrashi, Ledian Memushaj, Taulant Xhaka (YC86), Bekim Balaj (58' Eros Grezda), Myrto Uzuni. (Coach: Christian Panucci (ITA)).
Turkey: Mert Günok, Gökhan Gönül (46' Mehmet Çelik), Hasan-Ali Kaldirim, Kaan Ayhan, Merih Demiral, Emre Belözoglu (65' Dorukhan Toköz), Mahmut Tekdemir, Okay Yokuslu (YC47), Hakan Çalhanoglu, Burak Yilmaz (88' Deniz Türüç), Cenk Tosun (YC30). (Coach: Senol Günes (TUR)).
Goals: Turkey: 0-1 Burak Yilmaz (21'), 0-2 Hakan Çalhanoglu (55').
Referee: Tobias Stieler (GER)   Attendance: 11.730

22-03-2019   Estadi Nacional, Andorra la Vella: Andorra – Iceland 0-2 (0-1)
Andorra: Josep Antonio Gómes Moreira, Ildefons Lima Solà, Marc Vales González, Moisés San Nicolás Schellens, Marc Rebés Ruiz (YC82), Jesús "Chus" Rubio Gómez (YC40) (87' Julià "Juli" Sánchez Soto), Max Llovera González Adrio, Joan Cervós Moro, Márcio Vieira De Vasconcelos (YC20), Cristián Martínez Alejo (YC47) (81' Ludovic Clemente Garcés "Ludo"), Alexandre Martínez Palau (71' Jordi Aláez Peña). (Coach: Jesús Luis Álvarez De Eulate Güergue "Koldo" (AND)).
Iceland: Hannes Halldórsson, Ragnar Sigurdsson, Birkir Sævarsson, Ari Skúlason, Birkir Bjarnason, Kári Árnason, Aron Gunnarsson (63' Rúnar Sigurjónsson), Jóhann Berg Gudmundsson (83' Arnór Ingvi Traustason), Gylfi Sigurdsson, Arnór Sigurdsson, Alfred Finnbogason (70' Vidar Kjartansson). (Coach: Erik Hamrén (SWE)).
Goals: Iceland: 0-1 Birkir Bjarnason (22'), 0-2 Vidar Kjartansson (80').
Referee: Sandro Schärer (SUI)   Attendance: 1.854

22-03-2019   Stadionul Zimbru, Chisinau: Moldova – France 1-4 (0-3)
Moldova: Alexei Koselev, Ion Jardan, Veaceslav Posmac, Oleg Reabciuk, Eugen Cebotaru, Artur Ionita, Alexandru Antoniuc (73' Vladimir Ambros (YC83)), Radu Gînsari, Catalin Carp, Eugeniu Cociuc (46' Artiom Rozgoniuc), Ion Nicolaescu (59' Vitalie Damascan (YC78)). (Coach: Alexandru Spiridon (MOL)).
France: Hugo Lloris, Layvin Kurzawa, Raphaël Varane (YC34), Samuel Umtiti, Benjamin Pavard, Blaise Matuidi (73' Florian Thauvin), Paul Pogba, N'Golo Kanté, Olivier Giroud (81' Nabil Fekir), Antoine Griezmann (73' Thomas Lemar), Kylian Mbappé (YC90+1). (Coach: Didier Deschamps (FRA)).
Goals: Moldova: 1-4 Vladimir Ambros (89').
France: 0-1 Antoine Griezmann (24'), 0-2 Raphaël Varane (27'), 0-3 Olivier Giroud (36'), 0-4 Kylian Mbappé (87').
Referee: Aleksandar Stavrev (MCD)   Attendance: 10.042

25-03-2019   Yeni Eskisehir Stadyumu, Eskisehir: Turkey – Moldova 4-0 (2-0)
Turkey: Mert Günok, Hasan-Ali Kaldirim, Kaan Ayhan, Mehmet Çelik, Merih Demiral, Mahmut Tekdemir, Hakan Çalhanoglu (66' Yusuf Yazici), Deniz Türüç (78' Efecan Karaca), Dorukhan Toköz (84' Emre Belözoglu), Burak Yilmaz, Cenk Tosun. (Coach: Senol Günes (TUR)).
Moldova: Alexei Koselev, Ion Jardan, Veaceslav Posmac, Dinu Graur, Oleg Reabciuk (YC64), Eugen Cebotaru, Artur Ionita (YC65), Radu Gînsari (73' Alexandru Antoniuc), Artiom Rozgoniuc (YC26), Catalin Carp (46' Iaser Turcan), Vladimir Ambros (57' Ion Nicolaescu). (Coach: Alexandru Spiridon (MOL)).
Goals: Turkey: 1-0 Hasan-Ali Kaldirim (24'), 2-0 Cenk Tosun (26'), 3-0 Cenk Tosun (53'), 4-0 Kaan Ayhan (70').
Referee: Serhiy Mykolayovych Boyko (UKR)   Attendance: 29.456
(Burak Yilmaz missed a penalty kick in the 53rd minute)

25-03-2019   Estadi Nacional, Andorra la Vella: Andorra – Albania 0-3 (0-1)
Andorra: Josep Antonio Gómes Moreira (YC82), Ildefons Lima Solà (YC6), Marc Vales González (84' Marc Pujol Pons), Moisés San Nicolás Schellens, Marc Rebés Ruiz, Jesús "Chus" Rubio Gómez (YC59), Max Llovera González Adrio, Víctor Rodríguez Soria, Márcio Vieira de Vasconcelos, Cristián Martínez Alejo (YC73) (74' Jordi Aláez Peña), Ludovic Clemente Garcés "Ludo" (67' Joan Cervós Moro). (Coach: Jesús Luis Álvarez de Eulate Güergue "Koldo" (AND)).
Albania: Etrit Berisha, Elseid Hysaj, Berat Djimsiti, Naser Aliji, Ardian Ismajli, Migjen Basha (87' Ledian Memushaj), Taulant Xhaka (67' Amir Abrashi (YC83)), Ergys Kaçe, Armando Sadiku, Eros Grezda (70' Bekim Balaj), Myrto Uzuni. (Coach: Ervin Bulku (ALB)).
Goals: Albania: 0-1 Armando Sadiku (21'), 0-2 Bekim Balaj (87'), 0-3 Amir Abrashi (90+6').
Referee: Filip Glova (SVK)   Attendance: 1.373

25-03-2019   Stade de France, Saint Denis: France – Iceland 4-0 (1-0)
France: Hugo Lloris, Layvin Kurzawa (85' Presnel Kimpembe), Raphaël Varane, Samuel Umtiti, Benjamin Pavard, Blaise Matuidi, Paul Pogba, N'Golo Kanté (80' Thomas Lemar), Olivier Giroud (90' Moussa Sissoko), Antoine Griezmann (YC90+1), Kylian Mbappé. (Coach: Didier Deschamps (FRA)).
Iceland: Hannes Halldórsson, Ragnar Sigurdsson, Birkir Sævarsson (84' Ari Skúlason), Hördur Magnússon, Sverrir Ingason, Birkir Bjarnason (YC51), Kári Árnason, Aron Gunnarsson, Rúnar Sigurjónsson (57' Arnór Ingvi Traustason), Gylfi Sigurdsson, Albert Gudmundsson (62' Alfred Finnbogason). (Coach: Erik Hamrén (SWE)).
Goals: France: 1-0 Samuel Umtiti (12'), 2-0 Olivier Giroud (68'), 3-0 Kylian Mbappé (78'), 4-0 Antoine Griezmann (84').
Referee: István Kovács (ROM)   Attendance: 64.538

08-06-2019   Laugardalsvöllur, Reykjavik: Iceland – Albania 1-0 (1-0)
Iceland: Hannes Halldórsson, Ragnar Sigurdsson, Ari Skúlason, Hjörtur Hermannsson, Birkir Bjarnason, Kári Árnason, Aron Gunnarsson, Jóhann Berg Gudmundsson (56' Arnór Ingvi Traustason), Rúnar Sigurjónsson (YC33) (81' Arnór Sigurdsson), Gylfi Sigurdsson, Vidar Kjartansson (63' Kolbeinn Sigthórsson). (Coach: Erik Hamrén (SWE)).
Albania: Etrit Berisha, Ermir Lenjani, Freddie Veseli (YC89), Elseid Hysaj, Kastriot Dermaku (YC88), Ardian Ismajli, Amir Abrashi, Migjen Basha (YC22) (68' Ergys Kaçe), Taulant Xhaka (72' Emanuele Ndoj), Sokol Çikalleshi (80' Armando Sadiku), Bekim Balaj. (Coach: Edoardo Reja (ITA)).
Goal: Iceland: 1-0 Jóhann Berg Gudmundsson (22').
Referee: Bobby Madden (SCO)   Attendance: 8.968

438

08-06-2019   Stadionul Zimbru, Chisinau: Moldova – Andorra 1-0 (1-0)
Moldova: Alexei Koselev, Igor Armas, Ion Jardan, Stefan Efros, Oleg Reabciuk, Alexandru
Suvorov (50' Eugen Cebotaru), Artur Ionita (YC38,YC46), Alexandru Antoniuc (64' Eugeniu
Cociuc), Radu Gînsari, Catalin Carp (YC79), Vitalie Damascan (80' Alexandru Boiciuc).
(Coach: Alexandru Spiridon (MOL)).
Andorra: Josep Antonio Gómes Moreira, Ildefons Lima Solà (YC90+4), Marc Vales González,
Moisés San Nicolás Schellens, Marc Rebés Ruiz (YC33) (69' Sergio "Sergi" Moreno Marín),
Jesús "Chus" Rubio Gómez (71' Alexandre Martínez Palau), Max Llovera González Adrio,
Joan Cervós Moro, Márcio Vieira de Vasconcelos, Ludovic Clemente Garcés "Ludo", Jordi
Aláez Peña (82' Aarón Sánchez Alburquerque). (Coach: Jesús Luis Álvarez de Eulate Güergue
"Koldo" (AND)).
Goal: Moldova: 1-0 Igor Armas (8').
Referee: Bojan Pandzic (SWE)   Attendance: 6.712

08-06-2019   Konya Büyüksehir Belediye Stadyumu, Konya: Turkey – France 2-0 (2-0)
Turkey: Mert Günok, Hasan-Ali Kaldirim, Kaan Ayhan, Mehmet Çelik, Merih Demiral
(YC45+2), Mahmut Tekdemir (YC39), Irfan Can Kahveci (80' Ozan Tufan), Cengiz Ünder
(85' Yusuf Yazici), Dorukhan Toköz (90' Abdülkadir Ömür), Burak Yilmaz, Kenan Karaman.
(Coach: Senol Günes (TUR)).
France: Hugo Lloris, Lucas Digne (46' Ferland Mendy), Raphaël Varane, Samuel Umtiti
(YC45+2), Benjamin Pavard, Blaise Matuidi (46' Kingsley Coman (YC86)), Moussa Sissoko,
Paul Pogba, Olivier Giroud (72' Wissam Ben Yedder), Antoine Griezmann, Kylian Mbappé.
(Coach: Didier Deschamps (FRA)).
Goals: Turkey: 1-0 Kaan Ayhan (30'), 2-0 Cengiz Ünder (40').
Referee: Damir Skomina (SLO)   Attendance: 36.783

11-06-2019   Elbasan Arena, Elbasan: Albania – Moldova 2-0 (0-0)
Albania: Etrit Berisha, Mërgim Mavraj, Ermir Lenjani (59' Odise Roshi), Freddie Veseli,
Elseid Hysaj, Ardian Ismajli, Amir Abrashi, Ergys Kaçe (84' Kristi Qose), Ylber Ramadani
(YC90+3), Armando Sadiku (58' Sokol Çikalleshi), Myrto Uzuni. (Coach: Edoardo Reja
(ITA)).
Moldova: Alexei Koselev, Igor Armas (YC56), Ion Jardan (76' Dinu Graur), Stefan Efros,
Oleg Reabciuk, Eugen Cebotaru, Alexandru Suvorov (74' Eugeniu Cociuc), Alexandru
Antoniuc, Radu Gînsari, Catalin Carp (YC75), Vitalie Damascan (70' Alexandru Boiciuc).
(Coach: Alexandru Spiridon (MOL)).
Goals: Albania: 1-0 Sokol Çikalleshi (66'), 2-0 Ylber Ramadani (90+3').
Referee: Ville Nevalainen (FIN)   Attendance: 5.004

439

11-06-2019   Estadi Nacional, Andorra la Vella: Andorra – France 0-4 (0-3)
Andorra: Josep Antonio Gómes Moreira, Ildefons Lima Solà, Marc Vales González, Moisés San Nicolás Schellens, Marc Rebés Ruiz, Jesús "Chus" Rubio Gómez (YC11), Max Llovera González Adrio, Joan Cervós Moro (81' Víctor Rodríguez Soria), Márcio Vieira de Vasconcelos, Jordi Aláez Peña (85' Julià "Juli" Sánchez Soto), Alexandre Martínez Palau (58' Jordi Rubio Gómez). (Coach: Jesús Luis Álvarez de Eulate Güergue "Koldo" (AND)).
France: Hugo Lloris, Kurt Zouma (YC77), Clément Lenglet, Léo Dubois, Ferland Mendy, Paul Pogba (YC81), Florian Thauvin (81' Thomas Lemar), Tanguy NDombèlé (64' Moussa Sissoko), Antoine Griezmann, Wissam Ben Yedder (73' Olivier Giroud), Kylian Mbappé. (Coach: Didier Deschamps (FRA)).
Goals: France: 0-1 Kylian Mbappé (11'), 0-2 Wissam Ben Yedder (30'), 0-3 Florian Thauvin (45+1'), 0-4 Kurt Zouma (60').
Referee: Fran Jovic (CRO)   Attendance: 3.187

11-06-2019   Laugardalsvöllur, Reykjavik: Iceland – Turkey 2-1 (2-1)
Iceland: Hannes Halldórsson, Ragnar Sigurdsson, Ari Skúlason (69' Hördur Magnússon), Hjörtur Hermannsson, Birkir Bjarnason (YC72), Kári Árnason, Emil Hallfredsson (YC18), Aron Gunnarsson, Jóhann Berg Gudmundsson (80' Arnór Ingvi Traustason), Gylfi Sigurdsson, Jón Bödvarsson (64' Kolbeinn Sigthórsson). (Coach: Erik Hamrén (SWE)).
Turkey: Mert Günok, Hasan-Ali Kaldirim, Kaan Ayhan (YC55), Mehmet Çelik (YC56), Merih Demiral, Hakan Çalhanoglu, Irfan Can Kahveci (63' Abdülkadir Ömür), Ozan Tufan, Dorukhan Toköz (YC23) (85' Güven Yalçin), Burak Yilmaz (YC52), Kenan Karaman (46' Yusuf Yazici). (Coach: Senol Günes (TUR)).
Goals: Iceland: 1-0 Ragnar Sigurdsson (21'), 2-0 Ragnar Sigurdsson (32').
Turkey: 2-1 Dorukhan Toköz (40').
Referee: Szymon Marciniak (POL)   Attendance: 9.680

07-09-2019   Laugardalsvöllur, Reykjavik: Iceland – Moldova 3-0 (1-0)
Iceland: Hannes Halldórsson, Ragnar Sigurdsson, Ari Skúlason, Hjörtur Hermannsson, Birkir Bjarnason (78' Rúnar Sigurjónsson), Kári Árnason, Aron Gunnarsson, Gylfi Sigurdsson, Arnór Ingvi Traustason, Kolbeinn Sigthórsson (63' Emil Hallfredsson), Jón Bödvarsson (84' Vidar Kjartansson). (Coach: Erik Hamrén (SWE)).
Moldova: Alexei Koselev, Igor Armas (YC90+3), Victor Mudrac, Dinu Graur, Oleg Reabciuk, Eugen Cebotaru, Alexandru Suvorov, Artur Ionita, Radu Gînsari (80' Constantin Sandu), Catalin Carp (YC42) (67' Iaser Turcan), Vadim Cemîrtan (65' Maxim Cojocaru (I)). (Coach: Semen Altman (UKR)).
Goals: Iceland: 1-0 Kolbeinn Sigthórsson (31'), 2-0 Birkir Bjarnason (55'), 3-0 Jón Bödvarsson (77').
Referee: JOÃO Pedro da Silva PINHEIRO (POR)   Attendance: 8.338

07-09-2019   Stade de France, Saint Denis: France – Albania 4-1 (2-0)
France: Hugo Lloris, Raphaël Varane, Clément Lenglet, Lucas Hernández (80' Lucas Digne),
Benjamin Pavard, Blaise Matuidi, Thomas Lemar (84' Nabil Fekir), Corentin Tolisso, Olivier
Giroud, Antoine Griezmann, Kingsley Coman (77' Jonathan Ikoné). (Coach: Didier
Deschamps (FRA)).
Albania: Thomas Strakosha, Mërgim Mavraj, Elseid Hysaj, Berat Djimsiti, Ardian Ismajli,
Amir Abrashi (73' Taulant Xhaka (YC78)), Odise Roshi, Keidi Bare, Ylber Ramadani (53'
Klaus Gjasula (YC86)), Bekim Balaj (61' Sokol Çikalleshi), Myrto Uzuni. (Coach: Edoardo
Reja (ITA)).
Goals: France: 1-0 Kingsley Coman (8'), 2-0 Olivier Giroud (27'), 3-0 Kingsley Coman (68'),
4-0 Jonathan Ikoné (85').
Albania: 4-1 Sokol Çikalleshi (90' penalty).
Referee: JESÚS GIL Manzano (ESP)   Attendance: 77.655
(*Antoine Griezmann missed a penalty kick in the 36th minute*)

07-09-2019   Vodafone Park, Istanbul: Turkey – Andorra 1-0 (0-0)
Turkey: Mert Günok, Mehmet Çelik, Çaglar Söyüncü (YC78), Merih Demiral, Cengiz Umut
Meras (61' Ozan Tufan), Emre Belözoglu (YC71), Hakan Çalhanoglu (80' Emre Kilinç), Irfan
Can Kahveci, Yusuf Yazici (YC90), Cenk Tosun, Güven Yalçin (46' Kenan Karaman).
(Coach: Senol Günes (TUR)).
Andorra: Josep Antonio Gómes Moreira, Ildefons Lima Solà, Marc Vales González (YC20),
Moisés San Nicolás Schellens (YC50), Marc Rebés Ruiz, Max Llovera González Adrio, Joan
Cervós Moro, Víctor Rodríguez Soria (YC47) (63' Marc García Renom), Márcio Vieira de
Vasconcelos (87' Emili Josep García Miramontes), Cristián Martínez Alejo, Ludovic Clemente
Garcés "Ludo" (79' Jordi Aláez Peña (YC90)). (Coach: Jesús Luis Álvarez de Eulate Güergue
"Koldo" (AND)).
Goal: Turkey: 1-0 Ozan Tufan (89').
Referee: Donald Robertson (SCO)   Attendance: 42.600

10-09-2019   Elbasan Arena, Elbasan: Albania – Iceland 4-2 (1-0)
Albania: Thomas Strakosha (YC81), Ermir Lenjani (62' Odise Roshi (YC85)), Elseid Hysaj
(73' Amir Abrashi), Berat Djimsiti (66' Freddie Veseli), Kastriot Dermaku, Ardian Ismajli,
Ledian Memushaj, Klaus Gjasula, Keidi Bare, Sokol Çikalleshi (YC56), Rey Manaj. (Coach:
Edoardo Reja (ITA)).
Iceland: Hannes Halldórsson, Ragnar Sigurdsson, Ari Skúlason, Hjörtur Hermannsson, Birkir
Bjarnason (71' Hördur Magnússon), Kári Árnason (YC37), Emil Hallfredsson (56' Kolbeinn
Sigthórsson), Aron Gunnarsson, Rúnar Sigurjónsson, Gylfi Sigurdsson, Jón Bödvarsson (85'
Vidar Kjartansson). (Coach: Erik Hamrén (SWE)).
Goals: Albania: 1-0 Kastriot Dermaku (32'), 2-1 Elseid Hysaj (52'), 3-2 Odise Roshi (79'), 4-2
Sokol Çikalleshi (83').
Iceland: 1-1 Gylfi Sigurdsson (47'), 2-2 Kolbeinn Sigthórsson (58').
Referee: Ivan Kruzliak (SVK)   Attendance: 8.652

10-09-2019   Stade de France, Saint Denis: France – Andorra 3-0 (1-0)
France: Hugo Lloris, Lucas Digne, Raphaël Varane, Clément Lenglet, Léo Dubois, Moussa Sissoko, Corentin Tolisso, Jonathan Ikoné (63' Thomas Lemar), Olivier Giroud (72' Wissam Ben Yedder), Antoine Griezmann, Kingsley Coman (85' Nabil Fekir). (Coach: Didier Deschamps (FRA)).
Andorra: Josep Antonio Gómes Moreira, Ildefons Lima Solà, Marc Vales González, Moisés San Nicolás Schellens, Marc Rebés Ruiz, Jesús "Chus" Rubio Gómez (YC51), Max Llovera González Adrio, Joan Cervós Moro, Márcio Vieira de Vasconcelos (86' Sergio "Sergi" Moreno Marín), Cristián Martínez Alejo (69' Jordi Aláez Peña), Ludovic Clemente Garcés "Ludo" (80' Jordi Rubio Gómez). (Coach: Jesús Luis Álvarez de Eulate Güergue "Koldo" (AND)).
Goals: France: 1-0 Kingsley Coman (18'), 2-0 Clément Lenglet (52'), 3-0 Wissam Ben Yedder (90+1').
Referee: Mykola Balakin (UKR)   Attendance: 55.383
(Antoine Griezmann missed a penalty kick in the 28th minute)

10-09-2019   Stadionul Zimbru, Chisinau: Moldova – Turkey 0-4 (0-1)
Moldova: Alexei Koselev, Victor Mudrac, Dinu Graur, Iaser Turcan, Stefan Efros, Oleg Reabciuk, Eugen Cebotaru, Alexandru Suvorov (75' Artiom Rozgoniuc), Artur Ionita (81' Mihail Ghecev), Radu Gînsari (68' Vadim Cemîrtan), Constantin Sandu. (Coach: Semen Altman (UKR)).
Turkey: Mert Günok, Kaan Ayhan, Mehmet Çelik, Merih Demiral, Cengiz Umut Meras, Irfan Can Kahveci (80' Yusuf Yazici), Deniz Türüç, Ozan Tufan, Dorukhan Toköz (87' Abdülkadir Parmak), Cenk Tosun, Kenan Karaman (70' Hakan Çalhanoglu). (Coach: Senol Günes (TUR)).
Goals: Turkey: 0-1 Cenk Tosun (37'), 0-2 Deniz Türüç (57'), 0-3 Cenk Tosun (79'), 0-4 Yusuf Yazici (88').
Referee: Davide Massa (ITA)   Attendance: 8.281

11-10-2019   Estadi Nacional, Andorra la Vella: Andorra – Moldova 1-0 (0-0)
Andorra: Josep Antonio Gómes Moreira, Ildefons Lima Solà, Marc Vales González, Moisés San Nicolás Schellens, Jesús "Chus" Rubio Gómez (YC32), Max Llovera González Adrio, Joan Cervós Moro (YC84), Márcio Vieira de Vasconcelos, Cristián Martínez Alejo (YC45+2) (61' Jordi Aláez Peña), Ludovic Clemente Garcés "Ludo" (73' Marc Rebés Ruiz). (Coach: Jesús Luis Álvarez de Eulate Güergue "Koldo" (AND)).
Moldova: Alexei Koselev, Veaceslav Posmac, Dinu Graur, Anatolie Prepelita, Oleg Reabciuk, Eugen Cebotaru (YC40), Alexandru Suvorov (YC76), Artur Ionita, Maxim Mihaliov (72' Alexandru Dedov), Radu Gînsari (YC37,YC55), Alexandru Boiciuc. (Coach: Semen Altman (UKR)).
Goal: Andorra: 1-0 Marc Vales González (63').
Referee: Jonathan Lardot (BEL)   Attendance: 947

11-10-2019   Laugardalsvöllur, Reykjavik: Iceland – France 0-1 (0-0)
Iceland: Hannes Halldórsson, Ragnar Sigurdsson (YC43), Ari Skúlason, Birkir Bjarnason, Kári
Árnason, Jóhann Berg Gudmundsson (16' Jón Bödvarsson), Rúnar Sigurjónsson (YC63) (73'
Alfred Finnbogason), Gylfi Sigurdsson, Victor Pálsson, Arnór Ingvi Traustason (81' Arnór
Sigurdsson), Kolbeinn Sigthórsson. (Coach: Erik Hamrén (SWE)).
France: Steve Mandanda, Lucas Digne, Raphaël Varane, Clément Lenglet, Benjamin Pavard
(YC68), Blaise Matuidi, Moussa Sissoko, Corentin Tolisso (YC87), Olivier Giroud (YC29)
(78' Wissam Ben Yedder), Antoine Griezmann, Kingsley Coman (88' Jonathan Ikoné).
(Coach: Didier Deschamps (FRA)).
Goal: France: 0-1 Olivier Giroud (66' penalty).
Referee: Gianluca Rocchi (ITA)   Attendance: 9.719

11-10-2019   Ülker Stadyumu FB Sükrü Saracoglu Saracoglu Spor Kompleksi, Istanbul:
              Turkey – Albania 1-0 (0-0)
Turkey: Mert Günok, Kaan Ayhan (YC26) (46' Çaglar Söyüncü), Mehmet Çelik, Merih
Demiral (YC7), Cengiz Umut Meras, Emre Belözoglu (66' Irfan Can Kahveci), Mahmut
Tekdemir, Hakan Çalhanoglu, Ozan Tufan (YC69) (80' Yusuf Yazici), Burak Yilmaz, Cenk
Tosun. (Coach: Senol Günes (TUR)).
Albania: Thomas Strakosha, Ermir Lenjani (57' Odise Roshi), Freddie Veseli, Berat Djimsiti
(YC86), Kastriot Dermaku (YC4), Ardian Ismajli, Ledian Memushaj (YC12) (72' Amir
Abrashi (YC83)), Klaus Gjasula (YC90+6), Keidi Bare (YC7), Sokol Çikalleshi (83' Bekim
Balaj), Rey Manaj. (Coach: Edoardo Reja (ITA)).
Goal: Turkey: 1-0 Cenk Tosun (90').
Referee: Ovidiu Hategan (ROM)   Attendance: 41.438

14-10-2019   Stade de France, Saint Denis: France – Turkey 1-1 (0-0)
France: Steve Mandanda, Raphaël Varane, Clément Lenglet, Lucas Hernández (YC49),
Benjamin Pavard, Blaise Matuidi (76' Thomas Lemar), Moussa Sissoko, Corentin Tolisso,
Antoine Griezmann (YC81), Wissam Ben Yedder (72' Olivier Giroud), Kingsley Coman (87'
Jonathan Ikoné). (Coach: Didier Deschamps (FRA)).
Turkey: Mert Günok, Mehmet Çelik (53' Kaan Ayhan), Çaglar Söyüncü, Merih Demiral,
Cengiz Umut Meras, Mahmut Tekdemir, Okay Yokuslu (46' Hakan Çalhanoglu), Irfan Can
Kahveci (YC86), Ozan Tufan (81' Cenk Tosun (YC85)), Burak Yilmaz, Kenan Karaman
(YC86). (Coach: Senol Günes (TUR)).
Goals: France: 1-0 Olivier Giroud (76').
Turkey: 1-1 Kaan Ayhan (82').
Referee: Dr. Felix Brych (GER)   Attendance: 72.154

14-10-2019   Laugardalsvöllur, Reykjavik: Iceland – Andorra 2-0 (1-0)
Iceland: Hannes Halldórsson, Ragnar Sigurdsson (68' Sverrir Ingason), Jón Fjóluson, Ari Skúlason, Birkir Bjarnason (70' Emil Hallfredsson), Gylfi Sigurdsson, Victor Pálsson (YC80), Arnór Ingvi Traustason, Arnór Sigurdsson, Kolbeinn Sigthórsson, Alfred Finnbogason (64' Jón Bödvarsson). (Coach: Erik Hamrén (SWE)).
Andorra: Josep Antonio Gómes Moreira, Ildefons Lima Solà (YC65), Marc Vales González, Moisés San Nicolás Schellens, Marc Rebés Ruiz (YC90+4), Max Llovera González Adrio, Joan Cervós Moro, Víctor Rodríguez Soria, Márcio Vieira de Vasconcelos (60' Ricard Fernández Betriu "Cucu"), Jordi Aláez Peña (87' Sebastiá Gómez Pérez), Alexandre Martínez Palau (80' Marc García Renom). (Coach: Jesús Luis Álvarez de Eulate Güergue "Koldo" (AND)).
Goals: Iceland: 1-0 Arnór Sigurdsson (38'), 2-0 Kolbeinn Sigthórsson (65').
Referee: Tamás Bognár (HUN)   Attendance: 7.169
(Gylfi Sigurdsson missed a penalty kick in the 73rd minute)

14-10-2019   Stadionul Zimbru, Chisinau: Moldova – Albania 0-4 (0-3)
Moldova: Alexei Koselev, Veaceslav Posmac, Victor Mudrac (YC29) (31' Artiom Rozgoniuc), Dinu Graur (YC38), Anatolie Prepelita (YC81), Oleg Reabciuk (YC62), Eugen Cebotaru (YC58), Alexandru Suvorov (60' Alexandru Boiciuc), Artur Ionita, Eugeniu Sidorenco (80' Constantin Sandu), Gheorghe Anton. (Coach: Semen Altman (UKR)).
Albania: Thomas Strakosha, Freddie Veseli, Berat Djimsiti, Kastriot Dermaku, Lorenc Trashi, Ardian Ismajli (89' Marash Kumbulla), Amir Abrashi, Klaus Gjasula (YC82), Keidi Bare (YC46) (89' Lindon Selahi), Sokol Çikalleshi (YC57) (76' Odise Roshi), Rey Manaj. (Coach: Edoardo Reja (ITA)).
Goals: Albania: 0-1 Sokol Çikalleshi (22'), 0-2 Keidi Bare (34'), 0-3 Lorenc Trashi (40'), 0-4 Rey Manaj (90').
Referee: Chris Kavanagh (ENG)   Attendance: 4.367

14-11-2019   Türk Telekom Stadyumu, Istanbul: Turkey – Iceland 0-0
Turkey: Mert Günok, Mehmet Çelik (YC90+4) (90+4' Ömer Bayram), Çaglar Söyüncü, Merih Demiral, Cengiz Umut Meras, Mahmut Tekdemir, Okay Yokuslu (YC82), Hakan Çalhanoglu (87' Kaan Ayhan), Ozan Tufan (YC8), Cengiz Ünder (YC90+1) (81' Yusuf Yazici), Burak Yilmaz. (Coach: Senol Günes (TUR)).
Iceland: Hannes Halldórsson, Ragnar Sigurdsson, Ari Skúlason (85' Mikael Anderson), Birkir Bjarnason, Kári Árnason, Gylfi Sigurdsson, Victor Pálsson, Arnór Ingvi Traustason (YC35) (63' Hördur Magnússon), Kolbeinn Sigthórsson (YC83), Alfred Finnbogason (24' Arnór Sigurdsson), Jón Bödvarsson. (Coach: Erik Hamrén (SWE)).
Referee: Anthony Taylor (ENG)   Attendance: 48.329

444

14-11-2019   Elbasan Arena, Elbasan: Albania – Andorra 2-2 (1-1)
Albania: Etrit Berisha, Freddie Veseli, Berat Djimsiti, Lorenc Trashi (46' Elseid Hysaj),
Ardian Ismajli, Odise Roshi, Ledian Memushaj, Emanuele Ndoj (60' Keidi Bare), Ylber
Ramadani (73' Taulant Seferi Sulejmanov), Bekim Balaj (YC90), Rey Manaj. (Coach:
Edoardo Reja (ITA)).
Andorra: Josep Antonio Gómes Moreira, Emili Josep García Miramontes, Marc Vales
González, Moisés San Nicolás Schellens, Jesús "Chus" Rubio Gómez (YC19) (71' Víctor
Rodríguez Soria), Max Llovera González Adrio (YC44), Joan Cervós Moro (YC90+3), Sergio
"Sergi" Moreno Marín, Cristián Martínez Alejo (79' Ricard Fernández Betriu "Cucu"),
Ludovic Clemente Garcés "Ludo" (YC43), Jordi Aláez Peña (89' Alexandre Martínez Palau).
(Coach: Jesús Luis Álvarez de Eulate Güergue "Koldo" (AND)).
Goals: Albania: 1-0 Bekim Balaj (6'), 2-2 Rey Manaj (55').
Andorra: 1-1 Cristián Martínez Alejo (18'), 1-2 Cristián Martínez Alejo (48').
Referee: Kristo Tohver (EST)   Attendance: 4.260

14-11-2019   Stade de France, Saint Denis: France – Moldova 2-1 (1-1)
France: Steve Mandanda, Lucas Digne (YC73), Raphaël Varane, Clément Lenglet, Benjamin
Pavard, N'Golo Kanté, Corentin Tolisso, Olivier Giroud, Antoine Griezmann, Kingsley Coman
(88' Thomas Lemar), Kylian Mbappé. (Coach: Didier Deschamps (FRA)).
Moldova: Alexei Koselev, Igor Armas, Ion Jardan (YC54) (68' Dinu Graur), Veaceslav
Posmac (YC77), Artur Craciun (YC38), Artur Ionita, Radu Gînsari (74' Nicolae Milinceanu),
Vadim Rata (YC34) (81' Artur Patras), Catalin Carp, Eugeniu Cociuc, Sergiu Platica. (Coach:
Engin Firat (TUR)).
Goals: France: 1-1 Raphaël Varane (35'), 2-1 Olivier Giroud (79' penalty).
Moldova: 0-1 Vadim Rata (9').
Referee: Gediminas Mazeika (LTU)   Attendance: 64.367

17-11-2019   Air Albania Stadium, Tirana: Albania – France 0-2 (0-2)
Albania: Etrit Berisha, Ermir Lenjani (46' Odise Roshi), Freddie Veseli, Elseid Hysaj (YC20)
(82' Lorenc Trashi), Berat Djimsiti, Kastriot Dermaku, Klaus Gjasula, Kristi Qose (46' Ledian
Memushaj), Keidi Bare, Bekim Balaj, Rey Manaj. (Coach: Edoardo Reja (ITA)).
France: Steve Mandanda, Raphaël Varane, Benjamin Mendy (75' Lucas Digne), Clément
Lenglet (YC26), Presnel Kimpembe, Léo Dubois (88' Benjamin Pavard), Moussa Sissoko,
Corentin Tolisso, Olivier Giroud, Antoine Griezmann, Wissam Ben Yedder (85' Nabil Fekir).
(Coach: Didier Deschamps (FRA)).
Goals: France: 0-1 Corentin Tolisso (9'), 0-2 Antoine Griezmann (30').
Referee: Slavko Vincic (SLO)   Attendance: 19.228

17-11-2019   Estadi Nacional, Andorra la Vella: Andorra – Turkey 0-2 (0-2)
Andorra: Josep Antonio Gómes Moreira (87' Ferran Pol Perez), Ildefons Lima Solà (YC43),
Marc Vales González (YC77), Moisés San Nicolás Schellens, Marc Rebés Ruiz, Max Llovera
González Adrio (YC51), Joan Cervós Moro, Cristián Martínez Alejo, Ludovic Clemente
Garcés "Ludo" (85' Jordi Rubio Gómez), Jordi Aláez Peña (71' Víctor Rodríguez Soria),
Alexandre Martínez Palau. (Coach: Jesús Luis Álvarez de Eulate Güergue "Koldo" (AND)).
Turkey: Ugurcan Çakir, Ömer Bayram, Kaan Ayhan (YC53), Nazim Sangaré, Merih Demiral
(80' Yildirim Mert Çetin), Ozan Kabak, Hakan Çalhanoglu (60' Berkay Özcan), Ozan Tufan,
Yusuf Yazici, Enes Ünal, Ahmed Kutucu (85' Emre Kilinç). (Coach: Senol Günes (TUR)).
Goals: Turkey: 0-1 Enes Ünal (17'), 0-2 Enes Ünal (21' penalty).
Referee: Ivan Kruzliak (SVK)   Attendance: 2.357

17-11-2019   Stadionul Zimbru, Chisinau: Moldova – Iceland 1-2 (0-1)
Moldova: Alexei Koselev, Igor Armas, Maxim Focsa, Artur Craciun (YC34), Artur Ionita (YC76), Radu Gînsari (83' Dinu Graur), Vadim Rata (YC49), Catalin Carp (90' Andrei Cojocari), Eugeniu Cociuc, Sergiu Platica, Nicolae Milinceanu (60' Vitalie Damascan). (Coach: Engin Firat (TUR)).
Iceland: Hannes Halldórsson, Ragnar Sigurdsson, Ari Skúlason, Sverrir Ingason, Birkir Bjarnason (YC19) (87' Hördur Magnússon), Gylfi Sigurdsson, Victor Pálsson (YC43), Arnór Sigurdsson, Mikael Anderson (55' Samúel Kári Fridjónsson (YC90+4)), Kolbeinn Sigthórsson (29' Vidar Kjartansson), Jón Bödvarsson. (Coach: Erik Hamrén (SWE)).
Goals: Moldova: 1-1 Nicolae Milinceanu (56').
Iceland: 0-1 Birkir Bjarnason (17'), 1-2 Gylfi Sigurdsson (65').
Referee: Pavel Královec (CZE)   Attendance: 6.742
(*Gylfi Sigurdsson missed a penalty kick in the 78th minute*)

GROUP   I

21-03-2019	Astana	Kazakhstan – Scotland	3-0 (2-0)
21-03-2019	Nicosia	Cyprus – San Marino	5-0 (4-0)
21-03-2019	Brussels	Belgium – Russia	3-1 (2-1)
24-03-2019	Nur-Sultan	Kazakhstan – Russia	0-4 (0-2)
24-03-2019	Serravalle	San Marino – Scotland	0-2 (0-1)
24-03-2019	Nicosia	Cyprus – Belgium	0-2 (0-2)
08-06-2019	Saransk	Russia – San Marino	9-0 (4-0)
08-06-2019	Brussels	Belgium – Kazakhstan	3-0 (2-0)
08-06-2019	Glasgow	Scotland – Cyprus	2-1 (0-0)
11-06-2019	Nur-Sultan	Kazakhstan – San Marino	4-0 (1-0)
11-06-2019	Brussels	Belgium – Scotland	3-0 (1-0)
11-06-2019	Nizhny Novgorod	Russia – Cyprus	1-0 (1-0)
06-09-2019	Nicosia	Cyprus – Kazakhstan	1-1 (1-1)
06-09-2019	Serravalle	San Marino – Belgium	0-4 (0-1)
06-09-2019	Glasgow	Scotland – Russia	1-2 (1-1)
09-09-2019	Kaliningrad	Russia – Kazakhstan	1-0 (0-0)
09-09-2019	Serravalle	San Marino – Cyprus	0-4 (0-2)
09-09-2019	Glasgow	Scotland – Belgium	0-4 (0-3)
10-10-2019	Nur-Sultan	Kazakhstan – Cyprus	1-2 (1-0)
10-10-2019	Brussels	Belgium – San Marino	9-0 (6-0)
10-10-2019	Moscow	Russia – Scotland	4-0 (0-0)
13-10-2019	Nur-Sultan	Kazakhstan – Belgium	0-2 (0-1)
13-10-2019	Nicosia	Cyprus – Russia	0-5 (0-2)
13-10-2019	Glasgow	Scotland – San Marino	6-0 (3-0)
16-11-2019	Nicosia	Cyprus – Scotland	1-2 (0-1)
16-11-2019	Saint Petersburg	Russia – Belgium	1-4 (0-3)
16-11-2019	Serravalle	San Marino – Kazakhstan	1-3 (0-3)
19-11-2019	Brussels	Belgium – Cyprus	6-1 (4-1)
19-11-2019	Serravalle	San Marino – Russia	0-5 (0-2)
19-11-2019	Glasgow	Scotland – Kazakhstan	3-1 (0-1)

FINAL STANDING

Pos	Team	Pld	W	D	L	GF	GA	GD	Pts
1	Belgium	10	10	0	0	40	3	+37	30
2	Russia	10	8	0	2	33	8	+25	24
3	Scotland	10	5	0	5	16	19	-3	15
4	Cyprus	10	3	1	6	15	20	-5	10
5	Kazakhstan	10	3	1	6	13	17	-4	10
6	San Marino	10	0	0	10	1	51	-50	0

Belgium and Russia qualified for final tournament.

21-03-2019   Astana Arena, Astana: Kazakhstan – Scotland 3-0 (2-0)
Kazakhstan: Dmytro Nepogodov, Sergiy Maliy, Evgeni Postnikov, Gafurzhan Suyombaev (YC90+5), Temirlan Erlanov (81' Eldos Akhmetov), Islambek Kuat, Alexander Merkel (YC38), Yan Vorogovskiy, Baktiyor Zaynutdinov (84' Serikzhan Muzhikov), Yuri Pertsukh, Roman Murtazaev (68' Bauyrzhan Turysbek). (Coach: Michal Bílek (CZE)).
Scotland: Scott Bain, Graeme Shinnie (YC83), David Bates, Scott McKenna, James Forrest (81' Marc McNulty, Liam Palmer, Stuart Armstrong, Callum McGregor, John McGinn (70' Scott McTominay), Oliver Burke, Oliver McBurnie (61' Johnny Russell). (Coach: Alex McLeish (SCO)).
Goals: Kazakhstan: 1-0 Yuri Pertsukh (6'), 2-0 Yan Vorogovskiy (10'), 3-0 Baktiyor Zaynutdinov (51').
Referee: Srdjan Jovanovic (SRB)   Attendance: 27.641

21-03-2019   Neo GSP Stadium, Nicosia: Cyprus – San Marino 5-0 (4-0)
Cyprus: Costas Panayi, Kostas Laifis, Nicholas Ioannou, Ioannis Kousoulos, Giorgos Efrem, Jason Demetriou (65' Giorgios Merkis), Kostakis Artymatas, Anthony Georgiou, Fotis Papoulis (54' Matija Spoljaric), Nestoras Mitides, Pieros Sotiriou (27' Andreas Makris). (Coach: Ran Ben Shimon (ISR)).
San Marino: Elia Benedettini, Davide Simoncini (YC18), Mirko Palazzi (YC71), Manuel Battistini, Michele Cevoli, Mattia Giardi (YC20) (74' Lorenzo Lunadei), Enrico Golinucci (YC20), Marcello Mularoni, Filippo Berardi, Danilo Rinaldi (46' Adolfo José Hirsch), Nicola Nanni (46' Matteo Vitaioli). (Coach: Franco Varrella (ITA)).
Goals: Cyprus: 1-0 Pieros Sotiriou (19' penalty), 2-0 Pieros Sotiriou (23' penalty), 3-0 Ioannis Kousoulos (26'), 4-0 Giorgos Efrem (31'), 5-0 Kostas Laifis (56').
Referee: Juri Frischer (EST)   Attendance: 3.175

21-03-2019   King Baudouin Stadium, Brussels: Belgium – Russia 3-1 (2-1)
Belgium: Thibaut Courtois, Jan Vertonghen, Toby Alderweireld, Dedryck Boyata, Timothy Castagne, Leander Dendoncker, Youri Tielemans, Eden Hazard, Dries Mertens (YC89), Thorgan Hazard (84' Nacer Chadli), Michy Batshuayi. (Coach: ROBERT MARTÍNEZ Montoliú (ESP)).
Russia: Guilherme Alvim Marinato, Fedor Kudryashov, Kirill Nababkin, Mário Fernandes, Georgi Dzhikiya, Yuriy Zhirkov, Denis Cheryshev (65' Fedor Chalov), Daler Kuzyaev (26' Anton Miranchuk), Aleksandr Golovin (YC18,YC90), Ilzat Akhmetov, Artem Dzyuba (77' Fedor Smolov). (Coach: Stanislav Cherchesov (RUS)).
Goals: Belgium: 1-0 Youri Tielemans (14'), 2-1 Eden Hazard (45' penalty), 3-1 Eden Hazard (88').
Russia: 1-1 Denis Cheryshev (16').
Referee: Ovidiu Hategan (ROM)   Attendance: 34.245

24-03-2019   Astana Arena, Nur-Sultan: Kazakhstan – Russia 0-4 (0-2)
Kazakhstan: Dmytro Nepogodov, Yuriy Logvinenko (29' Yan Vorogovskiy), Sergiy Maliy, Eldos Akhmetov (YC64), Abzal Beysebekov, Gafurzhan Suyombaev (YC50), Islambek Kuat (YC59), Alexander Merkel, Baktiyor Zaynutdinov (YC90+3), Yuri Pertsukh (85' Georgiy Zhukov), Roman Murtazaev (59' Bauyrzhan Turysbek). (Coach: Michal Bílek (CZE)).
Russia: Guilherme Alvim Marinato, Fedor Kudryashov, Andrei Semyonov, Mário Fernandes, Georgi Dzhikiya, Aleksey Ionov (61' Vladislav Ignatyev), Yuri Gazinskiy, Magomed Ozdoev, Denis Cheryshev (YC70), Ilzat Akhmetov (72' Aleksey Miranchuk), Artem Dzyuba (82' Fedor Chalov). (Coach: Stanislav Cherchesov (RUS)).
Goals: Russia: 0-1 Denis Cheryshev (19'), 0-2 Denis Cheryshev (45+2'), 0-3 Artem Dzyuba (52'), 0-4 Abzal Beysebekov (62' *own goal*).
Referee: Slavko Vincic (SLO)   Attendance: 29.582

24-03-2019   Stadio Olimpico di Serravalle, Serravalle: San Marino – Scotland 0-2 (0-1)
San Marino: Elia Benedettini, Davide Simoncini (86' Lorenzo Lunadei), Mirko Palazzi, Manuel Battistini, Michele Cevoli, Enrico Golinucci, Adolfo José Hirsch (78' Andrea Grandoni), Alessandro Golinucci, Marcello Mularoni, Filippo Berardi (YC90+4), Matteo Vitaioli (61' Nicola Nanni). (Coach: Franco Varrella (ITA)).
Scotland: Scott Bain, Stephen O'Donnell, Andrew Robertson, Callum Paterson (37' Marc McNulty), David Bates, Scott McKenna, Kenny McLean, Stuart Armstrong (71' James Forrest), Callum McGregor (57' Scott McTominay (YC90+1)), Ryan Fraser, Johnny Russell. (Coach: Alex McLeish (SCO)).
Goals: Scotland: 0-1 Kenny McLean (4'), 0-2 Johnny Russell (74').
Referee: Manuel Schüttengruber (AUT)   Attendance: 4.077

24-03-2019   Neo GSP Stadium, Nicosia: Cyprus – Belgium 0-2 (0-2)
Cyprus: Rafael Urko Pardo Goas, Giorgios Merkis, Dossa Júnior (46' Anthony Georgiou), Kostas Laifis, Nicholas Ioannou, Ioannis Kousoulos, Giorgos Efrem (75' Matija Spoljaric), Renato Joao Inacio Margaça, Kostakis Artymatas, Fotis Papoulis, Minas Antoniou (81' Andreas Makris). (Coach: Ran Ben Shimon (ISR)).
Belgium: Thibaut Courtois, Thomas Vermaelen, Jan Vertonghen, Toby Alderweireld, Timothy Castagne, Leander Dendoncker, Youri Tielemans, Eden Hazard, Dries Mertens (57' Adnan Januzaj), Thorgan Hazard (68' Yannick Carrasco), Michy Batshuayi (89' Dennis Praet). (Coach: ROBERT MARTÍNEZ Montoliú (ESP)).
Goals: Belgium: 0-1 Eden Hazard (10'), 0-2 Michy Batshuayi (18').
Referee: François Letexier (FRA)   Attendance: 8.728

08-06-2019   Mordovia Arena, Saransk: Russia – San Marino 9-0 (4-0)
Russia: Guilherme Alvim Marinato, Fedor Kudryashov, Andrei Semyonov, Mário Fernandes, Georgi Dzhikiya, Magomed Ozdoev, Roman Zobnin (73' Dmitry Barinov), Aleksandr Golovin, Aleksey Miranchuk (61' Aleksey Ionov), Anton Miranchuk (60' Fedor Smolov), Artem Dzyuba. (Coach: Stanislav Cherchesov (RUS)).
San Marino: Elia Benedettini, Fabio Vitaioli, Mirko Palazzi (51' Luca Censoni), Manuel Battistini, Andrea Grandoni, Michele Cevoli, Enrico Golinucci, Alessandro Golinucci (64' Lorenzo Lunadei), Marcello Mularoni (YC17), Matteo Vitaioli, Danilo Rinaldi (YC11) (56' Fabio Tomassini). (Coach: Franco Varrella (ITA)).
Goals: Russia: 1-0 Michele Cevoli (25' own goal), 2-0 Artem Dzyuba (31' penalty), 3-0 Fedor Kudryashov (36'), 4-0 Anton Miranchuk (41'), 5-0 Artem Dzyuba (73'), 6-0 Artem Dzyuba (76'), 7-0 Fedor Smolov (77'), 8-0 Fedor Smolov (83'), 9-0 Artem Dzyuba (88').
Referee: Mohammed Al-Hakim (SWE)   Attendance: 42.241
(Artem Dzyuba missed a penalty kick in the 76th minute)

08-06-2019   King Baudouin Stadium, Brussels: Belgium – Kazakhstan 3-0 (2-0)
Belgium: Thibaut Courtois, Vincent Kompany (78' Thomas Vermaelen), Jan Vertonghen, Toby Alderweireld, Timothy Castagne, Axel Witsel, Kevin De Bruyne (68' Youri Tielemans), Eden Hazard, Dries Mertens, Romelu Lukaku (72' Michy Batshuayi), Thorgan Hazard. (Coach: ROBERT MARTÍNEZ Montoliú (ESP)).
Kazakhstan: Dmytro Nepogodov, Sergiy Maliy, Abzal Beysebekov (YC37), Temirlan Yerlanov, Aleksandr Marochkin, Islambek Kuat (YC45+2) (78' Askhat Tagybergen), Georgiy Zhukov, Maxim Fedin (66' Abat Aymbetov), Yan Vorogovskiy (YC75), Yuri Pertsukh, Toktar Zhangylyshbay (46' Bauyrzhan Islamkhan). (Coach: Michal Bílek (CZE)).
Goals: Belgium: 1-0 Dries Mertens (11'), 2-0 Timothy Castagne (14'), 3-0 Romelu Lukaku (50').
Referee: Irfan Peljto (BIH)   Attendance: 37.155

08-06-2019   Hampden Park, Glasgow: Scotland – Cyprus 2-1 (0-0)
Scotland: David Marshall, Charlie Mulgrew, Stephen O'Donnell, Andrew Robertson, Scott McKenna, James Forrest, Kenny McLean, Callum McGregor (YC45) (88' Stuart Armstrong), Ryan Fraser, John McGinn (79' Scott McTominay), Eamonn Brophy (73' Oliver Burke). (Coach: Steve Clarke (SCO)).
Cyprus: Rafael Urko Pardo Goas, Kostas Laifis, Nicholas Ioannou (YC26), Ioannis Kousoulos, Giorgos Efrem, Renato Joao Inacio Margaça, Kostakis Artymatas (YC74), Michalis Ioannou (66' Anthony Georgiou), Pieros Sotiriou, Andreas Makris (80' Ioannis Pittas), Matija Spoljaric (70' Ioannis Kosti). (Coach: Ran Ben Shimon (ISR)).
Goals: Scotland: 1-0 Andrew Robertson (61'), 2-1 Oliver Burke (89').
Cyprus: 1-1 Ioannis Kousoulos (87').
Referee: Ola Hobber Nilsen (NOR)   Attendance: 31.277

11-06-2019   Astana Arena, Nur-Sultan: Kazakhstan – San Marino 4-0 (1-0)
Kazakhstan: Dmytro Nepogodov, Dmitriy Shomko (YC90), Sergiy Maliy, Gafurzhan
Suyombaev, Temirlan Yerlanov (YC31), Islambek Kuat (84' Yuri Pertsukh), Bauyrzhan
Islamkhan, Askhat Tagybergen, Yan Vorogovskiy, Bauyrzhan Turysbek (70' Toktar
Zhangylyshbay), Abat Aymbetov (58' Maxim Fedin). (Coach: Michal Bílek (CZE)).
San Marino: Elia Benedettini, Fabio Vitaioli, Cristian Brolli (YC64), Davide Cesarini (77'
Manuel Battistini), Andrea Grandoni, Luca Censoni (YC48), Michael Battistini (46' Enrico
Golinucci), Marcello Mularoni, Lorenzo Lunadei, Matteo Vitaioli (84' Marco Bernardi),
Nicola Nanni. (Coach: Franco Varrella (ITA)).
Goals: Kazakhstan: 1-0 Islambek Kuat (45+1'), 2-0 Maxim Fedin (62'), 3-0 Gafurzhan
Suyombaev (65'), 4-0 Bauyrzhan Islamkhan (79').
Referee: Bartosz Frankowski (POL)   Attendance: 18.652

11-06-2019   King Baudouin Stadium, Brussels: Belgium – Scotland 3-0 (1-0)
Belgium: Thibaut Courtois, Vincent Kompany (90' Thomas Vermaelen), Jan Vertonghen,
Toby Alderweireld, Thomas Meunier, Axel Witsel, Kevin De Bruyne (YC34), Youri
Tielemans (78' Dries Mertens), Eden Hazard, Romelu Lukaku, Thorgan Hazard (90' Yannick
Carrasco). (Coach: ROBERT MARTÍNEZ Montoliú (ESP)).
Scotland: David Marshall, Charlie Mulgrew, Stephen O'Donnell, Scott McKenna, Greg
Taylor, Kenny McLean, Stuart Armstrong (32' Ryan Fraser), Callum McGregor, Oliver Burke,
Scott McTominay (YC52), Johnny Russell (67' James Forrest). (Coach: Steve Clarke (SCO)).
Goals: Belgium: 1-0 Romelu Lukaku (45+1'), 2-0 Romelu Lukaku (57'), 3-0 Kevin De Bruyne
(90+2').
Referee: Petr Ardeleánu (CZE)   Attendance: 32.482

11-06-2019   Nizhny Novgorod Stadium, Nizhny Novgorod: Russia – Cyprus 1-0 (1-0)
Russia: Guilherme Alvim Marinato, Fedor Kudryashov (YC73), Andrei Semyonov, Mário
Fernandes, Georgi Dzhikiya, Aleksey Ionov (90+2' Ilzat Akhmetov), Magomed Ozdoev,
Roman Zobnin (78' Dmitry Barinov), Aleksandr Golovin (YC45+2), Anton Miranchuk (64'
Aleksey Miranchuk), Artem Dzyuba. (Coach: Stanislav Cherchesov (RUS)).
Cyprus: Rafael Urko Pardo Goas, Kostas Laifis, Nicholas Ioannou, Ioannis Kousoulos, Ioannis
Kosti, Andreas Avraam (71' Ioannis Pittas), Renato Joao Inacio Margaça (YC63), Kostakis
Artymatas, Anthony Georgiou (46' Giorgos Efrem), Pieros Sotiriou, Andreas Makris (YC20)
(81' Matija Spoljaric). (Coach: Ran Ben Shimon (ISR)).
Goal: Russia: 1-0 Aleksey Ionov (38').
Referee: Marco Di Bello (ITA)   Attendance: 42.228

06-09-2019   Neo GSP Stadium, Nicosia: Cyprus – Kazakhstan 1-1 (1-1)
Cyprus: Costas Panayi, Giorgios Merkis, Konstantinos Mintikkis (YC7), Kostas Laifis
(YC90+4), Chambos Kyriakou, Nicholas Ioannou (YC15), Ioannis Kousoulos (YC45+2),
Giorgos Efrem (73' Ioannis Kosti), Grigoris Kastanos (58' Anthony Georgiou), Fotis Papoulis
(90' Ioannis Pittas), Pieros Sotiriou. (Coach: Ran Ben Shimon (ISR)).
Kazakhstan: Dmytro Nepogodov, Sergiy Maliy (YC51), Gafurzhan Suyombaev (YC85),
Temirlan Yerlanov, Aleksandr Marochkin, Islambek Kuat, Bauyrzhan Islamkhan (65' Maxim
Fedin), Askhat Tagybergen (82' Georgiy Zhukov), Yan Vorogovskiy, Yuri Pertsukh, Aleksey
Shchetkin (87' Abat Aymbetov). (Coach: Michal Bílek (CZE)).
Goals: Cyprus: 1-1 Pieros Sotiriou (39').
Kazakhstan: 0-1 Aleksey Shchetkin (2').
Referee: Mattias Gestranius (FIN)   Attendance: 5.639

06-09-2019   Stadio Olimpico di Serravalle, Serravalle: San Marino – Belgium 0-4 (0-1)
San Marino: Simone Benedettini, Davide Simoncini (YC41), Mirko Palazzi, Cristian Brolli, Manuel Battistini (YC78), Andrea Grandoni, Mattia Giardi (67' Alex Gasperoni), Enrico Golinucci (66' Alessandro Golinucci), Marcello Mularoni, Filippo Berardi (74' Matteo Vitaioli), Nicola Nanni. (Coach: Franco Varrella (ITA)).
Belgium: Thibaut Courtois, Jan Vertonghen, Toby Alderweireld, Thomas Meunier, Jason Denayer, Kevin De Bruyne (76' Dennis Praet), Yannick Carrasco, Adnan Januzaj (56' Nacer Chadli), Youri Tielemans, Michy Batshuayi, Divock Origi (55' Dries Mertens). (Coach: ROBERT MARTÍNEZ Montoliú (ESP)).
Goals: Belgium: 0-1 Michy Batshuayi (43' penalty), 0-2 Dries Mertens (57'), 0-3 Nacer Chadli (63'), 0-4 Michy Batshuayi (90+2').
Referee: Horatiu Fesnic (ROM)   Attendance: 2.523

06-09-2019   Hampden Park, Glasgow: Scotland – Russia 1-2 (1-1)
Scotland: David Marshall, Charlie Mulgrew, Liam Cooper (YC46), Stephen O'Donnell, Andrew Robertson, James Forrest (62' Kenny McLean (YC70)), Callum McGregor, Ryan Fraser, John McGinn (62' Ryan Christie), Scott McTominay (78' Matt Phillips), Oliver McBurnie. (Coach: Steve Clarke (SCO)).
Russia: Guilherme Alvim Marinato, Fedor Kudryashov, Andrei Semyonov, Mário Fernandes, Georgi Dzhikiya, Yuriy Zhirkov, Aleksey Ionov (80' Aleksandr Erokhin), Magomed Ozdoev, Roman Zobnin (YC55) (66' Dmitry Barinov (YC70)), Aleksandr Golovin (89' Ilzat Akhmetov (YC90)), Artem Dzyuba. (Coach: Stanislav Cherchesov (RUS)).
Goals: Scotland: 1-0 John McGinn (11').
Russia: 1-1 Artem Dzyuba (40'), 1-2 Stephen O'Donnell (59' own goal).
Referee: Anastasios Sidiropoulos (GRE)   Attendance: 32.432

09-09-2019   Kaliningrad Stadium, Kaliningrad: Russia – Kazakhstan 1-0 (0-0)
Russia: Guilherme Alvim Marinato, Andrei Semyonov, Mário Fernandes, Georgi Dzhikiya, Yuriy Zhirkov, Magomed Ozdoev, Denis Cheryshev (55' Fedor Kudryashov), Aleksandr Golovin, Anton Miranchuk (58' Aleksey Ionov), Ilzat Akhmetov (63' Roman Zobnin), Artem Dzyuba. (Coach: Stanislav Cherchesov (RUS)).
Kazakhstan: Dmytro Nepogodov, Dmitriy Shomko, Sergiy Maliy, Abzal Beysebekov, Temirlan Yerlanov, Aleksandr Marochkin, Aybol Abiken, Georgiy Zhukov (62' Bauyrzhan Islamkhan), Maxim Fedin (77' Serikzhan Muzhikov), Yuri Pertsukh, Aleksey Shchetkin (90' Abat Aymbetov). (Coach: Michal Bílek (CZE)).
Goal: Russia: 1-0 Mário Fernandes (89').
Referee: Nikola Dabanovic (MNE)   Attendance: 31.818

09-09-2019   Stadio Olimpico di Serravalle, Serravalle: San Marino – Cyprus 0-4 (0-2)
San Marino: Simone Benedettini, Fabio Vitaioli (YC72), Davide Simoncini, Andrea Grandoni, Alessandro D'Addario, Alex Gasperoni (61' José Adolfo Hirsch), Alessandro Golinucci, Filippo Berardi, Lorenzo Lunadei, Matteo Vitaioli (61' Michele Cevoli), Fabio Tomassini (62' Nicola Nanni). (Coach: Franco Varrella (ITA)).
Cyprus: Costas Panayi, Kostas Laifis, Chambos Kyriakou, Nicholas Ioannou, Ioannis Kousoulos, Ioannis Pittas (74' Grigoris Kastanos), Ioannis Kosti, Kostakis Artymatas, Fotis Papoulis (46' Anthony Georgiou), Pieros Sotiriou, Matija Spoljaric (62' Michalis Ioannou). (Coach: Ran Ben Shimon (ISR)).
Goals: Cyprus: 0-1 Ioannis Kousoulos (2'), 0-2 Fotis Papoulis (39'), 0-3 Ioannis Kousoulos (73'), 0-4 Kostakis Artymatas (75').
Referee: Iwan Arwel Griffith (WAL)   Attendance: 662

09-09-2019   Hampden Park, Glasgow: Scotland – Belgium 0-4 (0-3)
Scotland: David Marshall, Charlie Mulgrew, Liam Cooper, Stephen O'Donnell (YC59), Andrew Robertson, Robert Snodgrass, Matt Phillips (77' Johnny Russell), Kenny McLean, Callum McGregor (68' Stuart Armstrong), Ryan Christie (86' John McGinn), Scott McTominay (YC61). (Coach: Steve Clarke (SCO)).
Belgium: Thibaut Courtois, Thomas Vermaelen (YC79), Jan Vertonghen, Toby Alderweireld, Thomas Meunier (90' Benito Raman), Nacer Chadli (78' Yannick Carrasco), Kevin De Bruyne, Leander Dendoncker, Youri Tielemans (86' Yari Verschaeren), Dries Mertens, Romelu Lukaku. (Coach: ROBERT MARTÍNEZ Montoliú (ESP)).
Goals: Belgium: 0-1 Romelu Lukaku (9'), 0-2 Thomas Vermaelen (24'), 0-3 Toby Alderweireld (32'), 0-4 Kevin De Bruyne (82').
Referee: Pawel Gil (POL)   Attendance: 25.524

10-10-2019   Astana Arena, Nur-Sultan: Kazakhstan – Cyprus 1-2 (1-0)
Kazakhstan: Dmytro Nepogodov, Sergiy Maliy, Gafurzhan Suyombaev (YC4), Temirlan Yerlanov (YC39), Aleksandr Marochkin, Aybol Abiken (YC50) (80' Maxim Fedin), Islambek Kuat (YC64) (90' Askhat Tagybergen), Bauyrzhan Islamkhan (YC26), Yan Vorogovskiy, Yuri Pertsukh (YC72), Toktar Zhangylyshbay (61' Sergey Khizhnichenko). (Coach: Michal Bílek (CZE)).
Cyprus: Costas Panayi, Giorgios Merkis (YC26) (62' Matija Spoljaric), Konstantinos Mintikkis (YC44) (46' Pangiotis Zachariou), Kostas Laifis, Chambos Kyriakou, Nicholas Ioannou, Ioannis Kousoulos, Ioannis Kosti, Kostakis Artymatas, Fotis Papoulis (88' Renato Joao Inacio Margaça), Pieros Sotiriou. (Coach: Ran Ben Shimon (ISR)).
Goals: Kazakhstan: 1-0 Temirlan Yerlanov (34').
Cyprus: 1-1 Pieros Sotiriou (73'), 1-2 Nicholas Ioannou (84').
Referee: Craig Pawson (ENG)   Attendance: 11.769

10-10-2019   King Baudouin Stadium, Brussels: Belgium – San Marino 9-0 (6-0)
Belgium: Thibaut Courtois, Thomas Vermaelen, Jan Vertonghen, Toby Alderweireld, Timothy Castagne, Nacer Chadli, Hans Vanaken, Youri Tielemans, Eden Hazard (63' Yannick Carrasco), Dries Mertens (YC51) (63' Yari Verschaeren), Romelu Lukaku (76' Christian Benteke). (Coach: ROBERT MARTÍNEZ Montoliú (ESP)).
San Marino: Simone Benedettini, Davide Simoncini (YC90+1), Mirko Palazzi, Cristian Brolli, Manuel Battistini, Andrea Grandoni (78' Lorenzo Lunadei), Mattia Giardi (46' José Adolfo Hirsch), Enrico Golinucci, Marcello Mularoni (YC82), Filippo Berardi (46' Alessandro Golinucci), Nicola Nanni. (Coach: Franco Varrella (ITA)).
Goals: Belgium: 1-0 Romelu Lukaku (28'), 2-0 Nacer Chadli (31'), 3-0 Cristian Brolli (35'*own goal*), 4-0 Romelu Lukaku (41'), 5-0 Toby Alderweireld (43'), 6-0 Youri Tielemans (45+1'), 7-0 Christian Benteke (79'), 8-0 Yari Verschaeren (84' penalty), 9-0 Timothy Castagne (90').
Referee: Anastasios Papapetrou (GRE)   Attendance: 34.504

452

10-10-2019   Luzhniki Stadium, Moscow: Russia – Scotland 4-0 (0-0)
Russia: Guilherme Alvim Marinato, Fedor Kudryashov, Andrei Semyonov, Mário Fernandes, Georgi Dzhikiya, Yuriy Zhirkov (66' Denis Cheryshev), Aleksey Ionov (79' Ilzat Akhmetov), Magomed Ozdoev, Dmitry Barinov, Aleksandr Golovin, Artem Dzyuba (87' Nikolay Komlichenko). (Coach: Stanislav Cherchesov (RUS)).
Scotland: David Marshall, Charlie Mulgrew, Michael Devlin, Andrew Robertson, John Fleck (YC41) (82' Stuart Armstrong), Robert Snodgrass, Liam Palmer, Callum McGregor, Ryan Fraser (68' Ryan Christie), John McGinn, Oliver Burke (46' Lawrence Shankland). (Coach: Steve Clarke (SCO)).
Goals: Russia: 1-0 Artem Dzyuba (57'), 2-0 Magomed Ozdoev (60'), 3-0 Artem Dzyuba (70'), 4-0 Aleksandr Golovin (84').
Referee: Jakob Kehlet (DEN)   Attendance: 65.703

13-10-2019   Astana Arena, Nur-Sultan: Kazakhstan – Belgium 0-2 (0-1)
Kazakhstan: Dmytro Nepogodov, Dmitriy Shomko, Sergiy Maliy (YC57), Abzal Beysebekov (YC83), Olzhas Kerymzhanov, Gafurzhan Suyombaev (61' Yan Vorogovskiy), Aleksandr Marochkin, Aybol Abiken (YC90+2), Bauyrzhan Islamkhan, Georgiy Zhukov (YC36) (84' Toktar Zhangylyshbay), Maxim Fedin (71' Yuri Pertsukh). (Coach: Michal Bílek (CZE)).
Belgium: Thibaut Courtois, Thomas Vermaelen (90+2' Brandon Mechele), Jan Vertonghen, Toby Alderweireld, Thomas Meunier, Axel Witsel (YC82), Dennis Praet, Eden Hazard, Dries Mertens (78' Yannick Carrasco), Thorgan Hazard, Michy Batshuayi (YC11) (78' Christian Benteke). (Coach: ROBERT MARTÍNEZ Montoliú (ESP)).
Goals: Belgium: 0-1 Michy Batshuayi (21'), 0-2 Thomas Meunier (53').
Referee: Gediminas Mazeika (LTU)   Attendance: 26.801

13-10-2019   Neo GSP Stadium, Nicosia: Cyprus – Russia 0-5 (0-2)
Cyprus: Costas Panayi (40' Rafael Urko Pardo Goas), Giorgios Merkis, Kostas Laifis (RC27), Chambos Kyriakou, Nicholas Ioannou, Ioannis Kousoulos, Ioannis Kosti, Kostakis Artymatas, Pangiotis Zachariou (36' Renato Joao Inacio Margaça), Michalis Ioannou, Matija Spoljaric (79' Fotis Papoulis). (Coach: Ran Ben Shimon (ISR)).
Russia: Guilherme Alvim Marinato, Fedor Kudryashov, Andrei Semyonov, Sergey Petrov (38' Vyacheslav Karavaev (YC45+1)), Georgi Dzhikiya, Aleksey Ionov (78' Zelimkhan Bakaev), Magomed Ozdoev, Denis Cheryshev, Aleksandr Golovin, Ilzat Akhmetov (61' Daler Kuzyaev), Artem Dzyuba. (Coach: Stanislav Cherchesov (RUS)).
Goals: Russia: 0-1 Denis Cheryshev (9'), 0-2 Magomed Ozdoev (23'), 0-3 Artem Dzyuba (79'), 0-4 Aleksandr Golovin (89'), 0-5 Denis Cheryshev (90+2').
Referee: Srdjan Jovanovic (SRB)   Attendance: 9.439

13-10-2019   Hampden Park, Glasgow: Scotland – San Marino 6-0 (3-0)
Scotland: Jon McLaughlin, Michael Devlin, Stuart Findlay, Andrew Robertson, James Forrest, Liam Palmer, Callum McGregor (70' Johnny Russell), John McGinn (70' Stuart Armstrong), Ryan Christie, Scott McTominay (YC25), Lawrence Shankland. (Coach: Steve Clarke (SCO)).
San Marino: Aldo Simoncini, Cristian Brolli, Manuel Battistini, Alessandro D'Addario (46' Andrea Grandoni), Alex Gasperoni, Mattia Giardi (YC34) (46' José Adolfo Hirsch), Alessandro Golinucci (YC53), Luca Censoni, Marcello Mularoni, Filippo Berardi (80' Luca Ceccaroli), Nicola Nanni. (Coach: Franco Varrella (ITA)).
Goals: Scotland: 1-0 John McGinn (12'), 2-0 John McGinn (27'), 3-0 John McGinn (45+1'), 4-0 Lawrence Shankland (65'), 5-0 Stuart Findlay (67'), 6-0 Stuart Armstrong (87').
Referee: Jérôme Brisard (FRA)   Attendance: 20.699

453

16-11-2019   Neo GSP Stadium, Nicosia: Cyprus – Scotland 1-2 (0-1)
Cyprus: Rafael Urko Pardo Goas, Giorgios Merkis, Chambos Kyriakou (77' Dimitris Theodorou), Andreas Karo (42' Grigoris Kastanos), Nicholas Ioannou, Ioannis Kousoulos, Ioannis Kosti, Giorgos Efrem (74' Matija Spoljaric), Jason Demetriou (YC58), Fotis Papoulis, Pieros Sotiriou. (Coach: Ran Ben Shimon (ISR)).
Scotland: David Marshall, Declan Gallagher, Scott McKenna (YC47), Greg Taylor (YC58), Ryan Jack, James Forrest (72' Oliver Burke), Liam Palmer (YC90+1), Callum McGregor (YC14), John McGinn (YC56), Ryan Christie (90+2' Michael Devlin), Steven Naismith (62' Oliver McBurnie). (Coach: Steve Clarke (SCO)).
Goals: Cyprus: 1-1 Giorgos Efrem (47').
Scotland: 0-1 Ryan Christie (12'), 1-2 John McGinn (53').
Referee: Harald Lechner (AUT)   Attendance: 7.595

16-11-2019   Krestovsky Stadium, Saint Petersburg: Russia – Belgium 1-4 (0-3)
Russia: Guilherme Alvim Marinato, Andrei Semyonov, Mário Fernandes, Sergey Petrov (YC3), Georgi Dzhikiya, Yuriy Zhirkov (50' Zelimkhan Bakaev), Aleksey Ionov, Magomed Ozdoev, Roman Zobnin (62' Daler Kuzyaev), Aleksey Miranchuk, Artem Dzyuba (80' Nicolay Komlichenko). (Coach: Stanislav Cherchesov (RUS)).
Belgium: Thibaut Courtois, Thomas Vermaelen (67' Jason Denayer), Toby Alderweireld, Dedryck Boyata, Timothy Castagne, Axel Witsel, Kevin De Bruyne, Eden Hazard, Dries Mertens (52' Youri Tielemans), Romelu Lukaku (77' Michy Batshuayi), Thorgan Hazard. (Coach: ROBERT MARTÍNEZ Montoliú (ESP)).
Goals: Russia: 1-4 Georgi Dzhikiya (79').
Belgium: 0-1 Thorgan Hazard (19'), 0-2 Eden Hazard (33'), 0-3 Eden Hazard (40'), 0-4 Romelu Lukaku (72').
Referee: Artur Soares Dias (POR)   Attendance: 53.317

16-11-2019   Stadio Olimpico di Serravalle, Serravalle: San Marino – Kazakhstan 1-3 (0-3)
San Marino: Simone Benedettini, Davide Simoncini (YC85), Mirko Palazzi (YC54), Cristian Brolli, Manuel Battistini, Andrea Grandoni (80' Luca Ceccaroli (YC90)), Enrico Golinucci, Alessandro Golinucci (60' Lorenzo Lunadei), Marcello Mularoni, Filippo Berardi, Nicola Nanni (64' José Adolfo Hirsch). (Coach: Franco Varrella (ITA)).
Kazakhstan: Dmytro Nepogodov, Dmitriy Shomko, Sergiy Maliy, Gafurzhan Suyombaev, Aleksandr Marochkin, Islambek Kuat, Bauyrzhan Islamkhan, Askhat Tagybergen (YC44) (66' Maxim Fedin), Yan Vorogovskiy (18' Dmitry Miroshnichenko (YC31)), Baktiyor Zaynutdinov, Aleksey Shchetkin (73' Abat Aymbetov). (Coach: Michal Bílek (CZE)).
Goals: San Marino: 1-3 Filippo Berardi (77').
Kazakhstan: 0-1 Baktiyor Zaynutdinov (6'), 0-2 Gafurzhan Suyombaev (22'), 0-3 Aleksey Shchetkin (26').
Referee: Ali Palabiyik (TUR)   Attendance: 643

19-11-2019   King Baudouin Stadium, Brussels: Belgium – Cyprus 6-1 (4-1)
Belgium: Simon Mignolet, Toby Alderweireld, Jason Denayer, Elias Cobbaut, Kevin De Bruyne (68' Dennis Praet), Hans Vanaken, Yannick Carrasco, Youri Tielemans, Eden Hazard (64' Yari Verschaeren), Christian Benteke (80' Divock Origi), Thorgan Hazard. (Coach: ROBERT MARTÍNEZ Montoliú (ESP)).
Cyprus: Neofytos Michael, Giorgios Merkis (YC19), Chambos Kyriakou, Christos Wheeler, Nicholas Ioannou (67' Ioannis Kousoulos), Kypros Christoforou, Ioannis Kosti (81' Fotis Papoulis), Kostakis Artymatas, Grigoris Kastanos, Pieros Sotiriou, Matija Spoljaric (79' Giorgos Efrem). (Coach: Ran Ben Shimon (ISR)).
Goals: Belgium: 1-1 Christian Benteke (16'), 2-1 Kevin De Bruyne (36'), 3-1 Kevin De Bruyne (41'), 4-1 Yannick Carrasco (44'), 5-1 Kypros Christoforou (51' *own goal*), 6-1 Christian Benteke (68').
Cyprus: 0-1 Nicholas Ioannou (14').
Referee: Jørgen Burchardt (DEN)   Attendance: 40.568

19-11-2019   Stadio Olimpico di Serravalle, Serravalle: San Marino – Russia 0-5 (0-2)
San Marino: Aldo Simoncini, Fabio Vitaioli, Davide Simoncini (YC33), Mirko Palazzi (YC53), Alessandro D'Addario (64' Fabio Tomassini), Alex Gasperoni (46' Manuel Battistini), Mattia Giardi, Luca Censoni (YC45), Filippo Berardi, Lorenzo Lunadei, Marco Bernardi (61' José Adolfo Hirsch (YC90+3)). (Coach: Franco Varrella (ITA)).
Russia: Anton Shunin, Fedor Kudryashov, Maksim Belyaev, Sergey Petrov, Georgi Dzhikiya, Aleksey Ionov (59' Aleksandr Golovin), Magomed Ozdoev (YC53) (59' Roman Zobnin), Daler Kuzyaev, Aleksey Miranchuk (65' Nikolay Komlichenko), Zelimkhan Bakaev, Artem Dzyuba. (Coach: Stanislav Cherchesov (RUS)).
Goals: Russia: 0-1 Daler Kuzyaev (3'), 0-2 Sergey Petrov (19'), 0-3 Aleksey Miranchuk (49'), 0-4 Aleksey Ionov (56'), 0-5 Nikolay Komlichenko (78').
Referee: Thorvaldur Árnason (ISL)   Attendance: 1.604

19-11-2019   Hampden Park, Glasgow: Scotland – Kazakhstan 3-1 (0-1)
Scotland: David Marshall, Declan Gallagher (YC66), Scott McKenna, Greg Taylor, Ryan Jack, James Forrest, Liam Palmer, Callum McGregor, John McGinn (90+2' Stuart Armstrong), Ryan Christie (83' John Fleck), Steven Naismith (78' Oliver Burke). (Coach: Steve Clarke (SCO)).
Kazakhstan: Dmytro Nepogodov, Yuriy Logvinenko, Dmitriy Shomko, Sergiy Maliy, Gafurzhan Suyombaev, Aleksandr Marochkin (YC67), Aybol Abiken (YC43), Bauyrzhan Islamkhan (YC22) (75' Maxim Fedin), Baktiyor Zaynutdinov, Yuri Pertsukh (74' Islambek Kuat (YC81)), Aleksey Shchetkin (83' Abat Aymbetov). (Coach: Michal Bílek (CZE)).
Goals: Scotland: 1-1 John McGinn (48'), 2-1 Steven Naismith (64'), 3-1 John McGinn (90+1').
Kazakhstan: 0-1 Baktiyor Zaynutdinov (34').
Referee: Bas Nijhuis (HOL)   Attendance: 19.515

GROUP J

23-03-2019	Sarajevo	Bosnia-Herzegovina – Armenia	2-1 (1-0)
23-03-2019	Udine	Italy – Finland	2-0 (1-0)
23-03-2019	Vaduz	Liechtenstein – Greece	0-2 (0-1)
26-03-2019	Yerevan	Armenia – Finland	0-2 (0-1)
26-03-2019	Zenica	Bosnia-Herzegovina – Greece	2-2 (2-0)
26-03-2019	Parma	Italy – Liechtenstein	6-0 (4-0)
08-06-2019	Yerevan	Armenia – Liechtenstein	3-0 (2-0)
08-06-2019	Tampere	Finland – Bosnia-Herzegovina	2-0 (0-0)

08-06-2019	Athens	Greece – Italy	0-3 (0-3)
11-06-2019	Athens	Greece – Armenia	2-3 (0-2)
11-06-2019	Turin	Italy – Bosnia-Herzegovina	2-1 (0-1)
11-06-2019	Vaduz	Liechtenstein – Finland	0-2 (0-1)
05-09-2019	Yerevan	Armenia – Italy	1-3 (1-1)
05-09-2019	Zenica	Bosnia-Herzegovina – Liechtenstein	5-0 (1-0)
05-09-2019	Tampere	Finland – Greece	1-0 (0-0)
08-09-2019	Yerevan	Armenia – Bosnia-Herzegovina	4-2 (1-1)
08-09-2019	Tampere	Finland – Italy	1-2 (1-0)
08-09-2019	Athens	Greece – Liechtenstein	1-1 (1-0)
12-10-2019	Zenica	Bosnia-Herzegovina – Finland	4-1 (2-0)
12-10-2019	Rome	Italy – Greece	2-0 (0-0)
12-10-2019	Vaduz	Liechtenstein – Armenia	1-1 (0-1)
15-10-2019	Turku	Finland – Armenia	3-0 (1-0)
15-10-2019	Athens	Greece – Bosnia-Herzegovina	2-1 (1-1)
15-10-2019	Vaduz	Liechtenstein – Italy	0-5 (0-1)
15-11-2019	Yerevan	Armenia – Greece	0-1 (0-1)
15-11-2019	Helsinki	Finland – Liechtenstein	3-0 (1-0)
15-11-2019	Zenica	Bosnia-Herzegovina – Italy	0-3 (0-2)
18-11-2019	Athens	Greece – Finland	2-1 (0-1)
18-11-2019	Palermo	Italy – Armenia	9-1 (4-0)
18-11-2019	Vaduz	Liechtenstein – Bosnia-Herzegovina	0-3 (0-0)

FINAL STANDING

Pos	Team	Pld	W	D	L	GF	GA	GD	Pts
1	Italy	10	10	0	0	37	4	+33	30
2	Finland	10	6	0	4	16	10	+6	18
3	Greece	10	4	2	4	12	14	-2	14
4	Bosnia-Herzegovina	10	4	1	5	20	17	+3	13
5	Armenia	10	3	1	6	14	25	-11	10
6	Liechtenstein	10	0	2	8	2	31	-29	2

Italy and Finland qualified for final tournament.

23-03-2019   Stadion Grbavica, Sarajevo: Bosnia-Herzegovina – Armenia 2-1 (1-0)
Bosnia-Herzegovina: Ibrahim Sehic, Ervin Zukanovic, Ermin Bicakcic, Eldar Civic (YC40), Darko Todorovic, Miralem Pjanic, Edin Visca, Goran Zakaric (65' Deni Milosevic), Muhamed Besic, Rade Krunic (83' Amer Gojak), Edin Dzeko (87' Elvir Koljic). (Coach: Robert Prosinecki (CRO)).
Armenia: Aram Ayrapetyan, Gagik Dagbashyan, André Calisir, Varazdat Haroyan, Henrikh Mkhitaryan, Karlen Mkrtchyan, Kamo Hovhannisyan, Artak Grigoryan, Gevorg Ghazaryan (81' Aras Özbiliz), Alexander Karapetyan (67' Norberto Alejandro Briasco Balekian), Sargis Adamyan (67' Edgar Babayan). (Coach: Armen Gyulbudaghyants (ARM)).
Goals: Bosnia-Herzegovina: 1-0 Rade Krunic (33'), 2-0 Deni Milosevic (80').
Armenia: 2-1 Henrikh Mkhitaryan (90+3' penalty).
Referee: Jakob Kehlet (DEN)   Attendance: 10.000

23-03-2019   Dacia Arena, Udine: Italy – Finland 2-0 (1-0)
Italy: Gianluigi Donnarumma, Leonardo Bonucci, Giorgio Chiellini, Cristiano Biraghi (90+1'
Leonardo Spinazzola), Cristiano Piccini (YC81), Marco Verratti (YC63) (85' Nicolò Zaniolo),
Jorginho, Nicolò Barella, Ciro Immobile (80' Fabio Quagliarella), Federico Bernardeschi,
Moise Kean. (Coach: Roberto Mancini (ITA)).
Finland: Lukás Hrádecky, Juha Pirinen, Paulus Arajuuri, Joona Toivio, Albin Granlund (90'
Pyry Soiri), Sauli Väisänen, Tim Sparv (YC63), Kasper Hämäläinen (70' Lassi Lappalainen),
Robin Lod, Glen Kamara, Teemu Pukki (83' Rasmus Karjalainen). (Coach: Markku Kanerva
(FIN)).
Goals: Italy: 1-0 Nicolò Barella (7'), 2-0 Moise Kean (74').
Referee: Orel Grinfeld (ISR)   Attendance: 24.000

23-03-2019   Rheinpark Stadion, Vaduz: Liechtenstein – Greece 0-2 (0-1)
Liechtenstein: Benjamin Büchel, Martin Rechsteiner, Daniel Kaufmann, Nicolas Hasler (86'
Noah Frick), Maximilian Göppel, Martin Büchel (67' Aron Sele), Michele Polverino, Sandro
Wieser, Sandro Wolfinger, Dennis Salanovic, Robin Gubser (76' Seyhan Yildiz). (Coach:
Helgi Kolvidsson (ISL)).
Greece: Odisseas Vlachodimos, Dimitrios Siovas, Michalis Bakakis, Leonardo Koutris,
Andreas Samaris, Kostas Fortounis (83' Efthimios Koulouris), Zeca, Dimitrios Kourbelis,
Georgios Masouras, Kostas Mitroglou (23' Anastasios Donis (YC73)), Anastasios Bakasetas
(71' Dimitrios Kolovos). (Coach: Angelos Anastasiadis (GRE)).
Goals: Greece: 0-1 Kostas Fortounis (45+1'), 0-2 Anastasios Donis (80').
Referee: Alexandre Boucaut (BEL)   Attendance: 2.711

26-03-2019   Vazgen Sargsyan anvan Hanrapetakan Marzadasht, Yerevan:
              Armenia – Finland 0-2 (0-1)
Armenia: Aram Ayrapetyan, Gagik Dagbashyan, André Calisir (YC39), Varazdat Haroyan
(YC90+2), Henrikh Mkhitaryan, Kamo Hovhannisyan, Artak Grigoryan, Aras Özbiliz (67'
Tigran Barseghyan), Edgar Babayan (YC40) (74' Petros Avetisyan), Gevorg Ghazaryan,
Norberto Alejandro Briasco Balekian (YC54) (59' Alexander Karapetyan). (Coach: Armen
Gyulbudaghyants (ARM)).
Finland: Lukás Hrádecky (YC66), Juha Pirinen, Paulus Arajuuri, Joona Toivio, Albin
Granlund, Tim Sparv (YC71), Kasper Hämäläinen (57' Pyry Soiri), Robin Lod (87' Robert
Taylor), Glen Kamara (YC36), Fredrik Jensen (69' Rasmus Schüller), Teemu Pukki. (Coach:
Markku Kanerva (FIN)).
Goals: Finland: 0-1 Fredrik Jensen (14'), 0-2 Pyry Soiri (78').
Referee: Nikola Dabanovic (MNE)   Attendance: 12.900

26-03-2019   Bilino Polje Stadium, Zenica: Bosnia-Herzegovina – Greece 2-2 (2-0)
Bosnia-Herzegovina: Ibrahim Sehic, Toni Sunjic, Ervin Zukanovic, Ermin Bicakcic, Sead
Kolasinac (YC90+1), Miralem Pjanic (RC65), Edin Visca, Gojko Cimirot (90+3' Rade
Krunic), Muhamed Besic, Edin Dzeko (90' Amer Gojak), Haris Duljevic (80' Deni Milosevic).
(Coach: Robert Prosinecki (CRO)).
Greece: Odisseas Vlachodimos, Dimitrios Siovas, Sokratis Papastathopoulos, Michalis Bakakis
(80' Efthimios Koulouris), Leonardo Koutris, Andreas Samaris, Kostas Fortounis, Zeca,
Andreas Bouchalakis (46' Georgios Masouras), Dimitrios Kourbelis (YC14) (67' Dimitrios
Kolovos), Anastasios Donis (YC17). (Coach: Angelos Anastasiadis (GRE)).
Goals: Bosnia-Herzegovina: 1-0 Edin Visca (10'), 2-0 Miralem Pjanic (15').
Greece: 2-1 Kostas Fortounis (64' penalty), 2-2 Dimitrios Kolovos (85').
Referee: Danny Makkelie (HOL)   Attendance: 10.500

26-03-2019   Stadio Ennio Tardini, Parma: Italy – Liechtenstein 6-0 (4-0)
Italy: Salvatore Sirigu, Leonardo Bonucci (79' Armando Izzo (YC90+2)), Leonardo
Spinazzola, Alessio Romagnoli, Gianluca Mancini, Marco Verratti, Jorginho (57' Nicolò
Zaniolo), Stefano Sensi, Fabio Quagliarella (72' Leonardo Pavoletti), Matteo Politano, Moise
Kean. (Coach: Roberto Mancini (ITA)).
Liechtenstein: Benjamin Büchel, Daniel Kaufmann (RC45+2), Nicolas Hasler (YC34),
Maximilian Göppel, Jens Hofer, Michele Polverino, Sandro Wieser, Sandro Wolfinger, Aron
Sele (46' Andreas Malin), Dennis Salanovic (82' Martin Büchel), Simon Kühne (68' Livio
Meier). (Coach: Helgi Kolvidsson (ISL)).
Goals: Italy: 1-0 Stefano Sensi (17'), 2-0 Marco Verratti (32'), 3-0 Fabio Quagliarella (35'
penalty), 4-0 Fabio Quagliarella (45+3' penalty), 5-0 Moise Kean (69'), 6-0 Leonardo Pavoletti
(76').
Referee: Kirill Levnikov (RUS)   Attendance: 19.834

08-06-2019   Vazgen Sargsyan anvan Hanrapetakan Marzadasht, Yerevan:
              Armenia – Liechtenstein 3-0 (2-0)
Armenia: Aram Ayrapetyan, Hovhannes Hambardzumyan, Varazdat Haroyan, Taron
Voskanyan, Henrikh Mkhitaryan, Karlen Mkrtchyan (76' Artak Grigoryan), Kamo
Hovhannisyan, Petros Avetisyan (78' Rumyan Hovsepyan (YC82)), Gevorg Ghazaryan,
Alexander Karapetyan (73' Edgar Babayan), Tigran Barseghyan. (Coach: Armen
Gyulbudaghyants (ARM)).
Liechtenstein: Thomas Hobi, Nicolas Hasler, Maximilian Göppel, Andreas Malin, Jens Hofer,
Michele Polverino, Martin Büchel, Sandro Wolfinger (85' Daniel Brändle), Aron Sele (81'
Livio Meier), Dennis Salanovic, Yanick Frick (46' Simon Kühne). (Coach: Helgi Kolvidsson
(ISL)).
Goals: Armenia: 1-0 Gevorg Ghazaryan (2'), 2-0 Alexander Karapetyan (18'), 3-0 Tigran
Barseghyan (90+1').
Referee: Nikola Popov (BUL)   Attendancce: 9.200

08-06-2019   Tampere Stadium, Tampere: Finland – Bosnia-Herzegovina 2-0 (0-0)
Finland: Lukás Hrádecky, Paulus Arajuuri, Joona Toivio, Albin Granlund (38' Jukka Raitala),
Jere Uronen, Tim Sparv, Petteri Forsell (63' Lassi Lappalainen), Robin Lod, Glen Kamara,
Teemu Pukki, Simon Skrabb (84' Rasmus Schüller). (Coach: Markku Kanerva (FIN)).
Bosnia-Herzegovina: Ibrahim Sehic, Toni Sunjic, Ervin Zukanovic, Ermin Bicakcic, Eldar
Civic, Edin Visca (YC86), Gojko Cimirot, Muhamed Besic (79' Amer Gojak), Elvis Saric
(YC49), Edin Dzeko, Haris Duljevic (69' Rijad Bajic). (Coach: Robert Prosinecki (CRO)).
Goals: Finland: 1-0 Teemu Pukki (56'), 2-0 Teemu Pukki (68').
Referee: Daniel Stefanski (POL)   Attendance: 16.103

08-06-2019   Olympiako Stadio Spyros Louis, Athens: Greece – Italy 0-3 (0-3)
Greece: Vassilis Barkas, Dimitrios Siovas, Sokratis Papastathopoulos, Kostas Manolas, Kostas
Stafylidis, Andreas Samaris (YC18) (77' Anastasios Bakasetas), Kostas Fortounis, Zeca,
Dimitrios Kolovos (46' Charis Mavrias), Dimitrios Kourbelis (46' Emmanouil "Manolis"
Siopis), Georgios Masouras (YC45+1). (Coach: Angelos Anastasiadis (GRE)).
Italy: Salvatore Sirigu, Leonardo Bonucci, Giorgio Chiellini, Emerson (68' Mattia De Sciglio),
Alessandro Florenzi, Marco Verratti (YC43) (81' Lorenzo Pellegrini), Jorginho, Nicolò
Barella, Lorenzo Insigne, Andrea Belotti (84' Federico Bernardeschi), Federico Chiesa.
(Coach: Roberto Mancini (ITA)).
Goals: Italy: 0-1 Nicolò Barella (23'), 0-2 Lorenzo Insigne (30'), 0-3 Leonardo Bonucci (33').
Referee: Anthony Taylor (ENG)   Attendance: 19.828

458

11-06-2019   Olympiako Stadio Spyros Louis, Athens: Greece – Armenia 2-3 (0-2)
Greece: Odisseas Vlachodimos, Dimitrios Siovas, Sokratis Papastathopoulos (YC76), Leonardo Koutris, Andreas Samaris (75' Emmanouil "Manolis" Siopis), Kostas Fortounis, Zeca (YC72), Charis Mavrias (17' Giannis Kotsiras), Dimitrios Pelkas (YC19) (68' Dimitrios Kolovos), Georgios Masouras (YC81), Efthimios Koulouris. (Coach: Angelos Anastasiadis (GRE)).
Armenia: Aram Ayrapetyan, Hovhannes Hambardzumyan, Varazdat Haroyan, Hayk Ishkhanyan, Henrikh Mkhitaryan, Karlen Mkrtchyan (YC29) (55' Rumyan Hovsepyan), Kamo Hovhannisyan, Artak Grigoryan, Gevorg Ghazaryan (83' Petros Avetisyan), Alexander Karapetyan (YC69) (70' Edgar Babayan (YC90+6)), Tigran Barseghyan. (Coach: Armen Gyulbudaghyants (ARM)).
Goals: Greece: 1-2 Zeca (54'), 2-3 Kostas Fortounis (87').
Armenia: 0-1 Alexander Karapetyan (8'), 0-2 Gevorg Ghazaryan (33'), 1-3 Tigran Barseghyan (74').
Referee: Kristo Tohver (EST)   Attendance: 7.011

11-06-2019   Allianz Stadium, Torino: Italy – Bosnia-Herzegovina 2-1 (0-1)
Italy: Salvatore Sirigu, Leonardo Bonucci, Giorgio Chiellini, Emerson, Gianluca Mancini (66' Mattia De Sciglio), Marco Verratti, Jorginho (YC14), Nicolò Barella, Fabio Quagliarella (46' Federico Chiesa), Lorenzo Insigne, Federico Bernardeschi (81' Andrea Belotti). (Coach: Roberto Mancini (ITA)).
Bosnia-Herzegovina: Ibrahim Sehic, Ervin Zukanovic, Ermin Bicakcic, Eldar Civic (YC44) (72' Bojan Nastic), Darko Todorovic, Miralem Pjanic, Edin Visca, Muhamed Besic (YC43), Elvis Saric (YC62), Amer Gojak (81' Gojko Cimirot), Edin Dzeko (YC90+2). (Coach: Robert Prosinecki (CRO)).
Goals: Italy: 1-1 Lorenzo Insigne (49'), 2-1 Marco Verratti (86').
Bosnia-Herzegovina: 0-1 Edin Dzeko (32').
Referee: XAVIER ESTRADA Fernández (ESP)   Attendance: 30.077

11-06-2019   Rheinpark Stadion, Vaduz: Liechtenstein – Finland 0-2 (0-1)
Liechtenstein: Thomas Hobi, Martin Rechsteiner, Daniel Kaufmann, Nicolas Hasler, Jens Hofer, Sandro Wieser (46' Michele Polverino), Marcel Büchel (YC32) (54' Martin Büchel), Sandro Wolfinger (77' Daniel Brändle), Aron Sele, Dennis Salanovic, Simon Kühne. (Coach: Helgi Kolvidsson (ISL)).
Finland: Lukás Hrádecky, Jukka Raitala (87' Leo Väisänen), Paulus Arajuuri, Joona Toivio, Jere Uronen, Tim Sparv (61' Rasmus Schüller), Robin Lod, Glen Kamara, Lassi Lappalainen (74' Pyry Soiri), Teemu Pukki, Benjamin Källman. (Coach: Markku Kanerva (FIN)).
Goals: Finland: 0-1 Teemu Pukki (37'), 0-2 Benjamin Källman (57').
Referee: Jens Maae (DEN)   Attendance: 2.160

06-09-2019   Vazgen Sargsyan anvan Hanrapetakan Marzadasht, Yerevan:
Armenia – Italy 1-3 (1-1)
Armenia: Aram Ayrapetyan, Hovhannes Hambardzumyan, André Calisir, Varazdat Haroyan,
Henrikh Mkhitaryan, Karlen Mkrtchyan, Kamo Hovhannisyan, Artak Grigoryan (57' Rumyan
Hovsepyan), Gevorg Ghazaryan (YC26) (82' Edgar Babayan), Alexander Karapetyan
(YC26,YC45+1), Tigran Barseghyan (YC48) (57' Sargis Adamyan). (Coach: Armen
Gyulbudaghyants (ARM)).
Italy: Gianluigi Donnarumma, Leonardo Bonucci, Emerson, Alessandro Florenzi, Alessio
Romagnoli, Marco Verratti (YC26), Jorginho, Nicolò Barella (YC59) (69' Stefano Sensi),
Andrea Belotti, Federico Bernardeschi (83' Kevin Lasagna), Federico Chiesa (61' Lorenzo
Pellegrini). (Coach: Roberto Mancini (ITA)).
Goals: Armenia: 1-0 Alexander Karapetyan (11').
Italy: 1-1 Andrea Belotti (28'), 1-2 Lorenzo Pellegrini (77'), 1-3 Aram Ayrapetyan (80' *own
goal*).
Referee: Daniel Siebert (GER)   Attendance: 13.680

05-09-2019   Bilino Polje Stadium, Zenica: Bosnia-Herzegovina – Liechtenstein 5-0 (1-0)
Bosnia-Herzegovina: Ibrahim Sehic, Toni Sunjic (25' Marko Mihojevic), Ervin Zukanovic,
Sead Kolasinac, Darko Todorovic, Miralem Pjanic (83' Stjepan Loncar), Edin Visca, Deni
Milosevic (55' Haris Duljevic), Rade Krunic, Amer Gojak, Edin Dzeko. (Coach: Robert
Prosinecki (CRO)).
Liechtenstein: Benjamin Büchel, Martin Rechsteiner, Daniel Kaufmann, Nicolas Hasler,
Maximilian Göppel, Andreas Malin, Marcel Büchel (YC69), Sandro Wieser (85' Daniel
Brändle), Dennis Salanovic, Livio Meier (64' Sandro Wolfinger), Robin Gubser (74' Aron
Sele (YC76)). (Coach: Helgi Kolvidsson (ISL)).
Goals: Bosnia-Herzegovina: 1-0 Amer Gojak (11'), 2-0 Andreas Malin (80' *own goal*), 3-0
Edin Dzeko (85'), 4-0 Edin Visca (87'), 5-0 Amer Gojak (89').
Referee: Glenn Nyberg (SWE)   Attendance: 3.825

05-09-2019   Tampere Stadium, Tampere: Finland – Greece 1-0 (0-0)
Finland: Lukás Hrádecky, Jukka Raitala, Paulus Arajuuri, Joona Toivio, Jere Uronen, Tim
Sparv (YC57), Robin Lod, Glen Kamara (YC72), Jasse Tuominen (87' Fredrik Jensen), Teemu
Pukki (85' Rasmus Karjanainen), Pyry Soiri (90+3' Rasmus Schüller). (Coach: Markku
Kanerva (FIN)).
Greece: Vassilis Barkas, Vasilios Torosidis (YC39) (70' Michalis Bakakis), Sokratis
Papastathopoulos, Kostas Manolas, Kostas Stafylidis, Andreas Bouchalakis, Dimitrios Kolovos
(60' Dimitrios Pelkas (YC66)), Dimitrios Kourbelis (YC45), Georgios Masouras, Efthimios
Koulouris (76' Evangelos Pavlidis (YC90+2)), Marios Vrousai. (Coach: John van 't Schip
(HOL)).
Goal: Finland: 1-0 Teemu Pukki (52' penalty).
Referee: JUAN MARTÍNEZ Munuera (ESP)   Attendance: 16.163

460

08-09-2019   Vazgen Sargsyan anvan Hanrapetakan Marzadasht, Yerevan:
Armenia – Bosnia-Herzegovina 4-2 (1-1)
Armenia: Aram Ayrapetyan (YC85), Hovhannes Hambardzumyan, Varazdat Haroyan, Hayk
Ishkhanyan, Henrikh Mkhitaryan, Karlen Mkrtchyan (75' Artak Grigoryan), Kamo
Hovhannisyan (83' Arman Hovhannisyan), Rumyan Hovsepyan (77' Erik Vardanyan), Gevorg
Ghazaryan (YC33), Tigran Barseghyan, Sargis Adamyan. (Coach: Armen Gyulbudaghyants
(ARM)).
Bosnia-Herzegovina: Ibrahim Sehic, Ervin Zukanovic, Ermin Bicakcic, Sead Kolasinac, Darko
Todorovic (85' Rijad Bajic), Miralem Pjanic (YC72), Edin Visca (YC25) (64' Haris Duljevic),
Gojko Cimirot, Muhamed Besic (YC45) (80' Stjepan Loncar), Amer Gojak, Edin Dzeko
(YC72). (Coach: Robert Prosinecki (CRO)).
Goals: Armenia: 1-0 Henrikh Mkhitaryan (3'), 2-1 Henrikh Mkhitaryan (66'), 3-2 Hovhannes
Hambardzumyan (77'), 4-2 Stjepan Loncar (90+5' own goal).
Bosnia-Herzegovina: 1-1 Edin Dzeko (13'), 2-2 Amer Gojak (70').
Referee: Benoît Bastien (FRA)   Attendance: 12.457

08-09-2019   Tampere Stadium, Tampere: Finland – Italy 1-2 (0-0)
Finland: Lukás Hrádecky, Paulus Arajuuri (YC74), Joona Toivio, Albin Granlund (82' Pyry
Soiri), Jere Uronen, Sauli Väisänen (YC78), Rasmus Schüller (YC57) (87' Joni Kauko
(YC90+3)), Robin Lod, Glen Kamara, Lassi Lappalainen (75' Jasse Tuominen), Teemu Pukki.
(Coach: Markku Kanerva (FIN)).
Italy: Gianluigi Donnarumma (YC71), Leonardo Bonucci, Francesco Acerbi, Emerson (8'
Alessandro Florenzi), Armando Izzo, Jorginho (YC21), Stefano Sensi, Nicolò Barella, Lorenzo
Pellegrini, Ciro Immobile (76' Andrea Belotti), Federico Chiesa (72' Federico Bernardeschi).
(Coach: Roberto Mancini (ITA)).
Goals: Finland: 1-1 Teemu Pukki (72' penalty).
Italy: 0-1 Ciro Immobile (59'), 1-2 Jorginho (79' penalty).
Referee: Bobby Madden (SCO)   Attendance: 16.292

08-09-2019   Olympiako Stadio Spyros Louis, Athens: Greece – Liechtenstein 1-1 (1-0)
Greece: Vassilis Barkas, Sokratis Papastathopoulos, Kostas Manolas, Michalis Bakakis, Kostas
Tsimikas, Ioannis Fetfatzidis (68' Evangelos Pavlidis), Andreas Samaris, Andreas Bouchalakis
(62' Zeca (YC87)), Georgios Masouras (YC37) (86' Dimitris Giannoulis), Efthimios
Koulouris, Marios Vrousai. (Coach: John van 't Schip (HOL)).
Liechtenstein: Benjamin Büchel, Martin Rechsteiner (82' Jens Hofer), Daniel Kaufmann,
Nicolas Hasler, Maximilian Göppel, Andreas Malin, Marcel Büchel, Sandro Wieser, Dennis
Salanovic, Livio Meier (YC54) (64' Daniel Brändle), Robin Gubser (56' Seyhan Yildiz).
(Coach: Helgi Kolvidsson (ISL)).
Goals: Greece: 1-0 Georgios Masouras (33').
Liechtenstein: 1-1 Dennis Salanovic (85').
Referee: Alexander Harkam (AUT)   Attendance: 3.445

12-10-2019   Bilino Polje Stadium, Zenica: Bosnia-Herzegovina – Finland 4-1 (2-0)
Bosnia-Herzegovina: Ibrahim Sehic, Ermin Bicakcic, Adnan Kovacevic, Sead Kolasinac, Miralem Pjanic (76' Rade Krunic), Edin Visca (18' Izet Hajrovic), Gojko Cimirot, Zoran Kvrzic, Elvis Saric (71' Mato Jajalo (YC84)), Amer Gojak, Armin Hodzic (YC75). (Coach: Robert Prosinecki (CRO)).
Finland: Lukás Hrádecky, Jukka Raitala (YC53), Paulus Arajuuri (30' Sauli Väisänen), Joona Toivio, Jere Uronen (YC51), Tim Sparv (71' Joni Kauko), Robin Lod, Glen Kamara, Jasse Tuominen, Teemu Pukki (YC88), Pyry Soiri (46' Joel Pohjanpalo). (Coach: Markku Kanerva (FIN)).
Goals: Bosnia-Herzegovina: 1-0 Izet Hajrovic (29'), 2-0 Miralem Pjanic (37' penalty), 3-0 Miralem Pjanic (58'), 4-0 Armin Hodzic (73').
Finland: 4-1 Joel Pohjanpalo (79').
Referee: Ivan Kruzliak (SVK)   Attendance: 8.193

12-10-2019   Stadio Olimpico, Roma: Italy – Greece 2-0 (0-0)
Italy: Gianluigi Donnarumma, Leonardo Bonucci, Danilo D'Ambrosio, Francesco Acerbi, Leonardo Spinazzola, Marco Verratti, Jorginho, Nicolò Barella (87' Nicolò Zaniolo), Ciro Immobile (79' Andrea Belotti), Lorenzo Insigne, Federico Chiesa (39' Federico Bernardeschi). (Coach: Roberto Mancini (ITA)).
Greece: Alexandros Paschalakis, Dimitrios Siovas, Michalis Bakakis, Kostas Stafylidis, Pantelis Hatzidiakos (YC14), Zeca, Andreas Bouchalakis (YC62) (75' Dimitris Giannoulis), Dimitrios Kourbelis, Anastasios Bakasetas (79' Petros Mantalos), Efthimios Koulouris (YC27) (67' Anastasios Donis), Dimitris Limnios. (Coach: John van 't Schip (HOL)).
Goals: Italy: 1-0 Jorginho (63' penalty), 2-0 Federico Bernardeschi (78').
Referee: Sergei Karasev (RUS)   Attendance: 56.274

12-10-2019   Rheinpark Stadion, Vaduz: Liechtenstein – Armenia 1-1 (0-1)
Liechtenstein: Benjamin Büchel, Martin Rechsteiner, Daniel Kaufmann, Nicolas Hasler (YC90+5), Maximilian Göppel, Andreas Malin, Marcel Büchel, Michele Polverino (83' Aron Sele), Dennis Salanovic (YC10), Livio Meier (70' Seyhan Yildiz), Robin Gubser (67' Yanik Frick). (Coach: Helgi Kolvidsson (ISL)).
Armenia: Aram Ayrapetyan, Hovhannes Hambardzumyan, Varazdat Haroyan (YC30), Hayk Ishkhanyan, Arman Hovhannisyan (YC48), Rumyan Hovsepyan (YC53) (83' Artur Miranyan), Gevorg Ghazaryan (88' Aras Özbiliz), Marcos Pizzelli (60' Gor Malakyan), Alexander Karapetyan, Tigran Barseghyan, Sargis Adamyan. (Coach: Armen Gyulbudaghyants (ARM)).
Goals: Liechtenstein: 1-1 Yanik Frick (72').
Armenia: 0-1 Tigran Barseghyan (19').
Referee: István Kovács (ROM)   Attendance: 2.285

15-10-2019   Veritas Stadion, Turku: Finland – Armenia 3-0 (1-0)
Finland: Lukás Hrádecky, Jukka Raitala, Joona Toivio, Jere Uronen, Sauli Väisänen, Joni Kauko, Robin Lod, Glen Kamara (87' Rasmus Schüller), Fredrik Jensen (53' Joel Pohjanpalo), Lassi Lappalainen (61' Pyry Soiri), Teemu Pukki. (Coach: Markku Kanerva (FIN)).
Armenia: Aram Ayrapetyan, Hovhannes Hambardzumyan (YC39), Varazdat Haroyan (YC76), Hayk Ishkhanyan, Arman Hovhannisyan, Artak Grigoryan (72' Gor Malakyan), Rumyan Hovsepyan, Gevorg Ghazaryan (77' Edgar Babayan), Alexander Karapetyan, Tigran Barseghyan (65' Aras Özbiliz), Sargis Adamyan (YC54). (Coach: Armen Gyulbudaghyants (ARM)).
Goals: Finland: 1-0 Fredrik Jensen (31'), 2-0 Teemu Pukki (61'), 3-0 Teemu Pukki (88').
Referee: JESÚS GIL Manzano (ESP)   Attendance: 7.231

15-10-2019   Olympiako Stadio Spyros Louis, Athens:
Greece – Bosnia-Herzegovina 2-1 (1-1)
Greece: Alexandros Paschalakis, Michalis Bakakis (YC90+4), Kostas Stafylidis, Dimitris
Giannoulis, Pantelis Hatzidiakos, Petros Mantalos (60' Georgios Masouras (YC90)), Dimitrios
Kourbelis, Konsyantinos Galanopoulos, Anastasios Bakasetas, Evangelos Pavlidis (70'
Efthimios Koulouris (YC90+2)), Dimitris Limnios (84' Ioannis Fetfayzidis). (Coach: John van
't Schip (HOL)).
Bosnia-Herzegovina: Ibrahim Sehic, Ermin Bicakcic, Adnan Kovacevic, Sead Kolasinac,
Miralem Pjanic, Gojko Cimirot (YC32) (46' Mato Jajalo), Zoran Kvrzic (YC76), Elvis Saric
(63' Haris Duljevic), Amer Gojak, Izet Hajrovic, Armin Hodzic (71' Rijad Bajic). (Coach:
Robert Prosinecki (CRO)).
Goals: Greece: 1-0 Evangelos Pavlidis (30'), 2-1 Adnan Kovacevic (88' own goal).
Bosnia-Herzegovina: 1-1 Amer Gojak (35').
Referee: Felix Zwayer (GER)   Attendance: 4.512

15-10-2019   Rheinpark Stadion, Vaduz: Liechtenstein – Italy 0-5 (0-1)
Liechtenstein: Benjamin Büchel, Martin Rechsteiner (YC2), Daniel Kaufmann, Nicolas Hasler,
Seyhan Yildiz (83' Sandro Wolfinger), Maximilian Göppel, Jens Hofer, Martin Büchel,
Michele Polverino (56' Noah Frick), Dennis Salanovic, Robin Gubser (63' Yanik Frick).
(Coach: Helgi Kolvidsson (ISL)).
Italy: Salvatore Sirigu, Cristiano Biraghi (88' Leonardo Bonucci), Giovanni Di Lorenzo,
Alessio Romagnoli, Gianluca Mancini, Marco Verratti, Bryan Cristante, Vincenzo Grifo,
Nicolò Zaniolo (63' Stephen El Shaarawy), Andrea Belotti, Federico Bernardeschi (74' Sandro
Tonali (YC84)). (Coach: Roberto Mancini (ITA)).
Goals: Italy: 0-1 Federico Bernardeschi (2'), 0-2 Andrea Belotti (70'), 0-3 Alessio Romagnoli
(77'), 0-4 Stephen El Shaarawy (82'), 0-5 Andrea Belotti (90+2').
Referee: Andris Treimanis (LAT)   Attendance: 5.087

15-11-2019   Vazgen Sargsyan anvan Hanrapetakan Marzadasht, Yerevan:
Armenia – Greece 0-1 (0-1)
Armenia: Aram Ayrapetyan, Hovhannes Hambardzumyan, André Calisir, Hayk Ishkhanyan,
Taron Voskanyan (83' Petros Avetisyan), Kamo Hovhannisyan, Artak Grigoryan, Rumyan
Hovsepyan (YC77) (78' Artak Yedigaryan (YC84)), Erik Vardanyan (59' Artur Sarkisov),
Alexander Karapetyan, Tigran Barseghyan (YC39). (Coach: Abraham Khashmanyan (ARM)).
Greece: Odisseas Vlachodimos, Michalis Bakakis, Kostas Stafylidis (YC41), Dimitris
Giannoulis (YC21), Pantelis Hatzidiakos, Petros Mantalos (YC45+1) (66' Georgios
Masouras), Dimitrios Kourbelis, Konstantinos Galanopoulos, Anastasios Bakasetas (81'
Anastasios Donis), Evangelos Pavlidis (74' Efthimios Koulouris), Dimitris Limnios. (Coach:
John van 't Schip (HOL)).
Goal: Greece: 0-1 Dimitris Limnios (35').
Referee: Pawel Raczkowski (POL)   Attendance: 6.450

15-11-2019   Telia 5G -areena, Helsinki: Finland – Liechtenstein 3-0 (1-0)
Finland: Lukás Hrádecky, Jukka Raitala, Juha Pirinen, Paulus Arajuuri, Joona Toivio, Tim Sparv (71' Joni Kauko), Robin Lod, Glen Kamara, Jasse Tuominen, Teemu Pukki (84' Rasmus Karjalainen), Pyry Soiri (78' Simon Skrabb). (Coach: Markku Kanerva (FIN)).
Liechtenstein: Benjamin Büchel, Martin Rechsteiner, Nicolas Hasler, Maximilian Göppel, Andreas Malin, Martin Büchel, Michele Polverino (73' Robin Gubser), Daniel Brändle, Dennis Salanovic, Livio Meier (90+1' Aron Sele), Yanik Frick (84' Ridvan Kardesoglu). (Coach: Helgi Kolvidsson (ISL)).
Goals: Finland: 1-0 Jasse Tuominen (21'), 2-0 Teemu Pukki (64' penalty), 3-0 T. Pukki (75').
Referee: Benoît Bastien (FRA)   Attendance: 9.804

15-11-2019   Bilino Polje Stadium, Zenica: Bosnia-Herzegovina – Italy 0-3 (0-2)
Bosnia-Herzegovina: Ibrahim Sehic, Ermin Bicakcic, Adnan Kovacevic (YC79), Sead Kolasinac, Miralem Pjanic (77' Mato Jajalo), Edin Visca (61' Armin Hodzic), Gojko Cimirot, Zoran Kvrzic, Muhamed Besic (61' Elvis Saric), Rade Krunic, Edin Dzeko. (Coach: Robert Prosinecki (CRO)).
Italy: Gianluigi Donnarumma (88' Pierluigi Gollini), Leonardo Bonucci (YC65), Francesco Acerbi, Emerson, Alessandro Florenzi, Jorginho, Nicolò Barella, Sandro Tonali, Lorenzo Insigne (86' Gaetano Castrovilli), Andrea Belotti, Federico Bernardeschi (YC25) (75' Stephen El Shaarawy). (Coach: Roberto Mancini (ITA)).
Goals: Italy: 0-1 Francesco Acerbi (21'), 0-2 Lorenzo Insigne (37'), 0-3 Andrea Belotti (52').
Referee: Sandro Schärer (SUI)   Attendance: 8.355

18-11-2019   Olympiako Stadio Spyros Louis, Athens: Greece – Finland 2-1 (0-1)
Greece: Odisseas Vlachodimos, Michalis Bakakis, Kostas Stafylidis, Dimitris Giannoulis, Pantelis Hatzidiakos, Petros Mantalos (90+3' Georgios Masouras), Dimitrios Kourbelis (YC34), Konstantinos Galanopoulos (73' Andreas Bouchalakis), Anastasios Bakasetas, Evangelos Pavlidis (64' Efthimios Koulouris), Dimitris Limnios. (Coach: John van 't Schip (HOL)).
Finland: Jesse Joronen, Jukka Raitala, Joona Toivio (YC31) (59' Thomas Lam), Sauli Väisänen, Leo Väisänen, Rasmus Schüller (77' Fredrik Jensen), Joni Kauko (YC71), Robin Lod, Glen Kamara, Teemu Pukki, Simon Skrabb (78' Pyry Soiri). (Coach: Markku Kanerva (FIN)).
Goals: Greece: 1-1 Petros Mantalos (47'), 2-1 Konstantinos Galanopoulos (70').
Finland: 0-1 Teemu Pukki (27').
Referee: Aleksei Eskov (RUS)   Attendance: 5.453

18-11-2019   Stadio Renzo Barbera, Palermo: Italy – Armenia 9-1 (4-0)
Italy: Salvatore Sirigu (77' Alex Meret), Leonardo Bonucci (69' Armando Izzo), Cristiano Biraghi, Giovanni Di Lorenzo, Alessio Romagnoli, Jorginho, Nicolò Barella (46' Riccardo Orsolini), Nicolò Zaniolo, Sandro Tonali, Ciro Immobile, Federico Chiesa. (Coach: Roberto Mancini (ITA)).
Armenia: Aram Ayrapetyan, Artak Yedigaryan (82' Petros Avetisyan), Hovhannes Hambardzumyan, André Calisir, Varazdat Haroyan (YC34), Hayk Ishkhanyan (69' Artur Sarkisov), Kamo Hovhannisyan, Artak Grigoryan (60' Artem Simonyan), Edgar Babayan, Alexander Karapetyan, Tigran Barseghyan. (Coach: Abraham Khashmanyan (ARM)).
Goals: Italy: 1-0 Ciro Immobile (8), 2-0 Nicolò Zaniolo (9'), 3-0 Nicolò Barella (29'), 4-0 Ciro Immobile (33'), 5-0 Nicolò Zaniolo (64'), 6-0 Alessio Romagnoli (72'), 7-0 Jorginho (75' penalty), 8-0 Riccardo Orsolini (78'), 9-1 Federico Chiesa (81').
Armenia: 8-1 edgar Babayan (79').
Referee: TIAGO Bruno Lopes MARTINS (POR)   Attendance: 27.752

18-11-2019   Rheinpark Stadion, Vaduz: Liechtenstein – Bosnia-Herzegovina 0-3 (0-0)
Liechtenstein: Benjamin Büchel, Martin Rechsteiner, Nicolas Hasler, Maximilian Göppel, Andreas Malin, Martin Büchel, Michele Polverino (67' Noah Frommelt), Daniel Brändle, Sandro Wolfinger, Dennis Salanovic (46' Seyhan Yildiz), Yanik Frick (YC56) (82' Robin Gubser). (Coach: Helgi Kolvidsson (ISL)).
Bosnia-Herzegovina: Kenan Piric, Ermin Bicakcic, Marko Mihojevic (70' Edin Dzeko), Eldar Civic, Samir Memisevic, Mato Jajalo, Elvis Saric, Haris Hajradinovic (64' Muhamed Besic), Izet Hajrovic, Armin Hodzic, Haris Duljevic (46' Dino Hotic). (Coach: Robert Prosinecki (CRO)).
Goals: Bosnia-Herzegovina: 0-1 Eldar Civic (57'), 0-2 Armin Hodzic (64'), 0-3 Armin Hodzic (72').
Referee: Halis Özkahya (TUR)   Attendance: 2.993

QUALIFICATION PLAY-OFFS

The play-offs of the UEFA Euro 2020 qualifying tournament dedided the last four teams that qualified for the UEFA Euro 2020 final tournament to be staged across Europe in June and July 2021. Unlike previous editions, the participants of the play-offs were not decided based on results from the qualifying group stage. Instead, 16 teams that failed to qualify through their group were selected based on their performance in the 2018-2019 UEFA Nations League. The sixteen teams were then divided info four paths, each containing four teams, with each play-off path featuring two single-leg semi-finals and one single-leg final. The four play-off path winners joined the twenty teams that had already qualified for UEFA Euro 2020. The matches took place on 8 October and 12 November 2020. The matches were originally scheduled for March 2020, but were postponed by UEFA due to the COVID-19 pandemic in Europe.

PATH A

SEMI-FINALS

08-10-2020   Laugardalsvöllur, Reykjavik: Iceland – Romania 2-1 (2-0)
Iceland: Hannes Halldórsson, Ragnar Sigurdsson (YC62), Kári Árnason (86' Sverrir Ingason), Hördur Magnússon, Birkir Bjarnason, Aron Gunnarsson, Jóhann Berg Gudmundsson (83' Rúnar Sigurjónsson), Gylfi Sigurdsson, Victor Pálsson, Arnór Ingvi Traustason, Alfred Finnbogason (75' Kolbeinn Sigthórsson). (Coach: Erik Hamrén (SWE)).
Romania: Ciprian Tatarusanu, Camora, Mihai Balasa, Andrei Burca, Cristian Manea, Ciprian Deac (46' Gabriel Iancu (YC90+5)), Nicolae Stanciu (87' Alexandru Cicâldau), Alexandru Maxim (YC36) (80' Claudiu Keserü), Alexandru Cretu, Denis Alibec (46' George Puscas), Alexandru Mitrita (46' Ianis Hagi). (Coach: Mirel Radoi (ROM)).
Goals: Iceland: 1-0 Gylfi Sigurdsson (16'), 2-0 Gylfi Sigurdsson (34').
Romania: 2-1 Alexandru Maxim (63' penalty).
Referee: Damir Skomina (SVN)   Attendance: 60

465

08-10-2020   Vasil Levski National Stadium, Sofia: Bulgaria – Hungary 1-3 (0-1)
Bulgaria: Plamen Iliev, Cicinho, Vasil Bozhikov, Georgi Terziev, Anton Nedyalkov, Galin Ivanov (31' Georgi Yomov), Kristiyan Malinov, Todor Nedelev (81' Dominik Yankov), Yanis Karabelyov, Bozhidar Kraev (79' Ismail Isa), Birsent Karagaren (58' Kiril Despodov). (Coach: Georgi Dermendzhiev (BUL)).
Hungary: Péter Gulácsi, Attila Fiola (82' Endre Botka), Ádám Lang (YC55), Willi Orban, Attila Szalai, Dávid Sigér, Zsolt Kalmár (70' Szilveszter Hangya), Roland Sallai, Ádám Nagy (82' Dániel Gazdag (YC88)), Ádám Szalai (59' Nemanja Nikolic), Filip Holender (70' Loïc Négo). (Coach: Marco Rossi (ITA)).
Goals: Bulgaria: 1-3 Georgi Yomov (89').
Hungary: 0-1 Willi Orban (17'), 0-2 Zsolt Kalmár (47'), 0-3 Nemanja Nikolic (75').
Referee: Szymon Marciniak (POL)   Attendance: 1.929

FINAL

12-11-2020   Puskás Aréna, Budapest: Hungary – Iceland 2-1 (0-1)
Hungary: Péter Gulácsi, Attila Fiola (61' Gergö Lovrencsics), Endre Botka, Willi Orban, Attila Szalai (YC63), Zsolt Kalmár (61' Dávid Sigér), Roland Sallai, Ádám Nagy (84' Loïc Négo), Dominik Szoboszlai, Ádám Szalai (84' Norbert Könyves), Filip Holender (71' Nemanja Nikolic). (Coach: Marco Rossi (ITA)).
Iceland: Hannes Halldórsson, Ragnar Sigurdsson, Kári Árnason, Hördur Magnússon, Birkir Bjarnason, Aron Gunnarsson (83' Ari Skúlason), Jóhann Berg Gudmundsson (73' Jón Bödvarsson), Rúnar Sigurjónsson (87' Sverrir Ingason (YC90+5)), Gylfi Sigurdsson (YC5), Victor Pálsson, Alfred Finnbogason (73' Albert Gudmundsson). (Coach: Erik Hamrén (SWE)).
Goals: Hungary: 1-1 Loïc Négo (88'), 2-1 Dominik Szoboszlai (90+2').
Iceland: 0-1 Gylfi Sigurdsson (11').
Referee: Björn Kuipers (HOL)

Winner Hungary entered Group F in the Final Tournament.

PATH B

SEMI-FINALS

08-10-2020   Stadion Grbavica, Sarajevo:
Bosnia-Herzegovina – Northern Ireland 1-1 (1-0,1-1) (AET)
Bosnia-Herzegovina: Ibrahim Sehic, Sead Kolasinac (YC47) (118' Haris Hajradinovic), Sinisa
Sanicanin, Anel Ahmedhodzic, Branimir Cipetic, Miralem Pjanic (YC100), Edin Visca, Gojko
Cimirot (106' Stjepan Loncar), Rade Krunic (88' Dino Hotic), Amir Hadziahmetovic (YC19)
(83' Amer Gojak), Edin Dzeko. (Coach: Dusan Bajevic (BIH)).
Northern Ireland: Bailey Peacock-Farrell, Jonny Evans, Craig Cathcart, Stuart Dallas, Jamal
Lewis, Steven Davis (YC108), Niall McGinn (82' Jordan Jones, 120+1' Conor Washington),
Corry Evans (73' Gavin Whyte), Paddy McNair (90+3' Jordan Thompson, 120+1' Liam
Boyce), George Saville, Josh Magennis (90+3' Kyle Lafferty). (Coach: Ian Baraclough
(ENG)).
Goals: Bosnia-Herzegovina: 1-0 Rade Krunic (13').
Northern Ireland: 1-1 Niall McGinn (53').
Referee: Antonio Mateu Lahoz (ESP)   Attendance: 1.800
Penalties: 1 Miralem Pjanic   1 Stuart Dallas
                  * Haris Hajradinovic   2 Kyle Lafferty
                  * Edin Visca   * George Saville
                  2 Dino Hotic   3 Conor Washingon
                  3 Edin Dzeko   4 Liam Boyce

*Match, originally scheduled to be played at Bilino Polje, Zenica, was later moved to Stadion
Grbavica, Sarajavo.*

08-10-2020   Tehelné pole, Bratislava: Slovakia – Republic of Ireland 0-0 (AET)
Slovakia: Marek Rodák, Peter Pekarík, Róbert Mazán, Denis Vavro (112' Norbert Gyömbér),
Martin Valjent, Marek Hamsík (YC114), Juraj Kucka (86' Ján Gregus), Jaroslav Mihalík (74'
Lukás Haraslín), Albert Rusnák (86' Róbert Mak), Patrik Hrosovský, Ondrej Duda (YC101)
(108' Róbert Bozeník). (Coach: Pavel Hapal (CZE)).
Republic of Ireland: Darren Randolph, Enda Stevens, Shane Duffy (YC68), John Egan, Matt
Doherty, Jamie McCarthy (60' Alan Browne), Conor Hourihane (YC20), James McClean
(YC48) (60' Robbie Brady), Jeff Hendrick, David McGoldrick (112' Shane Long), Callum
Robinson (99' Callum O'Dowda). (Coach: Stephen Kenny (IRL)).
Referee: Clément Turpin (FRA)
Penalties: 1 Marek Hamsík   1 Conor Hourihane
                  2 Patrik Hrosovský   2 Robbie Brady
                  3 Lukás Haraslín   * Alan Browne
                  4 Ján Gregus   * Matt Doherty

FINAL

12-11-2020   Windsor Park, Belfast: Northern Ireland – Slovakia 1-2 (0-1,1-1) (AET)
Northern Ireland: Bailey Peacock-Farrell, Jonny Evans, Craig Cathcart (99' Tom Flanagan), Stuart Dallas, Jamal Lewis, Steven Davis, Niall McGinn (76' Kyle Lafferty), Paddy McNair (104' Shane Ferguson), George Saville (65' Jordan Thompson), Josh Magennis (77' Liam Boyce (YC117)), Conor Washington (66' Gavin Whyte). (Coach: Ian Baraclough (ENG)).
Slovakia: Marek Rodák (YC117), Tomás Hubocan, Peter Pekarík, Lubomír Satka, Milan Skriniar, Marek Hamsík (106' Ján Gregus), Juraj Kucka, Róbert Mak (65' Michal Duris), Albert Rusnák (118' Norbert Gyömbér), Stanislav Lobotka (65' Patrik Hrosovský), Ondrej Duda (YC66) (85' Samuel Mráz). (Coach: Stefan Tarkovic (SVK)).
Goals: Northern Ireland: 1-1 Milan Skriniar (87' own goal).
Slovakia: 0-1 Juraj Kucka (17'), 1-2 Michal Duris (110').
Referee: Dr. Felix Brych (GER)   Attendance: 1.060

Winner Slovakia entered Group E in the Final Tournament.

PATH   C
SEMI-FINALS

08-10-2020   Hampden Park, Glasgow: Scotland – Israel 0-0 (AET)
Scotland: David Marshall, Liam Cooper, Declan Gallagher, Stephen O'Donnell (113' Kenny McLean), Andrew Robertson, Ryan Jack (83' Ryan Fraser (YC105+2)), Callum McGregor, John McGinn (YC58), Scott McTominay, Oliver McBurnie (73' Lawrence Shankland), Lyndon Dykes (91' Callum Paterson (YC119)). (Coach: Steve Clarke (SCO)).
Israel: Ofir Marciano, Sheran Yeini, Eitan Tibi, Hatem Abd Elhamed, Eli Dasa, Bibras Natcho (YC12) (69' Mohammad Abu Fani), Eyal Golasa (101' Ilay Eliyau Elmkies), Nir Bitton (YC55), Manor Solomon, Eran Zahavi, Mounas Dabour (83' Shon Weissman (YC87)). (Coach: Willibald Ruttensteiner (AUT)).
Referee: Ovidiu Hategan (ROM)
Penalties: 1 John McGinn   * Eran Zahavi
                 2 Callum McGregor   1 Nir Bitton
                 3 Scott McTominay   2 Shon Weissman
                 4 Lawrence Shankland   3 Mohammed Abu Fani
                 5 Kenny McLean

08-10-2020   Ullevaal Stadion, Oslo: Norway – Serbia 1-2 (0-0,1-1) (AET)
Norway: Rune Jarstein, Tore Reginiussen (91' Stefan Strandberg), Omar Elabdellaoui (116' Morten Thorsby), Haitam Aleesami (106' Martin Linnes), Kristoffer Ajer, Stefan Johansen (67' Joshua King), Markus Henriksen (46' Mathias Normann (YC47)), Martin Ødegaard (111' Mohamed Elyounoussi), Sander Berge, Alexander Sørloth, Erling Håland. (Coach: Lars Lagerbäck (SWE)).
Serbia: Predrag Rajkovic, Aleksandar Kolarov, Stefan Mitrovic, Mihailo Ristic (YC60), Nikola Milenkovic, Darko Lazovic (106' Mijat Gacinovic), Nemanja Gudelj, Filip Djuricic (80' Sergej Milinkovic-Savic), Nemanja Maksimovic (80' Luka Milivojevic (YC90+4)), Dusan Tadic (YC118) (119' Sasa Lukic), Aleksandar Mitrovic. (Coach: Ljubisa Tumbakovic (SRB)).
Goals: Norway: 1-1 Mathias Normann (88').
Serbia: 0-1 Sergej Milinkovic-Savic (81'), 1-2 Sergej Milinkovic-Savic (102').
Referee: Daniele Orsato (ITA)   Attendance: 200

FINAL

12-11-2020   Stadion Rajko Mitic, Belgrade: Serbia – Scotland 1-1 (0-0,1-1) (AET)
Serbia: Predrag Rajkovic, Stefan Mitrovic (108' Uros Spajic), Nikola Milenkovic (YC11),
Darko Lazovic, Nemanja Gudelj (YC49), Filip Kostic (59' Filip Mladenovic), Sasa Lukic,
Sergej Milinkovic-Savic (71' Aleksandar Katai), Nemanja Maksimovic (70' Luka Jovic),
Dusan Tadic, Aleksandar Mitrovic. (Coach: Ljubisa Tumbakovic (SRB)).
Scotland: David Marshall, Declan Gallagher (YC44), Stephen O'Donnell (117' Leigh
Griffiths), Andrew Robertson, Kieran Tierney, Ryan Jack, Callum McGregor, John McGinn
(83' Kenny McLean), Ryan Christie (87' Callum Paterson), Scott McTominay, Lyndon Dykes
(83' Oliver McBurnie). (Coach: Steve Clarke (SCO)).
Goals: Serbia: 1-1 Luka Jovic (90').
Scotland: 0-1 Ryan Christie (52').
Referee: Antonio Mateu Lahoz (ESP)
Penalties: 1 Leigh Griffiths   1 Dusan Tadic
                 2 Callum McGregor   2 Luka Jovic
                 3 Scott McTominay   3 Nemanja Gudelj
                 4 Oliver McBurnie   4 Aleksandar Katai
                 5 Kenny McLean   * Aleksandar Mitrovic

Winner Scotland entered Group D in the Final Tournament.

PATH D
SEMI-FINALS

08-10-2020   Boris Paichadze Dinamo Arena, Tbilisi: Georgia – Belarus 1-0 (1-0)
Georgia: Giorgi Loria, Guram Kashia, Solomon Kverkvelia, Otar Kakabadze (82' Jemal
Tabidze), Lasha Dvali, Jaba Kankava (YC52), Nika Kvekveskiri (YC38), Tornike Okriashvili
(89' Giorgi Kvilitaia (YC90+4)), Otar Kiteishvili (65' Valeriane Gvilia), Khvicha
Kvaratskhelia (89' Saba Lobzhanidze), Valeri Qazaishvili (YC69) (81' Levan Shengelia).
(Coach: Vladimir Weiss (SVK)).
Belarus: Egor Khatkevich, Maksim Bordachev (74' Kirill Pechenin), Aleksandr Martinovich,
Nikita Naumov (YC33), Nikolay Zolotov, Pavel Nekhaychik, Andrey Khachaturyan (46' Ivan
Maevski), Evgeniy Yablonskiy (63' Maksim Skavysh), Max Ebong Ngome, Ivan Bakhar (63'
Dmitriy Podstrelov), Vitaly Lisakovich (70' Denis Laptev). (Coach: Mikhail Markhel (BLS)).
Goal: Georgia: 1-0 Tornike Okriashvili (7' penalty).
Referee: Cüneyt Çakir (TUR)

08-10-2020   Tose Proeski National Arena, Skopje: North Macedonia – Kosovo 2-1 (2-1)
North Macedonia: Stole Dimitrievski (YC90+3), Stefan Ristovski (YC73) (88' Tihomir
Kostadinov), Visar Musliu, Darko Velkovski, Egzon Bejtulai (YC14) (51' Kire Ristevski),
Arijan Ademi (YC38) (80' Stefan Spirovski), Boban Nikolov, Enis Bardhi, Goran Pandev (81'
Ivan Trickovski), Ilija Nestorovski (YC37) (89' Aleksandar Trajkovski), Egzjan Alioski
(YC56). (Coach: Igor Angelovski (MKD)).
Kosovo: Aro Muric, Fidan Aliti, Florent Hadërgjonaj, Mërgim Vojvoda (64' Edon Zhegrova),
Ibrahim Dresevic, Herolind Shala (87' Leart Paqarada), Valon Berisha, Arber Zeleni, Bersant
Celina (75' Lirim Kastrati), Benjamin Kololli, Atdhe Nuhiu (46' Elbasan Rashani (YC84)).
(Coach: Bernard Challandes (SUI)).
Goals: North Macedonia: 1-0 Benjamin Kololli (16' own goal), 2-1 Darko Velkovski (33').
Kosovo: 1-1 Florent Hadërgjonaj (29').
Referee: Danny Makkelie (HOL)

FINAL

12-11-2020   Boris Paichadze Dinamo Arena, Tbilisi: Georgia – North Macedonia 0-1 (0-0)
Georgia: Giorgi Loria, Guram Kashia (YC75) (88' Jambul Jighauri), Solomon Kverkvelia, Otar Kakabadze, Lasha Dvali (90+2' Zuriko Davitashvili), Jaba Kankava, Nika Kvekveskiri, Tornike Okriashvili (YC78), Valeriane Gvilia (80' Giorgi Papunashvili), Valeri Qazaishvili (90+2' Davit Khocholava), Nika Kacharava (80' Elguja Lobjanidze). (Coach: Vladimir Weiss (SVK)).
North Macedonia: Stole Dimitrievski, Stefan Ristovski (89' Gjoko Zajkov), Visar Musliu, Darko Velkovski, Egzon Bejtulai, Arijan Ademi (67' Stefan Spirovski), Egzjan Alioski, Boban Nikolov (YC62) (84' Tihomir Kostadinov (YC90+3)), Eljif Elmas, Goran Pandev, Ilija Nestorovski (YC82) (89' Ivan Trickovski). (Coach: Igor Angelovski (MKD)).
Goal: North Macedonia: 0-1 Goran Pandev (56').
Referee: Anthony Taylor (ENG)

Winner North Macedonia entered Group C in the Final Tournament.

FINAL   TOURNAMENT

GROUP   STAGE

GROUP   A

11-06-2021   Stadio Olimpico, Roma: Turkey – Italy 0-3 (0-0)
Turkey: Ugurcan Çakir, Zeki Çelik, Merih Demiral, Çaglar Söyüncü (YC88), Umut Meras, Okay Yokuslu (65' Irfan Can Kahveci), Yusuf Yazici (46' Cengiz Ünder), Ozan Tufan (64' Kaan Ayhan), Kenan Karaman (76' Halil Dervisoglu (YC90)), Hakan Çalhanoglu, Burak Yilmaz. (Coach: Senol Günes (TUR)).
Italy: Gianluigi Donnarumma, Alessandro Florenzi (46' Giovanni Di Lorenzo), Leonardo Bonucci, Giorgio Chiellini, Leonardo Spinazzola, Nicolò Barella, Jorginho, Manuel Locatelli (74' Bryan Cristante), Domenico Berardi (85' Federico Bernardeschi), Ciro Immobile (81' Andrea Belotti), Lorenzo Insigne (81' Federico Chiesa). (Coach: Roberto Mancini (ITA)).
Goals: Italy: 0-1 Merih Demiral (53' own goal), 0-2 Ciro Immobile (66'), 0-3 Lorenzo Insigne (79').
Referee: Danny Makkelie (HOL)   Attendance: 12.916

12-06-2021   Baku Olympic Stadium, Baku: Wales – Switzerland 1-1 (0-0)
Wales: Danny Ward, Ben Davies, Chris Mepham, Connor Roberts, Joe Rodon, Aaron Ramsey (90+3' Ethan Ampadu), Joe Allen, Joe Morrell, Daniel James (75' David Brooks), Gareth Bale, Kieffer Moore (YC47). (Coach: Rob Page (WAL)).
Switzerland: Yann Sommer, Fabian Schär (YC30), Kevin Mbabu (YC63), Manuel Akanji, Nico Elvedi, Ricardo Rodríguez, Granit Xhaka, Remo Freuler, Xherdan Shaqiri (66' Denis Zakaria), Breel Embolo, Haris Seferovic (84' Mario Gavranovic). (Coach: Vladimir Petkovic (BIH)).
Goals: Wales: 1-1 Kieffer Moore (74').
Switzerland: 0-1 Breel Embolo (49').
Referee: Clément Turpin (FRA)   Attendance: 8.782

16-06-2021 Baku Olympic Stadium, Baku: Turkey – Wales 0-2 (0-1)
Turkey: Ugurcan Çakir, Çaglar Söyüncü, Umut Meras (72' Mert Müldür), Kaan Ayhan, Zeki
Çelik, Cengiz Ünder (83' Irfan Can Kahveci), Hakan Çalhanoglu (YC90+2), Okay Yokuslu
(46' Merih Demiral), Ozan Tufan (46' Yusuf Yazici), Burak Yilmaz (YC90+2), Kenan
Karaman (75' Halil Dervisoglu). (Coach: Senol Günes (TUR)).
Wales: Danny Ward, Ben Davies (YC90+2), Chris Mepham (YC90+2), Connor Roberts, Joe
Rodon, Aaron Ramsey (85' Harry Wilson), Joe Allen (73' Ethan Ampadu), Joe Morrell, Daniel
James (90+4' Neco Williams), Gareth Bale, Kieffer Moore. (Coach: Rob Page (WAL)).
Goals: Wales: 0-1 Aaron Ramsey (42'), 0-2 Connor Roberts (90+5').
Referee: Artur Soares Dias (POR)   Attendance: 19.762

Gareth Bale missed a penalty kick (61').

16-06-2021 Stadio Olimpico, Roma: Italy – Switzerland 3-0 (1-0)
Italy: Gianluigi Donnarumma, Giorgio Chiellini (24' Francesco Acerbi), Giovanni Di Lorenzo,
Leonardo Bonucci, Leonardo Spinazzola, Jorginho, Manuel Locatelli (86' Matteo Pessina),
Nicolò Barella (86' Bryan Cristante), Ciro Immobile, Domenico Berardi (70' Rafael Tolói),
Lorenzo Insigne (69' Federico Chiesa). (Coach: Roberto Mancini (ITA)).
Switzerland: Yann Sommer, Fabian Schär (57' Steven Zuber), Kevin Mbabu (58' Silvan
Widmer), Manuel Akanji, Nico Elvedi, Ricardo Rodríguez, Granit Xhaka, Remo Freuler (84'
Djibril Sow), Xherdan Shaqiri (76' Ruben Vargas), Breel Embolo (YC79), Haris Seferovic
(46' Mario Gavranovic (YC49)). (Coach: Vladimir Petkovic (BIH)).
Goals: Italy: 1-0 Manuel Locatelli (26'), 2-0 Manuel Locatelli (52'), 3-0 Ciro Immobile (89').
Referee: Sergei Karasev (RUS)   Attendance: 12.445

20-06-2021 Baku Olympic Stadium, Baku: Switzerland – Turkey 3-1 (2-0)
Switzerland: Yann Sommer, Manuel Akanji, Nico Elvedi, Ricardo Rodríguez, Silvan Widmer
(90+2' Kevin Mbabu), Granit Xhaka (YC78), Remo Freuler, Steven Zuber (85' Loris Benito),
Xherdan Shaqiri (75' Ruben Vargas), Breel Embolo (85' Admir Mehmedi), Haris Seferovic
(75' Mario Gavranovic). (Coach: Vladimir Petkovic (BIH)).
Turkey: Ugurcan Çakir, Çaglar Söyüncü (YC76), Kaan Ayhan (63' Okay Yokuslu), Zeki Çelik
(YC75), Merih Demiral, Mert Müldür, Cengiz Ünder (80' Kenan Karaman), Hakan
Çalhanoglu (YC70) (86' Dorukhan Toköz), Irfan Can Kahveci (80' Orkun Kökçü), Ozan
Tufan (63' Yusuf Yazici), Burak Yilmaz. (Coach: Senol Günes (TUR)).
Goals: Switzerland: 1-0 Haris Seferovic (6'), 2-0 Xherdan Shaqiri (26'), 3-1 Xherdan Shaqiri
(68').
Turkey: 2-1 Irfan Can Kahveci (62').
Referee: Slavko Vincic (SVN)   Attendance: 17.138

20-06-2021 Stadio Olimpico, Roma: Italy – Wales 1-0 (1-0)
Italy: Gianluigi Donnarumma (89' Salvatore Sirigu), Alessandro Bastoni, Emerson, Leonardo
Bonucci (46' Francesco Acerbi), Rafael Tolói, Jorginho (75' Bryan Cristante), Marco Verratti,
Matteo Pessina (YC79) (87' Gaetano Castrovilli), Andrea Belotti, Federico Chiesa, Federico
Bernardeschi (75' Giacomo Raspadori). (Coach: Roberto Mancini (ITA)).
Wales: Danny Ward, Chris Gunter (YC79), Connor Roberts, Joe Rodon, Neco Williams (86'
Ben Davies), Aaron Ramsey, Ethan Ampadu (RC55), Joe Allen (YC51) (86' Dylan Levitt), Joe
Morrell (60' Kieffer Moore), Daniel James (74' Harry Wilson), Gareth Bale (86' David
Brooks). (Coach: Rob Page (WAL)).
Goal: Italy: 1-0 Matteo Pessina (39').
Referee: Ovidiu Hategan (ROM)   Attendance: 11.541

471

STANDINGS

Pos	Team	Pld	W	D	L	GF	GA	GD	Pts
1	Italy	3	3	0	0	7	0	+7	9
2	Wales	3	1	1	1	3	2	+1	4
3	Switzerland	3	1	1	1	4	5	-1	4
4	Turkey	3	0	0	3	1	8	-7	0

Italy, Wales and Switzerland qualified for the Knockout phase.

GROUP B

12-06-2021   Parken Stadium, Copenhagen: Denmark – Finland 0-1 (0-0)
Denmark: Kasper Schmeichel, Andreas Christensen, Joakim Mæhle, Simon Kjær (63' Jannik Vestergaard), Christian Eriksen (43' Mathias Jensen), Daniel Wass (76' Jens Stryger), Pierre-Emile Højbjerg, Thomas Delaney (76' Andreas Cornelius), Jonas Wind (63' Andreas Olsen), Martin Braithwaite, Yussuf Poulsen. (Coach: Kasper Hjulmand (DEN)).
Finland: Lucas Hrádecký, Daniel O'Shaughnessy, Jere Uronen, Joona Toivio, Jukka Raitala (90' Leo Väisänen), Paulus Arajuuri, Glen Kamara, Robin Lod (YC4), Tim Sparv (YC51) (76' Rasmus Schüller), Joel Pohjanpalo (84' Marcus Forss), Teemu Pukki (76' Joni Kauko). (Coach: Markku Kanerva (FIN)).
Goal: 0-1 Joel Pohjanpalo (60').
Referee: Anthony Taylor (ENG)   Attendance: 15.200

Pierre-Emile Højbjerg missed a penalty kick (74').

Match was suspended due to a medical emergency which involved Cristian Eriksen. The player went to hospital and was in stable condition. Following the request made by players of both teams, UEFA ageed to restart the match at 20:30 CET. The last 4 minutes of the first half were played; there was then a 5-minute half-time break followed by the second half.

12-06-2021   Krestovsky Stadium, Saint Petersburg: Belgium – Russia 3-0 (2-0)
Belgium: Thibaut Courtois, Dedryck Boyata, Jan Vertonghen (76' Thomas Vermaelen), Leander Dendoncker, Timothy Castagne (27' Thomas Meunier), Toby Alderweireld, Dries Mertens (72' Eden Hazard), Thorgan Hazard, Yannick Carrasco (77' Dennis Praet), Youri Tielemans, Romelu Lukaku. (Coach: ROBERT MARTÍNEZ Montoliú (ESP)).
Russia: Anton Shunin, Andrey Semenov, Georgi Dzhikiya, Mário Fernandes, Yuri Zhirkov (43' Vyacheslav Karavaev), Aleksandr Golovin, Daler Kuzyaev (29' Denis Cheryshev, 63' Aleksei Miranchuk), Dmitri Barinov (46' Igor Diveev), Magomed Ozdoev, Roman Zobnin (63' Maksim Mukhin), Artem Dzyuba. (Coach: Stanislav Cherchesov (RUS)).
Goals: 1-0 Romelu Lukaku (10'), 2-0 Thomas Meunier (34'), 3-0 Romelu Lukaku (88').
Referee: Antonio Mateu Lahoz (ESP)   Attendance: 26.264

16-06-2021   Krestovsky Stadium, Saint Petersburg: Finland – Russia 0-1 (0-1)
Finland: Lucas Hrádecký, Daniel O'Shaughnessy (YC90), Jere Uronen, Joona Toivio (84'
Fredrik Jensen), Jukka Raitala (75' Pyry Soiri), Paulus Arajuuri, Glen Kamara (YC22),
Rasmus Schüller (67' Joni Kauko), Robin Lod, Joel Pohjanpalo, Teemu Pukki (75' Lassi
Lappalainen). (Coach: Markku Kanerva (FIN)).
Russia: Matvei Safonov, Georgi Dzhikiya (YC88), Igor Diveev, Mário Fernandes (26'
Vyacheslav Karavaev), Aleksandr Golovin, Daler Kuzyaev, Dmitri Barinov (YC27), Magomed
Ozdoev (YC34) (61' Rifat Zhemaletdinov), Roman Zobnin, Aleksei Miranchuk (85' Maksim
Mukhin), Artem Dzyuba (85' Alexandr Sobolev). (Coach: Stanislav Cherchesov (RUS)).
Goal: Russia: 0-1 Aleksei Miranchuk (45+2').
Referee: Danny Makkelie (HOL)   Attendance: 24.540

17-06-2021   Parken Stadium, Copenhagen: Denmark – Belgium 1-2 (1-0)
Denmark: Kasper Schmeichel, Andreas Christensen, Jannik Vestergaard (84' Andreas Olsen),
Joakim Mæhle, Simon Kjær, Daniel Wass (YC59) (61' Jens Stryger), Mikkel Damsgaard
(YC69) (72' Andreas Cornelius), Pierre-Emile Højbjerg, Thomas Delaney (72' Mathias Jensen
(YC81)), Martin Braithwaite, Yussuf Poulsen (61' Christian Nørgaard). (Coach: Kasper
Hjulmand (DEN)).
Belgium: Thibaut Courtois, Jan Vertonghen, Jason Denayer, Leander Dendoncker (59' Axel
Witsel), Thomas Meunier, Toby Alderweireld, Dries Mertens (46' Kevin De Bruyne), Thorgan
Hazard (YC90+4) (90+4' Thomas Vermaelen), Yannick Carrasco (59' Eden Hazard), Youri
Tielemans, Romelu Lukaku. (Coach: ROBERT MARTÍNEZ Montoliú (ESP)).
Goals: Denmark: 1-0 Yussuf Poulsen (2').
Belgium: 1-1 Thorgan Hazard (55'), 1-2 Kevin De Bruyne (70').
Referee: Björn Kuipers (HOL)   Attendance: 23.395

21-06-2021   Parken Stadium, Copenhagen: Russia – Denmark 1-4 (0-1)
Russia: Matvei Safonov, Fedor Kudryashov (YC28) (67' Vyacheslav Karavaev), Georgi
Dzhikiya, Igor Diveev (YC75), Mário Fernandes, Aleksandr Golovin, Daler Kuzyaev (67'
Maksim Mukhin), Magomed Ozdoev (61' Rifat Zhemaletdinov), Roman Zobnin, Aleksei
Miranchuk (61' Alexandr Sobolev), Artem Dzyuba. (Coach: Stanislav Cherchesov (RUS)).
Denmark: Kasper Schmeichel, Andreas Christensen, Jannik Vestergaard, Joakim Mæhle,
Simon Kjær, Daniel Wass (60' Jens Stryger), Mikkel Damsgaard (72' Christian Nørgaard),
Pierre-Emile Højbjerg, Thomas Delaney (YC57) (85' Mathias Jensen), Martin Braithwaite (85'
Andreas Cornelius), Yussuf Poulsen (60' Kasper Dolberg). (Coach: Kasper Hjulmand (DEN)).
Goals: Russia: 1-2 Artem Dzyuba (70' penalty).
Denmark: 0-1 Mikkel Damsgaard (38'), 0-2 Yussuf Poulsen (59'), 1-3 Andreas Christensen
(79'), 1-4 Joakim Mæhle (82').
Referee: Clément Turpin (FRA)   Attendance: 23,644

21-06-2021   Krestovsky Stadium, Saint Petersburg: Finland – Belgium 0-2 (0-0)
Finland: Lucas Hrádecký, Daniel O'Shaughnessy, Jere Uronen (70' Nikolai Alho), Joona
Toivio, Jukka Raitala, Paulus Arajuuri, Glen Kamara, Robin Lod (90+1' Marcus Forss), Tim
Sparv (59' Rasmus Schüller), Joel Pohjanpalo (70' Joni Kauko), Teemu Pukki (90+1' Fredrik
Jensen). (Coach: Markku Kanerva (FIN)).
Belgium: Thibaut Courtois, Dedryck Boyata, Jason Denayer, Thomas Vermaelen, Axel Witsel,
Eden Hazard, Kevin De Bruyne (90+1' Hans Vanaken), Nacer Chadli, Jeremy Doku (75'
Michy Batshuayi), Leandro Trossard (75' Thomas Meunier), Romelu Lukaku (84' Christian
Benteke). (Coach: ROBERT MARTÍNEZ Montoliú (ESP)).
Goals: Belgium: 0-1 Lucas Hrádecký (74' own goal), 0-2 Romelu Lukaku (81').
Referee: Dr. Felix Brych (GER)   Attendance: 18,545

STANDINGS

Pos	Team	Pld	W	D	L	GF	GA	GD	Pts
1	Belgium	3	3	0	0	7	1	+6	9
2	Denmark	3	1	0	2	5	4	+1	3
3	Finland	3	1	0	2	1	3	-2	3
4	Russia	3	1	0	2	2	7	-5	3

Belgium and Denmark qualified for the Knockout phase.

GROUP   C

13-06-2021   Arena Nationala, Bucharest: Austria – North Macedonia 3-1 (1-1)
Austria: Daniel Bachmann, Aleksandar Dragovic (46' Philipp Lienhart), Andreas Ulmer, David Alaba, Martin Hinteregger, Stefan Lainer (YC85), Christoph Baumgartner (58' Michael Gregoritsch), Konrad Laimer (90+3' Julian Baumgartlinger), Marcel Sabitzer, Xaver Schlager (90+4' Stefan Ilsanker), Sasa Kalajdzic (59' Marko Arnautovic). (Coach: Franco Foda (GER)).
North Macedonia: Stole Dimitrievski, Darko Velkoski, Stefan Ristovski, Visar Musliu (86' Milan Ristovski), Arijan Ademi, Boban Nikolov (63' Egzon Bejtulai), Egzjan Alioski (YC52), Eljif Elmas, Enis Bardi (82' Ivan Trickovski), Aleksandar Trajkovski (YC42) (63' Tihomir Kostadinov), Goran Pandev. (Coach: Igor Angelovski (MKD)).
Goals: 1-0 Stefan Lainer (18'), 1-1 Goran Pandev (28'), 2-1 Michael Gregoritsch (78'), 3-1 Marko Arnautovic (89').
Referee: Andreas Ekberg (SWE)   Attendance: 9.082

13-06-2021   Johan Cruijff ArenA, Amsterdam: Netherlands – Ukraine 3-2 (0-0)
Netherlands: Maarten Stekelenburg, Daley Blind (64' Nathan Aké), Denzel Dumfries, Jurriën Timber (88' Joël Veltman), Patrick van Aanholt (64' Owen Wijndal), Stefan de Vrij, Frenkie de Jong, Georginio Wijnaldum, Marten de Roon, Memphis Depay (90+1' Donyell Malen), Wout Weghorst (88' Luuk de Jong). (Coach: Frank de Boer (HOL)).
Ukraine: Georgiy Bushchan, Oleksandr Karavaev, Illia Zabarnyi, Mykola Matvienko, Vitali Mykolenko, Oleksandr Zinchenko, Oleksandr Zubkov (13' Marlos Romero Bonfim, 64' Mykola Shaparenko), Ruslan Malinovskyi, Sergiy Sydorchuk (YC90+3), Andrey Yarmolenko, Roman Yaremchuk. (Coach: Andriy Shevchenko (UKR)).
Goals: 1-0 Georginio Wijnaldum (52'), 2-0 Wout Weghorst (58'), 2-1 Andrey Yarmolenko (75'), 2-2 Roman Yaremchuk (79'), 3-2 Denzel Dumfries (85').
Referee: Dr. Felix Brych (GER)   Attendance: 15.837

17-06-2021   Arena Nationala, Bucharest: Ukraine – North Macedonia 2-1 (2-0)
Ukraine: Georgiy Bushchan, Oleksandr Karavaev, Illia Zabarnyi, Mykola Matvienko, Vitali Mykolenko, Mykola Shaparenko (YC43) (78' Sergiy Sydorchuk), Oleksandr Zinchenko, Ruslan Malinovskyi (90+2' Eduard Sobol), Taras Stepanenko, Andrey Yarmolenko (70' Viktor Tsygankov), Roman Yaremchuk (70' Artem Besedin). (Coach: Andriy Shevchenko (UKR)).
North Macedonia: Stole Dimitrievski, Darko Velkoski (YC59) (85' Ivan Trickovski), Stefan Ristovski, Visar Musliu, Arijan Ademi (85' Kire Ristevski), Boban Nikolov (46' Aleksandar Trajkovski), Egzjan Alioski, Eljif Elmas, Enis Bardi (77' Daniel Avramovski (YC83)), Stefan Spirovski (46' Darko Churlinov), Goran Pandev. (Coach: Igor Angelovski (MKD)).
Goals: Ukraine: 1-0 Roman Yaremchuk (29'), 2-0 Roman Yaremchuk (34').
North Macedonia: 2-1 Egzjan Alioski (57').
Referee: Fernando Andres Rapallini (ARG)   Attendance: 10.001

Egzjan Alioski missed a penalty kick (57').
Ruslan Malinovskyi missed a penalty kick (84').

17-06-2021   Johan Cruijff ArenA, Amsterdam: Netherlands – Austria 2-0 (1-0)
Netherlands: Maarten Stekelenburg, Daley Blind (64' Nathan Aké), Denzel Dumfries, Matthijs de Ligt, Patrick van Aanholt (65' Owen Wijndal), Stefan de Vrij, Frenkie de Jong, Georginio Wijnaldum, Marten de Roon (YC14) (74' Ryan Gravenberch), Memphis Depay (82' Luuk de Jong), Wout Weghorst (64' Donyell Malen). (Coach: Frank de Boer (HOL)).
Austria: Daniel Bachmann (YC67), Aleksandar Dragovic (84' Philipp Lienhart), Andreas Ulmer, David Alaba (YC10), Martin Hinteregger, Stefan Lainer, Christoph Baumgartner (70' Valentino Lazaro), Konrad Laimer (62' Florian Grillitsch), Marcel Sabitzer, Xaver Schlager (84' Karim Onisiwo), Michael Gregoritsch (61' Sasa Kalajdzic). (Coach: Franco Foda (GER)).
Goals: Netherlands: 1-0 Memphis Depay (11' penalty), 2-0 Denzel Dumfries (67').
Referee: Orel Grinfeld (ISR)   Attendance: 15.243

21-06-2021   Johan Cruijff ArenA, Amsterdam: North Macedonia – Netherlands 0-3 (0-1)
North Macedonia: Stole Dimitrievski, Darko Velkoski, Stefan Ristovski (YC18), Visar Musliu (YC48), Arijan Ademi (78' Boban Nikolov), Egzjan Alioski (YC65), Eljif Elmas, Enis Bardi (78' Vlatko Stojanovski), Aleksandar Trajkovski (68' Ferhan Hasani), Goran Pandev (68' Tihomir Kostadinov (YC84)), Ivan Trickovski (56' Darko Churlinov). (Coach: Igor Angelovski (MKD)).
Netherlands: Maarten Stekelenburg, Daley Blind, Denzel Dumfries (46' Steven Berghuis), Matthijs de Ligt, Patrick van Aanholt, Stefan de Vrij (46' Jurriën Timber), Frenkie de Jong (78' Cody Gakpo), Georginio Wijnaldum, Ryan Gravenberch, Donyell Malen (66' Quincy Promes), Memphis Depay (66' Wout Weghorst). (Coach: Frank de Boer (HOL)).
Goals: Netherlands: 0-1 Memphis Depay (24'), 0-2 Georginio Wijnaldum (50'), 0-3 Georginio Wijnaldum (58').
Referee: István Kovács (ROM)   Attendance: 15.227

21-06-2021   Arena Nationala, Bucharest: Ukraine – Austria 0-1 (0-1)
Ukraine: Georgiy Bushchan, Oleksandr Karavaev, Illia Zabarnyi, Mykola Matvienko, Vitali Mykolenko (85' Artem Besedin), Mykola Shaparenko (68' Marlos Romero Bonfim), Oleksandr Zinchenko, Ruslan Malinovskyi (46' Viktor Tsygankov), Sergiy Sydorchuk, Andrey Yarmolenko, Roman Yaremchuk. (Coach: Andriy Shevchenko (UKR)).
Austria: Daniel Bachmann, Aleksandar Dragovic, David Alaba, Martin Hinteregger, Stefan Lainer, Christoph Baumgartner (32' Alessandro Schöpf), Florian Grillitsch, Konrad Laimer (72' Stefan Ilsanker), Marcel Sabitzer, Xaver Schlager, Marko Arnautovic (90' Sasa Kalajdzic). (Coach: Franco Foda (GER)).
Goal: Austria: 0-1 Christoph Baumgartner (21').
Referee: Cüneyt Çakir (TUR)   Attendance: 10.472

STANDINGS

Pos	Team	Pld	W	D	L	GF	GA	GD	Pts
1	Netherlands	3	3	0	0	8	2	+6	9
2	Austria	3	2	0	1	4	3	+1	6
3	Ukraine	3	1	0	2	4	5	-1	3
4	North Macedonia	3	0	1	2	2	8	-6	0

Netherlands, Austria and Ukraine qualified for the Knockout phase.

GROUP   D

13-06-2021   Wembley Stadium, London: England – Croatia 1-0 (0-0)
England: Jordan Pickford, John Stones, Kieran Trippier, Kyle Walker, Tyrone Mings, Declan Rice, Kalvin Phillips, Mason Mount, Phil Foden (YC64) (71' Marcus Rashford), Harry Kane (82' Jude Bellingham), Raheem Sterling (90+2' Dominic Calvert-Lewin). (Coach: Gareth Southgate (ENG)).
Croatia: Dominik Livakovic, Domagoj Vida, Duje Caleta-Car (YC42), Josko Gvardiol, Sime Vrsaljko, Ivan Perisic, Luka Modric, Marcelo Brozovic (YC66) (70' Nikola Vlasic), Mateo Kovacic (YC48) (85' Mario Pasalic), Andrej Kramaric (70' Josip Brekalo), Ante Rebic (78' Bruno Petkovic). (Coach: Zlatko Dalic (CRO)).
Goal: England: 1-0 Raheem Sterling (57').
Referee: Daniele Orsato (ITA)   Attendance: 18.497

14-06-2021   Hampden Park, Glasgow: Scotland – Czech Republic 0-2 (0-1)
Scotland: David Marshall, Andy Robertson, Grant Hanley, Jack Hendry (67' Callum McGregor), Liam Cooper, Stephen O'Donnell (79' James Forrest), John McGinn, Ryan Christie (46' Ché Adams), Scott McTominay, Stuart Armstrong (67' Ryan Fraser), Lyndon Dykes (79' Kevin Nisbet). (Coach: Steve Clarke (SCO)).
Czech Republic: Tomás Vaclík, Jan Boríl, Ondrej Celustka, Tomás Kalas, Vladimir Coufal, Alex Král (67' Tomás Holes), Jakub Jankto (72' Adam Hlozek), Lukás Masopust (72' Matej Vydra), Tomás Soucek, Vladimír Darida (87' Petr Sevcík), Patrik Schick (87' Michael Krmencík). (Coach: Jaroslav Silhavý (CZE)).
Goals: Czech Republic: 0-1 Patrik Schick (42'), 0-2 Patrik Schick (52').
Referee: Daniel Siebert (GER)   Attendance: 9.847

18-06-2021   Hampden Park, Glasgow: Croatia – Czech Republic 1-1 (0-1)
Croatia: Dominik Livakovic, Dejan Lovren (YC35), Domagoj Vida, Josko Gvardiol, Sime
Vrsaljko, Ivan Perisic, Josip Brekalo (46' Luka Ivanusec), Luka Modric, Mateo Kovacic (87'
Marcelo Brozovic), Andrej Kramaric (62' Nikola Vlasic), Ante Rebic (46' Bruno Petkovic).
(Coach: Zlatko Dalic (CRO)).
Czech Republic: Tomás Vaclík, Jan Boríl (YC82), Ondrej Celustka, Tomás Holes (63' Alex
Král), Tomás Kalas, Vladimír Coufal, Jakub Jankto (74' Petr Sevcík), Lukás Masopust (YC50)
(63' Adam Hlozek (YC90+3)), Tomás Soucek, Vladimír Darida (87' Antonín Barák), Patrik
Schick (74' Michael Krmencík). (Coach: Jaroslav Silhavý (CZE)).
Goals: Croatia: 1-1 Ivan Perisic (47').
Czech Republic: 0-1 Patrik Schick (37' penalty).
Referee: Carlos Del Cerro Grande (ESP)   Attendance: 5.607

18-06-2021   Wembley Stadium, London: England – Scotland 0-0
England: Jordan Pickford, John Stones, Luke Shaw, Reece James, Tyrone Mings, Declan Rice,
Kalvin Phillips, Mason Mount, Phil Foden (63' Jack Grealish), Harry Kane (74' Marcus
Rashford), Raheem Sterling. (Coach: Gareth Southgate (ENG)).
Scotland: David Marshall, Andy Robertson, Grant Hanley, Kieran Tierney, Stephen O'Donnell
(YC87), Billy Gilmour (76' Stuart Armstrong), Callum McGregor, John McGinn (YC15),
Scott McTominay, Ché Adams (86' Kevin Nisbet), Lyndon Dykes. (Coach: Steve Clarke
(SCO)).
Referee: Antonio Mateu Lahoz (ESP)   Attendance: 20.306

22-06-2021   Hampden Park, Glasgow: Croatia – Scotland 3-1 (1-1)
Croatia: Dominik Livakovic, Dejan Lovren (YC26), Domagoj Vida, Josip Juranovic, Josko
Gvardiol (70' Borna Barisic), Ivan Perisic (81' Ante Rebic), Luka Modric, Marcelo Brozovic,
Mateo Kovacic, Nikola Vlasic (76' Luka Ivanusec), Bruno Petkovic (70' Andrej Kramaric).
(Coach: Zlatko Dalic (CRO)).
Scotland: David Marshall, Andy Robertson, Grant Hanley (33' Scott McKenna (YC34)),
Kieran Tierney, Stephen O'Donnell (84' Nathan Patterson), Callum McGregor, John McGinn,
Scott McTominay, Stuart Armstrong (70' Ryan Fraser), Ché Adams (84' Kevin Nisbet),
Lyndon Dykes. (Coach: Steve Clarke (SCO)).
Goals: Croatia: 1-0 Nikola Vlasic (17'), 2-1 Luka Modric (62'), 3-1 Ivan Perisic (77').
Scotland: 1-1 Callum McGregor (42').
Referee: Fernando Andres Rapallini (ARG)   Attendance: 9.896

22-06-2021   Wembley Stadium, London: Czech Republic – England 0-1 (0-1)
Czech Republic: Tomás Vaclík, Jan Boríl (YC61), Ondrej Celustka, Tomás Holes (84' Matej Vydra), Tomás Kalas, Vladimír Coufal, Jakub Jankto (46' Petr Sevcík), Lukás Masopust (64' Adam Hlozek), Tomás Soucek, Vladimír Darida (64' Alex Král), Patrik Schick (75' Tomás Pekhart). (Coach: Jaroslav Silhavý (CZE)).
England: Jordan Pickford, Harry Maguire, John Stones (79' Tyrone Mings), Kyle Walker, Luke Shaw, Bukayo Saka (84' Jadon Sancho), Declan Rice (46' Jordan Henderson), Jack Grealish (67' Jude Bellingham), Kalvin Phillips, Harry Kane, Raheem Sterling (67' Marcus Rashford). (Coach: Gareth Southgate (ENG)).
Goal: England: 0-1 Raheem Sterling (12').
Referee: Artur Soares Dias (POR)   Attendance: 19.104

STANDINGS

Pos	Team	Pld	W	D	L	GF	GA	GD	Pts
1	England	3	2	1	0	2	0	+2	7
2	Croatia	3	1	1	1	4	3	+1	4
3	Czech Republic	3	1	1	1	3	2	+1	4
4	Scotland	3	0	1	2	1	5	-4	1

England, Croatia and Czech Republic qualified for the Knockout phase.

GROUP   E

14-06-2021   Krestovsky Stadium, Saint Petersburg: Poland – Slovakia 1-2 (0-1)
Poland: Wojciech Szczesny, Bartosz Bereszynski, Jan Bednarek, Kamil Glik, Maciej Rybus (74' Tymoteusz Puchacz), Grzegorz Krychowiak (YC22,YC62), Kamil Józwiak, Karol Linetty (74' Przemyslaw Frankowski), Mateusz Klich (85' Jakub Moder), Piotr Zielinski (85' Karol Swiderski), Robert Lewandowski. (Coach: PAULO Manuel Carvalho de SOUSA (POR)).
Slovakia: Martin Dúbravka, Lubomír Satka, Milan Skriniar, Peter Pekarík (79' Martin Koscelník), Tomás Hubocan (YC20), Jakub Hromada (79' Patrik Hrosovský), Juraj Kucka, Lukás Haraslín (87' Michal Duris), Marek Hamsík, Ondrej Duda (90+2' Ján Gregus), Róbert Mak (87' Tomás Suslov). (Coach: Stefan Tarkovic (SVK)).
Goals: 0-1 Wojciech Szczesny (18' own goal), 1-1 Karol Linetty (46'), 1-2 Milan Skriniar (69').
Referee: Ovidiu Hategan (ROM)   Attendance: 12.862

14-06-2021   La Cartuja, Seville: Spain – Sweden 0-0
Spain: UNAI SIMÓN Mendibil, Aymeric LAPORTE, JORDI ALBA Ramos, PAU Francisco TORRES, Daniel "DANI" OLMO Carvajal (74' GERARD Moreno Balagueró), Jorge Resurrección Merodio "KOKE" (87' FABIÁN Ruiz Peña), Marcos LLORENTE Moreno, Rodrigo Hernández Cascante "RODRI" (66' THIAGO ALCÁNTARA do Nascimento), Álvaro Borja MORATA Martín (66' PABLO SARABIA García), FERRÁN TORRES García (74' MIKEL OYARZABAL Ugarte), Pedro González López "PEDRI". (Coach: LUIS ENRIQUE Martínez García (ESP)).
Sweden: Robin Olsen, Ludwig Augustinsson, Marcus Danielsson, Mikael Lustig (YC55) (75' Emil Krafth), Victor Lindelöf, Albin Ekdal, Emil Forsberg (84' Pierre Bengtsson), Kristoffer Olsson (84' Jens-Lys Cajuste), Sebastian Larsson, Alexander Isak (69' Viktor Claesson), Marcus Berg (69' Robin Quaison). (Coach: Janne Andersson (SWE)).
Referee: Slavko Vincic (SVN)   Attendance: 10.559

18-06-2021   Krestovsky Stadium, Saint Petersburg: Sweden – Slovakia 1-0 (0-0)
Sweden: Robin Olsen, Ludwig Augustinsson (88' Pierre Bengtsson), Marcus Danielsson, Mikael Lustig, Victor Lindelöf, Albin Ekdal (88' Gustav Svensson), Emil Forsberg (90+3' Emil Krafth), Kristoffer Olsson (YC23) (64' Viktor Claesson), Sebastian Larsson, Alexander Isak, Marcus Berg (64' Robin Quaison). (Coach: Janne Andersson (SWE)).
Slovakia: Martin Dúbravka (YC76), Lubomír Satka, Martin Koscelník, Milan Skriniar, Peter Pekarík (64' Lukás Haraslín), Tomás Hubocan (84' Dávid Hancko), Juraj Kucka, Marek Hamsík (77' László Bénes), Ondrej Duda (YC80), Patrik Hrosovský (84' Michal Duris), Róbert Mak (77' Vladimír Weiss (YC87)). (Coach: Stefan Tarkovic (SVK)).
Goal: Sweden: 1-0 Emil Forsberg (77' penalty).
Referee: Daniel Siebert (GER)   Attendance: 11.525

19-06-2021   La Cartuja, Sevilla: Spain – Poland 1-1 (1-0)
Spain: UNAI SIMÓN Mendibil, Aymeric LAPORTE, JORDI ALBA Ramos, PAU Francisco TORRES (YC81), Daniel "DANI" OLMO Carvajal (61' FERRÁN TORRES García), Jorge Resurrección Merodio "KOKE" (68' PABLO SARABIA García), Marcos LLORENTE Moreno, Rodrigo Hernández Cascante "RODRI" (YC90+4), Álvaro Borja MORATA Martín (87' MIKEL OYARZABAL Ugarte), GERARD Moreno Balagueró (68' FABIÁN Ruiz Peña), Pedro González López "PEDRI". (Coach: LUIS ENRIQUE Martínez García (ESP)).
Poland: Wojciech Szczesny, Bartosz Bereszynski, Jan Bednarek (85' Pawel Dawidowicz), Kamil Glik, Tymoteusz Puchacz, Jakub Moder (YC57) (85' Karol Linetty), Kamil Józwiak (YC59), Mateusz Klich (YC36) (55' Kacper Kozlowski), Piotr Zielinski, Karol Swiderski (68' Przemyslaw Frankowski), Robert Lewandowski (YC90+3). (Coach: PAULO Manuel Carvalho de SOUSA (POR)).
Goals: Spain: 1-0 Álvaro Borja MORATA Martín (25').
Poland: 1-1 Robert Lewandowski (54').
Referee: Daniele Orsato (ITA)   Attendance: 11.742

GERARD Moreno Balagueró missed a penalty kick (58').

23-06-2021   La Cartuja, Sevilla: Slovakia – Spain 0-5 (0-2)
Slovakia: Martin Dúbravka, Lubomír Satka, Milan Skriniar (YC90+4), Peter Pekarík, Tomás Hubocan, Jakub Hromada (46' Stanislav Lobotka), Juraj Kucka, Lukás Haraslín (69' Tomás Suslov), Marek Hamsík (90' László Bénes), Ondrej Duda (YC12) (46' Michal Duris), Róbert Mak (69' Vladimír Weiss). (Coach: Stefan Tarkovic (SVK)).
Spain: UNAI SIMÓN Mendibil, Aymeric LAPORTE, César AZPILICUETA Tanco (77' MIKEL OYARZABAL Ugarte), ERIC GARCÍA Martret (71' PAU Francisco TORRES), JORDI ALBA Ramos (YC60), Jorge Resurrección Merodio "KOKE", PABLO SARABIA García, Sergio BUSQUETS Burgos (YC40) (71' THIAGO ALCÁNTARA do Nascimento), Álvaro Borja MORATA Martín (66' FERRÁN TORRES García), GERARD Moreno Balagueró (77' ADAMA TRAORÉ Diarra), Pedro González López "PEDRI". (Coach: LUIS ENRIQUE Martínez García (ESP)).
Goals: Spain: 0-1 Martin Dúbravka (30' own goal), 0-2 Aymeric LAPORTE (45+3'), 0-3 PABLO SARABIA García (56'), 0-4 FERRÁN TORRES García (67'), 0-5 Juraj Kucka (71' own goal).
Referee: Björn Kuipers (HOL)   Attendance: 11.204

Álvaro Borja MORATA Martín missed a penalty kick (12').

479

23-06-2021   Krestovsky Stadium, Saint Petersburg: Sweden – Poland 3-2 (1-0)
Sweden: Robin Olsen, Ludwig Augustinsson, Marcus Danielsson (YC10), Mikael Lustig (68'
Emil Krafth), Victor Lindelöf, Albin Ekdal, Emil Forsberg (78' Viktor Claesson), Kristoffer
Olsson, Sebastian Larsson, Alexander Isak (68' Marcus Berg), Robin Quaison (55' Dejan
Kulusevski). (Coach: Janne Andersson (SWE)).
Poland: Wojciech Szczesny, Bartosz Bereszynski, Jan Bednarek, Kamil Glik (YC83),
Tymoteusz Puchacz (46' Przemyslaw Frankowski), Grzegorz Krychowiak (YC74) (78'
Przemyslaw Placheta), Kamil Józwiak (61' Jakub Swierczok), Mateusz Klich (73' Kacper
Kozlowski), Piotr Zielinski, Karol Swiderski, Robert Lewandowski. (Coach: PAULO Manuel
Carvalho de SOUSA (POR)).
Goals: Sweden: 1-0 Emil Forsberg (2'), 2-0 Emil Forsberg (59'), 3-2 Viktor Claesson (90+3').
Poland: 2-1 Robert Lewandowski (61'), 2-2 Robert Lewandowski (84').
Referee: Michael Oliver (ENG)   Attendance: 14.252

STANDINGS

Pos	Team	Pld	W	D	L	GF	GA	GD	Pts
1	Sweden	3	2	1	0	4	2	+2	7
2	Spain	3	1	2	0	6	1	+5	5
3	Slovakia	3	1	0	2	2	7	-5	3
4	Poland	3	0	1	2	4	6	-2	1

Sweden and Spain qualified for the Knockout phase.

GROUP F

15-06-2021   Puskás Aréna, Budapest: Hungary – Portugal 0-3 (0-0)
Hungary: Péter Gulácsi, Attila Fiola (88' Kevin Varga), Attila Szalai, Endre Botka, Gergö
Lovrencsics, Willi Orbán (YC86), Ádám Nagy (88' Roland Varga), András Schäfer (65' Loïc
Négo (YC80)), László Kleinheisler (78' Dávid Sigér), Roland Sallai (77' Szabolcs Schön),
Ádám Szalai. (Coach: Marco Rossi (ITA)).
Portugal: RUI Pedro dos Santos PATRÍCIO, Képler Laveran Lima Ferreira "PEPE", NÉLSON
Cabral SEMEDO, RAPHAËL Adelino José GUERREIRO, RÚBEN Santos Gato Alves DIAS
(YC38), BERNARDO Mota Veiga de Carvalho e SILVA (71' Rafael Alexandre Fernandes
Ferreira "RAFA" da SILVA), BRUNO Miguel Borges FERNANDES (89' JOÃO Filipe Iria
Santos MOUTINHO), DANILO Luís Hélio PEREIRA, WILLIAM Silva de CARVALHO (81'
RENATO Júnior Luz SANCHES), CRISTIANO RONALDO dos Santos Aveiro, DIOGO
"JOTA" José Teixeira da Silva (81' ANDRÉ Miguel Valente da SILVA). (Coach:
FERNANDO Manuel Fernandes da Costa SANTOS (POR)).
Goals: Portugal: 0-1 RAPHAËL Adelino José GUERREIRO (84'), 0-2 CRISTIANO
RONALDO dos Santos Aveiro (87' penalty), 0-3 CRISTIANO RONALDO dos Santos Aveiro
(90+2').
Referee: Cüneyt Çakir (TUR)   Attendance: 55.662

15-06-2021   Allianz Arena, München: France – Germany 1-0 (1-0)
France: Hugo Lloris, Benjamin Pavard, Lucas Hernández, Presnel Kimpembe, Raphaël Varane, Adrien Rabiot (90+5' Ousmane Dembèlé), N'Golo Kanté, Paul Pogba, Antoine Griezmann, Karim Benzema (89' Corentin Tolisso), Kylian Mbappé. (Coach: Didier Deschamps (FRA)).
Germany: Manuel Neuer, Antonio Rüdiger, Mats Hummels, Matthias Ginter (88' Emre Can), Robin Gosens (88' Kevin Volland), Ilkay Gündogan, Joshua Kimmich (YC7), Kai Havertz (74' Leroy Sané), Toni Kroos, Serge Gnabry (74' Timo Werner), Thomas Müller. (Coach: Joachim Löw (GER)).
Goal: France: 1-0 Mats Hummels (20' own goal).
Referee: Carlos Del Cerro Grande (ESP)   Attendance: 13.000

19-06-2021   Puskás Aréna, Budapest: Hungary – France 1-1 (1-0)
Hungary: Péter Gulácsi, Attila Fiola, Attila Szalai, Endre Botka (YC52), Loïc Négo, Willi Orbán, Ádám Nagy, András Schäfer (75' Tamás Cseri), László Kleinheisler (84' Gergö Lovrencsics), Roland Sallai, Ádám Szalai (26' Nemanja Nikolic). (Coach: Marco Rossi (ITA)).
France: Hugo Lloris, Benjamin Pavard (YC10), Lucas Digne, Presnel Kimpembe, Raphaël Varane, Adrien Rabiot (57' Ousmane Dembèlé, 87' Thomas Lemar), N'Golo Kanté, Paul Pogba (76' Corentin Tolisso), Antoine Griezmann, Karim Benzema (76' Olivier Giroud), Kylian Mbappé. (Coach: Didier Deschamps (FRA)).
Goals: Hongary: 1-0 Attila Fiola (45+2').
France: 1-1 Antoine Griezmann (66').
Referee: Michael Oliver (ENG)   Attendance: 55.998

19-06-2021   Allianz Arena, München: Portugal – Germany 2-4 (1-2)
Portugal: RUI Pedro dos Santos PATRÍCIO, Képler Laveran Lima Ferreira "PEPE", NÉLSON Cabral SEMEDO, RAPHAËL Adelino José GUERREIRO, RÚBEN Santos Gato Alves DIAS, BERNARDO Mota Veiga de Carvalho e SILVA (46' RENATO Júnior Luz SANCHES), BRUNO Miguel Borges FERNANDES (64' JOÃO Filipe Iria Santos MOUTINHO), DANILO Luís Hélio PEREIRA, WILLIAM Silva de CARVALHO (58' Rafael Alexandre Fernandes Ferreira "RAFA" da SILVA), CRISTIANO RONALDO dos Santos Aveiro, DIOGO "JOTA" José Teixeira da Silva (83' ANDRÉ Miguel Valente da SILVA). (Coach: FERNANDO Manuel Fernandes da Costa SANTOS (POR)).
Germany: Manuel Neuer, Antonio Rüdiger, Mats Hummels (63' Emre Can), Matthias Ginter (YC77), Robin Gosens (63' Marcel Halstenberg), Ilkay Gündogan (73' Niklas Süle), Joshua Kimmich, Kai Havertz (YC66) (73' Leon Goretzka), Toni Kroos, Serge Gnabry (87' Leroy Sané), Thomas Müller. (Coach: Joachim Löw (GER)).
Goals: Portugal: 1-0 CRISTIANO RONALDO dos Santos Aveiro (15'), 2-4 DIOGO "JOTA" José Teixeira da Silva (67').
Germany: 1-1 RÚBEN Santos Gato Alves DIAS (35' own goal), 1-2 RAPHAËL Adelino José GUERREIRO (39' own goal), 1-3 Kai Havertz (51'), 1-4 Robin Gosens (60').
Referee: Anthony Taylor (ENG)   Attendance: 12.926

23-06-2021   Puskás Aréna, Budapest: Portugal – France 2-2 (1-1)
Portugal: RUI Pedro dos Santos PATRÍCIO, Képler Laveran Lima Ferreira "PEPE", NÉLSON Cabral SEMEDO (79' José DIOGO DALOT Teixeira), RAPHAËL Adelino José GUERREIRO, RÚBEN Santos Gato Alves DIAS, BERNARDO Mota Veiga de Carvalho e SILVA (72' BRUNO Miguel Borges FERNANDES), DANILO Luís Hélio PEREIRA (46' JOÃO Maria Lobo Alves PALHINHA Gonçalves), JOÃO Filipe Iria Santos MOUTINHO (73' RÚBEN Diogo da Silva NEVES), RENATO Júnior Luz SANCHES (88' SÉRGIO Miguel Relvas de OLIVEIRA), CRISTIANO RONALDO dos Santos Aveiro, DIOGO "JOTA" José Teixeira da Silva. (Coach: FERNANDO Manuel Fernandes da Costa SANTOS (POR)).
France: Hugo Lloris (YC27), Jules Koundé, Lucas Hernández (YC36) (46' Lucas Digne, 52' Adrien Rabiot), Presnel Kimpembe (YC83), Raphaël Varane, Corentin Tolisso (66' Kingsley Coman), N'Golo Kanté, Paul Pogba, Antoine Griezmann (YC39) (87' Moussa Sissoko), Karim Benzema, Kylian Mbappé. (Coach: Didier Deschamps (FRA)).
Goals: Portugal: 1-0 CRISTIANO RONALDO dos Santos Aveiro (30' penalty), 2-2 CRISTIANO RONALDO dos Santos Aveiro (60' penalty).
France: 1-1 Karim Benzema (45+2' penalty), 1-2 Karim Benzema (47').
Referee: Antonio Mateu Lahoz (ESP)   Attendance: 54.886

23-06-2021   Allianz Arena, München: Germany – Hungary 2-2 (0-1)
Germany: Manuel Neuer, Antonio Rüdiger, Mats Hummels, Matthias Ginter (82' Kevin Volland), Robin Gosens (82' Jamal Musiala), Ilkay Gündogan (YC29) (58' Leon Goretzka), Joshua Kimmich, Kai Havertz (67' Timo Werner), Toni Kroos, Leroy Sané (YC61), Serge Gnabry (67' Thomas Müller). (Coach: Joachim Löw (GER)).
Hungary: Péter Gulácsi, Attila Fiola (YC66) (88' Nemanja Nikolic), Attila Szalai, Endre Botka (YC28), Loïc Négo, Willi Orbán, Ádám Nagy, András Schäfer, László Kleinheisler (89' Gergö Lovrencsics), Roland Sallai (75' Szabolcs Schön), Ádám Szalai (YC64) (82' Kevin Varga). (Coach: Marco Rossi (ITA)).
Goals: Germany: 1-1 Kai Havertz (66'), 2-2 Leon Goretzka (84').
Hungary: 0-1 Ádám Szalai (11'), 1-2 András Schäfer (68').
Referee: Sergei Karasev (RUS)   Attendance: 12.413

STANDINGS

Pos	Team	Pld	W	D	L	GF	GA	GD	Pts
1	France	3	1	2	0	4	3	+1	5
2	Germany	3	1	1	1	6	5	+1	4
3	Portugal	3	1	1	1	7	6	+1	4
4	Hungary	3	0	2	1	3	6	-3	2

France, Germany and Portugal qualified for the Knockout phase.

RANKING OF THIRD-PLACE TEAMS

Pos	Grp	Team	Pld	W	D	L	GF	GA	GD	Pts
1	F	Portugal	3	1	1	1	7	6	+1	4
2	D	Czech Republic	3	1	1	1	3	2	+1	4
3	A	Switzerland	3	1	1	1	4	5	-1	4
4	C	Ukraine	3	1	0	2	4	5	-1	3
5	B	Finland	3	1	0	2	1	3	-2	3
6	E	Slovakia	3	1	0	2	2	7	-5	3

Portugal, Czech Republic, Switzerland and Ukraine as the four best third-place teams qualified for the Knockout phase.

KNOCKOUT PHASE

ROUND OF 16

26-06-2021   Johan Cruijff ArenA, Amsterdam: Wales – Denmark 0-4 (0-1)
Wales: Danny Ward, Ben Davies, Chris Mepham, Connor Roberts (40' Neco Williams), Joe Rodon (YC26), Aaron Ramsey, Joe Allen, Joe Morrell (59' Harry Wilson (RC90)), Daniel James (78' David Brooks (YC80)), Gareth Bale (YC90+3), Kieffer Moore (YC40) (78' Tyler Roberts). (Coach: Rob Page (WAL)).
Denmark: Kasper Schmeichel, Andreas Christensen, Jannik Vestergaard, Jens Stryger (77' Nicolai Boilesen), Joakim Mæhle, Simon Kjær (77' Joachim Andersen), Mikkel Damsgaard (60' Christian Nørgaard), Pierre-Emile Højbjerg, Thomas Delaney (60' Mathias Jensen), Kasper Dolberg (69' Andreas Cornelius), Martin Braithwaite. (Coach: Kasper Hjulmand (DEN)).
Goals: Denmark: 0-1 Kasper Dolberg (27'), 0-2 Kasper Dolberg (48'), 0-3 Joakim Mæhle (88'), 0-4 Martin Braithwaite (90+4').
Referee: Daniel Siebert (GER)   Attendance: 14.645

26-06-2021   Wembley Stadium, London: Italy – Austria 2-1 (0-0,0-0) (AET)
Italy: Gianluigi Donnarumma, Francesco Acerbi, Giovanni Di Lorenzo (YC50), Leonardo Bonucci, Leonardo Spinazzola, Jorginho, Marco Verratti (67' Manuel Locatelli), Nicolò Barella (YC51) (67' Matteo Pessina), Ciro Immobile (84' Andrea Belotti), Domenico Berardi (84' Federico Chiesa), Lorenzo Insigne (108' Bryan Cristante). (Coach: Roberto Mancini (ITA)).
Austria: Daniel Bachmann, Aleksandar Dragovic (YC120+1), David Alaba, Martin Hinteregger (YC103), Stefan Lainer (114' Christopher Trimmel), Christoph Baumgartner (90' Alessandro Schöpf), Florian Grillitsch (106' Louis Schaub), Konrad Laimer (114' Stefan Ilsanker), Marcel Sabitzer, Xaver Schlager (106' Michael Gregoritsch), Marko Arnautovic (YC2) (97' Sasa Kalajdzic). (Coach: Franco Foda (GER)).
Goals: Italy: 1-0 Federico Chiesa (95'), 2-0 Matteo Pessina (105').
Austria: 2-1 Sasa Kalajdzic (114').
Referee: Anthony Taylor (ENG)   Attendance: 18.910

27-06-2021   Puskás Aréna, Budapest: Netherlands – Czech Republic 0-2 (0-0)
Netherlands: Maarten Stekelenburg, Daley Blind (81' Jurriën Timber), Denzel Dumfries
(YC46), Matthijs de Ligt (RC52), Patrick van Aanholt (81' Steven Berghuis), Stefan de Vrij,
Frenkie de Jong (YC84), Georginio Wijnaldum, Marten de Roon (73' Wout Weghorst),
Donyell Malen (57' Quincy Promes), Memphis Depay. (Coach: Frank de Boer (HOL)).
Czech Republic: Tomás Vaclík, Ondrej Celustka, Pavel Kaderábek, Tomás Holes (85' Alex
Král), Tomás Kalas, Vladimír Coufal (YC56), Antonín Barák (90+2' Michal Sadílek), Lukás
Masopust (79' Jakub Jankto), Petr Sevcík (85' Adam Hlozek), Tomás Soucek, Patrik Schick
(90+2' Michal Krmencík). (Coach: Jaroslav Silhavý (CZE)).
Goals: Czech Republic: 0-1 Tomás Holes (68'), 0-2 Patrik Schick (80').
Referee: Sergei Karasev (RUS)   Attendance: 52.834

27-06-2021   La Cartuja, Sevilla: Belgium – Portugal 1-0 (1-0)
Belgium: Thibaut Courtois, Jan Vertonghen, Thomas Meunier, Thomas Vermaelen (YC72),
Toby Alderweireld (YC81), Axel Witsel, Eden Hazard (87' Yannick Carrasco), Kevin De
Bruyne (48' Dries Mertens), Thorgan Hazard (90+5' Leander Dendoncker), Youri Tielemans,
Romelu Lukaku. (Coach: ROBERT MARTÍNEZ Montoliú (ESP)).
Portugal: RUI Pedro dos Santos PATRÍCIO, José DIOGO DALOT Teixeira (YC51), Képler
Laveran Lima Ferreira "PEPE" (YC77), RAPHAËL Adelino José GUERREIRO, RÚBEN
Santos Gato Alves DIAS, BERNARDO Mota Veiga de Carvalho e SILVA (55' BRUNO
Miguel Borges FERNANDES), JOÃO Maria Lobo Alves PALHINHA Gonçalves (YC45) (78'
DANILO Luís Hélio PEREIRA), JOÃO Filipe Iria Santos MOUTINHO (55' JOÃO FÉLIX
Sequeira), RENATO Júnior Luz SANCHES (78' SÉRGIO Miguel Relvas de OLIVEIRA),
CRISTIANO RONALDO dos Santos Aveiro, DIOGO "JOTA" José Teixeira da Silva (70'
ANDRÉ Miguel Valente SILVA). (Coach: FERNANDO Manuel Fernandes da Costa
SANTOS (POR)).
Goal: Belgium: 1-0 Thorgan Hazard (42').
Referee: Dr. Felix Brych (GER)   Attendance: 11.504

28-06-2021   Parken Stadium, Copenhagen: Croatia – Spain 3-5 (1-1,3-3) (AET)
Croatia: Dominik Livakovic, Domagoj Vida, Duje Caleta-Car (YC84), Josip Juranovic (73'
Josip Brekalo), Josko Gvardiol, Luka Modric (114' Luka Ivanusec), Marcelo Brozovic
(YC73), Mateo Kovacic (79' Ante Budimir), Nikola Vlasic (79' Mario Pasalic), Ante Rebic
(67' Mislav Orsic), Bruno Petkovic (46' Andrej Kramaric). (Coach: Zlatko Dalic (CRO)).
Spain: UNAI SIMÓN Mendibil, Aymeric LAPORTE, César AZPILICUETA Tanco, ERIC
GARCÍA Martret (71' PAU Francisco TORRES), José Luis GAYÀ Peña (77' JORDI ALBA
Ramos), Jorge Resurrección Merodio "KOKE" (78' FABIÁN Ruiz Peña), PABLO SARABIA
García (71' Daniel "DANI" OLMO Carvajal), Sergio BUSQUETS Burgos (101' Rodrigo
Hernández Cascante "RODRI")), Álvaro Borja MORATA Martín, FERRÁN TORRES García
(88' MIKEL OYARZABAL Ugarte), Pedro González López "PEDRI". (Coach: LUIS
ENRIQUE Martínez García (ESP)).
Goals: Croatia: 1-0 Pedro González López "PEDRI" (20' own goal), 2-3 Mislav Orsic (85'),
3-3 Mario Pasalic (90+2').
Spain: 1-1 PABLO SARABIA García (38'), 1-2 César AZPILICUETA Tanco (57'), 1-3
FERRÁN TORRES García (77'), 3-4 Álvaro Borja MORATA Martín (100'), 3-5 MIKEL
OYARZABAL Ugarte (103').
Referee: Cüneyt Çakir (TUR)   Attendance: 22.771

28-06-2021   Arena Nationala, Bucharest: France – Switzerland 3-3 (0-1,3-3) (AET)
France: Hugo Lloris, Benjamin Pavard (YC91), Clément Lenglet (46' Kingsley Coman (YC88), 111' Marcus Thuram), Presnel Kimpembe, Raphaël Varane (YC30), Adrien Rabiot, N'Golo Kanté, Paul Pogba, Antoine Griezmann (88' Moussa Sissoko), Karim Benzema (94' Olivier Giroud), Kylian Mbappé. (Coach: Didier Deschamps (FRA)).
Switzerland: Yann Sommer, Manuel Akanji (YC108), Nico Elvedi (YC32), Ricardo Rodríguez (YC61) (87' Admir Mehmedi), Silvan Widmer (73' Kevin Mbabu), Granit Xhaka (YC76), Remo Freuler, Steven Zuber (79' Christian Fassnacht), Xherdan Shaqiri (73' Mario Gavranovic), Breel Embolo (79' Ruben Vargas), Haris Seferovic (97' Fabian Schär). (Coach: Vladimir Petkovic (BIH)).
Goals: France: 1-1 Karim Benzema (57'), 2-1 Karim Benzema (59'), 3-1 Paul Pogba (75').
Switzerland: 0-1 Haris Seferovic (15'), 3-2 Haris Seferovic (81'), 3-3 Mario Gavranovic (90').
Referee: Fernando Andres Rapallini (ARG)   Attendance: 22.642
Penalties: 1 Mario Gavranovic   1 Paul Pogba
               2 Fabian Schär   2 Olivier Giroud
               3 Manuel Akanji   3 Marcus Thuram
               4 Ruben Vargas   4 Presnel Kimpembe
               5 Admir Mehmedi   * Kylian Mbappé

Ricardo Rodríguez missed a penalty kick (55').

29-06-2021   Wembley Stadium: England – Germany 2-0 (0-0)
England: Jordan Pickford, Harry Maguire (YC77), John Stones, Kieran Trippier, Kyle Walker, Luke Shaw, Bukayo Saka (69' Jack Grealish), Declan Rice (YC8) (87' Jordan Henderson), Kalvin Phillips (YC45), Harry Kane, Raheem Sterling. (Coach: Gareth Southgate (ENG)).
Germany: Manuel Neuer, Antonio Rüdiger, Mats Hummels, Matthias Ginter (YC25) (87' Emre Can), Robin Gosens (YC72) (87' Leroy Sané), Joshua Kimmich, Kai Havertz, Leon Goretzka, Toni Kroos, Thomas Müller (90+2' Jamal Musiala), Timo Werner (69' Serge Gnabry). (Coach: Joachim Löw (GER)).
Goal: England: 1-0 Raheem Sterling (75'), 2-0 Harry Kane (86').
Referee: Danny Makkelie (HOL)   Attendance: 41.973

29-06-2021   Hampden Park, Glasgow: Sweden – Ukraine 1-2 (1-1,1-1) (AET)
Sweden: Robin Olsen, Ludwig Augustinsson (83' Pierre Bengtsson), Marcus Danielsson (RC98), Mikael Lustig (83' Emil Krafth), Victor Lindelöf, Albin Ekdal, Dejan Kulusevski (YC69) (97' Robin Quaison), Emil Forsberg (YC85), Kristoffer Olsson (101' Filip Helander), Sebastian Larsson (97' Viktor Claesson), Alexander Isak (97' Marcus Berg). (Coach: Janne Andersson (SWE)).
Ukraine: Georgiy Bushchan, Oleksandr Karavaev, Illia Zabarnyi, Mykola Matvienko, Sergiy Krivtsov, Mykola Shaparenko (61' Ruslan Malinovskyi), Oleksandr Zinchenko, Sergiy Sydorchuk (118' Roman Bezus), Taras Stepanenko (95' Evgeniy Makarenko), Andrey Yarmolenko (YC79) (105' Artem Dovbyk (YC120+2)), Roman Yaremchuk (91' Artem Besedin, 101' Viktor Tsygankov). (Coach: Andriy Shevchenko (UKR)).
Goals: Sweden: 1-1 Emil Forsberg (43').
Ukraine: 0-1 Oleksandr Zinchenko (27'), 1-2 Artem Dovbyk (120+1).
Referee: Daniele Orsato (ITA)   Attendance: 9.221

QUARTER-FINALS

02-07-2021   Krestovsky Stadium, Saint Petersburg:
Switzerland – Spain 1-1 (0-1,1-1) (AET)
Switzerland: Yann Sommer, Manuel Akanji, Nico Elvedi, Ricardo Rodríguez, Silvan Widmer (YC67) (100' Kevin Mbabu), Denis Zakaria (100' Fabian Schär), Remo Freuler (RC77), Steven Zuber (90+2' Christian Fassnacht), Xherdan Shaqiri (81' Djibril Sow), Breel Embolo (23' Ruben Vargas), Haris Seferovic (81' Mario Gavranovic (YC120+1)). (Coach: Vladimir Petkovic (BIH)).
Spain: UNAI SIMÓN Mendibil, Aymeric LAPORTE (YC90+3), César AZPILICUETA Tanco, JORDI ALBA Ramos, PAU Francisco TORRES (113' THIAGO ALCÁNTARA do Nascimento), Jorge Resurrección Merodio "KOKE" (90+1' Marcos LLORENTE Moreno), PABLO SARABIA García (46' Daniel "DANI" OLMO Carvajal), Sergio BUSQUETS Burgos, Álvaro Borja MORATA Martín (54' GERARD Moreno Balagueró), FERRÁN TORRES García (91' MIKEL OYARZABAL Ugarte), Pedro González López "PEDRI" (119' Rodrigo Hernández Cascante "RODRI"). (Coach: LUIS ENRIQUE Martínez García (ESP)).
Goals: Switzerland: 1-1 Xherdan Shaqiri (68').
Spain: 0-1 Denis Zakaria (8' own goal).
Referee: Michael Oliver (ENG)   Attendance: 24.764
Penalties: * Sergio BUSQUETS Burgos   1 Mario Gavranovic
           1 Daniel "DANI" OLMO Carvajal   * Fabian Schär
           * Rodrigo Hernández Cascante "RODRI"   * Manuel Akanji
           2 GERARD Moreno Balagueró   * Ruben Vargas
           3 MIKEL OYARZABAL Ugarte

02-07-2021   Allianz Arena, München: Belgium – Italy 1-2 (1-2)
Belgium: Thibaut Courtois, Jan Vertonghen, Thomas Meunier (69' Nacer Chadli, 73' Dennis Praet), Thomas Vermaelen, Toby Alderweireld, Axel Witsel, Kevin De Bruyne, Thorgan Hazard, Youri Tielemans (YC21) (69' Dries Mertens), Jeremy Doku, Romelu Lukaku. (Coach: ROBERT MARTÍNEZ Montoliú (ESP)).
Italy: Gianluigi Donnarumma, Giorgio Chiellini, Giovanni Di Lorenzo, Leonardo Bonucci, Leonardo Spinazzola (79' Emerson), Jorginho, Marco Verratti (YC20) (74' Bryan Cristante), Nicolò Barella, Ciro Immobile (75' Andrea Belotti), Federico Chiesa (90+1' Rafael Tolói), Lorenzo Insigne (79' Domenico Berardi (YC90)). (Coach: Roberto Mancini (ITA)).
Goals: Belgium: 1-2 Romelu Lukaku (45+2' penalty).
Italy: 0-1 Nicolò Barella (31'), 0-2 Lorenzo Insigne (44').
Referee: Slavko Vincic (SVN)   Attendancce: 12.984

03-07-2021   Baku Olympic Stadium, Baku: Czech Republic – Denmark 1-2 (0-2)
Czech Republic: Tomás Vaclík, Jan Boril, Ondrej Celustka (65' Jakub Brabec), Tomás Holes (46' Jakub Jankto), Tomás Kalas (YC86), Vladimír Coufal, Antonín Barák, Lukás Masopust (46' Michal Krmencík (YC84)), Petr Sevcík (79' Vladimír Darida), Tomás Soucek, Patrik Schick (79' Matej Vydra). (Coach: Jaroslav Silhavý (CZE)).
Denmark: Kasper Schmeichel, Andreas Christensen (81' Joachim Andersen), Jannik Vestergaard, Jens Stryger (70' Daniel Wass), Joakim Mæhle, Simon Kjær, Mikkel Damsgaard (59' Christian Nørgaard), Pierre-Emile Højbjerg, Thomas Delaney (81' Mathias Jensen), Kasper Dolberg (59' Yussuf Poulsen), Martin Braithwaite. (Coach: Kasper Hjulmand (DEN)).
Goals: Czech Republic: 1-2 Patrik Schick (49').
Denmark: 0-1 Thomas Delaney (5'), 0-2 Kasper Dolberg (42').
Referee: Björn Kuipers (HOL)   Attendance: 16.306

03-07-2021   Stadio Olimpico, Roma: Ukraine – England 0-4 (0-1)
Ukraine: Georgiy Bushchan, Oleksandr Karavaev, Illia Zabarnyi, Mykola Matvienko, Sergiy Krivtsov (35' Viktor Tsygankov), Vitali Mykolenko, Mykola Shaparenko, Oleksandr Zinchenko, Sergiy Sydorchuk (64' Evgeniy Makarenko), Andrey Yarmolenko, Roman Yaremchuk. (Coach: Andriy Shevchenko (UKR)).
England: Jordan Pickford, Harry Maguire, John Stones, Kyle Walker, Luke Shaw (65' Kieran Trippier), Declan Rice (57' Jordan Henderson), Jadon Sancho, Kalvin Phillips (65' Jude Bellingham), Mason Mount, Harry Kane (73' Dominic Calvert-Lewin), Raheem Sterling (65' Marcus Rashford). (Coach: Gareth Southgate (ENG)).
Goals: England: 0-1 Harry Kane (4'), 0-2 Harry Maguire (46'), 0-3 Harry Kane (50'), 0-4 Jordan Henderson (63').
Referee: Dr. Felix Brych (GER)   Attendance: 11.880

SEMI-FINALS

06-07-2021   Wembley Stadium, London: Italy – Spain 1-1 (0-0,1-1) (AET)
Italy: Gianluigi Donnarumma, Emerson (73' Rafael Tolói (YC97)), Giorgio Chiellini, Giovanni Di Lorenzo, Leonardo Bonucci (YC118), Jorginho, Marco Verratti (73' Matteo Pessina), Nicolò Barella (85' Manuel Locatelli), Ciro Immobile (61' Domenico Berardi), Federico Chiesa (107' Federico Bernardeschi), Lorenzo Insigne (85' Andrea Belotti). (Coach: Roberto Mancini (ITA)).
Spain: UNAI SIMÓN Mendibil, Aymeric LAPORTE, César AZPILICUETA Tanco (85' Marcos LLORENTE Moreno), ERIC GARCÍA Martret (109' PAU Francisco TORRES), JORDI ALBA Ramos, Daniel "DANI" OLMO Carvajal, Jorge Resurrección Merodio "KOKE" (70' Rodrigo Hernández Cascante "RODRI"), Sergio BUSQUETS Burgos (YC51) (106' THIAGO ALCÁNTARA do Nascimento), FERRÁN TORRES García (61' Álvaro Borja MORATA Martín), MIKEL OYARZABAL Ugarte (70' GERARD Moreno Balagueró), Pedro González López "PEDRI". (Coach: LUIS ENRIQUE Martínez García (ESP)).
Goals: Italy: 1-0 Federico Chiesa (60').
Spain: 1-1 Álvaro Borja MORATA Martín (80').
Referee: Dr. Felix Brych (GER)   Attendance: 57.811

Penalties:		
* Manuel Locatelli	* Daniel "DANI" OLMO Carvajal
1 Andrea Belotti	1 GERARD Moreno Balagueró
2 Leonardo Bonucci	2 THIAGO ALCÁNTARA do Nascimento
3 Federico Bernardeschi	* Álvaro Borja MORATA Martín
4 Jorginho	

07-07-2021   Wembley Stadium, London: England – Denmark 2-1 (1-1,1-1) (AET)
England: Jordan Pickford, Harry Maguire (YC49), John Stones, Kyle Walker, Luke Shaw, Bukayo Saka (69' Jack Grealish, 106' Kieran Trippier), Declan Rice (95' Jordan Henderson), Kalvin Phillips, Mason Mount (95' Phil Foden), Harry Kane, Raheem Sterling. (Coach: Gareth Southgate (ENG)).
Denmark: Kasper Schmeichel, Andreas Christensen (79' Joachim Andersen), Jannik Vestergaard (105' Jonas Wind), Jens Stryger (67' Daniel Wass (YC72)), Joakim Mæhle, Simon Kjær, Mikkel Damsgaard (67' Yussuf Poulsen), Pierre-Emile Højbjerg, Thomas Delaney (88' Mathias Jensen), Kasper Dolberg (67' Christian Nørgaard), Martin Braithwaite. (Coach: Kasper Hjulmand (DEN)).
Goals: England: 1-1 Simon Kjær (39' own goal), 2-1 Harry Kane (104').
Denmark: 0-1 Mikkel Damsgaard (30').
Referee: Danny Makkelie (HOL)   Attendance: 64.950

Harry Kane missed a penalty kick (104').

FINAL

11-07-2021   Wembley Stadium, London: Italy – England 1-1 (0-1,1-1) (AET)
Italy: Gianluigi Donnarumma, Emerson (118' Alessandro Florenzi), Giorgio Chiellini (YC90+6), Giovanni Di Lorenzo, Leonardo Bonucci (YC55), Jorginho (YC114), Marco Verratti (96' Manuel Locatelli), Nicolò Barella (YC47) (54' Bryan Cristante), Ciro Immobile (54' Domenico Berardi), Federico Chiesa (86' Federico Bernardeschi), Lorenzo Insigne (YC84) (91' Andrea Belotti). (Coach: Roberto Mancini (ITA)).
England: Jordan Pickford, Harry Maguire (YC106), John Stones, Kieran Trippier (70' Bukayo Saka), Kyle Walker (120' Jadon Sancho), Luke Shaw, Declan Rice (74' Jordan Henderson, 120' Marcus Rashford), Kalvin Phillips, Mason Mount (99' Jack Grealish), Harry Kane, Raheem Sterling. (Coach: Gareth Southgate (ENG)).
Goals: Italy: 1-1 Leonardo Bonucci (67').
England: 0-1 Luke Shaw (2').
Referee: Björn Kuipers (HOL)   Attendance: 67.173
Penalties: 1 Domenico Berardi   1 Harry Kane
                * Andrea Belotti   2 Harry Maguire
                2 Leonardo Bonucci   * Marcus Rashford
                3 Federico Bernardeschi   * Jadon Sancho
                * Jorginho   * Bukayo Saka

*** Italy were European Champions ***

488

GOALSCORERS TOURNAMENT 2019-2021:

Goals	Players
16	Harry Kane (ENG), CRISTIANO RONALDO dos Santos Aveiro (POR)
11	Romelu Lukaku (BEL), Raheem Sterling (ENG), Georginio Wijnaldum (HOL), Eran Zahavi (ISR)
10	Teemu Pukki (FIN), Artem Dzyuba (RUS), Aleksandar Mitrovic (SRB)
9	Patrik Schick (CZE), Robert Lewandowski (POL)
8	Serge Gnabry (GER), Memphis Depay (HOL)
7	Marko Arnautovic (AUT), Álvaro Borja MORATA Martín (ESP), John McGinn (SCO)
6	Olivier Giroud (FRA), Claudiu Keserü (ROM), Roman Yaremchuk (UKR)
5	Kevin De Bruyne (BEL), Eden Hazard (BEL), Ivan Perisic (CRO), Kasper Dolberg (DEN), Christian Eriksen (DEN), Leon Goretzka (GER), Gylfi Sigurdsson (ISL), Ciro Immobile (ITA), Lorenzo Insigne (ITA), Joshua King (NOR), George Puscas (ROM), Denis Cheryshev (RUS), Emil Forsberg (SWE), Robin Quaison (SWE), Cenk Tosun (TUR)
4	Sokol Çikalleshi (ALB), Michy Batshuayi (BEL), Amer Gojak (BIH), Bruno Petkovic (CRO), Nikola Vlasic (CRO), Ioannis Kousoulos (CYP), Pieros Sotiriou (CYP), Martin Braithwaite (DEN), Christian Gytkjær (DEN), Yussuf Poulsen (DEN), Ross Barkley (ENG), SERGIO RAMOS García (ESP), RODRIGO Moreno Machado (ESP), Karim Benzema (FRA), Antoine Griezmann (FRA), Moanes Dabour (ISR), Nilolò Barella (ITA), Andrea Belotti (ITA), Vedat Muriqi (KOS), Elif Elmas (MCD), Alexander Sørloth (NOR), Krzysztof Piatek (POL), Haris Seferovic (SUI), Josip Ilicic (SVN), Viktor Claesson (SWE)
3	Tigran Barseghyan (ARM), Aleksandre Karapetyan (ARM), Henrikh Mkhitaryan (ARM), Christian Benteke (BEL), Thorgan Hazard (BEL), Edin Dzeko (BIH), Armin Hodzic (BIH), Miralem Pjanic (BIH), Luka Modric (CRO), Robert Skov (DEN), Marcus Rashford (ENG), Francisco "PACO" ALCÁCER Garcia (ESP), GERARD Moreno Balagueró (ESP), MIKEL OYARZABAL Ugarte (ESP), PABLO SARABIA García (ESP), Kingsley Coman (FRA), Kylian Mbappé (FRA), Ilkay Gündogan (GER), Toni Kroos (GER), Marco Reus (GER), Leroy Sané (GER), Kostas Fortounis (GRE), Willi Orbán (HUN), Birkir Bjarnason (ISL), Kolbeinn Sigthórsson (ISL), Jorginho (ITA), Baktiyar Zaynutdinov (KAZ), Gerson Rodrigues (LUX), David Turpal (LUX), Goran Pandev (MKD), Josh Magennis (NIR), Bjørn Maars Johnsen (NOR), BERNARDO Mota Veiga de Carvalho e SILVA (POR), Cedric Itten (SUI), Xherdan Shaqiri (SUI), Róbert Bozeník (SVK), Marek Hamsík (SVK), Juraj Kucka (SVK), Alexander Isak (SWE), Kaan Ayhan (TUR), Ruslan Malinovskiy (UKR), Viktor Tsygankov (UKR), Andriy Yarmolenko (UKR), Kieffer Moore (WAL), Aaron Ramsey (WAL)
2	Bekim Balaj (ALB), Rey Manaj (ALB), Cristián Martínez Alejo (AND), Gevorg Ghazaryan (ARM), Michael Gregoritsch (AUT), Stefan Lainer (AUT), Valentino Lazaro (AUT), Marcel Sabitzer (AUT), Mahir Emreli (AZE), Ramil Sheydaev (AZE), Toby Alderweireld (BEL), Timothy Castagne (BEL), Nacer Chadli (BEL), Dries Mertens (BEL), Thomas Meunier (BEL), Youri Tielemans (BEL), Rade Krunic (BIH), Edin Visca (BIH), Vasil Bozhikov (BUL), Georgios Efrem (CYP), Nicholas Ioannou (CYP), Mikkel Damsgaard (DEN), Thomas Delaney (DEN), Joakim Mæhle (DEN), Jadon Sancho (ENG), FERRÁN TORRES García (ESP),

	Jesús NAVAS González (ESP), Fredrik Jensen (FIN), Joel Pohjanpalo (FIN), Wissam Ben Yedder (FRA), Raphaël Varane (FRA), Kai Havertz (GER), Timo Werner (GER), Ryan Babel (HOL), Denzel Dumfries (HOL), Máté Pátkai (HUN), Ádám Szalai (HUN), Dominik Szoboszlai (HUN), Ragnar Sigurdsson (ISL), Federico Bernardeschi (ITA), Leonardo Bonucci (ITA), Moise Kean (ITA), Manuel Locatelli (ITA), Matteo Pessina (ITA), Fabio Quagliarella (ITA), Alessio Romagnoli (ITA), Federico Chiesa (ITA), Marco Verratti (ITA), Nicolò Zaniolo (ITA), Aleksey Shchetkin (KAZ), Gafurzhan Suyombaev (KAZ), Valon Berisha (KOS), Milot Rashica (KOS), Arvydas Novikovas (LTU), Ezgjan Alioski (MKD), Enis Bardhi (MKD), Stefan Mugosa (MNE), Niall McGinn (NIR), WILLIAM Silva de CARVALHO (POR), GONÇALO Manuel Gabchinho GUEDES (POR), Alexandru Mitrita (ROM), Aleksandr Golovin (RUS), Aleksei Ionov (RUS), Aleksei Miranchuk (RUS), Magomed Ozdoev (RUS), Fedor Smolov (RUS), Ryan Christie (SCO), Luka Jovic (SRB), Sergey Milinkovic-Savic (SRB), Nemanja Radonjic (SRB), Dusan Tadic (SRB), Breel Embolo (SUI), Mario Gavranovic (SUI), Granit Xhaka (SUI), Denis Zakaria (SUI), Domen Crnigoj (SVN), Andraz Sporar (SVN), Benjamin Verbic (SVN), Miha Zajc (SVN), Marcus Berg (SWE), Sebastian Larsson (SWE), Enes Ünal (TUR), Yevhen Konoplyanka (UKR), Oleksandr Zinchenko (UKR), Gareth Bale (WAL)
1	Amir Abrashi (ALB), Keidi Bare (ALB), Kastriot Dermaku (ALB), Elseid Hysaj (ALB), Ylber Ramadani (ALB), Odise Roshi (ALB), Armando Sadiku (ALB), Lorenc Trashi (ALB), Marc Vales González (AND), Edgar Babayan (ARM), Hovhannes Hambardzumyan (ARM), David Alaba (AUT), Christoph Baumgartner (AUT), Guido Burgstaller (AUT), Martin Hinteregger (AUT), Sasa Kalajdzic (AUT), Konrad Laimer (AUT), Stefan Posch (AUT), Tamkin Khalilzade (AZE), Yannick Carrasco (BEL), Thomas Vermaelen (BEL), Yari Verschaeren (BEL), Eldar Civic (BIH), Izet Hajrovic (BIH), Deni Milosevic (BIH), Stanislaw Drahun (BLS), Nikita Naumov (BLS), Maksim Skavysh (BLS), Igor Stasevich (BLS), Kristian Dimitrov (BUL), Ismail Isa (BUL), Todor Nedelev (BUL), Ivelin Popov (BUL), Georgi Yomov (BUL), Borna Barisic (CRO), Andrej Kramaric (CRO), Dejan Lovren (CRO), Mislav Orsic (CRO), Mario Pasalic (CRO), Ante Rebic (CRO), Kostakis Artymatas (CYP), Konstantinos Laifis (CYP), Fotios Papoulis (CYP), Jakub Brabec (CZE), Ondrej Celustka (CZE), Vladimír Darida (CZE), Tomás Holes (CZE), Jakub Jankto (CZE), Alex Král (CZE), Lukás Masopust (CZE), Zdenek Ondrásek (CZE), Tomás Soucek (CZE), Andreas Christensen (DEN), Henrik Dalsgaard (DEN), Pierre-Emile Højbjerg (DEN), Mathias Jørgensen (DEN), Tammy Abraham (ENG), Jordan Henderson (ENG), Michael Keane (ENG), Harry Maguirre (ENG), Mason Mount (ENG), Alex Oxlade-Chamberlain (ENG), Luke Shaw (ENG), Harry Winks (ENG), César AZPILICUETA Tanco (ESP), Daniel "DANI" OLMO Carvajal (ESP), FABIÁN Ruiz Peña (ESP), José Luis GAYÀ Peña (ESP), Aymeric LAPORTE (ESP), Santiago "SANTI" CAZORLA González (ESP), SAÚL Ñíguez Esclapez (ESP), Pau Francisco TORRES (ESP), Erik Sorga (EST), Konstantin Vassiljev (EST), Rógvi Baldvinsson (FAR), Viljormur Davidsen (FAR), Klæmint Olsen (FAR), Jákup Thomsen (FAR), Benjamin Källman (FIN), Pyry Soiri (FIN), Jasse Tuominen (FIN), Jonathan Ikoné (FRA), Clément Lenglet (FRA), Paul Pogba (FRA), Florian Thauvin (FRA), Corentin Tolisso (FRA),

Samuel Umtiti (FRA), Kurt Zouma (FRA), Vato Arveladze (GEO), Valerian
Gvilia (GEO), Jaba Kankava (GEO), Giorgi Kharaishvili (GEO), Giorgi
Kvilitaia (GEO), Saba Lobzhanidze (GEO), Tornike Okriashvili (GEO),
Giorgi Papunashvili (GEO), Julian Brandt (GER), Matthias Ginter (GER),
Robin Gosens (GER), Marcel Halstenberg (GER), Nico Schulz (GER), Lee
Casciaro (GIB), Roy Chipolina (GIB), Reece Styche (GIB), Anastasios
Donis (GRE), Konstantinos Galanopoulos (GRE), Dimitris Kolovos (GRE),
Dimitris Limnios (GRE), Petros Mantalos (GRE), Giorgos Masouras
(GRE), Vangelis Pavlidis (GRE), Zeca (GRE), Nathan Aké (HOL), Myron
Boadu (HOL), Virgil van Dijk (HOL), Frenkie de Jong (HOL), Luuk de
Jong (HOL), Matthijs de Ligt (HOL), Donyell Malen (HOL), Wout
Weghorst (HOL), Attila Fiola (HUN), Dávid Holman (HUN), Zsolt Kalmár
(HUN), Mihály Korhut (HUN), Loïc Négo (HUN), Nemanja Nikolic
(HUN), András Schäfer (HUN), Robbie Brady (IRL), Matt Doherty (IRL),
Shane Duffy (IRL), Jeff Hendrick (IRL), Conor Hourihane (IRL), David
McGoldrick (IRL), Jón Dadi Bödvarsson (ISL), Jóhann Berg Gudmundsson
(ISL), Vidar Örn Kjartansson (ISL), Arnór Sigurdsson (ISL), Bibras Natcho
(ISR), Francesco Acerbi (ITA), Federico Cheisa (ITA), Stephan El
Shaarawy (ITA), Riccardo Orsolini (ITA), Leonardo Pavoletti (ITA),
Lorenzo Pellegrini (ITA), Stefano Sensi (ITA), Maxim Fedin (KAZ),
Bauyrzhan Islamkhan (KAZ), Islambek Kuat (KAZ), Yuriy Pertsukh
(KAZ), Yan Vorogovskiy (KAZ), Temirlan Yerlanov (KAZ), Florent
Hadergjonaj (KOS), Atdhe Nuhiu (KOS), Elba Rashani (KOS), Amir
Rrahmani (KOS), Mërgim Vojvoda (KOS), Arbër Zeneli (KOS), Vladimirs
Kamess (LAT), Mārcis Oss (LAT), Yanik Frick (LIE), Dennis Salanovic
(LIE), Vytautas Andriuskevicius (LTU), Fedor Cernych (LTU), Donatas
Kazlauskas (LTU), Leandro Barreiro (LUX), Arijan Ademi (MKD), Boban
Nikolov (MKD), Vlatko Stojanovski (MKD), Darko Velkovski (MKD),
Steve Berg (MLT), Paul Fenech (MLT), Kyrian Nwoko (MLT), Marko
Vesovic (MNE), Vladimir Ambros (MOL), Igor Armas (MOL), Nicolae
Milinceanu (MOL), Vadim Rata (MOL), Steven Davis (NIR), Jonny Evans
(NIR), Paddy McNair (NIR), Michael Smith (NIR), Conor Washington
(NIR), Sander Berge (NOR), Tarik Elyounoussi (NOR), Iver Fossum
(NOR), Stefan Johansen (NOR), Ola Kamara (NOR), Mathias Normann
(NOR), Martin Ødegaard (NOR), Tore Reginiussen (NOR), Przemyslaw
Frankowski (POL), Kamil Glik (POL), Jacek Góralski (POL), Kamil
Grosicki (POL), Damian Kadzior (POL), Grzegorz Krychowiak (POL),
Karol Linetty (POL), Arkadiusz Milik (POL), Sebastian Szymanski (POL),
DANILO Luís Hélio PEREIRA (POR), BRUNO Miguel Borges
FERNANDES (POR), DIOGO "JOTA" José Teixeira da Silva (POR),
GONÇALO Mendes PACIÊNCIA (POR), Luís Miguel Afonso Fernandes
"PIZZI" (POR), RAPHAËL Adelino José GUERREIRO (POR), Florin
Andone (ROM), Alexandru Chipciu (ROM), Ciprian Deac (ROM), Dennis
Man (ROM), Alexandru Maxim (ROM), Georgi Dzhikiya (RUS), Mário
Fernandes (RUS), Nikolay Komlichenko (RUS), Fedor Kudryashov (RUS),
Daler Kuzyaev (RUS), Anton Miranchuk (RUS), Sergei Petrov (RUS),
Stuart Armstrong (SCO), Oliver Burke (SCO), Stuart Findlay (SCO),
Callum McGregor (SCO), Kenny McLean (SCO), Steven Naismith (SCO),
Andrew Robertson (SCO), Johnny Russell (SCO), Lawrence Shankland
(SCO), Adem Ljajic (SRB), Nikola Milenkovic (SRB), Filippo Berardi
(SMR), Loris Benito (SUI), Christian Fassnacht (SUI), Edimilson Fernandes

	(SUI), Remo Freuler (SUI), Admir Mehmedi (SUI), Ricardo Rodríguez (SUI), Fabian Schär (SUI), Ruben Vargas (SUI), Steven Zuber (SUI), Ondrej Duda (SVK), Michal Duris (SVK), Dávid Hancko (SVK), Stanislav Lobotka (SVK), Róbert Mak (SVK), Albert Rusnák (SVK), Milan Skriniar (SVK), Roman Bezjak (SVN), Tim Matavz (SVN), Aljaz Struna (SVN), Sebastian Andersson (SWE), Marcus Danielson (SWE), John Guidetti (SWE), Victor Lindelöf (SWE), Mattias Svanberg (SWE), Hakan Çalhanoglu (TUR), Irfan Can Kahveci (TUR), Hasan Ali Kaldirim (TUR), Dorukhan Toköz (TUR), Ozan Tufan (TUR), Deniz Türüç (TUR), Cengiz Ünder (TUR), Yusuf Yazici (TUR), Burak Yilmaz (TUR), Artem Besedin (UKR), Artem Dovbyk (UKR), Marlos (UKR), David Brooks (WAL), Daniel James (WAL), Connor Roberts (WAL), Harry Wilson (WAL)
1 own goal	Aram Ayrapetyan (ARM) for Italy, Martin Hinteregger (AUT) for North Macedonia, Pavel Pashaev (AZE) for Wales, Adnan Kovacevic (BIH) for Greece, Stjepan Loncar (BIH) for Armenia, Kypros Christoforou (CYP) for Belgium, Tomás Kalas (CZE) for England, Simon Kjær (DEN) for England, Pedro González López "PEDRI" (ESP) for Croatia, Teitur Gestsson (FAR) for Spain, Lukás Hrádecký (FIN) for Belgium, Mats Hummels (GER) for France, Jonathan Tah (GER) for Netherlands, Joseph Chipolina (GIB) for Republic of Ireland, Abzal Beysebekov (KAZ) for Russia, Benjamin Kololli (KOS) for North Macedonia, Mërgim Vojvoda (KOS) for England, Pāvels Steinbors (LAT) for Austria, Igors Tarasovs (LAT) for Slovenia, Andreas Malin (LIE) for Bornia-Herzegovina, Gerson Rodrigues (LUX) for Ukraine, Egzon Bejtulai (MKD) for Austria, Darko Velkovski (MKD) for Latvia, Andrei Agius (MLT) for Sweden, Boris Kopitovic (MNE) for Czech Republic, Aleksandar Sofranac (MNE) for England, Håvard Nordtveit (NOR) for Sweden, Wojciech Szczesny (POL) for Slovakia, RAPHAËL Adelino José GUERREIRO (POR) for Germany, RÚBEN Santos Gato Alves DIAS (POR) for Germany, Adrian Rus (ROM) for Spain, Stephen O'Donnell (SCO) for Russia, Cristian Brolli (SMR) for Belgium, Michele Cevoli (SMR) for Russia, Denis Zakaria (SUI) for Spain, Martin Dúbravka (SVK) for Spain, Juraj Kucka (SVK) for Spain, Milan Skriniar (SVK) for Northern Ireland, Merih Demiral (TUR) for Italy, James Lawrence (WAL) for Croatia.

UEFA Euro 2024

QUALIFYING ROUND

GROUP A

25-03-2023	Glasgow	Scotland – Cyprus	3-0 (1-0)
25-03-2023	Málaga	Spain – Norway	3-0 (1-0)
28-03-2023	Batumi	Georgia – Norway	1-1 (0-1)
28-03-2023	Glasgow	Scotland – Spain	2-0 (1-0)
17-06-2023	Oslo	Norway – Scotland	1-2 (0-0)
17-06-2023	Larnaca	Cyprus – Georgia	1-2 (1-1)
20-06-2023	Oslo	Norway – Cyprus	3-1 (1-0)
20-06-2023	Glasgow	Scotland – Georgia	2-0 (1-0)
08-09-2023	Tbilisi	Georgia – Spain	1-7 (0-4)
08-09-2023	Larnaca	Cyprus – Scotland	0-3 (0-3)
12-09-2023	Oslo	Norway – Georgia	2-1 (2-0)
12-09-2023	Granada	Spain – Cyprus	6-0 (2-0)
12-10-2023	Larnaca	Cyprus – Norway	0-4 (0-1)
12-10-2023	Sevilla	Spain – Scotland	2-0 (0-0)
15-10-2023	Tbilisi	Georgia – Cyprus	4-0 (0-0)
15-10-2023	Oslo	Norway – Spain	0-1 (0-0)
16-11-2023	Tbilisi	Georgia – Scotland	2-2 (1-0)
16-11-2023	Kolossi	Cyprus – Spain	1-3 (0-3)
19-11-2023	Glasgow	Scotland – Norway	3-3 (2-2)
19-11-2023	Valladolid	Spain – Georgia	3-1 (1-1)

FINAL STANDING

Pos	Team	Pld	W	D	L	GF	GA	GD	Pts
1	Spain	8	7	0	1	25	5	+20	21
2	Scotland	8	5	2	1	17	8	+9	17
3	Norway	8	3	2	3	14	12	+2	11
4	Georgia	8	2	2	4	12	18	-6	8
5	Cyprus	8	0	0	8	3	28	-25	0

Spain and Scotland qualified for the Final Tournament in Germany.

Georgia advanced to the play-offs due to their performance in the 2022-23 UEFA Nations League.

25-03-2023   Hampden Park, Glasgow: Scotland – Cyprus 3-0 (1-0)
Scotland: Angus Gunn, Grant Hanley, Andy Robertson, Kieran Tierney, Ryan Porteous (YC74), Aaron Hickey (79' Nathan Patterson), Ryan Jack (67' Ryan Christie), Stuart Armstrong (YC14) (67' Scott McTominay), Callum McGregor, John McGinn, Ché Adams (58' Lyndon Dykes). (Coach: Steve Clarke (SCO)).
Cyprus: Dimitris Demetriou, Valentin Roberge, Kostas Laifis, Chambos Kyriakou (68' Charalampos Charalampous), Nikolas Ioannou (YC53,YC90+5), Ioannis Kousoulos (46' Danilo Spoljaric), Kostakis Artymatas, Alexandros Gogic (79' Loizos Loizou), Grigoris Kastanos (YC32) (79' Marinos Tzionis), Minas Antoniou, Ioannis Pittas (68' Andronikos Kakoullis). (Coach: Temur Ketsbaia (GEO)).
Goals: Scotland: 1-0 John McGinn (21'), 2-0 Scott McTominay (87'), 3-0 Scott McTominay (90+3').
Referee: Duje Strukan (CRO)   Attendance: 48.195

25-03-2023   Estadio La Rosaleda, Málaga: Spain – Norway 3-0 (1-0)
Spain: Kepa, Nacho, Dani Carvajal, Aymeric Laporte, Alejandro Balde, Mikel Merino (82' Fabián Ruiz), Dani Olmo (68' Yéremy Pino), Rodri, Gavi (58' Mikel Oyarzabal), Iago Aspas (58' Dani Ceballos), Álvaro Morata (81' Joselu). (Coach: Luis de la Fuente (ESP)).
Norway: Ørjan Nyland, Stefan Strandberg, Birgir Meling (75' Fredrik Bjørkan), Leo Østigård, Marcus Pedersen (75' Julian Ryerson), Mohamed Elyounoussi (74' Jørgen Strand Larsen), Fredrik Aursnes, Patrick Berg, Martin Ødegaard (YC42), Sander Berge (74' Ola Solbakken), Alexander Sørloth (YC51) (87' Ola Brynhildsen). (Coach: Ståle Solbakken (NOR)).
Goals: Spain: 1-0 Dani Olmo (13'), 2-0 Joselu (84'), 3-0 Joselu (85').
Referee: Benoît Bastien (FRA)   Attendance: 29.214

28-03-2023   Batumi Arena, Batumi: Georgia – Norway 1-1 (0-1)
Georgia: Giorgi Mamardashvili, Guram Kashia, Solomon Kvirkvelia, Otar Kakabadze, Jemal Tabidze (59' Budu Zivzivadze), Irakli Azarovi (YC53) (70' Giorgi Gocholeishvili (YC90+4)), Nika Kvekveskiri, Giorgi Aburjania (YC72) (90' Luka Gagnidze), Zuriko Davitashvili (60' Saba Lobzhanidze), Khvicha Kvaratskhelia, Georges Mikautadze (90' Giorgi Beridze). (Coach: Willy Sagnol (FRA)).
Norway: Ørjan Nyland, Stefan Strandberg, Birgir Meling (YC89), Leo Østigård, Marcus Pedersen (90+5' Julian Ryerson), Mohamed Elyounoussi (77' Sander Berge), Fredrik Aursnes, Patrick Berg (90+5' Kristian Thorstvedt), Martin Ødegaard, Alexander Sørloth, Ola Solbakken (YC79) (82' Ola Brynhildsen). (Coach: Ståle Solbakken (NOR)).
Goals: Georgia: 1-1 Georges Mikautadze (60').
Norway: 0-1 Alexander Sørloth (15').
Referee: Andris Treimanis (LVA)   Attendance: 20.300

28-03-2023   Hampden Park, Glasgow: Scotland – Spain 2-0 (1-0)
Scotland: Angus Gunn (YC76), Grant Hanley, Andy Robertson (YC27), Kieran Tierney (75'
Liam Cooper), Ryan Porteous, Aaron Hickey (82' Nathan Patterson), Callum McGregor, John
McGinn (83' Lewis Ferguson), Ryan Christie (74' Kenny McLean), Scott McTominay
(YC90+6), Lyndon Dykes (YC34) (89' Lawrence Shankland). (Coach: Steve Clarke (SCO)).
Spain: Kepa, Iñigo Martínez, David García, José Gayà, Pedro Porro (46' Dani Carvajal
(YC68)), Dani Ceballos (79' Gavi), Mikel Merino (57' Iago Aspas (YC84)), Rodri, Yéremy
Pino, Joselu (66' Borja Iglesias), Mikel Oyarzabal (46' Nico Williams). (Coach: Luis de la
Fuente (ESP)).
Goals: Scotland: 1-0 Scott McTominay (7'), 2-0 Scott McTominay (51').
Referee: Sandro Schärer (SUI)   Attendance: 47.976

*Sandro Schärer suffered an injury. He was replaced by the fourth oficial Lukas Fähndrich
(SUI) at half-time.*

17-06-2023   Ullevaal Stadion, Oslo: Norway – Scotland 1-2 (0-0)
Norway: Ørjan Nyland, Stefan Strandberg, Birgir Meling, Julian Ryerson, Leo Østigård,
Fredrik Aursnes (84' Kristian Thorstvedt), Patrick Berg (84' Jørgen Strand Larsen), Martin
Ødegaard, Alexander Sørloth (79' Mohamed Elyounoussi), Ola Solbakken (63' Sander Berge),
Erling Haaland (84' Mats Møller Dæhli). (Coach: Ståle Solbakken (NOR)).
Scotland: Angus Gunn, Andy Robertson, Kieran Tierney (YC53) (65' Liam Cooper), Jack
Hendry (YC40), Ryan Porteous (YC60) (79' Kenny McLean), Aaron Hickey, Callum
McGregor (78' Billy Gilmour), John McGinn (YC37) (90+1' Dominic Hyam), Ryan Christie
(78' Stuart Armstrong), Scott McTominay, Lyndon Dykes. (Coach: Steve Clarke (SCO)).
Goals: Norway: 1-0 Erling Haaland (61' penalty).
Scotland: 1-1 Lyndon Dykes (87'), 1-2 Kenny McLean (88').
Referee: Matej Jug (SVN)   Attendance: 25.791

17-06-2023   AEK Arena – Georgios Karapatakis, Larnaca:
               Cyprus – Georgia 1-2 (1-1)
Cyprus: Joël Mall, Anderson Correia, Kostas Laifis, Andreas Karo (YC16) (63' Marios
Antoniades, Ioannis Kousoulos, Alexandros Gogic (YC52), Grigoris Kastanos, Charalampos
Charalampous (78' Giannis Satsias), Minas Antoniou (YC56), Ioannis Pittas (78' Dimitris
Christofi), Marinos Tzionis (60' Loizos Loizou). (Coach: Temur Ketsbaia (GEO)).
Georgia: Giorgi Mamardashvili, Guram Kashia, Otar Kakabadze (YC17), Luka Lochoshvili
(87' Lasha Dvali), Giorgi Gocholeishvili (74' Saba Lobzhanidze), Irakli Azarovi, Nika
Kvekveskiri (74' Luka Gagnidze), Otar Kiteishvili, Giorgi Chakvetadze (74' Zuriko
Davitashvili), Khvicha Kvaratskhelia, Georges Mikautadze (88' Budu Zivzivadze). (Coach:
Willy Sagnol (FRA)).
Goals: Cyprus: 1-1 Ioannis Pittas (39' penalty).
Georgia: 0-1 Georges Mikautadze (31'), 1-2 Zuriko Davitashvili (84').
Referee: Fábio Veríssimo (POR)   Attendance: 3.763

20-06-2023   Ullevaal Stadion, Oslo: Norway – Cyprus 3-1 (1-0)
Norway: Ørjan Nyland, Stefan Strandberg, Birgir Meling, Julian Ryerson (59' Brice Wembangomo), Leo Østigård, Fredrik Aursnes (YC18) (88' Kristoffer Velde), Patrick Berg (74' Kristian Thorstvedt), Martin Ødegaard, Alexander Sørloth, Ola Solbakken (58' Sander Berge), Erling Haaland (88' Bård Finne (YC89)). (Coach: Ståle Solbakken (NOR)).
Cyprus: Joël Mall, Anderson Correia, Kostas Laifis, Nikolas Ioannou, Ioannis Kousoulos (90+2' Giannis Satsias), Kostas Pileas (61' Stelios Andreou), Alexandros Gogic, Grigoris Kastanos, Charalampos Charalampous (62' Marinos Tzionis), Minas Antoniou (62' Loizos Loizou), Ioannis Pittas (YC37) (70' Dimitris Christofi). (Coach: Temur Ketsbaia (GEO)).
Goals: Norway: 1-0 Ola Solbakken (12'), 2-0 Erling Haaland (56' penalty), 3-0 Erling Haaland (60').
Cyprus: 3-1 Grigoris Kastanos (90+3').
Referee: Aleksandar Stavrev (MKD)   Attendance: 23.643

20-06-2023   Hampden Park, Glasgow: Scotland – Georgia 2-0 (1-0)
Scotland: Angus Gunn, Andy Robertson (YC67), Kieran Tierney (78' John Souttar), Jack Hendry, Ryan Porteous, Aaron Hickey (YC45+4), Callum McGregor (78' Ryan Jack), John McGinn (90+2' Ryan Christie), Scott McTominay, Billy Gilmour (86' Kenny McLean), Lyndon Dykes (79' Kevin Nisbet). (Coach: Steve Clarke (SCO)).
Georgia: Giorgi Mamardashvili, Guram Kashia, Solomon Kvirkvelia, Otar Kakabadze, Lasha Dvali (56' Giorgi Gocholeishvili (YC68)), Nika Kvekveskiri (56' Budu Zivzivadze), Saba Lobzhanidze (64' Zuriko Davitashvili), Otar Kiteishvili, Luka Gagnidze (YC75), Khvicha Kvaratskhelia, Georges Mikautadze. (Coach: Willy Sagnol (FRA)).
Goals: Scotland: 1-0 Callum McGregor (6'), 2-0 Scott McTominay (47').
Referee: István Vad (II) (HUN)   Attendance: 50.062

Khvicha Kvaratskhelia missed a penalty kick (90+4').

08-09-2023   Boris Paichadze Dinamo Arena, Tbilisi: Georgia – Spain 1-7 (0-4)
Georgia: Giorgi Mamardashvili, Guram Kashia (YC50), Solomon Kvirkvelia, Giorgi Gocholeishvili (77' Saba Sazonov), Irakli Azarovi (60' Lasha Dvali), Giorgi Aburjania (YC45+2) (46' Giorgi Chakvetadze (YC63)), Saba Lobzhanidze (46' Zuriko Davitashvili), Otar Kiteishvili (YC60), Luka Gagnidze (46' Anzor Mekvabishvili), Khvicha Kvaratskhelia (YC82), Georges Mikautadze. (Coach: Willy Sagnol (FRA)).
Spain: Unai Simón, Dani Carvajal, Aymeric Laporte, José Gayà, Robin Le Normand, Fabián Ruiz, Dani Olmo (44' Lamine Yamal), Rodri (72' Martín Zubimendi (YC79)), Gavi (YC45+1) (58' Mikel Merino), Álvaro Morata (72' Joselu), Marco Asensio (44' Nico Williams). (Coach: Luis de la Fuente (ESP)).
Goals: Georgia: 1-4 Giorgi Chakvetadze (49').
Spain: 0-1 Álvaro Morata (22'), 0-2 Solomon Kvirkvelia (27' own goal), 0-3 Dani Olmo (38'), 0-4 Álvaro Morata (40'), 1-5 Álvaro Morata (66'), 1-6 Nico Williams (68'), 1-7 Lamine Yamal (74').
Referee: Daniel Siebert (GER)   Attendance: 51.694

08-09-2023   AEK Arena – Georgios Karapatakis, Larnaca:
Cyprus – Scotland 0-3 (0-3)
Cyprus: Joël Mall, Valentin Roberge, Anderson Correia (YC8), Kostas Laifis, Chambos
Kyriakou (80' Alexandros Gogic), Andreas Karo, Ioannis Kousoulos (46' Michalis Ioannou
(YC84)), Grigoris Kastanos, Charalampos Charalampous (84' Andronikos Kakoullis), Pieros
Sotiriou (46' Ioannis Pittas (YC57)), Minas Antoniou (80' Stelios Andreou). (Coach: Temur
Ketsbaia (GEO)).
Scotland: Angus Gunn, Andy Robertson, Kieran Tierney, Jack Hendry, Ryan Porteous, Aaron
Hickey (83' Nathan Patterson), Callum McGregor, John McGinn (83' Stuart Armstrong), Scott
McTominay (90' Ryan Christie), Billy Gilmour (67' Kenny McLean), Ché Adams (67'
Lyndon Dykes). (Coach: Steve Clarke (SCO)).
Goals: Scotland: 0-1 Scott McTominay (6'), 0-2 Ryan Porteous (16'), 0-3 John McGinn (30').
Referee: Balász Berke (HUN)   Attendance: 6.633

12-09-2023   Ullevaal Stadion, Oslo: Norway – Georgia 2-1 (2-0)
Norway: Ørjan Nyland, Stefan Strandberg, Kristoffer Ajer, Fredrik Bjørkan, Leo Østigård,
Fredrik Aursnes, Patrick Berg, Martin Ødegaard, Erling Haaland, Jørgen Strand Larsen (71'
Sander Berge), Antonio Nusa (71' Ola Solbakken). (Coach: Ståle Solbakken (NOR)).
Georgia: Giorgi Mamardashvili, Guram Kashia, Solomon Kvirkvelia, Giorgi Gocholeishvili
(46' Vladimir Mamuchashvili), Irakli Azarovi, Aleksandre Kalandadze, Otar Kiteishvili,
Giorgi Kochorashvili (76' Anzor Mekvabishvili), Zuriko Davitashvili (YC64) (67' Giorgi
Chakvetadze), Khvicha Kvaratskhelia, Georges Mikautadze (67' Budu Zivzivadze (YC82)).
(Coach: Willy Sagnol (FRA)).
Goals: Norway: 1-0 Erling Haaland (25'), 2-0 Martin Ødegaard (33').
Georgia: 2-1 Budu Zivzivadze (90+1').
Referee: Nikola Dabanovic (MNE)   Attendance: 23.665

12-09-2023   Estadio Nuevo Los Cármenes, Granada: Spain – Cyprus 6-0 (2-0)
Spain: Unai Simón, Dani Carvajal, Aymeric Laporte, José Gayà (61' Alejandro Balde), Robin
Le Normand, Mikel Merino, Rodri, Gavi (76' Álex Baena), Álvaro Morata (46' Joselu), Nico
Williams (46' Yéremy Pino (YC69)), Lamine Yamal (61' Ferran Torres). (Coach: Luis de la
Fuente (ESP)).
Cyprus: Joël Mall, Anderson Correia, Kostas Laifis, Chambos Kyriakou (46' Michalis
Ioannou), Andreas Karo, Ioannis Kousoulos (55' Marinos Tzionis), Stelios Andreou (90+1'
Andreas Panayiotou Filiotis), Alexandros Gogic, Grigoris Kastanos (YC45+3), Charalampos
Charalampous (62' Kostas Pileas), Pieros Sotiriou (62' Ioannis Pittas). (Coach: Temur
Ketsbaia (GEO)).
Goals: Spain: 1-0 Gavi (18'), 2-0 Mikel Merino (33'), 3-0 Joselu (70'), 4-0 Ferran Torres (73'),
5-0 Álex Baena (77'), 6-0 Ferran Torres (83').
Referee: Simone Sozza (ITA)   Attendance: 17,311

12-10-2023   AEK Arena – Georgios Karapatakis, Lanarca:
Cyprus – Norway 0-4 (0-1)
Cyprus: Joël Mall, Anderson Correia, Chambos Kyriakou (54' Danilo Spoljaric), Andreas
Karo, Ioannis Kousoulos (YC46) (79' Stavros Gavriel), Stelios Andreou, Alexandros Gogic,
Grigoris Kastanos (79' Pavlos Correa), Hector Kyprianou, Charalampos Charalampous (60'
Kostas Pileas), Andronikos Kakoullis (54' Marios Elia). (Coach: Temur Ketsbaia (GEO)).
Norway: Ørjan Nyland, Birger Meling, Kristoffer Ajer, Julian Ryerson, Leo Østigård, Fredrik
Aursnes (88' Bård Finne), Martin Ødegaard (77' Kristian Thorstvedt), Sander Berge,
Alexander Sørloth (63' Antonio Nusa), Ola Solbakken (63' Oscar Bobb), Erling Haaland (77'
Jørgen Strand Larsen). (Coach: Ståle Solbakken (NOR)).
Goals: Norway: 0-1 Alexander Sørloth (33'), 0-2 Erling Haaland (65'),
0-3 Erling Haaland (72'), 0-4 Fredrik Aursnes (81').
Referee: Donatas Rumsas (LTU)   Attendance: 7.206

12-10-2023   Estadio La Cartuja, Sevilla: Spain – Scotland   2-0 (0-0)
Spain: Unai Simón (YC60), Dani Carvajal (YC59) (67' Jesús Navas), Aymeric Laporte
(YC90), Robin Le Normand, Alejandro Balde (46' Fran García), Mikel Merino (YC45+4) (67'
Oihan Sancet), Rodri, Gavi, Álvaro Morata (84' Joselu), Mikel Oyarzabal (46' Bryan
Zaragoza), Ferran Torres. (Coach: Luis de la Fuente (ESP)).
Scotland: Angus Gunn, Andy Robertson (44' Nathan Patterson (YC50)), Scott McKenna, Jack
Hendry (YC84), Ryan Porteous (87' Billy Gilmour), Aaron Hickey, Callum McGregor (87'
Kenny McLean), John McGinn, Ryan Christie (79' Stuart Armstrong), Scott McTominay,
Lyndon Dykes (YC36) (79' Ché Adams). (Coach: Steve Clarke (SCO)).
Goals: Spain: 1-0 Álvaro Morata (73'), 2-0 Oihan Sancet (86').
Referee: Serdar Gözübüyük (HOL)   Attendance: 45.623

15-10-2023   Mikheil Meskhis sakhelobis Stadioni, Tbilisi:
               Georgia – Cyprus   4-0 (0-0)
Georgia: Giorgi Mamardashvili, Guram Kashia, Solomon Kvirkvelia, Luka Lochoshvili, Irakli
Azarovi (71' Levan Shengelia), Vladimir Mamuchashvili, Otar Kiteishvili (85' Nika
Kvekveskiri), Giorgi Kochorashvili, Giorgi Chakvetadze (YC45) (71' Zuriko Davitashvili),
Budu Zivzivadze (59' Georges Mikautadze), Khvicha Kvaratskhelia (85' Anzor
Mekvabishvili). (Coach: Willy Sagnol (FRA)).
Cyprus: Joël Mall, Chambos Kyriakou (62' Charalampos Charalampous), Andreas Karo
(YC48), Nikolas Ioannou (87' Anderson Correia), Ioannis Kousoulos, Stelios Andreou (46'
Minas Antoniou), Dimitris Christofi (YC29) (71' Andronikos Kakoullis), Alexandros Gogic,
Grigoris Kastanos (71' Loizos Loizou), Danilo Spoljaric, Hector Kyprianou. (Coach: Temur
Ketsbaia (GEO)).
Goals: Georgia: 1-0 Otar Kiteishvili (46'), 2-0 Khvicha Kvaratskhelia (58'),
3-0 Levan Shengelia (82'), 4-0 Georges Mikautadze (90+5' penalty).
Referee: Robert Jones (ENG)   Attendance: 15.871

15-10-2023   Ullevaal Stadion, Oslo: Norway – Spain   0-1 (0-0)
Norway: Ørjan Nyland, Stefan Strandberg (77' Kristoffer Ajer), Birger Meling, Julian Ryerson
(YC40), Leo Østigård, Fredrik Aursnes (77' Kristian Thorstvedt), Patrick Berg (58' Antonio
Nusa), Martin Ødegaard, Sander Berge, Oscar Bobb (YC31) (58' Alexander Sørloth), Erling
Haaland. (Coach: Ståle Solbakken (NOR)).
Spain: Unai Simón, Dani Carvajal, Aymeric Laporte (YC56), Robin Le Normand (YC30) (46'
David García), Fran García, Fabián Ruiz, Rodri (YC86), Gavi (79' Oihan Sancet), Álvaro
Morata (YC61) (89' Joselu), Ferran Torres (71' Alfonso Pedraza), Ansu Fati (46' Mikel
Oyarzabal). (Coach: Luis de la Fuente (ESP)).
Goal: Spain: 0-1 Gavi (49').
Referee: Tobias Stieler (GER)   Attendance: 25.885

16-11-2023   Boris Paichadze Dinamo Arena, Tbilisi: Georgia – Scotland   2-2 (1-0)
Georgia: Giorgi Mamardashvili, Guram Kashia, Solomon Kvirkvelia (YC59), Otar Kakabadze,
Luka Lochoshvili (78' Aleksandre Kalandadze), Nika Kvekveskiri (69' Anzor Mekvabishvili),
Giorgi Kochorashvili (YC82), Giorgi Chakvetadze (78' Zuriko Davitashvili), Levan Shengelia
(72' Irakli Azarovi), Khvicha Kvaratskhelia (YC90+1), Georges Mikautadze (69' Budu
Zivzivadze). (Coach: Willy Sagnol (FRA)).
Scotland: Zander Clark, Scott McKenna, Greg Taylor (79' Stuart Armstrong (YC90+5)), Ryan
Porteous, Nathan Patterson (YC8) (79' Anthony Ralston), Callum McGregor, John McGinn,
Ryan Christie (YC37) (46' Lewis Ferguson), Scott McTominay, Billy Gilmour (46' Kenny
McLean), Lyndon Dykes (86' Lawrence Shankland). (Coach: Steve Clarke (SCO)).
Goals: Georgia: 1-0 Khvicha Kvaratskhelia (15'), 2-1 Khvicha Kvaratskhelia (57').
Scotland: 1-1 Scott McTominay (49'), 2-2 Lawrence Shankland (90+3').
Referee: Aleksandar Stavrev (MKD)   Attendance: 44.595
16-11-2023   Alphamega Stadium, Kolossi: Cyprus – Spain   1-3 (0-3)

Cyprus: Joël Mall, Anderson Correia (YC17) (46' Kostas Pileas), Kostas Laifis, Chambos Kyriakou (46' Charalampos Charalampous), Andreas Karo (YC59) (66' Ioannis Kousoulos (YC77)), Nikolas Ioannou, Stelios Andreou, Alexandros Gogic, Grigoris Kastanos, Hector Kyprianou (46' Danilo Spoljaric (YC87)), Ioannis Pittas (61' Andronikos Kakoullis). (Coach: Temur Ketsbaia (GEO)).

Spain: David Raya, Jesús Navas (66' Dani Carvajal), Álex Grimaldo, Robin Le Normand (46' David García), Pau Torres, Mikel Merino (46' Aleix García), Martín Zubimendi, Gavi, Joselu, Mikel Oyarzabal (40' Rodrigo Riquelme (YC82)), Lamine Yamal (73' Ferran Torres). (Coach: Luis de la Fuente (ESP)).

Goals: Cyprus: 1-3 Kostas Pileas (75').
Spain: 0-1 Lamine Yamal (5'), 0-2 Mikel Oyarzabal (22'), 0-3 Joselu (28').
Referee: Mykola Balakin (UKR)   Attendance: 9.667

19-11-2023   Hampden Park, Glasgow: Scotland – Norway 3-3 (2-2)
Scotland: Zander Clark, Scott McKenna (YC79), Jack Hendry, Greg Taylor, Nathan Patterson, Kenny McLean (70' Lewis Ferguson), Stuart Armstrong (70' Ryan Christie), Callum McGregor (89' Lawrence Shankland), John McGinn (79' Ryan Jack), Scott McTominay, Jacob Brown (70' Lyndon Dykes). (Coach: Steve Clarke (SCO)).

Norway: Egil Selvik, Kristoffer Ajer (YC10), Julian Ryerson, Fredrik Bjørkan, Leo Østigård, Fredrik Aursnes (60' Mohamed Elyounoussi), Patrick Berg (YC45), Sander Berge (YC59), Aron Dønnum (60' Kristian Thorstvedt), Oscar Bobb (89' Marcus Pedersen), Jørgen Strand Larsen. (Coach: Ståle Solbakken (NOR)).

Goals: Scotland: 1-1 John McGinn (13' penalty), 2-2 Leo Østigård (33' own goal), 3-2 Stuart Armstrong (59').
Norway: 0-1 Aron Dønnum (3'), 1-2 Jørgen Strand Larsen (20'), 3-3 Mohamed Elyounoussi (86').
Referee: Horatiu Fesnic (ROM)   Attendance: 48.138

19-11-2023   Estadio Municipal José Zorrilla, Valladolid: Spain – Georgia 3-1 (1-1)
Spain: Unai Simón, Dani Carvajal, Iñigo Martínez (YC90+4), José Gayà, Robin Le Normand, Fabián Ruiz, Rodri (YC56) (86' Martín Zubimendi), Gavi (26' Oihan Sancet), Álvaro Morata, Ferran Torres (65' Lamine Yamal), Nico Williams (86' Rodrigo Riquelme). (Coach: Luis de la Fuente (ESP)).

Georgia: Giorgi Mamardashvili, Guram Kashia (YC83), Solomon Kvirkvelia, Otar Kakabadze (89' Vladimir Mamuchashvili), Luka Lochoshvili, Irakli Azarovi (77' Giorgi Gocholeishvili), Nika Kvekveskiri (59' Anzor Mekvabishvili), Giorgi Kochorashvili, Giorgi Chakvetadze (89' Sandro Altunashvili), Khvicha Kvaratskhelia (YC75), Georges Mikautadze (59' Zuriko Davitashvili). (Coach: Willy Sagnol (FRA)).

Goals: Spain: 1-0 Robin Le Normand (4'), 2-1 Ferran Torres (55'), 3-1 Luka Lochoshvili (72' own goal).
Georgia: 1-1 Khvicha Kvaratskhelia (10').
Referee: Ovidiu Alin Hategan (ROM)   Attendance: 24.146

GROUP B

24-03-2023	Sain-Denis	France – Netherlands	4-0 (3-0)
24-03-2023	Faro/Loulé (POR)	Gibraltar – Greece	0-3 (0-2)
27-03-2023	Rotterdam	Netherlands – Gibraltar	3-0 (1-0)
27-03-2023	Dublin	Republic of Ireland – France	0-1 (0-0)
16-06-2023	Faro/Loulé (POR)	Gibraltar – France	0-3 (0-2)
16-06-2023	Athens	Greece – Republic of Ireland	2-1 (1-1)

19-06-2023	Saint-Denis	France – Greece	1-0 (0-0)
19-06-2023	Dublin	Republic of Ireland – Gibraltar	3-0 (0-0)
07-09-2023	Paris	France – Republic of Ireland	2-0 (1-0)
07-09-2023	Eindhoven	Netherlands – Greece	3-0 (3-0)
10-09-2023	Athens	Greeece – Gibraltar	5-0 (2-0)
10-09-2023	Dublin	Republic of Ireland – Netherlands	1-2 (1-1)
13-10-2023	Amsterdam	Netherlands – France	1-2 (0-1)
13-10-2023	Dublin	Republic of Ireland – Greece	0-2 (0-2)
16-10-2023	Faro/Loulé (POR)	Gibraltar – Republic of Ireland	0-4 (0-2)
16-10-2023	Athens	Greece – Netherlands	0-1 (0-0)
18-11-2023	Nice	France – Gibraltar	14-0 (7-0)
18-11-2023	Amsterdam	Netherlands – Republic of Ireland	1-0 (1-0)
21-11-2023	Faro/Loulé (POR)	Gibraltar – Netherlands	0-6 (0-3)
21-11-2023	Athens	Greece – France	2-2 (0-1)

FINAL STANDING

Pos	Team	Pld	W	D	L	GF	GA	GD	Pts
1	France	8	7	1	0	29	3	+26	22
2	Netherlands	8	6	0	2	17	7	+10	18
3	Greece	8	4	1	3	14	8	+6	13
4	Republic of Ireland	8	2	0	6	9	10	-1	6
5	Gibraltar	8	0	0	8	0	41	-41	0

France and Netherlands qualified for the Final Tournament in Germany.

Greece advanced to the play-offs due to their performance in the 2022-23 UEFA Nations League.

24-03-2023   Stade de France, Saint-Denis: France – Netherlands   4-0 (3-0)
France: Mike Maignan, Theo Hernández (YC90), Dayot Upamecano (YC90+4), Ibrahima Konaté (YC71), Jules Koundé, Adrien Rabiot (YC45) (89' Khéphren Thuram), Aurélien Tchouaméni (76' Eduardo Camavinga), Antoine Griezmann (77' Youssouf Fofana), Kingsley Coman (67' Moussa Diaby), Kylian Mbappé, Randal Kolo Muani (77' Olivier Giroud). (Coach: Didier Deschamps (FRA)).
Netherlands: Jasper Cillessen, Nathan Aké, Virgil van Dijk, Lutsharel Geertruida (YC65) (87' Tyrell Malacia), Jurriën Timber, Georginio Wijnaldum, Marten de Roon (67' Daley Blind (YC79)), Kenneth Taylor (33' Wout Weghorst), Xavi Simons (68' Davy Klaassen), Steven Berghuis (68' Donyell Malen), Memphis Depay. (Coach: Ronald Koeman (HOL)).
Goals: France: 1-0 Antoine Griezmann (3'), 2-0 Dayot Upamecano (8'), 3-0 Kylian Mbappé (21'), 4-0 Kylian Mbappé (88').
Referee: Maurizio Mariani (ITA)   Attendance: 77.328

Memphis Depay missed a penalty kick (90+5').

24-03-2023   Estádio Do Algarve, Faro/Loulé (POR): Gibraltar – Greece 0-3 (0-2)
Gibraltar: Dayle Coleing, Bernardo Lopes, Jack Sergeant, Jayce Olivero, Roy Chipolina, Ethan
Britto (85' Ethan Jolley), Liam Walker, Graeme Torrilla (62' Aymen Mouelhi), Julian
Valarino (62' James Coombes), Kian Ronan (86' Joseph Chipolina), Lee Casciaro (85' Reece
Styche). (Coach: Julio Ribas (URU)).
Greece: Odisseas Vlachodimos, George Baldock, Pantelis Hatzidiakos, Kostas Tsimikas
(YC71) (86' Dimitris Giannoulis), Konstantinos Mavropanos, Petros Mantalos, Anastasios
Bakasetas (71' Kostas Fortounis), Manolis Siopis, Dimitrios Pelkas (63' Giannis
Konstantelias), Georgios Masouras (85' Tasos Chatzigiovanis), Georgios Giakoumakis (63'
Vangelis Pavlidis). (Coach: Gustavo Poyet (URU)).
Goals: Greece: 0-1 Georgios Masouras (11'), 0-2 Manolis Siopis (45'),
0-3 Anastasios Bakasetas (58').
Referee: Rohit Saggi (NOR)   Attendance: 390

*Gibraltar played their home matches at Estádio Do Algarve, Faro/Loulé, Portugal, due to the
redevelopment of their regular stadium Victoria Stadium, Gibraltar.*

27-03-2023   De Kuip, Rotterdam: Netherlands – Gibraltar 3-0 (1-0)
Netherlands: Jasper Cillessen, Nathan Aké, Virgil van Dijk, Denzel Dumfries, Matthijs de Ligt
(76' Tyrell Malacia), Georginio Wijnaldum (46' Cody Gakpo), Mats Wieffer (63' Daley
Blind), Xavi Simons, Steven Berghuis (46' Donyell Malen), Memphis Depay (63' Davy
Klaassen), Wout Weghorst. (Coach: Ronald Koeman (HOL)).
Gibraltar: Dayle Coleing, Bernardo Lopes, Jack Sergeant, Jayce Olivero, Roy Chipolina, Ethan
Britto, Liam Walker (RC51), Graeme Torrilla (86' Niels Hartman), Kian Ronan (76' Aymen
Mouelhi), James Coombes (65' Ethan Jolley), Lee Casciaro (YC12) (86' Julian Valarino).
(Coach: Julio Ribas (URU)).
Goals: Netherlands: 1-0 Memphis Depay (23'), 2-0 Nathan Aké (50'), 3-0 Nathan Aké (82').
Referee: Morten Krogh Hansen (DEN)   Attendance: 36.327

27-03-2023   Avica Stadium, Dublin: Republic of Ireland – France 0-1 (0-0)
Republic of Ireland: Gavin Bazunu, Séamus Coleman, John Egan (YC90), Matt Doherty
(YC65) (77' James McClean), Dara O'Shea (77' Alan Browne), Nathan Collins, Josh Cullen,
Jayson Molumby (YC77) (86' Michael Obafemi), Jason Knight (77' Mikey Johnston),
Chiedozie Ogbene, Evan Ferguson (65' Adam Idah (YC88)). (Coach: Stephen Kenny (IRL)).
France: Mike Maignan, Benjamin Pavard (YC22) (81' Jules Koundé), Theo Hernández, Dayot
Upamecano, Ibrahima Konaté, Adrien Rabiot (81' Aurélien Tchouaméni), Eduardo
Camavinga, Olivier Giroud (65' Moussa Diaby), Antoine Griezmann, Kylian Mbappé, Randal
Kolo Muani (90+4' Marcus Thuram). (Coach: Didier Deschamps (FRA)).
Goal: France: 0-1 Benjamin Pavard (50').
Referee: Artur Soares Dias (POR)   Attendance: 50.219

16-06-2023   Estádio Do Algarve, Faro/Loulé (POR): Gibraltar – France 0-3 (0-2)
Gibraltar: Dayle Coleing, Bernardo Lopes, Jack Sergeant, Jayce Olivero, Roy Chipolina, Ethan
Britto, Kian Ronan (72' Scott Wiseman), Ayoub El Hmidi (60' Aymen Mouelhi), Nicholas
Pozo (84' Joseph Chipolina), Niels Hartman (60' Louie Annesley), Lee Casciaro (60' Tjay De
Barr). (Coach: Julio Ribas (URU)).
France: Brice Samba, Benjamin Pavard, Theo Hernández, Ibrahima Konaté (84' Axel Disasi),
Wesley Fofana, Aurélien Tchouaméni, Eduardo Camavinga (79' Youssouf Fofana), Olivier
Giroud (65' Randal Kolo Muani), Antoine Griezmann (65' Christopher Nkunku), Kingsley
Coman (65' Ousmane Dembélé), Kylian Mbappé. (Coach: Didier Deschamps (FRA)).
Goals: France: 0-1 Olivier Giroud (3'), 0-2 Kylian Mbappé (45+3' penalty),
0-3 Aymen Mouelhi (78' own goal).
Referee: Yevhen Aranovskyi (UKR)   Attendance: 4.065

16-06-2023   OPAP Arena, Athens: Greece – Republic of Ireland 2-1 (1-1)
Greece: Odisseas Vlachodimos, George Baldock, Pantelis Hatzidiakos, Kostas Tsimikas,
Konstantinos Mavropanos, Petros Mantalos (YC35) (90' Manolis Siopis), Dimitrios Kourbelis,
Anastasios Bakasetas (YC76) (90+4' Giorgos Tzavellas (YC90+6)), Dimitrios Pelkas (YC65)
(71' Taxiarchis Fountas), Georgios Masouras, Vangelis Pavlidis (71' Georgios Giakoumakis).
(Coach: Gustavo Poyet (URU)).
Republic of Ireland: Gavin Bazunu, John Egan (YC88), Darragh Lenihan (89' Troy Parrott),
Matt Doherty (RC90+5), Nathan Collins, Callum O'Dowda (53' James McClean (YC76)),
Josh Cullen, Jayson Molumby (81' Michael Obafemi), Will Smallbone (53' Jason Knight),
Adam Idah (46' Mikey Johnston), Evan Ferguson. (Coach: Stephen Kenny (IRL)).
Goals: Greece: 1-0 Anastasios Bakasetas (15' penalty), 2-1 Georgios Masouras (49').
Republic of Ireland: 1-1 Nathan Collins (27').
Referee: Harald Lechner (AUT)   Attendance: 17.452

19-06-2023   Stade de France, Saint-Denis: France – Greece 1-0 (0-0)
France: Mike Maignan, Theo Hernández, Dayot Upamecano, Ibrahima Konaté, Jules Koundé,
Aurélien Tchouaméni, Eduardo Camavinga, Antoine Griezmann (86' Christopher Nkunku),
Kingsley Coman (77' Ousmane Dembélé), Kylian Mbappé, Randal Kolo Muani (86' Olivier
Giroud). (Coach: Didier Deschamps (FRA)).
Greece: Odisseas Vlachodimos, George Baldock, Pantelis Hatzidiakos (YC69), Kostas
Tsimikas, Konstantinos Mavropanos (YC50,RC69), Petros Mantalos, Dimitrios Kourbelis
(YC70) (86' Andreas Bouchalakis), Anastasios Bakasetas (71' Panagiotis Retsos), Manolis
Siopis (YC49) (66' Taxiarchis Fountas), Georgios Masouras (71' Konstantinos Koulierakis),
Georgios Giakoumakis (66' Vangelis Pavlidis). (Coach: Gustavo Poyet (URU)).
Goal: France: 1-0 Kylian Mbappé (56' penalty).
Referee: Antonio Mateu Lahoz (ESP)   Attendance: 76.500

19-06-2023   Aviva Stadium, Dublin: Republic of Ireland – Gibraltar 3-0 (0-0)
Republic of Ireland: Gavin Bazunu, John Egan, Dara O'Shea, Nathan Collins (46' Mikey
Johnston), James McClean, Jamie McGrath, Josh Cullen, Will Smallbone (72' Alan Browne),
Jason Knight (85' Jeff Hendrick), Michael Obafemi (58' Troy Parrott), Evan Ferguson (84'
Adam Idah). (Coach: Stephen Kenny (IRL)).
Gibraltar: Dayle Coleing, Bernardo Lopes, Jack Sergeant (YC35) (46' Scott Wiseman), Jayce
Olivero, Roy Chipolina (43' Aymen Mouelhi), Ethan Britto (73' Scott Ballantine), Louie
Annesley, Kian Ronan, Ayoub El Hmidi (46' Tjay De Barr), Nicholas Pozo (68' Ethan Jolley
(YC70)), Niels Hartman. (Coach: Julio Ribas (URU)).
Goals: Republic of Ireland: 1-0 Mikey Johnston (52'), 2-0 Evan Ferguson (59'),
3-0 Adam Idah (90+2').
Referee: Marian Alexandru Barbu (ROM)   Attendance: 42.156

07-09-2023   Parc des Princes, Paris: France – Republic of Ireland   2-0 (1-0)
France: Mike Maignan, Lucas Hernández (72' William Saliba), Theo Hernández (YC21),
Dayot Upamecano, Jules Koundé (89' Benjamin Pavard), Adrien Rabiot, Aurélien
Tchouaméni, Olivier Giroud (26' Marcus Thuram), Antoine Griezmann (YC87) (89' Eduardo
Camavinga), Ousmane Dembélé (72' Kingsley Coman), Kylian Mbappé. (Coach: Didier
Deschamps (FRA)).
Republic of Ireland: Gavin Bazunu, Enda Stevens (46' James McClean), Shane Duffy, John
Egan, Nathan Collins, Alan Browne, Josh Cullen (YC47), Jayson Molumby (67' Dara
O'Shea), Jason Knight, Chiedozie Ogbene (84' Festy Ebosele), Adam Idah (67' Will Keane,
78' Aaron Connolly). (Coach: Stephen Kenny (IRL)).
Goals: France: 1-0 Aurélien Tchouaméni (19'), 2-0 Marcus Thuram (48').
Referee: Urs Schnyder (SUI)   Attendance: 43.995

07-09-2023   Philips Stadion, Eindhoven: Netherlands – Greece   3-0 (3-0)
Netherlands: Mark Flekken, Daley Blind, Nathan Aké (YC43) (46' Stefan de Vrij), Virgil van
Dijk (YC90+1), Denzel Dumfries (85' Matthijs de Ligt), Lutsharel Geertruida, Marten de Roon
(65' Tijjani Reijnders), Frenkie de Jong (77' Joey Veerman), Xavi Simons, Wout Weghorst,
Cody Gakpo (65' Noa Lang). (Coach: Ronald Koeman (HOL)).
Greece: Odisseas Vlachodimos, Pantelis Hatzidiakos, Panagiotis Retsos, Kostas Tsimikas
(YC44), Lazaros Rota (69' Dimitris Giannoulis), Petros Mantalos (YC75), Dimitrios Kourbelis
(YC68) (69' Konstantinos Koulierakis), Anastasios Bakasetas (77' Andreas Bouchalakis),
Manolis Siopis (YC11), Georgios Masouras (69' Taxiarchis Fountas), Vangelis Pavlidis (73'
Georgios Giakoumakis). (Coach: Gustavo Poyet (URU)).
Goals: Netherlands: 1-0 Marten de Roon (17'), 2-0 Cody Gakpo (31'),
3-0 Wout Weghorst (39').
Referee: Michael Oliver (ENG)   Attendance: 32.079

10-09-2023   OPAP Arena, Athens: Greece – Gibraltar   5-0 (2-0)
Greece: Odisseas Vlachodimos, Dimitris Giannoulis, Pantelis Hatzidiakos, Konstantinos
Mavropanos, Lazaros Rota (84' Tasos Chatzigiovanis), Andreas Bouchalakis (68' Giannis
Papanikolaou), Anastasios Bakasetas, Dimitrios Pelkas (84' Sotirioa Alexandropoulos),
Georgios Masouras, Taxiarchis Fountas (68' Fotis Ioannidis), Vangelis Pavlidis (68' Georgios
Giakoumakis). (Coach: Gustavo Poyet (URU)).
Gibraltar: Dayle Coleing, Aymen Mouelhi (90' Ethan Santos), Jack Sergeant, Ethan Jolley,
Roy Chipolina, Ethan Britto, Liam Walker, Kian Ronan, Nicholas Pozo (YC58) (90' Lee
Casciaro), Niels Hartman (84' Mohamed Badr), Tjay De Barr. (Coach: Julio Ribas (URU)).
Goals: Greece: 1-0 Dimitrios Pelkas (9'), 2-0 Konstantinos Mavropanos (23'), 3-0 Georgios
Masouras (70'), 4-0 Konstantinos Mavropanos (82'), 5-0 Georgios Masouras (90+1').
Referee: Manfredas Lukjancukas (LTU)   Attendance: 9.774

10-09-2023   Aviva Stadium, Dublin: Republic of Ireland – Netherlands   1-2 (1-1)
Republic of Ireland: Gavin Bazunu (YC19), Shane Duffy, John Egan (73' Jamie McGrath),
Matt Doherty (87' Festy Ebosele), Nathan Collins, James McClean (64' Ryan Manning), Alan
Browne (73' Will Smallbone), Josh Cullen, Jason Knight (YC67) (87' Sinclair Armstrong),
Chiedozie Ogbene (YC42), Adam Idah. (Coach: Stephen Kenny (IRL)).
Netherlands: Mark Flekken, Daley Blind (46' Wout Weghorst (YC87)), Nathan Aké, Virgil
van Dijk, Denzel Dumfries, Matthijs de Ligt, Frenkie de Jong, Mats Wieffer (YC16) (46'
Tijjani Reijnders), Xavi Simons (89' Steven Berghuis), Donyell Malen (81' Teun
Koopmeiners), Cody Gakpo (YC67) (81' Noa Lang). (Coach: Ronald Koeman (HOL)).
Goals: Republic of Ireland: 1-0 Adam Idah (4' penalty).
Netherlands: 1-1 Cody Gakpo (19' penalty), 1-2 Wout Weghorst (56').
Referee: Irfan Peljto (BIH)   Attendance: 49.807

503

13-10-2023   Johan Cruijff Arena, Amsterdam: Netherlands – France   1-2 (0-1)
Netherlands: Bart Verbruggen, Nathan Aké (80' Micky van de Ven), Virgil van Dijk, Denzel
Dumfries (YC51) (62' Jeremie Frimpong), Lutsharel Geertruida, Quilindschy Hartman, Marten
de Roon (46' Mats Wieffer), Joey Veerman (YC29), Tijjani Reijnders, Xavi Simons (80'
Steven Bergwijn), Wout Weghorst (38' Donyell Malen). (Coach: Ronald Koeman (HOL)).
France: Mike Maignan, Jonathan Clauss (80' Malo Gusto), Lucas Hernández, Theo Hernández,
Ibrahima Konaté, Adrien Rabiot, Aurélien Tchouaméni (YC90+4), Antoine Griezmann (87'
Youssouf Fofana), Kingsley Coman (71' Olivier Giroud), Kylian Mbappé (YC90+6), Randal
Kolo Muani (80' Marcus Thuram). (Coach: Didier Deschamps (FRA)).
Goals: Netherlands: 1-2 Quilindschy Hartman (83').
France: 0-1 Kylian Mbappé (7'), 0-2 Kylian Mbappé (53').
Referee: Felix Zwayer (GER)   Attendance: 51.310

13-10-2023   Aviva Stadium, Dublin: Republic of Ireland – Greece   0-2 (0-2)
Republic of Ireland: Gavin Bazunu, Shane Duffy, Matt Doherty, Liam Scales, Nathan Collins
(46' Ryan Manning), Alan Browne (70' Mikey Johnston), Josh Cullen, Will Smallbone
(YC10) (70' Callum Robinson), Jason Knight, Chiedozie Ogbene (85' Adam Idah), Evan
Ferguson. (Coach: Stephen Kenny (IRL)).
Greece: Odisseas Vlachodimos, Panagiotis Retsos, Kostas Tsimikas, Konstantinos
Mavropanos, Lazaros Rota, Petros Mantalos, Dimitrios Kourbelis (64' Andreas Bouchalakis
(YC75)), Anastasios Bakasetas (87' Manolis Siopis), Dimitrios Pelkas (YC56) (64' Tasos
Chatzigiovanis), Georgios Masouras (87' Konstantinos Koulierakis), Georgios Giakoumakis
(70' Fotis Ioannidis). (Coach: Gustavo Poyet (URU)).
Goals: Greece: 0-1 Georgios Giakoumakis (20'), 0-2 Georgios Masouras (45+4').
Referee: Glenn Nyberg (SWE)   Attendance: 41.239

16-10-2023   Estádio Do Algarve, Faro/Loulé (POR):
          Gibraltar – Republic of Ireland   0-4 (0-2)
Gibraltar: Dayle Coleing, Aymen Mouelhi, Jack Sergeant (YC84), Jayce Olivero (68' Lee
Casciaro), Roy Chipolina (83' Evan De Haro), Ethan Britto, Louie Annesley (YC53), Liam
Walker, Kian Ronan (83' Joseph Chipolina), Nicholas Pozo (68' James Coombes), Tjay De
Barr (68' Ayoub El Hmidi). (Coach: Julio Ribas (URU)).
Republic of Ireland: Gavin Bazunu, Shane Duffy, Matt Doherty (YC72), Ryan Manning, Liam
Scales (74' Dara O'Shea), Jamie McGrath (YC88), Josh Cullen (74' Jayson Molumby), Jason
Knight, Chiedozie Ogbene (83' Mark Sykes), Mikey Johnston (66' Callum Robinson), Evan
Ferguson (66' Adam Idah). (Coach: Stephen Kenny (IRL)).
Goals: Republic of Ireland: 0-1 Evan Ferguson (8'), 0-2 Mikey Johnston (28'),
0-3 Matt Doherty (61'), 0-4 Callum Robinson (80').
Referee: Christian-Petru Ciochirca (AUT)   Attendance: 4.000

504

16-10-2023   OPAP Arena, Athens: Greece – Netherlands   0-1 (0-0)
Greece: Odisseas Vlachodimos, Panagiotis Retsos (YC77), Kostas Tsimikas, Konstantinos Mavropanos, Lazaros Rota, Konstantinos Koulierakis (60' Manolis Siopis), Petros Mantalos (YC29) (82' Vangelis Pavlidis (YC86)), Dimitrios Kourbelis (YC13) (60' Andreas Bouchalakis), Anastasios Bakasetas (60' Taxiarchis Fountas), Georgios Masouras (77' Georgios Giakoumakis), Fotis Ioannidis. (Coach: Gustavo Poyet (URU) (RC90)).
Netherlands: Bart Verbruggen, Nathan Aké, Virgil van Dijk, Denzel Dumfries, Lutsharel Geertruida (YC13) (46' Donyell Malen), Quilindschy Hartman (74' Micky van de Ven), Tijjani Reijnders, Mats Wieffer (81' Marten de Roon), Xavi Simons (YC51) (62' Joey Veerman), Wout Weghorst (62' Brian Brobbey), Steven Bergwijn. (Coach: Ronald Koeman (HOL)).
Goal: Netherlands: 0-1 Virgil van Dijk (90+3' penalty).
Referee: Alejandro Hernández Hernández (ESP)   Attendance: 24.967

Wout Weghorst missed a penalty kick (28').

18-11-2023   Allianz Riveira, Nice: France – Gibraltar   14-0 (7-0)
France: Mike Maignan, Jonathan Clauss, Theo Hernández, Dayot Upamecano (81' William Saliba), Jean-Clair Todibo, Adrien Rabiot (66' Boubacar Kamara), Warren Zaïre-Emery (19' Youssouf Fofana), Antoine Griezmann, Kingsley Coman (66' Ousmane Dembélé), Marcus Thuram (66' Olivier Giroud), Kylian Mbappé. (Coach: Didier Deschamps (FRA)).
Gibraltar: Dayle Coleing, Joseph Chipolina (61' Jayce Olivero), Aymen Mouelhi, Jack Sergeant, Roy Chipolina, Ethan Santos (RC18), Liam Walker (61' Ethan Jolley), Evan De Haro, Nicholas Pozo, Lee Casciaro, Tjay De Barr (81' James Coombes). (Coach: Julio Ribas (URU)).
Goals: France: 1-0 Ethan Santos (3' own goal), 2-0 Marcus Thuram (4'), 3-0 Warren Zaïre-Emery (16'), 4-0 Kylian Mbappé (30' penalty), 5-0 Jonathan Clauss (34'), 6-0 Kingsley Coman (36'), 7-0 Youssouf Fofana (37'), 8-0 Adrien Rabiot (63'), 9-0 Kingsley Coman (65'), 10-0 Ousmane Dembélé (73'), 11-0 Kylian Mbappé (74'), 12-0 Kylian Mbappé (82'), 13-0 Olivier Giroud (89), 14-0 Olivier Giroud (90+1').
Referee: John Brooks (ENG)   Attendance: 32.758

18-11-2023   Johan Cruijff Arena, Amsterdam:
    Netherlands – Republic of Ireland   1-0 (1-0)
Netherlands: Bart Verbruggen, Daley Blind, Stefan de Vrij, Virgil van Dijk, Denzel Dumfries, Quilindschy Hartman, Jerdy Schouten (90' Marten de Roon), Tijjani Reijnders (90' Teun Koopmeiners), Xavi Simons (80' Donyell Malen), Wout Weghorst, Cody Gakpo (69' Joey Veerman). (Coach: Ronald Koeman (HOL)).
Republic of Ireland: Gavin Bazunu, Matt Doherty (77' Mikey Johnston), Ryan Manning, Dara O'Shea (90' Troy Parrott), Liam Scales, Nathan Collins, Alan Browne, Josh Cullen, Jason Knight (77' Jayson Molumby (YC90)), Callum Robinson (46' Adam Idah), Evan Ferguson (55' Jamie McGrath). (Coach: Stephen Kenny (IRL)).
Goal: Netherlands: 1-0 Wout Weghorst (11').
Referee: Marco Di Bello (ITA)   Attendance: 51.811

21-11-2023 Estádio Do Algarve, Faro/Loulé (POR):
Gibraltar – Netherlands 0-6 (0-3)
Gibraltar: Dayle Coleing, Joseph Chipolina (66' Mohamed Badr), Aymen Mouelhi, Jack Sergeant, Jayce Olivero, Roy Chipolina, Liam Walker (66' Ayoub El Hmidi), Evan De Haro (YC83), Nicholas Pozo (14' Ethan Jolley), Lee Casciaro (66' James Coombes), Tjay De Barr (82' Dylan Peacock). (Coach: Julio Ribas (URU)).
Netherlands: Bart Verbruggen, Stefan de Vrij, Virgil van Dijk (46' Jorrel Hato), Jordan Teze (YC45), Quilindschy Hartman (63' Xavi Simons), Teun Koopmeiners, Calvin Stengs, Joey Veerman (46' Tijjani Reijnders), Mats Wieffer, Wout Weghorst (46' Thijs Dallinga), Donyell Malen (77' Cody Gakpo). (Coach: Ronald Koeman (HOL)).
Goals: Netherlands: 0-1 Calvin Stengs (10'), 0-2 Mats Wieffer (23'), 0-3 Teun Koopmeiners (38'), 0-4 Calvin Stengs (50'), 0-5 Calvin Stengs (62'), 0-6 Cody Gakpo (81').
Referee: Arda Kardesler (TUR)   Attendance: 2.280

21-11-2023 OPAP Arena, Athens: Greece – France 2-2 (0-1)
Greece: Odisseas Vlachodimos, Dimitris Giannoulis, Pantelis Hatzidiakos, Panagiotis Retsos (YC40), Konstantinos Mavropanos, Lazaros Rota (85' Manolis Saliakas), Andreas Bouchalakis (YC34), Anastasios Bakasetas (85' Giannis Konstantelias), Georgios Masouras (77' Vangelis Pavlidis), Konstantinos Galanopoulos (67' Sotirios Alexandropoulos), Fotis Ioannidis (YC75) (77' Zeca). (Coach: Gustavo Poyet (URU)).
France: Brice Samba, Lucas Hernández (85' Axel Disasi), Theo Hernández, Jules Koundé (64' Jonathan Clauss), William Saliba, Adrien Rabiot, Youssouf Fofana (YC55), Olivier Giroud (70' Marcus Thuram), Antoine Griezmann (YC90+2), Ousmane Dembélé (YC34) (64' Kingsley Coman), Randal Kolo Muani (64' Kylian Mbappé). (Coach: Didier Deschamps (FRA)).
Goals: Greece: 1-1 Anastasios Bakasetas (56'), 2-1 Fotis Ioannidis (61').
France: 0-1 Randal Kolo Muani (42'), 2-2 Youssouf Fofana (74').
Referee: Daniel Siebert (GER)   Attendance: 24.820

GROUP C

23-03-2023	Napoli	Italy – England	1-2 (0-2)
23-03-2023	Skopje	North Macedonia – Malta	2-1 (0-0)
26-03-2023	London	England – Ukraine	2-0 (2-0)
26-03-2023	Ta'Qali	Malta – Italy	0-2 (0-2)
16-06-2023	Ta'Qali	Malta – England	0-4 (0-3)
16-06-2023	Skopje	North Macedonia – Ukraine	2-3 (2-0)
19-06-2023	Trnava (SVK)	Ukraine – Malta	1-0 (0-0)
19-06-2023	Manchester	England – North Macedonia	7-0 (3-0)
09-09-2023	Wroclaw (POL)	Ukraine – England	1-1 (1-1)
09-09-2023	Skopje	North Macedonia – Italy	1-1 (0-0)
12-09-2023	Milano	Italy – Ukraine	2-1 (2-1)
12-09-2023	Ta'Qali	Malta – North Macedonia	0-2 (0-2)
14-10-2023	Praha (CZE)	Ukraine – North Macedonia	2-0 (1-0)
14-10-2023	Bari	Italy – Malta	4-0 (2-0)
17-10-2023	London	England – Italy	3-1 (1-1)
17-10-2023	Ta'Qali	Malta – Ukraine	1-3 (1-2)
17-11-2023	London	England – Malta	2-0 (1-0)
17-11-2023	Roma	Italy – North Macedonia	5-2 (3-0)
20-11-2023	Skopje	North Macedonia – England	1-1 (1-0)
20-11-2023	Leverkusen (GER)	Ukraine – Italy	0-0

FINAL STANDING

Pos	Team	Pld	W	D	L	GF	GA	GD	Pts
1	England	8	6	2	0	22	4	+18	20
2	Italy	8	4	2	2	16	9	+7	14
3	Ukraine	8	4	2	2	11	8	+3	14
4	North Macedonia	8	2	2	4	10	20	-10	8
5	Malta	8	0	0	8	2	20	-18	0

England and Italy qualified for the Final Tournament in Germany.

Ukraine advanced to the play-offs due to their performance in the 2022-23 UEFA Nations League.

23-03-2023   Stadio Diego Armando Maradona, Napoli: Italy – England 1-2 (0-2)
Italy: Gianluigi Donnarumma, Rafael Tolói, Ffrancesco Acerbi (YC90+2), Leonardo Spinazzola, Giovanni Di Lorenzo (YC53), Marco Verratti (88' Gianluca Scamacca), Jorginho (YC61) (69' Sandro Tonali), Nicolò Barella (62' Bryan Cristante), Lorenzo Pellegrini (69' Wilfried Gnonto), Domenico Berardi (62' Matteo Politano), Mateo Retegui. (Coach: Roberto Mancini (ITA)).
England: Jordan Pickford, Kyle Walker (YC71), Harry Maguire (YC57), John Stones, Luke Shaw (YC78,YC80), Jack Grealish (69' Phil Foden, 81' Kieran Trippier), Kalvin Phillips, Declan Rice (YC29), Jude Bellingham (85' Conor Gallagher), Harry Kane, Bukayo Saka (85' Reece James). (Coach: Gareth Southgate (ENG)).
Goals: Italy: 1-2 Mateo Retegui (56').
England: 0-1 Declan Rice (13'), 0-2 Harry Kane (44' penalty).
Referee: Srdjan Jovanovic (SRB)   Attendance: 44.536

23-03-2023   Tose Proeski National Arena, Skopje:
North Macedonia – Malta 2-1 (0-0)
North Macedonia: Stole Dimitrievski, Stefan Ristovski, Visar Musliu, Gjoko Zajkov (90+2' Kire Ristevski), Darko Velkovski (58' Darko Churlinov), Ezgjan Alioski (YC47) (79' Stefan Askovski), Enis Bardhi (YC45+3), Eljif Elmas, Jani Atanasov (YC90+7), Aleksandar Trajkovski (58' Ilija Nestorovski), Bojan Miovski (YC61) (78' Milan Ristovski). (Coach: Blagoja Milevski (MKD)).
Malta: Henry Bonello, Steve Borg (YC89), Cain Attard (YC90+7), Ferdinando Apap, Bjorn Kristensen (YC44) (77' Yannick Yankam), Ryan Camenzuli (77' Juan Corbalan), Teddy Teuma (YC63) (84' Brandon Paiber), Matthew Guillaumier, Joseph Mbong, Alexander Satariano (84' Jodi Jones), Paul Mbong (67' Shaun Dimech). (Coach: Michele Marcolini (ITA)).
Goals: North Macedonia: 1-0 Eljif Elmas (66'), 2-0 Darko Churlinov (72').
Malta: 2-1 Yannick Yankam (85').
Referee: Kristo Tohver (EST)   Attendance: 9.991

26-03-2023   Wembley Stadium, London: England – Ukraine   2-0 (2-0)
England: Jordan Pickford, Kyle Walker, Harry Maguire, John Stones, Ben Chilwell, Jordan Henderson, James Maddison (85' Jack Grealish), Declan Rice, Jude Bellingham (85' Conor Gallagher), Harry Kane (81' Ivan Toney), Bukayo Saka. (Coach: Gareth Southgate (ENG)).
Ukraine: Anatoliy Trubin, Oleksandr Zinchenko, Oleksandr Svatok, Mykola Matvienko, Vitaliy Mykolenko (62' Eduard Sobol), Taras Stepanenko (90' Yevgen Konoplyanka), Ruslan Malinovskyi (YC69), Oleksandr Karavayev (61' Vitaliy Buyalskyi), Mykhaylo Mudryk (61' Viktor Tsygankov), Georgiy Sudakov, Roman Yaremchuk (74' Artem Dovbyk). (Coach: Ruslan Rotan (UKR)).
Goals: England: 1-0 Harry Kane (37'), 2-0 Bukayo Saka (40').
Referee: Serdar Gözübüyük (HOL)   Attendance: 83.947

26-03-2023   Ta'Qali National Stadium, Ta'Qali: Malta – Italy   0-2 (0-2)
Malta: Henry Bonello, Steve Borg, Cain Attard (63' Zach Muscat), Ferdinando Apap (83' James Brown), Juan Corbalan, Matthew Guillaumier, Yannick Yankam, Nikolai Muscat (76' Teddy Teuma), Joseph Mbong, Jodi Jones (76' Shaun Dimech), Alexander Satariano (64' Kyrian Nwoko). (Coach: Michele Marcolini (ITA)).
Italy: Gianluigi Donnarumma, Emerson, Giovanni Di Lorenzo (YC36) (46' Matteo Darmian), Alessio Romagnoli, Giorgio Scalvini (YC54) (83' Rafael Tolói), Bryan Cristante, Matteo Pessina, Sandro Tonali (67' Marco Verratti), Matteo Politano, Mateo Retegui (66' Gianluca Scamacca), Wilfried Gnonto (22' Vincenzo Grifo). (Coach: Roberto Mancini (ITA)).
Goals: Italy: 0-1 Mateo Retegui (15'), 0-2 Matteo Pessina (27').
Referee: Georgi Kabakov (BUL)   Attendance: 16.015

16-06-2023   Ta'Qali National Stadium, Ta'Qali: Malta – England   0-4 (0-3)
Malta: Henry Bonello, Steve Borg, Zach Muscat, Cain Attard (87' Juan Corbalan), Ferdinando Apap, Bjorn Kristensen (YC49) (60' Nikolai Muscat), Teddy Teuma, Matthew Guillaumier (46' Yannick Yankam), Kyrian Nwoko (60' Alexander Satariano), Joseph Mbong, Jodi Jones (76' Jurgen Degabriele). (Coach: Michele Marcolini (ITA)).
England: Jordan Pickford, Kieran Trippier, Harry Maguire, Luke Shaw (60' Tyrone Mings), Trent Alexander-Arnold, Marc Guéhi, Jordan Henderson (60' Marcus Rashford), James Maddison (69' Eberechi Eze), Declan Rice, Harry Kane (60' Callum Wilson), Bukayo Saka (46' Phil Foden). (Coach: Gareth Southgate (ENG)).
Goals: England: 0-1 Ferdinando Apap (9' own goal), 0-2 Trent Alexander-Arnold (28'), 0-3 Harry Kane (31' penalty), 0-4 Callum Wilson (83' penalty).
Referee: Igor Pajac (CRO)   Attendance: 16.277

16-06-2023   Tose Proeski National Arena, Skopje:
                North Macedonia – Ukraine   2-3 (2-0)
North Macedonia: Stole Dimitrievski, Stefan Ristovski (YC8), Visar Musliu (YC54,YC72), Gjoko Zajkov, Arijan Ademi (64' Jani Atanasov), Ezgjan Alioski, Enis Bardhi, Eljif Elmas, Ilija Nestorovski (65' Milan Ristovski), Stefan Askovski (64' Vladica Brdarovski, 90+1' Dorian Babunski), Aleksandar Trajkovski (75' Ljupco Doriev). (Coach: Blagoja Milevski (MKD)). (Not used sub: Damjan Shishkovski (YC90+5)).
Ukraine: Anatoliy Trubin, Mykola Matvienko, Oleksandr Tymchyk (46' Yukhym Konoplya), Vitaliy Mykolenko (YC90+5), Illya Zabarnyi, Taras Stepanenko, Andrey Yarmolenko (66' Ruslan Malinovskyi), Mykhaylo Mudryk (90' Sergiy Sydorchuk), Georgiy Sudakov, Viktor Tsygankov (90+3' Oleksandr Zubkov), Artem Dovbyk (YC45+1) (46' Vladyslav Vanat). (Coach: Serhiy Rebrov (UKR)).
Goals: North Macedonia: 1-0 Enis Bardhi (31' penalty), 2-0 Eljif Elmas (39').
Ukraine: 2-1 Illya Zabarnyi (62'), 2-2 Yukhym Konoplya (67'), 2-3 Viktor Tsygankov (83').
Referee: Lukas Fähndrich (SUI)   Attendance: 14.370

508

19-06-2023   CITY ARENA – Stadión Antona Malatinského, Trnava (SVK):
Ukraine – Malta   1-0 (0-0)
Ukraine: Anatoliy Trubin, Sergiy Kryvtsov, Mykola Matvienko (46' Vitaliy Mykolenko), Yukhym Konoplya, Illya Zabarnyi, Taras Stepanenko, Andrey Yarmolenko (81' Sergiy Sydorchuk), Ruslan Malinovskyi (YC56) (63' Vitaliy Buyalskyi), Georgiy Sudakov, Viktor Tsygankov (90+5' Oleksandr Svatok), Vladyslav Vanat (YC43) (63' Artem Dovbyk). (Coach: Serhiy Rebrov (UKR)).
Malta: Henry Bonello (45+3' Matthew Grech), Steve Borg (YC70), Jean Borg (YC51), Ryan Camenzuli, Teddy Teuma (87' Jake Grech (I)), Matthew Guillaumier, Yannick Yankam, Zach Muscat, Kyrian Nwoko (46' Alexander Satariano), Joseph Mbong (87' Jurgen Degabriele), Jodi Jones (62' Shaun Dimech). (Coach: Michele Marcolini (ITA)).
Goal: Ukraine: 1-0 Viktor Tsygankov (72' penalty).
Referee: Ruddy Buquet (FRA)   Attendance: 7.543

Andrey Yarmolenko missed a penalty kick (52').

Due to the Russian invasion of Ukraine, Ukraine were required to play their home matches at neutral venues until further notice.

19-06-2023   Old Trafford, Manchester: England – North Macedonia   7-0 (3-0)
England: Jordan Pickford, Kyle Walker, Harry Maguire, John Stones, Luke Shaw, Trent Alexander-Arnold, Jordan Henderson (58' Conor Gallagher), Declan Rice (YC41) (59' Kalvin Phillips (YC77)), Harry Kane (74' Callum Wilson), Marcus Rashford (58' Jack Grealish), Bukayo Saka (59' Phil Foden). (Coach: Gareth Southgate (ENG)).
North Macedonia: Stole Dimitrievski, Stefan Ristovski (46' Egzon Bejtulai (YC72)), Gjoko Zajkov (57' Nikola Serafimov), Darko Velkovski, Arijan Ademi (58' Jani Atanasov), Ezgjan Alioski, Enis Bardhi (67' David Babunski), Eljif Elmas, Ilija Nestorovski, Stefan Askovski, Aleksandar Trajkovski (57' Dorian Babunski). (Coach: Blagoja Milevski (MKD)).
Goals: England: 1-0 Harry Kane (29'), 2-0 Bukayo Saka (38'), 3-0 Marcus Rashford (45'), 4-0 Bukayo Saka (47'), 5-0 Bukayo Saka (51'), 6-0 Kalvin Phillips (64'), 7-0 Harry Kane (73' penalty).
Referee: István Kovács (ROM)   Attendance: 70.708

09-09-2023   Tarczynski Arena, Wroclaw (POL): Ukraine – England   1-1 (1-1)
Ukraine: Georgiy Bushchan, Oleksandr Zinchenko (76' Vitaliy Buyalskyi), Mykola Matvienko (46' Sergiy Kryvtsov), Vitaliy Mykolenko, Yukhym Konoplya, Illya Zabarnyi, Taras Stepanenko (YC22), Mykhaylo Mudryk (90' Yegor Nazaryna), Georgiy Sudakov (65' Sergiy Sydorchuk), Roman Yaremchuk (YC43) (65' Artem Dovbyk), Viktor Tsygankov. (Coach: Serhiy Rebrov (UKR)).
England: Jordan Pickford, Kyle Walker, Harry Maguire (YC86), Ben Chilwell, Marc Guéhi, Jordan Henderson, James Maddison (YC34) (65' Phil Foden), Declan Rice, Jude Bellingham (65' Marcus Rashford), Harry Kane, Bukayo Saka (86' Conor Gallagher). (Coach: Gareth Southgate (ENG)).
Goals: Ukraine: 1-0 Oleksandr Zinchenko (26').
England: 1-1 Kyle Walker (41').
Referee: Georgi Kabakov (BUL)   Attendance: 39.000

509

09-09-2023　　　　Tose Proeski National Arena, Skopje:
North Macedonia – Italy　1-1 (0-0)
North Macedonia: Stole Dimitrievski, Visar Musliu, Gjoko Zajkov, Jovan Manev (YC68), Ezgjan Alioski, Enis Bardhi, Eljif Elmas, Jani Atanasov (90+1' Ahmed Iljazovski), Agon Elezi (74' Isnik Alimi (YC88)), Stefan Askovski (74' Bojan Dimoski), Bojan Miovski. (Coach: Blagoja Milevski (MKD)).
Italy: Gianluigi Donnarumma, Giovanni Di Lorenzo, Federico Dimarco (YC70) (82' Cristiano Biraghi), Gianluca Mancini (59' Giorgio Scalvini), Alessandro Bastoni, Bryan Cristante, Mattia Zaccagni (82' Wilfried Gnonto), Nicolò Barella, Sandro Tonali (YC75) (89' Giacomo Raspadori), Ciro Immobile, Matteo Politano (46' Nicolò Zaniolo (YC79)). (Coach: Luciano Spalletti (ITA)).
Goals: North Macedonia: 1-1 Enis Bardhi (81').
Italy: 0-1 Ciro Immobile (47').
Referee: François Letexier (FRA)　　　　　　Attendance: 28.126

12-09-2023　　　　Stadio Giuseppe Meazza, Milano: Italy – Ukraine　2-1 (2-1)
Italy: Gianluigi Donnarumma, Giovanni Di Lorenzo, Federico Dimarco (58' Cristiano Biraghi), Alessandro Bastoni, Giorgio Scalvini, Mattia Zaccagni (58' Wilfried Gnonto), Nicolò Barella (84' Bryan Cristante), Manuel Locatelli, Davide Frattesi, Nicolò Zaniolo (72' Riccardo Orsolini), Giacomo Raspadori (72' Mateo Retegui) (Coach: Luciano Spalletti (ITA)).
Ukraine: Georgiy Bushchan, Sergiy Kryvtsov, Oleksandr Zinchenko (75' Vitaliy Buyalskyi), Vitaliy Mykolenko (YC38), Yukhym Konoplya (YC62), Illya Zabarnyi (YC78), Taras Stepanenko (YC76) (84' Sergiy Sydorchuk), Andrey Yarmolenko (58' Mykhaylo Mudryk), Georgiy Sudakov, Viktor Tsygankov (75' Vladyslav Vanat), Artem Dovbyk (58' Roman Yaremchuk). (Coach: Serhiy Rebrov (UKR)).
Goals: Italy: 1-0 Davide Frattesi (12'), 2-0 Davide Frattesi (29').
Ukraine: 2-1 Andrey Yarmolenko (41').
Referee: Alejandro Hernández Hernández (ESP)　　　　Attendance: 58.386

12-09-2023　　　　Ta'Qali National Stadium, Ta'Qali: Malta – North Macedonia　0-2 (0-2)
Malta: Henry Bonello, Steve Borg (YC39), Enrico Pepe, Zach Muscat, Bjorn Kristensen (46' Yannick Yankam), Ryan Camenzuli (YC66), Teddy Teuma (YC27), Matthew Guillaumier (89' Brandon Paiber), Kyrian Nwoko (72' Paul Mbong), Joseph Mbong (46' Cain Attard), Jodi Jones (46' Luke Montebello). (Coach: Michele Marcolini (ITA)).
North Macedonia: Damjan Shishkovski (YC85), Visar Musliu, Gjoko Zajkov (79' Nikola Serafimov), Jovan Manev (YC87), Ezgjan Alioski, Isnik Alimi, Enis Bardhi, Eljif Elmas, Jani Atanasov (80' Agon Elezi), Bojan Dimoski (86' Stefan Askovski), Bojan Miovski (90+3' Milan Ristovski). (Coach: Blagoja Milevski (MKD)).
Goals: North Macedonia: 0-1 Eljif Elmas (5'), 0-2 Jovan Manev (41').
Referee: Henrik Nalbandyan (ARM)　　　　　　Attendance: 3.158

14-10-2023　　　　epet ARENA, Praha (CZE): Ukraine – North Macedonia　2-0 (1-0)
Ukraine: Anatoliy Trubin, Oleksandr Zinchenko (YC90+6) (76' Sergiy Sydorchuk), Mykola Matvienko, Vitaliy Mykolenko, Yukhym Konoplya, Illya Zabarnyi, Taras Stepanenko, Oleksandr Zubkov (68' Ruslan Malinovskyi (YC69)), Mykhaylo Mudryk (88' Oleksandr Karavayev), Georgiy Sudakov (87' Oleksandr Svatok), Artem Dovbyk (76' Roman Yaremchuk). (Coach: Serhiy Rebrov (UKR)).
North Macedonia: Stole Dimitrievski, Visar Musliu, Nikola Serafimov (YC90+2), Jovan Manev (46' Darko Churlinov), Ezgjan Alioski, Enis Bardhi, Eljif Elmas, Jani Atanasov (63' Arijan Ademi (YC90+4)), Agon Elezi (74' Ljupco Doriev), Stefan Askovski (46' Bojan Dimoski), Bojan Miovski (84' Aleksandar Trajkovski). (Coach: Blagoja Milevski (MKD)).
Goals: Ukraine: 1-0 Georgiy Sudakov (30'), 2-0 Oleksandr Karavayev (90+5').
Referee: Slavko Vincic (SVN)　　　　　　Attendance: 12.939

510

14-10-2023   Stadio Comunale San Nicola, Bari: Italy – Malta   4-0 (2-0)
Italy: Gianluigi Donnarumma, Matteo Darmian, Federico Dimarco (79' Destiny Udogie),
Gianluca Mancini, Alessandro Bastoni, Giacomo Bonaventura (87' Cristiano Biraghi), Nicolò
Barella (65' Davide Frattesi), Manuel Locatelli, Domenico Berardi (65' Riccardo Orsolini),
Moise Kean (79' Gianluca Scamacca), Giacomo Raspadori. (Coach: Luciano Spalletti (ITA)).
Malta: Henry Bonello, Enrico Pepe, Zach Muscat, Ferdinando Apap (YC54), Bjorn Kristensen
(66' Nikolai Muscat), Ryan Camenzuli, Matthew Guillaumier, Yannick Yankam (YC53) (84'
Kyrian Nwoko), Luke Montebello (55' Alexander Satariano), Joseph Mbong (66' Cain Attard),
Paul Mbong (YC44) (84' Brandon Paiber). (Coach: Michele Marcolini (ITA)).
Goals: Italy: 1-0 Giacomo Bonaventura (23'), 2-0 Domenico Berardi (45+1'),
3-0 Domenico Berardi (64'), 4-0 Davide Frattesi (90+3').
Referee: Duje Strukan (CRO)   Attendance: 56.186

17-10-2023   Wembley Stadium, London: England – Italy   3-1 (1-1)
England: Jordan Pickford, Kyle Walker, Kieran Trippier, Harry Maguire, John Stones (63'
Marc Guéhi), Kalvin Phillips (YC9) (70' Jordan Henderson), Declan Rice, Phil Foden, Jude
Bellingham (85' Jack Grealish), Harry Kane, Marcus Rashford. (Coach: Gareth Southgate
(ENG)).
Italy: Gianluigi Donnarumma, Francesco Acerbi (63' Alessandro Bastoni), Giovanni Di
Lorenzo (YC30), Destiny Udogie (YC10) (63' Federico Dimarco), Giorgio Scalvini (YC65),
Bryan Cristante, Nicolò Barella, Davide Frattesi, Stephan El Shaarawy (87' Riccardo Orsolini),
Domenico Berardi (78' Giacomo Raspadori), Gianluca Scamacca (63' Moise Kean). (Coach:
Luciano Spalletti (ITA)).
Goals: England: 1-1 Harry Kane (32' penalty), 2-1 Marcus Rashford (57'),
3-1 Harry Kane (77').
Italy: 0-1 Gianluca Scamacca (15').
Referee: Clément Turpin (FRA)   Attendance: 83.194

17-10-2023   Ta'Qali National Stadium, Ta'Qali: Malta – Ukraine   1-3 (1-2)
Malta: Henry Bonello, Steve Borg, Enrico Pepe, Jean Borg, Ryan Camenzuli, Matthew
Guillaumier, Yannick Yankam (86' Stephen Pisani (YC90+3)), Nikolai Muscat (69' Bjorn
Kristensen), Kyrian Nwoko (68' Alexander Satariano), Joseph Mbong (79' Cain Attard), Paul
Mbong (86' Luke Montebello). (Coach: Michele Marcolini (ITA)).
Ukraine: Anatoliy Trubin, Oleksandr Zinchenko (87' Oleksandr Pikhalyonok), Mykola
Matvienko (YC31) (46' Oleksandr Svatok), Vitaliy Mykolenko, Illya Zabarnyi, Sergiy
Sydorchuk, Oleksandr Karavayev (76' Oleksandr Zubkov (YC90+3)), Mykhaylo Mudryk,
Georgiy Sudakov (67' Yegor Nazaryna), Artem Dovbyk, Vladyslav Vanat (67' Yukhym
Konoplya). (Coach: Serhiy Rebrov (UKR)).
Goals: Malta: 1-0 Paul Mbong (12').
Ukraine: 1-1 Ryan Camenzuli (38' own goal), 1-2 Artem Dovbyk (43' penalty),
1-3 Mykhaylo Mudryk (85').
Referee: Morten Krogh Hansen (DEN)   Attendance: 3.547

17-11-2023 Wembley Stadium, London: England – Malta 2-0 (1-0)
England: Jordan Pickford, Kieran Trippier, Harry Maguire, Fikayo Tomori (YC26) (46'
Bukayo Saka), Trent Alexander-Arnold, Marc Guéhi, Jordan Henderson (61' Declan Rice),
Phil Foden, Conor Gallagher (46' Kyle Walker), Harry Kane (YC28), Marcus Rashford (61'
Cole Palmer). (Coach: Gareth Southgate (ENG)).
Malta: Henry Bonello, Steve Borg, Enrico Pepe, Jean Borg (79' Zach Muscat), Ryan
Camenzuli, Teddy Teuma, Matthew Guillaumier (YC39) (59' Bjorn Kristensen), Kemar Reid
(79' Kyrian Nwoko), Yannick Yankam, Joseph Mbong (86' Cain Attard), Paul Mbong (YC23)
(59' Jodi Jones). (Coach: Michele Marcolini (ITA)).
Goals: England: 1-0 Enrico Pepe (8' own goal), 2-0 Harry Kane (75').
Referee: Luís Godinho (POR)   Attendance: 81.388

17-11-2023 Stadio Olimpico, Roma: Italy – North Macedonia 5-2 (3-0)
Italy: Gianluigi Donnarumma, Matteo Darmian, Francesco Acerbi (YC89), Federico Dimarco,
Federico Gatti, Giacomo Bonaventura (62' Davide Frattesi), Jorginho (62' Bryan Cristante),
Nicolò Barella, Domenico Berardi (76' Stephan El Shaarawy), Federico Chiesa (62' Nicolò
Zaniolo (YC72)), Giacomo Raspadori (90' Gianluca Scamacca). (Coach: Luciano Spalletti
(ITA)).
North Macedonia: Stole Dimitrievski, Visar Musliu, Nikola Serafimov (YC87), Jovan Manev
(46' Stefan Askovski (YC81)), Arijan Ademi (46' Jani Atanasov), Ezgjan Alioski, Enis
Bardhi, Eljif Elmas (72' Darko Churlinov), Agon Elezi (64' Isnik Alimi), Bojan Dimoski,
Bojan Miovski (46' Milan Ristovski (YC84)). (Coach: Blagoja Milevski (MKD)).
Goals: Italy: 1-0 Matteo Darmian (17'), 2-0 Federico Chiesa (41'), 3-0 Federico Chiesa
(45+2'), 4-2 Giacomo Raspadori (81'), 5-2 Stephan El Shaarawy (90+3').
North Macedonia: 3-1 Jani Atanasov (52'), 3-2 Jani Atanasov (74').
Referee: Felix Zwayer (GER)   Attendance: 56.364

Jorginho missed a penalty kick (40').

20-11-2023 Tose Proeski National Arena, Skopje:
                         North Macedonia – England 1-1 (1-0)
North Macedonia: Stole Dimitrievski, Visar Musliu, Nikola Serafimov, Jovan Manev, Ezgjan
Alioski, Isnik Alimi (75' Tihomir Kostadinov), Enis Bardhi, Eljif Elmas (YC17), Jani
Atanasov (90+1' Agon Elezi), Bojan Dimoski (86' Stefan Askovski), Bojan Miovski (75'
Milan Ristovski). (Coach: Blagoja Milevski (MKD)).
England: Jordan Pickford, Kyle Walker, Harry Maguire, Trent Alexander-Arnold (YC56) (84'
Kalvin Phillips), Marc Guéhi, Rico Lewis (YC40), Jack Grealish (84' Marcus Rashford),
Declan Rice, Phil Foden, Ollie Watkins (58' Harry Kane), Bukayo Saka (84' Cole Palmer).
(Coach: Gareth Southgate (ENG)).
Goals: North Macedonia: 1-0 Enis Bardhi (41').
England: 1-1 Jani Atanasov (59' own goal).
Referee: Filip Glova (SVK)   Attendance: 27.982

Enis Bardhi missed a penalty kick (41').

20-11-2023   BayArena, Leverkusen (GER): Ukraine – Italy   0-0
Ukraine: Anatoliy Trubin, Oleksandr Zinchenko (86' Danylo Sikan), Oleksandr Svatok (90+1'
Ruslan Malinovskyi), Vitaliy Mykolenko, Yukhym Konoplya (YC79) (86' Oleksandr
Tymchyk), Illya Zabarnyi, Taras Stepanenko (80' Oleksandr Pikhalyonok), Mykhaylo Mudryk,
Georgiy Sudakov, Viktor Tsygankov (80' Oleksandr Zubkov), Artem Dovbyk. (Coach: Serhiy
Rebrov (UKR)).
Italy: Gianluigi Donnarumma, Francesco Acerbi, Giovanni Di Lorenzo, Federico Dimarco,
Alessandro Buongiorno (YC7), Jorginho (71' Bryan Cristante), Nicolò Barella, Davide
Frattesi, Nicolò Zaniolo (71' Matteo Politano, 90+1' Matteo Darmian), Federico Chiesa (80'
Moise Kean), Giacomo Raspadori (46' Gianluca Scamacca). (Coach: Luciano Spalletti (ITA)).
Referee: Jesús Gil Manzano (ESP)   Attendance: 26.403

GROUP D

25-03-2023	Yerevan	Armenia – Turkey	1-2 (1-1)
25-03-2023	Split	Croatia – Wales	1-1 (1-0)
28-03-2023	Bursa	Turkey – Croatia	0-2 (0-2)
28-03-2023	Cardiff	Wales – Latvia	1-0 (1-0)
16-06-2023	Riga	Latvia – Turkey	2-3 (0-1)
16-06-2023	Cardiff	Wales – Armenia	2-4 (1-2)
19-06-2023	Yerevan	Armenia – Latvia	2-1 (1-0)
19-06-2023	Samsun	Turkey – Wales	2-0 (0-0)
08-09-2023	Rijeka	Croatia – Latvia	5-0 (3-0)
08-09-2023	Eskisehir	Turkey – Armenia	1-1 (0-0)
11-09-2023	Yerevan	Armenia – Croatia	0-1 (0-1)
11-09-2023	Riga	Latvia – Wales	0-2 (0-1)
12-10-2023	Riga	Latvia – Armenia	2-0 (1-0)
12-10-2023	Osijek	Croatia – Turkey	0-1 (0-1)
15-10-2023	Konya	Turkey – Latvia	4-0 (0-0)
15-10-2023	Cardiff	Wales – Croatia	2-1 (0-0)
18-11-2023	Yerevan	Armenia – Wales	1-1 (1-1)
18-11-2023	Riga	Latvia – Croatia	0-2 (0-2)
21-11-2023	Zagreb	Croatia – Armenia	1-0 (1-0)
21-11-2023	Cardiff	Wales – Turkey	1-1 (1-0)

FINAL STANDING

Pos	Team	Pld	W	D	L	GF	GA	GD	Pts
1	Turkey	8	5	2	1	14	7	+7	17
2	Croatia	8	5	1	2	13	4	+9	16
3	Wales	8	3	3	2	10	10	0	12
4	Armenia	8	2	2	4	9	11	-2	8
5	Latvia	8	1	0	7	5	19	-14	3

Turkey and Croatia qualified for the Final Tournament in Germany.

Wales advanced to the play-offs due to their performance in the 2022-23 UEFA Nations League.

25-03-2023   Vazgan Sargsyan anvan Hanrapetakan Marzadasht, Yerevan:
Armenia – Turkey 1-2 (1-1)
Armenia: Arsen Beglaryan, Varazdat Haroyan (YC71), Taron Voskanyan (28' Styopa
Mkrtchyan (YC45), 54' Khoren Bayramyan), Nair Tiknizyan, Georgiy Harutyunyan, Kamo
Hovhannisyan, Tigran Barseghyan (YC80), Lucas Zelarayán (75' Sargis Adamyan), Eduard
Spertsyan (YC48), Ugochukwu Iwu, Norberto Briasco (76' Vahan Bichakhchyan). (Coach:
Oleksandr Petrakov (UKR)).
Turkey: Mert Günok, Onur Bulut (YC42), Çaglar Söyüncü (YC38), Merih Demiral (YC42)
(46' Salih Özcan), Ozan Kabak, Hakan Çalhanoglu, Ferdi Kadioglu (74' Eren Elmali), Orkun
Kökçü (73' Ismail Yüksek (YC90+1)), Cenk Tosun (46' Kerem Aktürkoglu), Enes Ünal (85'
Umut Nayir), Cengiz Ünder. (Coach: Stefan Kuntz (GER)).
Goals: Armenia: 1-0 Ozan Kabak (10' own goal).
Turkey: 1-1 Orkun Kökçü (34'), 1-2 Kerem Aktürkoglu (64').
Referee: José María Sánchez Martínez (ESP)   Attendance: 14.125

25-03-2023   Stadion Poljud, Split: Croatia – Wales 1-1 (1-0)
Croatia: Dominik Livakovic, Borna Sosa, Josip Juranovic (YC31), Josip Sutalo, Josko
Gvardiol, Luka Modric (90+2' Lovro Majer), Ivan Perisic, Marcelo Brozovic, Mateo Kovacic
(76' Mario Pasalic), Andrej Kramaric (76' Nikola Vlasic), Marko Livaja (53' Petar Musa).
(Coach: Zlatko Dalic (CRO)).
Wales: Danny Ward, Connor Roberts, Joe Rodon, Ethan Ampadu (YC25), Neco Williams,
Chris Mepham, Aaron Ramsey (64' Wes Burns), Dan James (64' Nathan Broadhead), Joe
Morrell (90+2' Jordan James), Harry Wilson (64' Sorba Thomas), Kieffer Moore (70' Tom
Bradshaw). (Coach: Rob Page (WAL)).
Goals: Croatia: 1-0 Andrej Kramaric (28').
Wales: 1-1 Nathan Broadhead (90+3').
Referee: João Pedro Pinheiro (POR)   Attendance: 33.474

28-03-2023   Yüzüncü Yil Atatürk Sütas Stadyumu, Bursa:
Turkey – Croatia 0-2 (0-2)
Turkey: Mert Günok, Zeki Çelik, Çaglar Söyüncü, Merih Demiral, Hakan Çalhanoglu (38'
Ismail Yüksek), Salih Özcan, Ferdi Kadioglu, Orkun Kökçü (67' Arda Güler), Enes Ünal (81'
Umut Nayir), Cengiz Ünder (81' Cenk Tosun), Kerem Aktürkoglu (67' Baris Yilmaz). (Coach:
Stefan Kuntz (GER)).
Croatia: Dominik Livakovic (YC62), Borna Barisic, Josip Sutalo, Josip Stanisic, Josko
Gvardiol (YC69), Luka Modric (84' Lovro Majer), Ivan Perisic (90+2' Luka Ivanusec),
Marcelo Brozovic, Mateo Kovacic, Mario Pasalic (65' Josip Juranovic), Andrej Kramaric (84'
Petar Musa). (Coach: Zlatko Dalic (CRO)).
Goals: Turkey: 1-0 Mateo Kovacic (20'), 2-0 Mateo Kovacic (45+4').
Referee: Andreas Ekberg (SWE)   Attendance: 37.750

28-03-2023   Cardiff City Stadium, Cardiff: Wales – Latvia 1-0 (1-0)
Wales: Danny Ward, Connor Roberts, Joe Rodon, Ethan Ampadu, Neco Williams, Chris
Mepham, Aaron Ramsey (90+2' Ollie Cooper), Dan James (73' Nathan Broadhead), Joe
Morrell, Harry Wilson (YC35) (90+4' Ben Cabango), Kieffer Moore. (Coach: Rob Page
(WAL)).
Latvia: Pāvels Steinbors, Roberts Savalnieks, Mārcis Oss, Andrejs Ciganiks (70' Renārs
Varslavāns), Vladislavs Sorokins (YC44) (46' Raivis Jurkovskis), Antonijs Cernomordijs
(YC58), Artūrs Zjuzins (YC62) (83' Aleksejs Saveljevs), Jānus Ikaunieks (59' Alvis
Jaunzems), Kristers Tobers, Vladislavs Gutkovskis, Roberts Uldrikis (82' Raimonds Krollis).
(Coach: Dainis Kazakevics (LVA)).
Goal: Wales: 1-0 Kieffer Moore (41').
Referee: Giorgi Kruashvili (GEO)   Attendance: 32.806

514

16-06-2023   Stadions Skonto, Riga: Latvia – Turkey   2-3 (0-1)
Latvia: Nils Purins, Roberts Savalnieks, Mārcis Oss (YC34), Andrejs Ciganiks (76' Eduards
Daskevics), Raivis Jurkovskis, Daniels Balodis, Eduards Emsis (YC51,YC83), Kristers Tobers
(YC66), Alvis Jaunzems (80' Dāvis Ikaunieks), Vladislavs Gutkovskis (76' Raimonds Krollis),
Roberts Uldrikis (86' Marko Regza). (Coach: Dainis Kazakevics (LVA)).
Turkey: Mert Günok, Abdülkerim Bardakçi, Zeki Çelik (YC32) (71' Eren Elmali), Merih
Demiral, Hakan Çalhanoglu, Ferdi Kadioglu (YC41) (89' Ozan Kabak), Orkun Kökçü (78'
Salih Özcan), Arda Güler (71' Baris Yilmaz), Umut Nayir, Cengiz Ünder, Kerem Aktürkoglu
(89' Irfan Kahveci). (Coach: Stefan Kuntz (GER)).
Goals: Latvia: 1-1 Eduards Emsis (51'), 2-2 Kristers Tobers (90+4').
Turkey: 0-1 Abdülkerim Bardakçi (22'), 1-2 Cengiz Ünder (61'), 90+5' Irfan Kahveci 2-3.
Referee: Tamás Bognár (HUN)   Attendance: 6.287.

16-06-2023   Cardiff City Stadium, Cardiff: Wales – Armenia   2-4 (1-2)
Wales: Danny Ward, Ben Davies, Connor Roberts, Joe Rodon (67' Neco Williams (YC85)),
Ethan Ampadu, Chris Mepham (YC70), Aaron Ramsey (67' Joe Morrell), Dan James (82'
Nathan Broadhead), Harry Wilson (82' Tom Bradshaw), Kieffer Moore (RC78), Brennan
Johnson (70' David Brooks). (Coach: Rob Page (WAL)).
Armenia: Ognjen Cancarevic (YC78), André Calisir (62' Varazdat Haroyan), Nair Tiknizyan
(YC70), Styopa Mkrtchyan (YC84), Georgiy Harutyunyan, Artak Dashyan, Tigran Barseghyan
(62' Vahan Bichakhchyan), Lucas Zelarayán (76' Norberto Briasco (YC90+7)), Eduard
Spertsyan, Ugochukwu Iwu, Grant-Leon Ranos (YC68) (88' Artur Serobyan). (Coach:
Oleksandr Petrakov (UKR)).
Goals: Wales: 1-0 Dan James (10'), 2-3 Harry Wilson (72').
Armenia: 1-1 Lucas Zelarayán (19'), 1-2 Grant-Leon Ranos (30'), 1-3 Grant-Leon Ranos (66'),
2-4 Lucas Zelarayán (75').
Referee: Georgi Kabakov (BUL)   Attendance: 32.774

19-06-2023   Vazgan Sargsyan anvan Hanrapetakan Marzadasht, Yerevan:
                    Armenia – Latvia   2-1 (1-0)
Armenia: Ognjen Cancarevic, Varazdat Haroyan (YC10), Nair Tiknizyan, Styopa Mkrtchyan,
Georgiy Harutyunyan, Artak Dashyan, Lucas Zelarayán (77' Artur Serobyan), Eduard
Spertsyan, Ugochukwu Iwu (90+5' Hovhannes Harutyunyan), Norberto Briasco (33' Vahan
Bichakhchyan), Grant-Leon Ranos (77' Tigran Barseghyan). (Coach: Oleksandr Petrakov
(UKR)).
Latvia: Nils Purins, Roberts Savalnieks, Mārcis Oss (69' Elvis Stuglis), Andrejs Ciganiks (64'
Eduards Daskevics), Raivis Jurkovskis, Daniels Balodis, Aleksejs Saveljevs (YC18), Kristers
Tobers (YC89), Alvis Jaunzems (YC51) (65' Maksims Tonisevs), Vladislavs Gutkovskis (65'
Raimonds Krollis), Roberts Uldrikis (YC81) (85' Marko Regza). (Coach: Dainis Kazakevics
(LVA)).
Goals: Armenia: 1-0 Nair Tiknizyan (35'), 2-1 Tigran Barseghyan (90+1' penalty).
Latvia: 1-1 Styopa Mkrtchyan (67' own goal).
Referee: Peter Královic (SVK)   Attendance: 13.450

515

19-06-2023   Samsun Yeni 19 Mayis Stadyumu, Samsun: Turkey – Wales   2-0 (0-0)
Turkey: Mert Günok, Abdülkerim Bardakçi, Zeki Çelik (YC16) (60' Eren Elmali), Merih
Demiral (YC47), Hakan Çalhanoglu, Salih Özcan (61' Arda Güler), Ferdi Kadioglu (73' Irfan
Kahveci (YC75)), Orkun Kökçü (89' Salih Uçan), Cengiz Ünder (YC51), Kerem Aktürkoglu
(46' Umut Nayir), Baris Yilmaz. (Coach: Stefan Kuntz (GER)).
Wales: Danny Ward, Connor Roberts (YC58), Joe Rodon, Ethan Ampadu, Neco Williams,
Chris Mepham, Aaron Ramsey (84' Jordan James), Dan James (62' Tom Bradshaw), Joe
Morrell (RC41), Harry Wilson (84' Nathan Broadhead), Brennan Johnson (46' Ben Cabango).
(Coach: Rob Page (WAL)).
Goals: Turkey: 1-0 Umut Nayir (72'), 2-0 Arda Güler (80').
Referee: Fabio Maresca (ITA)   Attendance: 28.766

Hakan Çalhanoglu missed a penalty kick (64').

08-09-2023   Stadion HNK Rijeka, Rijeka: Croatia – Latvia 5-0 (3-0)
Croatia: Dominik Livakovic, Borna Sosa (67' Borna Barisic), Josip Juranovic, Josip Sutalo,
Josko Gvardiol (46' Domagoj Vida), Luka Modric (61' Nikola Vlasic), Ivan Perisic, Marcelo
Brozovic (61' Mario Pasalic), Luka Ivanusec, Andrej Kramaric, Bruno Petkovic (67' Petar
Musa). (Coach: Zlatko Dalic (CRO)).
Latvia: Nils Purins, Kaspars Dubra, Roberts Savalnieks (56' Raimonds Krollis), Andrejs
Ciganiks (YC81), Vladislavs Sorokins, Antonijs Cernomordijs, Jānis Ikaunieks (76' Eduards
Daskevics), Eduards Emsis, Kristers Tobers (86' Aleksejs Saveljevs), Alvis Jaunzems (86'
Dāvis Ikaunieks), Roberts Uldrikis. (Coach: Dainis Kazakevics (LVA)).
Goals: Croatia: 1-0 Bruno Petkovic (3'), 2-0 Luka Ivanusec (13'), 3-0 Bruno Petkovic (44'),
4-0 Andrej Kramaric (68'), 5-0 Mario Pasalic (78').
Referee: Philip Farrugia (MLT)   Attendance: 8.152

08-09-2023   Yeni Eskisehir Stadyumu, Eskisehir: Turkey – Armenia 1-1 (0-0)
Turkey: Mert Günok, Zeki Çelik (61' Mert Müldür), Çaglar Söyüncü (YC79), Merih Demiral
(YC90+2), Cenk Özkaçar (72' Onut Bulut), Hakan Çalhanoglu, Orkun Kökçü, Ismail Yüksek
(61' Irfan Kahveci), Cengiz Ünder, Kerem Aktürkoglu (80' Bertug Yildirim (YC86)), Baris
Yilmaz (61' Halil Dervisoglu). (Coach: Stefan Kuntz (GER)).
Armenia: Ognjen Cancarevic (YC74), Varazdat Haroyan (YC82), Nair Tiknizyan (90+1'
Kamo Hovhannisyan), Styopa Mkrtchyan, Georgiy Harutyunyan, Artak Dashyan, Lucas
Zelarayán (83' Norberto Briasco), Vahan Bichakhchyan (YC27) (62' Artur Serobyan), Eduard
Spertsyan, Ugochukwu Iwu, Grant-Leon Ranos (62' Sargis Adamyan). (Coach: Oleksandr
Petrakov (UKR)).
Goals: Turkey: 1-1 Bertug Yildirim (88').
Armenia: 0-1 Artak Dashyan (49').
Referee: Daniele Orsato (ITA)   Attendance: 31,740

11-09-2023   Vazgan Sargsyan anvan Hanrapetakan Marzadasht, Yerevan:
Armenia – Croatia   0-1 (0-1)
Armenia: Ognjen Cancarevic, André Calisir, Nair Tiknizyan, Styopa Mkrtchyan, Georgiy Harutyunyan, Artak Dashyan, Lucas Zelarayán, Vahan Bichakhchyan (58' Artur Serobyan), Eduard Spertsyan, Ugochukwu Iwu (58' Kamo Hovhannisyan), Grant-Leon Ranos (68' Norberto Briasco). (Coach: Oleksandr Petrakov (UKR)).
Croatia: Dominik Livakovic, Borna Barisic, Josip Sutalo, Josip Stanisic (YC29), Josko Gvardiol (YC21), Luka Modric, Ivan Perisic, Marcelo Brozovic, Luka Ivanusec (74' Lovro Majer), Andrej Kramaric (69' Mario Pasalic), Bruno Petkovic (84' Petar Musa). (Coach: Zlatko Dalic (CRO)).
Goal: Croatia: 0-1 Andrej Kramaric (13').
Referee: Clément Turpin (FRA)   Attendance: 14.233

11-09-2023   Stadions Skonto, Riga: Latvia – Wales   0-2 (0-1)
Latvia: Roberts Ozols, Kaspars Dubra (YC27), Roberts Savalnieks (YC59), Andrejs Ciganiks (YC90+7), Antonijs Cernomordijs, Jānis Ikaunieks (YC64), Eduards Emsis (YC78), Kristers Tobers (YC89), Alvis Jaunzems (86' Eduards Daskevics), Roberts Uldrikis (86' Marko Regza), Raimonds Krollis. (Coach: Dainis Kazakevics (LVA)).
Wales: Danny Ward, Ben Davies, Connor Roberts, Joe Rodon, Ethan Ampadu, Neco Williams (YC52), Chris Mepham (YC90+3), Aaron Ramsey (49' David Brooks), Harry Wilson, Jordan James, Brennan Johnson (87' Tom Bradshaw). (Coach: Rob Page (WAL)).
Goals: Wales: 0-1 Aaron Ramsey (29' penalty), 0-2 David Brooks (90+6').
Referee: Michal Ocenás (SVK)   Attendance: 6,464

12-10-2023   Stadions Skonto, Riga: Latvia – Armenia   2-0 (1-0)
Latvia: Roberts Ozols, Roberts Savalnieks (88' Vladislavs Sorokins), Mārcis Oss (YC31,YC52), Andrejs Ciganiks, Daniels Balodis, Jānis Ikaunieks, Eduards Emsis (YC65), Aleksejs Saveljevs, Alvis Jaunzems (88' Dāvis Ikaunieks), Eduards Daskevics (55' Kaspars Dubra), Roberts Uldrikis (82' Marko Regza). (Coach: Dainis Kazakevics (LVA)).
Armenia: Ognjen Cancarevic, Varazdat Haroyan (YC31), Nair Tiknizyan, Styopa Mkrtchyan (59' Grant-Leon Ranos), Georgiy Harutyunyan, Artak Dashyan, Tigran Barseghyan (69' Edgar Sevikyan), Lucas Zelarayán (82' Vahan Bichakhchyan), Eduard Spertsyan, Ugochukwu Iwu, Norberto Briasco (69' Artur Serobyan). (Coach: Oleksandr Petrakov (UKR)).
Goals: Latvia: 1-0 Jānis Ikaunieks (39'), 2-0 Daniels Balodis (68').
Referee: Rade Obrenovic (SVN)   Attendance: 5.128

12-10-2023   Opus Arena, Osijek: Croatia – Turkey   0-1 (0-1)
Croatia: Dominik Livakovic, Borna Barisic (YC34) (80' Borna Sosa), Josip Sutalo, Josip Stanisic, Josko Gvardiol, Luka Modric (YC89), Marcelo Brozovic (YC12), Mateo Kovacic (80' Dion Beljo), Mario Pasalic (62' Lovro Majer), Josip Brekalo (63' Nikola Vlasic), Petar Musa (63' Bruno Petkovic (YC89)). (Coach: Zlatko Dalic (CRO)).
Turkey: Ugurcan Çakir (YC67), Abdülkerim Bardakçi, Samet Akaydin, Cenk Özkaçar, Hakan Çalhanoglu, Irfan Kahveci (65' Yunus Akgün (YC90+2)), Salih Özcan, Ferdi Kadioglu, Ismail Yüksek (86' Kaan Ayhan (YC90+1)), Kerem Aktürkoglu (86' Kenan Yildiz), Baris Yilmaz (YC16) (74' Bertug Yildirim (YC90)). (Coach: Vincenzo Montella (ITA)).
Goal: Turkey: 0-1 Baris Yilmaz (30').
Referee: Anthony Taylor (ENG)   Attendance: 12.812

15-10-2023   Medas Konya Büyüksehir Stadyumu, Konya: Turkey – Latvia   4-0 (0-0)
Turkey: Ugurcan Çakir, Abdülkerim Bardakçi (YC64), Samet Akaydin, Cenk Özkaçar, Hakan Çalhanoglu (86' Kaan Ayhan), Salih Özcan (YC17) (68' Berkan Kutlu), Ferdi Kadioglu (46' Zeki Çelik), Ismail Yüksek, Yunus Akgün (76' Yusuf Sari), Kerem Aktürkoglu (YC64), Baris Yilmaz (75' Cenk Tosun). (Coach: Vincenzo Montella (ITA)). (Not used sub: Irfan Kahveci (YC86)).
Latvia: Roberts Ozols (YC51), Kaspars Dubra, Roberts Savalnieks, Andrejs Ciganiks, Daniels Balodis, Jānis Ikaunieks, Aleksejs Saveljevs (46' Eduards Emsis (YC49)), Kristers Tobers (YC64), Alvis Jaunzems (86' Dāvis Ikaunieks), Eduards Daskevics (YC56) (59' Raimonds Krollis), Roberts Uldrikis (75' Marko Regza). (Coach: Dainis Kazakevics (LVA)).
Goals: Turkey: 1-0 Yunus Akgün (58'), 2-0 Cenk Tosun (84'), 3-0 Kerem Aktürkoglu (88'), 4-0 Cenk Tosun (90+2').
Referee: Enea Jorgji (ALB)   Attendance: 35.925

15-10-2023   Cardiff City Stadium, Cardiff: Wales – Croatia   2-1 (0-0)
Wales: Danny Ward, Ben Davies, Connor Roberts, Joe Rodon, Ethan Ampadu, Neco Williams, Chris Mepham, Harry Wilson (81' Nathan Broadhead), David Brooks (57' Dan James), Jordan James (YC86), Kieffer Moore. (Coach: Rob Page (WAL)).
Croatia: Dominik Livakovic, Domagoj Vida (YC22), Borna Barisic (59' Borna Sosa), Josip Juranovic (46' Josip Stanisic), Josko Gvardiol, Luka Modric, Marcelo Brozovic (YC89), Mateo Kovacic, Josip Brekalo (46' Mario Pasalic), Lovro Majer, Petar Musa (46' Dion Beljo). (Coach: Zlatko Dalic (CRO)).
Goals: Wales: 1-0 Harry Wilson (47'), 2-0 Harry Wilson (60').
Croatia: 2-1 Mario Pasalic (75').
Referee: Davide Massa (ITA)   Attendance: 31.240

18-11-2023   Vazgan Sargsyan anvan Hanrapetakan Marzadasht, Yerevan: Armenia – Wales   1-1 (1-1)
Armenia: Ognjen Cancarevic, André Calisir, Varazdat Haroyan (YC54), Nair Tiknizyan, Georgiy Harutyunyan, Artak Dashyan, Lucas Zelarayán, Vahan Bichakhchyan (72' Edgar Sevikyan), Eduard Spertsyan, Ugochukwu Iwu (63' Hovhannes Harutyunyan), Grant-Leon Ranos (72' Artur Miranyan). (Coach: Oleksandr Petrakov (UKR)).
Wales: Danny Ward, Ben Davies, Connor Roberts (78' Nathan Broadhead), Joe Rodon, Ethan Ampadu (YC55), Neco Williams, Chris Mepham (YC32), Harry Wilson (66' Dan James), David Brooks (50' Brennan Johnson), Jordan James (YC79), Kieffer Moore. (Coach: Rob Page (WAL)).
Goals: Armenia: 1-0 Lucas Zelarayán (5').
Wales: 1-1 Nair Tiknizyan (45+2' own goal).
Referee: Benoît Bastien (FRA)   Attendance: 14.271

18-11-2023   Stadions Skonto, Riga: Latvia – Croatia   0-2 (0-2)
Latvia: Roberts Ozols, Roberts Savalnieks, Andrejs Ciganiks, Antonijs Cernomordijs, Daniels Balodis, Jānis Ikaunieks, Aleksejs Saveljevs (YC65), Kristers Tobers (YC31), Alvis Jaunzems (89' Raivis Jurkovskis), Eduards Daskevics (89' Dmitrijs Zelenkovs), Roberts Uldrikis (83' Raimonds Krollis). (Coach: Dainis Kazakevics (LVA)).
Croatia: Dominik Livakovic, Martin Erlic, Josip Sutalo, Josip Stanisic, Josko Gvardiol, Luka Modric (86' Martin Baturina), Marcelo Brozovic, Luka Ivanusec (61' Mario Pasalic), Lovro Majer, Ante Budimir, Andrej Kramaric (80' Marco Pasalic). (Coach: Zlatko Dalic (CRO)).
Goals: Croatia: 0-1 Lovro Majer (7'), 0-2 Andrej Kramaric (16').
Referee: Urs Schnyder (SUI)   Attendance: 6,747

21-11-2023   Stadion Maksimir, Zagreb: Croatia – Armenia 1-0 (1-0)
Croatia: Dominik Livakovic, Borna Sosa, Josip Sutalo, Josip Stanisic (50' Josip Juranovic),
Josko Gvardiol, Luka Modric, Marcelo Brozovic, Luka Ivanusec (46' Mario Pasalic), Lovro
Majer (84' Luka Sucic), Ante Budimir (84' Martin Baturina), Andrej Kramaric (69' Marco
Pasalic). (Coach: Zlatko Dalic (CRO)).
Armenia: Ognjen Cancarevic, André Calisir, Nair Tiknizyan, Styopa Mkrtchyan, Georgiy
Harutyunyan, Kamo Hovhannisyan (86' Erik Piloyan (YC87)), Lucas Zelarayán (46' Vahan
Bichakhchyan), Hovhannes Harutyunyan (70' Artak Dashyan), Eduard Spertsyan, Edgar
Sevikyan (70' Artur Serobyan), Grant-Leon Ranos (73' Artur Miranyan). (Coach: Oleksandr
Petrakov (UKR)).
Goal: Croatia: 1-0 Ante Budimir (43').
Referee: Ivan Kruzliak (SVK)   Attendance: 20.398

21-11-2023   Cardiff City Stadiu, Cardiff: Wales – Turkey 1-1 (1-0)
Wales: Danny Ward, Ben Davies (YC68), Tom Lockyer, Connor Roberts (YC90+5), Joe
Rodon, Ethan Ampadu, Neco Williams (84' Kieffer Moore), Harry Wilson (80' Dan James),
Jordan James, Nathan Broadhead (62' David Brooks), Brennan Johnson (YC22). (Coach: Rob
Page (WAL)).
Turkey: Ugurcan Çakir (33' Altay Bayindir (YC90+5)), Abdülkerim Bardakçi, Samet
Akaydin, Cenk Özkaçar (46' Zeki Çelik (YC72)), Salih Özcan (YC89), Abdülkadir Ömür (33'
Yusuf Yazici (YC53)), Ferdi Kadioglu, Ismail Yüksek, Kerem Aktürkoglu (YC82), Yusuf Sari
(79' Kaan Ayhan), Baris Yilmaz (59' Kenan Yildiz). (Coach: Vincenzo Montella (ITA)).
Goals: Wales: 1-0 Neco Williams (7').
Turkey: 1-1 Yusuf Yazici (70' penalty).
Referee: Matej Jug (SVN)   Attendance: 32.291

GROUP E

24-03-2023	Praha	Czech Republic – Poland	3-1 (2-0)
24-03-2023	Chisinau	Moldova – Faroe Islands	1-1 (0-1)
27-03-2023	Chisinau	Moldova – Czech Republic	0-0
27-03-2023	Warszawa	Poland – Albania	1-0 (1-0)
17-06-2023	Tirana	Albania – Moldova	2-0 (0-0)
17-06-2023	Tórshavn	Faroe Islands – Czech Republic	0-3 (0-2)
20-06-2023	Tórshavn	Faroe Islands – Albania	1-3 (1-1)
20-06-2023	Chisinau	Moldova – Poland	3-2 (0-2)
07-09-2023	Praha	Czech Republic – Albania	1-1 (0-0)
07-09-2023	Warszawa	Poland – Faroe Islands	2-0 (0-0)
10-09-2023	Tórshavn	Faroe Islands – Moldova	0-1 (0-0)
10-09-2023	Tirana	Albania – Poland	2-0 (1-0)
12-10-2023	Tirana	Albania – Czech Republic	3-0 (1-0)
12-10-2023	Tórshavn	Faroe Islands – Poland	0-2 (0-1)
15-10-2023	Plzen	Czech Republic – Faroe Islands	1-0 (0-0)
15-10-2023	Warszawa	Poland – Moldova	1-1 (0-1)
17-11-2023	Chisinau	Moldova – Albania	1-1 (0-1)
17-11-2023	Warszawa	Poland – Czech Republic	1-1 (1-0)
20-11-2023	Tirana	Albania – Faroe Islands	0-0
20-11-2023	Olomouc	Czech Republic – Moldova	3-0 (1-0)

FINAL STANDING

Pos	Team	Pld	W	D	L	GF	GA	GD	Pts
1	Albania	8	4	3	1	12	4	+8	15
2	Czech Republic	8	4	3	1	12	6	+6	15
3	Poland	8	3	2	3	10	10	0	11
4	Moldova	8	2	4	2	7	10	-3	10
5	Faroe Islands	8	0	2	6	2	13	-11	2

Albania and Czech Republic qualified for the Final Tournament in Germany.

Poland advanced to the play-offs due to their performance in the 2022-23 UEFA Nations League.

24-03-2023   Fortuna Arena, Praha: Czech Republic – Poland   3-1 (2-0)
Czech Republic: Jirí Pavlenka, Jakub Brabec (YC36), Vladimír Coufal (69' David Doudera), David Jurásek (89' Jaroslav Zelený), Tomás Holes, Tomás Soucek (YC22), Alex Král, Ladislav Krejcí, Jan Kuchta (70' Antonín Barák), Adam Hlozek (89' Vaclav Cerný), Tomás Cvancara (65' Mojmír Chytil). (Coach: Jaroslav Silhavý (CZE)).
Poland: Wojciech Szczesny, Jan Bednarek, Matty Cash (9' Robert Gumny), Jakub Kiwior, Michal Karbownik (46' Michal Skóras), Piotr Zielinski, Karol Linetty (76' Damian Szymanski), Przemyslaw Frankowski, Krystian Bielik (46' Karol Swiderski), Sebastian Szymanski (64' Nicola Zalewski), Robert Lewandowski. (Coach: Fernando Santos (POR)).
Goals: Czech Republic: 1-0 ladislav Krejcí (1'), 2-0 Tomás Cvancara (3'), 3-0 Jan Kuchta (64').
Poland: 3-1 Damian Szymanski (87').
Referee: Anastasios Sidiropoulos (GRE)   Attendance: 19.045

24-03-2023   Stadionul Zimbru, Chisinau: Moldova – Faroe Islands   1-1 (0-1)
Moldova: Dorian Railean, Veaceslav Posmac, Victor Mudrac (73' Serafim Cojocari), Artur Craciun (YC45+1), Ioan-Calin Revenco, Vadim Rata, Mihail Caimacov, Sergiu Platica (72' Victor Stîna), Vitalie Damascan, Ion Nicolaescu, Virgiliu Postolachi (46' Nichita Motpan). (Coach: Serghei Clescenco (MDA)).
Faroe Islands: Mattias Lamhauge (YC85), Odmar Færø (79' Heini Vatnsdal (YC85)), Viljormur í Davidsen, Gunnar Vatnhamar (YC50), Sølvi Vatnhamar, René Joensen, Meinhard Olsen (79' Ári Jónsson (YC90+5)), Patrik Johannesen (63' Noah Mneney (YC86)), Jákup Andreasen, Mads Mikkelsen (71' Gilli Rólantsson (YC78)), Klæmint Olsen (79' Páll Klettskarð). (Coach: Håkan Ericson (SWE)).
Goals: Moldova: 1-1 Ion Nicolaescu (87' penalty).
Faroe Islands: 0-1 Mads Mikkelsen (27').
Referee: Nicholas Walsh (SCO)   Attendance: 4,732

520

27-03-2023   Stadionul Zimbru, Chisinau: Moldova – Czech Republic   0-0
Moldova: Dorian Railean, Veaceslav Posmac, Victor Mudrac, Artur Craciun, Ioan-Calin
Revenco (83' Sergiu Platica), Serafim Cojocari, Vadim Rata, Mihail Caimacov (YC90+4),
Nichita Motpan (59' Virgiliu Postolachi), Vitalie Damascan (14' Maxim Cojocaru), Ion
Nicolaescu (82' Victor Stîna). (Coach: Serghei Clescenco (MDA)).
Czech Republic: Jirí Pavlenka, Jakub Brabec, Vladimír Coufal (YC48), Václav Jemelka, David
Jurásek, Tomás Holes, Antonín Barák (73' Petr Sevcík (YC88)), Tomás Soucek, Jan Kuchta
(73' Mojmír Chytil), Adam Hlozek (82' Ondrej Lingr), Tomás Cvancara. (Coach: Jaroslav
Silhavý (CZE)).
Referee: Daniel Schlager (GER)   Attendance: 5.120

27-03-2023   Stadion Narodowy, Warszawa: Poland – Albania   1-0 (1-0)
Poland: Wojciech Szczesny, Bartosz Salamon (YC75), Jan Bednarek, Jakub Kiwior, Piotr
Zielinski, Karol Linetty (YC66) (78' Damian Szymanski (YC90+4)), Przemyslaw Frankowski,
Nicola Zalewski (68' Michal Skóras), Jakub Kaminski, Robert Lewandowski, Karol Swiderski
(88' Sebastian Szymanski). (Coach: Fernando Santos (POR)).
Albania: Thomas Strakosha, Elseid Hysaj (YC45), Iván Balliu Campeny, Marash Kumbulla,
Enea Mihaj, Klaus Gjasula (88' Qazim Laçi (YC90)), Ylber Ramadani, Kristjan Asllani (75'
Nedim Bajrami), Sokol Çikalleshi (75' Taulant Seferi), Jasir Asani (70' Anis Mehmeti), Myrto
Uzuni. (Coach: Sylvinho (BRA)).
Goal: 10' Karol Swiderski (41').
Referee: Slavko Vincic (SVN)   Attendance: 56.227

17-06-2023   Air Albania Stadium, Tirana: Albania – Moldova   2-0 (0-0)
Albania: Etrit Berisha, Elseid Hysaj, Berat Djimsiti, Ardian Ismajli, Mario Mitaj (YC21), Keidi
Bare (68' Kristjan Asllani), Ylber Ramadani, Nedim Bajrami (88' Ernest Muçi), Sokol
Çikalleshi, Jasir Asani (67' Anis Mehmeti), Myrto Uzuni (88' Taulant Seferi). (Coach:
Sylvinho (BRA)).
Moldova: Dorian Railean, Veaceslav Posmac, Victor Mudrac, Artur Craciun, Oleg Reabciuk,
Ioan-Calin Revenco (73' Serafim Cojocari), Vladyslav Baboglo (YC69) (73' Sergiu Platica),
Vadim Rata, Nichita Motpan (55' Victor Stîna), Vitalie Damascan (56' Maxim Cojocaru), Ion
Nicolaescu (65' Virgiliu Postolachi). (Coach: Serghei Clescenco (MDA)).
Goals: Albania: 1-0 Jasir Asani (51'), 2-0 Nedim Bajrami (76').
Referee: Dennis Hilger (HOL)   Attendance: 20,944

17-06-2023   Tórsvøllur, Tórshavn: Faroe Islands – Czech Republic   0-3 (0-2)
Faroe Islands: Teitur Gestsson, Odmar Færø, Heini Vatnsdal, Viljormur í Davidsen, Gilli
Rólantsson (YC65) (83' Hannes Agnarsson), Gunnar Vatnhamar, Sølvi Vatnhamar (84' Stefan
Radosavljevic), René Joensen, Jákup Andreasen (83' Rógvi Baldvinsson), Jóannes Bjartalíð
(58' Hanus Sørensen), Petur Knudsen (58' Jóan Símun Edmundsson). (Coach: Håkan Ericson
(SWE)).
Czech Republic: Jirí Pavlenka, Vladimír Coufal, David Jurásek, Tomás Holes, Vaclav Cerný
(81' Michal Sadílek), Tomás Soucek, Alex Král (89' Lukás Sadílek), Ladislav Krejcí, Václav
Jurecka (81' Jan Matousek), Jan Kuchta (69' Mojmír Chytil), Adam Hlozek (69' Lukás
Provod). (Coach: Jaroslav Silhavý (CZE)).
Goals: Czech Republic: 0-1 Ladislav Krejcí (15'), 0-2 Vaclav Cerný (44'),
0-3 Vaclav Cerný (75').
Referee: Arda Kardesler (TUR)   Attendance: 2.232

521

20-06-2023   Tórsvøllur, Tórshavn: Faroe Islands – Albania 1-3 (1-1)
Faroe Islands: Teitur Gestsson, Odmar Færø, Heini Vatnsdal, Viljormur í Davidsen, Gunnar Vatnhamar (80' Brandur Hendriksson), Hanus Sørensen, Sølvi Vatnhamar (80' Stefan Radosavljevic), René Joensen (YC49) (65' Petur Knudsen), Jákup Andreasen (46' Jóannes Bjartalíð), Jóan Símun Edmudsson (65' Andrass Johansen), Klæmint Olsen. (Coach: Håkan Ericson (SWE)).
Albania: Etrit Berisha, Elseid Hysaj, Berat Djimsiti, Ardian Ismajli, Mario Mitaj, Ylber Ramadani, Nedim Bajrami (75' Ernest Muçi), Kristjan Asllani (89' Keidi Bare), Sokol Çikalleshi (67' Myrto Uzuni), Taulant Seferi (89' Armando Sadiku), Jasir Asani (75' Anis Mehmeti). (Coach: Sylvinho (BRA)).
Goals: Faroe Islands: 1-1 Odmar Færø (45+1').
Albania: 0-1 Nedim Bajrami (20'), 1-2 Kristjan Asllani (51'), 1-3 Ernest Muçi (90+1').
Referee: Chrysovalantis Theouli (CYP)   Attendance: 2.507

Sokol Çikalleshi missed a penalty kick (32').

20-06-2023   Stadionul Zimbru, Chisinau: Moldova – Poland 3-2 (0-2)
Moldova: Dorian Railean (YC89), Veaceslav Posmac, Victor Mudrac, Artur Craciun, Oleg Reabciuk (YC90+2), Ioan-Calin Revenco, Vladyslav Baboglo (YC51), Cristian Dros (46' Nichita Motpan), Maxim Cojocaru, Vitalie Damascan (46' Virgiliu Postolachi), Ion Nicolaescu (YC81) (85' Serafim Cojocari). (Coach: Serghei Clescenco (MDA)).
Poland: Wojciech Szczesny, Tomasz Kedziora, Jan Bednarek, Jakub Kiwior, Piotr Zielinski, Przemyslaw Frankowski (64' Bartosz Bereszynski), Damian Szymanski (83' Karol Linetty), Sebastian Szymanski, Nicola Zalewski (65' Jakub Kaminski), Robert Lewandowski, Arkadiusz Milik (73' Karol Swiderski). (Coach: Fernando Santos (POR)).
Goals: Moldova: 1-2 Ion Nicolaescu (48'), 2-2 Ion Nicolaescu (79'),
3-2 Vladyslav Baboglo (85').
Poland: 0-1 Arkadiusz Milik (12'), 0-2 Robert Lewandowski (34').
Referee: Filip Glova (SVK)   Attendance: 9.442

07-09-2023   Fortuna Arena, Praha: Czech Republic – Albania 1-1 (0-0)
Czech Republic: Jirí Pavlenka, Jakub Brabec, Vladimír Coufal, Tomás Holes, Vaclav Cerný (70' Adam Hlozek), Lukás Provod (YC90+6), Tomás Soucek, Alex Král, Ladislav Krejcí (86' Mojmír Chytil (YC90+7)), Jan Kuchta (71' Václav Jurecka), Tomás Cvancara (87' Ondrej Lingr). (Coach: Jaroslav Silhavý (CZE)).
Albania: Etrit Berisha, Elseid Hysaj, Berat Djimsiti, Ardian Ismajli (YC90+7), Mario Mitaj, Ylber Ramadani, Nedim Bajrami (YC67) (85' Klaus Gjasula), Kristjan Asllani (69' Keidi Bare), Sokol Çikalleshi (58' Mirlind Daku), Taulant Seferi (84' Myrto Uzuni), Jasir Asani (YC52) (69' Arbnor Muja). (Coach: Sylvinho (BRA)).
Goals: Czech Republic: 1-0 Vaclav Cerný (56').
Albania: 1-1 Nedim Bajrami (66').
Referee: Anthony Taylor (ENG)   Attendance: 18.641

07-09-2023   Stadion Nadorowy, Warszawa: Poland – Faroe Islands 2-0 (0-0)
Poland: Wojciech Szczesny, Bartosz Bereszynski (59' Sebastian Szymanski), Tomasz
Kedziora, Jan Bednarek, Jakub Kiwior, Grzegorz Krychowiak (YC22) (80' Damian
Szymanski), Piotr Zielinski, Jakub Kaminski (88' Kamil Grosicki), Robert Lewandowski,
Arkadiusz Milik (59' Karol Swiderski), Michal Skóras (46' Pawel Wszolek (YC90+2)).
(Coach: Fernando Santos (POR)).
Faroe Islands: Mattias Lamhauge, Odmar Færø, Viljormur í Davidsen, Sonni Nattestad
(YC58), Hørður Askham, Gilli Rólantsson (74' Jóannes Danielsen), Gunnar Vatnhamar (88'
Stefan Radosavljevic), Sølvi Vatnhamar, René Joensen (74' Jákup Andreasen), Jóannes
Bjartalíð (61' Brandur Hendriksson), Jóan Símun Edmudsson (62' Klæmint Olsen). (Coach:
Håkan Ericson (SWE)).
Goals: Poland: 1-0 Robert Lewandowski (73' penalty), 2-0 Robert Lewandowski (83').
Referee: David Smajc (SVN)   Attendance: 54.129

10-09-2023   Tórsvøllur, Tórshavn: Faroe Islands – Moldova 0-1 (0-0)
Faroe Islands: Mattias Lamhauge, Odmar Færø, Viljormur í Davidsen, Gilli Rólantsson (46'
René Joensen), Gunnar Vatnhamar, Brandur Hendriksson, Jákup Andreasen (YC71) (80'
Hørður Askham), Jóannes Bjartalíð, Jóan Símun Edmudsson (64' Hannes Agnarsson),
Klæmint Olsen (80' Stefan Radosavljevic), Andrass Johansen (64' Sølvi Vatnhamar). (Coach:
Håkan Ericson (SWE)).
Moldova: Dorian Railean, Veaceslav Posmac, Denis Marandici, Artur Craciun, Ioan-Calin
Revenco, Vladyslav Baboglo, Vadim Rata (YC59) (77' Serafim Cojocari), Victor Stîna (46'
Virgiliu Postolachi), Nichita Motpan (YC10) (90+3' Victor Bogaciuc), Vitalie Damascan (46'
Maxim Cojocaru), Ion Nicolaescu (77' Mihai Platica). (Coach: Serghei Clescenco (MDA)).
Goals: Moldova: 0-1 Vadim Rata (53').
Referee: Vassilios Fotias (GRE)   Attendance: 2.710

10-09-2023   Air Albania Stadium, Tirana: Albania – Poland 2-0 (1-0)
Albania: Thomas Strakosha (YC59), Elseid Hysaj, Berat Djimsiti, Ardian Ismajli, Mario Mitaj,
Ylber Ramadani, Nedim Bajrami (80' Klaus Gjasula), Kristjan Asllani (YC45+8) (70' Keidi
Bare), Sokol Çikalleshi (YC45+1) (62' Mirlind Daku (YC63)), Jasir Asani (70' Arbnor Muja
(YC75)), Myrto Uzuni (62' Taulant Seferi (YC86)). (Coach: Sylvinho (BRA)). (Not used sub:
Frédéric Veseli (YC64)).
Poland: Wojciech Szczesny, Bartosz Bereszynski (YC45+8) (70' Karol Linetty), Tomasz
Kedziora (YC79), Jan Bednarek (YC8) (34' Mateusz Wieteska (YC88)), Matty Cash, Jakub
Kiwior, Grzegorz Krychowiak (YC60) (70' Michal Skóras), Piotr Zielinski, Sebastian
Szymanski (61' Karol Swiderski), Jakub Kaminski (YC45+7) (61' Kamil Grosicki), Robert
Lewandowski. (Coach: Fernando Santos (POR)).
Goals: 1-0 Jasir Asani (37'), 2-0 Mirlind Daku (62').
Referee: José María Sánchez Martínez (ESP) Attendance: 21.900

12-10-2023   Air Albania Stadium, Tirana: Albania – Czech Republic 3-0 (1-0)
Albania: Etrit Berisha, Elseid Hysaj, Berat Djimsiti, Arlind Ajeti, Mario Mitaj, Ylber
Ramadani, Nedim Bajrami (YC60) (67' Ernest Muçi), Kristjan Asllani, Sokol Çikalleshi (67'
Mirlind Daku), Taulant Seferi (86' Klaus Gjasula), Jasir Asani (54' Arbnor Muja). (Coach:
Sylvinho (BRA)).
Czech Republic: Jirí Pavlenka, Jakub Brabec, Vladimír Coufal (YC40), David Jurásek (86'
David Doudera), Tomás Holes (46' Lukás Provod (YC62)), Vaclav Cerný (64' Adam Hlozek),
Tomás Soucek, Michal Sadílek, Ladislav Krejcí, Jan Kuchta (64' Tomás Cvancara), Mojmír
Chytil (YC25,YC39). (Coach: Jaroslav Silhavý (CZE)).
Goals: Albania: 1-0 Jasir Asani (9'), 2-0 Taulant Seferi (51'), 3-0 Taulant Seferi (73').
Referee: Danny Makkelie (HOL)   Attendance: 20.917
12-10-2023   Tórsvøllur, Tórshavn: Faroe Islands – Poland 0-2 (0-1)

Faroe Islands: Mattias Lamhauge, Odmar Færø (YC90+4), Viljormur í Davidsen, Hørður Askham (RC48), Gunnar Vatnhamar, Sølvi Vatnhamar (90' Stefan Radosavljevic), Brandur Hendriksson (76' Ári Jónsson (YC85)), René Joensen, Jákup Andreasen (83' Jóannes Danielsen), Jóannes Bjartalíð (76' Andrass Johansen), Jóan Símun Edmudsson (76' Pætur Petersen). (Coach: Håkan Ericson (SWE)).

Poland: Wojciech Szczesny, Tomasz Kedziora, Matty Cash (YC16) (59' Pawel Wszolek), Jakub Kiwior, Patryk Peda, Piotr Zielinski (87' Filip Marchwinski), Przemyslaw Frankowski, Patryk Dziczek (82' Jakub Piotrowski (YC90+3)), Bartosz Slisz (YC90+4), Sebastian Szymanski (59' Karol Swiderski), Arkadiusz Milik (YC43) (59' Adam Buksa). (Coach: Michal Probierz (POL)).

Goals: Poland: 0-1 Sebastian Szymanski (4'), 0-2 Adam Buksa (65').

Referee: Allard Lindhout (HOL)   Attendance: 3.220

15-10-2023   Stadion Doosan Aréna, Plzen: Czech Republic – Faroe Islands 1-0 (0-0)
Czech Republic: Ales Mandous, David Jurásek (57' Lukás Provod), Tomás Holes, Vaclav Cerný (YC75) (77' Václav Jurecka), Tomás Soucek, Ondrej Lingr (YC36) (90+1' Jakub Brabec), Michal Sadílek, Ladislav Krejcí, David Doudera (77' Lukás Masopust (YC88)), Adam Hlozek, Tomás Cvancara (56' Jan Kuchta). (Coach: Jaroslav Silhavý (CZE)).

Faroe Islands: Mattias Lamhauge (YC40), Odmar Færø (YC90+5), Viljormur í Davidsen, Sonni Nattestad (YC75), Ári Jónsson (58' Jóannes Bjartalíð), Andrias Edmundsson, Sølvi Vatnhamar (84' Andrass Johansen), Brandur Hendriksson (YC82), René Joensen, Jákup Andreasen (84' Klæmint Olsen), Pætur Petersen (77' Jóan Símun Edmudsson). (Coach: Håkan Ericson (SWE)).

Goal: Czech Republic: 1-0 Tomás Soucek (76' penalty).

Referee: Rohit Saggi (NOR)   Attendance: 9.115

15-10-2023   Stadion Narodowy, Warszawa: Poland – Moldova 1-1 (0-1)
Poland: Wojciech Szczesny, Tomasz Kedziora (84' Kamil Grosicki), Jakub Kiwior, Patryk Peda, Pawel Wszolek (71' Jakub Kaminski), Piotr Zielinski, Przemyslaw Frankowski (YC47), Patryk Dziczek (46' Bartosz Slisz), Sebastian Szymanski (71' Filip Marchwinski), Arkadiusz Milik (71' Adam Buksa), Karol Swiderski. (Coach: Michal Probierz (POL)).

Moldova: Dorian Railean (YC85), Denis Marandici (YC45+4), Artur Craciun, Oleg Reabciuk (YC17), Ioan-Calin Revenco (70' Sergiu Platica (YC82)), Vladyslav Baboglo, Vadim Rata (79' Serafim Cojocari), Nichita Motpan (70' Mihai Platica), Maxim Cojocaru (YC21) (60' Vitalie Damascan), Ion Nicolaescu (79' Victor Bogaciuc), Virgiliu Postolachi (YC42). (Coach: Serghei Clescenco (MDA)).

Goals: Poland: 1-1 Karol Swiderski (53').
Moldova: 0-1 Ion Nicolaescu (26').

Referee: Artur Soares Dias (POR)   Attendance: 51.672

524

17-11-2023   Stadionul Zimbru, Chisinau: Moldova – Albania   1-1 (0-1)
Moldova: Dorian Railean, Veaceslav Posmac, Artur Craciun, Oleg Reabciuk, Ioan-Calin Revenco (46' Maxim Cojocaru), Vladyslav Baboglo, Vadim Rata (YC11), Mihail Caimacov (YC54) (76' Serafim Cojocari), Nichita Motpan (68' Vitalie Damascan), Ion Nicolaescu (76' Victor Stîna), Virgiliu Postolachi. (Coach: Serghei Clescenco (MDA)).
Albania: Etrit Berisha, Elseid Hysaj, Berat Djimsiti, Ardian Ismajli, Mario Mitaj (YC9), Ylber Ramadani, Nedim Bajrami (80' Klaus Gjasula), Kristjan Asllani, Sokol Çikalleshi (62' Mirlind Daku (YC86)), Taulant Seferi, Jasir Asani (90+2' Arbnor Muja). (Coach: Sylvinho (BRA)).
Goals: Moldova: 1-1 Vladyslav Baboglo (87').
Albania: 0-1 Sokol Çikalleshi (25' penalty).
Referee: William Collum (SCO)   Attendance: 9.537

17-11-2023   Stadion Narodowy, Warszawa: Poland – Czech Republic   1-1 (1-0)
Poland: Wojciech Szczesny, Jan Bednarek, Pawel Bochniewicz (YC36) (58' Patryk Peda, 85' Sebastian Szymanski), Jakub Kiwior, Przemyslaw Frankowski, Damian Szymanski (73' Kamil Grosicki), Bartosz Slisz, Jakub Piotrowski, Nicola Zalewski, Robert Lewandowski, Karol Swiderski (46' Adam Buksa). (Coach: Michal Probierz (POL)).
Czech Republic: Jindrich Stanek, Jakub Brabec (YC63), Vladimír Coufal, David Zima, Tomás Holes, Lukás Provod (75' Ondrej Lingr), Tomás Soucek, Michal Sadílek (90+1' Alex Král), David Doudera, Jan Kuchta (46' Adam Hlozek), Mojmír Chytil (46' Tomás Cvancara). (Coach: Jaroslav Silhavý (CZE)).
Goals: Poland: 1-0 Jakub Piotrowski (38').
Czech Republic: 1-1 Tomás Soucek (49').
Referee: Daniele Orsato (ITA)   Attendance: 56.310

20-11-2023   Air Albania Stadium, Tirana: Albania – Faroe Islands   0-0
Albania: Thomas Strakosha, Berat Djimsiti, Iván Balliu Campeny, Ardian Ismajli, Mario Mitaj, Keidi Bare (61' Qazim Laçi), Nedim Bajrami, Kristjan Asllani, Jasir Asani (74' Ernest Muçi), Myrto Uzuni (61' Arbnor Muçolli), Mirlind Daku (74' Sokol Çikalleshi (YC74)). (Coach: Sylvinho (BRA)).
Faroe Islands: Mattias Lamhauge (34' Bárður á Reynatrøð), Odmar Færø, Viljormur í Davidsen, Gunnar Vatnhamar, Jóannes Danielsen (YC90), Andrias Edmundsson, Brandur Hendriksson (63' Sølvi Vatnhamar), René Joensen (YC38), Jákup Andreasen, Jóannes Bjartalíð, Jóan Símun Edmudsson (86' Pætur Petersen). (Coach: Håkan Ericson (SWE)).
Referee: Sven Jablonski (GER)   Attendance: 21.456

20-11-2023   Andruv stadion, Olomouc: Czech Republic – Moldova   3-0 (1-0)
Czech Republic: Jindrich Stanek, David Zima, Martin Vitík, Tomás Holes, Lukás Masopust, Lukás Provod (77' Ondrej Lingr), Tomás Soucek, Michal Sadílek (58' Alex Král), David Doudera, Tomás Chorý (86' Mojmír Chytil), Adam Hlozek (58' Vasil Kusej (YC90+2)). (Coach: Jaroslav Silhavý (CZE)).
Moldova: Dorian Railean, Veaceslav Posmac (YC45), Artur Craciun, Oleg Reabciuk, Ioan-Calin Revenco (YC24) (46' Maxim Cojocaru), Vladyslav Baboglo (YC47,YC55), Vadim Rata (78' Victor Stîna (YC90+1)), Mihail Caimacov (YC30) (59' Mihai Platica), Nichita Motpan (46' Vitalie Damascan), Ion Nicolaescu (65' Serafim Cojocari), Virgiliu Postolachi. (Coach: Serghei Clescenco (MDA)).
Goals: Czech Republic: 1-0 David Doudera (14'), 2-0 Tomás Chorý (72'), 3-0 Tomás Soucek (90').
Referee: Sandro Schärer (SUI)   Attendance: 11.653

GROUP F

24-03-2023	Linz	Austria – Azerbaijan	4-1 (2-0)
24-03-2023	Solna	Sweden – Belgium	0-3 (0-1)
27-03-2023	Linz	Austria – Estonia	2-1 (0-1)
27-03-2023	Solna	Sweden – Azerbaijan	5-0 (1-0)
17-06-2023	Baku	Azerbaijan – Estonia	1-1 (0-1)
17-06-2023	Brussels	Belgium – Austria	1-1 (0-1)
20-06-2023	Vienna	Austria – Sweden	2-0 (0-0)
20-06-2023	Tallinn	Estonia – Belgium	0-3 (0-2)
09-09-2023	Baku	Azerbaijan – Belgium	0-1 (0-1)
09-09-2023	Tallinn	Estonia – Sweden	0-5 (0-3)
12-09-2023	Brussels	Belgium – Estonia	5-0 (2-0)
12-09-2023	Solna	Sweden – Austria	1-3 (0-0)
13-10-2023	Tallinn	Estonia – Azerbaijan	0-2 (0-2)
13-10-2023	Vienna	Austria – Belgium	2-3 (0-1)
16-10-2023	Baku	Azerbaijan – Austria	0-1 (0-0)
16-10-2023	Brussels	Belgium – Sweden	1-1 (1-1)
16-11-2023	Baku	Azerbaijan – Sweden	3-0 (2-0)
16-11-2023	Tallinn	Estonia – Austria	0-2 (0-2)
19-11-2023	Brussels	Belgium – Azerbaijan	5-0 (4-0)
19-11-2023	Solna	Sweden – Estonia	2-0 (1-0)

FINAL STANDING

Pos	Team	Pld	W	D	L	GF	GA	GD	Pts
1	Belgium	8	6	2	0	22	4	+18	20
2	Austria	8	6	1	1	17	7	+10	19
3	Sweden	8	3	1	4	14	12	+2	10
4	Azerbaijan	8	2	1	5	7	17	-10	7
5	Estonia	8	0	1	7	2	22	-20	1

Belgium and Austria qualified for the Final Tournament in Germany.

Estonia advanced to the play-offs due to their performance in the 2022-23 UEFA Nations League.

24-03-2023   Raiffeisen Arena, Linz: Austria – Azerbaijan 4-1 (2-0)
Austria: Heinz Lindner, Gernot Trauner (74' Andreas Ulmer), Phillipp Mwene, Kevin Danso,
Max Wöber (YC15) (34' Stefan Posch), Marcel Sabitzer (74' Dejan Ljubicic), Konrad Laimer,
Christoph Baumgartner, Nicolas Seiwald, Patrick Wimmer (68' Florian Kainz), Michael
Gregoritsch (68' Junior Adamu). (Coach: Ralf Rangnick (GER)).
Azerbaijan: Yusif Imanov, Baxtiyar Hasanalizade (46' Anton Krivotsyuk), Behlul
Mustafazade, Hojjat Haghverdi, Elvin Cafarquliyev (YC32) (46' Azar Aliyev), Richard
Almeida (YC45+3) (77' Aleksey Isaev), Emin Mahmudov (YC45), Eddy Israfilov (YC49) (59'
Elvin Camalov), Ramil Seydayev, Renat Dadashov (YC81), Ozan Kökçü (46' Namiq
Alasgarov). (Coach: Gianni De Biasi (ITA)).
Goals: Austria: 1-0 Marcel Sabitzer (27'), 2-0 Michael Gregoritsch (29'),
3-0 Marcel Sabitzer (50'), 4-1 Christoph Baumgartner (69').
Azerbaijan: 3-1 Emin Mahmudov (64').
Referee: Bartosz Frankowski (POL)   Attendance: 16.500

24-03-2023   Friends Arena, Solna: Sweden – Belgium 0-3 (0-1)
Sweden: Robin Olsen, Victor Lindelöf (YC78), Ludwig Augustinsson (85' Gabriel
Gudmundsson), Linus Wahlqvist, Hjalmar Ekdal, Emil Forsberg (73' Victor Claesson),
Kristoffer Olsson (YC38) (64' Viktor Gyökeres), Samuel Gustafson (YC62), Mattias
Svanberg, Dejan Kulusevski (YC90+4), Alexander Isak (73' Zlatan Ibrahimovic). (Coach:
Janne Andersson (SWE)).
Belgium: Thibaut Courtois, Jan Vertonghen, Timothy Castagne, Wout Faes, Arthur Theate
(86' Alexis Saelemaekers), Kevin De Bruyne, Yannick Carrasco (90' Loïs Openda), Amadou
Onana, Romelu Lukaku (85' Sebastian Bornauw), Leandro Trossard (61' Orel Mangala), Dodi
Lukébakio (61' Johan Bakayoko). (Coach: Domenico Tedesco (ITA)).
Goals: Belgium: 0-1 Romelo Lukaku (35'), 0-2 Romelo Lukaku (49'),
0-3 Romelo Lukaku (83').
Referee: Orel Grinfeld (ISR)   Attendance: 49.296

27-03-2023   Raiffeisen Arena, Linz: Austria – Estonia 2-1 (0-1)
Austria: Heinz Lindner, Phillipp Mwene, Stefan Posch (82' Karim Onisiwo), Kevin Danso,
Flavius Daniliuc (46' David Alaba), Konrad Laimer, Dejan Ljubicic (46' Junior Adamu),
Christoph Baumgartner (90+2' Romano Schmid), Nicolas Seiwald, Patrick Wimmer (61'
Florian Kainz), Michael Gregoritsch. (Coach: Ralf Rangnick (GER)).
Estonia: Karl Hein, Joonas Tamm, Karol Mets, Artur Pikk (90+1' Georgi Tunjov), Maksim
Paskotsi (YC34), Konstantin Vassiljev, Vlasiy Sinyavskiy (YC80), Martin Miller (78' Rocco
Shein), Mattias Käit (YC57), Sergei Zenjov (90+1' Sten Reinkort), Rauno Sappinen (84'
Henrik Ojamaa). (Coach: Thomas Häberli (SUI)).
Goals: Austria: 1-1 Florian Kainz (68'), 2-1 Michael Gregoritsch (88').
Estonia: 0-1 Rauno Sappinen (25').
Referee: Enea Jorgji (ALB)   Attendance: 16.500

Michael Gregoritsch missed a penalty kick (17').

27-03-2023   Friend Arena, Solna: Sweden – Azerbaijan 5-0 (1-0)
Sweden: Robin Olsen, Victor Lindelöf, Linus Wahlqvist, Gabriel Gudmundsson, Hjalmar
Ekdal (46' Isak Hien), Emil Forsberg (71' Jesper Karlström), Samuel Gustafson, Mattias
Svanberg, Dejan Kulusevski (82' Jesper Karlsson), Viktor Gyökeres (YC24) (87' Anthony
Elanga), Alexander Isak (70' Victor Claesson). (Coach: Janne Andersson (SWE)).
Azerbaijan: Emil Balayev, Behlul Mustafazade, Hojjat Haghverdi (73' Calal Hüseynov),
Anton Krivotsyuk, Toral Bayramov, Elvin Cafarquliyev (YC28) (74' Namiq Alasgarov),
Richard Almeida, Emin Mahmudov, Aleksey Isaev (YC45) (82' Musa Qurbanly), Ramil
Seydayev, Renat Dadashov. (Coach: Gianni De Biasi (ITA)).
Goals: Sweden: 1-0 Emil Forsberg (38'), 2-0 Behlul Mustafazade (65' own goal),
3-0 Viktor Gyökeres (79'), 4-0 Jesper Karlsson (88'), 5-0 Anthony Elanga (89').
Referee: Stéphanie Frappart (FRA)   Attendance: 23.674

17-06-2023   Dalga Arena, Baku: Azerbaijan – Estonia 1-1 (0-1)
Azerbaijan: Sharudin Mahammadaliyev, Badavi Hüseynov, Behlul Mustafazade, Hojjat
Haghverdi (46' Qismat Aliyev), Elvin Cafarquliyev (46' Toral Bayramov (YC72)), Emin
Mahmudov, Elvin Camalov (46' Anton Krivotsyuk), Aleksey Isaev (80' Filip Ozobic), Ramil
Seydayev, Mahir Emreli, Renat Dadashov (80' Musa Qurbanly). (Coach: Gianni De Biasi
(ITA)).
Estonia: Karl Hein, Karol Mets (YC42), Märten Kuusk, Marco Lukka (83' Taijo Teniste),
Rasmus Peetson, Konstantin Vassiljev, Vlasiy Sinyavskiy, Martin Miller, Mattias Käit
(YC90+2), Henri Anier (56' Henrik Ojamaa), Rauno Sappinen (83' Sten Reinkort). (Coach:
Thomas Häberli (SUI)).
Goals: Azerbaijan: 1-1 Anton Krivotsyuk (62').
Estonia: 0-1 Rauno Sappinen (27').
Referee: Ondrej Berka (CZE)   Attendance: 3.900

17-06-2023   Stade Roi Baudouin, Brussels: Belgium – Austria 1-1 (0-1)
Belgium: Thibaut Courtois, Timothy Castagne, Wout Faes, Arthur Theate, Yannick Carrasco
(76' Loïs Openda), Leander Dendoncker (84' Ameen Al-Dakhil), Youri Tielemans, Orel
Mangala (75' Aster Vranckx), Romelu Lukaku (YC90+4), Dodi Lukébakio (69' Johan
Bakayoko), Jérémy Doku (84' Mike Trésor). (Coach: Domenico Tedesco (ITA)).
Austria: Alexander Schlager (YC90+1), David Alaba, Philipp Lienhart, Stefan Posch (YC53),
Max Wöber (YC32) (46' Phillipp Mwene), Xaver Schlager (YC69) (87' Dejan Ljubicic),
Christoph Baumgartner, Nicolas Seiwald, Patrick Wimmer (60' Florian Kainz), Marko
Arnautovic (60' Marcel Sabitzer), Michael Gregoritsch (87' Karim Onisiwo). (Coach: Ralf
Rangnick (GER)).
Goals: Belgium: 1-1 Romelu Lukaku (62').
Austria: 0-1 Orel Mangala (21' own goal).
Referee: Jérôme Brisard (FRA)   Attendance: 39.237

20-06-2023   Ernst-Happel-Stadion, Vienna: Austria – Sweden 2-0 (0-0)
Austria: Alexander Schlager, David Alaba, Phillipp Mwene, Philipp Lienhart, Stefan Posch
(YC12) (45+8' Max Wöber), Xaver Schlager (71' Florian Grillitsch), Christoph Baumgartner
(90+1' Dejan Ljubicic), Nicolas Seiwald, Patrick Wimmer (59' Marcel Sabitzer), Michael
Gregoritsch, Junior Adamu (45+8' Marko Arnautovic). (Coach: Ralf Rangnick (GER)).
Sweden: Robin Olsen, Martin Olsson, Victor Lindelöf, Linus Wahlqvist, Isak Hien, Hjalmar
Ekdal (45+9' Jesper Karlström), Emil Forsberg (77' Jesper Karlsson), Samuel Gustafson,
Mattias Svanberg (87' Victor Claesson), Dejan Kulusevski (87' Anthony Elanga), Alexander
Isak (76' Viktor Gyökeres). (Coach: Janne Andersson (SWE)).
Goals: Austria: 1-0 Christoph Baumgartner (81'), 2-0 Christoph Baumgartner (89').
Referee: Marco Guida (ITA)   Attendance: 46.300

20-06-2023   A. Le Coq Arena, Tallinn: Estonia – Belgium   0-3 (0-2)
Estonia: Karl Hein, Taijo Teniste (79' Sten Reinkort), Karol Mets, Märten Kuusk, Rasmus
Peetson, Vlasiy Sinyavskiy (YC23), Martin Miller (74' Rocco Shein), Mattias Käit, Markus
Poom (61' Henri Anier), Henrik Ojamaa (YC27) (46' Georgi Tunjov (YC73)), Rauno
Sappinen (74' Erik Sorga). (Coach: Thomas Häberli (SUI)).
Belgium: Matz Sels, Jan Vertonghen (58' Ameen Al-Dakhil), Timothy Castagne (YC4), Wout
Faes, Arthur Theate (88' Olivier Deman), Yannick Carrasco, Youri Tielemans, Aster Vranckx
(YC22) (57' Orel Mangala), Romelu Lukaku (69' Michy Batshuayi), Mike Trésor (57' Jérémy
Doku), Johan Bakayoko. (Coach: Domenico Tedesco (ITA)).
Goals: Belgium: 0-1 Romelu Lukaku (37'), 0-2 Romelu Lukaku (40'),
0-3 Johan Bakayoko (90').
Referee: John Beaton (SCO)   Attendance: 11.772

09-09-2023   Dalga Arena, Baku: Azerbaijan – Belgium   0-1 (0-1)
Azerbaijan: Sharudin Mahammadaliyev, Behlul Mustafazade, Rahil Mammadov, Anton
Krivotsyuk, Toral Bayramov (62' Mahir Emreli), Elvin Cafarquliyev (85' Yusif Nabiyev),
Emin Mahmudov, Cosqun Diniyev (84' Filip Ozobic), Aleksey Isaev (62' Emil Safarov),
Ramil Seydayev (YC78), Renat Dadashov (61' Musa Qurbanly). (Coach: Gianni De Biasi
(ITA)).
Belgium: Koen Casteels, Jan Vertonghen, Timothy Castagne, Wout Faes, Arthur Theate,
Yannick Carrasco (84' Loïs Openda), Youri Tielemans (66' Orel Mangala), Amadou Onana,
Romelu Lukaku (66' Michy Batshuayi (YC90+3)), Leandro Trossard (79' Dodi Lukébakio),
Johan Bakayoko (66' Jérémy Doku (YC90+2)). (Coach: Domenico Tedesco (ITA)).
Goal: Belgium: 0-1 Yannick Carrasco (38').
Referee: Nenad Minakovic (SRB)   Attendance: 4.500

09-09-2023   A. Le Coq Arena, Tallinn: Estonia – Sweden   0-5 (0-3)
Estonia: Karl Hein, Joonas Tamm, Karol Mets (YC14), Rasmus Peetson (69' Märten Kuusk),
Maksim Paskotsi, Konstantin Vassiljev (84' Markus Poom), Vlasiy Sinyavskiy (46' Artur
Pikk), Martin Miller, Mattias Käit, Henri Anier (46' Sergei Zenjov), Henrik Ojamaa (46' Erik
Sorga). (Coach: Thomas Häberli (SUI)).
Sweden: Robin Olsen, Victor Lindelöf, Linus Wahlqvist (79' Emil Holm), Isak Hien (YC21)
(46' Carl Starfelt), Emil Forsberg (79' Jesper Karlsson), Samuel Gustafson, Ken Sema, Dejan
Kulusevski, Jens-Lys Cajuste, Viktor Gyökeres (64' Robin Quaison), Alexander Isak (64'
Victor Claesson). (Coach: Janne Andersson (SWE)).
Goals: Sweden: 0-1 Viktor Gyökeres (18'), 0-2 Dejan Kulusevski (24'),
0-3 Alexander Isak (39'), 0-4 Robin Quaison (75'), 0-5 Victor Claesson (90+2').
Referee: Horatiu Fesnic (ROM)   Attendance: 11.411

12-09-2023   Stade Roi Baudouin, Brussels: Belgium – Estonia   5-0 (2-0)
Belgium: Koen Casteels, Jan Vertonghen (84' Zeno Debast), Timothy Castagne (66' Hugo
Siquet), Wout Faes, Arthur Theate, Yannick Carrasco (59' Dodi Lukébakio), Orel Mangala,
Amadou Onana, Romelu Lukaku (61' Loïs Openda), Leandro Trossard (66' Charles De
Ketelaere (YC70)), Jérémy Doku. (Coach: Domenico Tedesco (ITA)).
Estonia: Karl Hein, Joonas Tamm, Nikita Baranov, Karol Mets (YC41), Artur Pikk, Maksim
Paskotsi, Konstantin Vassiljev (61' Georgi Tunjov), Mattias Käit (76' Martin Miller), Markus
Poom (46' Rocco Shein), Henri Anier (67' Sergei Zenjov), Henrik Ojamaa (61' Vlasiy
Sinyavskiy). (Coach: Thomas Häberli (SUI)).
Goals: Belgium: 1-0 Jan Vertonghen (4'), 2-0 Leandro Trossard (18'),
3-0 Romelu Lukaku (56'), 4-0 Romelu Lukaku (58'), 5-0 Charles De Ketelaere (88').
Referee: Bartosz Frankowski (POL)   Attendance: 24.127

12-09-2023   Friends Arena, Solna: Sweden – Austria 1-3 (0-0)
Sweden: Robin Olsen, Victor Lindelöf, Linus Wahlqvist (75' Emil Holm), Isak Hien, Albin
Ekdal (64' Samuel Gustafson), Emil Forsberg (64' Jesper Karlsson (YC71)), Ken Sema, Dejan
Kulusevski, Jens-Lys Cajuste (75' Victor Claesson), Viktor Gyökeres, Alexander Isak (83'
Robin Quaison). (Coach: Janne Andersson (SWE)).
Austria: Alexander Schlager, David Alaba, Phillipp Mwene (YC45) (72' Max Wöber), Philipp
Lienhart, Stefan Posch, Marcel Sabitzer, Konrad Laimer (87' Matthias Seidl), Xaver Schlager
(87' Florian Grillitsch), Nicolas Seiwald, Marko Arnautovic (72' Patrick Wimmer), Michael
Gregoritsch (84' Karim Onisiwo). (Coach: Ralf Rangnick (GER)).
Goals: Sweden: 1-3 Emil Holm (90').
Austria: 0-1 Michael Gregoritsch (53'), 0-2 Marko Arnautovic (56'),
0-3 Marko Arnautovic (69' penalty).
Referee: Serdar Gözübüyük (HOL)   Attendance: 43.228

13-10-2023   A. Le Coq Arena, Tallinn: Estonia – Azerbaijan 0-2 (0-2)
Estonia: Karl Hein, Artur Pikk (YC18), Märten Kuusk, Rasmus Peetson, Maksim Paskotsi,
Konstantin Vassiljev (63' Sergei Zenjov), Martin Miller (63' Vlasiy Sinyavskiy), Mattias Käit
(YC68), Markus Poom (63' Martin Vetkal (YC90+1)), Georgi Tunjov (74' Bogdan Vastsuk),
Henri Anier (85' Ken Kallaste). (Coach: Thomas Häberli (SUI)).
Azerbaijan: Sharudin Mahammadaliyev, Hojjat Haghverdi, Rahil Mammadov (YC40) (64'
Baxtiyar Hasanalizade), Anton Krivotsyuk, Toral Bayramov (75' Qismat Aliyev), Elvin
Cafarquliyev, Emin Mahmudov (YC22) (75' Filip Ozobic), Cosqun Diniyev, Aleksey Isaev
(69' Elvin Camalov), Ramil Seydayev, Mahir Emreli (YC45+1) (70' Renat Dadashov).
(Coach: Gianni De Biasi (ITA)).
Goals: Azerbaijan: 0-1 Toral Bayramov (9'), 0-2 Ramil Seydayev (45+4' penalty).
Referee: Robert Schröder (GER)   Attendance: 5.652

13-10-2023   Ernst-Happel-Stadion, Vienna: Austria – Belgium 2-3 (0-1)
Austria: Alexander Schlager, Philipp Lienhart, Kevin Danso (66' Samson Baidoo), Max
Wöber (71' Alexander Prass), Florian Grillitsch (YC15), Konrad Laimer (YC77), Xaver
Schlager, Christoph Baumgartner (66' Muhammed Cham), Nicolas Seiwald (YC40), Patrick
Wimmer (YC54) (79' Marcel Sabitzer), Manprit Sarkaria (66' Sasa Kalajdzic). (Coach: Ralf
Rangnick (GER)).
Belgium: Matz Sels, Jan Vertonghen, Timothy Castagne (YC63), Wout Faes, Arthur Theate,
Orel Mangala (YC24) (64' Youri Tielemans), Amadou Onana (YC35,YC78), Romelu Lukaku
(YC78), Dodi Lukébakio (71' Johan Bakayoko, 87' Arthur Vermeeren), Loïs Openda (46'
Yannick Carrasco), Jérémy Doku (88' Mandela Keita). (Coach: Domenico Tedesco (ITA)).
Goals: Austria: 1-3 Konrad Laimer (72'), 2-3 Marcel Sabitzer (84' penalty).
Belgium: 0-1 Dodi Lukébakio (12'), 0-2 Dodi Lukébakio (55'), 0-3 Romelu Lukaku (58').
Referee: Jesús Gil Manzano (ESP)   Attendance: 47.000

16-10-2023   Tofiq Bahramov adina Respublika stadionu, Baku:
Azerbaijan – Austria 0-1 (0-0)
Azerbaijan: Sharudin Mahammadaliyev (YC90+2), Hojjat Haghverdi, Rahil Mammadov, Anton Krivotsyuk (YC84), Toral Bayramov (YC88), Elvin Cafarquliyev (83' Qismat Aliyev), Emin Mahmudov, Cosqun Diniyev (YC57) (65' Emil Safarov), Aleksey Isaev (78' Mahir Emreli), Ramil Seydayev (YC90+3), Renat Dadashov (83' Musa Qurbanly). (Coach: Gianni De Biasi (ITA)).
Austria: Alexander Schlager, Philipp Lienhart, Max Wöber, Florian Kainz (46' Patrick Wimmer), Florian Grillitsch, Konrad Laimer, Xaver Schlager, Romano Schmid (46' Marcel Sabitzer (YC90+3)), Alexander Prass (46' Christoph Baumgartner (YC53)), Nicolas Seiwald, Sasa Kalajdzic (82' Guido Burgstaller (YC90+2,YC90+4). (Coach: Ralf Rangnick (GER)).
Goal: Austria: 0-1 Marcel Sabitzer (48' penalty).
Referee: Aristotelis Diamantopoulos (GRE)   Attendance: 4.446

16-10-2023   Stade Roi Baudouin, Brussels: Belgium – Sweden 1-1 (1-1)
Belgium: Matz Sels, Jan Vertonghen, Timothy Castagne, Wout Faes, Arthur Theate, Yannick Carrasco, Youri Tielemans, Orel Mangala, Charles De Ketelaere, Romelu Lukaku, Johan Bakayoko. (Coach: Domenico Tedesco (ITA)).
Sweden: Robin Olsen, Victor Lindelöf, Ludwig Augustinsson, Filip Helander, Linus Wahlqvist, Albin Ekdal, Emil Forsberg, Mattias Svanberg (YC36), Dejan Kulusevski, Jens-Lys Cajuste, Viktor Gyökeres. (Coach: Janne Andersson (SWE)).
Goals: Belgium: 1-1 Romelu Lukaku (31' penalty).
Sweden: 0-1 Viktor Gyökeres (15').
Referee: Maurizio Mariani (ITA)   Attendance: N/A

The match was abandoned for security reasons at half-time with the scoreline at 1-1.
Two Swedish supporters were killed in a terrorist shooting in Brussels prior to the match.
The scoreline at the time was later confirmed as the final result.

The attendance of the match was not announced due to the abandonment.

16-11-2023   Tofiq Bahramov adina Respublika stadionu, Baku:
Azerbaijan – Sweden 3-0 (2-0)
Azerbaijan: Sharudin Mahammadaliyev (YC72), Behlul Mustafazade (RC57), Rahil Mammadov, Anton Krivotsyuk (YC90+2), Toral Bayramov (81' Mahir Emreli), Elvin Cafarquliyev, Emin Mahmudov, Cosqun Diniyev (81' Elvin Camalov), Aleksey Isaev (75' Qismat Aliyev), Ramil Seydayev (YC29) (75' Eddy Israfilov), Renat Dadashov (66' Hojjat Haghverdi). (Coach: Gianni De Biasi (ITA)).
Sweden: Robin Olsen, Victor Lindelöf, Filip Helander, Linus Wahlqvist (60' Emil Krafth), Emil Forsberg, Samuel Gustafson (60' Victor Claesson), Ken Sema, Mattias Svanberg, Dejan Kulusevski (YC47), Jens-Lys Cajuste (YC52) (75' Robin Quaison), Viktor Gyökeres. (Coach: Janne Andersson (SWE)).
Goals: Azerbaijan: 1-0 Emin Mahmudov (3'), 2-0 Renat Dadashov (6'), 3-0 Emin Mahmudov (89').
Referee: Esther Staubli (SUI)   Attendance: 5.570

16-11-2023   A. Le Coq Arena, Tallinn: Estonia – Austria 0-2 (0-2)
Estonia: Karl Hein, Joonas Tamm, Karol Mets, Maksim Paskotsi, Bogdan Vastsuk (71' Sergei Zenjov), Vlasiy Sinyavskiy, Martin Miller (71' Artur Pikk), Markus Poom (83' Rasmus Peetson), Georgi Tunjov (60' Rocco Shein), Martin Vetkal, Henri Anier (60' Oliver Jürgens). (Coach: Thomas Häberli (SUI)).
Austria: Alexander Schlager, David Alaba, Philipp Lienhart, Stefan Posch, Max Wöber, Marcel Sabitzer (89' Florian Kainz), Konrad Laimer (46' Marko Arnautovic), Xaver Schlager (76' Matthias Seidl), Christoph Baumgartner (63' Romano Schmid), Nicolas Seiwald, Michael Gregoritsch (63' Sasa Kalajdzic). (Coach: Ralf Rangnick (GER)).
Goals: Austria: 0-1 Konrad Laimer (26'), 0-2 Philipp Lienhart (39').
Referee: Nikola Dabanovic (MNE)   Attendance: 4,488

19-11-2023   Stade Roi Baudouin, Brussels: Belgium – Azerbaijan 5-0 (4-0)
Belgium: Koen Casteels, Jan Vertonghen (84' Ameen Al-Dakhil), Timothy Castagne, Wout Faes, Arthur Theate (YC22) (60' Alexis Saelemaekers), Orel Mangala, Aster Vranckx (YC45) (46' Youri Tielemans), Romelu Lukaku (46' Loïs Openda), Leandro Trossard, Jérémy Doku, Johan Bakayoko (60' Yannick Carrasco). (Coach: Domenico Tedesco (ITA)).
Azerbaijan: Sharudin Mahammadaliyev (YC86), Hojjat Haghverdi, Rahil Mammadov, Anton Krivotsyuk, Toral Bayramov, Elvin Cafarquliyev (46' Qismat Aliyev), Emin Mahmudov (77' Elvin Camalov), Eddy Israfilov (YC20,YC24), Aleksey Isaev (46' Cosqun Diniyev), Mahir Emreli (46' Nariman Akhundzade), Renat Dadashov (64' Rüstam Ahmadzade). (Coach: Gianni De Biasi (ITA)).
Goals: Belgium: 1-0 Romelu Lukaku (17'), 2-0 Romelu Lukaku (26'),
3-0 Romelu Lukaku (30'), 4-0 Romelu Lukaku (37'), 5-0 Leandro Trossard (90').
Referee: Gergö Bogár (HUN)   Attendance: 30.276

19-11-2023   Friends Arena, Solna: Sweden – Estonia 2-0 (1-0)
Sweden: Robin Olsen, Victor Lindelöf, Ludwig Augustinsson, Emil Krafth, Filip Helander (YC72), Albin Ekdal (72' Hugo Larsson), Emil Forsberg (72' Mattias Svanberg), Victor Claesson (85' Robin Quaison), Dejan Kulusevski, Jens-Lys Cajuste (85' Kristoffer Olsson), Viktor Gyökeres. (Coach: Janne Andersson (SWE)).
Estonia: Karl Hein, Joonas Tamm (62' Märten Kuusk (YC69)), Karol Mets, Artur Pikk (84' Alex Tamm), Rasmus Peetson, Maksim Paskotsi, Bogdan Vastsuk (56' Vlasiy Sinyavskiy), Mattias Käit, Markus Poom (YC90+1), Georgi Tunjov (56' Sergei Zenjov), Oliver Jürgens (62' Henri Anier). (Coach: Thomas Häberli (SUI)).
Goals: Sweden: 1-0 Victor Claesson (22'), 2-0 Emil Forsberg (55').
Referee: Fabio Maresca (ITA)   Attendance: 11.201

GROUP G

24-03-2023	Razgrad	Bulgaria – Montenegro	0-1 (0-0)
24-03-2023	Beograd	Serbia – Lithuania	2-0 (1-0)
27-03-2023	Budapest	Hungary – Bulgaria	3-0 (3-0)
27-03-2023	Podgorica	Montenegro – Serbia	0-2 (0-0)
17-06-2023	Kaunas	Lithuania – Bulgaria	1-1 (1-1)
17-06-2023	Podgorica	Montenegro – Hungary	0-0
20-06-2023	Razgrad	Bulgaria – Serbia	1-1 (0-0)
20-06-2023	Budapest	Hungary – Lithuania	2-0 (1-0)
07-09-2023	Kaunas	Lithuania – Montenegro	2-2 (0-0)

07-09-2023	Beograd	Serbia – Hungary	1-2 (1-2)
10-09-2023	Podgorica	Montenegro – Bulgaria	2-1 (1-0)
10-09-2023	Kaunas	Lithuania – Serbia	1-3 (1-3)
14-10-2023	Sofia	Bulgaria – Lithuania	0-2 (0-1)
14-10-2023	Budapest	Hungary – Serbia	2-1 (2-1)
17-10-2023	Kaunas	Lithuania – Hungary	2-2 (2-0)
17-10-2023	Beograd	Serbia – Montenegro	3-1 (1-1)
16-11-2023	Sofia	Bulgaria – Hungary	2-2 (1-1)
16-11-2023	Podgorica	Montenegro – Lithuania	2-0 (1-0)
19-11-2023	Budapest	Hungary – Montenegro	3-1 (0-1)
19-11-2023	Leskovac	Serbia – Bulgaria	2-2 (1-0)

FINAL STANDING

Pos	Team	Pld	W	D	L	GF	GA	GD	Pts
1	Hungary	8	5	3	0	16	7	+9	18
2	Serbia	8	4	2	2	15	9	+6	14
3	Montenegro	8	3	2	3	9	11	-2	11
4	Lithuania	8	1	3	4	8	14	-6	6
5	Bulgaria	8	0	4	4	7	14	-7	4

Hungary and Serbia qualified for the Final Tournament in Germany.

24-03-2023   Huvepharma Arena, Razgrad: Bulgaria – Montenegro 0-1 (0-0)
Bulgaria: Daniel Naumov, Petko Hristov, Valentin Antov, Hristiyan Petrov (60' Yanis Karabelyov), Ilian Iliev (59' Nikola Iliev), Ilia Gruev, Ivan Yordanov (85' Georgi Rusev), Filip Krastev (76' Radoslav Kirilov), Yoan Stoyanov, Spas Delev (85' Marin Petkov), Kiril Despodov. (Coach: Mladen Krstajic (SRB)).
Montenegro: Milan Mijatovic, Marko Vesovic, Stefan Savic (YC43), Risto Radunovic, Igor Vujacic, Adam Marusic (83' Stefan Mugosa), Aleksandar Scekic, Marko Bakic (46' Stevan Jovetic), Vukan Savicevic, Sead Haksabanovic (46' Vladimir Jovovic, 79' Stefan Loncar), Nikola Krstovic (71' Milutin Osmajic). (Coach: Miodrag Radulovic (MNE)).
Goal: Montenegro: 0-1 Nikola Krstovic (70').
Referee: Aliyar Aghayev (AZE)   Attendance: 9.180

24-03-2023   Stadion Rajko Mitic, Beograd: Serbia – Lithuania 2-0 (1-0)
Serbia: Vanja Milinkovic-Savic, Strahinja Erakovic, Strahinja Pavlovic, Nemanja Gudelj, Filip Kostic, Sasa Lukic (72' Ivan Ilic), Marko Grujic, Dusan Tadic (72' Lazar Samardzic), Aleksandar Mitrovic (81' Dejan Joveljic), Andrija Zivkovic (80' Nikola Milenkovic), Dusan Vlahovic (63' Sergej Milinkovic-Savic). (Coach: Dragan Stojkovic (SRB)).
Lithuania: Dziugas Bartkus, Edvinas Girdvainis, Markas Beneta (86' Rolandas Baravykas), Kipras Kazukolovas, Fiodor Cernych, Domantas Simkus, Justas Lasickas, Eligijus Jankauskas (62' Arvydas Novikovas), Paulius Golubickas (62' Vykintas Slivka (YC90+3)), Gvidas Gineitis (80' Danielis Romanovskis), Gytis Paulauskas (80' Karolis Laukzemis). (Coach: Edgaras Jankauskas (LTU)).
Goals: Serbia: 1-0 Dusan Tadic (16'), 2-0 Dusan Vlahovic (53').
Referee: Lawrence Visser (BEL)   Attendance: 21.125

27-03-2023   Puskás Aréna, Budapest: Hungary – Bulgaria 3-0 (3-0)
Hungary: Dénes Dibusz, Ádám Lang, Willi Orbán, Attila Szalai, Bendegúz Bolla (87' Loïc
Négo), Milos Kerkez (87' Zsolt Kalmár), Roland Sallai (73' Kevin Csoboth),
Ádám Nagy (73' László Kleinheisler), Dominik Szoboszlai, Martin Ádám (59' Barnabás
Varga). (Coach: Marco Rossi (ITA)).
Bulgaria: Daniel Naumov, Plamen Galabov, Ivaylo Markov (46' Hristiyan Petrov), Valentin
Antov, Yanis Karabelyov (46' Filip Krastev), Ilia Gruev (85' Stanislav Shopov), Yoan
Stoyanov, Spas Delev (46' Georgi Rusev), Kiril Despodov (57' Radoslav Kirilov), Marin
Petkov, Nikola Iliev. (Coach: Mladen Krstajic (SRB)).
Goals: Hungary: 1-0 Bálint Vécsei (7'), 2-0 Dominik Szoboszlai (26'), 3-0 Martin Ádám (39').
Referee: Halil Umut Meler (TUR)   Attendance: 53.000

27-03-2023   Stadion Pod Goricom, Podgorica: Montenegro – Serbia 0-2 (0-0)
Montenegro: Milan Mijatovic, Marko Vesovic, Zarko Tomasevic (41' Nikola Sipcic), Stefan
Savic, Igor Vujacic, Adam Marusic, Aleksandar Scekic (76' Stefan Loncar), Vukan Savicevic
(70' Vladimir Jovovic), Stevan Jovetic (71' Milutin Osmajic), Sead Haksabanovic (77' Driton
Camaj), Nikola Krstovic (YC26). (Coach: Miodrag Radulovic (MNE)).
Serbia: Vanja Milinkovic-Savic, Filip Mladenovic (YC87), Nikola Milenkovic, Strahinja
Pavlovic, Nemanja Gudelj, Filip Djuricic (46' Dusan Vlahovic), Marko Grujic (81' Sasa
Lukic), Sergej Milinkovic-Savic, Ivan Ilic (46' Andrija Zivkovic (YC58)), Dusan Tadic (89'
Strahinja Erakovic), Aleksandar Mitrovic (85' Uros Racic). (Coach: Dragan Stojkovic (SRB)).
Goals: Serbia: 0-1 Dusan Vlahovic (78'), 0-2 Dusan Vlahovic (90+6').
Referee: Clément Turpin (FRA)   Attendance: 9.831

17-06-2023   Dariaus ir Giréno stadionas, Kaunas: Lithuania – Bulgaria 1-1 (1-1)
Lithuania: Edvinas Gertmonas, Edvinas Girdvainis, Markas Beneta (78' Artemijus
Tutyskinas), Rokas Lekiatas, Fiodor Cernych (38' Gytis Paulauskas (YC45)), Ovidijus
Verbickas (46' Klaudijus Upstas), Modestas Vorobjovas, Justas Lasickas (RC17), Eligijus
Jankauskas (79' Gratas Sirgedas), Deividas Sesplaukis (21' Pijus Sirvys), Gvidas Gineitis
(YC90+2). (Coach: Edgaras Jankauskas (LTU)).
Bulgaria: Ivan Dyulgerov, Valentin Antov, Alex Petkov, Patrick-Gabriel Galchev (81' Yoan
Stoyanov), Ivaylo Chochev, Ilia Gruev, Stanislav Shopov (46' Ivan Yordanov), Spas Delev
(46' Nikola Iliev), Kiril Despodov (74' Georgi Rusev (YC83)), Martin Minchev (63' Iliyan
Stefanov), Marin Petkov. (Coach: Mladen Krstajic (SRB)).
Goals: Lithuania: 1-0 Edvinas Girdvainis (15').
Bulgaria: 1-1 Marin Petkov (27').
Referee: Jakob Alexander Sundberg (DEN)   Attendance: 14.230

17-06-2023   Stadion Pod Goricom, Podgorica: Montenegro – Hungary 0-0
Montenegro: Milan Mijatovic, Marko Vesovic (YC15) (72' Marko Vukcevic), Zarko
Tomasevic, Stefan Savic (YC90+4), Igor Vujacic (YC34), Andrija Vukcevic, Aleksandar
Scekic (61' Milos Raickovic (YC63)), Marko Jankovic, Vukan Savicevic (82' Stefan Loncar),
Stevan Jovetic (83' Sead Haksabanovic), Nikola Krstovic (72' Milutin Osmajic). (Coach:
Miodrag Radulovic (MNE)).
Hungary: Dénes Dibusz, Ádám Lang, Willi Orbán, Attila Szalai, Bendegúz Bolla (88' Endre
Botka), Milos Kerkez, Roland Sallai (YC50) (59' Kevin Csoboth (YC70)), Ádám Nagy,
Dominik Szoboszlai, Martin Ádám (59' Barnabás Varga), Callum Styles (72' Zsolt Kalmár).
(Coach: Marco Rossi (ITA)).
Referee: Jesús Gil Manzano (ESP)   Attendance: 6.761

534

20-06-2023   Huvepharma Arena, Razgrad: Bulgaria – Serbia 1-1 (0-0)
Bulgaria: Ivan Dyulgerov (YC81), Petko Hristov, Valentin Antov, Viktor Popov (86' Patrick-Gabriel Galchev), Ivaylo Chochev (66' Filip Krastev), Andrian Kraev, Ilia Gruev, Kiril Despodov (78' Spas Delev), Georgi Rusev (YC62) (86' Simeon Petrov), Marin Petkov (YC42), Nikola Iliev (66' Iliyan Stefanov). (Coach: Mladen Krstajic (SRB)).
Serbia: Vanja Milinkovic-Savic, Nikola Milenkovic (YC70), Strahinja Pavlovic (YC88), Nemanja Gudelj, Filip Kostic (71' Filip Mladenovic), Sasa Lukic (58' Djordje Jovanovic), Sergej Milinkovic-Savic, Nemanja Maksimovic (81' Marko Grujic), Dusan Tadic, Andrija Zivkovic (71' Darko Lazovic), Dejan Joveljic (YC81). (Coach: Dragan Stojkovic (SRB)).
Goals: Bulgaria: 1-0 Kiril Despodov (47').
Serbia: 1-1 Darko Lazovic (90+6').
Referee: Craig Pawson (ENG)   Attendance: 6.700

20-06-2023   Puskás Aréna, Budapest: Hungaria – Lithuania 2-0 (1-0)
Hungary: Dénes Dibusz, Endre Botka, Willi Orbán (YC54), Attila Szalai, Milos Kerkez (78' János Ferenczi), Dániel Gazdag (78' Ádám Lang), Roland Sallai (88' Péter Baráth), Ádám Nagy, Dominik Szoboszlai (YC89), Callum Styles (60' László Kleinheisler), Barnabás Varga (60' Martin Ádám). (Coach: Marco Rossi (ITA)).
Lithuania: Edvinas Gertmonas, Linas Klimavicius, Rokas Lekiatas, Kipras Kazukolovas, Artemijus Tutyskinas (YC50) (63' Markas Beneta), Gratas Sirgedas (46' Pijus Sirvys), Eligijus Jankauskas (YC56) (86' Danielis Romanovskis), Deividas Sesplaukis (78' Armandas Kucys), Karolis Uzela (YC39) (46' Modestas Vorobjovas), Gvidas Gineitis, Gytis Paulauskas. (Coach: Edgaras Jankauskas (LTU)).
Goals: Hungary: 1-0 Barnabás Varga (32'), 2-0 Roland Sallai (83').
Referee: António Nobre (POR)   Attendance: 58.274

07-09-2023   Dariaus ir Giréno stadionas, Kaunas: Lithuania – Montenegro 2-2 (0-0)
Lithuania: Edvinas Gertmonas, Edvinas Girdvainis (YC29), Markas Beneta (46' Pijus Sirvys), Rokas Lekiatas, Arvydas Novikovas (81' Donatas Kazlauskas), Ovidijus Verbickas (90+2' Linas Klimavicius), Justas Lasickas, Eligijus Jankauskas (68' Fiodor Cernych), Paulius Golubickas (68' Vykintas Slivka), Gvidas Gineitis, Gytis Paulauskas. (Coach: Edgaras Jankauskas (LTU)).
Montenegro: Milan Mijatovic, Zarko Tomasevic, Stefan Savic, Risto Radunovic, Adam Marusic, Aleksandar Scekic (53' Stefan Loncar), Marko Jankovic (77' Viktor Djukanovic), Vladimir Jovovic (72' Uros Djurdjevic (YC84)), Vukan Savicevic (46' Driton Camaj), Stefan Mugosa (46' Stevan Jovetic), Nikola Krstovic. (Coach: Miodrag Radulovic (MNE)).
Goals: Lithuania: 1-0 Gytis Paulauskas (71'), 2-2 Fiodor Cernych (90+4').
Montenegro: 1-1 Nikola Krstovic (78'), 1-2 Stefan Savic (89').
Referee: Mohammed Al-Hakim (SWE)   Attendance: 11.328

07-09-2023   Stadion Rajko Mitic, Beograd: Serbia – Hungary 1-2 (1-2)
Serbia: Vanja Milinkovic-Savic, Milos Veljkovic, Strahinja Pavlovic, Nemanja Gudelj, Filip Kostic (46' Filip Mladenovic), Nemanja Radonjic (46' Andrija Zivkovic), Sergej Milinkovic-Savic, Nemanja Maksimovic (64' Nikola Milenkovic), Dusan Tadic (86' Ivan Ilic), Aleksandar Mitrovic, Dusan Vlahovic (87' Luka Jovic). (Coach: Dragan Stojkovic (SRB)).
Hungary: Dénes Dibusz, Loïc Négo, Ádám Lang, Willi Orbán, Attila Szalai (YC89), Milos Kerkez (70' Attila Fiola), Roland Sallai (90+4' Kevin Csoboth), Ádám Nagy (77' Mihály Kata), Dominik Szoboszlai, Callum Styles, Barnabás Varga (YC67) (77' Martin Ádám). (Coach: Marco Rossi (ITA)).
Goals: Serbia: 1-0 Attila Szalai (10' own goal).
Hungary: 1-1 Barnabás Varga (34'), 1-2 Willi Orbán (36').
Referee: Juan Martínez Munuera (ESP)   Attendance: 6.924

10-09-2023   Stadion Pod Goricom, Podgorica: Montenegro – Bulgaria 2-1 (1-0)
Montenegro: Milan Mijatovic, Stefan Savic, Igor Vujacic (YC24,YC59), Adam Marusic,
Andrija Vukcevic, Nikola Sipcic (26' Zarko Tomasevic), Marko Bakic (YC81) (84' Stefan
Mugosa), Marko Jankovic (84' Marko Vukcevic), Stefan Loncar, Uros Djurdjevic (YC45+3)
(46' Stevan Jovetic), Nikola Krstovic (YC59) (76' Driton Camaj). (Coach: Miodrag Radulovic
(MNE)).
Bulgaria: Ivan Dyulgerov, Valentin Antov, Kristian Dimitrov (74' Preslav Borukov), Dimo
Krastev, Viktor Popov (YC67), Patrick-Gabriel Galchev (63' Yoan Stoyanov), Andrian Kraev
(64' Dominik Yankov), Ilia Gruev, Lukas Petkov (83' Ivaylo Chochev), Kiril Despodov,
Georgi Rusev (46' Spas Delev). (Coach: Mladen Krstajic (SRB) (YC90)).
Goals: Montenegro: 1-0 Stefan Savic (45+1'), 2-1 Stevan Jovetic (90+6').
Bulgaria: 1-1 Preslav Borukov (79').
Referee: Harm Osmers (GER)   Attendance: 4.232

Spas Delev missed a penalty kick (61').

10-09-2023   Dariaus ir Giréno stadionas, Kaunas: Lithuania – Serbia 1-3 (1-3)
Lithuania: Edvinas Gertmonas, Edvinas Girdvainis (46' Kipras Kazukolovas), Markas Beneta
(71' Pijus Sirvys), Rokas Lekiatas, Fiodor Cernych (YC23), Vykintas Slivka, Ovidijus
Verbickas (46' Arvydas Novikovas), Justas Lasickas, Paulius Golubickas (46' Matijus
Remeikis), Gvidas Gineitis, Gytis Paulauskas (YC35) (78' Eligijus Jankauskas). (Coach:
Edgaras Jankauskas (LTU)).
Serbia: Vanja Milinkovic-Savic, Filip Mladenovic (84' Nemanja Radonjic), Milos Veljkovic,
Srdjan Babic, Nikola Milenkovic, Nemanja Gudelj, Sergej Milinkovic-Savic (YC84) (88' Uros
Racic), Ivan Ilic, Dusan Tadic (85' Lazar Samardzic), Aleksandar Mitrovic (72' Dusan
Vlahovic), Andrija Zivkovic (YC38) (72' Stefan Mitrovic (YC90+1)). (Coach: Dragan
Stojkovic (SRB)).
Goals: Lithuania: 1-3 Gytis Paulauskas (45').
Serbia: 0-1 Aleksandar Mitrovic (21'), 0-2 Aleksandar Mitrovic (32'),
0-3 Aleksandar Mitrovic (43').
Referee: Sascha Stegemann (GER)   Attendance: 8.586

14-10-2023   Stadion Vasil Levski, Sofia: Bulgaria – Lithuania 0-2 (0-1)
Bulgaria: Ivan Dyulgerov, Valentin Antov (YC8) (46' Simeon Petrov), Kristian Dimitrov,
Viktor Popov, Ivaylo Chochev (46' Lukas Petkov (YC60)), Andrian Kraev (YC21,YC42), Ilia
Gruev (YC68), Spas Delev 79' Hristo Ivanov), Kiril Despodov (YC71), Preslav Borukov (46'
Georgi Rusev), Marin Petkov (85' Ivan Turitsov). (Coach: Mladen Krstajic (SRB)).
Lithuania: Emilijus Zubas, Linas Klimavicius, Rokas Lekiatas, Pijus Sirvys (85' Markas
Beneta), Fiodor Cernych (70' Arvydas Novikovas), Vykintas Slivka (78' Eligijus Jankauskas),
Modestas Vorobjovas, Justas Lasickas, Edgaras Utkus, Gvidas Gineitis (YC19) (70' Matijus
Remeikis), Gytis Paulauskas (85' Faustas Steponavicius). (Coach: Edgaras Jankauskas (LTU)).
Goals: Lithuania: 0-1 Pijus Sirvys (45'), 0-2 Pijus Sirvys (55').
Referee: Giorgi Kruashvili (GEO)   Attendance: 6.916

14-10-2023   Puskás Aréna, Budapest: Hungary – Serbia   2-1 (2-1)
Hungary: Dénes Dibusz, Attila Fiola (74' Endre Botka (YC90+3)), Loïc Négo (63' Bendegúz
Bolla), Ádám Lang, Attila Szalai, Milos Kerkez, Roland Sallai (74' Mihály Kata), Ádám Nagy,
Dominik Szoboszlai, Callum Styles (63' Zsolt Kalmár (YC90+3,YC90+7)), Barnabás Varga
(YC77) (84' Martin Ádám). (Coach: Marco Rossi (ITA)).
Serbia: Vanja Milinkovic-Savic (YC90+7), Aleksa Terzic (46' Filip Kostic), Nikola
Milenkovic (YC76), Strahinja Erakovic (46' Dusan Tadic), Strahinja Pavlovic, Nemanja
Gudelj, Mijat Gacinovic (67' Filip Djuricic), Sasa Lukic (84' Petar Ratkov), Sergej
Milinkovic-Savic, Aleksandar Mitrovic, Andrija Zivkovic (75' Nemanja Radonjic). (Coach:
Dragan Stojkovic (SRB)).
Goals: Hungary: 1-0 Barnabás Varga (20'), 2-1 Roland Sallai (34').
Serbia: 1-1 Strahinja Pavlovic (33').
Referee: François Letexier (FRA)   Attendance: 58.215

17-10-2023   Dariaus ir Giréno stadionas, Kaunas: Lithuania – Hungary   2-2 (2-0)
Lithuania: Emilijus Zubas, Edvinas Girdvainis, Rokas Lekiatas (YC42), Pijus Sirvys (76'
Markas Beneta), Fiodor Cernych (65' Eligijus Jankauskas), Vykintas Slivka (90' Arvydas
Novikovas), Modestas Vorobjovas, Justas Lasickas (YC90), Edgaras Utkus (YC55) (64'
Kipras Kazukolovas (YC70)), Gvidas Gineitis, Gytis Paulauskas. (Coach: Edgaras Jankauskas
(LTU)).
Hungary: Dénes Dibusz, Attila Fiola (YC74), Loïc Négo (62' Kevin Csoboth), Ádám Lang,
Attila Szalai, Milos Kerkez (46' Zsolt Nagy), Dániel Gazdag (46' Callum Styles), Roland
Sallai (90+2' Bendegúz Bolla), Ádám Nagy, Dominik Szoboszlai (YC55), Barnabás Varga
(90+2' Martin Ádám). (Coach: Marco Rossi (ITA)).
Goals: Lithuania: 1-0 Fiodor Cernych (20'), 2-0 Pijus Sirvys (36').
Hungary: 2-1 Dominik Szoboszlai (67' penalty), 2-2 Barnabás Varga (82').
Referee: Juxhin Xhaja (ALB)   Attendance: 5.349

17-10-2023   Stadion Rajko Mitic, Beograd: Serbia – Montenegro   3-1 (1-1)
Serbia: Vanja Milinkovic-Savic, Filip Mladenovic (46' Filip Kostic), Milos Veljkovic, Nikola
Milenkovic, Strahinja Pavlovic, Nemanja Gudelj (YC49) (68' Nemanja Maksimovic), Sasa
Lukic (79' Lazar Samardzic), Ivan Ilic (46' Sergej Milinkovic-Savic), Dusan Tadic,
Aleksandar Mitrovic, Andrija Zivkovic (90' Srdjan Babic). (Coach: Dragan Stojkovic (SRB)).
Montenegro: Milan Mijatovic, Zarko Tomasevic (YC89), Stefan Savic (YC58), Adam
Marusic, Andrija Vukcevic (31' Risto Radunovic), Marko Tuci (85' Milos Raickovic), Marko
Jankovic (85' Milutin Osmajic), Edvin Kuc (85' Stefan Mugosa), Stevan Jovetic, Driton Camaj
(72' Vladimir Jovovic (YC88)), Nikola Krstovic. (Coach: Miodrag Radulovic (MNE)).
Goals: Serbia: 1-0 Aleksandar Mitrovic (9'), 2-1 Aleksandar Mitrovic (74'),
3-1 Dusan Tadic (77').
Montenegro: 1-1 Stevan Jovetic (36').
Referee: Szymon Marciniak (POL)   Attendance: 25.884

16-11-2023   Stadion Vasil Levski, Sofia: Bulgaria – Hungary 2-2 (1-1)
Bulgaria: Daniel Naumov, Anton Nedyalkov, Valentin Antov (YC8,YC37), Alex Petkov, Viktor Popov, Ivaylo Chochev (43' Zhivko Atanasov (YC81)), Ilia Gruev, Filip Krastev, Spas Delev (83' Stanislav Ivanov), Kiril Despodov (83' Georgi Rusev), Martin Minchev (72' Aleksandar Kolev (YC86)). (Coach: Ilian Iliev).
Hungary: Dénes Dibusz, Loïc Négo (81' Zsolt Kalmár), Endre Botka (YC42) (81' Dániel Gazdag), Ádám Lang, Attila Szalai, Milos Kerkez (YC44,YC57), Ádám Nagy, Dominik Szoboszlai, Martin Ádám (74' András Németh), Callum Styles, Kevin Csoboth (59' Zsolt Nagy). (Coach: Marco Rossi (ITA)).
Goals: Bulgaria: 1-1 Spas Delev (24'), 2-1 Kiril Despodov (79' penalty).
Hungary: 0-1 Martin Ádám (10'), 2-2 Alex Petkov (90+7' own goal).
Referee: Daniel Stefanski (POL)   Attendance: 230

16-11-2023   Stadion Pod Goricom, Podgorica: Montenegro – Lithuania 2-0 (1-0)
Montenegro: Milan Mijatovic, Marko Vesovic, Risto Radunovic (YC34), Igor Vujacic (YC28), Slobodan Rubezic (YC32), Marko Jankovic (79' Stefan Loncar), Edvin Kuc (YC87), Stevan Jovetic (69' Marko Vukcevic), Driton Camaj (YC72) (75' Viktor Djukanovic), Nikola Krstovic (79' Dusan Bakic), Milutin Osmajic. (Coach: Miodrag Radulovic (MNE)).
Lithuania: Edvinas Gertmonas, Edvinas Girdvainis, Rokas Lekiatas, Pijus Sirvys (63' Klaudijus Upstas), Fiodor Cernych (81' Danielis Romanovskis), Vykintas Slivka, Modestas Vorobjovas (YC41) (63' Arvydas Novikovas), Justas Lasickas (YC76), Edgaras Utkus (YC57) (63' Artūr Dolznikov), Gvidas Gineitis, Gytis Paulauskas. (Coach: Edgaras Jankauskas (LTU)).
Goals: Montenegro: 1-0 Edvin Kuc (3'), 2-0 Stevan Jovetic (48').
Referee: Artur Soares Dias (POR)   Attendance: 3.647

19-11-2023   Puskás Aréna, Budapest: Hungary – Montenegro 3-1 (0-1)
Hungary: Dénes Dibusz (YC78), Ádám Lang, Zsolt Nagy (YC86), Attila Szalai, Bendegúz Bolla (46' Loïc Négo), Botond Balogh, Dániel Gazdag (YC35) (46' Zsolt Kalmár), Ádám Nagy (90+4' Soma Szuhodovszki), Dominik Szoboszlai (YC26), Martin Ádám (78' András Németh), Callum Styles (64' Krisztofer Horváth). (Coach: Marco Rossi (ITA)).
Montenegro: Milan Mijatovic (58' Filip Djukic), Marko Vesovic (YC47) (54' Marko Vukcevic), Stefan Savic (YC18), Igor Vujacic (YC70), Andrija Vukcevic, Slobodan Rubezic (YC34) (76' Milos Raickovic (YC88)), Marko Jankovic (70' Andrija Radulovic), Edvin Kuc (YC90+2), Stevan Jovetic, Driton Camaj (YC13) (70' Nikola Krstovic), Milutin Osmajic. (Coach: Miodrag Radulovic (MNE)).
Goals: Hungary: 1-1 Dominik Szoboszlai (66'), 2-1 Dominik Szoboszlai (68'), 3-1 Ádám Nagy (90+3').
Montenegro: 0-1 Slobodan Rubezic (36').
Referee: Danny Makkelie (HOL)   Attendance: 59.600

19-11-2023 Gradski stadion Dubocica, Leskovac: Serbia – Bulgaria 2-2 (1-0)
Serbia: Vanja Milinkovic-Savic, Milos Veljkovic, Srdjan Babic, Nikola Milenkovic, Nemanja Gudelj, Filip Djuricic (62' Dusan Vlahovic), Filip Kostic (85' Nemanja Maksimovic), Sasa Lukic (YC51) (76' Ivan Ilic), Dusan Tadic, Aleksandar Mitrovic (85' Filip Mladenovic), Andrija Zivkovic (76' Nemanja Radonjic). (Coach: Dragan Stojkovic (SRB)).
Bulgaria: Daniel Naumov, Zhivko Atanasov, Ivan Turitsov, Alex Petkov (YC3), Viktor Popov, Andrian Kraev (77' Ivaylo Chochev), Ilia Gruev, Filip Krastev (77' Preslav Borukov), Aleksandar Kolev (77' Ilian Iliev), Kiril Despodov (90' Svetoslav Kovachev), Martin Minchev (46' Georgi Rusev). (Coach: Ilian Iliev).
Goals: Serbia: 1-0 Milos Veljkovic (17'), 2-2 Srdjan Babic (82').
Bulgaria: 1-1 Georgi Rusev (59'), 1-2 Kiril Despodov (69').
Referee: Erik Lambrechts (BEL)   Attendance: 7.325

GROUP H

23-03-2023	Astana	Kazakhstan – Slovenia	1-2 (1-0)
23-03-2023	København	Denmark – Finland	3-1 (1-0)
23-03-2023	Serravalle	San Marino – Northern Ireland	0-2 (0-1)
26-03-2023	Astanan	Kazakhstan- Denmark	3-2 (0-2)
26-03-2023	Ljubljana	Slovenia – San Marino	2-0 (0-0)
26-03-2023	Belfast	Northern Ireland – Finland	0-1 (0-1)
16-06-2023	Helsinki	Finland – Slovenia	2-0 (1-0)
16-06-2023	København	Denmark – Northern Ireland	1-0 (0-0)
16-06-2023	Parma (ITA)	San Marino – Kazakhstan	0-3 (0-1)
19-06-2023	Helsinki	Finland – San Marino	6-0 (2-0)
19-06-2023	Belfast	Northern Ireland – Kazakhstan	0-1 (0-0)
19-06-2023	Ljubljana	Slovenia – Denmark	1-1 (1-1)
07-09-2023	Astana	Kazakhstan – Finland	0-1 (0-0)
07-09-2023	København	Denmark – San Marino	4-0 (3-0)
07-09-2023	Ljubljana	Slovenia – Northern Ireland	4-2 (3-1)
10-09-2023	Astana	Kazakhstan – Northern Ireland	1-0 (1-0)
10-09-2023	Helsinki	Finland – Denmark	0-1 (0-0)
10-09-2023	Serravalle	San Marino – Slovenia	0-4 (0-2)
14-10-2023	Belfast	Northern Ireland – San Marino	3-0 (2-0)
14-10-2023	Ljubljana	Slovenia – Finland	3-0 (2-0)
14-10-2023	København	Denmark – Kazakhstan	3-1 (2-0)
17-10-2023	Helsinki	Finland – Kazakhstan	1-2 (1-0)
17-10-2023	Belfast	Northern Ireland – Slovenia	0-1 (0-1)
17-10-2023	Serravalle	San Marino – Denmark	1-2 (0-1)
17-11-2023	Astana	Kazakhstan – San Marino	3-1 (1-0)
17-11-2023	Helsinki	Finland – Northern Ireland	4-0 (1-0)
17-11-2023	København	Denmark – Slovenia	2-1 (1-1)
20-11-2023	Belfast	Northern Ireland – Denmark	2-0 (0-0)
20-11-2023	Serravalle	San Marino – Finland	1-2 (0-0)
20-11-2023	Ljubljana	Slovenia – Kazakhstan	2-1 (1-0)

539

FINAL STANDING

Pos	Team	Pld	W	D	L	GF	GA	GD	Pts
1	Denmark	10	7	1	2	19	10	+9	22
2	Slovenia	10	7	1	2	20	9	+11	22
3	Finland	10	6	0	4	18	10	+8	18
4	Kazakhstan	10	6	0	4	16	12	+4	18
5	Northern Ireland	10	3	0	7	9	13	-4	9
6	San Marino	10	0	0	10	3	31	-28	0

Denmark and Slovenia qualified for the Final Tournament in Germany.

Finland and Kazakhstan advanced to the play-offs due to their performances in the 2022-23 UEFA Nations League.

23-03-2023   <u>Astana Arena, Astana</u>: Kazakhstan – Slovenia   1-2 (1-0)
<u>Kazakhstan</u>: Igor Shatskiy, Sergiy Maliy, Mikhail Gabyshev (68' Bagdat Kairov), Yan Vorogovskiy, Marat Bystrov <u>(YC55)</u> (79' Temirlan Erlanov), Aleksandr Marochkin, Aslan Darabaev (79' Abzal Beysebekov), Askhat Tagybergen, Ramazan Orazov <u>(YC66)</u>, Maksim Samorodov (63' Bauyrzhan Islamkhan), Abat Aymbetov (63' Bakhtiyor Zaynutdinov). (Coach: Magomed Adiev (RUS)).
<u>Slovenia</u>: Jan Oblak, Miha Blazic (5' David Brekalo), Jure Balkovec (46' Miha Zajc), Petar Stojanovic <u>(YC45+1)</u>, Zan Karnicnik, Jaka Bijol, Benjamin Verbic (70' Sandi Lovric), Jon Gorenc Stankovic, Adam Gnezda Cerin, Zan Celar (70' Zan Vipotnik), Benjamin Sesko. (Coach: Matjaz Kek (SVN)).
<u>Goals</u>: Kazakhstan: 1-0 Maksim Samorodov (24').
Slovenia: 1-1 David Brekalo (47'), 1-2 Zan Vipotnik (78').
<u>Referee</u>: Glenn Nyberg (SWE)   <u>Attendance</u>: 27.122

23-03-2023   <u>Parken, København</u>: Denmark – Finland   3-1 (1-0)
<u>Denmark</u>: Kasper Schmeichel, Simon Kjær, Andreas Christensen (18' Victor Nelsson), Joakim Mæhle <u>(YC18)</u> (65' Jens Stryger Larsen), Alexander Bah, Christian Nørgaard <u>(YC49)</u>, Pierre-Emile Højbjerg, Mathias Jensen (77' Philip Billing), Mikkel Damsgaard (65' Mohamed Daramy), Martin Braithwaite (77' Jonas Wind), Rasmus Højlund. (Coach: Kasper Hjulmand (DEN)).
<u>Finland</u>: Lukás Hrádecký, Nikolai Alho, Richard Jensen (74' Tuomas Ollila <u>(YC78)</u>), Robert Ivanov, Leo Väisänen, Robin Lod (73' Marcus Forss), Glen Kamara, Kaan Kairinen, Teemu Pukki, Joel Pohjanpalo, Oliver Antman <u>(YC33)</u> (72' Anssi Suhonen). (Coach: Markku Kanerva (FIN)).
<u>Goals</u>: Denmark: 1-0 Rasmus Højlund (21'), 2-1 Rasmus Højlund (82'),
3-1 Rasmus Højlund (90+3').
Finland: 1-1 Oliver Antman (53').
<u>Referee</u>: Daniel Siebert (GER)   <u>Attendance</u>: 35.851

23-03-2023 Stadio Olimpico di Serravalle, Serravalle:
San Marino – Northern Ireland 0-2 (0-1)
San Marino: Elia Benedettini, Mirko Palazzi (46' Alessandro Tosi), Roberto Di Maio, Manuel Battistini, Filippo Fabbri, Dante Rossi (46' Michele Cevoli), Alessandro Golinucci, Lorenzo Capicchioni (72' Michael Battistini), Lorenzo Lazzari, Filippo Berardi (60' Danilo Rinaldi), Nicola Nanni (85' Matteo Vitaioli). (Coach: Fabrizio Costantini (SMR)).

Northern Ireland: Bailey Peacock-Farrell, Craig Cathcart, Paddy McNair, Jamal Lewis (74' Shane Ferguson), Ciaron Brown (YC43) (82' Isaac Price), Daniel Ballard (67' Cameron McGeehan), Conor Bradley, George Saville (73' Jordan Thompson), Shea Charles, Conor Washington (67' Josh Magennis), Dion Charles. (Coach: Michael O'Neill (NIR)).
Goals: Northern Ireland: 0-1 Dion Charles (24'), 0-2 Dion Charles (55').
Referee: Gergö Bogár (HUN)   Attendance: 2.099

26-03-2023 Astana Arena, Astana: Kazakhstan – Denmark 3-2 (0-2)
Kazakhstan: Igor Shatskiy (YC90+4), Sergiy Maliy (46' Temirlan Erlanov), Abzal Beysebekov (83' Aslan Darabaev), Mikhail Gabyshev (34' Lev Skvortsov), Yan Vorogovskiy, Aleksandr Marochkin, Nuraly Alip, Askhat Tagybergen, Ramazan Orazov, Bakhtiyor Zaynutdinov (79' Bauyrzhan Islamkhan), Maksim Samorodov (78' Abat Aymbetov (YC90,YC90+6)). (Coach: Magomed Adiev (RUS)).
Denmark: Kasper Schmeichel, Simon Kjær, Joakim Mæhle (83' Rasmus Kristensen), Victor Nelsson, Alexander Bah (64' Jens Stryger Larsen), Christian Nørgaard, Pierre-Emile Højbjerg, Mathias Jensen (65' Philip Billing), Mikkel Damsgaard (65' Mohamed Daramy), Jonas Wind (87' Martin Braithwaite), Rasmus Højlund (YC90+3). (Coach: Kasper Hjulmand (DEN)).
Goals: Kazakhstan: 1-2 Bakhtiyor Zaynutdinov (73' penalty), 2-2 Askhat Tagybergen (86'), 3-2 Abat Aymbetov (89').
Denmark: 0-1 Rasmus Højlund (21'), 0-2 Rasmus Højlund (35').
Referee: Novak Simovic (SRB)   Attendance: 28.697

26-03-2023 Stadion Stozice, Ljubljana: Slovenia – San Marino 2-0 (0-0)
Slovenia: Jan Oblak, Petar Stojanovic, David Brekalo, Zan Karnicnik (58' Jure Balkovec), Jaka Bijol (36' Vanja Drkusic), Miha Zajc (82' Jon Gorenc Stankovic), Benjamin Verbic (82' Tomi Horvat), Sandi Lovric, Adam Gnezda Cerin, Andrés Vombergar (58' Zan Vipotnik), Benjamin Sesko. (Coach: Matjaz Kek (SVN)).
San Marino: Elia Benedettini, Michele Cevoli, Alessandro D'Addario (YC45), Alessandro Tosi, Filippo Fabbri (YC54) (72' Simone Franciosi (YC78)), Dante Rossi (46' Roberto Di Maio), Alessandro Golinucci, Michael Battistini, Lorenzo Lunadei (73' Matteo Vitaioli), Filippo Berardi (58' Lorenzo Lazzari), Nicola Nanni (86' Danilo Rinaldi). (Coach: Fabrizio Costantini (SMR)).
Goals: Slovenia: 1-0 Benjamin Sesko (56'), 2-0 Roberto Di Maio (60' own goal).
Referee: Nathan Verboomen (BEL)   Attendance: 10.282

26-03-2023 Windsor Park, Belfast: Northern Ireland – Finland 0-1 (0-1)
Northern Ireland: Bailey Peacock-Farrell, Craig Cathcart, Paddy McNair, Jamal Lewis, Ciaron Brown, Daniel Ballard (50' Josh Magennis), Conor Bradley, Jordan Thompson (79' George Saville), Shea Charles (79' Isaac Price), Conor Washington (69' Gavin Whyte), Dion Charles (YC74). (Coach: Michael O'Neill (NIR)).
Finland: Lukás Hrádecký, Nikolai Alho (87' Robert Taylor), Richard Jensen (YC48) (52' Matti Peltola), Robert Ivanov, Leo Väisänen, Rasmus Schüller, Robin Lod, Glen Kamara, Anssi Suhonen (70' Pyry Soiri (YC90+4)), Teemu Pukki (70' Marcus Forss), Benjamin Källman (87' Joel Pohjanpalo). (Coach: Markku Kanerva (FIN)).
Goal: Finland: 0-1 Benjamin Källman (28').
Referee: Ivan Kruzliak (SVK)   Attendance: 17.936

541

16-06-2023   Helsingin olympiastadion, Helsinki: Finland – Slovenia   2-0 (1-0)
Finland: Lukás Hrádecký, Nikolai Alho (71' Jere Uronen), Richard Jensen (65' Matti Peltola), Robert Ivanov, Arttu Hoskonen, Rasmus Schüller (79' Glen Kamara), Ilmari Niskanen (YC66), Kaan Kairinen, Teemu Pukki (65' Daniel Håkans), Joel Pohjanpalo, Oliver Antman (79' Anssi Suhonen). (Coach: Markku Kanerva (FIN)).
Slovenia: Vid Belec, Jure Balkovec, Petar Stojanovic (78' Benjamin Verbic), David Brekalo, Zan Karnicnik, Jaka Bijol, Miha Zajc (78' Timi Elsnik), Sandi Lovric (65' Jan Mlakar), Adam Gnezda Cerin, Andraz Sporar (YC55) (65' Zan Vipotnik), Benjamin Sesko (86' Zan Celar). (Coach: Matjaz Kek (SVN)).
Goals: Finland: 1-0 Joel Pohjanpalo (13'), 2-0 Oliver Antman (64').
Referee: Guillermo Cuadra Fernández (ESP)   Attendance: 32.560

16-06-2023   Parken, København: Denmark – Northern Ireland   1-0 (0-0)
Denmark: Kasper Schmeichel, Simon Kjær, Andreas Christensen, Joachim Andersen, Joakim Mæhle (73' Jens Stryger Larsen), Christian Eriksen, Pierre-Emile Højbjerg, Martin Braithwaite (73' Mikkel Damsgaard), Jonas Wind (80' Rasmus Kristensen), Andreas Skov Olsen (80' Jesper Lindstrøm), Rasmus Højlund (90+2' Mohamed Daramy). (Coach: Kasper Hjulmand (DEN)).
Northern Ireland: Bailey Peacock-Farrell, Jonny Evans (YC76), Paddy McNair (YC71), Ciaron Brown, Trai Hume (YC88), Conor Bradley (77' Conor McMenamin), George Saville, Ali McCann (YC72) (85' Callum Marshall), Isaac Price (77' Dale Taylor), Shea Charles (69' Jordan Thompson), Shayne Lavery (69' Dion Charles). (Coach: Michael O'Neill (NIR)).
Goal: Denmark: 1-0 Jonas Wind (47').
Referee: Daniel Stefanski (POL)   Attendance: 35.701

16-06-2023   Stadio Ennio Tardini, Parma (ITA): San Marino – Kazakhstan   0-3 (0-1)
San Marino: Elia Benedettini, Roberto Di Maio, Manuel Battistini, Alessandro Tosi (65' Adolfo Hirsch), Filippo Fabbri (82' Michele Cevoli), Dante Rossi, Alessandro Golinucci, Lorenzo Capicchioni (YC67) (81' Matteo Vitaioli), Lorenzo Lazzari (YC70), Filippo Berardi (65' Luca Ceccaroli), Nicola Nanni (80' Michael Battistini). (Coach: Fabrizio Costantini (SMR)).
Kazakhstan: Igor Shatskiy, Abzal Beysebekov (57' Bakhtiyor Zaynutdinov (YC72)), Mikhail Gabyshev (78' Lev Skvortsov), Yan Vorogovskiy (78' Timur Dosmagambetov), Marat Bystrov, Aleksandr Marochkin, Nuraly Alip, Islambek Kuat (YC89), Askhat Tagybergen (71' Arman Kenesov), Ramazan Orazov, Maksim Samorodov (71' Elkhan Astanov). (Coach: Magomed Adiev (RUS)).
Goals: Kazakhstan: 0-1 Yan Vorogovskiy (37'), 0-2 Askhat Tagybergen (64' penalty), 0-3 Bakhtiyor Zaynutdinov (90+5').
Referee: Anastasios Papapetrou (GRE)   Attendance: 528

The match was played at Stadio Ennio Tardini, Parma, Italy, due to the redevelopment of the San Marion's regular stadium Stadio Olimpico di Serravalle, Serravalle.

19-06-2023   Helsingin olympiastadion, Helsinki: Finland – San Marino 6-0 (2-0)
Finland: Lukás Hrádecký, Nikolai Alho (81' Pyry Soiri), Jere Uronen (46' Noah Pallas),
Robert Ivanov, Diogo Tomas, Rasmus Schüller (60' Robert Taylor), Glen Kamara, Anssi
Suhonen, Joel Pohjanpalo (60' Teemu Pukki), Benjamin Källman, Oliver Antman (61' Daniel
Håkans). (Coach: Markku Kanerva (FIN)).
San Marino: Elia Benedettini, Roberto Di Maio (89' Simone Franciosi), Alessandro
D'Addario, Alessandro Tosi (YC51) (78' Manuel Battistini), Filippo Fabbri, Dante Rossi,
Alessandro Golinucci, Michael Battistini (79' Enrico Golinucci), Lorenzo Lunadei (67'
Marcello Mularoni), Filippo Berardi (66' Matteo Vitaioli), Nicola Nanni. (Coach: Fabrizio
Costantini (SMR)).
Goals: Finland: 1-0 Glen Kamara (16'), 2-0 Benjamin Källman (39'), 3-0 Daniel Håkans (65'),
4-0 Daniel Håkans (72'), 5-0 Daniel Håkans (74'), 6-0 Teemu Pukki (76').
Referee: Genc Nuza (KOS)   Attendance: 32.812

19-06-2023   Windsor Park, Belfast: Northern Ireland – Kazakhstan 0-1 (0-0)
Northern Ireland: Bailey Peacock-Farrell, Jonny Evans (64' Conor McMenamin), Craig
Cathcart, Paddy McNair, Trai Hume, George Saville (YC66), Jordan Thompson (84' Ciaron
Brown), Ali McCann (71' Dale Taylor), Isaac Price, Shea Charles, Dion Charles (72' Shayne
Lavery). (Coach: Michael O'Neill (NIR)).
Kazakhstan: Igor Shatskiy, Abzal Beysebekov, Mikhail Gabyshev (68' Lev Skvortsov), Yan
Vorogovskiy, Marat Bystrov, Aleksandr Marochkin, Nuraly Alip (YC67), Askhat Tagybergen
(YC70) (81' Erkin Tapalov), Ramazan Orazov (81' Elkhan Astanov), Bakhtiyor Zaynutdinov
(75' Islambek Kuat), Maksim Samorodov (80' Abat Aymbetov). (Coach: Magomed Adiev
(RUS)).
Goal: Kazakhstan: 0-1 Abat Aymbetov (88').
Referee: Roi Reinshreiber (ISR)   Attendance: 18.002

19-06-2023   Stadion Stozice, Ljubljana: Slovenia – Denmark 1-1 (1-1)
Slovenia: Matevz Vidovsek, Erik Janza, Petar Stojanovic, David Brekalo (YC75), Zan
Karnicnik, Jaka Bijol, Timi Elsnik, Adam Gnezda Cerin, Andraz Sporar (81' Zan Vipotnik),
Jan Mlakar (90+3' Benjamin Verbic), Benjamin Sesko. (Coach: Matjaz Kek (SVN)).
Denmark: Kasper Schmeichel, Simon Kjær, Mathias "Zanka" Jørgensen (YC69), Jens Stryger
Larsen (84' Victor Kristiansen), Andreas Christensen, Alexander Bah, Christian Eriksen,
Pierre-Emile Højbjerg, Jonas Wind (58' Mikkel Damsgaard), Andreas Skov Olsen (71' Yussuf
Poulsen), Rasmus Højlund (71' Martin Braithwaite). (Coach: Kasper Hjulmand (DEN)).
Goals: Slovenia: 1-0 Andraz Sporar (25').
Denmark: 1-1 Rasmus Højlund (42').
Referee: François Letexier (FRA)   Attendance: 14.382

07-09-2023   Astana Arena, Astana: Kazakhstan – Finland 0-1 (0-0)
Kazakhstan: Igor Shatskiy, Yan Vorogovskiy (82' Timur Dosmagambetov), Marat Bystrov,
Aleksandr Marochkin, Nuraly Alip, Lev Skvortsov (67' Erkin Tapalov), Aslan Darabaev (67'
Ramazan Orazov), Islambek Kuat, Askhat Tagybergen, Bakhtiyor Zaynutdinov (82' Islam
Chesnokov (YC87)), Abat Aymbetov (46' Maksim Samorodov (YC60)). (Coach: Magomed
Adiev (RUS)).
Finland: Lukás Hrádecký, Nikolai Alho, Richard Jensen, Robert Ivanov, Arttu Hoskonen,
Rasmus Schüller (67' Glen Kamara), Ilmari Niskanen, Kaan Kairinen, Teemu Pukki (67'
Benjamin Källman), Joel Pohjanpalo, Oliver Antman (85' Robert Taylor). (Coach: Markku
Kanerva (FIN)).
Goal: Finland: 0-1 Oliver Antman (78').
Referee: Radu Petrescu (ROM)   Attendance: 30.019

543

07-09-2023   Parken, København: Denmark – San Marino   4-0 (3-0)
Denmark: Kasper Schmeichel, Simon Kjær, Jens Stryger Larsen, Joachim Andersen, Joakim Mæhle, Christian Eriksen, Pierre-Emile Højbjerg (59' Rasmus Højlund), Mathias Jensen (59' Morten Hjulmand), Jesper Lindstrøm (72' Nicolai Vallys), Jonas Wind (82' Yussuf Poulsen), Andreas Skov Olsen (59' Martin Braithwaite). (Coach: Kasper Hjulmand (DEN)).
San Marino: Elia Benedettini, Roberto Di Maio, Manuel Battistini (66' Alessandro D'Addario), Alessandro Tosi (90' Andrea Magi), Simone Franciosi, Dante Rossi, Alessandro Golinucci, Luca Ceccaroli (46' Matteo Vitaioli), Lorenzo Capicchioni, Lorenzo Lazzari (86' Marcello Mularoni), Fabio Tomassini (66' Adolfo Hirsch). (Coach: Fabrizio Costantini (SMR)).
Goals: Denmark: 1-0 Pierre-Emile Højbjerg (26'), 2-0 Joakim Mæhle (28'), 3-0 Jonas Wind (40'), 4-0 Christian Eriksen (90+3').
Referee: Vitalijs Spasjonnikovs (LVA)   Attendance: 36.262

07-09-2023   Stadion Stozice, Ljubljana: Slovenia – Northern Ireland   4-2 (3-1)
Slovenia: Jan Oblak, Erik Janza (85' Jure Balkovec), Petar Stojanovic, David Brekalo (YC90+5), Zan Karnicnik, Jaka Bijol, Timi Elsnik (90' Sandi Lovric), Adam Gnezda Cerin, Andraz Sporar, Jan Mlakar (74' Jasmin Kurtic), Benjamin Sesko (85' Zan Vipotnik). (Coach: Matjaz Kek (SVN)).
Northern Ireland: Bailey Peacock-Farrell, Jonny Evans, Paddy McNair, Ciaron Brown (21' Craig Cathcart, 76' Paul Smyth), Trai Hume, George Saville, Conor McMenamin, Isaac Price (YC48) (64' Ali McCann (YC90+3)), Shea Charles (YC57), Matty Kennedy (46' Conor Washington), Dion Charles (46' Josh Magennis). (Coach: Michael O'Neill (NIR)).
Goals: Slovenia: 1-0 Andraz Sporar (3'), 2-1 Jonny Evans (17' own goal), 3-1 Benjamin Sesko (42'), 4-2 Andraz Sporar (56').
Northern Ireland: 1-1 Isaac Price (7'), 3-2 Jonny Evans (53').
Referee: Marco Guida (ITA)   Attendance: 12.587

10-09-2023   Astana Arena, Astana: Kazakhstan – Northern Ireland   1-0 (1-0)
Kazakhstan: Igor Shatskiy, Abzal Beysebekov (71' Aslan Darabaev), Yan Vorogovskiy (46' Timur Dosmagambetov (YC87)), Marat Bystrov (YC90), Aleksandr Marochkin, Nuraly Alip, Askhat Tagybergen (YC73), Erkin Tapalov (71' Sergiy Maliy), Ramazan Orazov, Bakhtiyor Zaynutdinov (88' Abat Aymbetov), Maksim Samorodov (YC30) (56' Islambek Kuat (YC77)). (Coach: Magomed Adiev (RUS)). (Not used sub: Elkhan Astanov (YC90+7)).
Northern Ireland: Bailey Peacock-Farrell, Jonny Evans, Paddy McNair (YC90+5), Daniel Ballard (YC83), Trai Hume, George Saville (46' Jordan Thompson (YC90+7)), Conor McMenamin (46' Paul Smyth), Ali McCann (70' Josh Magennis), Shea Charles, Matty Kennedy (63' Jordan Jones), Conor Washington (81' Dion Charles). (Coach: Michael O'Neill (NIR) (YC90)).
Goal: Kazakhstan: 1-0 Maksim Samorodov (27').
Referee: Daniel Schlager (GER)   Attendance: 28.458

544

10-09-2023   Helsingin olympiastadion, Helsinki: Finland – Denmark   0-1 (0-0)
Finland: Lukás Hrádecký, Nikolai Alho (62' Pyry Soiri), Robert Ivanov (YC18), Arttu
Hoskonen, Matti Peltola, Rasmus Schüller (62' Oliver Antman), Glen Kamara, Ilmari
Niskanen (12' Jere Uronen (YC53)), Kaan Kairinen, Teemu Pukki (62' Joel Pohjanpalo
(YC79)), Benjamin Källman (84' Robert Taylor). (Coach: Markku Kanerva (FIN)).
Denmark: Kasper Schmeichel, Andreas Christensen, Joachim Andersen (YC90+4), Rasmus
Kristensen (YC13) (80' Victor Kristiansen), Joakim Mæhle, Christian Eriksen, Christian
Nørgaard (YC62) (75' Thomas Delaney), Pierre-Emile Højbjerg, Jesper Lindstrøm (46'
Rasmus Højlund), Jonas Wind (66' Yussuf Poulsen (YC73)), Andreas Skov Olsen (80' Simon
Kjær). (Coach: Kasper Hjulmand (DEN)).
Goal: Denmark: 0-1 Pierre-Emile Højbjerg (86').
Referee: Szymon Marciniak (POL)   Attendance: 32.571

10-09-2023   Stadio Olimpico di Serravalle, Serravalle:
                    San Marino – Slovenia   0-4 (0-2)
San Marino: Elia Benedettini, Roberto Di Maio (88' Michele Cevoli), Alessandro D'Addario,
Alessandro Tosi (YC7) (46' Lorenzo Capicchioni), Simone Franciosi, Dante Rossi, Alessandro
Golinucci, Manuel Battistini (YC31) (74' Lorenzo Lunadei), Marcello Mularoni (46' Andrea
Magi), Lorenzo Lazzari, Matteo Vitaioli (YC24) (60' Mattia Stefanelli). (Coach: Fabrizio
Costantini (SMR)).
Slovenia: Jan Oblak, Miha Blazic (12' Vanja Drkusic), Petar Stojanovic (YC41) (66' Jure
Balkovec), Zan Karnicnik, Jaka Bijol, Sandi Lovric, Timi Elsnik (72' Jasmin Kurtic), Adam
Gnezda Cerin, Andraz Sporar (72' Luka Zahovic), Jan Mlakar, Zan Vipotnik (66' Benjamin
Verbic). (Coach: Matjaz Kek (SVN)).
Goals: Slovenia: 0-1 Zan Vipotnik (4'), 0-2 Jan Mlakar (16'), 0-3 Sandi Lovric (61'),
0-4 Zan Karnicnik (67').
Referee: Mykola Balakin (UKR)   Attendance: 844

14-10-2023   Windsor Park, Belfast: Northern Ireland – San Marino   3-0 (2-0)
Northern Ireland: Conor Hazard, Jonny Evans (63' Isaac Price), Paddy McNair (YC90+4),
Jamal Lewis (YC43) (79' Brodie Spencer), Daniel Ballard, Trai Hume, Jordan Thompson,
Shea Charles, Josh Magennis (63' Conor Washington (YC64)), Paul Smyth (63' Callum
Marshall), Dale Taylor (79' Conor McMenamin). (Coach: Michael O'Neill (NIR)).
San Marino: Elia Benedettini, Roberto Di Maio, Manuel Battistini, Simone Franciosi (46'
Alessandro D'Addario), Filippo Fabbri, Dante Rossi, Alessandro Golinucci, Lorenzo
Capicchioni (76' Luca Ceccaroli), Lorenzo Lazzari (88' Lorenzo Lunadei), Matteo Vitaioli
(60' Marcello Mularoni), Nicola Nanni. (Coach: Fabrizio Costantini (SMR)).
Goals: Northern Ireland: 1-0 Paul Smyth (5'), 2-0 Josh Magennis (11'),
3-0 Conor McMenamin (81').
Referee: Bram Van Driessche (BEL)   Attendance: 17.886

14-10-2023   Stadion Stozice, Ljubljana: Slovenia – Finland   3-0 (2-0)
Slovenia: Jan Oblak, Erik Janza (YC10), Miha Blazic, Petar Stojanovic (90+4' Jon Gorenc
Stankovic), Zan Karnicnik, Jaka Bijol, Timi Elsnik, Adam Gnezda Cerin, Andraz Sporar (80'
Jasmin Kurtic), Jan Mlakar (80' Benjamin Verbic), Benjamin Sesko (60' Zan Vipotnik).
(Coach: Matjaz Kek (SVN)).
Finland: Lukás Hrádecký, Nikolai Alho, Jere Uronen, Robert Ivanov (77' Marcus Forss), Leo
Väisänen, Arttu Hoskonen, Rasmus Schüller (46' Daniel Håkans), Glen Kamara, Kaan
Kairinen, Teemu Pukki, Benjamin Källman (YC34) (46' Joel Pohjanpalo). (Coach: Markku
Kanerva (FIN)).
Goals: Slovenia: 1-0 Benjamin Sesko (16' penalty), 2-0 Benjamin Sesko (28'),
3-0 Erik Janza (90+2').
Referee: Daniele Orsato (ITA)   Attendance: 15.823

14-10-2023   Parken, København: Denmark – Kazakhstan   3-1 (2-0)
Denmark: Kasper Schmeichel, Simon Kjær (YC27), Andreas Christensen (YC23), Joachim
Andersen, Joakim Mæhle, Christian Eriksen, Pierre-Emile Højbjerg, Robert Skov (69' Rasmus
Kristensen), Kasper Dolberg (69' Yussuf Poulsen), Jonas Wind (83' Christian Nørgaard),
Rasmus Højlund (90+1' Jesper Lindstrøm). (Coach: Kasper Hjulmand (DEN)).
Kazakhstan: Igor Shatskiy, Abzal Beysebekov (62' Islambek Kuat), Timur Dosmagambetov
(46' Yan Vorogovskiy), Marat Bystrov, Aleksandr Marochkin, Bagdat Kairov, Nuraly Alip
(YC85), Ramazan Orazov, Bakhtiyor Zaynutdinov (75' Aslan Darabaev), Maksim Samorodov
(80' Islam Chesnokov), Abat Aymbetov (46' Askhat Tagybergen). (Coach: Magomed Adiev
(RUS)).
Goals: Denmark: 1-0 Jonas Wind (36'), 2-0 Robert Skov (45+1'), 3-0 Robert Skov (48').
Kazakhstan: 3-1 Yan Vorogovskiy (58').
Referee: Michael Oliver (ENG)   Attendance: 35.845

17-10-2023   Helsingin olympiastadion, Helsinki: Finland – Kazakhstan   1-2 (1-0)
Finland: Lukás Hrádecký, Nikolai Alho (88' Pyry Soiri), Richard Jensen (88' Jere Uronen),
Robert Ivanov (YC72), Arttu Hoskonen, Robert Taylor (77' Benjamin Källman), Glen
Kamara, Kaan Kairinen, Daniel Håkans, Teemu Pukki (77' Marcus Forss), Joel Pohjanpalo.
(Coach: Markku Kanerva (FIN)).
Kazakhstan: Igor Shatskiy, Abzal Beysebekov (YC90+5) (55' Islambek Kuat (YC81)), Yan
Vorogovskiy, Marat Bystrov (87' Temirlan Erlanov), Aleksandr Marochkin (YC27), Bagdat
Kairov (86' Lev Skvortsov (YC90+3)), Nuraly Alip, Askhat Tagybergen (86' Erkin Tapalov),
Ramazan Orazov (YC90+5), Bakhtiyor Zaynutdinov, Maksim Samorodov (YC79) (85' Abat
Aymbetov). (Coach: Magomed Adiev (RUS)).
Goals: Finland: 1-0 Robert Taylor (28').
Kazakhstan: 1-1 Bakhtiyor Zaynutdinov (77' penalty), 1-2 Bakhtiyor Zaynutdinov (89').
Referee: Irfan Peljto (BIH)   Attendance: 30.375

17-10-2023   Windsor Park, Belfast: Northern Ireland – Slovenia   0-1 (0-1)
Northern Ireland: Bailey Peacock-Farrell, Jonny Evans (YC87), Eoin Toal, Jamal Lewis, Trai
Hume, Jordan Thompson (YC59) (63' Isaac Price), Bradley Lyons (86' Conor McMenamin),
Shea Charles (YC4,YC58), Josh Magennis (46' Conor Washington), Paul Smyth (YC60) (63'
Dion Charles), Dale Taylor (62' George Saville). (Coach: Michael O'Neill (NIR)).
Slovenia: Jan Oblak, Erik Janza (84' Benjamin Verbic), Miha Blazic, Petar Stojanovic, Zan
Karnicnik, Jaka Bijol, Timi Elsnik (YC37), Adam Gnezda Cerin, Andraz Sporar (YC56) (76'
Jasmin Kurtic), Jan Mlakar (75' Sandi Lovric), Benjamin Sesko. (Coach: Matjaz Kek (SVN)).
Goal: Slovenia: 0-1 Adam Gnezda Cerin (5').
Referee: István Kovács (ROM)   Attendance: 16.332

17-10-2023   Stadio Olimpico di Serravalle, Serravalle:
               San Marino – Denmark   1-2 (0-1)
San Marino: Elia Benedettini, Michele Cevoli (74' Matteo Vitaioli), Alessandro D'Addario
(55' Lorenzo Capicchioni (YC83)), Alessandro Tosi, Filippo Fabbri (YC70) (88' Simone
Franciosi), Dante Rossi, Alessandro Golinucci, Michael Battistini (56' Manuel Battistini),
Marcello Mularoni (YC90+7), Lorenzo Lazzari (75' Roberto Di Maio (YC88)), Nicola Nanni.
(Coach: Fabrizio Costantini (SMR)).
Denmark: Kasper Schmeichel, Simon Kjær, Joachim Andersen (YC65), Joakim Mæhle (90+2'
Rasmus Kristensen), Elias Jelert (62' Robert Skov), Christian Eriksen, Christian Nørgaard,
Pierre-Emile Højbjerg, Jesper Lindstrøm (62' Yussuf Poulsen), Mohamed Daramy (62' Jonas
Wind), Rasmus Højlund (YC70) (90+2' Mathias Jensen). (Coach: Kasper Hjulmand (DEN)).
Goals: San Marino: 1-1 Alessandro Golinucci (61').
Denmark: 0-1 Rasmus Højlund (42'), 1-2 Yussuf Poulsen (70').
Referee: Viktor Kopiyevskyi (UKR)   Attendance: 2.984

546

17-11-2023 Astana Arena, Astana: Kazakhstan – San Marino 3-1 (1-0)
Kazakhstan: Igor Shatskiy, Sergiy Maliy, Abzal Beysebekov, Timur Dosmagambetov (62' Yan Vorogovskiy), Marat Bystrov (54' Temirlan Erlanov (YC88)), Aleksandr Marochkin, Bagdat Kairov (54' Lev Skvortsov), Aleksandr Zuev (74' Erkin Tapalov), Ramazan Orazov (55' Arman Kenesov (YC63)), Islam Chesnokov, Abat Aymbetov. (Coach: Magomed Adiev (RUS)).
San Marino: Elia Benedettini, Roberto Di Maio (46' Simone Franciosi), Manuel Battistini, Alessandro Tosi, Filippo Fabbri (YC88), Dante Rossi, Alessandro Golinucci, Marcello Mularoni (YC50) (90+5' Lorenzo Lunadei), Lorenzo Capicchioni (90+4' Enrico Golinucci), Lorenzo Lazzari (77' Samuel Pancotti (YC90+1)), Nicola Nanni (27' Matteo Vitaioli). (Coach: Fabrizio Costantini (SMR)).
Goals: Kazakhstan: 1-0 Islam Chesnokov (19'), 2-0 Islam Chesnokov (51'), 3-1 Abat Aymbetov (90+2' penalty).
San Marino: 2-1 Simone Franciosi (60').
Referee: Haral Lechner (AUT)   Attendance: 30.100

17-11-2023 Helsingin olympiastadion, Helsinki:
Finland – Northern Ireland 4-0 (1-0)
Finland: Lukás Hrádecký, Nikolai Alho (83' Noah Pallas), Miro Tenho, Robert Ivanov, Matti Peltola, Rasmus Schüller (72' Robin Lod), Glen Kamara, Fredrik Jensen (60' Teemu Pukki), Kaan Kairinen, Daniel Håkans (72' Robert Taylor), Joel Pohjanpalo (83' Lucas Lingman). (Coach: Markku Kanerva (FIN)).
Northern Ireland: Conor Hazard, Paddy McNair, Eoin Toal, Jamal Lewis, Daniel Ballard, Trai Hume (85' Michael Forbes), George Saville, Jordan Thompson (77' Brodie Spencer), Isaac Price (85' Callum Marshall), Dion Charles (60' Josh Magennis), Ross McCausland (59' Conor Washington). (Coach: Michael O'Neill (NIR)).
Goals: Finland: 1-0 Joel Pohjanpalo (42' penalty), 2-0 Daniel Håkans (48'), 3-0 Teemu Pukki (74'), 4-0 Robin Lod (88').
Referee: Aliyar Aghayev (AZE)   Attendance: 28.711

17-11-2023 Parken, København: Denmark – Slovenia 2-1 (1-1)
Denmark: Kasper Schmeichel, Jannik Vestergaard, Andreas Christensen, Joachim Andersen, Joakim Mæhle, Victor Kristiansen (86' Rasmus Kristensen), Thomas Delaney (75' Morten Hjulmand), Christian Nørgaard (YC32) (46' Mathias Jensen), Pierre-Emile Højbjerg, Yussuf Poulsen (90+1' Jesper Lindstrøm), Jonas Wind (86' Kasper Dolberg). (Coach: Kasper Hjulmand (DEN)).
Slovenia: Jan Oblak, Erik Janza (62' Vanja Drkusic), Miha Blazic, Zan Karnicnik, Jaka Bijol, Benjamin Verbic (73' Sandi Lovric), Timi Elsnik (YC32) (62' Jasmin Kurtic), Adam Gnezda Cerin, Jan Mlakar (86' Miha Zajc), Zan Vipotnik, Benjamin Sesko (73' Jon Gorenc Stankovic). (Coach: Matjaz Kek (SVN)).
Goals: Denmark: 1-0 Joakim Mæhle (26'), 2-1 Thomas Delaney (54').
Slovenia: 1-1 Erik Janza (30').
Referee: José María Sánchez Martínez (ESP)   Attendance: 35.608

547

20-11-2023   Windsor Park, Belfast: Northern Ireland – Denmark   2-0 (0-0)
Northern Ireland: Conor Hazard, Paddy McNair, Eoin Toal, Jamal Lewis, Ciaron Brown, Trai
Hume (YC33), George Saville (YC28) (82' Jordan Thompson), Isaac Price (78' Paul Smyth),
Shea Charles, Dion Charles (87' Conor Washington), Dale Taylor (78' Conor McMenamin).
(Coach: Michael O'Neill (NIR)).
Denmark: Kasper Schmeichel, Andreas Christensen, Joachim Andersen (YC90+2), Rasmus
Kristensen, Victor Kristiansen, Mathias Jensen (61' Thomas Delaney), Morten Hjulmand (73'
Jonas Wind), Matthew O'Riley (61' Pierre-Emile Højbjerg (YC90)), Jesper Lindstrøm (56'
Yussuf Poulsen), Kasper Dolberg, Mohamed Daramy (61' Jannik Vestergaard). (Coach:
Kasper Hjulmand (DEN)).
Goals: Northern Ireland: 1-0 Isaac Price (60'), 2-0 Dion Charles (81').
Referee: Jérôme Brisard (FRA)   Attendance: 17.366

20-11-2023   Stadio Olimpico di Serravalle, Serravalle:
                             San Marino – Finland   1-2 (0-0)
San Marino: Aldo Simoncini, Mirko Palazzi, Alessandro D'Addario, Alessandro Tosi (YC56),
Simone Franciosi, Dante Rossi (78' Manuel Battistini (YC90+1)), Alessandro Golinucci,
Marcello Mularoni (78' Tommaso Zafferani (YC90+4)), Lorenzo Capicchioni (YC68),
Lorenzo Lazzari (90+2' Andrea Magi), Matteo Vitaioli (YC24) (62' Filippo Berardi). (Coach:
Fabrizio Costantini (SMR)).
Finland: Viljami Sinisalo, Pyry Soiri (71' Jere Uronen), Richard Jensen (YC90+6), Arttu
Hoskonen, Tomas Galvez (YC35), Robert Taylor, Robin Lod (46' Joel Pohjanpalo), Glen
Kamara (70' Kaan Kairinen), Lucas Lingman, Daniel Håkans (71' Benjamin Källman), Teemu
Pukki (79' Fredrik Jensen). (Coach: Markku Kanerva (FIN)).
Goals: San Marino: 1-2 Filippo Berardi (90+7' penalty).
Finland: 0-1 Pyry Soiri (50'), 0-2 Pyry Soiri (58').
Referee: Manfredas Lukjancukas (LTU)   Attendance: 1.427

20-11-2023   Stadion Stozice, Ljubljana: Slovenia – Kazakhstan   2-1 (1-0)
Slovenia: Jan Oblak, Erik Janza (87' Vanja Drkusic), Miha Blazic, Petar Stojanovic (90+2' Jon
Gorenc Stankovic), Zan Karnicnik, Jaka Bijol, Timi Elsnik, Adam Gnezda Cerin, Andraz
Sporar (87' Jasmin Kurtic), Jan Mlakar (72' Benjamin Verbic (YC86)), Benjamin Sesko.
(Coach: Matjaz Kek (SVN)).
Kazakhstan: Igor Shatskiy, Sergiy Maliy (YC79), Abzal Beysebekov (82' Erkin Tapalov), Yan
Vorogovskiy (YC40), Marat Bystrov, Aleksandr Marochkin, Nuraly Alip (YC90), Islambek
Kuat (YC61) (64' Arman Kenesov), Ramazan Orazov, Maksim Samorodov (90+2' Abat
Aymbetov), Islam Chesnokov (81' Ivan Sviridov). (Coach: Magomed Adiev (RUS)).
Goals: Slovenia: 1-0 Benjamin Sesko (41' penalty), 2-1 Benjamin Verbic (86').
Kazakhstan: 1-1 Ramazan Orazov (48').
Referee: Szymon Marciniak (POL)   Attendance: 16.432

548

GROUP I

25-03-2023	Novi Sad (SRB)	Belarus – Switzerland	0-5 (0-3)
25-03-2023	Tel Aviv	Israel – Kosovo	1-1 (0-1)
25-03-2023	Andorra la Vella	Andorra – Romania	0-2 (0-1)
28-03-2023	Pristina	Kosovo – Andorra	1-1 (0-0)
28-03-2023	Bucuresti	Romania – Belarus	2-1 (2-0)
28-03-2023	Lancy	Switzerland – Israel	3-0 (1-0)
16-06-2023	Andorra la Vella	Andorra – Switzerland	1-2 (0-2)
16-06-2023	Budapest (HUN)	Belarus – Israel	1-2 (1-0)
16-06-2023	Pristina	Kosovo – Romania	0-0
19-06-2023	Budapest	Belarus – Kosovo	2-1 (0-0)
19-06-2023	Jerusalem	Israel – Andorra	2-1 (1-0)
19-06-2023	Luzern	Switzerland – Romania	2-2 (2-0)
09-09-2023	Andorra la Vella	Andorra – Belarus	0-0
09-09-2023	Pristina	Kosovo – Switzerland	2-2 (0-1)
09-09-2023	Bucuresti	Romania – Israel	1-1 (1-0)
12-09-2023	Tel Aviv	Israel – Belarus	1-0 (0-0)
12-09-2023	Bucuresti	Romania – Kosovo	2-0 (0-0)
12-09-2023	Sion	Switzerland – Andorra	3-0 (0-0)
12-10-2023	Andorra la Vella	Andorra – Kosovo	0-3 (0-1)
12-10-2023	Budapest (HUN)	Belarus – Romania	0-0
15-10-2023	St. Gallen	Switzerland – Belarus	3-3 (1-0)
15-10-2023	Bucuresti	Romania – Andorra	4-0 (3-0)
12-11-2023	Pristina	Kosovo – Israel	1-0 (1-0)
15-11-2023	Felcsút (HUN)	Israel – Switzerland	1-1 (0-1)
18-11-2023	Budapest (HUN)	Belarus – Andorra	1-0 (0-0)
18-11-2023	Felcsút (HUN)	Israel – Romania	1-2 (1-1)
18-11-2023	Basel	Switzerland – Kosovo	1-1 (0-0)
21-11-2023	Andorra la Vella	Andorra – Israel	0-2 (0-1)
21-11-2023	Pristina	Kosovo – Belarus	0-1 (0-1)
21-11-2023	Bucuresti	Romania – Switzerland	1-0 (0-0)

FINAL STANDING

Pos	Team	Pld	W	D	L	GF	GA	GD	Pts
1	Romania	10	6	4	0	16	5	+11	22
2	Switzerland	10	4	5	1	22	11	+11	17
3	Israel	10	4	3	3	11	11	0	15
4	Belarus	10	3	3	4	9	14	-5	12
5	Kosovo	10	2	5	3	10	10	0	11
6	Andorra	10	0	2	8	3	20	-17	2

Romania and Switzerland qualified for the Final Tournament in Germany.

Israel advanced to the play-offs due to their performance in the 2022-23 UEFA Nations League.

25-03-2023   Stadion Karadjordje, Novi Sad (SRB): Belarus – Switzerland   0-5 (0-3)
Belarus: Andrey Kudravets, Denis Polyakov, Zakhar Volkov, Roman Yuzepchuk (33' Artem
Bykov), Vladislav Malkevich, Aleksandr Selyava (80' Valeriy Bocherov), Yuriy Kovalev (46'
Ivan Bakhar), Evgeniy Yablonskiy (YC25) (46' Vladislav Klimovich), Maks Ebong (YC84),
Denis Grechikho, Vladimir Khvashchinskiy (YC11) (61' Vladislav Morozov). (Coach: Georgi
Kondratjev (BLS)).
Switzerland: Yann Sommer, Ricardo Rodríguez, Silvan Widmer, Nico Elvedi, Manuel Akanji
(82' Cédric Zesiger), Granit Xhaka (YC48) (66' Fabian Rieder), Remo Freuler, Renato Steffen
(58' Zeki Amdouni), Denis Zakaria, Ruben Vargas (66' Christian Fassnacht), Cedric Itten
(YC40) (58' Noah Okafor). (Coach: Murat Yakin (SUI)).
Goals: Switzerland: 0-1 Renato Steffen (4'), 0-2 Renato Steffen (17'),
0-3 Renato Steffen (29'), 0-4 Granit Xhaka (62'), 0-5 Zeki Amdouni (65').
Referee: Alejandro Hernández Hernández (ESP)   Attendance: 0

*Due to the Belarusian country's involvement in the Russian invasion of Ukraine, Belarus were
required to play their home matches at neutral venues and behind closed doors until further
notice.*

25-03-2023   Bloomfield Stadium, Tel Aviv: Israel – Kosovo   1-1 (0-1)
Israel: Omri Glazer, Miguel Vítor (YC41), Eli Dasa, Raz Shlomo (YC86), Doron Leidner (88'
Danny Gruper), Dor Peretz, Neta Lavi, Dolev Haziza (YC64) (67' Mohamad Kna'an (YC77)),
Oscar Gloukh (79' Tai Baribo), Shon Weissman (88' Bibras Natcho), Manor Solomon.
(Coach: Alon Hazan (ISR)).
Kosovo: Aro Muric, Leart Paqarada, Amir Rrahmani, Mirlind Kryeziu (YC43), Mërgim
Vojvoda (88' Florent Hadergjonaj), Ibrahim Dresevic (YC84) (88' Valon Berisha), Bersant
Celina, Milot Rashica, Florent Muslija (79' Arber Zeneli), Edon Zhegrova (67' Betim Fazliji),
Vedat Muriqi. (Coach: Alain Giresse (FRA)).
Goals: Israel: 1-1 Dor Peretz (56').
Kosovo: 0-1 Eli Dasa (36' own goal).
Referee: William Collum (SCO)   Attendance: 28.935

25-03-2023   Estadi Nacional, Andorra la Vella: Andorra – Romania   0-2 (0-1)
Andorra: Iker Álvarez, Marc Valés (60' Joel Guillén), Moisés San Nicolás (86' Marc García),
Marc Rebés (YC59,YC61), Chus Rubio, Max Llovera (YC12), Joan Cervós (86' Marc Pujol),
Albert Alavedra, Márcio Vieira, Álex Martínez (72' Éric Vales), Berto Rosas Ubach (72'
Cucu). (Coach: Koldo Álvarez (AND)).
Romania: Ionut Radu, Andrei Burca, Radu Dragusin (YC88), Andrei Ratiu, Nicolae Stanciu
(78' Florin Tanase), Razvan Marin (YC23) (65' Tudor Baluta), Deian Sorescu, Darius Olaru
(65' Marius Marin), Olimpiu Morutan (73' Alex Dobre), Denis Alibec, Dennis Man (73'
Octavian Popescu (YC78)). (Coach: Edward Iordanescu (ROM)).
Goals: Romania: 0-1 Dennis Man (34'), 0-2 Denis Alibec (49').
Referee: Dario Bel (CRO)   Attendance: 2.927

550

28-03-2023 Stadiumi Fadil Vokrri, Pristina: Kosovo – Andorra 1-1 (0-0)
Kosovo: Aro Muric, Leart Paqarada (46' Donat Rrudhani), Amir Rrahmani, Florent
Hadergjonaj, Mirlind Kryeziu (YC23), Valon Berisha (46' Edon Zhegrova (YC60)), Arber
Zeneli (75' Zymer Bytyqi), Bersant Celina (75' Florent Muslija), Milot Rashica, Betim Fazliji,
Vedat Muriqi. (Coach: Alain Giresse (FRA)).
Andorra: Iker Álvarez, Jordi Rubio (69' Álex Martínez), Marc Valés (YC7), Chus Rubio, Max
Llovera, Joan Cervós (90+1' Víctor Bernat), Albert Alavedra, Joel Guillén, Marc García (78'
Moisés San Nicolás), Éric Vales, Berto Rosas Ubach (90+1' Marc Pujol). (Coach: Koldo
Álvarez (AND)).
Goals: Kosovo: 1-0 Edon Zhegrova (59').
Andorra: 1-1 Berto Rosas Ubach (61').
Referee: Sebastian Gishamer (AUT)   Attendance: 12.600

28-03-2023 Arena Nationala, Bucuresti: Romania – Belarus 2-1 (2-0)
Romania: Ionut Radu, Andrei Burca, Cristian Manea, Raul Oprut, Radu Dragusin, Nicolae
Stanciu (YC62) (77' Marius Marin), Razvan Marin, Tudor Baluta (44' Alexandru Cicaldau
(YC66)), Olimpiu Morutan (66' Alex Dobre), Denis Alibec (78' Florin Tanase), Dennis Man
(65' Octavian Popescu (YC74)). (Coach: Edward Iordanescu (ROM)).
Belarus: Maksim Plotnikov, Ruslan Khadarkevich (YC63), Zakhar Volkov, Vladislav
Malkevich (YC49), Aleksandr Selyava, Artem Bykov, Yuriy Kovalev (85' Denis Grechikho),
Evgeniy Yablonskiy (65' Vladislav Klimovich), Maks Ebong (YC55), Vladimir
Khvashchinskiy (46' Roman Yuzepchuk), Ivan Bakhar (78' Vladislav Morozov). (Coach:
Georgi Kondratjev (BLS)).
Goals: Romania: 1-0 Nicolae Stanciu (17'), 2-0 Andrei Burca (19').
Belarus: 2-1 Vladislav Morozov (86').
Referee: Allard Lindhout (HOL)   Attendance: 27.837

28-03-2023 Stade de Genève, Lancy: Switzerland – Israel 3-0 (1-0)
Switzerland: Yann Sommer, Ricardo Rodríguez (85' Edimilson Fernandes), Silvan Widmer
(YC90), Nico Elvedi, Manuel Akanji, Granit Xhaka, Remo Freuler, Denis Zakaria (74' Fabian
Rieder), Ruben Vargas (74' Christian Fassnacht), Cedric Itten (68' Noah Okafor), Zeki
Amdouni (69' Renato Steffen). (Coach: Murat Yakin (SUI)).
Israel: Omri Glazer, Miguel Vítor, Eli Dasa (YC38), Raz Shlomo, Doron Leidner, Dor Peretz
(73' Gavriel Kanichowsky), Neta Lavi, Dolev Haziza (53' Sagiv Yehezkel (YC57)), Mahmoud
Jaber (54' Oscar Gloukh), Manor Solomon, Tai Baribo (63' Shon Weissman). (Coach: Alon
Hazan (ISR)).
Goals: Switzerland: 1-0 Ruben Vargas (39'), 2-0 Zeki Amdouni (47'),
3-0 Silvan Widmer (52').
Referee: Nikola Dabanovic (MNE)   Attendance: 14.819

16-06-2023 Estadi Nacional, Andorra la Vella: Andorra – Switzerland 1-2 (0-2)
Andorra: Iker Álvarez, Moisés San Nicolás, Marc Rebés (65' Márcio Vieira), Chus Rubio (23'
Marc García), Max Llovera, Joan Cervós, Albert Alavedra, Joel Guillén (86' Ildefons Lima),
Jordi Aláez (64' Álex Martínez), Éric Vales, Berto Rosas Ubach (64' Cucu). (Coach: Koldo
Álvarez (AND)).
Switzerland: Gregor Kobel, Ricardo Rodríguez, Nico Elvedi, Manuel Akanji, Xherdan Shaqiri
(61' Renato Steffen), Granit Xhaka, Remo Freuler, Edimilson Fernandes, Denis Zakaria (74'
Djibril Sow), Ruben Vargas (61' Steven Zuber), Zeki Amdouni (61' Andi Zeqiri). (Coach:
Murat Yakin (SUI)).
Goals: Andorra: 1-2 Márcio Vieira (67').
Switzerland: 0-1 Remo Freuler (7'), 0-2 Zeki Amdouni (32').
Referee: Balász Berke (HUN)   Attendance: 2.490

16-06-2023   Szusza Ferenc Stadion, Budapest (HUN): Belarus – Israel 1-2 (1-0)
Belarus: Sergey Ignatovich, Sergey Politevich (YC84), Denis Polyakov, Roman Yuzepchuk, Kirill Pechenin, Aleksandr Selyava (YC29) (57' Evgeniy Yablonskiy), Artem Bykov, Yuriy Kovalev (YC40) (64' Valeriy Bocherov), Maks Ebong (79' Pavel Savitskiy), Kirill Kaplenko (79' Vladislav Klimovich), Vladislav Morozov (46' Ivan Bakhar). (Coach: Georgi Kondratjev (BLS)).
Israel: Omri Glazer, Ofir Davidzada (YC68), Eli Dasa (78' Sagiv Yehezkel), Shon Goldberg, Raz Shlomo, Ramzi Safuri (57' Oscar Gloukh (YC90+6)), Dor Peretz (66' Gavriel Kanichowsky), Mohammad Abu Fani, Manor Solomon, Tai Baribo (46' Shon Weissman), Liel Abada (46' Dolev Haziza). (Coach: Alon Hazan (ISR)).
Goals: Belarus: 1-0 Maks Ebong (16').
Israel: 1-1 Shon Weissman (85' penalty), 1-2 Oscar Gloukh (90+2').
Referee: Jarred Gillett (AUS)   Attendance: 0

16-06-2023   Stadiumi Fadil Vokrri, Pristina: Kosovo – Romania 0-0
Kosovo: Aro Muric, Fidan Aliti, Leart Paqarada, Amir Rrahmani, Mërgim Vojdoda, Ibrahim Dresevic (YC49) (73' Hekuran Kryeziu (YC86)), Bersant Celina, Milot Rashica (46' Edon Zhegrova), Florent Muslija (82' Jetmir Topalli), Betim Fazliji, Vedat Muriqi. (Coach: Alain Giresse (FRA)).
Romania: Horatiu Moldovan, Mario Camora (23' Deian Sorescu), Andrei Burca, Cristian Manea, Radu Dragusin, Nicolae Stanciu (86' Ianis Hagi), Marius Marin, Tudor Baluta, George Puscas (YC81) (86' Denis Alibec), Florinel Coman (62' Valentin Mihaila), Dennis Man (61' Olimpiu Morutan). (Coach: Edward Iordanescu (ROM)).
Referee: Danny Makkelie (HOL)   Attendance: 11.000

19-06-2023   Szusza Ferenc Stadion, Budapest (HUN): Belarus – Kosovo 2-1 (0-0)
Belarus: Sergey Ignatovich, Denis Polyakov, Zakhar Volkov, Roman Yuzepchuk (62' Yuriy Kovalev), Kirill Pechenin (88' Vladislav Malkevich), Pavel Savitskiy (63' Vladislav Morozov), Artem Bykov (YC86), Evgeniy Yablonskiy (89' Vladislav Klimovich), Maks Ebong, Kirill Kaplenko, Valeriy Bocherov (65' Aleksandr Selyava). (Coach: Georgi Kondratjev (BLS)).
Kosovo: Aro Muric, Fidan Aliti, Leart Paqarada (25' Ermal Krasniqi), Amir Rrahmani, Mërgim Vojdoda, Ibrahim Dresevic (46' Edon Zhegrova), Bersant Celina (79' Florian Loshaj), Florent Muslija, Betim Fazliji (53' Hekuran Kryeziu (YC90)), Donat Rrudhani, Vedat Muriqi. (Coach: Alain Giresse (FRA)).
Goals: Belarus: 1-0 Vladislav Morozov (73'), 2-0 Maks Ebong (75').
Kosovo: 2-1 Vedat Muriqi (87' penalty).
Referee: Julian Weinberger (AUT)   Attendance: 0

19-06-2023   Teddi Malcha Stadium, Jerusalem: Israel – Andorra 2-1 (1-0)
Israel: Omri Glazer, Eli Dasa, Shon Goldberg, Raz Shlomo (YC79), Roy Revivo, Ramzi Safuri (57' Oscar Gloukh), Neta Lavi, Dolev Haziza (57' Sagiv Yehezkel), Gavriel Kanichowsky (76' Mohammad Abu Fani), Shon Weissman (YC26) (75' Tai Baribo), Manor Solomon. (Coach: Alon Hazan (ISR)).
Andorra: Iker Álvarez, Moisés San Nicolás (YC60), Max Llovera (YC16), Joan Cervós, Albert Alavedra, Joel Guillén (YC85), Márcio Vieira (81' Marc Rebés), Marc García (89' Álex Martínez), Jordi Aláez (81' Izan Fernández), Éric Vales (90' Marc Pujol), Berto Rosas Ubach (67' Cucu). (Coach: Koldo Álvarez (AND)).
Goals: Israel: 1-0 Raz Shlomo (42'), 2-1 Manor Solomon (61').
Andorra: 1-1 Berto Rosas Ubach (52').
Referee: Dragomir Draganov (BUL)   Attendance: 13.300

19-06-2023   Swissporarena, Luzern: Switzerland – Romania 2-2 (2-0)
Switzerland: Yann Sommer, Ricardo Rodríguez, Nico Elvedi, Manuel Akanji (YC40), Xherdan Shaqiri (90+1' Uran Bislimi), Granit Xhaka, Remo Freuler, Edimilson Fernandes (YC23) (90+1' Fabian Schär), Denis Zakaria (75' Djibril Sow), Ruben Vargas (75' Renato Steffen (YC90+8)), Zeki Amdouni (59' Haris Seferovic). (Coach: Murat Yakin (SUI)).
Romania: Horatiu Moldovan, Ionut Nedelcearu, Andrei Burca, Cristian Manea, Radu Dragusin, Nicolae Stanciu, Ianis Hagi (YC26) (57' Valentin Mihaila), Deian Sorescu (YC45+1) (73' Darius Olaru), Vladimir Screciu (84' Alexandru Cicâldau), Denis Alibec (73' George Puscas), Florinel Coman (58' Olimpiu Morutan (YC90+4)). (Coach: Edward Iordanescu (ROM)).
Goals: Switzerland: 1-0 Zeki Amdouni (28'), 2-0 Zeki Amdouni (41').
Romania: 2-1 Valentin Mihaila (89'), 2-2 Valentin Mihaila (90+2').
Referee: Daniele Orsato (ITA)   Attendance: 14.400

09-09-2023   Estadi Nacional, Andorra la Vella: Andorra – Belarus 0-0
Andorra: Iker Álvarez, Marc Valés, Moisés San Nicolás, Max Llovera, Joan Cervós, Albert Alavedra, Márcio Vieira (59' Marc Rebés (YC81)), Marc Pujol (YC51) (59' Éric Vales), Jordi Aláez (84' Marc García), Álex Martínez (60' Cucu), Berto Rosas Ubach (90+5' Ildefons Lima). (Coach: Koldo Álvarez (AND) (YC81)).
Belarus: Maksim Plotnikov, Sergey Politevich (YC48), Denis Polyakov, Zakhar Volkov, Kirill Pechenin (88' Vladislav Malkevich), Pavel Savitskiy, Artem Bykov (65' Yuriy Kovalev), Nikita Korzun, Maks Ebong (YC29), Artem Kontsevoy (79' Ivan Bakhar), Vitaliy Lisakovich (YC57) (65' Vladislav Morozov (YC76)). (Coach: Carlos Alós (ESP)). (Not used sub: Sergey Ignatovich (YC90+1)).
Referee: Eldorjan Hamiti (ALB)   Attendance: 1.026

09-09-2023   Stadiumi Fadil Vokrri, Pristina: Kosovo – Switzerland 2-2 (0-1)
Kosovo: Aro Muric, Fidan Aliti (YC39), Leart Paqarada, Amir Rrahmani (YC79), Mërgim Vojdoda (YC90+2), Valon Berisha (46' Edon Zhegrova), Bernard Berisha (54' Ermal Krasniqi), Milot Rashica (81' Meriton Korenica), Florian Loshaj (YC42) (68' Florent Hadergjonaj), Betim Fazliji (46' Florent Muslija), Vedat Muriqi. (Coach: Primoz Gliha (SVN)).
Switzerland: Yann Sommer, Ricardo Rodríguez, Fabian Schär, Manuel Akanji, Xherdan Shaqiri (84' Noah Okafor), Granit Xhaka, Remo Freuler (84' Djibril Sow), Edimilson Fernandes, Denis Zakaria, Ruben Vargas (63' Dan Ndoye), Zeki Amdouni (63' Cedric Itten). (Coach: Murat Yakin (SUI)).
Goals: Kosovo: 1-1 Vedat Muriqi (65'), 2-2 Vedat Muriqi (90+4').
Switzerland: 0-1 Remo Freuler (14'), 1-2 Amir Rrahmani (79' own goal).
Referee: Jakob Kehlet (DEN)   Attendance: 12.700

09-09-2023   Arena Nationala, Bucuresti: Romania – Israel 1-1 (1-0)
Romania: Horatiu Moldovan, Andrei Burca, Cristian Manea, Radu Dragusin (YC61), Nicolae Stanciu (88' Alexandru Cicâldau), Nicusor Bancu, Razvan Marin, Marius Marin (YC56) (64' Darius Olaru), Deian Sorescu (56' Olimpiu Morutan), Denis Alibec (65' George Puscas (YC85)), Florinel Coman (57' Valentin Mihaila). (Coach: Edward Iordanescu (ROM)).
Israel: Omri Glazer, Miguel Vítor, Eli Dasa, Shon Goldberg (77' Stav Lemkin), Roy Revivo, Dor Peretz (73' Mohammad Abu Fani), Neta Lavi, Oscar Gloukh, Sagiv Yehezkel (73' Gavriel Kanichowsky (YC89)), Manor Solomon, Dor Turgeman (62' Shon Weissman). (Coach: Alon Hazan (ISR)).
Goals: Romania: 1-0 Denis Alibec (27').
Israel: 1-1 Oscar Gloukh (53').
Referee: Slavko Vincic (SVN)   Attendance: 49.193

553

12-09-2023   Bloomfield Stadium, Tel Aviv: Israel – Belarus   1-0 (0-0)
Israel: Omri Glazer, Miguel Vítor, Eli Dasa (78' Thai Baribo), Stav Lemkin, Roy Revivo, Dor Peretz (YC56) (65' Mohammad Abu Fani), Neta Lavi (72' Ramzi Safuri), Oscar Gloukh, Shon Weissman (65' Dor Turgeman (YC89)), Sagiv Yehezkel (65' Gavriel Kanichowsky), Manor Solomon. (Coach: Alon Hazan (ISR)).
Belarus: Maksim Plotnikov, Sergey Politevich, Denis Polyakov, Sergey Karpovich (79' Yuriy Kovalev), Zakhar Volkov (YC90+8), Kirill Pechenin (59' Vladislav Malkevich), Nikita Korzun (79' Artem Bykov), Kirill Kaplenko, Artem Kontsevoy (69' Pavel Savitskiy (YC90+7)), Valeriy Bocherov (59' Aleksandr Selyava), Vladislav Morozov. (Coach: Carlos Alós (ESP)).
Goal: Israel: 1-0 Gavriel Kanichowsky (90+3').
Referee: Ricardo de Burgos Bengoetxea (ESP)   Attendance: 28.435

12-09-2023   Arena Nationala, Bucuresti: Romania – Kosovo   2-0 (0-0)
Romania: Horatiu Moldovan, Andrei Burca (YC9) (63' Razvan Marin), Radu Dragusin, Andrei Ratiu, Nicolae Stanciu, Nicusor Bancu (YC52), Alexandru Cicâldau (77' Darius Olaru), Ianis Hagi (72' Olimpiu Morutan), Vladimir Screciu, George Puscas (YC34) (46' Denis Alibec), Florinel Coman (71' Valentin Mihaila). (Coach: Edward Iordanescu (ROM)).
Kosovo: Aro Muric, Fidan Aliti, Leart Paqarada, Amir Rrahmani (YC34), Mërgim Vojdoda (YC52) (81' Ismajl Beka), Valon Berisha (54' Florent Muslija), Bernard Berisha (YC14) (82' Albion Rrahmani), Milot Rashica (54' Florent Hadergjonaj), Florian Loshaj (YC59), Edon Zhegrova (64' Ibrahim Dresevic), Vedat Muriqi (YC19,YC43). (Coach: Primoz Gliha (SVN) (YC45)). (Not used sub: Visar Bekaj (YC90+6)).
Goals: Romania: 1-0 Nicolae Stanciu (83'), 2-0 Valentin Mihaila (90+3').
Referee: Willy Delajod (FRA)   Attendance: 29.982

Nicolae Stanciu missed a penalty kick (61').

12-09-2023   Stade de Tourbillon, Sion: Switzerland – Andorra   3-0 (0-0)
Switzerland: Yvon Mvogo, Ricardo Rodríguez, Nico Elvedi, Manuel Akanji (YC69), Xherdan Shaqiri (90+3' Michel Aebischer), Granit Xhaka, Remo Freuler (YC22) (66' Djibril Sow), Renato Steffen, Ruben Vargas (90+4' Uran Bislimi), Cedric Itten (81' Noah Okafor), Zeki Amdouni (66' Dan Ndoye). (Coach: Murat Yakin (SUI) (YC70)). (Not used sub: Yann Sommer (YC69)).
Andorra: Iker Álvarez, Ildefons Lima (23' Cucu, 88' Víctor Bernat), Marc Valés (76' Márcio Vieira), Moisés San Nicolás, Marc Rebés, Max Llovera, Joan Cervós (88' Izan Fernández), Albert Alavedra, Joel Guillén (YC69), Marc García, Éric Vales (YC68) (76' Jordi Aláez). (Coach: Koldo Álvarez (AND)).
Goals: Switzerland: 1-0 Cedric Itten (49'), 2-0 Granit Xhaka (84'), 3-0 Xherdan Shaqiri (90+3' penalty).
Referee: Elchin Masiyev (AZE)   Attendance: 9.000

554

12-10-2023   Estadi Nacional, Andorra la Vella: Andorra – Kosovo   0-3 (0-1)
Andorra: Iker Álvarez, Marc Valés, Moisés San Nicolás, Marc Rebés (75' Márcio Vieira),
Chus Rubio, Max Llovera (88' Kiko Pomares), Joan Cervós, Jordi Aláez (YC14) (56' Marc
García), Éric Vales (YC44) (56' Marc Pujol (YC80)), Cucu, Izan Fernández (75' Aarón
Sánchez (YC88)). (Coach: Koldo Álvarez (AND)).
Kosovo: Aro Muric, Fidan Aliti, Florent Hadergjonaj, Mërgim Vojdoda (YC14), Kreshnik
Hajrizi (46' Zymer Bytyqi), Lumbardh Dellova (YC78), Milot Rashica, Florent Muslija (75'
Altin Zeqiri), Florian Loshaj (46' Betim Fazliji), Qendrim Zyba (76' Bernard Berisha), Albion
Rrahmani (66' Meriton Korenica). (Coach: Primoz Gliha (SVN)).
Goals: Kosovo: 0-1 Milot Rashica (26'), 0-2 Milot Rashica (71'), 0-3 Altin Zeqiri (83').
Referee: Nicholas Walsh (SCO)   Attendance: 1,207

12-10-2023   Szusza Ferenc Stadion, Budapest (HUN): Belarus – Romania   0-0
Belarus: Sergey Ignatovich (YC73), Sergey Politevich, Denis Polyakov, Zakhar Volkov,
Roman Yuzepchuk (73' Sergey Karpovich), Kirill Pechenin, Nikita Korzun, Vladislav
Klimovich (83' Valeriy Gromyko), Maks Ebong (73' Valeriy Bocherov), Artem Kontsevoy
(90+1' Egor Karpitskiy), Vladislav Morozov (73' Ivan Bakhar (YC75)). (Coach: Carlos Alós
(ESP)).
Romania: Horatiu Moldovan, Andrei Burca, Radu Dragusin, Andrei Ratiu, Nicolae Stanciu
(84' Valentin Mihaila), Nicusor Bancu, Razvan Marin, Vladimir Screciu (77' Darius Olaru),
Denis Alibec (62' Ianis Hagi), Dennis Man (61' Olimpiu Morutan), Denis Dragus (77' Louis
Munteanu). (Coach: Edward Iordanescu (ROM)).
Referee: Espen Eskås (NOR)   Attendance: 0

15-10-2023   Kybunpark, St. Gallen: Switzerland – Belarus   3-3 (1-0)
Switzerland: Yann Sommer, Ricardo Rodríguez (73' Ulisses Garcia), Fabian Schär, Manuel
Akanji, Jordan Lotomba, Xherdan Shaqiri, Granit Xhaka, Remo Freuler, Renato Steffen (73'
Dan Ndoye), Djibril Sow (62' Zeki Amdouni), Cedric Itten (62' Andi Zeqiri (YC77)). (Coach:
Murat Yakin (SUI)).
Belarus: Sergey Ignatovich, Sergey Politevich (YC4), Denis Polyakov, Sergey Karpovich,
Zakhar Volkov, Vladislav Malkevich (83' Vladislav Klimovich (YC90+2)), Nikita Korzun
(YC90+4) (90+5' Aleksandr Pavlovets), Maks Ebong, Artem Kontsevoy (46' Dmitri
Antilevski), Valeriy Bocherov (65' Vladislav Morozov), Ivan Bakhar (YC85) (64' Kirill
Pechenin (YC90)). (Coach: Carlos Alós (ESP)).
Goals: Switzerland: 1-0 Xherdan Shaqiri (28'), 2-3 Manuel Akanji (89'),
3-3 Zeki Amdouni (90').
Belarus: 1-1 Maks Ebong (61'), 1-2 Denis Polyakov (69'), 1-3 Dmitri Antilevski (84').
Referee: João Pedro Pinheiro (POR)   Attendance: 17.000

15-10-2023   Arena Nationala, Bucuresti: Romania – Andorra   4-0 (3-0)
Romania: Horatiu Moldovan, Andrei Burca, Radu Dragusin (46' Adrián Rus), Nicolae Stanciu
(65' Marius Marin), Nicusor Bancu, Razvan Marin (YC9) (59' Alexandru Cicâldau), Ianis
Hagi (65' Denis Alibec), Deian Sorescu, Olimpiu Morutan, Florinel Coman, Daniel Bîrligea
(59' Valentin Mihaila). (Coach: Edward Iordanescu (ROM)).
Andorra: Iker Álvarez, Marc Valés, Moisés San Nicolás (YC19,YC90+1), Marc Rebés (86'
Marc Pujol), Chus Rubio (YC37) (65' Éric de Pablos), Max Llovera, Joan Cervós, Márcio
Vieira (YC9), Marc García (YC42) (86' Kiko Pomares), Éric Vales (76' Jordi Rubio), Aarón
Sánchez (YC12) (65' Víctor Bernat (YC84)). (Coach: Koldo Álvarez (AND)).
Goals: Romania: 1-0 Nicolae Stanciu (23'), 2-0 Ianis Hagi (28'), 3-0 Razvan Marin (44' pen),
4-0 Florinel Coman (50').
Referee: Kristo Tohver (EST)   Attendance: 21.723

555

12-11-2023   Stadiumi Fadil Vokrri, Pristina: Kosovo – Israel   1-0 (1-0)
Kosovo: Aro Muric (YC78), Fidan Aliti, Lumbardh Dellova, Bernard Berisha, Milot Rashica (78' Kreshnik Hajrizi), Florent Muslija (62' Elbasan Rashani), Florian Loshaj (46' Zymer Bytyqi), Qendrim Zyba (YC45+2), Ilir Krasniqi (YC88), Vedat Muriqi (66' Meriton Korenica), Lirim R.Kastrati (46' Ermal Krasniqi). (Coach: Primoz Gliha (SVN) (YC90)).
Israel: Omri Glazer, Miguel Vítor (YC84), Eli Dasa (72' Idan Gorno), Shon Goldberg, Roy Revivo (YC23,YC90+4), Dor Peretz (72' Ramzi Safuri), Gadi Kinda (46' Dor Turgeman), Neta Lavi (62' Mohammad Abu Fani), Oscar Gloukh, Eran Zahavi, Sagiv Yehezkel (22' Gavriel Kanichowsky). (Coach: Alon Hazan (ISR)).
Goal: Kosovo: 1-0 Milot Rashica (41').
Referee: Ivan Kruzliak (SVK)   Attendance: 5.245

Match was originally scheduled to be played on 15th October 2023, but was postponed until 12th November 2023 due to the Israel-Hamas war.

15-11-2023   Puskás Akadémia Pancho Aréna, Felcsút (HUN):
                   Israel – Switzerland   1-1 (0-1)
Israel: Omri Glazer, Ofir Davidzada (YC53), Eli Dasa (65' Eran Zahavi), Shon Goldberg, Raz Shloma, Ramzi Safuri (YC26) (46' Gavriel Kanichowsky), Neta Lavi (65' Dan Glazer), Mohammad Abu Fani (YC24), Dor Turgeman, Anan Khalaili (81' Shon Weissman), Idan Gorno (65' Oscar Gloukh). (Coach: Alon Hazan (ISR)).
Switzerland: Yann Sommer, Ricardo Rodríguez, Manuel Akanji (YC90+2), Cédric Zesiger (YC90+2), Granit Xhaka, Remo Freuler, Edimilson Fernandes (RC90+4), Denis Zakaria (YC45), Ruben Vargas (77' Renato Steffen (YC90+3)), Noah Okafor (68' Andi Zeqiri (YC80), 90+5' Eray Cömert), Zeki Amdouni (69' Dan Ndoye). (Coach: Murat Yakin (SUI)).
Goals: Israel: 1-1 Shon Weissman (88').
Switzerland: 0-1 Ruben Vargas (36').
Referee: Anthony Taylor (ENG)   Attendance: 2.024

The match was originally scheduled to be played on 12th October 2023 at Bloomfield Stadium, Tel Aviv, but was postponed to 15th November 2023 due to the Israel-Hamas war.

Israel played their remaining home matches at a neutral venue.

18-11-2023   Szusza Ferenc Stadion, Budapest (HUN): Belarus – Andorra   1-0 (0-0)
Belarus: Sergey Ignatovich, Sergey Karpovich (63' Ivan Bakhar), Aleksandr Pavlovets, Zakhar Volkov, Kirill Pechenin (74' Denis Laptev (YC90+6)), Egor Parkhomenko, Vladislav Klimovich (46' Artem Kontsevoy), Maks Ebong, Kirill Kaplenko (63' Valeriy Gromyko), Dmitri Antilevski, Vladislav Morozov (63' Maksim Skavysh). (Coach: Carlos Alós (ESP)).
Andorra: Iker Álvarez, Marc Valés, Marc Rebés (YC45+1) (66' Éric Vales), Max Llovera, Joan Cervós, Éric de Pablos (90' Jordi Rubio), Kiko Pomares (87' Ot Remolins Planes), Márcio Vieira (YC72) (88' Marc Pujol), Jordi Aláez, Álex Martínez (YC70), Cucu (66' Aarón Sánchez). (Coach: Koldo Álvarez (AND)).
Goal: Belarus: 1-0 Denis Laptev (83').
Referee: Bulat Sariyev (KAZ)   Attendance: 0

18-11-2023   Puskás Akadémia Pancho Aréna, Felcsút (HUN):
Israel – Romania 1-2 (1-1)
Israel: Omri Glazer, Miguel Vítor (YC37), Eli Dasa (62' Gavriel Kanichowsky), Shon
Goldberg, Roy Revivo (76' Thai Baribo (YC83)), Dor Peretz, Neta Lavi (62' Mohammad Abu
Fani), Oscar Gloukh, Eran Zahavi (YC90+1), Dor Turgeman, Anan Khalaili (76' Idan Gorno).
(Coach: Alon Hazan (ISR)).
Romania: Horatiu Moldovan, Andrei Burca, Radu Dragusin, Andrei Ratiu (YC78), Nicolae
Stanciu (87' Adrián Rus), Nicusor Bancu, Razvan Marin (87' Alexandru Cicâldau), Ianis Hagi
(65' Florinel Coman (YC71)), Vladimir Screciu (77' Marius Marin), George Puscas, Denis
Dragus (65' Valentin Mihaila (RC84)). (Coach: Edward Iordanescu (ROM)).
Goals: Israel: 1-0 Eran Zahavi (2').
Romania: 1-1 George Puscas (10'), 1-2 Ianis Hagi (63').
Referee: François Letexier (FRA)   Attendance: 2.921

18-11-2023   St. Jakob-Park, Basel: Switzerland – Kosovo 1-1 (0-0)
Switzerland: Yann Sommer, Nico Elvedi, Manuel Akanji, Ulisses Garcia, Eray Cömert (84'
Filip Ugrinic), Xherdan Shaqiri (84' Renato Steffen), Granit Xhaka (YC58), Remo Freuler (66'
Michel Aebischer), Denis Zakaria (YC76), Ruben Vargas (75' Zeki Amdouni), Noah Okafor
(75' Dan Ndoye). (Coach: Murat Yakin (SUI)).
Kosovo: Visar Bekaj, Fidan Aliti, Florent Hadergjonaj (73' Muhamet Hyseni), Mërgim
Vojdoda, Lumbardh Dellova, Elbasan Rashani (YC29) (46' Altin Zeqiri), Zymer Bytyqi
(YC16) (46' Lirim R.Kastrati), Bernard Berisha (66' Meriton Korenica), Florent Muslija,
Qendrim Zyba (86' Kreshnik Hajrizi), Ilir Krasniqi. (Coach: Primoz Gliha (SVN)).
Goals: Switzerland: 1-0 Ruben Vargas (47').
Kosovo: 1-1 Muhamet Hyseni (82').
Referee: António Nobre (POR)   Attendance: 33.000

21-11-2023   Estadi Nacional, Andorra la Vella: Andorra – Israel 0-2 (0-1)
Andorra: Iker Álvarez, Marc Valés, Moisés San Nicolás, Max Llovera, Joan Cervós (YC90+1),
Ian Olivera, Márcio Vieira (87' Marc Rebés), Jordi Aláez (74' Álex Martínez), Éric Vales
(YC44) (87' Marc Pujol (YC88)), Cucu (YC37) (57' Aarón Sánchez), Izan Fernández (57'
Marc García). (Coach: Koldo Álvarez (AND)).
Israel: Daniel Peretz, Ofir Davidzada, Raz Shloma, Stav Lekmin (46' Ofri Arad), Dor Peretz
(61' Don Glazer), Gadi Kinda (YC88) (89' Ramzi Safuri), Gavriel Kanichowsky, Avishay
Cohen, Dean David, Thai Baribo (74' Shon Weissman), Anan Khalaili (46' Idan Gorno).
(Coach: Alon Hazan (ISR)).
Goals: Israel: 0-1 Joan Cervós (29' own goal), 0-2 Gadi Kinda (81').
Referee: Sascha Stegemann (GER)   Attendance: 568

21-11-2023   Stadiumi Fadil Vokrri, Pristina: Kosovo – Belarus 0-1 (0-1)
Kosovo: Visar Bekaj, Fidan Aliti, Florent Hadergjonaj (83' Alba Ajdini), Mërgim Vojdoda
(YC86), Lumbardh Dellova, Elbasan Rashani (56' Altin Zeqiri (YC83)), Zymer Bytyqi (46'
Muhamet Hyseni (YC61)), Bernard Berisha (67' Lirim Kastrati (YC87)), Florent Muslija,
Qendrim Zyba (56' Meriton Korenica (YC78)), Ilir Krasniqi. (Coach: Primoz Gliha (SVN)).
Belarus: Pavel Pavlyuchenko (YC90+1), Sergey Politevich, Denis Polyakov, Zakhar Volkov,
Roman Yuzepchuk (90+1' Sergey Karpovich), Vladislav Malkevich (YC30), Nikita Korzun
(YC90+4), Maks Ebong (73' Artem Kontsevoy), Kirill Kaplenko (57' Valeriy Bocherov),
Maksim Skavysh (YC45) (56' Denis Laptev (YC87)), Dmitri Antilevski (74' Vladislav
Klimovich). (Coach: Carlos Alós (ESP)).
Goal: Belarus: 0-1 Dmitri Antilevski (43').
Referee: Georgi Kabakov (BUL)   Attendance: 5.026

557

21-11-2023   Arena Nationala, Bucuresti: Romania – Switzerland   1-0 (0-0)
Romania: Horatiu Moldovan, Andrei Burca, Radu Dragusin, Andrei Ratiu, Nicolae Stanciu
(83' Darius Olaru), Nicusor Bancu (YC90+5), Alexandru Cicâldau (64' Razvan Marin),
Marius Marin (YC2), Olimpiu Morutan (YC48) (65' Ianis Hagi (YC90+3)), Denis Alibec (83'
George Puscas), Florinel Coman (72' Denis Dragus). (Coach: Edward Iordanescu (ROM)).
Switzerland: Yvon Mvogo, Ricardo Rodríguez, Nico Elvedi, Manuel Akanji (YC90+3),
Ulisses Garcia (62' Filip Ugrinic), Xherdan Shaqiri (62' Renato Steffen), Granit Xhaka
(YC54), Michel Aebischer (84' Remo Freuler), Ruben Vargas (81' Andi Zeqiri), Noah Okafor
(62' Zeki Amdouni), Dan Ndoye. (Coach: Murat Yakin (SUI)).
Goal: Romania: 1-0 Denis Alibec (50').
Referee: Davide Massa (ITA)   Attendance: 50.224

GROUP J

23-03-2023	Zenica	Bosnia and Herzegovina – Iceland	3-0 (2-0)
23-03-2023	Lisboa	Portugal – Liechtenstein	4-0 (1-0)
23-03-2023	Trnava	Slovakia – Luxembourg	0-0
26-03-2023	Vaduz	Liechtenstein – Iceland	0-7 (0-2)
26-03-2023	Luxembourg City	Luxembourg – Portugal	0-6 (0-4)
26-03-2023	Bratislava	Slovakia – Bosnia and Herzegovina	2-0 (2-0)
17-06-2023	Luxembourg City	Luxembourg – Liechtenstein	2-0 (0-0)
17-06-2023	Reykjavík	Iceland – Slovakia	1-2 (1-1)
17-06-2023	Lisboa	Portugal – Bosnia and Herzegovina	3-0 (1-0)
20-06-2023	Zenica	Bosnia and Herzegovina – Luxembourg	0-2 (0-1)
20-06-2023	Reykjavík	Iceland – Portugal	0-1 (0-0)
20-06-2023	Vaduz	Liechtenstein – Slovakia	0-1 (0-1)
08-09-2023	Zenica	Bosnia and Herzegovina – Liechtenstein	2-1 (2-1)
08-09-2023	Luxembourg City	Luxembourg – Iceland	3-1 (1-0)
08-09-2023	Bratislava	Slovakia – Portugal	0-1 (0-1)
11-09-2023	Reykjavík	Iceland – Bosnia and Herzegovina	1-0 (0-0)
11-09-2023	Faro/Loulé	Portugal – Luxembourg	9-0 (4-0)
11-09-2023	Bratislava	Slovakia – Liechtenstein	3-0 (3-0)
13-10-2023	Reykjavík	Iceland – Luxembourg	1-1 (1-0)
13-10-2023	Vaduz	Liechtenstein – Bosnia and Herzegovina	0-2 (0-2)
13-10-2023	Porto	Portugal – Slovakia	3-2 (2-0)
16-10-2023	Zenica	Bosnia and Herzegovina – Portugal	0-5 (0-5)
16-10-2023	Reykjavík	Iceland – Liechtenstein	4-0 (2-0)
16-10-2023	Luxembourg City	Luxembourg – Slovakia	0-1 (0-0)
16-11-2023	Vaduz	Liechtenstein – Portugal	0-2 (0-0)
16-11-2023	Luxembourg City	Luxembourg – Bosnia and Herzegovina	4-1 (2-0)
16-11-2023	Bratislava	Slovakia – Iceland	4-2 (2-1)
19-11-2023	Zenica	Bosnia and Herzegovina – Slovakia	1-2 (0-0)
19-11-2023	Vaduz	Liechtenstein – Luxembourg	0-1 (0-0)
19-11-2023	Lisboa	Portugal – Iceland	2-0 (1-0)

FINAL STANDING

Pos	Team	Pld	W	D	L	GF	GA	GD	Pts
1	Portugal	10	10	0	0	36	2	+34	30
2	Slovakia	10	7	1	2	17	8	+9	22
3	Luxembourg	10	5	2	3	13	19	-6	17
4	Iceland	10	3	1	6	17	16	+1	10
5	Bosnia and Herzegovina	10	3	0	7	9	20	-11	9
6	Liechtenstein	10	0	0	10	1	28	-27	0

Portugal and Slovakia qualified for the Final Tournament in Germany.

Luxembourg, Iceland and Bosnia and Herzegovina all advanced to the play-offs due to their performances in the 2022-23 UEFA Nations League.

23-03-2023   Stadion Bilino Polje, Zenica:
Bosnia and Herzegovina – Iceland   3-0 (2-0)
Bosnia and Herzegovina: Ibrahim Sehic, Sinisa Sanicanin, Anel Ahmedhodzic, Jusuf Gazibegovic, Amar Dedic (YC64) (71' Dennis Hadzikadunic), Hrvoje Milicevic, Rade Krunic, Amir Hadziahmetovic (72' Sanjin Prcic), Benjamin Tahirovic (YC45+4) (83' Gojko Cimirot), Smail Prevljak (67' Kenan Kodro), Ermedin Demirovic (82' Nemanja Bilbija). (Coach: Faruk Hadzibegic (BIH)).
Iceland: Alex Rúnarsson, Hörður Magnússon, Victor Pálsson (YC19), Daniel Grétarsson, Davíð Kristján Ólafsson, Jóhann Guðmundsson (YC45+4), Arnór Traustason (82' Stefán Teitur Thórðarson), Arnór Sigurðsson (67' Mikael Anderson), Hákon Haraldsson (YC17), Alfreð Finnbogason (83' Andri Guðjohnsen), Jón Dagur Thorsteinsson (66' Mikael Egill Ellertsson). (Coach: Arnar Viðarsson).
Goals: Bosnia and Herzegovina: 1-0 Rade Krunic (14'), 2-0 Rade Krunic (40'), 3-0 Amar Dedic (63').
Referee: Donatas Rumsas (LTU)   Attendance: 9.234

23-03-2023   Estádio José Alvalade, Lisboa: Portugal – Liechtenstein   4-0 (1-0)
Portugal: Rui Patrício, João Cancelo, Raphaël Guerreiro, Rúben Dias, Gonçalo Inácio, Danilo Pereira (67' Rúben Neves), Bruno Fernandes (89' João Mário), João Palhinha, Bernardo Silva (78' Vitinha), Cristiano Ronaldo (78' Gonçalo Ramos), João Félix (67' Rafael Leão). (Coach: Roberto Martínez (ESP)).
Liechtenstein: Benjamin Büchel, Sandro Wolfinger (80' Seyhan Yildiz), Andreas Malin (38' Simon Lüchinger), Jens Hofer, Lars Traber, Nicolas Hasler, Sandro Wieser, Aron Sele (80' Niklas Beck), Livio Meier (60' Fabio Wolfinger), Noah Frommelt, Philipp Gaßner (60' Jakob Lorenz). (Coach: René Pauritsch (AUT)).
Goals: Portugal: 1-0 João Cancelo (8'), 2-0 Bernardo Silva (47'), 3-0 Cristiano Ronaldo (51' penalty), 4-0 Cristiano Ronaldo (63').
Referee: Espen Eskås (NOR)   Attendance: 45.378

23-03-2023   City Aréna – Stadión Antona Malatinského, Trnava:
Slovakia – Luxembourg 0-0
Slovakia: Martin Dúbravka, Peter Pekarík (82' Mical Tomic), Norbert Gyömbér, Lubomir
Satka, Dávid Hancko, Juraj Kucka, Stanislav Lobotka, Ondrej Duda (80' László Bénes), Lukás
Haraslín, Tomás Suslov (73' Robert Mak), Róbert Polievka (73' Róbert Bozeník). (Coach:
Francesco Calzona (ITA)).
Luxembourg: Anthony Moris, Lars Gerson (YC57), Maxime Chanot, Mica Pinto, Florian
Bohnert (84' Timothé Rupil), Christopher Martins, Danel Sinani (84' Sébastien Thill), Leandro
Barreiro, Mathias Olesen (64' Vincent Thill), Gerson Rodrigues, Yvandro Borges Sanches (63'
Laurent Jans (YC90+4)). (Coach: Luc Holtz (LUX)).
Referee: Rade Obrenovic (SVN)   Attendance: 3.523

26-03-2023   Rheinpark Stadion, Vaduz: Liechtenstein – Iceland 0-7 (0-2)
Liechtenstein: Benjamin Büchel, Sandro Wolfinger (72' Seyhan Yildiz), Jens Hofer, Lars
Traber, Nicolas Hasler, Sandro Wieser (YC64) (77' Niklas Beck), Aron Sele (YC90+1), Livio
Meier (46' Fabio Wolfinger (YC60)), Noah Frommelt, Simon Lüchinger (46' Andrin Netzer),
Philipp Gaßner (68' Noah Frick). (Coach: René Pauritsch (AUT)).
Iceland: Alex Rúnarsson, Hörður Magnússon (65' Alfons Sampsted), Victor Pálsson, Davíð
Kristján Ólafsson, Aron Gunnarsson (74' Ísak Bergmann Jóhannesson), Jóhann Guðmundsson
(46' Mikael Anderson), Arnór Sigurðsson (65' Mikael Egill Ellertsson), Stefán Teitur
Thórðarson, Hákon Haraldsson, Alfreð Finnbogason (YC56) (65' Andri Guðjohnsen), Jón
Dagur Thorsteinsson. (Coach: Arnar Viðarsson).
Goals: Iceland: 0-1 Davíð Kristján Ólafsson (3'), 0-2 Hákon Haraldsson (38'),
0-3 Aron Gunnarsson (48'), 0-4 Aron Gunnarsson (68'), 0-5 Aron Gunnarsson (73' penalty),
0-6 Andri Guðjohnsen (85'), 0-7 Mikael Egill Ellertsson (87').
Referee: Jakob Kehlet (DEN)   Attendance: 1.692

26-03-2023   Stade de Luxembourg, Luxembourg City:
Luxembourg – Portugal 0-6 (0-4)
Luxembourg: Anthony Moris, Lars Gerson (46' Dirk Carlson), Maxime Chanot, Laurent Jans,
Mica Pinto, Marvin Martins (YC37) (46' Florian Bohnert), Christopher Martins (YC74) (82'
Sébastien Thill), Danel Sinani (46' Mathias Olesen), Leandro Barreiro (YC82), Gerson
Rodrigues, Vincent Thill (YC32) (70' Yvandro Borges Sanches). (Coach: Luc Holtz (LUX)).
Portugal: Rui Patrício, Rúben Dias, Diogo Dalot, Nuno Mendes, António Silva, Danilo Pereira,
Bruno Fernandes (75' Rafael Leão), João Palhinha (87' Diogo Jota), Bernardo Silva (64'
Rúben Neves), Cristiano Ronaldo (YC57) (65' Gonçalo Ramos), João Félix (75' Otávio).
(Coach: Roberto Martínez (ESP)).
Goals: Portugal: 0-1 Cristiano Ronaldo (9'), 0-2 João Félix (15'), 0-3 Bernardo Silva (18'),
0-4 Cristiano Ronaldo (31'), 0-5 Otávio (77'), 0-6 Rafael Leão (88').
Referee: Radu Petrescu (ROM)   Attendance: 9.231

Rafael Leão missed a penalty kick (85').

560

26-03-2023 Stadión Tehelné pole, Bratislava:
Slovakia – Bosnia and Herzegovina 2-0 (2-0)
Slovakia: Martin Dúbravka, Peter Pekarík, Norbert Gyömbér, Denis Vavro, Dávid Hancko, Juraj Kucka, Stanislav Lobotka (90+2' Patrik Hrosovský), Ondrej Duda (69' László Bénes), Lukás Haraslín (90+2' Matús Bero), Robert Mak (58' Tomás Suslov), Róbert Polievka (69' Adam Zrelák). (Coach: Francesco Calzona (ITA)).
Bosnia and Herzegovina: Ibrahim Sehic, Sinisa Sanicanin, Anel Ahmedhodzic, Jusuf Gazibegovic, Amar Dedic, Hrvoje Milicevic (46' Gojko Cimirot), Rade Krunic, Amir Hadziahmetovic (63' Sanjin Prcic), Benjamin Tahirovic (74' Miroslav Stevanovic), Smail Prevljak (63' Edin Dzeko), Ermedin Demirovic. (Coach: Faruk Hadzibegic (BIH)).
Goals: Slovakia: 1-0 Robert Mak (13'), 2-0 Lukás Haraslín (40').
Referee: Marco Di Bello (ITA) Attendance: 6.052

17-06-2023 Stade de Luxembourg, Luxembourg City:
Luxembourg – Liechtenstein 2-0 (0-0)
Luxembourg: Anthony Moris, Maxime Chanot (YC79), Laurent Jans (YC22) (46' Florian Bohnert), Marvin Martins (90' Eldin Dzogovic), Enes Mahmutovic, Christopher Martins, Danel Sinani, Leandro Barreiro, Vincent Thill (46' Gerson Rodrigues), Alessio Curci (46' Mathias Olesen), Yvandro Borges Sanches (90' Timothé Rupil). (Coach: Luc Holtz (LUX)).
Liechtenstein: Benjamin Büchel, Maximilian Göppel (75' Fabio Wolfinger), Andreas Malin (YC77), Niklas Beck, Lars Traber, Nicolas Hasler (24' Sandro Wolfinger), Aron Sele, Dennis Salanovic, Livio Meier (55' Andrin Netzer), Simon Lüchinger (YC27) (75' Jens Hofer), Ferhat Saglam (55' Seyhan Yildiz). (Coach: Konrad Fünfstück (GER)).
Goals: Luxembourg: 1-0 Danel Sinani (59'), 2-0 Gerson Rodrigues (89').
Referee: Oleksiy Derevinskyi (UKR) Attendance: 6.806

17-06-2023 Laugardalsvöllur, Reykjavík: Iceland – Slovakia 1-2 (1-1)
Iceland: Alex Rúnarsson, Hörður Magnússon (YC67), Victor Pálsson, Sverrir Ingason, Alfons Sampsted (81' Sævar Atli Magnússon), Valgeir Lunddal Friðriksson, Jóhann Guðmundsson, Alfreð Finnbogason (63' Hákon Haraldsson), Albert Guðmundsson, Jón Dagur Thorsteinsson (63' Mikael Egill Ellertsson), Willum Willumsson. (Coach: Åge Hareide (NOR)).
Slovakia: Martin Dúbravka, Peter Pekarík (YC26), Milan Skriniar, Denis Vavro, Dávid Hancko, Marek Hamsík (81' Matús Bero), Juraj Kucka, Stanislav Lobotka, Robert Mak (57' Tomás Suslov), Ivan Schranz (81' Dávid Duris), Róbert Polievka (57' Róbert Bozeník). (Coach: Francesco Calzona (ITA)).
Goals: Iceland: 1-1 Alfreð Finnbogason (41' penalty).
Slovakia: 0-1 Juraj Kucka (27'), 1-2 Tomás Suslov (69').
Referee: Donald Robertson (SCO) Attendance: 7.555

17-06-2023   Estádio do Sport Libao e Benfica, Lisboa:
           Portugal – Bosnia and Herzegovina 3-0 (1-0)
Portugal: Diogo Costa, João Cancelo, Raphaël Guerreiro (78' Nélson Semedo), Rúben Dias, António Silva, Danilo Pereira (YC51), Bruno Fernandes, João Palhinha (87' Diogo Jota), Bernardo Silva (87' Otávio), Cristiano Ronaldo, João Félix (62' Rúben Neves). (Coach: Roberto Martínez (ESP)).
Bosnia and Herzegovina: Ibrahim Sehic, Sead Kolasinac (79' Jusuf Gazibegovic), Sinisa Sanicanin, Anel Ahmedhodzic, Amar Dedic, Adrian Barisic (71' Said Hamulic), Miralem Pjanic (YC41) (78' Sanjin Prcic), Miroslav Stevanovic, Gojko Cimirot, Amir Hadziahmetovic (71' Benjamin Tahirovic (YC84)), Edin Dzeko (79' Dal Varesanovic). (Coach: Faruk Hadzibegic (BIH)).
Goals: Portugal: 1-0 Bernardo Silva (44'), 2-0 Bruno Fernandes (77'), 3-0 Bruno Fernandes (90+3').
Referee: Davide Massa (ITA)   Attendance: 55.058

20-06-2023   Stadion Bilino Polje, Zenica:
           Bosnia and Herzegovina – Luxembourg 0-2 (0-1)
Bosnia and Herzegovina: Ibrahim Sehic, Sead Kolasinac, Sinisa Sanicanin, Amar Dedic, Adrian Barisic, Miralem Pjanic, Miroslav Stevanovic (72' Luka Menalo), Gojko Cimirot (72' Smail Prevljak), Benjamin Tahirovic (46' Amir Hadziahmetovic), Edin Dzeko (YC88), Kenan Kodro (46' Saïd Hamulic). (Coach: Faruk Hadzibegic (BIH)).
Luxembourg: Anthony Moris (YC87), Maxime Chanot, Laurent Jans, Florian Bohnert (YC55), Enes Mahmutovic, Christopher Martins (YC63), Danel Sinani (90+2' Dejvid Sinani), Leandro Barreiro, Mathias Olesen, Alessio Curci (58' Marvin Martins (YC86)), Yvandro Borges Sanches (83' Dirk Carlson). (Coach: Luc Holtz (LUX)).
Goals: Luxembourg: 0-1 Yvandro Borges Sanches (4'), 0-2 Danel Sinani (74').
Referee: Gal Leibovitz (ISR)   Attendance: 8.600

Amir Hadziahmetovic missed a penalty kick (56').

20-06-2023   Laugardalsvöllur, Reykjavík: Iceland – Portugal 0-1 (0-0)
Iceland: Alex Rúnarsson, Hörður Magnússon, Victor Pálsson, Sverrir Ingason, Valgeir Lunddal Friðriksson (79' Alfons Sampsted), Jóhann Guðmundsson, Arnór Traustason (75' Ísak Bergmann Jóhannesson), Alfreð Finnbogason (YC45+1) (75' Sævar Atli Magnússon), Albert Guðmundsson (YC45), Jón Dagur Thorsteinsson (YC74) (79' Hákon Haraldsson), Willum Willumsson (YC70,YC81). (Coach: Åge Hareide (NOR)).
Portugal: Diogo Costa, Pepe, João Cancelo (67' Raphaël Guerreiro), Rúben Dias, Diogo Dalot (YC27), Danilo Pereira (84' Otávio), Rúben Neves (67' Gonçalo Inácio), Bruno Fernandes (84' Vitinha), Bernardo Silva (YC74) (90+3' Diogo Jota), Cristiano Ronaldo (YC83), Rafael Leão. (Coach: Roberto Martínez (ESP)).
Goal: Portugal: 0-1 Cristiano Ronaldo (89').
Referee: Daniel Siebert (GER)   Attendance: 9.517

20-06-2023   Rheinpark Stadion, Vaduz: Liechtenstein – Slovakia   0-1 (0-1)
Liechtenstein: Benjamin Büchel, Sandro Wolfinger (62' Lukas Graber), Maximilian Göppel, Jens Hofer, Niklas Beck (YC31), Lars Traber, Aron Sele (90' Julien Hasler), Fabio Wolfinger (62' Livio Meier), Dennis Salanovic, Simon Lüchinger (77' Colin Haas), Ferhat Saglam (77' Philipp Gaßner). (Coach: Konrad Fünfstück (GER)).
Slovakia: Martin Dúbravka, Peter Pekarík, Milan Skriniar, Denis Vavro (89' Norbert Gyömbér), Dávid Hancko, Marek Hamsík (77' Matús Bero), Juraj Kucka, Stanislav Lobotka (89' Patrik Hrosovský), Tomás Suslov, Robert Mak (63' Dávid Duris), Róbert Polievka (77' Dávid Strelec). (Coach: Francesco Calzona (ITA)).
Goals: Slovakia: 0-1 Denis Vavro (45+1').
Referee: Yigal Frid (ISR)   Attendance: 2.316

08-09-2023   Stadion Bilino Polje, Zenica:
                Bosnia and Herzegovina – Liechtenstein   2-1 (2-1)
Bosnia and Herzegovina: Ibrahim Sehic, Sead Kolasinac (YC57), Dennis Hadzikadunic, Amar Dedic, Miralem Pjanic (77' Amir Hadziahmetovic), Hrvoje Milicevic, Rade Krunic (YC60) (90+3' Saïd Hamulic), Adi Nalic (64' Benjamin Tahirovic), Edin Dzeko, Nemanja Bilbija (77' Jusuf Gazibegovic), Ermedin Demirovic (90+3' Kenan Kodro). (Coach: Meho Kodro (BIH)).
Liechtenstein: Benjamin Büchel, Sandro Wolfinger (84' Fabio Wolfinger), Maximilian Göppel, Andreas Malin (YC74), Niklas Beck, Lars Traber, Sandro Wieser (69' Livio Meier), Aron Sele, Dennis Salanovic (82' Andrin Netzer), Simon Lüchinger (YC76) (83' Julien Hasler), Ferhat Saglam (74' Fabio Luque Notaro). (Coach: Konrad Fünfstück (GER)).
Goals: Bosnia and Herzegovina: Edin Dzeko (3'), 2-0 Simon Lüchinger (18' own goal).
Liechtenstein: 2-1 Sandro Wolfinger (21').
Referee: Sayat Karabayev (KAZ)   Attendance: 6.189

08-09-2023   Stade de Luxembourg, Luxembourg City:
                Luxembourg – Iceland   3-1 (1-0)
Luxembourg: Anthony Moris, Maxime Chanot, Mica Pinto, Marvin Martins (64' Florian Bohnert), Enes Mahmutovic (YC13) (64' Lars Gerson), Christopher Martins (YC15), Danel Sinani, Leandro Barreiro, Mathias Olesen (64' Laurent Jans), Alessio Curci (81' Vincent Thill), Yvandro Borges Sanches (90+3' Aiman Dardari). (Coach: Luc Holtz (LUX)).
Iceland: Alex Rúnarsson, Hörður Magnússon (YC39,YC73), Victor Pálsson, Kolbeinn Finnsson, Valgeir Lunddal Friðriksson, Jóhann Guðmundsson, Arnór Traustason, Hákon Haraldsson (YC56), Alfreð Finnbogason (79' Mikael Anderson), Jón Dagur Thorsteinsson (79' Ísak Bergmann Jóhannesson (YC85)), Sævar Atli Magnússon (46' Orri Óskarsson). (Coach: Åge Hareide (NOR)).
Goals: Luxembourg: 1-0 Maxime Chanot (9' penalty), 2-0 Yvandro Borges Sanches (70'), 3-1 Danel Sinani (89').
Iceland: 2-1 Hákon Haraldsson (88').
Referee: Goga Kikacheishvili (GEO)   Attendance: 7.427

08-09-2023   Stadión Tehelné pole, Bratislava: Slovakia – Portugal   0-1 (0-1)
Slovakia: Martin Dúbravka, Peter Pekarík, Milan Skriniar, Denis Vavro, Dávid Hancko, Juraj Kucka (75' László Bénes), Stanislav Lobotka (83' Patrik Hrosovský), Ondrej Duda (YC53), Lukás Haraslín (83' Dávid Duris), Ivan Schranz (YC35) (63' Tomás Suslov), Róbert Polievka (64' Róbert Bozeník). (Coach: Francesco Calzona (ITA)).
Portugal: Diogo Costa, João Cancelo (62' Nélson Semedo), Rúben Dias, Diogo Dalot, António Silva, Bruno Fernandes, João Palhinha, Bernardo Silva, Vitinha (63' Otávio), Cristiano Ronaldo (YC62), Rafael Leão (63' Pedro Neto). (Coach: Roberto Martínez (ESP)).
Goal: Portugal: 0-1 Bruno Fernandes (43').
Referee: Glenn Nyberg (SWE)   Attendance: 21.473

11-09-2023   Laugardalsvöllur, Reykjavík:
                    Iceland – Bosnia and Herzegovina 1-0 (0-0)
Iceland: Alex Rúnarsson, Victor Pálsson, Hjörtur Hermannsson, Kolbeinn Finnsson, Alfons
Sampsted, Jóhann Guðmundsson, Arnór Traustason (YC70), Mikael Anderson (76' Jón Dagur
Thorsteinsson), Hákon Haraldsson, Willum Willumsson (76' Alfreð Finnbogason), Orri
Óskarsson. (Coach: Åge Hareide (NOR)).
Bosnia and Herzegovina: Ibrahim Sehic, Sead Kolasinac, Dennis Hadzikadunic (YC29), Jusuf
Gazibegovic (82' Luka Menalo), Amar Dedic (86' Eldar Civic), Hrvoje Milicevic (YC81),
Rade Krunic, Amir Hadziahmetovic (68' Miralem Pjanic), Benjamin Tahirovic (81' Nemanja
Bilbija), Edin Dzeko, Ermedin Demirovic (67' Kenan Kodro). (Coach: Meho Kodro (BIH)).
Goal: Iceland: 1-0 Alfreð Finnbogason (90+1').
Referee: Lawrence Visser (BEL)   Attendance: 5.229

11-09-2023   Estádio Do Algarve, Faro/Loulé: Portugal – Luxembourg 9-0 (4-0)
Portugal: Diogo Costa, Nélson Semedo (61' João Cancelo), Rúben Dias, Diogo Dalot, Gonçalo
Inácio, Danilo Pereira (75' Rúben Neves), Bruno Fernandes, Bernardo Silva (61' Ricardo
Horta), Diogo Jota, Rafael Leão (75' Otávio), Gonçalo Ramos (61' João Félix). (Coach:
Roberto Martínez (ESP)).
Luxembourg: Anthony Moris, Maxime Chanot (78' Seid Korac), Laurent Jans, Mica Pinto (54'
Vincent Thill (YC54)), Florian Bohnert (46' Lars Gerson (YC76)), Enes Mahmutovic (YC65),
Danel Sinani, Leandro Barreiro, Timothé Rupil (46' Sébastien Thill), Alessio Curci (46' Dirk
Carlson), Yvandro Borges Sanches. (Coach: Luc Holtz (LUX)).
Goals: Portugal: 1-0 Gonçalo Inácio (12'), 2-0 Gonçalo Ramos (18'), 3-0 Gonçalo Ramos
(34'), 4-0 Gonçalo Inácio (45+4'), 5-0 Diogo Jota (58'), 6-0 Ricardo Horta (67'),
7-0 Diogo Jota (77'), 8-0 Bruno Fernandes (83'), 9-0 João Félix (88').
Referee: John Brooks (ENG)   Attendance: 18.932

11-09-2023   Stadión Tehelné pole, Bratislava: Slovakia – Liechtenstein 3-0 (3-0)
Slovakia: Martin Dúbravka, Norbert Gyömbér, Milan Skriniar, Dávid Hancko (86' Vernon De
Marco (YC87)), Michal Tomic (YC45+2) (69' Peter Pekarík), Stanislav Lobotka (76' Patrik
Hrosovský (YC77)), Ondrej Duda (77' Matús Bero), Lukás Haraslín, László Bénes, Robert
Mak (70' Lubomír Tupta), Róbert Bozeník. (Coach: Francesco Calzona (ITA)).
Liechtenstein: Benjamin Büchel, Sandro Wolfinger (63' Livio Meier), Maximilian Göppel,
Andreas Malin (90' Martin Marxer), Niklas Beck, Lars Traber, Sandro Wieser (YC28), Aron
Sele, Dennis Salanovic (63' Andrin Netzer), Simon Lüchinger (90' Colin Haas), Ferhat Saglam
(73' Severin Schlegel). (Coach: Konrad Fünfstück (GER)).
Goals: Slovakia: 1-0 Dávid Hancko (1'), 2-0 Ondrej Duda (3'), 3-0 Robert Mak (6').
Referee: Sander van der Eijk (HOL)   Attendance: 13.679

13-10-2023   Laugardalsvöllur, Reykjavík: Iceland – Luxembourg 1-1 (1-0)
Iceland: Alex Rúnarsson, Victor Pálsson, Sverrir Ingason (YC66), Kolbeinn Finnsson (YC75),
Alfons Sampsted, Arnór Traustason, Arnór Sigurðsson (85' Mikael Anderson), Ísak Bergmann
Jóhannesson (70' Gylfi Sigurðsson), Hákon Haraldsson, Willum Willumsson (70' Jón Dagur
Thorsteinsson), Orri Óskarsson (70' Alfreð Finnbogason). (Coach: Åge Hareide (NOR)).
Luxembourg: Anthony Moris (YC90+4), Maxime Chanot (YC82), Mica Pinto (85' Olivier
Thill), Enes Mahmutovic (YC21), Dirk Carlson, Eldin Dzogovic (46' Laurent Jans),
Christopher Martins (YC64), Danel Sinani, Leandro Barreiro, Vincent Thill (61' Mathias
Olesen), Alessio Curci (YC44) (46' Gerson Rodrigues). (Coach: Luc Holtz (LUX)).
Goals: Iceland: 1-0 Orri Óskarsson (23').
Luxembourg: 1-1 Gerson Rodrigues (46').
Referee: Sebastian Gishamer (AUT)   Attendance: 4.568

13-10-2023   Rheinpark Stadion, Vaduz:
                    Liechtenstein – Bosnia and Herzegovina   0-2 (0-2)
Liechtenstein: Benjamin Büchel, Sandro Wolfinger (33' Severin Schlegel, 90+7' Julien
Hasler), Maximilian Göppel, Andreas Malin (71' Martin Marxer), Jens Hofer, Sandro Wieser,
Marcel Büchel, Aron Sele, Dennis Salanovic (YC33) (90+7' Livio Meier), Simon Lüchinger,
Fabio Luque Notaro (71' Kenny Kindle). (Coach: Konrad Fünfstück (GER)).
Bosnia and Herzegovina: Ibrahim Sehic, Sead Kolasinac (86' Eldar Civic), Dennis
Hadzikadunic, Amar Dedic (90+3' Jusuf Gazibegovic), Adrian Barisic (78' Renato Gojkovic),
Miralem Pjanic (78' Amir Hadziahmetovic), Miroslav Stevanovic, Gojko Cimirot, Amar
Rahmanovic, Edin Dzeko (86' Nemanja Bilbija), Ermedin Demirovic. (Coach: Savo Milosevic
(SRB)).
Goals: Bosnia and Herzegovina: 0-1 Amar Rahmanovic (13'), 0-2 Miroslav Stevanovic (41').
Referee: Damian Sylwestrzak (POL)   Attendance: 5.874

13-10-2023   Estádio Do Dragão, Porto: Portugal – Slovakia   3-2 (2-0)
Portugal: Diogo Costa, João Cancelo, Rúben Dias, Diogo Dalot, António Silva, Bruno
Fernandes (YC57), João Palhinha (YC75) (86' Otávio), Bernardo Silva (86' Rúben Neves),
Cristiano Ronaldo, Rafael Leão (65' João Félix), Gonçalo Ramos (87' Diogo Jota). (Coach:
Roberto Martínez (ESP)).
Slovakia: Martin Dúbravka, Peter Pekarík (YC31) (76' Michal Tomic), Milan Skriniar, Denis
Vavro, Dávid Hancko, Juraj Kucka (46' László Bénes), Stanislav Lobotka, Ondrej Duda
(YC61), Robert Mak (46' Tomás Suslov (YC85)), Ivan Schranz (87' Dávid Duris), Róbert
Bozeník (65' Róbert Polievka). (Coach: Francesco Calzona (ITA)). (Not used subs: Norbert
Gyömbér (YC90+4), Patrik Hrosovský (YC90+4)).
Goals: Portugal: 1-0 Gonçalo Ramos (18'), 2-0 Cristiano Ronaldo (29' penalty),
3-1 Cristiano Ronaldo (72').
Slovakia: 2-1 Dávid Hancko (69'), 3-2 Stanislav Lobotka (80').
Referee: Anastasios Sidiropoulos (GRE)   Attendance: 46.601

16-10-2023   Stadion Bilino Polje, Zenica:
                    Bosnia and Herzegovia – Portugal   0-5 (0-5)
Bosnia and Herzegovina: Ibrahim Sehic (72' Nikola Vasilj), Sead Kolasinac (YC88), Dennis
Hadzikadunic (YC83), Amar Dedic, Adrian Barisic (72' Renato Gojkovic), Miralem Pjanic,
Miroslav Stevanovic (66' Saïd Hamulic), Gojko Cimirot, Amar Rahmanovic (46' Amir
Hadziahmetovic), Edin Dzeko, Ermedin Demirovic (46' Jusuf Gazibegovic). (Coach: Savo
Milosevic (SRB)).
Portugal: Diogo Costa, João Cancelo, Rúben Dias, Diogo Dalot, Gonçalo Inácio, Danilo
Pereira, Otávio (85' João Neves), Bruno Fernandes (79' Rúben Neves), Cristiano Ronaldo (66'
Diogo Jota), Rafael Leão (66' Pedro Neto), João Félix (79' Vitinha). (Coach: Roberto Martínez
(ESP)).
Goals: Portugal: 0-1 Cristiano Ronaldo (5' penalty), 0-2 Cristiano Ronaldo (20'),
0-3 Bruno Fernandes (25'), 0-4 João Cancelo (32'), 0-5 João Félix (41').
Referee: Halil Umut Meler (TUR)   Attendance: 13.047

16-10-2023   Laugarsalsvöllur, Reykjavík: Iceland – Liechtenstein   4-0 (2-0)
Iceland: Elías Ólafsson, Victor Pálsson, Sverrir Ingason, Kolbeinn Finnsson, Alfons Sampsted, Gylfi Sigurðsson (58' Ísak Bergmann Jóhannesson), Arnór Traustason (80' Aron Gunnarsson), Hákon Haraldsson, Alfreð Finnbogason (57' Orri Óskarsson (YC68)), Jón Dagur Thorsteinsson (80' Andri Guðjohnsen), Willum Willumsson (57' Mikael Anderson). (Coach: Åge Hareide (NOR)).
Liechtenstein: Benjamin Büchel, Maximilian Göppel, Martin Marxer (YC51), Lars Traber, Sandro Wieser, Marcel Büchel (71' Jakob Lorenz), Aron Sele (YC59), Dennis Salanovic (90+1' Kenny Kindle), Livio Meier (71' Andrin Netzer), Simon Lüchinger (75' Niklas Beck), Julian Hasler (90+1' Fabio Luque Notaro). (Coach: Konrad Fünfstück (GER)).
Goals: Iceland: 1-0 Gylfi Sigurðsson (22' penalty), 2-0 Alfreð Finnbogason (44'), 3-0 Gylfi Sigurðsson (49'), 4-0 Hákon Haraldsson (63').
Referee: Abdulkadir Bitigen (TUR)   Attendance: 4.317

Sandro Wieser missed a penalty kick (45+5').

16-10-2023   Stade de Luxembourg, Luxembourg City:
                    Luxembourg – Slovakia   0-1 (0-0)
Luxembourg: Anthony Moris, Lars Gerson, Maxime Chanot, Laurent Jans (YC27) (88' Dirk Carlson), Marvin Martins, Christopher Martins, Danel Sinani (YC74), Leandro Barreiro, Mathias Olesen (YC90+3), Gerson Rodrigues, Vincent Thill (YC26) (88' Alessio Curci). (Coach: Luc Holtz (LUX)).
Slovakia: Martin Dúbravka, Peter Pekarík (YC29) (90+4' Norbert Gyömbér), Milan Skriniar, Denis Vavro, Dávid Hancko, Juraj Kucka, Stanislav Lobotka, Ondrej Duda (88' Patrik Hrosovský (YC90+1)), Tomás Suslov (YC90), Ivan Schranz (63' Dávid Duris), Róbert Polievka (63' Róbert Bozeník (YC79)). (Coach: Francesco Calzona (ITA)).
Goal: Slovakia: 0-1 Dávid Duris (77').
Referee: José María Sánchez Martínez (ESP)   Attendance: 9.386

16-11-2023   Rheinpark Stadion, Vaduz: Liechtenstein – Portugal   0-2 (0-0)
Liechtenstein: Benjamin Büchel, Maximilian Göppel, Andreas Malin, Niklas Beck (64' Liam Kranz), Lars Traber, Sandro Wieser, Marcel Büchel, Aron Sele (77' Jens Hofer), Dennis Salanovic (90+1' Martin Marxer), Simon Lüchinger (YC24) (46' Livio Meier), Julian Hasler (64' Philipp Ospelt). (Coach: Konrad Fünfstück (GER)).
Portugal: José Sá, João Cancelo (87' João Mário), Toti Gomes, António Silva, Rúben Neves, Bruno Fernandes (68' Vitinha), Bernardo Silva (60' Ricardo Horta), Cristiano Ronaldo (67' Bruma), Diogo Jota (YC90+5), João Félix (87' João Neves), Gonçalo Ramos. (Coach: Roberto Martínez (ESP)).
Goals: Portugal: 0-1 Cristiano Ronaldo (46'), 0-2 João Cancelo (57').
Referee: Mohammed Al-Hakim (SWE)   Attendance: 5.749

16-11-2023   Stade de Luxembourg, Luxembourg City:
Luxembourg – Bosnia and Herzegovina   4-1 (2-0)
Luxembourg: Anthony Moris, Maxime Chanot (64' Lars Gerson), Marvin Martins, Florian
Bohnert (75' Sébastien Thill), Enes Mahmutovic (YC61) (84' Seid Korac), Dirk Carlson,
Christopher Martins (YC24) (84' Olivier Thill (YC89)), Danel Sinani, Leandro Barreiro,
Mathias Olesen (75' Edvin Muratovic), Gerson Rodrigues. (Coach: Luc Holtz (LUX)).
Bosnia and Herzegovina: Nikola Vasilj, Adnan Kovacevic, Renato Gojkovic (YC45+4), Nihad
Mujakic, Amar Dedic (YC71), Miroslav Stevanovic (46' Ermedin Demirovic), Gojko Cimirot
(YC28), Rade Krunic (YC88), Amir Hadziahmetovic (YC26) (46' Haris Hajradinovic
(YC69)), Haris Tabakovic (80' Smail Prevljak), Saïd Hamulic (79' Jusuf Gazibegovic).
(Coach: Savo Milosevic (SRB)).
Goals: Luxembourg: 1-0 Mathias Olesen (6'), 2-0 Gerson Rodrigues (30' penalty),
3-0 Nihad Mujakic (55' own goal), 4-1 Gerson Rodrigues (90+5').
Bosnia and Herzegovina: 3-1 Renato Gojkovic (90+3').
Referee: Andris Treimanis (LVA)   Attendance: 8.520

16-11-2023   Stadión Tehelné pole, Bratislava: Slovakia – Iceland   4-2 (2-1)
Slovakia: Martin Dúbravka (YC88), Norbert Gyömbér, Milan Skriniar, Denis Vavro, Dávid
Hancko, Juraj Kucka, Stanislav Lobotka, Ondrej Duda (79' László Bénes), Lukás Haraslín (65'
Tomás Suslov), Ivan Schranz (79' Dávid Duris), Róbert Bozeník (89' Róbert Polievka).
(Coach: Francesco Calzona (ITA)).
Iceland: Elías Ólafsson, Victor Pálsson, Sverrir Ingason, Kolbeinn Finnsson, Alfons Sampsted,
Jóhann Guðmundsson, Arnór Traustason (25' Stefan Teitur Thórðarson), Arnór Sigurðsson
(61' Aron Gunnarsson), Kristian Hlynsson (46' Ísak Bergmann Jóhannesson), Willum
Willumsson (73' Alfreð Finnbogason), Orri Óskarsson (73' Andri Guðjohnsen). (Coach: Åge
Hareide (NOR)).
Goals: Slovakia: 1-1 Juraj Kucka (30'), 2-1 Ondrej Duda (36' penalty),
3-1 Lukás Haraslín (47'), 4-1 Lukás Haraslín (55').
Iceland: 0-1 Orri Óskarsson (17'), 4-2 Andri Guðjohnsen (74').
Referee: Craig Pawson (ENG)   Attendance: 21.548

19-11-2023   Stadion Bilino Polje, Zenica:
Bosnia and Herzegovina – Slovakia   1-2 (0-0)
Bosnia and Herzegovina: Kenan Piric, Renato Gojkovic (YC35,YC63), Dennis Hadzikadunic,
Nihad Mujakic, Jusuf Gazibegovic, Gojko Cimirot (78' Nermin Zolotic), Haris Hajradinovic
(87' Almedin Ziljkic), Ivan Basis (YC48), Smail Prevljak (YC58) (59' Nemanja Bilbija),
Ermedin Demirovic, Saïd Hamulic (87' Dal Varesanovic). (Coach: Savo Milosevic (SRB)).
Slovakia: Marek Rodák, Peter Pekarík, Lubomír Satka, Milan Skriniar, Dávid Hancko, Patrik
Hrosovský, Ondrej Duda (85' Jakub Kadák), László Bénes (66' Juraj Kucka), Tomás Suslov
(85' Erik Jirka), Róbert Mak (75' Lubomír Tupta), Róbert Bozeník (YC52) (76' Róbert
Polievka). (Coach: Francesco Calzona (ITA)).
Goals: Bosnia and Herzegovina: 1-0 Patrik Hrosovský (49' own goal).
Slovakia: 1-1 Róbert Bozeník (52'), 1-2 Lubomír Satka (71').
Referee: Julina Weinberger (AUT)   Attendance: 3.800

567

19-11-2023   Rheinpark Stadion, Vaduz: Liechtenstein – Luxembourg   0-1 (0-0)
Liechtenstein: Benjamin Büchel, Sandro Wolfinger (63' Niklas Beck), Maximilian Göppel, Andreas Malin (YC69), Jens Hofer (63' Liam Kranz), Lars Traber (75' Severin Schlegel), Sandro Wieser (YC7), Marcel Büchel, Dennis Salanovic, Livio Meier (YC73) (75' Andrin Netzer), Julien Hasler (9' Philipp Ospelt). (Coach: Konrad Fünfstück (GER)).
Luxembourg: Anthony Moris, Maxime Chanot, Laurent Jans (90' Marvin Martins), Dirk Carlson, Seid Korac (57' Enes Mahmutovic), Sébastien Thill (57' Florian Bohnert), Danel Sinani (RC5), Leandro Barreiro, Mathias Olesen, Gerson Rodrigues, Vincent Thill (75' Edvin Muratovic). (Coach: Luc Holtz (LUX)).
Goal: Luxembourg: 0-1 Gerson Rodrigues (69').
Referee: Stéphanie Frappart (FRA)   Attendance: 2.241

19-11-2023   Estádio José Alvalade, Lisboa: Portugal – Iceland   2-0 (1-0)
Portugal: Diogo Costa, João Cancelo (87' João Neves), Rúben Dias, João Mário (63' Raphaël Guerreiro), Gonçalo Inácio, Otávio (75' Vitinha), Bruno Fernandes, João Palhinha (YC54), Bernardo Silva (62' Ricardo Horta), Cristiano Ronaldo, João Félix (YC84) (87' Bruma). (Coach: Roberto Martínez (ESP)).
Iceland: Hákon Valdimarsson, Guðmundur Thórarinsson, Victor Pálsson, Sverrir Ingason, Hjörtur Hermannsson, Jóhann Guðmundsson (YC54), Arnór Sigurðsson, Ísak Bergmann Jóhannesson (YC28) (62' Arnór Traustason), Alfreð Finnbogason (46' Orri Óskarsson), Jón Dagur Thorsteinsson (YC32) (62' Andri Guðjohnsen), Willum Willumsson (YC46) (62' Mikael Egill Ellertsson). (Coach: Åge Hareide (NOR)).
Goals: Portugal: 1-0 Bruno Fernandes (37'), 2-0 Ricardo Horta (66').
Referee: Anastasios Papapetrou (GRE)   Attendance: 45.655

QUALIFICATION PLAY-OFFS

The play-offs of the UEFA Euro 2024 qualifying tournament decided the last three places in the UEFA Euro 2024 final tournament in Germany. The twelve participants of the play-offs were selected based on their performances in the 2022-2023 UEFA Nations League. The teams were divided into three paths, each containing four teams, with each play-off featuring two single-leg semi-finals, and one single-leg final. The three play-off path winners joined the hosts, Germany, and the twenty other teams who had already qualified for UEFA Euro 2024.

PATH A – SEMI-FINALS

21-03-2024   Stadion Narodowy, Warszawa: Poland – Estonia 5-1 (1-0)
Poland: Wojciech Szczesny, Jan Bednarek, Pawel Dawidowicz, Jakub Kiwior, Piotr Zielinski (72' Sebastian Szymanski), Przemyslaw Frankowski (46' Matty Cash, 56' Tymoteusz Puchacz (YC60)), Bartosz Slisz, Jakub Piotrowski (73' Jakub Moder), Nicola Zalewski, Robert Lewandowski, Karol Swiderski (72' Adam Buksa). (Coach: Michal Probierz (POL)).
Estonia: Karl Hein, Ragnar Klavan, Ken Kallaste (67' Artur Pikk), Joonas Tamm, Karol Mets, Maksim Paskotsi (YC15,YC27), Markus Soomets (82' Mihkel Ainsalu), Martin Vetkal, Kevor Palumets (67' Markus Poom), Alex Tamm (31' Kristo Hussar), Oliver Jürgens (67' Mark Anders Lepik). (Coach: Thomas Häberli (SUI)).
Goals: Poland: 1-0 Przemyslaw Frankowski (22'), 2-0 Piotr Zielinski (50'), 3-0 Jakub Piotrowski (70'), 4-0 Karol Mets (74' own goal), 5-0 Sebastian Szymanski (76').
Estonia: 5-1 Martin Vetkal (78').
Referee: Slavko Vincic (SVN)   Attendance: 53,868.

568

21-03-2024   Cardiff City Stadium, Cardiff: Wales – Finland 4-1 (2-1)
Wales: Danny Ward, Ben Davies, Connor Roberts, Joe Rodon, Ethan Ampadu, Neco Williams, Chris Mepham (YC74), Harry Wilson (YC65) (90' Nathan Broadhead), David Brooks (61' Kieffer Moore (YC90+5)), Jordan James (YC54), Brennan Johnson (73' Dan James). (Coach: Rob Page (WAL)).
Finland: Lucas Hrádecký, Nikolai Alho (87' Ilmari Niskanen), Miro Tenho (YC50), Robert Ivanov, Matti Peltola, Rasmus Schüller (73' Kaan Kairinen), Robin Lod (YC22) (73' Oliver Antman), Glen Kamara, Daniel Håkans (YC68), Teemu Pukki (78' Fredrik Jensen), Joel Pohjanpalo (78' Benjamin Källman). (Coach: Markku Kanerva (FIN)).
Goals: Wales: 1-0 David Brooks (3'), 2-0 Neco Williams (38'), 3-1 Brennan Johnson (47'), 4-1 Dan James (86').
Finland: 2-1 Teemu Pukki (45').
Referee: István Kovács (ROM)   Attendance: 32,162.

FINAL

26-03-2024   Cardiff City Stadium, Cardiff: Wales – Poland 0-0 (AET)
Wales: Danny Ward, Ben Davies, Connor Roberts (84' David Brooks, 112' Nathan Broadhead), Joe Rodon, Ethan Ampadu, Neco Williams, Chris Mepham (YC98,YC120+1), Harry Wilson, Jordan James (YC55), Kieffer Moore, Brennan Johnson (70' Dan James). (Coach: Rob Page (WAL)).
Poland: Wojciech Szczesny, Jan Bednarek (80' Bartosz Salamon), Pawel Dawidowicz, Jakub Kiwior, Piotr Zielinski (101' Sebastian Szymanski), Przemyslaw Frankowski, Bartosz Slisz, Jakub Piotrowski (YC50) (105' Taras Romanczuk), Nicola Zalewski (YC72), Robert Lewandowski, Karol Swiderski (80' Krzysztof Piatek). (Coach: Michal Probierz (POL)).
Referee: Daniele Orsato (ITA)   Attendance: 31,876.
Penalties: 1 Robert Lewandowski   1 Ben Davies
            2 Sebastian Szymanski   2 Kieffer Moore
            3 Przemyslaw Frankowski   3 Harry Wilson
            4 Nicola Zalewski   4 Neco Williams
            5 Krzysztof Piatek   * Dan James

Poland entered Group D in the Final Tournament.

569

PATH B

SEMI-FINALS

21-03-2024   Szusza Ferenc Stadion, Budapest (HUN): Israel – Iceland 1-4 (1-2)
Israel: Omri Glazer, Miguel Vítor, Elazar Dasa, Sean Goldberg, Roy Revivo (RC73), Dor
Peretz (70' Mohammad Abu Fani), Gadi Kinda (62' Ramzi Safuri), Gavriel Kanichowsky (46'
Oscar Gloukh), Eran Zahavi (YC73), Dor Turgeman, Anan Khalaili (71' Liel Abada). (Coach:
Alon Hazan (ISR)).
Iceland: Hákon Valdimarsson, Guðmundur Thórarinsson, Victor Pálsson, Sverrir Ingason,
Daniel Leo Grétarsson, Arnór Traustason (62' Ísak Bergmann Jóhannesson), Arnór Sigurðsson
(77' Mikael Anderson), Hakon Arnar Haraldsson, Albert Thor Gudmundsson, Willum
Willumsson (46' Jón Dagur Thorsteinsson), Orri Óskarsson (62' Andri Guðjohnsen). (Coach:
Åge Hareide (NOR)).
Goals: Israel: 1-0 Eran Zahavi (31' penalty).
Iceland: 1-1 Albert Thor Gudmundsson (39'), 1-2 Arnór Traustason (42'),
1-3 Albert Thor Gudmundsson (83'), 1-4 Albert Thor Gudmundsson (87').
Referee: Anthony Taylor (ENG)   Attendance: 1,226.

Eran Zahavi missed a penalty kick (80').

*Due to the Israel-Hamas war, Israel were required to play their home matches at neutral
venues until further notice.*

21-03-2024   Stadion Bilino Polje, Zenica:
                    Bosnia and Herzegovina – Ukraine 1-2 (0-0)
Bosnia and Herzegovina: Ibrahim Sehic, Sead Kolasinac (YC9), Dennis Hadzikadunic, Anel
Ahmedhodzic (YC79) (82' Adnan Kovacevic (YC90+4)), Jusuf Gazibegovic (YC26), Amar
Dedic (68' Eldar Civic), Gojko Cimirot, Haris Hajradinovic (82' Miralem Pjanic), Rade Krunic
(90+2' Amar Rahmanovic), Edin Dzeko, Ermedin Demirovic. (Coach: Savo Milosevic (SRB)).
Ukraine: Andriy Lunin (YC90+7), Oleksandr Zinchenko (76' Ruslan Malinovskyi), Mykola
Matviyenko (YC16), Vitaliy Mykolenko, Yukhym Konoplya (YC58), Illya Zabarnyi,
Oleksandr Zubkov (76' Oleksii Hutsuliak), Mykhaylo Mudryk, Georgiy Sudakov, Volodymyr
Brazhko (81' Roman Yaremchuk (YC90+1)), Artem Dovbyk (90+2' Maksym Talovierov).
(Coach: Serhiy Rebrov (UKR)).
Goals: Bosnia and Herzegovina: 1-0 Mykola Matviyenko (56' own goal).
Ukraine: 1-1 Roman Yaremchuk (85'), 1-2 Artem Dovbyk (88').
Referee: Felix Zwayer (GER)   Attendance: 10,992.

FINAL

26-03-2024   Tarczynski Arena, Wroclaw (POL): Ukraine – Iceland 2-1 (0-1)
Ukraine: Andriy Lunin, Mykola Matviyenko, Vitaliy Mykolenko, Yukhym Konoplya, Illya
Zabarnyi, Ruslan Malinovskyi (YC42) (64' Oleksandr Zinchenko (YC90+2)), Mykhaylo
Mudryk, Georgiy Sudakov, Volodymyr Brazhko, Roman Yaremchuk (72' Artem Dovbyk),
Viktor Tsyhankov (88' Maksym Talovierov). (Coach: Serhiy Rebrov (UKR)).
Iceland: Hákon Valdimarsson, Guðmundur Thórarinsson (63' Kolbeinn Finnsson), Victor
Pálsson, Sverrir Ingason (YC56), Daniel Leo Grétarsson, Johann Berg Gudmundsson (YC90),
Arnór Traustason, Hakon Arnar Haraldsson (YC21) (87' Mikael Anderson), Albert Thor
Gudmundsson, Jón Dagur Thorsteinsson (87' Mikael Egill Ellertsson), Andri Guðjohnsen (64'
Orri Óskarsson). (Coach: Åge Hareide (NOR)).
Goals: Ukraine: 1-1 Viktor Tsyhankov (54'), 2-1 Mykhaylo Mudryk (84').
Iceland: 0-1 Albert Thor Gudmundsson (30').
Referee: Clément Turpin (FRA)   Attendance: 29,310.

*Due to the Russian invasion of Ukraine, Ukraine were required to play their home matches at
neutral venues until further notice.*

Ukraine entered Group E in the Final Tournament.

PATH C – SEMI-FINALS

21-03-2024   Boris Paichadze Dinamo Arena, Tbilisi:
Georgia – Luxembourg 2-0 (1-0)
Georgia: Giorgi Mamardashvili, Guram Kashia (YC90+2), Solomon Kvirkvelia, Otar
Kakabadze, Lasha Dvali, Otar Kiteishvili, Giorgi Kochorashvili (86' Jaba Kankava (YC87)),
Giorgi Chakvetadze (77' Nika Kvekveskiri (YC78)), Budu Zivzivadze (YC21) (86' Giorgi
Kvilitaia), Levan Shengelia (72' Giorgi Tsitaishvili), Georges Mikautadze (77' Zuriko
Davitashvili). (Coach: Willy Sagnol (FRA)).
Luxembourg: Anthony Moris, Maxime Chanot (RC56), Laurent Jans, Michael Pinto (YC24)
(42' Marvin Martins (YC82)), Florian Bohnert (YC90+2), Enes Mahmutovic (90+1' Edvin
Muratovic), Christopher Martins (YC87), Leandro Barreiro (YC66), Mathias Olesen (YC90+6)
(77' Olivier Thill), Gerson Rodrigues (YC54) (90+1' Seid Korac), Yvandro Borges Sanches
(77' Alessio Curci). (Coach: Luc Holtz (LUX)).
Goals: Georgia: 1-0 Budu Zivzivadze (40'), 2-0 Budu Zivzivadze (63').
Referee: José María Sánchez Martínez (ESP)   Attendance: 51,404.

21-03-2024   OPAP Arena, Athens: Greece – Kazakhstan 5-0 (4-0)
Greece: Odisseas Vlachodimos, George Baldock (67' Lazaros Rota), Pantelis Hatzidiakos
(YC30) (46' Panagiotis Retsos), Konstantinos Tsimikas, Konstantinos Mavropanos, Petros
Mantalos, Dimitrios Kourbelis, Anastasios Bakasetas (74' Andreas Bouchalakis), Dimitris
Pelkas (64' Giorgos Giakoumakis), Georgios Masouras, Fotis Ioannidis (64' Giannis
Konstantelias). (Coach: Gustavo Poyet (URU)).
Kazakhstan: Igor Shatskiy, Abzal Beysebekov (46' Adilet Sadybekov (YC54)), Yan
Vorogovskiy (YC17), Temirlan Erlanov (YC68), Marat Bystrov, Aleksandr Marochkin,
Bagdat Kairov (46' Erkin Tapalov), Baktiyor Zaynutdinov, Maksim Samorodov (77' Abat
Aymbetov), Islam Chesnokov (68' Aleksandr Zuev), Elkhan Astanov (46' Ramazan Orazov
(YC67)). (Coach: Magomed Adiev (RUS)).
Goals: Greece: 1-0 Anastasios Bakasetas (9' penalty), 2-0 Dimitris Pelkas (15'),
3-0 Fotis Ioannidis (37'), 4-0 Dimitrios Kourbelis (40'), 5-0 Erkin Tapalov (86' own goal).
Referee: Danny Makkelie (HOL)   Attendance: 25,200.

FINAL

26-03-2024   Boris Paichadze Dinamo Arena, Tbilisi: Georgia – Greece 0-0 (AET)
Georgia: Giorgi Mamardashvili, Guram Kashia, Solomon Kvirkvelia (YC50), Otar Kakabadze,
Lasha Dvali, Otar Kiteishvili (104' Nika Kvekveskiri), Giorgi Kochorashvili, Giorgi
Chakvetadze (104' Zuriko Davitashvili), Budu Zivzivadze (YC42) (75' Georges Mikautadze),
Levan Shengelia (86' Giorgi Tsitaishvili), Khvicha Kvaratskhelia (109' Giorgi Kvilitaia).
(Coach: Willy Sagnol (FRA)). (Not used sub: Giorgi Loria (RC45+3)).
Greece: Odisseas Vlachodimos, George Baldock (YC6) (60' Lazaros Rota (YC90+3)), Pantelis
Hatzidiakos (YC35) (105' Panagiotis Retsos), Konstantinos Tsimikas, Konstantinos
Mavropanos (YC44), Petros Mantalos (99' Andreas Bouchalakis), Dimitrios Kourbelis (67'
Emmanouil Siopis), Anastasios Bakasetas, Dimitris Pelkas (61' Giannis Konstantelias
(YC90)), Georgios Masouras, Fotis Ioannidis (90' Giorgos Giakoumakis). (Coach: Gustavo
Poyet (URU)).
Referee: Szymon Marciniak (POL)   Attendance: 44,000.
Penalties: 1 Giorgi Kochorashvili   * Anastasios Bakasetas
            2 Zuriko Davitashvili 1 Georgios Masouras
            * Georges Mikautadze   2 Andreas Bouchalakis
            3 Lasha Dvali   * Giorgos Giakoumakis
            4 Nika Kvekveskiri

Georgia entered Group F in the Final Tournament.

FINAL TOURNAMENT

GROUP STAGE

GROUP A

14-06-2024   Fußball Arena München, München: Germany – Scotland 5-1 (3-0)
Germany: Manuel Neuer, Antonio Rüdiger, Jonathan Tah (YC62), Maximilian Mittelstädt,
Toni Kroos (80' Emre Can), Ilkay Gündogan, Robert Andrich (YC31) (46' Pascal Groß),
Joshua Kimmich, Kai Havertz (63' Niclas Füllkrug), Florian Wirtz (63' Leroy Sané), Jamal
Musiala (74' Thomas Müller). (Coach: Julian Nagelsmann (GER)).
Scotland: Angus Gunn, Andrew Robertson, Kieran Tierney (77' Scott McKenna), Jack
Hendry, Anthony Ralston (YC48), Ryan Porteous (RC45), Callum McGregor (67' Billy
Gilmour), John McGinn (67' Kenny McLean), Ryan Christie (82' Lawrence Shankland), Scott
McTominay, Che Adams (46' Grant Hanley). (Coach: Steve Clarke (SCO)).
Goals: Germany: 1-0 Florian Wirtz (10'), 2-0 Jamal Musiala (19'),
3-0 Kai Havertz (45+1' penalty), 4-0 Niclas Füllkrug (68'), 5-1 Emre Can (90+3').
Scotland: 4-1 Antonio Rüdiger (87' own goal).
Referee: Clément Turpin (FRA)   Attendance: 65,052.

15-06-2024   RheinEnergieStadion, Cologne: Hungary – Switzerland 1-3 (0-2)
Hungary: Peter Gulácsi, Attila Fiola, Ádám Lang (46' Bendeguz Bolla (YC87)), Willi Orbán, Attila Szalai (YC69) (79' Marton Dárdai), Milos Kerkez (79' Martin Ádám), Roland Sallai, Ádám Nagy (67' László Kleinheisler), Dominik Szoboszlai, Andras Schäfer, Barnabas Varga. (Coach: Marco Rossi (ITA)).
Switzerland: Yann Sommer, Ricardo Rodríguez, Fabian Schär, Silvan Widmer (YC5) (68' Leonidas Stergiou), Manuel Akanji, Granit Xhaka, Remo Freuler (YC59) (86' Vincent Sierro), Michel Aebischer, Ruben Vargas (74' Breel Embolo), Kwadwo Duah (68' Zeki Amdouni), Dan Ndoye (86' Fabian Rieder). (Coach: Murat Yakin (SUI)).
Goals: Hungary: 1-2 Barnabas Varga (66').
Switzerland: 0-1 Kwadwo Duah (12'), 0-2 Michel Aebischer (45'), 1-3 Breel Embolo (90+3').
Referee: Slavko Vincic (SVN)   Attendance: 41,676.

19-06-2024   MHPArena, Stuttgart: Germany – Hungary 2-0 (1-0)
Germany: Manuel Neuer, Antonio Rüdiger (YC27), Jonathan Tah, Maximilian Mittelstädt (YC89), Toni Kroos, Ilkay Gündogan (84' Deniz Undav), Robert Andrich (71' Emre Can), Joshua Kimmich, Kai Havertz (58' Niclas Füllkrug), Florian Wirtz (58' Leroy Sané), Jamal Musiala (72' Chris Führich). (Coach: Julian Nagelsmann (GER)).
Hungary: Peter Gulácsi, Attila Fiola, Willi Orbán, Bendeguz Bolla (75' Martin Ádám), Marton Dárdai, Milos Kerkez (75' Zsolt Nagy), Roland Sallai (87' Kevin Csoboth), Ádám Nagy (64' László Kleinheisler), Dominik Szoboszlai (YC90+3), Andras Schäfer, Barnabas Varga (YC23) (87' Daniel Gazdag). (Coach: Marco Rossi (ITA)).
Goals: Germany: 1-0 Jamal Musiala (22'), 2-0 Ilkay Gündogan (67').
Referee: Danny Makkelie (HOL)   Attendance: 54,000.

19-06-2024   RheinEnergieStadion, Cologne: Scotland – Switzerland 1-1 (1-1)
Scotland: Angus Gunn, Grant Hanley, Andrew Robertson, Kieran Tierney (61' Scott McKenna (YC68)), Jack Hendry, Anthony Ralston, Callum McGregor, John McGinn (YC71) (90' Ryan Christie), Scott McTominay (YC51), Billy Gilmour (79' Kenny McLean), Che Adams (90+1' Lawrence Shankland). (Coach: Steve Clarke (SCO)).
Switzerland: Yann Sommer, Ricardo Rodríguez (YC31), Fabian Schär, Silvan Widmer (86' Leonidas Stergiou), Manuel Akanji, Xherdan Shaqiri (60' Breel Embolo), Granit Xhaka, Remo Freuler (75' Vincent Sierro (YC86)), Michel Aebischer, Ruben Vargas (75' Fabian Rieder), Dan Ndoye (86' Zeki Amdouni). (Coach: Murat Yakin (SUI)).
Goals: Scotland: 1-0 Scott McTominay (13').
Switzerland: 1-1 Xherdan Shaqiri (26').
Referee: Ivan Kruzliak (SVK)   Attendance: 42,711.

23-06-2024   Frankfurt Arena, Frankfurt am Main: Switzerland – Germany 1-1 (1-0)
Switzerland: Yann Sommer, Ricardo Rodríguez, Fabian Schär, Silvan Widmer (YC81), Manuel Akanji, Granit Xhaka (YC66), Remo Freuler, Michel Aebischer, Fabian Rieder (65' Ruben Vargas), Breel Embolo (65' Kwadwo Duah), Dan Ndoye (YC25) (65' Zeki Amdouni). (Coach: Murat Yakin (SUI)).
Germany: Manuel Neuer, Antonio Rüdiger, Jonathan Tah (YC38) (61' Nico Schlotterbeck), Maximilian Mittelstädt (61' David Raum), Toni Kroos, Ilkay Gündogan, Robert Andrich (65' Maximilian Beier), Joshua Kimmich, Kai Havertz, Florian Wirtz (76' Leroy Sané), Jamal Musiala (76' Niclas Füllkrug). (Coach: Julian Nagelsmann (GER)).
Goals: Switzerland: 1-0 Dan Ndoye (28').
Germany: 1-1 Niclas Füllkrug (90+2').
Referee: Daniele Orsato (ITA)   Attendance: 46,685.

23-06-2024   MHPArena, Stuttgart: Scotland – Hungary 0-1 (0-0)
Scotland: Angus Gunn, Grant Hanley, Andrew Robertson (89' Lewis Morgan), Scott McKenna, Jack Hendry, Anthony Ralston (83' Kenny McLean), Callum McGregor, John McGinn (76' Stuart Armstrong), Scott McTominay (YC50), Billy Gilmour (83' Ryan Christie), Che Adams (76' Lawrence Shankland). (Coach: Steve Clarke (SCO)).
Hungary: Peter Gulácsi, Endre Botka, Willi Orbán (YC26), Bendeguz Bolla (86' Kevin Csoboth (YC90+12)), Marton Dárdai (74' Attila Szalai), Milos Kerkez (86' Zsolt Nagy), Roland Sallai, Callum Styles (YC18) (61' Ádám Nagy), Dominik Szoboszlai, Andras Schäfer (YC44), Barnabas Varga (74' Martin Ádám). (Coach: Marco Rossi (ITA)).
Goal: Hungary: 0-1 Kevin Csoboth (90+10').
Referee: Facundo Tello (ARG)   Attendance: 54,000.

STANDINGS

Pos	Team	Pld	W	D	L	GF	GA	GD	Pts
1	Germany (H)	3	2	1	0	8	2	+6	7
2	Switzerland	3	1	2	0	5	3	+2	5
3	Hungary	3	1	0	2	2	5	-3	3
4	Scotland	3	0	1	2	2	7	-5	1

Germany and Switzerland qualified for the Knock-out Stage.

GROUP B

15-06-2024   Olympiastadion, Berlin: Spain – Croatia 3-0 (3-0)
Spain: Unai Simón, Nacho, Dani Carvajal, Robin Le Normand, Marc Cucurella, Fabián Ruiz, Rodri (YC78) (86' Martín Zubimendi), Pedri (59' Dani Olmo), Álvaro Morata (67' Mikel Oyarzabal), Nico Williams (68' Mikel Merino), Lamine Yamal (86' Ferran Torres). (Coach: Luis de la Fuente (ESP)).
Croatia: Dominik Livakovic, Marin Pongracic, Josip Sutalo, Josip Stanisic, Josko Gvardiol, Luka Modric (65' Mario Pasalic), Marcelo Brozovic, Mateo Kovacic (65' Luka Sucic), Lovro Majer, Ante Budimir (56' Ivan Perisic), Andrej Kramaric (72' Bruno Petkovic). (Coach: Zlatko Dalic (CRO)).
Goals: Spain: 1-0 Álvaro Morata (29'), 2-0 Fabián Ruiz (32'), 3-0 Dani Carvajal (45+2').
Referee: Michael Oliver (ENG)   Attendance: 68,844.

Bruno Petkovic missed a penalty kick (80').

15-06-2024   BVB Stadion Dortmund, Dortmund: Italy – Albania 2-1 (2-1)
Italy: Gianluigi Donnarumma, Giovanni Di Lorenzo, Federico Dimarco (83' Matteo Darmian), Alessandro Bastoni, Riccardo Calafiori (YC51), Jorginho, Nicolò Barella (90+2' Michael Folorunsho), Lorenzo Pellegrini (YC21) (77' Bryan Cristante), Davide Frattesi, Gianluca Scamacca (83' Mateo Retegui), Federico Chiesa (77' Andrea Cambiaso). (Coach: Luciano Spalletti (ITA)).
Albania: Thomas Strakosha, Elseid Hysaj, Berat Djimsiti, Arlind Ajeti, Mario Mitaj, Ylber Ramadani, Nedim Bajrami (87' Ernest Muçi), Kristjan Asllani, Tauljant Seferi (68' Qazim Laçi), Jasir Asani (68' Arber Hoxha (YC74)), Armando Broja (YC51) (77' Rey Manaj). (Coach: Sylvinho (BRA)).
Goals: Italy: 1-1 Alessandro Bastoni (11'), 2-1 Nicolò Barella (16').
Albania: 0-1 Nedim Bajrami (1').
Referee: Felix Zwayer (GER)   Attendance: 60,512.

19-06-2024   Volksparkstadion, Hamburg: Croatia – Albania 2-2 (0-1)
Croatia: Dominik Livakovic, Josip Juranovic, Josip Sutalo, Josko Gvardiol, Luka Modric, Ivan Perisic (84' Borna Sosa), Marcelo Brozovic (46' Mario Pasalic), Mateo Kovacic, Lovro Majer (46' Luka Sucic), Andrej Kramaric (84' Martin Baturina), Bruno Petkovic (69' Ante Budimir). (Coach: Zlatko Dalic (CRO)). (Not used sub: Ivica Ivusic (YC87)).
Albania: Thomas Strakosha, Elseid Hysaj (YC76), Berat Djimsiti, Arlind Ajeti, Mario Mitaj, Qazim Laçi (73' Klaus Gjasula (YC90+7)), Ylber Ramadani (85' Arber Hoxha), Nedim Bajrami, Kristjan Asllani, Jasir Asani (64' Tauljant Seferi), Rey Manaj (85' Mirlind Daku (YC90+3)). (Coach: Sylvinho (BRA)).
Goals: Croatia: 1-1 Andrej Kramaric (74'), 2-1 Klaus Gjasula (76' own goal).
Albania: 0-1 Qazim Laçi (11'), 2-2 Klaus Gjasula (90+5').
Referee: François Letexier (FRA)   Attendance: 46,784.

20-06-2024   Arena AufSchalke, Gelsenkirchen: Spain – Italy 1-0 (0-0)
Spain: Unai Simón, Dani Carvajal (YC90+6), Aymeric Laporte, Robin Le Normand (YC69), Marc Cucurella, Fabián Ruiz (90+4' Mikel Merino), Rodri (YC45+1), Pedri (71' Álex Baena), Álvaro Morata (78' Mikel Oyarzabal), Nico Williams (78' Ayoze Pérez), Lamine Yamal (71' Ferran Torres). (Coach: Luis de la Fuente (ESP)).
Italy: Gianluigi Donnarumma (YC15), Giovanni Di Lorenzo, Federico Dimarco, Alessandro Bastoni, Riccardo Calafiori, Jorginho (46' Bryan Cristante (YC46)), Nicolò Barella, Lorenzo Pellegrini (82' Giacomo Raspadori), Davide Frattesi (46' Andrea Cambiaso), Gianluca Scamacca (64' Mateo Retegui), Federico Chiesa (64' Mattia Zaccagni). (Coach: Luciano Spalletti (ITA)).
Goal: Spain: 1-0 Riccardo Calafiori (55' own goal).
Referee: Slavko Vincic (SVN)   Attendance: 49,528.

24-06-2024   Merkur Sopiel-Arena, Düsseldorf: Albania – Spain 0-1 (0-1)
Albania: Thomas Strakosha, Berat Djimsiti, Arlind Ajeti, Ivan Balliu, Mario Mitaj, Qazim Laçi (70' Medon Berisha (YC89)), Ylber Ramadani, Nedim Bajrami (YC66) (70' Arber Hoxha), Kristjan Asllani, Jasir Asani (81' Ernest Muçi), Rey Manaj (59' Armando Broja). (Coach: Sylvinho (BRA)).
Spain: David Raya, Jesús Navas, Aymeric Laporte (46' Robin Le Normand), Álex Grimaldo, Dani Vivian (YC90), Mikel Merino, Martín Zubimendi, Joselu (72' Álvaro Morata), Mikel Oyarzabal (62' Fermín López), Dani Olmo (84' Álex Baena), Ferran Torres (72' Lamine Yamal). (Coach: Luis de la Fuente (ESP)).
Goal: Spain: 0-1 Ferran Torres (13').
Referee: Glenn Nyberg (SWE)   Attendance: 46,586.

24-06-2024   Red Bull Arena, Leipzig: Croatia – Italy 1-1 (0-0)
Croatia: Dominik Livakovic, Marin Pongracic (YC78), Josip Sutalo, Josip Stanisic (YC82),
Josko Gvardiol, Luka Modric (YC60) (81' Lovro Majer), Marcelo Brozovic (YC90+1), Mateo
Kovacic (70' Luka Ivanusec (YC73)), Mario Pasalic (46' Ante Budimir), Luka Sucic (YC24)
(70' Ivan Perisic), Andrej Kramaric (90' Josip Juranovic). (Coach: Zlatko Dalic (CRO)).
Italy: Gianluigi Donnarumma, Matteo Darmian (81' Mattia Zaccagni), Giovanni Di Lorenzo,
Federico Dimarco (57' Federico Chiesa), Alessandro Bastoni, Riccardo Calafiori (YC90+3),
Jorginho (81' Nicolo Fagioli (YC90+6)), Nicolò Barella, Lorenzo Pellegrini (46' Davide
Frattesi), Giacomo Raspadori (75' Gianluca Scamacca), Mateo Retegui. (Coach: Luciano
Spalletti (ITA)).
Goals: Croatia: 1-0 Luka Modric (55').
Italy: 1-1 Mattia Zaccagni (90+8').
Referee: Danny Makkelie (HOL)   Attendance: 38,322.

Luka Modric missed a penalty kick (54').

STANDINGS

Pos	Team	Pld	W	D	L	GF	GA	GD	Pts
1	*Spain*	*3*	*3*	*0*	*0*	*5*	*0*	*+5*	*9*
2	*Italy*	*3*	*1*	*1*	*1*	*3*	*3*	*0*	*4*
3	Croatia	3	0	2	1	3	6	-3	2
4	Albania	3	0	1	2	3	5	-2	1

Spain and Italy qualified for the Knock-out Stage.

GROUP C

16-06-2024   MHPArena, Stuttgart: Slovenia – Denmark 1-1 (0-1)
Slovenia: Jan Oblak, Erik Janza, Petar Stojanovic (YC53) (67' Benjamin Verbic), Vanja
Drkusic, Zan Karnicnik, Jaka Bijol, Timi Elsnik (75' Jon Gorenc Stankovic), Adam Gnezda
Cerin, Andraz Sporar (90+4' David Brekalo), Jan Mlakar (75' Zan Celar (YC84)), Benjamin
Sesko (90+4' Jasmin Kurtic). (Coach: Matjaz Kek (SVN)).
Denmark: Kasper Schmeichel, Jannik Vestergaard, Andreas Christensen, Joachim Andersen,
Alexander Bah, Victor Kristiansen (77' Joakim Mæhle), Christian Eriksen, Pierre-Emile
Højbjerg (83' Christian Nørgaard), Morten Hjulmand (YC49) (89' Thomas Delaney), Jonas
Wind (83' Kasper Dolberg), Rasmus Højlund (83' Yussuf Poulsen). (Coach: Kasper Hjulmand
(DEN)).
Goals: Slovenia: 1-1 Erik Janza (77').
Denmark: 0-1 Christian Eriksen (17').
Referee: Sandro Schärer (SUI)   Attendance: 54,000.

16-06-2024   Arena AufSchalke, Gelsenkirchen: Serbia – England 0-1 (0-1)
Serbia: Predrag Rajkovic, Milos Veljkovic, Nikola Milenkovic, Starhinja Pavlovic, Nemanja
Gudelj (YC39) (46' Ivan Ilic), Filip Kostic (43' Filip Mladenovic), Sasa Lukic (61' Luka
Jovic), Sergej Milinkovic-Savic, Aleksandar Mitrovic (61' Dusan Tadic (YC75)), Andrija
Zivkovic (74' Veljko Birmancevic), Dusan Vlahovic. (Coach: Dragan Stojkovic (SRB)).
England: Jordan Pickford, Kyle Walker, Kieran Trippier, John Stones, Marc Guéhi, Trent
Alexander-Arnold (69' Conor Callagher), Declan Rice, Jude Bellingham (86' Kobbie Mainoo),
Harry Kane, Phil Foden, Bukayo Saka (76' Jarrod Bowen). (Coach: Gareth Southgate (ENG)).
Goal: England: 0-1 Jude Bellingham (13').
Referee: Daniele Orsato (ITA)   Attendance: 48,953.

20-06-2024   Allianz Arena, München: Slovenia – Serbia 1-1 (0-0)
Slovenia: Jan Oblak, Erik Janza (YC87), Petar Stojanovic (76' Benjamin Verbic), Vanja
Drkusic, Zan Karnicnik, Jaka Bijol, Timi Elsnik (90+1' David Brekalo), Adam Gnezda Cerin,
Andraz Sporar, Jan Mlakar (64' Jon Gorenc Stankovic), Benjamin Sesko (76' Zan Vipotnik
(YC90+4)). (Coach: Matjaz Kek (SVN)).
Serbia: Predrag Rajkovic, Filip Mladenovic (YC25) (46' Mijat Gacinovic (YC90+3)), Milos
Veljkovic, Nikola Milenkovic, Starhinja Pavlovic, Sasa Lukic (YC54) (64' Sergej Milinkovic-
Savic), Ivan Ilic, Dusan Tadic (82' Lazar Samardzic), Aleksandar Mitrovic, Andrija Zivkovic
(82' Veljko Birmancevic), Dusan Vlahovic (64' Luka Jovic (YC90+2)). (Coach: Dragan
Stojkovic (SRB)).
Goals: Slovenia: 1-0 Zan Karnicnik (69').
Serbia: 1-1 Luka Jovic (90+5').
Referee: István Kovács (ROM)   Attendance: 63,028.

20-06-2024   Frankfurt Arena, Frankfurt am Main: Denmark – England 1-1 (1-1)
Denmark: Kasper Schmeichel, Jannik Vestergaard (YC27), Andreas Christensen, Joachim
Andersen, Joakim Mæhle (YC73), Victor Kristiansen (57' Alexander Bah), Christian Eriksen
(82' Andreas Skov Olsen), Pierre-Emile Højbjerg, Morten Hjulmand (83' Christian Nørgaard
(YC87)), Jonas Wind (57' Mikkel Damsgaard), Rasmus Højlund (67' Yussuf Poulsen).
(Coach: Kasper Hjulmand (DEN)).
England: Jordan Pickford, Kyle Walker, Kieran Trippier, John Stones, Marc Guéhi, Trent
Alexander-Arnold (54' Conor Callagher (YC62)), Declan Rice, Jude Bellingham, Harry Kane
(70' Ollie Watkins), Phil Foden (69' Jarrod Bowen), Bukayo Saka (69' Eberechi Eze). (Coach:
Gareth Southgate (ENG)).
Goals: Denmark: 1-1 Morten Hjulmand (34').
England: 0-1 Harry Kane (18').
Referee: Artur Soares Dias (POR)   Attendance: 46,177.

25-06-2024   RheinEnergieStadion, Cologne: England – Slovenia 0-0
England: Jordan Pickford, Kyle Walker, Kieran Trippier (YC17) (84' Trent Alexander-
Arnold), John Stones, Marc Guéhi (YC68), Declan Rice, Conor Callagher (46' Kobbie
Mainoo), Jude Bellingham, Harry Kane, Phil Foden (YC77) (89' Anthony Gordon), Bukayo
Saka (71' Cole Palmer). (Coach: Gareth Southgate (ENG)).
Slovenia: Jan Oblak, Erik Janza (YC22) (90+1' Jure Balkovec), Petar Stojanovic, Vanja
Drkusic, Zan Karnicnik, Jaka Bijol (YC72), Timi Elsnik, Adam Gnezda Cerin, Andraz Sporar
(86' Zan Celar), Jan Mlakar (86' Jon Gorenc Stankovic), Benjamin Sesko (75' Josip Ilicic).
(Coach: Matjaz Kek (SVN)).
Referee: Clément Turpin (FRA)   Attendance: 41,536.

25-06-2024   Allianz Arena, München: Denmark – Serbia 0-0
Denmark: Kasper Schmeichel, Jannik Vestergaard, Andreas Christensen, Joachim Andersen,
Joakim Mæhle, Alexander Bah (77' Thomas Delaney), Christian Eriksen (88' Yussuf Poulsen),
Pierre-Emile Højbjerg, Morten Hjulmand (YC30) (77' Victor Kristiansen), Jonas Wind
(YC27) (46' Andreas Skov Olsen), Rasmus Højlund (59' Kasper Dolberg). (Coach: Kasper
Hjulmand (DEN)).
Serbia: Predrag Rajkovic, Milos Veljkovic, Nikola Milenkovic (YC4), Starhinja Pavlovic,
Nemanja Gudelj (46' Luka Jovic), Srdjan Mijailovic (73' Filip Mladenovic), Sasa Lukic (87'
Sergej Milinkovic-Savic), Ivan Ilic (67' Dusan Vlahovic), Lazar Samardzic (46' Dusan Tadic),
Aleksandar Mitrovic (YC83), Andrija Zivkovic. (Coach: Dragan Stojkovic (SRB)).
Referee: François Letexier (FRA)   Attendance: 64,288.

STANDINGS

Pos	Team	Pld	W	D	L	GF	GA	GD	Pts
1	England	3	1	2	0	2	1	+1	5
2	Denmark	3	0	3	0	2	2	0	3
3	Slovenia	3	0	3	0	2	2	0	3
4	Serbia	3	0	2	1	1	2	-1	2

England, Denmark and Slovenia qualified for the Knock-out Stage.

GROUP D

16-06-2024   Volksparkstadion, Hamburg: Poland – Netherlands 1-2 (1-1)
Poland: Wojciech Szczesny, Bartosz Salamon (86' Bartosz Bereszynski), Jan Bednarek, Jakub Kiwior, Piotr Zielinski (78' Jakub Piotrowski), Przemyslaw Frankowski, Taras Romanczuk (55' Bartosz Slisz), Sebastian Szymanski (46' Jakub Moder), Nicola Zalewski, Kacper Urbanski (55' Karol Swiderski), Adam Buksa. (Coach: Michal Probierz (POL)).
Netherlands: Bart Verbruggen, Stefan de Vrij, Nathan Aké (87' Mickey van de Ven), Virgil van Dijk, Denzel Dumfries, Jerdy Schouten, Joey Veerman (YC15) (62' Georginio Wijnaldum), Tijjani Reijnders, Xavi Simons (62' Donyell Malen), Memphis Depay (81' Wout Weghorst), Cody Gakpo (81' Jeremie Frimpong). (Coach: Ronald Koeman (HOL)).
Goals: Poland: 1-0 Adam Buksa (16').
Netherlands: 1-1 Cody Gakpo (29'), 1-2 Wout Weghorst (83').
Referee: Artur Soares Dias (POR)   Attendance: 48,117.

17-06-2024   Merkur Spiel-Arena, Düsseldorf: Austria – France 0-1 (0-1)
Austria: Patrick Pentz, Philipp Mwene (YC33) (88' Alexander Prass), Stefan Posch, Kevin Danso (YC90+3), Max Wöber (YC16) (59' Gernot Trauner), Marcel Sabitzer, Florian Grillitsch (60' Patrick Wimmer), Konrad Laimer (YC84) (90+1' Romano Schmid), Christoph Baumgartner (YC80), Nicolas Seiwald, Michael Gregoritsch (59' Marko Arnautovic). (Coach: Ralf Rangnick (GER)).
France: Mike Maignan, Theo Hernández, Dayotchanculle Upamecano, Jules Koundé, William Saliba, Ngolo Kanté, Adrien Rabiot (71' Eduardo Camavinga), Antoine Griezmann (90+1' Youssouf Fofana), Ousmane Dembélé (YC56) (71' Randal Kolo Muani), Marcus Thuram, Kylian Mbappé (YC90) (90' Olivier Giroud). (Coach: Didier Deschamps (FRA)).
Goal: France: 0-1 Max Wöber (38' own goal).
Referee: Jesús Gil Manzano (ESP)   Attendance: 46,425.

21-06-2024   Olympiastadion, Berlin: Poland – Austria 1-3 (1-1)
Poland: Wojciech Szczesny (YC77), Jan Bednarek, Pawel Dawidowicz, Jakub Kiwior, Piotr Zielinski (87' Kacper Urbanski), Przemyslaw Frankowski, Bartosz Slisz (YC53) (75' Kamil Grosicki), Jakub Piotrowski (46' Jakub Moder (YC62)), Nicola Zalewski, Adam Buksa (60' Karol Swiderski), Krzysztof Piatek (60' Robert Lewandowski (YC64)). (Coach: Michal Probierz (POL)).
Austria: Patrick Pentz, Gernot Trauner (59' Kevin Danso), Philipp Mwene (63' Alexander Prass), Philipp Lienhart, Stefan Posch, Marcel Sabitzer, Florian Grillitsch (46' Patrick Wimmer (YC56)), Konrad Laimer, Christoph Baumgartner (81' Romano Schmid), Nicolas Seiwald, Marko Arnautovic (YC70) (81' Michael Gregoritsch). (Coach: Ralf Rangnick (GER)).
Goals: Poland: 1-1 Krzysztof Piatek (30').
Austria: 0-1 Gernot Trauner (9'), 1-2 Christoph Baumgartner (66'), 1-3 Marko Arnautovic (78' penalty).
Referee: Halil Umut Meler (TUR)   Attendance: 69,455.

21-06-2024   Red Bull Arena, Leipzig: Netherlands – France 0-0
Netherlands: Bart Verbruggen, Stefan de Vrij, Nathan Aké, Virgil van Dijk, Denzel Dumfries, Jeremie Frimpong (73' Lutsharel Geertruida), Jerdy Schouten (YC31) (73' Georginio Wijnaldum), Tijjani Reijnders, Xavi Simons (73' Joey Veerman), Memphis Depay (79' Wout Weghorst), Cody Gakpo. (Coach: Ronald Koeman (HOL)).
France: Mike Maignan, Theo Hernández, Dayotchanculle Upamecano, Jules Koundé, William Saliba, Ngolo Kanté, Adrien Rabiot, Aurelien Tchouaméni, Antoine Griezmann, Ousmane Dembélé (75' Kingsley Coman), Marcus Thuram (75' Olivier Giroud). (Coach: Didier Deschamps (FRA)).
Referee: Anthony Taylor (ENG)   Attendance: 38,531.

25-06-2024   Olympiastadion, Berlin: Netherlands – Austria 2-3 (0-1)
Netherlands: Bart Verbruggen, Stefan de Vrij, Nathan Aké (65' Mickey van de Ven), Virgil van Dijk, Lutsharel Geertruida, Jerdy Schouten, Joey Veerman (35' Xavi Simons), Tijjani Reijnders (65' Georginio Wijnaldum), Memphis Depay, Donyell Malen (72' Wout Weghorst), Cody Gakpo. (Coach: Ronald Koeman (HOL)).
Austria: Patrick Pentz, Philipp Lienhart (62' Christoph Baumgartner), Stefan Posch (YC32), Maximilian Wöber, Marcel Sabitzer, Florian Grillitsch (64' Leopold Querfeld (YC90+4)), Romano Schmid (90+2' Andreas Weimann), Alexander Prass, Nicolas Seiwald, Patrick Wimmer (YC33) (63' Konrad Laimer), Marko Arnautovic (78' Michael Gregoritsch). (Coach: Ralf Rangnick (GER)).
Goals: Netherlands: 1-1 Cody Gakpo (47'), 2-2 Memphis Depay (75').
Austria: 0-1 Donyell Malen (6' own goal), 1-2 Romano Schmid (59'),
2-3 Marcel Sabitzer (80').
Referee: Ivan Kruzliak (SVK)   Attendance: 68,363.

25-06-2024   BVB Stadion Dortmund, Dortmund: France – Poland 1-1 (0-0)
France: Mike Maignan, Theo Hernández, Dayotchanculle Upamecano, Jules Koundé, William Saliba, Ngolo Kanté (61' Antoine Griezmann), Adrien Rabiot (YC43) (61' Eduardo Camavinga), Aurelien Tchouaméni (81' Youssouf Fofana), Ousmane Dembélé (86' Randal Kolo Muani), Kylian Mbappé, Bradley Barcola (61' Olivier Giroud). (Coach: Didier Deschamps (FRA)).
Poland: Lukasz Skorupski, Jan Bednarek, Pawel Dawidowicz (YC89), Jakub Kiwior, Piotr Zielinski, Przemyslaw Frankowski, Jakub Moder, Sebastian Szymanski (68' Karol Swiderski (YC90+2)), Nicola Zalewski (YC24) (68' Michal Skóras), Kacper Urbanski, Robert Lewandowski. (Coach: Michal Probierz (POL)).
Goals: France: 1-0 Kylian Mbappé (56' penalty).
Poland: 1-1 Robert Lewandowski (79' penalty).
Referee: Marco Guida (ITA)   Attendance: 59,728.

STANDINGS

Pos	Team	Pld	W	D	L	GF	GA	GD	Pts
1	Austria	3	2	0	1	6	4	+2	6
2	France	3	1	2	0	2	1	+1	5
3	Netherlands	3	1	1	1	4	4	0	4
4	Poland	3	0	1	2	3	6	-3	1

Austria, France and Netherlands qualified for the Knock-out Stage.

GROUP E

17-06-2024   Allianz Arena, München: Romania – Ukraine 3-0 (1-0)
Romania: Florin Nita, Nicusor Bancu, Andrei Burca, Radu Dragusin, Andrei Ratiu, Nicolae
Stanciu (87' Bogdan Racovitan), Razvan Marin (YC79), Florinel Coman (62' Valentin
Mihaila), Marius Marin (75' Adrian Rus), Dennis Man (62' Ianis Hagi), Denis Dragus (75'
George Puscas). (Coach: Edward Iordanescu (ROM)).
Ukraine: Andriy Lunin, Oleksandr Zinchenko, Mykola Matviyenko, Yukhym Konoplya
(YC67) (72' Oleksandr Tymchyk), Illya Zabarnyi, Taras Stepanenko (62' Volodymyr
Brazhko), Mykola Shaparenko (63' Roman Yaremchuk), Mykhaylo Mudryk, Georgiy Sudakov
(83' Ruslan Malinovskyi), Viktor Tsyhankov (63' Andriy Yarmolenko), Artem Dovbyk.
(Coach: Serhiy Rebrov (UKR)).
Goals: Romania: 1-0 Nicolae Stanciu (29'), 2-0 Razvan Marin (53'), 3-0 Denis Dragus (57').
Referee: Glenn Nyberg (SWE)   Attendance: 61,591.

17-06-2024   Frankfurt Arena, Frankfurt am Main: Belgium – Slovakia 0-1 (0-1)
Belgium: Koen Casteels, Timothy Castagne, Wout Faes, Zeno Debast, Kevin De Bruyne, Orel
Mangala (YC29) (57' Johan Bakayoko), Amadou Onana, Romelu Lukaku, Leandro Trossard
(74' Youri Tielemans (YC76)), Yannick Carrasco (84' Dodi Lukébakio (YC85)), Jérémy Doku
(84' Loïs Openda). (Coach: Domenico Tedesco (ITA)).
Slovakia: Martin Dúbravka, Peter Pekarík, Milan Skriniar, Denis Vavro, Dávid Hancko, Juraj
Kucka, Stanislav Lobotka, Ondrej Duda (90+4' Adam Obert), Ivan Schranz (YC41) (81' David
Duris), Luka Haraslín (70' Tomás Suslov), Róbert Bozeník (70' David Strelec). (Coach:
Francesco Calzona (ITA)).
Goal: Slovakia: 0-1 Ivan Schranz (7').
Referee: Halil Umut Meler (TUR)   Attendance: 45,181.

21-06-2024   Merkur Spiel-Arena, Düsseldorf: Slovakia – Ukraine 1-2 (1-0)
Slovakia: Martin Dúbravka, Peter Pekarík, Milan Skriniar, Denis Vavro, Dávid Hancko (67'
Tomás Suslov), Juraj Kucka, Stanislav Lobotka, Ondrej Duda (60' Laszlo Bénes), Ivan
Schranz (86' Leo Sauer), Luka Haraslín (67' Adam Obert), Róbert Bozeník (60' David
Strelec). (Coach: Francesco Calzona (ITA)).
Ukraine: Anatolii Trubin, Oleksandr Zinchenko, Mykola Matviyenko, Oleksandr Tymchyk,
Illya Zabarnyi, Andriy Yarmolenko (67' Oleksandr Zubkov), Mykola Shaparenko (90+2'
Maksym Talovierov), Mykhaylo Mudryk (85' Ruslan Malinovskyi), Georgiy Sudakov,
Volodymyr Brazhko (85' Sergey Sydorchuk), Artem Dovbyk (67' Roman Yaremchuk
(YC84)). (Coach: Serhiy Rebrov (UKR)).
Goals: Slovakia: 1-0 Ivan Schranz (17').
Ukraine: 1-1 Mykola Shaparenko (54'), 1-2 Roman Yaremchuk (80').
Referee: Michael Oliver (ENG)   Attendance: 43,910.

22-06-2024   RheinEnergieStadion, Cologne: Belgium – Romania 2-0 (1-0)
Belgium: Koen Casteels, Jan Vertonghen, Timothy Castagne, Wout Faes, Arthur Theate (77'
Zeno Debast), Kevin De Bruyne, Youri Tielemans (72' Orel Mangala), Amadou Onana,
Romelu Lukaku, Dodi Lukébakio (YC35) (56' Leandro Trossard), Jérémy Doku (72' Yannick
Carrasco). (Coach: Domenico Tedesco (ITA)).
Romania: Florin Nita, Nicusor Bancu (YC59), Andrei Burca, Radu Dragusin, Andrei Ratiu
(90' Deian Sorescu), Nicolae Stanciu, Razvan Marin, Marius Marin (YC65) (68' Darius
Olaru), Dennis Man, Valentin Mihaila (68' Ianis Hagi), Denis Dragus (81' Denis Alibec).
(Coach: Edward Iordanescu (ROM)).
Goals: Belgium: 1-0 Youri Tielemans (2'), 2-0 Kevin De Bruyne (80').
Referee: Szymon Marciniak (POL)   Attendance: 42,535.

580

26-06-2024   Frankfurt Arena, Frankfurt am Main: Slovakia – Romania 1-1 (1-1)
Slovakia: Martin Dúbravka, Peter Pekarík (90+2' Norbert Gyömbér), Milan Skriniar, Denis Vavro, Dávid Hancko, Juraj Kucka, Stanislav Lobotka, Ondrej Duda (YC90+1) (90+2' Matús Bero), Ivan Schranz (78' David Duris), Luka Haraslín (70' Tomás Suslov), David Strelec (70' Róbert Bozeník). (Coach: Francesco Calzona (ITA)).
Romania: Florin Nita, Nicusor Bancu (YC45+3), Andrei Burca (YC45+1), Radu Dragusin, Andrei Ratiu, Nicolae Stanciu, Razvan Marin (86' Adrian Rus), Ianis Hagi (66' Dennis Man), Florinel Coman (58' Deian Sorescu), Marius Marin, Denis Dragus (67' George Puscas (YC88)). (Coach: Edward Iordanescu (ROM)).
Goals: Slovakia: 1-0 Ondrej Duda (24').
Romania: 1-1 Razvan Marin (37' penalty).
Referee: Daniel Siebert (GER)   Attendance: 45,033.

26-06-2024   MHPArena, Stuttgart: Ukraine – Belgium 0-0
Ukraine: Anatolii Trubin, Oleksandr Svatok (81' Andriy Yarmolenko), Mykola Matviyenko, Oleksandr Tymchyk, Vitalii Mykolenko (58' Oleksandr Zinchenko), Illya Zabarnyi, Mykola Shaparenko (70' Vladyslav Vanat), Georgiy Sudakov, Volodymyr Brazhko (70' Taras Stepanenko), Roman Yaremchuk (70' Ruslan Malinovskyi), Artem Dovbyk (YC69). (Coach: Serhiy Rebrov (UKR)).
Belgium: Koen Casteels, Jan Vertonghen, Timothy Castagne, Wout Faes (YC43), Arthur Theate, Kevin De Bruyne, Youri Tielemans (62' Orel Mangala), Amadou Onana, Romelu Lukaku (90' Lois Openda), Leandro Trossard (62' Yannick Carrasco), Jérémy Doku (77' Johan Bakayoko). (Coach: Domenico Tedesco (ITA)).
Referee: Anthony Taylor (ENG)   Attendance: 54,000.

STANDINGS

Pos	Team	Pld	W	D	L	GF	GA	GD	Pts
1	Romania	3	1	1	1	4	3	+1	4
2	Belgium	3	1	1	1	2	1	+1	4
3	Slovakia	3	1	1	1	3	3	0	4
4	Ukraine	3	1	1	1	2	4	-2	4

Romania, Belgium and Slovakia qualified for the Knock-out Stage.

GROUP F

18-06-2024   BVB Stadion Dortmund, Dortmund: Turkey – Georgia 3-1 (1-1)
Turkey: Mert Günok, Kaan Ayhan (79' Merih Demiral), Abdülkerim Bardakçi (YC35), Samet Akaydin, Mert Müldür (85' Zeki Çelik), Hakan Çalhanoglu (YC89) (90+2' Salih Özcan), Ferdi Kadioglu, Orkun Kökçu, Arda Güler (79' Yusuf Yazici), Baris Yilmaz, Kenan Yildiz (85' Kerem Aktürkoglu). (Coach: Vincenzo Montella (ITA)).
Georgia: Giorgi Mamardashvili, Guram Kashia, Solomon Kvirkvelia (YC55) (85' Budu Zivzivadze), Otar Kakabadze, Lasha Dvali, Giorgi Kochorashvili, Giorgi Chakvetadze (74' Zuriko Davitashvili), Giorgi Tsitaishvili (74' Luka Lochoshvili), Anzor Mekvabishvili (89' Sandro Altunashvili), Khvicha Kvaratskhelia, Georges Mikautadze. (Coach: Willy Sagnol (FRA)).
Goals: Turkey: 1-0 Mert Müldür (25'), 2-1 Arda Güler (65'), 3-1 Kerem Aktürkoglu (90+7').
Georgia: 1-1 Georges Mikautadze (32').
Referee: Facundo Tello (ARG)   Attendance: 59,127.

18-06-2024   Red Bull Arena, Leipzig: Portugal – Czech Republic 2-1 (0-0)
Portugal: Diogo Costa, Pepe, João Cancelo (90' Nélson Semedo), Rúben Dias, Diogo Dalot
(63' Gonçalo Inácio), Nuno Mendes (90' Pedro Neto), Bruno Fernandes, Bernardo Silva,
Vitinha (90' Francisco Conceição (YC90+3)), Cristiano Ronaldo, Rafael Leão (YC39) (63'
Diogo Jota). (Coach: Roberto Martínez (ESP)).
Czech Republic: Jindrich Stanek, Vladimir Coufal, Tomás Holes (90+3' Tomás Chorý),
Ladislav Krejcí, David Doudera, Robin Hranác, Lukás Provod (79' Antonin Barák), Tomás
Soucek, Pavel Sulc (79' Petr Sevcík), Patrik Schick (YC57) (61' Mojmír Chytil), Jan Kuchta
(60' Ondrej Lingr). (Coach: Ivan Hasek (CZE)).
Goals: Portugal: 1-1 Robin Hranác (69' own goal), 2-1 Francisco Conceição (90+2').
Czech Republic: 0-1 Lukás Provod (62').
Referee: Marco Guida (ITA)   Attendance: 38,421.

22-06-2024   Volksparkstadion, Hamburg: Georgia – Czech Republic 1-1 (1-0)
Georgia: Giorgi Mamardashvili, Guram Kashia (YC36), Solomon Kvirkvelia (82' Giorgi
Gvelesiani (YC82)), Otar Kakabadze, Lasha Dvali, Giorgi Kochorashvili (YC90+5), Giorgi
Tsitaishvili (62' Luka Lochoshvili), Anzor Mekvabishvili (YC83), Zuriko Davitashvili (62'
Giorgi Chakvetadze), Khvicha Kvaratskhelia (82' Saba Lobjanidze), Georges Mikautadze (88'
Giorgi Kvilitaia). (Coach: Willy Sagnol (FRA)).
Czech Republic: Jindrich Stanek, Vladimir Coufal (YC18), Tomás Holes (YC53), Ladislav
Krejcí, Robin Hranác, David Jurásek (YC47) (81' Petr Sevcík), Vaclav Cerný (55' Matej
Jurásek), Lukás Provod (YC40) (81' Antonin Barák), Tomás Soucek (YC81), Patrik Schick
(68' Mojmír Chytil), Adam Hlozek (55' Ondrej Lingr). (Coach: Ivan Hasek (CZE)).
Goals: Georgia: 1-0 Georges Mikautadze (45+4' penalty).
Czech Republic: 1-1 Patrik Schick (59').
Referee: Daniel Siebert (GER)   Attendance: 46,524.

22-06-2024   BVB Stadion Dortmund, Dortmund: Turkey – Portugal 0-3 (0-2)
Turkey: Altay Bayindir, Kaan Ayhan (58' Ismail Yüksek), Abdülkerim Bardakçi (YC25),
Samet Akaydin (YC42) (75' Merih Demiral), Zeki Çelik (YC42), Hakan Çalhanoglu, Ferdi
Kadioglu, Orkun Kökçu (46' Yusuf Yazici), Yunus Akgün (70' Arda Güler), Kerem
Aktürkoglu (58' Kenan Yildiz), Baris Yilmaz. (Coach: Vincenzo Montella (ITA)).
Portugal: Diogo Costa, Pepe (83' António Silva), João Cancelo (68' Nélson Semedo), Rúben
Dias, Nuno Mendes, Bruno Fernandes, João Palhinha (YC45) (46' Rúben Neves), Bernardo
Silva, Vitinha (88' João Neves), Cristiano Ronaldo, Rafael Leão (YC39) (46' Pedro Neto).
(Coach: Roberto Martínez (ESP)).
Goals: Portugal: 0-1 Bernardo Silva (21'), 0-2 Samet Akaydin (28' own goal),
0-3 Bruno Fernandes (56').
Referee: Felix Zwayer (GER)   Attendance: 61,047.

26-06-2024   Arena AufSchalke, Gelsenkirchen: Georgia – Portugal 2-0 (1-0)
Georgia: Giorgi Mamardashvili, Guram Kashia, Giorgi Gvelesiani (76' Solomon Kvirkvelia),
Otar Kakabadze, Lasha Dvali, Luka Lochoshvili (63' Giorgi Tsitaishvili), Otar Kiteishvili,
Giorgi Kochorashvili, Giorgi Chakvetadze (81' Anzor Mekvabishvili (YC85)), Khvicha
Kvaratskhelia (82' Zuriko Davitashvili), Georges Mikautadze. (Coach: Willy Sagnol (FRA)).
Portugal: Diogo Costa, Diogo Dalot, António Silva (66' Nélson Semedo), Gonçalo Inácio,
Danilo Pereira, João Palhinha (46' Rúben Neves (YC53)), João Neves (75' Matheus Nunes),
Cristiano Ronaldo (YC28) (66' Gonçalo Ramos), João Félix, Pedro Neto (YC44) (75' Diogo
Jota), Francisco Conceição. (Coach: Roberto Martínez (ESP)).
Goals: Georgia: 1-0 Khvicha Kvaratskhelia (2'), 2-0 Georges Mikautadze (57' penalty).
Referee: Sandro Schärer (SUI)   Attendance: 49,616.

26-06-2024   Volksparkstadion, Hamburg: Czech Republic – Turkey 1-2 (0-0)
Czech Republic: Jindrich Stanek (55' Matej Kovár), Vladimir Coufal, Tomás Holes, Ladislav Krejcí (YC90+1), Robin Hranác, David Jurásek (81' Matej Jurásek), Antonin Barák (YC11,YC20), Lukás Provod (75' Ondrej Lingr), Tomás Soucek (YC90+8), Mojmír Chytil (55' Jan Kuchta), Adam Hlozek (55' Tomás Chorý (RC90+8)). (Coach: Ivan Hasek (CZE)).
(Not used subs: Vitezslav Jaros (YC84), Lukás Cerv (YC85), Patrik Schick (YC34)).
Turkey: Mert Günok (YC64), Samet Akaydin (YC85), Merih Demiral, Mert Müldür (YC81), Hakan Çalhanoglu (YC66) (87' Orkun Kökçu (YC90+5)), Salih Özcan (YC31) (46' Kaan Ayhan (YC90+5)), Ferdi Kadioglu, Ismail Yüksek (YC49) (63' Okay Yokuslu), Arda Güler (YC90+8) (75' Cenk Tosun), Baris Yilmaz, Kenan Yildiz (YC37) (76' Kerem Aktürkoglu). (Coach: Vincenzo Montella (ITA)). (not used sub: Ugurcan Çakir (YC68)).
Goals: Czech Republic: 1-1 Tomás Soucek (66').
Turkey: 0-1 Hakan Çalhanoglu (51'), 1-2 Cenk Tosun (90+4').
Referee: István Kovács (ROM)   Attendance: 47,683.

STANDINGS

Pos	Team	Pld	W	D	L	GF	GA	GD	Pts
1	Portugal	3	2	0	1	5	3	+2	6
2	Turkey	3	2	0	1	5	5	0	6
3	Georgia	3	1	1	1	4	4	0	4
4	Czech Republic	3	0	1	2	3	5	-2	1

Portugal, Turkey and Georgia qualified for the Knock-out Stage.

RANKING OF THIRD-PLACED TEAMS

Pos	Grp	Team	Pld	W	D	L	GF	GA	GD	Pts
1	D	Netherlands	3	1	1	1	4	4	0	4
2	F	Georgia	3	1	1	1	4	4	0	4
3	E	Slovakia	3	1	1	1	3	3	0	4
4	C	Slovenia	3	0	3	0	2	2	0	3
5	A	Hungary	3	1	0	2	2	5	-3	3
6	B	Croatia	3	0	2	1	3	6	-3	2

Netherlands, Georgia, Slovakia and Slovenia all qualified for the Knock-out phase as the four third-placed teams with the best records.

KNOCK-OUT PHASE

ROUND OF 16

29-06-2024   Olympiastadion, Berlin: Switzerland – Italy 2-0 (1-0)
Switzerland: Yann Sommer, Ricardo Rodríguez, Fabian Schär, Manuel Akanji, Granit Xhaka, Remo Freuler, Michel Aebischer (90+2' Renato Steffen), Ruben Vargas (71' Steven Zuber), Fabian Rieder (71' Leonidas Stergiou), Breel Embolo (77' Kwadwo Duah), Dan Ndoye (77' Vincent Sierro). (Coach: Murat Yakin (SUI)).
Italy: Gianluigi Donnarumma, Matteo Darmian (75' Andrea Cambiaso), Giovanni Di Lorenzo, Gianluca Mancini (YC57), Alessandro Bastoni, Bryan Cristante (75' Lorenzo Pellegrini), Nicolò Barella (YC35) (64' Mateo Retegui), Nicolo Fagioli (86' Davide Frattesi), Stephan El Shaarawy (YC45) (46' Mattia Zaccagni), Gianluca Scamacca, Federico Chiesa. (Coach: Luciano Spalletti (ITA)).
Goals: Switzerland: 1-0 Remo Freuler (37'), 2-0 Ruben Vargas (46').
Referee: Szymon Marciniak (POL)   Attendance: 68,172.

29-06-2024   BVB Stadion Dortmund, Dortmund: Germany – Denmark 2-0 (0-0)
Germany: Manuel Neuer, Antonio Rüdiger, David Raum (81' Benjamin Henrichs), Nico Schlotterbeck, Toni Kroos, Ilkay Gündogan (65' Niclas Füllkrug), Robert Andrich (64' Emre Can), Joshua Kimmich, Kai Havertz, Leroy Sané (88' Waldemar Anton), Jamal Musiala (81' Florian Wirtz). (Coach: Julian Nagelsmann (GER)).
Denmark: Kasper Schmeichel, Jannik Vestergaard, Andreas Christensen (81' Jacob Bruun Larsen), Joachim Andersen (YC57), Joakim Mæhle (YC60), Alexander Bah (81' Victor Kristiansen), Thomas Delaney (69' Christian Nørgaard), Christian Eriksen, Pierre-Emile Højbjerg, Andreas Skov Olsen (69' Yussuf Poulsen), Rasmus Højlund (81' Jonas Wind). (Coach: Kasper Hjulmand (DEN)).
Goals: Germany: 1-0 Kai Havertz (53' penbalty), 2-0 Jamal Musiala (68').
Referee: Michael Oliver (ENG)   Attendance: 61,612.

30-06-2024   Arena AufSchalke, Gelsenkirchen:
England – Slovakia 2-1 (0-1,1-1) (AET)
England: Jordan Pickford, Kyle Walker, Kieran Trippier (66' Cole Palmer), John Stones, Marc Guéhi (YC3), Declan Rice, Jude Bellingham (YC17) (105' Ezri Konsa), Kobbie Mainoo (YC7) (84' Eberechi Eze), Harry Kane (105' Conor Callagher), Phil Foden (90+4' Ivan Toney), Bukayo Saka. (Coach: Gareth Southgate (ENG)).
Slovakia: Martin Dúbravka, Peter Pekarík (YC77) (108' Lubomir Tupta), Milan Skriniar (YC45+1), Denis Vavro (YC108), Dávid Hancko, Juraj Kucka (YC13) (81' Matús Bero), Stanislav Lobotka, Ondrej Duda (81' Laszlo Bénes), Ivan Schranz (90+3' Norbert Gyömbér (YC114)), Luka Haraslín (61' Tomás Suslov (YC120+2)), David Strelec (62' Róbert Bozeník). (Coach: Francesco Calzona (ITA)).
Goals: England: 1-1 Jude Bellingham (90+5'), 2-1 Harry Kane (91').
Slovakia: 0-1 Ivan Schranz (25').
Referee: Halil Umut Meler (TUR)   Attendance: 47,244.

30-06-2024 RheinEnergieStadion, Cologne: Spain – Georgia 4-1 (1-1)
Spain: Unai Simón, Dani Carvajal (81' Jesús Navas), Aymeric Laporte, Robin Le Normand, Marc Cucurella (66' Álex Grimaldo), Fabián Ruiz (81' Mikel Merino), Rodri, Pedri (52' Dani Olmo), Álvaro Morata (YC44) (67' Mikel Oyarzabal), Nico Williams, Lamine Yamal. (Coach: Luis de la Fuente (ESP)).
Georgia: Giorgi Mamardashvili, Guram Kashia, Giorgi Gvelesiani (79' Nika Kvekveskiri), Otar Kakabadze, Lasha Dvali, Luka Lochoshvili (63' Giorgi Tsitaishvili), Otar Kiteishvili (41' Sandro Altunashvili), Giorgi Kochorashvili, Giorgi Chakvetadze (63' Zuriko Davitashvili (YC71)), Khvicha Kvaratskhelia, Georges Mikautadze (79' Budu Zivzivadze). (Coach: Willy Sagnol (FRA)).
Goals: Spain: 1-1 Rodri (39'), 2-1 Fabián Ruiz (51'), 3-1 Nico Williams (75'), 4-1 Dani Olmo (83').
Georgia: 0-1 Robin Le Normand (18' own goal).
Referee: François Letexier (FRA)   Attendance: 42,233.

01-07-2024 Merkur Spiel-Arena, Düsseldorf: France – Belgium 1-0 (0-0)
France: Mike Maignan, Theo Hernández, Dayotchanculle Upamecano, Jules Koundé, William Saliba, Ngolo Kanté, Adrien Rabiot (YC24), Aurelien Tchouaméni (YC14), Antoine Griezmann (YC23), Marcus Thuram (62' Randal Kolo Muani), Kylian Mbappé. (Coach: Didier Deschamps (FRA)).
Belgium: Koen Casteels, Jan Vertonghen (YC76), Timothy Castagne (88' Charles De Ketelaere), Wout Faes, Arthur Theate, Kevin De Bruyne, Amadou Onana, Romelu Lukaku, Yannick Carrasco (88' Dodi Lukébakio), Lois Openda (63' Orel Mangala (YC90+3)), Jérémy Doku. (Coach: Domenico Tedesco (ITA)).
Goal: France: 1-0 Jan Vertonghen (85' own goal).
Referee: Glenn Nyberg (SWE)   Attendance: 46,810.

01-07-2024 Frankfurt Arena, Frankfurt am Main: Portugal – Slovenia 0-0 (AET)
Portugal: Diogo Costa, Pepe (117' Rúben Neves), João Cancelo (YC107) (117' Nélson Semedo), Ruben Dias, Nuno Mendes, Bruno Bernardes, João Palhinha, Bernardo Silva, Vitinha (65' Diogo Jota), Cristiano Ronaldo, Rafael Leão (76' Francisco Conceição). (Coach: Roberto Martínez (ESP)).
Slovenia: Jan Oblak, Jure Balkovec (YC107), Petar Stojanovic (86' Benjamin Verbic), Vanja Drkusic (YC32), Zan Karnicnik (YC37), Jaka Bijol (YC106), Timi Elsnik (105' Josip Ilicic), Adam Gnezda Cerin, Andraz Sporar (75' Zan Celar), Jan Mlakar (74' Jon Gorenc Stankovic (YC101)), Benjamin Sesko. (Coach: Matjaz Kek (SVN)).
Referee: Daniele Orsato (ITA)   Attendance: 46,576.
Penalties: * Josip Ilicic   1 Cristiano Ronaldo
             * Jure Balkovec   2 Fernandes
             * Benjamin Verbic   3 Bruno Silva

Cristiano Ronaldo missed a penalty kick (105').

02-07-2024   Allianz Arena, München: Romania – Netherlands 0-3 (0-1)
Romania: Florin Nita, Vasile Mogos (38' Bogdan Racovitan), Andrei Burca, Radu Dragusin, Andrei Ratiu, Nicolae Stanciu (YC81) (88' Darius Olaru), Razvan Marin, Ianis Hagi (72' Denis Alibec), Marius Marin (YC67) (72' Alexandru Cicaldau), Dennis Man, Denis Dragus (72' Valentin Mihaila). (Coach: Edward Iordanescu (ROM)).
Netherlands: Bart Verbruggen, Stefan de Vrij, Nathan Aké (69' Mickey van de Ven), Virgil van Dijk, Denzel Dumfries (YC78), Jerdy Schouten (69' Joey Veerman), Tijjani Reijnders, Xavi Simons, Memphis Depay (90+2' Daley Blind), Steven Bergwijn (46' Donyell Malen (YC90+4)), Cody Gakpo (84' Wout Weghorst). (Coach: Ronald Koeman (HOL)).
Goals: Netherlands: 0-1 Cody Gakpo (20'), 0-2 Donyell Malen (83'), 0-3 Donyell Malen (90+3').
Referee: Felix Zwayer (GER)   Attendance: 65,012.

02-07-2024   Red Bull Arena, Leipzig: Austria – Turkey 1-2 (0-1)
Austria: Patrick Pentz, Philipp Mwene (46' Alexander Prass), Philipp Lienhart (YC52) (64' Maximilian Wöber), Stefan Posch, Kevin Danso, Marcel Sabitzer, Konrad Laimer (64' Florian Grillitsch), Christoph Baumgartner, Romano Schmid (YC38) (46' Michael Gregoritsch), Nicolas Seiwald, Marko Arnautovic. (Coach: Ralf Rangnick (GER)).
Turkey: Mert Günok, Kaan Ayhan, Abdulkerim Bardakci, Merih Demiral, Mert Müldür, Ferdi Kadioglu, Orkun Kökçu (YC11) (83' Irfan Kahveci), Ismail Yüksek (YC42) (58' Salih Özcan), Arda Güler (78' Kerem Aktürkoglu), Baris Yilmaz, Kenan Yildiz (78' Okay Yokuslu). (Coach: Vincenzo Montella (ITA)).
Goals: Austria: 1-2 Michael Gregoritsch (66').
Turkey: 0-1 Merih Demiral (1'), 0-2 Merih Demiral (59').
Referee: Artur Soares Dias (POR)   Attendance: 38,305.

QUARTER-FINALS

05-07-2024   MHPArena, Stuttgart: Spain – Germany 2-1 (0-0,1-1) (AET)
Spain: Unai Simón (YC82), Dani Carvajal (YC100,YC120+6)), Aymeric Laporte, Robin Le Normand (YC29) (46' Nacho), Marc Cucurella, Fabián Ruiz (YC120+1) (102' Joselu), Rodri (YC110), Pedri (8' Dani Olmo), Álvaro Morata (80' Mikel Oyarzabal), Nico Williams (80' Mikel Merino), Lamine Yamal (63' Ferran Torres (YC74)). (Coach: Luis de la Fuente (ESP)).
Germany: Manuel Neuer, Antonio Rüdiger (YC13), Jonathan Tah (80' Thomas Müller), David Raum (YC28) (Maximilian Mittelstädt (YC73)), Toni Kroos (YC67), Ilkay Gündogan (57' Niclas Füllkrug), Emre Can (46' Robert Andrich (YC56)), Joshua Kimmich, Kai Havertz (90' Waldemar Anton), Leroy Sané (46' Florian Wirtz (YC94)), Jamal Musiala. (Coach: Julian Nagelsmann (GER)). (Not used subs: Nico Schlotterbeck (YC90), Deniz Undav (YC113)).
Goals: Spain: 1-0 Dani Olmo (51'), 2-1 Mikel Merino (119').
Germany: 1-1 Florian Wirtz (89').
Referee: Anthony Taylor (ENG)   Attendance: 54,000.

05-07-2024   Volksparkstadion, Hamburg: Portugal – France 0-0 (AET)
Portugal: Diogo Costa, Pepe, João Cancelo (74' Nélson Semedo), Ruben Dias, Nuno Mendes, Bruno Bernandes (75' Francisco Conceição), João Palhinha (YC79) (90+2' Rúben Neves), Bernardo Silva, Vitinha (119' Matheus Nunes), Cristiano Ronaldo, Rafael Leão (105' João Félix). (Coach: Roberto Martínez (ESP)).
France: Mike Maignan, Theo Hernández, Dayotchanculle Upamecano, Jules Koundé, William Saliba (YC84), Ngolo Kanté, Aurelien Tchouaméni, Eduardo Camavinga (90' Youssouf Fofana), Antoine Griezmann (67' Ousmane Dembélé), Kylian Mbappé (105' Bradley Barcola), Randal Kolo Muani (86' Marcus Thuram). (Coach: Didier Deschamps (FRA)).
Referee: Michael Oliver (ENG)   Attendance: 47,789.
Penalties: 1 Ousmane Dembélé   1 Cristiano Ronaldo
            2 Youssouf Fofana   2 Bernardo Silva
            3 Jules Koundé   * João Félix
            4 Bradley Barcola   3 Nuno Mendes
            5 Theo Hernández

06-07-2024   Merkur Spiel-Arena, Düsseldorf:
                  England – Switzerland 1-1 (0-0,1-1) (AET)
England: Jordan Pickford, Kyle Walker, Kieran Trippier (78' Eberechi Eze), John Stones, Ezri Konsa (78' Cole Palmer), Declan Rice, Jude Bellingham, Kobbie Mainoo (78' Luke Shaw), Harry Kane (YC67) (109' Ivan Toney), Phil Foden (115' Trent Alexander-Arnold), Bukayo Saka. (Coach: Gareth Southgate (ENG)).
Switzerland: Yann Sommer, Ricardo Rodríguez, Fabian Schär (YC32), Manuel Akanji, Granit Xhaka, Remo Freuler (118' Zeki Amdouni), Michel Aebischer (118' Vincent Sierro), Ruben Vargas (64' Silvan Widmer (YC85)), Fabian Rieder (63' Steven Zuber), Breel Embolo (109' Xherdan Shaqiri), Dan Ndoye (98' Denis Zakaria). (Coach: Murat Yakin (SUI)).
Goals: England: 1-1 Bukayo Saka (80').
Switzerland: 0-1 Breel Embolo (75').
Referee: Daniele Orsato (ITA)   Attendance: 46,907.
Pernalties: 1 Cole Palmer   * Manuel Akanji
            2 Jude Bellingham   1 Fabian Schär
            3 Bukayo Saka   2 Xherdan Shaqiri
            4 Ivan Toney   3 Zeki Amdouni
            5 Trent Alexander-Arnold

06-07-2024   Olympiastadion, Berlin: Netherlands – Turkey 2-1 (0-1)
Netherlands: Bart Verbruggen, Stefan de Vrij, Nathan Aké (YC55) (73' Mickey van de Ven), Virgil van Dijk (YC64), Denzel Dumfries, Jerdy Schouten, Tijjani Reijnders (73' Joey Veerman), Xavi Simons (YC30) (87' Joshua Zirkzee), Memphis Depay (87' Jeremie Frimpong), Steven Bergwijn (46' Wout Weghorst (YC90+6)), Cody Gakpo. (Coach: Ronald Koeman (HOL)).
Turkey: Mert Günok, Kaan Ayhan (89' Semih Kiliçsoy), Abdulkerim Bardakci, Samet Akaydin (82' Cenk Tosun (YC90+3)), Mert Müldür (82' Zeki Çelik), Hakan Çalhanoglu, Salih Özcan (77' Okay Yokuslu), Ferdi Kadioglu, Arda Güler, Baris Yilmaz, Kenan Yildiz (77' Kerem Aktürkoglu). (Coach: Vincenzo Montella (ITA)). (Not used sub: Bertu Yildirim (RC90+6)).
Goals: Netherlands: 1-1 Stefan de Vrij (70'), 2-1 Mert Müldür (76' own goal).
Turkey: 0-1 Samet Akaydin (35').
Referee: Clément Turpin (FRA)   Attendance: 70,091.

SEMI-FINALS

09-07-2024   Allianz Arena, München: Spain – France 2-1 (2-1)
Spain: Unai Simón, Jesús Navas (YC14) (58' Dani Vivian), Nacho, Aymeric Laporte, Marc
Cucurella, Fabián Ruiz, Rodri, Álvaro Morata (76' Mikel Oyarzabal), Dani Olmo (76' Mikel
Merino), Nico Williams (90+4' Martín Zubimendi), Lamine Yamal (YC90+1) (90+3' Ferran
Torres). (Coach: Luis de la Fuente (ESP)).
France: Mike Maignan, Theo Hernández, Dayotchanculle Upamecano, Jules Koundé, William
Saliba, Ngolo Kanté (62' Antoine Griezmann), Adrien Rabiot (62' Eduardo Camavinga
(YC89)), Aurelien Tchouaméni (YC60), Ousmane Dembélé (79' Oliver Giroud), Kylian
Mbappé, Randal Kolo Muani (63' Bradley Barcola). (Coach: Didier Deschamps (FRA)).
Goals: Spain: 1-1 Lamine Yamal (21'), 2-1 Dani Olmo (25').
France: 0-1 Randal Kolo Muani (9').
Referee: Slavko Vincic (SVN)   Attendance: 62,042.

10-07-2024   BVB Stadion Dortmund, Dortmund: Netherlands – England 1-2 (1-1)
Netherlands: Bart Verbruggen, Stefan de Vrij, Nathan Aké, Virgil van Dijk (YC87), Denzel
Dumfries (YC17) (90+3' Joshua Zirkzee), Jerdy Schouten, Tijjani Reijnders, Xavi Simons
(YC90+1) (90+3' Brian Brobbey), Memphis Depay (35' Joey Veerman), Donyell Malen (46'
Wout Weghorst), Cody Gakpo. (Coach: Ronald Koeman (HOL)).
England: Jordan Pickford, Kyle Walker, Kieran Trippier (YC90+4) (46' Luke Shaw), John
Stones, Marc Guéhi, Declan Rice, Jude Bellingham (YC72), Kobbie Mainoo (90+3' Conor
Gallagher), Harry Kane (81' Ollie Watkins), Phil Foden (80' Cole Palmer), Bukayo Saka
(YC86) (90+3' Ezri Konsa). (Coach: Gareth Southgate (ENG)).
Goals: Netherlands: 1-0 Xavi Simons (7').
England: 1-1 Harry Kane (18' penalty), 1-2 Watkins (90+1').
Referee: Felix Zwayer (GER)   Attendance: 60,926.

FINAL

14-07-2024   Olympiastadion, Berlin: Spain – England 2-1 (0-0)
Spain: Unai Simón, Dani Carvajal, Aymeric Laporte, Robin Le Normand (83' Nacho), Marc
Cucurella, Fabián Ruiz, Rodri (46' Martín Zubimendi), Álvaro Morata (68' Mikel Oyarzabal),
Dani Olmo (YC31), Nico Williams, Lamine Yamal (89' Mikel Merino). (Coach: Luis de la
Fuente (ESP)).
England: Jordan Pickford, Kyle Walker, John Stones (YC53), Luke Shaw, Marc Guéhi, Declan
Rice, Jude Bellingham, Kobbie Mainoo (70' Cole Palmer), Harry Kane (61' Ollie Watkins
(YC90+2)), Phil Foden (89' Ivan Toney), Bukayo Saka. (Coach: Gareth Southgate (ENG)).
Goals: 47' Nico Williams 1-0, 73' Cole Palmer 1-1, 86' Mikel Oyarzabal 2-1.
Referee: François Letexier (FRA)   Attendance: 65,600.

*** Spain were European Champions ***

GOALSCORERS TOURNAMENT 2023-2024:

Goals	Players
14	Romelu Lukaku (BEL)
11	Harry Kane (ENG)
10	Kylina Mbappé (FRA), Cristiano Ronaldo (POR)
8	Scott McTominay (SCO)
7	Rasmus Højlund (DEN), Bruno Fernandes (POR)
6	Georges Mikautadze (GEO), Cody Gakpo (HOL), Erling Haaland (NOR), Zeki Amdouni (SUI)
5	Marcel Sabitzer (AUT), Andrej Kramaric (CRO), Bukayo Saka (ENG), Álvaro Morata (ESP), Dani Olmo (ESP), Khvicha Kvaratskhelia (GEO), Georgios Masouras (GRE), Barnabás Varga (HUN), Gerson Rodrigues (LUX), Aleksandar Mitrovic (SRB), Benjamin Sesko (SVN)
4	Nedim Bajrami (ALB), Christoph Baumgartner (AUT), Michael Gregoritsch (AUT), Tomás Soucek (CZE), Joselu (ESP), Ferran Torres (ESP), Daniel Håkans (FIN), Anastasios Bakasetas (GRE), Wout Weghorst (HOL), Dominik Szoboszlai (HUN), Albert Thor Gudmundsson (ISL), Bakhtiyar Zaynutdinov (KAZ), Ion Nicolaescu (MDA), Robert Lewandowski (POL), Bernardo Silva (POR), Nicolae Stanciu (ROM), Ruben Vargas (SUI)
3	Jasir Asani (ALB), Lucas Zelarayán (ARM), Marko Arnautovic (AUT), Emin Mahmudov (AZE), Max Ebong (BLS), Kiril Despodov (BUL), Václav Cerný (CZE), Jonas Wind (DEN), Lamine Yamal (ESP), Nico Williams (ESP), Oliver Antman (FIN), Teemu Pukki (FIN), Olivier Giroud (FRA), Budu Zivzivadze (GEO), Jamal Musiala (GER), Calvin Stengs (HOL), Hákon Arnar Haraldsson (ISL), Alfreð Finnbogason (ISL), Aron Gunnarsson (ISL), Davide Frattesi (ITA), Abat Aymbetov (KAZ), Vedat Muriqi (KOS), Milot Rashica (KOS), Pijus Sirvys (LTU), Danel Sinani (LUX), Enis Bardhi (MKD), Elif Elmas (MKD), Stevan Jovetic (MNE), Dion Charles (NIR), João Cancelo (POR), João Félix (POR), Gonçalo Ramos (POR), Denis Alibec (ROM), Razvan Marin (ROM), Valentin Mihaila (ROM), John McGinn (SCO), Dusan Vlahovic (SRB), Remo Freuler (SUI), Xherdan Shaqiri (SUI), Renato Steffen (SUI), Ondrej Duda (SVK), Lukás Haraslín (SVK), Ivan Schranz (SVK), Erik Janza (SVN), Andraz Sporar (SVN), Viktor Gyökeres (SWE), Kerem Aktürkoglu (TUR), Cenk Tosun (TUR), Viktor Tsyhankov (UKR), Harry Wilson (WAL)
2	Taulant Seferi (ALB), Berto Rosas Ubach (AND), Grant-Leon Ranos (ARM), Konrad Laimer (AUT), Dodi Lukébakio (BEL), Leandro Trossard (BEL), Rade Krunic (BIH), Dmitri Antilevski (BLS), Vladislav Morozov (BLS), Mateo Kovacic (CRO), Mario Pasalic (CRO), Bruno Petkovic (CRO), Ladislav Krejcí (CZE), Christian Eriksen (DEN), Pierre-Emile Højbjerg (DEN), Joakim Mæhle (DEN), Robert Skov (DEN), Jude Bellingham (ENG), Marcus Rashford (ENG), Mikel Merino (ESP), Mikel Oyarzabal (ESP), Fabián Ruiz (ESP), Gavi (ESP), Rauno Sappinen (EST), Benjamin Källman (FIN), Joel Pohjanpalo (FIN), Pyry Soiri (FIN), Kingsley Coman (FRA), Youssouf Fofana (FRA), Randal Kolo Muani (FRA), Marcus Thuram (FRA), Niclas Füllkrug (GER), Kai Havertz (GER), Florian Wirtz (GER), Fotis Ioannidis (GRE), Konstantinos Mavropanos (GRE), Dimitrios Pelkas (GRE), Nathan Aké (HOL), Memphis Depay (HOL), Donyell Malen (HOL), Martin Ádám (HUN), Roland Sallai (HUN), Evan Ferguson (IRL), Adam Idah (IRL), Mikey Johnston (IRL), Andri Guðjohnsen (ISL), Orri Óskarsson (ISL), Gylfi Sigurðsson (ISL), Oscar Gloukh (ISR), Shon Weissman (ISR), Eran Zahavi (ISR), Domenico Berardi

	(ITA), Federico Chiesa (ITA), Mateo Retegui (ITA), Islam Chesnokov (KAZ), Maksim Samorodov (KAZ), Askhat Tagybergen (KAZ), Yan Vorogovsky (KAZ), Fedor Cernych (LTU), Gytis Paulauskas (LTU), Yvandro Borges Sanches (LUX), Vladislav Baboglo (MDA), Jani Atanasov (MKD), Nikola Krstovic (MNE), Stefan Savic (MNE), Isaac Price (NIR), Alexander Sørloth (NOR), Adam Buksa (POL), Jakub Piotrowski (POL), Karol Swiderski (POL), Sebastian Szymanski (POL), Ricardo Horta (POR), Gonçalo Inácio (POR), Diogo Jota (POR), Ianis Hagi (ROM), Dusan Tadic (SRB), Breel Embolo (SUI), Granit Xhaka (SUI), Dávid Hancko (SVK), Juraj Kucka (SVK), Róbert Mak (SVK), Zan Karnicnik (SVN), Zan Vipotnik (SVN), Viktor Claesson (SWE), Emil Forsberg (SWE), Merih Demiral (TUR), Arda Güler (TUR), Artem Dovbyk (UKR), Mykhailo Mudryk (UKR), Viktor Tsyhankov (UKR), Roman Yaremchuk (UKR), David Brooks (WAL), Daniel James (WAL), Neco Williams (WAL)
1	Kristjan Asllani (ALB), Sokol Çikalleshi (ALB), Mirlind Daku (ALB), Klaus Gjasula (ALB), Qazim Laçi (ALB), Ernest Muçi (ALB), Márcio Vieira (AND), Tigran Barceghyan (ARM), Artak Dashyan (ARM), Nair Tiknizyan (ARM), Florian Kainz (AUT), Philipp Lienhart (AUT), Romano Schmid (AUT), Gernot Trauner (AUT), Toral Bayramov (AZE), Renat Dadashov (AZF), Anton Krivotsyuk (AZE), Ramil Seydayev (AZE), Johan Bakayoko (BEL), Yannick Carrasco (BEL), Kevin De Bruyne (BEL), Charles De Ketelaere (BEL), Youri Tielemans (BEL), Jan Vertonghen (BEL), Amar Dedic (BIH), Edin Dzeko (BIH), Renato Gojkovic (BIH), Amar Rahmanovic (BIH), Miroslav Stevanovic (BIH), Denis Laptev (BLS), Denis Polyakov (BLS), Preslav Borukov (BUL), Spas Delev (BUL), Marin Petkov (BUL), Georgi Rusev (BUL), Ante Budimir (CRO), Luka Ivanusec (CRO), Lovro Majer (CRO), Luka Modric (CRO), Grigoris Kastanos (CYP), Kostas Pileas (CYP), Ioannis Pittas (CYP), Tomás Chorý (CZE), Tomás Cvancara (CZE), David Doudera (CZE), Jan Kuchta (CZE), Lukás Provod (CZE), Patrik Schick (CZE), Thomas Delaney (DEN), Morten Hjulmand (DEN), Yussuf Poulsen (DEN), Trent Alexander-Arnold (ENG), Cole Palmer (ENG), Kalvin Phillips (ENG), Declan Rice (ENG), Kyle Walker (ENG), Ollie Watkins (ENG), Callum Wilson (ENG), Álex Baena (ESP), Dani Carvajal (ESP), Oihan Sancet (ESP), Robin Le Normand (ESP), Rodri (ESP), Martin Vetkal (EST), Glen Kamara (FIN), Robin Lod (FIN), Robert Taylor (FIN), Jonathan Clauss (FRA), Ousmane Dembélé (FRA), Antoine Griezmann (FRA), Benjamin Pavard (FRA), Adrien Rabiot (FRA), Aurélien Tchouaméni (FRA), Dayot Upamecano (FRA), Warren Zaïre-Emery (FRA), Mads Boe Mikkelsen (FRO), Odmar Færø (FRO), Giorgi Chakvetadze (GEO), Zuriko Davitashvili (GEO), Otar Kiteishvili (GEO), Levan Shengelia (GEO), Emre Can (GER), Ilkay Gündogan (GER), Giorgos Gaikoumakis (GRE), Dimitrios Kourbelis (GRE), Manolis Siopis (GRE), Marten de Roon (HOL), Quilindschy Hartman (HOL), Teun Koopmeiners (HOL),Virgil van Dijk (HOL), Xavi Simons (HOL), Stefan de Vrij (HOL), Mats Wieffer (HOL), Kevin Csoboth (HUN), Ádám Nagy (HUN), Willi Orbán (HUN), Bálint Vécsei (HUN), Nathan Collins (IRL), Matt Doherty (IRL), Callum Robinson (IRL), Mikael Egill Ellertsson (ISL), Davíð Kristján Ólafsson (ISL), Arnór Ingvi Traustason (ISL), Gabi Kanichowsky (ISR), Gadi Kinda (ISR), Dor Peretz (ISR), Raz Shlomo (ISR), Manor Solomon (ISR), Nicolò Barella (ITA), Alessandro Bastoni (ITA), Giacomo Bonaventura (ITA), Matteo Darmian (ITA), Stephan El Sharaawy (ITA), Ciro Immobile (ITA), Matteo Pessina (ITA), Giacomo Raspadori (ITA), Gianluca Scamacca (ITA), Mattia Zaccagni (ITA), Ramazan Orazov (KAZ), Muhamet Hyseni (KOS), Altin Zeqiri (KOS),

	Edon Zhegrova (KOS), Sandro Wolfinger (LIE), Edvinas Girdvainis (LTU), Maxime Chanot (LUX), Mathias Olesen (LUX), Daniles Balodis (LVA), Eduards Emsis (LVA), Jānis Ikaunieks (LVA), Kristers Tobers (LVA), Vadim Rata (MDA), Paul Mbong (MLT), Yannick Yankam (MLT), Darko Churlinov (MKD), Jovan Manev (MKD), Edvin Kuc (MNE), Slobodan Rubezic (MNE), Jonny Evans (NIR), Josh Magennis (NIR), Conor McMenamin (NIR), Paul Smyth (NIR), Fredrik Aursnes (NOR), Aron Dønnum (NOR), Mohamed Elyounoussi (NOR), Martin Ødegaard (NOR), Ola Solbakken (NOR), Jørgen Strand Larsen (NOR), Przemyslaw Frankowski (POL), Arkadiusz Milik (POL), Krzysztof Piatek (POL), Jakub Piotrowski (POL), Damian Szymanski (POL), Piotr Zielinski (POL), Francisco Conceição (POR), Rafael Leão (POR), Otávio (POR), Andrei Burca (ROM), Florinel Coman (ROM), Denis Dragus (ROM), Dennis Man (ROM), George Puscas (ROM), Stuart Armstrong (SCO), Lyndon Dykes (SCO), Callum McGregor (SCO), Kenny McLean (SCO), Ryan Porteous (SCO), Lawrence Shankland (SCO), Filippo Berardi (SMR), Simone Franciosi (SMR), Alessandro Golinucci (SMR), Srdjan Babic (SRB), Luka Jovicv (SRB), Darko Lazovic (SRB), Strahinja Pavlovic (SRB), Milos Veljkovic (SRB), Michel Aebischer (SUI), Manuel Akanji (SUI), Kwadwo Duah (SUI), Cedric Itten (SUI), Dan Ndoye (SUI), Silvan Widmer (SUI), Róbert Bozeník (SVK), Dávid Duris (SVK), Stanislav Lobotka (SVK), Lubomír Satka (SVK), Tomás Suslov (SVK), Denis Vavro (SVK), David Brekalo (SVN), Adam Gnezda Cerin (SVN), Sandi Lovric (SVN), Jan Mlakar (SVN), Benjamin Verbic (SVN), Anthony Elanga (SWE), Emil Holm (SWE), Alexander Isak (SWE), Jesper Karlsson (SWE), Dejan Kulusevski (SWE), Robin Quaison (SWE), Samet Akaydin (TUR), Yunus Akgün (TUR), Baris Alper Yilmaz (TUR), Abdülkerim Bardakçi (TUR), Hakan Çalhanoglu (TUR), Irfan Kahveci (TUR), Orkun Kökçu (TUR), Mert Müldür (TUR), Umut Nayir (TUR), Cengoz Ünder (TUR), Yusuf Yazici (TUR), Bertug Yildirim (TUR), Oleksandr Karavayev (UKR), Yukhym Konoplya (UKR), Mykola Shaparenko (UKR), Georgiy Sudakov (UKR), Andriy Yarmolenko (UKR), Illya Zabarnyi (UKR), Oleksandr Zinchenko (UKR), Natham Broadhead (WAL), Brennan Johnson (WAL), Kieffer Moore (WAL), Aaron Ramsey (WAL), Neco Williams (WAL)
1 own goal	Klaus Gjasula (ALB) for Croatia Joan Cervós (AND) for Israel Styopa Mkrtchyan (ARM) for Latvia Nair Tiknizyan (ARM) for Wales Maximilain Wöber (AUT) for France Behlul Mustafazade (AZE) for Sweden Orel Mangala (BEL) for Austria Jan Vertonghen (BEL) for France Nihad Mujakoc (BIH) for Luxembourg Aleks Petkov (BUL) for Hungary Robin Hranác (CZE) for Portugal Robin Le Normand (ESP) for Georgia Karol Mets (EST) for Poland Solomon Kvirkvelia (GEO) for Spain Luka Lochoshvili (GEO) for Spain Antonio Rüdiger (GER) for Scotland Aymen Mouelhi (GIB) for France Ethan Santos (GIB) for France Donyell Malen (HOL) for Austria Attila Szalai (HUN) for Serbia

	Eli Dasa (ISR) for Kosovo
	Riccardo Calafiori (ITA) for Spain
	Yerkin Tapalov (KAZ) for Greece
	Amir Rrahmani (KOS) for Switzerland
	Simon Lüchtinger (LIE) for Bosnia and Herzegovina
	Ferdinandi Apap (MLT) for England
	Ryan Camenzuli (MLT) for Ukraine
	Enrico Pepe (MLT) for England
	Jani Atanasov (MKD) for England
	Jonny Evans (NIR) for Slovenia
	Leo Østigård (NOR) for Scotland
	Roberto Di Maio (SMR) for Slovenia
	Patrik Hrosovský (SVK) for Bosnia and Herzegovina
	Samet Akaydin (TUR) for Portugal
	Ozan Kabak (TUR) for Armenia
	Mert Müldür (TUR) for Netherlands
	Mykola Matviyenko (UKR) for Bosnia and Herzegovina